(ex·ploring)

SERIES

1. Investigating in a systematic way: examining. 2. Searching into or ranging over for the purpose of disc⌐

Microsoft®

Office 365® Excel™ 2019

COMPREHENSIVE

Series Editor **Mary Anne Poatsy**

Mulbery | Davidson

Pearson

Vice President of Courseware Portfolio Management: Andrew Gilfillan
Executive Portfolio Manager: Samantha Lewis
Team Lead, Content Production: Laura Burgess
Content Producer: Alexandrina Wolf
Development Editor: Barbara Stover
Portfolio Management Assistant: Bridget Daly
Director of Product Marketing: Brad Parkins
Director of Field Marketing: Jonathan Cottrell
Product Marketing Manager: Heather Taylor
Field Marketing Manager: Bob Nisbet
Product Marketing Assistant: Liz Bennett
Field Marketing Assistant: Derrica Moser
Senior Operations Specialist: Maura Garcia
Senior Art Director: Mary Seiner
Interior and Cover Design: Pearson CSC
Cover Photo: Courtesy of Shutterstock® Images
Senior Product Model Manager: Eric Hakanson
Manager, Digital Studio: Heather Darby
Digital Content Producer, MyLab IT: Becca Golden
Course Producer, MyLab IT: Amanda Losonsky
Digital Studio Producer: Tanika Henderson
Full-Service Project Management: Pearson CSC (Amy Kopperude)
Composition: Pearson CSC

Credits and acknowledgments borrowed from other sources and reproduced, with permission, in this textbook appear on the appropriate page within text.

ISBN 10:   0-13-545275-9
ISBN 13: 978-0-13-545275-2

2 2019

Dedications

For my husband, Ted, who unselfishly continues to take on more than his share to support me throughout the process; and for my children, Laura, Carolyn, and Teddy, whose encouragement and love have been inspiring.

Mary Anne Poatsy

I dedicate this book to my nephew Peyton and nieces MaKynlee and Tenley. I further dedicate this book to the loving memory of Aunt Barbara.

Keith Mulbery

I dedicate this book to my beautiful wife Sarah. Thank you for your love, support, and amazing home-cooked meals. Your love is still my greatest achievement.

Jason Davidson

About the Authors

Mary Anne Poatsy, Series Editor, Common Features Author

Mary Anne is a senior faculty member at Montgomery County Community College, teaching various computer application and concepts courses in face-to-face and online environments. She holds a B.A. in Psychology and Education from Mount Holyoke College and an M.B.A. in Finance from Northwestern University's Kellogg Graduate School of Management.

Mary Anne has more than 20 years of educational experience. She has taught at Gwynedd Mercy College, Bucks County Community College, and Muhlenberg College. She also engages in corporate training. Before teaching, she was Vice President at Shearson Lehman in the Municipal Bond Investment Banking Department.

Dr. Keith Mulbery, Excel Author

Dr. Keith Mulbery is the Department Chair and a Professor in the Information Systems and Technology Department at Utah Valley University (UVU), where he currently teaches systems analysis and design, and global and ethical issues in information systems and technology. He has also taught computer applications, C# programming, and management information systems. Keith served as Interim Associate Dean, School of Computing, in the College of Technology and Computing at UVU.

Keith received the Utah Valley State College Board of Trustees Award of Excellence in 2001, School of Technology and Computing Scholar Award in 2007, and School of Technology and Computing Teaching Award in 2008. He has authored more than 17 textbooks, served as Series Editor for the Exploring Office 2007 series, and served as developmental editor on two textbooks for the Essentials Office 2000 series.

Keith received his B.S. and M.Ed. in Business Education from Southwestern Oklahoma State University and earned his Ph.D. in Education with an emphasis in Business Information Systems at Utah State University. His dissertation topic was computer-assisted instruction using Prentice Hall's Train and Assess IT program (the predecessor to MyITLab) to supplement traditional instruction in basic computer proficiency courses.

Jason Davidson, Excel Author

Jason Davidson is a faculty member in the Lacey School of Business at Butler University, where he teaches Advanced Web Design, Data Networks, Data Analysis and Business Modeling, and introductory information systems courses. He has served as a co-author on the Exploring series since 2013. Prior to joining the faculty at Butler, he worked in the technical publishing industry using his background in media development. Along with teaching, he currently serves as an IT consultant for regional businesses in the Indianapolis area. He holds a B.A. in Media Arts from Butler University and an M.B.A. from Morehead State University. He lives in Indianapolis, Indiana, with his wife Sarah, and in his free time enjoys road biking, photography, and spending time with his family.

Dr. Robert T. Grauer, Creator of the Exploring Series

Bob Grauer is an Associate Professor in the Department of Computer Information Systems at the University of Miami, where he is a multiple winner of the Outstanding Teaching Award in the School of Business, most recently in 2009. He has written numerous COBOL texts and is the vision behind the Exploring Office series, with more than three million books in print. His work has been translated into three foreign languages and is used in all aspects of higher education at both national and international levels. Bob Grauer has consulted for several major corporations including IBM and American Express. He received his Ph.D. in Operations Research in 1972 from the Polytechnic Institute of Brooklyn.

Brief Contents

Contents

■ CHAPTER EIGHT Statistical Functions: Analyzing Statistics 494

■ CHAPTER NINE Multiple-Sheet Workbook Management: Ensuring Quality Control 540

■ CHAPTER TEN Power Add-Ins: Managing Data 608

Acknowledgments

The Exploring team would like to acknowledge and thank all the reviewers who helped us throughout the years by providing us with their invaluable comments, suggestions, and constructive criticism.

A. D. Knight
Northwestern State University
Natchitoches–Louisiana

Aaron Montanino
Davenport University

Adriana Lumpkin
Midland College

Alan S. Abrahams
Virginia Tech

Alexandre C. Probst
Colorado Christian University

Ali Berrached
University of Houston–Downtown

Allen Alexander
Delaware Technical & Community College

Amy Rutledge
Oakland University

Andrea Marchese
Maritime College
State University of New York

Andrew Blitz
Broward College; Edison State College

Angel Norman
University of Tennessee–Knoxville

Angela Clark
University of South Alabama

Ann Rovetto
Horry–Georgetown Technical College

Astrid Todd
Guilford Technical Community College

Audrey Gillant
Maritime College, State University of New York

Barbara Stover
Marion Technical College

Barbara Tollinger
Sinclair Community College

Ben Brahim Taha
Auburn University

Beverly Amer
Northern Arizona University

Beverly Fite
Amarillo College

Biswadip Ghosh
Metropolitan State University of Denver

Bonita Volker
Tidewater Community College

Bonnie Homan
San Francisco State University

Brad West
Sinclair Community College

Brian Kovar
Kansas State University

Brian Powell
West Virginia University

Carmen Morrison
North Central State College

Carol Buser
Owens Community College

Carol Roberts
University of Maine

Carol Wiggins
Blinn College

Carole Pfeiffer
Southeast Missouri State University

Carolyn Barren
Macomb Community College

Carolyn Borne
Louisiana State University

Cathy Poyner
Truman State University

Charles Hodgson
Delgado Community College

Chen Zhang
Bryant University

Cheri Higgins
Illinois State University

Cheryl Brown
Delgado Community College

Cheryl Hinds
Norfolk State University

Cheryl Sypniewski
Macomb Community College

Chris Robinson
Northwest State Community College

Cindy Herbert
Metropolitan Community College–Longview

Craig J. Peterson
American InterContinental University

Craig Watson
Bristol Community College

Dana Hooper
University of Alabama

Dana Johnson
North Dakota State University

Daniela Marghitu
Auburn University

David Noel
University of Central Oklahoma

David Pulis
Maritime College, State University of New York

David Thornton
Jacksonville State University

Dawn Medlin
Appalachian State University

Debby Keen
University of Kentucky

Debra Chapman
University of South Alabama

Debra Hoffman
Southeast Missouri State University

Derrick Huang
Florida Atlantic University

Diana Baran
Henry Ford Community College

Diane Cassidy
The University of North Carolina at Charlotte

Diane L. Smith
Henry Ford Community College

Dick Hewer
Ferris State College

Don Danner
San Francisco State University

Don Hoggan
Solano College

Don Riggs
SUNY Schenectady County Community College

Doncho Petkov
Eastern Connecticut State University

Donna Ehrhart
Genesee Community College

Elaine Crable
Xavier University

Elizabeth Duett
Delgado Community College

Erhan Uskup
Houston Community College–Northwest

Eric Martin
University of Tennessee

Erika Nadas
Wilbur Wright College

Evelyn Schenk
Saginaw Valley State University

Floyd Winters
Manatee Community College

Frank Lucente
Westmoreland County Community College

G. Jan Wilms
Union University

Gail Cope
Sinclair Community College

Gary DeLorenzo
California University of Pennsylvania

Gary Garrison
Belmont University

Gary McFall
Purdue University

George Cassidy
Sussex County Community College

Gerald Braun
Xavier University

Gerald Burgess
Western New Mexico University

Gladys Swindler
Fort Hays State University

Gurinder Mehta
Sam Houston State University

Hector Frausto
California State University Los Angeles

Heith Hennel
Valencia Community College

Henry Rudzinski
Central Connecticut State University

Irene Joos
La Roche College

Iwona Rusin
Baker College; Davenport University

J. Roberto Guzman
San Diego Mesa College

Jacqueline D. Lawson
Henry Ford Community College

Jakie Brown, Jr.
Stevenson University

James Brown
Central Washington University

James Powers
University of Southern Indiana

Jane Stam
Onondaga Community College

Janet Bringhurst
Utah State University

Janice Potochney
Gateway Community College

Jean Luoma
Davenport University

Jean Welsh
Lansing Community College

Jeanette Dix
Ivy Tech Community College

Jennifer Day
Sinclair Community College

Jill Canine
Ivy Tech Community College

Jill Young
Southeast Missouri State University

Jim Chaffee
The University of Iowa Tippie College of Business

Joanne Lazirko
University of Wisconsin–Milwaukee

Jodi Milliner
Kansas State University

John Hollenbeck
Blue Ridge Community College

John Meir
Midlands Technical College

John Nelson
Texas Christian University

John Seydel
Arkansas State University

Judith A. Scheeren
Westmoreland County Community College

Judith Brown
The University of Memphis

Juliana Cypert
Tarrant County College

Kamaljeet Sanghera
George Mason University

Karen Priestly
Northern Virginia Community College

Karen Ravan
Spartanburg Community College

Karen Tracey
Central Connecticut State University

Kathleen Brenan
Ashland University

Ken Busbee
Houston Community College

Kent Foster
Winthrop University

Kevin Anderson
Solano Community College

Kim Wright
The University of Alabama

Kirk Atkinson
Western Kentucky University

Kristen Hockman
University of Missouri–Columbia

Kristi Smith
Allegany College of Maryland

Laura Marcoulides
Fullerton College

Laura McManamon
University of Dayton

Laurence Boxer
Niagara University

Leanne Chun
Leeward Community College

Lee McClain
Western Washington University

Lewis Cappelli
Hudson Valley Community College

Linda D. Collins
Mesa Community College

Linda Johnsonius
Murray State University

Linda Lau
Longwood University

Linda Theus
Jackson State Community College

Linda Williams
Marion Technical College

Lisa Miller
University of Central Oklahoma

Lister Horn
Pensacola Junior College

Lixin Tao
Pace University

Loraine Miller
Cayuga Community College

Lori Kielty
Central Florida Community College

Lorna Wells
Salt Lake Community College

Lorraine Sauchin
Duquesne University

Lucy Parakhovnik
California State University–Northridge

Lynn Baldwin
Madison College

Lynn Keane
University of South Carolina

Lynn Mancini
Delaware Technical Community
College

Lynne Seal
Amarillo College

Mackinzee Escamilla
South Plains College

Marcia Welch
Highline Community College

Margaret McManus
Northwest Florida State College

Margaret Warrick
Allan Hancock College

Marilyn Hibbert
Salt Lake Community College

Mark Choman
Luzerne County Community College

Mary Beth Tarver
Northwestern State University

Mary Duncan
University of Missouri–St. Louis

Maryann Clark
University of New Hampshire

Melissa Nemeth
Indiana University–Purdue University
Indianapolis

Melody Alexander
Ball State University

Michael Douglas
University of Arkansas at Little Rock

Michael Dunklebarger
Alamance Community College

Michael G. Skaff
College of the Sequoias

Michele Budnovitch
Pennsylvania College of Technology

Mike Jochen
East Stroudsburg University

Mike Michaelson
Palomar College

Mike Scroggins
Missouri State University

Mimi Spain
Southern Maine Community College

Muhammed Badamas
Morgan State University

NaLisa Brown
University of the Ozarks

Nancy Grant
Community College of Allegheny
County–South Campus

Nanette Lareau
University of Arkansas Community
College–Morrilton

Nikia Robinson
Indian River State University

Pam Brune
Chattanooga State Community College

Pam Uhlenkamp
Iowa Central Community College

Patrick Smith
Marshall Community and Technical College

Paul Addison
Ivy Tech Community College

Paul Hamilton
New Mexico State University

Paula Ruby
Arkansas State University

Peggy Burrus
Red Rocks Community College

Peter Ross
SUNY Albany

Philip H. Nielson
Salt Lake Community College

Philip Valvalides
Guilford Technical Community College

Ralph Hooper
University of Alabama

Ranette Halverson
Midwestern State University

Richard Blamer
John Carroll University

Richard Cacace
Pensacola Junior College

Richard Hewer
Ferris State University

Richard Sellers
Hill College

Rob Murray
Ivy Tech Community College

Robert Banta
Macomb Community College

Robert Dus˘ek
Northern Virginia Community College

Robert G. Phipps, Jr.
West Virginia University

Robert Sindt
Johnson County Community College

Robert Warren
Delgado Community College

Robyn Barrett
St. Louis Community College–Meramec

Rocky Belcher
Sinclair Community College

Roger Pick
University of Missouri at Kansas City

Ronnie Creel
Troy University

Rosalie Westerberg
Clover Park Technical College

Ruth Neal
Navarro College

Sandra Thomas
Troy University

Sheila Gionfriddo
Luzerne County Community College

Sherrie Geitgey
Northwest State Community College

Sherry Lenhart
Terra Community College

Shohreh Hashemi
University of Houston–Downtown

Sophia Wilberscheid
Indian River State College

Sophie Lee
California State University–Long Beach

Stacy Johnson
Iowa Central Community College

Stephanie Kramer
Northwest State Community College

Stephen Z. Jourdan
Auburn University at Montgomery

Steven Schwarz
Raritan Valley Community College

Sue A. McCrory
Missouri State University

Sumathy Chandrashekar
Salisbury University

Susan Fuschetto
Cerritos College

Susan Medlin
UNC Charlotte

Susan N. Dozier
Tidewater Community College

Suzan Spitzberg
Oakton Community College

Suzanne M. Jeska
County College of Morris

Sven Aelterman
Troy University

Sy Hirsch
Sacred Heart University

Sylvia Brown
Midland College

Tanya Patrick
Clackamas Community College

Terri Holly
Indian River State College

Terry Ray Rigsby
Hill College

Thomas Rienzo
Western Michigan University

Tina Johnson
Midwestern State University

Tommy Lu
Delaware Technical Community College

Troy S. Cash
Northwest Arkansas Community College

Vicki Robertson
Southwest Tennessee Community

Vickie Pickett
Midland College

Vivianne Moore
Davenport University

Weifeng Chen
California University of Pennsylvania

Wes Anthony
Houston Community College

William Ayen
University of Colorado at Colorado Springs

Wilma Andrews
Virginia Commonwealth University

Yvonne Galusha
University of Iowa

Special thanks to our content development and technical team:

Barbara Stover

Lisa Bucki

Lori Damanti

Sallie Dodson

Morgan Hetzler

Ken Mayer

Joyce Nielsen

Chris Parent

Sean Portnoy

Steven Rubin

LeeAnn Bates
MyLab IT content author

Becca Golden
Media Producer

Jennifer Hurley
MyLab IT content author

Kevin Marino
MyLab IT content author

Ralph Moore
MyLab IT content author

Jerri Williams
MyLab IT content author

The Exploring Series and You

Exploring is Pearson's Office Application series that requires students like you to think "beyond the point and click." In this edition, the *Exploring* experience has evolved to be even more in tune with the student of today. With an emphasis on Mac compatibility, critical thinking, and continual updates to stay in sync with the changing Microsoft Office 365, and by providing additional valuable assignments and resources, the *Exploring* series is able to offer you the most usable, current, and beneficial learning experience ever.

The goal of *Exploring* is, as it has always been, to go farther than teaching just the steps to accomplish a task—the series provides the theoretical foundation for you to understand when and why to apply a skill. As a result, you achieve a deeper understanding of each application and can apply this critical thinking beyond Office and the classroom.

New to This Edition

Continual eText Updates: This edition of *Exploring* is written to Microsoft® Office 365®, which is constantly updating. In order to stay current with the software, we are committed to twice annual updates of the eText and Content Updates document available as an instructor resource for text users.

Focus on Mac: Mac usage is growing, and even outstripping PC usage at some four-year institutions. In response, new features such as Mac Tips, On a Mac step boxes, Mac Troubleshooting, and Mac tips on Student Reference Cards help ensure Mac users have a flawless experience using *Exploring*.

Expanded Running Case: In this edition, the Running Case has been expanded to all applications, with one exercise per chapter focusing on the New Castle County Technical Services case, providing a continuous and real-world project for students to work on throughout the semester.

Pre-Built Learning Modules: Pre-built inside MyLab IT, these make course setup a snap. The modules are based on research and instructor best practices, and can be easily customized to meet your course requirements.

Critical Thinking Modules: Pre-built inside MyLab IT, these pair a Grader Project with a critical thinking quiz that requires students to first complete a hands-on project, then reflect on what they did and the data or information they interacted with, to answer a series of objective critical thinking questions. These are offered both at the chapter level for regular practice, as well as at the Application level where students can earn a Critical Thinking badge.

What's New for MyLab IT Graders

Graders with WHY: All Grader project instructions now incorporate the scenario and the WHY to help students critically think and understand why they're performing the steps in the project.

Hands-On Exercise Assessment Graders: A new Grader in each chapter that mirrors the Hands-On Exercise. Using an alternate scenario and data files, this new Grader is built to be more instructional and features Learning Aids such as Read (eText), Watch (video), and Practice (guided simulation) in the Grader report to help students learn, remediate, and resubmit.

Auto-Graded Critical Thinking Quizzes:

- Application Capstones that allow students to earn a Critical Thinking badge
- Chapter-level quizzes for each Mid-Level Exercise Grader project

Improved Mac Compatibility in Graders: All Graders are tested for Mac compatibility and any that can be made 100% Mac compatible are identified in the course. This excludes Access projects as well as any that use functionality not available in Mac Office.

Autograded Integrated Grader Projects: Based on the discipline-specific integrated projects, covering Word, Excel, PowerPoint, and Access in various combinations.

Final Solution Image: Included with Grader student downloads, final output images allows students to visualize what their solution should look like.

What's New for MyLab IT Simulations

Updated Office 365, 2019 Edition Simulations: Written by the *Exploring* author team, ensures one-to-one content to directly match the Hands-On Exercises (Simulation Training) and mirror them with an alternate scenario (Simulation Assessment).

Student Action Visualization: Provides a playback of student actions within the simulation for remediation by students and review by instructors when there is a question about why an action is marked as incorrect.

Series Hallmarks

The **How/Why Approach** helps students move beyond the point and click to a true understanding of how to apply Microsoft Office skills.

- **White Pages/Yellow Pages** clearly distinguish the theory (white pages) from the skills covered in the Hands-On Exercises (yellow pages) so students always know what they are supposed to be doing and why.

- **Case Study** presents a scenario for the chapter, creating a story that ties the Hands-On Exercises together and gives context to the skills being introduced.

- **Hands-On Exercise Videos** are tied to each Hands-On Exercise and walk students through the steps of the exercise while weaving in conceptual information related to the Case Study and the objectives as a whole.

An **Outcomes focus** allows students and instructors to know the higher-level learning goals and how those are achieved through discreet objectives and skills.

- **Outcomes** presented at the beginning of each chapter identify the learning goals for students and instructors.

- **Enhanced Objective Mapping** enables students to follow a directed path through each chapter, from the objectives list at the chapter opener through the exercises at the end of the chapter.
  - **Objectives List:** This provides a simple list of key objectives covered in the chapter. This includes page numbers so students can skip between objectives where they feel they need the most help.
  - **Step Icons:** These icons appear in the white pages and reference the step numbers in the Hands-On Exercises, providing a correlation between the two so students can easily find conceptual help when they are working hands-on and need a refresher.
  - **Quick Concepts Check:** A series of questions that appear briefly at the end of each white page section. These questions cover the most essential concepts in the white pages required for students to be successful in working the Hands-On Exercises. Page numbers are included for easy reference to help students locate the answers.
  - **Chapter Objectives Review:** Located near the end of the chapter and reviews all important concepts covered in the chapter. Designed in an easy-to-read bulleted format.

- **MOS Certification Guide** for instructors and students to direct anyone interested in prepping for the MOS exam to the specific locations to find all content required for the test.

End-of-Chapter Exercises offer instructors several options for assessment. Each chapter has approximately 11–12 exercises ranging from multiple choice questions to open-ended projects.

- **Multiple Choice, Key Terms Matching, Practice Exercises, Mid-Level Exercises, Running Case, Disaster Recovery, and Capstone Exercises** are at the end of all chapters.
  - **Enhanced Mid-Level Exercises** include a **Creative Case** (for PowerPoint and Word), which allows students some flexibility and creativity, not being bound by a definitive solution, and an **Analysis Case** (for Excel and Access), which requires students to interpret the data they are using to answer an analytic question.

- **Application Capstone** exercises are included in the book to allow instructors to test students on the contents of a single application.

The Exploring Series and MyLab IT

The *Exploring Series* has been a market leader for more than 20 years, with a hallmark focus on both the *how* and *why* behind what students do within the Microsoft Office software. In this edition, the pairing of the text with MyLab IT Simulations, Graders, Objective Quizzes, and Resources as a fully complementary program allows students and instructors to get the very most out of their use of the *Exploring Series*.

To maximize student results, we recommend pairing the text content with MyLab IT, which is the teaching and learning platform that empowers you to reach every student. By combining trusted author content with digital tools and a flexible platform, MyLab personalizes the learning experience and helps your students learn and retain key course concepts while developing skills that future employers are seeking in their candidates.

Solving Teaching and Learning Challenges

Pearson addresses these teaching and learning challenges with *Exploring* and MyLab IT 2019.

Reach Every Student

MyLab IT 2019 delivers trusted content and resources through easy-to-use, Prebuilt Learning Modules that promote student success. Through an authentic learning experience, students become sharp critical thinkers and proficient in Microsoft Office, developing essential skills employers seek.

Practice and Feedback: What do I do when I get stuck or need more practice?

MyLab IT features **Integrated Learning Aids** within the Simulations and now also within the Grader Reports, allowing students to choose to Read (via the eText), Watch (via an author-created hands-on video), or Practice (via a guided simulation) whenever they get stuck. These are conveniently accessible directly within the simulation training so that students do not have to leave the graded assignment to access these helpful resources. The **Student Action Visualization** captures all the work students do in the Simulation for both Training and Assessment and allows students and instructors to watch a detailed playback for the purpose of remediation or guidance when students get stuck. MyLab IT offers **Grader project reports** for coaching, remediation, and defensible grading. Score Card Detail allows you to easily see where students were scored correctly or incorrectly, pointing out how many points were deducted on each step. Live Comments Report allows you and the students to see the actual files the student submitted with mark-ups/comments on what they missed and now includes Learning Aids to provide immediate remediation for incorrect steps.

Application, Motivation, and Employability Skills: Why am I taking this course, and will this help me get a job?

Students want to know that what they are doing in this class is setting them up for their ultimate goal—to get a job. With an emphasis on **employability skills** like critical thinking and other soft skills, **digital badges** to prove student proficiency in Microsoft skills and critical thinking, and **MOS Certification practice materials** in MyLab IT, the *Exploring Series* is putting students on the path to differentiate themselves in the job market, so that they can find and land a job that values their schools once they leave school.

Application: How do I get students to apply what they've learned in a meaningful way?

The *Exploring Series* and MyLab IT offer instructors the ability to provide students with authentic formative and summative assessments. The realistic and hi-fidelity **simulations** help students feel like they are working in the real Microsoft applications and allow them to explore, use 96% of Microsoft methods, and do so without penalty. The **Grader projects** allow students to gain real-world context as they work live in the application, applying both an understanding of how and why to perform certain skills to complete a project. New **Critical Thinking quizzes** require students to demonstrate their understanding of why, by answering questions that force them to analyze and interpret the project they worked on to answer a series of objective questions. The new **Running Case** woven through all applications requires students to apply their knowledge in a realistic way to a long-running, semester-long project focused on the same company.

Ease of Use: I need a course solution that is easy to use for both me and my students

MyLab IT 2019 is the easiest and most accessible in its history. With new **Prebuilt Learning** and **Critical Thinking Modules** course set-up is simple! **LMS integration capabilities** allow users seamless access to MyLab IT with single sign-on, grade sync, and asset-level deep linking. Continuing a focus on accessibility, MyLab IT includes an **integrated Accessibility Toolbar** with translation feature for students with disabilities, as well as a **Virtual Keyboard** that allows students to complete keyboard actions entirely on screen. There is also an enhanced focus on Mac compatibility with even more Mac-compatible Grader projects,

Developing Employability Skills

High-Demand Office Skills are taught to help students gain these skills and prepare for the Microsoft Office Certification exams (MOS). The MOS objectives are covered throughout the content, and a MOS Objective Appendix provides clear mapping of where to find each objective. Practice exams in the form of Graders and Simulations are available in MyLab IT.

Badging Digital badges are available for students in Introductory and Advanced Microsoft Word, Excel, Access, and PowerPoint. This digital credential is issued to students upon successful completion (90%+ score) of an Application Capstone Badging Grader project. MyLab IT badges provide verified evidence that learners have demonstrated specific skills and competencies using Microsoft Office tools in a real project and help distinguish students within the job pool. Badges are issued through the Acclaim system and can be placed in a LinkedIn ePortfolio, posted on social media (Facebook, Twitter), and/or included in a résumé. Badges include tags with relevant information that allow students to be discoverable by potential employers, as well as search for jobs for which they are qualified.

> "The badge is a way for employers to actually verify that a potential employee is actually somewhat fluent with Excel."—Bunker Hill Community College Student

The new **Critical Thinking Badge** in MyLab IT for 2019 provides verified evidence that learners have demonstrated the ability to not only complete a real project, but also analyze and problem-solve using Microsoft Office applications. Students prove this by completing an objective quiz that requires them to critically think about the project, interpret data, and explain why they performed the actions they did in the project. Critical Thinking is a hot button issue at many institutions and is highly sought after in job candidates, allowing students with the Critical Thinking Badge to stand out and prove their skills.

Soft Skills Videos are included in MyLab IT for educators who want to emphasize key employability skills such as Accepting Criticism and Being Coachable, Customer Service, and Resume and Cover Letter Best Practices.

Resources

Instructor Teaching Resources

Supplements Available to Instructors at www.pearsonhighered.com/exploring	Features of the Supplement
Instructor's Manual	Available for each chapter and includes: • List of all Chapter Resources, File Names, and Where to Find • Chapter Overview • Class Run-Down • Key Terms • Discussion Questions • Practice Projects & Applications • Teaching Notes • Additional Web Resources • Projects and Exercises with File Names • Solutions to Multiple Choice, Key Terms Matching, and Quick Concepts Checks
Solutions Files, Annotated Solution Files, Scorecards	• Available for all exercises with definitive solutions • Annotated Solution Files in PDF feature callouts to enable easy grading • Scorecards to allow for easy scoring for hand-grading all exercises with definitive solutions, and scoring by step adding to 100 points.
Rubrics	For Mid-Level Exercises without a definitive solution. Available in Microsoft Word format, enabling instructors to customize the assignments for their classes
Test Bank	Approximately 75–100 total questions per chapter, made up of multiple-choice, true/false, and matching. Questions include these annotations: • Correct Answer • Difficulty Level • Learning Objective Alternative versions of the Test Bank are available for the following LMS: Blackboard CE/Vista, Blackboard, Desire2Learn, Moodle, Sakai, and Canvas
Computerized TestGen	TestGen allows instructors to: • Customize, save, and generate classroom tests • Edit, add, or delete questions from the Test Item Files • Analyze test results • Organize a database of tests and student results
PowerPoint Presentations	PowerPoints for each chapter cover key topics, feature key images from the text, and include detailed speaker notes in addition to the slide content. PowerPoints meet accessibility standards for students with disabilities. Features include, but are not limited to: • Keyboard and Screen Reader access • Alternative text for images • High color contrast between background and foreground colors

Scripted Lectures	• A lecture guide that provides the actions and language to help demonstrate skills from the chapter • Follows the activity similar to the Hands-On Exercises but with an alternative scenario and data files
Prepared Exams	• An optional Hands-On Exercise that can be used to assess students' ability to perform the skills from each chapter, or across all chapters in an application. • Each Prepared Exam folder includes the needed data files, instruction file, solution, annotated solution, and scorecard.
Outcome and Objective Maps	• Available for each chapter to help you determine what to assign • Includes every exercise and identifies which outcomes, objectives, and skills are included from the chapter
MOS Mapping, MOS Online Appendix	• Based on the Office 2019 MOS Objectives • Includes a full mapping of where each objective is covered in the materials • For any content not covered in the textbook, additional material is available in the Online Appendix document
Transition Guide	A detailed spreadsheet that provides a clear mapping of content from Exploring Microsoft Office 2016 to Exploring Microsoft Office 365, 2019 Edition
Content Updates Guide	A living document that features any changes in content based on Microsoft Office 365 changes as well as any errata
Assignment Sheets	Document with a grid of suggested student deliverables per chapter that can be passed out to students with columns for Due Date, Possible Points, and Actual Points
Sample Syllabus	Syllabus templates set up for 8-week, 12-week, and 16-week courses
Answer Keys for Multiple Choice, Key Terms Matching, and Quick Concepts Check	Answer keys for each objective, matching, or short-answer question type from each chapter

Student Resources

Supplements Available to Students at www.pearsonhighered.com/exploring	**Features of the Supplement**
Student Data Files	All data files needed for the following exercises, organized by chapter: • Hands-On Exercises • Practice Exercises • Mid-Level Exercises • Running Case • Disaster Recovery Case • Capstone Exercise
MOS Certification Material	• Based on the Office 2019 MOS Objectives • Includes a full mapping of where each objective is covered in the materials • For any content not covered in the textbook, additional material is available in the Online Appendix document

Microsoft®

Office 365®

Excel™ 2019

COMPREHENSIVE

Office 365 Common Features

LEARNING OUTCOME

You will apply skills common across the Microsoft Office suite to create and format documents and edit content in Office 365 applications.

OBJECTIVES & SKILLS: After you read this chapter, you will be able to:

CASE STUDY | Spotted Begonia Art Gallery

You are an administrative assistant for Spotted Begonia, a local art gallery. The gallery does a lot of community outreach to help local artists develop a network of clients and supporters. Local schools are invited to bring students to the gallery for enrichment programs.

As the administrative assistant for Spotted Begonia, you are responsible for overseeing the production of documents, spreadsheets, newspaper articles, and presentations that will be used to increase public awareness of the gallery. Other clerical assistants who are familiar with Microsoft Office will prepare the promotional materials, and you will proofread, make necessary corrections, adjust page layouts, save and print documents, and identify appropriate templates to simplify tasks. Your experience with Microsoft Office is limited, but you know that certain fundamental tasks that are common to Word, Excel, and PowerPoint will help you accomplish your oversight task. You are excited to get started with your work!

Taking the First Step

Dean Drobot/Shutterstock

THE SPOTTED BEGONIA ART GALLERY

May 6, 2021

Ms. Jane Hernandez
Executive Director
ABC Arts Foundation
432 Main Street
Detroit, MI 48201

RE: DISCOVER THE ARTIST IN YOU! PROGRAM

Dear Ms. Hernandez,

We are pleased to invite you and your coworkers to our *Discover the Artist in You!* Children's Art Festival on June 6th at 2pm at the gallery. Light refreshments will be served. Please see the enclosed flyer.

The Spotted Begonia Art Gallery is pleased that the ABC Arts Foundation has accepted our funding proposal for the *Discover the Artist in You!* Program. The *Discover the Artist in You!* Program will introduce elementary students to local artists and will give those students a chance to create their own art projects under the guidance of those artists. We look forward to partnering with you to provide this program to more than 500 local elementary students!

Please RSVP by June 1st to ejhazelton@sbag.org with the number attending. Please let me know if you have any questions.

Thank you,

Emma J. Hazelton

Arts Education Outreach Coordinator
Spotted Begonia Art Gallery
387 Pine Hill Road
Pontiac, MI 48340

Sirtravelalot/Shutterstock

JUNE 6, 2021

DISCOVER THE ARTIST IN YOU!

Children's Art Festival
Come and Discover the Artist in You! at our fifth annual Children's Art Festival. Participate in a wide range of interactive programs designed for families with children ages 3 – 12.

Spotted Begonia Art Gallery

Paint a T-Shirt.

Decorate a Bird House.

Design a Garden Fairy.

EVENT LOCATION
387 Pine Hill Road
Pontiac, MI 48340

(248) 555-3434

Noon – 4 PM

Spotted Begonia Art Gallery   www.sbag.org

FIGURE 1.1 Spotted Begonia Art Gallery Documents

CASE STUDY | Spotted Begonia Art Gallery

Starting Files	Files to be Submitted
cf01h1Letter.docx	**cf01h1Letter_LastFirst.docx**
Seasonal Event Flyer Template	**cf01h3Flyer_LastFirst.docx**

MyLab IT Grader An alternate version of this project is available as a MyLab IT Grader Assessment

Get Started with Office Applications

Organizations around the world rely heavily on Microsoft Office software to produce documents, spreadsheets, presentations, and databases. **Microsoft Office** is a productivity software suite that includes a set of software applications, each one specializing in a specific type of output. There are different versions of Office. Office 365 is purchased as a monthly or annual subscription and is fully installed on your PC, tablet, and phone. With Office 365, you receive periodic updates of new features and security measures. Office 365 also includes access to OneDrive storage. Office 2019 is a one-time purchase and fully installed on your PC. Periodic upgrades are not available. Both Office 365 and Office 2019 have versions that run on a Mac.

All versions of Microsoft Office include Word, Excel, and PowerPoint, as well as some other applications. Some versions of Office also include Access. Office 365 for Mac and Office for Mac include Word, Excel, and PowerPoint, but not Access. **Microsoft Word** (Word) is a word processing application, used to produce all sorts of documents, including memos, newsletters, reports, and brochures. **Microsoft Excel** (Excel) is a financial spreadsheet program, used to organize records, financial transactions, and business information in the form of worksheets. **Microsoft PowerPoint** (PowerPoint) is presentation software, used to create dynamic presentations to inform and persuade audiences. Finally, **Microsoft Access** (Access) is a database program, used to record and link data, query databases, and create forms and reports. The choice of which software application to use really depends on what type of output you are producing. Table 1.1 describes the major tasks of the four primary applications in Microsoft Office.

TABLE 1.1	Microsoft Office Applications
Office Application	**Application Characteristics**
Word	Word processing software used with text and graphics to create, edit, and format documents.
Excel	Spreadsheet software used to store quantitative data and to perform accurate and rapid calculations, what-if analyses, and charting, with results ranging from simple budgets to sophisticated financial and statistical analyses.
PowerPoint	Presentation graphics software used to create slide shows for presentation by a speaker or delivered online, to be published as part of a website, or to run as a stand-alone application on a computer kiosk.
Access	Relational database software used to store data and convert it into information. Database software is used primarily for decision making by businesses that compile data from multiple records stored in tables to produce informative reports.

These programs are designed to work together, so you can integrate components created in one application into a file created by another application. For example, you could integrate a chart created in Excel into a Word document or a PowerPoint presentation, or you could export a table created in Access into Excel for further analysis. You can use two or more Office applications to produce your intended output.

In addition, Microsoft Office applications share common features. Such commonality gives a similar feel to each software application so that learning and working with each Office software application is easier. This chapter focuses on many common features that the Office applications share. Although Word is primarily used to illustrate many examples, you are encouraged to open and explore Excel and PowerPoint (and to some degree, Access) to examine the same features in those applications. As a note, most of the content in this chapter and book are for the Windows-based Office applications. Some basic information about Office for Mac is included in TIP boxes and in the Step boxes when there are significant differences to point out.

In this section, you will learn how to log in with your Microsoft account, open an application, and open and save a file. You will also learn to identify interface components common to Office software applications, such as the ribbon, Backstage view, and the Quick Access Toolbar. You will experience Live Preview. You will learn how to get help with an application. You will also learn about customizing the ribbon and using Office add-ins.

Starting an Office Application

Microsoft Office applications are launched from the Start menu. Select the Start icon ⊞ to display the Start menu and select the app tile for the application in which you want to work (see Figure 1.2). Note: The Start menu in Figure 1.2 may show different tiles and arrangement of tiles than what is on your Start menu. If the application tile you want is not on the Start menu, you can open the program from the list of all apps on the left side of the Start menu, or alternatively, you can use search on the taskbar. Just type the name of the program in the search box and press Enter. The program will open automatically.

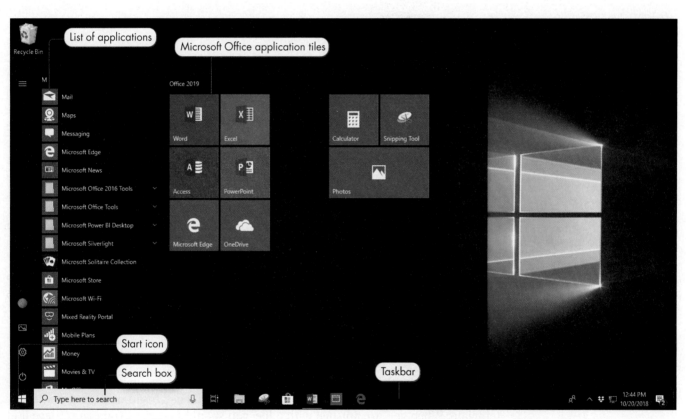

FIGURE 1.2 Windows Start Menu

Use Your Microsoft Account

When you have a Microsoft account, you can sign in to any Windows computer and you will be able to access the saved settings associated with your Microsoft account. That means any computer can have the same familiar look that you are used to seeing on your home or school computers and devices. Your Microsoft account will automatically sign in to all the apps and services that use a Microsoft account, such as OneDrive and Outlook. If you share your computer with another user, each user can have access to his or her own Microsoft account, and can easily switch between accounts by logging out of one Microsoft account and logging in to another Microsoft account. You can switch accounts within an application as well.

To switch between accounts in an application such as Word, complete the following steps:

1. Click the profile name at the top-right of the application.
2. Select Switch account.
3. Select an account from the list, if the account has already been added to the computer, or add a new account.

On a Mac, to switch between accounts in an application, complete the following steps:

1. Click the application menu (Word, Excel, etc.), click Sign Out, and then click Sign Out again.
2. Click File, click New From Template, and then click Sign in at top of the left pane.
3. Click Sign in again, type your user email, click Next, type password, and then click Sign in.

Use OneDrive

Having a Microsoft account also provides additional benefits, such as being connected to all of Microsoft's resources on the Internet. These resources include an Outlook email account and access to OneDrive cloud storage. *Cloud storage* is a technology used to store files and work with programs that are stored in a central location on the Internet. *OneDrive* is a Microsoft app used to store, access, and share files and folders on the Internet. OneDrive is the default storage location when saving Office files. Because OneDrive stores files on the Internet, when a document has been saved in OneDrive the most recent version of the document will be accessible when you log in from any computer connected to the Internet. Files and folders saved to OneDrive can be available offline and accessed through File Explorer—Windows' file management system. Moreover, changes made to any document saved to OneDrive will be automatically updated across all devices, so each device you access with your Windows account will all have the same version of the file.

OneDrive enables you to collaborate with others. You can share your documents with others or edit a document on which you are collaborating. You can even work with others simultaneously on the same document.

STEP 1 ▶ Working with Files

When working with an Office application, you can begin by opening an existing file that has already been saved to a storage medium or you can begin work on a new file or template. When you are finished with a file, you should save it, so you can retrieve it at another time.

Create a New File

After opening an Office application, you will be presented with template choices. Use the Blank document (workbook, presentation, database, etc.) template to start a new blank file. You can also create a new Office file from within an application by selecting New from the File tab.

The File tab is located at the far left of the ribbon. When you select the File tab, you see *Backstage view*. Backstage view is where you manage your files and the data about them—creating, saving, printing, sharing, inspecting for accessibility, compatibility, and other document issues, and accessing other setting options. The File tab and Backstage view is where you do things "to" a file, whereas the other tabs on the ribbon enable you to do things "in" a file.

Save a File

Saving a file enables you to open it for additional updates or reference later. Files are saved to a storage medium such as a hard drive, flash drive, or to OneDrive.

The first time you save a file, you indicate where the file will be saved and assign a file name. It is best to save the file in an appropriately named folder so you can find it easily later. Thereafter, you can continue to save the file with the same name and location using the Save command. If the file is saved in OneDrive, any changes to the file will be automatically saved. You do not have to actively save the document. If you want more control over when changes to your document are saved, you have the option to turn this feature off (or back on) with the AutoSave feature in the Quick Access Toolbar.

There are instances where you will want to rename the file or save it to a different location. For example, you might reuse a budget saved as an Excel worksheet, modifying it for another year, and want to keep a copy of both the old and revised budgets. In this instance, you would save the new workbook with a new name, and perhaps save it in a different folder. To do so, use the Save As command, and continue with the same procedure to save a new file: navigating to the new storage location and changing the file name. Figure 1.3 shows a typical Save As pane that enables you to select a location before saving the file. Notice that OneDrive is listed as well as This PC. To navigate to a specific location, use Browse.

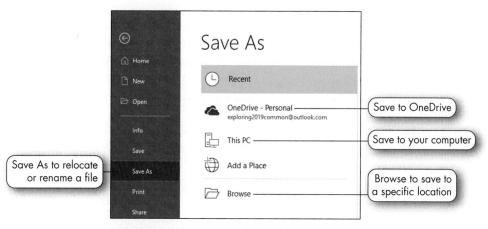

FIGURE 1.3 Save As in Backstage View

> **To save a file with a different name and/or file location, complete the following steps:**
>
> 1. Click the File tab.
> 2. Click Save As.
> 3. Select a location or click Browse to navigate to the file storage location.
> 4. Type the file name.
> 5. Click Save.

STEP 2 ▶ Open a Saved File

Often you will need to work on an existing file that has been saved to a storage location. This may be an email attachment that you have downloaded to a storage device, a file that has been shared with you in OneDrive, or a file you have previously created. To open an existing file, navigate in File Explorer to the folder or drive where the document is stored, and then double-click the file name to open the file. The application and the file will open. Alternatively, if the application is already open, from Backstage view, click Open, and then click Browse, This PC, or OneDrive to locate and open the file (see Figure 1.4).

> **MAC TIP:** To open an existing file, navigate in Finder to the folder or drive where the document is stored and double-click the file name to open the file.

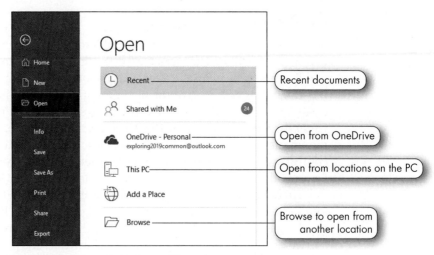

FIGURE 1.4 Open in Backstage View

Office simplifies the task of reopening files by providing a Recent documents list with links to your most recently used files, as shown in Figure 1.5. When opening the application, the Recent list displays in the center pane. The Recent list changes to reflect only the most recently opened files, so if it has been quite some time since you worked with a particular file, or if you have worked on several other files in between and you do not see your file listed, you can click More documents (or Workbooks, Presentations, etc).

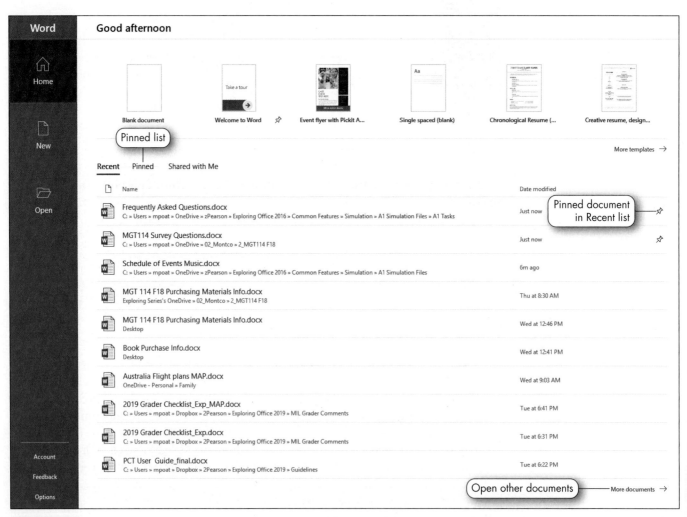

FIGURE 1.5 Recent Documents List

Using Common Interface Components

When you open any Office application, you will first notice the title bar and ribbon (see Figure 1.6) at the top of the document. These features enable you to identify the document, provide easy access to frequently used commands, and controls the window in which the document displays. The **title bar** identifies the current file name and the application in which you are working. It also includes control buttons that enable you to minimize, restore down, or close the application window. The Quick Access Toolbar, on the left side of the title bar, enables you to turn AutoSave on or off, save the file, undo or redo editing, and customize the Quick Access Toolbar. Located just below the title bar is the ribbon. The **ribbon** is the command center of Office applications containing tabs, groups, and commands. If you are working with a large project, you can maximize your workspace by temporarily hiding the ribbon. There are several methods that can be used to hide and then redisplay the ribbon:

- Double-click any tab name to collapse; click any tab name to expand
- Click the Collapse Ribbon arrow at the far-right side of the ribbon
- Use the Ribbon Display Option on the right side of the Title bar. These controls enable you to not only collapse or expand the ribbon, but also to choose whether you want to see the tabs or no tabs at all.

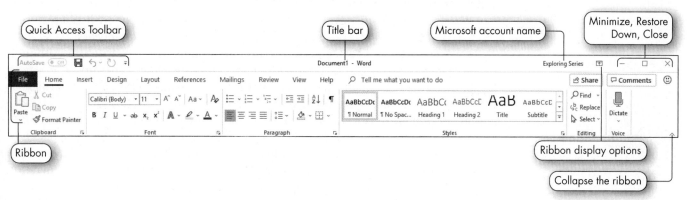

FIGURE 1.6 The Title Bar, Quick Access Toolbar, and Document Controls

Use the Ribbon

The main organizational grouping on the ribbon is tabs. The **tab** name indicates the type of commands located on the tab. On each tab, the ribbon displays several task-oriented groups. A **group** is a subset of a tab that organizes similar commands together. A **command** is a button or task within a group that you select to perform a task (see Figure 1.7). The ribbon with the tabs and groups of commands is designed to provide efficient functionality. For that reason, the Home tab displays when you first open a file in an Office software application and contains groups with the most commonly used commands for that application. For example, because you often want to change the way text is displayed, the Home tab in an Office application includes a Font group, with commands related to modifying text. Similarly, other tabs contain groups of related actions, or commands, many of which are unique to each Office application. The active tab in Figure 1.7 is the Home tab.

> **MAC TIP:** Office for Mac does not display group names in the ribbon by default. On a Mac, to display group names on the ribbon, click the application name menu (Word, Excel, PowerPoint) and select Preferences. Click View and click to select Show group titles in the Ribbon section of the View dialog box.

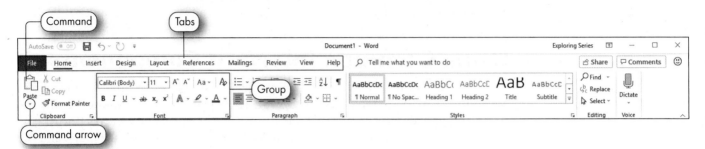

FIGURE 1.7 The Ribbon

As shown in Figure 1.7, some ribbon commands, such as Paste in the Clipboard group, contain two parts: the main command and an arrow. The arrow may be below or to the right of the main command, depending on the command, window size, or screen resolution. When selected, the arrow brings up additional commands or options associated with the main command. For example, selecting the Paste arrow enables you to access the Paste Options commands, and the Font color arrow displays a set of colors from which to choose. Instructions in the *Exploring* series use the command name to instruct you to click the main command to perform the default action, such as click Paste. Instructions include the word *arrow* when you need to select the arrow to access an additional option, such as click the Paste arrow.

Office applications enable you to work with objects such as images, shapes, charts, and tables. When you include such objects in a project, they are considered separate components that you can manage independently. To work with an object, you must first select it. When an object is selected, the ribbon is modified to include one or more **contextual tabs** that contain groups of commands related to the selected object. These tabs are designated as Tool tabs; for example, Picture Tools is the contextual tab that displays when a picture is selected. When the object is no longer selected, the contextual tab disappears.

Word, PowerPoint, Excel, and Access all share a similar ribbon structure. Although the specific tabs, groups, and commands vary among the Office programs, the way in which you use the ribbon and the descriptive nature of tab titles is the same, regardless of which program you are using. For example, if you want to insert a chart in Excel, a header in Word, or a shape in PowerPoint, those commands are found on the Insert tab in those programs. The first thing you should do as you begin to work with an Office application is to study the ribbon. Look at all tabs and their contents. That way, you will have a good idea of where to find specific commands, and how the ribbon with which you are currently working differs from one that you might have used in another application.

STEP 3 Use a Dialog Box and Gallery

Some commands and features do not display on the ribbon because they are not as commonly used. For example, you might want to apply a special effect such as Small caps or apply character spacing to some text. Because these effects are not found on the ribbon, they will most likely be found in a **dialog box** (in this case, the Font dialog box). When you open a dialog box, you gain access to more precise or less frequently used commands. Dialog boxes are accessed by clicking a **Dialog Box Launcher** ⌐, found in the lower right corner of some ribbon groups. Figure 1.8 shows the Font group Dialog Box Launcher and the Font dialog box.

> **MAC TIP:** Dialog box launchers are not available in Office for Mac. Instead, click a menu option such as Format, Edit, or Insert for additional options.

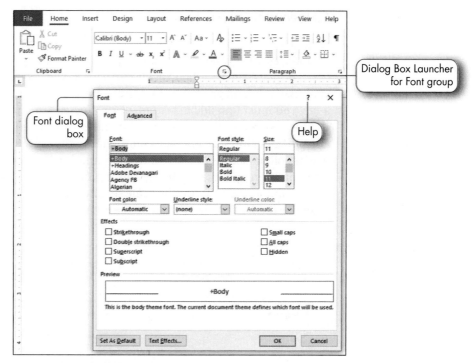

FIGURE 1.8 The Font Dialog Box in Word

TIP: GETTING HELP WITH DIALOG BOXES
You will find commands or options in a dialog box that you are not familiar with. Click the Help button that displays as a question mark in the top-right corner of the dialog box. The subsequent Help window offers suggestions or assistance in implementing the relevant feature.

Similarly, some formatting and design options are too numerous to include in the ribbon's limited space. For example, the Styles group displays on the Home tab of the Word ribbon. Because there are more styles than can easily display at once, the Styles group can be expanded to display a gallery of additional styles. A ***gallery*** is an Office feature that displays additional formatting and design options. Galleries in Excel and PowerPoint provide additional choices of chart styles and slide themes, respectively. Figure 1.9 shows an example of a PowerPoint Themes gallery. From the ribbon, you can display a gallery of additional choices by clicking More ⬇, which is located at the bottom right of the group's scroll bar found in some ribbon selections (see Figure 1.9).

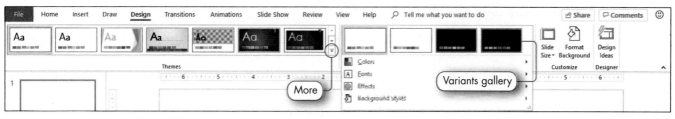

FIGURE 1.9 The Variants Gallery in PowerPoint

When editing a document, worksheet, or presentation, it is helpful to see the results of formatting changes before you make final selections. The feature that displays a preview of the results of a selection is called ***Live Preview***. For example, you might be considering modifying the color of an image in a document or worksheet. As you place the pointer over a color selection in a ribbon gallery or group, the selected image will temporarily display the color to which you are pointing. Similarly, you can get a preview of how theme designs would display on PowerPoint slides by pointing to specific themes in the PowerPoint Themes group and noting the effect on a displayed slide. When you click the item, the selection is applied. Live Preview is available in various ribbon selections among the Office applications.

Customize the Ribbon

Although the ribbon is designed to put the tasks you need most in an easily accessible location, there may be tasks that are specific to your job or hobby that are on various tabs, or not displayed on the ribbon at all. In this case, you can personalize the ribbon by creating your own tabs and group together the commands you want to use. To add a command to a tab, you must first add a custom group. You can create as many new tabs and custom groups with as many commands as you need. You can also create a custom group on any of the default tabs and add commands to the new group or hide any commands you use less often (see Figure 1.10). Keep in mind that when you customize the ribbon, the customization applies only to the Office program in which you are working at the time. If you want a new tab with the same set of commands in both Word and PowerPoint, for example, the new tab would need to be created in each application.

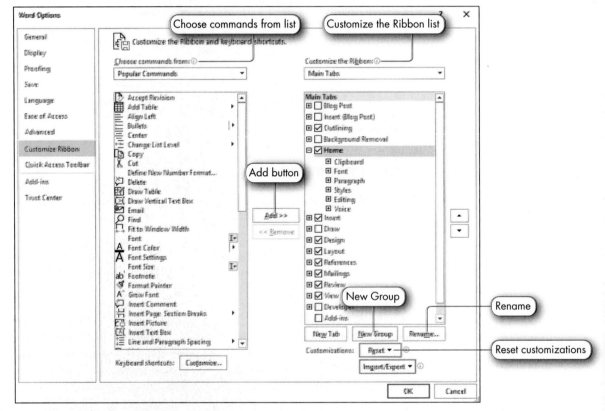

FIGURE 1.10 Customize the Ribbon in Word

There are several ways to access the Customize the Ribbon options:

- Right-click in an empty space in the ribbon and select Customize the Ribbon on the shortcut menu.
- Click the File tab, select Options, and then select Customize Ribbon.
- Click the Customize Quick Access Toolbar button, select More Commands, and then select Customize Ribbon.

The left side of the Customize the Ribbon window displays popular commands associated with the active application, but all available commands can be displayed by selecting All Commands in the *Choose commands from* list. On the right side of the Customize the Ribbon window is a list of the Main Tabs and Groups in the active application. You can also access the contextual Tool tabs by selecting the arrow in the Customize the Ribbon list and selecting Tool Tabs.

To customize the ribbon by adding a command to an existing tab, complete the following steps:

1. Click the File tab, click Options, and then select Customize Ribbon. (Alternatively, follow the other steps above to access the Customize the Ribbon window.)
2. Click the tab name that you want to add a group to under the Customize the Ribbon list. Ensure a blue background displays behind the tab name. Note that checking or unchecking the tab is not selecting the tab for this feature.
3. Click New Group. New Group (Custom) displays as a group on the selected tab.
4. Click Rename and give the new group a meaningful name.
5. Click the command to be added under the Choose commands from list.
6. Click Add.
7. Repeat as necessary, click OK when you have made all your selections.

On a Mac, to customize the ribbon, complete the following steps:

1. Click the Word menu (or whichever application you are working in) and select Preferences.
2. Click Ribbon & Toolbar in the Authoring and Proofing Tools (or in Excel, Authoring).
3. Click the plus sign at the bottom of the Main Tabs box and select New Group.
4. Click the Settings icon and click Rename. Give the new group a meaningful name. Click Save.
5. Continue using steps 5 and 6 in the PC step box above.

To revert all tabs or to reset select tabs to original settings, click Reset, and then click Reset all customizations or Reset only selected Ribbon tab (refer to Figure 1.10).

STEP 4 ▸ Use and Customize the Quick Access Toolbar

The **Quick Access Toolbar (QAT)**, located at the top-left corner of every Office application window (refer to Figure 1.6), provides one-click access to commonly executed tasks. By default, the QAT includes commands for saving a file and for undoing or redoing recent actions. You can recover from a mistake by clicking Undo on the QAT. If you click the Undo command arrow on the QAT, you can select from a list of previous actions in order of occurrence. The Undo list is not maintained when you close a file or exit the application, so you can only erase an action that took place during the current Office session. You can also Redo (or Replace) an action that you have just undone.

You can also customize the QAT to include commands you frequently use (see Figure 1.11). One command you may want to add is Quick Print. Rather than clicking

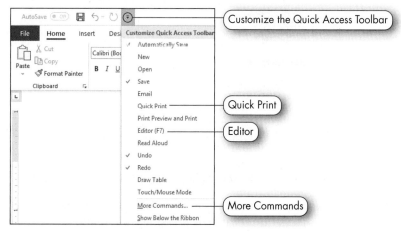

FIGURE 1.11 Customize the Quick Access Toolbar

the File tab, selecting Print, and then selecting various print options, you can add Quick Print to the QAT so that with one click you can print your document with the default Print settings. Other convenient commands can be added, such as Editor to run a spell check of the document.

You customize the QAT by selecting Customize Quick Access Toolbar arrow on the right side of the displayed QAT commands or by right-clicking an empty area on the QAT, and then selecting or deselecting the options from the displayed list of commands. Alternatively, you can right-click any command on the ribbon and select Add to Quick Access Toolbar from the shortcut menu.

To remove a command from the QAT, right-click the command and select Remove from Quick Access Toolbar. If you want to move the QAT to display under the ribbon, select Customize Quick Access Toolbar and click Show below the Ribbon.

STEP 5 ## Use a Shortcut Menu

In Office, you can usually accomplish the same task in several ways. Although the ribbon and QAT provide efficient access to commands, in some situations you might find it more convenient to access the same commands on a shortcut menu. A ***shortcut menu*** is a context-sensitive menu that displays commands and options relevant to the active object. Shortcut menus are accessed by selecting text or an object or by placing the insertion point in a document and pressing the right mouse button or pressing the right side of a trackpad. (On a Mac, press the Control key when you tap the mouse or use a two-finger tap on a trackpad). The shortcut menu will always include options to cut, copy, and paste. In addition, a shortcut menu features tasks that are specifically related to the document content where the insertion point is placed. For example, if your insertion point is on a selected word or group of words, the shortcut menu would include tasks such as to find a synonym or add a comment. If the active object is a picture, the shortcut menu includes options to group objects, provide a caption, or wrap text. As shown in Figure 1.12, when right-clicking a slide thumbnail in PowerPoint, the shortcut menu displays options to add a new slide, duplicate or delete slides, or to change slide layout.

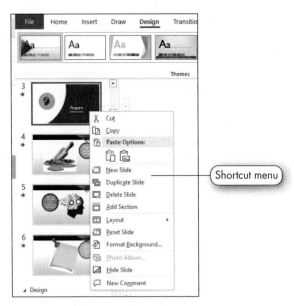

FIGURE 1.12 A Shortcut Menu in PowerPoint

Use Keyboard Shortcuts

Another way to simplify initiating commands is to use ***keyboard shortcuts***. Keyboard shortcuts are created by pressing combinations of two or more keys to initiate a software command. Keyboard shortcuts are viewed as being more efficient because you do not have to take your fingers off the keyboard. Some of the most common keyboard shortcuts in Office include Ctrl+C (Copy), Ctrl+X (Cut), Ctrl+V (Paste), and Ctrl+Z (Undo). Pressing Ctrl+Home moves the insertion point to the beginning of a Word document, to cell A1 in Excel, or to the first PowerPoint slide. To move to the end of those files, press Ctrl+End. There are many other keyboard shortcuts. To discover a keyboard shortcut for a command, point to a command icon on the ribbon to display the ScreenTip. If a keyboard shortcut exists, it will display in the ScreenTip. Many similar keyboard shortcuts exist for Office for Mac applications; however, press the Command key rather than the Ctrl key, such as Command+C for Copy.

TIP: USING KEYTIPS

Another way to use shortcuts, especially those that do not have a keyboard shortcut, is to press Alt to display KeyTips. You can use KeyTips to do tasks quickly without using the mouse by pressing a few keys—no matter where you are in an Office program. You can get to every command on the ribbon by using an access key—usually by pressing two to four keys sequentially. To stop displaying KeyTips, press Alt again.

Getting Help

No matter whether you are a skilled or a novice user of an Office application, there are times when you need help in either finding a certain ribbon command or need additional assistance or training for a task. Fortunately, there are features included in every Office application to offer you support.

STEP 6 ## Use the Tell Me Box

To the right of the last ribbon tab is a magnifying glass icon and the phrase "Tell me what you want to do." This is the **_Tell me box_** (see Figure 1.13). Use Tell me to enter words and phrases to search for help and information about a command or task you want to perform. Alternatively, use Tell me for a shortcut to a command or, in some instances (like Bold), to complete the action for you. Tell me can also help you research or define a term you entered. Perhaps you want to find an instance of a word in your document and replace it with another word but cannot locate the Find command on the ribbon. As shown in Figure 1.13, you can type _find_ in the Tell me box and a list of commands related to the skill will display, including Find & Select and Replace. Find & Select gives options for the Find command. If you click Replace, the Find and Replace dialog box opens without you having to locate the command on the ribbon.

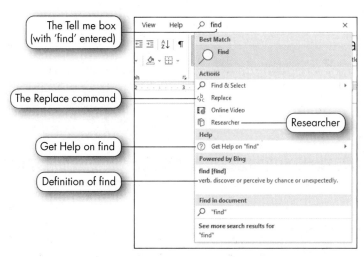

FIGURE 1.13 The Tell Me Box

Should you want to read about the feature instead of applying it, you can click *Get Help on "find,"* which will open Office Help for the feature. Another feature is Smart Lookup on the References tab. This feature opens the Smart Lookup pane that shows results from various online sources based on the search term. ***Smart Lookup*** provides information about tasks or commands in Office and can also be used to search for general information on a topic, such as *President George Washington*. Smart Lookup is also available on the shortcut menu when you right-click text as well as on the References tab in Word. Depending on your search, Researcher may display instead of, or in addition to, Smart Lookup. Researcher can be used to find quotes, citable sources, and images. Researcher is shown in Figure 1.13.

Use the Help Tab

If you are looking for additional help or training on certain features in any Microsoft Office application, you can access this support on the Help tab (see Figure 1.14). The Help command opens the Help pane with a list of tutorials on a variety of application-specific topics. Show Training displays application-specific training videos in the Help pane. Besides Help and Show Training, the Help tab also includes means to contact Microsoft support and to share your feedback. If you are using Office 365, you receive periodic updates with new features as they are released. To learn more about these features, or simply to discover what a new or previous update includes, use the What's New command. What's New brings you to a webpage that discusses all the newly added features organized by release date. You can also access What's New by clicking Account in Backstage view.

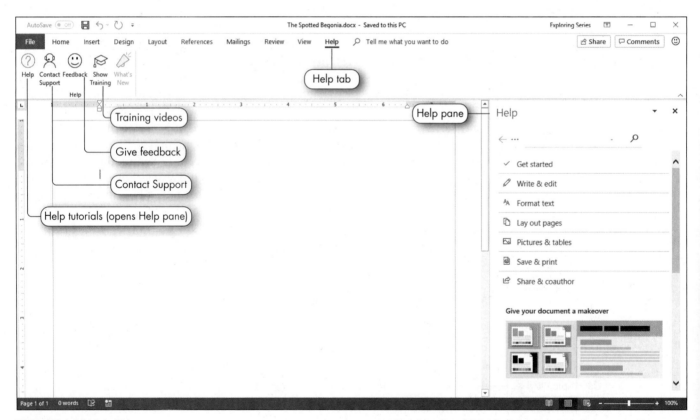

FIGURE 1.14 Help Tab

Use Enhanced ScreenTips

As you use the commands on the ribbon, there may be some that you would like to know more about its purpose, or would like assurance that you are selecting the correct command. For quick summary information on the name and purpose of a command button, point to the command until an **Enhanced ScreenTip** displays, with the name and a brief description of the command. If applicable, a keyboard shortcut is also included. Some ScreenTips include a *Tell me more* option for additional help. The Enhanced ScreenTip, shown for **Format Painter** in Figure 1.15, provides a short description of the command in addition to the steps that discuss how to use Format Painter. Use Format Painter to copy all applied formatting from one set of text to another.

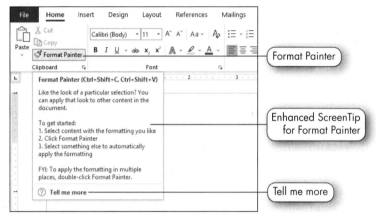

FIGURE 1.15 Enhanced ScreenTip

TIP: COPY FORMAT WITH FORMAT PAINTER
Use Format Painter to quickly apply the same formatting, such as color, font style, and size to other text. Format Painter can also be used to copy border styles to shapes. Format Painter is available in Word, Excel, and PowerPoint, and can be extremely useful when applying multiple formats to other text. Using Format Painter also ensures consistency in appearance between sets of text. To copy formatting to one location, single-click Format Painter, and then click where you want the format applied. To copy formatting to multiple locations, double-click Format Painter. Press Esc or click Format Painter again to turn off the command.

Installing Add-ins

As complete as the Office applications are, you still might want an additional feature that is not a part of the program. Fortunately, there are Microsoft and third-party programs called add-ins that you can add to the program. An **add-in** is a custom program that extends the functionality of a Microsoft Office application (see Figure 1.16). For example, in PowerPoint, you could add capability for creating diagrams, access free images, or obtain assistance with graphic design. In Excel, add-ins could provide additional functionality that can help with statistics and data mining. In Word, add-ins could provide survey or resume-creating capabilities. Some add-ins will be available for several applications. For example, the Pickit image app shown in Figure 1.16 is available for Word and PowerPoint. You can access add-ins through the My Add-ins or Get Add-ins commands on the Insert tab. Some templates may come with an add-in associated with it. Some add-ins are available for free, whereas others may have a cost.

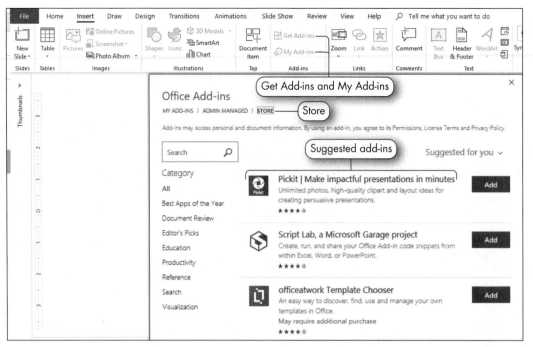

FIGURE 1.16 Add-ins for PowerPoint

Quick Concepts

1. Explain the benefits of logging in with your Microsoft account. ***p. 5***

2. Describe when you would use Save and when you would use Save As when saving a document. ***p. 7***

3. Explain how the ribbon is organized. ***p. 9***

4. Describe the Office application features that are available to assist you in getting help with a task. ***p. 15***

Hands-On Exercises

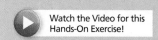
Watch the Video for this Hands-On Exercise!

Skills covered: Open a Saved File • Save a File • Use a Shortcut Menu • Use the Tell me Box

1 Get Started with Office Applications

The Spotted Begonia Art Gallery just hired several new clerical assistants to help you develop materials for the various activities coming up throughout the year. A coworker sent you a letter and asked for your assistance in making a few minor formatting changes. The letter is an invitation to the *Discover the Artist in You!* program Children's Art Festival. To begin, you will open Word and open an existing document. You will use the Shortcut menu to make simple changes to the document. Finally, you will use the Tell me box to apply a style to the first line of text.

STEP 1 OPEN AND SAVE A FILE

You start Microsoft Word and open an event invitation letter that you will later modify. You rename the file to preserve the original and to save the changes you will make later. Refer to Figure 1.17 as you complete Step 1.

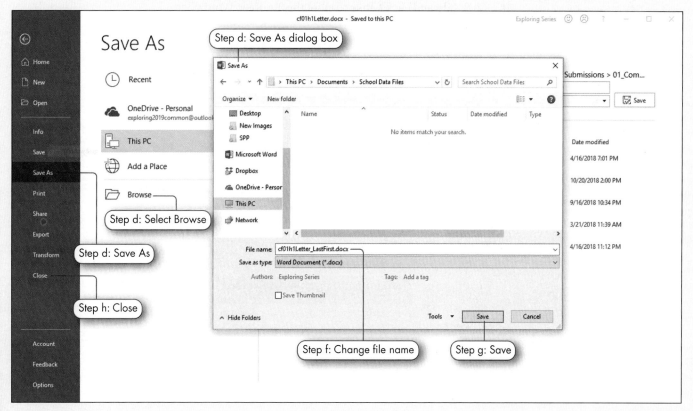

FIGURE 1.17 The Save As Dialog Box

a. Open the Word document *cf01h1Letter*.

The event invitation letter opens.

> **TROUBLESHOOTING:** When you open a file from the student files associated with this book, you may see an Enable Content warning in the Message Bar. This is a security measure to alert a user when there is potentially unsafe content in the file you want to open. You may be confident of the trustworthiness of the files for this book, and should click Enable Content to begin working on the file.

b. Click the **File tab**, click **Save As**, and then click **Browse** to display the Save As dialog box.

Because you will change the name of an existing file, you use the Save As command to give the file a new name. On a Mac, click the File menu and click Save As.

c. Navigate to the location where you are saving your files.

If you are saving the file in a different location than that of your data files, then you will also change the location of where the file is saved.

d. Click in the **File name box** (or the Save As box in Office for Mac) and type **cf01h1Letter_LastFirst**.

You save the document with a different name to preserve the original file.

When you save files, use your last and first names. For example, as the Common Features author, I would name my document "cf01h1Letter_PoatsyMaryAnne."

e. Click **Save**.

> **TROUBLESHOOTING:** If you make any major mistakes in this exercise, you can close the file, open *cf01h1Letter* again, and then start this exercise over.

The file is now saved as cf01h1Letter_LastFirst. Check the title bar of the document to confirm that the file has been saved with the correct name.

f. Click **File** and click **Close** to close the file. Keep Word open.

STEP 2 OPEN A SAVED FILE AND USE THE RIBBON

You now have time to modify the letter, so you open the saved file. You use ribbon commands to modify parts of the letter. Refer to Figure 1.18 as you complete Step 2.

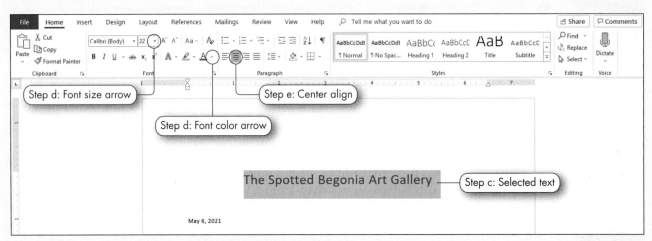

FIGURE 1.18 Use Ribbon Commands to Modify Text

a. Click the **File tab** and click **Open** from the left menu.

The Open window displays.

b. Click **cf01h1Letter_LastFirst** from the list of Recent documents on the right side of the Open window.

The letter you saved earlier opens and is ready to be modified.

c. Place the insertion point in the left margin just before the first line of text *The Spotted Begonia Art Gallery* so an angled right-pointing arrow displays and click.

This is an efficient way of selecting an entire line of text. Alternatively, you can drag the pointer across the text while holding down the left mouse button to select the text.

d. Click the **Font color arrow** in the Font group on the Home tab and select **Blue** in the Standard Colors section. With the text still selected, click the **Font Size arrow** in the Font group and select **22**.

You have changed the color and size of the Art Gallery's name.

e. Click **Center** in the Paragraph group.

f. Click **File** and click **Save**.

Because the file has already been saved, and the name and location are not changing, you use the Save command to save the changes.

USE A DIALOG BOX AND GALLERY

Some of the modifications you want to make to the letter require using tasks that are in dialog boxes and galleries. You will use a Dialog Box Launcher and More to expand the galleries to access the needed commands and features. Refer to Figure 1.19 as you complete Step 3.

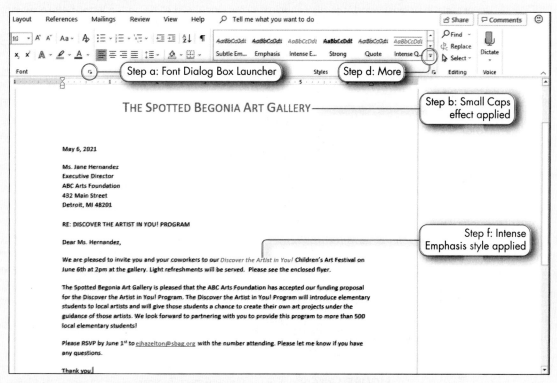

FIGURE 1.19 Use a Dialog Box and Gallery

a. Select the text **The Spotted Begonia Art Gallery**, if it is not already selected. Click the **Font Dialog Box Launcher** in the Font group.

The Font dialog box displays.

> **MAC TROUBLESHOOTING:** Office for Mac does not have Dialog Box Launchers. Instead, open a menu and select an option. For example, to access Font options that display in the Font Dialog Box, click the Format menu, and then click Font.

b. Click the **Small caps check box** in the Effects section to select it and click **OK**.

The Small caps text effect is applied to the selected text.

c. Place the insertion point immediately to the left of the text *Discover the Artist in You!* in the first sentence of the paragraph beginning *We are pleased*. Hold the left mouse button down and drag the pointer to select the text up to and including the exclamation point.

> **TROUBLESHOOTING:** Be sure the file you are working on is displayed as a full window. Otherwise, use the vertical scroll bar to bring the paragraph into view.

d. Click **More** in the Styles group to display the Styles gallery. (On a Mac, click the right gallery arrow or click the down arrow to view more options.)

e. Point to Heading 1 style.

Notice how Live Preview shows how that effect will look on the selected text.

f. Click **Intense Emphasis**.

The Intense Emphasis style is applied to the program name.

g. Click **File** and click **Save**.

STEP 4 USE AND CUSTOMIZE THE QUICK ACCESS TOOLBAR

You make a change to the document and immediately change your mind. You use the Undo button on the QAT to revert to the original word. You also anticipate checking the spelling on the letter before sending it out. Because you use Spell Check often, you decide to add the command to the QAT. Finally, you realize that you could be saving the document more efficiently by using Save on the QAT. Refer to Figure 1.20 as you complete Step 4.

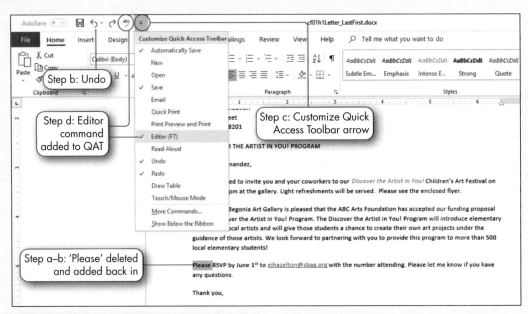

FIGURE 1.20 Customize the Quick Access Toolbar

a. Scroll down so the third paragraph beginning with *Please RSVP* is visible. Double-click **Please** and press **Delete** on the keyboard.

Please is deleted from the letter, but you decide to add it back in.

b. Click **Undo** on the QAT.

Please displays again.

c. Click the **Customize Quick Access Toolbar arrow** on the right side of the QAT.

A list of commands that can be added to the QAT displays.

d. Click **Editor**.

The Editor icon displays on the QAT so you can check for spelling, grammar, and writing issues.

e. Click **Save** on the QAT.

The letter inviting Ms. Hernandez also extends the invitation to her coworkers. Ms. Hazelton has asked that you use a different word for coworkers, so you use a shortcut menu to find a synonym. Refer to Figure 1.21 as you complete Step 5.

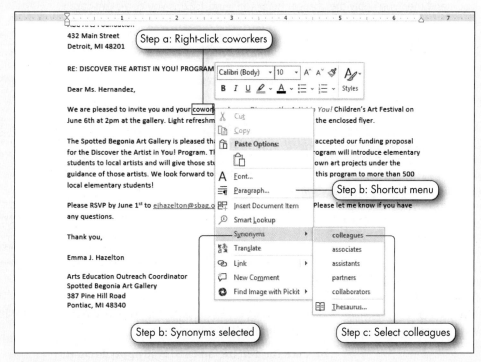

FIGURE 1.21 Use the Shortcut Menu to Find a Synonym

a. Point to and right-click the word **coworkers** in the first sentence of the letter that starts with *We are pleased*.

A shortcut menu displays.

MAC TROUBLESHOOTING: To open a shortcut menu, use Control+click.

---

b. Select **Synonyms** on the shortcut menu.

A list of alternate words for coworkers displays.

c. Select **colleagues** from the list.

The synonym *colleagues* replaces the word *coworkers*.

d. Click **Save** on the QAT.

You would like to apply the Intense Effect style you used to format *Discover the Artist in You!* to other instances of the program name in the second paragraph. You think there is a more efficient way of applying the same format to other text, but you do not know how to complete the task. Therefore, you use the Tell me box to search for the command and then you apply the change. Refer to Figure 1.22 as you complete Step 6.

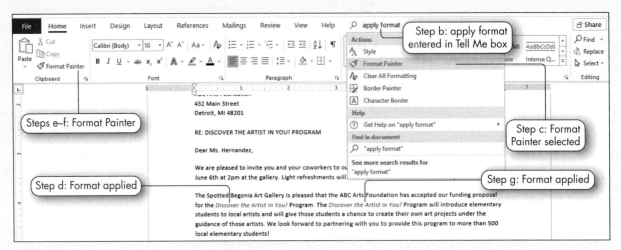

FIGURE 1.22 Use the Tell Me Box

a. Click anywhere in the text **Discover the Artist in You!** in the first sentence of the letter that starts with *We are pleased.*

b. Click the **Tell me box** and type **apply format**.

   The Tell me box displays a list of options related to apply format.

c. Select **Format Painter** from the list of options in the Tell Me results.

   Notice that the Format Painter command in the Clipboard group is selected and a paint-brush is added to the insertion point ▲I.

d. Drag the pointer over the first instance of **Discover the Artist in You!** in the second line of the second paragraph beginning with *The Spotted Begonia.*

   The Intense Emphasis style was applied to the selected text.

> **TROUBLESHOOTING:** If the format is not applied to the text, move to the next step, but double-click Format Painter and apply the format to both instances of Discover the Artist in You!

e. Point to **Format Painter** in the Clipboard group and read the Enhanced ScreenTip.

   You notice that to apply formatting to more than one selection, you must double-click Format Painter, but because you need to apply the format to only one more set of text, you will single-click the command.

f. Click **Format Painter** in the Clipboard group.

g. Drag the pointer over the second instance of **Discover the Artist in You!** in the second paragraph beginning with *The Spotted Begonia.*

   You used the Format Painter to copy the formatting applied to text to other text.

> **TROUBLESHOOTING:** Press Esc on the keyboard to turn off Format Painter if you had to double-click Format Painter in Step d above.

h. Save and close the document. You will submit this file to your instructor at the end of the last Hands-On Exercise.

Format Document Content

In the process of creating a document, worksheet, or presentation, you will most likely make some formatting changes. You might center a title, or format budget worksheet totals as currency. You can change the font so that typed characters are larger or in a different style. You might even want to bold text to add emphasis. Sometimes, it may be more efficient to start with a document that has formatting already applied or apply a group of coordinated fonts, font styles, and colors. You might also want to add, delete, or reposition text. Inserting and formatting images can add interest to a document or illustrate content. Finally, no document is finished until all spelling and grammar has been checked and all errors removed.

In this section, you will explore themes and templates. You will learn to use the Mini Toolbar to quickly make formatting changes. You will learn how to select and edit text, as well as check your grammar and spelling. You will learn how to move, copy, and paste text, and how to insert pictures. And, finally, you will learn how to resize and format pictures and graphics.

Using Templates and Applying Themes

You can enhance your documents by using a template or applying a theme. A ***template*** is a predesigned file that incorporates formatting elements and layouts and may include content that can be modified. A ***theme*** is a collection of design choices that includes colors, fonts, and special effects used to give a consistent look to a document, workbook, or presentation. Microsoft provides high-quality templates and themes, designed to make it faster and easier to create professional-looking documents.

STEP 1 ### Open a Template

When you launch any Office program and click New, the screen displays thumbnail images of a sampling of templates for that application (see Figure 1.23). Alternatively, if you are already working in an application, click the File tab and select New on the Backstage

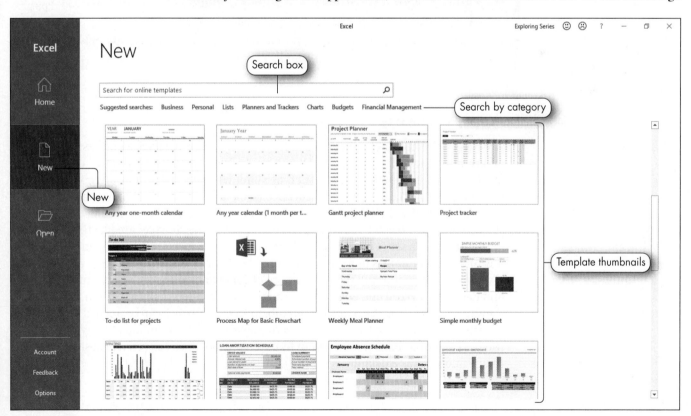

FIGURE 1.23 Templates in Excel

Navigation Pane. One benefit of starting with a template is if you know only a little bit about the software, with only a few simple changes you would have a well-formatted document that represents your specific needs. Even if you know a lot about the program, starting with a template can be much more efficient than if you designed it yourself from a blank file. Templates in Excel often use complex formulas and formatting to achieve a dynamic workbook that would automatically adjust with only a few inputs. Using a resume template in Word greatly simplifies potentially complex formatting, enabling you to concentrate on just inputting your personal experiences. PowerPoint templates can include single element slides (such as organization charts) but also include comprehensive presentations on topics such as Business Plans or a Quiz show game presentation similar to *Jeopardy!*

The Templates list is composed of template groups available within each Office application. The search box enables you to locate other templates that are available online. When you select a template, you can view more information about the template, including author information, a general overview about the template, and additional views (if applicable).

To search for and use a template, complete the following steps:

1. Open the Microsoft Office application with which you will be working. Or, if the application is already open, click File and click New.
2. Type a search term in the *Search for online templates box* or click one of the Suggested searches.
3. Scroll through the template options or after selecting a search term, use the list at the right to narrow your search further.
4. Select a template and review its information in the window that opens.
5. Click Create to open the template in the application.

On a Mac, to search for and use a template, complete the following steps:

1. Open the Microsoft Office application with which you will be working. Or, if the application is already open, click the File menu and click New from Template.
2. Continue with steps 2 through 5 in the PC steps above.

STEP 2 Apply a Theme

Applying a theme enables you to visually coordinate various page elements. Themes are different for each of the Office applications. In Word, a theme is a set of coordinating fonts, colors, and special effects, such as shadowing or glows, that are combined into a package to provide a stylish appearance (see Figure 1.24). In PowerPoint, a theme is a file that includes the formatting elements such as a background, a color scheme, and slide layouts that position content placeholders. Themes in Excel are like those in Word in that they are a set of coordinating fonts, colors, and special effects. Themes also affect any SmartArt or charts in a document, workbook, or presentation. Access also has a set of themes that coordinate the appearance of fonts and colors for objects such as Forms and Reports. In Word and PowerPoint, themes are accessed from the Design tab. In Excel, they are accessed from the Page Layout tab. In Access, themes can be applied to forms and reports and are accessed from the respective object's Tools Design tab. In any application, themes can be modified with different fonts, colors, or effects, or you can design your own theme and set it as a default.

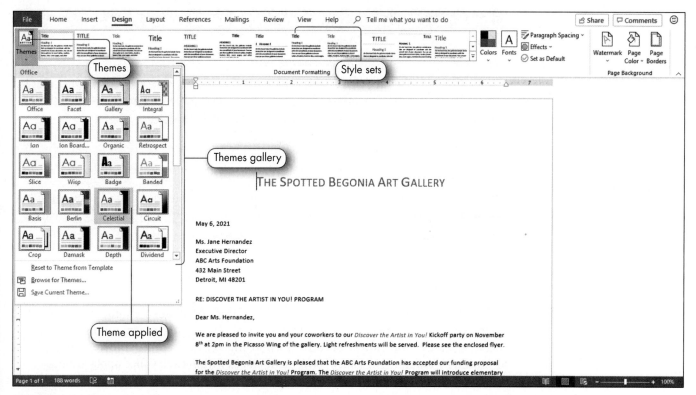

FIGURE 1.24 Themes in Word

Modifying Text

Formatting and modifying text in documents, worksheets, or presentations is an essential function when using Office applications. Centering a title, formatting cells, or changing the font color or size are tasks that occur frequently. In all Office applications, the Home tab provides tools for editing text.

STEP 3 ## Select Text

Before making any changes to existing text or numbers, you must first select the characters. A common way to select text or numbers is to place the pointer before the first character of the text you want to select, hold down the left mouse button, and then drag to highlight the intended selection. Note that in Word and PowerPoint when the pointer is used to select text in this manner, it takes on the shape of the letter *I*, called the *I-beam* $\boxed{\text{I}}$.

Sometimes it can be difficult to precisely select a small amount of text, such as a few letters or a punctuation mark. Other times, the task can be overwhelmingly large, such as when selecting an entire multi-page document. Or, you might need to select a single word, sentence, or paragraph. In these situations, you should use one of the shortcuts to selecting large or small blocks of text. The shortcuts shown in Table 1.2 are primarily applicable to text in Word and PowerPoint. When working with Excel, you will more often need to select multiple cells. To select multiple cells, drag the selection when the pointer displays as a large white plus sign $\boxed{\Leftrightarrow}$.

Once you have selected the text, besides applying formatting, you can delete or simply type over to replace the text.

TABLE 1.2 Shortcut Selection in Word and PowerPoint

Item Selected	Action
One word	Double-click the word.
One line of text	Place the pointer at the left of the line, in the margin area. When the pointer changes to an angled right-pointing arrow, click to select the line.
One sentence	Press and hold Ctrl and click in the sentence to select it.
One paragraph	Triple-click in the paragraph.
One character to the left of the insertion point	Press and hold Shift and press the left arrow on the keyboard.
One character to the right of the insertion point	Press and hold Shift and press the right arrow on the keyboard.
Entire document	Press and hold Ctrl and press A on the keyboard.

Format Text

At times, you will want to make the font size larger or smaller, change the font color, or apply other font attributes, for example, to emphasize key information such as titles, headers, dates, and times. Because formatting text is commonplace, Office places formatting commands in many convenient places within each Office application.

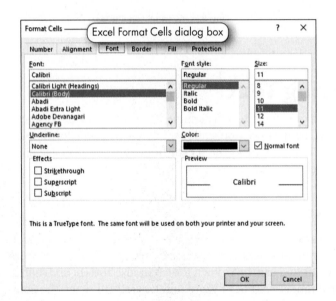

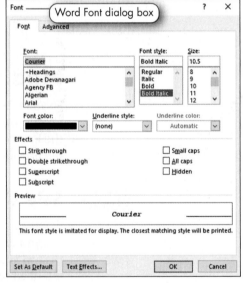

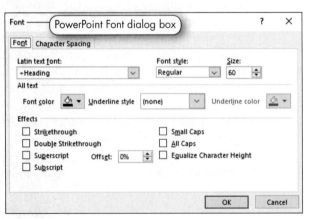

FIGURE 1.25 The Font Dialog Boxes

You can find the most common formatting commands in the Font group on the Home tab. As noted earlier, Word, Excel, and PowerPoint all share very similar Font groups that provide access to tasks related to changing the font, size, and color. Remember that you can place the pointer over any command icon to view a summary of the command's purpose, so although the icons might appear cryptic at first, you can use the pointer to quickly determine the purpose and applicability to your potential text change.

If the font change that you plan to make is not included as a choice on the Home tab, you may find what you are looking for in the Font dialog box. If you are making many formatting choices at once, using the Font dialog box may be more efficient. Depending on the application, the contents of the Font dialog box vary slightly, but the purpose is consistent—providing access to choices related to modifying characters (refer to Figure 1.25).

The way characters display onscreen or print in documents, including qualities such as size, spacing, and shape, is determined by the font. When you open a Blank document, you are opening the Normal template with an Office theme and the Normal style. The Office theme with Normal Style includes the following default settings: Calibri font, 11-point font size, and black font color. These settings remain in effect unless you change them. Some formatting commands, such as Bold and Italic, are called **toggle commands**. They act somewhat like a light switch that you can turn on and off. Once you have applied bold formatting to text, the Bold command is highlighted on the ribbon when that text is selected. To undo bold formatting, select the bold formatted text and click Bold again.

Use the Mini Toolbar

You have learned that you can always use commands on the Home tab of the ribbon to change selected text within a document, worksheet, or presentation. Although using the ribbon to select commands is simple enough, the **Mini Toolbar** provides another convenient way to accomplish some of the same formatting changes. When you select or right-click any amount of text within a worksheet, document, or presentation, the Mini Toolbar displays (see Figure 1.26) along with the shortcut menu. The Mini Toolbar provides access to the most common formatting selections, as well as access to styles and list options. Unlike the QAT, you cannot add or remove options from the Mini Toolbar. To temporarily remove the Mini Toolbar from view, press Esc. You can permanently disable the Mini Toolbar so that it does not display in any open file when text is selected by selecting Options on the File tab. Ensure the General tab is selected and deselect *Show Mini Toolbar on selection* in the User Interface options section.

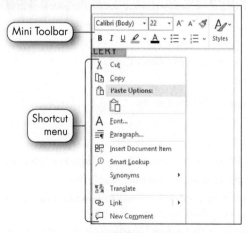

FIGURE 1.26 The Mini Toolbar and Shortcut Menu

Relocating Text

On occasion, you may want to relocate a section of text from one area of a Word document to another. Or suppose that you have included text on a PowerPoint slide that you believe would be more appropriate on a different slide. Or perhaps an Excel formula should be copied from one cell to another because both cells should show totals in a similar manner. In all these instances, you would use the cut, copy, and paste features found in the Clipboard group on the Home tab. The **Office Clipboard** is an area of memory reserved to temporarily hold selections that have been cut or copied and enables you to paste the selections to another location.

STEP 4 ## Cut, Copy, and Paste Text

To **cut** means to remove a selection from the original location and place it in the Office Clipboard. To **copy** means to duplicate a selection from the original location and place a copy in the Office Clipboard. To **paste** means to place a cut or copied selection into another location in a document. It is important to understand that cut or copied text remains in the Office Clipboard even after you paste it to another location. The Office Clipboard can hold up to 24 items at one time.

> **To cut or copy text, and paste to a new location, complete the following steps:**
>
> 1. Select the text you want to cut or copy.
> 2. Click the appropriate command in the Clipboard group either to cut or copy the selection.
> 3. Click the location where you want the cut or copied text to be placed. The location can be in the current file or in another open file within most Office applications.
> 4. Click Paste in the Clipboard group on the Home tab.

You can paste the same item multiple times, because it will remain in the Office Clipboard until you power down your computer or until the Office Clipboard exceeds 24 items. It is best practice to complete the paste process as soon after you have cut or copied text.

In addition to using the commands in the Clipboard group, you can also cut, copy, and paste by using the Mini Toolbar, a shortcut menu (right-clicking), or by keyboard shortcuts. These methods are listed in Table 1.3.

TABLE 1.3	Cut, Copy, and Paste Options
Command	**Actions**
Cut	• Click Cut in Clipboard group. • Right-click selection and select Cut. • Press Ctrl+X.
Copy	• Click Copy in Clipboard group. • Right-click selection and select Copy. • Press Ctrl+C.
Paste	• Click in destination location and select Paste in Clipboard group. • Click in destination location and press Ctrl+V. • Right-click in destination location and select one of the choices under Paste Options in the shortcut menu. • Click Clipboard Dialog Box Launcher to open Clipboard pane. Click in destination location. With Clipboard pane open, click the arrow beside the intended selection and select Paste.

Use the Office Clipboard

When you cut or copy selections, they are placed in the Office Clipboard. Regardless of which Office application you are using, you can view the Office Clipboard by clicking the Clipboard Dialog Box Launcher, as shown in Figure 1.27.

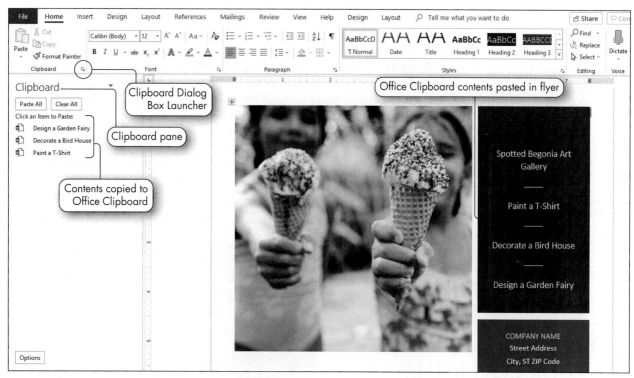

FIGURE 1.27 The Office Clipboard

Unless you specify otherwise when beginning a paste operation, the most recently added item to the Office Clipboard is pasted. If you know you will be cutting or copying and then pasting several items, rather than doing each individually, you can cut or copy all the items to the Office Clipboard, and then paste each or all Office Clipboard items to the new location. This is especially helpful if you are pasting the Office Clipboard items to a different Office file. Just open the new file, display the Clipboard pane, and select the item in the list to paste it into the document. The Office Clipboard also stores graphics that have been cut or copied. You can delete items from the Office Clipboard by clicking the arrow next to the selection in the Clipboard pane and selecting Delete. You can remove all items from the Office Clipboard by clicking Clear All. The Options button at the bottom of the Clipboard pane enables you to control when and where the Office Clipboard is displayed. Close the Clipboard pane by clicking the Close button in the top-right corner of the pane or by clicking the arrow in the title bar of the Clipboard pane and selecting Close.

Reviewing a Document

As you create or edit a file, and certainly as you finalize a file, you should make sure no spelling or grammatical errors exist. It is important that you carefully review your document for any spelling or punctuation errors, as well as any poor word choices before you send it along to someone else to read. Word, Excel, and PowerPoint all provide standard tools for proofreading, including a spelling and grammar checker and a thesaurus.

STEP 5 | Check Spelling and Grammar

Word and PowerPoint automatically check your spelling and grammar as you type. If a word is unrecognized, it is flagged as misspelled or grammatically incorrect. Misspellings are identified with a red wavy underline, and grammatical or word-usage errors (such as using *bear* instead of *bare*) have a blue double underline. Excel does not check spelling as you type, so it is important to run the spelling checker in Excel. Excel's spelling checker will review charts, pivot tables, and textual data entered in cells.

Although spelling and grammar is checked along the way, you may find it more efficient to use the spelling and grammar feature when you are finished with the document. The Check Document command is found on the Review tab in the Proofing group in Word. In Excel and PowerPoint the Spelling command is on the Review tab in the Proofing group. When it is selected, the Editor pane will open on the right. For each error, you are offered one or more suggestions as a correction. You can select a suggestion and click Change, or if it is an error that is made more than one time throughout the document, you can select Change All (see Figure 1.28). If an appropriate suggestion is not made, you can always enter a correction manually.

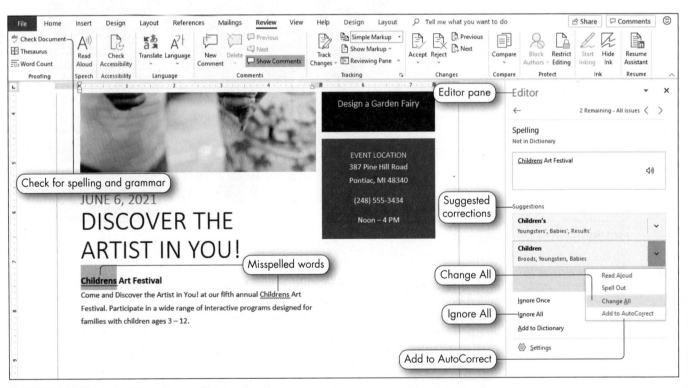

FIGURE 1.28 Using the Editor Pane to Correct Spelling

It is important to understand that the spelling and grammar check is not always correct, so you still need to proof a document thoroughly and review the errors carefully. For example, you might have a word that is truly misspelled in its context, but perhaps is still a valid word in the dictionary. Spell check might not pick it up as a misspelled word, but a careful read through would probably pick it up. There are times when the spelling and grammar check will indicate a word is misspelled and it really is not. This often happens with names or proper nouns or with new technical terms that may not be in the application's dictionary. In these instances, you can choose to Ignore, Ignore All, or Add. Choosing Ignore will skip the word without changing it. If you know there are multiple instances of that word throughout the document, you can choose Ignore All, and it will skip all instances of the word. Finally, if it is a word that is spelled correctly and that you use it often, you can choose to Add it to the dictionary, so it will not be flagged as an error in future spell checks.

If you right-click a word or phrase that is identified as a potential error, you will see a shortcut menu similar to that shown in Figure 1.29. The top of the shortcut menu will identify the type of error, whether it is spelling or grammar. A pane opens next to the shortcut menu with a list of options to correct the misspelling. These would be the same options that would display in the Editor pane if you ran the Spelling & Grammar command from the ribbon. Click on any option to insert it into the document. Similarly, you have the choices to Add to Dictionary or Ignore All. Each alternative also has options to Read Aloud or Add to AutoCorrect.

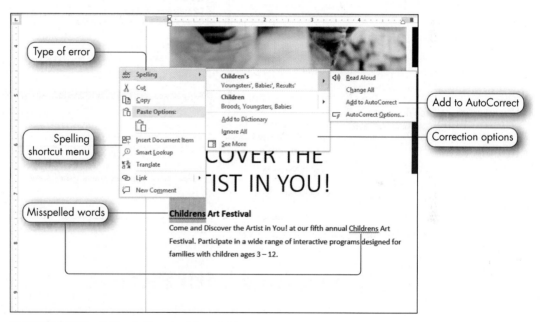

FIGURE 1.29 Spell Check Shortcut Menu options

You can use AutoCorrect to correct common typing errors, misspelled words, and capitalization errors, as well as to insert symbols (see Figure 1.30). There is a standard list of common errors and suggested replacements that is used in Excel, Word, and PowerPoint. So, if you type a word that is found in the Replace column, it will automatically be replaced with the replacement in the With column. For example, if you typed *accross* it would automatically correct to *across*. If you typed (tm) it would automatically change to the trademark symbol ™. You can add or delete terms and manage AutoCorrect by selecting Options from the File tab, and then in the Options dialog box, select Proofing and then click AutoCorrect Options.

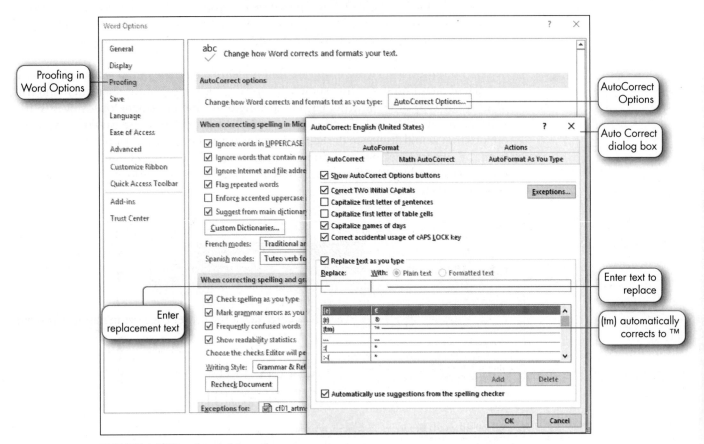

FIGURE 1.30 Proofing and AutoCorrect

Working with Pictures

Documents, worksheets, and presentations can include much more than just words and numbers. You can add energy and additional description to a project by including pictures and other graphic elements. A **picture** is just that—a digital photo. A picture can also be considered an illustration. Illustrations can also be shapes, icons, SmartArt, and Charts. While each of these types of illustrative objects have definitive differences, they are all handled basically the same when it comes to inserting and resizing. For the purposes of simplicity, the following discussion focuses on pictures, but the same information can be applied to any illustrative object you include in your document, worksheet, or presentation.

STEP 6 Insert Pictures

In Word, Excel, and PowerPoint, you can insert pictures from your own library of digital photos you have saved on your hard drive, OneDrive, or another storage medium. If you want a wider variety of pictures to choose from, you can search directly inside the Office program you are using for an online picture using Bing. Pictures and Online Pictures are found on the Insert tab.

To insert an online picture, complete the following steps:

1. Click in the file where you want the picture to be placed.
2. Click the Insert tab.
3. Click Online Pictures in the Illustrations group.
4. Type a search term in the Bing search box and press Enter.
5. Select an image and click Insert.

When the picture is inserted into a document, the Picture Tools Format tab displays. You can use these tools to modify the picture as needed.

TIP: CREATIVE COMMONS LICENSE

The Bing search filters are set to use the Creative Commons license system so the results display images that have been given a Creative Commons license. These are images and drawings that can be used more freely than images found directly on websites. Because there are different levels of Creative Commons licenses, you should read the Creative Commons license for each image you use to avoid copyright infringement.

STEP 7 ▶ Modify a Picture

Once you add a picture to your document, you may need to resize or adjust it. Before you make any changes to a picture, you must first select it. When the picture is selected, eight sizing handles display on the corners and in the middle of each edge (see Figure 1.31) and the Picture Tools tab displays on the ribbon. To adjust the size while maintaining the proportions, place your pointer on one of the corner sizing handles, and while holding the left mouse button down, drag the pointer on an angle upward or downward to increase or decrease the size, respectively. If you use one of the center edge sizing handles, you will

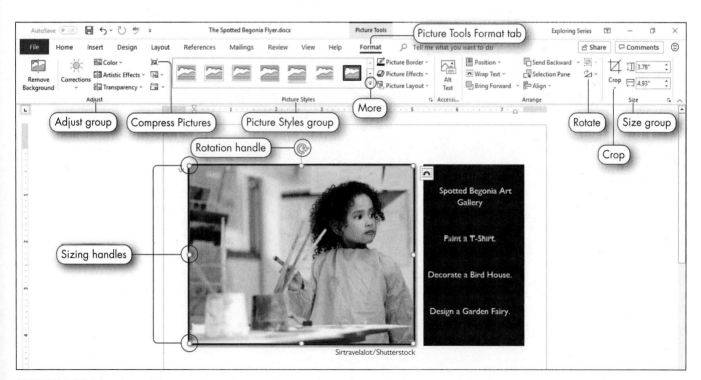

FIGURE 1.31 Formatting a Picture

stretch or shrink the picture out of proportion. In addition to sizing handles, a rotation handle displays at the top of the selected image. Use this to turn the image. For more precise controls, use the Size and Rotate commands on the Picture Tools Format tab. When a picture is selected, the Picture Tools Format tab includes options for modifying a picture. You can apply a picture style or effect, as well as add a picture border, from selections in the Picture Styles group. Click More to view a gallery of picture styles. As you point to a style, the style is shown in Live Preview, but the style is not applied until you select it. Options in the Adjust group simplify changing a color scheme, applying creative artistic effects, and even adjusting the brightness, contrast, and sharpness of an image (refer to Figure 1.31).

If a picture contains areas that are not necessary, you can crop it, which is the process of trimming edges that you do not want to display. The Crop tool is located on the Picture Tools Format tab (refer to Figure 1.31). Even though cropping enables you to adjust the amount of a picture that displays, it does not actually delete the portions that are cropped out. Therefore, you can later recover parts of the picture, if necessary. Cropping a picture does not reduce the file size of the picture or the document in which it displays. If you want to permanently remove the cropped portions of a figure and reduce the file size, you must compress the picture. Compress Pictures is found in the Adjust group on the Picture Tools Format tab (refer to Figure 1.31).

Quick Concepts

5. Discuss the differences between themes and templates. ***p. 25***

6. Discuss several ways text can be modified. ***p. 27***

7. Explain how the Office Clipboard is used when relocating text. ***p. 31***

8. Explain how to review a document for spelling and grammar. ***p. 32***

9. Explain why it is important to use the corner sizing handles of a picture when resizing. ***p. 35***

Hands-On Exercises

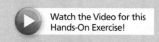 Watch the Video for this Hands-On Exercise!

Skills covered: Open a Template • Apply a Theme • Select Text • Format Text • Cut, Copy, and Paste Text • Check Spelling and Grammar • Insert a Picture • Modify a Picture

2 Format Document Content

As the administrative assistant for the Spotted Begonia Art Gallery, you want to create a flyer to announce the *Discover the Artist in You!* Children's Art Festival. You decide to use a template to help you get started more quickly and to take advantage of having a professionally formatted document without knowing much about Word. You will modify the flyer created with the template by adding and formatting your own content and changing out the photo.

STEP 1 OPEN A TEMPLATE

To facilitate making a nice-looking flyer, you review the templates that are available in Microsoft Word. You search for flyers and finally choose one that is appropriate for the event, knowing that you will be able to replace the photo with your own. Refer to Figure 1.32 as you complete Step 1.

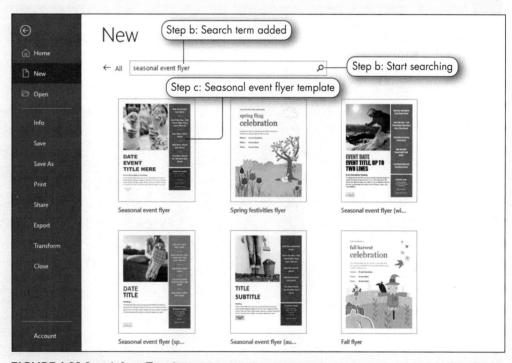

FIGURE 1.32 Search for a Template

a. Ensure Word is open. Click **File** and click **New**.

b. Type the search term **seasonal event flyer** in the *Search for online templates* box to search for event flyer templates. Click **Start searching**.

Your search results in a selection of event flyer templates.

c. Locate the Seasonal event flyer template as shown in Figure 1.32 and click to select it.

The template displays in a preview.

   d. Click **Create** to open the flyer template.

      The flyer template that you selected opens in Word.

   e. Click **Save** on the QAT.

      Because this is the first time you save the flyer file, clicking Save on the QAT opens the Save As window, in which you must indicate the location of the file and the file name.

   f. Click **Browse** to navigate to where you save your files. Save the document as **cf01h2Flyer_LastFirst**.

STEP 2 **APPLY A THEME**

You want to change the theme of the template for a different font effect and theme color that matches more of the Spotted Begonia Art Gallery's other documents. Refer to Figure 1.33 as you complete Step 2.

FIGURE 1.33 Select and Edit Text

   a. Click the **Design tab** and click **Themes** in the Document Formatting group.

      The Themes gallery displays.

   b. Point to a few themes and notice how the template changes with each different theme.

   c. Click **Gallery**.

      The Gallery theme is applied, changing the color of the banners, and modifying the font and font size.

   d. Save the document.

You will replace the template text to create the flyer, adding information such as a title, date, and description. After adding the text to the document, you will modify the formatting of the organization name in the flyer. Refer to Figure 1.34 as you complete Step 3.

FIGURE 1.34 Edit Placeholder Text

a. Scroll to see the **Date placeholder** in the main body of the text, click, and then type **June 6, 2021** in the placeholder.

b. Click the **Event Title Here placeholder** and type **Discover the Artist in You!** in the placeholder.

c. Press **Enter** and continue typing **Spotted Begonia Art Gallery**.

d. Click the **Event Description Heading placeholder** and type **Childrens Art Festival**. (Ignore the misspelling for now.)

e. Select each text placeholder in the bottom box of the right table column and replace the content in each text placeholder with the content from the right column below.

Placeholder	Text Typed Entry
Company Name	**Event Location**
Street Address City ST Zip Code	**387 Pine Hill Road Pontiac, MI 48340**
Telephone	**(248) 555-3434**
Web Address	**Noon – 4 PM**
Dates and Times	**Delete the text**

You modify the placeholders to customize the flyer.

f. Select the title text **Discover the Artist in You!**. Click the **Font arrow** on the Mini Toolbar. Select **Franklin Gothic Medium**.

The font is changed.

> **TROUBLESHOOTING:** If the Mini Toolbar does not display after selecting the text, right-click the selected text and select the font Franklin Gothic Medium.

g. Select the text **June 6, 2021**. Click the **Font Size arrow** on the Mini Toolbar. Select **26** on the Font Size menu.

The font size is changed to 26 pt.

h. Click **Save** on the QAT to save the document.

STEP 4 CUT, COPY, AND PASTE TEXT

You add descriptive text about the event. You then decide to move some of the text to the banner panel on the right. You also copy the sponsor's name to the top of the banner. Finally, you delete some unwanted placeholders. Refer to Figure 1.35 as you complete Step 4.

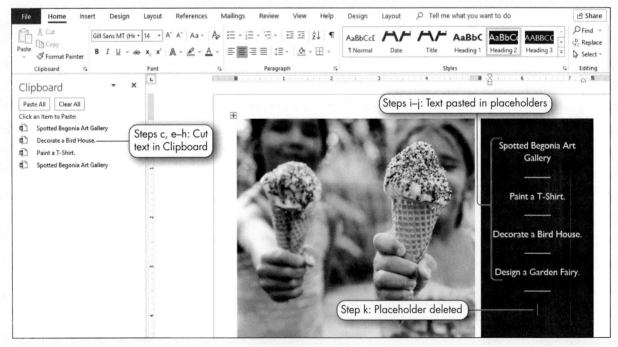

FIGURE 1.35 Use the Clipboard Commands

a. Select the **placeholder text** below Childrens Art Festival that begins with *To get started* and press **Delete**. Enter the following text and ignore any intentional misspellings. They will be corrected later.

Come and Discover the Artist in You! at our fifth annual Childrens Art Festival. Participate in a wide range of interactive programs designed for families with children ages 3–12. Paint a T-Shirt. Decorate a Bird House. Design a Garden Fairy.

b. Click the **YOUR LOGO HERE placeholder** and press **Delete**.

c. Select the text **Spotted Begonia Art Gallery**. Right-click the selected text and click **Cut** from the shortcut menu.

d. Scroll to the top of the flyer. Click the **Add Key Event Info Here! placeholder** in the right column. Click the **Home tab** and click **Paste** in the Clipboard group to paste the previously cut text.

The text is now moved to the banner.

e. Click the **Clipboard Dialog Box Launcher**.

The Office Clipboard displays. The cut text displays in the Clipboard pane.

MAC TROUBLESHOOTING: For Step e, use Command+X. Select the Don't be Shy . . . placeholder text and press Command+V. Repeat for Steps f and g below, using Command+X to cut the indicated text, and Command+V to paste the text in the two placeholders below Paint a T-Shirt.

---

f. Scroll to the paragraph at the bottom of the flyer beginning with Come and Discover. Select the text **Paint a T-Shirt.** (include the period) and press **Ctrl+X**.

Notice that the cut text selection is in the Office Clipboard.

g. Select the text **Decorate a Bird House.** from the text you entered in Step a and press **Ctrl+X**.

h. Select the text **Design a Garden Fairy.** from the text you entered in Step a and press **Ctrl+X**.

The Office Clipboard displays the three cut selections of text.

i. Scroll to the top of the flyer. Select the **Don't Be Shy . . . placeholder text** and click **Paint a T-Shirt** from the Office Clipboard.

The text in the Office Clipboard is pasted in a new location.

j. Repeat Step i, replacing **One More Point Here! placeholder text** with **Decorate a Bird House** and **Add More Great Info Here placeholder text** with **Design a Garden Fairy**.

k. Select the last **placeholder text** in the banner and press **Delete**.

l. Click **Clear All** in the Clipboard pane and close the Office Clipboard. Save the document.

Because this flyer will be seen by the public, it is important to check the spelling and grammar in your document. Refer to Figure 1.36 as you complete Step 5.

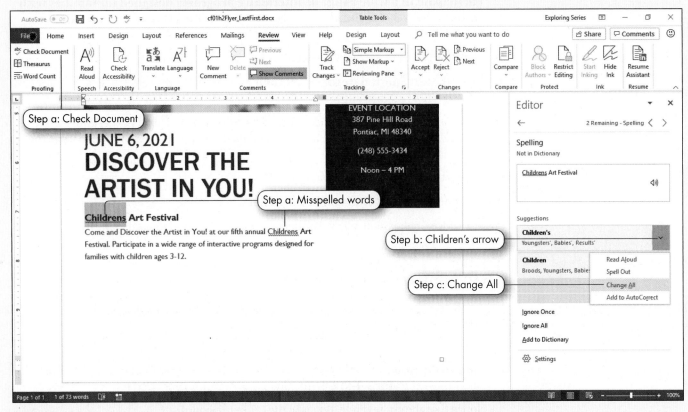

FIGURE 1.36 Check Spelling and Grammar

a. Press **Ctrl+Home**. Click the **Review tab** and click **Check Document** in the Proofing group.

The Editor pane opens and two spelling errors are identified.

b. Click Spelling in the Corrections box and click the **arrow** to the right of Children's in the Editor pane.

c. Select **Change All** to accept the suggested change to *Children's* in the Spelling pane for all instances. Make any other changes as needed. Click **OK** to close the dialog box.

The spelling and grammar check is complete.

d. Save the document.

You want to change the template image to an image that better reflects the children's event being held at the gallery. You use an image the Art Gallery director has provided you. Refer to Figure 1.37 as you complete Step 6.

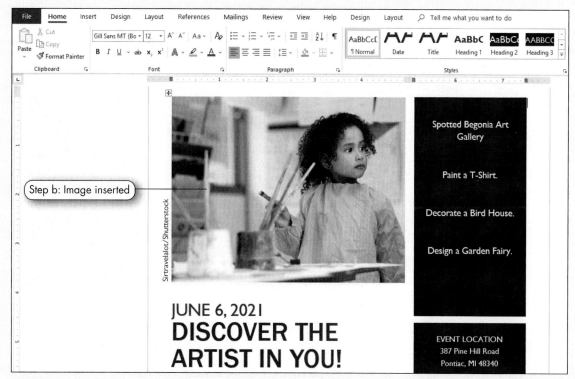

FIGURE 1.37 Insert Picture

a. Scroll to the top of the flyer. Click the **image** to select it and press **Delete**.

You have deleted the image you want to replace.

b. Click **Pictures** in the Illustrations group on the Home tab. Navigate to your Student Data files and select *cf01h2Art.jpg*. Click **Insert**.

The new image is placed in the document.

c. Save the document.

You want to make the picture stand out better, so you decide to add a border frame around the image. Refer to Figure 1.38 as you complete Step 7.

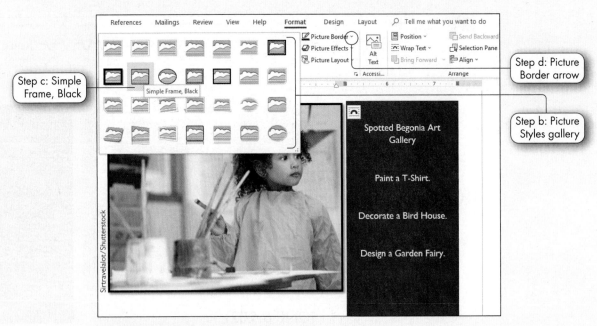

FIGURE 1.38 Modify a Picture

a. Click the **picture** if it is not already selected.

The Picture Tools Format tab displays on the ribbon and sizing handles display around the image. The Table Tools Design and Layout tabs also display. The flyer template uses a table to place the elements. Selecting the picture also selects the table.

b. Click the **Format tab** and click **More** in the Picture Styles group.

A gallery of Picture Styles displays.

c. Point to a few different Picture Styles to see the effects in Live Preview and select **Simple Frame, Black**. Keep the image selected.

A black border is applied around the image.

d. Click the **Picture Border arrow** and select **Pink, Accent 2, Darker 50%** under Theme Colors.

The border color is changed to coordinate with the colors on the flyer.

e. Save the document. Keep the document open if you plan to continue with the next Hands-On Exercise. If not, close the document and exit Word.

Modify Document Layout and Properties

When working with a document, before you send or print it, you will want to view the final product to make sure that your margins and page layout are as they should be. Moreover, you might want to add some details in a header or footer, or in document properties to help identify the author and contents of the document to help in later searches. Although you can always print a document using the default printer settings, you may want to change printer settings or page layout settings before printing.

In this section, you will explore how to view and edit document properties. You will learn about views and how to change a document view to suit your needs. In addition, you will learn how to modify the page layout, including page orientation and margins as well as how to add headers and footers. Finally, you will explore Print Preview and the various printing options available to you.

STEP 1 ▶ Changing Document Views

As you prepare or read a document, you may find that you want to change the way you view it. A section of your document may be easier to view when you can see it magnified, or you might want to display more of your document than what is showing onscreen. You can also select a different *view*, the way a file appears onscreen, to make working on your project easier.

Change Document Views Using the Ribbon

Views for Word, Excel, and PowerPoint are available on the View tab. Each application has views that are specific to that application. PowerPoint and Excel each have a Normal view, which is the typical view used to create and view presentation slides and workbooks. Word's Print Layout view is like Normal view in that it is the view used to create documents. Print Layout view is useful when you want to see both the document text and such features margins and page breaks. Table 1.4 outlines the other views in each application. Access does not have a View tab, but rather incorporates unique views that are visible when working with any Access object.

TABLE 1.4	Office Views	
Application	**View**	**Description**
Word	Print Layout	The default view used when creating documents.
	Read Mode	All editing commands are hidden. Arrows on the left and right sides of the screen are used to move through the pages of the document.
	Web Layout	All page breaks are removed. Use this view to see how a document will display as a webpage.
	Outline View	If Style Headings are used in a document, the document is organized by level. Otherwise, the document will display with each paragraph as a separate bullet.
	Draft View	A pared-down version of Print Layout view.
Excel	Normal	The default view used when creating worksheets.
	Page Break Preview	Displays a worksheet with dashed lines that indicate automatic page breaks. Used to adjust page breaks manually.
	Page Layout	Displays the worksheet headers and margins.
	Custom Views	Create custom views.
PowerPoint	Normal	The default view used when creating presentations.
	Outline View	Displays a presentation as an outline using titles and main text from each slide.
	Slide Sorter	Displays presentation slides in thumbnail form making it easier to sort and organize slide sequence.
	Notes Page	Makes the Notes pane, which is located under the Slide pane, visible. You can type notes that apply to the current slide. Notes do not display during a presentation.
	Reading View	Displays the presentation in full screen like Slide Show.

Change Document Views Using the Status Bar

The **status bar**, located at the bottom of the program window, displays information relevant to the application and document on which you are working, as well as some commands. On the left side of the status bar is application- and document-specific information. When you work with Word, the status bar informs you of the number of pages and words in an open document. Excel shows the status of the file and a Macro recording command. The PowerPoint status bar shows the slide number and total number of slides in the presentation. Word and PowerPoint also display a proofing icon that looks like an opened book. An x in the icon indicates there are proofing errors that need to be fixed 📖. Clicking the icon will start the spelling and grammar check.

Other pertinent document information for PowerPoint and Excel display on the right side of the status bar. The Excel status bar displays summary information, such as average and sum, of selected cells, and the PowerPoint status bar provides access to slide notes.

The right side of the status bar also includes means for changing the view and for changing the zoom size of onscreen file contents. The view buttons (see Figure 1.39) on the status bar of each application enable you to change the view of the open file. These views correspond to the most commonly used views in each application.

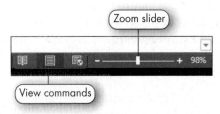

FIGURE 1.39 The Status Bar

The **Zoom slider** is a horizontal bar on the right side of the status bar that enables you to increase or decrease the size of the document onscreen. You can drag the tab along the slider in either direction to increase or decrease the magnification of the file (refer to Figure 1.39). Be aware, however, that changing the size of text onscreen does not change the font size when the file is printed or saved.

STEP 2 Changing the Page Layout

When you prepare a document or worksheet, you are concerned with the way the project appears onscreen and possibly in print. The Layout tab in Word and the Page Layout tab in Excel provide access to a full range of options such as margin settings and page orientation. PowerPoint does not have a Page Layout tab, because its primary purpose is displaying contents onscreen rather than in print.

Because a document or workbook is most often designed to be printed, you may need to adjust margins and change the page orientation, or to center a worksheet vertically or horizontally on a page for the best display. In addition, perhaps the document text should be aligned in columns. You will find these and other common page settings in the Page Setup group on the Layout (or Page Layout) tab. For less common settings, such as determining whether headers should print on odd or even pages, you use the Page Setup dialog box.

Change Margins

A *margin* is the area of blank space that displays to the left, right, top, and bottom of a document or worksheet. Margins display when you are in Print Layout or Page Layout view (see Figure 1.40), or in Backstage view previewing a document to print. There are Normal, Wide, and Narrow default margin settings for Word and Excel. Word also includes Moderate and Mirrored margins. If you want more customized margin settings, use the Custom Margins option at the bottom of the Margins gallery to display the Page Setup dialog box.

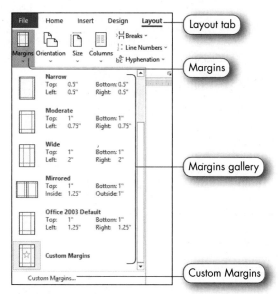

FIGURE 1.40 Page Margins in Word

To change margins in Word and Excel, complete the following steps:
1. Click the Layout (or Page Layout) tab.
2. Click Margins in the Page Setup group.
3. Do one of the following:
   - Select a preset margin option.
   - Click Custom Margins (refer to Figure 1.40) and set the custom margin settings. Click OK to accept the custom margin settings.

Change Page Orientation

Documents and worksheets can be displayed or printed in different page orientations. A page in *portrait orientation* is taller than it is wide. A page in *landscape orientation* is wider than it is tall. Word documents are usually displayed in portrait orientation, whereas Excel worksheets are often more suited to landscape orientation. In PowerPoint, you can change the orientation of slides as well as notes and handouts. Orientation is also an option in the Print page of Backstage view.

Use the Page Setup Dialog Box

Page Orientation settings for Word and Excel are found in the Layout (or Page Layout) tab in the Page Setup group. The Page Setup group contains Margins and Orientation settings as well as other commonly used page options for each Office application. Some are unique to Excel, and others are more applicable to Word. Other less common settings are available in the Page Setup dialog box only, displayed when you click the Page Setup Dialog Box Launcher. The Page Setup dialog box includes options for customizing margins, selecting page orientation, centering horizontally or vertically, printing gridlines, and creating headers and footers. Figure 1.41 shows both the Excel and Word Page Setup dialog boxes.

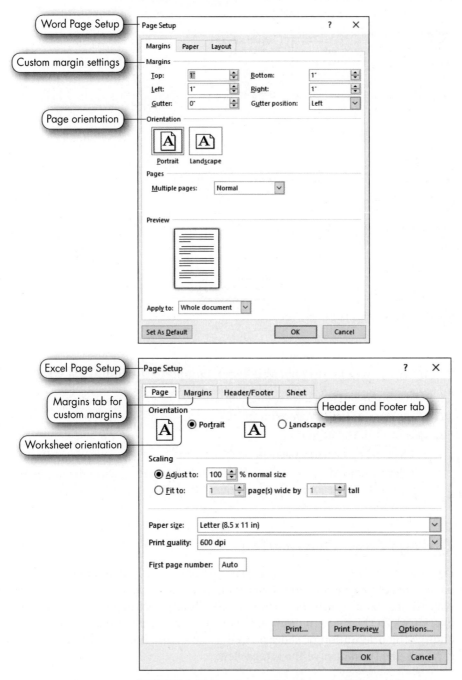

FIGURE 1.41 Page Setup Dialog Boxes in Word and Excel

Although PowerPoint slides are generally set to landscape orientation, you can change to portrait orientation by accessing the Slide Size controls on the Design tab and selecting Custom Slide Size. When choosing to print Notes Pages, Outline, or Handouts, the page orientation can be changed in Print Settings in Backstage view.

STEP 3 › Creating a Header and a Footer

The purpose of including a header or footer is to better identify the document and give it a professional appearance. A ***header*** is a section in the top margin of a document. A ***footer*** is a section in the bottom margin of a document. Generally, page numbers, dates, author's name, or file name are included in Word documents or PowerPoint presentations. Excel worksheets might include the name of a worksheet tab, as well. Company logos are often displayed in a header or footer. Contents in a header or footer will appear on each page of the document, so you only have to specify the content once, after which it displays automatically on all pages. Although you can type the text yourself at the top or bottom of every page, it is time-consuming, and the possibility of making a mistake is great.

Header and footer commands are found on the Insert tab. In Word, you can choose from a predefined gallery of headers and footers as shown in Figure 1.42. To create your own unformatted header or footer, select Edit Header (or Edit Footer) at the bottom of the gallery. You can only add footers to PowerPoint slides (see Figure 1.42). You can apply footers to an individual slide or to all slides. To add date and time or a slide number, check each option to apply. Check the Footer option to add in your own content. In PowerPoint, the location of a footer will depend on the template or theme applied to the presentation. For some templates and themes, the footer will display on the side of the slide rather than at the bottom. Headers and footers are available for PowerPoint Notes and Handouts. Select the Notes and Handouts tab in the Header and Footer dialog box and enter in the content

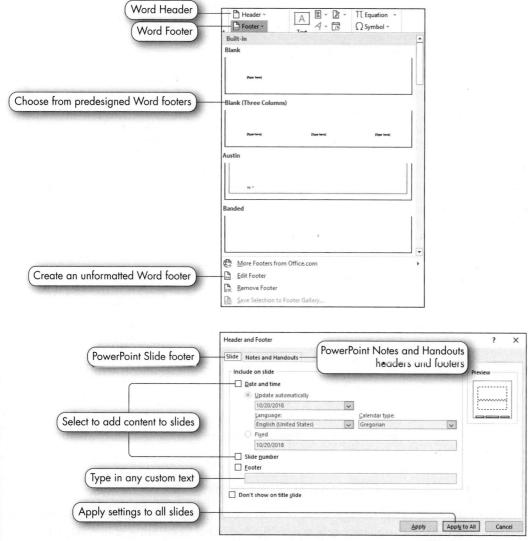

FIGURE 1.42 Insert Footer in Word and PowerPoint

similarly to how you would enter footer information on slides. In Excel, headers and footers are separated into left, center, and right sections. You can type your own contents or use a predefined header or footer element, such as date, file name, or sheet name.

After typing a header or a footer, it can be formatted like any other text. It can be formatted in any font or font size. In Word or Excel, when you want to leave the header and footer area and return to the document, click Close Header and Footer or double-click in the body of the document.

STEP 4 Configuring Document Properties

Recall that Backstage view is a component of Office that provides a collection of commands related to a file. Earlier in this chapter, you used Backstage view to open and save a file and template and to customize ribbon settings. Using Backstage view, you can also view or specify settings related to protection, permissions, versions, and properties of a file. A file's properties include the author, file size, permissions, and date modified. Backstage view also includes options for customizing program settings, signing in to your Office account, and exiting the application. In addition to creating a new document and opening and saving a document, you use Backstage view to print, share, export, and close files.

All the features of Backstage view are accessed by clicking the File tab and then selecting Info in the Backstage Navigation Pane (see Figure 1.43). The Info page will occupy the entire application window, hiding the file with which you are working. You can return to the file in a couple of ways. Either click the Back arrow in the top-left corner or press Esc on the keyboard.

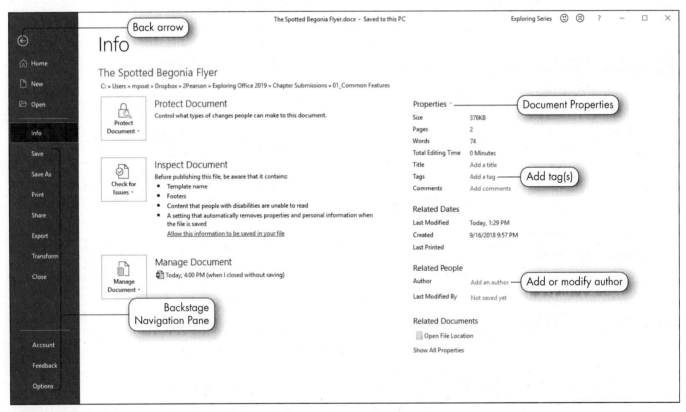

FIGURE 1.43 Backstage View and Document Properties

View and Edit Document Properties

The Info page of Backstage view is where you can protect, inspect, and manage your document as well as manage specific document properties. It is good to include information that identifies a document, such as the author and title. You can also add one or more tags (refer to Figure 1.43). A ***tag*** is a data element or metadata that is added as a document property. Like a keyword, you can search for a file based on tags you assign a document. For example, suppose you apply a tag of *Picasso* to all documents you create that are associated with that artist. Later, you can use that keyword as a search term, locating all associated documents. Statistical information related to the current document such as file size, number of pages, and total words are located on the Info page of Backstage view.

STEP 5 Previewing and Printing a File

When you want to print an Office file, you can select from various print options, including the number of copies and the specific pages to print. It is a good idea to look at how your document or worksheet will appear before you print it. When you select Print from Backstage view, the file previews on the right, with print settings located in the center of the Backstage view. Figure 1.44 shows a typical Backstage Print view. If you know that the page setup is correct and that there are no unique print settings to select, you can simply print without adjusting any print settings.

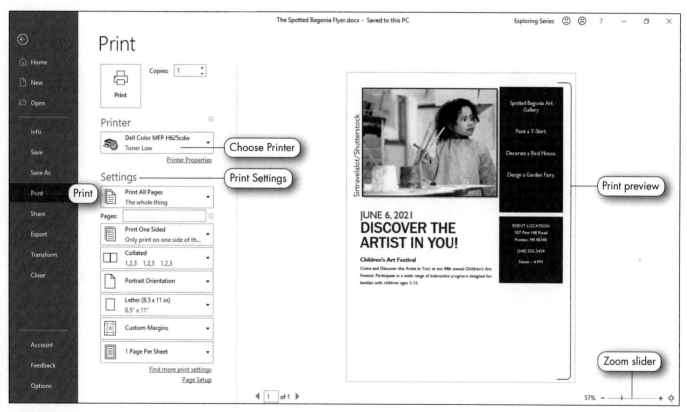

FIGURE 1.44 Backstage Print View in Word

> **TIP: CHANGING THE SIZE OF PRINT PREVIEW**
> Sometimes the preview image of your document shows only a part of the document page or shows a smaller image of the document page. You can change the size of the print preview by using the zoom slider in the bottom-right corner of the preview (refer to Figure 1.44).

Other options in the Backstage Print view vary depending on the application in which you are working. For example, PowerPoint's Backstage Print view includes options for printing slides and handouts in various configurations and colors, whereas Excel's focuses on worksheet selections and Word's includes document options. Regardless of the Office application, you will be able to access Settings options from Backstage view, including page orientation (landscape or portrait), margins, and paper size. To print a file, click the Print button (refer to Figure 1.44).

10. Discuss why you would need to change the view of a document. *p. 45*

11. Discuss the various ways you can change a page layout. *p. 46*

12. Explain what functions and features are included in Backstage view. *p. 50*

13. Discuss some document properties and explain why they are helpful. *p. 50*

Hands-On Exercises

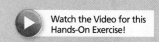

3 Modify Document Layout and Properties

You continue to work on the flyer. You will review and add document properties, and prepare the document to print and distribute by changing the page setup. You will also add a footer with Spotted Begonia's information. As the administrative assistant for the Spotted Begonia Art Gallery, you must be able to search for and find documents previously created. You know that by adding tags to your flyer you will more easily be able to find it later. Finally, you will explore printing options.

STEP 1 **CHANGE THE DOCUMENT VIEW**

To get a better perspective on how your flyer would look if posted to the Gallery's website, you explore the Web Layout view available in Word. Refer to Figure 1.45 as you complete Step 1.

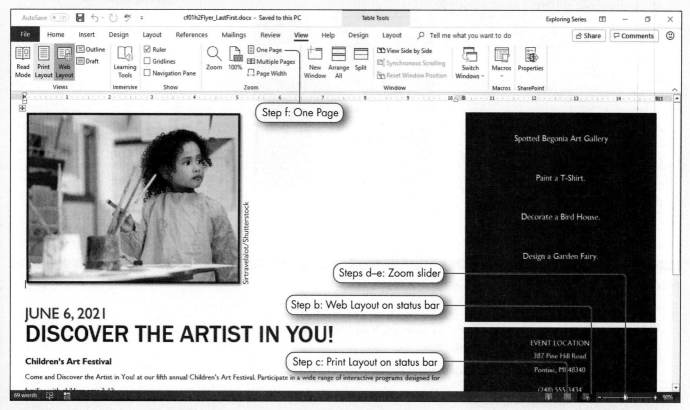

FIGURE 1.45 The Flyer in Web Layout View

a. Open *cf01h2Flyer_LastFirst* if you closed it at the end of Hands-On Exercise 2, and save it as **cf01h3Flyer_LastFirst**, changing h2 to h3.

b. Click **Web Layout** on the status bar. Observe the changes to the view.

   The view is changed to Web Layout and simulates how the document would display on the Web.

c. Click **Print Layout** on the status bar. Observe the changes to the view.

   The document has returned to Print Layout view.

d. Drag the **Zoom slider** to the left so you can see the full page of the flyer.

e. Drag the **Zoom slider** to the right to zoom in on the image.

f. Click the **View tab** and click **One Page** in the Zoom group.

The entire flyer is displayed.

CHANGE THE PAGE LAYOUT

You show the flyer to the Program Director. You both wonder whether changing the orientation and margin settings will make the flyer look better when it is printed. You change the orientation setting, but ultimately revert to Portrait orientation. You modify the margins in Portrait orientation to improve the spacing around the edges of the page. Refer to Figure 1.46 as you complete Step 2.

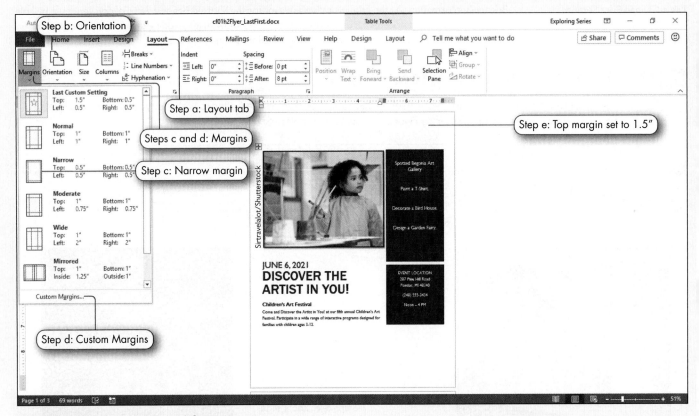

FIGURE 1.46 Change Margins and Orientation

a. Click the **Layout tab** and click **Orientation** in the Page Setup group. Select **Landscape**.

The document is now wider than it is tall.

b. Click **Orientation** and select **Portrait**.

The document returns to Portrait orientation.

c. Click **Margins** in the Page Setup group. Select **Narrow**.

The document margins were changed to Narrow. The Narrow margin allows for better spacing horizontally, but you would like the flyer to be centered better vertically on the page.

d. Click **Margins** and select **Custom Margins**.

The Page Setup dialog box opens.

e. Change the Top margin to **1.5"** Click OK.

   f. Click the **View tab** and click **One Page** in the Zoom group.

   The document looks well balanced on the page.

   g. Save the document.

INSERT A HEADER AND A FOOTER

You decide to add the Gallery's name and website URL to the flyer as a footer so anyone who is looking for more information on the Spotted Begonia Art Gallery can access the website. Refer to Figure 1.47 as you complete Step 3.

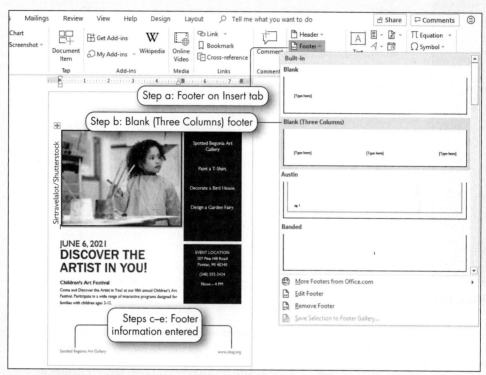

FIGURE 1.47 Insert a Footer

   a. Click the **Insert tab** and click **Footer** in the Header & Footer group.

   A footer gallery displays.

   b. Click the **Blank (Three Columns) footer**.

   You select a footer with three areas to add your own information.

   c. Click **[Type here]** on the left side of the footer. Type **Spotted Begonia Art Gallery**.

   d. Click **[Type here]** on the center of the footer. Press **Delete**.

   e. Click **[Type here]** on the right side of the footer. Type **www.sbag.org**.

   f. Click **Close Header and Footer** in the Close group.

   The footer information is entered.

   g. Save the document.

STEP 4 ENTER DOCUMENT PROPERTIES

You add document properties, which will help you locate the file in the future when performing a search of your files. Refer to Figure 1.48 as you complete Step 4.

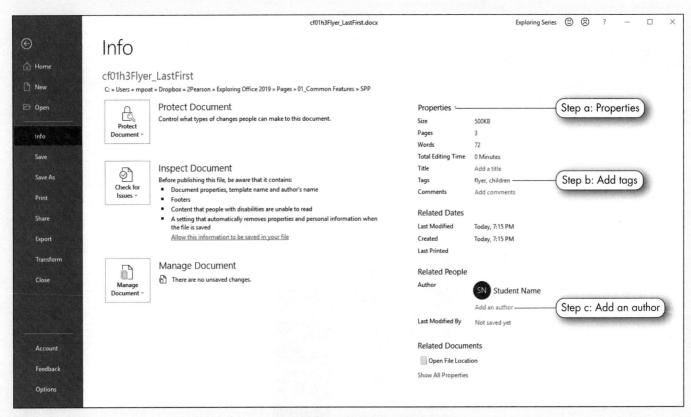

FIGURE 1.48 Enter Document Properties

   a. Click the **File tab** and click Info on the Backstage Navigation Pane. Locate Properties at the top of the right section of Backstage view.

   b. Click the **Add a tag box** and type **flyer, children**.

> **MAC TROUBLESHOOTING:** On a Mac, to add a tag click the File menu and select Properties. Click the Summary tab and enter text in the Keywords box.

   You added tag properties to the flyer.

   c. Click the **Add an Author box** and type your first and last name.

   You added an Author property to the flyer.

   d. Click **Save** in the Backstage Navigation Pane.

STEP 5 ▶ PREVIEW A FILE AND CHANGE PRINT SETTINGS

You have reviewed and almost finalized the flyer. You want to look at how it will appear when printed. You also want to look over Print Settings to ensure they are correct. Refer to Figure 1.49 as you complete Step 5.

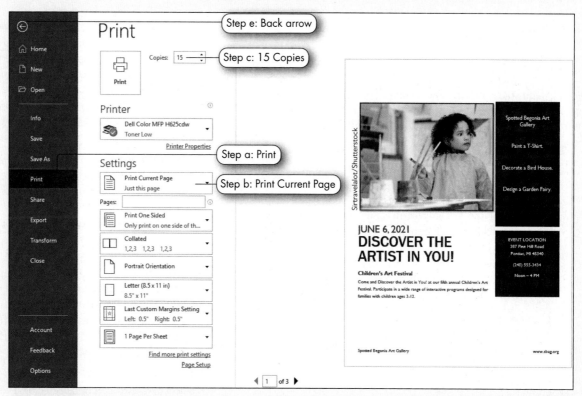

FIGURE 1.49 Backstage Print View

a. Click **Print** in the Backstage Navigation Pane.

It is always a good idea before printing to use Print Preview to check how a file will look when printed.

b. Click **Print All Pages arrow** and select **Print Current Page**.

You notice that the template created extra pages. You only want to print the current page.

c. Select the **1** in the Copies box and type **15**.

The orientation and custom margins settings match what was done previously. Even though you will not print the document now, the print settings will be saved when you save the document.

d. Click the **Back arrow**,

e. Save and close the file. Based on your instructor's directions, submit the following:

cf01h1Letter_LastFirst
cf01h3Flyer_LastFirst

Chapter Objectives Review

After reading this chapter, you have accomplished the following objectives:

1. Start an Office application.

- Use your Microsoft account: Your Microsoft account connects you to all of Microsoft's Internet-based resources.
- Use OneDrive: OneDrive is an app used to store, access, and share files and folders on the Internet. OneDrive is the default storage location for Microsoft Office files. OneDrive is incorporated directly in File Explorer.

2. Work with files.

- Create a new file: You can create a document as a blank document or from a template.
- Save a file: Saving a file enables you to open it later for additional updates or reference. Files are saved to a storage medium such as a hard drive, CD, flash drive, or to OneDrive.
- Open a saved file: You can open an existing file using the Open dialog box. Recently saved files can be accessed using the Recent documents list.

3. Use common interface components.

- Use the ribbon: The ribbon, the long bar located just beneath the title bar containing tabs, groups, and commands, is the command center of Office applications.
- Use a dialog box and gallery: Some commands are not on the ribbon. To access these commands, you need to open a dialog box with a Dialog Box Launcher. A gallery displays additional formatting and design options for a command. Galleries are accessed by clicking More at the bottom of a gallery scroll bar
- Customize the ribbon: You can personalize the ribbon by creating your own tabs and custom groups with commands you want to use. You can create a custom group and add to any of the default tabs.
- Use and Customize the Quick Access Toolbar: The Quick Access Toolbar, located at the top-left corner of any Office application window, provides one-click access to commonly executed tasks, such as saving a file or undoing recent actions.
- You can add additional commands to the QAT.
- Use a Shortcut menu: When you right-click selected text or objects, a context-sensitive menu displays with commands and options relating to the selected text or object.
- Use keyboard shortcuts: Keyboard shortcuts are keyboard equivalents for software commands. Universal keyboard shortcuts in Office include Ctrl+C (Copy), Ctrl+X (Cut), Ctrl+V (Paste), and Ctrl+Z (Undo). Not all commands have a keyboard shortcut. If one exists, it will display in the command ScreenTip.

4. Get help.

- Use the Tell me box: The Tell me box not only links to online resources and technical support but also provides quick access to commands.

Use the Help tab:
- Use the Help tab: The Help tab includes resources for written and video tutorials and training, a means to contact Microsoft Support, and a way to share feedback. What's New displays a webpage that discusses all newly added features organized by release date.
- Use Enhanced ScreenTips: An Enhanced ScreenTip describes a command and provides a keyboard shortcut, if applicable.

5. Install add-ins.

- Add-ins are custom programs or additional commands that extend the functionality of a Microsoft Office program.

6. Use templates and apply themes.

- Open a template: Templates are a convenient way to save time when designing a document. A gallery of template options displays when you start any application. You can also access a template when you start a new document, worksheet, presentation, or database.
- Apply a theme: Themes are a collection of design choices that include colors, fonts, and special effects used to give a consistent look to a document, workbook, or presentation.

7. Modify text.

- Select text: Text can be selected by a variety of methods. You can drag to highlight text and select individual words or groups of text with shortcuts.
- Format text: You can change the font, font color, size, and many other attributes.
- Use the Mini Toolbar: The Mini Toolbar provides instant access to common formatting commands after text is selected.

8. Relocate text.

- Cut, copy, and paste text: To cut means to remove a selection from the original location and place it in the Office Clipboard. To copy means to duplicate a selection from the original location and place a copy in the Office Clipboard. To paste means to place a cut or copied selection into another location.
- Use the Office Clipboard: When you cut or copy selections, they are placed in the Office Clipboard. You can paste the same item multiple times; it will remain in the Office Clipboard until you exit all Office applications or until the Office Clipboard exceeds 24 items.

9. Review a document.

- Check spelling and grammar: As you type, Office applications check and mark spelling and grammar errors (Word only) for later correction. The Thesaurus enables you to search for synonyms. Use AutoCorrect to correct common typing errors and misspelled words and to insert symbols.

10. Work with pictures.

- Insert a picture: You can insert pictures from your own library of digital photos saved on your hard drive, OneDrive, or another storage medium, or you can initiate a Bing search for online pictures directly inside the Office program you are using.
- Modify a picture: To resize a picture, drag a corner-sizing handle; never resize a picture by dragging a center sizing handle. You can apply a picture style or effect, as well as add a picture border, from selections in the Picture Styles group.

11. Change document views.

- Change document views using the ribbon: The View tab offers views specific to the individual application. A view is how a file will be seen onscreen.
- Change document views using the status bar: In addition to information relative to the open file, the Status bar provides access to View and Zoom level options.

12. Change the page layout.

- Change margins: A margin is the area of blank space that displays to the left, right, top, and bottom of a document or worksheet.
- Change page orientation: Documents and worksheets can be displayed in different page orientations. Portrait orientation is taller than it is wide; landscape orientation is wider than it is tall.
- Use the Page Setup dialog box: The Page Setup dialog box includes options for customizing margins, selecting page orientation, centering horizontally or vertically, printing gridlines, and creating headers and footers.

13. Create a header and a footer.

- A header displays at the top of each page.
- A footer displays at the bottom of each page.

14. Configure Document Properties.

- View and edit document properties: Information that identifies a document, such as the author, title, or tags can be added to the document's properties. Those data elements are saved with the document as metadata, but do not appear in the document as it displays onscreen or is printed.

15. Preview and print a file.

- It is important to preview your file before printing.
- Print options can be set in Backstage view and include page orientation, the number of copies, and the specific pages to print.

Key Terms Matching

Match the key terms with their definitions. Write the key term letter by the appropriate numbered definition.

a.	Add-in	**k.**	Mini Toolbar
b.	Backstage view	**l.**	Office Clipboard
c.	Cloud storage	**m.**	OneDrive
d.	Footer	**n.**	Quick Access Toolbar
e.	Format Painter	**o.**	Ribbon
f.	Group	**p.**	Status bar
g.	Header	**q.**	Tag
h.	Margin	**r.**	Tell me box
i.	Microsoft Access	**s.**	Template
j.	Microsoft Office	**t.**	Theme

1. _____ A productivity software suite including a set of software applications, each one specializing in a type of output. **p. 4**

2. _____ The long bar located just beneath the title bar containing tabs, groups, and commands. **p. 9**

3. _____ A custom program or additional command that extends the functionality of a Microsoft Office program. **p. 17**

4. _____ A collection of design choices that includes colors, fonts, and special effects used to give a consistent look to a document, workbook, or presentation. **p. 25**

5. _____ A data element or metadata that is added as a document property. **p. 51**

6. _____ A component of Office that provides a concise collection of commands related to an open file and includes save and print options. **p. 6**

7. _____ A tool that displays near selected text that contains formatting commands. **p. 29**

8. _____ Relational database software used to store data and convert it into information. **p. 4**

9. _____ A feature in a document that consists of one or more lines at the bottom of each page. **p. 49**

10. _____ A predesigned file that incorporates formatting elements, such as a theme and layouts, and may include content that can be modified. **p. 25**

11. _____ A feature that enables you to search for help and information about a command or task you want to perform and will also present you with a shortcut directly to that command. **p. 15**

12. _____ A tool that copies all formatting from one area to another. **p. 17**

13. _____ Stores up to 24 cut or copied selections for use later in your computing session. **p. 30**

14. _____ A task-oriented section of a ribbon tab that contains related commands. **p. 9**

15. _____ An online app used to store, access, and share files and folders. **p. 6**

16. _____ Provides handy access to commonly executed tasks, such as saving a file and undoing recent actions. **p. 13**

17. _____ The long bar at the bottom of the screen that houses the Zoom slider and various View buttons. **p. 46**

18. _____ The area of blank space that displays to the left, right, top, and bottom of a document or worksheet **p. 47**

19. _____ A technology used to store files and to work with programs that are stored in a central location on the Internet. **p. 6**

20. _____ A feature in a document that consists of one or more lines at the top of each page. **p. 49**

Multiple Choice

1. In Word or PowerPoint, a quick way to select an entire paragraph is to:
   - (a) place the pointer at the left of the line, in the margin area, and click.
   - (b) triple-click inside the paragraph.
   - (c) double-click at the beginning of the paragraph.
   - (d) press Ctrl+C inside the paragraph.

2. When you want to copy the format of a selection but not the content, you should:
   - (a) double-click Copy in the Clipboard group.
   - (b) right-click the selection and click Copy.
   - (c) click Copy Format in the Clipboard group.
   - (d) click Format Painter in the Clipboard group.

3. Which of the following is *not* a benefit of using One Drive?
   - (a) Save your folders and files to the cloud.
   - (b) Share your files and folders with others.
   - (c) Hold video conferences with others.
   - (d) Simultaneously work on the same document with others.

4. What does a red wavy underline in a document or presentation mean?
   - (a) A word is misspelled or not recognized by the Office dictionary.
   - (b) A grammatical mistake exists.
   - (c) An apparent formatting error was made.
   - (d) A word has been replaced with a synonym.

5. Which of the following is *true* about headers and footers?
   - (a) They can be inserted from the Layout tab.
   - (b) Headers and footers only appear on the last page of a document.
   - (c) Headers appear at the top of every page in a document.
   - (d) Only page numbers can be included in a header or footer.

6. You can get help when working with an Office application in which one of the following areas?
   - (a) The Tell me box
   - (b) The Status bar
   - (c) Backstage view
   - (d) The Quick Access Toolbar

7. To access commands that are not on the ribbon, you need to open which of the following?
   - (a) Gallery
   - (b) Dialog box
   - (c) Shortcut menu
   - (d) Mini Toolbar

8. To create a document without knowing much about the software, you should use which of the following?
   - (a) Theme
   - (b) Live Preview
   - (c) Template
   - (d) Design Style

9. Which is the preferred method for resizing a picture so that it keeps its proportions?
   - (a) Use the rotation handle
   - (b) Use a corner-sizing handle
   - (c) Use a side-sizing handle
   - (d) Use the controls in the Adjust group

10. Which is *not* a description of a tag in a Word document?
    - (a) A data element
    - (b) Document metadata
    - (c) Keyword
    - (d) Document title

Practice Exercises

1 Designing Webpages

You have been asked to make a presentation at the next Montgomery County, PA Chamber of Commerce meeting. With the Chamber's continued emphasis on growing the local economy, many small businesses are interested in establishing a Web presence. The business owners would like to know more about how webpages are designed. In preparation for the presentation, you will proofread and edit your PowerPoint file. You decide to insert an image to enhance your presentation and use an add-in to include a map and contact information for the Chamber of Commerce. Refer to Figure 1.50 as you complete this exercise.

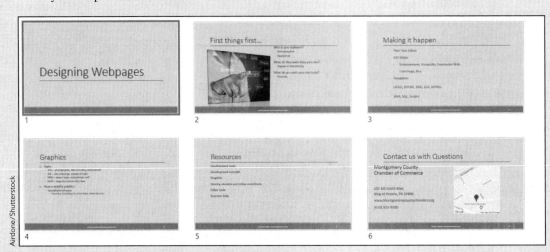

FIGURE 1.50 Designing Webpages Presentation

   a. Open the PowerPoint presentation *cf01p1Design*.

   b. Click the **File tab**, click **Save As**, and then save the file as **cf01p1Design_LastFirst**.

   c. Click the **Design tab** and click **More** in the Themes group. Scroll through the themes to find and select **Retrospect theme**. Select the **third Variant** in the Variants group. Close the Design Ideas pane if it opens.

   d. Click **Slide 2** in the Slides pane on the left. Double-click to select **Resources** on the slide title. Use the Mini Toolbar to click the **Font Color arrow**. Select **Orange, Accent 2** in the Theme Colors group. Click **Bold** on the Mini Toolbar.

   e. Click **Slide 3** in the Slides pane. Click the **Pictures icon** in the left content placeholder. Browse to the student data files, locate and select *cf01p1Website.jpg*, and then click **Insert**. Close the Design Ideas pane if it opens.

   f. Select the picture. Click the **Format tab** and click **More** in the Picture Styles group to open the Pictures Style Gallery. Click the **Reflected Perspective Right**. Click the **Height box** in the Size group and type **4**. Press **Enter**. Place the pointer over the image to display a 4-headed arrow and drag to position the image so it is centered vertically in the open space.

   g. Click the **Home tab** and click the **Clipboard Dialog Box Launcher**. Click **Slide 7** and select all the placeholder content. Right-click the selected text and click **Cut** from the shortcut menu.

> **TROUBLESHOOTING:** If there is content in the Office Clipboard, click Clear All to remove all previously cut or copied items from the Office Clipboard.

> **MAC TROUBLESHOOTING:** On a Mac, select the text and press Control+X. Click Slide 4 and press Control+V. Repeat for Step h. Skip to Step j.

   h. Click **Slide 5** and select all the placeholder content. Press **Ctrl+X**.

   i. Click **Slide 4** and click the **content placeholder**. Click **Paste All** in the Office Clipboard. Close the Office Clipboard.

j. Click **Slide Sorter** on the status bar. Click **Slide 5** and press **Delete**. Click **Slide 6** and press **Delete**. Drag **Slide 2** to the right of **Slide 5**. Click the **View tab** and click **Normal**.

k. Click **Slide 6** in the Slides pane. Click the **Insert tab**, point to **My Add-ins** in the Add-ins group, and read the Enhanced Screen Tip to find out more about Add-ins. Click **My Add-ins**, click the **Store tab**, and then in the search box, type **map**. Press **Enter**.

l. Click **Add** to add OfficeMaps - Insert maps quick and easy!

m. Click Open OfficeMaps on the Insert tab. Click in the Enter a location box and type the address shown on Slide 6. Click Insert Map. Close the OfficeMaps pane.

n. Select the map, click the **Height box** in the Size group, and type **4**. Press **Enter**. Position the map attractively in the slide.

o. Click **Slide 1**. Click **Header & Footer** in the Text group on the Insert tab. Click the **Slide number check box** to select it. Click the **Footer box** to select it and type **Business Owners Association Presentation**. Click **Don't show on title slide check box** to select it. Click **Apply to All**.

p. Click the **Review tab** and click **Spelling** in the Proofing group. In the Spelling pane, click **Change** or **Ignore** to make changes as needed. The words *KompoZer* and *Nvu* are not misspelled, so you should ignore them when they are flagged. Click **OK** when you have finished checking spelling.

q. Click the **File tab.** Click the **Add a Tag box** and type **business, BOA, web design**.

r. Click **Print**. Click the **Full Page Slides arrow** and select **6 Slides Horizontal** to see a preview of all the slides as a handout.

> **MAC TROUBLESHOOTING:** Click the File menu, click Print, and then click Show Details. In the Print dialog box, click the Layout arrow and select Handouts (6 slides per page).

s. Click the **Portrait Orientation arrow** and select **Landscape Orientation**. Click the **Back arrow**.

t. Save and close the file. Based on your instructor's directions, submit cf01p1Design_LastFirst.

2 Upscale Bakery

You have always been interested in baking and have worked in the field for several years. You now have an opportunity to devote yourself full time to your career as the CEO of a company dedicated to baking cupcakes and pastries. One of the first steps in getting the business off the ground is developing a business plan so that you can request financial support. You will use Word to develop your business plan. Refer to Figure 1.51 as you complete this exercise.

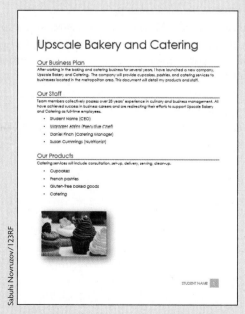

FIGURE 1.51 Upscale Bakery Business Plan

a. Open the Word document *cf01p2Business*. Click the **File tab**, click **Save As**, and save the file as **cf01p2Business_LastFirst**.

b. Click the **Design tab**, click **Themes**, and then select **Slice**.

c. Select the paragraphs beginning with *Our Staff* and ending with *(Nutritionist)*. Click the **Home tab** and click **Cut** in the Clipboard group. Click to the left of *Our Products* and click **Paste**.

d. Select the text **Your name** in the first bullet in the *Our Staff* section and replace it with your first and last names. Select the entire bullet list in the *Our Staff* section. On the Mini Toolbar, click the **Font Size arrow** and select **11**.

e. Click **Format Painter** in the Clipboard group. Drag the Format Painter pointer across all four *Our Products* bullets to change the bullets' font size to 11 pt.

f. Click the **Tell me box** and type **footer**. Click **Add a Footer**, scroll to locate the **Integral footer**, and click to add it to the page. Keep the footer open.

g. Right-click the **page number box** in the footer. Click the **Shading arrow** in the Paragraph group on the Home tab and select **White Background 1 Darker 50%**. Click **Close Header and Footer** on the Header & Footer Tools Design tab.

h. Triple-click to select the last line in the document, which says *Insert and position picture here*, and press **Ctrl+X**. Click the **Insert tab** and click **Online Pictures** in the Illustrations group.

i. Click in the **Bing Image search box**, type **Cupcakes**, and then press **Enter**.

j. Select any **cupcake image** and click **Insert**. Do not deselect the image.

k. Ensure the Picture Tools Format tab is active, and in the Picture Styles group, select the **Drop Shadow Rectangle**.

> **TROUBLESHOOTING:** If you are unable to find a cupcake image in Bing, you can use *cf01p2Cupcake* from the student data files.

l. Click the **Size Dialog Box Launcher** and ensure that Lock aspect ratio is selected. Click **OK**. Click the **Shape width box** in the Size group and change the width to **2.5**.

m. Click outside the picture.

n. Press **Ctrl+Home**. Click **Customize Quick Access Toolbar** and select **Spelling & Grammar** (ignore if present). Click **Spelling & Grammar** from the QAT. Correct the spelling error and click **OK**.

o. Click the **View tab** and select **Draft** in the Views group. Click **Print Layout** in the Views group and click **One Page** in the Zoom group.

p. Click the **Layout tab** and click **Margins** in the Page Setup group. Change to **Moderate Margins**.

q. Click the **File tab**. In the Properties section, click in Add a tag box and add the tag **business plan**. Click **Add an author** and add your first and last name to the Author property. Right-click the **current author** (should say Exploring Series) and click **Remove Person**.

r. Click **Print** in Backstage view. Notice the author name has changed in the footer. Change the number of copies to **2**. Click the **Back arrow**.

s. Save and close the file. Based on your instructor's directions, submit cf01p2Business_LastFirst.

1 Reference Letter

MyLab IT Grader

You are an instructor at a local community college. A student asked you to provide her with a letter of reference for a job application. You have used Word to prepare the letter, but now you want to make a few changes before it is finalized.

a. Open the Word document *cf01m1RefLetter* and save it as **cf01m1RefLetter_LastFirst**.

b. Change the theme to **Gallery**. Point to Colors in the Document Formatting group and read the Enhanced ScreenTip. Click **Colors** and select **Red**.

c. Insert a **Blank footer**. Type **410 Wellington Parkway, Huntsville, AL 35611**. Center the footer. Close the footer.

d. Place the insertion point at the end of Professor Smith's name in the signature line. Press **Enter** twice. Insert a picture from your files using *cf01m1College.png*. Resize the image to **1"** tall. Click **Color** in the Adjust group and select **Dark Red, Accent color 1 Light**. Click **Center** in the Paragraph group on Home tab.

e. Press **Ctrl+Home**. Select the **date** and point to several font sizes on the Mini Toolbar. Use Live Preview to view them. Click **12**.

f. Right-click the word **talented** in the second paragraph starting with *Stacy is a* and click **Synonyms** from the shortcut menu. Replace *talented* with **gifted**.

g. Move the last paragraph—beginning with *In my opinion*—to position it before the second paragraph—beginning with *Stacy is a gifted*.

h. Press **Ctrl+Home**. Use Spelling & Grammar to correct all errors. Make any spelling and grammar changes that are suggested. Stacy's last name is spelled correctly.

i. Change the margins to **Narrow**.

j. Customize the QAT to add **Print Preview and Print**. Preview the document as it will appear when printed. Stay in Backstage view.

k. Click **Info** in Backstage view. Add the tag **reference** to the Properties for the file in Backstage view.

l. Save and close the file. Based on your instructor's directions, submit cf01m1RefLetter_LastFirst.

2 Medical Monitoring

MyLab IT Grader

You are enrolled in a Health Informatics study program in which you learn to manage databases related to health fields. For a class project, your instructor requires that you monitor your blood pressure, recording your findings in an Excel worksheet. You have recorded the week's data and will now make a few changes before printing the worksheet for submission.

a. Open the Excel workbook *cf01m2Tracker* and save it as **cf01m2Tracker_LastFirst**.

b. Change the theme to **Crop**.

c. Click in the cell to the right of *Name* and type your first and last names. Press **Enter**.

d. Select **cells H1, I1, J1**, and **K1**. Cut the selected cells and paste to **cell C2**. Click **cell A1**.

e. Press **Ctrl+A**. Use Live Preview to see how different fonts will look. Change the font of the worksheet to **Arial**.

f. Add the Spelling feature to the QAT and check the spelling for the worksheet to ensure that there are no errors.

g. Select **cells E22, F22**, and **G22**. You want to increase the decimal places for the values in cells so that each value shows one place to the right of the decimal. Use **Increase Decimal** as the search term in the Tell me box. Click **Insert Decimal** in the results to increase the decimal place to **1**.

h. Press **Ctrl+Home** and insert an **Online Picture** of your choice related to blood pressure. Resize and position the picture so that it displays in an attractive manner. Apply the **Drop Shadow Rectangle** picture style to the image.

i. Insert a footer. Use the Page Number header and footer element in the center section. Use the File Name header and footer element in the right section of the footer. Click in a cell on the worksheet. Return to Normal view.

j. Change the orientation to **Landscape**. Change the page margins so Left and Right are **1.5"** and Top and Bottom and **1"**. Center on page both vertically and horizontally. Close the dialog box.

k. Add **blood pressure** as a tag and adjust print settings to print two copies. You will not actually print two copies unless directed by your instructor.

l. Save and close the file. Based on your instructor's directions, submit cf01m2Tracker_LastFirst.

Running Case

New Castle County Technical Services

New Castle County Technical Services (NCCTS) provides technical support for companies in the greater New Castle County, Delaware, area. The company has been in operation since 2011 and has grown to become one of the leading technical service companies in the area. NCCTS has prided itself on providing great service at reasonable costs, but as you begin to review the budget for next year and the rates your competitors are charging, you are realizing that it may be time to increase some rates. You have prepared a worksheet with suggested rates and will include those rates in a memo to the CFO. You will format the worksheet, copy the data to the Office Clipboard, and use the Office Clipboard to paste the information into a memo. You will then modify the formatting of the memo, check the spelling, and ensure the document is ready for distribution before sending it on to the CFO.

a. Open the Excel workbook *cf01r1NCCTSRates* and save as **cf01r1NCCTSRates_LastFirst**.

b. Select **cells A4:C4**. Click **More** in the Styles group on the Home tab and select **Heading 2**.

c. Select **cells A5:C5**. Press **Ctrl** and select cells **A7:C7**. Change the font color to **Red** in Standard Colors.

d. Select **cells A5:C10** and increase the font size to **12**.

e. Select cells **A4:C10**. Open the **Office Clipboard**. Clear the Office clipboard if items display. Click **Copy** in the Clipboard group. Keep Excel open.

f. Open the Word document *cf01r1NCCTSMemo* and save it as **cf01r1NCCTSMemo_LastFirst**.

g. Change Your Name in the From: line to your own name.

h. Press **Ctrl+Home**. Insert image *cf01r1Logo.jpg*. Resize the height to **1"**.

i. Change the document theme to **Retrospect**.

j. Place insertion point in the blank line above the paragraph beginning with *Please*.

k. Open Office Clipboard and click the item in the Office Clipboard that was copied from the NCCTS Rates workbook. Clear then close the **Office Clipboard**.

l. Check the spelling. Correct all grammar and spelling mistakes.

m. Increase left and right margins to **1.5"**.

n. Insert a footer and click **Edit Footer**. Click **Document Info** in the Insert group on the Header and Footer Tools Design tab. Click **File Name**. Click **Close Header and Footer**.

o. Enter **2022**, **rates** as tags.

p. Save and close the files. Based on your instructor's directions, submit the following files:
cf01r1NCCTSMemo_LastFirst
cf01r1NCCTSRates_LastFirst

Disaster Recovery

Resume Enhancement

You are applying for a new position and you have asked a friend to look at your resume. She has a better eye for details than you do, so you want her to let you know about any content or formatting errors. She has left some instructions pointing out where you can improve the resume. Open the Word document *cf01d1Resume* and save it as **cf01d1Resume_LastFirst**. Add your name, address, phone and email in the placeholders at the top of the document. Change the theme of the resume to Office. Bold all the job titles and dates held. Italicize all company names and locations. Use Format Painter to copy the formatting of the bullets in the Software Intern description and apply them to the bullets in the other job description. Bold the name of the university and location. Apply italics to the degree and date. Change the margins to Narrow. Add resume as a tag. Check the spelling and grammar. Save and close the file. Based on your instructor's directions, submit cf01d1Resume_LastFirst.

Capstone Exercise

Social Media Privacy

You have been asked to create a presentation about protecting privacy on social media sites. You have given the first draft of your presentation to a colleague to review. She has come up with several suggestions that you need to incorporate before you present.

Open and Save Files

You will open, review, and save a PowerPoint presentation.

1. Open the PowerPoint presentation *cf01c1SocialMedia* and save it as **cf01c1SocialMedia_LastFirst**.

Apply a Theme and Change the View

You generally develop a presentation using a blank theme, and then when most of the content is on the slides, you add a different theme to provide some interest.

2. Apply the **Quotable theme** to the presentation and use the **Purple variant**.
3. Change to **Slide Sorter view**. Drag **Slide 2** to become **Slide 3** and drag **Slide 8** to become **Slide 6**.
4. Return to **Normal view**.

Select Text, Move Text, and Format Text

You make some changes to the order of text and change some word choices.

5. Click **Slide 5** and cut the second bullet. Paste it so it is the first bullet.
6. Right-click the second use of **regularly** in the first bullet to find a synonym. Change the word to **often**.
7. Double-click **location** in the fourth bullet. Drag it so it comes after *Disable* and add a space between the two words. Delete the word **of** so the bullet reads *Disable location sharing*.
8. Use the Mini Toolbar to format **Never** in the fifth bullet in italics.

Insert and Modify a Picture

You think Slide 2 has too much empty space and needs a picture. You insert a picture and add a style to give it a professional look.

9. Click **Slide 2** and insert the picture *cf01c1Sharing.jpg* from your data files.
10. Resize the picture height to **4.5"**.
11. Apply the **Rounded Diagonal Corner, White Picture Style**.

Use the Tell me Box

You also want to center the picture on Slide 2 vertically. You use the Tell Me box to help with this. You also need help to change a bulleted list on Slide 5 to SmartArt because many of your slides use SmartArt. You know that there is a way to convert text to SmartArt, but you cannot remember where it is. You use the Tell me box to help you with this function, too.

12. Ensure the picture on Slide 2 is still selected. Type **Align** in the Tell me box. Click **Align Objects** and select **Align Middle**.
13. Select the bulleted text on **Slide 5**. Use the Tell me box to search **SmartArt**.
14. Click the first instance of Convert text to SmartArt from your search and click **More SmartArt Graphics** to convert the text to a **Lined List**.

Insert Header and Footer

You want to give the audience printed handouts of your presentation, so you add a header and footer to the handouts, with page numbers and information to identify you and the topic.

15. Add **page numbers** to all Handouts.
16. Add **Social Media Privacy** as a Header in all Handouts.
17. Add **your name** as a Footer in all Handouts.

Customize the Quick Access Toolbar

You know to review the presentation for spelling errors. Because you run spell check regularly, you add a button on the QAT. You also add a button to preview and print your presentation for added convenience.

18. Add **Spelling** to the QAT.
19. Add **Print Preview and Print** to the QAT.

Check Spelling and Change View

Before you call the presentation complete, you will correct any spelling errors and view the presentation as a slide show.

20. Press **Ctrl+Home** and check the spelling.
21. View the slide show. Click after reviewing the last slide to return to the presentation.

Use Print Preview, Change Print Layout, and Adjust Document Properties

You want to print handouts of the presentation so that 3 slides will appear on one page.

22. Click the **Print Preview and Print command** on the QAT to preview the document as it will appear when printed.

23. Change Full Page Slides to **3 Slides**.

> **MAC TROUBLESHOOTING:** Click the File menu and click Print. Click Show Details. Click Layout and choose Handouts (3 slides per page).

24. Change the Page Orientation to **Landscape**.

25. Adjust the print settings to print **two** copies. You will not actually print two copies unless directed by your instructor.

26. Change document properties to add **social media** as a tag and change the author name to your own.

27. Save and close the file. Based on your instructor's directions, submit cf01c1SocialMedia_LastFirst.

Introduction to Excel

LEARNING OUTCOME You will create and format a basic Excel worksheet.

OBJECTIVES & SKILLS: After you read this chapter, you will be able to:

CASE STUDY | Celebrity Musician's Souvenir Shop

Melissa Rogers, the merchandise manager for Celebrity Musician's Souvenir Shop, asked you to calculate the retail price, sale price, and profit analysis for selected items on sale for the upcoming concert. Using markup rates that Melissa provided, you will calculate the retail price—the amount the souvenir shop charges its customers for the products. In addition, you will calculate sale prices based on discount rates. Finally, you will calculate the profit margin to determine the percentage of the final sale price over the cost.

YanLev/Shutterstock

Creating and Formatting a Worksheet

After you create the initial pricing spreadsheet, you will be able to change values and see that the formulas update the results automatically. In addition, you will insert data for additional sale items or delete an item based on the manager's decision. After inserting formulas, you will format the data in the worksheet to have a professional appearance.

J6 : fx =(H6-C6)/H6

	A	C	D	E	F	G	H	I	J	K	L
1			Celebrity Musician's Souvenir Shop								
2			9/1/2021								
3											
4	Product	Cost	Markup Rate	Markup Amount	Retail Price	Percent Off	Sale Price	Profit Amount	Profit Margin		
5	Apparel										
6	Hat	$ 7.95	109.5%	$ 8.71	$ 16.66	15%	$ 14.16	$ 6.21	43.8%		
7	Hoodie	$ 27.25	125.0%	$ 34.06	$ 61.31	20%	$ 49.05	$ 21.80	44.4%		
8	T-shirt	$ 7.10	315.5%	$ 22.40	$ 29.50	10%	$ 26.55	$ 19.45	73.3%		
9	Souvenirs										
10	Mug	$ 5.00	200.0%	$ 10.00	$ 15.00	15%	$ 12.75	$ 7.75	60.8%		
11	Souvenir Program	$ 9.95	101.0%	$ 10.05	$ 20.00	25%	$ 15.00	$ 5.05	33.7%		
12	Travel Mug	$ 7.00	200.0%	$ 14.00	$ 21.00	15%	$ 17.85	$ 10.85	60.8%		
13											

September   Formulas   ⊕

Ready   160%

	Product	Cost	Markup Rate	Markup Amount	Retail Price	Percent Off	Sale Price	Profit Amount	Profit Margin
4	Product	Cost	Markup Rate	Markup Amount	Retail Price	Percent Off	Sale Price	Profit Amount	Profit Margin
5	Apparel								
6	Hat	7.95	1.095	=C6*D6	=C6+E6	0.15	=F6*(1-G6)	=H6-C6	=(H6-C6)/H6
7	Hoodie	27.25	1.25	=C7*D7	=C7+E7	0.2	=F7*(1-G7)	=H7-C7	=(H7-C7)/H7
8	T-shirt	7.1	3.155	=C8*D8	=C8+E8	0.1	=F8*(1-G8)	=H8-C8	=(H8-C8)/H8
9	Souvenirs								
10	Mug	5	2	=C10*D10	=C10+E10	0.15	=F10*(1-G10)	=H10-C10	=(H10-C10)/H10
11	Souvenir Program	9.95	1.01	=C11*D11	=C11+E11	0.25	=F11*(1-G11)	=H11-C11	=(H11-C11)/H11
12	Travel Mug	7	2	=C12*D12	=C12+E12	0.15	=F12*(1-G12)	=H12-C12	=(H12-C12)/H12
13									
14									
15									
16									

September   Formulas   ⊕

Ready   130%

FIGURE 1.1 Completed Souvenir Shop Worksheet

CASE STUDY | Celebrity Musician's Souvenir Shop

Starting File	File to be Submitted
e01h1Souvenirs	e01h5Souvenirs_LastFirst

MyLab IT Grader An alternate version of this project is available as a MyLab IT Grader Assessment

Introduction to Spreadsheets

Organizing, calculating, and evaluating quantitative data are important skills required today for personal and managerial decision making. You track expenses for your household budget, maintain a savings plan, and determine what amount you can afford for a house or car payment. Retail managers create and analyze their organizations' annual budgets, sales projections, and inventory records.

A *spreadsheet* is an electronic file that contains a grid of columns and rows to organize related data and to display results of calculations, enabling interpretation of quantitative data for decision making. When you make changes, the formula results recalculate automatically and accurately.

In this section, you will learn how to design spreadsheets. You will also explore the Excel window. Then, you will enter text, values, and dates in a spreadsheet. In addition, you will correct spelling errors and find and replace data.

Exploring the Excel Window

In Excel, a *worksheet* is a spreadsheet that usually contains descriptive labels, numeric values, formulas, functions, and charts. A *workbook* is a collection of one or more related worksheets contained within a single file. Storing multiple worksheets within one workbook helps organize related data together in one file and enables you to perform calculations among the worksheets. For example, you can create a budget workbook of 13 worksheets, one for each month to store income and expenses and a final worksheet to calculate totals across the entire year.

Identify Excel Window Elements

Figure 1.2 identifies elements in the Excel window, and Table 1.1 lists and describes the Excel window elements.

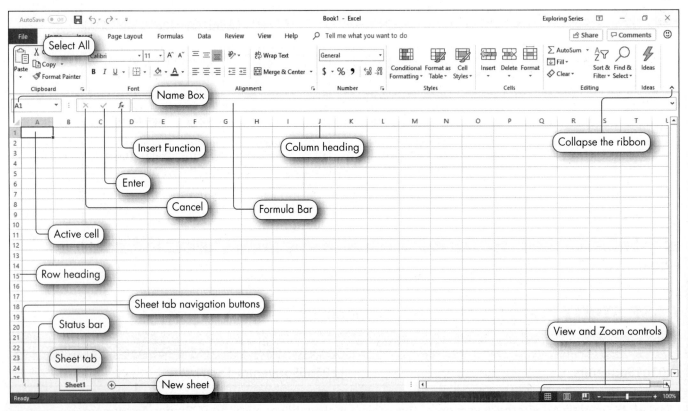

FIGURE 1.2 Excel Window

TABLE 1.1	Excel Elements	
Element		**Description**
Name Box		A rectangular area located below the ribbon that displays the address (or name) of the active cell, selected chart, or selected table. Use the Name Box to go to a cell, chart, or table; select a range; or assign a name to one or more cells.
Cancel	☒	A command to the left of the Formula Bar used to cancel data being entered or edited into the active cell. As you enter or edit data in a cell, the Cancel command changes from gray to red when you position the pointer over it.
Enter	☑	A command to the left of the Formula Bar used to accept data typed in the active cell and keep the current cell active. As you enter or edit data in a cell, the Enter command changes from gray to blue when you position the pointer over it.
Insert Function	*fx*	A command that displays the Insert Function dialog box to search for and select a function to insert into the active cell. The Insert Function command changes from gray to green when you position the pointer over it.
Formula Bar		A bar below the ribbon and to the right of the Insert Function command that shows the contents (text, value, date, formula, or function) stored in the active cell. You enter or edit cell contents here.
Select All	�	The triangle at the intersection of the row and column headings in the top-left corner of the worksheet used to select everything contained in the active worksheet.
Column heading		The letter above each column in a worksheet.
Row heading		The number to the left of a row in a worksheet.
Active cell		The currently selected cell in a worksheet. It is indicated by a dark green border.
Sheet tab		A label that looks like a file folder tab, located between the bottom of the worksheet and the status bar, that shows the name of a worksheet contained in the workbook. When you create a new Excel workbook, the default worksheet is named Sheet1.
New sheet	⊕	Button used to insert a new worksheet to the right of the current worksheet.
Sheet tab scroll buttons	◀ ▶	Buttons to the left of the sheet tabs used to scroll through sheet tabs; not all the sheet tabs are displayed at the same time. Use the left scroll button to scroll through sheets to the left; use the right scroll button to scroll through sheets to the right.
View controls	⊞ ▣ ⊡	Buttons on the right side of the status bar that control how a worksheet displays. *Normal view*, the default, displays the worksheet without showing margins, headers, footers, and page breaks. *Page Layout view* displays margins, header and footer area, and a ruler. *Page Break Preview* displays page breaks within the worksheet.

Identify Columns, Rows, and Cells

A worksheet contains columns and rows, with each column and row assigned a heading. Columns are assigned alphabetic headings from columns A to Z, continuing from AA to AZ, and then from BA to BZ until XFD, which is the last of the possible 16,384 columns. Rows have numeric headings ranging from 1 to 1,048,576. Depending on your screen resolution, you may see more or fewer columns and rows than what are shown in the figures in this book.

The intersection of a column and a row is a *cell*; a total of more than 17 billion cells are available in a worksheet. Each cell has a *cell address*, a unique identifier starting with its column letter and then its row number. For example, the cell at the intersection of column C and row 6 is cell C6 (see Figure 1.3). The active cell is the current cell. Excel displays a dark green border around the active cell in the worksheet, and the Name Box shows the cell address of the active cell, which is C6 in Figure 1.3. The contents of the active cell, or the formula used to calculate the results of the active cell, appear in the Formula Bar. Cell references are useful in formulas or in navigation.

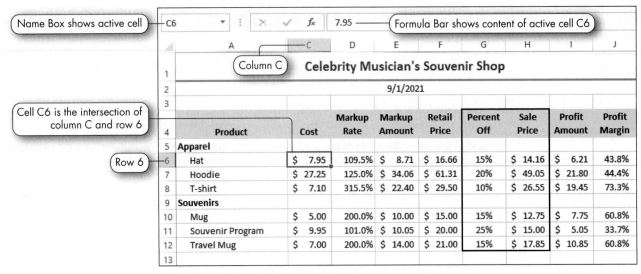

FIGURE 1.3 Columns, Rows, and Cells

Navigate in and Among Worksheets

To move to a new cell, use the pointer or the arrow keys on the keyboard. If you work in a large worksheet, use the vertical and horizontal scroll bars to display another area of the worksheet and click in the desired cell to make it the active cell.

The worksheet that is currently displayed is called the ***active sheet***. The sheet tab for the active sheet is bold green with a green horizontal line below the tab name. Use the sheet tabs at the bottom of the workbook window (above the status bar) to display the contents of another worksheet within the workbook. Once a sheet is the active sheet, you can then navigate within that worksheet.

The keyboard contains several keys that can be used in isolation or in combination with other keys to navigate in a worksheet. Table 1.2 lists the keyboard navigation methods.

TABLE 1.2 Keystrokes and Actions

PC Keystroke	Mac Keystroke	Used to
▲	↑	Move up one cell in the same column.
▼	↓	Move down one cell in the same column.
◄	←	Move left one cell in the same row.
►	→	Move right one cell in the same row.
Tab	Tab	Move right one cell in the same row.
Page Up	fn ↑	Move the active cell up one screen.
Page Down	fn ↓	Move the active cell down one screen.
Home	fn ←	Move the active cell to column A of the current row.
Ctrl+Home	Control fn ←	Make cell A1 the active cell.
Ctrl+End	Control fn →	Make the lower right active corner of the worksheet—the intersection of the last column and row that contains data—the active cell. Does not move to cell XFD1048576 unless that cell contains data.
Ctrl+Page Down	Option ↓	Move to the next sheet on the right side of the active sheet.
Ctrl+Page Up	Option ↑	Move to the next sheet on the left side of the active sheet.
F5 or Ctrl+G		Open the Go To dialog box to enter any cell address.

Go To is a helpful navigation feature when working in large workbooks. Use Go To to navigate to a specific cell, particularly when that cell is not visible onscreen or is many columns or rows away. For example, you might want to go to the cell containing the profit margin for the Travel Mug in the Souvenir Shop workbook. Use the Go To dialog box or the Go To Special dialog box.

> **To use the Go To dialog box, complete the following steps:**
>
> 1. Click Find & Select in the Editing group on the Home tab.
> 2. Select Go To on the menu to open the Go To dialog box (see Figure 1.4).
> 3. Select a range name from the Go to list, or type a cell address (such as B5) or a range such as B5:B10 in the Reference box.
> 4. Click OK.

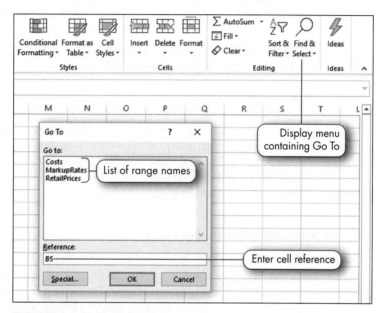

FIGURE 1.4 Go To Dialog Box

If you enter a specific cell address in the Go To dialog box, Excel will make it the active cell. If you select a range name from the list or if you type a range address (such as G5:G12) in the Go To dialog box, Excel will select the entire range defined by the name or addresses. For more specific options, select the Go To Special option. The Go To Special dialog box opens so that you can go to a cell containing comments, constants, formulas, blanks, and so on. Use Help to learn more about the options in this dialog box.

TIP: USING THE NAME BOX
You can enter a cell address, such as G12, in the Name Box and press Enter to go to that cell.

Entering and Editing Cell Data

You should plan the structure of a worksheet before you start entering data. Using the Souvenir Shop case presented at the beginning of the chapter as an example, use the following steps to plan the worksheet design, enter and format data, and complete the workbook. Refer to Figure 1.1 for the completed workbook.

Plan the Worksheet Design

1. **State the purpose of the worksheet.** The purpose of the Souvenir Shop worksheet is to store data about products on sale and to calculate the retail price based on the markup, the sales price based on a discount rate, and the profit margin.

2. **Decide what outputs are required to achieve the purpose of the worksheet.** Outputs are the calculated results. For the Souvenir Shop worksheet, the outputs include columns to calculate the retail price (i.e., the original price you charge your customers), the sale price (the price you charge when the product is on sale), and the profit margin. Some worksheets contain an *output area*, the range of cells in the worksheet to contain formulas dependent on the values in the input area.

3. **Decide what input values are required to achieve the desired output.** Input values are the initial values, such as variables and assumptions. You would change these values to see what type of effects different values have on the end results. For the Souvenir Shop worksheet, the input values include the costs Souvenir Shop pays the manufacturers, the markup rates, and the proposed discount rates for the sale. In some worksheets, you should create an *input area*, a range of cells in the worksheet to store and change the variables used in calculations. For example, if you use the same Markup Rate and same Percent Off for all products, it would be easier to create an input area at the top of the worksheet. Then you could change the values in one location rather than in several locations.

Enter and Format the Data

4. **Enter the labels, values, and formulas in Excel.** Use the design plan (steps 2–3) as you enter labels, input values, and formulas. In the Souvenir Shop worksheet, descriptive labels (the product names) in the first column indicate that the values on a specific row pertain to a specific product. Descriptive labels at the top of each column, such as Cost and Retail Price, describe the values in the respective column. Enter the values and formulas. Change some values to test that your formulas produce correct results. If necessary, correct any errors in the formulas to produce correct results. For the Souvenir Shop worksheet, change some of the original costs and markup rates to ensure the calculated retail price, selling price, and profit margin percentage results update correctly.

5. **Format the numeric values in the worksheet.** Align decimal points in columns of numbers and add number formats and styles. In the Souvenir Shop worksheet, you will use Accounting Number Format and the Percent Style to format the numerical data. Adjust the number of decimal places based on the data.

6. **Format the descriptive titles and labels.** Add bold and color to headings so that they stand out. Apply other formatting to headings and descriptive labels to achieve a professional appearance. In the Souvenir Shop worksheet, you will center the main title over all the columns, bold and center column labels over the columns, and apply other formatting.

Complete the Workbook

7. **Document the workbook as thoroughly as possible.** Include the current date, your name as the workbook author, assumptions, and purpose of the workbook. Some people provide this documentation in a separate worksheet within the workbook. You can also add some documentation in the Properties section when you click the File tab.

8. **Save and share the completed workbook.** Preview and prepare printouts for distribution in meetings, send an electronic copy of the workbook to those who need it, or upload the workbook to a shared network drive or in the cloud.

TIP: TEMPLATES AND THEMES

To save time designing a workbook, consider using an Excel template that contains some of the text, formulas, and formatting. You can then enter specific values and text, and customize the worksheet. You can apply a theme to a workbook to provide a consistent appearance with a unique set of fonts, colors, and other visual effects on worksheet data, shapes, charts, and objects. The Page Layout tab contains commands to change Themes, Colors, Fonts, and Effects.

STEP 1 Enter Text

Text is any combination of letters, numbers, symbols, and spaces not used in calculations. Excel treats phone numbers, such as 617-555-1234 as text entries. You enter text for a worksheet title to describe the contents of the worksheet, as row and column labels to describe data, and as cell data. In Figure 1.5, the cells in column A contain text, such as Class. Text aligns at the left side of the cell by default.

As soon as you begin typing text into a cell, the **AutoComplete** feature searches for and automatically displays any other text in the same column that matches the letters you type. The left side of Figure 1.5 shows Spreadsheet Apps was typed in cell A3. When you start to type *Sp* in cell A4, AutoComplete displays *Spreadsheet Apps* because a text entry in the same column already starts with *Sp*. Press Enter to accept the repeated label, or continue typing to enter a different label, such as Spanish II. When you press Enter, the next cell down in the same column becomes the active cell. However, if you press Ctrl+Enter or click Enter (the check mark between the Name Box and the Formula Bar) after entering data in a cell, the cell remains the active cell.

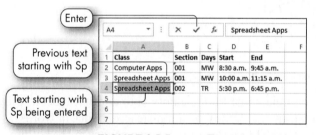
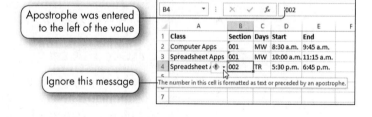

FIGURE 1.5 Entering Text

TIP: ENTER A NUMBER AS TEXT

If you want to enter a numeric value as text, type an apostrophe and the number, such as '002. The right side of Figure 1.5 shows that '002 was entered in cell B4 to start the text with a 0. Otherwise, Excel would have eliminated the zeros in the class section number. Ignore the error message that displays when you intentionally use an apostrophe to enter a number that is not actually a value.

Check the Spelling in a Worksheet

Unlike Word, which displays a red wavy line below misspelled words, Excel does not display any visual indicators for potentially misspelled words. After entering and editing text in a worksheet, you should use the Spelling tool to detect and correct misspelled words.

To check the spelling of text in a worksheet, complete the following steps:

1. Make cell A1 the active cell. If you want to check the spelling in several worksheets, click the first sheet tab and hold Shift to select the last sheet tab; otherwise, only the active sheet will be checked.

2. Click the Review tab and click Spelling in the Proofing group to open the Spelling dialog box (see Figure 1.6). The Spelling dialog box opens, and the potentially misspelled word is displayed in the Not in Dictionary box. The Suggestions box contains a list of potentially correct words.

3. Select the correct word in the Suggestions box and click Change. If the correct word is not listed, click Cancel and correct the misspelled word manually. Start Spelling again to check the rest of the worksheet. If the word is spelled correctly but is not in the dictionary, click Ignore Once to ignore the current occurrence or click Ignore All to ignore all occurrences of the word. You can also click Add to Dictionary to add the word to the dictionary.

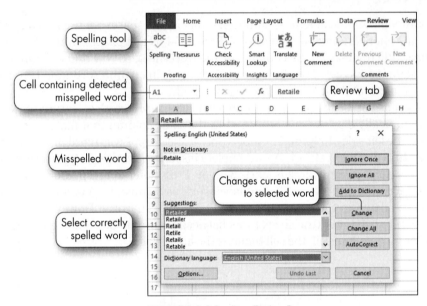

FIGURE 1.6 Spelling Dialog Box

STEP 2 ▶ **Use Auto Fill to Complete a Sequence**

Although AutoComplete helps to complete text that is identical to another label in the same column, *Auto Fill* is a feature that enables you to complete a sequence of words or values and is implemented by using the *fill handle* (a small green square in the bottom-right corner of the active cell). For example, if you enter January in a cell, use Auto Fill to fill in the rest of the months in adjacent cells so that you do not have to type the rest of the month names. Auto Fill can help you complete other sequences, such as quarters (Qtr 1, etc.), weekdays, and weekday abbreviations after you type the first item in the sequence. Figure 1.7 shows the results of filling in months, abbreviated months, quarters, weekdays, abbreviated weekdays, numeric series, and increments of 5.

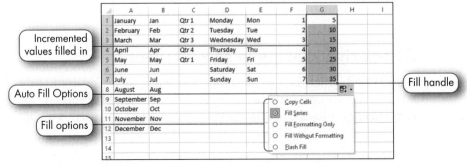

FIGURE 1.7 Auto Fill Examples

> **To use Auto Fill to complete a text or numeric series, complete the following steps:**
>
> 1. Type the first text, such as January, in the starting cell or type the first value, such as 1 (refer to Figure 1.7).
> 2. Make sure the original text or value is the active cell.
> 3. Point to the fill handle until the pointer changes to a thin black plus sign.
> 4. Drag the fill handle to repeat the content in other cells (e.g., through cell A12).

Immediately after you use Auto Fill, Excel displays Auto Fill Options in the bottom-right corner of the filled data (refer to Figure 1.7). Click Auto Fill Options to display several fill options: Copy Cells, Fill Series, Fill Formatting Only, Fill Without Formatting, or Flash Fill. The menu will also include other options, depending on the cell content: Fill Months for completing months; Fill Weekdays for completing weekdays; and Fill Days, Fill Weekdays, Fill Months, Fill Years to complete dates. Select Fill Formatting Only when you want to copy the formats but not complete a sequence. Select Fill Without Formatting when you want to complete the sequence but do not want to format the rest of the sequence. For example, if the first cell contains a top border, use Fill Without Formatting to prevent Auto Fill from formatting the rest of the cells with a top border.

For a single value, Auto Fill will copy that value. Use Auto Fill Options and select Fill Series to change the numbers to be in sequential order, starting with the original value you typed. For nonconsecutive numeric sequences, you must specify the first two values in sequence. To use Auto Fill to fill a sequence of number patterns (such as 5, 10, 15, 20, as shown in Figure 1.7), type the first two numbers in the sequence of adjoining cells, select those two cells, and then drag the fill handle to fill in the rest of the sequence.

> **TIP: FLASH FILL**
> Flash Fill is a similar feature to Auto Fill in that it can quickly fill in data for you; however, *Flash Fill* is a feature that uses data in previous columns as you type in a new label as a pattern in an adjoining column to determine what to fill in. For example, in Figure 1.8 column M contains a list of first and last names (such as Penny Sumpter in cell M2), but you want to have a column of just first names. To do this, type Penny's name in cell N2, click Fill in the Editing group on the Home tab and select Flash Fill to fill in the rest of column N with people's first names based on the data entered in column M. After you use Flash Fill, the status bar displays *Flash Fill Changed Cells: 3*, where 3 indicates the number of cells filled in.

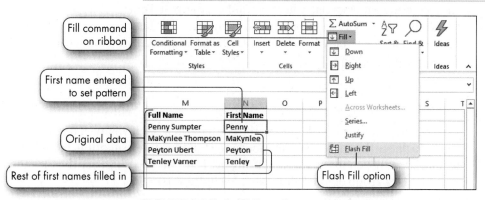

FIGURE 1.8 Flash Fill Examples

STEP 3 **Enter Values**

Values are numbers that represent a quantity or a measurable amount. Excel usually distinguishes between text and value data based on what you enter. The primary difference between text and value entries is that value entries can be the basis of calculations, whereas text cannot. In Figure 1.3, the data below the Cost, Markup Rate, and Percent Off labels are values. Values align at the right side of the cell by default. After entering values, align decimal places and apply formatting by adding characters, such as $ or %. Entering values is the same process as entering text: Type the value in a cell and click Enter or press Enter.

Enter Dates and Times

You can enter dates and times in a variety of formats. You should enter a static date to document when you create or modify a workbook or to document the specific point in time when the data were accurate, such as on a balance sheet or income statement. Later, you will learn how to use formulas to enter dates that update to the current date. In Figure 1.9, the data in column A contains the date 9/1/2021, but in different formats. Dates are values, so they align at the right side of a cell. The data in column C contains the time 2:30 PM, but in different formats.

	A	B	C	D
1	9/1/2021		2:30 PM	
2	Wednesday, September 1, 2021		2:30:00 PM	
3	9/1		14:30	
4	9/1/21		14:30:00	
5	09/01/21			
6	1-Sep			
7	1-Sep-21			
8	September 1, 2021			
9				

FIGURE 1.9 Date and Time Examples

Excel displays dates differently from the way it stores dates. Excel stores dates as serial numbers starting at 1 for January 1, 1900. For example, 9/1/2021 is stored as 44440, and 10/1/2021 is stored as 44470. Because Excel stores dates as serial numbers, you can create formulas to calculate the number of days between dates. When you subtract 9/1/2021 from 10/1/2021, the result is 30 days.

Edit and Clear Cell Contents

After entering data in a cell, you may want to change it. For example, you may want to edit a label to make it more descriptive, such as changing a label from Ceramic Mug to Souvenir Mug, or changing a value from 500 to 5000. There are several methods to edit cell contents:

- Double-click the cell.
- Click in the Formula Bar.
- Press F2.

You may want to clear or delete the contents in a cell if you no longer require data in a cell. To delete the contents of the active cell but keep the formatting, press Delete. If you want to clear the content and formatting or clear other settings, use the Clear command in the Editing group on the Home tab (see Figure 1.10).

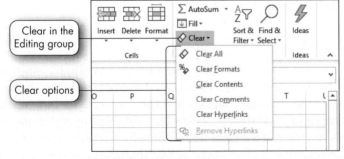

FIGURE 1.10 Clear Options

STEP 4 Find and Replace Data

When you work with a large dataset in Excel or a workbook with multiple worksheets, you can search through it to find a value or specific label. For example, you can search through the Souvenir Shop worksheet to find all occurrences of 0.15. Use the Find & Select tool to find data and select data.

> **To find data, complete the following steps:**
>
> 1. Click Find & Select in the Editing group on the Home tab.
> 2. Select Find to open the Find and Replace dialog box.
> 3. Enter data you want to find in the Find what box.
> 4. Click Options if you want to specify conditions. The dialog box expands to display options to narrow the search (see Figure 1.11).
>   - Click Format to specify a number, alignment, font, fill, or border format.
>   - Click the Within arrow to specify where to find the data: within the current sheet or within the entire workbook.
>   - Click the Match case check box to select it to identify cells that contain the same capitalization style as the data you entered.
> 5. Click Find All or Find Next to locate the data with the conditions you specified.

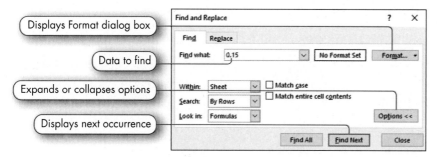

FIGURE 1.11 Find Options

- Displays Format dialog box
- Data to find
- Expands or collapses options
- Displays next occurrence

> **MAC TIP:** The Mac version of Excel does not have a Find All option.

If you click Find All, the dialog box will list the workbook, sheet, cell, and exact value. The bottom of the dialog box specifies the number of cells where the data is found, such as 37 cell(s) found. In the worksheet, Excel makes the first occurrence it finds as the active cell. If you click Find Next, Excel makes the next occurrence it finds as the active cell. The dialog box does not display a list of the other occurrences.

Instead of just finding data, you may want to find and replace it. For example, you can search to find all occurrences of the 0.15 discount rate and replace those occurrences with a 0.17 discount rate.

> **To find and replace data, compete the following steps:**
>
> 1. Click Find & Select in the Editing group on the Home tab.
> 2. Select Replace to open the Find and Replace dialog box.
> 3. Enter data you want to find in the Find what box and enter the replacement data in the Replace with box (see Figure 1.12).
> 4. Click Options if you want to specify conditions. You can specify specific formatting for both the data to find and the data to replace.
> 5. Click Replace All to replace all occurrences, click Replace to replace the current occurrence only, click Find All, or click Find Next to review the data before replacing it.

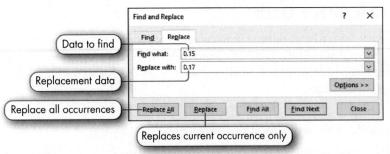

FIGURE 1.12 Find and Replace Options

Quick Concepts ✓

1. Describe two situations in which you could create workbooks to store and calculate data. *p. 72*

2. Describe how Excel indicates which cell is the active cell. *p. 73*

3. List the steps you should perform before entering data into a worksheet. *p. 76*

4. Explain the difference between Auto Fill and Flash Fill. *pp. 78–79*

Hands-On Exercises

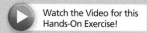

Skills covered: Go to a Cell •
Enter Text • Check the Spelling
in a Worksheet • Use Auto Fill
to Complete a Sequence • Enter
Values • Enter a Date • Clear Cell
Contents • Find and Replace Data

1 Introduction to Spreadsheets

As the assistant manager of the Celebrity Musician's Souvenir Shop, you will create a worksheet that shows
the cost (the amount Souvenir Shop pays its suppliers), the markup percentage (the percentage over cost),
and the retail selling price. You also will list the discount percentage (such as 25% off) for each product, the
sale price, and the profit margin percentage.

STEP 1 ENTER TEXT AND CHECK THE SPELLING IN A WORKSHEET

Now that you have planned the Souvenir Shop worksheet, you are ready to enter the rest of the product names in
the first column. Although you should check the spelling as a final step before distributing a workbook, it is also a good
practice to check spelling after entering or editing a lot of text. Refer to Figure 1.13 as you complete Step 1.

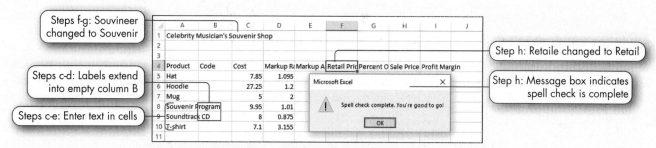

Steps f-g: Souvineer changed to Souvenir

Steps c-d: Labels extend into empty column B

Steps c-e: Enter text in cells

Step h: Retaile changed to Retail

Step h: Message box indicates spell check is complete

FIGURE 1.13 Text Entered in Cells

---

a. Open *e01h1Souvenirs* and save it as **e01h1Souvenirs_LastFirst**.

   When you save files, use your last and first names. For example, as the Excel author, I
   would name my workbook "e01h1Souvenirs_MulberyKeith."

> **TROUBLESHOOTING:** If you make any major mistakes in this exercise, you can close the file,
> open *e01h1Souvenirs* again, and then start this exercise over.

b. Press **Ctrl+G**, type **A8** in the Reference box, and then click **OK**.

   You used the Go To dialog box to make cell A8 the active cell.

c. Type **Souvenir Program** and press **Enter**.

   Cell A9 becomes the active cell. The text Souvenir Program does not completely fit
   in cell A8, and some of the text displays in cell B8. However, the text is stored only in
   cell A8. If you make cell B8 the active cell, the Formula Bar is empty, indicating that
   nothing is stored in that cell.

d. Type **Soundtrack CD** in **cell A9** and press **Enter**.

   When you start typing S in cell A9, AutoComplete displays a ScreenTip suggesting a
   previous text entry starting with S—Souvenir Program—but keep typing Soundtrack CD
   instead.

e. Type **T-shirt** in **cell A10** and press **Enter**.

   You just entered the product labels to describe the data in each row.

> **TROUBLESHOOTING:** If you make an error, click in the cell containing the error and retype the label, or press F2 to edit the cell contents, move the insertion point using the arrow keys, press Backspace or Delete to delete the incorrect characters, type the correct characters, and press Enter. If you type a label in an incorrect cell, click the cell and press Delete.

f. Press **Ctrl+Home** to make **cell A1** the active cell, click the **Review tab**, and then click **Spelling** in the Proofing group.

The Spelling dialog box opens, indicating that *Souvineer* is not in the dictionary. *Souvenir*, the first word in the Suggestions box, is the correct word.

g. Click **Change** to change the misspelled word to Souvenir.

Retaile is detected as not being in the dictionary.

h. Select **Retail**, the third word in the Suggestions box, click **Change.** Correct any other misspelled words and click **OK** when prompted.

i. Click **Save** on the Quick Access Toolbar.

If your file is saved on OneDrive, it will be automatically saved if AutoSave is On. Otherwise, you should manually save your workbook periodically. That way if your system unexpectedly shuts down, you will not lose your work.

STEP 2 USE AUTO FILL TO COMPLETE A SEQUENCE

Product codes help to identify products with a unique number. Therefore, you will assign a product code for each product on sale at the Souvenir Shop. You will assign consecutive numbers 101 to 106. After typing the first code number, you will use Auto Fill to complete the rest of the series. Refer to Figures 1.14 and 1.15 as you complete Step 2.

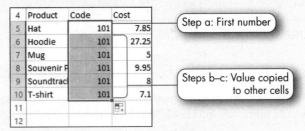

FIGURE 1.14 Auto Fill Copied Original Value

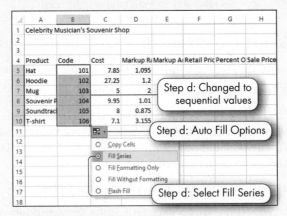

FIGURE 1.15 Auto Fill Sequence

a. Click **cell B5**, type **101**, and then press **Ctrl+Enter**.

Pressing Ctrl+Enter or clicking Enter to the left of the Formula Bar keeps cell B5 the active cell.

b. Position the pointer on the fill handle in the bottom-right corner of **cell B5**.

The pointer looks like a black plus sign when you point to a fill handle.

c. Double-click the **cell B5 fill handle**.

Excel copies 101 as the item number for the rest of the products. Excel stops inserting item numbers in column B when it detects the last label in cell A10 (refer to Figure 1.14). The product names no longer overlap into column B after you enter data into cells B8 and B9. The data in cells A8 and A9 are hidden and will fully display if the column width is adjusted.

d. Click **Auto Fill Options** and select **Fill Series**. Save the workbook.

Excel changes the duplicate values to continue sequentially in a series of numbers.

STEP 3 ENTER VALUES, ENTER DATES, AND CLEAR CONTENTS

Now that you have entered the descriptive labels and item numbers, you will enter the percentage off as a decimal value for each product. You want to provide a date to indicate when the sale starts. Refer to Figure 1.16 as you complete Step 3.

	A	B	C	D	E	F	G	H	I	J
1	Celebrity Musician's Souvenir Shop									
2	9/1/2021		Step e: Date				Steps a–b: Percentage Off values			
3										
4	Product	Code	Cost	Markup Ra	Markup A	Retail Pric	Percent O	Sale Price	Profit Margin	
5	Hat	101	7.85	1.095			0.15			
6	Hoodie	102	27.25	1.2			0.2			
7	Mug	103	5	2			0.05			
8	Souvenir P	104	9.95	1.01			0.25			
9	Soundtracl	105	8	0.875			0.3			
10	T-shirt	106	7.1	3.155			0.05			
11										

FIGURE 1.16 Values and a Date Entered in Cells

a. Click **cell G5**, type **0.15**, and then press **Enter**.

Although you could have entered .15 without the 0, in this book, 0 will be shown before the decimal point to clearly indicate a decimal value. However, you can type just the decimal value such as .15 and get the same results. You entered the percentage off rate as a decimal (0.15) instead of a percentage (15%). You will apply Percent Style later, but now you will concentrate on data entry.

b. Type the remaining values in **cells G6** through **G10** as shown in Figure 1.16.

To improve your productivity, use the number keypad (if available) on the right side of your keyboard. It is much faster to type values and press Enter on the number keypad rather than to use the numbers at the top of the keyboard. Make sure Num Lock is active before using the number keypad to enter values.

c. Click **cell A2**, type **9/1**, and then press **Enter**.

Because you entered 9/1 without a preceding =, Excel treats 9/1 as a date rather than dividing 9 by 1. The date aligns on the right cell margin by default. Excel displays 1-Sep instead of 9/1.

d. Click **cell A2**, click the **Home tab**, click **Clear** in the Editing group, and then select **Clear Formats**.

The date formatting is cleared, and the date displays as the serial number. Later in this chapter, you will learn how to apply different date formats. For now, you will type the date differently.

e. Type **9/1/2021** in **cell A2** and press **Ctrl+Enter**. Save the workbook.

When you retype the date, Excel detects the data entry is a date and displays the date rather than the serial number. The date now displays as 9/1/2021 instead of 44440.

> **TROUBLESHOOTING:** If you did not use Clear Formats and typed 9/1/2021 in cell A2, Excel retains the previous date format and displays 1-Sep again. Repeat Step d, ensuring that you select Clear Formats, and then repeat Step e.

STEP 4 FIND AND REPLACE DATA

To motivate the Souvenir Shop customers to buy more products, you want to change the percentage off from 5% (0.05) to 10% (0.10). Although the Souvenir Shop worksheet contains a small dataset, where you could easily find the 0.05 rate, you will use the Find and Replace feature so that you do not miss any occurrences. Refer to Figure 1.17 as you complete Step 4.

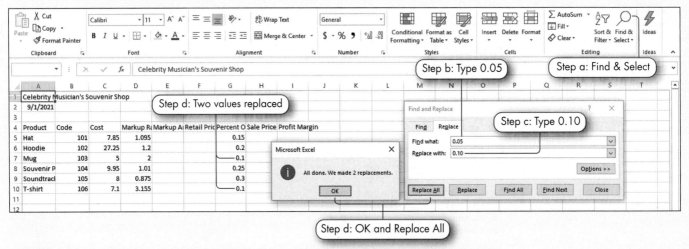

FIGURE 1.17 Data Replaced in the Worksheet

a. Go to **cell A1**, click **Find & Select** in the Editing group on the Home tab, and then select **Replace**.

The Find and Replace dialog box opens with the Replace tab options displayed.

> **MAC TROUBLESHOOTING:** Click Edit, point to Find, and then click Find.

b. Type **0.05** in the Find what box.

You want to find all occurrences of the 0.05 rate.

> **TROUBLESHOOTING:** Make sure you include the decimal place and 0 in the correct location to avoid finding and replacing the wrong rate.

c. Press **Tab** and type **0.10** in the Replace with box.

You want the replacement value to be 0.10.

d. Click **Replace All** and click **OK** when prompted. Click **Close** in the Find and Replace dialog box.

Excel found two occurrences of 0.05 and replaced them with 0.10.

e. Save the workbook. Keep the workbook open if you plan to continue with the next Hands-On Exercise. If not, close the workbook, and exit Excel.

Mathematical Operations and Formulas

A *formula* combines cell references, arithmetic operations, values, and/or functions used in a calculation. Formulas transform static numbers into meaningful results that update as values change. In the Souvenir Shop product sales worksheet, you will create formulas to calculate the retail price, sale price, and profit margin (refer to Figure 1.1).

In this section, you will learn how to use mathematical operations in Excel formulas. You will refresh your memory of the mathematical order of operations and learn how to construct formulas using cell references so that when the value of an input cell changes, the result of the formula changes without you having to modify the formula.

Creating Formulas

Formulas help you analyze how results change as the input data changes. You can change the value of your assumptions or inputs and explore the results quickly and accurately. For example, if the vendor increases the cost of the souvenir mugs, how does that affect your retail selling price?

STEP 1 Use Cell References in Formulas

Use cell references instead of values in formulas where possible so if the value of the cell changes, the results of the formulas will update and reflect the change in input. You may include values in an input area—such as dates, salary, or costs—that you will need to reference in formulas. Referencing these cells in your formulas, instead of typing the value of the cell to which you are referring, keeps your formulas accurate if you change values to perform a what-if analysis.

To enter a formula in the active cell, type = followed by the arithmetic expression, using cell references instead of values. If you type B2+B3 without the equal sign, Excel does not recognize that you entered a formula and stores the "formula" as text. You can enter cell references in uppercase, such as =B2+B3, or lowercase, such as =b2+b3. Excel changes the cell references to uppercase automatically.

> **TIP: EXCEL INTELLISENSE FORMULA AUTOCOMPLETE**
> When you start typing a cell reference immediately after the equal sign (such as =B), Excel Intellisense Formula AutoComplete displays a list of functions that start with that letter. Keep typing the cell reference (such as =B4) and complete the rest of the formula.

Figure 1.18 shows a worksheet containing input values and results of formulas. For example, cell E2 contains the formula =B2+B3. Excel uses 10, the value stored in cell B2, and adds it to 2, the value stored in cell B3. The result of 12 displays in cell E2 instead of the actual formula. The Formula Bar displays the formula contained in the active cell.

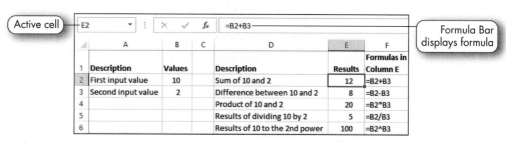

FIGURE 1.18 Formula Results

In Figure 1.18, cell B2 contains 10, and cell B3 contains 2. Cell E2 contains =B2+B3 but shows the result 12. If you change the value of cell B3 to 5, cell E2 displays the new result, which is 15. However, if you had typed actual values in the formula, $^-10+2$, the formula would still show a result of 12, and you would have to edit the formula to =10+5, even though the value in cell B3 was changed to 5. Using values in formulas can cause problems if you forget to edit the formula or if you create a typographical error when editing the formula. Where possible, design worksheets in such a way as to be able to place those values that might change as input values. Referencing cells with input values in formulas instead of using the values themselves will avoid having to modify the formulas if an input value changes later.

TIP: WHEN TO USE A VALUE IN A FORMULA

Use cell references instead of actual values in formulas, unless the value will never change. For example, if you want to calculate how many total months are in a specified number of years, enter a formula such as =B5*12, where B5 contains the number of years. You might want to change the number of years; therefore, type that value in cell B5. However, every year always has 12 months, so you can use the value 12 in the formula.

Copy a Formula

After you enter a formula in a cell, duplicate the formula without retyping the formula for other cells that require a similar formula. Previously, you learned about the Auto Fill feature that enables you to use the fill handle to fill in a series of values, months, quarters, and weekdays. You can also drag the fill handle to copy the formula in the active cell to adjacent cells down a column or across a row, depending on how the data are organized. Cell references in copied formulas adjust based on their relative locations to the original formula.

Use Semi-Selection to Create a Formula

To decrease typing time and ensure accuracy, use *semi-selection*, a process of selecting a cell or range of cells for entering cell references as you create formulas. Semi-selection is often called *pointing* because you use the pointer to select cells as you build the formula. Some people prefer using the semi-selection method instead of typing a formula so that they can make sure they use the correct cell references as they build the formula.

To use the semi-selection technique to create a formula, complete the following steps:

1. Type = to start a formula.
2. Click the cell that contains the value to use in the formula. A moving marquee appears around the cell you select, and Excel displays the cell reference in the formula.
3. Type a mathematical operator.
4. Continue clicking cells, selecting ranges, and typing operators to finish the formula. Use the scroll bars if the cell is in a remote location in the worksheet or click a worksheet tab to see a cell in another worksheet.
5. Press Enter to complete the formula.

STEP 2 **Apply the Order of Operations**

The ***order of operations*** (also called *order of precedence*) is a set of rules that control the sequence in which arithmetic operations are performed, which affects the result of the calculation. Excel performs mathematical calculations left to right in this order: **P**arentheses, **E**xponentiation, **M**ultiplication or **D**ivision, and finally **A**ddition or **S**ubtraction. Some people remember the order of operations with the phrase *Please Excuse My Dear Aunt Sally.*

Table 1.3 lists the primary order of operations. Use Help to learn about the complete order of operations.

TABLE 1.3	Order of Operations	
Order	**Description**	**Symbols**
1	Parentheses	( )
2	Exponentiation	^
3	Multiplication and Division	* and / (respectively)
4	Addition and Subtraction	+ and − (respectively)

Use parentheses to make sure a lower-order operation occurs first. For example, if you want to add the values stored in cells A1 and A2 and multiply that result by the value stored in cell A3, enclose parentheses around the addition operation: =(A1+A2)*A3. Without parentheses, =A1+A2*A3, the first calculation multiplies the values stored in A2 and A3. That result is then added to the value stored in cell A1, because multiplication has a higher order of operation than addition.

Figure 1.19 shows formulas, the sequence in which calculations occur, description of the calculations, and the formula results. The highlighted results are the final formula results. This figure illustrates the arithmetic symbols and the how parentheses affect the formula results.

	A	B	C	D	E	F
1	**Input**		**Formula**	**Sequence**	**Description**	**Result**
2	2		=A2+A3*A4+A5	1	3 (cell A3) * 4 (cell A4)	12
3	3			2	2 (cell A2) + 12 (order 1)	14
4	4			3	14 (order 2) + 5 (cell A5)	19
5	5					
6			=(A2+A3)*(A4+A5)	1	2 (cell A2) + 3 (cell A3)	5
7				2	4 (cell A4) + 5 (cell A5)	9
8				3	5 (order 1) * 9 (order 2)	45
9						
10			=A2/A3+A4*A5	1	2 (cell A2) / 3 (cell A3)	0.666667
11				2	4 (cell A4) * 5 (cell A5)	20
12				3	0.666667 (order 1) + 20 (order 2)	20.66667
13						
14			=A2/(A3+A4)*A5	1	3 (cell A3) + 4 (cell A4)	7
15				2	2 (cell A2) / 7 (order 1)	0.285714
16				3	0.285714 (order 2) * 5 (cell A5)	1.428571
17						
18			=A2^2+A3*A4%	1	4 (cell A4) is converted to percentage	0.04
19				2	2 (cell A2) to the power of 2	4
20				3	3 (cell A3) * 0.04 (order 1)	0.12
21				4	4 (order 2) + 0.12 (order 3)	4.12

FIGURE 1.19 Formula Results Based on Order of Operations

STEP 3 ▸ Display Cell Formulas

Excel shows the result of the formula in the cell (see the top half of Figure 1.20); however, you can display the formulas instead of the calculated results in the cells (see the bottom half of Figure 1.20). Displaying the cell formulas may help you double-check all your formulas at one time or troubleshoot a problem with a formula instead of looking at each formula individually. To display cell formulas, press Ctrl and the grave accent (`) key between the Tab and Esc keys or click Show Formulas in the Formula Auditing group on the Formulas tab. Repeat the process to hide formulas and display results again.

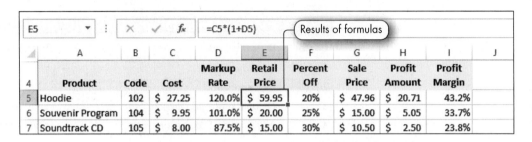

FIGURE 1.20 Formulas and Formula Results

Quick Concepts

5. Describe the importance of the order of operations. Provide an example where the outcome is affected using and not using parentheses. ***p. 89***

6. Explain why you should use cell references instead of typing values in formulas. ***p. 87***

7. Explain when it would be useful to display formulas instead of formula results in a worksheet. ***p. 90***

Hands-On Exercises

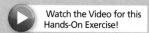

Skills covered: Use Cell References in Formulas • Copy a Formula • Use Semi-Selection to Create a Formula • Apply the Order of Operations • Display Cell Formulas

2 Mathematical Operations and Formulas

In Hands-On Exercise 1, you created the Souvenir Shop worksheet by entering text, values, and a date for items on sale. Now you will insert formulas to calculate the missing results—specifically, the retail (before sale) price, sale price, and profit margin. You will use cell references in your formulas, so when you change a referenced value, the formula results will update automatically.

STEP 1 USE CELL REFERENCES IN A FORMULA, COPY A FORMULA, AND USE SEMI-SELECTION TO CREATE A FORMULA

The first formula you create will calculate the markup amount. The markup is based on the cost and markup rate. After you enter the formula for the first product, you will copy the formula down the column to calculate the markup amount for the other products. Then, you will use the semi-selection method to calculate the retail price, which is the price you charge customers. It is the sum of the cost and the markup amount. Refer to Figure 1.21 as you complete Step 1.

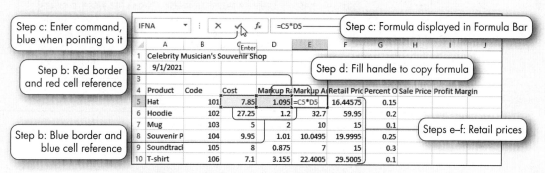

FIGURE 1.21 Markup Amount and Retail Price Formulas

a. Open *e01h1Souvenirs_LastFirst* if you closed it at the end of Hands-On Exercise 1 and save it as **e01h2Souvenirs_LastFirst**, changing h1 to h2.

b. Click **cell E5** and type **=C5*D5**, but do not press Enter.

Note the cell references in the formula match colored borders around the cells. This helps to identify cells as you construct your formulas (refer to Figure 1.21).

c. Click **Enter** to enter the formula.

Multiplying 7.85 (the cost in cell C5) by 1.095 (the markup rate in cell D5) equals 8.59575. You are marking up the hat by $8.60 over your cost. View the formula in the Formula Bar to check it for accuracy.

> **TROUBLESHOOTING:** If the result is not correct, with cell E5 active, check the Formula Bar to make sure the formula contains the correct cell references and the asterisk for multiplication. Correct any errors.

d. Position the pointer on the **cell E5 fill handle**. When the pointer changes from a white plus sign to a thin black plus sign, double-click the **fill handle**.

Excel copies the Markup Amount formula down the column for the remaining products. Excel stops copying the formula when it detects the last row in the dataset.

e. Click **cell F5**. Type **=**, click **cell C5**, type **+**, click **cell E5**, and click **Enter**.

You used the semi-selection method to add 7.85 (the cost) plus 8.59575 (the markup amount) to equal 16.44575 (the retail price).

f. Double-click the **cell F5 fill handle** and save the workbook.

Excel copies the Retail Price formula through cell F10.

APPLY THE ORDER OF OPERATIONS

The products are on sale this week, so you want to calculate the sale prices. For example, the hat is on sale for 15% off the retail price. After calculating the sale price, you will calculate the profit margin. The formulas you create will apply the order of operations. Refer to Figure 1.22 as you complete Step 2.

I5   *fx* =(H5-C5)/H5

	A	B	C	D	E	F	G	H	I	J	K
1	Celebrity Musician's Souvenir Shop										
2	9/1/2021										
3											
4	Product	Code	Cost	Markup Ra	Markup A	Retail Pric	Percent O	Sale Price	Profit Margin		
5	Hat	101	7.85	1.095	8.59575	16.44575	0.15	13.97889	0.438439		
6	Hoodie	102	27.25	1.2	32.7	59.95	0.2	47.96	0.431818		
7	Mug	103	5	2	10	15	0.1	13.5	0.62963		
8	Souvenir P	104	9.95	1.01	10.0495	19.9995	0.25	14.99963	0.33665		
9	Soundtrac	105	8	0.875	7	15	0.3	10.5	0.238095		
10	T-shirt	106	7.1	3.155	22.4005	29.5005	0.1	26.55045	0.732585		
11											
12											

Step f: Formula entered in cell I5

Steps f–g: Results =(Sale Price-Cost)/Sale Price

Steps b–c: Results =Retail Price*(1-Percent Off)

FIGURE 1.22 Sale Price and Profit Margin Formulas

a. Click **cell H5**.

b. Type **=F5*(1-G5)** and press **Ctrl+Enter** to keep the current cell as the active cell.

The result is 13.97889. The formula first subtracts 0.15 (the percentage off) from 1, which is 0.85. Then Excel multiplies 16.44575 (the value in cell F5) by 0.85 to get 13.97889 (the retail price).

> **TROUBLESHOOTING:** If your result is different, check the formula for correct cell references, mathematical operators, and parentheses.

c. Double-click the **cell H5 fill handle** to copy the formula down column H.

d. Click **cell H6** and view the Formula Bar.

The original formula was =F5*(1-G5). The copied formula in cell H6 is adjusted to =F6*(1-G6) so that it calculates the sales price based on the data in row 6.

e. Click **cell I5**.

f. Type **=(H5-C5)/H5** and click **Enter**.

Profit margin is (Sale Price – Cost)/Sale Price. The Souvenir Shop paid $7.85 for the hat and sells it for $13.98. The $6.13 profit is divided by the $13.98 sale price, which gives a profit margin of 0.438484, which will be formatted later as a percentage (43.8%).

g. Double-click the **cell I5 fill handle** to copy the formula down the column. Save the workbook.

DISPLAY CELL FORMULAS

You want to display the formulas in the worksheet to check for accuracy. In addition, you want to see how the prices and profit margins are affected when you change three original values. For example, the supplier might notify you that the cost to you will increase. Refer to Figures 1.23 and 1.24 as you complete Step 3.

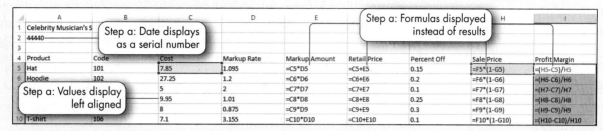

FIGURE 1.23 Formulas Displayed in the Worksheet

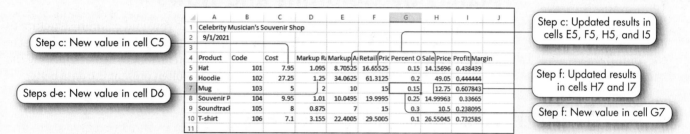

FIGURE 1.24 Results of Changed Values

a. Press **Ctrl+`** (the grave accent mark).

The workbook displays the formulas rather than the formula results (refer to Figure 1.23). This is helpful when you want to review several formulas at one time.

b. Click the **Formulas tab** and click **Show Formulas** in the Formula Auditing group.

Alternatively, you can press Ctrl+`. The workbook now displays the formula results in the cells again.

c. Click **cell C5**, type **7.95**, and then press **Enter**.

The results of the markup amount, retail price, sale price, and profit margin formulas change based on the new cost.

d. Click **cell D6** and press **F2**.

The insertion point blinks to the right of 1.2.

e. Type **5** and press **Enter**.

You added 5, so the new markup rate is 1.25. The results of the markup amount, retail price, sale price, and profit margin formulas change based on the new markup rate.

f. Click **cell G7**, type **0.15**, and then press **Ctrl+Enter**.

The results of the sale price and profit margin formulas change based on the new percentage off rate. Note that the retail price did not change because that formula is not based on the markup rate.

g. Save the workbook. Keep the workbook open if you plan to continue with the next Hands-On Exercise. If not, close the workbook, and exit Excel.

Worksheet Structure and Clipboard Tasks

Although you plan worksheets before entering data, you can insert a new row to accommodate new data, delete a column that you no longer want, hide a column of confidential data before printing worksheets for distribution, or adjust the size of columns and rows so that the data fit better. Furthermore, you may decide to move data to a different location in the same worksheet, or even to a different worksheet. In some instances, you will create a copy of data entered so that you can explore different values and compare the results of the original dataset and the copied and edited dataset.

In this section, you will learn how to make changes to columns and rows. You will also learn how to select ranges, move data to another location, copy data to another range, and use the Paste Special feature.

Managing Columns and Rows

As you enter and edit worksheet data, you can adjust the row and column structure to accommodate new data or remove unnecessary data. You can add rows and columns to add new data and delete data, columns, and rows that you no longer need. Adjusting the height and width of rows and columns, respectively, can often present the data better.

STEP 1 ▶ Insert Cells, Columns, and Rows

After you construct a worksheet, you can insert cells, columns, or rows to accommodate new data. For example, you can insert a new column to perform calculations or insert a new row to list a new product. To insert a new column or row, make a cell the active cell on that column or row, use the Insert arrow in the Cells group on the Home tab (see Figure 1.25), and then select Insert Sheet Columns or Insert Sheet Rows. Alternatively, you can use a shortcut menu: Right-click the column (letter) or row (number) heading and select Insert from the shortcut menu. Excel inserts a new blank column to the left of the current column and moves the remaining columns to the right. When you insert a new row, Excel moves the remaining rows down.

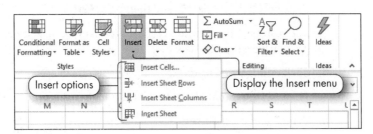

FIGURE 1.25 Insert Menu

Inserting a cell is helpful when you realize that you left out an entry after you have entered a lot of data. Instead of inserting a new row or column, you just want to move the existing content down or over to enter the missing value. You can insert a single cell in a row or column. When you insert cells, rows, and columns, cell addresses in formulas adjust automatically.

If you click Insert in the Cells group, the default action inserts a cell at the current location, which moves existing data down *in that column only*. For more options for inserting cells, use the Insert arrow in the Cells group on the Home tab and select Insert Cells to display the Insert dialog box (see Figure 1.26). You can then insert cells and shift existing cells to the right or down.

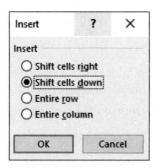

FIGURE 1.26 Insert Dialog Box

STEP 2 ## Delete Cells, Columns, and Rows

If you no longer require data in a cell, column, or row, you should delete it. For example, you can delete a row containing a product you no longer carry. In these situations, you are deleting the entire cell, column, or row, not just the contents of the cell to leave empty cells. As with inserting new cells, columns, or rows, any affected formulas adjust the cell references automatically.

To delete a column or row, select the column or row heading for the column or row you want to delete and use Delete in the Cells group on the Home tab. Alternatively, make any cell within the column or row you want to delete the active cell, click the Delete arrow in the Cells group on the Home tab (see Figure 1.27), and then select Delete Sheet Columns or Delete Sheet Rows. Another alternative is to right-click the column letter or row number for the column or row you want to delete and select Delete from the shortcut menu.

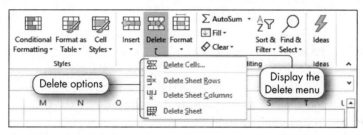

FIGURE 1.27 Delete Menu

Clicking Delete in the Cells group immediately deletes the active cell, which moves existing data up in that column only. To delete a cell or range of cells, select Delete Cells to display the Delete dialog box (see Figure 1.28). Select the option to shift cells left or up.

FIGURE 1.28 Delete Dialog Box

STEP 3 ## Adjust Column Width

After you enter data in a column, you often will adjust the ***column width***—the horizontal measurement of a column in a table or a worksheet. For example, in the worksheet you created in Hands-On Exercises 1 and 2, the labels in column A displayed into column B when those adjacent cells were empty. However, after you typed values in column B, the labels in column A appeared cut off. You should widen column A to show the full name of your products. Excel provides two ways to widen a column to accommodate the longest text or value in a column:

- Point to the right vertical border of the column heading. When the pointer displays as a two-headed arrow, double-click the border.
- Click Format in the Cells group on the Home tab (see Figure 1.29) and select AutoFit Column Width.

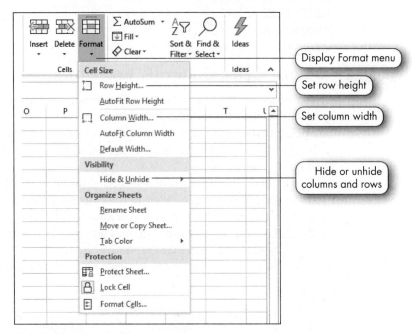

FIGURE 1.29 Format Menu

Sometimes, widening the column to fit the longest text or value makes the column too wide for the remaining data. In those cases, specify an exact column width by using one of these methods:

- Drag the vertical border to the left to decrease the column width or to the right to increase the column width. As you drag the vertical border, Excel displays a Screen-Tip specifying the width (see Figure 1.30) from 0 to 255 characters and in pixels.
- Click Format in the Cells group on the Home tab (refer to Figure 1.29), select Column Width, type a value that represents the maximum number of characters to display in the Column width box in the Column Width dialog box, and then click OK.

	A	B	C	D	E	F	G	H	I
1	Celebrity Musician's Souvenir Shop								
2	9/1/2021								
3									
4	Product	Code	Cost	Markup R	Markup A	Retail Pric	Percent O	Sale Price	Profit Margin
5	Hat	101	7.95	1.095	8.70525	16.65525	0.15	14.15696	0.438439
6	Hoodie	102	27.25	1.25	34.0625	61.3125	0.2	49.05	0.444444
7	Mug	103	5	2	10	15	0.15	12.75	0.607843
8	Souvenir P	104	9.95	1.01	10.0495	19.9995	0.25	14.99963	0.33665
9	Soundtrac	105	8	0.875	7	15	0.3	10.5	0.238095
10	T-shirt	106	7.1	3.155	22.4005	29.5005	0.1	26.55045	0.732585
11									

Current column width — G7 — fx — 0.15

Width: 12.00 (89 pixels)

ScreenTip displaying column width

Column width when you release the mouse button

Pointer as you drag the boundary on the right side of a column heading

FIGURE 1.30 Increasing Column Width

Adjust Row Height

You can adjust the ***row height***—the vertical measurement of the row—similarly to how you change column width by double-clicking the border between row numbers or by selecting Row Height or AutoFit Row Height from the Format menu (refer to Figure 1.29). In Excel, row height is a value between 0 and 409 based on point size (abbreviated as *pt*) and pixels. Whether you are measuring font sizes or row heights, one point size is equal to 1/72 of an inch. The row height should be taller than the font size. For example, with an 11 pt font size, the default row height is 15.

Hide and Unhide Columns and Rows

Sometimes a worksheet might contain data that you do not want to display, such as employee IDs or birthdates, or assumptions, or internal notes. You can hide columns or rows that contain the sensitive data before printing a copy to distribute or displaying the worksheet on a screen during a meeting.

However, the column or row is not deleted. If you hide column B, you will see columns A and C side by side. If you hide row 3, you will see rows 2 and 4 together. Figure 1.31 shows that column B and row 3 are hidden. Excel displays a double line between column headings or row headings to indicate that columns or rows are hidden.

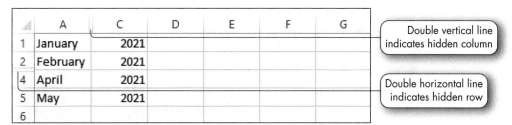

FIGURE 1.31 Hidden Columns and Rows

To hide a column or row, complete the following steps:

1. Select a cell or cells in the column or row you want to hide.
2. Click Format in the Cells group on the Home tab (refer to Figure 1.29).
3. Point to Hide & Unhide.
4. Select Hide Columns or Hide Rows, depending on what you want to hide.

Alternatively, you can right-click the column or row heading(s) you want to hide and select Hide. You can hide multiple columns or multiple rows at the same time. To select adjacent columns (such as columns B through E) or adjacent rows (such as rows 2 through 4), drag across the adjacent column or row headings and use the Hide command. To hide nonadjacent columns or rows, press and hold Ctrl while you click the desired column or row headings, and then use the Hide command. To unhide, select the columns or rows on both sides of the hidden column or row and select Unhide Columns or Unhide Rows, respectively.

Selecting, Moving, Copying, and Pasting Data

You may already know the basics of selecting, cutting, copying, and pasting data in other programs, such as Word. The overall process is the same in Excel. However, some of the techniques differ slightly as you work with cells, columns, and rows of data in Excel.

STEP 4 ▶ ## Select a Range

A **range** refers to a group of adjacent or contiguous cells in a worksheet. A range may be as small as a single cell or as large as the entire worksheet. It may consist of a row or part of a row, a column or part of a column, or multiple rows or columns, but the range will always be a rectangular shape, as you must select the same number of cells in each row or column for the entire range. A range is specified by indicating the top-left and bottom-right cells in the selection. For example, in Figure 1.32, the date is a single-cell range in cell A2, the Mug product data are stored in the range A7:H7, the cost values are stored in the range C5:C10, and the sales prices and profit margins are stored in range G5:H10. A **nonadjacent range** contains multiple ranges, such as D5:D10 and F5:F10, that are not positioned in a contiguous cluster in the worksheet. At times, you will select nonadjacent ranges so that you can apply the same formatting at the same time, such as formatting the nonadjacent range D5:D10 and F5:F10 with Percent Style.

Table 1.4 lists methods to select ranges, including nonadjacent ranges.

FIGURE 1.32 Sample Ranges

TABLE 1.4	Selecting Ranges
To Select	**Do This**
A range	Drag until you select the entire range. Alternatively, click the first cell in the range, press and hold Shift, and click the last cell in the range.
An entire column	Click the column heading.
Column of data (current cell to last cell containing data in the column)	Press Ctrl+Shift+down arrow. (On a Mac, press Shift+Command+arrow.)
An entire row	Click the row heading.
Row of data (current cell to last cell on the row containing data)	Press Ctl+Shift+right arrow. (On a Mac, press Shift+Command+arrow.)
Current range containing data, including headings	Click in the range of data and press Ctrl+A. (On a Mac, press Command+A.)
All cells in a worksheet	Click Select All or press Ctrl+A twice.
Nonadjacent range	Select the first range, press and hold Ctrl, and select additional range(s).

A green border surrounds a selected range. Any command you execute will affect the entire range. The range remains selected until you select another range or click in any cell in the worksheet.

Move a Range

You can move cell contents from one range to another. For example, you can move an input area from the right side of the worksheet to above the output range. When you move a range containing text and values, the text and values do not change. However, any formulas that refer to cells in that range will update to reflect the new cell addresses.

To move a range, complete the following steps:

1. Select the range.
2. Click Cut in the Clipboard group (see Figure 1.33). Unlike cutting data in other Microsoft Office applications, the data you cut in Excel remain in their locations until you paste them elsewhere. A moving dashed green border surrounds the selected range and the status bar displays *Select destination and press ENTER or choose Paste*.
3. Ensure the destination range—the range where you want to move the data—is the same size or greater than the size of the cut range.
4. Click in the top-left corner of the destination range and click Paste (see Figure 1.33). If any cells within the destination range contain data, Excel overwrites that data when you use the Paste command.

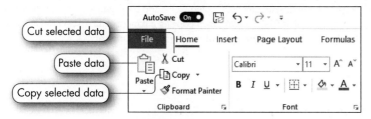

FIGURE 1.33 Cut, Copy, Paste

STEP 5 Copy and Paste a Range

You may want to copy cell contents from one range to another. When you copy a range, the original data remain in their original locations. For example, you can copy your January budget to another worksheet to use as a model for creating your February budget. Cell references in copied formulas adjust based on their relative locations to the original data. Furthermore, you want to copy formulas from one range to another range. In this situation, where you cannot use the fill handle, you will use the Copy and Paste functions to copy the formula.

The process for copying a range is similar to moving a range. Instead of using the Cut command, use the Copy command after selecting the range. Then, when you use the Paste command, Excel overwrites any data if any cells within the destination range contain data. Figure 1.34 shows a selected range (A4:H10) and a copy of the range (J4:Q10). The original range still has the moving dashed green border, and the pasted copied range is selected with a solid green border. Press Esc to turn off the moving dashed border.

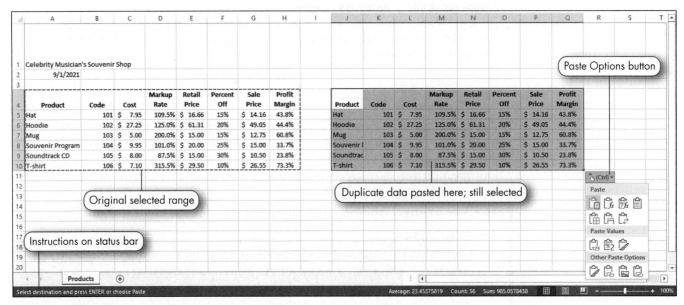

FIGURE 1.34 Copied and Pasted Range

TIP: INSERT COPIED CELLS
Instead of inserting a blank column or row, cutting, and then pasting the data in the new column or row, you can simplify the process. Select the data and click Cut. Right-click the upper-left cell where you want the data to be moved, select Insert Copied Cells, and then select Shift Cells Right when copying a column of data or Shift Cells Down when copying a row of data. Excel inserts a column or row and pastes the data at the same time without overwriting existing data.

TIP: COPY AS PICTURE
Click the Copy arrow in the Clipboard group to select Copy as Picture. This option copies an image of the selected data. When you use Paste, the copied data becomes an object that can be modified like other pictures. It is like taking a screenshot of a selected range. However, when you copy the data as an image, you cannot edit individual cell data in the image.

STEP 6 **Use Paste Options**

Sometimes you want to paste data in a different format than they are in the Clipboard. For example, you can preserve the results of calculations before changing the original data by pasting the data as values. Immediately after you click Paste, the **Paste Options button** displays near the bottom-right corner of the pasted data. Click the arrow to select a different result for the pasted data (refer to Figure 1.34).

Instead of using the Paste Options button, the Paste arrow in the Clipboard group contains many different paste options. To display more information about a paste option, point to it on the Paste gallery (see Figure 1.35).

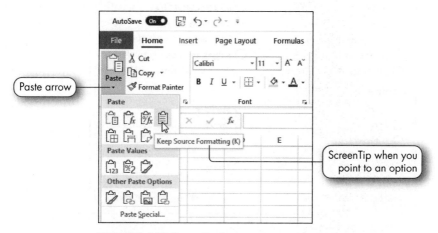

FIGURE 1.35 Paste Options

Table 1.5 lists and describes some of the options in the Paste gallery that opens when you click the Paste arrow in the Clipboard group or the Paste Options button that displays immediately after you use Paste. Paste options enable you to paste content or attributes, such as a formula or format.

TABLE 1.5 Paste Options

Icon	Option Name	Paste Description
	Paste	Cell contents and all formatting from copied cells.
	Formulas	Formulas, but no formatting, from copied cells.
	Formulas & Number Formatting	Formulas and number formatting, such as Currency, but no font formatting, such as font color, fill color, or borders.
	Keep Source Formatting	Cell contents and formatting from copied cells.
	No Borders	Cell contents, number formatting, and text formatting except borders.
	Keep Source Column Widths	Cell contents, number and text formatting, and the column width of the source data when pasting in another column.
	Transpose	Transposes data from rows to columns and columns to rows.
	Values	Unformatted values that are the results of formulas, not the actual formulas.
	Values & Number Formatting	Values that are the results of formulas, not the actual formulas; preserves number formatting but not text formatting.
	Values & Source Formatting	Values that are the results of formulas, not the actual formulas; preserves number and text formatting.
	Formatting	Number and text formatting only from the copied cells; no cell contents.
	Paste Link	Creates a reference to the source cells (such as =$G$15), not the cell contents; preserves number formatting but not text formatting.
	Picture	Creates a picture image of the copied data; pasted data is not editable.
	Linked Picture	Creates a picture with a reference to the copied cells; if the original cell content changes, so does the picture.
	Paste Special	Opens the Paste Special dialog box (see Figure 1.36).

FIGURE 1.36 Paste Special Dialog Box

TIP: TRANSPOSING COLUMNS AND ROWS

You can transpose the columns and rows so that the data in the first column appear as column labels across the first row, or the column labels in the first row appear in the first column. Figure 1.37 shows the original data with the months in column A and the utility costs in columns B, C, and D. In the transposed data, the months are shown in the first row, and each row contains utility information. The original formats (bold and right-aligned) are copied in the transposed data.

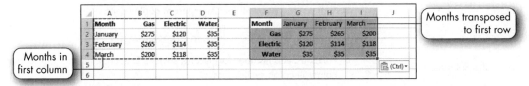

Months in first column

Months transposed to first row

FIGURE 1.37 Transposed Data

TIP: COPY EXCEL DATA TO OTHER PROGRAMS

You can copy Excel data and use it in other applications, such as in a Word document or in a PowerPoint presentation. For example, you can perform statistical analyses in Excel and copy the data into a research paper in Word. Alternatively, you can create a budget in Excel and copy the data into a PowerPoint slide show for a meeting. After selecting and copying a range in Excel, you must decide how you want the data to appear in the destination application. Use the Paste arrow in the destination application to see a gallery of options or to select the Paste Special option. For example, you can paste the Excel data as a worksheet object, as unformatted text, or in another format.

Quick Concepts

8. Give an example of when you would delete a column versus when you would hide a column. *pp. 95, 97*

9. When should you adjust column widths instead of using the default width? *p. 95*

10. Discuss how you would use a paste option. *pp. 100–102*

Hands-On Exercises

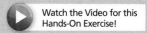
Skills covered: Insert a Column • Insert and Delete Rows • Adjust Column Width • Adjust Row Height • Hide a Column • Select a Range • Move a Range • Copy and Paste a Range • Use Paste Options

3 Worksheet Structure and Clipboard Tasks

You want to insert a column to calculate the amount of markup and delete a row containing data you no longer require. You also want to adjust column widths to display the labels in the columns. In addition, Melissa asked you to enter data for a new product. Because it is almost identical to an existing product, you will copy the original data and edit the copied data to save time. You also want to experiment with the Paste Special option to see the results of using it in the Souvenir Shop workbook.

STEP 1 INSERT A COLUMN

You decide to add a column to display the profit. Because profit is a dollar amount, you want to keep the profit column close to another column of dollar amounts. Therefore, you will insert a new column before the profit margin column. Refer to Figure 1.38 as you complete Step 1.

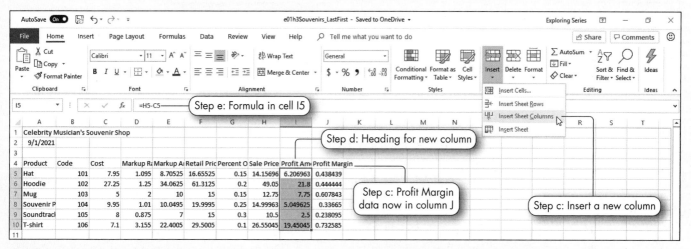

FIGURE 1.38 Profit Amount Column Inserted

a. Open *e01h2Souvenirs_LastFirst* if you closed it at the end of Hands-On Exercise 2 and save it as **e01h3Souvenirs_LastFirst**, changing h2 to h3.

b. Click any cell in **column I**.

You want to insert a column between the Sale Price and Profit Margin columns.

c. Click the **Insert arrow** in the Cells group on the Home tab and select **Insert Sheet Columns**.

You inserted a new blank column I. The contents in the original column I are now in column J.

d. Click **cell I4**, type **Profit Amount**, and then press **Enter**.

e. Ensure the active cell is **cell I5**. Enter the formula **=H5-C5**. Double-click the **cell I5 fill handle**. Save the workbook.

You calculated the profit amount by subtracting the original cost from the sale price and then copied the formula down the column. The profit for the soundtrack CD is $2.50.

You decide to insert new rows for product information and category names. Furthermore, you decided not to include the Soundtrack CD for this week's list of sale items, so you want to delete the row containing that data. Refer to Figure 1.39 as you complete Step 2.

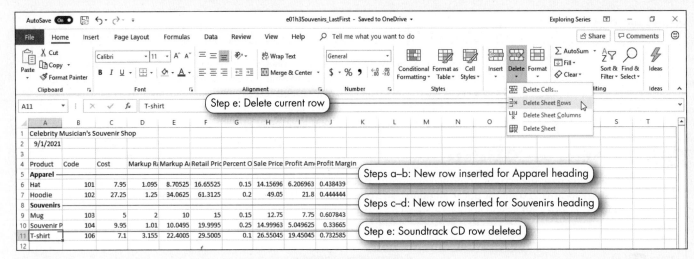

FIGURE 1.39 Category Rows Inserted and the Soundtrack CD Row Deleted

a. Right-click the **row 5 heading** and select **Insert** from the shortcut menu.

You inserted a new blank row 5, which is selected. The original rows of data move down a row each.

> **MAC TROUBLESHOOTING:** Use Control+click when instructed to right-click in the instructions.

b. Click **cell A5**. Type **Apparel** and press **Ctrl+Enter**. Click **Bold** in the Font group.

c. Right-click the **row 8 heading** and select **Insert** from the shortcut menu.

You inserted a new blank row 8. The data that was originally on row 8 is now on row 9.

d. Click **cell A8**. Type **Souvenirs** and press **Ctrl+Enter**. Click **Bold** in the Font group.

You typed and applied bold formatting to the category name Souvenirs above the list of souvenir products.

e. Click **cell A11**, click the **Delete arrow** in the Cells group, and then select **Delete Sheet Rows**. Save the workbook.

The Soundtrack CD row is deleted, and the remaining row moves up one row.

> **TROUBLESHOOTING:** If you accidentally delete the wrong row or accidentally select Delete Sheet Columns instead of Delete Sheet Rows, click Undo on the Quick Access Toolbar to restore the deleted row or column. Then complete Step e again.

ADJUST COLUMN WIDTH, ADJUST ROW HEIGHT, AND HIDE A COLUMN

As you review your worksheet, you notice that the text in column A appears cut off. You will increase the width of that column to display the entire product names. In addition, you want to make row 1 taller so that the title stands out. Finally, you decide to hide the column containing the codes because the managers are more interested in the monetary values than the codes. Refer to Figure 1.40 as you complete Step 3.

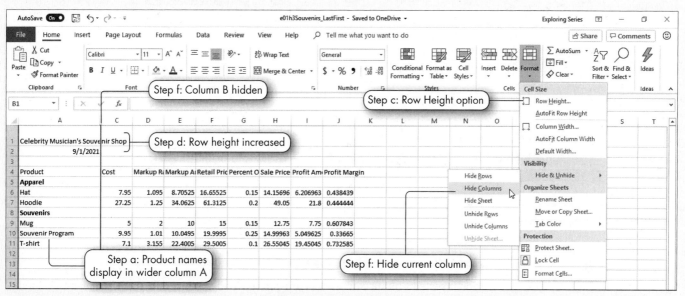

FIGURE 1.40 Column Width and Row Height Changed; Codes Column Hidden

a. Point to the **right border** of column A. When the pointer looks like a double-headed arrow with a solid black vertical line, double-click the **border**.

Excel increased the width of column A based on the cell containing the longest content (the title in cell A1). You decide to adjust the column width to the longest product name instead.

b. Point to the **right border** of column A until the double-headed arrow appears. Drag the border to the left until the ScreenTip displays **Width: 23.00 (166 pixels)**. Release the mouse button.

You decreased the column width to 23 for column A. The longest product name is visible. You will adjust the other column widths after you apply formats to the column headings in Hands-On Exercise 4.

c. Click **cell A1**. Click **Format** in the Cells group and select **Row Height**.

The Row Height dialog box opens so that you can adjust the height of the current row.

d. Type **30** in the Row height box and click **OK**.

You increased the height of the row that contains the worksheet title so that it is more prominent.

e. Click the **column B heading**.

f. Click **Format** in the Cells group, point to **Hide & Unhide**, and then select **Hide Columns**. Save the workbook.

Excel hides column B, the column containing the Codes. You see a gap in column heading letters A and C, indicating column B is hidden instead of deleted.

You want to move the T-shirt product to be immediately after the Hoodie product. Before moving the T-shirt row, you will insert a blank row between the Hoodie and Souvenirs. Refer to Figure 1.41 as you complete Step 4.

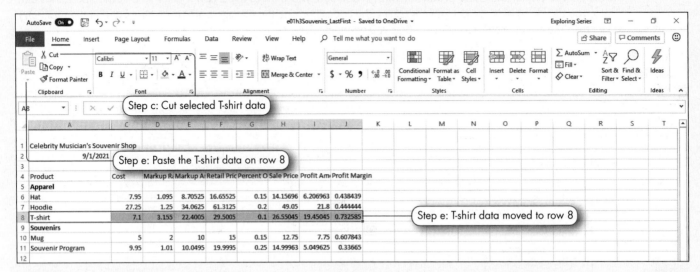

FIGURE 1.41 T-shirt Row Moved

a. Right-click the **row 8 heading** and select **Insert** from the menu.

You inserted a blank row so that you can move the T-shirt data to be between the Hoodie and Souvenirs rows.

b. Select the **range A12:J12**.

You selected the range of cells containing the T-shirt data.

c. Click **Cut** in the Clipboard group.

A moving dashed green border outlines the selected range. The status bar displays the message *Select destination and press ENTER or choose Paste.*

d. Click **cell A8**.

This is the first cell in the destination range. If you cut and paste a row without inserting a new row first, Excel will overwrite the original row of data, which is why you inserted a new row in step a.

e. Click **Paste** in the Clipboard group and save the workbook.

The T-shirt product data is now located on row 8.

STEP 5 ▶ COPY AND PASTE A RANGE

In addition to selling ceramic mugs, Melissa ordered travel mugs. She asked you to enter the data for the new product. Because most of the data is the same as the current mug, you will copy the original mug data, edit the product name, and change the cost to reflect the cost of the second type of mug. Refer to Figure 1.42 as you complete Step 5.

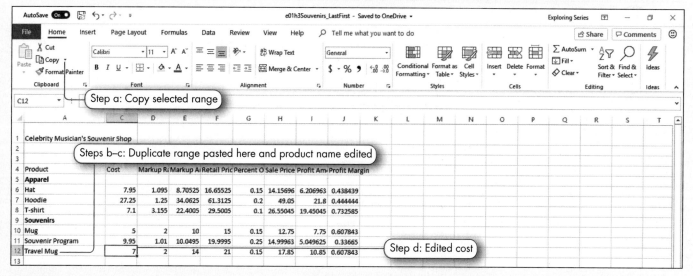

FIGURE 1.42 Mug Data Copied and Edited

a. Select the **range A10:J10** and click **Copy** in the Clipboard group.

You copied the row containing the Mug product data to the Clipboard.

b. Click **cell A12**, click **Paste** in the Clipboard group, and then press **Esc**.

The pasted range is selected in row 12.

c. Click **cell A12**, press **F2** to activate Edit Mode, press **Home**, type **Travel**, press **Spacebar**, and then press **Enter**.

You edited the product name to display Travel Mug.

d. Change the value in **cell C12** to **7**. Save the workbook.

The formulas calculate the results based on the $7 cost for the Travel Mug.

During your lunch break, you want to experiment with some of the Paste options. Particularly, you are interested in pasting Formulas and Value & Source Formatting. First, you will apply bold and a font color to the title to help you test these Paste options. Refer to Figure 1.43 as you complete Step 6.

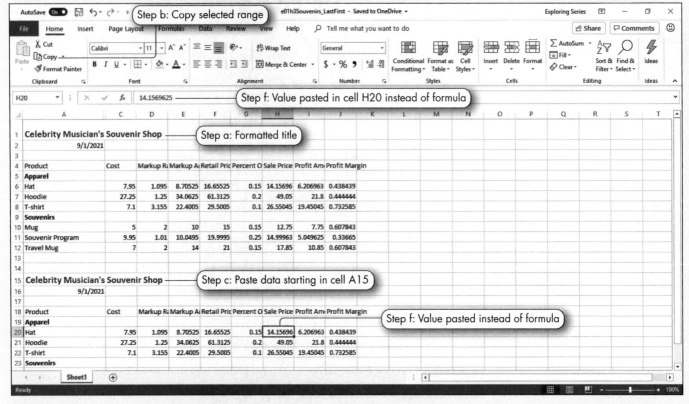

FIGURE 1.43 Results of Paste Options

a. Click **cell A1**. Click the **Font Size arrow** in the Font group and select **14**, click **Bold**, click the **Font Color arrow**, and then select **Dark Red** in the Standard Colors section.

b. Select the **range A1:J12** and click **Copy** in the Clipboard group.

c. Click **cell A15**, the top-left corner of the destination range.

d. Click the **Paste arrow** in the Clipboard group and point to **Formulas**, the second icon from the left in the Paste group.

   Without clicking the command, Excel shows you a preview of what that option would do. The pasted copy would not contain the font formatting you applied to the title or the bold on the two category names. In addition, the pasted date would appear as a serial number. The formulas would be maintained.

e. Position the pointer over **Values & Source Formatting**, the first icon from the right in the Paste Values group.

   This option would preserve the formatting, but it would convert the formulas into the current value results.

f. Click **Values & Source Formatting** and press **Esc**. Click **cell H6** to see a formula and click **cell H20**.

   Cell H6 contains a formula, but in the pasted version, the equivalent cell H20 has converted the formula result into an actual value. If you were to change the original cost in cell C20, the contents of cell H20 would not change. In a working environment, this is useful only if you want to capture the exact value in a point in time before making changes to the original data.

g. Save the workbook. Keep the workbook open if you plan to continue with the next Hands-On Exercise. If not, close the workbook, and exit Excel.

Worksheet Formatting

After entering data and formulas, you should format the worksheet. A professionally formatted worksheet—through adding appropriate symbols, aligning decimals, and using fonts and colors to make data stand out—makes finding and analyzing data easy. You can apply different formats to accentuate meaningful details or to draw attention to specific ranges in a worksheet.

In this section, you will learn to apply a cell style, different alignment options, including horizontal and vertical alignment, text wrapping, and indent options. In addition, you will learn how to format different types of values.

Applying Cell Styles, Cell Alignment, and Font Options

Visual clues, created by formatting changes, can differentiate parts of the worksheet. For example, the title may be centered in 16 pt size; column labels may be bold, centered, and Dark Blue font; and input cells may be formatted differently from output cells. The Font group on the Home tab contains the Font, Font Size, Bold, Italic, Underline, and Font Color commands. In addition to these commands, you will use other options in the Font, Alignment, and Styles groups to format data in a worksheet.

STEP 1 ▷ Apply Cell Styles

You can apply formats individually, or you can apply a group of formats by selecting a cell style. A *cell style* is a collection of format characteristics that provides a consistent appearance within a worksheet and among similar workbooks. A cell style controls the following formats: font, font color, font size, borders, fill colors, alignment, and number formatting. When you click Cell Styles in the Styles group on the Home tab, the Cell Styles gallery displays (see Figure 1.44). Position the pointer over a style name to see a Live Preview of how the style will affect the selected cell or range. The gallery provides a variety of built-in styles to apply to cells in your worksheet to make it easy to apply consistent formatting.

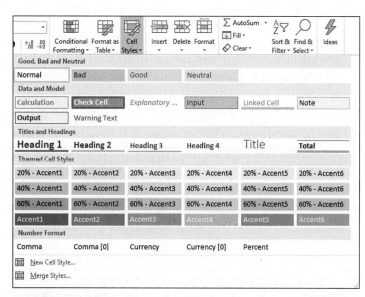

FIGURE 1.44 Cell Styles

Merge Cells

Often, a worksheet title is centered over the columns of data in the worksheet. Use Merge and Center to combine selected cells together into one cell. When the cells are merged horizontally, only data in the far-left cell are merged. When cells are merged vertically, only data in the top-left cell is maintained. Any other data in the merged cells are deleted.

You can use Merge and Center to center main titles over the columns of data in the worksheet, and you can merge and center category titles over groups of related columns. You can also merge cells on adjacent rows. Table 1.6 lists the four options when you click the Merge & Center arrow.

TABLE 1.6	Merge Options
Option	**Results**
Merge & Center	Merges selected cells and centers data into one cell.
Merge Across	Merges the selected cells but keeps text left aligned or values right aligned.
Merge Cells	Merges a range of cells and keeps original alignment.
Unmerge Cells	Separates a merged cell into multiple cells again.

STEP 2 ▶ Change Cell Alignment

Alignment refers to how data are positioned in the boundaries of a cell. Each type of data has a default alignment. *Horizontal alignment* specifies the position of data between the left and right cell margins. Text aligns at the left cell margin, and dates and values align at the right cell margin. You should change the alignment of cell contents to improve the appearance of data within the cells. For example, you can apply center horizontal alignment to center column labels over the values in a column. *Vertical alignment* specifies the position of data between the top and bottom cell margins. Bottom Align is the default vertical alignment. While this alignment is not noticeable with the default row height, if you increase the row height to accommodate text in another cell on that row, data might not appear aligned properly across the row. In that situation, consider applying Top Align or Middle Align to see if that improves readability.

The Alignment group on the Home tab contains the vertical and horizontal alignment options. The vertical and horizontal alignments applied to the active cell display with a green background on the ribbon. In Figure 1.45, cell I4 is formatted with Bottom Align vertical alignment and Center horizontal alignment, as indicated by the light green background of those commands on the ribbon.

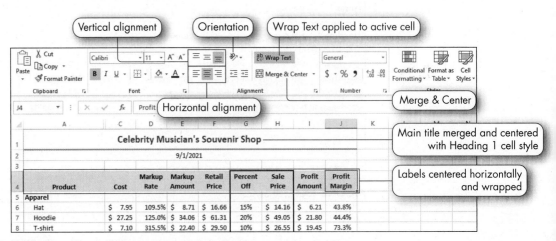

FIGURE 1.45 Cell Style and Alignment Settings Applied

The Format Cells dialog box contains options for changing horizontal and ver
alignment, text wrapping, merging cells, and rotating data in cells. In addition, you
shrink data to fit within the cell and change the text direction in the cell. To oper
Format Cells dialog box, click the Dialog Box Launcher in the Alignment group or
Home tab.

> **MAC TIP:** Office for Mac does not have Dialog Box Launchers. Instead, use the Format menu.

> **TIP: CHANGE TEXT ORIENTATION**
> People sometimes rotate headings in cells. More text may fit when it is rotated at an angle, rotated
> or rotated down. To rotate data in a cell, click Orientation in the Alignment group on the Home t
> and select an option, such as Angle Clockwise.

Wrap Text

Use **wrap text** to word-wrap data on multiple lines within a cell by adjusting the row
to fit the cell contents within the column width. Excel wraps the text on two or mos
within the cell. In Figure 1.45, the Markup Rate and Percent Off labels on row 4 are-
ples of wrapped text. The Wrap Text option is in the Alignment group on the Ho).
Wrap Text has a light green background because the text is wrapped in the active.

> **TIP: LINE BREAK IN A CELL**
> If a long text label does not fit well in a cell even after you have applied wrap text, you can insert
> line break to display the text label on multiple lines within the cell. To insert a line break while yo
> typing a label, press Alt+Enter where you want to start the next line of text within the cell. On a
> press Option+Enter.

STEP 3 ## Increase and Decrease Indent

Cell content is left-aligned or right-aligned based on the default data type. Howerou
can **indent** the cell contents to offset the data from its current alignment. For examext
is left-aligned, but you can indent it to offset it from the left side. Indenting helps otsee
the hierarchical structure of data. Accountants often indent the word Totals in fcial
statements so that it stands out from a list of items above the total row. Values aght-
aligned by default, but you can indent a value to offset it from the right side of cell.
In Figure 1.46, the specific products (Hat, Hoodie, T-shirt, Mug, Souvenir Progrand
Travel Mug) are indented. Use the Increase Indent or Decrease Indent in the Alinent
group to adjust the indent of data in a cell.

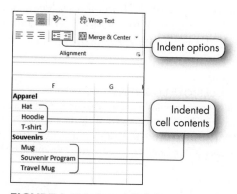

FIGURE 1.46 Indented Cell Contents

STEP 4 Apply Borders and Fill Color

A worksheet with a lot of text and numbers will be hard to read without some formatting to help emphasize headings, important data, input and output areas, etc. You can apply a border or fill color to accentuate data in a worksheet. A ***border*** is a line that surrounds a cell or a range of cells. Use borders to offset some data from the rest of the worksheet data. Borders are applied by using the Border command in the Font group on the Home tab. The Border arrow displays different options, and for more control, select More Borders to display the Format Cells dialog box with additional border options. In Figure 1.47, a border surrounds the range G4:H12. To remove a border, select No Border from the Borders menu.

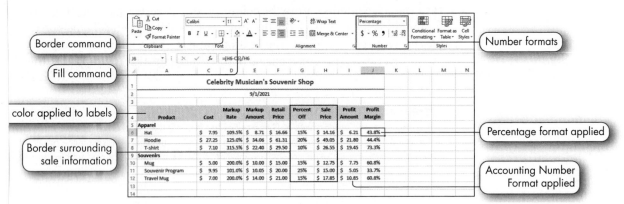

FIGURE 1.47 Borders, Fill Color, and Number Formats

Add some color to your worksheets to emphasize data or headers by applying a fill color. ***Fill color*** is a background color that displays behind data in a cell so that the data stand out. Choose a fill color that contrasts with the font color. For example, if the font color is Black, Text 1, select White or Yellow fill color. If the font color is White, Background 1, select a dark fill color such as Dark Blue. The color palette contains two sections: Theme Colors and Standard Colors. The Theme Colors section displays variations of colors that match the current theme applied in the worksheet. The Standard Colors section contains basic colors that do not change with the theme. When you click the Fill Color arrow in the Font group on the Home tab, a color palette displays. If you want to remove a fill color, select No Fill from the bottom of the palette. Select More Colors to open the Colors dialog box and use the Standard tab or Custom tab to select a color. In Figure 1.47, the column labels in row 4 are formatted with Blue-Gray, Text 2, Lighter 80% fill color to complement the Blue-Gray, Text 2 font color for the title in cell A1.

Applying Number Formats

Values have no special formatting when you enter data. However, you can ap *number formats*, settings that control how a value is displayed in a cell. The defa number format is General, which displays values as you originally enter them. Genei number format does not align decimal points in a column or include symbols, such ; dollar signs, percent signs, or commas. Applying number formats provides context for th values, such as displaying currency symbols for monetary values and percent signs foi percentages, and make the data easier to read.

STEP 5 ▶ Apply a Number Format

The Number group on the Home tab contains commands for applying Accounting Number Format, Percent Style, and Comma Style numbering formats. The *Accounting Number Format* and *Currency format* both display the dollar sign, commas for every three digits on the left side of the decimal point, align decimal points, and display two digits to the right of the deci-mal point; however, the placement of the dollar sign differs. In Accounting Number Format, the dollar sign aligns on the left side of the cell; in Currency format, the dollar sign is immedi-ately to the left of the value. You can click the Accounting Number Format arrow and select other denominations, such as English pounds or euros. For other number formats, click the Number Format arrow and select the numbering format you want to use. Figure 1.47 shows the Accounting Number Format applied to the ranges C6:C12, E6:F12, and H6:I12. Percent Style is applied to the ranges D6:D12, G6:G12, and J6:J12.

Applying a different number format changes the way the number displays in a cell, but the format does not change the stored value. If, for example, you enter 123.456 into a cell and format the cell with the Currency number type, the value shows as $123.46 onscreen where the value is rounded to the nearest cent, but Excel uses the full value 123.456 when performing calculations.

Table 1.7 lists and describes the primary number formats in Excel. Figure 1.48 shows different number formats applied to the value 1234.567 and the special Zip+4 and phone number formats.

TABLE 1.7 Number Formats

Format Style	Display
General	The default number format.
Number	A number with or without the comma separator and with any number of decimal places. Negative numbers can be displayed with parentheses and/or red.
Currency format	A number, the dollar sign immediately to the left of the number, a comma for every three digits on the left side of the decimal point, and two digits to the right of the decimal point. Negative values are preceded by a minus sign. Zero displays as $0.00.
Accounting Number Format	A number, the dollar sign on the left side of the cell, a comma for every three digits on the left side of the decimal point, and two digits to the right of the decimal point. Negative values are enclosed in parentheses by default. Zero displays as a dollar sign and a hyphen.
Comma Style	The *Comma Style* formats with a comma for every three digits on the left side of the decimal point and displays two digits to the right of the decimal point.
Date	A serial number formatted as a date.
Time	A number formatted for time.
Percent Style	The *Percent Style* formats a value as if it was multiplied by 100 and with a percent symbol.
Fraction	A number formatted as a fraction.
Scientific	A number as a decimal fraction followed by a whole number exponent of 10; for example, the number 12345 would display as 1.23E+04.
Text	Treats data as text, even if it contains numbers.
Special	A number with editing characters, such as the parentheses and hyphen in a phone number, hyphen in a Zip Code+4, and the hyphens in a Social Security number.
Custom	Predefined customized number formats or special symbols to create your own customized number format.

▲	A	B	C	D	E	F
1	General	1234.567		Original Value	9171234567	
2	Number	1234.57		Phone Number Format	(917) 123-4567	
3	Currency	$1,234.57				
4	Accounting	$ 1,234.57		Original Value	102821234	
5	Comma	1,234.57		Zip + 4 Number Format	10282-1234	
6	Percent	123457%				

FIGURE 1.48 Number Formats

TIP: CUSTOM NUMBER FORMATS

You can create a custom format if the built-in formats do not meet your needs by accessing the Custom Format options in the Format Cells dialog box. Select Custom in the Category list (see Figure 1.49) and select the custom format. Use Help to learn how to create custom number formats.

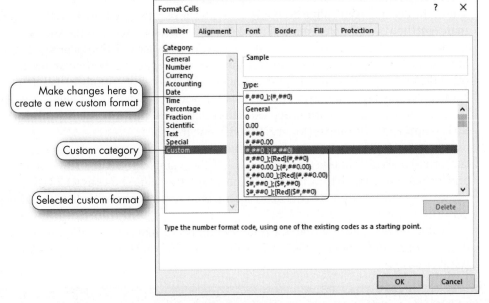

Make changes here to create a new custom format

Custom category

Selected custom format

FIGURE 1.49 Custom Number Formats

Increase and Decrease Decimal Places

After applying a number format, you will usually adjust the number of decimal places that display. For example, if you have an entire column of monetary values formatted in Accounting Number Format, Excel displays two decimal places by default. If the entire column of values contains whole dollar values and no cents, displaying *.00* down the column looks cluttered. Decrease the number of decimal places to show whole numbers only. By default, Percent Style displays percentages as whole numbers. However, for greater precision, you can increase the number of decimal places displayed to one or two. Use Increase Decimal or Decrease Decimal in the Number group on the Home tab to adjust the number of decimal points for a value.

TIP: FORMAT PAINTER

Use Format Painter in the Clipboard group on the Home tab to copy formats (alignment, fill color, border, number format, text wrapping, and number formats) to other cells in the workbook.

Quick Concepts

11. Discuss when you would use Merge and Center in a worksheet. *p. 110*

12. Explain why you would wrap text in a cell. *p. 111*

13. Explain why you would increase the number of decimal places for values formatted with Percent Style. *p. 114*

Hands-On Exercises

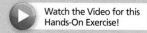

Skills covered: Apply a Cell Style • Merge Cells • Change Cell Alignment • Wrap Text • Increase Indent • Apply a Border • Apply Fill Color • Apply Number Formats • Increase and Decrease Decimal Places

4 Worksheet Formatting

In the first three Hands-On Exercises, you entered data about products on sale, created formulas to calculate markup and profit, and inserted new rows and columns. You are ready to format the Souvenir Shop worksheet. Specifically, you will apply a cell style, merge and center the title, align text, format values, and apply other formatting to enhance the readability of the worksheet.

STEP 1 APPLY A CELL STYLE AND MERGE CELLS

To make the title stand out, you want to apply a cell style and center it over all the data columns. You will use the Merge & Center command to merge cells and center the title at the same time. Refer to Figure 1.50 as you complete Step 1.

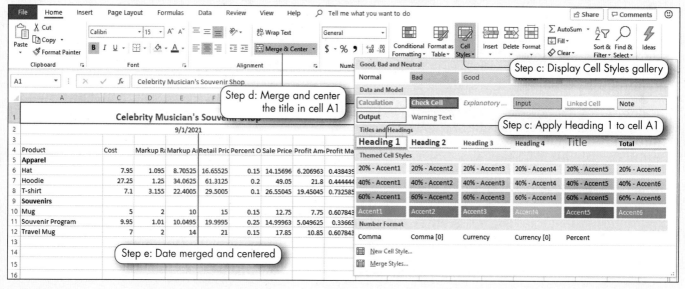

FIGURE 1.50 Cell Style Applied and Cells Merged

a. Open *e01h3Souvenirs_LastFirst* if you closed it at the end of Hands-On Exercise 3 and save it as **e01h4Souvenirs_LastFirst**, changing h3 to h4.

b. Select the **range A15:J26** and press **Delete**.

You maintained a copy of your Paste Special results in the e01h3Souvenirs_LastFirst workbook, but you do not need it to continue.

c. Select the **range A1:J1**, click **Cell Styles** in the Styles group on the Home tab, and then click **Heading 1** from the gallery.

You applied the Heading 1 style to the range A1:J1. This style formats the contents with 15-pt font size, Blue-Gray, Text 2 font color, and a thick blue bottom border.

d. Click **Merge & Center** in the Alignment group.

Excel merges cells in the range A1:J1 into one cell and centers the title horizontally within the merged cell, which is cell A1.

> **TROUBLESHOOTING:** If you merge too many or not enough cells, unmerge the cells and start again. To unmerge cells, click in the merged cell. The Merge & Center command is shaded in green when the active cell is merged. Click Merge & Center to unmerge the cell. Then select the correct range to merge and use Merge & Center again.

e. Select the **range A2:J2**. Click **Merge & Center** in the Alignment group. Save the workbook.

> **TROUBLESHOOTING:** If you try to merge and center data in the range A1:I2, Excel will keep the top-left data only and delete the date. To merge separate data on separate rows, you must merge and center data separately.

CHANGE CELL ALIGNMENT AND WRAP TEXT

You want to center the title vertically between the top and bottom cell margins. In addition, you will center the column labels horizontally between the left and right cell margins and wrap the text in the column labels to avoid columns that are too wide for the data (such as Profit Margin). Refer to Figure 1.51 as you complete Step 2.

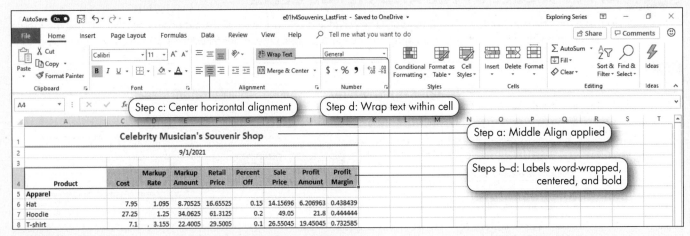

FIGURE 1.51 Alignment Options Applied to the Title and Column Labels

a. Click **cell A1**, which contains the title, and click **Middle Align** in the Alignment group.

   Middle Align vertically centers data between the top and bottom edges of the cell.

b. Select the **range A4:J4** to select the column labels.

c. Click **Center** in the Alignment group and click **Bold** in the Font group to format the selected column labels.

   The column labels are centered horizontally between the left and right edges of each cell.

d. Click **Wrap Text** in the Alignment group. Save the workbook.

   The multiple-word column labels (such as Markup Rate and Profit Margin) are now visible on two lines within each cell.

STEP 3 ▶ INCREASE INDENT

You decide to indent the labels within each category to better display which products are in the Apparel and Souvenirs categories. Refer to Figure 1.52 as you complete Step 3.

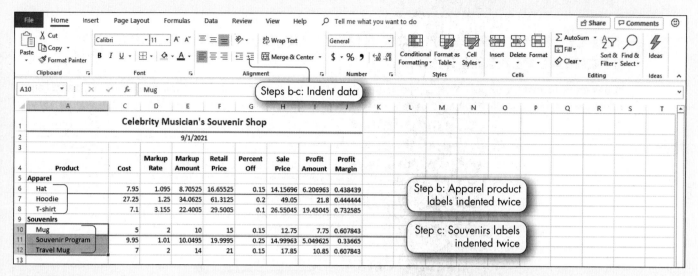

FIGURE 1.52 Product Names Indented

a. Select the **range A6:A8**, the cells containing Apparel products labels.

b. Click **Increase Indent** in the Alignment group twice.

The three selected product names are indented below the Apparel heading.

c. Select the **range A10:A12** and click **Increase Indent** twice. Save the workbook.

The three selected product names are indented below the Souvenirs heading.

STEP 4 ▶ APPLY A BORDER AND FILL COLOR

You want to apply a light blue-gray fill color to highlight the column labels. In addition, you want to emphasize the percentage off and sale prices by applying a border around that range. Refer to Figure 1.53 as you complete Step 4.

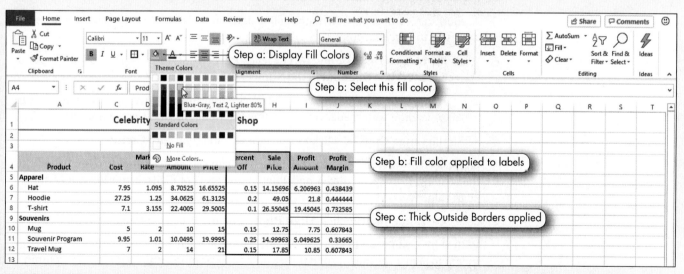

FIGURE 1.53 Border and Fill Color Applied

a. Select the **range A4:J4** and click the **Fill Color arrow** in the Font group.

b. Click **Blue-Gray, Text 2, Lighter 80%** in the Theme Colors section (second row, fourth column).

You applied a fill color that complements the Heading 1 cell style applied to the title.

c. Select the **range G4:H12**, click the **Border arrow** in the Font group, and then select **Thick Outside Borders**. Click **cell A4**. Save the workbook.

You applied a border around the selected cells.

APPLY NUMBER FORMATS AND INCREASE AND DECREASE DECIMAL PLACES

You want to format the values to improve readability and look more professional. You will apply number formats and adjust the number of decimal points displayed. Refer to Figure 1.54 as you complete Step 5.

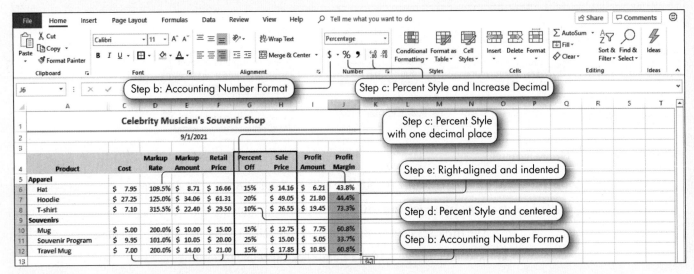

FIGURE 1.54 Number Formats and Decimal Places

a. Select the **ranges C6:C12**, **E6:F12**, and **H6:I12**.

   To apply the same format to nonadjacent ranges, hold Ctrl while selecting each range.

b. Click **Accounting Number Format** in the Number group.

   Accounting Number Format aligns dollar signs on the left side of the cell and aligns values on the decimal point.

c. Select the **ranges D6:D12** and **J6:J12**, click **Percent Style** in the Number group, and then click **Increase Decimal** in the Number group.

   You formatted the selected values with Percent Style and displayed one decimal place to avoid misleading your readers by displaying the values as whole percentages.

d. Select the **range G6:G12**, click **Percent Style**, and then click **Center**.

   Because all the percentages are two digits, you can center the values to align them below the heading. If the percentages had different numbers of digits, centering would not align values correctly.

e. Select the **range J6:J12**, click **Align Right**, and then click **Increase Indent**.

   With values, you want to keep the decimal points aligned, but you can then use Increase Indent to adjust the indent so that the values appear more centered below the column labels.

f. Save the workbook. Keep the workbook open if you plan to continue with the next Hands-On Exercise. If not, close the workbook, and exit Excel.

Worksheet Management, Page Setup, and Printing

When you start a new blank workbook in Excel, the workbook contains one worksheet named Sheet1. However, you can add additional worksheets. The individual worksheets are saved under one workbook file name. Having multiple worksheets in one workbook is helpful to keep related items together. After creating and formatting worksheets, consider if you will use these for your own purposes or if you will distribute the workbook electronically or as printouts to other people. If you plan to distribute a workbook to others, you should set up the worksheets so that they can print attractively and meaningfully on a printout.

In this section, you will copy, move, and rename worksheets. You will also select options on the Page Layout tab; specifically, you will use the Page Setup, Scale to Fit, and Sheet Options groups. After selecting page setup options, you will learn how to print the worksheet.

Managing Worksheets

Creating a multiple-worksheet workbook takes some planning and maintenance. Worksheet tab names should reflect the contents of the respective worksheets. In addition, you can insert, copy, move, and delete worksheets within the workbook. You can even apply background color to the worksheet tabs so that they stand out onscreen. Figure 1.55 shows a workbook in which the sheet tabs have been renamed, colors have been applied to worksheet tabs, and a worksheet tab has been right-clicked so that the shortcut menu displays.

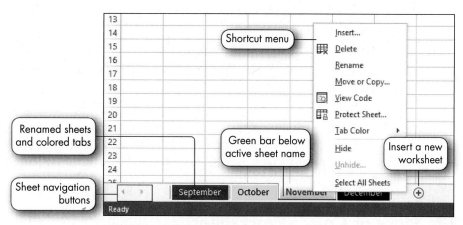

FIGURE 1.55 Worksheet Tabs

If a color has been applied to the sheet tab, the tab shows in the full color when it is not active. When that sheet is active, the sheet tab color is a gradient of the selected color. Regardless of whether a tab color has been applied, the active sheet tab has a green horizontal bar below the sheet name, and the sheet name is bold and green.

TIP: USING OTHER SHORTCUT MENUS
Right-click a sheet tab scroll arrow to display a list of worksheets. You can then make another worksheet active by selecting the name from the menu. Press Ctrl and click the left sheet tab scroll button to display the first sheet tab. Press Ctrl and click the right sheet tab scroll button to display the last sheet tab.

Insert and Delete a Worksheet

Sometimes you want more than one worksheet in the workbook. For example, you can create one worksheet for each month to track your monthly income and expenses for one year. When tax time comes around, you have all your data stored in one workbook file. Adding worksheets within one workbook enables you to save related sheets of data together. Excel provides several methods to insert a new sheet; choose one of these methods:

- Click New sheet to the right of the last worksheet tab to insert a sheet to the right of the active sheet.
- Click the Insert arrow in the Cells group on the Home tab and select Insert Sheet to insert a sheet to the left of the active sheet.
- Right-click any sheet tab, select Insert from the shortcut menu (refer to Figure 1.55), click Worksheet in the Insert dialog box, and then click OK to insert a sheet to the left of the active sheet. You can also use the Insert dialog box to insert worksheets based on Microsoft Office templates, such as the Cashflow analysis template. The inserted worksheets contain formatted text, default values, and formulas to save you time in planning and setting up worksheets.
- Press Shift+F11.

> **MAC TIP:** Use the shortcut menu to insert a sheet. A dialog box does not open.

When you insert a new blank worksheet, the default name is Sheet with a number, such as Sheet2. The next sheet would be Sheet3, and so on. Even if you rename or delete worksheets, the additional sheet names will continue incrementing the number.

If you no longer require the data in a worksheet, delete the worksheet. Doing so will eliminate extra data in a file and reduce file size. You can choose either of the following methods to delete a worksheet:

- Click the Delete arrow in the Cells group on the Home tab and select Delete Sheet.
- Right-click any sheet tab and select Delete from the shortcut menu (refer to Figure 1.55).

Make sure you save a workbook before deleting sheets in case you decide you want the worksheet data after all. If the sheet you are deleting contains data, Excel displays a warning: *Microsoft Excel will permanently delete this sheet. Do you want to continue?* When you try to delete a blank sheet, Excel will not display a warning; it will immediately delete the sheet.

STEP 1 ▶ Move or Copy a Worksheet

After creating a worksheet, you can copy it to use as a template or starting point for similar data. For example, if you create a worksheet for your September budget, you can copy the worksheet and easily edit the data on the copied worksheet to enter data for your October budget. Copying the entire worksheet saves you a lot of time in entering and formatting the new worksheet, and it preserves the column widths and row heights. You can rearrange the sheet tabs to be in a different sequence by moving a worksheet within the workbook. You can also move a worksheet to a new workbook or to another workbook that is open. For example, you can move worksheets created by different sales representatives into a consolidated sales workbook.

To copy or move a worksheet, complete the following steps:

1. Right-click the sheet tab of the worksheet you want to copy or click Format in the Cells group on the Home tab.
2. Select Move or Copy from the shortcut menu or Move or Copy Sheet from the ribbon menu to display the Move or Copy dialog box (see Figure 1.56).
3. Click the To book arrow. The list options include (new book), the name of the current workbook, and the names of other open workbooks. The default option is the current workbook. Select which book you want to contain the original or copy of the active worksheet.
4. Select a sheet in the Before sheet list, which displays the names of the worksheets in the workbook you selected in Step 3. If you selected (new book), no worksheets are listed. If you select the current workbook or another open workbook, the list displays the names of the worksheets in left-to-right sequence in that workbook. The default selected sheet is the first sheet in the respective workbook.
5. Click the Create a copy check box to select it if you want to make a copy of it. By default, the check box is not selected; leave the check box empty if you want to move the worksheet.
6. Click OK.

FIGURE 1.56 Move or Copy Dialog Box

> **TIP: DRAGGING TO COPY OR MOVE SHEETS**
> You can also move a worksheet within the existing workbook by clicking and dragging the sheet tab to the left or right of other sheet tabs. As you drag a sheet tab, the pointer resembles a piece of paper. A triangle displays between sheet tabs to indicate where the sheet will be placed when you release the mouse button. To copy a worksheet, press and hold Ctrl as you drag a sheet tab. A plus sign displays on the pointer to indicate that you are copying the sheet.

When you copy a worksheet within the same workbook, the tab for the copied sheet contains the name of the original sheet and a number. For example, if you copy a sheet named Sales, the copied sheet name is Sales (2). However, if you copy a worksheet to a new book or another open workbook, the copied sheet name is identical to the original sheet name.

Rename a Worksheet

The default worksheet name Sheet1 does not describe the contents of the worksheet. It is good practice to rename worksheet tabs to reflect the sheet contents. Although you can have spaces in worksheet names, keep the names short for readability. Excel provides three different methods for renaming a worksheet:

- Double-click a sheet tab, type the new name, and then press Enter.
- Click the sheet tab for the sheet you want to rename, click Format in the Cells group on the Home tab, select Rename Sheet, type the new sheet name, and then press Enter.
- Right-click the sheet tab, select Rename from the shortcut menu (refer to Figure 1.55), type the new sheet name, and then press Enter.

Selecting Page Setup Options

The Page Setup group on the Page Layout tab contains options to set the margins, select orientation, specify page size, select the print area, and apply other options (see Figure 1.57). The Scale to Fit group contains options for adjusting the scaling of the spreadsheet on the printed page. Table 1.8 lists and describes the commands in the Page Setup group.

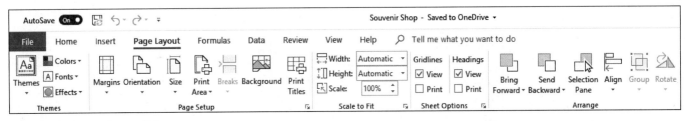

FIGURE 1.57 Page Layout Tab

TABLE 1.8	**Page Setup Commands**
Command	**Description**
Margins	Displays a menu to select predefined margin settings. The default margins are 0.75" top and bottom and 0.7" left and right. If you require different margins, select Custom Margins.
Orientation	Displays orientation options. The default page orientation is portrait, which displays a worksheet vertically. Landscape orientation displays a worksheet horizontally.
Size	Displays a list of standard paper sizes. The default size is 8½" by 11".
Print Area	Designates the selected range to print instead of printing the entire worksheet.
Breaks	Displays a menu to insert or remove page breaks.
Background	Enables you to select an image to appear as the background behind the worksheet data when viewed onscreen (backgrounds do not appear when the worksheet is printed).
Print Titles	Enables you to select column headings and row labels to repeat on multiple-page printouts.

> **TIP: APPLYING PAGE SETUP OPTIONS TO MULTIPLE WORKSHEETS**
> When you apply Page Setup options, those settings apply to the current worksheet only. However, you can apply page setup options, such as margins or a header, to multiple worksheets at the same time. To select adjacent sheets, click the first sheet tab, press and hold Shift, and click the last sheet tab to group the worksheets together. To select nonadjacent sheets, press and hold Ctrl as you click each sheet tab. Then choose the Page Setup options to apply to the selected sheets. When you are done, right-click a sheet tab and select Ungroup Sheets.

STEP 2 **Specify Page Options**

To apply several page setup options at once or to access options not found on the ribbon, click the Page Setup Dialog Box Launcher. The Page Setup dialog box organizes options into four tabs: Page, Margins, Header/Footer, and Sheet. All tabs contain Print and Print Preview buttons.

The Page tab (see Figure 1.58) contains options to select the orientation and paper size. Select Portrait for worksheets that have more rows than columns and select Landscape for worksheets that have more columns than rows. In addition, the Page tab contains scaling options that are similar to the options in the Scale to Fit group on the Page Layout tab. You use scaling options to increase or decrease the size of characters on a printed page, similar to using a zoom setting on a photocopy machine. Use the *Fit to* option to force the data to print on a specified number of pages. Be careful when using the Fit to option to make sure the printed text is still large enough to read. Otherwise, if you fit too much data on a printed page, the text may be too small to read.

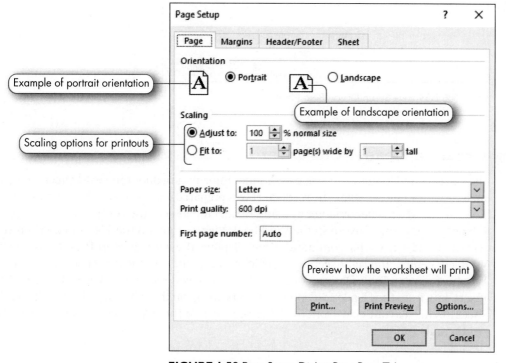

FIGURE 1.58 Page Setup Dialog Box: Page Tab

Set Margin Options

The Margins tab (see Figure 1.59) contains options for setting the specific margins. In addition, it contains options to center the worksheet data horizontally or vertically on the page that are used to balance worksheet data equally between the left and right margins or top and bottom margins, respectively.

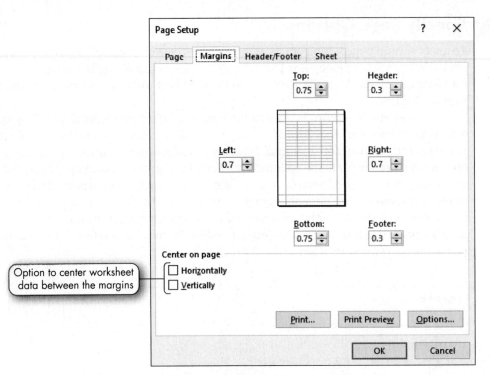

FIGURE 1.59 Page Setup Dialog Box: Margins Tab

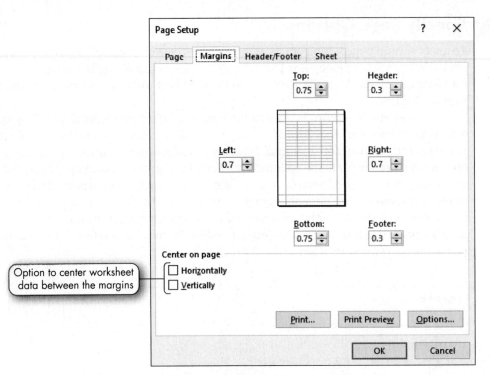
Option to center worksheet data between the margins

STEP 3 ▶ Create a Header or Footer

Use headers and footers to provide additional information about the worksheet. You can include your name, the date the worksheet was prepared, and page numbers, for example. You can insert a header or footer by using Header & Footer in the Text group on the Insert tab or by using Page Layout in the Workbook Views group on the Views tab. When you use the Header & Footer command, Excel displays the worksheet in Page Layout view with left, center, and right sections. The insertion point is in the center section, and the Header & Footer Tools Design contextual tab displays (see Figure 1.60). Enter text or insert data from the Header & Footer Elements group on the tab. If you display the worksheet in Page Layout view from the View tab, click in the *Add header* area to display the contextual tab.

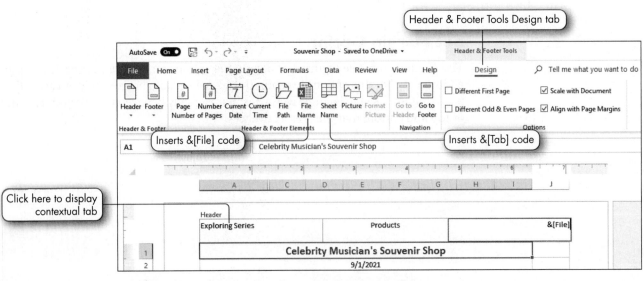

Header & Footer Tools Design tab

Inserts &[File] code

Inserts &[Tab] code

Click here to display contextual tab

FIGURE 1.60 Headers & Footer Tools Design Contextual Tab

To hide the header or footer and display the worksheet in Normal view, make any cell the active cell and use Normal in the Workbook Views group on the View tab or click Normal on the status bar. You can also create a header by clicking Page Layout in the Workbook Views group to display the header area.

Another way to insert a header or footer is to use the Header/Footer tab in the Page Setup dialog box (see Figure 1.61). This method is efficient when you want to insert headers or footers and select other page setup options from within the dialog box. Use the Header or Footer arrows to choose from several preformatted entries, or use Custom Header or Custom Footer to display the Header or the Footer dialog box, respectively, to insert text and other objects.

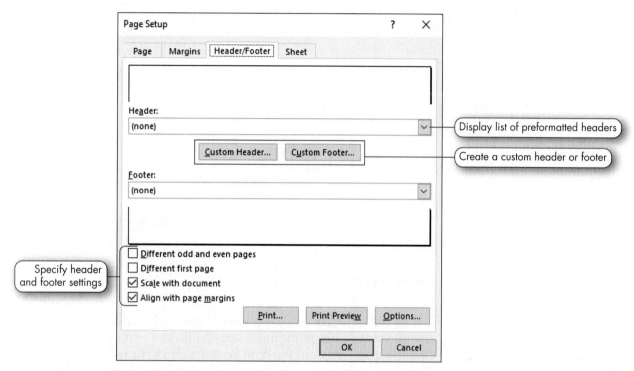

FIGURE 1.61 Page Setup Dialog Box: Header/Footer Tab

You can create different headers or footers on different pages, such as one header with the file name on odd-numbered pages and a header containing the date on even-numbered pages. Select the *Different odd and even pages* check box in the Page Setup dialog box (refer to Figure 1.61).

You can have a different header or footer on the first page from the rest of the printed pages, or you might not want a header or footer to show up on the first page but want the header or footer to display on the remaining pages. Select the *Different first page* check box in the Page Setup dialog box to specify a different first page header or footer.

TIP: DIFFERENT PAGE SETUP OPTIONS AND HEADERS
If you applied different orientation, scaling, and margins to different worksheets, do not group the worksheets to create headers or footers. Doing so would apply identical page settings to all the grouped worksheets. When you have different settings for different worksheets, create the headers or footers individually on each sheet.

Select Sheet Options

The Sheet tab (see Figure 1.62) contains options for setting the print area, print titles, print options, and page order. Some of these options are also located in the Sheet Options group on the Page Layout tab.

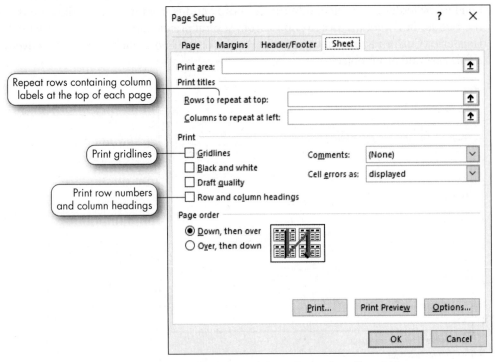

FIGURE 1.62 Page Setup Dialog Box: Sheet Tab

By default, Excel displays gridlines onscreen to show you each cell's margins, but the gridlines do not print unless you specifically select the Gridlines check box in the Page Setup dialog box or the Print Gridlines check box in the Sheet Options group on the Page Layout tab. In addition, Excel displays row and column headings onscreen. However, these headings do not print unless you click the *Row and column headings* check box in the Page Setup dialog box or click the Print Headings check box in the Sheet Options group on the Page Layout tab. For most worksheets, you do not need to print gridlines and row/column headings; however, when you want to display and print cell formulas instead of formula results, consider printing the gridlines and row/column headings. Doing so will help you analyze your formulas. The gridlines help you see the cell boundaries, and the headings help you identify what data are in each cell. Displaying gridlines helps separate data on a printout to increase readability.

> **TIP: REPEATING ROWS AND COLUMNS (TITLES)**
> If worksheet contains too many rows to print on one page, click Print Titles in the Page Setup group to open the Page Setup dialog box with the Sheet tab options displayed. Select the *Rows to repeat at top* box and select the row(s) containing column labels. The rows containing the descriptive column labels will repeat at the top of each printed page so that you can easily know what data is in each column. Likewise, if the worksheet has too many columns to print across on one page, select the *Columns to repeat at left* box and select the column(s) so that the row labels will display on the left side of each printed page.

STEP 4 Previewing and Printing a Worksheet

Backstage view displays print options and the worksheet in print preview mode. Print preview used before printing enables you to see if the data are balanced on the page or if data will print on multiple pages.

You can specify the number of copies to print and which printer to use to print the worksheet. The first option in the Settings area specifies what to print. The default option is Print Active Sheets. You can choose other options, such as Print Entire Workbook or Print Selection, or specify which pages to print. For example, you can select a range and display the print options to print only that range, or you can print only page 1 if it contains summary data.

The bottom of the Print window indicates how many pages will print. If the worksheet data flows just a little onto a second page, you can set smaller margins or adjust the scaling so that the data fits on one page. If the worksheet data fits on several pages, make sure the row and/or column labels repeat at the top and left of each printed page. You can also adjust column widths to improve the readability of the data and preview how the worksheet will print. A link to open the Page Setup dialog box is at the bottom of the print settings for easy access to make any of these adjustments.

TIP: PRINTING MULTIPLE WORKSHEETS

To print more than one worksheet at a time, select the sheets you want to print. To select adjacent sheets, click the first sheet tab, press and hold Shift, and then click the last sheet tab. To select nonadjacent sheets, press Ctrl as you click each sheet tab. When you display the Print options, Print Active Sheets is one of the default settings. If you want to print all worksheets within the workbook, change the setting to Print Entire Workbook.

Quick Concepts

14. Why would you insert several worksheets of data in one workbook instead of creating a separate workbook for each worksheet? *p. 120*

15. Why would you select a *Center on page* option in the Margins tab within the Page Setup dialog box if you have already set the margins? *p. 123*

16. List at least five elements you can insert in a header or footer. *p. 124*

17. Why would you want to print gridlines and row and column headings? *p. 126*

Hands-On Exercises

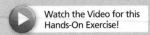
Skills covered: Copy a
Worksheet • Move a Worksheet •
Rename a Worksheet • Set
Page Orientation • Select Scaling
Options • Set Margin Options •
Create a Header or Footer •
View in Print Preview • Print a
Worksheet

5 Worksheet Management, Page Setup, and Printing

You are ready to complete the Souvenirs Shop worksheet. You want to copy the existing worksheet so that you display the results on the original sheet and display formulas on the duplicate sheet. Before printing the worksheet for your supervisor, you want to make sure the data will appear professional when printed. You will adjust some page setup options to put the finishing touches on the worksheet.

STEP 1 COPY, MOVE, AND RENAME A WORKSHEET

You want to copy the worksheet, move it to the right side of the original worksheet, and rename the duplicate worksheet so that you can show formulas on the duplicate sheet. Refer to Figure 1.63 as you complete Step 1.

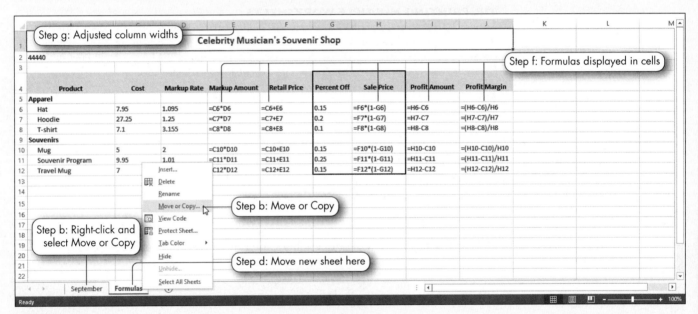

FIGURE 1.63 Two Worksheets

a. Open *e01h4Souvenirs_LastFirst* if you closed it at the end of Hands-On Exercise 4 and save it as **e01h5Souvenirs_LastFirst**, changing h4 to h5.

b. Right-click the **Sheet1 tab** at the bottom of the worksheet and select **Move or Copy**.

The Move or Copy dialog box opens so that you can move the existing worksheet or make a copy of it.

> **MAC TROUBLESHOOTING:** Press Control and click the Sheet1 tab.

c. Click the **Create a copy check box** to select it and click **OK**.

The duplicate worksheet is named Sheet1 (2) and is placed to the left of the original worksheet.

d. Drag the **Sheet1 (2) worksheet tab** to the right of the Sheet1 worksheet tab.

The duplicate worksheet is now on the right side of the original worksheet.

e. Double-click the **Sheet1 sheet tab**, type **September**, and then press **Enter**. Rename Sheet1 (2) as **Formulas**.

You renamed the original worksheet as September to reflect the September sales data, and you renamed the duplicate worksheet as Formulas to indicate that you will keep the formulas displayed on that sheet.

f. Press **Ctrl+`** to display the formulas in the Formulas worksheet.

g. Change these column widths in the Formulas sheet:

- Column A: **12.00**
- Columns C and D: **6.00**
- Columns E, F, H, I, and J: **7.00**
- Column G: **5.00**

You reduced the column widths so that the data will fit on a printout better.

h. Save the workbook.

STEP 2 ## SET PAGE ORIENTATION, SCALING, AND MARGIN OPTIONS

Because the worksheet has several columns, you decide to print it in landscape orientation. You want to set a 1″ top margin and center the data between the left and right margins. Furthermore, you want to make sure the data fits on one page on each sheet. Currently, if you were to print the Formulas worksheet, the data would print on two pages. Refer to Figure 1.64 as you complete Step 2.

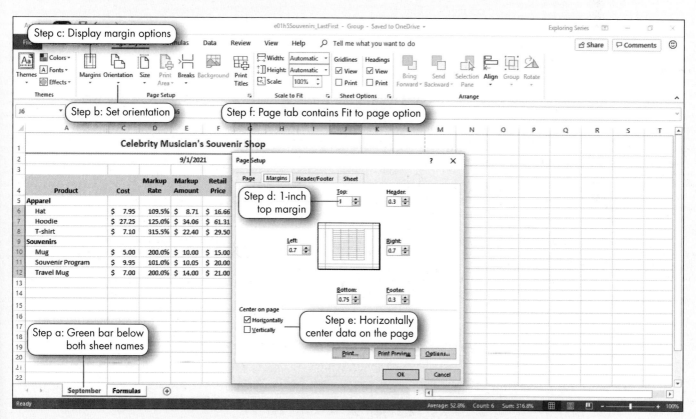

FIGURE 1.64 Page Setup Options Applied

a. Click the **September sheet tab**, press and hold **Ctrl**, and then click the **Formulas sheet tab**.

Both sheets are grouped and active, as indicated by the solid green bar below both sheet tab names. Anything you do on one sheet affects both sheets.

b. Click the **Page Layout tab**, click **Orientation** in the Page Setup group, and then select **Landscape** from the list.

Because both worksheets are active, both worksheets are formatted in landscape orientation.

c. Click **Margins** in the Page Setup group on the Page Layout tab and select **Custom Margins**.

The Page Setup dialog box opens with the Margins tab options displayed.

d. Click the **Top spin arrow** to display **1**.

Because both worksheets are grouped, the 1" top margin is set for both worksheets.

e. Click the **Horizontally check box** in the Center on page section to select it. Click **OK**.

Because both worksheets are grouped, the data on each worksheet are centered between the left and right margins.

f. Right-click the **Formulas sheet tab** and select **Ungroup Sheets**. With the Formulas sheet active, click the **Page Setup Dialog Box Launcher** in the Scale to Fit group, click **Fit to** in the Scaling section, and then click **OK**. Save the workbook.

The data on the September sheet fit on one page; however, the data on the Formulas sheet did not, so you used the Fit to option ensuring that the Formulas sheet data fits on one page.

> **TROUBLESHOOTING:** If you leave both sheets selected and use the Fit to option, the Fit to setting will apply to only the September sheet. Make sure that the Formulas sheet is active (not grouped) to use the Fit to option.

STEP 3 ▶ CREATE A HEADER

To document the grouped worksheets, you want to include your name, the sheet name, and the file name in a header. Refer to Figure 1.65 as you complete Step 3.

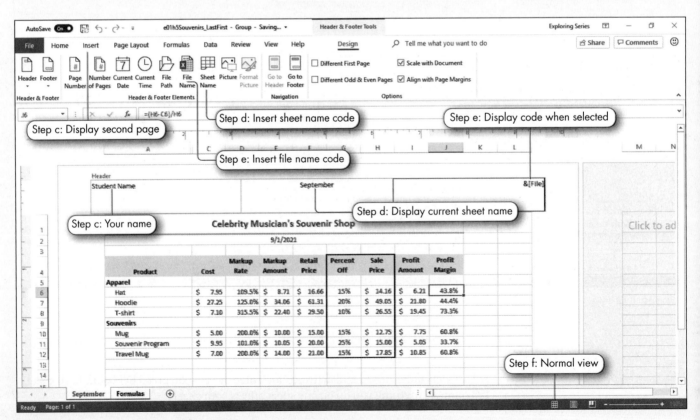

FIGURE 1.65 Header in Souvenir Shop Workbook

a. Click the **September sheet tab**, press and hold **Ctrl**, and then click the **Formulas sheet tab**.

b. Click the **Insert tab**, click **Text**, and then click **Header & Footer** in the Text group.

Excel displays the Header & Footer Tools Design contextual tab. The worksheet displays in Page Layout view, which displays the header area, margin space, and ruler. The insertion point is active in the center section of the header.

c. Click in the **left section** of the header and type your name.

d. Click in the **center section** of the header and click **Sheet Name** in the Header & Footer Elements group on the Design tab.

Excel inserts the code &[Tab]. This code displays the name of the worksheet. If you change the worksheet tab name, the header will reflect the new sheet name.

e. Click in the **right section** of the header and click **File Name** in the Header & Footer Elements group on the Design tab.

Excel inserts the code &[File]. This code displays the name of the file. Notice that &[Tab] in the center section now displays the current tab name, September. Because the worksheets were selected when you created the header, a header will display on both worksheets. The file name will be the same; however, the sheet names will be different.

f. Click in any cell in the worksheet and click **Normal** on the status bar.

Normal view displays the worksheet but does not display the header or margins.

g. Click **cell A1**, click the **Review tab**, and then click **Spelling** in the Proofing group. Correct all errors, if any, and click **OK** when prompted with the message, *Spell check complete. You're good to go!* Leave the worksheets grouped. Save the workbook.

You should always check the spelling immediately before distributing a workbook.

STEP 4 VIEW IN PRINT PREVIEW AND PRINT

Before printing the worksheets, you should preview it. Doing so helps you detect margin problems and other issues, such as a single row or column of data flowing onto a new page. Refer to Figure 1.66 as you complete Step 4.

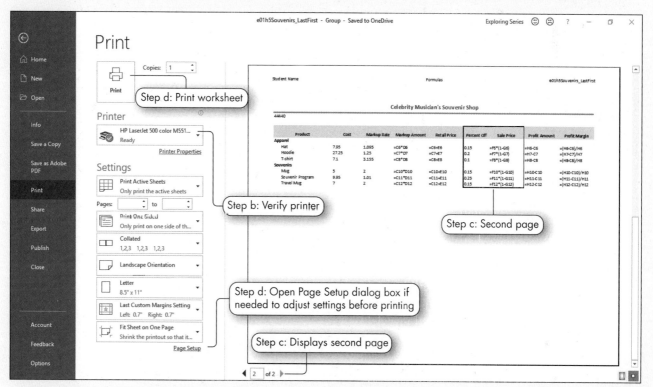

FIGURE 1.66 Worksheet in Print Preview

a. Click the **File tab** and click **Print**.

The Print Preview window displays options and a preview of the worksheet.

b. Verify the Printer box displays the printer that you want to use to print your worksheet, and verify the last Settings option displays Fit Sheet on One Page.

The bottom of the Print Preview window shows 1 of 2, indicating two pages will print.

c. Click **Next Page** to see the second page.

d. Click the **Back arrow** and save the workbook.

Although you did not print the worksheets, all the print options are saved.

e. Save and close the file. Exit Excel. Based on your instructor's directions, submit e01h5Souvenirs_LastFirst.

> **TROUBLESHOOTING:** Once the file is closed, the Formulas sheet may not display the formulas when you open the workbook again. If that happens, press Ctrl+` again.

Chapter Objectives Review

After reading this chapter, you have accomplished the following objectives:

1. Explore the Excel window.

- A worksheet is a single spreadsheet containing data. A workbook is a collection of one or more related worksheets contained in a single file.
- Identify Excel window elements: The Name Box displays the name of the current cell. The Formula Bar displays the contents of the current cell. The active cell is the current cell. A sheet tab shows the name of the worksheet.
- Identify columns, rows, and cells: Columns have alphabetical headings, such as A, B, C; rows have numbers, such as 1, 2, 3. A cell is the intersection of a column and row and is indicated with a column letter and a row number.
- Navigate in and among worksheets: Use the arrow keys to navigate within a sheet, or use the Go To command to go to a specific cell. Click a sheet tab to display the contents on another worksheet.

2. Enter and edit cell data.

- You should plan the worksheet design by stating the purpose, deciding what output you want, and then identifying what input values are required. Next, you enter and format data in a worksheet. Finally, you document, save, and then share a workbook.
- Enter text: Text may contain letters, numbers, symbols, and spaces. Text aligns at the left side of a cell.
- Check the spelling in a worksheet: After entering or editing text, check the spelling in the worksheet to identify and correct misspelled words.
- Use Auto Fill to complete a sequence: Auto Fill can automatically fill in sequences, such as month names or values, after you enter the first label or value. Double-click the fill handle to fill in the sequence.
- Enter values: Values are numbers that represent a quantity. Values align at the right side of a cell by default.
- Enter dates and times: Excel stores dates and times as serial numbers so that you can calculate the number of days between dates or times.
- Edit and clear cell contents: You can edit the contents of a cell to correct errors or to make labels more descriptive. Use the Clear option to clear the cell contents and/or formats.
- Find and replace data: Use Find to locate data within a worksheet. Use Find and Replace to find specific data and replace it with other data.

3. Create formulas.

- A formula is used to perform a calculation. The formula results display in the cell.
- Use cell references in formulas: Use references, such as =B5+B6, instead of values within formulas.
- Copy a formula: Double-click the fill handle to copy a formula down a column.

- Use semi-selection to create a formula: When building a formula, click a cell containing a value to enter that cell reference in the formula.
- Apply the order of operations: The most commonly used operators are performed in this sequence: Parentheses, exponentiation, multiplication, division, addition, and subtraction.
- Display cell formulas: Displaying cell formulas instead of formula results is helpful when you want to review several formulas for accuracy. You can display formulas by pressing Ctrl+`.

4. Manage columns and rows.

- Insert cells, columns, and rows: Insert a cell to move the remaining cells down or to the right in a specific column or row to enter missing data. Rows or columns can be inserted, moving the remaining rows or columns down or to the right, respectively.
- Delete cells, columns, and rows: Delete cells, columns, and rows you no longer want.
- Adjust column width: Double-click between the column headings to widen a column based on the longest item in that column, or drag the border between column headings to increase or decrease a column width.
- Adjust row height: Drag the border between row headings to increase or decrease the height of a row.
- Hide and unhide columns and rows: Hiding rows and columns protects confidential data from being displayed.

5. Select, move, copy, and paste data.

- Select a range: A range is a single cell or a rectangular block of cells. After selecting a range, you can copy, move, or format the cells in the range.
- Move a range: After selecting a range, cut it from its location. Then select the top-left corner of the destination range to make it the active cell and paste the range there.
- Copy and paste a range: You can copy a range within a worksheet, to another sheet within the workbook, or to a different workbook.
- Use Paste Options: Use the Paste Options button or the Paste arrow to specify how the data are pasted into the worksheet.

6. Apply cell styles, cell alignment, and font options.

- Apply cell styles: Cell styles contain a collection of formatting, such as font, font color, font size, fill, and borders. You can apply an Excel cell style to save formatting time.
- Merge cells: You can merge multiple cells into one cell. The Merge & Center command merges cells and then horizontally centers data between the left and right sides of the combined cell.

- Change cell alignment: You can change how data aligns between the top and bottom edges of the cell and between the left and right sides of the cell.
- Wrap text: Use the Wrap Text option to display text on multiple lines in order to avoid having extra-wide columns.
- Increase and decrease indent: To indicate hierarchy of data or to offset a label, increase or decrease how much the data are indented in a cell.
- Apply borders and fill color: Borders and fill colors help improve readability of worksheets. Borders are lines that surround one or more edges of a cell or range. Fill is a background color that displays behind the data in a cell.

7. Apply number formats.
- Apply a number format: The default number format is General, which does not apply any particular format to values. Apply appropriate formats to values to display the data with the correct symbols and decimal alignment. For example, Accounting Number Format is a common number format for monetary values.
- Increase and decrease decimal places: After applying a number format, you can increase or decrease the number of decimal places displayed.

8. Manage worksheets.
- Insert and delete a worksheet: You can insert new worksheets to include related data within one workbook, or you can delete extra worksheets you do not want.
- Move or copy a worksheet: Drag a sheet tab to rearrange the worksheets. You can copy a worksheet within a workbook or to another workbook.
- Rename a worksheet: The default worksheet tab name is Sheet1, but you should change the name to describe the contents of the worksheet.

9. Select page setup options.
- The Page Layout tab on the ribbon contains options for setting margins, selecting orientation, specifying page size, selecting the print area, and applying other settings.
- Specify page options: Page options include orientation, paper size, and scaling. The default orientation is portrait, but you can select landscape orientation for worksheets containing a lot of columns. Use scaling options to increase or decrease the magnification of data on a printout.
- Set margin options: You can set the left, right, top, and bottom margins. In addition, you can center worksheet data horizontally and vertically on a page.
- Create a header or footer: Insert a header or footer to display documentation, such as your name, date, time, and worksheet tab name. A header displays at the top of the page, and a footer displays at the bottom of a printout.
- Select sheet options: Sheet options control the print area, print titles, print options, and page order. You can specify that row of column headings repeat at the top of each printed page and the row headings repeat on the left side of each printed page.

10. Preview and print a worksheet.
- Before printing a worksheet, display a preview to ensure the data will print correctly. The Print Preview enables you to see if margins are correct or if isolated rows or columns will print on separate pages.
- After making appropriate adjustments, print the worksheet.

Key Terms Matching

Match the key terms with their definitions. Write the key term letter by the appropriate numbered definition.

a. Alignment

b. Auto Fill

c. Cell

d. Column width

e. Fill color

f. Fill handle

g. Formula

h. Formula Bar

i. Input area

j. Name Box

k. Order of operations

l. Output area

m. Range

n. Row height

o. Sheet tab

p. Text

q. Value

r. Workbook

s. Worksheet

t. Wrap text

1. _____ A spreadsheet that contains formulas, functions, values, text, and visual aids. **p. 72**

2. _____ A file containing related worksheets. **p. 72**

3. _____ A range of cells containing values for variables used in formulas. **p. 76**

4. _____ A range of cells containing results based on manipulating the variables. **p. 76**

5. _____ Identifies the address of the current cell. **p. 73**

6. _____ Displays the content (text, value, date, or formula) in the active cell. **p. 73**

7. _____ Displays the name of a worksheet within a workbook. **p. 73**

8. _____ The intersection of a column and a row. **p. 73**

9. _____ Includes letters, numbers, symbols, and spaces. **p. 77**

10. _____ A number that represents a quantity or an amount. **p. 79**

11. _____ Rules that control the sequence in which Excel performs arithmetic operations. **p. 89**

12. _____ Enables you to copy the contents of a cell or cell range or to continue a sequence by dragging the fill handle over an adjacent cell or range of cells. **p. 78**

13. _____ A small green square at the bottom-right corner of a cell. **p. 78**

14. _____ The horizontal measurement of a column. **p. 95**

15. _____ The vertical measurement of a row. **p. 97**

16. _____ A rectangular group of cells. **p. 98**

17. _____ The position of data between the cell margins. **p. 110**

18. _____ Formatting that enables a label to appear on multiple lines within the current cell. **p. 111**

19. _____ The background color appearing behind data in a cell. **p. 112**

20. _____ A combination of cell references, operators, values, and/or functions used to perform a calculation. **p. 87**

Multiple Choice

1. Cell A5 is the active cell. You want to make cell B10 the active cell. Which of the following is *not* a method for going to cell B10?

    (a) Use the Go To dialog box.

    (b) Type B10 in the Name Box and press Enter.

    (c) Use the scroll arrows on the keyboard.

    (d) Type B10 in the Formula Bar and press Enter.

2. Which step is *not* part of planning a worksheet design?

    (a) Decide what input values are required.

    (b) Enter labels, values, and formulas.

    (c) State the purpose of the worksheet.

    (d) Decide what outputs are required to achieve the purpose.

3. Cell A2 contains the regular price $100. Cell B2 contains the discount rate 15%. Cell C3 contains =A2*(1-B2) to calculate the sale price of $85. Which of the following formulas produces the same result?

    (a) =A2*(B2-1)

    (b) =A2-(A2*B2)

    (c) =A2*B2-1

    (d) =A2*1-B2

4. What should you do if you see pound signs (###) instead of values or results of formulas?

    (a) Increase the column width.

    (b) Increase the zoom percentage.

    (c) Delete the column.

    (d) Adjust the row height.

5. You just copied a range of data containing formulas. However, you want to preserve the formula results and the original number and text formatting in the pasted range. Which paste option would you select?

    (a) Formulas

    (b) Keep Source Formatting

    (c) Values & Source Formatting

    (d) Values & Number Formatting

6. The label *Souvenir Shop* is in cell A1, and *April Sales Report* is in cell B1. You select the range A1:E1 and click Merge & Center. What is the result?

    (a) Souvenir Shop is centered over the range A1:E1, and April Sales Report is moved to cell F1.

    (b) Excel does not let you merge and center a range of cells where those cells each contain data.

    (c) Souvenir Shop is combined with April Sales Report. The new combined label is then centered over the range A1:E1.

    (d) Souvenir Shop is centered over the range A1:E1, and April Sales Report is deleted.

7. What number format places a dollar sign on the left side of the cell, includes commas to separate thousands, displays two decimal places, and displays zero values as hyphens?

    (a) Currency Format

    (b) Monetary Number Format

    (c) Dollars and Cents Format

    (d) Accounting Number Format

8. You want to copy the March worksheet to use it to enter data for April. After you right-click the March sheet tab and select Move or Copy, you click OK in the Move or Copy dialog box without changing any settings. What happens?

    (a) A copy of the March sheet is inserted to the right of the original March sheet. The new sheet is named April automatically.

    (b) A copy of the March sheet is inserted to the left of the original March sheet. The new sheet is named March (1).

    (c) The March sheet is moved to the left of the first sheet tab. The worksheet is not copied.

    (d) The March sheet is moved to a new workbook named Book1. The March sheet no longer exists in the original workbook.

9. The Header & Footer Tools tab contains commands that insert codes into a header or footer. These codes enable the header or footer text to change automatically. You can insert a code for all of the following *except*:

    (a) Your Name.

    (b) File Name.

    (c) Sheet Name.

    (d) Page Number.

10. Assume that the data on a worksheet consume a whole printed page and two columns on a second page. You can do all of the following *except* what to force the data to print all on one page?

    (a) Decrease the Scale value

    (b) Increase the left and right margins

    (c) Decrease column widths

    (d) Decrease the font size

Practice Exercises

1 Mathematics and Formatting

You want to apply the skills you learned in this chapter. First, you will use Auto Fill to fill in a sequence of values in the input area and check the spelling in the worksheet to correct errors. You will copy the input and transpose the data vertically to improve readability and move the output range to the right side of the input area. You will adjust the worksheet by deleting an unnecessary row, adjusting column and row heights. Using input and output areas, you want to create several formulas with different arithmetic operators and explore the order of operations. Furthermore, you will copy a worksheet from another workbook, apply cell styles and alignment settings to improve the formatting, and then apply different number formats to compare the formatted values. Finally, you will apply page setup options to finalize your workbook. Refer to Figure 1.67 as you complete this exercise.

	A	B	C	D	E	F
1	Excel Formulas and Order of Precedence					
2						
3	Input Area:			Output Area:		
4	First Value	2		Sum of 1st and 2nd values	6	
5	Second Value	4		Difference between 4th and 1st values	6	
6	Third Value	6		Product of 2nd and 3rd values	24	
7	Fourth Value	8		Quotient of 3rd and 1st values	3	
8				2nd value to the power of 3rd value	4096	
9				1st value added to product of 2nd and 4th values and difference between sum and 3rd value	28	
10				Product of sum of 1st and 2nd and difference between 4th and 3rd values	12	
11				Product of 1st and 2nd added to product of 3rd and 4th values	56	
12						

Tabs: **Calculations** | Number Formats

	A	B	C	D	E	F
1	Original Values	Accounting	Currency	Comma	Number
2	12.3	$ 12.30	$12.30	12.30	12.30
3	12.34	$ 12.34	$12.34	12.34	12.34
4	123.456	$ 123.46	$123.46	123.46	123.46
5	1234.5	$1,234.50	$1,234.50	1,234.50	1234.50
6					

Tabs: Calculations | **Number Formats**

FIGURE 1.67 Math Review Worksheet

a. Open *e01p1Math* and save it as **e01p1Math_LastFirst**.

b. Click **cell C5**, type **0**, and then press **Ctrl+Enter**. Use Auto Fill to complete the series by doing the following:
   - Drag the **cell C5 fill handle** to **cell G5** to fill in the range with 0.
   - Click **Auto Fill Options** and select **Fill Series** to fill the series from 0 to 4.

c. Press **Ctrl+Home** to navigate to cell A1, click **Find & Select** in the Editing group on the Home tab, and then select **Replace**.
   - Type **Number** in the Find what box and type **Value** in the Replace with box.
   - Click **Replace All**, click **OK** in the message box, and then click **Close** in the dialog box.

d. Click the **Review tab**, click **Spelling** in the Proofing group, and then do the following:
   - Click **Change** when prompted to change Formules to Formulas.
   - Click **Change** when prompted to change Presedence to Precedence.
   - Click **OK** when prompted with *Spell check complete. You're good to go!*

e. Use copy and paste to transpose the input range from being organized horizontally to being organized vertically by doing the following:
   - Select the **range C4:G5**, click the **Home tab**, and then click **Copy** in the Clipboard group.
   - Click **cell A4**, click the **Paste arrow** in the Clipboard group, and then click **Transpose**.
   - Press **Esc**, select the **range C4:G5**, and then press **Delete**.

f. Select the **range A10:A19** (the output range), click **Cut** in the Clipboard group, click **cell D3**, and then click **Paste** to move the output range.

g. Click **cell A4**, click the **Delete arrow** in the Cells group, and then select **Delete Sheet Rows** to delete the Starting Value row.

Practice Exercises • Excel 2019   137

h. Click **cell A5**, click **Format** in the Cells group, and then select **Column Width**. Type **12.6** in the Column width box and click **OK**. Click **cell D5** and set the column width to **36**.

i. Click **cell D9**, click **Format** in the Cells group, select **Row Height**, type **45** in the Row height box, and then click **OK**. Select the **range D10:D11** and set the row height to **30**.

j. Click **cell E4**. Type **=B4+B5** and press **Enter**. Excel adds the value in cell B4 (1) to the value in cell B5 (2). The result (3) displays in cell E4, as described by the label in cell D4.

k. Enter the following formulas:
- Cell E5: **=B7-B4**
- Cell E6: **=B5*B6**
- Cell E7: **=B6/B4**
- Cell E8: **=B5^B6**

l. Type **=B4+B5*B7-B6** in **cell E9**. Calculate the answer: 2*4=8; 1+8=9; 9-3=6. Multiplication occurs first, followed by addition, and finally subtraction.

m. Type **=(B4+B5)*(B7-B6)** in **cell E10**. Calculate the answer: 1+2=3; 4-3=1; 3*1=3. This formula is almost identical to the previous formula; however, calculations in parentheses occur before the multiplication.

n. Type **=(B4*B5)+(B6*B7)** in **cell E11**. Calculate the answer: 1*2=2; 3*4=12; 2+12=14. Although multiplication would have occurred first without the parentheses, the parentheses help improve the readability of the formula.

o. Enter **2** in **cell B4**, **4** in **cell B5**, **6** in **cell B6**, and **8** in **cell B7**. Refer to Figure 1.67 to compare the updated formula results.

p. Double-click the **Sheet 1 tab**, type **Calculations**, and then press **Enter** to rename the sheet tab.

q. Open *e01p1Values*. Copy the worksheet to your e01p1Math_LastFirst workbook by doing the following:
- Right-click the **Number Formats sheet tab** and select **Move or Copy**.
- Click the **To book arrow** and select **e01p1Math_LastFirst.xlsx**.
- Select **(move to end)**, click the **Create a copy check box** to select it, and then click **OK**.
- Close the e01p1Values workbook without saving it.

r. Format the headings on row 1 of the Numbers Format worksheet by doing the following:
- Select the **range A1:E1**, click **Wrap Text** in the Alignment group, and then click **Center**.
- Click the **Fill Color arrow** in the Font group and select **Light Gray, Background 2** (the third color from the left on the first row).

s. Select the **range A2:A5**, click **Cell Styles** in the Styles group, and then click **Input**. Select the **range B2:E5** and apply the **Output cell style**.

t. Apply number formatting by doing the following:
- Select the **range B2:B5** and click **Accounting Number Format** in the Number group.
- Select the **range C2:C5**, click the **Number Format arrow**, and then select **Currency**.
- Select the **range D2:D5** and click **Comma Style** in the Number group.
- Select the **range E2:E5**, click the **Number Format arrow**, and then select **Number**.

u. Right-click the **Calculations sheet tab** and select **Select All Sheets** to group the sheets. Apply Page Setup options by doing the following:
- Click the **Page Layout tab**, click **Margins** in the Page Setup group, select **Custom Margins**, click the **Top spin arrow** to display **1**, and then click the **Horizontally check box** to select it.
- Click the **Header/Footer tab** within the Page Setup dialog box and click **Custom Footer**. Type your name in the Left section box, click **Insert Sheet Name** in the Center section box, click **Insert File Name** in the Right section box, and then click **OK**. Click **OK** to close the Page Setup dialog box.

v. Click the **File tab** and click **Print**. Verify that each worksheet will print on one page. Press **Esc** to close the Print Preview, and right-click the **Calculations sheet tab** and click **Ungroup Sheets**.

w. Save and close the file. Exit Excel. Based on your instructor's directions, submit e01p1Math_LastFirst.

2 Calendar Formatting

You want to create a calendar for October 2021. The calendar will enable you to practice alignment settings, including center, merge and center, and indents. In addition, you will adjust column widths and increase row height to create cells large enough to enter important information, such as birthdays. You will create a formula and use Auto Fill to complete the days of the week and the days within each week. To improve the appearance of the calendar, you will add fill colors, font colors, and borders. Refer to Figure 1.68 as you complete this exercise.

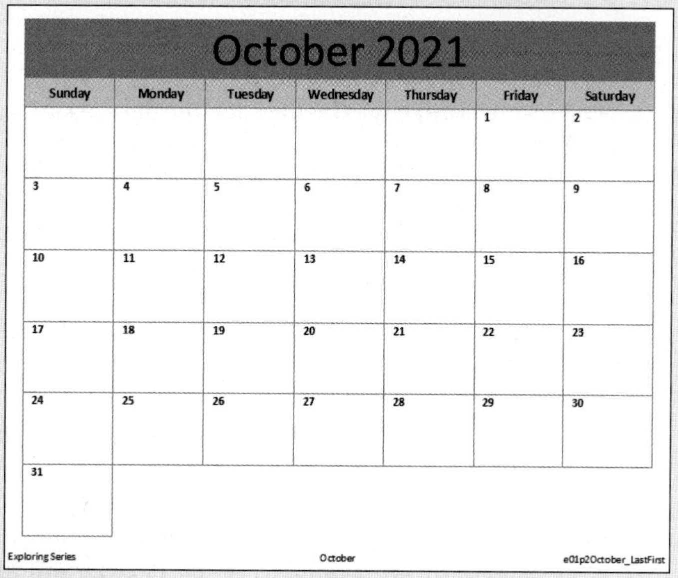

FIGURE 1.68 Calendar

a. Start Excel and create a new blank workbook. Save the workbook as **e01p2October_LastFirst**.

b. Type **'October 2021** (be sure to include the apostrophe before October) in **cell A1** and click **Enter** on the left side of the Formula Bar.

c. Format the title:
- Select the **range A1:G1** and click **Merge & Center** in the Alignment group.
- Change the font size to **48**.
- Click the **Fill Color arrow** and click **Orange, Accent 2** in the Theme Colors section of the color palette.
- Click **Middle Align** in the Alignment group.

d. Complete the days of the week:
- Type **Sunday** in **cell A2** and click **Enter** to the left side of the Formula Bar.
- Drag the **cell A2 fill handle** across the row through **cell G2** to use Auto Fill to complete the rest of the weekdays.
- Ensure that the **range A2:G2** is selected. Click the **Fill Color arrow** and select **Orange, Accent 2, Lighter 60%** in the Theme Colors section of the color palette.
- Click **Bold** in the Font group, click the **Font Size arrow**, and then select **14** to format the selected range.
- Click **Middle Align** and click **Center** in the Alignment group to format the selected range.

e. Complete the days of the month:
- Type **1** in **cell F3** and type **2 in cell G3**. Type **3** in **cell A4** and press **Ctrl+Enter**. Drag the **cell A4 fill handle** across the row through **cell G4**.
- Click **Auto Fill Options** near the bottom-right corner of the copied data and select **Fill Series** to change the numbers to 3 through 9.
- Type **=A4+7** in **cell A5** and press **Ctrl+Enter**. Usually you avoid numbers in formulas, but the number of days in a week is always 7. Drag the **cell A5 fill handle** down through **cell A8** to get the date for each Sunday in October.

- Keep the **range A5:A8** selected and drag the fill handle across through **cell G8**. This action copies the formulas to fill in the days in the month.
- Select the **range B8:G8** and press **Delete** to delete the extra days 32 through 37 because October has only 31 days.

f. Format the columns and rows:

- Select **columns A:G**. Click **Format** in the Cells group, select **Column Width**, type **16** in the Column width box, and then click **OK**.
- Select **row 2**. Click **Format** in the Cells group, select **Row Height**, type **30**, and then click **OK**.
- Select **rows 3:8**. Set the row height to **75**.

g. Apply borders around the cells:

- Select the **range A1:G8**. Click the **Borders arrow** in the Font group and select **More Borders** to display the Format Cells dialog box with the Border tab selected.
- Click the **Color arrow** and select **Orange, Accent 2**.
- Click **Outline** and **Inside** in the Presets section. Click **OK**. This action applies an orange border inside and outside the selected range.

h. Clear the border formatting around cells that do not have days:

- Select the **range B8:G8**.
- Click **Clear** in the Editing group and select **Clear All**. This action removes the borders around the cells after the last day of the month.

i. Format the days in the month:

- Select the **range A3:G8**. Click **Top Align** and **Align Left** in the Alignment group.
- Click **Increase Indent** in the Alignment group to offset the days from the border.
- Click **Bold** in the Font group, click the **Font Size arrow**, and then select **12**.

j. Double-click the **Sheet1 tab**, type **October**, and then press **Enter**.

k. Click in any cell in the worksheet, click the **Page Layout tab**, and then do the following:

- Click **Orientation** in the Page Setup group and select **Landscape**.
- Click **Margins** in the Page Setup group and select **Custom Margins**. Click the **Top margin spin arrow** to display **0.5**, click the **Bottom margin spin arrow** to display **0.5**, click the **Horizontally check box** to select it in the *Center on page* section, and then click **OK**.

l. Click the **Insert tab** and click **Header & Footer** in the Text group and do the following:

- Click **Go to Footer** in the Navigation group. Click in the **left side** of the footer and type your name.
- Click in the **center** of the footer and click **Sheet Name** in the Header & Footer Elements group on the Design tab.
- Click in the **right side** of the footer and click **File Name** in the Header & Footer Elements group on the Design tab.
- Click in any cell in the workbook, press **Ctrl+Home**, and then click **Normal** on the status bar.

m. Save and close the file. Exit Excel. Based on your instructor's directions, submit e01p2October_LastFirst.

Mid-Level Exercises

1 Guest House Rental Rates

ANALYSIS CASE

You manage a beach guesthouse in Ft. Lauderdale containing three types of rental units. Prices are based on off-peak and peak times of the year. You want to calculate the maximum daily revenue for each rental type, assuming all units are rented. In addition, you will calculate the discount rate for off-peak rental times. Finally, you will improve the appearance of the worksheet by applying font, alignment, and number formats.

a. Open *e01m1Rentals* and save it as **e01m1Rentals_LastFirst**.

b. Apply the **Heading 1 cell style** to the **range A1:G1** and the **20% - Accent1 cell style** to the **range A2:G2**.

c. Merge and center *Peak Rentals* in the **range C4:D4**, over the two columns of peak rental data. Apply **Dark Red fill color** and **White, Background 1 font color**.

d. Merge and center *Off-Peak Rentals* in the **range E4:G4** over the three columns of off-peak rental data. Apply **Blue fill color** and **White, Background 1 font color**.

e. Center horizontally and wrap the headings on row 5. Set the width of columns D and F to **10.0**. Horizontally center the data in the **range B6:B8**.

f. Create and copy the following formulas:
   - **Cell D6:** Calculate the Peak Rentals Maximum Revenue by multiplying the number of units (No. Units) by the Peak Rentals Daily Rate. Copy the formula from **cell D6** to the range **D7:D8**.
   - **Cell F6:** Calculate the Off-Peak Rentals Maximum Revenue by multiplying the number of units (No. Units) by the Off-Peak Rentals Daily Rate. Copy the formula from **cell F6** to the range **F7:F8**.
   - **Cell G6:** Calculate the Off-Peak Rentals Discount Rate by dividing the Off-Peak Rentals Daily Rate by the Peak Rentals Daily Rate (to get the off-peak percent of the peak rate) and then subtracting that from 1 (which represents 100%). For example, the off-peak daily rate for the studio apartment is .226075 (22.6%) off the peak daily rate. Copy the formula from **cell G6** to the **range G7:G8**.

g. Format the monetary values in the **range C6:F8** with **Accounting Number Format**. Format the **range G6:G8** with **Percent Style** with one decimal place.

h. Apply **Blue, Accent 1, Lighter 80% fill color** to the **range E5:G8**.

i. Select the **range C5:D8**, click the **Fill Color arrow** and select **More Colors**. Create a custom color with these settings: **Red 242**, **Green 220**, and **Blue 219**.

j. Answer the four questions below the worksheet data. Enter the answer to question 1 in **cell A15**, question 2 in **cell A18**, question 3 in **cell A21**, and question 4 in **cell A24**. If you change any values to answer the questions, change the values back to the original values.

k. Check the spelling in the worksheet and correct any errors in your answers.

l. Create a copy of the Rental Rates worksheet, place the new sheet to the right side of the original worksheet, and rename the new sheet **Formulas**. Display cell formulas on the Formulas sheet.

m. Select the two worksheet tabs and do the following:
   - Select landscape orientation.
   - Set **1"** top, bottom, left, and right margins. Center the data horizontally on the page.
   - Insert a footer with your name on the left side, the sheet name code in the center, and the file name code on the right side.
   - Apply the setting to fit to one page.

n. Click the **Formulas sheet tab** and set options to print gridlines and headings. Adjust the column widths to display all data.

o. Save and close the file. Exit Excel. Based on your instructor's directions, submit e01m1Rentals_LastFirst.

You are a real estate agent in Indianapolis. You track the real estate properties you list for clients. You want to analyze sales for selected properties. Yesterday, you prepared a workbook with a worksheet for recent sales data and another worksheet listing several properties. You want to calculate the number of days that the houses were on the market and their sales percentage of the list price. In one situation, the house was involved in a bidding war between two families who really wanted the house; therefore, the sale price exceeded the list price.

a. Open *e01m2Sales* and save it as **e01m2Sales_LastFirst**.

b. Delete the row that has incomplete sales data. The owners took their house off the market.

c. Type **2021-001** in **cell A5** and use Auto Fill to complete the series to assign a property ID to each property.

d. Calculate the number of days each house was on the market in **cell C5** by subtracting the date listed from the date sold. Copy the formula to the **range C6:C12**.

e. Format list prices and sold prices with **Accounting Number Format** with zero decimal places.

f. Calculate the sales price percentage of the list price in **cell H5** by dividing the sold price by the list price. Format the percentages with two decimal places. Copy the formula to the **range H6:H12**. The second house was listed for $500,250, but it sold for only $400,125. Therefore, the sale percentage of the list price is 79.99%.

g. Center horizontally and wrap the headings on row 4.

h. Insert a new column between the Date Sold and List Price columns. Do the following:
  • Move the Days on Market **range C4:C12** to the **range F4:F12**.
  • Delete the empty column C.

i. Edit the list date of the 41 Chestnut Circle house to be **4/22/2021**. Edit the list price of the house on Amsterdam Drive to be **$355,000**.

j. Select the property rows and set a **25 row height** and apply **Middle Align**.

k. Apply the **All Borders border style** to the **range A4:H12**. Adjust column widths as necessary.

l. Apply **Align Right** and increase indent twice the values in the **range E5:E12**.

m. Delete the Properties worksheet.

n. Insert a new worksheet and name it **Formulas**.

o. Click the **Select All button** to select all data on the Houses Sold worksheet and copy it to the Formulas worksheet.

p. Select the worksheet tabs and do the following:
  • Set landscape orientation.
  • Center the page horizontally and vertically between the margins.
  • Insert a footer with your name on the left side, the sheet tab code in the center, and the file name code on the right side.

q. Complete the following steps on the Formulas worksheet:
  • Hide the Date Listed and Date Sold columns.
  • Display cell formulas.
  • Set options to print gridlines and row and column headings.
  • Adjust column widths.

r. Display the Houses Sold worksheet and apply **120% scaling**.

s. Save and close the file. Exit Excel. Based on your instructor's directions, submit e01m2Sales_LastFirst.

Running Case

New Castle County Technical Services

New Castle County Technical Services (NCCTS) provides technical support for companies in the greater New Castle County, Delaware, area. You downloaded a dataset from the company database that contains a list of call cases closed during March. You want to calculate the number of days between the start and end dates and the amount owed per transaction. Then you will format the worksheet.

a. Open *e01r1NCCTS* and save it as **e01r1NCCTS_LastFirst**.

b. Insert a row above the first row and do the following:
  - Type **Billing Hours and Amounts** in **cell A1**.
  - Apply the **Orange, Accent2 cell style**.
  - Merge and center the title in the **range A1:K1**.
  - Bold the title and change the font size to **16 pt**.

c. Select the **range A2:K2**, apply the **40% - Accent2 cell style**, bold, and merge and center.

d. Find *Virus Detection* and replace it with **Virus Removal** throughout the worksheet.

e. Apply these formats to the **range A4:K4**: bold, wrap text, center horizontally, and **Orange, Accent 2, Lighter 60% fill color**.

f. Hide columns C and D that contain the RepID and CallTypeID.

g. Create and copy the following formulas:
  - **Cell J5**: Calculate the number of days each case was opened by subtracting the Opened Date from the Closed Date. Copy the formula to the **range J6:J36**.
  - **Cell K5**: Calculate the amount billed for each transaction by multiplying the Rate by the Hours Logged. Copy the formula to the **range K6:K36**.

h. Apply these number formats:
  - Apply the **Accounting Number Format** with **zero** decimal places to the **range F5:F36**.
  - Apply **Accounting Number Format** to the **range K5:K36**.
  - Apply **Comma Style** to the **range G5:G36**.

i. Set a width of **28** for column E.

j. Cut the **range G4:G36** (Hours Logged), right-click **cell K4**, and then select **Insert Cut Cells**.

k. Rename the sheet tab as **March Hours**. Change the sheet tab color to **Orange, Accent 2**.

l. Set **0.4"** left and right margins and center the worksheet data horizontally on the page. Set **90% scaling**.

m. Insert a footer with your name on the left side, the sheet name code in the center, and the file name code on the right side.

n. Save and close the file. Exit Excel. Based on your instructor's directions, submit e01r1NCCTS_LastFirst.

Disaster Recovery

Net Proceeds from House Sale

Daryl Patterson is a real estate agent. He wants his clients to have a realistic expectation of how much money they will receive when they sell their houses. Sellers know they pay a commission to the agent and pay off their existing mortgages; however, many sellers forget to consider they might have to pay some of the buyer's closing costs, title insurance, and prorated property taxes.

Daryl created a worksheet to enter values in an input area to calculate the estimated deductions at closing and calculate the estimated net proceeds the seller will receive; however, the worksheet contains errors. Open *e01d1Proceeds* and save it as **e01d1Proceeds_LastFirst**. Review the font formatting and alignment for consistency. Use the New Comment command in the Comments group on the Review tab to insert a comment in a cell. As you identify the errors, insert comments in the respective cells to explain the errors. Correct the errors, including formatting errors.

In the Output Area, the only entered value should be the title insurance policy. The other numbers should be results of formulas or a reference to a cell in the Input Area. The commission and closing costs are amounts based on the sale price and respective rates. The prorated property tax is the product of the annual property taxes and the months to prorate the taxes out of the entire year. The estimated net proceeds is calculated as the difference between the sale price and the total estimated deductions.

Apply Landscape orientation, 115% scaling, 1.5" top margin, and center horizontally. Insert your name on the left side of the header, the sheet name code in the center, and the file name code on the right side. Save and close the file. Exit Excel. Based on your instructor's directions, submit e01d1Proceeds_LastFirst.

Capstone Exercise

MyLab IT Grader

Theatre Ticket Sales

You work in the accounting division at Sugarhouse District Theatre, where touring Broadway plays and musicals are performed. You started a worksheet that lists the number of seats in each section (orchestra and the tiers) and the number of seats sold for a specific performance date. You will calculate the percentage of sold and unsold seats and gross revenue by section. You will format the worksheet to improve readability and copy the final worksheet to use as a template to enter data for the next day's performance.

Format the Title and Enter the Date

Your first task is to format the title by centering it over the data columns, enlarging the font size, and applying a different font color. Next, you will enter and format the performance date on the next row.

1. Open *e01c1TicketSales* and save it as **e01c1TicketSales_LastFirst**.
2. Merge and center the title over the **range A1:G1**, change the font size to **20**, and then apply **Purple font color**.
3. Type **4/16/2021** in **cell A2**, then apply the **Long Date number format**, apply the **Note cell style**, and then merge and center the date over the **range A2:G2**.

Format Seating Labels

Previously, you entered section labels Orchestra Front and Tiers to identify the seating sections. You will insert a new row for Orchestra Back, indent the specific seating sections to distinguish these labels from the main labels, and adjust the column width.

4. Insert a new row above row 9, between Right and Left. The new row is row 9. Copy the data from **cell A5** to **cell A9** and change the data in **cell A9** from Front to **Back**.
5. Indent twice the data in the **ranges A6:A8**, **A10:A12**, and **A14:A17**.
6. Change the width of **column A** to **18**.

Format Labels, Replace Text, and Checking Spelling

Previously, you applied Lavender fill and bold to the label in cell A4. You will use Format Painter to copy the formats to the other column labels on row 4. Then you will apply other alignment settings to the labels, replace *Purchased* with *Sold*, and check the spelling in the worksheet.

7. Use Format Painter to copy the formats in **cell A4** to the **range B4:G4**.
8. Wrap text and horizontally center the labels in the **range A4:G4** and set the height of row 4 to **30**.
9. Find all occurrences of *Purchased* and replace them with **Sold**.

10. Check the spelling in the worksheet and correct all spelling errors.

Insert Formulas and Apply Number Formats

You are ready to enter formulas in the last three columns to calculate the percentage of seats sold at the performance, percentage of unsold seats (i.e., empty), and the gross revenue for the sold seats.

11. Calculate the Percentage Sold in **cell E6** by dividing the Seats Sold by the Seats in Section. Copy the formula to the **range E7:E17**. Delete the formula in **cells E9** and **E13** because those are empty rows.
12. Calculate the Percentage Not Sold in **cell F6** by subtracting the Percentage Sold from 1. Copy the formula to the **range F7:F17**. Delete the formula in **cells F9** and **F13** because those are empty rows.
13. Calculate the Gross Revenue in **cell G6** by multiplying the Seats Sold by the Price Per Seat. Copy the formula to the range **G7:G17**. Delete the formula in **cells G9** and **G13** because those are empty rows.
14. Apply **Accounting Number Format** with zero decimal places to the **ranges D6:D17** and **G6:G17**.
15. Apply **Percentage Style** with one decimal place to the **range E6:F17**.

Move a Column, Adjust Alignment, and Add Borders

After reviewing the data, you decide to move the Price Per Seat to be to the left of the Gross Revenue data. In addition, you decide to center the values in the Seats in Section and Seats Sold columns.

16. Insert a new column G. Select and move the **range D4:D17** to the **range G4:G17**. Delete the empty column D.
17. Center horizontally the data in the **range B6:C17**.
18. Apply **Align Right** and indent twice the data in the **range D6:E17**.
19. Apply **Outside Borders** to the **range A4:G4**, the **range A5:G8**, **A9:G12**, and **A13:G17** one range at a time.

Format the Worksheet

To finalize the worksheet, you are ready to set a larger top margin, center the worksheet between the left and right margins, and insert a footer. Finally, you will rename the sheet tab, copy the worksheet, and delete some data to use a template for the next performance.

Capstone Exercise • Excel 2019   145

20. Set a **1"** top margin and center the worksheet horizontally between the left and right margins.

21. Insert a footer with your name on the left side, the sheet name code in the center, and the file name code on the right side.

22. Rename Sheet1 as **4-16-2021**.

23. Copy the worksheet, place the duplicate to the right, and rename it as **4-17-2021**.

24. Change the date in **cell A2** to **4/17/2021**. Keep the Long Date Format. Delete the values in the **range C6:C17**.

25. Save and close the file. Exit Excel. Based on your instructor's directions, submit e01c1TicketSales_LastFirst.

Formulas and Functions

LEARNING OUTCOME You will apply formulas and functions to calculate and analyze data.

OBJECTIVES & SKILLS: After you read this chapter, you will be able to:

CASE STUDY | Townsend Mortgage Company

You are an assistant to Erica Matheson, a mortgage broker at the Townsend Mortgage Company. Erica spends her days reviewing mortgage rates and trends, meeting with clients, and preparing paperwork. She relies on your expertise in using Excel to help analyze mortgage data.

Today, Erica provided you with sample mortgage data: loan number, house cost, down payment, mortgage rate, and the length of the loan in years. She has asked you to perform some basic calculations so that she can check the output provided by her system to verify that it is calculating results correctly. She wants you to calculate the amount financed, the periodic interest rate, the total number of payment periods, the percentage of the house cost financed, and the payoff year for each loan. In addition, you will calculate totals, averages, and other basic statistics.

Furthermore, she has asked you to complete another worksheet that uses functions to look up interest rates from a separate table, calculate the monthly payments, and determine how much (if any) the borrower will have to pay for private mortgage insurance (PMI).

Performing Quantitative Analysis

YanLev/Shutterstock

	A	B	C	D	E	F	G	H	I	J	K	L
1	**Townsend Mortgage Company**											
2												
3		**Input Area**										
4	Today's Date:	4/3/2021										
5	Pmts Per Year:	12										
6												
7	Loan #	House Cost	Down Payment	Amount Financed	Mortgage Rate	Rate Per Period	Years	# of Pmt Periods	% Financed	Date Financed	Payoff Year	
8	452786	$ 400,000	$ 80,000	$ 320,000	3.625%	0.302%	25	300	80.0%	5/1/2018	2043	
9	453000	$ 425,000	$ 60,000	$ 365,000	3.940%	0.328%	30	360	85.9%	11/3/2018	2048	
10	453025	$ 175,500	$ 30,000	$ 145,500	3.550%	0.296%	25	300	82.9%	4/10/2019	2044	
11	452600	$ 265,950	$ 58,000	$ 207,950	2.500%	0.208%	15	180	78.2%	10/14/2019	2034	
12	452638	$ 329,750	$ 65,000	$ 264,750	3.250%	0.271%	30	360	80.3%	2/4/2020	2050	
13												
14		**Summary Statistics**										
15	Statistics	House Cost	Down Payment	Amount Financed								
16	Total	$ 1,596,200	$ 293,000	$ 1,303,200								
17	Average	$ 319,240	$ 58,600	$ 260,640								
18	Median	$ 329,750	$ 60,000	$ 264,750								
19	Lowest	$ 175,500	$ 30,000	$ 145,500								
20	Highest	$ 425,000	$ 80,000	$ 365,000								
21	# of Mortgages	5	5	5								

FIGURE 2.1 Townsend Mortgage Company Worksheet

CASE STUDY | Townsend Mortgage Company

Starting File	File to be Submitted
e02h1Loans	**e02h3Loans_LastFirst**

MyLab IT Grader An alternate version of this project is available as a MyLab IT Grader Assessment

Formula Basics

When you increase your understanding of formulas, you can construct robust workbooks that perform a variety of calculations for quantitative analysis. Your ability to build sophisticated workbooks and to interpret the results increases your value to any organization. By now, you should be able to create simple formulas using cell references and mathematical operators and use the order of operations to control the sequence of calculations in formulas.

In this section, you will create formulas in which cell addresses change or remain fixed when you copy them.

Using Relative, Absolute, and Mixed Cell References in Formulas

When you copy a formula, Excel either adjusts or preserves the cell references in the copied formula based on how the cell references appear in the original formula. Excel uses three different ways to refer to a cell in a formula: relative, absolute, and mixed. Relative references change when a formula is copied. For example, if a formula containing the cell A1 is copied down one row in the column, the reference would become A2. In contrast, absolute references remain constant, no matter where they are copied. Mixed references are a combination of both absolute and relative, where part of the cell reference will change and part will remain constant.

When you create a formula that you will copy to other cells, ask yourself the following question: Do the cell references contain constant or variable values? In other words, should the cell reference adjust or always refer to the same cell location, regardless of where the copied formula is located?

STEP 1 ▷ **Use a Relative Cell Reference**

A *relative cell reference* is the default method of referencing in Excel. It indicates a cell's relative location on a worksheet, such as five rows up and one column to the left, from the original cell containing the formula. When you copy a formula containing a relative cell reference, the cells referred to in the copied formula change relative to the position of the copied formula. Regardless of where you paste the formula, the cell references in the copied formula maintain the same relative distance from the cell containing the copied formula, as the cell references the relative location to the original formula cell.

In Figure 2.2, the formulas in column G contain relative cell references. When you copy the original formula =D2-E2 from cell F2 down one row to cell F3, the copied formula changes to =D3-E3. Because you copy the formula to the next row in the column, the column letters in the formula stay the same, but the row numbers change to reflect the row to which you copied the formula. Using relative referencing is an effective time saving tool.

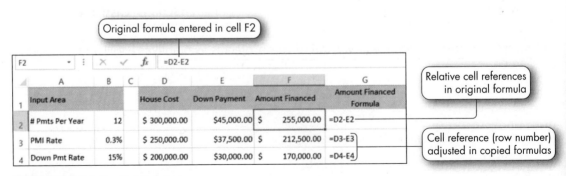

FIGURE 2.2 Relative Cell References

STEP 2 ▸ Use an Absolute Cell Reference

In many calculations, there are times in which a value should remain constant, such as an interest rate or payoff date. In these situations, absolute cell references are needed. An **absolute cell reference** provides a constant reference to a specific cell. When you copy a formula containing an absolute cell reference, the absolute cell reference in the copied formula does not change, regardless of where you copy the formula. An absolute cell reference is designated with a dollar sign before both the column letter and row number, such as $B$4.

In Figure 2.3, the down payment is calculated by multiplying the house cost by the 15% down payment rate. Each down payment calculation uses a different purchase price and constant down payment rate; therefore, an absolute reference is required for the down payment rate. Cell E2 contains =D2*$B$4 ($300,000*15.0%) to calculate the first borrower's down payment. When you copy the formula down to the next row, the copied formula in cell E3 is =D3*$B$4. The relative cell reference D2 changes to D3 (for the next house cost), and the absolute cell reference $B$4 remains the same to refer to the constant 15.0% down payment rate in cell B4. This formula ensures that the cell reference to the house cost changes for each row but that the house cost is always multiplied by the rate in cell B4.

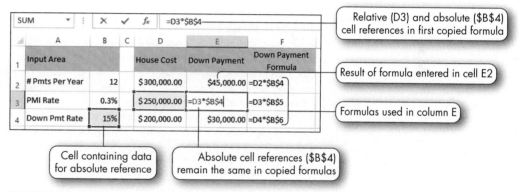

FIGURE 2.3 Relative and Absolute Cell References

TIP: INPUT AREA AND ABSOLUTE CELL REFERENCES

In Figure 2.3, values that can be modified, such as the down payment rate, are put in an input area. Generally, formulas use absolute references to the cells in the input area. For example, B4 is an absolute cell reference in all the down payment calculations. If the value in B4 is modified, Excel recalculates the amount of down payment for all the down payment formulas. By using cell references from an input area, you can perform what-if analyses very easily.

When utilizing the fill handle to copy a formula, if an error or unexpected result occurs, a good starting point for troubleshooting is checking cell references in the formula to determine if an absolute reference is needed. Figure 2.4 shows what happens if the down payment formula used a relative reference to cell B4. If the original formula in cell E2 is =D2*B4, the copied formula becomes =D3*B5 in cell E3. The relative cell reference to B4 changes to B5 when you copy the formula. Because cell B5 is empty, the $350,000 house cost in cell D3 is multiplied by 0, giving a $0 down payment, which is not a valid down payment amount.

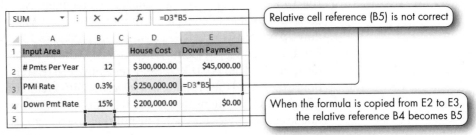

FIGURE 2.4 Error in Formula

TIP: THE F4 KEY
When using Windows, the function F4 key toggles through relative, absolute, and mixed references. Click a cell reference within a formula on the Formula Bar and press F4 to change it. For example, click in B4 in the formula =D2*B4. Press F4 and the relative cell reference (B4) changes to an absolute cell reference ($B$4). Press F4 again and $B$4 becomes a mixed reference (B$4); press F4 again and it becomes another mixed reference ($B4). Press F4 a fourth time and the cell reference returns to the original relative reference (B4). Note to laptop users: Many laptops assign shared functions to the F4 key. If your keyboard has two functions assigned to the F4 key, the Fn key and the F4 key must be pressed to toggle references.

STEP 3 ▸ **Use a Mixed Cell Reference**

A *mixed cell reference* combines an absolute cell reference with a relative cell reference. When you copy a formula containing a mixed cell reference, either the column letter or the row number that has the absolute reference remains fixed while the other part of the cell reference that is relative changes in the copied formula. $B4 and B$4 are examples of mixed cell references. In the reference $B4, the column B is absolute, and the row number is relative; when you copy the formula, the column letter B does not change, but the row number will change. In the reference B$4, the column letter B changes, but the row number, 4, does not change. To create a mixed reference, type the dollar sign to the left of the part of the cell reference you want to be absolute.

In the down payment formula, you can change the formula in cell E2 to be =D2*B$4. Because you are copying down the same column, only the row reference 4 must be absolute; the column letter stays the same. Figure 2.5 shows the copied formula =D3*B$4 in cell E3. In situations where you can use either absolute or mixed references, consider using mixed references to shorten the length of the formula.

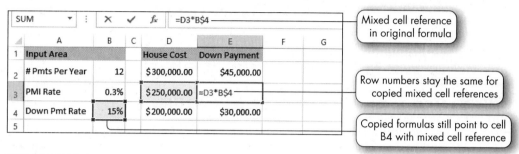

FIGURE 2.5 Relative and Mixed Cell References

MAC TIP: TOGGLING REFERENCES ON A MAC

For Apple users, the F4 key is reserved to launch the macOS dashboard. When using Excel on a Mac, the shortcut to toggle between relative, absolute, and mixed cell references is Command+T.

Quick Concepts

1. Describe what happens when you copy a formula containing a relative cell reference one row down. **p. 150**

2. Explain why you would use an absolute reference in a formula. **p. 151**

3. Describe the benefits of using a mixed reference. **p. 152**

Hands-On Exercises

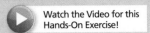
Skills covered: Use a Relative
Cell Reference • Use an Absolute
Cell Reference • Use a Mixed Cell
Reference

1 Formula Basics

Erica prepared a workbook containing data for five mortgages financed with the Townsend Mortgage
Company. The data include house cost, down payment, mortgage rate, number of years to pay off the
mortgage, and the financing date for each mortgage.

STEP 1 USE A RELATIVE CELL REFERENCE

You will calculate the amount financed by each borrower by creating a formula with relative cell references that
calculates the difference between the house cost and the down payment. After verifying the results of the amount
financed by the first borrower, you will copy the formula down the Amount Financed column to calculate the other
borrowers' amounts financed. Refer to Figure 2.6 as you complete Step 1.

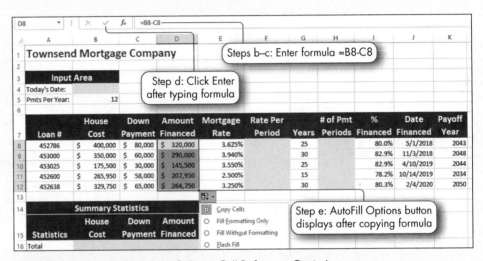

FIGURE 2.6 Formula Containing Relative Cell Reference Copied

a. Open *e02h1Loans* and save it as **e02h1Loans_LastFirst**.

   The workbook contains two worksheets: Details (for Hands-On Exercises 1 and 2) and
   Payment Info (for Hands-On Exercise 3). You will enter formulas in the shaded cells.

> **TROUBLESHOOTING:** If you make any major mistakes in this exercise, you can close the file,
> open *e02h1Loans* again, and then start this exercise over.

b. Click **cell D8** in the Details sheet. Type **=** and click **cell B8**, the cell containing the first
   borrower's house cost.

c. Type **-** and click **cell C8**, the cell containing the down payment by the first borrower.

d. Click **Enter** ✓ (the check mark between the Name Box and Formula Bar) to complete
   the formula.

   The first client borrowed $320,000, the difference between the house cost in cell B8 and
   the down payment in cell C8.

e. Double-click the **cell D8 fill handle**.

   You copied the formula down the Amount Financed column for each mortgage row.

f. Click **cell D9** and view the formula in the Formula Bar.

The formula in cell D8 is =B8-C8. The formula copied to cell D9 is =B9-C9. Because the original formula contained relative cell references, when you copy the formula to the next row, the row numbers for the cell references change. Each result represents the amount financed for that borrower.

g. Press ⬇ and look at the cell references in the Formula Bar to see how the references change for each formula you copied. Save the workbook with the new formula you created.

STEP 2 USE AN ABSOLUTE CELL REFERENCE

Column E contains the mortgage rate for each loan. Because the borrowers will make monthly payments, you will modify the given annual interest rate (APR) to a monthly rate by dividing it by 12 (the number of payments in one year) for each borrower. Refer to Figure 2.7 as you complete Step 2.

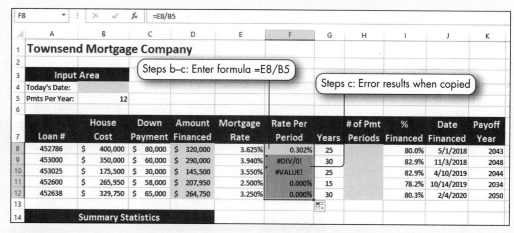

FIGURE 2.7 Formula Containing Incorrect Relative Cell Reference Copied

a. Click **cell F8**.

You will create a formula to calculate the monthly interest rate for the first borrower.

b. Type **=E8/B5** and click **Enter**.

Typically, you should avoid typing values directly in formulas. Therefore, you use a reference to cell B5, where the number of payments per year is placed in the input area, so that the company can change the payment period to bimonthly (24 payments per year) or quarterly (four payments per year) without adjusting each formula.

> **MAC TROUBLESHOOTING:** On a Mac there is no Enter key. When using a Mac, click the Return key or click Enter on the ribbon to complete a formula.

c. Double-click the **cell F8 fill handle**, click **cell F9**, and then view the results (see Figure 2.7).

An error icon displays to the left of cell F9, which displays #DIV/0!, and cell F10 displays #VALUE!. The original formula was =E8/B5. Because you copied the formula =E8/B5 down the column, the first copied formula is =E9/B6, and the second copied formula is =E10/B7. Although you want the mortgage rate cell reference (E8) to change (E9, E10, etc.) from row to row, you do not want the number of payments per year (cell B5) to change. You need all formulas to divide by the value stored in cell B5, so you will edit the formula to make B5 an absolute reference.

d. Click **Undo** in the Quick Access Toolbar to undo the Auto Fill process. With F8 as the active cell, click to the right of **cell B5** in the Formula Bar.

e. Press the function key **F4** and click **Enter** on the formula bar.

Excel changes the cell reference from B5 to $B$5, making it an absolute cell reference.

f. Double-click the **fill handle** to copy the formula down the Rate Per Period column. Click **cell F9** and view the formula in the Formula Bar.

The formula in cell F9 is =E9/$B$5. The reference to E9 is relative and the reference to B5 is absolute. The results of all the calculations in the Rate Per Period column are now correct.

g. Save the workbook.

STEP 3 USE A MIXED CELL REFERENCE

The next formula you create will calculate the total number of payment periods for each loan. Refer to Figure 2.8 as you complete Step 3.

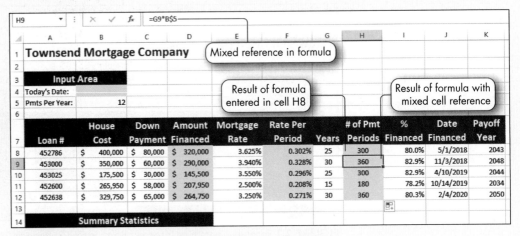

FIGURE 2.8 Formula Containing Mixed Cell Reference Copied

a. Click **cell H8** and type **=G8*B5**.

You will multiply the number of years (25) by the number of payment periods in one year (12) using cell references.

b. Press **F4** to make the B5 cell reference absolute and click **Enter**.

You want B5 to be absolute so that the cell reference remains B5 when you copy the formula. The product of 25 years and 12 months is 300 months or payment periods.

c. Copy the formula down the # of Pmt Periods column.

The first copied formula is =G9*$B$5, and the result is 360. You want to see what happens if you change the absolute reference to a mixed reference and copy the formula again. Because you are copying down a column, the column letter B can be relative because it will not change either way, but the row number 5 must be absolute.

d. Ensure that cell H8 is the active cell and click **Undo** on the Quick Access Toolbar to undo the copied formulas.

e. Click within the **$B$5 cell reference** in the Formula Bar. Press **F4** to change the cell reference to a mixed cell reference: B$5. Press **Ctrl+Enter** and copy the formula down the # of Pmt Periods column. Click **cell H9**.

The first copied formula is =G9*B$5 and the result is still 360. In this situation, using either an absolute reference or a mixed reference provides the same results.

f. Save the workbook. Keep the workbook open if you plan to continue with the next Hands-On Exercise . If not, close the workbook and exit Excel.

Function Basics

An Excel *function* is a predefined computation that simplifies creating a formula that performs a complex calculation. Excel contains more than 400 functions, which are organized into 14 categories. Table 2.1 lists and describes the primary function categories used in this chapter.

TABLE 2.1	Function Categories and Descriptions
Category	**Description**
Date & Time	Provides methods for manipulating date and time values.
Financial	Performs financial calculations, such as payments, rates, present value, and future value.
Logical	Performs logical tests and returns the value of the tests. Includes logical operators for combined tests, such as AND, OR, and NOT.
Lookup & Reference	Looks up values, creates links to cells, or provides references to cells in a worksheet.
Math & Trig	Performs standard math and trigonometry calculations.
Statistical	Performs common statistical calculations, such as averages and standard deviations.

When using functions, you must adhere to correct *syntax*, the rules that dictate the structure and components required to perform the necessary calculations. Start a function with an equal sign, followed by the function name, and then its arguments enclosed in parentheses.

- The function name describes the purpose of the function. For example, the function name SUM indicates that the function sums, or adds, values.

- A function's *arguments* are enclosed in parentheses and specify the inputs—such as cells, values, or arithmetic expressions—that are required to complete the operation. In some cases, a function requires multiple arguments separated by commas.

In this section, you will learn how to insert common functions using the keyboard and the Insert Function and Function Arguments dialog boxes.

Inserting a Function

To use a function in a calculation, after the equal sign, you must enter the function name. You can do this by simply typing the function name or you can locate the function from the Formulas tab or by using the Insert Function dialog box. (On a Mac, this is called the *Formula Builder.*) To insert a function by typing, first type an equal sign, and then begin typing the function name. *Formula AutoComplete* displays a list of functions and defined names that match letters as you type a formula. For example, if you type =SU, Formula AutoComplete displays a list of functions and names that start with *SU* (see Figure 2.9). You can double-click the function name from the list or continue typing the function name. To learn more about a function in the AutoComplete list, point to the name and read the screen tip that describes the function.

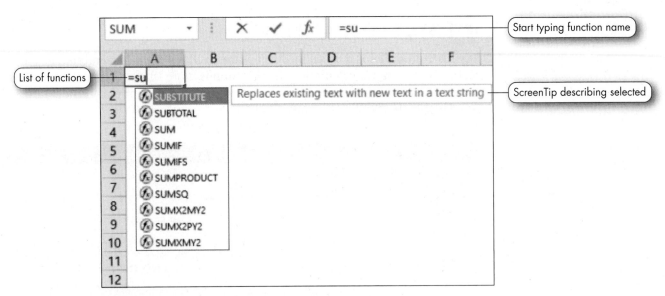

FIGURE 2.9 Formula AutoComplete

Recall that function syntax is the equal sign, function name, and function arguments that are enclosed in parentheses. After you type the function name and opening parenthesis, Excel displays the ***function ScreenTip***, a small pop-up description of the function's arguments. The argument you are currently entering is bold in the function ScreenTip (see Figure 2.10). Square brackets indicate optional arguments. For example, the SUM function requires the number1 argument, but the number2 argument is optional. Click the argument name in the function ScreenTip to select the actual argument in the formula you are creating if you want to make changes to the argument. When you are finished entering the required arguments, type a closing parenthesis and press Enter to end the function.

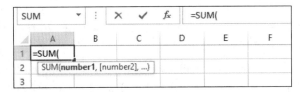

FIGURE 2.10 Function ScreenTip

You can also use the Insert Function dialog box to search for a function, select a function category, and select a function from the list (see Figure 2.11). The dialog box is helpful if you want to browse a list of functions, especially if you are not sure of the function you need and want to see descriptions.

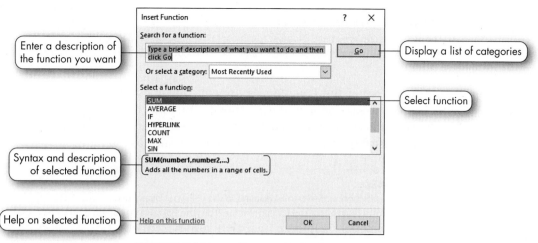

FIGURE 2.11 Insert Function Dialog Box

To display the Insert Function dialog box, click Insert Function f_x (located between the Name Box and the Formula Bar) or click Insert Function in the Function Library group on the Formulas tab. From within the dialog box, select a function category, such as Most Recently Used, and select a function to display the syntax and a brief description of that function. Click *Help on this function* to display details about the selected function. When using a Mac, *More help on this function* displays at the bottom of the Formula Builder.

When you find the function you want, click OK. The Function Arguments dialog box opens so that you can enter the arguments for that specific function (see Figure 2.12). Argument names in bold (such as number1 in the SUM function) are required. Argument names that are not bold (such as number2 in the SUM function) are optional. The function can operate without the optional argument, which is used when you need additional specifications to calculate a result.

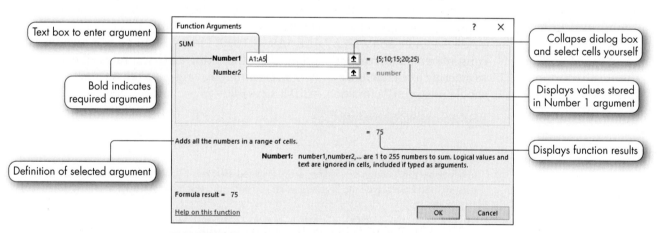

FIGURE 2.12 Function Arguments Dialog Box

Type the cell references in the argument boxes or click the collapse button to the right side of an argument box to collapse the dialog box and select the cell or range of cells in the worksheet to designate as that argument. If you click the collapse button to select a range, click the expand button to expand the dialog box again. You can also manually select the cells for the argument without clicking the collapse button. The collapse button is best used if the view of the cells for the arguments is obstructed. The value, or results, of a formula contained in the argument cell displays on the right side of the argument box (such as 5; 10; 15; 20; 25—the values stored in the range A1:A5 used for the number1 argument). If the argument is not valid, Excel displays an error description on the right side of the argument box.

The bottom of the Function Arguments dialog box displays a description of the function and a description of the argument containing the insertion point. As you enter arguments, the description changes to describe each argument, and the bottom of the dialog box also displays the result of the function, such as 75.

Inserting Basic Math and Statistics Functions

Excel includes commonly used math and statistical functions for a variety of calculations. For example, you can insert functions to calculate the total amount you spend on dining out in a month (SUM), the average amount you spend per month purchasing music online (AVERAGE), your highest electric bill (MAX), and your lowest time to run a mile this week (MIN).

STEP 1 Use the SUM Function

The *SUM function* totals values in one or more cells and displays the result in the cell containing the function. This function is more efficient to create when you want to add the values contained in three or more contiguous cells. For example, to add the contents of cells A2 through A14, you could enter =A2+A3+A4+A5+A6+A7+A8+A9+A10+A11+A12+A13+A14, which is time-consuming and increases the probability of entering an inaccurate cell reference, such as entering a cell reference twice or accidentally leaving out a cell reference. Instead, you should use the SUM function, =SUM(A2:A14).

=SUM(number1, [number2], . . .)

The SUM function contains one required argument (number1) that represents a range of cells to add. The range, such as A2:A14, specifies the first and last of an adjacent group of cells containing values to SUM. Excel will sum all cells within that range. The number2 optional argument is used when you want to sum values stored in nonadjacent cells or ranges, such as =SUM(A2:A14,F2:F14). The ellipsis in the function syntax indicates that you can add as many additional ranges as desired, separated by commas.

Figure 2.13 shows the result of using the SUM function in cell D2 to total scores in cells A2:A14 with the results (898).

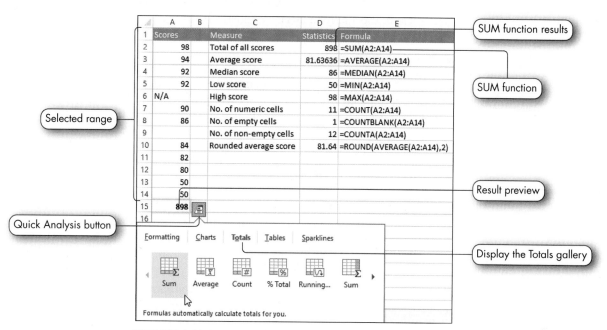

FIGURE 2.13 Function Results

TIP: AUTOSUM ARROW
If you click AutoSum in the Editing group on the Home tab or in the Function Library group on the Formulas tab, Excel inserts the SUM function. However, if you click the AutoSum arrow, Excel displays a list of basic functions to select: Sum, Average, Count Numbers, Max, and Min. If you want to insert another function, select More Functions from the list.

STEP 2 Use the AVERAGE Function

People often describe data based on central tendency, which means that values tend to cluster around a central value. Excel provides two functions to calculate central tendency: AVERAGE and MEDIAN. The *AVERAGE function* calculates the arithmetic mean, or average, for the values in a range of cells. You can use this function to calculate the class average on a biology test or the average number of points scored per game by a basketball player. In Figure 2.13, =AVERAGE(A2:A14) in cell D3 returns 81.63636 as the average test score. The AVERAGE function ignores empty cells and cells containing N/A or text.

=AVERAGE (number1,[number2], . . .)

STEP 3 Use the Median Function

The *MEDIAN function* finds the midpoint value, which is the value that one half of the data set is above or below. The median is particularly useful because extreme values often influence the arithmetic mean calculated by the AVERAGE function. In Figure 2.13, the two extreme test scores of 50 distort the average. The rest of the test scores range from 80 to 98. Cell D4 contains =MEDIAN(A2:A14). The median for test scores is 86, which indicates that half the test scores are above 86 and half the test scores are below 86. This statistic is more reflective of the data set than the average. The MEDIAN function ignores empty cells and cells containing N/A or text.

=MEDIAN(number1,[number2], . . .)

Use the MIN and MAX Functions

The **MIN function** analyzes an argument list to determine the lowest value, such as the lowest score on a test. Manually inspecting a range of values to identify the lowest value is inefficient, especially in large spreadsheets. In Figure 2.13, =MIN(A2:A14) in cell D5 identifies that 50 is the lowest test score.

=MIN(number1,[number2], . . .)

The **MAX function** analyzes an argument list to determine the highest value, such as the highest score on a test. In Figure 2.13, =MAX(A2:A14) in cell D6 identifies 98 as the highest test score.

=MAX(number1,[number2], . . .)

Use the COUNT Functions

Excel provides three basic count functions—COUNT, COUNTBLANK, and COUNTA—to count the cells in a range that meet a particular criterion. The **COUNT function** tallies the number of cells in a range that contain values you can use in calculations, such as numerical and date data, but excludes blank cells and text entries from the tally. In Figure 2.13, the selected range spans 13 cells; however, =COUNT(A2:A14) in cell D7 returns 11, the number of cells that contain numeric data. It does not count the cell containing the text *N/A* or the blank cell.

The **COUNTBLANK function** tallies the number of cells in a range that are blank. In Figure 2.13, =COUNTBLANK(A2:A14) in cell D8 identifies that one cell in the range A2:A14 is blank. The **COUNTA function** tallies the number of cells in a range that are not blank—that is, cells that contain data, whether a value, text, or a formula. In Figure 2.13, =COUNTA(A2:A14) in cell D9 returns 12, indicating that the range A2:A14 contains 12 cells that contain some form of data. It does not count the blank cell; however, it will count cells that contain text such as cell A6.

=COUNT(value1,[value2], . . .)

=COUNTBLANK(range)

=COUNTA(value1,[value2], . . .)

> **TIP: STATUS BAR STATISTICS: AVERAGE, COUNT, AND SUM**
> When you select a range of cells containing values, by default Excel displays the average, count, and sum of those values on the right side of the status bar. You can customize the status bar to show other selection statistics, such as the minimum and maximum values for a selected range. To display or hide selection statistics, right-click the status bar and select the statistic.

Perform Calculations with Quick Analysis Tools

Quick Analysis is a set of analytical tools you can use to apply formatting, create charts or tables, and insert basic functions. When you select a range of data, the Quick Analysis button displays adjacent to the bottom-right corner of the selected range. Click the Quick Analysis button to display the Quick Analysis gallery and select the analytical tool to meet your needs. Quick Analysis is only available for the PC version of Excel.

Figure 2.13 shows the Totals gallery options so that you can sum, average, or count the values in the selected range. Select % Total to display the percentage of the grand total of two or more columns. Select Running Total to provide a cumulative total at the bottom of multiple columns. Additional options can be seen by clicking the right expansion arrow.

> **TIP: ROUND VERSUS DECREASE DECIMAL POINTS**
> When you click Decrease Decimal in the Number group to display fewer or no digits after a decimal point, Excel still stores the original value's decimal places so that those digits can be used in calculations. If you would instead want to change the stored value to a specified number of decimal places, use the **ROUND function** =ROUND(number, num_digits).

Using Date Functions

In order to maximize the use of dates and date functions in Excel, it is important to understand how they are handled in the program. Excel assigns serial numbers to dates. The date January 1, 1900, is the equivalent to the number 1. The number 2 is the equivalent of January 2, 1900, and so on. Basically, Excel adds 1 to every serial number as each day passes. Therefore, the newer the date, the bigger the equivalent serial number. For example, assume today is January 1, 2021, and you graduate on May 6, 2021. To determine how many days until graduation, subtract today's date from the graduation date. Excel uses the serial numbers for these dates (44197 and 44322) to calculate the difference of 125 days.

STEP 5 ## Use the TODAY Function

The **TODAY function** returns the serial number for the current day displayed as a date. Excel updates the TODAY function results when you open or print the workbook. The TODAY() function does not require arguments, but you must include the parentheses. If you omit the parentheses, Excel displays #NAME? in the cell with a green triangle in the top-left corner of the cell. When you click the cell, an error icon displays that you can click for more information.

=TODAY()

> **TIP: STATIC DATES**
> When using the TODAY functions, the date will update every time the workbook is opened. If you do not want the date to update daily, it must be manually typed in a cell or it can be inserted using the shortcut Ctrl +;

Use the NOW Function

The **NOW function** uses the computer's clock to display the current date and military time. (Military time expresses time on a 24-hour period where 1:00 is 1 a.m. and 13:00 is 1 p.m.). The date and time will change every time the workbook is opened. Like the TODAY function, the NOW function does not require arguments, but you must include the parentheses. Omitting the parentheses creates a #NAME? error.

=NOW()

> **TIP: UPDATE THE DATE AND TIME**
> Both the TODAY and NOW functions display the date/time the workbook was last opened or last calculated. These functions do not continuously update the date and time while the workbook is open. To update the date and time, press F9 (Fn + F9 on Mac) or click the Formulas tab and click Calculate Now in the Calculation group.

Quick Concepts

4. Describe two different methods of entering a function directly in a cell. ***pp. 157–160***

5. Outline the type of data you enter in a Function Arguments dialog box; list four things the dialog box tells you. ***p. 159***

6. Explain the difference between the COUNT and the COUNTA functions. ***p. 162***

7. Explain the difference between using the TODAY function and manually entering a date in a cell. ***p. 163***

Hands-On Exercises

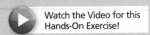
Skills covered: Insert a
Function • Insert a Function Using
Formula AutoComplete • Use
the Insert Function Dialog Box •
Use the SUM Function • Use the
AVERAGE and MEDIAN Functions •
Use the MIN and MAX Functions •
Use the COUNT Functions • Use
the TODAY Function

2 Function Basics

The Townsend Mortgage Company worksheet contains an area in which you will enter summary statistics. To complete the calculations first you will use the SUM function to determine the total value of all the homes, then you will use the AVERAGE function to determine the mean purchase price, then you will use the MEDIAN function to determine the median purchase price. After calculating the total value, average, and median you will use the MIN and MAX function to determine the highest and lowest home costs. Your last step will be to use the TODAY function to insert the current date in the worksheet. In addition, you will include the current date.

STEP 1 USE THE SUM FUNCTION

The first summary statistic you calculate is the total value of the houses bought by the borrowers. You will use the SUM function. Refer to Figure 2.14 as you complete Step 1.

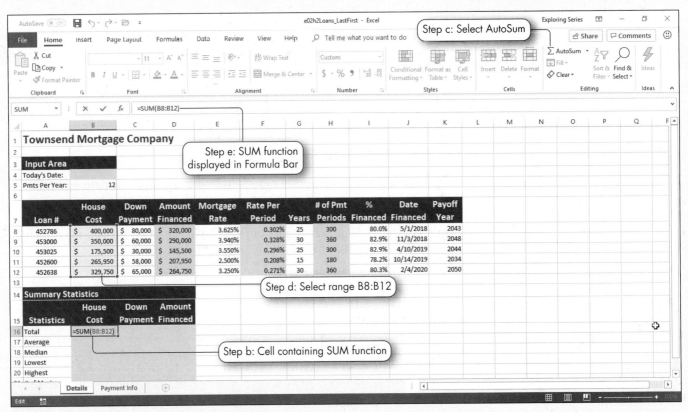

FIGURE 2.14 SUM Function Calculates Total House Cost

a. Open *e02h1Loans_LastFirst* if you closed it at the end of Hands-On Exercise 1 and save it as **e02h2Loans_LastFirst**, changing h1 to h2.

b. Ensure that the Details worksheet is active and click **cell B16**, the cell where you will enter a formula for the total house cost.

c. Click **AutoSum** ∑ AutoSum ▾ in the Editing group on the Home tab.

Excel anticipates the range of cells containing values you want to sum based on where you enter the formula—in this case, B8:B15. This is not the correct range, so you must enter the correct range.

> **TROUBLESHOOTING:** AutoSum, like some other commands in Excel, contains two parts: the main command button and an arrow. Click the main command button when instructed to click AutoSum. Click the arrow when instructed to click the AutoSum arrow for additional options. If you accidentally clicked the arrow instead of AutoSum, press Esc to cancel the SUM function from being completed and try Step c again.

d. Select the **range B8:B12**, the cells containing house costs.

As you use the semi-selection process, Excel enters the range in the SUM function.

> **TROUBLESHOOTING:** If you entered the function without changing the arguments, repeat Steps b–d or edit the arguments in the Formula Bar by deleting the default range, typing B8:B12 between the parentheses and pressing Enter.

e. Click **Enter**.

Cell B16 contains the function = SUM(B8:B12), and the result is $1,521,200.

f. Save the workbook.

STEP 2 ▶ USE THE AVERAGE FUNCTION

Before copying the functions to calculate the total down payments and amounts financed, you want to calculate the average house cost of the houses bought by the borrowers in your list. Calculating an average is a useful statistic because it provides insight into the overall center of your data. Refer to Figure 2.15 as you complete Step 2.

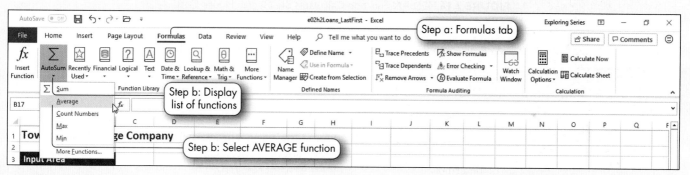

FIGURE 2.15 AVERAGE Function

a. Click the **Formulas tab** and click **cell B17**, the cell where you will display the average cost of the houses.

b. Click the **AutoSum arrow** in the Function Library group and select **Average**.

Excel selects cell B16, which is the total cost of the houses. You need to change the range.

c. Select the **range B8:B12**, the cells containing the house costs.

The function is =AVERAGE(B8:B12).

d. Press **Enter**, making cell B18 the active cell.

The average house cost is $304,240.

e. Save the workbook.

The average function can lead to misleading results if there are values that are statistical outliers. Homes with values extremely high or low compared to the majority of the mortgages being evaluated can lead to an average that does not truly represent the center of the mortgage data. You realize that extreme house costs may distort the average. Therefore, you decide to identify the median house cost to compare it to the average house cost. Refer to Figure 2.16 as you complete Step 3.

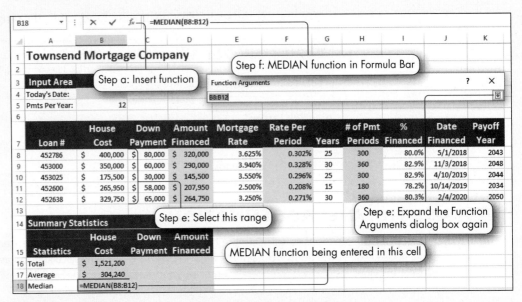

FIGURE 2.16 MEDIAN Function Calculates the Median House Cost

a. Ensure that cell B18 is the active cell. Click **Insert Function** to the left of the Formula bar.

The Insert Function dialog box opens. Use this dialog box to select the MEDIAN function.

b. Type **median** in the Search for a function box and click **Go**.

Excel displays a list of functions in the Select a function list. The MEDIAN function is selected at the top of the list; the bottom of the dialog box displays the syntax and the description.

c. Read the MEDIAN function description and click **OK**.

The Function Arguments dialog box opens. It contains one required argument, Number1, representing a range of cells containing values.

d. Click **Collapse Dialog Box** to the right of the Number1 box.

You collapsed the Function Arguments dialog box so that you can select the range.

e. Select the **range B8:B12** and click **Expand Dialog Box** in the Function Arguments dialog box.

The Function Arguments dialog box expands, displaying B8:B12 in the Number1 box.

f. Click **OK** to accept the function arguments and close the dialog box.

Half of the houses purchased cost more than the median, $329,750, and half of the houses cost less than this value. Notice the difference between the median and the average: The average is lower because it is affected by the lowest-priced house, $175,500.

g. Save the workbook.

STEP 4 USE THE MIN, MAX, AND COUNT FUNCTIONS

Erica wants to know the least and most expensive houses so that she can analyze typical customers of the Townsend Mortgage Company. You will use the MIN and MAX functions to obtain these statistics. In addition, you will use the COUNT function to tally the number of mortgages in the sample. Refer to Figure 2.17 as you complete Step 4.

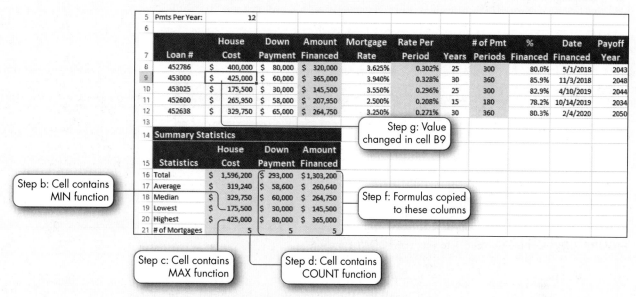

FIGURE 2.17 MIN, MAX, and COUNT Function Results

a. Click **cell B19**, the cell to display the cost of the least expensive house.

b. Click the **AutoSum arrow** in the Function Library group, select **Min**, select the **range B8:B12**, and then press **Enter**.

The MIN function identifies that the least expensive house is $175,500.

c. Click **cell B20**. Click the **AutoSum arrow** in the Function Library group, select **Max**, select the **range B8:B12**, and then press **Enter**.

The MAX function identifies that the highest-costing house is $400,000.

d. Click **cell B21**. Type **=COUNT(B8:B12)** and press **Enter**.

As you type the letter C, Formula AutoComplete suggests functions starting with C. As you continue typing, the list of functions narrows. After you type the beginning parenthesis, Excel displays the function ScreenTip, indicating the arguments for the function. The range B8:B12 contains five cells.

e. Select the **range B16:B21**.

You want to select the range of original statistics to copy the cells all at one time to the next two columns.

f. Drag the fill handle to the right by two columns to copy to the range C16:D21. Click **cell D21**.

Because you used relative cell references in the functions, the range in the function changes from =COUNT(B8:B12) to =COUNT(D8:D12).

g. Click **cell B9**, change the cell value to **425000**, and then click **Enter**.

The results of all formulas and functions change, including the total, average, and max house costs.

h. Save the workbook.

STEP 5 USE THE TODAY FUNCTION

Before finalizing the worksheet, you will insert the current date to document when the data was created. You will use the TODAY function to display the current date. Refer to Figure 2.18 as you complete Step 5.

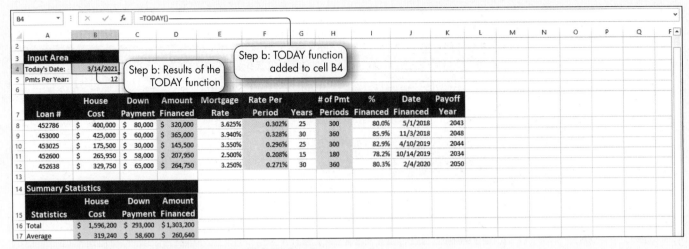

FIGURE 2.18 Insert the Current Date with the TODAY Function

a. Click **cell B4**, the cell to contain the current date.

b. Click **Date & Time** in the Function Library group, select **TODAY** to display the Function Arguments dialog box, and then click **OK** to close the dialog box.

The Function Arguments dialog box opens, although no arguments are necessary for this function. Excel displays TODAY() in the Edit formula bar, and inserts the current date in Short Date format, such as 3/14/2021, based on the computer system's date.

c. Click the **Format arrow** from the Cells group on the Home tab and select **AutoFit Column Width**.

d. Save the workbook. Keep the workbook open if you plan to continue with the next Hands-On Exercise. If not, close the workbook and exit Excel.

Logical, Lookup, and Financial Functions

As you prepare complex spreadsheets using functions, you will frequently use functions from three categories: lookup and reference, logical, and finance. Lookup and reference functions are useful when looking up a value in a list to identify the applicable value. Financial functions are useful to anyone who plans to take out a loan or invest money. Logical functions compare two or more situations and return results based on the comparison.

In this section, you will learn how to use the lookup, logical, and financial functions.

Using Lookup Functions

You can use lookup and reference functions to quickly find data associated with a specified value. For example, when you order merchandise on a website, the webserver looks up the shipping costs based on weight and distance; or at the end of a semester, your professor uses your average, such as 88%, as a reference to assign a letter grade, such as B+. There are numerous lookup functions in Excel that can be used to identify and return information based, in part, on how the data is organized.

STEP 1 ▸ Use the VLOOKUP Function

The *VLOOKUP function* accepts a value, looks for the value in the left column of a specified table array, and then returns another value located in the same row from a specified column. This is similar to a menu in which the item is in the left most column and the corresponding price is in the right column. Use VLOOKUP to search for exact matches or for the nearest value that is less than or equal to the search value, such as assigning a B grade for a class average between 80% and 89%. The VLOOKUP function has the following three required arguments and one optional argument: (1) lookup_value, (2) table_array, (3) col_index_num, and (4) range_lookup.

=VLOOKUP(lookup_value,table_array,col_index_num,[range_lookup])

Figure 2.19 shows a partial gradebook that contains a vertical lookup table, as well as the final scores and letter grades. The function in cell F3 is =VLOOKUP(E3,$A$3:$B$7,2). The data shown in Figure 2.19 is a small sample; however, the true value of VLOOKUP can be found in large datasets. When working with large datasets, it is time consuming and also error prone to look up information manually. Using VLOOKUP can quickly retrieve data no matter the size of the dataset.

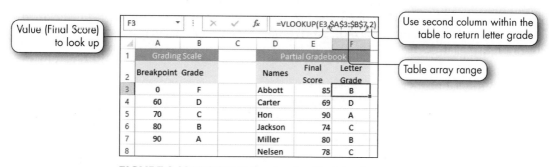

FIGURE 2.19 VLOOKUP Function for Gradebook

- The ***lookup value*** is the cell reference that contains the value to look up. The lookup value for the first student is cell E3, which contains 85.
- The ***table array*** is the range that contains the lookup table: $A$3:$B$7. The table array range must be absolute, and the value you want to look up must be located in the first column and cannot include column labels for the lookup table.
- The ***column index number*** is the column number in the lookup table that contains the return values. In this example, the column index number is 2, which corresponds to the letter grades in column B.

TIP: USING VALUES IN FORMULAS

You know to avoid using values in formulas because the input values in a worksheet cell might change. However, as shown in Figure 2.19, the value 2 is used in the col_index_number argument of the VLOOKUP function. The 2 refers to a particular column within the lookup table.

- The optional ***range_lookup*** determines how the VLOOKUP function handles lookup values that are not an exact match for the data in the table array. By default, the range_lookup is set to TRUE, which is appropriate to look up values in a range such as numeric grades in a gradebook and matching them to a letter grade. Omitting the optional argument or typing TRUE in it enables the VLOOKUP function to find the nearest value that is less than or equal in the table to the lookup value.

To look up an exact match, enter FALSE in the range_lookup argument. For example, if you are looking up product numbers, you must find an exact match to display the price. The function returns a value for the first lookup value that exactly matches the first column of the table array. If no exact match is found, the function returns #N/A.

Here is how the VLOOKUP function works:

1. The first argument of the function evaluates the value to be located in the left column of the table array.
2. Excel searches the first column of the table array until it (a) finds an exact match or (b) identifies the correct range if an exact match is not required.
3. If Excel finds an exact match, it moves across the table to the column designated by the column index number on that same row, and returns the value stored in that cell. If the last argument is TRUE or omitted, then Excel is looking for an approximate value (not an exact value). In Figure 2.19, the VLOOKUP function assigns letter grades based on final scores. Excel identifies the lookup value (85 in cell E3) and compares it to the values in the first column of the table array (range A3:B7). The last argument is omitted, so Excel tries to find 85. Excel detects that 85 is greater than 80 but is not greater than 90. Therefore, it stays on the 80 row. Excel looks at the second column (column index number of 2) and returns the letter grade of B. The B grade is then displayed in cell F3.

Create the Lookup Table

A *lookup table* is a range containing a table array of values. A table array is a range containing a table of values and text from which data can be retrieved. The table should contain at least two rows and two columns, not including headings. Figure 2.20 illustrates a college directory with three columns. The first column contains professors' names. You look up a professor's name in the first column to see his or her office (second column) and phone extension (third column).

Name	Office	Extension
Brazil, Estivan	GT 218b	7243
Fiedler, Zazilia	CS 417	7860
Lam, Kaitlyn	SC 124a	7031
Rodriquez, Lisa	GT 304	7592
Yeung, Braden	CS 414	7314

FIGURE 2.20 College Directory Lookup Table Analogy

It is important to plan the table so that it conforms to the way in which Excel can utilize the data in it. If the values you look up are exact values (i.e., range lookup = False), you can arrange the first column in any order. However, to look up an approximate value in a range (i.e., range lookup = True), such as the range 80–89, you must arrange data from the lowest to the highest value and include only the lowest value in the range (such as 80 is the lowest value for the range of a B grade) instead of the complete range (as demonstrated in Table 2.2). The lowest value for a category or in a series is the *breakpoint*. Table 2.3 shows how to construct the lookup table in Excel. The first column contains the breakpoints—such as 60, 70, 80, and 90—or the lowest values to achieve a particular grade. The lookup table contains one or more additional columns of related data to retrieve.

TABLE 2.2 Grading Scale

Range	Grade
90–100	A
80–89	B
70–79	C
60–69	D
Below 60	F

TABLE 2.3 Table Array

Range	Grade
0	F
60	D
70	C
80	B
90	A

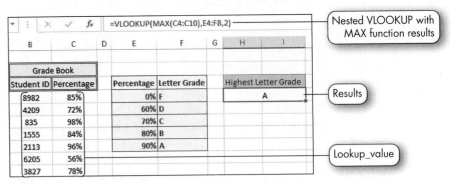

FIGURE 2.21 MAX Function Nested in VLOOKUP Function

Use the HLOOKUP Function

Lookup functions are not limited to only retrieving data from tables that are arranged in vertical tables. In situations in which data is better organized horizontally, you can design a lookup table where the first row contains the values for the basis of the lookup or the breakpoints, and additional rows contain data to be retrieved. This data must be arranged in ascending order from left to right. With a horizontal lookup table, use the *HLOOKUP function*. Table 2.4 shows the previous grades arranged horizontally for use with HLOOKUP.

TABLE 2.4	Horizontal Lookup Table				
Range	0	60	70	80	90
Grade	F	D	C	B	A

The syntax is similar to the syntax of the VLOOKUP function, except the third argument is row_index_num instead of col_index_num.

=HLOOKUP(lookup_value,table_array,row_index_num,[range_lookup])

STEP 2 ▶ Using the PMT Function

Excel contains several financial functions to enable you to perform calculations with monetary values. If you take out a loan to purchase a car, you need to know the monthly payment to determine if you can afford the car. The monthly payment depends on the price of the car, the down payment amount, and the terms of the loan. The decision is made easier by developing the worksheet in Figure 2.22 and by changing the various input values as indicated.

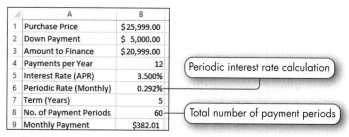

FIGURE 2.22 Car Loan assumptions

Creating a loan model enables you to evaluate options. You realize that the purchase of a $25,999 car might be prohibitive if you cannot afford the monthly payment of $382.01. Purchasing a less expensive car, coming up with a substantial down payment, taking out a longer-term loan, or finding a better interest rate can decrease your monthly payments.

The *PMT function* calculates payments for a loan with a fixed amount at a fixed periodic rate for a fixed time period. The PMT function uses three required arguments and two optional arguments: rate, nper, pv, fv, and type.

=PMT(rate,nper,pv,[fv],[type])

- The *rate* is the interest rate per payment period. Because the PMT function calculates a periodic (i.e., monthly) payment, the units of each of the arguments must be converted to that same periodic unit. Bank rates are usually given as annual rates, so the annual rate must be converted to the periodic rate—in this case, a monthly rate so the annual rate should be divided by 12. A quarterly payment would require the annual rate to be divided by 4. However, instead of calculating the periodic interest rate within the PMT function, you can calculate it in a separate cell and refer to that cell in the PMT function, as is done in cell B6 of Figure 2.22.

- The *nper* is the total number of payment periods. The term of a loan is usually stated in years; however, you need to convert the number of years to the number of periodic payments. For monthly payments, you make 12 payments per year. To calculate the nper, multiply the number of years by the number of payments in one year. You can either calculate the number of payment periods in the PMT function, or calculate the number of payment periods in cell B8 and use that calculated value in the PMT function.

- The *pv* is the present value of the loan. The result of the PMT function is a negative value because it represents your debt. However, you can display the result as a positive value by typing a minus sign in front of the present value cell reference in the PMT function.

> **TIP: FINANCIAL FUNCTIONS AND NEGATIVE VALUES**
> When utilizing the PMT and other financial functions in Excel, the results are often displayed as negative numbers. This happens because Excel understands accounting cash flow and the negative value represents a debt or outgoing monetary stream. It is important to understand why this happens and to understand in some situations this should be a positive number. This can be manipulated by changing the pv argument of the PMT function between positive and negative values or by adding a minus sign in front of the PMT function.

STEP 3 ▶ Using the IF Function

The most common logical function is the **IF function**, which tests specified criteria to see if it is true or false, then returns one value when a condition is met, or is true, and returns another value when the condition is not met, or is false. For example, a company gives a $500 bonus to employees who sold over $10,000 in merchandise in a week, but no bonus to employees who did not sell over $10,000 in merchandise. Figure 2.23 shows a worksheet containing the sales data for three representatives and their bonuses, if any.

The IF function has three arguments: (1) a condition that is tested to determine if it is either true or false, (2) the resulting value if the condition is true, and (3) the resulting value if the condition is false.

=IF(logical_test,[value_if_true],[value_if_false])

- The **logical test** is any value or expression that can be evaluated to TRUE or FALSE.
- The **value_if_true** is the value returned if the Logical_test is TRUE; if omitted, the word TRUE is returned.
- The **value_if_false** is the value returned if Logical_test is FALSE; if omitted, the word FALSE is returned.

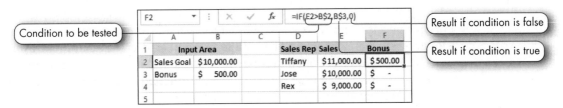

FIGURE 2.23 Function to Calculate Bonus

You might find it helpful to create two flowcharts to illustrate an IF function. First, construct a flowchart that uses words and numbers to illustrate the condition and results. For example, the left flowchart in Figure 2.24 tests to see if sales are greater than $10,000, and the $500 bonus if the condition is true or $0 if the condition is false. Then, create a second flowchart—similar to the one on the right side of Figure 2.24—that replaces the words and values with actual cell references. Creating these flowcharts can help you construct the IF function that is used in cell F2 in Figure 2.23.

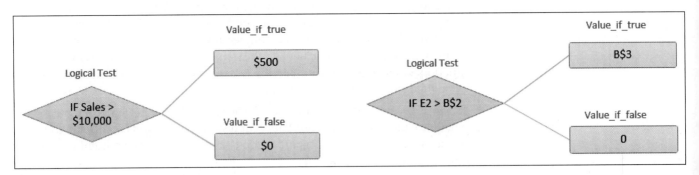

FIGURE 2.24 Flowcharts Illustrating IF Function

Design the Logical Test

The first argument for the IF function is the logical test. The logical test requires a comparison between at least two variables, such as the sales amount and the sales goal needed to receive a bonus. The comparison results are a true or false outcome. Either the sales amount meets the sales goal (true) or it does not meet the sales goal (false). Table 2.5 lists and describes in more detail the logical operators to make the comparison in the logical test.

In Figure 2.23, cell F2 contains an IF function where the logical test is E2>B$2, which determines if Tiffany's sales in cell E2 are greater than the sales goal in cell B2. Copying the function down the column will compare each sales representative's sales with the $10,000 value in cell B2.

TABLE 2.5 Comparison Operators	
Operator	**Description**
=	Equal to
<>	Not equal to
<	Less than
>	Greater than
<=	Less than or equal to
>=	Greater than or equal to

Design the Value_If_True and Value_If_False Arguments

The second and third arguments of an IF function are value_if_true and value_if_false. When Excel evaluates the logical test, the result is either true or false. If the logical test is true, the value_if_true argument executes. If the logical test is false, the value_if_false argument executes. Only one of these two arguments is executed; both arguments cannot be executed, because the logical test is either true or false but not both. The value_if_true and value_if_false arguments can contain text, cell references, formulas, or constants.

In Figure 2.23, cell F2 contains an IF function in which the value_if_true argument is B$3 and the value_if_false argument is 0. Because the logical test (E2>B$2) is true—that is, Tiffany's sales of $11,000 are greater than the $10,000 goal—the value_if_true argument is executed, and the result displays $500, the value that is stored in cell B3. Jose's sales of $10,000 are *not* greater than $10,000, and Rex's sales of $9,000 are *not* greater than $10,000; therefore, the value_if_false argument is executed and returns no bonus in cells F3 and F4.

> **TIP: AT LEAST TWO POSSIBLE RIGHT ANSWERS**
> In many situations, the IF function can have at least two constructions to produce the desired result. Since the logical test is a comparative expression, it can be written two ways. For example, comparing whether E2 is greater than B2 can be written using greater than (E2>B2), or the reverse can also be compared to see if B2 is less than E2 (B2<E2). Depending on the logical test, the value if true and value if false arguments will switch.

Figure 2.25 illustrates several IF functions, how they are evaluated, and their results. The input area contains values that are used in the logical tests and results. You can create this worksheet with the input area and IF functions to develop your understanding of how IF functions work.

	A	B	C
1	Input Values		
2	$ 1,000.00		
3	$ 2,000.00		
4	10%		
5	5%		
6	$ 250.00		
7			
8	IF Function	Evaluation	Result
9	=IF(A2=A3,A4,A5)	$1,000 is equal to $2,000: FALSE	5%
10	=IF(A2<A3,A4,A5)	$1,000 is less than $2,000: TRUE	10%
11	=IF(A2<>A3,"Not Equal","Equal")	$1,000 and $2,000 are not equal: TRUE	Not Equal
12	=IF(A2>A3,A2*A4,A2*A5)	$1,000 is greater than $2,000: FALSE	$ 50.00
13	=IF(A2>A3,A2*A4,MAX(A2*A5,A6))	$1,000 is greater than $2,000: FALSE	$ 250.00
14	=IF(A2*A4=A3*A5,A6,0)	$100 (A2*A4) is equal to $100 (A3*A5): TRUE	$ 250.00
15			

FIGURE 2.25 Sample IF Functions

- **Cell A9.** The logical test A2=A3 compares the values in cells A2 and A3 to see if they are equal. Because $1,000 is not equal to $2,000, the logical test is false. The value_if_false argument is executed, which displays 5%, the value stored in cell A5.

- **Cell A10.** The logical test A2<A3 determines if the value in cell A2 is less than the value in A3. Because $1,000 is less than $2,000, the logical test is true. The value_if_true argument is executed, which displays the value stored in cell A4, which is 10%.

- **Cell A11.** The logical test A2<>A3 determines if the values in cells A2 and A3 are not equal. Because $1,000 and $2,000 are not equal, the logical test is true. The value_if_true argument is executed, which displays the text Not Equal.

- **Cell A12.** The logical test A2>A3 is false. The value_if_false argument is executed, which multiplies the value in cell A2 ($1,000) by the value in cell A5 (5%) and displays $50. The parentheses in the value_if_true (A2*A4) and value_if_false (A2*A5) arguments are optional. They are not required but may help you read the function arguments better.

- **Cell A13.** The logical test A2>A3 is false. The value_if_false argument, which contains a nested MAX function, is executed. The MAX function, MAX(A2*A5,A6), multiplies the values in cells A2 ($1,000) and A5 (5%) and returns the higher of the product ($50) and the value stored in cell A6 ($250).

- **Cell A14.** The logical test A2*A4=A3*A5 is true. The contents of cell A2 ($1,000) are multiplied by the contents of cell A4 (10%) for a result of $100. That result is then compared to the result of A3*A5, which is also $100. Because the logical test is true, the function returns the value of cell A6 ($250).

TIP: USE TEXT IN AN IF FUNCTION

You can use text within a formula. For example, you can build a logical test comparing the contents of cell A1 to specific text, such as A1="Input Values". The IF function in cell A11 in Figure 2.25 uses "Not Equal" and "Equal" in the value_if_true and value_if_false arguments. When you use text in a formula or function, you must enclose the text in quotation marks. However, do not use quotation marks around formulas, cell references, or values.

Quick Concepts

8. Describe a situation in which an IF statement could be used. **p. 174**

9. Describe how you should structure a vertical lookup table if you need to look up values in a range. **p. 171**

10. Explain why the PMT function often produces negative results. **p. 173**

Hands-On Exercises

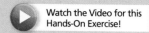
Skills covered: Use the
VLOOKUP Function • Use
the PMT Function • Use the IF
Function

3 Logical, Lookup, and Financial Functions

Erica wants you to complete another model that she might use for future mortgage data analysis. As you study the model, you realize you need to incorporate logical, lookup, and financial functions.

STEP 1 USE THE VLOOKUP FUNCTION

Rates vary based on the number of years to pay off the loan. Erica created a lookup table for three common mortgage terms and she entered the current APR for each item. The lookup table will provide efficiency later when the rates change. You will use the VLOOKUP function to display the correct rate for each customer based on the number of years of their respective loans. Refer to Figure 2.26 as you complete Step 1.

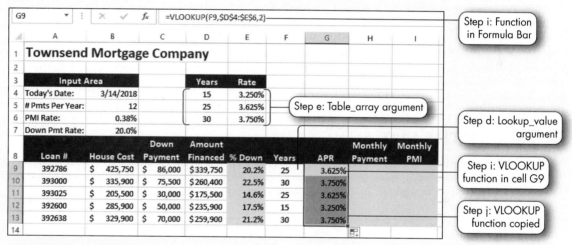

FIGURE 2.26 VLOOKUP Function to Determine APR

a. Open *e02h2Loans_LastFirst* if you closed it at the end of Hands-On Exercise 2 and save it as **e02h3Loans_LastFirst**, changing h2 to h3.

b. Click the **Payment Info worksheet tab** to display the worksheet containing the data to complete. Click **cell G9**, the cell that will store the APR for the first customer.

c. Click the **Formulas tab**, click **Lookup & Reference** in the Function Library group, and then select **VLOOKUP**.

The Function Arguments dialog box opens.

d. Ensure that the insertion point is in the Lookup_value box, click the **Collapse Dialog Box**, click **cell F9** to enter F9 in the Lookup_value box, and then click the **Expand Dialog Box** to return to Function Arguments dialog box.

Cell F9 contains the value you need to look up in the table: 25 years.

e. Press **Tab**, click **Collapse Dialog Box** to the right of the Table_array box, select the **range D4:E6**, and then click **Expand Dialog Box** to return to the Function Arguments dialog box.

This is the range that contains that data for the lookup table. The Years values in the table are arranged from lowest to highest.

Anticipate what will happen if you copy the formula down the column. What do you need to do to ensure that the cell references always point to the exact location of the table? If your answer is to make the table array cell references absolute, then you answered correctly.

f. Select the **range D4:E6** and press **F4** to make the range references absolute.

The Table_array box now contains $D$4:$E$6.

g. Press **Tab** and type **2** in the Col_index_num box.

The second column of the lookup table contains the Rates that you want to return and display in the cells containing the formulas.

h. Press **Tab** and type **False** in the Range_lookup box.

To ensure an exact match to look up in the table, you enter *False* in the optional argument.

i. Click **OK**.

The VLOOKUP function uses the first loan's term in years (25) to find an exact match in the first column of the lookup table, and then returns the corresponding rate from the second column, which is 3.625%.

j. Copy the formula down the column.

Spot-check the results to make sure the function returned the correct APR based on the number of years.

k. Save the workbook.

STEP 2 USE THE PMT FUNCTION

The worksheet now has all the necessary data for you to calculate the monthly payment for each loan: the APR, the number of years for the loan, the number of payment periods in one year, and the initial loan amount. You will use the PMT function to calculate the monthly payment. Refer to Figure 2.27 as you complete Step 2.

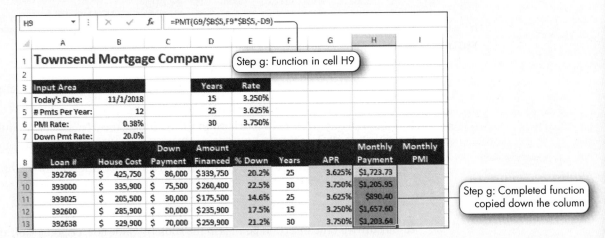

FIGURE 2.27 PMT Function to Calculate Monthly Payment

a. Click **cell H9**, the cell that will store the payment for the first customer.

b. Click **Financial** in the Function Library group, scroll through the list, and then select **PMT**.

The Function Arguments dialog box opens.

c. Enter **G9/B5** in the Rate box.

Think about what will happen if you copy the formula. The argument will be G10/B6 for the next customer. Are those cell references correct? G10 does contain the APR for the next customer, but B6 does not contain the correct number of payments in one year. Therefore, you need to make B5 an absolute cell reference because the number of payments per year does not vary.

d. Press **F4** to make the reference to cell B5 absolute.

e. Press **Tab** and type **F9*$B$5** in the Nper box.

You calculate the nper by multiplying the number of years by the number of payments in one year. You must make B5 an absolute cell reference so that it does not change when you copy the formula down the column.

f. Press **Tab** and type **-D9** in the Pv box.

The bottom of the dialog box indicates that the monthly payment is 1723.73008, or $1,723.73.

TROUBLESHOOTING: If the payment displays as a negative value, you probably forgot to type the minus sign in front of the D9 reference in the Pv box. Edit the function and type the minus sign in the correct place.

---

g. Click **OK**. Copy the formula down the column.

h. Save the workbook.

STEP 3 ▶ USE THE IF FUNCTION

Lenders often want borrowers to have a 20% down payment. If borrowers do not put in 20% of the cost of the house as a down payment, they pay a private mortgage insurance (PMI) fee. PMI serves to protect lenders from absorbing loss if the borrower defaults on the loan, and it enables borrowers with less cash to secure a loan. The PMI fee is about 0.38% of the amount financed. Some borrowers pay PMI for a few months or years until the outstanding balance owed is less than 80% of the appraised value of the property. The worksheet contains the necessary values in the input area. You use the IF function to determine which borrowers must pay PMI and how much they will pay. Refer to Figure 2.28 as you complete Step 3.

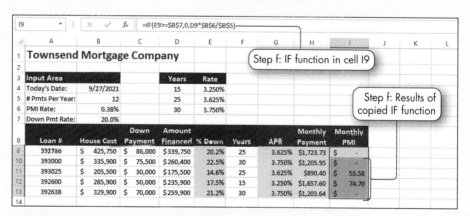

FIGURE 2.28 IF Function to Calculate Monthly PMI

a. Click **cell I9**, the cell that will store the PMI, if any, for the first customer.

b. Click **Logical** in the Function Library group and select **IF**.

The Function Arguments dialog box opens. You will enter the three arguments.

c. Type **E9>=$B$7** in the Logical_test box.

The logical test compares the down payment percentage to see if it is at least 20%, the threshold stored in B7. The customer's percentage cell reference is relative so that it will change when you copy it down the column; however, cell B7 must be absolute because it contains a value that should remain constant when the formula is copied to other cells.

d. Press **Tab** and type **0** in the Value_if_true box.

If the customer makes a down payment that is at least 20% of the purchase price, the customer does not pay PMI, so a value of 0 will display whenever the logical test is true. The first customer paid more than 20% of the purchase price, so he or she does not have to pay PMI.

e. Press **Tab** and type **D9*$B$6/$B$5** in the Value_if_false box.

If the logical test is false, the customer must pay PMI, which is calculated by multiplying the amount financed (D9) by the periodic PMI rate (the result of dividing the yearly PMI (B6) by the number of payments per year (B5)).

f. Click **OK** and copy the formula down the column.

The first, second, and fifth customers paid at least 20% of the purchase price, so they do not have to pay PMI. The third and fourth customers must pay PMI because their respective down payments were less than 20% of the purchase price.

> **TROUBLESHOOTING:** If the results are not as you expected, check the logical operators. People often mistype < and > or forget to type = for >= situations. Also check for the appropriate use of absolute or mixed cell references. Correct any errors in the original formula and copy the formula again.

g. Set the worksheets to print on one page and return to Normal View. Add a footer with your name on the left, sheet code in the middle, and the file name code on the right.

h. Save and close the file. Based on your instructor's directions, submit e02h3Loans_LastFirst.

Chapter Objectives Review

After reading this chapter, you have accomplished the following objectives:

1. Use relative, absolute, and mixed cell references in formulas.

- Use a relative cell address: A relative reference indicates a cell's location relative to the formula cell. When you copy the formula, the relative cell reference changes.
- Use an absolute cell reference: An absolute reference is a permanent pointer to a particular cell, indicated with $ before the column letter and the row number, such as $B$5. When you copy the formula, the absolute cell reference does not change.
- Use a mixed cell reference: A mixed reference contains part absolute and part relative reference, such as $B5 or B$5. Either the column or the row reference changes, while the other remains constant when you copy the formula.

2. Insert a function.

- A function is a predefined formula that performs a calculation. It contains the function name and arguments. Formula AutoComplete, function ScreenTips, and the Insert Function dialog box enable you to select and create functions. The Function Arguments dialog box guides you through the entering requirements for each argument.

3. Insert basic math and statistics functions.

- Use the SUM function: The SUM function calculates the total of a range of values. The syntax is =SUM(number1,[number2], . . .).
- Use the AVERAGE: The AVERAGE function calculates the arithmetic mean of values in a range.
- Use the MEDIAN function: The MEDIAN function identifies the midpoint value in a set of values.
- Use the MIN and MAX functions: The MIN function identifies the lowest value in a range, whereas the MAX function identifies the highest value in a range.
- Use the COUNT functions: The COUNT function tallies the number of cells in a range that contain values, whereas the COUNTBLANK function tallies the number of blank cells in a range, and COUNTA tallies the number of cells that are not empty.

- Perform calculations with Quick Analysis tools: With the Quick Analysis tools you can apply formatting, create charts or tables, and insert basic functions.

4. Use date functions.

- Use the TODAY function: The TODAY function displays the current date.
- Use the NOW function: The NOW function displays the current date and time.

5. Use lookup functions.

- Use the VLOOKUP function: The VLOOKUP function contains the required arguments lookup_value, table_array, and col_index_num and one optional argument, range_lookup.
- Create the lookup table: Design the lookup table using exact values or the breakpoints for ranges. If using breakpoints, the breakpoints must be in ascending order.
- Use the HLOOKUP function: The HLOOKUP function looks up values by row (horizontally) rather than by column (vertically).

6. Use the PMT function.

- The PMT function calculates periodic payments for a loan with a fixed interest rate and a fixed term. The PMT function requires the periodic interest rate, the total number of payment periods, and the original value of the loan.

7. Use the IF function.

- Design the logical test: The IF function is a logical function that evaluates a logical test using logical operators, such as <, >, and =, and returns one value if the condition is true and another value if the condition is false.
- Design the value_if_true and value_if_false arguments: The arguments can contain cell references, text, or calculations. If a logical test is true, Excel executes the value_if_true argument. If a logical test is false, Excel executes the value_if_false argument.
- You can nest or embed other functions inside one or more of the arguments of an IF function to create more complex formulas.

Key Terms Matching

Match the key terms with their definitions. Write the key term letter by the appropriate numbered definition.

a. Absolute cell reference

b. Argument

c. AVERAGE function

d. COUNT function

e. IF function

f. Logical test

g. Lookup table

h. MAX function

i. MEDIAN function

j. MIN function

k. Mixed cell reference

l. NOW function

m. PMT function

n. Relative cell reference

o. ROUND function

p. SUM function

q. Syntax

r. TODAY function

s. VLOOKUP function

1. _____ A set of rules that governs the structure and components for properly entering a function. **p. 169**

2. _____ Displays the current date. **p. 163**

3. _____ Indicates a cell's specific location; the cell reference does not change when you copy the formula. **p. 151**

4. _____ An input, such as a cell reference or value, needed to complete a function. **p. 157**

5. _____ Identifies the highest value in a range. **p. 162**

6. _____ Tallies the number of cells in a range that contain values. **p. 162**

7. _____ Looks up a value in a vertical lookup table and returns a related result from the lookup table. **p. 169**

8. _____ A range that contains data for the basis of the lookup and data to be retrieved. **p. 171**

9. _____ Calculates the arithmetic mean, or average, of values in a range. **p. 161**

10. _____ Identifies the midpoint value in a set of values. **p. 161**

11. _____ Displays the current date and time. **p. 163**

12. _____ Evaluates a condition and returns one value if the condition is true and a different value if the condition is false. **p. 174**

13. _____ Calculates the total of values contained in one or more cells. **p. 160**

14. _____ Calculates the periodic payment for a loan with a fixed interest rate and fixed term. **p. 173**

15. _____ Indicates a cell's location from the cell containing the formula; the cell reference changes when the formula is copied. **p. 150**

16. _____ Contains both an absolute and a relative cell reference in a formula; the absolute part does not change but the relative part does when you copy the formula. **p. 152**

17. _____ An expression that evaluates to true or false. **p. 174**

18. _____ Displays the lowest value in a range. **p. 162**

19. _____ Rounds a number to a specified number of digits. **p. 162**

Multiple Choice

1. If cell E15 contains the function =PMT(B$15/12,C7*12,-D8), what type of cell reference is B$15?

   (a) Relative reference
   (b) Absolute reference
   (c) Mixed reference
   (d) Syntax

2. What function would most efficiently accomplish the same thing as =(B5+C5+D5+E5+F5)?

   (a) =SUM(B5:F5)
   (b) =AVERAGE(B5:F5)
   (c) =MEDIAN(B5:F5)
   (d) =COUNT(B5:F5)

3. When you start to type =AV, what feature displays a list of functions and defined names?

   (a) Function ScreenTip
   (b) Formula AutoComplete
   (c) Insert Function dialog box
   (d) Function Arguments dialog box

4. A formula containing the entry =J$7 is copied to a cell three columns to the right and four rows down. How will the entry display in its new location?

   (a) =M$7
   (b) =J$7
   (c) =M11
   (d) =J$11

5. Which of the following functions should be used to insert the current date and time in a cell?

   (a) =TODAY()
   (b) =CURRENT()
   (c) =NOW()
   (d) =DATE

6. Which of the following is *not* a comparison operator?

   (a) <
   (b) >
   (c) &
   (d) <>

7. Which of the following is *not* true about the VLOOKUP function?

   (a) The col_index_num argument cannot be 1.
   (b) The lookup table must be in descending order.
   (c) The default match type is approximate.
   (d) The match type must be false when completing an exact match.

8. The function =PMT(C5,C7,-C3) is stored in cell C15. What must be stored in cell C5?

   (a) APR
   (b) Periodic interest rate
   (c) Loan amount
   (d) Number of payment periods

9. Which of the following is *not* an appropriate use of the MAX function?

   (a) =MAX(B3:B45)
   (b) =MAX(F1:G10)
   (c) =MAX(A8:A15,D8:D15)
   (d) =MAX(D15-C15)

10. What is the keyboard shortcut to create an absolute reference?

    (a) F2
    (b) F3
    (c) F4
    (d) Alt

Practice Exercises

1 Hamilton Heights Auto Sales

You are the primary loan manager for Hamilton Heights Auto Sales, an auto sales company located in Missouri. To most efficiently manage the auto loans your company finances, you have decided to create a spreadsheet to perform several calculations. You will insert the current date, calculate down payment and interest rates based on credit score, calculate periodic payment amounts, and complete the project with basic summary information. Refer to Figure 2.29 as you complete this exercise.

	A	B	C	D	E	F	G
1			**Hamilton Heights Auto Sales**				
2	Date	3/15/2021					
3			Auto Finance Worksheet				
4	Vin #	Purchase Price	Credit Rating	Down Payment	Amount Financed	Rate	Payment
5	619600647	$ 23,417.00	579	$ 2,341.70	$ 21,075.30	4.00%	$388.13
6	464119439	$ 23,732.00	763	$ -	$ 23,732.00	3.00%	$426.43
7	122140305	$ 44,176.00	657	$ 4,417.60	$ 39,758.40	3.50%	$723.27
8	276772526	$ 42,556.00	827	$ -	$ 42,556.00	2.75%	$759.96
9	335963723	$ 24,305.00	652	$ 2,430.50	$ 21,874.50	3.50%	$397.94
10	401292230	$ 27,847.00	676	$ 2,784.70	$ 25,062.30	3.50%	$455.93
11		$ 186,033.00			$ 29,009.75		
12							
13	Credit Score	APR		Down Payment	Credit Score Threshold		
14	500	4.00%		10%	750		
15	650	3.50%					
16	700	3.25%		Payments Per Year	Total # of Payments		
17	750	3.00%		12	60		
18	800	2.75%					
19	850	2.25%					
20							

FIGURE 2.29 Hamilton Heights Auto Sales

a. Open *e02p1AutoSales* and save it as **e02p1AutoSales_LastFirst**.

b. Click **cell B2**, click the **Formulas tab**, click **Date & Time** in the Function Library group, select **NOW**, and then click **OK** (**Done** on a Mac) to enter today's date in the cell.

c. Click **cell D5**, ensure the Formulas tab is displayed, click **Logical** in the Function Library group, and select **IF**.

d. Type **C5<=$E$14** in the Logical_test box, type **$D$14*B5** in the Value_if_true box, type **0** in the Value_if_false box, and then click **OK**.

   This uses the IF function to calculate the required down payment based on credit score. If the customer has a credit score higher than 750 a down payment is not required. All clients with credits scores lower than 750 must pay a required 10% down payment in advance.

e. Double-click the fill handle to copy the contents of **cell D5** down the column, click **Auto Fill Options** to the lower-right of the copied cells, and then select **Fill Without Formatting** to ensure that the **Bottom Double border** remains applied to cell D10.

f. Calculate the Amount Financed by doing the following:
   • Click **cell E5** and type **=B5-D5**.
   • Use **cell E5's fill handle** to copy the function down the column.
   • Apply **Bottom Double border** to cell E10.

g. Calculate the Rate by doing the following:
   • Click **cell F5**. Click **Lookup & Reference** in the Function Library group on the Formula tab, and select **VLOOKUP**.
   • Type **C5** in the Lookup_value box, type **$A$14:$B$19** in the Table_array box, type **2** in the Col_index_num box, and then click **OK**.
   • Double-click **cell F5's fill handle** to copy the function down the column.
   • Click **Auto Fill Options**, and select **Fill Without Formatting**.

h. Calculate the required periodic payment by doing the following:

- Click **cell G5**, click **Financial** in the Function Library Group, scroll down, and then select **PMT**.
- Type **F5/$D$17** in the Rate box, type **$E$17** in the Nper box, type **–E5** in the Pv box, and then click **OK**.
- Double-click **cell G5's** fill handle to copy the function down the column.
- Click the **Auto Fill Options button**, and select **Fill Without Formatting**.

i. Select the **range B5:B10**, click the **Quick Analysis button**, click **Totals**, and then select **Sum** from the Quick Analysis Gallery. (On a Mac, select the range B5:B10 and click AutoSum on the ribbon.)

j. Click **cell E11** and type **=AVERAGE(E5:E10)** to calculate the average amount financed.

k. Create a footer with your name on the left side, the sheet name code in the center, and the file name on the right side.

l. Save and close the workbook. Based on your instructor's directions, submit e02p1AutoSales_LastFirst.

2 Garten Realty

As the accounting manager for Garten Realty, you have the task of calculating monthly salaries including performance bonuses for the company's sales agents. Sales agents receive a base salary and a bonus based on the amount of sales generated. The bonus award is a percentage of the amount of sales generated and is calculated using a graduated scale based on years of service with the company. Refer to Figure 2.30 as you complete this exercise.

	A	B	C	D	E	F
1				Garten Realty		
2						
3	**Inputs and Constants**				**Bonus Data**	
4	Date:	3/15/2018		Sales	<3 Years of Service	>=3 Years of Service
5	Number of Agents	7		$ 50,000.00	1%	2%
6				$ 500,000.00	2%	4%
7				$ 1,000,000.00	4%	6%
8						
9	**Agent ID**	**Years of Service**	**Base Annual Salary**	**Total sales generated**	**Bonus**	**Monthly Take Home**
10	73822278	1	$ 68,621.00	$ 50,000.00	$ 500.00	$ 6,218.42
11	92261130	2	$ 65,411.00	$ 60,000.00	$ 600.00	$ 6,050.92
12	24697518	9	$ 68,308.00	$ 84,000.00	$ 1,680.00	$ 7,372.33
13	78235598	9	$ 68,855.00	$ 101,000.00	$ 2,020.00	$ 7,757.92
14	41061578	10	$ 47,316.00	$ 175,000.00	$ 3,500.00	$ 7,443.00
15	88306993	18	$ 43,441.00	$ 500,000.00	$ 20,000.00	$ 23,620.08
16	58569982	20	$ 64,665.00	$ 750,000.00	$ 30,000.00	$ 35,388.75
17						
18	**Statistics**					
19	Lowest Bonus	$ 500.00				
20	Average Bonus	$ 8,328.57				
21	Highest Bonus	$ 30,000.00				

Bonus_Calculation

FIGURE 2.30 Garten Realty

a. Open *e02p2Realty* and save it as **e02p2Realty_LastFirst**.

b. Click **cell B4**, click the **Formulas tab**, click **Date & Time** in the Function Library group, select **TODAY**, and then click **OK** to enter today's date in the cell.

c. Click **cell B5**, click the **AutoSum arrow** in the Function Library group, and then select **Count Numbers**. Select the **range A10:A16** and press **Enter**.

d. Click **cell E10**, type **=VLOOKUP(D10,$D$5:$F$7,IF(B10<3,2,3),TRUE)*D10**, press **Ctrl+Enter**, and then double-click the **fill handle**.

This nested function uses the IF function nested within the VLOOKUP function to determine which values should be used from the lookup table. The IF function is required because there are two different bonus values based on years of service.

e. Calculate each employee's monthly take-home pay by doing the following:

- Click **cell F10** and type **=C10/12+E10**.
- Press **Ctrl+Enter** and double-click the **cell F10 fill handle**.

f. Calculate basic summary statistics by doing the following:

- Click **cell B19**, click the **Formulas tab**, click the **AutoSum arrow**, and then select **MIN**.
- Select the **range E10:E16** and press **Enter**.
- Click **cell B20**, click the **AutoSum arrow**, select **AVERAGE**, select the **range E10:E16**, and then press **Enter**.
- Click **cell B21**, click the **AutoSum arrow**, select **MAX**, select the **range E10:E16**, and then press **Enter**.

g. Create a footer with your name on the left side, the sheet name in the center, and the file name code on the right side.

h. Save and close the workbook. Based on your instructor's directions, submit e02p2Realty_LastFirst.

Mid-Level Exercises

1 Metropolitan Zoo Gift Shop Weekly Payroll

As manager of the gift shop at the Metropolitan Zoo, you are responsible for managing the weekly payroll. Your assistant developed a partial worksheet, but you will enter the formulas to calculate the regular pay, overtime pay, gross pay, taxable pay, withholding tax, FICA, and net pay. In addition, you want to include total pay columns and calculate some basic statistics. As you construct formulas, make sure you use absolute and relative cell references correctly in formulas.

a. Open the *e02m1Payroll* workbook and save it as **e02m1Payroll_LastFirst**.

b. Study the worksheet structure and read the business rules in the Notes section.

c. Use IF functions to calculate the regular pay and overtime pay based on a regular 40-hour work-week in **cells E5** and **F5**. Pay overtime only for overtime hours. Calculate the gross pay in **cell G5** based on the regular and overtime pay. Abram's regular pay is $398. With eight overtime hours, Abram's overtime pay is $119.40.

d. Create a formula in **cell H5** to calculate the taxable pay. Multiply the number of dependents by the deduction per dependent and subtract that from the gross pay. With two dependents, Abram's taxable pay is $417.40.

e. Insert a VLOOKUP function in **cell I5** to identify and calculate the federal withholding tax. With a taxable pay of $417.40, Abram's tax rate is 25% and the withholding tax is $104.35. The VLOOKUP function returns the applicable tax rate, which you must then multiply by the taxable pay.

f. Calculate FICA in **cell J5** based on gross pay and the FICA rate, and calculate the net pay in **cell K5**.

g. Copy all formulas down their respective columns.

h. Use Quick Analysis tools to calculate the total regular pay, overtime pay, gross pay, taxable pay, withholding tax, FICA, and net pay on **row 17**. (On a Mac, this step must be completed using the AutoSum feature on the ribbon).

i. Apply **Accounting Number Format** to the **range C5:C16**. Apply **Accounting Number Format** to the first row of monetary data and to the total row. Apply the **Comma style** to the monetary values for the other employees. Underline the last employee's monetary values and use the Format Cells dialog box to apply Top and Double Bottom borders for the totals.

j. Insert appropriate functions to calculate the average, highest, and lowest values in the Summary Statistics area (the **range I21:K23**) of the worksheet. Format the # of hours calculations as **Number format** with one decimal and the remaining calculations with **Accounting Number Format**.

k. Insert a footer with your name on the left side, the sheet name in the center, and the file name code on the right side of both worksheets.

l. Save and close the workbook. Based on your instructor's directions, submit e02m1Payroll_LastFirst.

FROM SCRATCH

You have just graduated from college and before beginning your first professional job, you would like to purchase a new smartphone. You have the option to purchase the new phone in one payment or make monthly payments by taking advantage of a 36-month flex payment plan. The payment plan charges an APR of 1.75% for the service. Prior to making your payment decision, you would like to make a worksheet to calculate the monthly payment for *Consumer Reports'* top three smartphones for young professionals.

a. Start a new Excel workbook, save it as **e02m2SmartPhone_LastFirst**, and then rename Sheet1 **FlexPay**.

b. Type **Flex Pay Calculator** in cell A1. Apply **bold, 20 pt** font size, **Blue, Accent 1,** font color.

c. Type **Inputs** in **cell A2**. Apply **Thick Outside Borders** to the **range A2:C2**.

d. Type **APR** and **# of payments** in the **range A3:A4**, and adjust the column width as needed.

e. Type **1.75%** in **cell B3** and **36** in **cell B4**. Type **Outputs** in **cell A6**. Select the **range A6:C6** and apply **Thick Outside Borders**.

f. Type **Model** in **cell A7**, **Price** in **cell B7**, and **Payment** in **cell C7**. Next enter the price information listed below in the range A8:B10. Adjust the column width as needed and apply **Currency Number Format** to the **range B8:C10**.

Model	Price
iPhone X	**949.00**
Samsung Galaxy	**799.00**
LG V30	**650.00**

g. Use the PMT function in **cell C8** to calculate the monthly flex payment for the first option. Be sure to use the appropriate absolute, relative, or mixed cell references. Next use the fill handle to copy the function down, completing the **range C8:C10**.

h. Type **Highest payment**, **Average payment**, and **Lowest payment** in the **range A12:A14**. Resize column A as needed.

i. Use the MAX function in **cell B12** to calculate the highest flex payment, in **cell B13** use the AVERAGE function to calculate the average flex payment, and in **cell B14** use the MIN function to calculate the lowest flex payment.

j. Insert a footer with your name on the left side, the sheet name in the center, and the file name code on the right side of the worksheet.

k. Save and close the workbook. Based on your instructor's directions, submit e02m2SmartPhone_LastFirst.

Running Case

New Castle County Technical Services

New Castle County Technical Services (NCCTS) provides technical support services for a number of companies in New Castle County, Delaware. You previously downloaded a dataset from the company's database that contains a list of call cases that were closed during March, formatted the worksheet, and calculated the number of days each case was open and the amount owed per transaction. Since then, you added two worksheets, one for your customer list and one for the rates. In the March Hours worksheet, you inserted new columns to look up customer names and rates from the respective worksheets. You want to use this data to enter summary statistics to complete billing analysis for March.

a. Open *e02r1NCCTS* and save it as **e02r1NCCTS_LastFirst**.

b. Insert a **VLOOKUP** function in **cell C5**, to return the customer name based on the customer ID in column B and the lookup table in the Customers worksheet.

c. Copy the function from cell C5 to the **range C6:C36**.

d. Insert a **VLOOKUP** function in **cell F5** to look up Rates for CallTypeID in column D using the lookup table in the Rates worksheet. Copy the function from cell F5 to the **range F6:F36**.

e. Insert an IF function in **cell K5** to calculate the amount billed. If the hours logged is less than or equal to 10 (cell O12), multiply the rate by the hours worked. Otherwise multiply the rate by the hours worked and add a $100 premium (cell O13) to the bill. Copy the function from cell K5 to the **range K6:K36**.

f. Insert a function in **cell O5** to calculate the total hours logged in column J.

g. Insert a function in **cell O6** to calculate the total amount billed in column K.

h. Insert a function in **cell O7** to calculate the average days required to complete a service request (column I).

i. Insert a function in **cell O8** to calculate the fewest days open in column I.

j. Insert a function in **cell O9** to calculate the most days open in column I.

k. Insert a function in **cell E2** to add the current date and time to the worksheet.

l. Insert a footer with your name on the left side, the sheet name in the center, and the file name code on the right side of the worksheet. Return to Normal view.

m. Save and close the workbook. Based on your instructor's directions, submit e02r1NCCTS_LastFirst.

Disaster Recovery

Auto Finance

After many years of service your automobile has been diagnosed with a cracked engine block. It has been determined that the damage is too costly to repair so you have decided to purchase a new vehicle. Before purchasing the car, you want to create a worksheet to estimate the monthly payment based on the purchase price, APR, down payment, and years. Your monthly budget is $500 and you will used conditional logic to automatically determine if you can afford the cars you are evaluating. After completing the calculations for the first car option in row 12, you used the fill handle to copy the functions down completing the worksheet. Unfortunately, after using the fill handle you receive errors in your calculations. You need to locate and repair the errors in order to complete the worksheet. Open the workbook *e02d1CarLoan* and save it as **e02d1CarLoan_LastFirst**. Review the formula in cell B12. Add the appropriate mixed cell reference for the down payment located in cell D4 and use the fill handle to copy the formula down completing the column. Review the formula in cell C12. Add the appropriate mixed cell references for the APR and years financed located in cells D5 and D6. Next use the fill handle to copy the formula down completing the column. Include a footer with your name on the left side, the date in the center, and the file name on the right side. Save and close the workbook. Based on your instructor's directions, submit e02d1CarLoan_LastFirst.

Capstone Exercise

W.C. Hicks Appliances

You are an account manager for W.C. Hicks Appliances, a local appliance store that also provides financing, delivery, and installation. As part of your daily tasks, you create an Excel workbook that reports sales, payment plan information, and summary statistics.

Insert Current Date

In order to ensure proper documentation you want to insert the current date and time.

1. Open the *e02c1Appliances* workbook and save it as **e02c1Appliances_LastFirst**.
2. Insert a function in **cell B2** to display the current date and format as a **Long Date**.
3. Set column B's width to **Autofit**.

Create Item Lookup

Your first task is to use a lookup function based on the data in the range A18:C23 to determine the name of the item purchased and the corresponding price based on the provided SKU number.

4. Insert a function in **cell C5** to display the item named based on the provided inventory lookup information.
5. Copy the function from **cell C5** down through **C13** to complete column C.
6. Set column C's width to **12.5**.
7. Insert a function in **cell E5** to display the item price based on the provided inventory lookup information.
8. Copy the function from **cell E5** down through **E13** to complete column E.
9. Apply **Currency Number Format** to **column E**.

Determine Delivery Fee

You will calculate the total due for each customer's order. The total is the purchase price plus an optional $75.00 delivery charge.

10. Insert an IF function in **cell F5** to calculate the total due. If the customer has chosen home delivery, there is an additional delivery charge located in **cell B25**. Be sure to use appropriate relative and absolute cell references.

11. Copy the function from **cell F5** down through **F13** to complete column Gra F.
12. Apply **Currency format** to **column F**.

Calculate the Monthly Payment

Your next step is to calculate the periodic payment for each customer's purchase. The payments are based on the years financed in column G and the annual interest rate in cell B26. All accounts are paid on a monthly basis.

13. Insert the function in **cell H5** to calculate the first customer's monthly payment, using appropriate relative and absolute cell references.
14. Copy the formula down the column.
15. Insert a function in **cell H14** to calculate the total of all monthly payments in column H.
16. Apply **Currency Number Format** to **column H**.

Finalize the Workbook

You perform some basic statistical calculations and finalize the workbook with formatting and page setup options.

17. Insert a function in **cell H18** to calculate the total number of orders.
18. Insert a function in **cell H19** to calculate the lowest monthly payment in column H.
19. Insert a function in **cell H20** to calculate the average monthly payment in column H.
20. Insert a function in **cell H21** to calculate the highest monthly payment in column H.
21. Insert a function in **cell H22** to calculate the median monthly payment in column H.
22. Apply **Currency format** to the **range H19:H22**.
23. Insert a footer with your name on the left side, the sheet name in the center, and the file name on the right side.
24. Save and close the workbook. Based on your instructor's directions, submit e02c1Appliances_ LastFirst.

Excel

Charts

LEARNING OUTCOME You will create charts and insert sparklines to represent data visually.

OBJECTIVES & SKILLS: After you read this chapter, you will be able to:

CASE STUDY | Computer Job Outlook

You are an academic advisor for the School of Computing at a university in Seattle, Washington. You will visit high schools over the next few weeks to discuss the computing programs at the university and to inform students about the job outlook in the computing industry. Your assistant, Doug Demers, researched growing computer-related jobs in the *Occupational Outlook Handbook* published by the Bureau of Labor Statistics on the U.S. Department of Labor's website. Doug listed computer-related jobs that require a bachelor's degree, the number of those jobs in 2016, the projected number of jobs by 2026, the growth in percentage increase and number of jobs, and the 2017 median pay.

To prepare for your presentation to encourage students to select a computing major in your School of Computing, you will create several charts that depict the job growth in the computer industry. Each chart will provide different perspectives on the data. After you complete the charts, you will be able to use them in a variety of formats, such as presentations, fliers, and brochures.

Depicting Data Visually

YanLev/Shutterstock

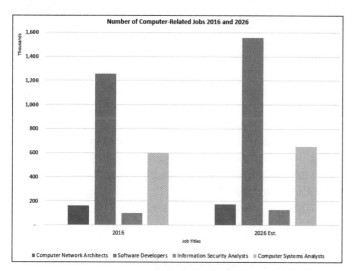

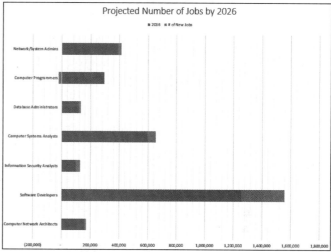

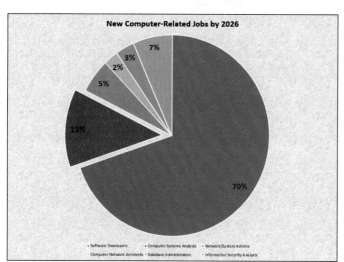

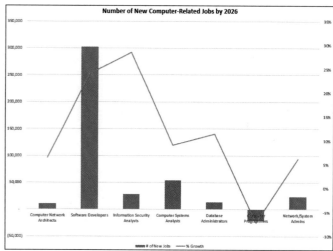

CHAPTER 3

FIGURE 3.1 Computer-Related Jobs Outlook

CASE STUDY | Computer Job Outlook

Starting File	File to be Submitted
e03h1Jobs	e03h3Jobs_LastFirst

MyLab IT Grader An alternate version of this project is available as a MyLab IT Grader Assessment

Chart Basics

A *chart* is a visual representation of numeric data that compares data and reveals trends or patterns to help people make informed decisions. An effective chart depicts data in a clear, easy-to-interpret manner and contains enough data to be useful without being overwhelming.

Review the structure of the worksheet—the column labels, the row labels, the quantitative data, and the calculated values. Before creating a chart, make sure the values or units in each column or row are consistent (such as number of jobs for a specific year) and that the row and column headings are descriptive (such as Computer Systems Analysts). Identify if the worksheet contains a single set of data (such as the number of jobs in 2026 by job title) or multiple sets of data (such as the number of jobs for two or more years by job title). If the worksheet contains multiple sets of data, decide which set or sets of data you want to focus on and include in the chart. As you review the data, make sure the dataset does not include any blank rows or columns. Otherwise, if you select a dataset with a blank row or column, the chart would display gaps represented by the blank row or column.

You can create different charts from the same dataset; each chart type tells a different story. Select a chart type that appropriately represents the data and tells the right story. For example, one chart might compare the number of computer-related jobs between 2016 and 2026, and another chart might indicate the percentage of new jobs by job title. Table 3.1 lists and describes the most commonly used chart types. Each chart type provides a unique perspective to the selected data.

TABLE 3.1	Common Chart Types	
Chart	**Chart Type**	**Description**
	Column chart	Displays values in vertical columns where the height represents the value; the taller the column, the larger the value. Categories display along the horizontal (category) axis.
	Bar chart	Displays values in horizontal bars where the length represents the value; the longer the bar, the larger the value. Categories display along the vertical (category) axis.
	Pie chart	Shows proportion of individual data points to the total or whole of all those data points.
	Line chart	Displays category data on the horizontal axis and value data on the vertical axis. Appropriate to show continuous data to depict trends over time, such as months, years, or decades.
	Combo	Combines two chart types (such as column and line) to plot different data types (such as values and percentages).

In this section, you will select the data source, use different methods for creating a chart, move and size a chart, and prepare a chart for distribution.

STEP 1 Creating a Basic Chart

After reviewing the data in a worksheet and deciding what story to represent, you are ready to create a chart. First, you select the data to be included in the chart, and then you select the type of chart to create. After the chart is created, you can move the chart, adjust the size of the chart, and prepare it for distribution.

Select the Data Source

The first step to creating a chart is to identify the range that contains the data you want to include in the chart. It is important that you decide the range first to ensure the chart contains the necessary values and text. After you identify the data source, select the values and text headings needed to create the chart. However, do not select worksheet titles or subtitles; doing so would add meaningless data to the chart.

> **TIP: SELECTING NONADJACENT RANGES FOR THE DATA SOURCE**
> The values and text that you want to use as the data source may be in nonadjacent ranges. It is important that you select the same start and end points for both ranges. For example, if you select the range A4:A7, you would need to select a range with the same row numbers, such as C4:C7. To select nonadjacent ranges as the data source, select the first range and press and hold Ctrl while you select the nonadjacent range. On a Mac, press Command.

Figure 3.2 shows worksheet data and the resulting chart. The range A4:C7 was selected as the data source to create the chart. An individual value in a cell that is plotted in a chart is a ***data point.*** The value 654,900 in cell C5 is a data point for the estimated number of Computer Systems Analysts in 2026. A ***data series*** is a group of related data points typically originated in columns in a worksheet that are plotted in a chart. For example, the values 654,900, 415,300, and 273,600 show the number of estimated jobs in the 2026 data series. Each data series is represented by a different color on the chart. For example, the 2016 data series is blue, and the 2026 data series is orange. Furthermore, the text row headings, such as Computer Systems Analysts, are used as categories.

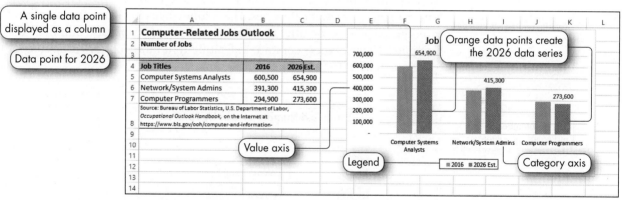

FIGURE 3.2 Dataset and Chart

Data are plotted on two axes. The ***x-axis***, also known as the *horizontal axis*, is the horizontal border that provides a frame of reference for measuring data left to right in a chart. The ***y-axis***, also known as the *vertical axis*, is the vertical border that provides a frame of reference for measuring data up and down in a chart. Excel refers to chart axes as the category axis and the value axis. The ***category axis*** is the axis that displays descriptive labels for the data points plotted in a chart. In Figure 3.2, the category axis displays on the x-axis using the text row headings. The ***value axis*** is the axis that displays incremental numbers to identify the approximate values of data points in a chart. In Figure 3.2, the value axis displays on the y-axis using increments for the number of jobs.

If you change the underlying data used in a chart, the chart automatically changes to reflect the new data. For example, if you change the value in cell C5 from 654,900 to 800,000, the 2026 column for Computer Systems Analysts becomes taller to reflect the higher value in the worksheet.

Use the Insert Tab to Create a Chart

The Charts group on the Insert tab contains commands for creating a variety of charts (see Figure 3.3). When you click a command, a gallery displays specific chart subtypes. For example, selecting Column or Bar Chart displays a gallery of 2-D and 3-D column and bar charts, such as clustered column, stacked column, and 100% stacked column. You should select the specific chart type that best achieves the purpose of the selected data source.

FIGURE 3.3 Charts Group on the Insert Tab

Create a Column Chart

A ***column chart*** compares values across categories, such as job titles, using vertical columns where the height represents the value of an individual data point. The taller the column is, the larger the value is. Column charts are most effective when they are limited to seven or fewer categories. The column chart in Figure 3.4 compares the number of projected jobs by job title. The Computer Systems Analysts column is taller than the Computer Programmers column, indicating that more jobs are projected for Computer Systems Analysts than Computer Programmers.

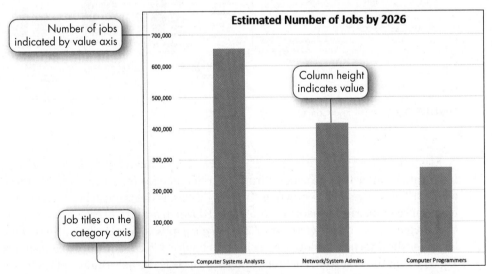

FIGURE 3.4 Column Chart

A ***clustered column chart*** compares groups or clusters of columns set side by side. The clustered column chart facilitates quick comparisons across data series, and it is effective for comparing several data points among categories. Figure 3.5 shows a clustered column chart where each yearly data series is assigned a color. This chart makes it easy to compare the predicted job growth from 2016 to 2026 for each job title, and then to compare the trends among job titles. The legend displays at the bottom of the chart to identify the color assigned to each data series in a chart. In this case, blue represents the 2016 data series, and orange represents the 2026 data series.

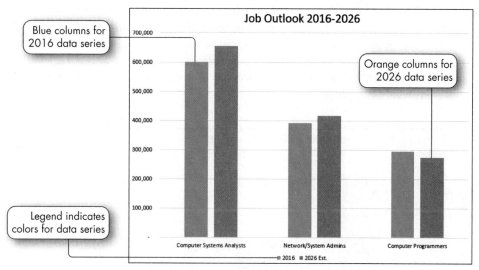

FIGURE 3.5 Clustered Column Chart

TIP: SELECTING HEADINGS FOR MULTIPLE DATA SERIES
When you create a chart that contains more than one data series, you must include the row and column headings. If you select only the values, Excel will display Series 1 and Series 2 in the legend. In that case, you would not know which color represents what data series.

A **stacked column chart** shows the relationship of individual data points to the whole category by stacking data in segments on top of each other in a column. Only one stacked column displays for each category. Each segment within the stacked column is color-coded for one data series. Use the stacked column chart to compare total values across categories, as well as to display the individual values. Figure 3.6 shows a stacked column chart in which a single column represents each year, and each column stacks color-coded data-point segments representing the different jobs. The stacked column chart compares the total number of computer-related jobs for each year. The height of each color-coded data point shows the relative contribution of each job to the total number of jobs for that year.

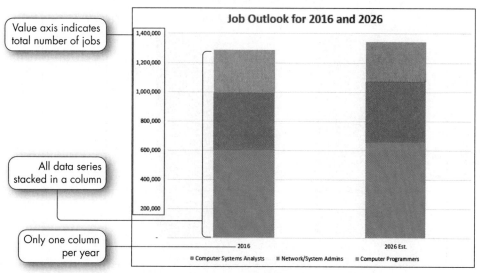

FIGURE 3.6 Stacked Column Chart

When you create a stacked column chart, make sure data are additive: Each column represents a sum of the data for each segment. Figure 3.6 correctly uses years as the category axis and the Jobs as data series. For each year, Excel sums the number of Jobs, and the columns display the total number of jobs. For example, the estimated total number of the three computer-related jobs in 2026 is about 1,344,000. Figure 3.7 shows a meaningless stacked column chart because the yearly number of jobs by job title is *not* additive. Adding the number of current actual jobs to the number of estimated jobs in the future does not make sense. It is incorrect to state that about 1,255,400 Computer Systems Analysts jobs exist; therefore, it is important to ensure the chart reflects a logical interpretation of data.

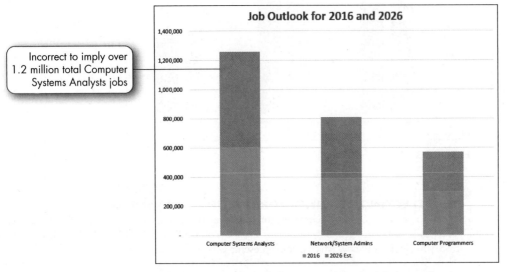

FIGURE 3.7 Incorrectly Constructed Stacked Column Chart

A **_100% stacked column chart_** converts individual data points (values) into percentages of the total value. Similar to a stacked column chart, each data series is a different color of the stack, though with a 100% stacked column chart, the data series is represented as a percentage of the whole, not as a discrete value. The total of each column is 100%. For example, the chart in Figure 3.8 illustrates that Computer Systems Analysts account for 47–49% of the computer-related jobs in both 2016 and 2026.

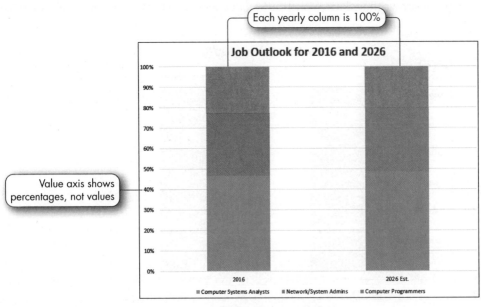

FIGURE 3.8 100% Stacked Column Chart

Move a Chart

When you create a chart, Excel displays the chart in the worksheet where the data is located, often on top of existing worksheet data. Therefore, you should move the chart so that it does not cover up data. With the chart selected, you can use the Cut and Paste commands to move the chart to a different location in the worksheet, or you can drag the chart to a different location. Before dragging a chart, point to the chart area to display the Chart Area ScreenTip, and when the pointer includes the white arrowhead and a four-headed arrow 🔀, drag the chart to the new location.

Instead of keeping the chart on the same worksheet as the data source, you can place the chart in a separate worksheet, called a *chart sheet*. A chart sheet contains a single full-size chart only; you cannot enter data and formulas on a chart sheet. Moving a chart to its own sheet enlarges the chart so that you can easily see the different components of the chart.

> **To move a chart to a new sheet, complete the following steps:**
>
> 1. Select the chart.
> 2. Click the Design tab and click Move Chart in the Location group (or right-click the chart and select Move Chart) to open the Move Chart dialog box (see Figure 3.9).
> 3. Select *New sheet* to move the chart to its own sheet and type a name for the chart sheet.
> 4. Click OK.

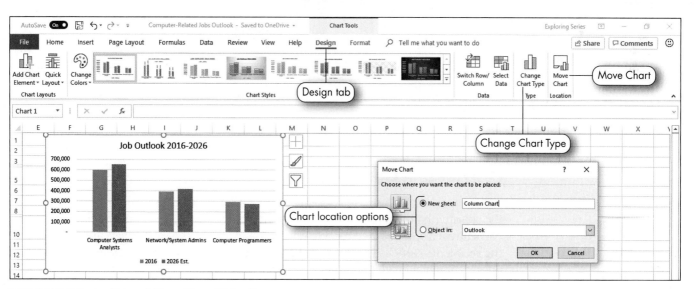

FIGURE 3.9 Design Tab and Move Chart Dialog Box

You can also move the chart as an object to another sheet within the same workbook or to a sheet within another open workbook. For example, you could move all charts to one worksheet to provide a visual summary of the data of key points contained in the workbook. To move a chart to another worksheet, click *Object in* within the Move Chart dialog box and select a worksheet to which you want to move the chart. After you move the chart to that worksheet, you can move it to a different location on that sheet.

Size a Chart

After moving a chart within a worksheet, you can adjust the size of the chart to fit in a range or to ensure the chart is appropriately sized. With the chart selected, you can set height and width of the chart using a *sizing handle*, which is one of eight circles that display around the four corners and outside middle edges of a chart when you select it. Use a middle sizing handle to change either the height or the width of the chart; use a corner-sizing handle to change both the height and width at the same time. When you position the pointer on a sizing handle, the pointer changes to a two-headed arrow so that you can drag the sizing handle to change the size the chart. Press and hold Shift as you drag a corner sizing handle to change the height and width proportionately.

One concern about using sizing handles to adjust the chart size is that the chart may become distorted if you later adjust row height, column width, or insert or delete rows or columns. If you anticipate making these types of changes, use the Shape Height and Shape Width settings in the Size group on the Format tab (see Figure 3.10) instead to change the size of the chart. Setting the height and width on the Format tab ensures the chart dimensions do not change if you adjust column widths or row heights or insert or delete columns or rows in the worksheet.

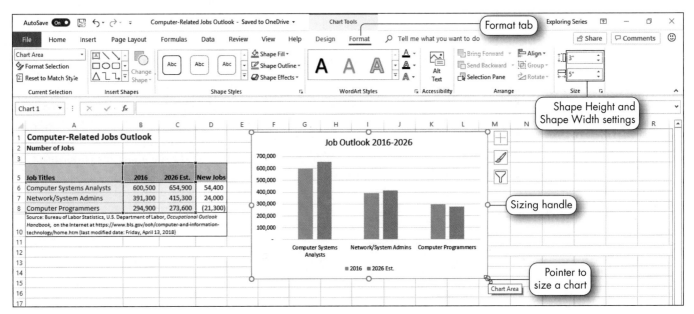

FIGURE 3.10 Sizing a Chart

Distribute a Chart

After you create a chart, you should prepare it for distribution. You may want to share the chart with others as a printout, on a shared drive, or as an email attachment. Even if you share a workbook electronically, you should ensure the worksheets are set up so that the recipients can easily print the chart if they want. Add any necessary identification information in a header or footer on the worksheet and chart sheets.

> **TIP: GROUPING SHEETS TO INSERT HEADERS AND FOOTERS**
> If you insert footers in a workbook containing both regular worksheets and chart sheets, you cannot group all sheets together and insert headers or footers. You can group all chart sheets together to insert a header or footer; then group all regular worksheets together to insert a header or footer.

Follow these guidelines to print a chart:

- If the data and chart are on the same worksheet, but you want to print only the data or only the chart, select the data or the chart, and then display the Print Preview window. Select the Print Selection setting to print spreadsheet data or ensure Print Selected Chart is selected to print the chart.

- To print both the data and chart, display the Print Preview window to ensure the data and chart fit appropriately on a page. Adjust the margins and scaling if needed to achieve the desired printout.

- If the chart is on a chart sheet, the chart is the only item on that worksheet. When you display Print Preview, the chart displays as a full-page chart within the margins.

Using Other Methods to Create Charts

The chart commands in the Chart group on the Insert tab are helpful when you know the exact type of chart you want to create. However, if you are unsure which type of chart would effectively represent the data, you can use the Recommended Charts command or Quick Analysis to review potential charts to depict the selected data source. In addition, you can change the chart type after creating the chart if you decide that another chart type will better depict the data.

STEP 2 ## Create a Recommended Chart

Use the Recommended Charts command in the Charts group on the Insert tab to display the Insert Chart dialog box (see Figure 3.11). This dialog box contains two tabs: Recommended Charts and All Charts. Excel analyzes the selected data and displays thumbnails of recommended charts. Click a thumbnail to see a larger visualization of how the selected data would look in that chart type. The dialog box displays a message indicating the purpose of the selected chart. When you click OK within the dialog box, Excel creates the type of chart you selected in the dialog box.

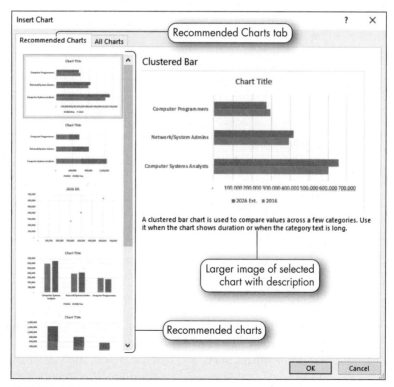

FIGURE 3.11 Insert Chart Dialog Box: Recommended Charts

Change the Chart Type

After you create a chart, you may decide that the data would be better represented by a different type of chart. For example, you might decide a bar chart would display the labels better than a column chart, or you might want to change a clustered bar chart to a stacked bar chart to provide a different perspective for the data. Use the Change Chart Type command to change a chart to a different type of chart. The Change Chart Type dialog box opens, which is similar to the Insert Chart dialog box that contains the Recommended Charts and All Charts tabs.

To change the type of an existing chart, complete the following steps:

1. Select the chart and click the Design tab.
2. Click Change Chart Type in the Type group to open the Change Chart Type dialog box.
3. Click a chart type on the left side of the Change Chart Type dialog box.
4. Click a chart subtype on the right side of the dialog box and click OK.

STEP 3 ## Create a Chart with Quick Analysis

Recall that when you select a range of adjacent cells (such as the range A5:C12) and position the pointer over that selected range, Excel displays Quick Analysis in the bottom-right corner of the selected area (see Figure 3.12). Quick Analysis does not display when you select nonadjacent ranges, such as ranges A6:A12 and D6:D12.

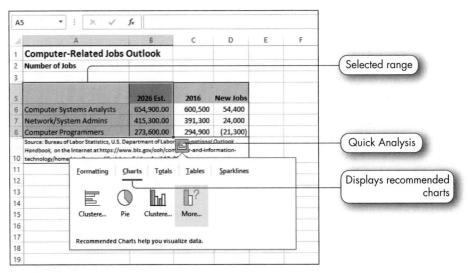

FIGURE 3.12 Quick Analysis Tool

Previously, you used the Quick Analysis tool to insert basic functions for a selected range. Another feature of Quick Analysis is that you can quickly create charts. Similar to Recommended Charts, you can use Quick Analysis to display recommended charts based on the data you selected. The thumbnails of recommended charts change based on the data you select.

MAC TIP: Quick Analysis is not available for Mac users. Use Recommended Charts or create a chart by using the Insert tab.

Create a Chart with Ideas

Similar to Quick Analysis and Recommended Charts, the new *Ideas feature* provides intelligent analysis of a dataset to recommend potentially useful charts. With the active cell in a dataset or with a range selected, click Ideas in the Ideas group on the Home tab. Ideas analyzes the data and provides visualizations of the data in a task pane. A *task pane* is a window of options specific to a feature in an Office application. The task pane name and options change based on the selected range, object, or feature. For Ideas to work best, the dataset should have single-row, unique headers, no blank cells within the header row and no blank columns or rows within the dataset. Figure 3.13 shows the Ideas task pane with recommended charts using a dataset.

MAC TIP: Ideas may not be available for Mac users.

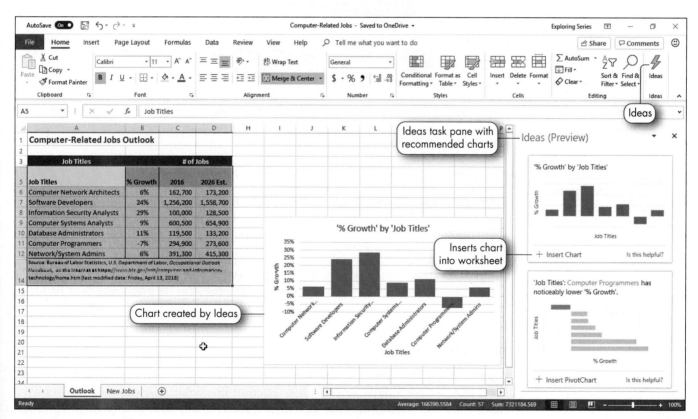

FIGURE 3.13 Charts Recommended by Ideas

Creating Other Charts

Column, bar, line, and pie charts are some of the most common chart types. Other frequently created charts include combo charts, X Y (scatter) charts, and area charts. For people who study the stock market, stock charts are useful.

Create a Bar Chart

A **bar chart** is similar to a column chart in that it compares values across categories. Unlike a column chart that displays values in vertical columns, a bar chart displays values using horizontal bars. The horizontal axis displays values, and the vertical axis displays categories (see Figure 3.14). Bar charts and column charts tell a similar story: they both compare categories of data. A bar chart is preferable when category names are long, such as *Computer Network Architects*. A bar chart displays category names in an easy-to-read format, whereas a column chart might display category names at an awkward angle or in a smaller font size. The overall decision between a column and a bar chart may come down to the fact that different data may look better with one chart type than the other.

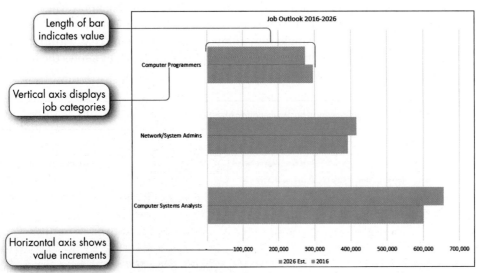

Length of bar indicates value

Vertical axis displays job categories

Horizontal axis shows value increments

FIGURE 3.14 Clustered Bar Chart

> **TIP: CLUSTERED, STACKED, AND 100% BAR CHARTS**
> Similar to column charts, you can create different types of bar charts. A **clustered bar chart** compares groups—or clusters—of bars displayed horizontally in groups. A **stacked bar chart** shows the relationship of individual data points to the whole category. A stacked bar chart displays only one bar for each category. Each category within the stacked bar is color-coded for one data series. A **100% stacked bar chart** converts individual data points (values) into percentages of the total value. Each data series is a different color of the stack, representing a percentage. The total of each bar is 100%.

Create a Line Chart

A **line chart** displays lines connecting data points to show trends over equal time periods. Excel displays each data series with a different line color. The category axis (x-axis) represents time, such as 10-year increments, whereas the value axis (y-axis) represents a value, such as money or quantity. A line chart enables you to detect trends because the line continues to the next data point. To show each data point, choose the Line with Markers chart type. Figure 3.15 shows a line chart indicating the number of majors from 2010 to 2025 (estimated) at five-year increments. The number of Arts majors remains relatively constant, but the number of Technology majors increases significantly over time, especially between the years 2015 and 2025.

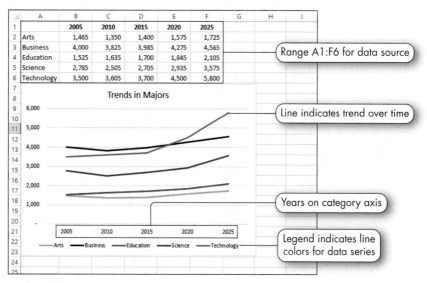

FIGURE 3.15 Line Chart

Create a Pie Chart

A *pie chart* shows each data point as a proportion to the whole data series. The pie chart displays as a circle, or "pie," where the entire pie represents the total value of the data series. Each slice represents a single data point. The larger the slice, the larger percentage that data point contributes to the whole. Use a pie chart when you want to convey percentages for up to seven data points in a data series. Including more than seven data points in a pie chart makes the chart look too cluttered or hard to interpret. Unlike column, bar, and line charts that typically chart multiple data series, pie charts represent a single data series only.

The pie chart in Figure 3.16 divides the pie representing the estimated number of new jobs into three slices, one for each job title. The size of each slice is proportional to the percentage of total computer-related jobs depicted in the worksheet for that year. For example, for the three jobs listed, Computer Systems Analysts account for 49% of the estimated total number of computer-related jobs in 2026. Excel creates a legend to indicate which color represents which pie slice.

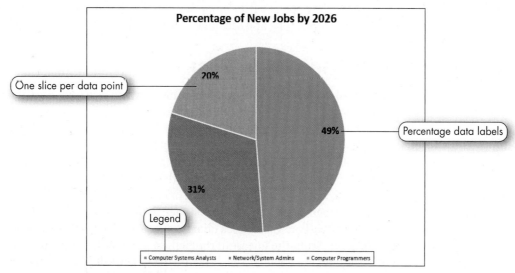

FIGURE 3.16 Pie Chart

STEP 4 Create a Combo Chart

A **combo chart** is a chart that combines two chart types, such as column and line charts. This type of chart is useful to show two different but related data types, such as quantities and percentages. Several types of combo charts are available. A combo chart can share the same axis or have a secondary axis. For example, Figure 3.17 shows a combo chart called *clustered column-line on its secondary axis* that combines a clustered column chart and a line chart to show the number of new jobs in columns and the percentage growth of new jobs in a line within the same chart (see Figure 3.17).

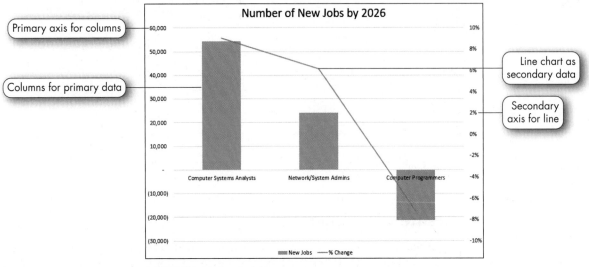

FIGURE 3.17 Combo Chart

When a combo chart has a primary and secondary axis, the primary axis displays on the left side, and the secondary axis displays on the right side. In Figure 3.17, the primary axis on the left side indicates the number of jobs, and the secondary axis on the right side indicates the percentage of new jobs. Combining two chart types (column and line) gives you a better understanding of the data. For example, you know that the 55,000 new Computer Systems Analysts jobs (indicated by the blue column) is about a 9% increase between 2016 and 2026 (indicated by the line).

For more control in designing a combo chart, you can create custom dual-axis combo charts. This method enables you to specify the chart type for each series and specify which series is displayed on the secondary axis. To create a custom combo chart, click Combo in the Charts group on the Insert tab and select Create Custom Combo Chart. The Insert Chart dialog box opens with Combo selected on the left side and the specific options for selecting the chart type and secondary axis on the right side of the dialog box.

Create Other Types of Charts

An **X Y (scatter) chart** shows a relationship between two numeric variables using their X and Y coordinates. Excel plots one variable on the horizontal x-axis and the other variable on the vertical y-axis. Scatter charts are often used to represent data in educational, scientific, and medical experiments. Figure 3.18 shows the relationship between the number of minutes students view a training video and their test scores. The more minutes of a video a student watches, the higher the test score.

A **stock chart** shows fluctuations in stock prices. Excel has four stock subtypes: High-Low-Close, Open-High-Low-Close, Volume-High-Low-Close, and Volume-Open-High-Low-Close. The High-Low-Close stock chart marks a stock's trading range on a given day with a vertical line from the lowest to the highest stock prices. Rectangles mark the opening and closing prices. Table 3.2 lists and describes some of the other types of charts you can create in Excel.

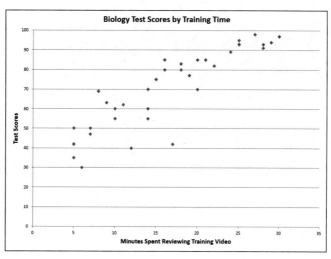

FIGURE 3.18 *X Y* (Scatter) Chart

TABLE 3.2	Other Chart Types	
Chart	Chart Type	Description
	Area chart	Similar to a line chart in that it shows trends over time; however, the area chart displays colors between the lines to help illustrate the magnitude of changes.
	Surface chart	Represents numeric data and numeric categories. Displays trends using two dimensions on a continuous curve.
	Radar chart	Uses each category as a spoke radiating from the center point to the outer edges of the chart. Each spoke represents each data series, and lines connect the data points between spokes, similar to a spider web. A radar chart compares aggregate values for several data series. For example, a worksheet could contain the number of specific jobs for 2018, 2019, 2020, and 2021. Each year would be a data series containing the individual data points (number of specific jobs) for that year. The radar chart would aggregate the total number of jobs per year for all four data series.
	Histogram	A histogram is similar to a column chart. The category axis shows bin ranges (intervals) where data is aggregated into bins, and the vertical axis shows frequencies. For example, your professor might want to show the number (frequency) of students who earned a score within each grade interval, such as 60–69, 70–79, 80–89, and 90–100.

Quick Concepts

1. Explain the importance of selecting row and column headings when selecting the data source for a chart. *p. 195*

2. Explain when you would create a bar chart instead of a column chart. *p. 204*

3. Explain why a professor would create a pie chart instead of a column chart to show overall class results for a test. *p. 205*

4. Describe the purpose of a combo chart. *p. 206*

Hands-On Exercises

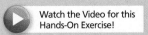

MyLab IT HOE1 Sim Training

Watch the Video for this Hands-On Exercise!

Skills covered: Select a Data Source • Use the Insert Tab to Create a Chart • Create a Column Chart • Move a Chart • Size a Chart • Create a Recommended Chart • Create a Bar Chart • Change the Chart Type • Create a Chart with Quick Analysis • Create a Pie Chart • Create a Combo Chart

1 Chart Basics

Doug Demers, your assistant, gathered data about seven computer-related jobs from the *Occupational Outlook Handbook* online. He organized the data into a structured worksheet that contains the job titles, the number of jobs in 2016, the projected number of jobs by 2026, and other data. Now you are ready to transform the data into charts to detect the trends.

STEP 1 ▷ CREATE A BASIC CHART

You want to compare the number of jobs in 2016 to the projected number of jobs in 2026 for the four highest-paid computer-related jobs. You decide to create a clustered column chart to depict this data. After you create this chart, you will move it to the right of the data and adjust its size. Refer to Figure 3.19 as you complete Step 1.

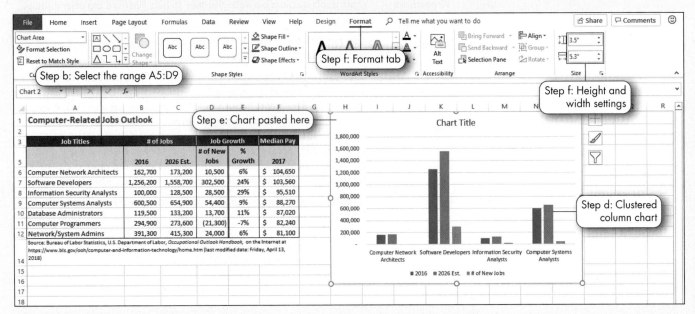

FIGURE 3.19 Clustered Column Chart

a. Open *e03h1Jobs* and save it as **e03h1Jobs_LastFirst**.

> **TROUBLESHOOTING:** If you make any major mistakes in this exercise, you can close the file, open *e03h1Jobs* again, and then start this exercise over.

b. Select the **range A5:D9** on the Outlook sheet.

You selected the job titles, the number of jobs in 2016, the projected number of jobs in 2026, and the number of estimated new jobs between 2016 and 2026 for the four highest-paid computer jobs listed. Because you are selecting three data series (three columns of numeric data), you must also select the column headings on row 5.

c. Click the **Insert tab** and click **Insert Column or Bar Chart** in the Charts group.

A gallery of column and bar charts displays. The thumbnails provide a visual of the different chart types.

d. Point to **Clustered Column** (the first thumbnail in the 2-D Column group) and click **Clustered Column**.

When you point to a thumbnail, Excel displays a ScreenTip describing what the chart does and when to use it. When you click the thumbnail, Excel inserts a chart in the middle of the worksheet. With the newly created chart selected, the Chart Tools Design and Format tabs display on the ribbon, and sizing handles display around the chart.

e. Click the **Home tab**, click **Cut** in the Clipboard group, click **cell H1**, and then click **Paste**.

You moved the chart from its original location so that the top-left corner is in cell H1.

f. Click the **Format tab**, click in the **Shape Height box** in the Size group, type **3.5**, and then press **Enter**. Click in the **Shape Width box** in the Size group, type **5.3**, and then press **Enter**.

You adjusted the height and width of the chart to make it easier to read. Save the workbook.

STEP 2 CREATE A RECOMMENDED CHART AND CHANGE THE CHART TYPE

You want to review potential charts to depict the number of jobs in 2016 and the number of new jobs that will be created by 2026. To help you decide which type of chart to create, you will use the Recommended Chart command to see different chart options. After creating a clustered bar chart, you decide to change it to a stacked bar chart to show the total number of jobs in 2026. Finally, you will move the bar chart to its own chart sheet. Refer to Figure 3.20 as you complete Step 2.

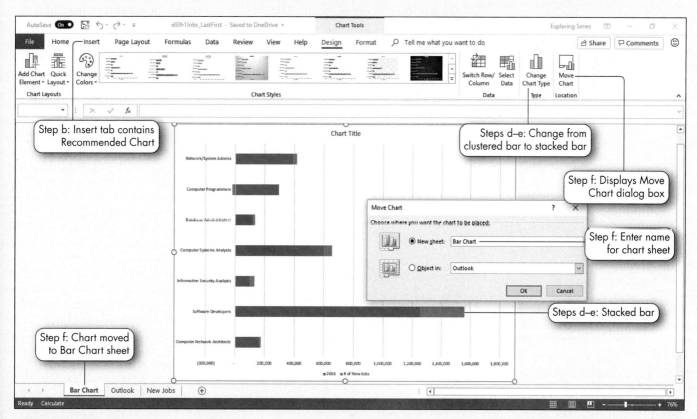

FIGURE 3.20 Stacked Bar Chart on Chart Sheet

a. Select the **range A5:B12**, press and hold **Ctrl**, and then select the **range D5:D12**.

You used Ctrl to select nonadjacent ranges: the job title labels, the number of jobs in 2016, and the number of new jobs. Because you selected nonadjacent ranges, each range must contain the same number of cells. For example, A5:A12, B5:B12, and D5:D12 are parallel ranges. Even though cell A5 is blank, you must include it to have a parallel range with the other two selected ranges that include cells on row 5.

> **TROUBLESHOOTING:** If you do not select parallel ranges, the chart you are about to create will not display correctly. Before continuing, make sure that both ranges A5:B12 and D5:D12 are selected. If not, deselect the ranges and select the correct ranges.

b. Click the **Insert tab** and click **Recommended Charts** in the Charts group.

The Insert Chart dialog box opens, displaying recommended charts based on the data you selected. The first recommended chart is a clustered bar chart. The right side of the dialog box shows how your data will be depicted with the selected chart type.

c. Click **OK**.

Excel inserts a clustered bar chart in the worksheet. You decide that clustered bars do not convey the story you want. You want to display the number of estimated new jobs in addition to the number of jobs in 2016 to show the total estimated number of jobs in 2026. Therefore, you decide to change from a clustered bar chart to a stacked bar chart.

d. Click **Change Chart Type** in the Type group on the Design tab.

The Change Chart Type dialog box opens. The left side of the dialog box lists all chart types. The top-right side displays thumbnails of various bar charts, and the lower section displays a sample of the selected chart. On a Mac, clicking Change Chart Type displays a menu.

e. Click **Stacked Bar** in the top center of the dialog box and click **OK**. Save the workbook.

Excel displays the number of jobs in 2016 in blue and stacks the number of new jobs in orange into one bar per job title. This chart tells the story of how the total projected number of jobs in 2026 is calculated: the number of existing jobs in 2016 and the number of new jobs. Because the estimated number of jobs is expected to decrease for Computer Programmers, the orange displays to the left of the blue bar.

f. Click **Move Chart** in the Location group on the Design tab, click **New sheet**, type **Bar Chart**, and then click **OK**. Save the workbook.

You moved the stacked bar chart to a new sheet called Bar Chart so that you can focus on just the chart. The chart is the only object in a chart sheet.

You decide to create a pie chart that depicts the percentage of new jobs by job title calculated from the total number of new jobs created for six job titles. You will use Quick Analysis because it is a simple way to create a standard pie chart. Because the number of programmers is expected to decrease, you will exclude that data from the pie chart. Refer to Figure 3.21 as you complete Step 4.

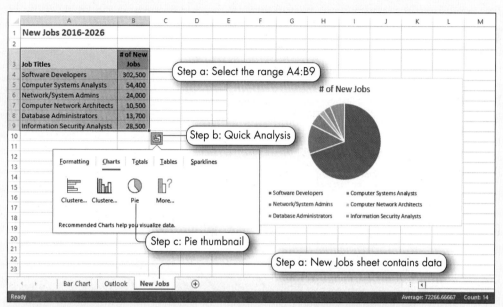

FIGURE 3.21 Pie Chart

a. Click the **New Jobs sheet tab** and select the **range A4:B9**.

 While you must select column headings when creating column and bar charts for multi data series, you do not select column headings when selecting data for a pie chart.

b. Click **Quick Analysis** at the bottom-right corner of the selected range and click **Charts**.

> **MAC TROUBLESHOOTING:** Quick Analysis is not available on Excel for Mac. Click the Insert tab, click Pie, click the first option below 2-D Pie and skip Step c.

 The Quick Analysis gallery displays recommended charts based on the selected range.

c. Click **Pie**.

 Each slice of the pie indicates the percentage of new jobs created by category. The pie chart clearly shows that Software Developers will account for over 50% of the new jobs created between 2016 and 2026.

d. Click **Move Chart** in the Location group on the Design tab, click **New sheet**, type **Pie Chart**, and then click **OK**. Save the workbook.

 Excel creates a new sheet called Pie Chart between the Outlook and New Jobs sheets.

You want to create a chart that shows the number of new jobs and the percentage of new jobs. Because the two data types are different, you will create a combo chart. Although the number of new jobs is higher for software developers, the percentage increase is higher for information security analysts. Refer to Figure 3.22 as you complete Step 5.

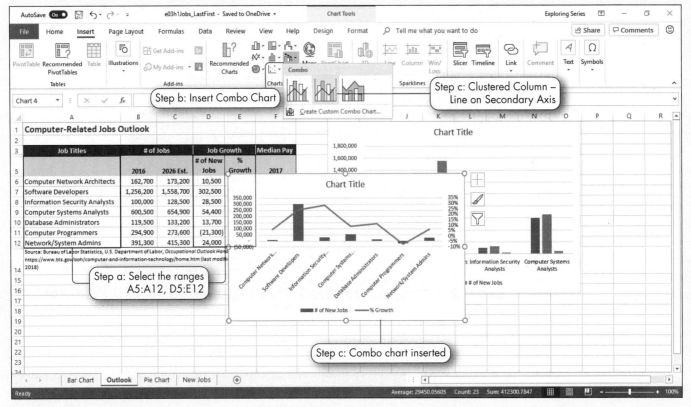

FIGURE 3.22 Combo Chart

a. Click the **Outlook sheet tab**, select the **range A5:A12**, press and hold **Ctrl**, then select the **range D5:E12**.

   You selected the job titles, number of new jobs, and percent growth data.

b. Click the **Insert tab** and click **Insert Combo Chart** in the Charts group.

   The Combo Chart gallery of thumbnails displays.

c. Click the **Clustered Column – Line on Secondary Axis thumbnail**, which is the middle thumbnail.

   Excel creates a combo chart based on the thumbnail you selected. The number of new jobs displays in blue columns, and the percentage growth displays as an orange line. Because the number of programming jobs is expected to decline, the orange line drops below 0.

d. Click **Move Chart** in the Location group on the Design tab, click **New sheet**, type **Combo Chart**, and then click **OK**.

e. Save the workbook. Keep the workbook open if you plan to continue with the next Hands-On Exercise. If not, close the workbook, and exit Excel.

Chart Elements

After creating a chart, you should add appropriate chart elements. A ***chart element*** is a component that completes or helps clarify the chart. Some chart elements, such as chart titles, should be included in every chart. Other elements are optional. When you point to a chart element, Excel displays a ScreenTip with the element name. Table 3.3 describes the chart elements, and Figure 3.23 illustrates several chart elements.

TABLE 3.3	Chart Elements
Element	**Description**
Axis title	Label that describes the category or value axes, such as In Millions of Dollars, to clarify the axis.
Chart area	Container for the entire chart and its elements.
Chart title	Heading that describes the entire chart.
Data label	Descriptive label that shows the exact value or name of a data point.
Data table	Grid that contains the data source values and labels; useful when the chart is on a different sheet from the data source.
Error bars	Visuals that indicate the standard error amount, a percentage, or a standard deviation for a data point or marker.
Gridlines	Horizontal or vertical lines that extend from the tick marks on the value axis across the plot area to guide the reader's eyes across the chart to identify values.
Legend	Box that contains a key to identify the color or pattern assigned to each data series.
Plot area	Region containing the graphical representation of the values in the data series; surrounded by two axes.
Trendline	Line that depicts trends or helps forecast future data, such as estimating future sales or number of births in a region. Add a trendline to column, bar, line, stock, scatter, and bubble charts. Excel analyzes the trends and displays a line indicating future values.

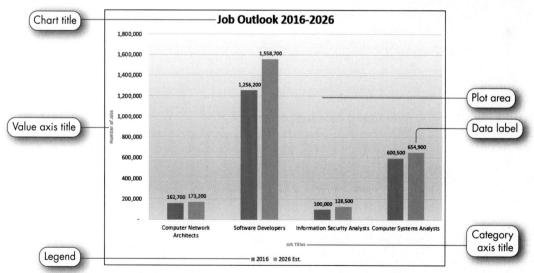

FIGURE 3.23 Chart Elements

In this section, you will learn how to add, edit, and format chart elements. Specifically, you will type a chart title, add axis titles, add data labels, and position the legend. Furthermore, you will learn how to format these elements as well as format axes, position the legend, and add gridlines. Finally, you will learn how to format the chart area, plot area, data series, and a data point.

Adding and Formatting Chart Elements

When you create a chart, one or more elements may display by default. For example, when you created the charts in Hands-On Exercise 1, Excel displayed a placeholder for the chart title and displayed a legend so that you know which color represents each data series. After you create a chart, you usually add elements to enhance the chart. Adding descriptive labels and a meaningful title provide information for the reader to comprehend the chart without knowing or seeing the underlying data. Finally, you can format the chart elements to improve the appearance of the chart.

When a chart is selected, two contextual tabs display: Design and Format. In addition, three icons display to the right of the chart. The top icon is Chart Elements, and when clicked displays a menu so that you can conveniently add or hide chart elements (see Figure 3.24). Click a check box to select and display that element. When you point to the right side of a chart element name on the menu, a triangle displays. Click the triangle to display a submenu specific for that chart element. Click Chart Elements again to hide the menu. Another way to add a chart element is to use the Add Chart Elements command in the Chart Layouts group on the Design tab.

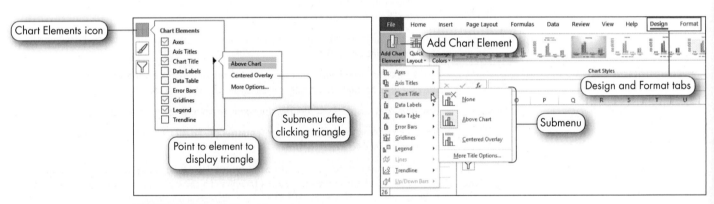

FIGURE 3.24 Add Chart Elements

MAC TIP: The Chart Elements, Chart Styles, and Chart Filters icons do not display next to a selected chart in Excel for Mac. Click the Chart Design tab and click Add Chart Elements to display a menu of chart elements. Select the chart element from that menu.

TIP: REMOVE AN ELEMENT
To remove an element, click Chart Elements and click a check box to deselect that element. Alternatively, use Add Chart Element in the Chart Layouts group on the Chart Tools Design tab, point to the element name, and then select None. You can also select a chart element and press Delete to remove it.

You must select a chart element before you apply additional formatting or change its settings. If a chart element is easily identified, such as the Chart Title, click the element to select it. If the element is hard to identify, such as the Plot Area, use the Chart Elements arrow in the Current Selection group on the Format tab and select the chart element from the list.

The Chart Elements menu includes a More option. When you select that option or when you double-click a chart element, a task pane displays on the right side of the screen. The task pane name and options change based on the selected chart element. Figure 3.25 shows the components of a task pane.

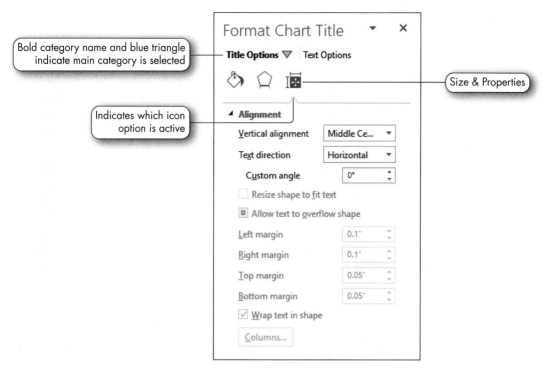

FIGURE 3.25 Format Chart Title Task Pane

TIP: ALTERNATIVE FOR OPENING FORMAT TASK PANES
Another way to display a task pane is to right-click the chart element and choose Format Element, where Element is the specific chart element, such as Format Chart Title. If you do not close a task pane after formatting a particular element, such as gridlines, and then click another chart element, the task pane will change so that you can format that chart element.

The top of a task pane displays the name of the task pane, such as Format Chart Title. Task panes contain a hierarchy of categories and subcategories to organize the options and settings. For example, category names such as Title Options and Text Options display below the task pane title. When you select a category, the category name is bold so that you know what category of options is displayed in the task pane.

Icons display below the category names. For example, Fill & Line, Effects, and Size & Properties icons display below the Title Options category name. A thin horizontal gray line separates the icons from the options. The line contains a partial triangle that points to the icon that is active to indicate which options are displayed. Figure 3.25 shows the triangle is pointing to Size & Properties. When you click an icon, the task pane displays specific options. For example, the Size & Properties options include vertical alignment and text direction.

After you select a chart element, you can format the chart element using commands in the Font group on the Home tab. For example, you can apply bold, increase the font size, and change the font color.

TIP: CHANGE THE FONT COLOR FOR CHART ELEMENTS
The default font color for the chart title, axes, axes titles, and legend is Black, Text 1, Lighter 35%. If you want these elements to stand out, change the color to Black, Text 1 or another solid color to improve the contrast, making it easier to read.

Apply a Quick Layout

Use Quick Layout to apply predefined layouts to a chart. Specifically, you can apply a layout to add several chart elements conveniently at one time. Select Quick Layout in the Chart Layouts group on the Design tab (see Figure 3.26). When you point to a thumbnail in the gallery, Excel displays a ScreenTip with the layout name, such as Layout 3, and a list of what chart elements are included. Each layout contains predefined chart elements and their positions. When you apply a layout, your chart does not retain any custom formatting that you might have previously applied. The chart is formatted with the predefined settings of the layout you select.

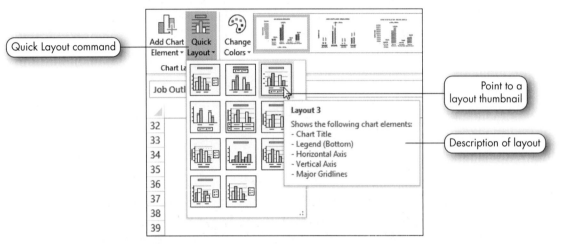

FIGURE 3.26 Quick Layout Gallery

STEP 1 Edit, Position, and Format Chart Titles

Excel includes the placeholder text *Chart Title* above a newly created chart. To give the chart a more meaningful or descriptive title, select the default chart title, type a descriptive title, and press Enter. For example, Houses Sold is too generic, but Houses Sold in Seattle in 2021 indicates the what (Houses), the where (Seattle), and the when (2021).

By default, the chart title displays centered above the plot area. Although this is a standard location for the chart, you can position the chart title elsewhere in the chart area by using the Chart Elements icon. Selecting Centered Overlay centers the chart title over the top of the plot area and increases the height of the plot area. However, only use this location if the overlay title does not hide data points in the plot area. You can also remove the chart title if you position the title immediately below the data source and plan to print both the data source and chart. Refer to Figure 3.24 to identify the chart title options. Use the Home tab to format the chart title.

> **TIP: LINKING A CHART TITLE OR AN AXIS TITLE TO A CELL**
> Instead of typing text directly in the Chart Title or Axis Title placeholder, you can link the title to a label in a cell. Click the Chart Title or Axis Title placeholder, type = in the Formula Bar, click the cell containing the label you want for the title, and then press Enter. The sheet name and cell reference, such as =Outlook!$A$1, displays in the Formula Bar. If you change the worksheet label, Excel will also change the chart title.

STEP 2 Add and Format Axis Titles

Axis titles help people understand charts by adding a brief description of the value or category axis. For example, if the values are abbreviated as 7 instead of 7,000,000, you should indicate the unit of measurement on the value axis as In Millions. To further clarify the labels on the category axis, include a category axis title, such as Job Titles. You can add the following types of axis titles:

- **Primary Horizontal:** Displays a title for the primary horizontal axis.
- **Primary Vertical:** Displays a title for the primary vertical axis.
- **Secondary Horizontal:** Displays a title for the secondary horizontal axis in a combo chart.
- **Secondary Vertical:** Displays a title for the secondary vertical axis in a combo chart.

The horizontal axis title displays below the category labels, and the rotated vertical axis title displays on the left side of the value axis. After adding an axis title, select the title, type the text for the title, and then press Enter similar to editing text for a chart title. Use the Home tab to format axis titles. If you want to further customize an axis title, use the Format Axis Title task pane.

Format the Axes

Based on the data source values and structure, Excel determines the start, incremental, and end values that display on the value axis when you create the chart. However, you can adjust the value axis so that the numbers displayed are simplified or fit better on the chart. For example, when working with large values such as 4,567,890, the value axis displays increments, such as 4,000,000 and 5,000,000. You can simplify the value axis by displaying values in millions, so that the values on the axis are 4 and 5 with the word Millions placed by the value axis to indicate the units.

Double-click the axis to open the Format Axis task pane (see Figure 3.27). Use the Axis Options to specify the bounds, units, display units, labels, and number formatting for an axis. Table 3.4 lists and describes some of the axis options. In addition, you can use the Home tab to format the axis.

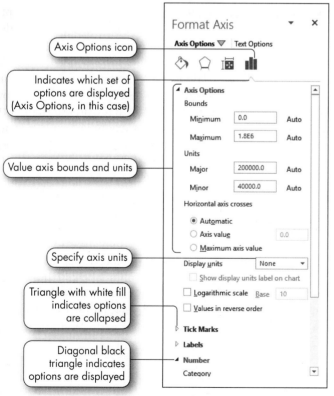

FIGURE 3.27 Format Axis Task Pane

TABLE 3.4 Axis Options

Option	Description
Bounds	Specifies the Minimum (lowest) and Maximum (highest) values displayed on the value axis. The Auto setting automatically determines the minimum and maximum values on the value axis. If you want to control the values, enter the values directly in the Minimum and Maximum boxes.
Units	Controls the intervals of values listed on the value axis. The Major setting controls the primary intervals, such as displaying values at every 50,000 units. The Minor setting controls more specific interval values, such as every 5,000 units, within the major units.
Display units	Specifies any conversion of values on the value axis. The default None setting does not convert values; the value axis displays the entire value, such as 1,500,000. Other settings include Hundreds, Thousands, Millions, and so on, in which zeros are dropped on large numbers on the value axis. For example, instead of displaying 1,500,000, you can select Millions to display 1.5 on the value axis to simplify the display of large numbers.
Tick Marks	Specifies the location of tick marks, which are tiny line extensions on the value axis intervals. The *Major type* setting displays a colored line extension at the major interval lines. The *Minor type* setting displays little lines at the minor unit intervals within the major intervals to further clarify values in the chart.
Labels	Specifies the location of the interval numbers on the value axis.
Number	Formats the values with a number format, the number of decimal places displayed, the format for displaying negative values, and other number formatting.

> **TIP: DISPLAYING OPTIONS WITHIN TASK PANES**
> A diagonal black triangle next to a category, such as Axis Options, indicates that all options in a category are displayed (expanded). A triangle with a white fill, such as the one next to Tick Marks, indicates that the category options are not displayed (collapsed).

STEP 3 Add, Position, and Format Data Labels

A data label is descriptive text that shows the exact value or name of a data point. Data labels indicate specific values for data points you want to emphasize. Typically, you add data labels only to specific data points, and not all data points. Use either Chart Elements or the Design tab to display data labels. When you click the Data Labels check box on the Chart Elements menu to display labels, you can then click the arrow to the right of the Data Labels item to select the position of the data labels. For example, you can specify Center or Outside End. Figure 3.23 shows a data label above each column for both the 2016 and 2026 data series.

To display data labels for only one data series, select that data series before selecting the Data Labels check box. Doing so focuses attention on that data series and keeps the plot area from being cluttered. For example, displaying data labels for just the 2026 data series focuses attention on the 2026 values.

Use the Format Data Labels task pane (see Figure 3.28) to customize and format the data labels. For example, you can select the type of data labels, such as Values or Percentages. In addition, you can select the position of the data label, such as Center or Inside End. Experiment with the data label positions to determine which position is easiest to read for your chart. Finally, click Number within the task pane to apply number formatting if the numeric data labels are not formatted properly. Use the Home tab to apply font formatting (such as font size and color) to the data labels.

Label contents

Label position options

FIGURE 3.28 Format Data Labels Task Pane

TIP: MOVING A DATA LABEL

Often one or more data labels will be positioned over a gridline, making it hard to read. To move a single data label, click the data label, which selects all data labels. Then click that data label again to select only that data label. Then you can drag the data label to a better location or individually format it.

When you create a pie chart, Excel generates a legend to identify the category labels for the different slice colors, but it does not display data labels. A best practice is to display Percentage data labels within or next to each slice. If you have more than five slices, consider also displaying the Category labels and removing the legend to avoid duplicating elements. Category data labels are easier to read than the small print in the legend. In addition, consider increasing the font size and applying bold so that the data labels are easy to read, particularly in a pie chart.

TIP: INSERTING AND FORMATTING SHAPES

The Format tab contains options to select a chart element, insert shapes, apply shape styles, apply WordArt styles, arrange objects, and specify the size of an object. In particular, you can insert a shape, such as a callout, to draw attention or place additional emphasis to a data point or data series in a chart. After inserting a shape, you can format the shape with a shape style, fill color, outline color, and shape effect.

Position and Format the Legend

When you create a multiple series chart, the legend displays, providing a key to the color-coded data series. Position the legend to the right, top, bottom, or left of the plot area, similar to choosing the position for a chart title using Chart Elements. The placement of the legend affects the plot area. For example, if you place the legend on the right side, the plot area is narrower. Make sure that the columns, bars, or lines appear proportionate and well balanced after you position the legend. Use the Format Legend task pane to customize and format the legend. Use the Home tab to format the legend. For example, select a larger font size and Black, Text 1 font color so that the legend is easier to read.

Add and Format Gridlines

Gridlines are horizontal or vertical lines that span across the plot area of the chart to help people identify the values plotted by the visual elements, such as a column. Excel displays horizontal gridlines for column, line, scatter, surface, and bubble charts and vertical gridlines for bar charts. Use either Chart Elements or Add Chart Elements in the Chart Layouts group on the Design tab to add gridlines.

Format gridlines by double-clicking a gridline to open the Format Major Gridlines task pane. You can change the line type, color, and width of the gridlines so that the gridlines help guide the reader's eye across the column, bar, line, and combo chart.

STEP 4 ## Format the Chart Area, Plot Area, and Data Series

Apply multiple settings, such as fill colors and borders, at once using the Format task pane for an element. To open a chart element's task pane, double-click the chart element. Figure 3.29 displays the Format Plot Area, Format Chart Area, and Format Data Series task panes with different fill options selected to display the different options that result. All three task panes include the same fill and border elements. For example, you change the fill color of a data series from blue to green to complement the green used in the worksheet data. After you select a fill option, such as *Gradient fill*, the remaining options change in the task pane.

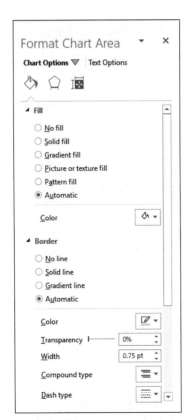 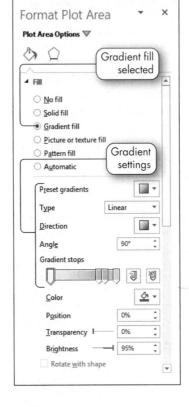 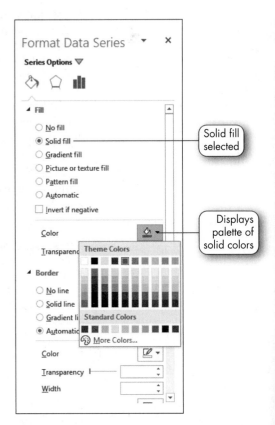

FIGURE 3.29 Format Task Panes

Include Alt Text

It is a good practice to apply some features that are accessibility compliant for people who have disabilities, such as vision or cognitive impairments, that may prevent them from seeing or comprehending the visual aid. In addition to assigning a meaningful name to a chart, you should provide **Alt Text**, also known as *alternative text*, which is a description that displays when a pointer moves over the chart or image. A screen reader can read the description to the user to help them understand the chart. To add Alt Text, click Alt Text in the Accessibility group on the Format tab. Alternatively, right-click the chart and select Edit Alt Text. The Alt Text task pane displays (see Figure 3.30). Enter a description of the chart in the text box and close the task pane.

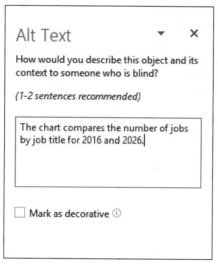

FIGURE 3.30 Alt Text Task Pane

Format a Data Point

Earlier in this chapter, you learned that a data point reflects a value in a single cell in a worksheet. You can select that single data point in a chart and format it differently from the rest of the data series. Select the data point you want to format, display the Format Data Point task pane, and make the changes you want.

In a pie chart, you can focus a person's attention on a particular slice by separating one or more slices from the rest of the chart in an ***exploded pie chart***. Figure 3.31 shows the Computer Network Architects slice is exploded 14%. You can explode a pie slice by selecting the slice and dragging it away from the pie.

To format a pie slice data point, complete the following steps:

1. Click within the pie chart, pause, and then select the slice you want to format.
2. Right-click the selected pie slice and select Format Data Point to open the Format Data Point task pane.
3. Click the Fill & Line icon and click the option (such as Solid fill) in the Fill category.
4. Click the Color arrow and select a color for a solid fill; select a Preset gradient, type, color, and other options for a gradient fill; or insert a picture or select a texture for a picture or texture fill.
5. Click the Series Options icon and drag the Point Explosion to the right to explode the selected pie slice.

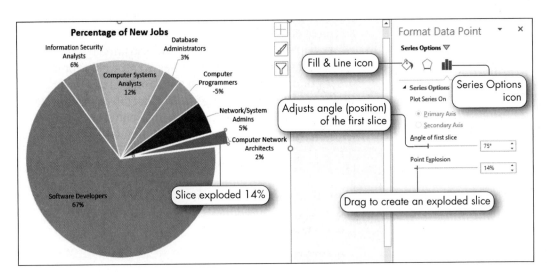

FIGURE 3.31 Format Data Point Task Pane

After you add data labels, long data labels for thin slices may display too close together. You can rotate the slices by changing the angle of the first slice until the data labels fit better in the chart area. Use the *Angle of first slice* option in the Format Data Point or Format Data Series task pane. As you increase the angle, the slices, along with their data labels, rotate clockwise.

Quick Concepts

5. Describe a situation when you would display the units in Millions, change the number category, and specify the decimal places for the value axis. ***pp. 217–218***

6. Explain the importance of including an Alt Text title and description for a chart. ***p. 221***

7. Explain why you would explode a slice on a pie chart. ***p. 221***

Hands-On Exercises

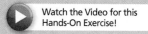

MyLab IT HOE2 Sim Training

Watch the Video for this
Hands-On Exercise!

Skills covered: Edit and
Format Chart Titles • Add and
Format Axis Titles • Format the
Axes • Add, Position, and Format
Data Labels • Format the Chart
Area • Add Alt Text • Format a
Data Point

2 Chart Elements

You want to enhance the computer job column, bar, and pie charts by adding some chart elements. You
will enter a descriptive chart title for each chart, add and format axis titles for the bar chart, add and format
data labels for the pie chart, and change fill colors in the pie chart.

STEP 1 · EDIT AND FORMAT CHART TITLES

When you created the column, bar, and pie charts in Hands-On Exercise 1, Excel displayed *Chart Title* at the top of
each chart. You will add a title that appropriately describes each chart. In addition, you will format the chart titles to be
easier to read by applying bold, enlarging the font sizes, and applying Black, Text 1 font color. Refer to Figure 3.32 as
you complete Step 1.

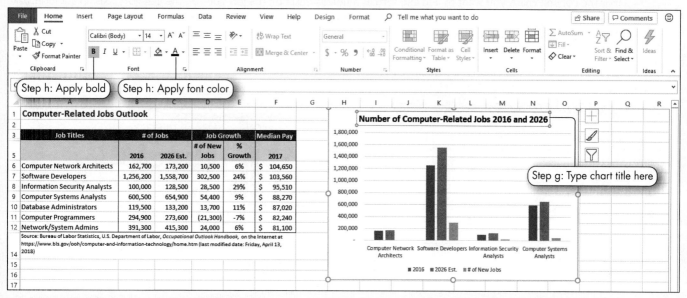

FIGURE 3.32 Formatted Chart Title

a. Open *e03h1Jobs_LastFirst* if you closed it at the end of the Hands-On Exercise 1, and save
it as **e03h2Jobs_LastFirst**, changing h1 to h2.

b. Make sure the Combo Chart sheet is the active sheet, select the **Chart Title placeholder**, type **Number of New Computer-Related Jobs by 2026** in the Formula Bar,
and then press **Enter**.

As you type a chart title, Excel displays the text in the Formula Bar. The text does not display in the chart title until after you press Enter.

> **TROUBLESHOOTING:** If you double-click a title and type directly into the title placeholder, do
> not press Enter after typing the new title. Doing so will add a blank line.

c. Click the **Home tab**, click **Bold** in the Font group, click the **Font Color arrow**, and
then select **Black, Text 1** (first row, second column in the Theme Colors section).

You applied font formats so that the chart title stands out.

d. Click the **Pie Chart sheet tab**, select the **Chart Title placeholder**, type **New Computer-Related Jobs by 2026** in the Formula Bar, and then press **Enter**.

e. Click the **Home tab**, click **Bold**, click the **Font Size arrow** and select **18**, and then click the **Font Color arrow** and select **Black, Text 1**.

You formatted the pie chart title so that it stands out.

f. Click the **Bar Chart sheet tab**, select the **Chart Title placeholder**, type **Projected Number of Jobs by 2026** in the Formula Bar, and then press **Enter**. Click **Bold**, click the **Font Size arrow**, and then select **18**. Click the **Font Color arrow** and click **Black, Text 1** font color to the chart title.

g. Click the **Outlook sheet tab**, select the **Chart Title placeholder**, type **Number of Computer-Related Jobs 2016 and 2026**, and then press **Enter**.

h. Click **Bold**, click the **Font Color arrow**, and then select **Dark Blue** in the Standard Colors section. Save the workbook.

You formatted the bar chart title to have a similar font color as the worksheet title.

STEP 2 ADD AND FORMAT AXIS TITLES AND FORMAT THE AXES

For the column chart, you want to add and format a title to describe the job titles on the category axis. In addition, you want to simplify the value axis values to avoid displaying *,000* for each increment and add the title *Thousands*. Refer to Figure 3.33 as you complete Step 2.

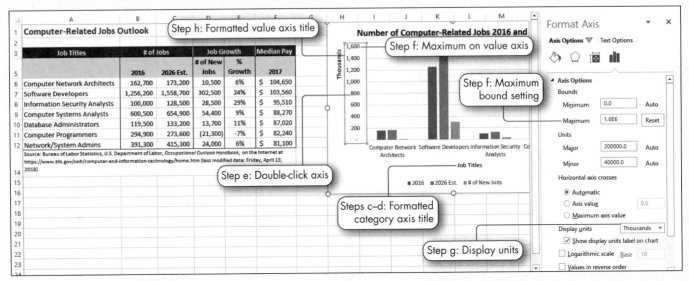

FIGURE 3.33 Formatted Axis Titles and Axes

a. Select the column chart on the Outlook worksheet and click **Chart Elements** to the right of the chart.

Excel displays the Chart Elements menu.

> **MAC TROUBLESHOOTING:** Click the Chart Design tab and click Add Chart Elements.

b. Point to **Axis Titles**, click the **Axis Titles arrow**, and then click the **Primary Horizontal check box** to select it. Click **Chart Elements** to close the menu.

Excel displays Axis Title below the horizontal axis.

c. Ensure that the Axis Title placeholder is selected, type **Job Titles**, and then press **Enter**.

d. Click the **Home tab**, click the **Font Color arrow**, and then click **Dark Blue** in the Standard Colors section.

e. Point to the **vertical axis**. When you see the ScreenTip, *Vertical (Value) Axis*, double-click the values on the vertical axis.

The Format Axis task pane opens for you to format the value axis.

f. Select **1.8E6** in the Maximum Bounds box, type **1.6E6**, and then press **Enter**.

You changed the maximum value on the value axis from 1,800,000 to 1,600,000.

g. Click the **Display units arrow** and select **Thousands**.

> **TROUBLESHOOTING:** If the Display units setting is not shown, click the Axis Options icon, and click Axis Options to display the options.

The axis now displays values such as 1,600 instead of 1,600,000. The title *Thousands* displays in the top-left corner of the value axis.

h. Click the **Home tab**, select the value axis title **Thousands**, and then apply **Dark Blue** font color in the Font group. Close the task pane. Save the workbook.

STEP 3 › ADD AND FORMAT DATA LABELS

The pie chart includes a legend to identify which color represents each computer-related job; however, it does not include numeric labels to help you interpret what percentage of all computer-related jobs will be hired for each position. You want to insert and format percentage value labels. Refer to Figure 3.34 as you complete Step 3.

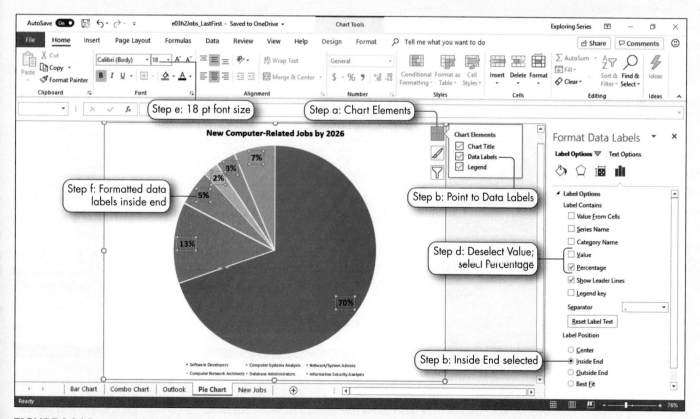

FIGURE 3.34 Formatted Data Labels

a. Click the **Pie Chart sheet tab** and click **Chart Elements**. (On a Mac, click Add Chart Element on the Chart Design tab.)

b. Click the **Data Labels arrow** and select **Inside End**. Close the Chart Elements menu.

You added data labels to the pie slices. The default data labels show the number of new jobs in the pie slices.

c. Right-click one of the data labels and select **Format Data Labels** to open the Format Data Labels task pane.

d. Click **Label Options**, click the **Percentage check box** to select it, and then click the **Value check box** to deselect it. Close the Format Data Labels task pane.

Typically, pie chart data labels show percentages instead of values.

e. Click **Bold** and change the font size to **18**. Save the workbook.

STEP 4 FORMAT THE CHART AREA, ADD ALT TEXT, AND FORMAT A DATA POINT

You want to apply a texture fill to the chart area to create a softer appearance around the chart. In addition, you want to change the fill color and explode for the Computer Systems Analysts slice. Refer to Figure 3.35 as you complete Step 4.

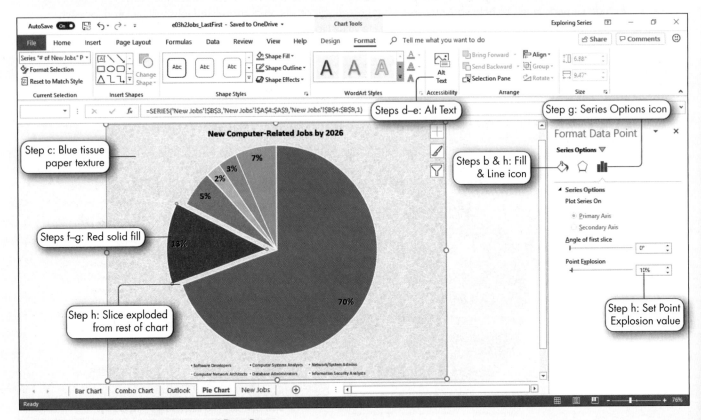

FIGURE 3.35 Formatted Chart Area and Data Point

a. Point to the **chart area** (the white space in the chart) and double-click when you see the Chart Area ScreenTip.

b. Click the **Fill & Line icon** in the Format Chart Area task pane and click **Fill**.

The task pane displays different fill options.

c. Click **Picture or texture fill**, click the **Texture arrow**, and then click **Blue tissue paper** (fourth row, second column).

The chart area now has the blue tissue paper texture fill.

d. Click the **Format tab** and click **Alt Text** in the Accessibility group.

The Alt Text task pane displays.

MAC TROUBLESHOOTING: Double-click the chart and click Edit Alt Text.

---

e. Type **Displays the percentage of new computer jobs by job title.** (including the period) in the text box. Close the Alt Text task pane.

You entered a description of the chart.

f. Click the **13% Computer Systems Analyst slice** (which is currently filled with Orange, Accent 2 color), pause, and then click the **Computer Systems Analyst slice** again to select just that data point (slice).

The first click selects all slices of the pie. The second click selects only the Computer Systems Analyst slice so that you can format that data point. Because you did not close the Format Chart Area task pane after Step c, Excel changes the task pane from Format Chart Area to Format Data Point when you select a data point.

g. Click the **Fill & Line icon**, click **Solid fill**, click the **Color arrow**, and then click **Red** in the Standard Colors section.

You changed the fill color from Orange, Accent 2 to Red.

h. Click the **Series Options icon** in the Format Data Point task pane and click the **Point Explosion increment** to **10%**. Close the task pane.

The Computer Systems Analyst slide is now exploded 10% to emphasize that slice.

i. Save the workbook. Keep the workbook open if you plan to continue with the next Hands-On Exercise. If not, close the workbook and exit Excel.

Chart Design and Sparklines

After you add and format chart elements, consider experimenting with other features to enhance a chart. The Chart Tools Design tab contains the Chart Styles and Data groups. These groups contain options to apply a different style or color scheme to a chart or manipulate the data that are used to build a chart. You can also use Chart Styles and Chart Filters to the right of a chart to change the design of a chart. Furthermore, as an alternative to regular charts, you can insert sparklines into cells to provide a quick visualization of a trend in a series of values.

In this section, you will learn how to apply chart styles and colors, filter chart data, and insert and customize miniature charts (sparklines) within individual cells.

STEP 1 ▶ Applying a Chart Style and Colors

After you create a chart and include the chart elements you want, you can change the appearance of the chart by applying a different chart style. A *chart style* is a collection of formatting that controls the colors of the chart area, plot area, and data series, as well as the font and font size of the titles. The colors and font attributes are based on the colors defined by the theme applied to the workbook. Selecting a different chart style can save you time from individually applying different colors to the various chart elements.

Figure 3.36 shows the options when you click Chart Styles to the right of the chart, and Figure 3.37 shows the Chart Styles gallery that displays from Chart Styles on the Design tab. The styles in the Chart Styles gallery reflect what is available for the currently selected chart, such as a pie chart. If you select a different type of chart, the gallery will display styles for that type of chart.

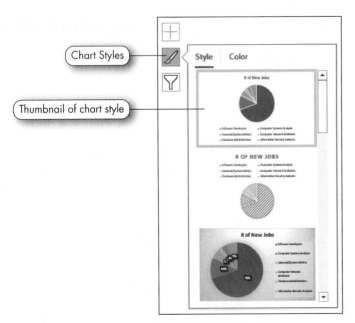

FIGURE 3.36 Chart Styles

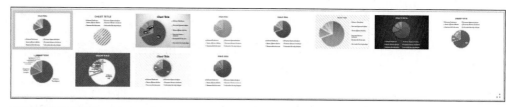

FIGURE 3.37 Chart Styles Gallery

Use Change Colors in the Chart Style group on the Design tab to select a different set of predefined colorful or monochromatic combinations of the colors defined by the workbook theme. The colorful set includes different colors, whereas the monochromatic colors displays different shades of the same color.

TIP: CHANGING THE WORKBOOK THEME

Explore how different themes impact the colors and formats in your charts by changing the workbook theme. Use Themes on the Page Layout tab to apply a different theme to the workbook, which controls the Change Colors palette and the colors, fonts, and other formatting applied to your charts. You can also customize a workbook theme to use the exact colors you want for the worksheet data as well as the chart elements.

Save a Chart as a Template

You can save a chart as a template to be able to create other charts with those chart elements, formats, and colors. Right-click the chart and select Save as Template from the menu. Enter a name for the chart template and save it. The chart template is available when you display the Insert Chart or the Change Chart Type dialog box and select Templates. If you use the chart template to create a chart in another workbook, Excel uses the chart template colors, not the workbook theme colors.

Modifying the Data Source

The data source is the range of worksheet cells that are used to construct a chart. Although you should select the data source carefully before creating a chart, you may decide to alter that data source after you create and format the chart. The Data group on the Design tab is useful for adjusting the data source. Furthermore, you can apply filters to display or hide a data series without adjusting the entire data source.

STEP 2 ### Change the Data Source

Use the Select Data command in the Data group on the Design tab to open the Select Data Source dialog box (see Figure 3.38). This dialog box is a way to filter which categories and data series are visible in your chart. Furthermore, this dialog box enables you to change the source data range, as well as add, edit, or remove data that is being used to create the chart. Specifically, use this dialog box to add any category labels you forgot to include when you selected the original data source before creating the chart or use this dialog box to remove a data series. For example, you can use this dialog box to remove the 2016 data series or the Software Developers category from being included in the chart.

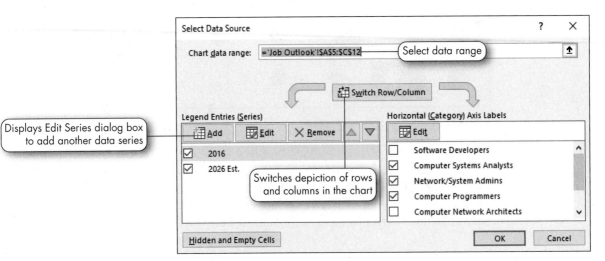

FIGURE 3.38 Select Data Source Dialog Box

Switch Row and Column Data

Recall earlier in the chapter that you learned that data in rows are used to create categories, and data in columns create data series. You can switch data used to create the horizontal axis and the legend to give a different perspective and to change the focus on the data. For example, after displaying years as data series to compare different years for categories, you can switch the data to show years on the category axis to compare job titles within the same year. In Figure 3.39, the chart on the left uses the job titles to build the category axis and the years to build the data series and legend. The chart on the right shows the results after switching the data: the job titles build the data series and legend, and the years display on the category axis. The Switch Row/Column command in the Data group on the Design tab switches how the rows and columns are depicted in the selected chart, or you can switch rows and columns from within the Select Data Source dialog box.

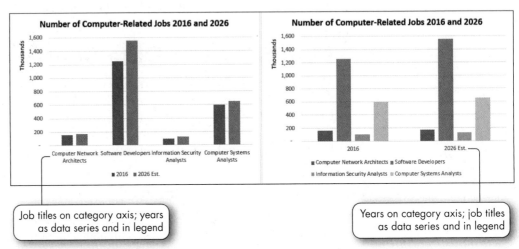

FIGURE 3.39 Original Chart and Chart with Switched Rows/Columns

Apply Chart Filters

A *chart filter* controls which data series and categories are visible in a chart. By default, all the data you selected to create the chart are used to construct the data series and categories. However, you can apply a chart filter to focus on particular data. For example, filter the chart to focus on just one job title at a time. Use Chart Filters to the right of the chart to display the options (see Figure 3.40). A check mark indicates the data series or categories currently displayed in the chart. Use the check boxes to select (display) or deselect (hide) a data series or a category.

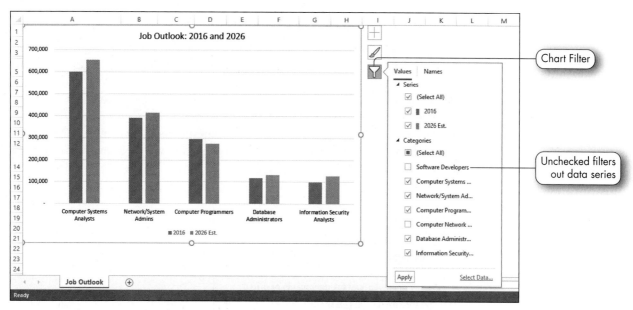

FIGURE 3.40 Chart Filter Options

> **MAC TIP:** The Chart Filters feature is not available on a Mac.

Creating and Customizing Sparklines

A *sparkline* is a small line, column, or win/loss chart contained in a single cell. The purpose of a sparkline is to present a simple visual illustration of data. Unlike a regular chart, a sparkline does not include any of the standard chart labels, such as a chart title, axis label, axis titles, legend, or data labels. Inserting sparklines next to data helps to create a visual "dashboard" to help you understand the data quickly without having to look at a full-scale chart.

Figure 3.41 shows three sample sparklines: line, column, and win/loss. The line sparkline shows trends over time, such as each student's trends in test scores. The column sparkline compares data, such as test averages for a class. The win/loss sparkline depicts the team's trends of wins and losses.

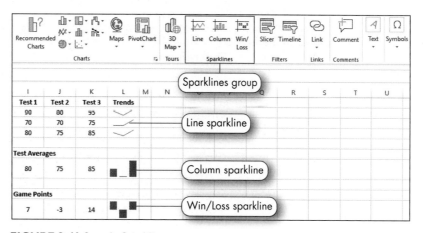

FIGURE 3.41 Sample Sparklines

STEP 3 **Insert a Sparkline**

Before creating a sparkline, identify the data range you want to depict (such as A2:C2 for the first person's test score) and where you want to place the sparkline (such as cell D2).

To insert a sparkline, complete the following steps:

1. Click the Insert tab.
2. Click Line, Column, or Win/Loss in the Sparklines group. The Create Sparklines dialog box opens (see Figure 3.42).
3. Type in the Data Range box or select the range of cell references containing the values you want to chart with the sparkline.
4. Enter or select the range where you want the sparkline to display in the Location Range box and click OK. The default cell location is the active cell unless you change it.

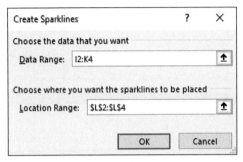

FIGURE 3.42 Create Sparklines Dialog Box

Customize a Sparkline

After you insert a sparkline, the Sparkline Tools Design tab displays (see Figure 3.43), with options to customize the sparkline. Table 3.5 lists and describes the groups on the Sparkline Tools Design tab.

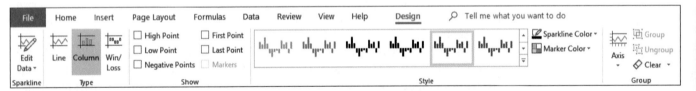

FIGURE 3.43 Sparkline Tools Design Tab

TABLE 3.5	Sparkline Tools Design Tab
Group	**Description**
Sparkline	Edits the location and data source for a group or individual data point that generates a group of sparklines or an individual sparkline.
Type	Changes the selected sparkline type (line, column, win/loss).
Show	Displays points, such as the high points, or markers within a sparkline.
Style	Changes the sparkline style, similar to a chart style, changes the sparkline color, or changes the marker color.
Group	Specifies the horizontal and vertical axis settings, groups objects together, ungroups objects, and clears sparklines.

Quick Concepts

8. Describe the relationship of a workbook theme, chart styles, and chart colors. *p. 219*
9. Explain why you would switch rows and columns in a chart. *p. 230*
10. Describe the purpose of inserting sparklines in a worksheet. *p. 231*

Hands-On Exercises

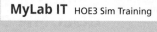

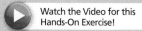
Skills covered: Apply a Chart Style • Change the Data Source • Switch Row and Column Data • Insert a Sparkline • Customize Sparklines

3 Chart Design and Sparklines

Now that you have completed the pie chart, you want to focus again on the bar chart. You are not satisfied with the overall design and want to try a different chart style. In addition, you want to include sparklines to show trends for all jobs between 2016 and 2026.

STEP 1 **APPLY A CHART STYLE**

You want to give more contrast to the bar chart. Therefore, you will apply the Style 2 chart style. That style changes the category axis labels to all capital letters and displays data labels inside each segment of each bar. Refer to Figure 3.44 as you complete Step 1.

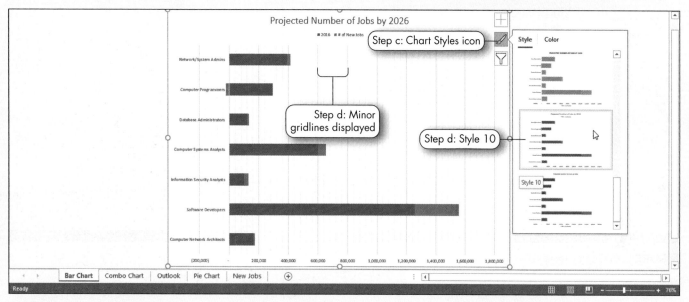

FIGURE 3.44 Chart Style Applied

a. Open *e03h2Jobs_LastFirst* if you closed it at the end of the Hands-On Exercise 2, and save it as **e03h3Jobs_LastFirst**, changing h2 to h3.

b. Click the **Bar Chart sheet tab**.

c. Click **Chart Styles** to the right of the chart.

   The gallery of chart styles opens.

> **MAC TROUBLESHOOTING:** Click the Design tab and click More in the Chart Styles group.

d. Scroll through the gallery and point to **Style 10**. When you see the ScreenTip that identifies *Style 10*, click **Style 10**. Click **Chart Styles** to close the gallery. Save the workbook.

   Excel applies the Style 10 chart style to the chart, which displays the minor gridlines in light gray between the major gridlines displayed in dark gray. The chart title font changes and is no longer bold using Style 10.

CHANGE THE DATA SOURCE AND SWITCH ROW AND COLUMN DATA

When you first created the clustered column chart, you included the number of new jobs as well as the number of 2016 jobs and the projected number of 2026 jobs. However, you decide that the number of new jobs is implied by comparing the 2016 to the 2026 jobs. Therefore, you want to change the data source to exclude the number of new jobs. In addition, you want to switch the data series from years to job titles for a different perspective. Refer to Figure 3.45 as you complete Step 2.

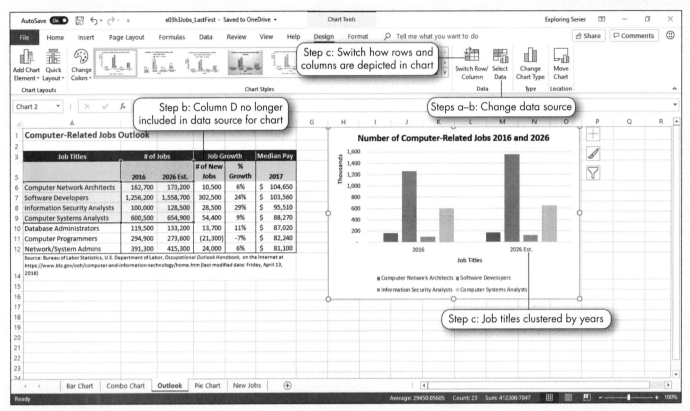

FIGURE 3.45 Chart Filters

a. Click the **Outlook sheet tab**, select the **column chart**, click the **Design tab**, and then click **Select Data**.

The Select Data Source dialog box opens.

b. Change D to **C** in =Outlook!$A$5:$D$9 in the Chart data range box and click **OK**.

The number of new jobs (gray) data series no longer displays in the clustered column chart.

c. Click **Switch Row/Column** in the Data group on the Design tab. Save the workbook.

The columns are arranged by clustering data series for each year rather than clustering the two years for each job title. The legend shows the color coding for the job titles data series.

STEP 3 INSERT AND CUSTOMIZE SPARKLINES

You want to insert sparklines to show the trends between 2016 and 2026. After inserting the sparklines, you want to display the high points to show that all jobs will have major increases by 2026. Refer to Figure 3.46 as you complete Step 3.

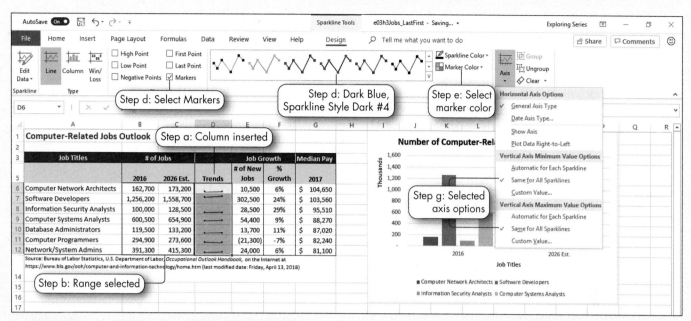

FIGURE 3.46 Sparkline Tools Design Tab

a. Click **cell D6** on the Outlook sheet, click the **Insert arrow** in the Cells group, and then select **Insert Sheet Columns**. Type **Trends** in **cell D5**.

   You inserted a new column so that you can place the sparklines close to the data you want to visualize.

b. Select the **range B6:C12**, click the **Insert tab**, and then click **Line** in the Sparklines group.

   The selected range is entered in the Data Range box in the Create Sparklines dialog box.

MAC TROUBLESHOOTING: Click Sparklines and click Line.

---

c. Select the **range D6:D12** to enter that range in the Location Range box. Click **OK**.

   Excel inserts sparklines in the range D6:D12 with each sparkline representing data on its respective row. The Sparkline Tools Design tab displays.

d. Click the **Markers check box** in the Show group to select it and click **Dark Blue, Sparkline Style Dark #4** in the Style group.

e. Click **Marker Color** in the Style group, point to **Markers**, and then select **Dark Red** in the Standard Colors section.

f. Click **Axis** in the Group group and click **Same for All Sparklines** in the Vertical Axis Minimum Value Options section. Click **Axis** again and click **Same for All Sparklines** in the Vertical Axis Maximum Value Options section.

   Because the sparklines look identical in trends, you changed the axis settings to set the minimum and maximum values as relative to the sparkline values in the entire selected range of rows rather than the default setting that bases the minimum and maximum for each row.

g. Save and close the file. Based on your instructor's directions, submit e03h3Jobs_LastFirst.

Chapter Objectives Review

After reading this chapter, you have accomplished the following objectives:

I. Create a basic chart.

- Select the data source: Select row and column headings to create column and bar charts. To select a nonadjacent range, press and hold Ctrl while selecting the ranges. Each value is a data point, and several related data points create a data series in a chart. A legend displays a key to identify the color for each data series. The category axis displays categories of data, and the value axis displays increments of the values used in the chart.

- Use the Insert tab to create a chart: Use commands in the Charts group to create charts. When you click a command, a menu displays specific chart types. Excel creates the selected chart using the data you selected.

- Create a column chart: A clustered column chart compares groups of side-by-side columns where the height of the column indicates its value. The taller the column, the larger the value. A stacked column chart shows relationships of individual data points to the whole. The row headings display on the category axis, and the value axis displays incremental numbers based on the values contained in the columns.

- Move a chart: Use the Cut and Paste commands to move a selected chart to a different area within a worksheet. Use Move Chart in the Location group on the Design tab to display the Move Chart dialog box. Select New sheet and enter a name to move the chart to a chart sheet. The chart is the only object on that sheet.

- Size a chart: If a chart is on a regular worksheet, you can adjust the chart size by dragging a sizing handle or specifying exact measurements in the Size group on the Format tab. Use the Size group on the Format tab to ensure the chart size does not change if you adjust row height, adjust column widths, or add or delete columns or rows.

- Distribute a chart: Before distributing a chart, ensure the worksheets are set up so that recipients can easily print the chart. To print a chart with its data series, the chart needs to be on the same worksheet as the data source. To ensure both the data and the chart print, make sure the chart is not selected. If the chart is on its own sheet or if you select the chart on a worksheet containing other data, the chart will print as a full-size chart.

2. Use other methods to create charts.

- Create a recommended chart: Use the Recommended Charts command in the Charts group on the Insert tab to display the Insert Chart dialog box. Excel displays a gallery of recommended charts based on the selected data. The dialog box displays a message indicating the purpose of the selected chart.

- Change the chart type: After creating a chart, you can change it to a different type by clicking Change Chart Type in the Type group on the Design tab.

- Create a chart with Quick Analysis: When you select a range of adjacent cells and position the pointer over that selected range, Excel displays Quick Analysis near the bottom-right corner of the selected area. Quick Analysis displays thumbnails of recommended charts based on the data you selected so that you can create a chart quickly.

- Create a chart with Ideas: The Ideas feature provides intelligent analysis of a dataset to recommend potentially useful charts. The Ideas task pane displays thumbnails of charts. Click Insert Chart to insert a recommended chart.

3. Create other charts.

- Create a bar chart: A bar chart compares values across categories using horizontal bars where the width of the bar indicates its value. The wider the bar, the larger the value. A stacked bar chart shows relationships of individual data points to the whole.

- Create a line chart: A line chart compares trends over time. Values are displayed on the value axis, and time periods are displayed on the category axis.

- Create a pie chart: A pie chart indicates the proportion to the whole for one data series. The size of the slice indicates the size of the value. The larger the pie slice, the larger the value.

- Create a combo chart: A combo chart combines elements of two chart types, such as column and line, to depict different data, such as individual data points compared to averages or percentages.

- Create other types of charts: An X Y (scatter) chart shows a relationship between two numeric variables. A stock chart shows fluctuations in prices of stock, such as between the opening and closing prices on a specific day.

4. Add and format chart elements.

- Click Chart Elements to the top-right of the selected chart to add elements. Chart elements include a chart title, axis titles, data labels, legend, gridlines, chart area, plot area, data series, and data point.

- Apply a Quick Layout: Applying a layout adds several chart elements conveniently at one time. Each layout specifies which chart elements are displayed and their locations.

- Edit, position, and format chart titles: The default chart title is Chart Title, but you should edit it to provide a descriptive title for the chart. Apply font formats, such as bold, font size, and font color, to the chart title. Position the chart title above the chart, centered and overlaid, or in other locations.

- Add and format axis titles: Display titles for the value and category axes to help describe the axes better. Use the Format Axis Title task pane to customize the axis title. When you click an icon at the top of the task pane, specific options display related to that category.

- Format the axes: Use the Format Axis task pane to set the minimum and maximum bounds, set the major and minor intervals on the value axis, change the unit of display for the value axis, display major and minor tick marks, specify location of the interval labels on the axis, and format numbers.
- Add, position, and format data labels: Data labels provide exact values for a data series. Select the position of the data labels and the content of the data labels. Use the Format Data Labels task pane to customize and format data labels.
- Position and format the legend: Position the legend to the right, top, bottom, or left of the plot area. Change the font size to adjust the label sizes within the legend.
- Add and format gridlines: Gridlines help the reader read across a column chart. Use the Format Major Gridlines task pane to change the line type, color, and width of the gridlines.
- Format the chart area, plot area, and data series: The Format task panes enable you to apply fill colors, select border colors, and apply other settings.
- Include Alt Text: Alternative text is used by a screen reader to help people understand the content of an object, such as a chart. Click Alt Text in the Accessibility group on the Design tab to display the Alt Text task pane. Enter a description of the chart in the text box within the task pane.
- Format a data point: Format a single data point, such as changing the fill color for a single pie slice or specifying the percentage to explode a slice in a pie chart.

5. Apply a chart style and colors.

- A chart style feature applies predetermined formatting, such as the background color and the data series color.
- Save a chart as a template: You can save a chart as a template to be able to create other charts with those chart elements, formats, and colors. The chart template is available when you display the Insert Chart or Change Chart Type dialog box and select Templates.

6. Modify the data source.

- Change the data source: Use the Select Data Source dialog box to filter chart data and change the range of data being used to create the chart.
- Switch row and column data: You can switch the way data is used to create a chart by switching data series and categories.
- Apply chart filters: Use the Select Data Source dialog box to modify the ranges used for the data series. When you deselect a series, Excel removes that series from the chart.

7. Create and customize sparklines.

- Insert a sparkline: A sparkline is a miniature chart in a cell representing a single data series. The Sparklines group on the Insert tab contains commands to insert a line, column, or win/loss sparkline.
- Customize a sparkline: Change the data source, location, and style. Display markers and change line or marker colors.

Key Terms Matching

Match the key terms with their definitions. Write the key term letter by the appropriate numbered definition.

a. Axis title

b. Bar chart

c. Category axis

d. Chart area

e. Chart title

f. Clustered column chart

g. Combo chart

h. Data label

i. Data point

j. Data series

k. Gridline

l. Legend

m. Line chart

n. Pie chart

o. Plot area

p. Sizing handle

q. Sparkline

r. Task pane

s. Value axis

t. X Y (scatter) chart

1. _____ A chart that groups columns side by side to compare data points among categories. **p. 196**

2. _____ A miniature chart contained in a single cell. **p. 231**

3. _____ A chart that shows trends over time in which the value axis indicates quantities and the horizontal axis indicates time. **p. 204**

4. _____ The label that describes the entire chart. **p. 213**

5. _____ The label that describes either the category axis or the value axis. **p. 213**

6. _____ The key that identifies the color or pattern fill assigned to each data series in a chart. **p. 213**

7. _____ A chart that compares categories of data horizontally. **p. 204**

8. _____ A chart that shows each data point in proportion to the whole data series. **p. 205**

9. _____ A numeric value that describes a single value on a chart. **p. 195**

10. _____ A chart that contains two chart types, such as column and line, to depict two types of data, such as individual data points and percentages. **p. 206**

11. _____ A circle that enables you to adjust the height or width of a selected chart. **p. 200**

12. _____ A horizontal or vertical line that extends from the horizontal or vertical axis through the plot area. **p. 213**

13. _____ A chart that shows the relationship between two variables. **p. 206**

14. _____ A group of related data points that display in row(s) or column(s) in a worksheet. **p. 195**

15. _____ A window that contains options specific to a selected text, an object or a feature, such as options to format and customize chart elements. **p. 203**

16. _____ A chart element that contains descriptive labels for the data points plotted in a chart. **p. 195**

17. _____ The section of a chart that contains graphical representation of the values in a data series. **p. 213**

18. _____ A container for the entire chart and all of its elements. **p. 213**

19. _____ An identifier that shows the exact value of a data point in a chart. **p. 213**

20. _____ The chart element that displays incremental numbers to identify approximate values, such as dollars or units, of data points in a chart. **p. 195**

Multiple Choice

1. Which type of chart is the *least* appropriate for depicting yearly rainfall totals for five cities for four years?
   - (a) Pie chart
   - (b) Line chart
   - (c) Column chart
   - (d) Bar chart

2. Why would Series 1 and Series 2 display in a chart legend?
   - (a) The data are contained in one column.
   - (b) The data are contained only in one row.
   - (c) Column headings were not selected when creating a chart.
   - (d) The selected headings are in non-adjacent cells to the values.

3. You moved a chart to its own chart sheet. What chart element can you add to provide a grid that contains a copy of the data source at the bottom of the chart?
   - (a) Axis title
   - (b) Data table
   - (c) Gridlines
   - (d) Error bars

4. You want to create a single chart that shows the proportion of yearly sales for five divisions for each year for five years. Which type of chart can accommodate your needs?
   - (a) Pie chart
   - (b) Surface chart
   - (c) Clustered column chart
   - (d) 100% stacked column chart

5. A combo chart displays the number of new jobs on the primary value axis, percentage growth on the secondary value axis, job titles in the category axis, "New Job Growth by 2026" as the chart title, but no legend. Which is the *least important* title to include in the chart?
   - (a) The chart title *New Job Growth by 2026*
   - (b) The primary value axis title *Number of New Jobs*
   - (c) The category axis *Job Titles*
   - (d) The secondary value axis title *Percentage Growth*

6. The value axis currently shows increments such as 50,000 and 100,000. What option would you select to display the values in increments of 50 and 100?
   - (a) Show Axis in Thousands
   - (b) More Primary Vertical Axis Title Options
   - (c) Show Axis in Millions
   - (d) Show Right to Left Axis

7. If you want to show exact values for a data series in a bar chart, which chart element should you display?
   - (a) Chart title
   - (b) Legend
   - (c) Value axis title
   - (d) Data labels

8. You applied a chart style to a clustered column chart. However, you want to experiment with other settings to change the colors used in the chart without individually changing colors. Which of the following *does not* apply changes to the entire chart?
   - (a) Change the workbook theme.
   - (b) Change colors in the Format Data Series task pane.
   - (c) Select a color set from the Change Colors palette.
   - (d) Change the colors for the workbook theme.

9. Currently, a column chart shows values on the value axis, years on the category axis, and state names in the legend. What should you do if you want to organize data with the states on the category axis and the years shown in the legend?
   - (a) Click Switch Row/Column in the Data group on the Design tab.
   - (b) Change the chart type to a clustered column chart.
   - (c) Click Layout 2 in the Chart Layouts group on the Design tab and apply a different chart style.
   - (d) Click Legend in the Labels group on the Layout tab and select Show Legend at Bottom.

10. You created a worksheet that tracks data for a basketball team. The range B10:F10 contains the difference in final points between your team and the other team. What is the recommended sparkline to create to represent this data?
    - (a) Line
    - (b) Column
    - (c) Win/Loss
    - (d) Plus/Minus

Practice Exercises

1 Loza Family Utility Expenses

Your cousin, Alexander Loza, wants to analyze her family's utility expenses for 2021. She gave you her files for the electric, gas, and water bills for the year. You created a worksheet that lists the individual expenses per month, along with yearly totals per utility type and monthly totals. You will create some charts to depict the data. Refer to Figure 3.47 as you complete this exercise.

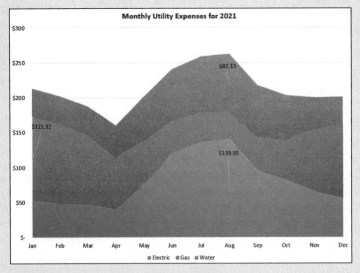

FIGURE 3.47 Loza Family Utility Expenses

a. Open *e03p1Utilities* and save it as **e03p1Utilities_LastFirst**.

b. Select the **range A4:E17**, click **Quick Analysis**, click **Charts**, and then select **Clustered Column**. If Quick Analysis displays two Clustered Column thumbnails, select the thumbnail that shows monthly totals in columns (not as a line).

> **MAC TROUBLESHOOTING:** Quick Analysis is not available on a Mac. Click the Insert tab and click Clustered Column.

c. Click **Chart Filters** to the right of the chart and do the following:
- Click the **Monthly Totals check box** to deselect it in the Series group
- Scroll through the Categories group and click the **Yearly Totals check box** to deselect it.
- Click **Apply** to remove totals from the chart. Click **Chart Filters** to close the menu.

> **MAC TROUBLESHOOTING:** Chart Filters is not available on a Mac.

d. Point to the **chart area**. When you see the Chart Area ScreenTip, drag the chart so that the top-left corner of the chart is in **cell A21**.

e. Click the **Format tab** and change the size by doing the following:
- Click in the **Shape Height box** in the Size group, type **3.5"**, and then press **Enter**.
- Click in the **Shape Width box** in the Size group, type **6"**, and then press **Enter**.

f. Click the **Design tab**, click **Quick Layout** in the Chart Layouts group, and then click **Layout 3**.

g. Select the **Chart Title placeholder**, type **Monthly Utility Expenses for 2021**, and then press **Enter**.

h. Click the chart and click **Style 6** in the Chart Styles group.

i. Click the **Home tab**, click **Copy** on the Clipboard group, click **cell A39**, and then click **Paste**. With the second chart selected, do the following:

- Click the **Design tab**, click **Change Chart Type** in the Type group, click **Line** on the left side of the dialog box, select **Line with Markers** in the top-center section, and then click **OK**.
- Click the **Electric data series line** to select it and click the **highest marker (August)** to select only that marker. Click **Chart Elements** and click the **Data Labels check box** to select it.

> **MAC TROUBLESHOOTING:** Click Add Chart Element, point to Data Labels, and then select Above.

- Double-click the **data label** to display the Format Data Labels task pane. Make sure Label Options is bold, click the **Label Options icon**, scroll through the task pane and click **Number**, scroll down, click the **Category arrow**, and then select **Accounting**.
- Click the **Gas data series line** to select it and click the **highest marker (January)** to select only that marker. With the Chart Elements menu displayed, click the **Data Labels check box** to select it.
- Click the **Water data series line** to select it and click the highest marker (August) to select only that marker. With the Chart Elements menu displayed, click the **Data Labels check box** to select it. Click **Chart Elements** to close the menu.
- Double-click the **Water data label** to display the Format Data Labels task pane. Make sure Label Options is bold, click the **Label Options icon**, scroll through the task pane and click **Number**, scroll down, click the **Category arrow**, and then select **Accounting**.
- Select the chart, copy it, and then paste it in **cell A57**.

j. Ensure that the third chart is selected and do the following:

- Click the **Design tab**, click **Change Chart Type** in the Type group, select **Area** on the left side, select **Stacked Area** in the top-center section of the dialog box, and then click **OK**.

> **MAC TROUBLESHOOTING:** Point to Line, scroll down if necessary, and then under 2-D Area, click Stacked Area.

- Click **Move Chart** in the Location group, click **New sheet**, type **Area Chart**, and then click **OK**.
- Select each data label and change the font size to **12**. Move each data label up closer to the top of the respective shaded area. Each label now has a line pointing to where the label had been originally. Apply **Accounting Number Format** to any data labels that did not retain this format.
- Select the **value axis** and change the font size to **12**.
- Right-click the **value axis** and select **Format Axis**. Scroll down in the Format Axis task pane, click **Number**, click in the **Decimal places box**, and then type **0**. Close the Format Axis task pane.
- Change the font size to **12** for the category axis and the legend.

k. Click the **Expenses sheet tab**, select the **line chart**, and do the following:

- Click the **Design tab**, click **Move Chart** in the Location group, click **New sheet**, type **Line Chart**, and then click **OK**.
- Change the font size to **12** for the value axis, category axis, data labels, and legend.
- Apply **Accounting Number Format** to any data labels that did not retain this format.
- Format the vertical axis with zero decimal places.
- Right-click the **chart area**, select **Format Chart Area**, click **Fill**, click **Gradient fill**, click the **Preset gradients arrow**, and then select **Light Gradient – Accent 1**. Close the Format Chart Area task pane.

l. Click the **Expenses sheet**, click the chart area of the **column chart**, click the **Format tab**, and then click **Alt Text** in the Accessibility group. Type **The chart compares the electric, gas, and water bills for each month in 2021.** (including the period) in the text box in the Alt Text task pane. Enter the same Alt Text for the other two charts.

m. Click the **Expenses sheet**, select the **range B5:D16**, and then do the following:

- Click the **Insert tab**, click **Line** in the Sparkline group, click in the **Location Range box**, type **B18:D18**, and then click **OK**.

> **MAC TROUBLESHOOTING:** Click Sparklines and click Line.

- Click the **High Point check box** to select it and click the **Low Point check box** to select it in the Show group with all three sparklines selected.
- Click the **Page Layout tab**. Change the **Width** and **Height** in the Scale to Fit group to **1 page**.

n. Create a footer with your name on the left side, the sheet name code in the center, and the file name code on the right of each sheet. You can group the Area Chart and Line Chart sheets to create the footer, but you must select the Expenses worksheet separately to apply a footer to that sheet.

o. Save and close the file. Based on your instructor's directions, submit e03p1Utilities_LastFirst.

2 Trends in Market Value of Houses on Pine Circle

You live in a house on Pine Circle, a quiet cul-de-sac in a suburban area. Recently, you researched the market value and square footage of the five houses on Pine Circle. Now, you want to create charts to visually depict the data to compare values for the houses in the cul-de-sac. Refer to Figure 3.48 as you complete this exercise.

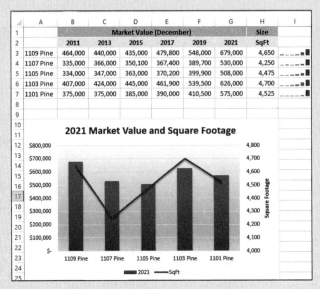

FIGURE 3.48 Market Values

a. Open *e03p2Pine* and save it as **e03p2Pine_LastFirst**.

b. Select the **range A2:E7**, click the **Insert tab**, and then click **Recommended Charts** in the Charts group. The dialog box shows two Line charts. Select the **Line chart** that shows the years on the category axis and click **OK**.

c. Click **Move Chart** in the Location group, click **New sheet**, type **Line**, and then click **OK**.

d. Click **Select Data** in the Data group on the Design tab, change E to **G** in the Chart data range so that it looks like **='Pine Circle'!$A$2:$G$7** and click **OK**.

e. Select the **Chart Title placeholder** and do the following:

- Type **Market Value of Pine Circle Houses** and press **Enter**.
- Apply bold to the chart title, change the font size to **20**, and then select **Olive Green, Accent 3, Darker 50% font color**.

f. Click the **value axis** on the left side of the chart and do the following:

- Change the font size to 12 and select **Olive Green, Accent 3, Darker 50% font color**.
- Double-click the **value axis** to open the Format Axis task pane.
- Make sure Axis Options is selected and that Text Options is selected. Type **300000** in the Minimum Bounds box and press **Enter**. The Maximum Bounds box should change to 700000 automatically.
- Scroll down in the Format Axis task pane and click **Number** to display those options.
- Click the **Category arrow** and select **Accounting**. Close the Format Axis task pane.

g. Click **Chart Elements**, click the **Axis Titles triangle**, and then click the **Primary Vertical check box** to select it. Type **December Market Values** in the Axis Title placeholder and press **Enter**.

> **MAC TROUBLESHOOTING:** Click the Chart Design tab, click Add Chart Elements, point to Axis Titles, and then click Primary Vertical.

h. Display the Chart Elements menu, click the **Gridlines triangle**, and then click the **Primary Minor Horizontal check box** to select it.

i. Click the blue **1109 Pine data series line**, click the **Data Labels check box** to select it, and then click **Chart Elements** to close the menu.

j. Click the data labels you just created, click the **Home tab**, click the **Font Color arrow**, and then select **Blue** in the Standard Colors section.

k. Select the category axis, change the font size to **12**, and then select **Olive Green, Accent 3, Darker 50% font color**.

l. Right-click the legend and select **Format Legend**. Click **Top** in the Legend Position section of the Format Legend task pane and close the task pane.

m. Right-click the **chart area** and select **Edit Alt Text**. Type **The line chart displays a line for each house from 2011 to 2021 at two-year increments.** (including the period) in the text box in the Alt Text task pane.

n. Click the **Pine Circle sheet tab** and select the **ranges A2:A7** and **G2:H7**.

o. Click the **Insert tab**, click **Insert Combo Chart** in the Charts group, and then select the **Clustered Column – Line on Secondary Axis thumbnail**.

p. Do the following to the combo chart:

- Move and resize the chart to fill the **range A10:H25**.
- Select the **Chart Title placeholder**, type **2021 Market Value and Square Footage**, and then press **Enter**.
- Double-click the value axis on the left side, make sure Axis Options is bold, click the **Axis Options icon**, scroll down in the Format Axis task pane, click **Number**, scroll down, click the **Category arrow**, and then select **Accounting**.
- Click **Chart Elements**, click the **Axis Titles triangle**, click the **Secondary Vertical check box** to select it, type **Square Footage**, and then press **Enter**. Close the Format Axis Title task pane.
- Click **Style 4** in the Chart Styles group.
- Double-click the plot area to display the Format Plot Area task pane, click the **Fill & Line icon**, click **Fill**, and then click **Gradient fill** to select it.

q. Right-click the **chart area** and select **Edit Alt Text**. Type **The combo chart displays the 2021 market value and square footage for each house on Pine Circle.** (including the period) in the text box in the Alt Text task pane.

r. Select the **range B3:G7**, click the **Insert tab**, click **Column** in the Sparklines group, make sure B3:G7 displays in the Data Range box, type **I3:I7** in the Location Range box, and then click **OK**.

s. Customize the sparklines by doing the following:

- Click **More** in the Style group and select **Orange, Sparkline Style Accent 6, Darker 25%**.
- Click **Last Point** in the Show group.

t. Create a footer with your name on the left side, the sheet name code in the center, and the file name code on the right of both sheets. You must create the footer on the chart sheet and the regular sheet separately.

u. Save and close the file. Based on your instructor's directions, submit e03p2Pine_LastFirst.

Mid-Level Exercises

1 Airport Passenger Counts

ANALYSIS CASE

As an analyst for the airline industry, you track the number of passengers at the top six major U.S. airports: Atlanta (ATL), Chicago (ORD), Los Angeles (LAX), Dallas/Fort Worth (DFW), Denver (DEN), and New York (JFK). You researched passenger data and created a worksheet that lists the number of total yearly passengers at the top six airports. To prepare for an upcoming meeting, you will create a clustered column chart to compare the number of passengers at each airport. Then, you will create a line chart that compares trends over time. Next, you will create a bar chart to compare the passenger count for the latest year of data available and then emphasize the airport with the largest number of passenger traffic. Finally, you want to insert sparklines to visually represent trends in passengers at each airport over the ten-year period. You can then refer to the sparklines and clustered column chart to answer critical-thinking questions.

a. Open *e03m1Airports* and save it as **e03m1Airports_LastFirst**.

b. Use Quick Analysis to create a clustered column chart for the **range A4:L10**. Cut the chart and paste it in **cell A15**.

c. Customize the column chart by doing the following:
   - Type **Passengers by Top U.S. Airports** as the chart title
   - Swap the data on the category axis and in the legend.
   - Set a **3.5" height** and **11.4" width**.
   - Apply the **Style 7 chart style**.

d. Adjust the value axis by doing the following:
   - Change the display units to **Millions** for the value axis.
   - Edit the axis title to display **Millions of Passengers**.

e. Display data labels above the columns for the 2016 data series only.

f. Apply the **Light Gradient - Accent 1 fill color** to the chart area.

g. Add Alt Text **The column chart displays the number of passengers in millions for the top six airports from 2006 to 2016.** (including the period).

h. Use the Page Layout tab to change the workbook theme to **Slice**.

i. Create a recommended clustered bar chart for the **range A5:A10** and **L5:L10** and move the chart to a chart sheet named **Bar Chart**.

j. Customize the bar chart by doing the following:
   - Change the chart color to **Monochromatic Palette 7**.
   - Enter **Passengers at Top 6 U.S. Airports in 2016** as the chart title.
   - Apply the **Style 5 chart style**.
   - Add Alt Text **Atlanta had the most passengers in 2016.** (including the period).

k. Modify the axes by doing the following:
   - Change the font size to **10** for the category axis and value axis.
   - Change the value axis Maximum Bound to **1.1E8**. (The Minimum Bound will change automatically.)

l. Format a data point and add gridlines by doing the following:
   - Format the Atlanta data point with solid **Dark Blue fill color**.
   - Add **Primary Minor Vertical gridlines**.

m. Create a line chart using **the range A4:L10** in the Passengers worksheet and move the chart to a chart sheet named **Line Chart**.

n. Add a chart title **Passengers at U.S. Airports 2006-2016** and bold the title.

o. Customize the line chart by doing the following:
   - Set the **Minimum Bound** at **4.0E7** for the value axis. The Maximum Bound should change to 1.1E8 automatically.
   - Display the value axis in **Millions**. Add a value axis title **In Millions**.
   - Change the font size to **10** for the value axis and category axis.
   - Move the legend to the top.

- Filter the chart by deselecting the odd-numbered years.
- Add the Alt Text **The line chart displays trends for top six U.S. airports from 2006 to 2016 at two-year intervals.** (including the period).

p. Display the Passenger worksheet and insert **Line sparklines** in the **range M5:M10** to illustrate the data in the **range B5:L10**. This should insert a sparkline to represent yearly data for each airport.

q. Customize the sparklines by doing the following:
- Show the high and low points in each sparkline.
- Apply **Black, Text 1 color** to the high point marker in each sparkline.

r. Display the Questions worksheet. Read the question in cell B2 and type the answer in **cell A2**. Read the rest of the questions in column B and type the correct answers in column A in the respective cells.

s. Group the Bar Chart and Line Chart sheets and insert a footer with your name on the left side, the sheet name code in the center, and the file name code on the right on all worksheets. Group the Passenger and Questions sheets and insert a footer with the same data. Change to Normal view.

t. Set the page formats for the Passenger worksheet:
- Select **Legal paper size** and **Landscape orientation**.
- Set **0.3"** left and right margins.
- Scale to fit to 1 page.

u. Save and close the file. Based on your instructor's directions, submit e03m1Airports_LastFirst.

2 | Grade Analysis

You are a teaching assistant for Dr. Elizabeth Croghan's BUS 101 Introduction to Business class. You have maintained her gradebook all semester, entering three test scores for each student and calculating the final average. You created a section called Final Grade Distribution that contains calculations to identify the number of students who earned an A, B, C, D, or F. Dr. Croghan wants you to create a chart that shows the percentage of students who earn each letter grade. Therefore, you decide to create and format a pie chart. You will also create a bar chart to show a sample of the students' test scores. Furthermore, Dr. Croghan wants to see if a correlation exists between attendance and students' final grades; therefore, you will create a scatter chart depicting each student's percentage of attendance with his or her respective final grade average.

a. Open *e03m2Grades* and save it as **e03m2Grades_LastFirst**.

b. Use the Insert tab to create a pie chart from the Final Grade Distribution data located below the student data in the **range F35:G39** and move the pie chart to its own sheet named **Final Grade Distribution**.

c. Customize the pie chart with these specifications:
- Apply the **Style 12 chart style.**
- Type **BUS 101 Final Grades: Fall 2021** for the chart title.
- Explode the A grade slice by **7%**.
- Change the F grade slice to **Dark Red**.
- Remove the legend.
- Add Alt Text **The pie chart shows the percentage of the class that earned each letter grade. Most students earned B and C grades.** (including the period).

d. Add data labels and customize the labels with these specifications:
- Display these data labels: **Percentage** and **Category Name** in the Inside End position. Remove other data labels.
- Change the font size to **20** and apply **Black, Text 1 font color**.

e. Create a clustered bar chart using the **ranges A5:D5** and **A18:D23** in the Grades worksheet and move the bar chart to its own sheet named **Sample Student Scores**.

f. Customize the bar chart with these specifications:
- Apply the **Style 5 chart style**.
- Type **Sample Student Test Scores** for the chart title.
- Format the plot area with the **Light Gradient - Accent 2 fill color**.
- Position the legend on the right side and change the font size to **11**.
- Format the Final Exam data series with **Blue-Gray, Text 2 fill color**.
- Add data labels in the Outside End position.
- Select the **category axis** and display the categories in reverse order in the Format Axis task pane so that O'Hair is listed at the top and Sager is listed at the bottom of the bar chart.
- Add Alt Text **The bar chart shows test scores for six students in the middle of the list. Quinn earned the highest scores on all tests.** (including the period).

g. Create a scatter chart using the **range E5:F31** in the Grades worksheet, the attendance record and final averages from the Grades worksheet. Cut the chart and paste it in **cell A42**. Adjust the width to **5.5"** and the height to **5.96"**.

h. Add Alt Text **The scatter chart shows the relationship of each student's final grade and his or her attendance record.** (including the period).

i. Apply these label settings to the scatter chart:
- Type **Final Average-Attendance Relationship** for the chart title and bold the title.
- Add the following primary horizontal axis title: **Percentage of Attendance**.
- Add the following primary vertical axis title: **Student Final Averages**.

j. Select the **vertical axis**. Change the Minimum Bound to **40**, the Maximum Bound to **100**, and select **Number** format with zero decimal places.

k. Select the **horizontal axis**. Change the Minimum Bound to **40** and the Maximum Bound to **100**.

l. Apply the **Parchment texture fill** to the plot area.

m. Add a **linear trendline** chart element.

n. Insert Column sparklines in the **range H6:H31** using the **range B6:D31** as the data source. Display the low points. Format the sparklines axis by using the same minimum value for all sparklines and the same maximum value for all sparklines. Change the row height to **22** for rows 6 through 31.

o. Insert a footer with your name on the left, the sheet name code in the center, and the file name code on the right on all the sheets. Group the two chart sheets together to insert the footer. Then insert the footer on the Grades sheet. Change to Normal view.

p. Save and close the file. Based on your instructor's directions, submit e03m2Grades_LastFirst.

Running Case

New Castle County Technical Services

New Castle County Technical Services (NCCTS) provides technical support services for a number of companies in New Castle County, Delaware. You previously created formulas to determine the number of days and hours logged and amount billed for each call. Since then, you have grouped the customers and call type data to determine some general trends. You will create charts to depict this summary data visually.

a. Open *e03r1NCCTS* and save it as **e03r1NCCTS_LastFirst**.

b. Create a pie chart using the range **G4:H14** on the Summary Stats worksheet.

c. Move the chart as an object in the Summary Charts worksheet. Move the chart so that it starts in **cell A3**. Set a **5.9"** height and **8"** width.

d. Apply the **Style 6 chart style**.

e. Change the chart title to **Total Days Open by Service Type** and apply **Black, Text 1 font color**.

f. Filter out VoIP Service, Security Camera Maintenance, and Other.

g. Remove the legend, apply the Percentage and Category Name data labels, and position the data labels on the Outside End.

h. Add Alt Text **The pie chart displays each service type as a percentage of all service types, excluding VoIP Service, Security Camera Maintenance, and Other.** (including the period).

i. Create a bar chart using the **ranges A4:A21** and **D4:D21** on the Summary Stats worksheet.

j. Move the chart as an object in the Summary Charts worksheet. Move the chart so that it starts in **cell N3**. Set a **5.9"** height and **7.3"** width.

k. Apply the **Style 6 chart style**.

l. Change the chart title to **Total Amount Billed by Customer** and apply **Black, Text 1 font color**.

m. Select The Trophy Factory data point and format it with **Dark Blue fill color** to stand out.

n. Format the value axis with zero decimal places.

o. Add Alt Text **The bar chart displays the amount billed to each customer for March.** (including the period).

p. Create a custom combo chart using the **ranges G4:H14** and **J4:J14** on the Summary Stats worksheet with Total Days Open as a Clustered Column chart on the Primary Axis, and Total Amount Billed as Line Chart on the Secondary Axis.

q. Move the chart to a chart sheet named **Billings vs. Days Open**.

r. Change the chart title to **Days Open vs Amount Billed by Service Type**.

s. Apply the **Style 5 Chart Style**.

t. Format the secondary value axis with zero decimal places.

u. Add a primary value axis title **Days Open**.

v. Add Alt Text **The combo chart displays the number of days open in columns and the amount billed by service type as a line.** (including the period).

w. Insert a footer with your name on the left side, the sheet name in the center, and the file name code on the right side of Summary Charts and Billings vs Days Open worksheets. Return to Normal view.

x. Save and close the workbook. Based on your instructor's directions, submit e03r1NCCTS_LastFirst.

Disaster Recovery

Harper County Houses Sold

You want to analyze the number of houses sold by type (e.g., rambler, two story) in each quarter in Harper County. You entered quarterly data for 2021, calculated yearly total number of houses sold by each type, and quarterly total number of houses sold. You asked an intern to create a stacked column chart for the data, but the chart contains a lot of errors.

Open *e03d1Houses* and save it as **e03d1Houses_LastFirst**. Identify the errors and poor design for the chart. Below the chart, list the errors and your corrections in a two-column format. Then correct the problems in the chart. Link the chart title to the cell containing the most appropriate label in the worksheet.

Add Alt Text **The stacked column chart displays quarterly sales by house types. Two-story houses had the most sales.** (including the period). Create a footer with your name, the sheet name code, and the file name code. Adjust the margins and scaling to print the worksheet data, including the error list, and the chart on one page. Save and close the file. Based on your instructor's directions, submit e03d1Houses_LastFirst.

Fitness Gym

You and a business partner opened a fitness gym three years ago. Your partner oversees managing the operations of the gym, ensuring the right equipment is on hand, maintenance is conducted, and the appropriate classes are being offered with the right trainers and staff. You oversee managing the business aspects, such as marketing, finance, and general personnel issues. The business is nearing the end of its third year. You have put together the financials, and now you want to show the data more visually because you know it will make more sense to your business partner that way. You want to create charts and insert sparklines that show the trends to discuss with your partner.

Create and Move a Basic Chart

You want to focus on just the expenses for the current year. Creating a pie chart will help your partner visualize the breakdown of all operating expenses for that year. After you create the chart, you will move it to a new chart sheet and add a meaningful title.

1. Open *e03c1Gym* and save as **e03c1Gym_LastFirst**.
2. Insert a 2-D pie chart using the **ranges A11:A19** and **D11:D19** on the Income worksheet and move the chart to a new chart sheet named **Expenses**. Move it to the right of the Membership sheet.
3. Change the chart title to **Expenses for Year 3** and change the font size to **20**.

Create a Chart and Apply Filter

Seeing how Payroll and Cost of Sales make up most of the expenses, you want to create a chart to focus on the other expenses. You create a clustered bar chart, filter out Payroll and Cost of Sales, add a title and move the chart to the Summary worksheet.

4. Insert a clustered bar chart using the **ranges A4:D4** and **A11:D19** on the Income worksheet. Move the chart as an object on the Summary worksheet. Cut the chart and paste it in **cell I1**.
5. Change the chart title to **Expenses (Without Payroll and Cost of Sales)**.
6. Select the category axis and use the Format Axis task pane to display categories in reverse order.
7. Apply a chart filter to remove Payroll and Cost of Sales.
8. Change the Maximum Bound to **25000**.

Add and Format Chart Elements

You decide to format the pie chart with data labels and remove the legend because there are too many categories for the legend to be effective. In addition, you want to add a gradient fill color to the chart area.

9. Display the Expenses sheet and remove the legend.

10. Add **Percentage** and **Category Name data labels** and choose **Best Fit** position for the labels. Change the data labels font size to **10**.
11. Explode the Education & Training slice by **12%**.
12. Add the **Light Gradient – Accent 2 fill color** to the chart area.

Create and Modify a Column Chart

You create another chart showing the Balance sheet items. You change the chart to a clustered column and switch the row and column data to focus on each balance sheet item. You move the chart to the Summary worksheet and give it a meaningful title.

13. Insert a stacked column chart using the **ranges A4:D4, A10:D10, A15:D15**, and **A16:D16** on the Balance sheet.
14. Change the chart type to **Clustered Column** and switch the rows and columns in the chart.
15. Change the title to **3-Year Balance Sheet**.
16. Move the column chart to the Summary worksheet. Cut the chart and paste it in **cell A1**.

Create and Format a Line Chart

You create one last chart to show the trend in Memberships. You modify the vertical axis and insert an axis title and move the legend. You change the chart style to add data points and change the chart color. You move the chart to the Summary worksheet.

17. Insert a line chart using the **range I3:L15** on the Membership worksheet.
18. Adjust the vertical axis so the Minimum Bound is **200** and display a vertical axis title **# of Memberships**.
19. Apply **Chart Style 4** and change colors to **Monochromatic Palette 8**.
20. Move the legend to the top of the chart and add the chart title **3-Year Membership Trends**.
21. Move chart to the Summary worksheet. Cut the chart and paste it in **cell A17**.

Add Alt Text

You remember that you should add Alt Text for each chart as a best practice for accessibility.

22. Display the pie chart and add Alt Text **Displays percentage of expenses for Year 3.** (including the period).
23. Display the column chart and add Alt Text **Displays total assets, total liabilities, and retained earnings.** (including the period).

24. Display the bar chart and add Alt Text **Displays expenses for three years without payroll or cost of sales.** (including the period).

25. Display the line chart and add Alt Text **Displays monthly trends in memberships for three years.** (including the period).

Insert Sparklines

Finally, you add sparklines to the Daily Attendance Trends. You add high points to emphasize which time of day is the most popular for your membership.

26. Select **range B16:F16** on the Membership worksheet. Insert **Column Sparklines** using data from the **range B6:F14**.

27. Display the **high points** for the sparklines.

28. Insert a footer with your name on the left side, the sheet name in the center, and the file name code on the right side of the Membership, Expenses, and Summary sheets. Return to Normal view.

29. Save and close the file. Based on your instructor's directions, submit e03c1Gym_LastFirst.

Excel

Datasets and Tables

LEARNING OUTCOME

You will demonstrate how to manage and analyze large sets of data.

OBJECTIVES & SKILLS: After you read this chapter, you will be able to:

CASE STUDY | Reid Furniture Store

Vicki Reid owns Reid Furniture Store in Portland, Oregon. She divided her store into four departments: Living room, Bedroom, Dining room, and Appliances. All merchandise is categorized into one of these four departments for inventory records and sales. Vicki has four sales representatives: Chantalle Desmarais, Jade Gallagher, Sebastian Gruenewald, and Ambrose Sardelis. The sales system tracks which sales representative processed each transaction.

The business has grown rapidly, and Vicki hired you to analyze the sales data to increase future profits. For example, which department generates the most sales? Who is the leading salesperson? Do most customers purchase or finance? Are sales promotions necessary to promote business, or will customers pay the full price?

You downloaded March 2021 data from the sales system into an Excel workbook. Because the dataset is large, you will convert the data into a table, sort, filter, and utilize conditional formatting to complete your analysis.

Managing Large Volumes of Data

CHAPTER 4

YanLev/Shutterstock

	A	B	C	D	E	F	G	H	I	J
1	Reid Furniture Store									
2	Monthly Transactions:			March 2021						
3	Down Payment Requirement:			25%						
4										
5	Trans_No	Operator	Sales_First	Sales_Last	Date	Department	Furniture	Pay_Type	Trans_Type	Amount
6	2021-001	KRM	Sebastian	Gruenewald	3/1/2021	Bedroom	Mattress	Finance	Promotion	2,788
7	2021-002	RKM	Sebastian	Gruenewald	3/1/2021	Bedroom	Mattress	Finance	Promotion	3,245
8	2021-003	MAP	Jade	Gallagher	3/1/2021	Living Room	Sofa, Loveseat, Chair Package	Finance	Promotion	10,000
9	2021-004	MAP	Jade	Gallagher	3/1/2021	Living Room	End Tables	Finance	Promotion	1,000
10	2021-005	MAP	Jade	Gallagher	3/1/2021	Appliances	Washer and Dryer	Finance	Promotion	2,750
11	2021-006	COK	Ambrose	Sardelis	3/1/2021	Living Room	Sofa, Loveseat, Chair Package	Finance	Promotion	12,000
12	2021-006	COK	Ambrose	Sardelis	3/1/2021	Living Room	Sofa, Loveseat, Chair Package	Finance	Promotion	12,000
13	2021-007	MAP	Jade	Gallagher	3/1/2021	Dining Room	Dining Room Table	Finance	Promotion	3,240
14	2021-008	COK	Chantalle	Desmarais	3/1/2021	Dining Room	Dining Room Table	Finance	Promotion	4,080
15	2021-009	KRM	Sebastian	Gruenewald	3/1/2021	Appliances	Washer and Dryer	Finance	Promotion	2,750
16	2021-010	MAP	Jade	Gallagher	3/2/2021	Dining Room	Dining Room Table and Chairs	Finance	Standard	6,780
17	2021-011	COK	Chantalle	Desmarais	3/2/2021	Dining Room	Dining Room Table and Chairs	Finance	Standard	10,000
18	2021-012	KRM	Ambrose	Sardelis	3/2/2021	Appliances	Washer	Paid in Full	Promotion	1,100
19	2021-013	COK	Chantalle	Desmarais	3/3/2021	Living Room	Recliners	Finance	Standard	2,430
20	2021-014	COK	Jade	Gallagher	3/3/2021	Dining Room	Dining Room Table and Chairs	Paid in Full	Standard	4,550
21	2021-015	MAP	Chantalle	Desmarais	3/3/2021	Living Room	Sofa, Loveseat, Chair Package	Finance	Standard	6,784
22	2021-016	MAP	Jade	Gallagher	3/4/2021	Appliances	Dishwasher	Paid in Full	Standard	640
23	2021-017	MAP	Jade	Gallagher	3/4/2021	Appliances	Refrigerator, Oven, Microwave Combo	Finance	Promotion	8,490
24	2021-018	KRM	Sebastian	Gruenewald	3/4/2021	Appliances	Refrigerator, Oven, Microwave Combo	Finance	Promotion	6,780
25	2021-018	KRM	Sebastian	Gruenewald	3/4/2021	Appliances	Refrigerator, Oven, Microwave Combo	Finance	Promotion	6,780

	A	B	C	D	E	F	G	H	I	J	K
1	Reid Furniture										
2	Monthly Transactions:			March 2021							
3	Down Payment Requirement:			25%							
4											
5	Trans_No	Date	Sales_First	Sales_Last	Department	Furniture		Pay_Type	Trans_Type	Amou	Down_Pa	Owe
6	2021-001	3/1/2021	Sebastian	Gruenewald	Bedroom	Mattress		Finance	Promotion	2,788	697.00	2,091.00
7	2021-002	3/1/2021	Sebastian	Gruenewald	Bedroom	Mattress		Finance	Promotion	3,245	811.25	2,433.75
8	2021-003	3/1/2021	Jade	Gallagher	Living Room	Sofa, Loveseat, Chair Package		Finance	Promotion	10,000	2,500.00	7,500.00
9	2021-004	3/1/2021	Jade	Gallagher	Living Room	End Tables		Finance	Promotion	1,000	250.00	750.00
10	2021-005	3/1/2021	Jade	Gallagher	Appliances	Washer and Dryer		Finance	Promotion	2,750	687.50	2,062.50
11	2021-006	3/1/2021	Ambrose	Sardelis	Living Room	Sofa, Loveseat, Chair Package		Finance	Promotion	12,000	3,000.00	9,000.00
12	2021-007	3/1/2021	Jade	Gallagher	Dining Room	Dining Room Table		Finance	Promotion	3,240	810.00	2,430.00
13	2021-008	3/1/2021	Chantalle	Desmarais	Dining Room	Dining Room Table		Finance	Promotion	4,080	1,020.00	3,060.00
14	2021-009	3/1/2021	Sebastian	Gruenewald	Appliances	Washer and Dryer		Finance	Promotion	2,750	687.50	2,062.50
15	2021-010	3/2/2021	Jade	Gallagher	Dining Room	Dining Room Table and Chairs		Finance	Standard	6,780	1,695.00	5,085.00
16	2021-011	3/2/2021	Chantalle	Desmarais	Dining Room	Dining Room Table and Chairs		Finance	Standard	10,000	2,500.00	7,500.00
17	2021-012	3/2/2021	Ambrose	Sardelis	Appliances	Washer		Paid in Full	Promotion	1,100	1,100.00	-
18	2021-013	3/3/2021	Chantalle	Desmarais	Living Room	Recliners		Finance	Standard	2,430	607.50	1,822.50
19	2021-014	3/3/2021	Jade	Gallagher	Dining Room	Dining Room Table and Chairs		Paid in Full	Standard	4,550	4,550.00	-
20	2021-015	3/3/2021	Chantalle	Desmarais	Living Room	Sofa, Loveseat, Chair Package		Finance	Standard	6,784	1,696.00	5,088.00
21	2021-016	3/4/2021	Jade	Gallagher	Appliances	Dishwasher		Paid in Full	Standard	640	640.00	-
22	2021-017	3/4/2021	Jade	Gallagher	Appliances	Refrigerator, Oven, Microwave Combo		Finance	Promotion	8,490	2,122.50	6,367.50
23	2021-018	3/4/2021	Sebastian	Gruenewald	Appliances	Refrigerator, Oven, Microwave Combo		Finance	Promotion	6,780	1,695.00	5,085.00
24	2021-019	3/5/2021	Jade	Gallagher	Living Room	Sofa		Paid in Full	Standard	2,500	2,500.00	-
25	2021-020	3/5/2021	Jade	Gallagher	Living Room	End Tables		Paid in Full	Standard	950	950.00	-

March Totals | March Individual

FIGURE 4.1 Managing Large Datasets

CASE STUDY | Reid Furniture Store

Starting File	File to be Submitted
e04h1Reid	e04h4Reid_LastFirst

MyLab IT Grader An alternate version of this project is available as a MyLab IT Grader Assessment

Large Datasets

So far, you have worked with worksheets that contain small datasets, a collection of structured, related data in a limited number of columns and rows. In reality, you will probably work with large datasets consisting of hundreds or thousands of rows and columns of data. When you work with small datasets, you can usually view most or all of the data without scrolling. When you work with large datasets, you probably will not be able to see the entire dataset onscreen even on a large, widescreen monitor set at high resolution. Figure 4.2 shows Reid Furniture Store's March 2021 sales transactions. Because it contains a lot of transactions, the entire dataset is not visible. You could decrease the zoom level to display more transactions; however, doing so decreases the text size onscreen, making it hard to read the data.

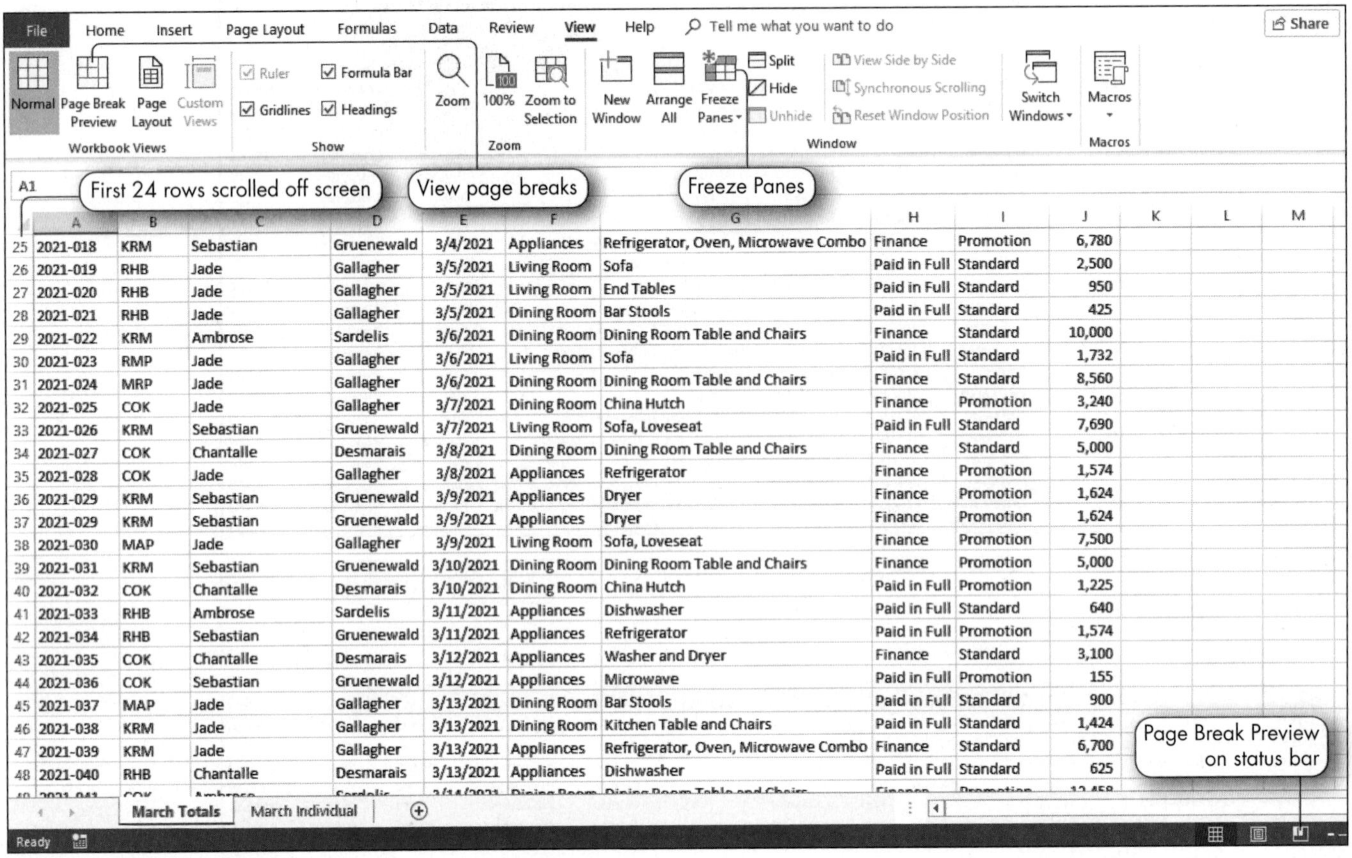

FIGURE 4.2 Large Dataset

As you work with larger datasets, realize that the data will not always fit on one page when it is printed. It will be helpful to keep the column and row labels always in view, even as you scroll throughout the dataset. You will want to preview the automatic page breaks and probably insert some manual page breaks in more desirable locations, or you might want to print only a selected range within the large dataset to distribute to others.

In this section, you will learn how to keep labels onscreen as you scroll through a large dataset. In addition, you will learn how to manage page breaks, print only a range instead of an entire worksheet, print row headings on the left and print column labels at the top of each page of a large dataset.

TIP: GO TO A SPECIFIC CELL

You can navigate through a large worksheet by using the Go To command. Click Find & Select in the Editing group on the Home tab and select Go To (or press F5 or Ctrl+G) to display the Go To dialog box, enter the cell address in the Reference box, and then press Enter to go to the cell. You can also click in the Name Box, type the cell reference, and then press Enter to go to a specific cell. (On a Mac, click the Edit menu, point to Find, and then select Go To).

Freezing Rows and Columns

When you scroll to parts of a dataset not initially visible, some rows and columns, such as headings, disappear from view. When the row and column labels scroll off the screen, it is hard to remember what each column or row represents. You can keep labels onscreen by freezing them. **Freezing** is the process of keeping rows and/or columns visible onscreen at all times even when you scroll through a large dataset. Table 4.1 describes the three freeze options.

TABLE 4.1	Freeze Options
Option	**Description**
Freeze Panes	Keeps both rows and columns above and to the left of the active cell visible as you scroll through a worksheet.
Freeze Top Row	Keeps only the top row visible as you scroll through a worksheet.
Freeze First Column	Keeps only the first column visible as you scroll through a worksheet.

To freeze one or more rows and columns, use the Freeze Panes option. Before selecting this option, make the active cell one row below and one column to the right of the rows and columns you want to freeze. For example, to freeze the first five rows and the first column, make cell B6 the active cell before clicking the Freeze Panes option. As Figure 4.3 shows, Excel displays a horizontal line below the last frozen row (row 5) and a vertical line to the right of the last frozen column (column F). Unfrozen rows (such as rows 6–20) are no longer visible as you scroll down.

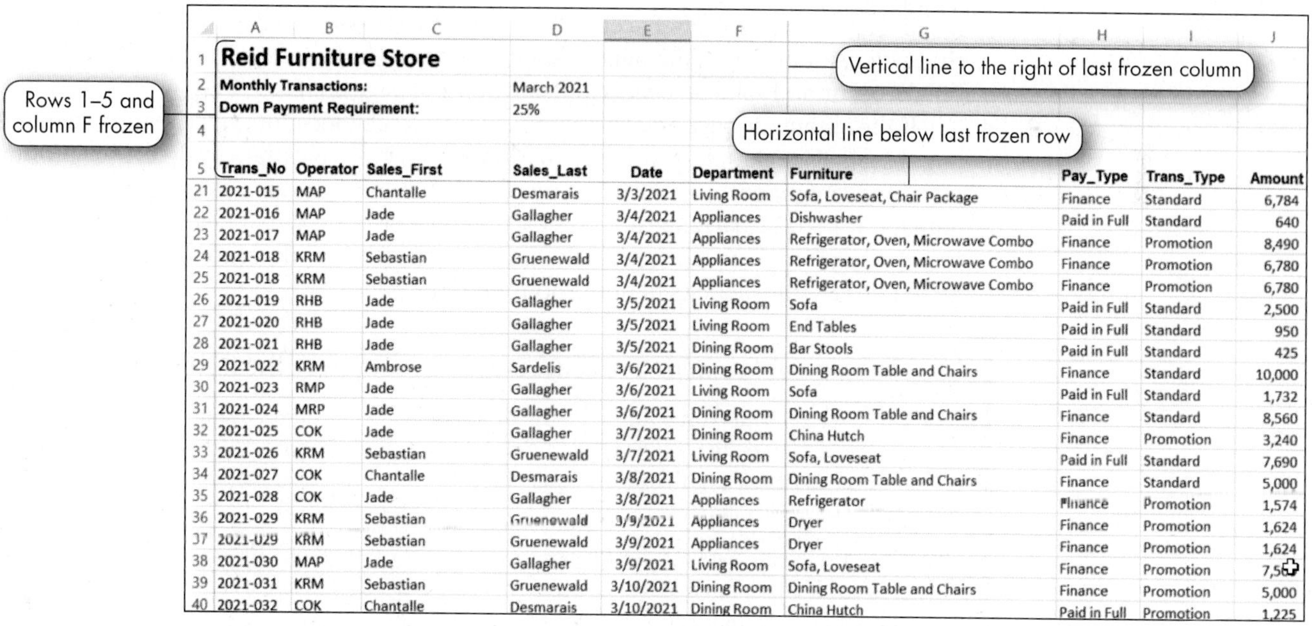

FIGURE 4.3 Freeze Panes Set

To unlock the rows and columns from remaining onscreen as you scroll, click Freeze Panes in the Window group and select Unfreeze Panes. After you unfreeze the panes, the Freeze Panes option displays on the menu instead of Unfreeze Panes.

When you freeze panes and press Ctrl+Home, the first unfrozen cell is the active cell instead of cell A1. For example, with column F and rows 1 through 5 frozen in Figure 4.3, pressing Ctrl+Home makes cell G6 the active cell. If you want to edit a cell in the frozen area, click the particular cell to make it active and edit the data.

Printing Large Datasets

For a large dataset, some columns and rows may print on several pages. Analyzing the data on individual printed pages is difficult when each page does not contain column and row labels. To prevent wasting paper, always use Print Preview. Doing so enables you to adjust page settings until you are satisfied with how the data will print.

The Page Layout tab (see Figure 4.4) contains options to prepare large datasets to print. Previously, you changed the page orientation, set different margins, and adjusted the scaling. In addition, you can manage page breaks, set the print area, and print titles using the Page Layout tab.

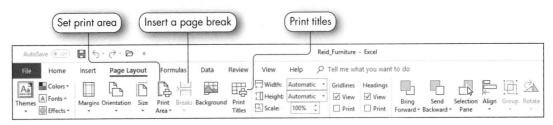

FIGURE 4.4 Page Setup Options

STEP 2 Display and Change Page Breaks

Based on the paper size, orientation, margins, and other settings, Excel identifies how much data can print on a page. Then it displays a *page break*, indicating where data will start on another printed page. To identify where these automatic page breaks will occur, click Page Break Preview on the status bar or in the Workbook Views group on the View tab. In Page Break Preview, Excel displays watermarks, such as Page 1, indicating the area that will print on a specific page. Blue dashed lines indicate where the automatic page breaks occur and solid blue lines indicate manual page breaks.

If the automatic page breaks occur in an undesirable location, you can insert a manual page break. For example, if you have a worksheet listing sales data by date, the automatic page break might occur within a group of rows for one date, such as between two rows of data for 3/1/2021. To make all rows for that date print on the same page, you can either insert a page break above the first data row for that date or decrease the margins so that all 3/1/2021 transactions fit at the bottom of the page.

> **To set a manual break at a specific location, complete the following steps:**
>
> 1. Click the cell that you want to be the first row and column on a new printed page. For example, if you click cell D50, you create a page for columns A through C, and then column D starts a new page.
> 2. Click the Page Layout tab.
> 3. Click Breaks in the Page Setup group and select Insert Page Break. Excel displays a solid blue line in Page Break Preview. Figure 4.5 shows a worksheet with both automatic and manual page breaks.

An alternative method is to use the pointer to adjust a page break by pointing to the page break line to see the two-headed arrow and dragging the line to the location where you want the page break to occur. If you want to remove a manual page break, click below the horizontal line indicating the page break or to the right of the vertical page break, click Breaks in the page Setup group and click Remove Page Break. You can also reset all page breaks by using the Breaks command in the Page Setup group.

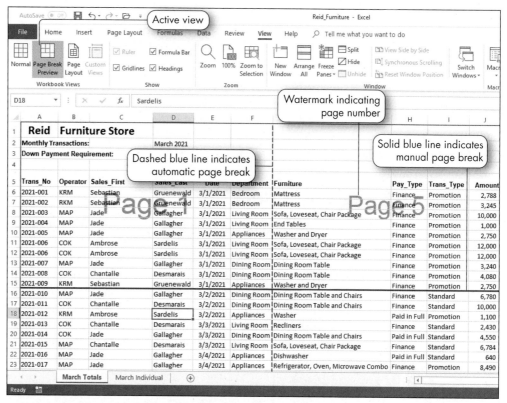

FIGURE 4.5 Page Breaks in Page Break Preview

Set and Clear a Print Area

The default Print settings send an entire dataset on the active worksheet to the printer. However, you might want to print only part of the worksheet data. If you display the worksheet in Page Break view, you can identify which page(s) you want to print. Then click the File tab and select Print. Under Settings, type the number(s) of the page(s) you want to print. For example, to print page 2 only, type 2 in the Pages text box and in the *to* text box.

You can further restrict what is printed by setting the ***print area***, which is the range of cells that will print. For example, you might want to print only an input area or just the transactions that occurred on a particular date. Begin by selecting the range you want to print, click the Page Layout tab, and then click Print Area in the Page Setup group. Next use the Set Print Area command to set the print area you want.

In Page Break Preview, the print area has a white background and solid blue border; the rest of the worksheet has a gray background (see Figure 4.6). In Normal view or Page Layout view, the print area is surrounded by thin gray lines.

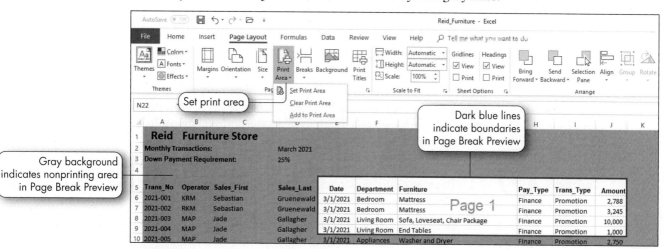

FIGURE 4.6 Print Area in Page Break Preview

To add print areas where each print area will print on a separate page, select the range you want to print, click Print Area, and then select Add to Print Area. You can clear the print area by clicking Print Area in the Page Setup group and selecting Clear Print Area.

> **TIP: PRINT A SELECTION**
> Another way to print part of a worksheet is to select the range you want to print. Click the File tab and click Print. Click the first arrow in the Settings section and select Print Selection. This provides additional flexibility compared to using a defined print area in situations in which you may be required to print materials outside a consistent range of cells.

STEP 4 ▶ Print Titles

When you print large datasets, it is helpful if every page contains descriptive column and row labels. When you click Print Titles in the Page Setup group on the Page Layout tab, Excel opens the Page Setup dialog box with the Sheet tab active so that you can select which row(s) and/or column(s) to repeat on each page of a printout (see Figure 4.7).

To repeat rows or columns at the top or left of each page when printed, select the row(s) that contain the labels or titles (such as row 5) in the *Rows to repeat at top* box to display $5:$5. To print the row labels at the left side of each page, select the column(s) that contain the labels or titles (such as column A) in the *Columns to repeat at left* box to display AA.

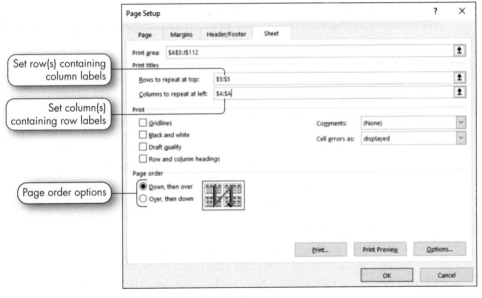

FIGURE 4.7 Sheet Tab Options

Control Print Page Order

Print order is the sequence in which the pages are printed. By default, the pages print in the following order: top-left section, bottom-left section, top-right section, and bottom-right section. However, you might want to print the entire top portion of the worksheet before printing the bottom portion. To change the print order, open the Page Setup dialog box, click the Sheet tab, and then select the desired Page order option (refer to Figure 4.7).

Quick Concepts

1. Explain the purpose of freezing panes in a worksheet. ***p. 253***

2. Describe a situation in which you would want to insert page breaks instead of using the automatic page breaks. ***p. 254***

3. Describe the steps you should take to ensure that column labels display on each printed page of a large dataset. ***p. 256***

Hands-On Exercises

MyLab IT HOE1 Sim Training

Watch the Video for this Hands-On Exercise!

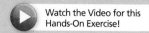

Skills covered: Freeze Rows and Columns • Display and Change Page Breaks • Set and Clear a Print Area • Print Titles

1 Large Datasets

You want to review the large dataset that shows the March transactions for Reid Furniture Store. You will view the data and adjust some page setup options so that you can print necessary labels on each page.

STEP 1 FREEZE ROWS AND COLUMNS

Before printing the March transaction dataset, you want to view the data. The dataset contains more rows than will display onscreen at the same time. You decide to freeze the column and row labels to stay onscreen as you scroll through the transactions. Refer to Figure 4.8 as you complete Step 1.

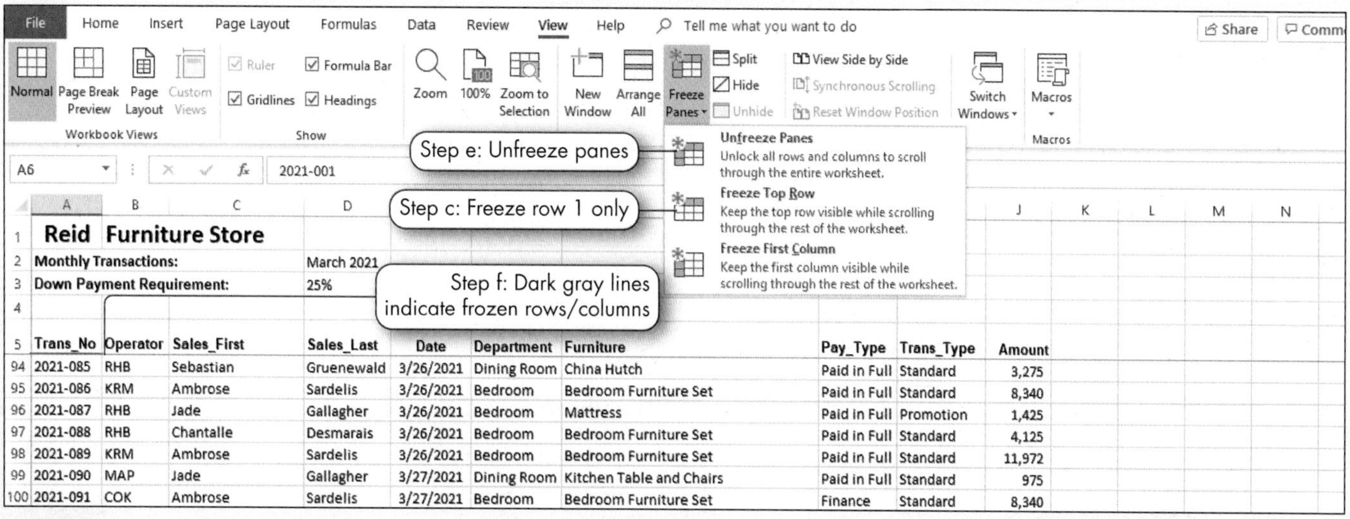

FIGURE 4.8 Freeze Panes Activated

a. Open *e04h1Reid* and save it as **e04h1Reid_LastFirst**. Ensure the March Totals worksheet is active.

> **TROUBLESHOOTING:** If you make any major mistakes in this exercise, you can close the file, open *e04h1Reid* again, and then start this exercise over.

The workbook contains two worksheets: March Totals (for Hands-On Exercises 1–3) and March Individual (for Hands-On Exercise 4)

b. Press **Page Down** five times to scroll through the dataset, note the column headers are not visible. Press **Ctrl+Home** to go back to the top of the worksheet.

After you press Page Down, the column labels in row 5 scroll off the screen, making it challenging to remember what type of data are in some columns.

c. Click the **View tab**, click **Freeze Panes** in the Window group, and then select **Freeze Top Row**.

A dark gray horizontal line displays between rows 1 and 2.

d. Press **Page Down** to scroll down through the worksheet.

As rows scroll off the top of the Excel window, the first row remains frozen onscreen. The title by itself is not helpful; you need to freeze the column labels as well.

e. Click **Freeze Panes** in the Window group and select **Unfreeze Panes**.

f. Click **cell B6**, the cell below the row and one column to the right of what you want to freeze. Click **Freeze Panes** in the Window group and select **Freeze Panes**.

Excel displays a vertical line between columns A and B, indicating that column A is frozen, and a horizontal line between rows 5 and 6, indicating the first five rows are frozen.

g. Press **Ctrl+G**, type **Q112** in the Reference box of the Go To dialog box, and then click **OK** to make cell Q112 the active cell.

Rows 6 through 96 and columns B and C are not visible because they scrolled off the screen. Note that the results may vary slightly based on screen resolution.

h. Save the workbook.

STEP 2 DISPLAY AND CHANGE PAGE BREAKS

You plan to print the dataset so that you and Vicki Reid can discuss the transactions in your weekly meeting. Because the large dataset requires more than one page to print, you want to see where the automatic page breaks are, and then insert a manual page break. Refer to Figure 4.9 as you complete Step 2.

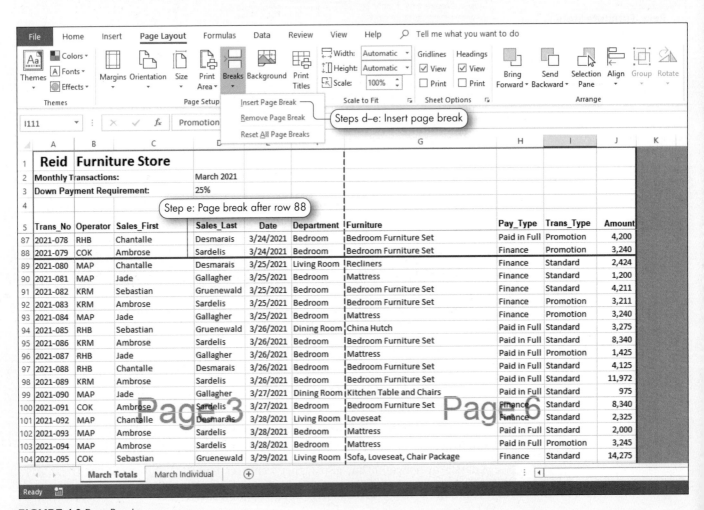

FIGURE 4.9 Page Breaks

a. Press **Ctrl+Home** to move to cell B6, the first cell in the unfrozen area. Click the **View tab** and click **Page Break Preview** in the Workbook Views group or on the status bar.

Excel displays blue dashed lines to indicate the automatic page breaks.

b. Scroll down until you see row 45 below the frozen column labels.

The automatic horizontal page break is in the middle of the transactions for 3/13/2021. You do not want transactions for a particular day to span between printed pages, so you want to move the page break up to keep all 3/13/2021 transactions together.

> **TROUBLESHOOTING:** Due to various screen resolutions, the page break may not appear after row 45. If the page break does not appear on row 45, click the blue page break line and drag it up to row 44.

c. Click **cell A45**, the first cell in a row that contains 3/13/2021 data and the cell to start the top of the second page.

d. Click the **Page Layout tab**, click **Breaks** in the Page Setup group, and then select **Insert Page Break**.

You inserted a page break between rows 44 and 45 so that the 3/13/2021 transactions will be on one page.

e. Click the blue page break line located above row 92 and drag it under row 88.

You inserted a page break between rows 88 and 89 to keep the 3/25/2021 transactions on the same page.

f. Save the workbook.

STEP 3 SET AND CLEAR A PRINT AREA

You want to focus on the transactions for only March 1, 2021. To avoid printing more data than you need, you will set the print area to print transactions for only that day. Refer to Figure 4.10 as you complete Step 3.

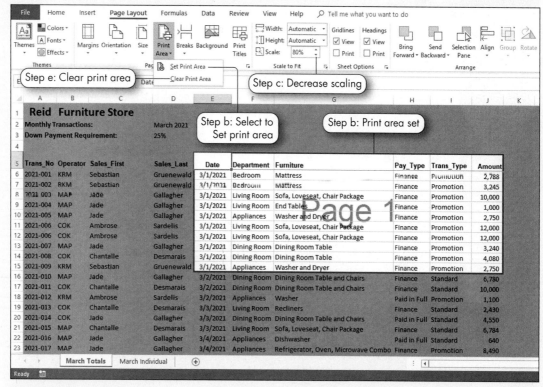

FIGURE 4.10 Print Area Set

a. Press **Ctrl+Home**. Select the **range E5:J15**, the range of data for March 1, 2021.

b. Click **Print Area** in the Page Setup group and select **Set Print Area**.

Excel displays the print area with a border. The rest of the worksheet displays with a gray background.

c. Click **cell E5** and click the **Scale arrow** down four times to display 80% in the Scale to Fit group. (Note on Mac: Scaling is found by clicking Page Setup.)

The selected print area will print on one page.

d. Press **Ctrl+P** to see that only the print area will print. Press **Esc**.

e. Click **Print Area** in the Page Setup group and select **Clear Print Area**.

When the print area is cleared, the thin gray outline defining the print area and the gray background disappears.

f. Save the workbook.

STEP 4 PRINT TITLES

Only the first page will print both transaction numbers and column labels. Pages 2 and 3 will print the remaining transaction numbers, page 4 will print the remaining column labels, and pages 5 and 6 will not print either label. You want to make sure the column and row labels print on all pages. Refer to Figure 4.11 as you complete Step 4.

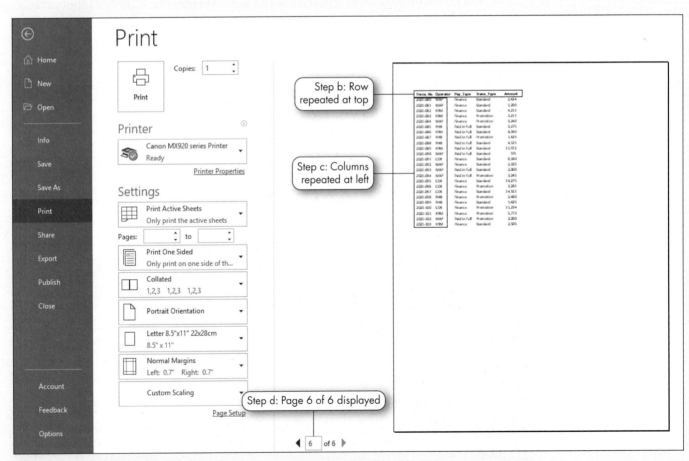

FIGURE 4.11 Print Titles

a. Click **Print Titles** in the Page Setup group.

The Page Setup dialog box opens, displaying the Sheet tab.

b. Click in the **Rows to repeat at top box** and click the **row 5 heading**.

You selected the fifth row, which contains the column labels.

c. Click in the **Columns to repeat at left box**, type **A:B**, click the **Over, then down Page order**, and then click **Print Preview** in the Page Setup box. (On a Mac, click OK and press Command+P.)

You have manually entered the columns that contain the heading you want to repeat. By choosing Over, then down Page order, the pages print from left to right.

d. Click **Next Page** at the bottom of the Print Preview. Click **Next Page** until the sixth page displays.

Figure 4.11 shows a preview of the sixth page. The column labels and the first two columns appear on all pages.

e. Click the back arrow and click Normal view. Save the workbook. Keep the workbook open if you plan to continue with the next Hands-On Exercise. If not, close the workbook, and exit Excel.

Excel Tables

All organizations maintain lists of data. Businesses maintain inventory lists, educational institutions maintain lists of students and faculty, and governmental entities maintain lists of contracts. Although more complicated related data should be stored in a database management program, such as Access, you can manage basic data structure in Excel tables. A ***table*** is a structured range that contains related data organized in a method that increases the capability to manage and analyze information.

In this section, you will learn table terminology and rules for structuring data. You will create a table from existing data, manage records and fields, and remove duplicates. You will then apply a table style to format the table.

Exploring the Benefits of Data Tables

When dealing with large datasets it is imperative that documents are strategically organized to maintain data integrity and ease of use. Thus far you have worked with the manipulation of data ranges, and while you can use many tools in Excel to analyze simple data ranges, tables provide many additional analytical and time saving benefits. Using tables in Excel can help create and maintain data structure. ***Data structure*** is the organization method used to manage multiple data points within a dataset. For example, a dataset of students may include names, grades, contact information, and intended majors of study. The data structure of this dataset would define how the information is stored, organized, and accessed. Although you can manage and analyze data structure as a range in Excel, a table provides many advantages:

- Column headings remain onscreen without having to use Freeze Panes.
- Table styles easily format table rows and columns with complementary fill colors.
- Calculated columns enable you to create and edit formulas that copy down the columns automatically.
- A calculated total row enables you to implement a variety of summary functions.
- You can use structured references instead of cell references in formulas.

Designing and Creating Tables

The Reid furniture data is entered in the worksheet as a range. Converting the range into a table will help further manipulate the data. A table is a group of related data organized in a series of rows and columns that is managed independently from any other data on the worksheet. Once a data range is converted into a table, each column represents a ***field***, which is an individual piece of data, such as last names or quantities sold. Each field should represent the smallest possible unit of data. For example, instead of a Name field, separate name data into First Name and Last Name fields. Instead of one large address field, separate address data into Street Address, City, State, and ZIP Code fields. Separating data into the smallest units possible enables you to manipulate the data in a variety of ways for output.

> **TIP: FLASH FILL**
>
> Flash Fill can be used to separate data such as first and last names across columns. To use Flash Fill to split data, enter the first name or value in the first column to the right of the original content. In the next row, type the first few letters of the next name and press Enter.

Each row in a table represents a ***record***, which is a collection of related data about one entity. For example, all data related to one particular transaction form a record in the Reid Furniture Store worksheet.

You should plan the structure before creating a table. The more thoroughly you plan, the fewer changes you will have to make to gain information from the data in the table after you create it. To help plan your table, follow these guidelines:

- Enter field (column) names on the top row of the table.
- Keep field names short, descriptive, and unique. No two field names should be identical.
- Format the field names so that they stand out from the data.
- Enter data for each record on a row below the field names.
- Do not leave blank rows between records or between the field names and the first record.
- Delete any blank columns between fields in the dataset.
- Make sure each record has something unique, such as a transaction number or ID.
- Insert at least one blank row and one blank column between the table and other data, such as the main titles. When you need multiple tables in one workbook, a best practice is to place each table on a separate worksheet.

STEP 1 ## Create a Table

By taking the time to create an organized data structure, you will ensure that the data can be used to identify specific information easily, is efficient to manage, and is scalable. When your worksheet data is structured correctly, you can easily create a table.

To create a table from existing data, complete the following steps:

1. Click within the existing range of data.
2. Click the Insert tab and click Table in the Tables group. The Create Table dialog box opens (see Figure 4.12), prompting you to enter the range of data.
   - Select the range for the *Where is the data for your table* box if Excel does not correctly predict the range.
   - Click the *My table has headers* check box if the existing range contains column labels.
3. Click OK to create the table.

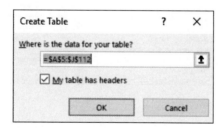

FIGURE 4.12 Create Table Dialog Box

If the results are not what you expect, an existing table can be converted back into a range. To convert a table back to a range, click within the table range, click the Table Tools Design tab, click Convert to Range in the Tools group, and then click Yes in the message box asking, *Do you want to convert the table to a normal range.*

TIP: QUICK ANALYSIS TABLE CREATION

You can also create a table by selecting a range, clicking the Quick Analysis button, clicking Tables (see Figure 4.13) in the Quick Analysis gallery, and then selecting Table. While Quick Analysis is efficient for tasks such as creating a chart, it may take more time to create a table because you must select the entire range first. Some people find that it is faster to create a table on the Insert tab. The Quick Analysis feature is only available for PC. (On a Mac, use the Insert tab to create a table.)

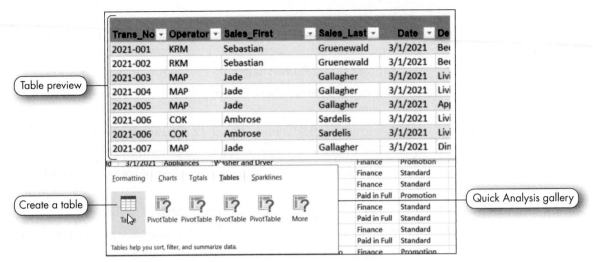

FIGURE 4.13 Quick Analysis Gallery

After you create a table, the Table Tools Design tab displays. Excel applies the default Table Style Medium 2 style to the table and each cell in the header row has filter arrows (see Figure 4.14).

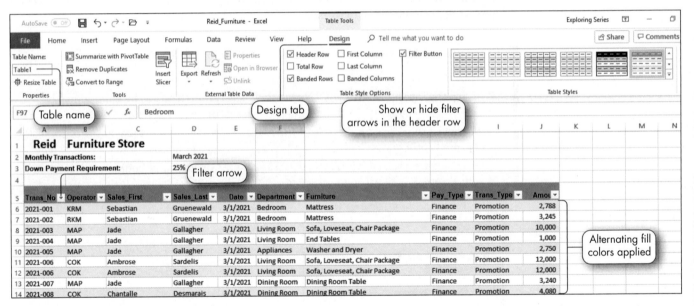

FIGURE 4.14 Excel Table in Default Format

Instead of converting a range to a table, you can create a table structure first and add data to it later. Select an empty range and follow the previously listed steps to create the range for the table. The default column headings are Column1, Column2, and so on. Click each default column heading and type a descriptive label. Then enter the data into each row of the newly created table.

STEP 2 ## Rename a Table

By default, when a table is created, Excel assigns a name automatically. For example, the first table created in a worksheet will be named Table1 (refer to figure 4.14). The default nomenclature does not provide descriptive information and, as a best practice, you should change the default name to something more meaningful. Not only does changing the name provide clarification, it also is a good practice for accessibility compliance. The name of the table can be changed using the Table Name box in the Properties group on the Table Tools Design tab. Once a name has been assigned to a table, it can be used when building functions in place of the traditional absolute references.

STEP 3 Add and Delete Fields

After creating a table, you can insert new fields. For example, you might want to add a field for product numbers to the Reid Furniture Store transaction table. To insert a new column in a table, select any data cell in a field that will be to the right of the new field. Then use the Insert Table Columns to the Left feature located on the Home tab in the Cells group.

If you want to add a field at the end of the right side of a table, click in the cell to the right of the last field name and type a label. Excel will extend the table to include that field and will format the cell as a field name.

You can also delete a field if you no longer need any data for that particular field. Although deleting records and fields is easy, you must make sure not to delete data erroneously. To delete a field in a table, select a cell in the field you want to delete and use the Delete Table Columns feature located on the Home tab in the Cells group. If you accidentally delete data, click Undo immediately.

STEP 4 Add, Edit, and Delete Records

After you begin storing data in your newly created table, you can add new records, such as a new client or a new item to an inventory table. One of the advantages to using tables in Excel is you can easily add, edit, or delete records within the dataset.

To add a record to a table, complete the following steps:

1. Click a cell in the record below which you want the new record inserted. If you want to add a new record below the last record, click the row containing the last record.
2. Click the Home tab and click the Insert arrow in the Cells group.
3. Select Insert Table Rows Above to insert a row above the current row or select Insert Table Row Below if the current row is the last one and you want a row below it.

You can also add a record to the end of a table by clicking in the row immediately below the table and typing. Excel will extend the table to include that row as a record in the table and will apply consistent formatting.

You might want to change data for a record. For example, when a client moves, you will change the client's address. You edit data in a table the same way you edit data in a regular worksheet cell.

Finally, you can delete records. For example, if you maintain an inventory of artwork in your house and sell a piece of art, delete that record from the table. To delete a record first select the record you want to remove. Next use the Delete Table Rows feature located on the Home tab in the Cells group to remove the entire row.

STEP 5 Remove Duplicate Rows

Due to clerical issues or human error, a table might contain duplicate records, which can give false results when totaling or performing other calculations on the dataset. For a small table, you might be able to scan the data to detect duplicate records and delete them manually. For large tables, it is more difficult and less time efficient to identify duplicate records by simply scanning the table with the eye. The Remove Duplicates command launches the Remove Duplicates dialog box (see Figure 4.15) which enables you to automatically locate and remove all duplicates. This feature is located on the Design tab. To remove duplicate records, select any cell in the table, click the Design tab, and click Remove Duplicates in the Tools group. Select the columns with duplicate values in the Remove Duplicates dialog box and click OK.

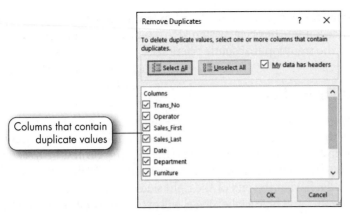

Columns that contain
duplicate values

FIGURE 4.15 Remove Duplicates Dialog Box

STEP 6 ▶ Applying a Table Style

When you create a table, it is automatically formatted with the default table style of alternating colored rows and bold format for the header row. A **Table style** controls the fill color of the header row (the row containing field names) and rows of records. In addition, table styles specify heading formats and border lines. You can change the table style to complement your organization's color scheme or to emphasize data in the header rows or columns. Click More in the Table Styles group to display the Table Styles gallery (see Figure 4.16). On a PC to see how a table style will format your table using Live Preview, point to a style in the Table Styles gallery. After you identify a style you want, select it to apply it to the table. (Note: Live Preview is unavailable on a Mac).

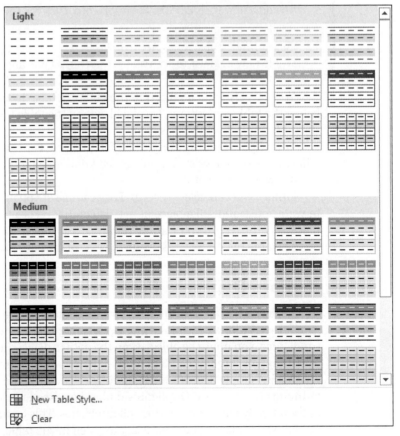

FIGURE 4.16 Table Styles Gallery

After you select a table style, you can control what the style formats. The Table Style Options group contains check boxes to select specific format actions in a table. Table 4.2 lists the options and the effect of each check box. Avoid over-formatting the table. Applying too many formatting effects may obscure the message you want to present with the data. Be sure to apply only formatting and options that best reflect the data. For example, add a total row only when you want to summarize key performance indicators in the data.

TABLE 4.2	Table Style Options
Check Box	**Action**
Header Row	Displays the header row (field names) when selected; removes field names when deselected. Header Row formatting takes priority over column formats.
Total Row	Displays a total row when selected. Total Row formatting takes priority over column formats.
First Column	Applies a different format to the first column so that the row headings stand out. First Column formatting takes priority over Banded Rows formatting.
Last Column	Applies a different format to the last column so that the last column of data stands out; effective for aggregated data, such as grand totals per row. Last Column formatting takes priority over Banded Rows formatting.
Banded Rows	Displays alternate fill colors for even and odd rows to help distinguish records.
Banded Columns	Displays alternate fill colors for even and odd columns to help distinguish fields.
Filter Button	Displays a filter button on the right side of each field name in the header row.

 **Quick Concepts**

4. List at least four guidelines for planning a table in Excel. ***pp. 262–263***

5. Discuss two reasons why you would convert a range of data into an Excel table. ***p. 262***

6. Describe a situation in which it would be beneficial to add a total row. ***p. 262***

Hands-On Exercises

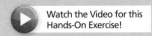
Skills covered: Create a Table • Rename a Table • Add and Delete Fields • Add, Edit, and Delete Records • Remove Duplicate Rows • Apply a Table Style

2 Excel Tables

You want to convert the March Totals data to a table. As you review the table, you will delete the unnecessary Operator field, add two new fields, insert a missing furniture sale transaction, and remove duplicate transactions. Finally, you will enhance the table appearance by applying a table style.

STEP 1 CREATE A TABLE

Although Reid Furniture Store's March transaction data are organized in an Excel worksheet, you know that you will have additional functionality if you convert the range to a table. Refer to Figure 4.17 as you complete Step 1.

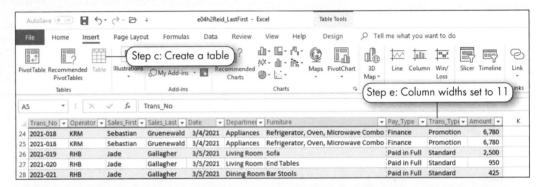

FIGURE 4.17 Range Converted to a Table

a. Open *e04h1Reid_LastFirst* if you closed it at the end of Hands-On Exercise 1, and save it as **e04h2Reid_LastFirst**, changing h1 to h2.

b. Unfreeze the panes and scroll through the data.

With a regular range of data, column labels scroll off the top of the screen if you do not freeze panes. When you scroll within a table, the table's header row remains onscreen by moving up to where the Excel column (letter) headings usually display. Note that it will not retain the bold formatting when scrolling.

c. Click in any cell within the transactional data, click the **Insert tab**, and then click **Table** in the Tables group.

The Create Table dialog box opens. The *Where is the data for your table?* box displays =$A$5:$J$112. Keep the *My table has headers* check box selected so that the headings on the fifth row become the field names for the table.

d. Click **OK** and click **cell A5**.

Excel creates a table from the data range and displays the Design tab, filter arrows, and alternating fill colors for the records.

e. **Ctrl** and click the field names, **Sales_First**, **Sales_Last**, **Department**, **Pay_Type**, and **Trans_Type**. Click the **Home tab**, click **Format** in the Cells group, and then select **Column Width**. Type 11 in the column width box and click **OK**.

f. Save the workbook.

RENAME THE TABLE

After creating the table, you will change the name from the default *Table 2* to a more descriptive title that meets your business standards. Refer to Figure 4.18 as you complete Step 2.

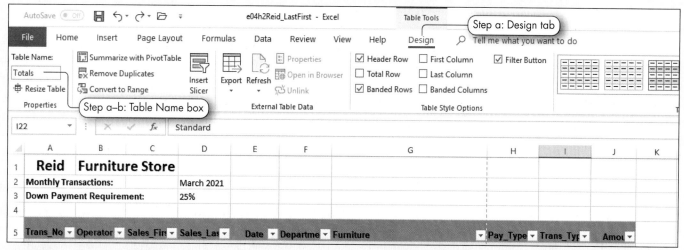

FIGURE 4.18 Rename the Table

a. Click the Design tab and click the **Table Name box** in the Properties group.

b. Type **Totals** in the Table Name box and press **Enter**.

You have given the table a custom name.

ADD AND DELETE FIELDS

The original range included a column for the data entry operators' initials. You will delete this column because you do not need it for your analysis. In addition, you want to add a field to display down payment amounts in the future. Refer to Figure 4.19 as you complete Step 3.

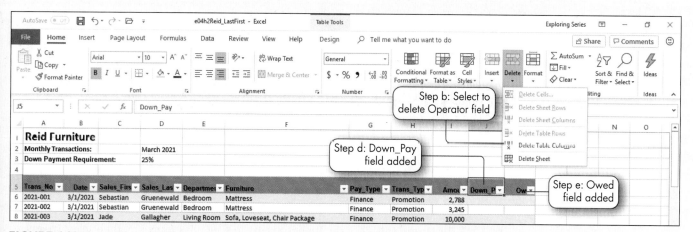

FIGURE 4.19 Newly Created Fields

a. Click any cell containing a value in the Operator column.

You need to make a cell active in the field you want to remove.

b. Click the **Home tab**, click the **Delete arrow** in the Cells group, and then select **Delete Table Columns**.

Excel deletes the Operator column and may adjust the width of other columns.

c. Set the widths of columns E, F, and G to **AutoFit**. Click **cell J5**, the first blank cell on the right side of the field names.

d. Type **Down_Pay** and press **Enter**.

Excel extends the table formatting to column J automatically. A filter arrow displays for the newly created field name, and alternating fill colors appear in the rows below the field name.

e. Click **cell K5**, type **Owed**, and then press **Enter**. Save the workbook.

STEP 4 ADD RECORDS

As you review the March transaction table, you notice that two transactions are missing: 2021-068 and 2021-104. After finding the paper invoices, you are ready to add records with the missing transaction data. Refer to Figure 4.20 as you complete Step 4.

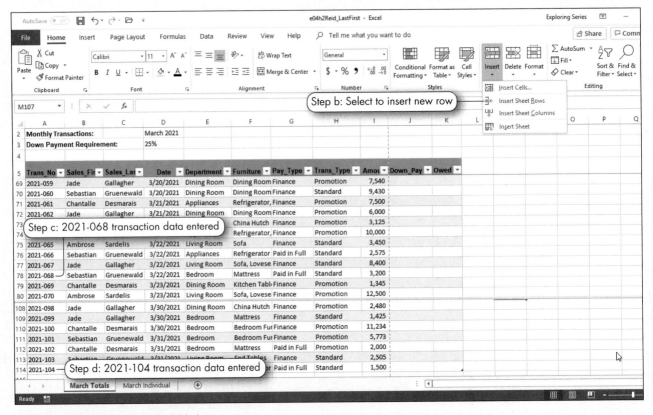

FIGURE 4.20 Missing Records Added

a. Click **cell A78**.

The missing record 2021-068 needs to be inserted between 2021-067 on row 77 and 2021-069 on row 78.

b. Click the **Home tab**, click the **Insert arrow** in the Cells group, and then select **Insert Table Rows Above**.

Excel inserts a new table row on row 78, between the 2021-067 and 2021-069 transactions.

c. Enter the following data in the respective fields on the newly created row:

2021-068, Sebastian, Gruenewald, 3/22/2021, Bedroom, Mattress, Paid in Full, Standard, 3200

d. Click **cell A114** and enter the following data in the respective fields:

2021-104, Ambrose, Sardelis, 3/31/2021, Appliances, Refrigerator, Paid in Full, Standard, 1500

When you start typing 2021-104 in the row below the last record, Excel immediately includes and formats row 114 as part of the table. Review Figure 4.20 to ensure that you inserted the records in the correct locations. In the figure, rows 81–109 are hidden to display both new records in one screenshot.

e. Save the workbook.

REMOVE DUPLICATE ROWS

You noticed that the 2021-006 transaction is duplicated on rows 11 and 12 and that the 2021-018 transaction is duplicated on rows 24 and 25. You think the table may contain other duplicate rows. To avoid having to look at the entire table row by row, you will have Excel find and remove the duplicate rows for you. Refer to Figure 4.21 as you complete Step 5.

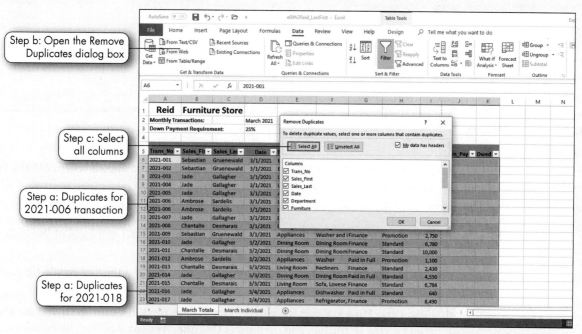

FIGURE 4.21 Remove Duplicate Records

a. Click a cell in the table. Scroll to see rows 11 and 12. Click the **Design tab**.

The records on rows 11 and 12 are identical. Rows 24 and 25 are also duplicates. You need to remove the extra rows.

b. Click **Remove Duplicates** in the Tools group.

The Remove Duplicates dialog box opens.

c. Ensure Select All is selected, ensure the *My data has headers* check box is selected, and then click **OK**.

Excel displays a message box indicating 5 *duplicate records found and removed; 104 unique values remain.*

d. Click **OK** in the message box. Click **cell A109** to view the last record in the table. Save the workbook.

Transaction 2021-104 is located on row 109 after the duplicate records are removed.

Now that you have finalized the fields and added missing records to the March transaction table, you want to apply a table style to format the table. Refer to Figure 4.22 as you complete Step 6.

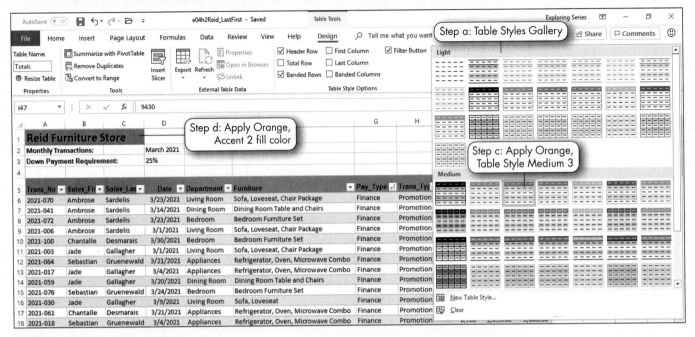

FIGURE 4.22 Table Style Applied

a. Click a cell in the table. Ensure the Design tab is displayed and click **More** in the Table Styles group to open the Table Styles gallery.

b. Point to the fourth style on the second row in the Light section.

Live Preview shows the table with the Orange, Table Style Light 10 style but does not apply it.

c. Select **Orange, Table Style Medium 3**, the third style on the first row in the Medium section.

d. Press **Ctrl+Home**. Select the **range A1:C1**, click the **Fill Color arrow** in the Font group on the Home tab, and then select **Orange, Accent 2** in the Theme colors.

You applied a fill color for the title to match the fill color of the field names on the header row in the table.

e. Save the workbook. Keep the workbook open if you plan to continue with the next Hands-On Exercise. If not, close the workbook, and exit Excel.

Table Manipulation

Along with maintaining data structure, tables have a variety of options to enhance and manipulate data, in addition to managing fields, adding records, and applying table styles. You can build formulas and functions, arrange records in different sequences to get different perspectives on the data, and restrict the onscreen appearance of data using filtering. For example, you can arrange the transactions by sales representative. Furthermore, you can display only particular records instead of the entire dataset to focus on a subset of the data. For example, you might want to focus on the financed transactions.

In this section, you will learn how to create structured references, and how to sort records by text, numbers, and dates in a table. In addition, you will learn how to filter data based on conditions you set.

STEP 1 Creating Structured References in Formulas

Your experience in building formulas involves using cell references, such as =SUM(B1:B15) or =H6*$B$3. Cell references in formulas help to identify where the content is on a worksheet but do not tell the user what the content represents. An advantage to Excel tables is that they use structured references to clearly indicate which type of data is used in the calculations. A *structured reference* is a tag, or the use of a table element such as a field heading, as a reference in a formula. As shown in Figure 4.23, structured references in formulas clearly indicate which type of data is used in the calculations.

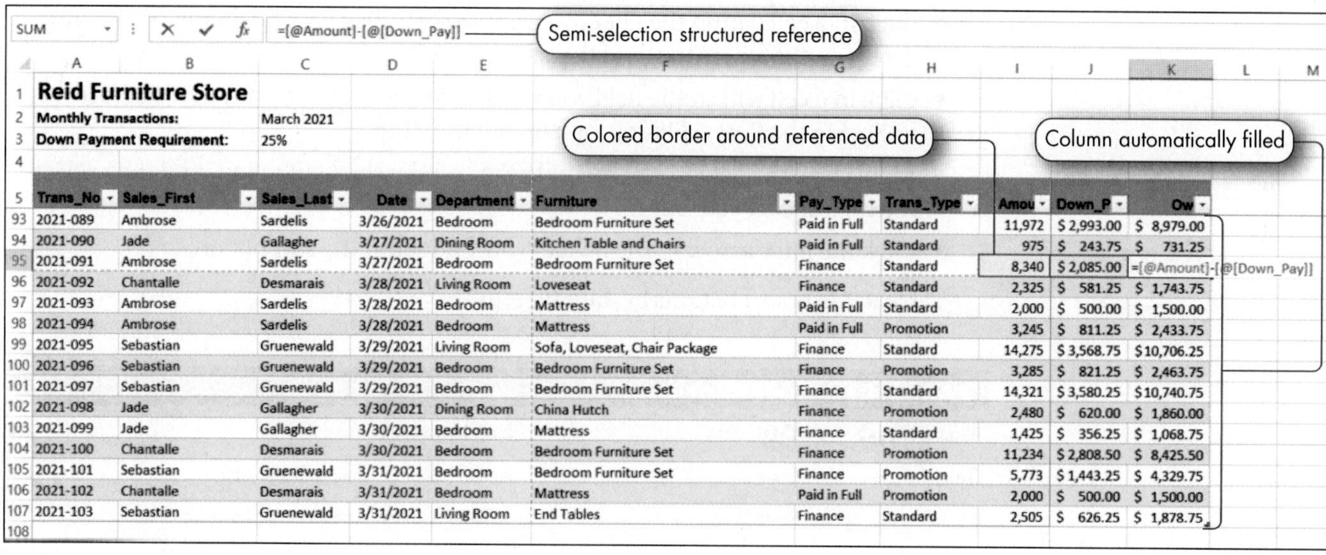

FIGURE 4.23 Structured Reference

When creating a formula in a table using structured references, field headings are set off by brackets around column headings or field names, such as =[Amount]–[Down_Pay]. The use of field headings without row references in a structured formula is called an *unqualified reference*. After you type the equal sign to begin the formula, type an opening bracket, and then Formula AutoComplete displays a list of field headings. Type or double-click the column name from the list and type the closing bracket. Excel displays a colored border around the referenced column that coordinates with the structured reference in the formula, similar to Excel identifying cell references and their worksheet placement. When you enter a formula using structured references, Excel copies the formula down the rest of the table column automatically, compared to typing references in formulas and using the fill handle to copy the formula down a column.

You can also use the semi-selection process to create a formula. As you click cells to enter a formula in a table, Excel builds a formula like this: =[@Amount]–[@Down_Pay], where the @ indicates the current row. If you use the semi-selection process to create a formula outside the table, the formula includes the table and field names, such as =Table1[@Amount]–Table1[@Down_Pay]. Table1 is the name of the table; Amount and Down_Pay are field names. This structured formula that includes references with a table name is called a ***fully qualified structured reference***. When you build formulas *within* a table, you can use either unqualified or fully qualified structured references. If you need to use table data in a formula *outside* the table boundaries, you must use fully qualified structured references.

Sorting Data

Sometimes if you rearrange the order of records, a new perspective is gained making the information easier to understand. In Figure 4.23, the March data is arranged by transaction number. You might want to arrange the transactions so that all of the transactions for a particular sales representative are together. ***Sorting*** is the process of arranging records by the value of one or more fields within a table. Sorting is not limited to data within tables; normal data ranges can be sorted as well.

STEP 2 ## Sort One Field

You can sort data in a table or a regular range in a worksheet. For example, you could sort by transaction date or department. You can sort by only one field using any of the following steps:

- Click in a cell within the field you want to sort, click Sort & Filter in the Editing group on the Home tab, and then select a sort option.
- Click in a cell within the field you want to sort and click Sort A to Z, Sort Z to A, or Sort in the Sort & Filter group on the Data tab.
- Right-click the field to sort, point to Sort on the shortcut menu, and then select the type of sort you want.
- Click the filter arrow in the header row and select the sort option.

Table 4.3 lists sort options by data type.

TABLE 4.3	Sort Options	
Data Type	**Options**	**Explanation**
Text	Sort A to Z	Arranges data in alphabetic order
	Sort Z to A	Arranges data in reverse alphabetic order
Dates	Sort Oldest to Newest	Displays data in chronological order, from oldest to newest
	Sort Newest to Oldest	Displays data in reverse chronological order, from newest to oldest
Values	Sort Smallest to Largest	Arranges values from the smallest value to the largest
	Sort Largest to Smallest	Arranges values from the largest value to the smallest
Color	Sort by Cell Color	Arranges data together for cells containing a particular fill color
	Sort by Font Color	Arranges data together for cells containing a particular font color

STEP 3 **Sort Multiple Fields**

After sorting by one field, if a second sort is applied, the original sort will be removed. However, at times, sorting by only one field does not yield the desired outcome. Using multiple level sorts enables like records in the primary sort to be further organized by additional sort levels. Always check the data to determine how many levels of sorting to apply. If your table contains several people with the same last name but different first names, you would first sort by the Last Name field, then sort by First Name field. All the people with the last name Desmarais would be grouped together and further sorted by first name, such as Amanda and then Bradley. Excel enables you to sort data on 64 different levels.

To perform a multiple level sort, complete the following steps:

1. Click in any cell in the table.
2. Click Sort in the Sort & Filter group on the Data tab to display the Sort dialog box.
3. Select the primary sort level by clicking the Sort by arrow, selecting the field to sort by, clicking the Order arrow, and then selecting the sort order from the list.
4. Click Add Level (On a Mac, click the plus icon), select the second sort level by clicking the Then by arrow, select the column to sort by, click the Order arrow, and then select the sort order from the list.
5. Continue to click Add Level and add sort levels until you have entered all sort levels (see Figure 4.24). Click OK.

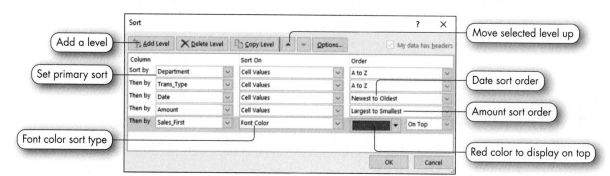

FIGURE 4.24 Sort Dialog Box

STEP 4 **Create a Custom Sort**

When sorting, Excel arranges data in alphabetic or numeric order. For example, days of the week are sorted alphabetically: Friday, Monday, Saturday, Sunday, Thursday, Tuesday, and Wednesday. However, if you want to sort the days of the week in the traditional sequence of Sunday to Saturday, then you would create a custom sort.

To create a custom sort sequence, complete the following steps:

1. Click Sort in the Sort & Filter group on the Data tab.
2. Click the Order arrow and select Custom List to display the Custom Lists dialog box (see Figure 4.25).
3. Select an existing sort sequence in the Custom lists box or select NEW LIST.
4. Type the entries in the sort sequence in the List entries box. Enter a comma between entries.
5. Click Add and click OK.

On a Mac, to create a custom sort sequence, complete the following steps:

1. Click the Excel menu.
2. Select Preferences and select Custom Lists in the Formulas and Lists group.
3. Enter the new list in the List entries box and click Add.
4. Close the Custom List dialog box.

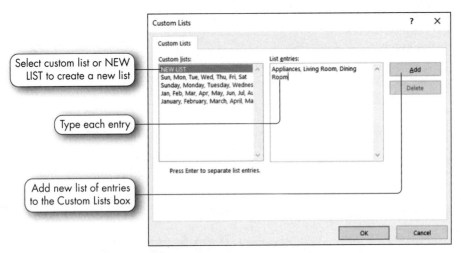

FIGURE 4.25 Custom Lists Dialog Box

Filtering Data

To display only a subset of the data available, for example, the data to show transactions for only a particular sales representative, you would apply a filter to achieve the desired results. In Excel, you can filter using various criteria such as date, value, text, and color. *Filtering* is the process of displaying only those records that meet certain conditions. When a filter is applied, the filter arrow displays a filter icon, indicating which field is filtered. Excel displays the row numbers in blue, indicating that you applied a filter. The missing row numbers indicate hidden rows of data. When you remove the filter, all the records display again.

To apply a filter, complete the following steps:

1. Click any cell in the range of data to be filtered.
2. Click the Data tab and click Filter in the Sort & Filter group to display the filter arrows (this step can be skipped if the data is in a table).
3. Click the filter arrow for the column you want to filter.
4. Deselect the Select All check box and select the check boxes for the text you want to remain visible in the dataset. Click OK.

Clear Filters

Filtering is nondestructive; you can remove the filters from one or more fields to expand the dataset again. To remove only one filter and keep the other filters, click the filter arrow for the field from which you want to clear the filter and select Clear Filter From. All filters can be removed by clicking Clear in the Sort & Filter group on the Data tab. As an alternate method, click Sort & Filter in the Editing group on the Home tab and select Clear.

STEP 5 ▶ Apply Text Filters

When you apply a filter to a text field, the filter menu displays each unique text item. You can select one or more text items from the list to be filtered. Once completed, only the selected text will be displayed. You can also select Text Filters to see a submenu of additional options, such as Begins With, Ends with, and Contains.

For example, Figure 4.26 shows the Sales_Last filter menu with two names selected. Excel displays records for these two reps only. The records for the other sales reps are hidden but not deleted.

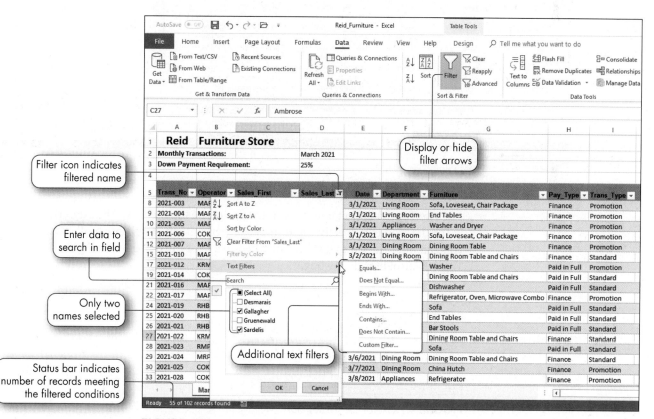

FIGURE 4.26 Filtered Text

STEP 6 ▶ Apply Number Filters

Excel contains a variety of number filters that enable you to display specific numbers, or a range of numbers such as above average or top 10 values. When you filter a field of numbers, you can select specific numbers. Or, you might want to filter numbers by a range, such as numbers greater than $5,000 or numbers between $4,000 and $5,000. If the field contains a large number of unique entries, you can click in the Search box and enter a value to display all matching records. For example, if you enter $7, the list will display only values that start with $7. The filter submenu enables you to set a variety of number filters. In Figure 4.27, the amounts are filtered to show only those that are above the average amount. In this example, Excel calculates the average amount as $4,512. Only records above that amount display.

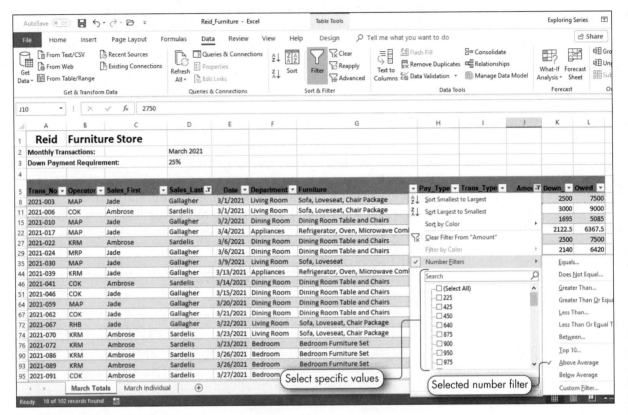

FIGURE 4.27 Filtered Numbers

The Top 10 option enables you to specify the top records. Although the option name is Top 10, you can specify the number or percentage of records to display. For example, you can filter the list to display only the top five or the bottom 7%. Figure 4.28 shows the Top 10 AutoFilter dialog box.

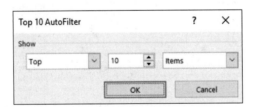

FIGURE 4.28 AutoFilter Dialog Box

STEP 7 Apply Date Filters

When you filter a field of dates, you can select specific dates or a date range, such as dates after 3/15/2021 or dates between 3/1/2021 and 3/7/2021. The submenu enables you to set a variety of date filters such as week, month, quarter, and year. For more specific date options, point to Date Filters, point to All Dates in the Period, and then select a period, such as Quarter 2 or October. Figure 4.29 shows the Date Filters menu.

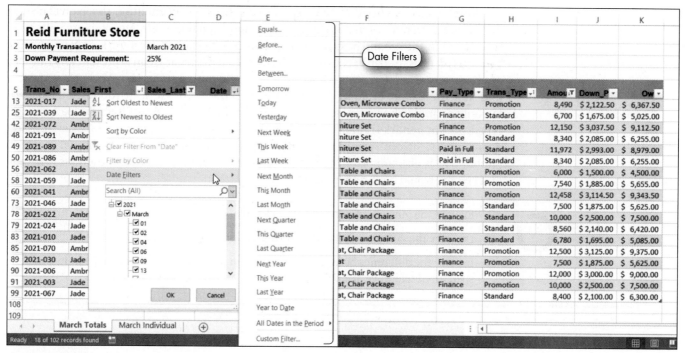

FIGURE 4.29 Date Filters

Apply a Custom Filter

Suppose as the manager of a furniture store, you are only interested in marketing directly to people who spent between $500 and $1,000 in the last month. To quickly identify the required data, you could use a custom AutoFilter. If you select options such as Greater Than or Between, Excel displays the Custom AutoFilter dialog box (see Figure 4.30). You can also select Custom Filter from the menu to display this dialog box, which is designed for more complex filtering requirements.

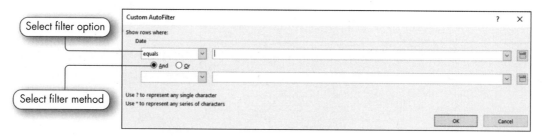

FIGURE 4.30 Custom AutoFilter Dialog Box

The dialog box indicates the column being filtered. To set the filters, click the arrows to select the comparison type, such as equals or contains. Click the arrow on the right to select a specific text, value, or date entry, or type the data yourself. For ranges of dates or values, click And, and then specify the comparison operator and value or date for the next condition row. For text, click Or. For example, if you want both Gallagher and Desmarais, you must select Or because each data entry contains either Gallagher or Desmarais but not both at the same time.

When filtering, you can use wildcards to help locate information in which there are multiple criteria and no custom filters. For example, to select all states starting with New, type *New* * in the second box; this will obtain results such as New York or New Mexico. The asterisk (*) is used in exchange for the text after "New" and can represent any number of characters. Therefore, this wildcard filter would return states New York, New Mexico, and New Hampshire because they all begin with the word "New." If you want a wildcard for only a single character, select Contains in the Custom Autofilters dialog box, and type a question mark (?) in place of the unknown character. For example, when filtering departments, "R?om" would return any department with *Room* in the name, as would "Room*." It is also important to note this feature is not case sensitive, therefore "R?om" and "r?om" would both return *Room*.

Quick Concepts

7. Explain the purpose of sorting data in a table. *p. 274*

8. Describe the difference between filtering and sorting data. *p. 276*

9. Explain the difference between an unqualified structured reference and a fully qualified structured reference. *p. 273*

Hands-On Exercises

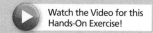

MyLab IT HOE3 Sim Training

▶ Watch the Video for this Hands-On Exercise!

Skills covered: Create a Structured Reference in a Formula • Sort One Field • Sort Multiple Fields • Create a Custom Sort • Apply Text Filters • Apply Number Filters • Apply Date Filters

3 Table Manipulation

You want to start analyzing the March transactions for Reid Furniture Store by calculating the totals owed, then sorting and filtering data in a variety of ways to help you understand the transactions better.

STEP 1 CREATE A STRUCTURED REFERENCE IN A FORMULA

First, you want to calculate the down payment owed by each customer. You will then calculate the total amount owed by subtracting the down payment from the total down payment. You will use structured references to complete these tasks. Refer to Figure 4.31 as you complete Step 1.

M	▼	:	× ✓ fx	=[Amount]-[Down_Pay]								

fx =[Amount]-[Down_Pay]

	A	B	C	D	E	F	G	H	I	J	K	L	M

Reid Furniture Store

| Monthly Transactions: | | | March 2021 | | | | | | | | |
| Down Payment Requirement: | | | 25% | | | | | | | | |

Step c: Structured reference

Trans_No ▼	Sales_Fir ▼	Sales_Las ▼	Date ▼	Department ▼	Furniture		Pay_Type ▼	Trans_Typ ▼	Amo ▼	Down_P ▼	Owed ▼
2021-001	Sebastian	Gruenewald	3/1/2021	Bedroom	Mattress		Finance	Promotion	2,788	697.00	=[Amount]-[Down_Pay]
2021-002	Sebastian	Gruenewald	3/1/2021	Bedroom	Mattress		Finance	Promotion	3,245	811.25	2,433.75
2021-003	Jade	Gallagher	3/1/2021	Living Room	Sofa, Loveseat, Chair Package		Finance	Promotion	10,000	2,500.00	7,500.00
2021-004	Jade	Gallagher	3/1/2021	Living Room	End Tables		Finance	Promotion	1,000	250.00	750.00
2021-005	Jade	Gallagher	3/1/2021	Appliances	Washer and Dryer		Finance	Promotion	2,750	687.50	2,062.50
2021-006	Ambrose	Sardelis	3/1/2021	Living Room	Sofa, Loveseat, Chair Package		Finance	Promotion	12,000	3,000.00	9,000.00
2021-007	Jade	Gallagher	3/1/2021	Dining Room	Dining Room Table		Finance	Promotion	3,240	810.00	2,430.00
2021-008	Chantalle	Desmarais	3/1/2021	Dining Room	Dining Room Table		Finance	Promotion	4,080	1,020.00	3,060.00
2021-009	Sebastian	Gruenewald	3/1/2021	Appliances	Washer and Dryer		Finance	Promotion	2,750	687.50	2,062.50
2021-010	Jade	Gallagher	3/2/2021	Dining Room	Dining Room Table and Chairs		Finance	Standard	6,780	1,695.00	5,085.00
2021-011	Chantalle	Desmarais	3/2/2021	Dining Room	Dining Room Table and Chairs		Finance	Standard	10,000	2,500.00	7,500.00
2021-012	Ambrose	Sardelis	3/2/2021	Appliances	Washer		Paid in Full	Promotion	1,100	275.00	825.00
2021-013	Chantalle	Desmarais	3/3/2021	Living Room	Recliners		Finance	Standard	2,430	607.50	1,822.50

Step c: Formula copied down

Step d: Comma Style applied

FIGURE 4.31 Create a Structured Reference

a. Open *e04h2Reid_LastFirst* if you closed it at the end of Hands-On Exercise 2. Save it as **e04h3Reid_LastFirst**, changing h2 to h3.

b. Click **cell J6**. Type **=** click **cell I6**, type *****. Click **cell D3**, press **F4**, and then press **Enter**.

The down payment required is 25% of the total purchase price. Structured reference format is used for Amount to create the formula that calculates the customer's down payment. Since the percentage in cell D3 (25%) is a constant it is entered as an absolute reference. Excel then copies the formula down the column.

c. Click **cell K6**. Enter the formula **=[Amount]-[Down_Pay]** and press **Enter**.

The formula calculates the total value owed for the transaction and copies the formula down the column.

d. Select the **range J6:K109** and apply the **Comma Style Number Format**.

e. Save the workbook.

You want to compare the number of transactions by sales rep, so you will sort the data by the Sales_Last field. After reviewing the transactions by sales reps, you want to arrange the transactions to show the one with the largest purchase first and the smallest purchase last. Refer to Figure 4.32 as you complete Step 2.

Step a: Sort alphabetically by last name

Step b: Sort amount from largest to smallest

	Trans_N ▾	Sales_Fir ▾	Sales_Las ▾	Date ▾	Department ▾	Furniture ▾	Pay_Type ▾	Trans_Typ ▾	Amou ▾	Down_P ▾	Ow ▾
5											
6	2021-073	Chantalle	Desmarais	3/24/2021	Living Room	Sofa, Loveseat, Chair Package	Finance	Standard	17,500	4,375.00	13,125.00
7	2021-097	Sebastian	Gruenewald	3/29/2021	Bedroom	Bedroom Furniture Set	Finance	Standard	14,321	3,580.25	10,740.75
8	2021-095	Sebastian	Gruenewald	3/29/2021	Living Room	Sofa, Loveseat, Chair Package	Finance	Standard	14,275	3,568.75	10,706.25
9	2021-056	Chantalle	Desmarais	3/19/2021	Living Room	Sofa, Loveseat, Chair Package	Finance	Standard	12,500	3,125.00	9,375.00
10	2021-070	Ambrose	Sardelis	3/23/2021	Living Room	Sofa, Loveseat, Chair Package	Finance	Promotion	12,500	3,125.00	9,375.00
11	2021-041	Ambrose	Sardelis	3/14/2021	Dining Room	Dining Room Table and Chairs	Finance	Promotion	12,458	3,114.50	9,343.50
12	2021-072	Ambrose	Sardelis	3/23/2021	Bedroom	Bedroom Furniture Set	Finance	Promotion	12,150	3,037.50	9,112.50
13	2021-006	Ambrose	Sardelis	3/1/2021	Living Room	Sofa, Loveseat, Chair Package	Finance	Promotion	12,000	3,000.00	9,000.00
14	2021-089	Ambrose	Sardelis	3/26/2021	Bedroom	Bedroom Furniture Set	Paid in Full	Standard	11,972	2,993.00	8,979.00
15	2021-100	Chantalle	Desmarais	3/30/2021	Bedroom	Bedroom Furniture Set	Finance	Promotion	11,234	2,808.50	8,425.50
16	2021-011	Chantalle	Desmarais	3/2/2021	Dining Room	Dining Room Table and Chairs	Finance	Standard	10,000	2,500.00	7,500.00
17	2021-003	Jade	Gallagher	3/1/2021	Living Room	Sofa, Loveseat, Chair Package	Finance	Promotion	10,000	2,500.00	7,500.00
18	2021-064	Sebastian	Gruenewald	3/21/2021	Appliances	Refrigerator, Oven, Microwave Combo	Finance	Promotion	10,000	2,500.00	7,500.00
19	2021-022	Ambrose	Sardelis	3/6/2021	Dining Room	Dining Room Table and Chairs	Finance	Standard	10,000	2,500.00	7,500.00

FIGURE 4.32 Sorted Data

a. Click the **Sales_Last filter arrow** and select **Sort A to Z**.

Excel arranges the transactions in alphabetic order by last name, starting with Desmarais. Within each sales rep, records display in their original sequence by transaction number. If you scan the records, you can see that Gallagher completed the most sales transactions in March. The up arrow icon on the Sales_Last filter arrow indicates that records are sorted in alphabetic order by that field.

b. Click the **Amount filter arrow** and select **Sort Largest to Smallest**.

The records are no longer sorted by Sales_Last. When you sort by another field, the previous sort is not saved. In this case, the transactions are arranged from the largest amount to the smallest amount, indicated by the down arrow icon in the Amount filter arrow.

c. Save the workbook.

You want to review the transactions by payment type (financed or paid in full). Within each payment type, you further want to compare the transaction type (Promotion or Standard). Finally, you want to compare costs within the sorted records by displaying the highest costs first. You will use the Sort dialog box to perform a three-level sort. Refer to Figure 4.33 as you complete Step 3.

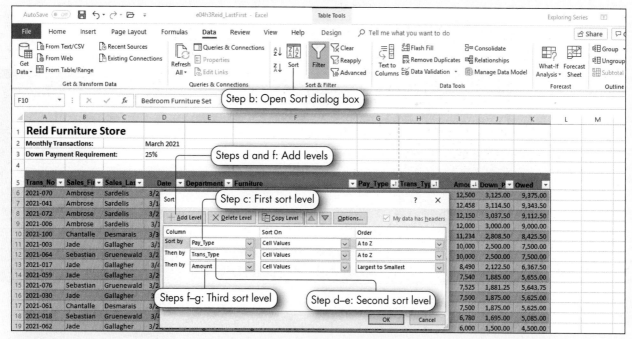

FIGURE 4.33 Three-Level Sort

a. Click inside the table and click the **Data tab**.

Both the Data and Home tabs contain commands to open the Sort dialog box.

b. Click **Sort** in the Sort & Filter group to open the Sort dialog box.

c. Click the **Sort by arrow** and select **Pay_Type**. Click the **Order arrow** and select **A to Z**.

You start by specifying the column for the primary sort. In this case, you want to sort the records first by the payment type column.

d. Click **Add Level**.

The Sort dialog box adds the Then by row, which adds a secondary sort.

e. Click the **Then by arrow** and select **Trans_Type**.

The default order is A to Z, which will sort in alphabetic order by Trans_Type. Excel will first sort the records by the Pay_Type (Finance or Paid in Full). Within each Pay_Type, Excel will further sort records by Trans_Type (Promotion or Standard).

f. Click **Add Level** to add another Then by row. Click the second **Then by arrow** and select **Amount**.

g. Click the **Order arrow** for the Amount sort and select **Largest to Smallest**.

Within the Pay_Type and Trans_Type sorts, this will arrange the records with the largest amount first in descending order to the smallest amount.

h. Click **OK** and scroll through the records. Save the workbook.

Most customers finance their purchases instead of paying in full. For the financed transactions, more than half were promotional sales. For merchandise paid in full, a majority of the transactions were standard sales, indicating that people with money do not necessarily wait for a promotional sale to purchase merchandise.

STEP 4 ▶ CREATE A CUSTOM SORT

For the month of March, you want to closely monitor sales of the Dining Room and Living Room departments. After completing the prior sort, you will add an additional level to create a custom sort of the department's data. Refer to Figure 4.34 as you complete Step 4.

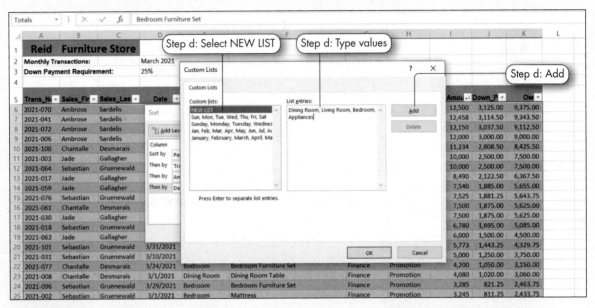

FIGURE 4.34 Custom Sort

a. Click inside the table and click **Sort** in the Sort & Filter group to open the Sort dialog box.

The Sort dialog box will open with the prior sort criteria displayed.

b. Click the last Then by (Amount) in the Sort dialog box created in the prior step and click **Add Level**.

c. Click the Then by arrow and select **Department**. Click the **Order arrow** and select **Custom List**.

This will open the Custom Lists dialog box, enabling you to manually specify the sort order.

> **MAC TROUBLESHOOTING:** Click the Excel menu and select Preferences. Click Custom Lists in the Formulas and Lists section.

d. Click **NEW LIST** in the Custom lists box, click the **List entries box**, and then type **Dining Room, Living Room, Bedroom, Appliances**. Click **Add**, click **OK**, and then click **OK** again to complete to return to the worksheet.

After completing the custom list, the data in column E will be sorted by Dining room, Living Room, Bedroom, and Appliances as the last step within the custom sort.

e. Save the workbook.

STEP 5 > APPLY TEXT FILTERS

You will filter the table to focus on Jade Gallagher's sales. You notice that she sells more merchandise from the Dining room department, so you will filter out the other departments. Refer to Figure 4.35 as you complete Step 5.

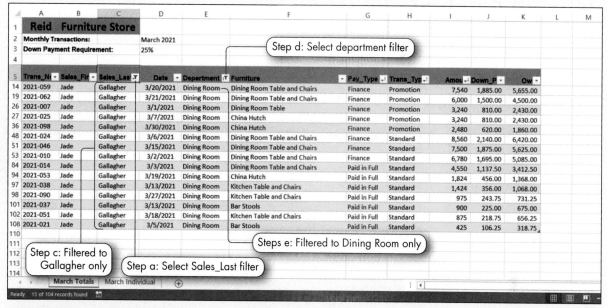

FIGURE 4.35 Apply Text Filters

a. Click the **Sales_Last filter arrow**.

The (Select All) check box is selected.

b. Click the **(Select All) check box** to deselect all last names.

c. Click the **Gallagher check box** to select it and click **OK**.

The status bar indicates that 33 out of 104 records meet the filtering condition. The Sales_Last filter arrow includes a funnel icon, indicating that this column is filtered.

d. Click the **Department filter arrow**.

e. Click the **(Select All) check box** to deselect all departments, click the **Dining Room check box** to focus on that department, and then click **OK**. Save the workbook.

The remaining 15 records show Gallagher's dining room sales for the month. The Department filter arrow includes a funnel icon, indicating that this column is also filtered.

Vicki is considering giving a bonus to employees who sold high-end dining room furniture during a specific time period (3/16/2021 to 3/31/2021). You want to determine if Jade Gallagher qualifies for this bonus. In particular, you are interested in how much gross revenue she generated for dining room furniture that cost at least $5,000 or more. Refer to Figure 4.36 as you complete Step 6.

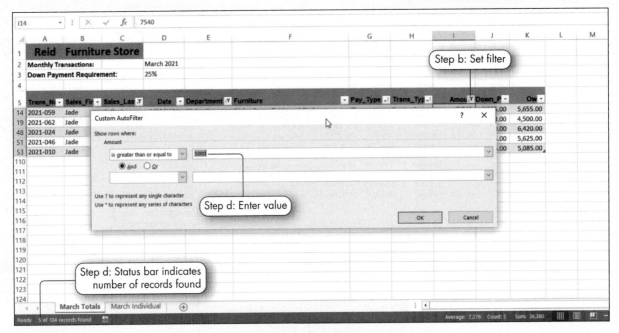

FIGURE 4.36 Filtered to Amounts Greater Than or Equal to $5,000

a. Select the **range I14:I108** of the filtered list and view the status bar.

   The average transaction amount is $3,754 with 15 transactions (i.e., 15 filtered records).

b. Click the **Amount filter arrow**.

c. Point to **Number Filters** and select **Greater Than** Or **Equal To**.

   The Custom AutoFilter dialog box opens.

d. Type **5000** in the box to the right of *is greater than or equal to* and click **OK**. Save the workbook.

   When typing numbers, you can type raw numbers such as 5000 or formatted numbers such as $5,000. Out of Gallagher's original 15 dining room transactions, only five transactions (one-third of her sales) were valued at $5,000 or more.

Finally, you want to study Jade Gallagher's sales records for the last half of the month. You will add a date filter to identify those sales records. Refer to Figure 4.37 as you complete Step 7.

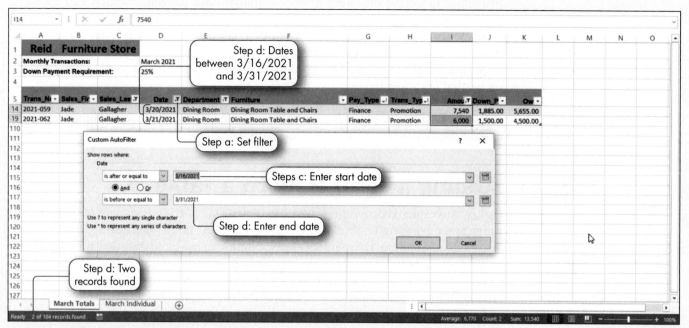

FIGURE 4.37 Filtered by Dates Between 3/16/2021 and 3/31/2021

a. Click the **Date filter arrow**.

b. Point to **Date Filters** and select **Between**.

The Custom AutoFilter dialog box opens. The default comparisons are *is after or equal to* and *is before or equal to*, ready for you to enter the date specifications.

c. Type **3/16/2021** in the box on the right side of *is after or equal to*.

You specified the starting date of the range of dates to include. You will keep the *And* option selected.

d. Type **3/31/2021** in the box on the right side of *is before or equal to*. Click **OK**.

Gallagher had only two dining room sales greater than $5,000 during the last half of March.

e. Save the workbook. Keep the workbook open if you plan to continue with the next Hands-On Exercise. If not, close the workbook, and exit Excel.

Table Aggregation and Conditional Formatting

In addition to sorting and filtering tables to analyze data, you might want to add fields that provide data aggregation such as Average or the total amount purchased. Furthermore, you might want to apply special formatting to cells that contain particular values or text using conditional formatting. For example, a sales manager might want to highlight employees that have reached their sales goal, or a professor might want to highlight test scores that fall below the average.

In this section, you will learn how to add a total row to a table along with learning about the five conditional formatting categories and how to apply conditional formatting to a range of values based on a condition you set.

STEP 1 ▷ Adding a Total Row to a Table

Earlier, you explored converting ranges to tables. One of the advantages of converting a range to a table is that a total row could be added. At times, aggregating data provides insightful information. For regular ranges of data, you use basic statistical functions, such as SUM, AVERAGE, MIN, and MAX, to provide summary analysis for a dataset. An Excel table provides the advantage of being able to display a total row automatically without creating the aggregate function yourself. A *total row* displays below the last row of records in an Excel table and enables you to display summary statistics, such as a sum of values displayed in a column.

> **To display and use the total row in a table, complete the following steps:**
>
> 1. Click any cell in the table.
> 2. Click the Design tab.
> 3. Click Total Row in the Table Style Options group. Excel displays the total row below the last record in the table. Excel displays Total in the first column of the total row.
> 4. Click a cell in the total row, click that cell's total row arrow, and then select the function result that you want. Excel calculates the summary statistics for values, but if the field is text, the only summary statistic that can be calculated is Count.
> 5. Click in the empty cell to add a summary statistic to another column for that field in the total row and click the arrow to select a function. Select None to remove the function.

Figure 4.38 shows the active total row with totals applied to the Amount, Down_Pay, and Owed fields. A list of functions displays to change the function for the last field.

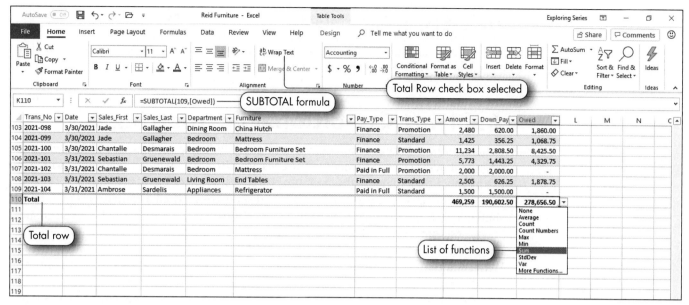

FIGURE 4.38 Total Row

The calculations on the total row use the SUBTOTAL function. The **SUBTOTAL function** calculates an aggregate value, such as totals or averages, for displayed values in a range, table, or database. If you click in a calculated total row cell, the SUBTOTAL function displays in the Formula Bar. The function for the total row looks like this: =SUBTOTAL(function_num,ref1). The function_num argument is a number that represents a function (see Table 4.4). The ref1 argument indicates the range of values to calculate. The SUBTOTAL function used to total the values in the Owed field would be =SUBTOTAL(109,[Owed]), where the number 109 represents the SUM function, and [Owed] represents the Owed field. A benefit of the SUBTOTAL function is that it subtotals data for filtered records, so you have an accurate total for the visible records.

=SUBTOTAL(function_num,ref1, . . .)

TABLE 4.4	Subtotal Function Numbers	
Function	**Function Number**	**Table Number**
AVERAGE	1	101
COUNT	2	102
COUNTA	3	103
MAX	4	104
MIN	5	105
PRODUCT	6	106
STDEV.S	7	107
STDEV.P	8	108
SUM	9	109
VAR.S	10	110
VAR.P	11	111

TIP: FILTERING DATA AND SUBTOTALS
If you filter the data and display the total row, the SUBTOTAL function's 109 argument ensures that only the displayed data are summed; data for hidden rows are not calculated in the aggregate function.

Applying Conditional Formatting

Conditional formatting enables you and your audience understand a dataset better because it adds a visual element to the cells. ***Conditional formatting*** applies formatting to any set of data to highlight or emphasize cells that meet specific conditions. The term is called *conditional* because the formatting displays only when a condition is met. This is similar logic to the IF function you have used. Remember with an IF function, you create a logical test that is evaluated. If the logical or conditional test is true, the function produces one result. If the logical or conditional test is false, the function produces another result. With conditional formatting, if the condition is true, Excel formats the cell automatically based on that condition; if the condition is false, Excel does not format the cell. If you change a value in a conditionally formatted cell, Excel examines the new value to see if it should apply the conditional format.

Table 4.5 lists and describes a number of different conditional formats that can be applied.

TABLE 4.5	Conditional Formatting Options
Options	**Description**
Highlight Cells Rules	Highlights cells with a fill color, font color, or border (such as Light Red Fill with Dark Red Text) if values are greater than, less than, between two values, equal to a value, or duplicate values; text that contains particular characters; or dates when a date meets a particular condition, such as *In the last 7 days*.
Top/Bottom Rules	Formats cells with values in the top 10 items, top 10%, bottom 10 items, bottom 10%, above average, or below average. You can change the exact values to format the top or bottom items or percentages, such as top 5 or bottom 15%.
Data Bars	Applies a gradient or solid fill bar in which the width of the bar represents the current cell's value compared relatively to other cells' values.
Color Scales	Formats different cells with different colors, assigning one color to the lowest group of values and another color to the highest group of values, with gradient colors to other values.
Icon Sets	Inserts an icon from an icon palette in each cell to indicate values compared to each other.

Another way to apply conditional formatting is with Quick Analysis. When you select a range and click the Quick Analysis button, the Formatting options display in the Quick Analysis gallery. Point to a thumbnail and Live Preview will show how it will affect the selected range (see Figure 4.39). You can also apply conditional formatting by clicking Conditional Formatting in the Styles group on the Home tab. Table 4.6 describes the conditional formatting options in the Quick Analysis gallery.

MAC TROUBLESHOOTING: Quick Analysis is not available for Mac users. Conditional Formatting can be applied by clicking the Home tab and selecting Conditional Formatting.

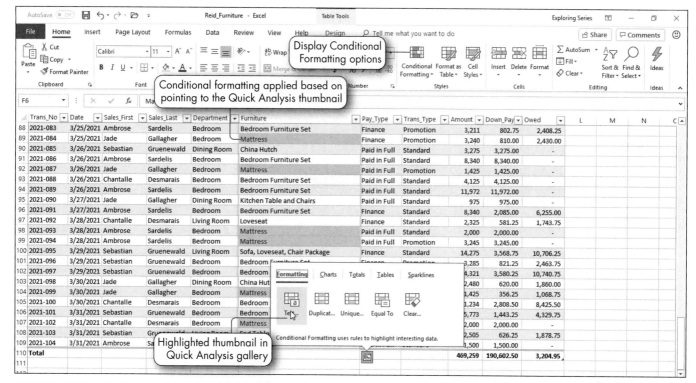

FIGURE 4.39 Quick Analysis Gallery to Apply Conditional Formatting

TABLE 4.6	Conditional Formatting Options in Quick Analysis Gallery
Options	**Description**
Text Contains	Formats cells that contain the text in the first selected cell. In Figure 4.39, the first selected cell contains Mattress. If a cell contains Mattress and Springs, Excel would format that cell also because it contains Mattress.
Duplicate Values	Formats cells that are duplicated in the selected range.
Unique Values	Formats cells that are unique; that is, no other cell in the selected range contains the same data.
Equal To	Formats cells that are exactly like the data contained in the first selected cell.
Clear Format	Removes the conditional formatting from the selected range.

STEP 2 ## Apply a Highlight Cells Rules

The Highlight Cells Rules category enables you to apply a highlight to cells that meet a condition, such as cells containing values greater than a particular value. This option contains predefined combinations of fill colors, font colors, and/or borders. For example, suppose you are a sales manager who developed a worksheet containing the sales for each day of a month. You are interested in sales between $5,000 and $10,000. You can apply a conditional format to cells that contain values within the desired range. To apply this conditional formatting, select Highlight Cells Rules, and then select Between. In the Between dialog box (see Figure 4.40), type 5000 in the first value box and 10000 in the second value box, select the type of conditional formatting, such as Light Red Fill with Dark Red Text, and then click OK to apply the formats. The results are displayed in Figure 4.41.

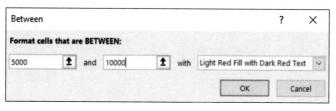

FIGURE 4.40 Between Dialog Box

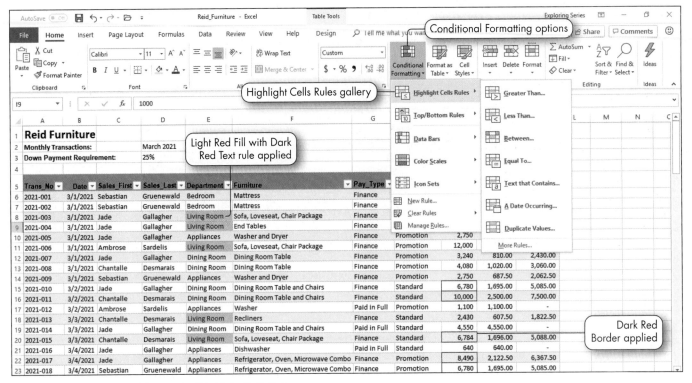

FIGURE 4.41 Conditional Formatting Highlight Cells Rules

STEP 3 | ## Specify Top/Bottom Rules

If you wanted to identify the top five sales to reward the sales associates or want to identify the bottom 15% of sales for more focused marketing, the Top/Bottom Rules category enables you to specify the top or bottom number, top or bottom percentage, or values that are above or below the average value in a specified range. In Figure 4.42, the Amount column is conditionally formatted to highlight the top five amounts. (The data has been sorted so the top 5 display at the top of the table.) Although the menu option is Top 10 Items, you can specify the exact number of items to format.

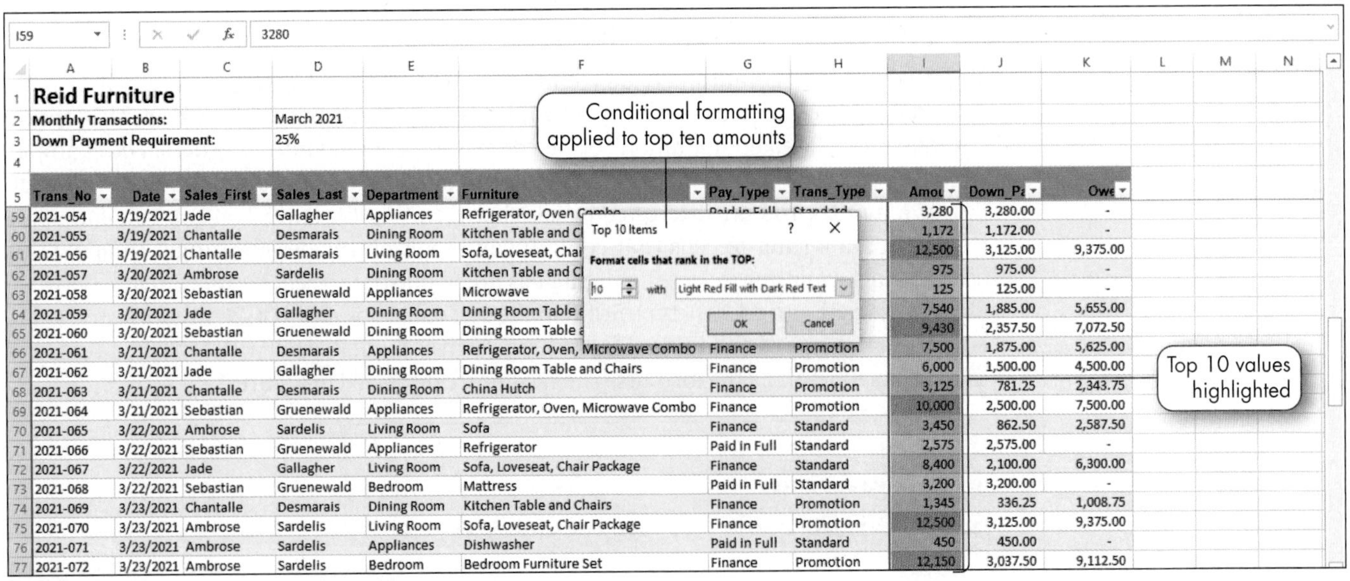

FIGURE 4.42 Top 10 Items Dialog Box

STEP 4 ▷ Display Data Bars, Color Scales, and Icon Sets

Data bars apply a gradient or solid fill bar in which the width of the bar represents the current cell's value compared relatively to other cells' values (see Figure 4.43). The width of the data bar represents the value in a cell, with a wider bar representing a higher value and a narrower bar a lower value. Excel locates the largest value and displays the widest data bar in that cell. Excel then finds the smallest value and displays the smallest data bar in that cell. Excel sizes the data bars for the remaining cells based on their values relative to the high and low values in the column. If you change the values, Excel updates the data bar widths. Excel uses the same color for each data bar, but each bar differs in size based on the value in the respective cells.

Color scales format cells with different colors based on the relative value of a cell compared to other selected cells. You can apply a two- or three-color scale. This scale assists in comparing a range of cells using gradations of those colors. The shade of the color represents higher or lower values. In Figure 4.43, for example, the red color scales display for the lowest values, the green color displays for the highest values, and gradients of yellow and orange represent the middle range of values in the Down_Pay column. Use color scales to understand variation in the data to identify trends, for example, to view good stock returns and weak stock returns.

Icon sets are symbols or signs that classify data into three, four, or five categories, based on the values in a range. Excel determines categories of value ranges and assigns an icon to each range. In Figure 4.43, a three-icon set was applied to the Owed column. Excel divided the range of values between the lowest value of $0 and the highest value of $13,125 into thirds. The red diamond icon displays for the cells containing values in the lowest third ($0 to $4,375), the yellow triangle icon displays for cells containing the values in the middle third ($4,376 to $8,750), and the green circle icon displays for cells containing values in the top third ($8,751 to $13,125). Most purchases fall into the lowest third.

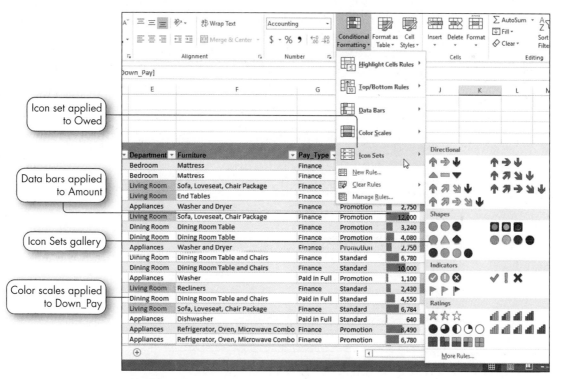

FIGURE 4.43 Data Bars, Color Scales, and Icon Sets

STEP 5 ▶ Creating a New Conditional Formatting Rule

The default conditional formatting categories provide a variety of options. Excel also enables you to create your own rules to specify different fill colors, borders, or other formatting if you do not want the default settings. Excel provides three ways to create a new rule:

- Click Conditional Formatting in the Styles group and select New Rule.
- Click Conditional Formatting in the Styles group, select Manage Rules to open the Conditional Formatting Rules Manager dialog box, and then click New Rule. (On a Mac, click the **+** icon to add a new rule.)
- Click Conditional Formatting in the Styles group, select a rule category such as Highlight Cells Rules, and then select More Rules.

When creating a new rule, the New Formatting Rule dialog box opens (see Figure 4.44) so that you can define the conditional formatting rule. First, select a rule type, such as *Format all cells based on their values*. The *Edit the Rule Description* section changes, based on the rule type you select. With the default rule type selected, you can specify the format style (2-Color Scale, 3-Color Scale, Data Bar, or Icon Sets). You can then specify the minimum and maximum values, the fill colors for color sets or data bars, or the icons for icon sets. After you edit the rule description, click OK to save the new conditional format.

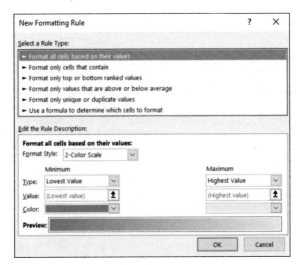

FIGURE 4.44 New Formatting Rule Dialog Box

If you select any rule type except the *Format all cells based on their values* rule, the dialog box contains a Format button. When you click Format, the Format Cells dialog box opens so that you can specify number, font, border, and fill formats to apply to your rule. (On a Mac, to access the Format Cells dialog box, select Classic in the Style box, click Format with, and then select Custom Format.)

Manage Rules

Periodically, conditional formatting rules may need to be updated, moved, or completely deleted. To edit or delete any conditional formatting rule that has been applied to data, use the features in the Manage Rules dialog box. To display the manage rules dialog box, click Conditional Formatting in the Styles group and select Manage rules (see Figure 4.45). You can display rules for data in a table, worksheet, or a selection of cells. To modify a setting of a conditional formatting rule, click Edit Rule. Use Delete Rule to remove conditional formats. You can also delete or clear rules from a worksheet, table, or selection by using Clear Rules in the Conditional Formatting command on the Home tab.

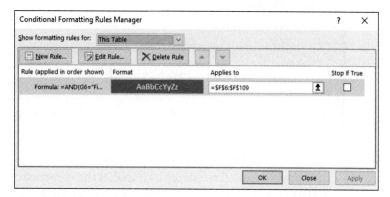

FIGURE 4.45 Conditional Formatting Rules Manager Dialog Box

Use Formulas in Conditional Formatting

Suppose you want to format merchandise amounts of financed items *and* amounts that are $10,000 or more. You can use a formula to create a conditional formatting rule to complete the task. Figure 4.46 shows the Edit Formatting Rule dialog box and the corresponding conditional formatting applied to cells.

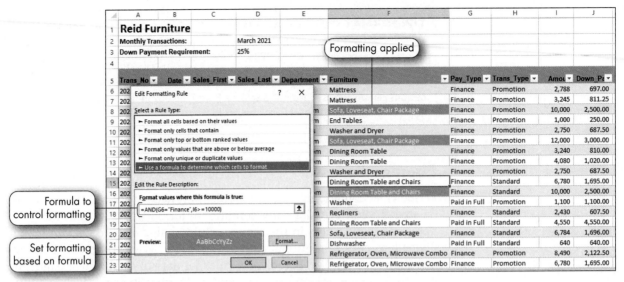

Formula to control formatting

Set formatting based on formula

FIGURE 4.46 Formula Rule Created and Applied

To create a formula-based conditional formatting rule, complete the following steps:

1. Select the data range.
2. Click the Home tab, click Conditional Formatting in the Styles group, and then click New Rule.
3. Select *Use a formula to determine which cells to format* and type the formula, using cell references in the first row, in the *Format values where this formula is true* box.
4. Click Format, select the desired formatting to be applied, and then click OK.

Once complete, Excel applies the general formula to the selected range, substituting the appropriate cell reference as it makes the comparisons. In the Figure 4.45 example, =AND(G6="Finance",I6>=10000) requires that the text in the Pay_Type column (column G) contain Finance and the Amount column (column I) contain a value that is greater than or equal to $10,000. The AND function requires that both logical tests be met to apply the conditional formatting. A minimum of two logical tests are required; however, you can include additional logical tests. Note that *all* logical tests must be true to apply the conditional formatting.

Quick Concepts

10. Describe the ways in which How is conditional formatting similar to an IF function. ***p. 290***

11. Describe a situation in which you would use conditional formatting. ***p. 290***

12. Describe how is data bar conditional formatting helpful when reviewing a column of data. ***p. 293***

Hands-On Exercises

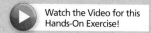
Skills covered: Add a Total Row • Apply Highlight Cells Rules • Specify Top/Bottom Rules • Display Data Bars, Color Scales, and Icon Sets • Create a New Conditional Formatting Rule • Use Formulas in Conditional Formatting • Manage Rules

4 Table Aggregation and Conditional Formatting

Vicki Reid wants to review the transactions with you. She is interested in Sebastian Gruenewald's sales record and the three highest transaction amounts. In addition, she wants to compare the down payment amounts visually. Finally, she wants you to analyze the amounts owed for sales completed by Sebastian.

STEP 1 ADD A TOTAL ROW

You want to see the monthly totals for the Amount, Down_Pay, and Owed columns. You will add a total row to calculate the values. Refer to Figure 4.47 as you complete Step 1.

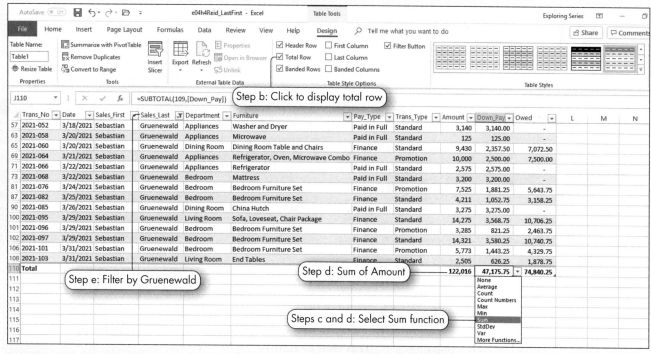

FIGURE 4.47 Add a Total Row

a. Open *e04h3Reid_LastFirst* if you closed it at the end of Hands-On Exercise 3. Save the workbook as **e04h4Reid_LastFirst**, changing h3 to h4.

b. Select the **March Individual worksheet**, click any cell inside the table, click the **Design tab**, and then click **Total Row** in the Table Style Options group.

Excel displays the total row after the last record. It sums the last field of values automatically. The total amount customers owe is 278,656.50.

c. Click the **Down_Pay cell** in row 110, click the **Total arrow**, and then select **Sum**.

You added a total to the Down_Pay field. The total amount of down payment collected is 190,602.50. The formula displays as =SUBTOTAL(109,[Down_Pay]) in the Formula Bar.

d. Click the **Amount cell** in row 110, click the **Total arrow**, and then select **Sum**.

You added a total to the Amount column. The total amount of merchandise sales is $469,259. The formula displays as =SUBTOTAL(109,[Amount]) in the Formula Bar.

e. Click the **Sales_Last filter arrow**, click the **Select All check box**, and then deselect the values. Click the **Gruenewald check box** to select it and click **OK**.

The total row values change to display the totals for only Gruenewald: $122,016 (Amount), 47,175.75 (Down_Pay), and 74,840.25 (Owed). This is an advantage of using the total row, which uses the SUBTOTAL function, as opposed to if you had inserted the SUM function manually. The SUM function would provide a total for all data in the column, not just the filtered data.

f. Click the **Data tab** and click **Clear** in the Sort & Filter group to remove all filters.

g. Save the workbook.

STEP 2 · **APPLY HIGHLIGHT CELLS RULES**

You want to identify Sebastian's sales for March without filtering the data. You will set a conditional format to apply a fill and font color so cells that document appliance sales stand out. Refer to Figure 4.48 as you complete Step 2.

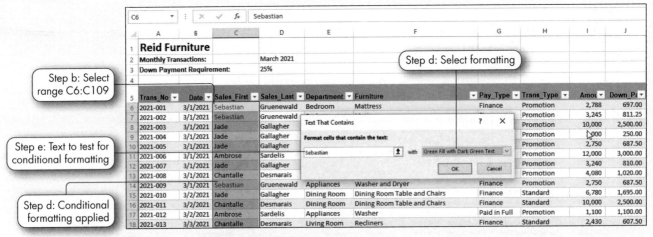

FIGURE 4.48 Highlight Cell Rules Dialog Box

a. Select the **range C6:C109**.

b. Click **Conditional Formatting** in the Styles group, point to **Highlight Cells Rules**, and then select **Text that Contains**.

The Text that Contains dialog box opens. (On a Mac, the New Formatting Rule box opens.)

c. Type **Sebastian** in the box, click the **with arrow**, and then select **Green Fill with Dark Green Text**. Click **OK**. Deselect the range and save the workbook.

Excel formats only cells that contain Sebastian with the fill and font color.

SPECIFY TOP/BOTTOM RULES

Vicki is now interested in identifying the highest three sales transactions in March. Instead of sorting the records, you will use the Top/Bottom Rules conditional formatting. Refer to Figure 4.49 as you complete Step 3.

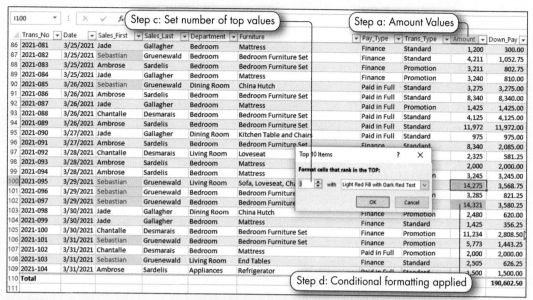

FIGURE 4.49 Top Three Amounts Conditionally Formatted

a. Select the **range I6:I109**, the range containing the amounts.

b. Click **Conditional Formatting** in the Styles group, point to **Top/Bottom Rules**, and then select **Top 10 Items**.

The Top 10 Items dialog box opens.

c. Click the arrow to display **3** and click **OK**.

d. Scroll through the worksheet to see the top three amounts. Save the workbook.

Vicki wants to compare all of the down payments. Data bars will add visual references that will enable her to quickly evaluate the data. Refer to Figure 4.50 as you complete Step 4.

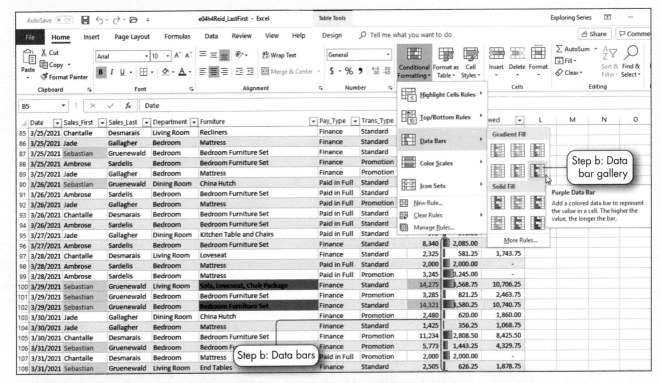

FIGURE 4.50 Data Bars Conditional Formatting

a. Select the **range J6:J109**, which contains the down payment amounts.

Excel displays a data bar in each cell. Note that one customer paid the full purchase price up front. In this case the down payment was 100% of the purchase price therefore the data bar fills the entire cell and the amount owed is 0.

b. Click **Conditional Formatting** in the Styles group, point to **Data Bars**, and then select **Purple Data Bar** in the Gradient Fill section. Scroll through the list and save the workbook.

CREATE A NEW CONDITIONAL FORMATTING RULE

Vicki's next request is to analyze the amounts owed by Sebastian's customers. In particular, she wants to highlight the merchandise for which more than $5,000 is owed. To do this, you realize you need to create a custom rule that evaluates both the Sales_First column and the Owed column. Refer to Figure 4.51 as you complete Step 5.

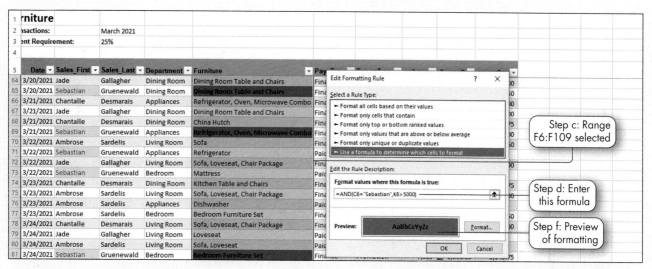

FIGURE 4.51 Custom Rule Created

a. Select the **range F6:F109**, which contains the furniture merchandise.

b. Click **Conditional Formatting** in the Styles group and select **New Rule**.

   The New Formatting Rule dialog box opens.

c. Select **Use a formula to determine which cells to format**.

MAC TROUBLESHOOTING: On a Mac, select Classic from the Style box and select Use a formula to determine which cells to format.

---

d. Type **=AND(C6="Sebastian",K6>5000)** in the *Format values where this formula is true* box.

   Because you are comparing the contents of cell C6 to text, you must enclose the text within quotation marks.

e. Click **Format** in the New Formatting Rule dialog box to open the Format Cells dialog box. On a Mac, select Custom Format in the Format with box to display the Format Cells dialog box.

f. Click the **Font tab** and click **Bold** in the Font style list. Click the **Border tab**, click the **Color arrow**, select **Blue, Accent 5**, and then click **Outline**. Click the **Fill tab**, click **Blue, Accent 5 background color** (the second color from the right on the first row), and then click **OK**.

   Figure 4.51 shows the Edit Formatting Rule dialog box, but the options are similar to the New Formatting Rule dialog box.

g. Click **OK** in the New Formatting Rule dialog box and scroll through the list to see which amounts owed are greater than $5,000 for Sebastian only.

TROUBLESHOOTING: If the results seem incorrect, click Conditional Formatting and select Manage Rules. Edit the rule you just created and make any corrections to the formula.

---

h. Save and close the file. Based on your instructor's directions, submit e04h4Reid_LastFirst.

Chapter Objectives Review

After reading this chapter, you have accomplished the following objectives:

1. Freeze rows and columns.
- The Freeze Panes setting freezes the row(s) above and the column(s) to the left of the active cell. When you scroll, those rows and columns remain onscreen.
- Use Unfreeze Panes to clear the frozen rows and columns.

2. Print large datasets.
- Display and change page breaks: Display the data in Page Break Preview to see the automatic page breaks. Dashed blue lines indicate automatic page breaks. You can insert manual page breaks, indicated by solid blue lines.
- Set and clear a print area: If you do not want to print an entire worksheet, select a range and set a print area.
- Print titles: Select rows to repeat at top and/or columns to repeat at left to print the column and row labels on every page of a printout of a large dataset.
- Control print page order: You can control the sequence in which the pages will print.

3. Explore the benefits of data tables.
- A table is a structured range that contains related data. Tables have several benefits over regular ranges. The column labels, called field names, display on the first row of a table. Each row is a complete set of data for one record.

4. Design and create tables.
- Plan a table before you create it. Create unique field names on the first row of the table and enter data below the field names, avoiding blank rows.
- Create a table: You can create a table from existing data. Excel applies Table Style formatting and assigns a name, such as Table1, to the table. When the active cell is within a table, the Table Tools Design tab displays.
- Rename a table: When a table is created, Excel assigns a generic name and enables you to edit the default to a more suitable name.
- Add and delete fields: You can insert and delete table rows and columns to adjust the structure of a table.
- Add, edit, and delete records: You can add table rows, edit records, and delete table rows.
- Remove duplicate rows: Use the Remove Duplicates dialog box to remove duplicate records in a table. Excel will display a dialog box telling you how many records are deleted.

5. Apply a table style.
- Table styles control the fill color of the header row and records within the table.

6. Create structured references in formulas.
- Structured references use tags as field headings that can be used in formulas in place of cell references.

7. Sort data.
- Sort one field: You can sort text in alphabetic or reverse alphabetic order, values from smallest to largest or largest to smallest, and dates from oldest to newest or newest to

oldest. Click the filter arrow and select the sort method from the list.
- Sort multiple fields: Open the Sort dialog box and add column levels and sort orders.
- Create a custom sort: You can create a custom sort for unique data, such as ensuring that the months sort in sequential order rather than alphabetic order.

8. Filter data.
- Filtering is the process of specifying conditions for displaying records in a table. Only records that meet those conditions display; the other records are hidden.
- Clear filters: If you do not need filters, you can clear the filters.
- Apply text filters: A text filter can find exact text, text that does not equal a condition, text that begins with a particular letter, and so forth.
- Apply number filters: A number filter can find exact values, values that do not equal a particular value, values greater than or equal to a value, and so on.
- Apply date filters: You can set filters to find dates before or after a certain date, between two dates, yesterday, next month, and so forth.
- Apply a custom filter: You can create a custom AutoFilter to filter values by options such as Greater Than, Less Than, or Before.

9. Add a total row to a table.
- You can display a total row after the last record. You can add totals or select a different function, such as Average.

10. Apply conditional formatting.
- After selecting text, click Formatting in the Quick Analysis gallery to apply a conditional format.
- Apply a highlight cells rule: This rule highlights cell contents with a fill color, font color, and/or border color where the contents match a particular condition.
- Specify top/bottom rules: These rules enable you to highlight the top or bottom x number of items or percentage of items.
- Display data bars, color scales, and icon sets: Data bars compare values within the selected range. Color scales indicate values that occur within particular ranges. Icon sets display icons representing a number's relative value compared to other numbers in the range.

11. Create a new conditional formatting rule.
- You can create conditional format rules. The New Formatting Rule dialog box enables you to select a rule type.
- Manage rules: Use the Conditional Formatting Rules Manager dialog box to edit and delete rules.
- Use formulas in conditional formatting: You can create rules based on content in multiple columns.

Key Terms Matching

Match the key terms with their definitions. Write the key term letter by the appropriate numbered definition.

a. Color scale
b. Conditional formatting
c. Data bar
d. Data Structure
e. Field
f. Filtering
g. Freezing
h. Fully qualified structured reference
i. Icon set
j. Page break

k. Print area
l. Print order
m. Record
n. Sorting
o. Structured reference
p. SUBTOTAL function
q. Table
r. Table style
s. Total Row
t. Unqualified reference

1. _____ A conditional format that displays a horizontal gradient or solid fill indicating the cell's relative value compared to other selected cells. **p. 293**

2. _____ The process of listing records or text in a specific sequence, such as alphabetically by last name. **p. 274**

3. _____ The process of specifying conditions to display only those records that meet those conditions. **p. 276**

4. _____ A set of rules that applies specific formatting to highlight or emphasize cells that meet specifications. **p. 290**

5. _____ A group of related fields representing one entity, such as data for one person, place, event, or concept. **p. 262**

6. _____ The rules that control the fill color of the header row, columns, and records in a table. **p. 266**

7. _____ An indication of where data will start on another printed page. **p. 254**

8. _____ A table row that appears below the last row of records in an Excel table and displays summary or aggregate statistics, such as a sum or an average. **p. 288**

9. _____ A conditional format that displays a particular color based on the relative value of the cell contents to the other selected cells. **p. 293**

10. _____ The sequence in which the pages are printed. **p. 256**

11. _____ A tag or use of a table element, such as a field label, as a reference in a formula. **p. 273**

12. _____ Symbols or signs that classify data into three, four, or five categories, based on the values in a range. **p. 293**

13. _____ The range of cells within a worksheet that will print. **p. 255**

14. _____ A predefined formula that calculates an aggregate value, such as totals, for values in a range, a table, or a database. **p. 289**

15. _____ An individual piece of data in a table, such as first name, last name, address, and phone number. **p. 288**

16. _____ A structure that organizes data in a series of records (rows), with each record made up of a number of fields (columns). **p. 273**

17. _____ The process of keeping rows and/or columns visible onscreen at all times, even when you scroll through a large dataset. **p. 253**

18. _____ The organization method used to manage multiple data points within a dataset. **p. 262**

19. _____ The use of headings without row references in a structured formula. **p. 273**

20. _____ A structured formula that includes references, for table name. **p. 273**

Multiple Choice

1. You have a large dataset that will print on several pages. You want to ensure that related records print on the same page with column and row labels visible and that confidential information is not printed. You should apply all of the following page setup options *except* which one to accomplish this task?

   (a) Set a print area.
   (b) Print titles.
   (c) Adjust page breaks.
   (d) Change the print page order.

2. You are working with a large worksheet. Your row headings are in column A. Which command(s) should be used to see the row headings and the distant information in columns X, Y, and Z?

   (a) Freeze Panes command
   (b) Hide Rows command
   (c) New Window command and cascade the windows
   (d) Split Rows command

3. Which statement is *not* a recommended guideline for designing and creating an Excel table?

   (a) Avoid naming two fields with the same name.
   (b) Ensure that no blank columns separate data columns within the table.
   (c) Leave one blank row between records in the table.
   (d) Include field names on the first row of the table.

4. Which of the following characters are wildcards in Excel? (Check all that apply.)

   (a) *
   (b) #
   (c) &
   (d) $

5. What should you do to ensure that records in a table are unique?

   (a) Do nothing; a logical reason probably exists to keep identical records.
   (b) Use the Remove Duplicates command.
   (c) Look at each row yourself and manually delete duplicate records.
   (d) Filter the data to show only unique records.

6. Which Conditional Formatting rule is best suited to highlight sales value greater than $5,000?

   (a) Equals
   (b) Between
   (c) Greater Than
   (d) Less Than

7. Which date filter option enables you to restrict the view to only dates between April 1, 2021, and April 30, 2021?

   (a) Equals
   (b) Before
   (c) After
   (d) Between

8. Which of the following is a fully qualified structured reference?

   (a) =[Purchase_Price]-[Down_Payment]
   (b) =Sales[@Purchase_Price]-Sales[@Down_Payment]
   (c) =Purchase_Price-Down_Payment
   (d) =[Sales]Purchase_Price-[Sales]Down_Payment

9. Which of the following is *not* an aggregate function that can be applied in a total row?

   (a) MAX
   (b) AVERAGE
   (c) COUNT
   (d) VLOOKUP

10. If you would like to set a conditional formatting rule based on the function =AND(G6="Finance", H7<7000), which formatting rule type is needed?

    (a) Format all cells based on their values.
    (b) Format only cells that contain.
    (c) Use a formula to determine which cells to format.
    (d) Format only values that are above or below average.

Practice Exercises

1 Institute for Study Abroad

You are an administrative assistant for the local university's Institute for Study Abroad. The institute for study abroad is responsible for the coordination and management of all students that plan to study overseas. As part of your duties, you have been asked to enhance a preexisting worksheet by creating an Excel table, applying filters, conditional formatting, adding tuition calculations, and making the document printer friendly. Refer to Figure 4.52 as you complete this exercise.

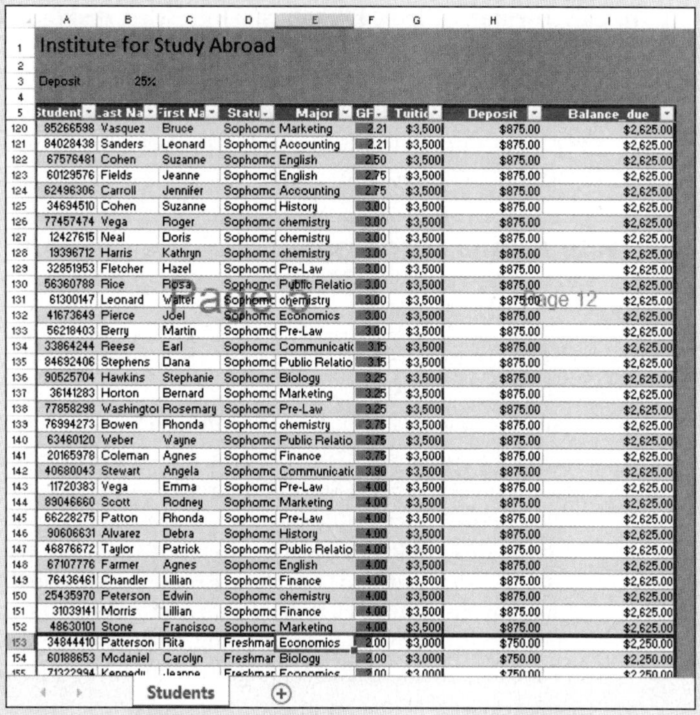

FIGURE 4.52 Institute for Study Abroad

a. Open *e04p1StudyAbroad* and save it as **e04p1StudyAbroad_LastFirst**.

b. Select the **range A5:G209**. Click the **Insert tab**, click **Table** in the Tables group. Be sure to click *My table has headers* and click **OK** in the Create Table dialog box.

c. Type **Students** in the Table Name box in the Properties group.

d. Click **cell A1** and click **cell A6**. Click the **View tab**, click **Freeze Panes** in the Window group, and then select Freeze Panes.

e. Click the **Data tab** and click **Remove Duplicates** in the Data Tools group. Click **OK** and then click **OK** again.

   Four Duplicate values should be found and removed.

f. Click **cell H5**, type **Deposit**, and then press **Enter**. Click **cell I5**, type **Balance_due**, and then press **Enter**.

g. Click **cell H6**, type **=$B$3*[Tuition]**, and then press **Enter**.

h. Click **cell I6**, type **=[Tuition]-[Deposit]**, and then press **Enter**.

i. Select the **range H5:I205**. Click the **Home tab**, click **Format** in the cells group, and then select **AutoFit Column Width**.

j. Click **Currency Number Format** in the Numbers group.

k. Select the **range F6:F205**. Click the **Quick Analysis box** located at the bottom of the selection, and select **Data Bars** in the Formatting group. (On a Mac, click the Home tab, click Conditional Formatting, and then select Data Bars.)

l. Click the **Design tab** and click **Total Row** in the Table Style Options group.

m. Select the **range A6:A205**. Click the **Home tab**, click **Conditional Formatting** in the Styles group, and then select **New Rule**. Click **Use a formula to determine which cells to format** and type **=AND(D6="Senior", F6<=2)**.

n. Click **Format**, click the **Fill tab**, and then select **Red** (last row, second from the left). Click **OK** and click **OK** again to apply the conditional formatting.

o. Click **cell F6**, click the **Data tab**, and then click **Sort** in the Sort & Filter group. Click the **Column arrow** and select **Status**. Click the **Order arrow** and select **Custom list**. Click **NEW LIST** in the Custom lists box and click the List entries box. Type **Senior, Junior, Sophomore, Freshman** in the List entries box.

> **MAC TROUBLESHOOTING:** Click the Excel menu and select Preferences. Click Custom Lists in the Formulas and Lists section.

p. Click **OK** to return to the Sort dialog box. Click **Add Level**, click the **Then by arrow**, and then select **GPA**. Click **OK**.

q. Prepare the Students worksheet for printing by doing the following:
- Select the **range A5:I206**, click the **Page Layout tab**, click **Print Area** in the Page Setup group, and then select **Set Print Area**.
- Click **Print Titles** in the Page Setup group, click the **Rows to repeat at top Collapse Dialog Box**, click the **row 5 header**, and then click **Expand Dialog Box**. Click **OK**.
- Click the **View tab** and click **Page Break Preview** in the Workbook Views group. Click the **Page Layout tab**. Click the row that contains the first student with Junior status (row 58), click **Breaks** in the Page Setup group, and then click Insert Page Break. Repeat the last step to add page breaks at each change in status (rows 110 and 153).

r. Save and close the file. Based on your instructor's directions, submit e04p1StudyAbroad_LastFirst.

2 Sunny Popcorn, Inc.

You are a financial analyst for Sunny Popcorn, Inc., and have been given the task of compiling a workbook to detail weekly sales information. The current information provides detailed sales rep information, flavors ordered, account type, and volume ordered. The owners are specifically interested in local sales that are generating at least $150.00 a week. To complete the document you will sort, filter, use table tools, and apply conditional formatting. Refer to Figure 4.53 as you complete this exercise.

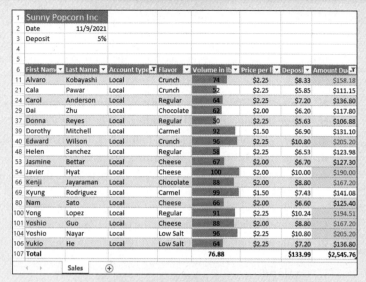

	First Name	Last Name	Account type	Flavor	Volume in lbs	Price per lb	Deposit	Amount Due
1	Sunny Popcorn Inc							
2	Date	11/9/2021						
3	Deposit	5%						
4								
5								
6	First Name	Last Name	Account type	Flavor	Volume in lbs	Price per lb	Deposit	Amount Due
11	Alvaro	Kobayashi	Local	Crunch	74	$2.25	$8.33	$158.18
21	Cala	Pawar	Local	Crunch	52	$2.25	$5.85	$111.15
24	Carol	Anderson	Local	Regular	64	$2.25	$7.20	$136.80
29	Dai	Zhu	Local	Chocolate	62	$2.00	$6.20	$117.80
37	Donna	Reyes	Local	Regular	50	$2.25	$5.63	$106.88
39	Dorothy	Mitchell	Local	Carmel	92	$1.50	$6.90	$131.10
40	Edward	Wilson	Local	Crunch	96	$2.25	$10.80	$205.20
48	Helen	Sanchez	Local	Regular	58	$2.25	$6.53	$123.98
53	Jasmine	Bettar	Local	Cheese	67	$2.00	$6.70	$127.30
54	Javier	Hyat	Local	Cheese	100	$2.00	$10.00	$190.00
66	Kenji	Jayaraman	Local	Chocolate	88	$2.00	$8.80	$167.20
69	Kyung	Rodriguez	Local	Carmel	99	$1.50	$7.43	$141.08
80	Nam	Sato	Local	Cheese	66	$2.00	$6.60	$125.40
100	Yong	Lopez	Local	Regular	91	$2.25	$10.24	$194.51
101	Yoshio	Guo	Local	Cheese	88	$2.00	$8.80	$167.20
104	Yoshio	Nayar	Local	Low Salt	96	$2.25	$10.80	$205.20
106	Yukio	He	Local	Low Salt	64	$2.25	$7.20	$136.80
107	Total				76.88		$133.99	$2,545.76

Sales ⊕

FIGURE 4.53 Sunny Popcorn Inc.

a. Open *e04p2Popcorn* and save it as **e04p2Popcorn_LastFirst**.

b. Click **cell C7**, ensure the Home tab is displayed, click the **Sort & Filter arrow** in the Editing group, and then select **Sort A to Z**.

c. Click the **Insert tab**, click **Table** in the Tables group, and then click **OK** in the Create Table dialog box.

d. Click **Orange, Table Style Medium 3** in the Table Styles group on the Design tab.

e. Click **cell G7**, type **=[Price per lb]*[Volume in lbs]*$B$3** and then press **Enter**.

f. Click **cell H7**, type **=[Price per lb]*[Volume in lbs]-[Deposit]** and then press **Enter**

g. Select the **range G7:H106**, click the **Home tab**, and then click **Currency Number Format** in the Number group.

h. Click the **Design tab** and click **Total Row** in the Table Style Options group.

i. Click the **Deposit Total Row arrow**, ensure **Sum** is selected, click the **Volume in lbs Total Row arrow**, and then select **Average**.

j. Click the **filter arrow** of the Account type column, click the **Select All check box** to deselect it, click **Local**, and then click **OK**. Click the **filter arrow** of Amount Due, select **Number Filters**, and then select Above Average.

k. Select the **range H11:H106**, click **Quick Analysis**, and then select **Greater Than**. Type **150.00** in the Format cells that are GREATER THAN box, select **Green Fill with Dark Green Text**, and then click **OK**. (On a Mac, click the Home tab, click Conditional Formatting, and then click **Highlight Cells Rules**. Select **Greater Than** and enter the parameters.)

> **MAC TROUBLESHOOTING:** Quick Analysis is not available for Mac. In order to apply conditional formatting click the Home tab and click Conditional Formatting.

l. Select the **range E11:E106**, click **Quick Analysis**, and then select **Data Bars**.

m. Click the **Page Layout tab**, click the **Scale box** in the Scale to Fit group, and then type **85%**. (On a Mac, click the Page Layout tab, click Page Setup, and then adjust the scale to 85%.)

n. Create a footer with your name on the left side, the sheet name code in the center, and the file name code on the right side.

o. Save and close the file. Based on your instructor's directions, submit e04p2Popcorn_LastFirst.

Mid-Level Exercises

1 Crafton's Pet Supplies

MyLab IT Grader

You are the inventory manager for Crafton's Pet Supplies. You are currently performing an analysis to determine inventory levels, as well as the total value of inventory on hand. Your last steps will be to check the report for duplicate entries and format for printing.

a. Open *e04m1Inventory* and save it as **e04m1Inventory_LastFirst**.

b. Freeze the panes so that the column labels do not scroll offscreen.

c. Convert the data to a table and name the table **Inventory2021**.

d. Apply **Red, Table Style Medium 3** to the table.

e. Sort the table by Warehouse (A to Z), then Department, and then by Unit Price (smallest to largest). Create a custom sort order for Department so that it appears in this sequence: Food & Health, Collars & Leashes, Toys, Clothes, Training, and Grooming.

f. Remove duplicate records from the table. Excel should find and remove one duplicate record.

g. Create an unqualified structured reference in column G to determine the value of the inventory on hand. To calculate the inventory on hand, multiply the **Unit Price** and the **Amount on Hand.**

h. Apply a **Total Row** to the Inventory2021 table; set the Amount on Hand to Average. Format the results to display with two decimal points.

i. Create a new conditional formatting rule that displays any Inventory Value for the Food & Health department with a value of $30,000 or more as **Red, Accent 2 fill color** with **White, Background 1** font color. There will be two qualifying entries.

j. Ensure the warehouse information is not broken up between pages when printed. Add a page break to make sure that each warehouse prints on its own consecutive page.

k. Set the worksheet to **Landscape orientation** and repeat row 1 labels on all pages.

l. Display the Inventory sheet in Page Break Preview.

m. Insert a footer with your name on the left side, the sheet name code in the center, and the file name code on the right side.

n. Save and close the file. Based on your instructor's directions, submit e04m1Inventory_LastFirst.

2 Riverwood Realty

MyLab IT Grader

You work as a real estate agent for Riverwood Realty, an independent real estate agency in Utah. As part of your end of year reports, you compile a list of homes that have sold in your sales region. To complete the report, you will create an Excel table, apply Filters, Sort, perform basic calculations using unqualified structured references, and then prepare the document to print.

a. Open *e04m2Homes* and save it as **e04m2Homes_LastFirst**.

b. Freeze the panes so that the column labels do not scroll offscreen.

c. Convert the data to a table and name the table Sales.

d. Apply **Purple, Table Style Dark 10** to the table.

e. Remove duplicate records from the table. Excel should find and remove eight duplicate records.

f. Add a new column in column I named **Days on Market**. Use unqualified structured references to calculate the days on market (Sale date – list date) in column I. Set column I's width to **18**.

g. Apply a **Total Row** to the Sales table; set the selling price and Days on Market totals to Average with one decimal point.

h. Use Quick Analysis to apply Top 10% conditional formatting to column F. On a Mac Quick Analysis is not available. Click the Home tab, click Conditional Formatting, click Top/Bottom Rules, and then select Top 10%.

i. Apply **3 Traffic Lights (Unrimmed)** conditional formatting icon set to column I. Set the icon to display green for homes that sold within 45 days, yellow for 46 to 90, and red to homes that took more than 90 days to sell.

j. Filter the data to only display sales by the **Selling Agent Hernandez**.

k. Sort the table in **Ascending order** by City (Column C).

l. Set the **range A1:I83** as the print area.

m. Save and close the file. Based on your instructor's directions, submit e04m2Homes_LastFirst.

Running Case

New Castle County Technical Services

New Castle County Technical Services (NCCTS) provides technical support services for a number of companies in New Castle County, Delaware. You previously created charts to depict summary data by service type, customer, and days open. Since then, you copied the charts as pictures to replace the actual charts so changes you make to the dataset will not alter the charts. However, you have a backup of the original charts in case you need to change them later. Now, you will sort the main dataset for analysis and prepare it to be printed on two pages. You will apply conditional formatting to highlight transactions that took more than 9 days to close and display data bars for the amount billed to give a quick visual for transaction amounts. You will also filter a copy of the dataset to set filters to further analyze the transactions. Finally, you will convert the summary sections into tables.

a. Open *e04r1NCCTS* and save it as **e04r1NCCTS_LastFirst**.

b. Freeze the fourth row and second column so that they do not scroll off the window on the March Hours worksheet.

c. Sort the data on the March Hours worksheet in alphabetic order by Call Type and within call type by Amount Billed from largest to smallest.

d. Apply conditional formatting that highlights over 9 days open in Light Red Fill with Dark Red Text.

e. Apply solid fill **Orange Data Bar** conditional formatting to the Amount Billed values.

f. Display the March Filtered worksheet and set a filter to display transactions with an Opened Date in March.

g. Set another filter to display transactions with an Amount Billed greater than or equal to $400.

h. Display the Summary Statistics worksheet. Create a table for the Summary Statistics by Customer dataset. As you create the table, adjust the table range to start on row 2.

i. Assign the name **Customer_Stats** to the table.

j. Apply **Orange, Table Style Medium 3**.

k. Add a total row to display the sum of the Total Amount Billed column to the table.

l. Select the **range A1:D20** in the Summary Stats worksheet and set it as a print area.

m. Create a table for the Summary Statistics by Call Type dataset below the first dataset. As you create the table, adjust the table range to start on row 27.

n. Assign the name **CallType_Stats** to the table.

o. Apply **Orange, Table Style Medium 3**.

p. Add a total row to display the sum of the Total Amount Billed column to the table.

q. Click **cell D27** and insert a table column to the left. Type **Hours per Day** in **cell D27**.

r. Insert a structured reference in a formula in **cell D28** that divides the Total Days Open by the Total Hours Logged.

s. Use Format Painter to copy the fill formatting from **cell D26** to **cell E26**.

t. Insert a footer with your name on the left side, the sheet name in the center, and the file name code on the right side of Summary Charts and Summary Statistics worksheets. Return to Normal view.

u. Save and close the workbook. Based on your instructor's directions, submit e04r1NCCTS_LastFirst.

Disaster Recovery

Dairy Farm

You are the product manager for Schaefer Dairy farm, a local organic farm that produces dairy products. Current inventory information is stored in an Excel worksheet and conditional formatting is used to indicate when a product has expired and should be discarded. Unfortunately, the conditional formatting rule that was created to indicate a product should be discarded has stopped working. You need to examine the existing conditional formatting rule and repair the error in order to identify the expired products. All products have a shelf life of 30 days.

Open *e04d1Dairy* and save it as **e04d1Dairy_LastFirst**. Review the shelf-life information referenced in cell D3. Note the 30-day shelf life was erroneously changed to 300. Enter the correct input to reflect the actual shelf life. Next, edit the custom conditional formatting rule applied to **column B** to reflect the correct shelf life referenced in cell D3. Rename the table **Products** and add a total row that calculates the total value of inventory in column D and counts the total number of products in column E.

Save and close the file. Based on your instructor's directions, submit e04d1Dairy_LastFirst.

IT Department Analysis

You have been hired as a student assistant in the IT department of your university. As part of your responsibilities, you have been asked to enhance the Excel workbook used to analyze the department's performance. The workbook contains records of all support issues resolved over the past year. You will convert the data to a table, format the table, sort and filter the table, insert calculations to evaluate key performance indicators, and then prepare the worksheet for printing

Prepare the Large Worksheet as a Table

You will freeze the panes so that labels remain onscreen. You also want to convert the data to a table so that you can apply table options.

1. Open the *e04c1TechSupport* workbook and save it as **e04c1TechSupport_LastFirst**.
2. Freeze Panes so the first row containing column headings (Row 5) on the SupportCalls worksheet will remain static when scrolling.
3. Convert the data to a table, name the table **SupportCalls**, and then apply the **Gold, Table Style Medium 12**.
4. Remove duplicate records.

Add a Structured Reference and a Total Row

To help the IT analyze productivity, you will use unqualified structured references to add a calculation to the table. You will also add a total row to provide basic summary data.

5. Add a new column to the table named **Duration**.
6. Create a formula using unqualified structured references to calculate the days required to resolve the incident (Date Resolved – Date created) and apply General Number Format.
7. Add a total row to display the Average days required to resolve an issue.

Sort and Filter the Table

To help the IT manager analyze the effectiveness of each support technician, you will create a custom sort to display Agents in alphabetic order, then by problem description, and then by incident duration.

8. Sort the table by Agent Name in alphabetic order, add a second level to sort by description, and then create a custom sort order as follows: Won't power on, Virus, Printing Issues, Software Update, Forgotten Password. Add a third level to sort by duration smallest to largest.
9. Filter the table to only display closed incidents as indicated in the status column.

Apply Conditional Formatting

The IT department has a 30-day threshold to resolve all technical incidents. You will use conditional formatting to identify issues that lasted or exceeded 30 days to resolve.

10. Use Quick Analysis to apply **Data Bars** conditional formatting to the column that contains duration. (On a Mac, click the Home tab and use Conditional Formatting to apply **Data Bars** to the column that contains the data.)
11. Create a conditional format that applies **Red fill** and White Background 1 font color to the incidents (column A) that required 30 or more days to resolve.

Prepare the Worksheet for Printing

The final report will be distributed in print for your end-of-the-year meeting. You will set page breaks and repeating column headings before printing.

12. Select **Landscape orientation** for all sheets and set appropriate margins so that the data will print on one page. Set the print scale to **85%**.
13. Change page breaks so agent information is not split between pages.
14. Set row 5 to repeat on each page that is printed.
15. Add a footer with your name on the left side, the sheet name code in the center, and the file name code on the right side.
16. Save and close the file. Based on your instructor's directions, submit e04c1TechSupport_LastFirst.

Subtotals, PivotTables, and PivotCharts

LEARNING OUTCOME   You will manage and analyze data by creating subtotals, PivotTables, and PivotCharts.

OBJECTIVES & SKILLS: After you read this chapter, you will be able to:

CASE STUDY | Ivory Halls Publishing Company

You are the vice president of the Sociology Division at Ivory Halls Publishing Company. Textbooks are classified by an overall discipline. Books are further classified by area. You will use these classifications to see which areas and disciplines have the highest and lowest sales. The worksheet contains wholesale and retail data.

     You want to analyze sales for books published in the Sociology Division. To do this, you will organize data by discipline and insert subtotal rows. You will also create PivotTables to gain a variety of perspectives of aggregated data. Finally, you will create a PivotChart to depict the aggregated data.

CHAPTER 5

Summarizing and Analyzing Data

YanLev/Shutterstock

Top-left subtotals table:

	Discipline	Area	Sales: Wholesale	Sales: Retail	Total Book Sales
79	Research/Stats	Data Analysis	$ 644,250	$ 4,704	$ 648,954
80	Research/Stats	Data Analysis	$ 675,000	$ 11,700	$ 686,700
81	Research/Stats	Data Analysis	$ 1,338,750	$ 13,653	$ 1,352,403
82	Research/Stats	Data Analysis	$ 815,625	$ 9,800	$ 825,425
83		**Data Analysis Total**	$ 3,473,625	$ 39,857	$ 3,513,482
84	Research/Stats	Research Methods	$ 640,220	$ 9,213	$ 649,433
85	Research/Stats	Research Methods	$ 1,927,500	$ 130,000	$ 2,057,500
86	Research/Stats	Research Methods	$ 2,311,100	$ 40,560	$ 2,351,660
87	Research/Stats	Research Methods	$ 3,016,575	$ 226,688	$ 3,243,263
88	Research/Stats	Research Methods	$ 526,125	$ 21,450	$ 547,575
89		**Research Methods Total**	$ 8,421,520	$ 427,911	$ 8,849,431
90	Research/Stats	Social Statistics	$ 2,569,675	$ 109,800	$ 2,679,475
91	Research/Stats	Social Statistics	$ 457,500	$ 8,190	$ 465,690
92	Research/Stats	Social Statistics	$ 2,946,875	$ 202,935	$ 3,149,810
93	Research/Stats	Social Statistics	$ 1,123,400	$ 1,950	$ 1,125,350
94	Research/Stats	Social Statistics	$ 1,413,125	$ 13,888	$ 1,427,013
95	Research/Stats	Social Statistics	$ 868,250	$ 13,200	$ 881,450
96		**Social Statistics Total**	$ 9,378,825	$ 349,963	$ 9,728,788
97	**Research/Stats Total**		$ 21,273,970	$ 817,731	$ 22,091,701

Top-right PivotTable:

	A	B	C	D	E	F
3	Sales by Discipline	Copyright Year				
4	Discipline	2018	2019	2020	2021	Grand Total
5	Aging/Death	$ 3,689,688	$ 1,391,874	$ 1,801,600	$ 5,977,074	$ 12,860,236
6	Criminal Justice	$ 951,068	$ 563,137	$ 2,022,000	$ 3,878,898	$ 7,415,103
7	Family	$ 565,451	$ 1,823,366	$ 2,138,209	$ 3,945,558	$ 8,472,584
8	Introductory		$ 5,123,050	$ 6,967,985	$ 5,758,835	$ 17,849,870
9	Miscellaneous	$ 264,819	$ 64,810	$ 327,045	$ 2,760,453	$ 3,417,127
10	Race/Class/Gender	$ 684,500	$ 3,535,415	$ 6,366,445	$12,369,071	$ 22,955,431
11	Research/Stats	$ 2,542,032	$ 2,112,753	$12,049,287	$ 5,354,588	$ 22,058,660
12	Social Problems	$ 1,403,664	$ 1,608,100	$ 2,926,145	$ 4,808,298	$ 10,746,207
13	Social Psychology	$ 2,360,666	$ 1,169,512	$ 3,404,641	$ 7,329,991	$ 14,264,810
14	**Grand Total**	$ 12,461,888	$17,392,017	$38,003,357	$52,182,766	$ 120,040,028

Bottom-left PivotTable (percentages):

	A	B	C	D	E	F
1	Edition	(All)				
3	Sales by Discipline	Copyright Year				
4	Discipline	2018	2019	2020	2021	Grand Total
5	Aging/Death	3.07%	1.16%	1.50%	4.98%	10.71%
6	Criminal Justice	0.79%	0.47%	1.68%	3.23%	6.18%
7	Family	0.47%	1.52%	1.78%	3.29%	7.06%
8	Introductory	0.00%	4.27%	5.80%	4.80%	14.87%
9	Miscellaneous	0.22%	0.05%	0.27%	2.30%	2.85%
10	Race/Class/Gender	0.57%	2.95%	5.30%	10.30%	19.12%
11	Research/Stats	2.12%	1.76%	10.04%	4.46%	18.38%
12	Social Problems	1.17%	1.34%	2.44%	4.01%	8.95%
13	Social Psychology	1.97%	0.97%	2.84%	6.11%	11.88%
14	**Grand Total**	10.38%	14.49%	31.66%	43.47%	100.00%

Bottom-right PivotTable and PivotChart:

	A	B
3	Row Labels	Sum of Total Book Sales
4	⊟ Family	
5	Santos	$ 3,207,290
6	Huang	$ 1,572,792
7	Hort	$ 1,403,250
8	Mitchell	$ 1,320,624
9	Sullivan	$ 565,567
10	Gagne	$ 421,614
11	**Grand Total**	$ 8,491,137

Sum of Total Book Sales

Family Discipline Book Sales

Discipline
Editor Last

- Family Santos
- Family Huang
- Family Hort
- Family Mitchell

FIGURE 5.1 Ivory Halls Publishing Company Subtotals, PivotTables, and PivotChart

CASE STUDY | Ivory Halls Publishing Company

Starting Files	Files to be Submitted
e05h1Sociology	e05h3Sociology_LastFirst
e05h4Sociology	e05h4Sociology_LastFirst

MyLab IT Grader An alternate version of this project is available as a MyLab IT Grader Assessment

Subtotals and Outlines

Data alone are meaningless; data translated into meaningful information increase your knowledge so that you can make well-informed decisions. Previously, you used analytical tools such as sorting, filtering, conditional formatting, tables, and charts. These tools help translate raw data into information so that you can identify trends, patterns, and anomalies in a dataset. Now you are ready to explore other functionalities that help you analyze larger amounts of data.

In this section, you will learn how to insert subtotals within a dataset. Then you will learn how to group data to create an outline, collapse and expand groups within the outline, and ungroup data to return them to their original state.

STEP 1 ▸ Subtotaling Data

You know how to calculate a total value or grand total for a column using the SUM function. However, at times you will want to calculate subtotals for each category of items within that column. In these situations, you use the Subtotals command to display a **subtotal**, a summary calculation, such as a total or average, of values for a category. For columns that contain values, select a function such as Sum, Min, Max, or Count. For text columns, use the Count function to count the number of rows within the category.

The Subtotal command inserts a **subtotal row**, which is a row that includes one or more aggregate functions for each category within a dataset. Using the Subtotal command preserves the dataset by inserting subtotal rows that can be quickly hidden or removed. Manually inserting subtotal rows would disrupt the dataset and potentially lead to errors. After you use the Subtotal command, you can compare the subtotals. Furthermore, when you use the Subtotals command, you can collapse and expand details without having to manually hide and unhide individual rows.

Before you use the Subtotal command, make sure the dataset does not contain blank rows or columns and that the dataset is not formatted as a table. Furthermore, because Excel inserts subtotal rows where the content changes in a column, you must first sort the dataset by a column containing categories. When you sort data into categories, Excel groups related data together. For example, sorting the sociology textbook dataset by the Discipline column enables you to subtotal sales for each discipline.

> **To add subtotals to a dataset, complete the following steps:**
>
> 1. Ensure that the dataset is not formatted as a table and sort the dataset using the column that you want to use to group the data.
> 2. Click in the dataset and click the Data tab.
> 3. Click Subtotal in the Outline group to open the Subtotal dialog box.
> 4. Click the *At each change in* arrow and select the column by which the data are sorted (see Figure 5.2).
> 5. Click the *Use function* arrow and select the function you want to apply.
> 6. Select the check boxes in the *Add subtotal to* list for each field you want to subtotal.
> 7. Select any other check boxes you want to use and click OK.

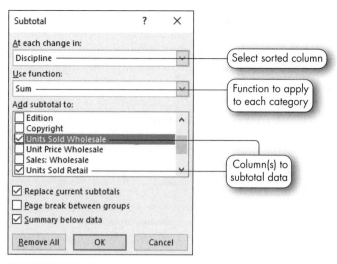

FIGURE 5.2 Subtotal Dialog Box

Figure 5.3 shows the results when subtotaling is applied. The highlighting was added for emphasis and is not automatically applied when you use the Subtotal command. The sociology textbook dataset is grouped by discipline. The Subtotal command inserts subtotals at a change in discipline. For example, Excel inserted subtotal rows on rows 79, 90, and 99, at the end of the Research/Stats, Social Problems, and Social Psychology disciplines, respectively.

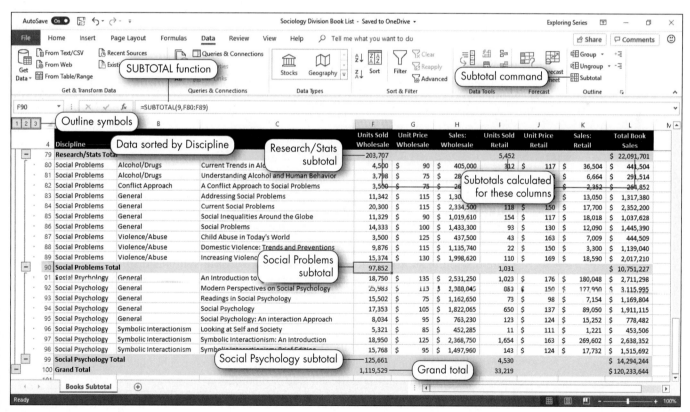

FIGURE 5.3 Subtotaled Data

In Figure 5.3, the Subtotal command calculates the number of books sold in the Units Sold Wholesale, Units Sold Retail, and the Total Book Sales columns for each discipline. Adding subtotals helps identify which disciplines contribute the highest revenue for the company and which disciplines produce the lowest revenue. You can then analyze the data to determine whether to continue publishing books in high revenue-generating areas or discontinue the publication of books in low-selling areas. A grand total row is inserted at the end of the dataset to display the total for each subtotaled column: Units Sold Wholesale, Units Sold Retail, and Total Book Sales.

TIP: SUBTOTAL FUNCTION

For each subtotal row, Excel inserts a SUBTOTAL function, a Math & Trig function that calculates a subtotal for values contained in a specified range. Cell F90 contains =SUBTOTAL(9,F80:F89) to sum the number of books sold contained in the range F80:F89. The first argument indicates which summary function is used to calculate the subtotal. In this case, the argument 9 sums all values in the range specified in the second argument. Use Excel Help to learn which values in the first argument represent other summary functions. Excel inserts the function and its arguments automatically so that you do not have to memorize what the arguments represent.

STEP 2 Add a Second Subtotal

You can add a second level of subtotals to a dataset. Adding a second level preserves the primary subtotals and adds another level of subtotals for subcategories. For the sociology book list, you can display subtotals for each discipline and the areas within each discipline by performing a two-level sort based on the primary and secondary categorical data.

After inserting the first subtotal based on the primary sort, open the Subtotal dialog box again. This time, for the *At a change in* setting, specify the column that you used for the secondary sort. Select the functions and columns to be subtotaled. Deselect the *Replace current subtotals* check box. That way, you preserve the original subtotal rows while you add the second set of subtotal rows.

TIP: REMOVING SUBTOTALS

The subtotal rows are temporary. To remove the rows of subtotals, display the Subtotals dialog box and click Remove All.

STEP 3 Collapse and Expand the Subtotals

The Subtotal command creates an ***outline***, a hierarchical structure that groups related detailed data in rows to summarize. When a dataset has been grouped into an outline, you can collapse the outlined data to show only main rows, such as subtotals, or expand the outlined data to show all the detailed rows. When you collapse the dataset, rows are hidden only; they are not deleted. Figure 5.4 shows a dataset that is collapsed to display the discipline subtotals and the grand total. Outline symbols display below the Name Box. The number of outline symbols depends on the total number of subtotals created.

In Figure 5.4, clicking the Level 1 outline symbol displays only the grand totals, clicking the Level 2 outline symbol displays the grand total and subtotals, and clicking the Level 3 outline symbol displays all details. Furthermore, you can expand the dataset to display the detailed rows in the subtotaled or outlined dataset by clicking the expand outline symbol (the plus sign), or you can collapse the dataset by clicking a collapse outline symbol (the minus sign) on the left side of a category.

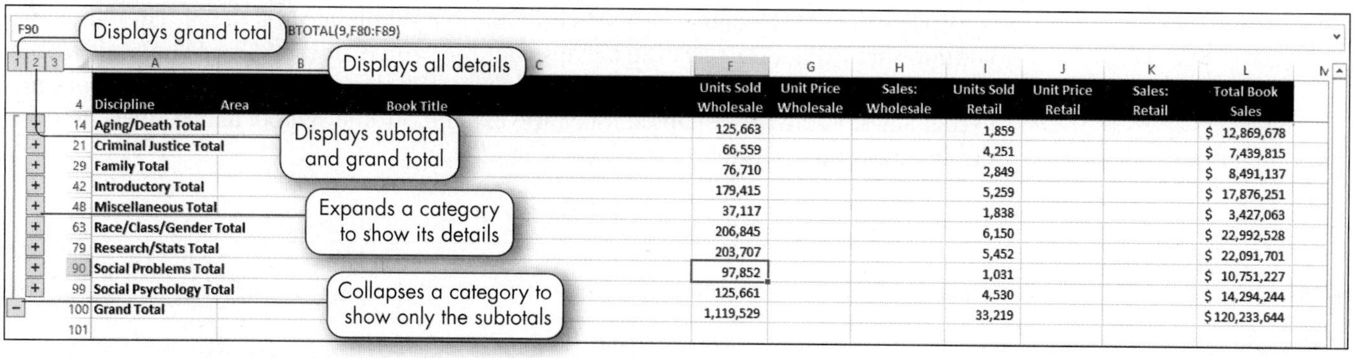

FIGURE 5.4 Subtotaled Data Collapsed

STEP 4 Grouping and Ungrouping Data

You can group related columns of data to create an outline so that you can collapse and expand the outlined columns similarly to collapsing and expanding outlined rows containing subtotals. Excel can create an automatic outline of columns if the dataset includes columns containing formulas or functions based on values in other columns. For example, the Units Sold: Wholesale and the Unit Price: Wholesale columns contain values used in the formula in the Sales: Wholesale column. You can group the Wholesale columns into a collapsible outline. Applying an outline to group columns of data enables you to hide columns of detailed data and focus on columns containing formulas or functions.

Select Auto Outline from the Group command in the Outline group on the Data tab to create an outline by columns. If Excel cannot create the outline, it displays the message box *Cannot create an outline*. After you apply the outline, the collapse outline symbol ⊟ displays above a column containing formulas. Click the collapse outline symbol to hide the columns containing values so that you can focus on just the column containing the formula. When you collapse outlined columns, the columns are hidden; they are not deleted. You can then click the expand outline symbol ⊞ to display the hidden columns again.

If Excel cannot create an automatic outline, you can create groups. *Grouping* is the process of joining rows or columns of related data together into a single entity so that groups can be collapsed or expanded for data analysis. After you create groups in the dataset, you can collapse a group to hide detail columns and show only the outside column or expand groups of related columns to view the internal columns of data. Grouping enables you to hide raw data while you focus on key calculated results.

> **To group data, complete the following steps:**
>
> 1. Select the rows or columns you want to group. For column groups, you often select columns containing details but not aggregate columns, such as totals or averages.
> 2. Click the Data tab.
> 3. Click Group in the Outline group.
> 4. Click Rows to group the data by rows or click Columns to group the data by columns if the Group dialog box opens and then click OK.

In Figure 5.5, the data is grouped by columns: Wholesale and Retail. The Wholesale columns are expanded. Click the collapse outline symbol above Sales: Wholesale to hide the wholesale columns and display only the Sales: Wholesale column. The Retail columns except Sales: Retail are collapsed. Click the expand outline symbol above Sales: Retail to display the retail columns.

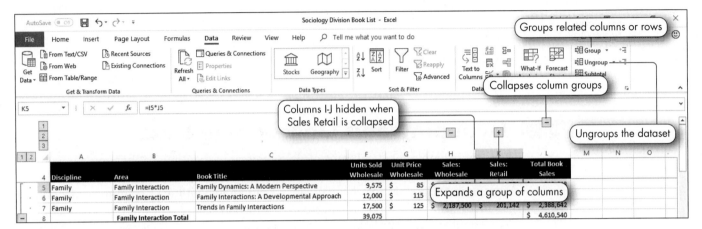

FIGURE 5.5 Grouped Data

TIP: REMOVING GROUPS

To remove groups, select all grouped columns or rows and click Ungroup in the Outline group on the Data tab.

Quick Concepts

1. Discuss why a dataset must be sorted by a category before using the Subtotal feature. *p. 314*

2. Describe the benefits of using the Subtotal command in a dataset. *p. 314*

3. Explain the purpose of grouping and outlining columns in a worksheet. *p. 317*

Hands-On Exercises

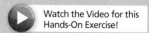
Skills covered: Subtotal Data • Add a Second Subtotal • Collapse and Expand the Subtotals • Group Data

1 Subtotals and Outlines

As vice president of the Sociology Division, you want to analyze the textbook publications. Each textbook falls within a general discipline, and each discipline is divided into several areas. The company tracks units sold, unit prices, and gross sales by two major types of sales: (1) wholesale sales to bookstores and (2) retail sales to individual customers. Your assistant applied Freeze Panes to keep the column headings in row 4 and the disciplines and areas in columns A and B visible regardless of where you scroll.

STEP 1 SUBTOTAL DATA

First, you sort the data by discipline and then by area. After sorting the data, you will insert subtotals for each discipline. You want to see the totals for the wholesale sales, retail sales, and total book sales. Refer to Figure 5.6 as you complete Step 1.

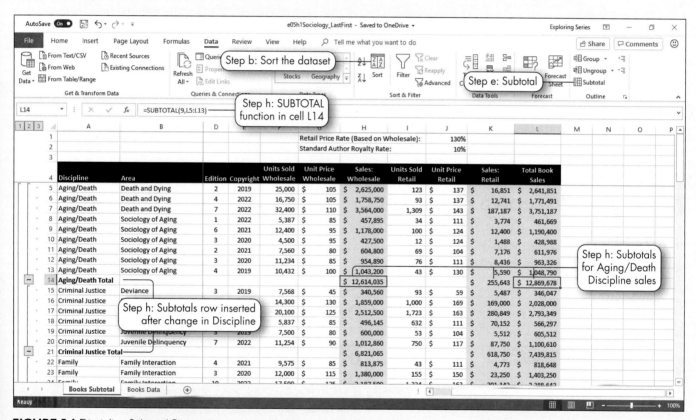

FIGURE 5.6 Discipline Subtotal Rows

a. Open *e05h1Sociology* and save it as **e05h1Sociology_LastFirst**.

> **TROUBLESHOOTING:** If you make any major mistakes in this exercise, you can close the file, open *e05h1Sociology* again, and then start this exercise over.

b. Make sure that **cell C5** is active in the Books Subtotal sheet. Click the **Data tab** and click **Sort** in the Sort & Filter group.

c. Click the **Sort by arrow** and select **Discipline** in the Sort dialog box.

d. Click **Add Level**, click the **Then by arrow**, and then select **Area**. Click **OK**.

Excel sorts the data by discipline in alphabetical order. Within each discipline, Excel sorts the data by area. The data are sorted first by disciplines so that you can apply subtotals to each discipline.

MAC TROUBLESHOOTING: On a Mac, Add Level looks like this: ➕.

---

e. Click **Subtotal** in the Outline group.

The Subtotal dialog box opens. The default *At each change in* is the Discipline column, and the default *Use function* is Sum. These settings are correct.

f. Click the **Sales: Wholesale check box** to select it in the *Add subtotal to* section.

g. Click the **Sales: Retail check box** to select it in the *Add subtotal to* section.

Excel selected the last column (Total Book Sales) automatically. You selected the other two sales columns to total. Leave the *Replace current subtotals* and *Summary below data* check boxes selected.

h. Click **OK**.

Excel inserts subtotal rows after each discipline category. The subtotal rows include discipline labels and subtotals for the Sales: Wholesale, Sales: Retail, and Total Book Sales columns. Outline symbols (1, 2, and 3) display below the Name Box so that you can collapse or expand the details in the subtotaled dataset.

i. Scroll to the right to see the subtotals and click **cell L14**. Save the workbook.

TROUBLESHOOTING: If your subtotals do not match the totals in Figure 5.6, open the Subtotal dialog box, click Remove All, click OK, and repeat Steps b through i again.

STEP 2 ▸ **ADD A SECOND SUBTOTAL**

Now you want to add another level to see subtotals for each area within each discipline. You already added subtotals for the primary category (Discipline). Now you will add a subtotal to the second category (Area). When you use the Subtotal dialog box, you will keep the original subtotals intact. Refer to Figure 5.7 as you complete Step 2.

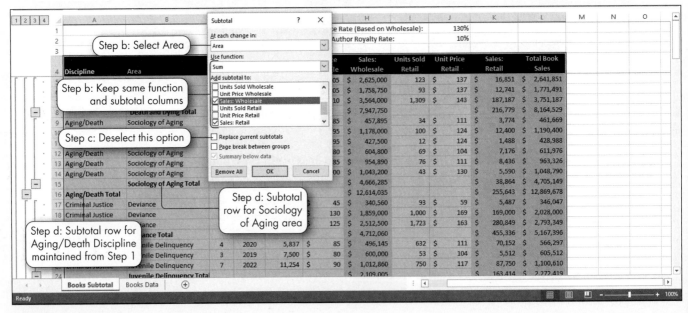

FIGURE 5.7 Discipline and Area Subtotal Rows

a. Click **Subtotal** in the Outline group to open the Subtotal dialog box again.

b. Click the **At each change in arrow** and select **Area**.

The *Use function* is still Sum, and Excel remembers the last columns you selected (Sales: Wholesale, Sales: Retail, and Total Book Sales) in the *Add subtotal to* section.

c. Click the **Replace current subtotals check box** to deselect it.

Deselecting this check box will keep the discipline subtotals.

d. Click **OK** and click **cell L15**. Save the workbook.

Excel inserts subtotal rows after each area. Your data have discipline subtotals and area subtotals. Four numbered outline symbols now display below the Name Box, indicating that you added another level of subtotals to the dataset.

STEP 3 COLLAPSE AND EXPAND THE SUBTOTALS

You want to compare wholesale, retail, and book sales among the disciplines and then among areas within a discipline. Refer to Figure 5.8 as you complete Step 3.

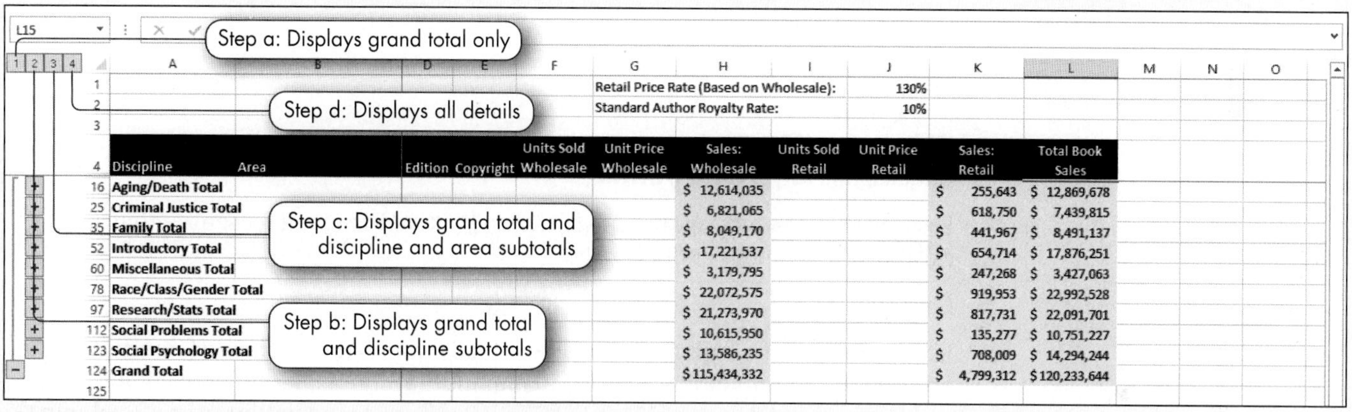

FIGURE 5.8 Collapsed Subtotals at Level 2

a. Click the **Level 1 outline symbol** in the top-left corner of the outline area (to the left of the column headings and below the Name Box).

You collapsed the outline to show the grand totals only for wholesale, retail, and total book sales.

b. Click the **Level 2 outline symbol** in the top-left corner of the outline area.

You expanded the outline to show the grand and discipline subtotals.

c. Click the **Level 3 outline symbol** in the top-left corner of the outline area.

You expanded the outline to show the grand, discipline, and area subtotals. Within the Introductory discipline, which area had the lowest sales? How do wholesale and retail sales compare? Are they proportionally the same within each area?

d. Click the **Level 4 outline symbol** in the top-left outline area. Save the workbook.

You expanded the outline to show all details again.

You want to apply an outline to the columns so that you can collapse or expand the Units Sold and Unit Price columns. You will use the collapse and expand outline symbols after outlining the dataset. Refer to Figure 5.9 as you complete Step 4.

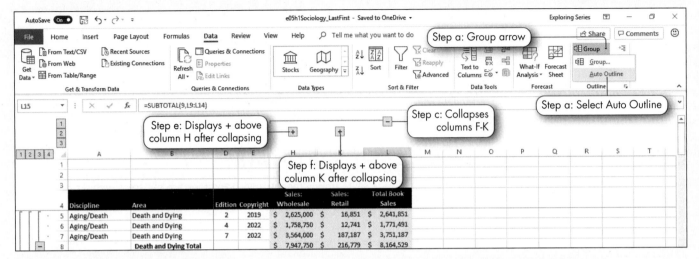

FIGURE 5.9 Groups of Columns Outlined

a. Make sure **cell L15** is the active cell. Click the **Group arrow** in the Outline group on the Data tab and select **Auto Outline**.

Excel displays the message box *Modify existing outline* because it recognizes that an existing row subtotals outline exists.

b. Click **OK**.

Excel maintains the outlined subtotal rows and outlines the columns. Horizontal lines and collapse buttons display above the columns that contain formulas (columns H, K, and L). The formula in cell H5 is =F5*G5, so Excel creates an outline to group columns F, G, and H. The formula in cell K5 is =I5*J5, so Excel creates an outline to group columns I, J, and K. It also creates a higher-level outline of columns F through K, because the formula in column L sums the values in columns H and K.

c. Click the **collapse outline symbol** ☐ above column L.

You collapsed columns F through K to display disciplines, areas, and total sales by title.

d. Click the **expand outline symbol** ☐ above column L.

You expanded the outline to show columns F through K again.

e. Click the **collapse outline symbol** above column H.

You collapsed the outline to hide columns F and G so you can focus on the wholesale sales without the distraction of the Units Sold Wholesale or Unit Price Wholesale columns.

f. Click the **collapse outline symbol** above column K.

You collapsed the outline to hide columns I and J so you can focus on the retail sales without the distraction of the Units Sold Retail or Unit Price Retail columns.

g. Save the workbook. Keep the workbook open if you plan to continue with the next Hands-On Exercise. If not, save and close the workbook, and exit Excel.

PivotTable Basics

So far, you subtotaled data by categories and grouped data to outline it for initial data analysis. However, you will want to use more sophisticated tools to analyze large amounts of data to make solid business decisions. Entering data is the easy part; retrieving data in a structured, meaningful way is more challenging. ***Data mining*** is the process of analyzing large volumes of data to discover patterns and identify trends in the data. Managers use data-mining techniques to address a variety of questions, such as which sociology discipline sold the most books with a 2021 copyright date? This type of question helps organizations prepare their marketing plans to capitalize on consumer spending patterns.

When you want to create a structured summary of a large dataset, you can create a ***PivotTable***, which is an interactive table that uses calculations to consolidate and summarize data from a data source into a separate table. PivotTables enable you to analyze data in a dataset without altering the dataset itself. PivotTables are dynamic: You can easily and quickly pivot, or rearrange, fields to analyze data from different viewpoints. Looking at data from different perspectives enables you to identify trends and patterns among the variables that might not be obvious from looking at hundreds or thousands of rows of data yourself.

Figure 5.10 shows a sample dataset and a corresponding PivotTable that summarizes sales for morning, afternoon, and evening for three days at an arts festival. The PivotTable provides an easy-to-interpret structure to analyze the data without modifying the original dataset.

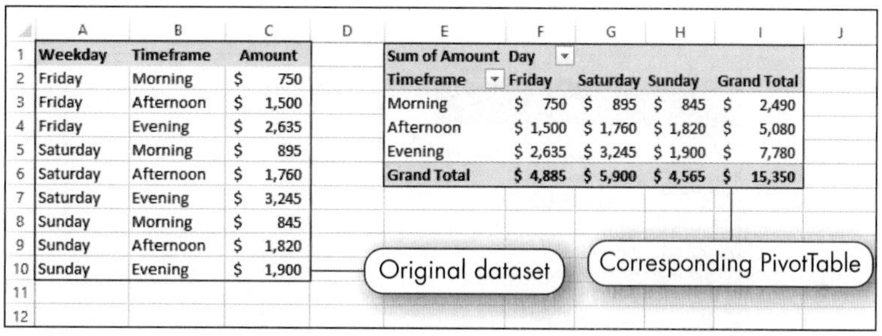

Weekday	Timeframe	Amount
Friday	Morning	$ 750
Friday	Afternoon	$ 1,500
Friday	Evening	$ 2,635
Saturday	Morning	$ 895
Saturday	Afternoon	$ 1,760
Saturday	Evening	$ 3,245
Sunday	Morning	$ 845
Sunday	Afternoon	$ 1,820
Sunday	Evening	$ 1,900

Sum of Amount	Day			
Timeframe	Friday	Saturday	Sunday	Grand Total
Morning	$ 750	$ 895	$ 845	$ 2,490
Afternoon	$ 1,500	$ 1,760	$ 1,820	$ 5,080
Evening	$ 2,635	$ 3,245	$ 1,900	$ 7,780
Grand Total	$ 4,885	$ 5,900	$ 4,565	$ 15,350

FIGURE 5.10 Sample Dataset and Corresponding PivotTable

In this section, you will create a PivotTable. You will learn how to organize and group data into rows and columns, remove and rearrange fields, and change the settings for value fields.

Creating a PivotTable

Before you create a PivotTable, ensure that the data is well structured by applying the rules for good table design. Use meaningful column labels, ensure data accuracy, and avoid blank rows and columns in the dataset. At least one column must have duplicate values for several records, such as the same discipline or area name, to create categories for organizing and summarizing data. Another column usually contains numeric values that can be aggregated to produce quantitative summaries, such as averages or sums.

TIP: PIVOTTABLE OR SUBTOTALS?

PivotTables are similar to subtotals because they both produce subtotals, but PivotTables provide more flexibility than subtotals. If you want complex subtotals cross-referenced by two or more categories with filtering and other specifications, create a PivotTable. Furthermore, using the Subtotals command inserts subtotals rows within the dataset, whereas creating a PivotTable does not change the dataset.

STEP 1 Create a Recommended PivotTable

You can create a recommended PivotTable from the Quick Analysis gallery or from the Recommended PivotTables command in the Tables group on the Insert tab. One benefit of these methods is that Excel displays previews of recommended PivotTables based on the data in the dataset. Creating a recommended PivotTable is beneficial when you first start using PivotTables so that you can see potential ways to depict the dataset before starting to create PivotTables from scratch.

To create a PivotTable using Quick Analysis, complete the following steps:

1. Right-click within a dataset and select Quick Analysis on the shortcut menu.
2. Click Tables in the Quick Analysis gallery.
3. Point to a PivotTable thumbnail to see a preview of the different recommended PivotTables (see Figure 5.11).
4. Click a PivotTable thumbnail to create the desired PivotTable.

MAC TIP: Quick Analysis is not available in Excel for Mac. To create a Recommended PivotTable, click Recommended PivotTable on the Insert tab.

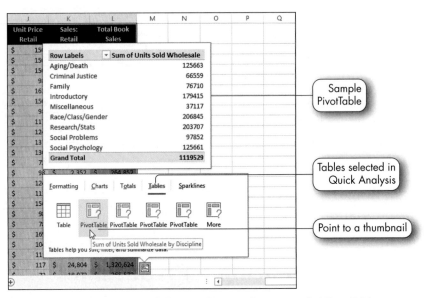

FIGURE 5.11 Quick Analysis Gallery to Create a Recommended PivotTable

Another way to create a PivotTable is to make sure the active cell is within the dataset and use the Recommended PivotTables command in the Tables group on the Insert tab. The Recommended PivotTables dialog box opens (see Figure 5.12). Point to a thumbnail on the left side to display a preview of the PivotTable. Click OK to create the desired PivotTable.

FIGURE 5.12 Recommended PivotTable Dialog Box

MAC TIP: Instead of displaying the Recommended PivotTables dialog box, Excel for Mac creates a PivotTable immediately without giving you other recommended PivotTables from which to choose.

Excel creates a PivotTable on a new worksheet (see Figure 5.13) with a generic sheet name, such as Sheet1. Excel assigns a generic name, such as PivotTable1, to the PivotTable until you assign a more meaningful name. The ribbon displays the PivotTable Tools Analyze and Design tabs. The PivotTable Fields task pane displays on the right side of the screen. The ***PivotTable Fields task pane*** is a task pane that displays the list of fields in a dataset and areas to place the fields to create the layout to organize data in columns, rows, values, and filters in a PivotTable.

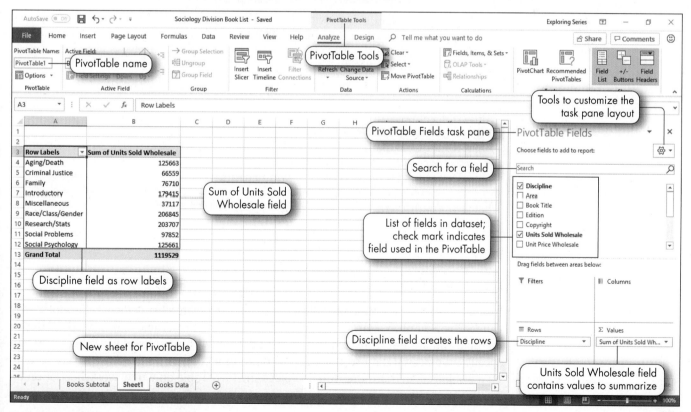

FIGURE 5.13 Recommended PivotTable

TIP: PIVOTTABLE FIELDS TASK PANE

If the PivotTable Fields task pane does not display when you click inside a PivotTable, click Field List in the Show group on the Analyze tab. This command is a toggle, so you can click it to show or hide the PivotTable Fields task pane.

The PivotTable Fields task pane contains two sections. The top section contains a list of the fields or column labels contained in the dataset. The fields are listed in the same order as the original dataset; however, you can alter the recommended layout by clicking Tools in the PivotTable Fields task pane. For example, you can select Sort A to Z to list the fields in alphabetical order in the PivotTable Fields task pane. If the data source has several fields, scroll through the list or click in the Search box and type a name of a field to find. For example, Figure 5.13 shows only 8 of the 12 fields from the dataset.

The bottom section of the PivotTable Fields task pane contains four areas where you can place fields to organize the layout of the PivotTable. Table 5.1 describes the four areas of a PivotTable.

TABLE 5.1	Areas of a PivotTable
Area	**Description**
Filters Area	Displays top-level filters above the PivotTable so that you can set filters to display results based on conditions you select.
Columns Area	Displays columns of summarized data for the selected field(s). When you drag a field to the Columns area, the PivotTable displays one column of data for each unique value contained in the dataset.
Rows Area	Groups the data into categories in the first column based on the selected field(s). Each unique text entry is listed only one time in alphabetical order in the first column regardless of how many times the text is present in the original dataset. These labels identify the content on each row.
Values Area	Displays summary statistics, such as totals or averages, for the selected field. The default function is SUM for quantitative fields. If you select a field containing labels, the default function is COUNT to count the number of text entries within each category.

TIP: NAMING A PIVOTTABLE

A best practice is to assign a name to a PivotTable, such as Wholesale Units Sold by Discipline because the default name such as PivotTable1 is not meaningful. Furthermore, it is a good practice to name a PivotTable so that the workbook is accessibility compliant for people who have disabilities, such as vision or cognitive impairments, that may prevent them from seeing or comprehending the visual aid. To name a PivotTable, click within the PivotTable and type a name in the PivotTable Name box in the PivotTable group on the Analyze tab.

Create a Blank PivotTable

Instead of using a recommended PivotTable, you can create a blank PivotTable and specify the data you want to analyze and where you want the PivotTable to be placed. With this method, you are not restricted to a current dataset within an Excel worksheet; you can specify an external data source such as data on a company's database server or data on a webpage. Furthermore, you can place the PivotTable on a new worksheet or on an existing worksheet.

> **To create a blank PivotTable, complete the following steps:**
>
> 1. Click inside the dataset in a worksheet.
> 2. Click the Insert tab and click PivotTable in the Tables group to open the Create PivotTable dialog box.
> 3. Select the data that you want to analyze: the current table or range, a different table or range, an external source, or a previously created data model.
> 4. Select where you want to place the PivotTable: New Worksheet or Existing Worksheet. If you click Existing Worksheet, specify the sheet tab name in the Location box.
> 5. Click OK to create the PivotTable.

The PivotTable Tools Analyze and Design tabs display, the PivotTable Fields task pane displays on the right side, and a blank PivotTable is located on the left side (see Figure 5.14). The top of the PivotTable Fields task pane displays the fields or column labels from the dataset.

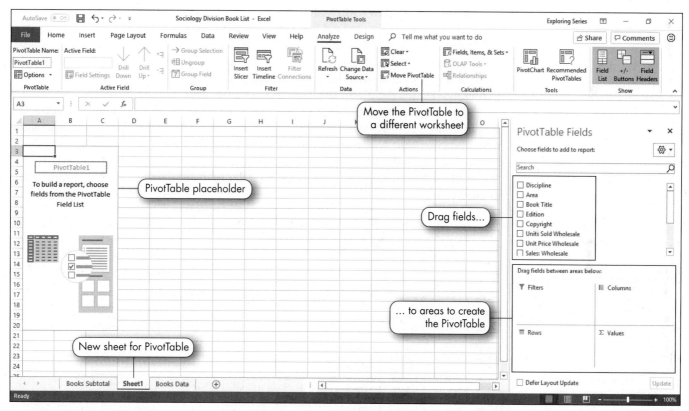

FIGURE 5.14 Blank PivotTable

TIP: MOVE A PIVOTTABLE

You can move a PivotTable to another worksheet. To move a PivotTable, click within the PivotTable, click Move PivotTable in the Actions group on the Analyze tab to open the Move PivotTable dialog box. Click New Worksheet or click Existing Worksheet and specify the existing sheet name and the cell in the top-left corner to locate the PivotTable, and then click OK.

STEP 2 Add Rows, Values, and Columns

You can add one or more fields to the PivotTable to provide a more detailed analysis. You can add fields to the Rows area to display details, columns for additional levels of depth, and values to aggregate the data. You have three ways to add fields in a PivotTable:

- Click the field's check box to select it in the *Choose fields to add to report* section. Excel adds the field to a PivotTable based on the type of data stored in the field. If the field contains text, Excel usually places that field in the Rows area. If the field contains a value, Excel usually places that field in the Values area. Excel makes the value an aggregate, such as Sum of Sales. If you place a text field, such as Book Title, in the Values area, Excel counts the number of records for each group listed in the Rows area.

- Drag the field from the *Choose fields to add to report* section and drop it in the Rows, Columns, or Values area.

- Right-click the field name in the *Choose fields to add to report* section and select Add to Row Labels, Add to Column Labels, or Add to Values.

> **MAC TIP:** In Excel for Mac, *Field Names* is the section name instead of *Choose fields to add to report*.

The sequence of the fields within the Rows area controls the hierarchy. For example, you can show the Areas within each Discipline for the Ivory Halls book list. To show this hierarchy, list the Discipline field first and Area field second in the Rows area. When you add multiple fields to the Values area, the PivotTable displays a column of aggregated values for each field. If you place a text field in the Values area, the PivotTable displays a count of the unique data in that field. You can add fields to the Columns area to provide greater aggregated details for the fields in the Values area.

Figure 5.15 shows a PivotTable that uses the Discipline and Area fields as rows, the Sum of Total Sales field as values, and the Copyright field as columns. Each discipline, area, and copyright year display only once in the PivotTable. This added level of detail enables you to see the total sales for each discipline and area based on its copyright year. The PivotTable includes grand totals for each discipline and area, as well as grand totals for each year.

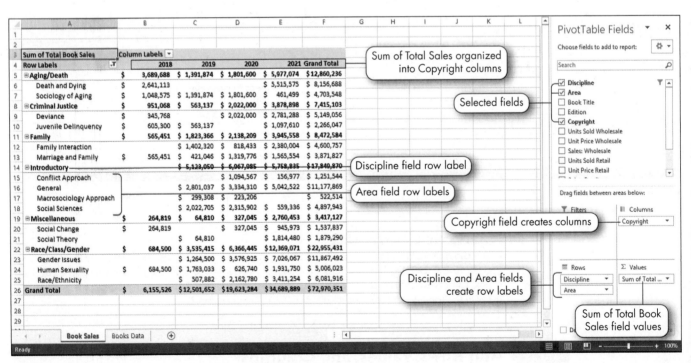

FIGURE 5.15 Fields added to the Rows, Columns, and Values Areas

Modifying a PivotTable

After you create a PivotTable, you can modify it to see the data from a different perspective. For example, you can collapse the PivotTable to show fewer details or expand it to show more details. In addition, you can remove fields to simplify a PivotTable. Finally, you can rearrange fields to organize the data differently in the PivotTable.

Collapse and Expand Categories

If you include two or more fields in the Rows area, the PivotTable displays more depth but may be overwhelming. You can hide or collapse the secondary field rows, as needed. To collapse a category, click Collapse on the left side of the category you want to collapse. Excel hides the subcategories for that category and shows only the aggregated totals for the category. Continue collapsing other categories as needed to focus on the details for a specific category. To expand a category, click Expand on the left side of the category label.

For example, if the PivotTable contains both Discipline and Area row labels, you can collapse areas for some disciplines. The collapse and expand buttons display to the left of the row labels (see Figure 5.16). If the buttons do not display, click +/− Buttons in the Show group on the Analyze tab. You can collapse all categories at one time by clicking Collapse Field in the Active Field group on the Analyze tab. To expand all categories at one time, click Expand Field

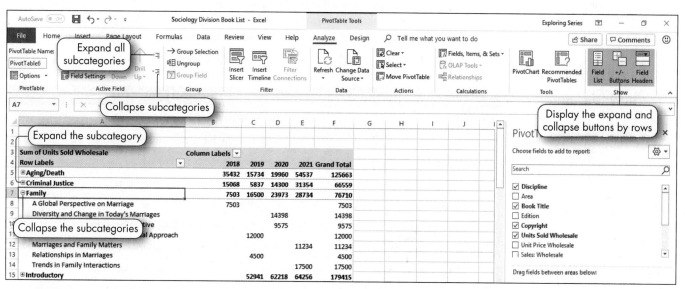

FIGURE 5.16 Collapse and Expand PivotTable

STEP 3 ## Remove Fields

As you continue adding and arranging fields, the PivotTable may contain too much data to be useful or the needs have changed, making it necessary to remove fields. You can remove fields to reduce the amount of data to analyze. Excel provides three methods to remove a field from a PivotTable:

- Click the field name in the *Drag fields between areas below* section and select Remove Field.

- Click the check box next to the field name to deselect it in the *Choose fields to add to report* section.

- Drag a field name in the *Drag fields between areas below* section outside the PivotTable Fields task pane.

You can reset a PivotTable back to a blank PivotTable and start over if the PivotTable gets too cluttered. To clear all fields from a PivotTable, click within the PivotTable, click Clear in the Actions group on the Analyze tab, and then select Clear All.

Rearrange Fields

A primary benefit of creating a PivotTable is that you can rearrange (or pivot) fields to view and summarize data from different perspectives or to create an easier layout to interpret data. PivotTables provide ease and flexibility in changing the layout and level of depth depicted. You can pivot the data by moving a field from the Columns area to the Row area. As you move fields from one area to another in the PivotTable Fields task pane, the PivotTable immediately reflects the new layout. For example, the PivotTable could include the Discipline and Copyright fields in the Rows area so that you can view details for each discipline by copyright year. You can move the Copyright field to the Columns area to create a more distinct analysis of revenue for each discipline by copyright year. Excel provides two methods to move a field within a PivotTable:

- Drag the field in the *Drag fields between areas below* section.
- Click the field arrow within the area and select Move to Report Filter, Move to Row Labels, Move to Column Labels, or Move to Values. (On a Mac, use the two-finger tap, select Move, and then select a Move option.)

You can also move a field within its area. Table 5.2 explains the Move options.

TABLE 5.2 Move Options	
Option	**Moves the Field . . .**
Move Up	Up one position in the hierarchy within the same area
Move Down	Down one position in the hierarchy within the same area
Move to Beginning	To the beginning of all fields in the same area
Move to End	To the end of all fields in the same area
Move to Report Filter	To the end of the Filters area of the PivotTable
Move to Row Labels	To the end of the Rows area of the PivotTable
Move to Column Labels	To the end of the Columns area of the PivotTable
Move to Values	To the end of the Values area of the PivotTable

STEP 4 ## Change Values Field Settings

Excel uses the SUM function as the default summary statistic for numeric fields and COUNT as the default statistic for text fields. However, you can select a different function for numeric fields. For example, you can calculate the average, lowest, or highest value within each group, or identify the lowest sales for each discipline/copyright year combination to see if the older books have decreased sales.

When you add a value field and select its summary statistic, the column label above the values includes the summary statistic function applied, such as *Sum of Total Sales by Book* or *Average of Total Sales by Book*, depending on the summary statistic applied to the values. Because the column label contains a lot of words, consider editing the value field setting to use a shorter column label. In addition, the aggregated values are not often formatted well. Therefore, you should apply an appropriate number format and specify the number of decimal places.

To modify value field settings, complete the following steps:

1. Click a value in the field in the PivotTable where you want to modify the value settings in the PivotTable.
2. Click Field Settings in the Active Field group on the Analyze tab. Alternatively, click the field's arrow in the Values area of the PivotTable Fields task pane and select Value Field Settings. (On a Mac, use the two-finger tap on the field in the area box and select Field Settings.)
3. Select options in the Value Field Settings dialog box (see Figure 5.17) or the PivotTable Field dialog box on a Mac.
4. Click OK.

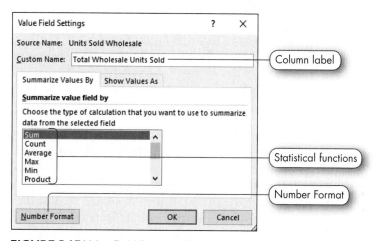

FIGURE 5.17 Value Field Settings Dialog Box

Use the Custom Name box to change the name that displays as the column label. For example, you can change the heading from *Sum of Total Sales* to *Total Book Sales*. You can select the statistical function used to summarize values in the *Summarize value field by* list. Click Number Format to open a simplified version of the Format Cells dialog box. Select a number type, such as Accounting, in the Category list; select other settings, such as the number of decimal places in the *Decimal places* box; and then click OK.

STEP 5 ▷ Use the GETPIVOTDATA Function

As you work with a data source on one worksheet, you may want to display a summary value from a PivotTable on another worksheet. You can use the **GETPIVOTDATA** function to obtain the summary data that is visible in a PivotTable. If you filter a PivotTable, the function result changes to reflect the updated visible data in the worksheet. If data is hidden in a PivotTable, the function returns #REF!

The function contains two required arguments: data_field and pivot_table. The data_field argument is the name of the field in the PivotTable that contains the data you want to retrieve. The pivot_table argument is a reference to the worksheet that contains the PivotTable and any cell within that PivotTable.

GETPIVOTDATA(data_field,pivot_table, [field1, item1, field2, item2], . . .)

Using Figure 5.15, you can Insert the GETPIVOTDATA function on the Books Data sheet, the worksheet containing the original data source. The function =GETPIVOTDATA("Total Book Sales",PivotTable!$A$4) obtains the total value from the Total Book Sales field using the PivotTable located in cell A4 in the PivotTable worksheet. The function returns the total $72,970,351, which is the grand total in cell F26.

You can use the optional arguments to pair field names and items that describe data to retrieve. Field1 refers to the name of a field in the PivotTable, and Item1 refers to a specific item within that field. For example, in the function =GETPIVOTDATA("Total Book Sales",PivotTable!$A$4,"Discipline","Family"), Discipline is a field within the PivotTable, and Family is the item for which you want to obtain a value. Using the data in Figure 5.15, the function returns $8,472,584, the total book sales for only the Family discipline.

TIP: INSERTING THE GETPIVOTDATA FUNCTION QUICKLY

Although the GETPIVOTDATA function is located within the Lookup & Reference function in the Function Library on the Formulas tab, you can quickly enter the function by typing the equal sign, clicking the cell within the PivotTable that contains the summary value you want, and then pressing Enter. Excel will insert the GETPIVOTDATA function with the correct arguments.

Refresh a PivotTable

Although PivotTables are powerful, they are not automatically updated if you make any changes to the underlying data in the data source. For example, if you change a sales value or delete a row in the data source, the PivotTable does not reflect the changed data. Unfortunately, this causes PivotTable summary statistics to become outdated with inaccurate results. To update the PivotTable, display the Analyze tab and click Refresh in the Data group to refresh the current PivotTable only, or click the Refresh arrow and select Refresh All to refresh all PivotTables in the workbook.

PivotTables should be current when you open a workbook. However, you can specify a setting to ensure that the PivotTables are updated when you open a workbook containing PivotTables. With the Analyze tab displayed, click the Options in the PivotTable group to open the PivotTable Options dialog box. Click the Data tab in the dialog box, select the *Refresh data when opening the file* check box, and then click OK.

TIP: CHANGE THE DATA SOURCE

If you add rows to the original data source, those rows may not be reflected in the PivotTable. To change the data source used to create the PivotTable, click Change Data Source in the Data group on the Analyze tab, select the new range containing the data to pivot, and click OK in the Change Data Source dialog box.

Quick Concepts

4. Explain the advantages of using a PivotTable instead of a subtotal. ***p. 323***

5. Explain the main benefit of creating a PivotTable using Quick Analysis or from the Recommended PivotTables dialog box over creating a blank PivotTable. ***p. 324***

6. Describe the four areas of a PivotTable. ***p. 326***

Hands-On Exercises

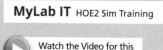

Skills covered: Create a Recommended PivotTable • Rename a PivotTable • Add Rows, Values, and Columns • Remove Fields • Rearrange Fields • Change Value Field Settings • Use the GETPIVOTDATA Function • Refresh a PivotTable

2 PivotTable Basics

After exhausting the possibilities of outlines and subtotals, you want to create a PivotTable to analyze the sociology book sales. You realize you can see the data from different perspectives, enabling you to have a stronger understanding of the sales by various categories.

STEP 1 ## CREATE A RECOMMENDED PIVOTTABLE

Because you want to keep the subtotals you created in the Books Subtotal worksheet, you will create a PivotTable from the Books Data worksheet. Refer to Figure 5.18 as you complete Step 1.

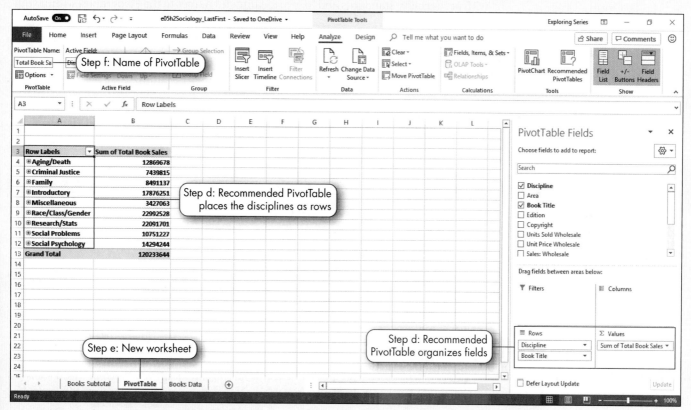

FIGURE 5.18 PivotTable for Total Book Sales

a. Open *e05h1Sociology_LastFirst* if you closed it at the end of Hands-On Exercise 1 and save it as **e05h2Sociology_LastFirst**, changing h1 to h2.

b. Click the **Books Data sheet tab**.

A PivotTable cannot be created using subtotaled data. To preserve the subtotals you created in Hands-On Exercise 1, you will use the dataset in the Books Data worksheet.

c. Click **cell A5**, click the **Insert tab**, and then click **Recommended PivotTables** in the Tables group. (On a Mac, click the **Insert tab**, click **PivotTable** and then click **OK**.)

The Recommended PivotTables dialog box opens.

d. Scroll the thumbnails of recommended PivotTables and click the **Sum of Total Book Sales by Discipline (+) thumbnail**. (Note: Point to each thumbnail to see the full name.) Click **OK**.

You selected this PivotTable to show the overall total book sales for each discipline. The dialog box shows a preview of the selected PivotTable.

> **MAC TROUBLESHOOTING:** Replace Step d with these steps: Drag Discipline in the PivotTable Field Name list to the Rows area, drag Book Title below Discipline in the Rows area, and then click the Total Book Sales check box to select it to display in the Values area.

e. Rename Sheet1 as **PivotTable**.

Excel inserts a new Sheet1 worksheet, which you renamed as PivotTable, with the PivotTable on the left side and the PivotTable Fields task pane on the right side.

f. Click the **PivotTable Name box** in the PivotTable group on the Analyze tab, type **Total Book Sales**, and then press **Enter**. Save the workbook.

You changed the name of the PivotTable from *PivotTable2* to *Total Book Sales* to comply with accessibility standards and to give meaningful names to the PivotTables within your workbook.

STEP 2 ▶ **ADD ROWS, VALUES, AND COLUMNS**

You want to compare sales combinations by discipline, copyright year, and edition. The Discipline field is already in the PivotTable, so you will add the Copyright Year and Edition fields. Refer to Figure 5.19 as you complete Step 2.

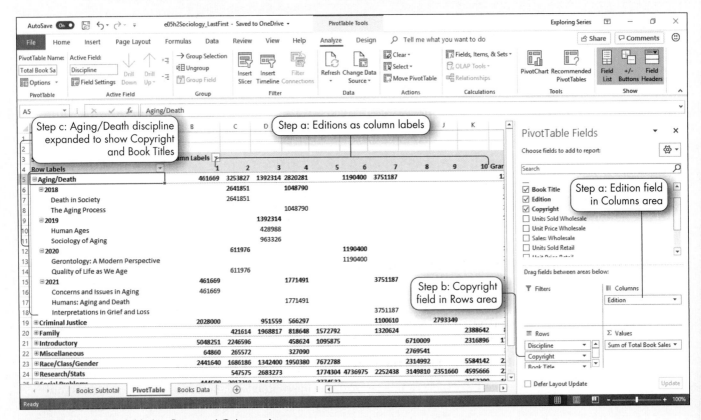

FIGURE 5.19 Fields Added to Rows and Columns Areas

a. Drag the **Edition field** in the *Choose fields to add to report* section to the Columns area in the PivotTable Fields task pane.

Excel displays the total book sales by a combination of discipline and edition. This enables you to compare sales of current editions within each discipline. Blanks appear in the PivotTable when a discipline does not have a specific edition. For example, the Family discipline does not have any first-edition books currently being published.

b. Drag the **Copyright field** in the *Choose fields to add to report* section between the Discipline and Book Title fields in the Rows area in the PivotTable Fields task pane.

The Copyright and Book Titles are not showing in the PivotTable because they are collapsed within the Discipline rows.

c. Click **Expand** for the Aging/Death discipline on the left side of the PivotTable. Save the workbook.

You expanded the Aging/Death discipline to show the copyright years and titles.

STEP 3 **REMOVE AND REARRANGE FIELDS**

Although it is informative to compare sales by edition, you think that the PivotTable contains too much detail, so you will remove the Edition field. In addition, the Rows area contains the Book Titles field, but those data are collapsed; therefore, you will remove it as well. After you remove the fields, you will rearrange other fields to simplify the PivotTable. Refer to Figure 5.20 as you complete Step 3.

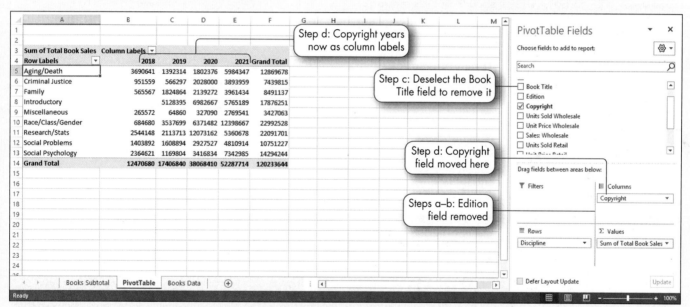

FIGURE 5.20 PivotTable After Removing and Rearranging Fields

a. Click the **Edition arrow** in the Columns area in the PivotTable Fields task pane.

Excel displays a menu of options to apply to this field.

> **MAC TROUBLESHOOTING:** Use two-finger tap on Edition in the Columns area to display a menu.

b. Select **Remove Field** on the menu.

You removed the Edition field from the PivotTable. Excel consolidates the sales into one sales column.

c. Click the **Book Title check box** to deselect it in the *Choose fields to add to report* section in the PivotTable Fields task pane.

You removed the Book Title field from the PivotTable.

d. Drag the **Copyright field** from the Rows area to the Columns area. Save the workbook.

> This arrangement consolidates the data. Instead of repeating the copyright years for each discipline, the copyright years are listed only once each at the top of the sales columns.

CHANGE THE VALUES FIELD SETTINGS

After selecting the PivotTable fields, you want to improve the appearance of the sociology textbook PivotTable. You will format the values with the Accounting Number Format and replace the generic Row Labels description with a label that indicates the sociology disciplines. Refer to Figure 5.21 as you complete Step 4.

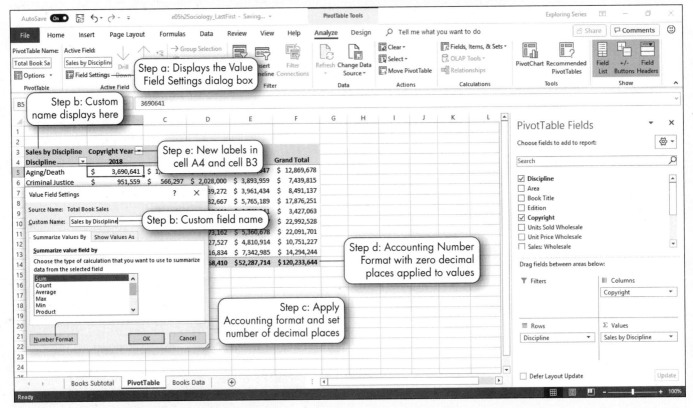

FIGURE 5.21 Formatted Values and Labels

a. Click **cell B5** and click **Field Settings** in the Active Field group on the Analyze tab.

> The Value Field Settings dialog box (on a Mac, PivotTable Fields dialog box) opens so that you can format the field.

b. Type **Sales by Discipline** in the Custom Name box. Leave Sum as the selected calculation type in the *Summarize value field by* section. (On a Mac, type **Sales by Discipline** in the Field Name box).

> You created a customized name for the calculated field and retained the calculation to sum the values. The Value Field Settings dialog box is still open so that you can format the field.

c. Click **Number Format**.

> Excel opens a Format Cells dialog box with only the Number tab.

d. Click **Accounting** in the Category list, change the Decimal places value to **0**, click **OK** in the Format Cells dialog box, and then click **OK** in the Value Field Settings dialog box.

> You formatted the values with Accounting Number Format with no decimal places, and the heading Sales by Discipline displays in cell A3.

e. Type **Discipline** in **cell A4** and type **Copyright Year** in **cell B3**.

You replaced the generic Row Labels heading with Discipline to describe the contents of the first column, and you replaced the Column Labels heading with Copyright Year. Although you can create custom names for values, you cannot create custom names for row and column labels. However, you can edit the labels directly in the cells.

f. Select the **range B4:E4** and center the labels horizontally. Save the workbook.

USE GETPIVOTDATA FUNCTION AND REFRESH A PIVOTTABLE

On the Books Data sheet, you want to insert a function that will display the total from the PivotTable. After consulting with the Accounting Department, you realize that the retail prices are incorrect. The unit retail prices are based on a percentage of the wholesale price. The retail unit price is 30% more than the wholesale unit price, but it should be 25%. You will edit the input cell in the original worksheet and refresh the PivotTable to see the corrected results. Refer to Figure 5.22 as you complete Step 5.

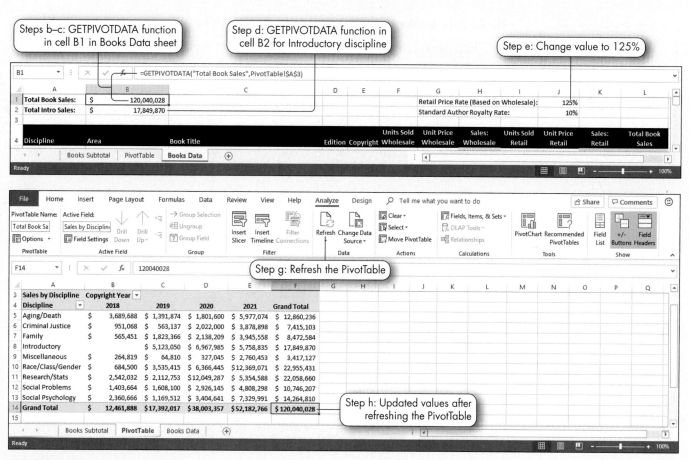

FIGURE 5.22 Refreshed PivotTable

a. Look at **cell F14**.

The current grand total is $120,233.644.

b. Click the **Books Data sheet tab** and click **cell B1**.

c. Type **=**, click the **PivotTable sheet tab**, click **cell F14**, and then press **Enter**.

Excel inserts =GETPIVOTDATA("Total Book Sales", PivotTable!$A$3) in cell B1 on the Books Data sheet tab and returns $120,233.644, the grand sum for the Total Book Sales field in cell F14 that you selected in the PivotTable.

d. Make sure **cell B2** is active in the Books Data sheet, type **=**, click the **PivotTable sheet tab**, click **cell F8**, and then press **Enter**.

=GETPIVOTDATA("Total Book Sales",PivotTable!$A$3,"Discipline","Introductory") is inserted in cell B2 on the Books Data sheet tab and returns $17,876,251, the total for the Introductory discipline in cell F8 that you selected in the PivotTable.

e. Click **cell J1**, type **125**, and then press **Enter**. Save the workbook.

You changed the retail price rate, which changes the results shown in columns J, K, and L in the Books Data worksheet. However, the PivotTable values are not updated yet.

f. Click the **PivotTable sheet tab**.

Notice that the PivotTable aggregate values did not change. The grand total is still $120,233,644. You must refresh the PivotTable.

g. Click the **Analyze tab** and click **Refresh** in the Data group.

Excel updates the PivotTable values based on the change you made in the Books Data worksheet. The grand total is now $120,040,028.

h. Click the **Books Data sheet tab** and look at **cell B1**.

The results of the GETPIVOTDATA function reflect the updated total from the PivotTable.

i. Save the workbook. Keep the workbook open if you plan to continue with the next Hands-On Exercise. If not, close the workbook and exit Excel.

PivotTable Options

As you have experienced, PivotTables consolidate and aggregate large amounts of data to facilitate data analysis. You can use the Analyze tab to customize the PivotTable. You can add filters, insert slicers, and insert a timeline to include or exclude data from being represented in a PivotTable. In addition, you can perform a variety of calculations and show specific calculation results. Furthermore, you can change the design to control the appearance of the PivotTable.

In this section, you will learn how to filter data in a PivotTable. In addition, you will create a calculated field and display subtotals. Finally, you will change overall the style of the PivotTable.

Sorting, Filtering, and Slicing a PivotTable

PivotTables display aggregated data for each category. You can sort the row and column labels to display in a different sequence. In addition, you can set a filter to exclude categories or values. You can specify a particular field to filter the PivotTable. Finally, you can include slicers to easily set filters to designate which specific data to include in the PivotTable.

Sort Data within a Field

The data within a Rows or Columns field are often sorted in alphabetical or chronological order. For example, Aging/Death is listed before Criminal Justice for the Discipline field row labels. You can use the Row Labels filter arrow to change the sort order. Alphabetical order may not be the logical sequence for data such as Morning, Afternoon, and Evening. To arrange the labels in that sequence, right-click a row label, select Move, and then select the direction, such as Move "Morning" to Beginning (see Figure 5.23). You can move labels to the beginning, end, up, or down.

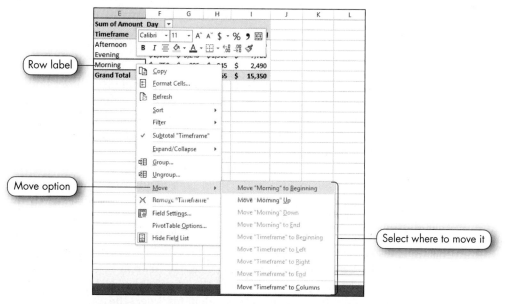

FIGURE 5.23 Moving Row Label

STEP 1 ▶ **Add Filters**

You can apply filters to show a subset of the PivotTable. Similar to applying filters to an Excel table, when you add filters in a PivotTable, the filters temporarily remove some data from view. The PivotTable displays only data that reflects the filters you enabled. For example, you can filter the PivotTable to show only aggregates for first- and second-edition books. When you add a field to the Filters area, Excel displays the filters above the PivotTable. The first field in the Filters area displays in cell A1 with a filter arrow in cell B1. Additional fields added to the Filters area display in the subsequent rows. After a field is listed in the Filters area, click the filter arrow in column B (such as in cell B1) to open the Filter menu and choose one of these options:

- Select the value in the list to filter the data by that value only.
- Click the Select Multiple Items check box if you want to select more than one value to filter the PivotTable. Click the check boxes by each value you want to set (see Figure 5.24).
- Type a value in the Search box if the list is long and you want to find a value quickly.

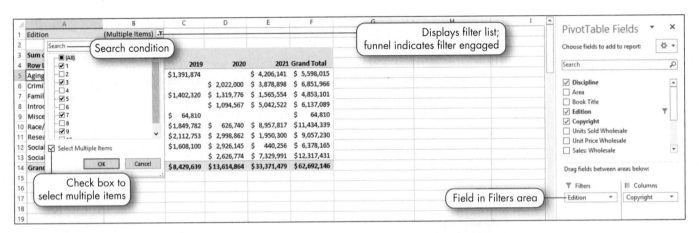

FIGURE 5.24 Filter Menu

The PivotTable displays a subset of the data that meet those conditions and calculates the summary statistics based on the filtered data rather than the complete dataset. The filter arrow displays an icon of a funnel when the PivotTable is being filtered. Cell B1 displays All when no filter is enabled, the value if one filter is enabled, or Multiple Items if more than one item is selected.

If you no longer want a filter, you can remove it. To remove the entire filter, drag the field from the Filters area in the PivotTable Fields task pane. To remove filter settings but keep the field in the Filters area for future filtering, click the Filter arrow in cell B1, select All and click OK.

You can apply filters for rows and columns. For example, you can apply date filters to display summary statistics for data occurring within a particular time frame or apply filters for values within a designated range. To apply row or column filters, click the Row Labels or Column Labels arrow in the PivotTable (see Figure 5.25), click the Select All check box on the menu to deselect all items, select the check boxes by the items you want to display, and then click OK.

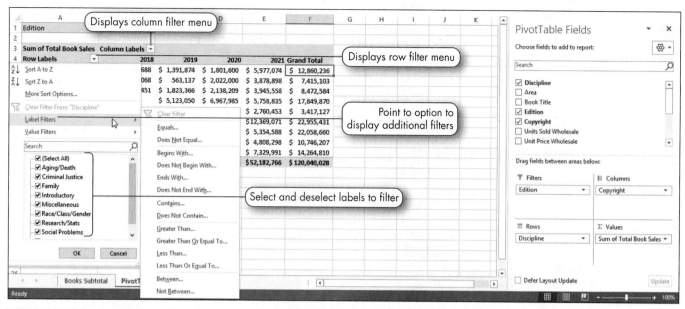

FIGURE 5.25 Row and Column Filtering

Insert a Slicer

You can insert a *slicer*, a small window containing one button for each unique item in a field so that you can filter the PivotTable quickly. The benefit of using slicers over the Filters area is that slicers display color-coded buttons to show which fields are being filtered, whereas using the filter arrows within the PivotTable do not show what fields are currently being filtered. The visual representation is easier to manipulate than adding more fields to the Filters area and setting each field's filter. Use Insert Slicer in the Filter group on the Analyze tab to open the Insert Slicers dialog box (see Figure 5.26). Select one or more field check boxes to display one or more slicers. For each field check box you select, Excel inserts a slicer into the worksheet. Because a slicer is an object similar to a chart, you can move it on the worksheet so that it does not overlap the data.

FIGURE 5.26 Insert Slicers Dialog Box

To filter the PivotTable by one category listed in the slicer, click that category. To filter multiple items, click Multi-Select first and select the categories. Slicer buttons are color-coded to indicate which categories are displayed and which categories are filtered out. In Figure 5.27, the Discipline field is filtered by Family, Introductory, and Social Problems. When you want to display all categories again, click Clear Filter in the top-right corner of the slicer to clear the filters for that field.

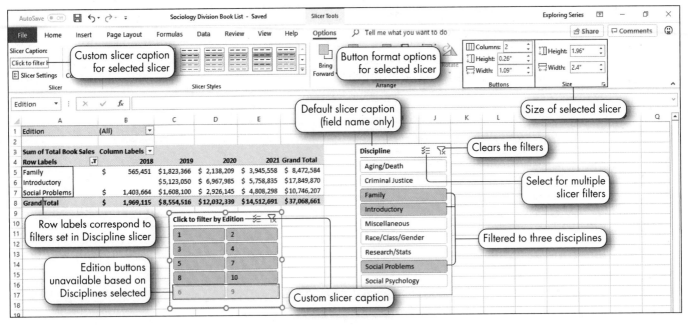

FIGURE 5.27 Slicers

TIP: UNAVAILABLE SLICER BUTTONS

When you insert multiple slicers and set filters in one slicer, some categories in the other slicers will change color, indicating those categories are not applicable based on the filters engaged by the first slicer.

Customize a Slicer

When you select a slicer, the Slicer Tools Options tab displays so that you can customize the slicer. The *slicer caption* is text that displays in the header at the top of the slicer window, similar to a title bar, to identify the data in the field. The default slicer caption displays the field name only. However, you can customize the slicer by changing its caption. In Figure 5.27, the caption for the Edition slicer displays an instruction to the user, whereas the caption for the Discipline slicer displays the default field name. Table 5.3 lists and describes the commands on the Slicer Tools Options tab. On a Mac, options to customize a slicer are located on the Slicer tab.

TABLE 5.3 Slicer Tools Commands

Group	Commands
Slicer	Change the slicer caption, display the Slicer Settings dialog box for further customization, and manage the PivotTable connected to the slicer. The Edition slicer has been sorted in ascending order. For example, the light blue items 6 and 9 do not apply to the selected disciplines.
Slicer Styles	Applies a style to the slicer by specifying the color of the filtered item in the slicer. For example, given the workbook theme, the default active filters appear in blue and unavailable items appear in light blue.
Arrange	Specifies the slicer's placement in relation to other groups, such as placing a slicer on top of other slicers.
Buttons	Defines how many columns are displayed in the selected slicer and the height and width of each button inside the slicer.
Size	Sets the height and width of the slicer window. For example, the Edition slicer's height is 1.96".

Insert a Timeline to Filter a PivotTable

When a PivotTable is based on a dataset that contains dates, you can filter data to a specific date or range of dates to analyze the data. Insert a **_PivotTable timeline_** to filter the data based on the date range you want. A PivotTable timeline is a small window that starts with the first date and ends with the last date in the data source. It contains horizontal tiles that you can filter data by day, month, quarter, or year.

To insert a timeline and filter data on a timeline in a PivotTable, complete the following steps:

1. Click the Analyze tab.
2. Click Insert Timeline in the Filter group to open the Insert Timelines dialog box, which displays field names of fields that contain date-formatted data.
3. Click a field check box to select it and click OK. Excel displays a timeline in the worksheet, and the Timeline Tools Options tab displays (see Figure 5.28) so that you can change the timeline caption, apply a style, adjust the size, and show items on the timeline.
4. Click the arrow by the current time level and select a time period: YEARS, QUARTERS, MONTHS, or DAYS. The timeline displays that time period.
5. Click a tile on the timeline to filter data. For example, click March 2021 to filter data in the PivotTable for that month. To select multiple time periods, click the tile representing the first time period and drag across the tiles to select consecutive time periods. For non-consecutive time periods (such as the 1st quarter of each year), press and hold Ctrl while you click various time periods on the timeline.
6. Click Clear Filter in the top-right corner of the timeline to clear a timeline.

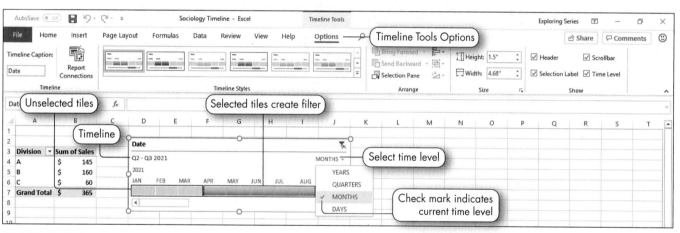

FIGURE 5.28 Timeline

Group PivotTable Data

You can group a subset of data within a PivotTable to analyze data. For example, you can group individual dates into quarters or months to simplify the PivotTable. One way to organize or group data by dates is to drag a date field to the Rows or Columns area in the PivotTable Fields task pane. The PivotTable automatically divides the aggregated data into those time periods.

To group values, dates, or times in a PivotTable, complete the following steps:

1. Select a cell that contains a numeric or date/time field in the PivotTable.
2. Click Group Field in the Group group on the Analyze tab to open the Grouping dialog box.
3. Enter values or dates in the Starting at and Ending at boxes.
4. Enter the interval value in the By box. For dates, select the date interval, such as months. Click OK.

Sometimes the row labels may list individual labels instead of category labels if the original data source does not include categories. However, you can create groups in the PivotTable. Press and hold Ctrl as you select the individual labels in the PivotTable and click Group Selection in the Group group on the Analyze tab. Excel displays a category name, such as Group 1, and inserts another field in the Rows area in the PivotTable Fields task pane. For example, if you select and group Aging/Death and Family, the Rows area will display Discipline2 for the new grouping and the original Discipline field name.

Use Help for more details and examples about grouping data and to learn how to ungroup data in a PivotTable.

STEP 3 ▶ Creating a Calculated Field

You can create a *calculated field*, which is a user-defined field that derives its value based on performing calculations in other fields in a PivotTable. The calculated field does not exist in the original dataset. For example, you can create a calculated field that converts totals to percentages for easier relative comparison among categories, or you can create a calculated field that determines the number of units sold generated by a 10% increase for the upcoming year.

To create a calculated field, complete the following steps:

1. Select a cell within the PivotTable and click the Analyze tab.
2. Click Fields, Items, & Sets in the Calculations group and select Calculated Field to display the Insert Calculated Field dialog box (see Figure 5.29).
3. Type a descriptive label for the calculated field in the Name box.
4. Build a formula starting with the equal sign (=). Instead of using cell references, double-click a field name to insert it in the formula and type operators, such as * to multiply. For example, = 'Total Book Sales'*.1 calculates a 10% royalty amount on the total book sales.
5. Click OK to insert the calculated field in the PivotTable. Format the numeric values in the calculated field column as needed.

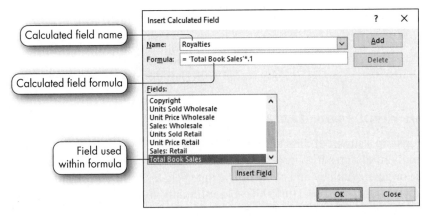

FIGURE 5.29 Insert Calculated Field Dialog Box

STEP 4 ▶ Show Values as Calculations

You can apply built-in custom calculations that display relationships between values in rows and columns in the PivotTable. To use a value as a calculation, insert the field in the Values area. You can repeat the field twice: once for the actual sum and a second time to perform the calculation. For example, you can show each value as a percentage of the grand total or each value's percentage of the row total.

To display values in relation to others, complete the following steps:

1. Click the field in the Values area of the PivotTable Fields task pane and select Value Field Settings (or click within the field in the PivotTable and click Field Settings in the Active Field group on the Analyze tab).
2. Click the Show Values As tab within the Value Field Settings dialog box.
3. Click the *Show values as* arrow and select the desired calculation type. Table 5.4 lists and describes some of the calculation options.
4. Select the *Base field* and the *Base item* if those options are available. These settings control which item within the designated field is used to base the calculations on.
5. Click Number Format to set number formats, click OK to close the Format Cells dialog box, and then click OK to close the Value Field Settings dialog box.

TABLE 5.4 Calculation Options

Option	Description
% of Grand Total	Displays each value as a percentage of the grand total.
% of Column Total	Displays each value as a percentage of the respective column total. The values in each column total 100%.
% of Row Total	Displays each value as a percentage of the respective row total. The values in each row total 100%.
% of Parent Row Total	Displays values as: (value for the item)/(value for the parent item on rows). Two fields should be contained in the Rows area where the first field is a parent of the second field. For example, if Discipline is the first field and Area is the second field, Family would be the parent for the Family Interaction and Marriage and Family areas. The calculation would divide the Family Interaction value by the total value in the Family parent row.
Running Total	Displays values as running totals.
Rank Smallest to Largest	Displays the rank of values in a specific field where 1 represents the smallest value.
Rank Largest to Smallest	Displays the rank of values in a specific field where 1 represents the largest value.

Figure 5.30 illustrates the use of the Total Sales field inserted three times in the Values area: (1) sum of the totals for each discipline and area, (2) % of Parent Row Total, and (3) % of Grand Total. The Discipline and Area fields are contained in the Rows area. The Disciplines are the parents to the respective Areas. In the % of Parent Row column, the Death and Dying sales ($3,751,187) are 66.92% of its Aging/Death parent sales of $5,606,170. The Sociology of Aging sales ($1,853,983) are 33.08% of the Aging/Death parent sales. The percentages for the areas within the Aging/Death discipline must add up to 100%. The Aging/Death discipline sales of $5,605,170 is 8.93% of its parent sales, the grand total of $62,796,185.

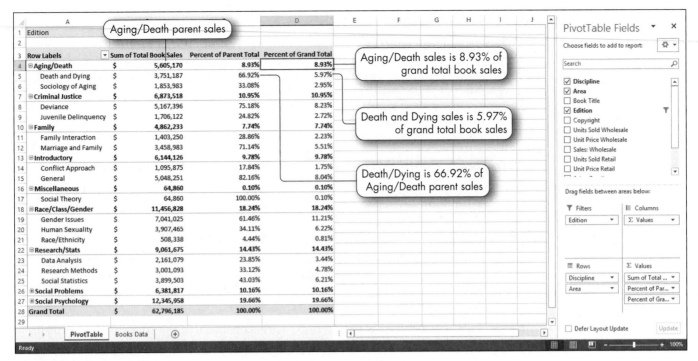

FIGURE 5.30 PivotTable Calculations

In the % of Grand Total column, each parent's sale is the percentage of the grand total, and each area's sales is a percentage of the grand total. The bold discipline (parent) percentages equal 100%, and the area percentages also equal 100% of the total sales.

Changing the PivotTable Design

Excel applies basic formatting to PivotTables. For example, it formats primary row labels in bold to distinguish those categories from the subcategories. In addition, the subtotals are bold to offset these values from the subcategory values. The PivotTable Tools Design tab contains commands for enhancing the format of a PivotTable (see Figure 5.31).

FIGURE 5.31 PivotTable Design Tab

STEP 5 **Change the PivotTable Style**

A *PivotTable style* controls bold formatting, font colors, shading colors, and border lines. For example, the default Light Blue, Pivot Style Light 16 displays a light blue fill color for the field filters in cells A1 and B1, the column and row labels, and the grand total row. If you change the workbook theme in the Page Layout tab, the PivotTable style will change to reflect the workbook theme colors.

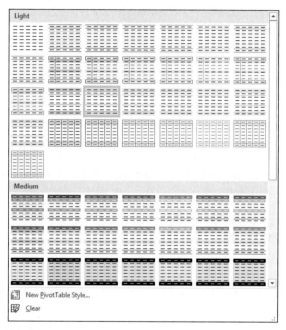

FIGURE 5.32 PivotTable Styles

The PivotTable Style Options group on the Design tab controls which areas of the PivotTable are affected by the style. Select Row Headers to apply special formatting for the first column. Column Headers to apply special formatting to the first row. Banded Rows to format odd and even rows differently, and Banded Columns to format odd and even columns differently.

Change the PivotTable Layout

The Layout group on the Design tab controls the layout of the PivotTable elements. These commands control whether subtotals and grand totals are displayed or hidden. You can customize the location of subtotals by clicking Subtotals in the Layout group on the Design tab. Displaying the subtotals at the top of the group draws attention to the totals and enables you to scroll to view all of the supporting data.

The Report Layout controls the overall format. You can select a compact, outline, or tabular layout. The Report Layout also controls whether item labels are repeated when multiple fields are located in the Rows area of the PivotTable Fields task pane. The Blank Rows command enables you to insert blank rows between items or remove blank rows.

Quick Concepts

7. Explain the purpose of applying a filter to a PivotTable and what type of filters you can apply. *p. 340*

8. Explain the purpose of inserting a slicer in a worksheet that contains a PivotTable. *p. 341*

9. Describe when you would create a calculated field in a PivotTable. *p. 344*

Hands-On Exercises

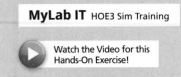
Skills covered: Add Filters •
Insert a Slicer • Customize a Slicer •
Create a Calculated Field • Show
Values as Calculations • Change
the PivotTable Style

3 PivotTable Options

The PivotTable you created enables you to review sales data by discipline for each copyright year. In addition, you have used the PivotTable to compare grand total sales among disciplines and grand totals by copyright year. Now you want to extend your analysis. You will calculate author royalties from the sales and impose filters to focus your attention on each analysis. Finally, you will apply a different style to the PivotTable.

STEP 1 ADD FILTERS

The level of success of the first two editions especially determines the likelihood of approving subsequent revisions and editions. To display aggregated sales for these editions, you will set a filter to remove the other editions so they are not included in the calculated sales data. After you review the first- and second-edition data, you will enable additional filters to review books published in the past two years. Refer to Figure 5.33 as you complete Step 1.

FIGURE 5.33 Filters Enabled

a. Open *e05h2Sociology_LastFirst* if you closed it at the end of Hands-On Exercise 2 and save it as **e05h3Sociology_LastFirst**, changing h2 to h3.

b. Make sure the PivotTable worksheet tab is active and drag the **Edition field** from the *Choose fields to add to report* section to the Filters area.

You can now filter the PivotTable based on the Edition field. Cell A1 displays the field name, and cell B1 displays All and the filter arrow.

c. Click the **Edition filter arrow** in **cell B1** and click the **Select Multiple Items check box** to select it. On a Mac, because Select Multiple Items is not available, skip this step.

The list displays a check box for each item.

d. Click the **All check box** to deselect it.

e. Click the **1** and **2 check boxes** to select them and click **OK**.

The summary statistics reflect sales data for only first- and second-edition publications. The filter arrow changes to a funnel icon in cell B1. Cell B1 also changes from All to Multiple Items, indicating that multiple items are included in the filter.

f. Click the **Copyright Year filter arrow** in **cell B3** and click the **Select All check box** to deselect it.

g. Click the **2020** and **2021 check boxes** to select them, click **OK**, and then save the workbook.

Excel filters out data for years that do not meet the condition you set. The filter arrow changes to a funnel icon in cell B3.

STEP 2 INSERT AND CUSTOMIZE A SLICER

You plan to distribute the workbook to colleagues who are not as skilled in Excel as you are. To help them set their own filters, you want to insert slicers. Refer to Figure 5.34 as you complete Step 2.

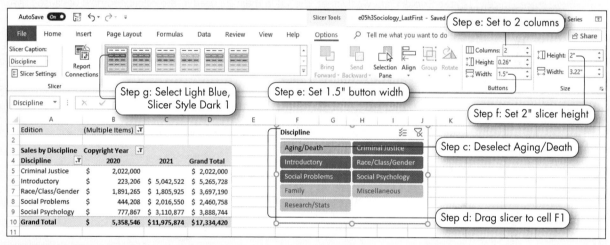

FIGURE 5.34 Discipline Slicer

a. Click **Insert Slicer** in the Filter group on the Analyze tab.

The Insert Slicers dialog box opens, listing each field name.

b. Click the **Discipline check box** to select it and click **OK**.

Excel inserts the Discipline slicer in the worksheet. Six slicer buttons are blue, indicating that those disciplines are selected. The grayed-out buttons at the bottom of the slicer indicate those disciplines are not applicable based on other engaged filters you set (first and second editions and 2020 and 2021 copyright years, respectively).

c. Press and hold **Ctrl** as you click **Aging/Death** in the Discipline slicer.

This deselects the Aging/Death discipline.

> **TROUBLESHOOTING:** Because several disciplines are selected, if you click Aging/Death instead of pressing Ctrl as you click it, you set Aging/Death as the only discipline. The others are filtered out. If this happens, immediately click Undo and repeat Step c.

d. Drag the slicer so that the top-left corner of the slicer is in **cell F1**.

You moved the slicer so that it does not cover up data in the PivotTable.

e. Change the **Columns** value to **2** in the Buttons group on the Options tab. Change the button **Width** to **1.5"** in the Buttons group.

The slicer now displays buttons in two columns. You changed the width of the buttons to 1.5" to display the full discipline names within the buttons.

f. Change the slicer Height to **2** in the Size group.

The slicer window is now only 2" tall.

g. Click **More** in the Slicer Styles group and click **Light Blue, Slicer Style Dark 1** (the first style in the Dark group). Save the workbook.

Based on the selected workbook theme, Light Blue, Slicer Style Dark 1 applies a dark blue fill color for selected disciplines, dark gray and black font for available but not currently selected disciplines, and light blue fill with medium blue font color for non-applicable disciplines.

STEP 3 ## CREATE A CALCULATED FIELD

You want to calculate the amount of the sales returned to the authors as royalties. Although the 10% royalty rate is stored in cell J2 in the Books Data worksheet, the value must be used in the calculated field because range names and cell references outside the PivotTable cannot be used. Refer to Figure 5.35 as you complete Step 3.

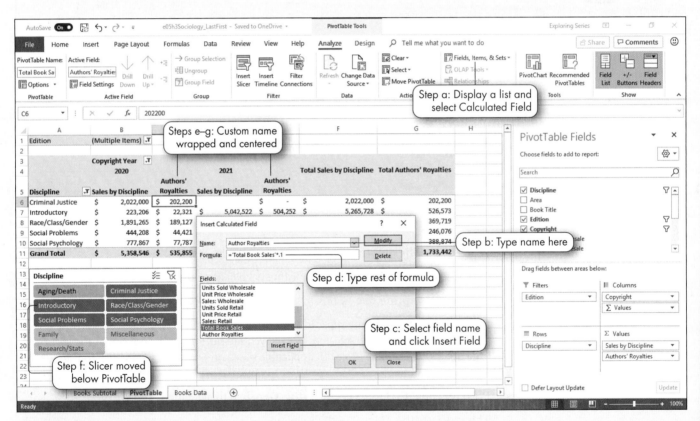

FIGURE 5.35 Calculated Field

a. Click within the PivotTable, click the **Analyze tab**, click **Fields, Items, & Sets** in the Calculations group, and then select **Calculated Field**.

The Insert Calculated Field dialog box opens.

b. Type **Author Royalties** in the Name box.

c. Scroll down the Fields list, click **Total Book Sales**, and then click **Insert Field**.

Excel starts to build the formula, which is currently = 'Total Book Sales'.

d. Type ***.1** at the end of the Formula box and click **OK**.

Excel adds Sum of Author Royalties calculated field columns, one for each copyright year category. It calculates the authors' royalties as 10% of the total sales for each copyright year.

e. Click **cell C5**, click **Field Settings** in the Active Field group on the Analyze tab, type **Authors' Royalties** in the Custom Name box in the Value Field Settings dialog box, and then click **OK**.

f. Move the slicer below the PivotTable so that the top-left corner is in **cell A13**.

g. Select **cells C5** and **E5**, click the **Home tab**, and then click **Center** and **Wrap Text** in the Alignment group. Click **Format** in the Cells group and select **Row Height**, type **30**, and click **OK**. Click **Format**, select **Column Width**, type **12**, and then click **OK**.

h. Save the workbook.

SHOW VALUES AS CALCULATIONS

You want to see which copyright year generated the largest sales for each discipline, which discipline contributes the largest percentage of the total sociology sales, and which introductory book has the largest sales contribution within that discipline. Refer to Figure 5.36 as you complete Step 4.

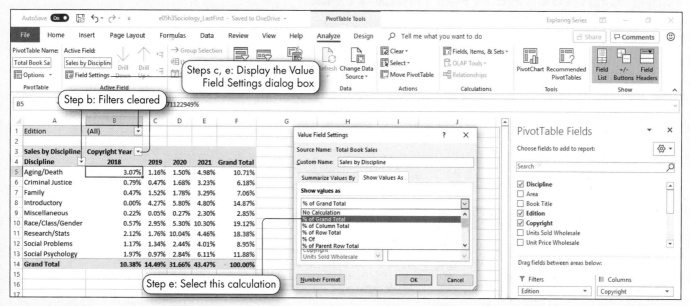

FIGURE 5.36 Percentage of Grand Total

a. Right click the **PivotTable sheet tab**, select **Move or Copy**, click **Books Data** in the *Before sheet* list, click the **Create a copy check box** to select it, and then click **OK**.

You copied the PivotTable worksheet to maintain the previous tasks you completed as evidence. You will work with the PivotTable (2) worksheet, which is the active worksheet.

b. Do the following to remove filters, slicer, and Authors' Royalties field:

- Click the **Edition filter** in **cell B1**, click the **All check box** to select it, and then click **OK** to clear the Edition filter and display all edition numbers again.
- Click the **Discipline filter** in **cell A5** and select **Clear Filter From "Discipline"**.
- Click the **Copyright Year filter** in **cell B3** and select **Clear Filter From "Copyright"**.
- Select the slicer and press **Delete**.
- Click **Authors' Royalties** in the Values area of the PivotTable Fields task pane and select **Remove Field**.

c. Click any value in the PivotTable, click the **Analyze tab**, and then click **Field Settings** in the Active Field group.

The Value Field Settings dialog box opens.

d. Click the **Show Values As tab**, click the **Show values as arrow**, select **% of Row Total**, and then click **OK**.

Excel displays each copyright year's values as percentages for that discipline. All disciplines except Introductory and Research/Stats had the highest percentage of sales for the books with a 2021 copyright. These two disciplines had their highest percentage of sales for books with a 2020 copyright.

e. Click the **Field Settings** in the Active Field group, click the **Show Values As tab** within the dialog box, click the **Show values as arrow**, select **% of Grand Total**, and then click **OK**. Save the workbook.

Refer to Figure 5.36. Each discipline's yearly value displays as a percentage of the total sales. Which discipline and for what copyright year produces the highest percentage of total sales? Answer: 2021 Race/Class/Gender with 10.30%, followed closely by the 2020 Research/Stats with 10.04%. In general, the Race/Class/Gender discipline contributed the highest percentage of the total sales with 19.12%.

STEP 5 CHANGE THE PIVOTTABLE STYLE

To enhance the readability of the sociology textbook PivotTable, you will change the PivotTable style. Refer to Figure 5.37 as you complete Step 5.

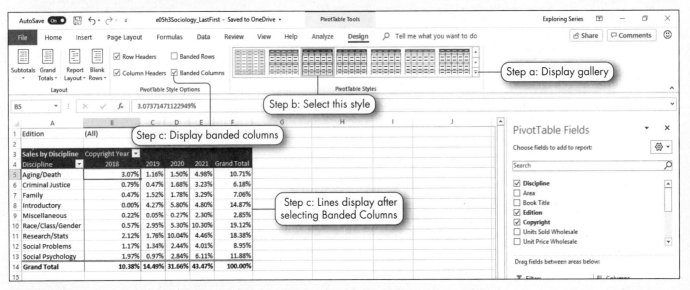

FIGURE 5.37 PivotTable Style Applied

a. Make sure the PivotTable (2) sheet tab is active. Click a cell within the PivotTable, click the **Design tab**, and then click **More** in the PivotTable Styles group.

The PivotTable Style gallery displays styles that you can apply.

b. Click **Light Blue, Pivot Style Medium 2** to apply a dark blue style to the PivotTable.

c. Click the **Banded Columns check box** to select it in the PivotTable Style Options group to add dark blue vertical lines between the columns.

d. Save and close the workbook. You will submit this file to your instructor at the end of the last Hands-On Exercise.

Data Modeling and PivotCharts

When you created a PivotTable earlier in this chapter, you created it from a dataset in a single worksheet. However, the data is often contained in multiple sources, such as multiple worksheets or databases. Excel enables you to use related data to create a PivotTable.

You can create PivotCharts, which like other charts you have created in Excel, provide visual representations of numeric data. Charts help reveal trends or patterns in the data because people can often interpret visual aids easier than reviewing an entire dataset.

In this section, you will select multiple datasets, create a relationship between the datasets, and then create a PivotTable. Finally, you will create and format a PivotChart.

Creating a Data Model

So far, you have been working with data from one table. Often, however, you will want to analyze data contained in multiple tables. A ***data model*** is a collection of related tables that contain structured data used to create a database. You can create a relationship between two or more Excel ranges that have been formatted as tables that have some commonality and relationship, similar to how you can create relationships among common tables in an Access database. You can then perform complex data analysis to make insightful decisions.

TIP: NAMING TABLES

Before creating relationships between tables, you should assign a meaningful name to each table. Assigning meaningful table names enables you to select the correct tables in the Create Relationships dialog box. Otherwise, Excel uses the default table names, such as Table1 and Table2, making it more challenging to decide which table to use to create the relationship.

STEP 1 ▶ **Create Relationships**

A ***relationship*** is an association or connection between two tables where both tables contain a common field of data. Similar to how a VLOOKUP function looks up data from a range to find matching data in another range, you can create relationships between tables. For example, you want to generate a report that contains sales representatives' names and their respective data, but the sales data is stored in SALES table, and the representatives' names are stored in the REPS table.

To combine the names and data into one report, you must establish a link (or relationship) between the two tables using the sales representatives' IDs. Both tables contain a field to store the representatives' IDs. While the field names do not have to be identical in both tables, both tables must contain the same type of data to build the relationship. The values in one table must be unique with no duplicates. For example, the ID field in the REPS table contains one value for each rep. In the SALES table, the RepID values are duplicated, indicating that each rep is responsible for multiple sales. The relationship between REPS and SALES is a one-to-many relationship where the ID is listed one time in the REPS table and many times in the SALES table. Figure 5.38 contains an entity-relationship diagram (ERD) that shows the relationship between the REPS table and SALES table.

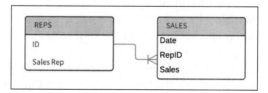

FIGURE 5.38 Relationships between Tables

To create a relationship between two tables in Excel, complete the following steps:

1. Click the Data tab and click Relationships in the Data Tools group to open the Manage Relationships dialog box.
2. Click New in the dialog box to open the Create Relationship dialog box (see Figure 5.39).
3. Click the Table arrow and select the name of a table. In a one-to-many relationship, select the table on the many side. The table in this example is SALES.
4. Click the Column (Foreign) arrow and select the name of the column that contains a relationship to the related or lookup table. For example, Rep ID is the column that relates to a column in the other table.
5. Click the Related Table arrow and select the name of the related or lookup table. For example, the related table is REPS.
6. Click the Related Column (Primary) arrow and select the name of the column that has unique values and is related to the other table. For example, the ID column in the REPS table relates to the Rep ID column in the SALES table.
7. Click OK in the Create Relationships dialog box and click Close in the Manage Relationships dialog box.

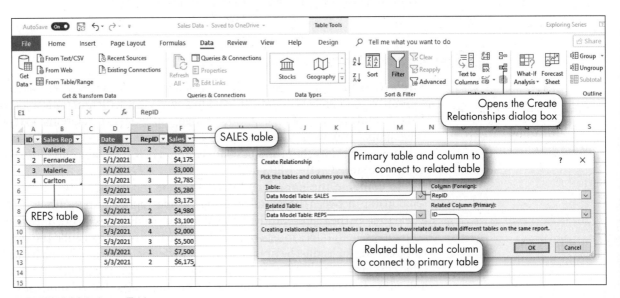

FIGURE 5.39 Relating Tables

You can create multiple relationships with one table similar to creating relationships among several tables in an Access database. To create multiple relationships, you must create a relationship between two tables at a time. Each combination of tables must have a common field. After creating the first relationship, repeat the process to create a relationship between two other tables.

If you want to edit the relationship, click Relationships in the Data Tools group to open the Manage Relationships dialog box. Select the relationship you want to edit, click Edit to open the Edit Relationships dialog box (which looks like the Create Relationships dialog box), make the changes, click OK, and then click Close.

STEP 2 Create a PivotTable from Related Tables

After you create a relationship between tables, you can create a PivotTable using fields from both tables. When selecting fields, use the common field. For example, if both tables contain sales representatives' IDs, you can use the actual names instead of their IDs for better descriptions in the PivotTable.

To create a PivotTable from the data model, complete the following steps:

1. Click within the primary table.
2. Click the Insert tab and click PivotTable in the Tables group to open the Create PivotTable dialog box (see Figure 5.40).
3. Make sure the primary table name is displayed in the Table/Range box.
4. Click the *Add this data to the Data Model* check box to select it and click OK.

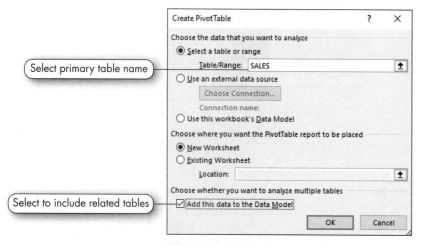

FIGURE 5.40 Create PivotTable Dialog Box

In the PivotTable Fields task pane, click All to display the names of all related tables. Click the table names to display the field names. You then can arrange the fields in the different area boxes at the bottom of the task pane (see Figure 5.41).

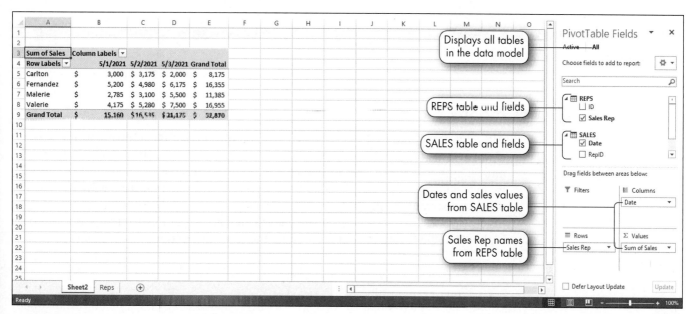

FIGURE 5.41 PivotTable Created from Related Tables

Data Modeling and PivotCharts • **Excel 2019**   355

STEP 3 Creating a PivotChart

A *PivotChart* is an interactive graphical representation of the data in a PivotTable. A PivotChart presents the consolidated data visually. When you change the position of a field in either the PivotTable or the PivotChart, the corresponding object changes as well. With the active cell within a PivotTable, click PivotChart in the Tools group on the Analyze tab.

Excel creates a PivotChart based on the current PivotTable settings—row labels, column labels, values, and filters. The PivotChart contains elements that enable you to set filters. The Rows area is replaced with Axis (Categories), and the Columns area is replaced with Legend (Series) when you select the PivotChart (see Figure 5.42). The PivotChart contains field buttons so that you can sort and filter the chart by that field. The field used for the Filters area remains a field to use to filter data within the PivotChart. The field used for Values in a PivotTable remains a field that builds the plot area within the PivotChart.

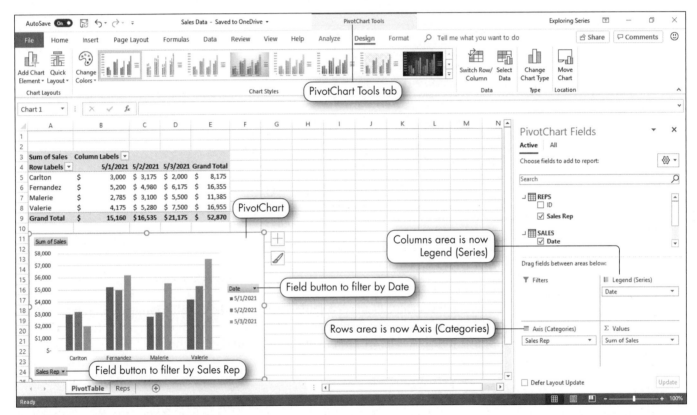

FIGURE 5.42 PivotTable and PivotChart

STEP 4 Modify the PivotChart

Although Excel creates the PivotChart based on the current PivotTable settings, you can change the settings using the PivotChart Fields task pane. Use the Filters arrows to sort and filter data used to design the chart. You can filter the category axis and the legend to exclude data from being depicted in the chart. Changes you make to the PivotChart also affect the corresponding PivotTable. For example, if you apply a filter to the PivotChart, Excel also filters the PivotTable. If you click Switch Rows/Column to change how the data is plotted in the PivotChart, Excel changes the rows and columns in the PivotTable.

If a PivotChart is designed from a PivotTable that contains two or more rows, you can double-click a data series in the PivotChart to drill down to show additional details. For example, if a PivotTable contains the Discipline and Copyright fields in the Rows area, you can collapse the Copyright rows in the PivotTable and then double-click one discipline column in the PivotChart to drill down to show data for different copyright years for that discipline. Use Help to learn more about drilling down in a PivotTable or a PivotChart.

TIP: DUPLICATE THE PIVOTTABLE

Instead of creating a PivotChart from an existing PivotTable, you can copy the PivotTable worksheet and use the duplicate PivotTable for the basis for creating the PivotChart. That way, you can modify the PivotChart settings without altering your original PivotTable.

The PivotChart Tools Analyze tab contains the same options that you used to customize a PivotTable. You can enter a name in the Chart Name box in the PivotChart group, insert slicers and timelines to filter the data depicted in the chart, and refresh the chart after changing the data source. In addition, the Actions group contains the Move Chart option so that you can move a PivotChart to a different worksheet.

The PivotChart Tools Design tab contains the Chart Layouts, Chart Styles, Data, Type, and Location groups, similar to the groups on the Chart Tools Design tab. Table 5.5 describes the commands in these groups.

TABLE 5.5	PivotChart Tools Design Tab
Group	**Commands**
Chart Layouts	Add chart elements (such as a chart title and data labels) and apply a layout to the PivotChart.
Chart Styles	Apply a different chart style to the PivotChart and then customize the chart by changing the color scheme.
Data	Switch how rows and columns of data are represented in the PivotChart and change the data source used to create the chart.
Type	Change the chart type, such as changing a column chart to a bar chart.
Location	Move the chart to a different sheet in the workbook.

The Chart Elements and Chart Styles buttons display to the right of a PivotChart when it is selected (see Figure 5.43). When you click Chart Elements, a menu displays to add or remove chart elements, such as the chart title, data labels, and legend. When you click Chart Styles, a gallery of chart styles displays so that you can apply a different style to the chart.

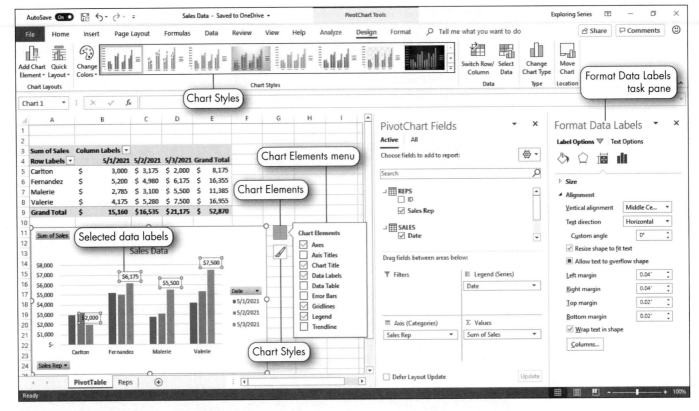

FIGURE 5.43 PivotChart Formatting

When you double-click a chart element, a task pane displays on the right side of the screen so that you can customize that element. For example, if you double-click a data label, the Format Data Labels task pane displays (refer to Figure 5.43).

If you double-click a column in a column chart or a bar in a bar chart, the Format Data Series task pane displays so that you can change the fill color. If you double-click a slice of a pie in a pie chart, the Format Data Point task pane displays so that you can change the fill color for that slice. Use Excel Help to learn more about customizing PivotCharts.

Quick Concepts

10. Explain when it is beneficial to create a relationship between two tables. **p. 353**

11. Describe the PivotTable areas used to create the elements in a PivotChart. **p. 358**

12. Explain what happens when you set filters and change fields used in a PivotChart. **p. 358**

Hands-On Exercises

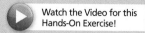
Skills covered: Create Relationships • Create a PivotTable from Related Tables • Create a PivotChart • Modify the PivotChart

4 Data Modeling and PivotCharts

You are converting the data into separate tables to improve the database design of the book's data. Your new workbook contains a Books table, an Editor table, and a Discipline table. The Books table uses numbers to code the editor assigned to each book and the discipline for each book. You will build relationships among these tables, create a PivotTable to analyze data by discipline and editor, and then create a PivotChart for the Family discipline.

STEP 1 CREATE RELATIONSHIPS

The BOOKS table contains codes instead of discipline categories, and a new column contains editor IDs. You will create relationships between the BOOKS table and the DISCIPLINE and EDITOR tables to build a data model. Refer to Figure 5.44 as you complete Step 1.

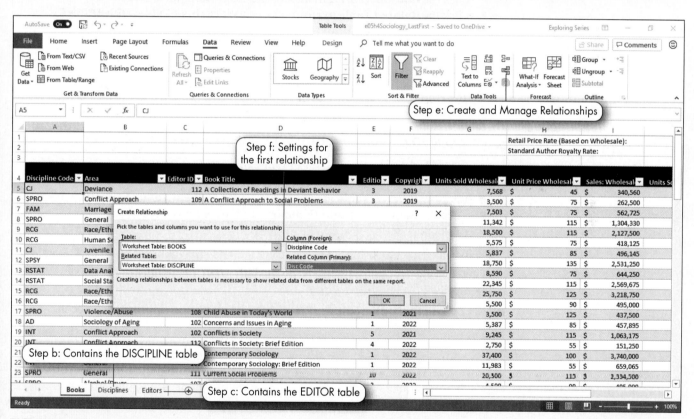

FIGURE 5.44 Relating Tables

MAC TROUBLESHOOTING: Creating and managing relationships is not supported in Excel for Mac.

---

a. Open *e05h4Sociology* and save it as **e05h4Sociology_LastFirst**.

The Books sheet tab contains the BOOKS table. Notice that the discipline category names have been replaced with discipline codes in the first column. The third column contains codes that represent editor names.

b. Click the **Disciplines sheet tab**.

The Disciplines sheet contains the DISCIPLINE table. Each discipline code and category name is listed only once. For example, FAM is the code for the Family discipline.

c. Click the **Editors sheet tab**.

The Editors sheet contains the EDITOR table. Each editor is listed only once. For example, 101 is Melissa Hort.

d. Click the **Books sheet tab** and click **cell A5**.

e. Click the **Data tab** and click **Relationships** in the Data Tools group.

The Manage Relationships dialog box opens.

f. Click **New** to open the Create Relationship dialog box and do the following:

- Click the **Table arrow** and select **Worksheet Table: BOOKS**.
- Click the **Column (Foreign) arrow** and select **Discipline Code**.
- Click the **Related Table arrow** and select **Worksheet Table: DISCIPLINE**.
- Click the **Related Column (Primary) arrow** and select **Disc Code**.
- Click **OK**.

You created a relationship between the BOOKS and DISCIPLINE tables based on the common data, the discipline codes. The Manage Relationships dialog box now displays the relationship you created. You will now add a second relationship before closing the dialog box.

g. Click **New** to open the Create Relationship dialog box and do the following:

- Click the **Table arrow** and select **Worksheet Table: BOOKS**.
- Click the **Column (Foreign)** and select **Editor ID**.
- Click the **Related Table arrow** and select **Worksheet Table: EDITOR**.
- Click the **Related Column (Primary)** and select **Editor ID**.
- Click **OK**.

You created a relationship between the BOOKS and EDITOR tables based on the common data, the Editor IDs. The Manage Relationships dialog box now displays the relationship you created.

h. Click **Close** to close the Manage Relationships dialog box and save the workbook.

CREATE A PIVOTTABLE FROM RELATED TABLES

Now that the BOOKS table is related to both the DISCIPLINE and EDITOR tables, you are ready to create a PivotTable using the three tables. Refer to Figure 5.45 as you complete Step 2.

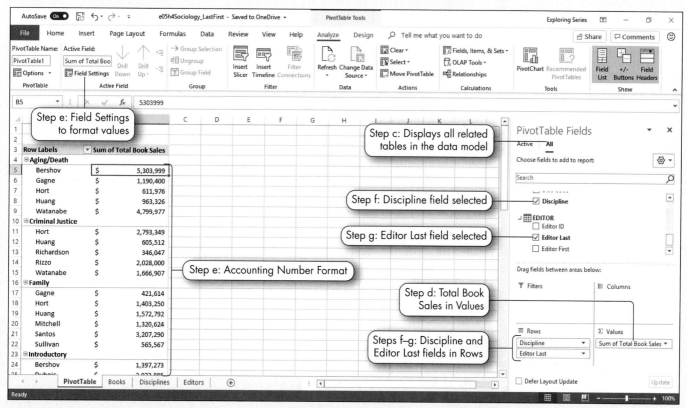

FIGURE 5.45 PivotTable for Related Tables

a. Click within the dataset on the Books sheet, click the **Insert tab**, and then click **PivotTable** in the Tables group.

The Create PivotTable dialog box opens with BOOKS as the selected Table/Range.

b. Click the **Add this data to the Data Model check box** to select it and click **OK**.

Excel inserts Sheet1 with a blank PivotTable on the left side.

c. Click **All** at the top of the PivotTable Fields task pane.

The PivotTable Fields task pane shows BOOKS, DISCIPLINE, and EDITOR table names.

d. Click **BOOKS** to display the fields in the BOOKS table, scroll through the fields, and then click the **Total Book Sales check box** to select it.

The Total Book Sales field is added to the Values area.

e. Click **Field Settings** in the Active Field group on the Analyze tab to open the Value Field Settings dialog box and complete the following steps:

- Click **Number Format** to open the Number Format dialog box.
- Click **Accounting** in the Category list.
- Change the **Decimal places** to **0**.
- Click **OK** in the Format Cells dialog box.
- Click **OK** in the Value Field Settings dialog box.

The value is formatted with Accounting Number Format with zero decimal places.

f. Click **DISCIPLINE** in the PivotTable Fields task pane to display the fields in the DISCIPLINE table and click the **Discipline check box** to select it.

The Discipline field is added to the Rows area.

g. Scroll down and click **EDITOR** in the task pane to display the fields in the EDITOR table and click the **Editor Last check box** to select it.

The Editor Last field is added below the Discipline field in the Rows area.

h. Double-click the **Sheet1 sheet tab**, type **PivotTable**, and then press **Enter**. Save the workbook.

You want to create a PivotChart to depict the sales data by editor for the Family discipline. Refer to Figure 5.46 as you complete Step 3.

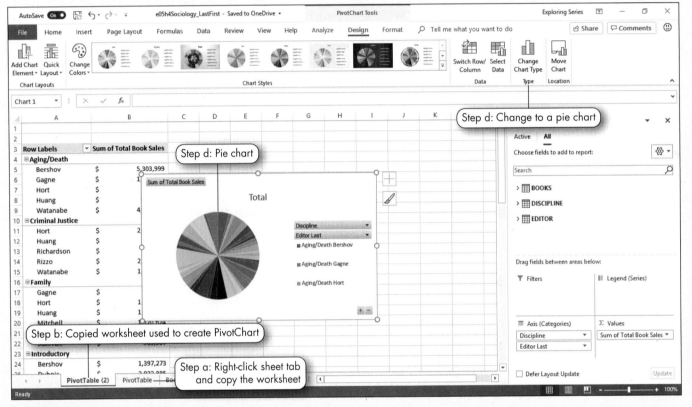

FIGURE 5.46 PivotChart Created

a. Right-click the **PivotTable sheet tab**, select **Move or Copy**, click the **Create a copy check box** to select it, and then click **OK**.

You created a copy of the PivotTable so that you can preserve that PivotTable settings, modify the duplicate PivotTable, and then create a PivotChart based on the modified PivotTable.

b. Ensure the PivotTable (2) sheet tab is active, click **PivotChart** in the Tools group on the Analyze tab to open the Insert Chart dialog box, and then click **OK**.

Excel creates a clustered column chart from the PivotTable.

c. Click the **Design tab**.

d. Click **Change Chart Type** in the Type group, click **Pie**, and then click **OK**. Save the workbook.

You changed the chart type from a clustered column chart to a pie chart.

The PivotChart depicts too many data points. You will set a filter to display data for the Family discipline only. You will add a descriptive chart title and display slices from largest to smallest. Finally, you will display percentage data labels. Refer to Figure 5.47 as you complete Step 4.

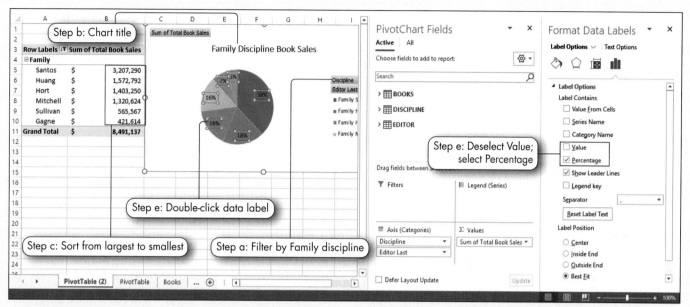

FIGURE 5.47 Modified PivotChart

a. Click the **Discipline arrow** within the PivotChart, click the **Select All check box** to deselect all disciplines, click the **Family check box**, and then click **OK**.

This action filtered both the PivotChart and the PivotTable to display only Family discipline data.

b. Click **Total** in the chart title and type **Family Discipline Book Sales**.

You changed the chart title to be more descriptive.

c. Click **cell B5** in the PivotTable, click the **Data tab**, and then click **Sort Largest to Smallest** in the Sort & Filter group.

This action sorts the values from largest to smallest in both the PivotTable and in the PivotChart.

d. Click the PivotChart, click **Chart Elements** on the right of the PivotChart, and then click the **Data Labels check box** to select it.

You added data labels to the PivotChart.

e. Double-click a data label to display the Format Data Labels task pane, click the **Value check box** to deselect the values, click the **Percentage check box**, and then close the task pane.

f. Cut the PivotChart and paste it in **cell C1**.

g. Save and close the file. Exit Excel. Based on your instructor's directions, submit the following:

e05h3Sociology_LastFirst

e05h4Sociology_LastFirst

Chapter Objectives Review

After reading this chapter, you have accomplished the following objectives:

1. Subtotal data.

- Use the Subtotal dialog box to insert subtotals, such as sums or averages, based on sorted data. This feature detects changes between categories arranged in rows to insert the subtotal rows.
- Add a second subtotal: You can keep the first subtotals and add a second subtotal for a subcategory by deselecting the *Replace current subtotals* check box in the Subtotals dialog box.
- Collapse and expand the subtotals: Use the outline level buttons to collapse the subtotals to the grand total, grand total and subtotals, or entire dataset. The collapse buttons collapse a category to hide detailed columns, and the expand buttons expand a category to display detailed columns.

2. Group and ungroup data.

- If the data contain columns of formulas based on other columns, use Auto Outline to create an outline based on the data structure. You can collapse and expand the outline. If you no longer want data to be grouped, select and ungroup the data.

3. Create a PivotTable.

- Create a Recommended PivotTable: Use Quick Analysis or Recommended PivotTable to provide recommended PivotTables. The PivotTable displays on a new worksheet, and the PivotTable Fields task pane displays. The task pane contains a list of fields in the dataset and areas to control the layout of the PivotTable.
- Create a blank PivotTable: Use the ribbon to create a blank PivotTable layout. You can then add fields to design the PivotTable.
- Add rows, values, and columns: Add fields to the Rows, Values, and Columns areas of the PivotTable Fields task pane. The order of the fields within the Rows area dictates the hierarchy. Add numeric fields to the Values area to display aggregated totals for that field. If you add a field containing text, the default calculation is to provide a count of data. Add columns to provide greater detail for the fields in the Values area.

4. Modify a PivotTable.

- Collapse and expand categories: Use the collapse and expand buttons to collapse and expand, respectively, details within a PivotTable.
- Remove fields: If a field is no longer useful, you can remove it from the PivotTable by selecting Remove Field.
- Rearrange fields: Drag fields from one area to another in the PivotTable Fields task pane to rearrange fields in the PivotTable.

- Change value field settings: You can select a function to calculate the statistics in the PivotTable. You can apply number formatting and specify a custom column heading.
- Use the GETPIVOTDATA function: Use this function to obtain a summary value from a PivotTable. This function is useful to enter on a worksheet containing the main data source so that you do not have to go back and forth between the data source and PivotTable worksheets as you review the data source.
- Refresh a PivotTable: Because PivotTables do not update automatically if you change the original dataset, you must refresh the PivotTable to update it based on the changes in the dataset.

5. Sort, filter, and slice a PivotTable.

- Sort data within a field: Use the Row Labels filter arrow to change the sort order of data within a PivotTable. If the sort order does not arrange data in the sequence you want, use the Move option to move a category within the PivotTable.
- Add filters: You can add a field to the Filters area of the PivotTable Fields task pane and set conditions to filter the PivotTable. You can also set row and column filters using the filter arrows within the PivotTable.
- Insert a slicer: A slicer is a small window containing the values for a field. Use the slicer buttons to set filters for that field.
- Customize a slicer: You can specify the slicer's style and size. You can specify how many columns of buttons appear in the slicer and the size of those buttons.
- Insert a timeline to filter a PivotTable: A timeline is a small window that enables you to filter a PivotTable to a particular time period, such as years, quarters, months, or dates.
- Group PivotTable data: You can group values or date/time data to structure a PivotTable. In addition, you can select and group labels in a PivotTable to create groups. Creating groups is helpful if the data source used to create the PivotTable did not have categories or groups.

6. Create a calculated field.

- A calculated field is a user-defined field based on other fields. You can use arithmetic operations, but you cannot use cell references or range names in the calculated field syntax.
- Show values as calculations: You can apply predefined calculations, such as % of Grand Total, for displaying the values in the PivotTable.

7. Change the PivotTable design.

- Change the PivotTable style: A PivotTable style controls bold formatting, font colors, shading colors, and border lines. The PivotTable Styles gallery displays thumbnails of styles from which to choose.
- Change the PivotTable layout: The layout commands control whether subtotals and grand totals are displayed, specifies the location of subtotals, and controls the overall layout.

8. Create a data model.

- Create relationships: You can create relationships between two or more related tables within one workbook. The relationship is based on a common field in the tables.
- Create a PivotTable from related tables: After creating the relationships, you can create a PivotTable that uses fields from the related tables. The PivotTable Fields task pane displays the names of the related tables in the data model.

9. Create a PivotChart.

- A PivotChart is similar to a regular chart, except it is based on the categories and structure of the PivotTable, not the original dataset. If you change the fields or sort order in either the PivotTable or the PivotChart, Excel automatically adjusts the corresponding pivot object.
- Modify the PivotChart: You can modify the PivotChart like a regular chart. You can add a chart title, change the chart type, and add chart elements such as data labels. In addition, you can apply a different style to a PivotChart. If you change the fields or set filters for the PivotChart, Excel applies those same changes to the related PivotTable. Finally, if a PivotChart is designed from a PivotTable containing multiple fields in the Rows area, you an collapse or drill down into categories.

Key Terms Matching

Match the key terms with their definitions. Write the key term letter by the appropriate numbered definition.

a. Calculated field
b. Columns area
c. Data mining
d. Data model
e. Filters area
f. GETPIVOTDATA

g. Grouping
h. Outline
i. PivotChart
j. PivotTable Fields task pane
k. PivotTable
l. PivotTable style

m. PivotTable timeline
n. Relationship
o. Rows area
p. Slicer
q. Slicer caption

r. Subtotal
s. Subtotal row
t. Values area

1. _____ An association created between two tables where both tables contain a common field of data. **p. 353**

2. _____ A hierarchical structure of data that you can group related data to summarize. **p. 316**

3. _____ A row that contains one or more aggregate calculations for each category within a dataset. **p. 314**

4. _____ A process of joining related rows or columns of related data into a single entity so that groups can be collapsed or expanded. **p. 317**

5. _____ The process of analyzing large volumes of data to identify trends and patterns in the data. **p. 323**

6. _____ An interactive table that uses calculations to consolidate and summarize data from a data source to enable a person to analyze the data in a dataset without altering the actual data. **p. 323**

7. _____ A user-defined field that performs a calculation based on other fields in a PivotTable. **p. 344**

8. _____ A window listing all unique items in a field so that the user can click a button to filter data by that item or value. **p. 341**

9. _____ A section within the PivotTable Fields task pane used to group data into categories in the first column based on selected field(s) in a PivotTable. **p. 326**

10. _____ A section within the PivotTable Fields task pane used to place a field to display summary statistics, such as totals or averages in a PivotTable. **p. 326**

11. _____ A section within the PivotTable Fields task pane used to place a field so that the user can then filter the data by that field. **p. 326**

12. _____ A section within the PivotTable Fields task pane used to display summarized data in vertical columns for the selected field(s) in a PivotTable. **p. 326**

13. _____ A graphical representation of aggregated data derived from a PivotTable. **p. 356**

14. _____ A window that displays the fields in a dataset and enables a user to specify what fields are used to create a layout to organize the data in columns, rows, values, and filters in a PivotTable. **p. 325**

15. _____ The text or field name that appears as a header or title at the top of a slicer to identify the data in that field. **p. 342**

16. _____ A small window that starts with the first date and ends with the last date in the data source. It contains horizontal tiles that you can click to filter data by day, month, quarter, or year. **p. 343**

17. _____ A collection of related tables that contain structured data used to create a database. **p. 353**

18. _____ A set of formatting that controls bold, font colors, shading colors, and border lines within a PivotTable. **p. 346**

19. _____ A summary calculation of values for a category. **p. 314**

20. _____ A function that returns a summary value from a PivotTable. **p. 331**

Multiple Choice

1. You want to apply a subtotal to a dataset containing names, departments, and salaries. What is the first step you need to do?

   (a) Filter the dataset by salaries

   (b) Select the function to be used for the subtotal

   (c) Insert new rows where you want the subtotal rows within the dataset

   (d) Sort the dataset by a field containing categories

2. Why would you click the collapse outline symbol above a column of outlined data?

   (a) You want to see more detailed columns that relate to the formula in that column.

   (b) You want to hide the detailed columns to focus on the result column.

   (c) You want to insert a subtotal row for a set of rows.

   (d) You want to delete columns containing values.

3. After creating a blank PivotTable, you click a field containing monetary amounts in the PivotTable Fields task pane. Where does Excel place that field?

   (a) Filters area

   (b) Columns area

   (c) Values area

   (d) Rows area

4. What is the default summary statistic for any value field added to a PivotTable?

   (a) Average

   (b) Count

   (c) Min

   (d) Sum

5. You created a PivotTable and changed some values in the dataset from which the PivotTable was created. How does this affect the PivotTable?

   (a) The PivotTable is updated automatically when you make changes to the dataset.

   (b) Changes in the dataset do not affect the PivotTable until you refresh the PivotTable.

   (c) You must create a new PivotTable if you want updated results in a PivotTable.

   (d) The PivotTable is deleted from the workbook because it is not up to date.

6. What settings should you select to apply a different color scheme and display a fill color for every other row or horizontal lines within the PivotTable?

   (a) Banded Rows and Banded Columns check boxes

   (b) Banded Columns check box and a different PivotTable style

   (c) Banded Rows check box and a different PivotTable style

   (d) A different PivotTable style only

7. Why would you create a slicer for a PivotTable?

   (a) To filter data in a PivotTable

   (b) To sort data for a field in a PivotTable

   (c) To slice the data into a timeline

   (d) To create a color-coded slice for each category

8. Which of the following is *not* used when creating a calculated field in a PivotTable?

   (a) Operands, such as multiplication (*)

   (b) Name of a field containing values

   (c) Another value to be used in the calculation

   (d) A cell reference to a value outside of the PivotTable

9. You created a PivotChart showing sales by quarter by sales rep. How do you remove a sales rep from the chart without deleting the data?

   (a) Make the employee's data points and axis titles invisible.

   (b) You cannot delete the rep from the chart without first deleting the data.

   (c) Filter the Sales Rep field in the PivotChart and deselect the employee's check box.

   (d) Hide that rep's row(s) in the underlying list, which automatically removes that rep from the chart.

10. You want to create a PivotTable that uses fields from two Excel tables. What is the first step?

    (a) Create a relationship on a common field between the two tables.

    (b) Create a PivotTable using one table and then add the second table to the PivotTable Fields task pane.

    (c) Merge the two tables into one large dataset before creating the PivotTable.

    (d) Create a subtotal for each table, copy and paste the two subtotals together, and then create the PivotTable.

Practice Exercises

1 January Restaurant Revenue

Anthony, a restaurant manager, tracks daily revenue for the lunch and dinner hours. He wants to analyze revenue by weekday for January. You will add subtotals of revenue by days of the week and by meal time for Anthony. In addition, he wants to analyze data by days of the week and quarters for the whole year. You will create a PivotTable and a PivotChart to organize the data. Refer to Figure 5.48 as you complete this exercise.

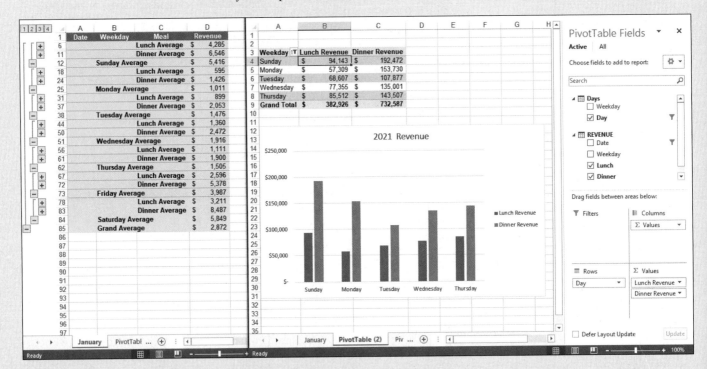

FIGURE 5.48 Revenue Subtotals, PivotTable, and PivotChart

a. Open *e05p1Revenue* and save it as **e05p1Revenue_LastFirst**.

b. Ensure that the January worksheet is active. Complete the following steps to sort the data:
- Click the **Data tab** and click **Sort** in the Sort & Filter group to open the Sort dialog box.
- Click the **Sort by arrow** and select **Weekday**.
- Click the **Order arrow** and select **Custom List** to open the Custom Lists dialog box. Select **Sunday, Monday, Tuesday** in the *Custom lists* section and click **OK**.
- Click **Add Level** in the Sort dialog box, click the **Then by arrow**, and then select **Meal**.
- Click the **Order arrow** for Meal, select **Z to A** to list Lunch before Dinner, and then click **OK**.

c. Click **Subtotal** in the Outline group. Complete the following steps in the Subtotal dialog box:
- Click the **At each change in arrow** and select **Weekday**.
- Click the **Use function arrow** and select **Average**.
- Keep the Revenue check box selected and click **OK**.

d. Click **Subtotal** in the Outline group, click the **At each change in arrow**, and then select **Meal**. Ensure the Average function and Revenue check box area selected. Click the **Replace current subtotals check box** to deselect it and click **OK**.

e. Click the **Level 2 outline symbol** in the top-left corner of the outline area to collapse the list to see the weekday and grand averages. Click the **Level 3 outline symbol** to expand the list to see weekday subtotals for lunch and dinner. Increase the width of column C so that the labels fully display. Which weekday produced the highest average dinner revenue? (Friday)

f. Click the **Yearly Data sheet tab**. The Revenue table lists lunch and dinner revenue for every day in 2021. The Weekday column is coded where 1 = Sunday and 7 = Saturday. Click the **Weekdays sheet tab**. The Days table contains two columns: the Weekday codes with their respective weekday in the Day column. Click the **Yearly Data sheet tab**.

g. Click the **Data tab**, click **Relationships** in the Data Tools group to open the Manage Relationships dialog box, and then complete the following steps:

- Click **New** to open the Create Relationship dialog box.
- Click the **Table arrow** and select **Worksheet Table: REVENUE** (the main table). Click the **Column (Foreign) arrow** and select **Weekday**.
- Click the **Related Table arrow** and select **Worksheet Table: DAYS**. Click the **Related Column (Primary) arrow** and select **Weekday**.
- Click **OK** to close the Create Relationship dialog box. Click **Close** to close the Manage Relationships dialog box.

h. Complete the following steps to create a PivotTable using the related tables:

- Click within the Yearly Data worksheet table. Click the **Insert tab** and click **PivotTable** in the Tables group to open the Create PivotTable dialog box.
- Click the **Add this data to the Data Model check box** in the *Choose whether you want to analyze multiple tables* section. Click **OK**. Double-click the **Sheet1 tab**, type **PivotTable**, and then press **Enter**.
- Click **All** at the top of the PivotTable Fields task pane to display all table names.
- Click **REVENUE** at the top of the task pane to display the fields for the Revenue table.
- Click the **Lunch** and **Dinner check boxes** to select them in the task pane. These fields are added to the Values area.
- Click **DAYS** the task pane to display the fields for the DAYS table.
- Click the **Day check box** to select it in the task pane. The Day field is added to the Rows area.

i. Modify the PivotTable by doing the following:

- Click the **Row Labels arrow** in **cell A3** and select **Sort A to Z**. (Note that this action sorts in sequential order by weekday, not alphabetical order by weekday name.)
- Type **Weekday** in **cell A3** and press **Enter**.
- Click the **Design tab**, click the **More button** in the PivotTable Styles group, and then select **Light Orange, Pivot Style Light 17**.
- Click the **Banded Rows check box** to select it in the PivotTable Style Options group.

j. Format the values by doing the following:

- Click **cell B4**, click the **Analyze tab**, and then click **Field Settings** in the Active Field group.
- Type **Lunch Revenue** in the Custom Name box.
- Click **Number Format**, click **Accounting**, click the **Decimal places arrow** to display **0**, click **OK** in the Format Cells dialog box, and then click **OK** in the Value Field Settings dialog box.
- Click **cell C4** and click **Field Settings** in the Active Field group.
- Type **Dinner Revenue** in the Custom Name box.
- Click **Number Format**, click **Accounting**, click the **Decimal places arrow** to display **0**, click **OK** in the Format Cells dialog box, and then click **OK** in the Value Field Settings dialog box.
- Click the **PivotTable Name box** in the PivotTable group on the Analyze tab, type **Weekday Revenue**, and then press **Enter**.

k. Insert a timeline by completing the following steps:

- Click **Insert Timeline** in the Filter group to open the Insert Timelines dialog box.
- Click the **Date check box** to select it and click **OK** to display the Date timeline. Move the Date timeline so that the top-left corner starts in **cell A13**.
- Click the **MONTHS arrow** in the Date timeline and select **QUARTERS**.
- Click the tile below **Q4** in the timeline to filter the data to reflect weekday totals for the fourth quarter only (October through December).

l. Click the **Yearly Data sheet tab**. Create a GETPIVOTDATA functions to display the total lunch and total dinner revenue for the filtered data by completing the following steps:

- Click **cell G2**, type **=**, click the **PivotTable sheet tab**, click **cell B11**, and then press **Enter**.
- Click **cell G3**, type **=**, click the **PivotTable sheet tab**, click **cell C11**, and then press **Enter**.

m. Create a PivotChart from the PivotTable by doing the following:

- Right-click the **PivotTable sheet tab**, select **Move or Copy**, click **PivotTable** in the *Before sheet* list, click the **Create a copy check box** to select it, and then click **OK**.
- Ensure that the PivotTable (2) sheet tab is active. Click the **Date timeline window** and press **Delete**.
- Click within the PivotTable, click the **Analyze tab**, click **PivotChart** in the Tools group, and then click **OK** in the Insert Chart dialog box to create a default clustered column chart.
- Click the **Day arrow** in the bottom-left corner of the PivotChart, click the **Friday** and **Saturday check boxes** to deselect these weekdays so that you can focus on the other days of the week where sales are lower. Click **OK**.
- Click the **Shape Height box** in the Size group on the Format tab, type **3.5"**, and then press **Enter**. Click in the **Shape Width box**, type **6"**, and then press **Enter**.
- Click **Chart Elements** on the right of the chart, click the **Chart Title check box**, and then click **Chart Elements** to close the menu.
- Click the **Chart Title placeholder**, type **2021 Revenue**, and then press **Enter**.
- Move the chart so that the top-left corner starts in **cell A12**.
- Click the **Analyze tab**, click the **Field Buttons arrow** in the Show/Hide group, and then select **Hide All** to hide the buttons within the chart area.

n. Create a footer with your name on the left side, the sheet name code in the center, and the file name code on the right side on each worksheet.

o. Save and close the file. Based on your instructor's directions, submit e05p1Revenue_LastFirst.

2 Lake View Regional Hospital

Alesha is the Nurse Manager for the Neuro Acute Care Division at Lake View Regional Hospital. The 12-hour nursing shifts are divided into day and night. Alesha collects patient data. She also notes how many nurses worked each shift. Because of your expertise in using Excel, she asked you to help consolidate the data. She is interested in the number of nurses per daily shift for August. Refer to Figure 5.49 as you complete this exercise.

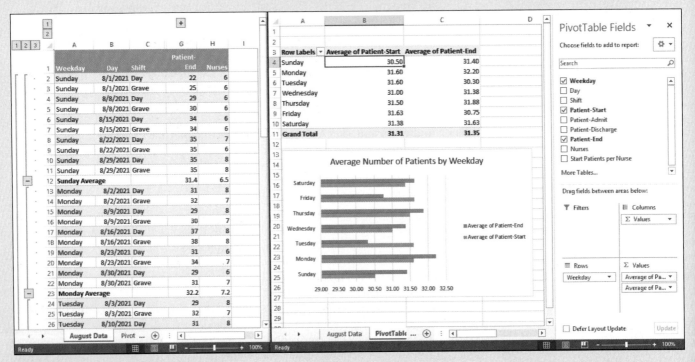

FIGURE 5.49 Lake View Regional Hospital

a. Open *e05p2Patients* and save it as **e05p2Patients_LastFirst**.

b. Ensure that the August Data worksheet is active. Complete the following steps to sort the data:
   - Click the **Data tab** and click **Sort** in the Sort & Filter group.
   - Click the **Sort by arrow** and select **Weekday**.
   - Click the **Order arrow** and select **Custom List** to open the Custom Lists dialog box. Select **Sunday, Monday, Tuesday** in the Custom lists section and click **OK**. Click **OK** in the Sort dialog box.

c. Click **Subtotal** in the Outline group. Complete the following steps in the Subtotal dialog box:
   - Click the **At each change in arrow** and select **Weekday**.
   - Click the **Use function arrow** and select **Average**.
   - Click the **Patient-End check box** to select it, keep the Nurses check box selected, and then click **OK**.

d. Click the **Group arrow** in the Outline group on the Data tab, select **Auto Outline**, and then click **OK**. Click **collapse** above column G to collapse the outline.

e. Click the **August Table sheet tab**, click the **Insert tab**, click **Recommended PivotTables** in the Tables group, click the **Sum of Patient-Start by Weekday and Shift thumbnail**, and then click **OK**.

f. Complete the following steps to modify the PivotTable:
   - Click the **Day check box** to select it in the task pane and add it to the Rows area. Click the **Patient-End check box** to select it and add it to the Values area.
   - Move the **Shift field** from the Columns area to the Filters area in the PivotTable Fields task pane.
   - Click the **Shift arrow** in **cell B1**, select **Day**, and then click **OK** to filter the records to show totals for only the day shifts.
   - Click the **PivotTable Name box** in the PivotTable group on the Analyze tab, type **Patients-Nurses**, and then press **Enter**.
   - Rename Sheet1 as **PivotTable**.

g. Complete the following steps to create a calculated field:
   - Click the **Analyze tab**, click **Fields, Items, & Sets** in the Calculations group, and then select **Calculated Field**.
   - Type **Start Patients per Nurse** in the Name box in the Insert Calculated Field dialog box.
   - Double-click **Patient-Start** in the Fields list. Type **/** and double-click **Nurses** in the Fields list. Click **OK**.
   - Click **cell D3**, click **Field Settings** in the Active Field group, click **Number Format**, click **Number** in the Category list, click the **Decimal places** setting to **0**, click **OK** in the Format Cells dialog box, and then click **OK** in the Value Field Settings dialog box.

h. Click **Insert Slicer** in the Filter group, click the **Weekday check box** to select it in the Insert Slicers dialog box, and then click **OK**.

i. Complete the following steps to customize the filter:
   - Move the filter to start in **cell F3**.
   - Click **More** in the Slicer Styles group on the Options tab and click **Light Blue, Slicer Style Dark 5**.
   - Change the Width to **1.5** in the Buttons group on the Options tab.
   - Press **Ctrl** and click **Sunday** and **Saturday** in the Weekday slicer to filter out these two days.

j. Click the **August Table sheet tab**. Create a GETPIVOTDATA functions to display the total Monday start patients and the total Friday end patients for the PivotTable by completing the following steps:
   - Click **cell K2**, type =, click the **PivotTable sheet tab**, click **cell B4**, and then press **Enter**.
   - Click **cell K3**, type =, click the **PivotTable sheet tab**, click **cell C26**, and then press **Enter**.

k. Copy the PivotTable sheet tab and place the PivotTable (2) sheet tab between the August Data and PivotTable sheet tabs. Ensure that the PivotTable (2) sheet is active and complete the following steps:

- Click the **Shift check box** to deselect it in the task pane. The Shift field is removed from the Filters area.
- Click the **Day check box** to deselect it in the task pane. The Day field is removed from the Rows area.
- Click **Multi-Select** in the Weekday slicer window, click **Sunday**, and then click **Saturday** so that all seven days will display.

l. Click in the PivotTable, click the **Analyze tab**, click **PivotChart** in the Tools group, and then complete the following steps:

- Click **Bar** in the Insert Chart dialog box and click **OK**.
- Click the **Sum of Start Patients per Nurse arrow** in the Values area of the task pane and select **Remove Field**.
- Click the **Sum of Patient-Start arrow** in the Values area of the task pane, select **Value Field Settings**, select **Average**, click **Number Format**, select **Number** in the Category list, click **OK** in the Format Cells dialog box, and then click **OK** in the Value Field Settings dialog box.
- Click the **Sum of Patient-End arrow** in the Values area of the task pane, select **Value Field Settings**, select **Average**, click **Number Format**, select **Number** in the Category list, click **OK** in the Format Cells dialog box, and then click **OK** in the Value Field Settings dialog box.
- Click the **Analyze tab**, click the **Field Buttons arrow** in the Show/Hide group, and then select **Hide All**.
- Click the **Chart Elements button** and click the **Chart Title check box** to select it. Click the **Chart Title placeholder**, type **Average Number of Patients by Weekday**, and then press **Enter**.
- Move the chart so that the top-left corner starts in **cell A13**. Change the chart width to **5.26"**.

m. Create a footer with your name on the left side, the sheet name code in the center, and the file name code on the right side on each worksheet.

n. Save and close the file. Based on your instructor's directions, submit e05p2Patients_LastFirst.

Mid-Level Exercises

1   Mountain View Realty

You are a real estate analyst who works for Mountain View Realty in the North Utah County area. You have consolidated a list of houses sold during the past few months and want to analyze the data. For a simple analysis, you will outline the data and use the Subtotal feature. You will then create two PivotTables and a PivotChart to perform more in-depth analysis.

a. Open *e05m1RealEstate* and save it as **e05m1RealEstate_LastFirst**.

b. Make sure the Sales Subtotals worksheet is the active sheet and insert the following formulas:
   - Insert a formula in **cell G2** to calculate the selling price percentage of the asking price, format it with **Percent Style** with **1** decimal place, and then copy the formula down the column.
   - Insert a formula in **cell J2** to calculate the number of days between the listing date and sale date. Copy the formula down the column.

c. Sort the list by city in alphabetical order, then by selling agent in alphabetical order, and finally by listing date in chronological order.

d. Use the Subtotal feature to calculate the average selling price, percentage of asking price, and days on market by city.

e. Apply an automatic outline to the columns and complete the following steps:
   - Collapse the outline to hide the listing and sale dates.
   - Click the outline symbol to display the grand average and city average rows only. Format the average days on market to zero decimal places.
   - Apply wrap text for **cells G1** and **J1**.
   - Select individually columns G and J and change the column width to **10.00**.
   - Change the row height to **24** for the first row.
   - Set a print area for the **range C1:J88**.

f. Go to **cell C101** in the Sales Subtotals worksheet. Read the questions and provide the appropriate answers in the respective highlighted cells in the **range G102:G106**. Apply **Accounting Number Format** with **0** decimal places to **cell G102**.

g. Click the **Sales Data sheet tab** and create a blank PivotTable on a new worksheet. Name the new worksheet **PivotTable**. Name the PivotTable **Average City Prices**.

h. Place the **City field** in Rows, the **Selling Agent field** in Columns, and the **Asking Price** and **Selling Price fields** as Values.

i. Modify the PivotTable by completing the following steps:
   - Display averages rather than sums with **Accounting Number Format** with **0** decimal places for the two value fields.
   - Pivot the data by moving the **City field** below the Values field in the Columns area and moving the **Selling Agents field** to Rows area.
   - Add a filter in **cell B3** to display only Alpine and Cedar Hills.

j. Complete the following steps to change the format of the PivotTable:
   - Change the widths of columns A, B, C, D, and E to **11**.
   - Change the widths of columns F and G to **14**.
   - Wrap text and center horizontally data in **cells B4, D4, F4,** and **G4**.
   - Apply the **Bottom Border** to the **range B4:E4**.
   - Change the label in **cell A5** to **Agent**. Change the height of row 4 to **40**.

k. Display the contents on the Sales Data worksheet. You realize that a selling price is incorrect. Change the selling price for Number 40 from *$140,000* to **$1,400,000**. Refresh the PivotTable. Adjust the column widths to match the instructions in Step j.

l. Display the contents on the Sales Data worksheet. Create a recommended PivotTable using the **Sum of Selling Price by City** thumbnail. Change the name of the new PivotTable worksheet to **Selling Price**. Make these changes to the new PivotTable:
   - Change the value to display averages not sums.
   - Apply the **Accounting Number Format** with **0** decimal places to the values.
   - Apply **Light Blue, Pivot Style Medium 2** to the PivotTable.

m. Create a column PivotChart from the PivotTable on the Selling Price worksheet. Move the chart to a chart sheet named **Sales Chart**. Complete the following steps for the chart:

  • Change the chart title to **Average Selling Price by City** and apply **Dark Blue font color**.
  • Remove the legend.
  • Apply **Dark Blue fill color** to the data series.

n. Create a footer with your name on the left side, the sheet name code in the center, and the file name code on the right side of all worksheets. Adjust page scaling if needed.

o. Save and close the file. Based on your instructor's directions, submit e05m1RealEstate_LastFirst.

2 Fiesta Collection

MyLab IT Grader

Your Aunt Laura has been collecting Fiesta dinnerware, a popular brand from the Homer Laughlin China Company, since 1986. You help her maintain an inventory. So far, you and Aunt Laura have created a table of color numbers, color names, year introduced, and year retired, if applicable. In a second table, you entered color numbers, item numbers, items, current value, and source. Previously, you helped her research current replacement costs from Homer Laughlin's website, Replacements, Ltd., and eBay; however, you believe the retired colors may be worth more now. Laura is especially interested in the values of retired colors so that she can provide this information for her insurance agent. You will build a PivotTable and add slicers to help her with the analysis.

a. Open *e05m2Fiesta* and save it as **e05m2Fiesta_LastFirst**.

b. Create a relationship between the Items table using the **Color Number field** and the Colors table using the **Color Number field**.

c. Create a blank PivotTable from within the Items table on the Collection worksheet to analyze multiple tables. Add the data to the data model. Place the PivotTable on a new worksheet and name the worksheet **Retired Colors**. Name the PivotTable **Retired**.

d. Display the names of both tables in the PivotTable Fields task pane.

e. Place the **Color field** in Rows and the sum of the **Replacement Value field** as Values.

f. Add a filter to display aggregates for retired colors only using the **Retired field**. Note that current colors do not have a retirement date, so you must filter out the blanks.

g. Apply the **Light Green, Pivot Style Medium 7**.

h. Format the values with **Accounting Number Format** with **2** decimal places. Create a custom name **Replacement Values**. Change *Row Labels* in **cell A3** to **Retired Colors**.

i. Add a column to show calculations by completing the following steps:

  • Add a second **Replacement Value field** below the current field in the Values area.
  • Select the option to display the values as percentages of the grand total.
  • Type the custom name **Percent of Total**.

j. Add a slicer for the **Color field**. Select these colors to display: **Apricot**, **Chartreuse**, **Lilac**, **Marigold**, **Pearl Gray**, and **Sapphire**.

k. Customize the slicer by completing the following steps:

  • Apply the **Light Green, Slicer Style Light 6 style**.
  • Display 3 columns within the slicer window.
  • Change the button width to **1.5"**. Move the slicer so that the top-left corner starts in **cell E2**.

l. Create a clustered column PivotChart and place it on a new chart sheet named **Retired PivotChart**.

m. Modify the chart by completing these steps:

  • Add the chart title **Replacement Value of Retired Items**.
  • Change the Lilac data point fill color to **Purple**.
  • Change the value axis font size to **11** and apply **Black, Text 1** font color.
  • Change the category axis font size to **11** and apply **Black, Text 1** font color.
  • Hide the field buttons on the PivotChart.

n. Create a footer with your name on the left side, the sheet name code in the center, and the file name code on the right side of all worksheets.

o. Save and close the file. Based on your instructor's directions, submit e05m2Fiesta_LastFirst.

New Castle County Technical Services

New Castle County Technical Services (NCCTS) provides technical support services for a number of companies in New Castle County, Delaware. You previously created charts to depict summary data by service type, customer, and days open. You copied the charts as pictures to replace the actual charts so changes you make to the dataset will not alter the charts. Then you sorted the main dataset for analysis and prepared it to be printed on two pages. You also applied conditional formatting to highlight transactions that took more than nine days to close and displayed data bars for the amount billed to give a quick visual for transaction amounts. Finally, you filtered a copy of the dataset and converted the summary sections into tables. Next, you will create a PivotTable and PivotChart to analyze agent performance in resolving disaster recovery support calls.

a. Open *e05r1NCCTS* and save it as **e05r1NCCTS_LastFirst**.

b. Use the **range A4:K39** on the March Hours worksheet and use the PivotChart command in the Charts group on the Insert tab to create a blank PivotChart and PivotTable on a new worksheet.

c. Name the worksheet **Disaster Recovery Analysis**.

d. Place the Call Type and Customer ID fields in Rows.

e. Place the Hours Logged, Days Open, and Amount Billed fields as Values.

f. Set the Hours Logged and Days Open fields to Summarize by Average. Apply **Number format** with **2** decimal places.

g. Assign the name **Summary Table** to the PivotTable.

h. Apply **Light Blue, Pivot Style Medium 20** to the PivotTable.

i. Insert a slicer based on Call Type. Place the top-left corner of the slicer in **cell F3**. Set a **3.5"** height and **2.5"** width for the slicer. Select the Disaster Recovery slice to filter the PivotTable.

j. Reposition the top-left corner of the PivotChart in **cell A10**.

k. Change the chart type to **Pie**.

l. Apply **Style 3** chart style.

m. Apply **Accounting Number Format** to the Amount Billed data.

n. Display the March Hours worksheet and create GETPIVOTDATA functions by completing these steps:

   - **Cell K1:** Display the average Disaster Recovery hours using the Average of Hours Logged on row 4 in the PivotTable.
   - **Cell K2:** Display the total Disaster Recovery amount billed using the Sum of Amount Billed on row 4 in the PivotTable.

o. Insert a footer with your name on the left side, the sheet name in the center, and the file name code on the right side.

p. Save and close the workbook. Based on your instructor's directions, submit e05r1NCCTS_LastFirst.

Disaster Recovery

Innovative Game Studio

You work as an assistant to Terry Park, the producer for a video game studio in Phoenix, Arizona. The company produces video games for various gaming consoles. The producer tracks salaries and performance for everyone on a particular team, which consists of artists, animators, programmers, and so forth. Terry tried to create a PivotTable to organize the data by department and then by title within department. He also wants to display total salaries by these categories and filter the data to show aggregates for team members who earned only Excellent and Good performance ratings. In addition, he wants to see what the percentages of total salaries for each job title are of each department's total salaries. For example, the total salary for Senior Artists is $263,300. That represents 50.27% of the Art Department's salary budget ($523,800) for Excellent- and Good-rated employees. However, the percentages are not displayed correctly. Terry called you in to correct his PivotTable.

Open *e05d1Games* and save it as **e05d1Games_LastFirst**. Identify the errors and make a list of these errors starting on row 41 in the PivotTable worksheet. Correct the errors and improve the format, including a medium Pivot Style, throughout the PivotTable. Create a footer with your name, the sheet name code, and the file name code. Save and close the file. Based on your instructor's directions, submit e05d1Games_LastFirst.

Capstone Exercise

Apartment Complexes

You manage several apartment complexes in Phoenix, Arizona. You created a dataset that lists details for each apartment complex, such as apartment number, including number of bedrooms, whether the unit is rented or vacant, the last remodel date, rent, and deposits. You will use the datasets to aggregate data to analyze the apartments at the complexes.

Sort, Subtotal, and Outline Data

You want to use the Subtotal feature to display the average total deposit by number of bedrooms for each apartment complex. Before using the Subtotal command, you will sort the dataset on the Summary worksheet first. After subtotaling the data, you will apply an automatic outline and consolidate the columns.

1. Open *e05c1Apartments* and save it as **e05c1Apartments_LastFirst**.

2. Select the Summary sheet. Sort the data by Apartment Complex in alphabetical order and further sort it by # Bed (the number of bedrooms) from smallest to largest.

3. Use the Subtotal feature to insert subtotal rows by Apartment Complex to calculate the average Total Deposit.

4. Add a second subtotal (without removing the first subtotal) by # Bed to calculate the average Total Deposit by the number of bedrooms.

5. Use the outline symbols to display only the subtotal rows.

6. Create an automatic outline and collapse the outline above Total Deposit.

Create a PivotTable

You want to create a PivotTable to determine the total monthly rental revenue for occupied apartments. After creating the initial PivotTable, you will format the values, set a filter, and name the PivotTable.

7. Display the Rentals sheet and create a blank Pivot-Table on a new worksheet. Do *not* add the data to the data model.

8. Place the **Apartment Complex** and **# Bed fields** in Rows and the **Rental Price field** as Values.

9. Format the Sum of Rent for **Accounting Number Format** with **0** decimal places and enter the custom name **Total Rent Collected**.

10. Select the **Occupied field** for the filter and set the filter to **Yes** to display data for occupied apartments.

11. Name the PivotTable **Rental Revenue** and change the name of Sheet1 to **Rental Revenue.**

Change Value Field Settings and Create a Calculated Field

Periodically, you increase the rental rates to account for increased operating costs. You want to perform a what-if analysis to calculate the total monthly rental revenue if the rates increase by 5% for the occupied apartments.

12. Insert a calculated field to multiply the Rental Price by 1.05.

13. Customize the calculated field by completing the following steps:

    *   Change the custom name to **New Rental Revenue**.

    *   Apply **Accounting Number Format** with **0** decimal places.

14. Select the **range B3:C3** and apply these formats: wrap text, **Align Right** horizontal alignment, **30** row height, and **15** column widths.

Apply a Style, Insert a Slicer, and Insert a Timeline

You want to apply a different PivotTable style to have a similar color scheme as the dataset. In addition, you will insert a slicer to facilitate filtering apartments by the number of bedrooms. Finally, you will insert a timeline so that you can filter data by year apartments were last remodeled.

15. Apply **Light Orange, Pivot Style Medium 10** to the PivotTable.

16. Display banded rows.

17. Insert a slicer for **# Bed** so that you can filter the dataset by number of bedrooms. Then complete the following steps to customize the slicer:

    *   Change the slicer caption to **# of Bedrooms**.

    *   Change the slicer height to **1.4"** and width to **1.75"**.

    *   Apply **Light Orange, Slicer Style Light 2**.

    *   Cut the slicer and paste it in **cell E2**.

18. Insert a timeline for the Last Remodel field and complete the following steps:

    *   Change the time period to **YEARS**.

    *   Apply **Light Orange, Timeline Style Light 2**.

    *   Change the timeline height to **1.4"** and width to **3.75"**.

Create a Relationship Between Tables, Create a PivotTable, and Create a PivotChart

The Databases sheet contains two tables. You will create a relationship between those tables and create a PivotTable using fields from both tables so that you can calculate the percentage of apartments within each complex that have 1-, 2- and 3-bedroom units.

> **MAC TROUBLESHOOTING:** Because Excel for Mac does not support relationships, you must use Excel for Windows to complete the rest of this exercise.

19. Display the Databases sheet.

20. Create a relationship between the **APARTMENTS table** using the **Code field** and the **COMPLEX table** using the **Code field**.

21. Create a PivotTable using the data model on a new sheet. Change the sheet name to **Bedrooms**. Select the **Apartment Name field** from the COMPLEX table for Rows, the **# Bed field** for Columns, and the **# Bed field** as Values.

22. Display the values as a percentage of row totals.

23. Create a Clustered Column PivotChart. Cut the chart and paste it in **cell A13**.

24. Customize the PivotChart by completing these steps:

   - Select the 3-bedroom data series and apply the **Black, Text 1, Lighter 50% solid fill color**.
   - Apply **Black, Text 1 font color** to the vertical axis and category axis.
   - Change the chart height to **3.4"** and the width to **5.2"**.
   - Hide the field buttons in the PivotChart.

Finalizing Your Workbook

You will finalize your workbook by adding a footer to the worksheets you changed and created.

25. Create a footer on all worksheets with your name, the sheet name code, and the file name code.

26. Save and close the file. Based on your instructor's directions, submit e05c1Apartments_LastFirst.

What-If Analysis

LEARNING OUTCOME You will demonstrate how to use decision-making tools.

OBJECTIVES & SKILLS: After you read this chapter, you will be able to:

CASE STUDY | Personal Finance: Buying Your First Home

After several years of living with friends after college, you have decided to purchase your first home. After doing some preliminary research on prices, you developed a spreadsheet to calculate your monthly mortgage payment, total amount to repay the loan, and the total amount of interest you will pay. Your total budget for the home is $150,000 including taxes, closing costs, and other miscellaneous fees. You plan to take $10,000 out of your savings account for a down payment. You are currently investigating loan interest rates at various banks and credit unions. You realize that you may need to find a less expensive home or increase your down payment to reach a monthly payment you can afford. Although you know a larger down payment will change the monthly payment, you want to be able to see the comparisons at the same time. In addition, you want to look at your budget to review the impact of purchasing a new home on your income and expenses.

CHAPTER 6

Using Decision-Making Tools

YanLev/Shutterstock

You will use Excel to help create a worksheet to analyze the variables that affect the mortgage payment, total amount to repay the loan, and the total interest paid. To help you make a decision, you will use several what-if analysis tools, each with specific purposes, benefits, and restrictions. With these tools, you will have a better understanding of how a mortgage payment will affect your overall budget.

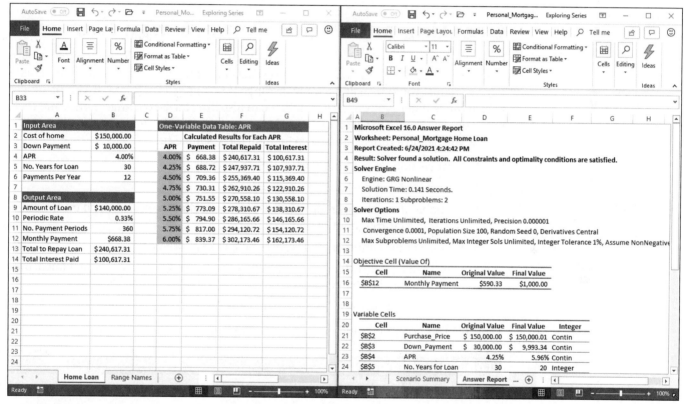

FIGURE 6.1 Home Loan Worksheet

CASE STUDY | Personal Finance: Buying Your First Home

Starting File	File to be Submitted
e06h1Mortgage	e06h4Mortgage_LastFirst

MyLab IT Grader An alternate version of this project is available as a MyLab IT Grader Assessment

Range Names

In order to complete the required mortgage analysis, you will use several financial functions in conjunction with analysis tools within Excel. To simplify entering ranges into these functions, you can use range names. A ***range name*** is a word or string of characters assigned to one or more cells. Think of range names in this way: Your college identifies you by your student ID; however, your professors call you by your name, which is easier to remember, such as Will or Valerie. Similarly, instead of using cell addresses, you can use descriptive range names in formulas. For example, when calculating a periodic mortgage payment using the PMT function, instead of using the function =PMT(B3,C3,-D3), you could assign easy to understand range names to the cell references modifying the function to =PMT(Periodic_Rate,Payments,-Cost). Another benefit of using range names is that they are absolute references, which helps ensure accuracy in your calculations.

In this section, you will work with range names. First, you will learn how to create and maintain range names. You then learn how to use a range name in a formula.

Creating and Maintaining Range Names

Each range name within a workbook must be unique. For example, you cannot assign the name *COST* to ranges on several worksheets or on the same sheet. After you create a range name, you may edit its name or range if a change is required. If you no longer need a range name, you can delete it. You can also insert a list of range names and their respective cell ranges in a workbook for documentation and future reference.

As you define a range name, keep in mind these simple rules:

- A range name can contain up to 255 characters.
- It must begin with a letter or an underscore.
- A combination of upper- or lowercase letters, numbers, periods, and underscores can be used throughout the range name.
- A range name cannot include spaces or special characters.
- You should create range names that describe the range of cells being named, but names cannot be identical to the cell contents.
- Keep the range names short to make them easier to use in formulas.

Table 6.1 lists acceptable and unacceptable range names.

TABLE 6.1	Range Names
Name	**Description**
Grades	Acceptable range name
Tax_Rate	Acceptable name with underscore
Rate_2021	Acceptable name with underscore and numbers
Commission Rate	Unacceptable name; cannot use spaces in names
Discount Rate %	Unacceptable name; cannot use special symbols or spaces
2021_Rate	Unacceptable name; cannot start with a number

STEP 1 ▷ **Define a Range Name**

There are several ways to create a named range. The easiest way is to use the Name Box. The Name Box is located to the left of the formula bar. In earlier chapters, you used the Name Box to navigate to a particular cell. To define a range name using the Name Box, ensure the cell or range of cells you want to name is the active cell, then type the range name in the Name Box, and then press Enter. Then, similar to navigating to any cell address, you can click the Name Box arrow to view the list of named ranges in the worksheet and select the range you want to navigate to. You can also use the Go To dialog box to go to the top-left cell in a range specified by a range name.

> **To create a range name, select the range you want to name, and complete one of the following steps:**
>
> - Click in the Name Box, type the range name, and then press Enter.
> - Click the Formulas tab, click Define Name in the Defined Names group to open the New Name dialog box (see Figure 6.2), type the range name in the Name Box, and then click OK. (If using a Mac, click the Formulas tab, click Define Name, and then click Define Name. As an alternative, click the Insert menu, click Name, and then select Define Name.)
> - Click the Formulas tab, click Name Manager in the Defined Names group to open the Name Manager dialog box, click New, type the range name in the Name Box, click OK, and then click Close.

For more options when defining a named range, you should use commands in the Defined Names group on the Formulas tab. When you click Define Name, the New Name dialog box displays (see Figure 6.2). In this dialog box, enter a name for the range, choose whether the name is applicable just for the worksheet or the entire workbook, and add a comment. If you are not already in the active cell, you can enter or navigate to the cell or range you want to define in the *Refers to* box. Another way to access the New Name dialog box is through the Name Manager. Click Name Manager in the Defined Names group on the Formulas tab and click New.

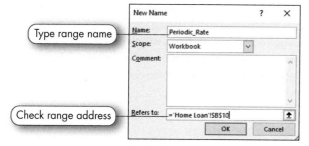

FIGURE 6.2 New Name Dialog Box

TIP: USE THE NAME BOX TO INSERT A FUNCTION

When the equal sign is typed in a cell, the name box will display a list of functions. Select the function you want to use from the list and the insert function dialog box will automatically open.

While using the Name box or the New Name dialog box is convenient, these methods are used to create one named range at a time. You can create several range names at the same time if your worksheet includes ranges with values and descriptive labels. First, select the range of cells containing the labels that you want to become names and the cells that contain the values to name, click *Create from Selection* in the Defined Names group on the Formulas tab, and then select an option in the Create Names from Selection dialog box (see Figure 6.3).

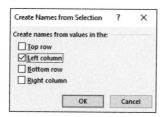

FIGURE 6.3 Create Names from Selection Dialog Box

STEP 2 〉 Edit or Delete a Range Name

At times you may want to add, update, or remove cells that are part of named ranges. You can use the Name Manager dialog box to edit, delete, and create range names as shown in Figure 6.4. To edit a range or range name, click the range name in the list and click Edit. In the Edit Name dialog box, edit the range name and click OK.

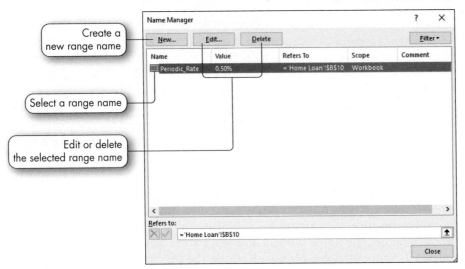

FIGURE 6.4 Name Manager Dialog Box

If you change a range name, any formulas that use the range name reflect the new name. For example, if a formula contains =Cost*Rate and you change the name Rate to tax_rate, Excel updates the formula to be =Cost*tax_rate. To delete a range name, open the Name Manager dialog box, select the name you want to delete, click Delete, and then click OK in the confirmation message box. If you delete a range name and a formula depends on that range name, Excel displays #NAME? for each formula that uses that name, indicating an Invalid Name error. This problem would need to be corrected in order to keep using the range name in the formula.

STEP 3 〉 Use Range Names in Formulas

Range names are more descriptive than letter and number cell references. You can use range names in formulas instead of cell references. By using named ranges in formulas, anyone reviewing the worksheet will have a clearer understanding of what a formula is calculating. Another benefit of using range names is that if you want to copy the formula, you do not have to make the cell reference absolute in the formula. For example, if cell C15 contains a purchase amount, and cell C5 contains the sales tax rate, instead of typing =C15*C5, you can type the range names in the formula, such as =Purchase*Tax_Rate. When you type a formula, Formula AutoComplete displays a list of range names, as well as functions, that start with the letters you use as you type (see Figure 6.5). Double-click the range name to insert it in the formula. If you use the semi-selection method, named ranges will be used automatically. Furthermore, range names will be used automatically if you are using the Insert Function dialog box. When adding a range name to a formula or function as an alternative to using AutoComplete, the Paste Name dialog box can be used. To access the Paste Name dialog box, press F3 on your keyboard.

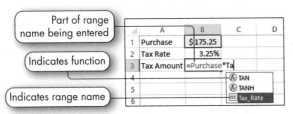

FIGURE 6.5 Range Names Inserted in a Formula

It is important to note that named ranges will not automatically be added to existing formulas. If you want to use named ranges in existing formulas, the original formula or function must be edited. Alternatively, defined named ranges can be automatically applied to existing formulas by using the Apply Names feature. To apply names to an existing formula click the Formulas tab, click Define Name in the Defined Names group, and select Apply Names. Select the range names you would like to apply to the formula and click OK.

STEP 4 Insert a List of Range Names

The number of range names that can be defined is limited by the available memory on your computer. Therefore, a modern computer with at least 8 gigabytes of RAM could have hundreds of defined range names. With this many defined range names, you may want to document the information in a workbook by inserting a list of range names. To insert a list of range names, display the Paste Name dialog box by pressing F3. Alternatively, select the first cell of the location to paste the information, click Use in Formula in the Defined Names group on the Formulas tab, and select Paste Names. The Paste Name dialog box opens (see Figure 6.6), listing all range names in the current workbook. Click Paste List to insert a list of range names in alphabetical order. The first column contains a list of range names and the second column contains the worksheet names and range locations. When you paste range names, the list will overwrite any existing data in a worksheet, so consider pasting the list on its own worksheet. If you add, edit, or delete range names, the list does not update automatically. To keep the list current, you need to paste the list again.

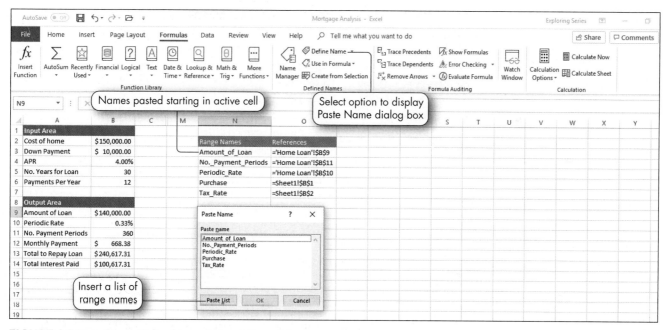

FIGURE 6.6 Paste Name Dialog Box and List of Range Names

Quick Concepts

1. Describe the benefits of using range names. *p. 382*

2. List at least five guidelines and rules for naming a range. *p. 382*

3. Describe the significance of inserting a list of range names in a worksheet. *p. 385*

Hands-On Exercises

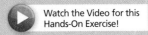
Skills covered: Define a Range Name • Edit or Delete a Range Name • Use Range Names in Formulas • Insert a List of Range Names

1 Range Names

You decide to simplify the PMT function you are using to calculate your mortgage by adding range names for the Amount of Loan, Periodic Rate, and No. of Payments instead of the actual cell references. After creating the range names, you will modify the names and create a list of range names.

STEP 1 CREATE A RANGE NAME

The PMT function required to calculate your mortgage payment requires multiple arguments. To make this function easier to understand you want to assign a range name to the Amount of Loan, Periodic Rate, and No. of Payments. Refer to Figure 6.7 as you complete Step 1.

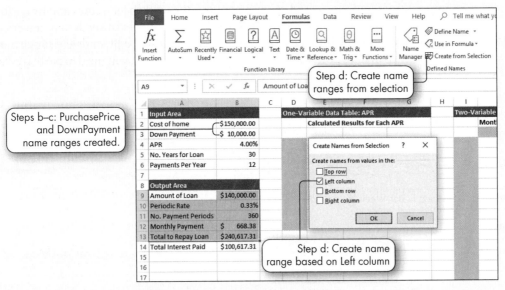

FIGURE 6.7 Range Name

a. Open *e06h1Mortgage* and save it as **e06h1Mortgage_LastFirst**.

> **TROUBLESHOOTING:** If you make any major mistakes in this exercise, you can close the file, open *e06h1Mortgage* again, and then start this exercise over.

b. Select **cell B2**. Click the **Name Box**, type **PurchasePrice**, and then press **Enter**.

   You manually assigned the range name PurchasePrice to cell B2.

c. Select **cell B3**. Click the **Name Box**, type **DownPayment**, and then press **Enter**.

d. Select the **range A9:B13**, click the **Formulas tab**, click **Create from Selection** in the Defined Names group, and then ensure the Left column check box is selected.

   Range names are automatically assigned to values based on the row labels in Column A.

e. Click **OK** in the Create Names from Selection dialog box.

   Range names are created for cells B9:B13 and when any cell in that range is selected, the name will display in the Name Box.

f. Save the workbook.

You noticed that a named range was created that was not necessary. You will use the Name Manager dialog box to view and delete the unneeded name range. You also will add underscores to the DownPayment and PurchasePrice range names. Refer to Figure 6.8 as you complete Step 2.

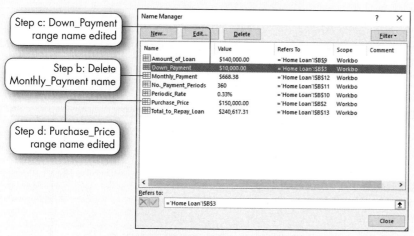

Step c: Down_Payment range name edited

Step b: Delete Monthly_Payment name

Step d: Purchase_Price range name edited

FIGURE 6.8 Editing Range Names

a. Click **Name Manager** in the Defined Names group on the Formulas tab.

The Name Manager dialog box opens.

> **MAC TROUBLESHOOTING:** To delete a range name on a Mac, click Define Name on the Formulas tab, select the range name from the Names in workbook box, and then click the minus sign to delete the name.

b. Select **Monthly_Payment** in the list of named ranges, click **Delete,** read the warning message box, and then click **OK** to confirm the deletion of the Monthly_Payment range name.

This range name applies to the cell that will contain the monthly payment function, which does not require a named range.

c. Select **DownPayment** and click **Edit.** Type **Down_Payment** in the Name box and click **OK**.

> **MAC TROUBLESHOOTING:** To edit a range name, open the Define Name dialog box. Click the range name in the Names in workbook box and make necessary changes to the range name in the *Enter a name for the data range* box.

d. Select **PurchasePrice** and click **Edit.** Type **Purchase_Price** in the Name box and click **OK**.

e. Click **Close**.

f. Save the workbook.

You will modify the PMT function by replacing the existing references with the corresponding range names. You will then apply existing range names to the Total Interest Paid formula. This will help interpret the PMT function as well as the total interest paid. Refer to Figure 6.9 as you complete Step 3.

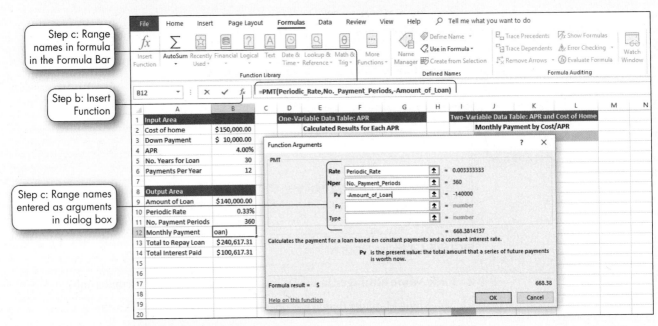

FIGURE 6.9 Range Names Inserted in a Formula

a. Click **cell B12**, the cell containing the PMT function.

b. Click **Insert Function** (between the Name Box and the Formula Bar) to open the Function Arguments dialog box.

c. Click in the **Rate box**, click **cell B10**, and then press **Tab**. Click **cell B11**, press **Tab**, and type **-**, and then click **B9**.

The new function is =PMT(Periodic_Rate,No._Payment_Periods,-Amount_of_Loan).

d. Click **OK**.

e. Select **cell B14**. Click the **Formulas tab,** click **Define Name** in the Defined Names group, and then click **Apply Names**.

f. Select **Amount_of_Loan** and **Total_to_Repay_Loan.**

g. Click **cell B14** and review the Total Interest paid formula in the Formula Bar. Note that range names have been applied to the corresponding cells.

h. Click **OK** and save the workbook.

To ensure continuity moving forward, you want to create a documentation worksheet that lists all of the range names in the workbook. Refer to Figure 6.10 as you complete Step 4.

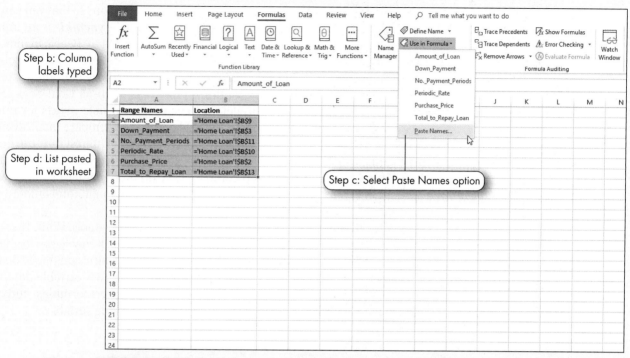

FIGURE 6.10 Range Names Inserted in a Formula

a. Click **New sheet** to the right of the Home Loan tab and double-click the default sheet name **Sheet1**. Type **Range Names** and press **Enter**.

You inserted and renamed the new worksheet to reflect the data you will add to it.

b. Type **Range Names** in **cell A1** and type **Location** in **cell B1**. Bold these headings.

These column headings will display above the list of range names.

c. Click **cell A2**, click **Use in Formula** in the Defined Names group on the Formulas tab, and then select **Paste Names**.

The Paste Name dialog box opens, displaying all of the range names in the workbook.

> **MAC TROUBLESHOOTING:** Paste Names is not available on a Mac. Type each range name and its cell address.

d. Click **Paste List**.

Excel pastes an alphabetical list of range names starting in cell A2. The second column displays the locations of the range names.

e. Increase the widths of columns A and B to fit the data.

f. Save the workbook. Keep the workbook open if you plan to continue with the next Hands-On Exercise. If not, close the workbook and exit Excel.

One- and Two-Variable Data Tables

You are now ready to explore Excel's powerful what-if analysis tools. *What-if analysis* enables you to experiment with different variables or assumptions so that you can observe and compare how these changes affect a related outcome. A *variable* is an input value that can change to other values to affect the results of a situation. People in almost every industry perform some type of what-if analysis to make educated decisions. Tools such as one-variable and two-variable data tables enable you to analyze bottom-line sensitivity to variable changes. Furthermore, optimization tools such as Goal Seek, Scenario Manager, and Solver enable you to determine specific variable inputs for outputs or goals. For example, you can use a one-variable data table to compare monthly mortgage payments. As you recall, monthly payments are based on the interest rate, the number of payment periods, and the amount of the loan. Holding the number of payment periods and loan amount constant, you can compare how different values of the interest rate (the one variable) affect the calculated results: monthly payment, total amount to repay the loan, and total interest paid.

Remember that these what-if analysis tools are just that—tools. While these tools do not provide the definitive, perfect solution to a problem, they will enable you to analyze and interpret data, but you or another human must make ultimate decisions based on the data.

In this section, you will learn how to create one- and two-variable data tables to perform what-if analysis. You will design the data tables, insert formulas, and complete the data tables to compare the results for different values of the variables.

Creating a One-Variable Data Table

Suppose you are applying for a mortgage and used the PMT function to determine what the monthly payment would be. You hear that interest rates are fluctuating and are uncertain how the varying interest rates would affect your monthly payment. You begin to insert different interest rates into the PMT function and write down the results. If you are just trying out one or two different interest rates, this may be an adequate method. However, if you want to compare the effect many different interest rates would have on a monthly payment, you could use a one-variable data table. A *one-variable data table* is a dynamic range that contains different values for one variable to compare how those values affect one or more calculated results. When setting up a one-variable data table, you must determine which one variable you want to use. After identifying the input variable, then you select one or more formulas that depend on that input variable for calculations.

STEP 1 Set Up One-Variable Substitution Values

Once you have determined the variable to manipulate, you will specify the substitution values. A *substitution value* is a value that replaces the original input value of a variable in a data table. For example, the original interest rate is 4.5%, but you might want to substitute 5%, 5.5%, 6%, 6.5%, and 7% in place of the 4.5% to see how these different interest rates affect the results.

To set up the one-variable data table, locate the range to create the one-variable data table. If you are inserting the one-variable data table on the same worksheet, leave at least one blank row and one blank column between the dataset and the data table. Enter the substitution values down one column or across one row. With one variable and several results, a vertical orientation for the substitution values is recommended because people often look for a value in the first column of a table and then read across to see corresponding values.

You can enter the substitution values yourself or use the Series dialog box to help complete a series of values (see Figure 6.11).

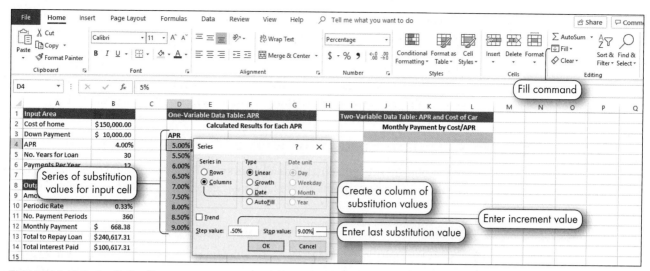

FIGURE 6.11 Series Dialog Box

To create a series of substitution values, complete the following steps:

1. Type the first substitution value (such as 5%) in a cell and keep that cell as the active cell.
2. Click the Home tab, click Fill in the Editing group, and then select Series to open the Series dialog box.
3. Click Rows to place the series of substitution values across a row or click Columns to place the series of substitution values down a column.
4. Enter the value increment in the *Step value* box and enter the ending value for the series in the *Stop value* box.
5. Click OK. Excel fills in a series of values.

TIP: AUTOFILL A SERIES OF SUBSTITUTION VALUES

Instead of using the Series dialog box, you can use AutoFill to complete a series of substitution values. To do this, enter the first two substitution values (such as 5% and 5.5%). Select the cells containing these two values and drag the fill handle down until the ScreenTip displays the last substitution value you want. Excel sets the increment pattern based on the difference between the first two values.

STEP 2 ▸ **Add Formulas to a One-Variable Data Table**

After you enter the substitution values in either a column or row, you must add one or more formulas that relate mathematically to the variable for which you are using substitution values. Although you can create formulas directly in the data table, referencing cells containing existing formulas outside the data table is preferable because the formulas are often already created. You can save time and reduce errors by referencing the original formula. The formula references must be entered in a specific location based on the location of the substitution values (see Table 6.2).

TABLE 6.2 Locations for Formula References

Location of Substitution Values	Enter the First Formula Reference	Enter Additional Formula References
Vertically in a column	On the row above and one column to the right of the first substitution value	To the right of the first formula reference
Horizontally in a row	On the row below and one column to the left of the first substitution value	Below the first formula reference

For example, assume you want to compare the effect of different interest rates on the monthly payment, the total amount repaid, and the total interest paid. As shown in Figure 6.12, you need to set up three columns to show the calculated results. The first formula reference for monthly payment (=B12) goes in cell E3. To compare the effects of substitution values on other results, the second formula reference for total repaid (=B13) goes in cell F3, and the third formula reference for total interest paid (=B14) goes in cell G3.

STEP 3 ▶ Calculate Results for a One-Variable Data Table

It is important that you enter the substitution values and formula references in the correct locations. This sets the left and top boundaries of the soon-to-be-completed data table.

To complete a one-variable data table, complete the following steps:

1. Select the data table boundaries, starting in the blank cell in the top-left corner of the data table. Drag down and to the right, if there is more than one column, to select the last blank cell at the intersection of the last substitution value and the last formula reference.

2. Click the Data tab, click What-If Analysis in the Forecast group, and then select Data Table to open the Data Table dialog box (see Figure 6.12).

3. Enter the cell reference of the cell containing the original variable for which you are substituting values. Since this is a one-variable data table, you will use either a Row input cell or a Column input cell, determined by how the substitution variables were placed in the data table. If you listed the substitution values in a row, enter the original variable cell reference in the Row input cell box. If you listed the substitution values in a column, enter the original variable cell reference in the Column input cell box. In Figure 6.12, for example, the substitution interest rates are listed in a column so you would click in the Column input cell box and then click cell B4 (the original interest rate variable). Note that the cell reference is automatically made absolute so that Excel always refers to the original input cell as it performs calculations in the data table.

4. Click OK.

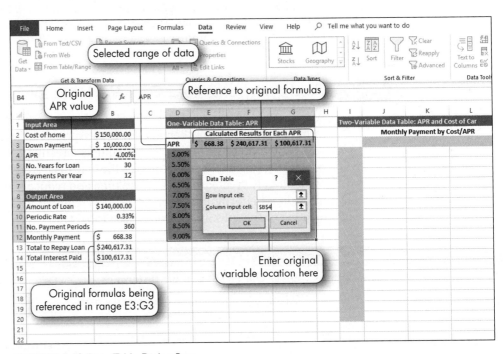

FIGURE 6.12 Data Table Dialog Box

When you create the one-variable data table, Excel uses the substitution values individually to replace the original variable's value, which is then used in the formulas to produce the results in the body of the data table. In Figure 6.13, the data table shows the substitution values of different interest rates, the calculated monthly payments (column E), total payments (column F), and total interest paid (column G) for the respective interest rates.

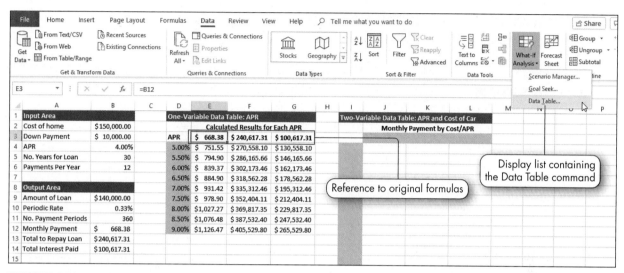

FIGURE 6.13 Completed Data Table

STEP 4 ▶ Format a One-Variable Data Table

The column headings displayed in data tables are the results of formulas used for the table calculations. You can also create custom formats to disguise the formula references as column labels. After creating the data table, you should format the values to reduce confusion. Although you are using a custom number format that displays text, Excel remembers that the actual contents are values derived from formulas.

> **To create custom formats, complete the following steps:**
>
> 1. Click in the cell containing a formula reference in the data table.
> 2. Click the Number Dialog Box Launcher in the Number group on the Home tab to open the Format Cells dialog box with the Number tab active.
> 3. Click Custom in the Category list.
> 4. Type the column heading in the Type box above the Type list. Enter the text within quotation marks, such as "Payment". Note that you must include the word to be displayed within quotation marks or the custom format will not display properly (see Figure 6.14).
> 5. Click OK.

You can then apply bold and center formatting to the column headings. If you see pound signs, adjust the column width or format with wrap text to accommodate the headings.

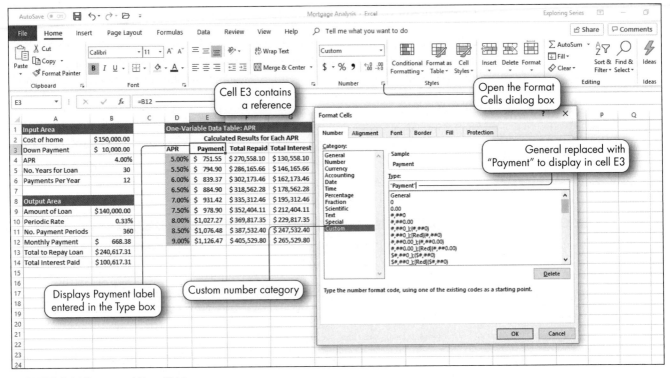

FIGURE 6.14 Formatted Data Table

Creating a Two-Variable Data Table

Although a one-variable data table is effective for comparing results for different values of one input, you might want to compare results of a calculation based on two variables. For example, you might want to compare the combined effects of various interest rates (such as 5%, 5.5%, and 6%) and different down payments (such as $10,000, $15,000, and $20,000) on the monthly payment. A **two-variable data table** is a structured range that contains different values for two variables to compare how these differing values affect the results for one calculated value.

STEP 5 ▶ Set Up Two-Variable Substitution Values

Create the two-variable data table separate from regular worksheet data. Similar to a one-variable data table, list substitution values for one variable in a column. Then, list substitution values for the second variable in the top row, as shown in Figure 6.15. Figure 6.15 shows substitution interest rates in the first column (range D4:D12) and substitution down payments in the first row (range E3:G3).

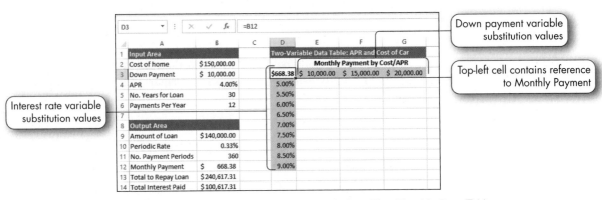

FIGURE 6.15 Substitution Values and Formula for a Two-Variable Data Table

Add a Formula to the Data Table

With the one-variable data table, you use one variable (interest rate) to compare multiple results: monthly payment, total to repay the loan, and total interest paid. The two-variable data table enables you to use two variables, but you are restricted to only one result. In the case of a home loan, you might want to focus on how changes in interest rates and down payments (the two variables) affect different monthly payments (the result). Enter the formula or reference to the original formula for the result in the blank cell in the top-left corner. For example, enter the cell reference for the monthly payment (=B12) in cell D3 as shown in Figure 6.15.

STEP 6 Calculate Results for a Two-Variable Data Table

After entering the substitution values and the reference to one formula result, you are ready to complete the table to see the results.

To finish a two-variable data table, complete the following steps:

1. Select the data table boundaries, starting in the top-left corner of the data table.
2. Click the Data tab, click What-If Analysis in the Forecast group, and then select Data Table. The Data Table dialog box opens.
3. Enter the cell that contains the original value for the substitution values in the first row in the Row input cell box. Enter the cell that contains the original value for the substitution values in the first column in the Column input cell box. Note that a two-variable data table is calculated based on two changing variables therefore row input and column inputs are required. For example, the original row (down payment) variable value is stored in cell B3, and the original column (APR) variable value is stored in cell B4.
4. Click OK.

After you complete the data table, to reduce confusion, you should format the results by applying a custom number format to the formula cell to display as a heading and add a merged heading above the row substitution values (see Figure 6.16).

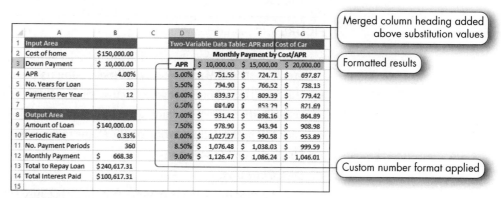

FIGURE 6.16 Completed and Formatted Two-Variable Data Table

Quick Concepts

4. Describe the benefit of using a one-variable data table. *p. 390*

5. Explain why it is preferable to reference formula cells outside of a one-variable data table versus entering the formula manually. *pp. 391–392*

6. Compare the uses of a one- and two-variable data table. *p. 394*

Hands-On Exercises

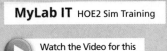

Skills covered: Set Up One-Variable Substitution Values • Add Formulas to a One-Variable Data Table • Calculate Results for a One-Variable Data Table • Format a One-Variable Data Table • Set Up Two-Variable Substitution Values • Add a Formula to the Data Table • Calculate Results for a Two-Variable Data Table

2 One- and Two-Variable Data Tables

As you consider different options for a home purchase, you want to use data tables to compare how different interest rates and prices will affect your monthly payment. You decide to create both one- and two-variable data tables to analyze the results.

STEP 1 ▶ SET UP ONE-VARIABLE SUBSTITUTION VALUES

You want to compare monthly mortgage payments, total amounts to repay a loan, and total interest you will pay based on several interest rates—the variable. The interest rates range from 4% to 6% in 0.25% increments. Your first step is to enter a series of substitution values for the interest rate. Refer to Figure 6.17 as you complete Step 1.

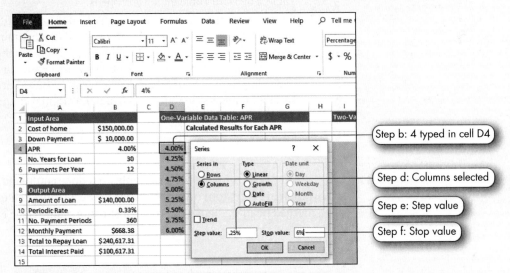

FIGURE 6.17 Substitution Values

a. Open *e06h1Mortgage_LastFirst* if you closed it at the end of Hands-On Exercise 1, and save it as **e06h2Mortgage_LastFirst**, changing h1 to h2.

b. Make the Home Loan worksheet active, click **cell D4**, type **4** and then press **Ctrl+Enter**.

   Cell D4 is the first cell containing a substitution value. Make sure cell D4 is still the active cell.

c. Click **Fill** in the Editing group on the Home tab and select **Series**.

   The Series dialog box opens.

d. Click **Columns**.

   You changed the *Series in* option to Columns because you want the series of substitution values listed vertically in column D.

e. Delete the existing value in the Step value box and type **0.25%**.

f. Type **6%** in the Stop value box and click **OK**.

   Excel fills in the series of values.

> **TROUBLESHOOTING:** If you forget to type the decimal point in Step e and/or the percent sign in Steps e or f, the series will be incorrect. If this happens, click Undo and repeat Steps c through f.

STEP 2 ▸ ADD FORMULAS TO A ONE-VARIABLE DATA TABLE

In the next steps, you will enter references to the monthly payment, total amount to repay the loan, and total interest formulas. Then, after entering the appropriate input cell reference, you will calculate the results of the one-variable data table. You will complete the table to compare the results for different interest rates ranging from 4% to 6%. Refer to Figure 6.18 as you complete Step 2.

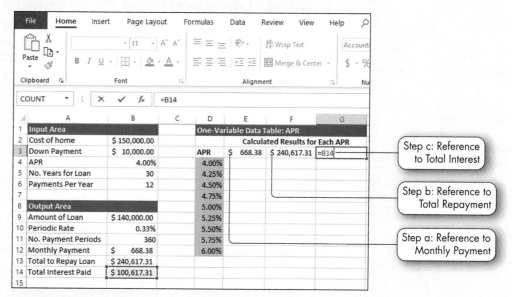

FIGURE 6.18 Complete the Data Table

a. Click **cell E3**, type **=B12**, and then press **Tab**.

You entered a reference to the original monthly payment formula in cell B12. When the results of cell B12 change, they are reflected in cell E3.

b. Type **=B13** in **cell F3** and press **Tab**.

You entered a reference to the original total amount to repay the loan.

c. Type **=B14** in **cell G3** and press **Enter**.

You entered a reference to the original total interest paid.

STEP 3 ▸ CALCULATE RESULTS FOR A ONE-VARIABLE DATA TABLE

In the next step, you will calculate the results of the one-variable data table. You will complete the table to compare the results for different interest rates ranging from 4% to 6%. Refer to Figure 6.19 as you complete Step 2.

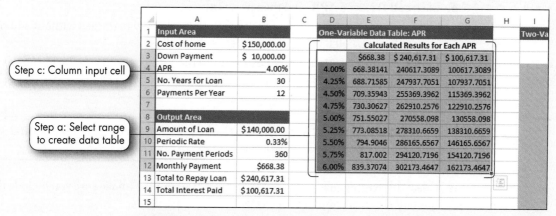

FIGURE 6.19 Complete the Data Table

a. Select the **range D3:G12**.

You select the entire range of the data table, starting in the blank cell in the top-left corner. Note that you did not select the titles or headings in cells D1:G2.

b. Click the **Data tab**, click **What-If Analysis** in the Forecast group, and then select **Data Table**.

c. Click in the **Column input cell box**, click **cell B4**, and then click **OK**. Save the workbook.

Because the APR substitution values are listed in a column in the data table, you reference cell B4 in the Column input box. Excel inserts the TABLE array function in the empty result cells and substitutes the values in range D4:D12 individually for the original APR to calculate the respective monthly payments, total amounts, and total interest payments. The higher the APR, the higher the monthly payment, total amount to repay the loan, and total interest.

STEP 4 ▶ FORMAT A ONE-VARIABLE DATA TABLE

You want to format the results to show dollar signs and to display rounded values to the nearest penny. In addition, you want to add column headings to provide more detail to the data table and add custom formats to the cells to appear as column headings. Refer to Figure 6.20 as you complete Step 3.

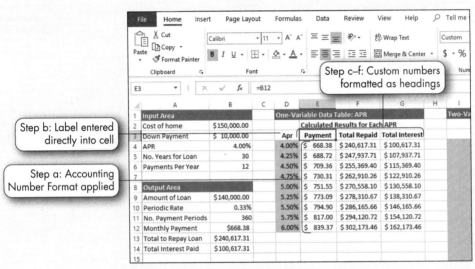

FIGURE 6.20 Formatted Data Table

a. Select the **range E4:G12**, click the **Home tab**, and then click **Accounting Number Format** in the Number group.

The values look more professional now that you have formatted them.

b. Click **cell D3**, type **APR**, and then press **Tab**.

Because cell D3 was empty, you can type the label directly in the cell without adding a custom format. Cell E3 should now be the active cell.

c. Click the **Number Dialog Box Launcher** in the Number group on the Home tab.

d. Select **Custom** in the Category list, scroll up through the Type list, and then select **General** in the list.

> **MAC TROUBLESHOOTING:** Click the Number Format arrow on the Home tab, and click More Number Formats. Click Custom in the Category box, then follow Step e.

e. Select the existing text in the Type box, type **"Payment"** (make sure you include the quotation marks), and then click **OK**.

The custom format is applied and Payment displays instead of =B12.

f. Repeat and adapt Steps c through e to enter the following custom number formats: **"Total Repaid"** for **cell F3** and **"Total Interest"** for **cell G3**.

> **TROUBLESHOOTING:** If you forget the quotation marks, the cell contents will contain a mix of numbers and characters. If this happens, open the Format Cells dialog box again and edit the contents of the Type box to display the text surrounded by quotation marks.

g. Center and bold the **range E3:G3**.

h. Save the workbook.

STEP 5 SUBSTITUTION VALUES AND ADD A FORMULA TO THE DATA TABLE

Now you want to focus on how a combination of interest rates and different costs will affect just the monthly payment. The interest rates range from 4% to 8% at .25% increments with costs of $150,000, $175,000, $200,000. Refer to Figure 6.21 as you complete Step 4.

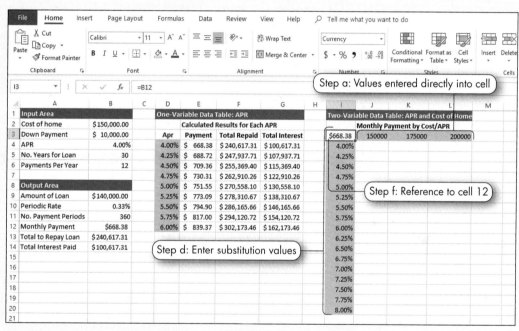

FIGURE 6.21 Substitution Values

a. Enter **150000**, **175000**, and **200000** in the **range J3:L3**. Format these values with **Accounting Number Format** with no decimals. Expand the column width as needed if pound signs (#) appear.

b. Click **cell I4**, type **4%**, and then press **Ctrl+Enter**.

c. Click **Fill** in the Editing group on the Home tab, select **Series**, and then click **Columns**.

d. Replace the existing value in the Step value box with **0.25%**, type **8%** in the Stop value box, and then click **OK**.

e. Format the **range I4:I20** with two decimal places.

f. Click **cell I3**, type **=B12**, and then press **Ctrl+Enter**. Resize column I as needed. Save the workbook.

You inserted the reference to the formula in the top-left cell of the two-variable data table. The cell displays pound signs, indicating the column is too narrow to display the value; you will apply a custom number format in Step 6.

Hands-On Exercise 2   **399**

You complete the data table, format the monthly payment results, and apply a custom number format to the cell containing the formula reference so that it displays the text APR. Refer to Figure 6.22 as you complete Step 6.

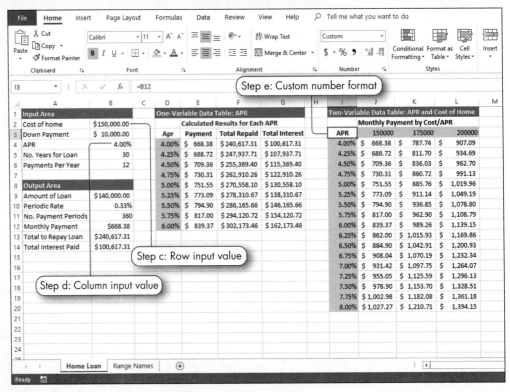

FIGURE 6.22 Completed Two-Variable Data Table

a. Select the **range I3:L20**.

b. Click the **Data tab**, click **What-If Analysis** in the Forecast group, and then select **Data Table**.

c. Click **cell B2** to enter that cell reference in the Row input cell box.

   Because you entered the purchase price substitution values in the top row of the data table, you entered the reference to the cell containing the original Cost of home in the Row input cell box.

d. Click in the **Column input cell box**, click **cell B4**, and then click **OK**.

   Because you entered the interest rate substitution values in the left column of the data table, you entered the reference to the cell containing the original APR variable in the Column input cell box.

e. Click **cell I3** and apply a Custom number format to display **APR**. Center and bold the contents in **cell I3**.

f. Save the workbook. Keep the workbook open if you plan to continue with the next Hands-On Exercise. If not, close the workbook and exit Excel.

Goal Seek and Scenario Manager

Although data tables are useful to compare effects of different values for one or two variables, other what-if analysis tools such as Goal Seek and Scenario Manager are better suited for other situations. For example, you might want to determine exactly the down payment required to acquire a desired payment. In this situation, you would not need all the data provided by a data table. You may also want to weigh the options between various values of down payments, purchase costs, and interest rates. If more than two variables are being analyzed, data tables would not be a viable option.

In this section, you will learn when and how to use two other what-if analysis tools, Goal Seek and Scenario Manager, to assist you in making decisions. These tools enable you to perform what-if analysis to make forecasts or predictions involving quantifiable data.

STEP 1 Determining Optimal Input Values Using Goal Seek

Suppose the most you can afford for a monthly payment on a mortgage is $800. How can you determine the down payment amount needed to meet that monthly payment? **Goal Seek** is a tool that identifies the necessary input value to obtain a desired goal by changing one variable. Goal Seek works backward to identify the exact value for a variable to reach your goal. In this case, you can use Goal Seek to determine the required down payment. Unlike variable data tables, Goal Seek manipulates only one variable and one result; it does not produce a list of values to compare. It is important to note that the result value that is calculated using Goal Seek is the Set Cell in the Goal Seek dialog box. This cell must contain a formula, such as the monthly payment calculation. The variable that is changed to find the optimized value is referred to as the Changing Cell. This cell must be a value, not a formula, which has a mathematical relationship with the cell containing the formula or goal.

> **To use Goal Seek, complete the following steps:**
>
> 1. Click What-If Analysis in the Forecast group on the Data tab.
> 2. Select Goal Seek to open the Goal Seek dialog box.
> 3. Enter the cell reference for the cell to be optimized in the *Set cell* box. This cell must contain a formula, such as the calculation for a monthly payment.
> 4. Enter the result you want to achieve (such as the $800 goal) in the *To value* box.
> 5. Enter the cell reference that contains the variable to adjust (such as the down payment) in the *By changing cell* box as shown in Figure 6.23.

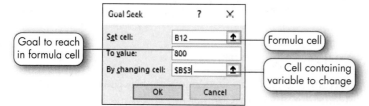

FIGURE 6.23 Goal Seek Dialog Box

Excel varies the input value until the desired result is achieved, if possible, and displays the Goal Seek Status dialog box. Click OK to accept the target value and change the value of the input cell you entered to the newly determined value. If you do not want to change the value permanently, click Cancel to keep the original input cell value instead of changing it. If Excel cannot determine a solution given the input cell and the desired results, it displays a message box.

Using Scenario Manager

So far you have used What-If Analysis tools to manipulate one- or two-variable tables; however, you may want to compare several variables and their combined effects on multiple calculated results. This type of analysis involves identifying and setting up *scenarios*, which are detailed sets of values that represent different possible situations. Business managers often create a best-case scenario, worst-case scenario, and most likely scenario to compare outcomes. For example, a best-case scenario could reflect an increase in units sold and lower production costs. A worst-case scenario could reflect fewer units sold and higher production costs.

Scenario Manager is a what-if analysis tool that enables you to define and manage up to 32 scenarios to compare their effects on calculated results. You can perform more sophisticated what-if analyses with Scenario Manager with the increased number of variables and results than with data tables. Each scenario represents different sets of what-if conditions to assess the outcome of spreadsheet models. Each scenario is stored under its own name and defines cells whose values change from scenario to scenario. Scenario Manager will display the results of each scenario in a formal report or directly on the worksheet. The Scenario Manager dialog box (see Figure 6.24) enables you to create, edit, and delete scenario names.

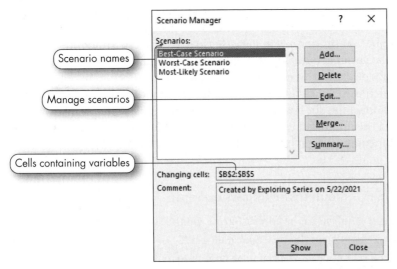

FIGURE 6.24 Scenario Manager Dialog Box

> **TIP: SCENARIOS ON DIFFERENT WORKSHEETS**
> When you create scenarios, Excel maintains those scenarios on the worksheet that was active when you created them. You can create scenarios for each worksheet in a workbook. The Scenario Manager dialog box displays only those scenarios you have created on the active worksheet.

STEP 2 Create and Add Scenarios

Before you start the Scenario Manager, identify cells that contain the variables you want to change or manipulate. For example, in evaluating home loans, you might want to manipulate the values for these variables: cost, down payment, interest rate, and the duration of the loan. You enter the cell references for these variables as the changing cells. After identifying the variables you want to change, identify one or more cells containing formulas that generate results you want to compare. Note these formulas must be directly impacted by the changing cell. For example, a scenario that calculates a monthly car payment using the PMT function may have changing cells that contain interest and total number of periods.

To create a scenario, complete the following steps:

1. Click What-If Analysis in the Forecast group on the Data tab.
2. Select Scenario Manager to open the Scenario Manager dialog box.
3. Click Add to open the Add Scenario dialog box (see Figure 6.25).
4. Enter a meaningful name in the Scenario name box.
5. Enter the input cells for the scenario in the Changing cells box. These are the cells containing variable values that Scenario Manager will adjust or change. Ranges can be used and commas are required between nonadjacent cells. The changing cells must be identical cell references across all scenarios.
6. Click in the Comment box. Excel enters the name of the person who created the scenarios in the Comment box; however, you can change the name and enter additional descriptions and rationales for the scenarios.
7. Click OK to open the Scenario Values dialog box (see Figure 6.26), which lists the changing cell references that you specified in the previous dialog box. For each respective changing cell, type the value you want to use for that particular scenario.

   After completing the first scenario, the process can be repeated to add additional scenarios. When creating a scenario, it is important to note the maximum number of changing variable cells is limited to 32.

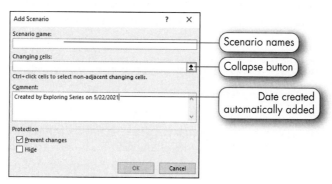

FIGURE 6.25 Add Scenario Dialog Box

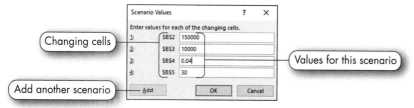

FIGURE 6.26 Scenario Values Dialog Box

STEP 3 ▶ **View and Edit Scenarios**

After you create the scenarios, you can view each of them. To view the scenarios, click What-If Analysis in the Forecast group on the Data tab, select Scenario Manager, select the name of the scenario you want to view in the Scenarios list, and then click Show. Excel places the defined values in the respective changing cells and displays the results on the worksheet.

After creating a scenario, you may also want to edit the original values. If you want to modify the parameters of a scenario, such as the name or input values, open the Scenario Manager dialog box, select the scenario you want to modify in the Scenarios list, and then click Edit. The Edit Scenario dialog box opens so that you can change the values. Click OK after making the necessary changes.

If you have scenarios in several worksheets or workbooks, you can combine them. Click Merge in the Scenario Manager dialog box to open the Merge Scenarios dialog box. Select the workbook and worksheet and click OK. Use Help to learn more about merging scenarios.

TIP: RANGE NAMES

To help you know what data to enter for the changing cells, assign a range name to the variable cells before using Scenario Manager. If you do this, the range names, rather than the cell references, display in the Scenario Values dialog box.

STEP 4 ## Generate a Scenario Summary Report

Although you can view the defined scenarios and their results individually, you will probably want to compare all scenarios in a table. A **Scenario Summary report** is an organized structured table of the scenarios, their input values, and their respective results. The summary report displays in the form of a worksheet outline and enables you to compare the results based on different values specified by the respective scenarios. While viewing a scenario displays the impact of the changing variable cells on the entire worksheet, in contrast, a Scenario Summary report only shows the impact of the changing variable cells on the result cells. For example, in Figure 6.27, the result cells are monthly payment (B12), Total to Repay Loan (B13), and Total Interest Paid (B14).

To create a Scenario Summary report, complete the following steps:

1. Open the Scenario Manager dialog box.
2. Click Summary to open the Scenario Summary dialog box (see Figure 6.27).
3. Click Scenario summary or click Scenario PivotTable report. Enter the reference for the cell(s) whose values change in the scenarios in the Result cells box.
4. Click OK. Excel creates the Scenario Summary on a new worksheet.

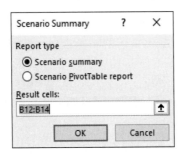

FIGURE 6.27 Scenario Summary Dialog Box

Excel can produce two types of reports: Scenario Summary and Scenario PivotTable. As shown in Figure 6.28 Scenario Summary reports display the results of each scenario in a new worksheet. The data reported in the summary are formatted without gridlines, and the report is easily printable. PivotTable reports summarize the data in a pivot table. This provides the same functionality as any other pivot table.

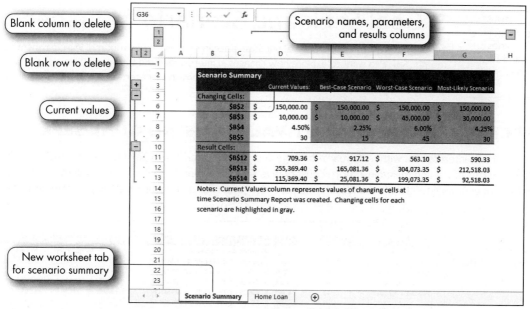

FIGURE 6.28 Scenario Summary

The Scenario Summary contains a column listing the changing and resulting cell references, current values and result values, and a column of values and results for each defined scenario. This organized structure enables you to compare the results as you analyze the scenarios. You should modify the structure and format the data for a more professional look. Typically, you would do the following:

- Delete the blank row 1 and the blank column A.
- Delete the Current Values column if it duplicates a defined scenario or if you do not want that data.
- Replace cell reference labels with descriptive labels in the first column.
- Delete the explanatory paragraph below the table and replace it with a narrative analysis relevant to the data.

> **TIP: UPDATED SCENARIO REPORTS**
> Unlike one- and two-variable data tables, which update results, if you change other values in the input area, scenario reports are not updated. If you change other values or assumptions, or if you add, edit, or delete scenarios, you will have to generate a new scenario report. To avoid this problem, do your best to double-check the scenarios to ensure they are perfect before you generate a Scenario Summary report.

Quick Concepts

7. Describe the limitations of Goal Seek. **p. 401**

8. Describe a situation in which you would choose to use Scenario Manager instead of Goal Seek. **p. 402**

9. Explain the benefits of using Scenario Manager. **p. 402**

Hands-On Exercises

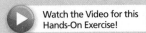

Skills covered: Determine Optimal Input Values Using Goal Seek • Create Scenarios • Add Scenarios • View and Edit Scenarios • Generate a Scenario Summary Report

3 Goal Seek and Scenario Manager

You want to determine the optimal purchase price in order to lower your mortgage payment to $600 per month. You also want to explore how changes in interest rate and total number of periods will impact your monthly payment. You will use Goal Seek and Scenario Manager to complete your analysis.

STEP 1 DETERMINE OPTIMAL INPUT VALUES USING GOAL SEEK

Given the current interest rate with a 30-year mortgage and your planned down payment, you want to identify the most that you can afford and maintain a more conservative $600.00 monthly payment. You will use Goal Seek to work backward from your goal to identify the ideal home purchase price. Refer to Figure 6.29 as you complete Step 1.

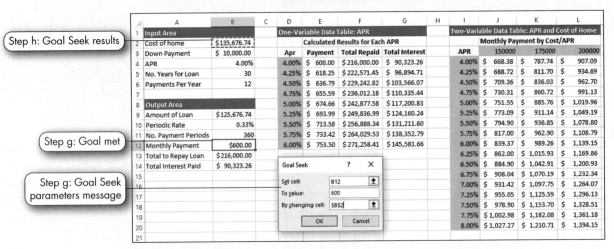

FIGURE 6.29 Goal Seek

a. Open the *e06h2Mortgage_LastFirst* workbook if you closed it at the end of Hands-On Exercise 2, and save it as **e06h3Mortgage_LastFirst**, changing h2 to h3.

b. Ensure the Home Loan worksheet is active. Click the **Data tab**.

c. Click **What-If Analysis** in the Forecast group and select **Goal Seek**.

   The Goal Seek dialog box opens.

d. Click **cell B12** to enter the cell reference for the monthly payment in the Set cell box.

   You indicated which cell contains the formula that produces the goal.

e. Click in the **To value box** and type **600**.

   You want the monthly payment to be $600.

f. Click in the **By changing cell box** and click **cell B2**, the cell containing the cost of the home.

   Cell B2 is the cell whose value will be determined using the Goal Seek analysis tool.

g. Click **OK**.

   The Goal Seek Status dialog box opens, indicating that it reached the target monthly payment goal of $600.

h. Click **OK** to accept the solution and to close the Goal Seek Status dialog box. Save the workbook.

To achieve a $600 monthly mortgage payment, you need to purchase a home that costs up to $135,676.74, instead of the original $150,000, assuming the other variables (down payment, interest rate, and term of loan) stay the same.

CREATE AND ADD SCENARIOS

You want to use Scenario Manager to explore different scenarios. Your first scenario is a best-case scenario with these parameters: $150,000 home, $10,000 down payment, special reduced interest financing for 15 years. Refer to Figure 6.30 as you complete Step 2.

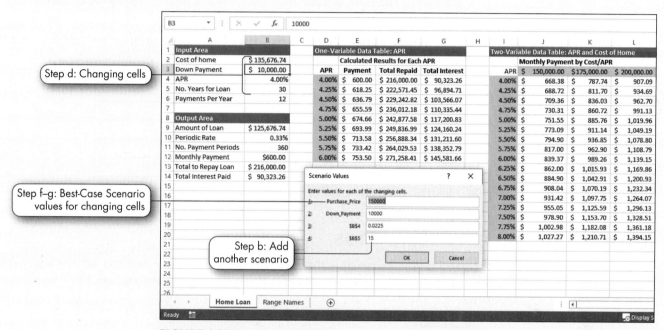

FIGURE 6.30 First Scenario's Values

a. Click **What-If Analysis** in the Forecast group on the Data tab and select **Scenario Manager**.

The Scenario Manager dialog box opens.

b. Click **Add**.

The Add Scenario dialog box opens so that you can assign a scenario name and select the changing cells.

c. Click in the **Scenario name box** and type **Best-Case Scenario**.

d. Delete existing contents in the Changing cells box and select the **range B2:B5**.

Excel enters this range in the Changing cells box. These are the variable cells cost of the home, down payment, interest rate, and term that will be changed in the various scenarios.

e. Ensure the Comment box displays your name and the date the scenario is created, such as "Created by Jason Davidson on 8/01/2021," and click **OK**.

The Scenario Values dialog box opens so that you can enter the parameters for the scenario.

f. Type **150000** in the Purchase_Price box and press **Tab** twice to accept the current $10,000 down payment.

You entered 150000 as the cost of the home.

g. Type **0.0225** in the $B$4 box, press **Tab**, and then type **15** in the $B$5 box.

h. Click **Add**, type **Worst-Case Scenario**, and then click **OK**.

The Changing cells box displays B2:B5, the range you selected for the first scenario.

Type the following values in the respective changing cells boxes:

Changing Cell Box	Value
Purchase_Price	150000
Down_Payment	45000
$B$4	6%
$B$5	45

For the cell $B$4 box, you can enter the value as a percentage (6%) or as a decimal equivalent (0.06).

i. Click **Add**, type **Most Likely Scenario** in the Add Scenario dialog box, and then click **OK**.

j. Type the following values in the respective changing cells boxes:

Changing Cell Box	Value
Purchase_Price	150000
Down_Payment	30000
$B$4	42.5%
$B$5	30

k. Click **OK**. Click **Close** and Save the workbook.

STEP 3 ▶ VIEW AND EDIT SCENARIOS

You will use Scenario Manager to view the results of the scenarios created in the prior step. You will then edit the Most Likely scenario to correct an error in the APR variable. Refer to Figure 6.31 as you complete Step 3.

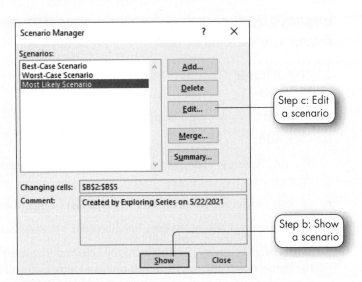

FIGURE 6.31 Edit Scenario

a. Click **What-If Analysis** in the Forecast group on the Data tab and select **Scenario Manager**.

b. Select the **Most Likely Scenario** and click **Show**.

Note that the monthly payment in cell B12 displays as $4,250.02 due to an input error in the prior step. The interest rate 4.25% was incorrectly entered as 42.5%.

c. Click **Edit** and click **OK**.

d. Ensure the Scenario Values Box is displayed. Click the third **Changing Cell** ($B$4) and type **0.0425**.

e. Click **OK,** select **Most Likely Scenario**, and then click **Show.**

The data in the worksheet will now reflect the corrected interest rate.

f. Click **Close**, resize column B as needed, and save the workbook.

GENERATE A SCENARIO SUMMARY REPORT

You want to generate a Scenario Summary report to compare the three home loan scenarios you created. Refer to Figure 6.32 as you complete Step 4.

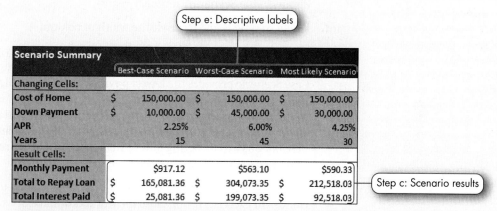

FIGURE 6.32 Scenario Summary

a. Click **What-If Analysis** in the Forecast group and select **Scenario Manager**.

b. Click **Summary**.

The Scenario Summary window opens displaying report options.

c. Select the **range B12:B14** to enter it in the Result cells box and click **OK**.

Excel generates the summary on a new worksheet named Scenario Summary. The report details the changes in payment amounts based on the variable inputs. The results are similar to Figure 6.32. You need to make a few deletions and add descriptive labels.

d. Delete the following:

- Column A
- Row 1
- Current Values column
- Notes in the **range A13:A15**

e. Type the following values in the respective changing cells boxes:

Cell	Label
A5	**Cost of Home**
A6	**Down Payment**
A7	**APR**
A8	**Years**
A10	**Monthly Payment**
A11	**Total to Repay Loan**
A12	**Total Interest Paid**

The labels describe data contained in each row. Now you can delete column B, which displays the cell references. Note: If range names are used with Scenario Manager, they will display in the Scenario Summary report.

f. Delete column B and increase the width of column A.

The Best-Case Scenario provides the highest monthly payment but pays off the loan in only 15 years. Based on the Scenario Summary report you learn that the Worst-Case Scenario provides the lowest payment but has the highest interest charges and longest repayment duration. You also learned the Best-Case Scenario has the highest payment but the shortest repayment duration and lowest interest charges. This leaves the Most-Likely Scenario, which offers a monthly payment in-between Best- and Worst-Case options while offering lower interest charges and a reduced repayment duration compared to the Worst-Case Scenario.

g. Save the workbook. Keep the workbook open if you plan to continue with the next Hands-On Exercise. If not, close the workbook and exit Excel.

Solver

While Scenario Manager is a useful analytic tool to evaluate potential outcomes, it lacks the ability to incorporate economic constraints as well as maximization and minimization calculation options. Due to the popularity of Microsoft Excel, there are numerous companies that produce software to enhance the already robust capabilities of the program. These supplemental programs are called *add-ins*. **Add-ins** are programs that can be added to Excel to provide enhanced functionality. **Solver** is an add-in application that searches for the best or optimum solution to a problem by manipulating the values for several variables within restrictions that you impose. You can use Solver to create optimization models. **Optimization models** find the highest, lowest, or exact value for one result by adjusting values for selected variables. Solver is one of the most sophisticated what-if analysis tools, and people use Solver in a variety of situations and industries. For example, a cellular phone manufacturing facility could use Solver to maximize the number of phones made or minimize the number of labor hours required while conforming to other production specifications. A financial planner might use Solver to help a family adjust their expenses to stay within their monthly income.

In this section, you will learn how to load the Solver add-in. Then, you will use Solver to set a target, select changing cells, and create constraints.

STEP 1 Loading the Solver Add-In

Because companies other than Microsoft create third-party add-ins, they are not active by default. Solver is a third-party add-in that you must load before you can use it.

To load Solver, complete the following steps:

1. Click the File tab and select Options.
2. Click Add-ins to see a list of active and inactive add-in applications. The Active Application Add-ins list displays currently enabled add-ins, and the Inactive Application Add-ins list displays add-ins that are not currently enabled.
3. Click the Manage arrow at the bottom of the dialog box, select Excel Add-ins, and then click Go to open the Add-ins dialog box (see Figure 6.33).
4. Click the Solver Add-in check box in the Add-ins available list and click OK.

On a Mac, to load Solver, complete the following steps:

1. Click the Tools menu, select Excel Add-ins.
2. Check Solver Add-in checkbox to select it and click OK.

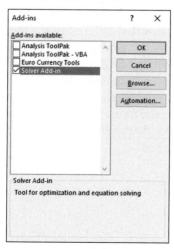

FIGURE 6.33 Add-Ins Dialog Box

When you load Solver, Excel displays Solver in the Analysis group on the Data tab (see Figure 6.34), where it remains until you remove the Solver add-in.

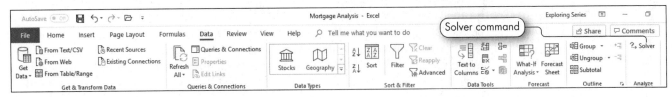

FIGURE 6.34 Solver on the Data Tab

> **TIP: SOLVER**
>
> If you are in a campus computer lab that resets software settings when you log off, you will have to load Solver each time you log into the lab's network. Furthermore, if you are working in a campus computer lab, your institution may prevent you from loading applications, such as Solver. Check with your instructor if your system in the lab prevents you from loading Solver.

Optimizing Results with Solver

Solver may be the best what-if analysis tool to solve complex linear and nonlinear problems. You can use it for complex equation solving and for constrained optimization, where a set of constraints is specified, and you want the outcome to be minimized or maximized. With Solver, you can change the values of several variables at once to achieve a result. For example, a business analyst might want to use Solver to maximize profits by changing selected variables while adhering to required limitations. Or a fulfillment company might want to determine the lowest shipping costs to transfer merchandise from a distribution center to retail stores. Along with the ability to maximize and minimize, Solver also can hit target goals similar to Goal Seek. For example, a production company may want to produce a certain quantity of products to reach a specific earnings goal while not exceeding production capabilities.

STEP 2 Identify the Objective Cell and Changing Cells

Before using Solver, review your spreadsheet as you specify the goal, identify one or more variables that can change to reach a goal, and determine the limitations of the model. You will use these data to specify three parameters in Solver: objective cell, changing cells, and constraints.

The ***objective cell*** specifies the cell that contains a formula that produces a value that you want to optimize (that is, maximize, minimize, or set to a value) by manipulating values of one or more variables. The formula in the objective cell relates directly or indirectly to the changing cells and constraints. Using the mortgage case study as an example, the objective cell is B14 (the cell containing the total interest paid formula), and your goal is to minimize the total interest.

The ***changing variable cell*** is a single cell or range of cells containing variables whose values change within the constraints until the objective cell reaches its optimum value. The changing variable cells typically contain values, not formulas, but these cells have a mathematical relationship to the formula in the objective. In the home loan example, the changing variable cells are B3 (down payment) and B5 (number of years). You can select up to 200 changing variable cells.

To specify the objective and changing cells, complete the following steps:

1. Click Solver in the Analysis group on the Data tab to open the Solver Parameters dialog box (see Figure 6.35).
2. Enter the cell containing the formula for which you want to optimize its value in the Set Objective box.
3. Click an option in the *To* section to specify what type of value you want to find for the target cell.
4. Click Max to maximize the value, Min to find the lowest value, or Value Of, and then specify the value in the Value Of box.
5. Enter the cell references that contain variables in the By Changing Variable Cells box. These are the variables that you want to change to reach the objective.

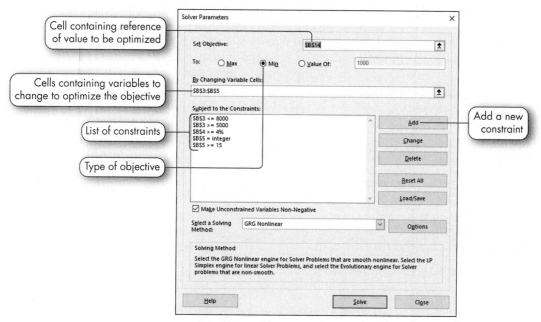

FIGURE 6.35 Solver Parameters Dialog Box

STEP 3 ▶ Define Constraints

Rules govern every business model, based on historical requirements, physical limitations, and other decisions. You may identify limitations through conversations with your supervisor, by reading policy statements, gathering information in meetings, and so on. Probably the most challenging process in using Solver is identifying all legitimate limitations. The **constraints** specify the restrictions or limitations imposed on a spreadsheet model as Solver determines the optimum value for the objective cell. Using the home loan example, a constraint might be the down payment must be between $5,000 and $8,000. After you enter data into Solver and run a report, you may gain knowledge of other limitations that you must build into the model.

One popular constraint operator is *integer*. This constraint requires the changing variable cell to be an integer, or whole number. For example, a manufacturing plant does not produce partial units such as 135.62 units, and a department store does not sell 18.32 shirts. To ensure that Solver produces realistic results, you should create integer constraints for these types of quantities. In Figure 6.35, the constraint $B$5 = integer limits the number of years for the loan to be a whole number.

Another often-overlooked constraint is the requirement that the value of a variable cell be greater than or equal to zero. Physically, it makes no sense to produce a negative number of products in any category. Mathematically, however, a negative value in a changing variable cell may produce a higher value for the objective cell. By default, the Make Unconstrained Variables Non-Negative check box is selected to ensure variable values are greater than or equal to zero. If you want to allow the lower end of a variable's value to be a negative value, you can create a constraint such as B2>=−100. That constraint takes priority over the Make Unconstrained Variables Non-Negative check box.

> **To add constraints to the Solver, complete the following steps:**
>
> 1. Click Add to the right of the Subject to the Constraints list in Solver Parameters to open the Add Constraint dialog box.
> 2. Enter the cell reference, the operator to test the cell reference, and the constraint the cell needs to match (see Figure 6.36). The cell reference contains a variable whose value you want to constrain or restrict to a particular value or range. The operator defines the relationship between the variable and the constraint. For example, cell B3 (the down payment) is restricted to being less than or equal to $8,000. Solver will not allow the down payment to be higher than this value.
> 3. Click OK to add the constraint and return to the Solver Parameters dialog box, or click Add to add the constraint and create another constraint.

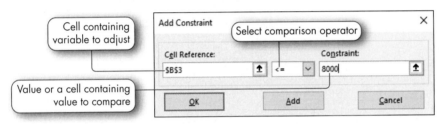

FIGURE 6.36 Add Constraint Dialog Box

To modify a constraint's definition, select the constraint in the Subject to the Constraints list and click Change. Make changes in the Change Constraint dialog box and click OK to update the definition. If you no longer need a constraint, select it in the Subject to the Constraints list and click Delete. Be careful when using Delete; Solver does not prompt you to confirm the deletion. Solver deletes the selected constraint immediately, and you cannot restore the deleted constraint.

STEP 4 Create a Solver Report

After defining the objective, changing variable cells, and constraints, select a solving method. Solver uses the selected solving method to determine which type of algorithms it executes to reach the objective. The Solver add-in for Excel contains these solving methods: GRG Nonlinear, Simplex LP, and Evolutionary. Look up *Solver* in Help to link to a specific set of descriptions of these methods. You can also review additional information and download additional add-ins on www.solver.com. For the purposes of this chapter, accept the default option, GRG Nonlinear.

You are now ready to use Solver to find a solution to the problem. Solver uses an iterative process of using different combinations of values in the changing variable cells to identify the optimum value for the objective cell. It starts with the current values and adjusts those values in accordance with the constraints. Once it finds the best solution, given the parameters you set, it identifies the values for the changing variable cells and shows you the optimum value in the objective value. If Solver cannot determine an optimum value, it does not enable you to generate summary reports.

Once activated, when Solver completes the iterative process, the Solver Results dialog box displays (see Figure 6.37). If it finds a solution, the Reports list displays available report types. If Solver cannot reach an optimal solution, no reports are available. Solutions are unattainable if a logic error exists or if the constraints do not allow sufficient elasticity to achieve a result. For example, a constraint between 10 and 11 may not allow sufficient flexibility, or a constraint greater than 20 but also less than 10 is illogical. If this happens, check each constraint for range constraints or errors in logic. Once a solution is found, you have the option of keeping the values or reverting to the original data. If you keep the changed values, Excel makes those changes to the actual worksheet. Do this if you are comfortable with those changes. If you want to maintain the original values, you should restore the original values. Along with adding the values to the worksheet, you can also generate a formal report if needed.

To create a Solver report, complete the following steps:

1. Click Solve in the Solver Parameters dialog box.
2. Click Keep Solver Solution to keep the changed objective and variable values, or click Restore Original Values to return to the original values in the worksheet.
3. Select a report from the Reports list. Generating a report is appropriate to see what changes Solver made while preserving the original values in the worksheet from Step 2.
4. Click OK to generate the summary on a separate worksheet.

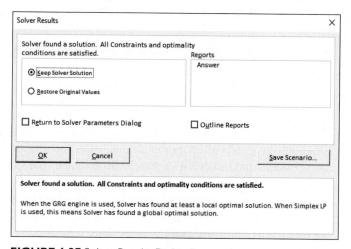

FIGURE 6.37 Solver Results Dialog Box

Solver creates a new worksheet for the Solver summary report containing four major sections (see Figure 6.38). The first section displays information about the Solver report. Specifically, it displays the report type, file name and worksheet containing the dataset, date and time the report was generated, Solver Engine details, and Solver Options that were set at the time the report was generated.

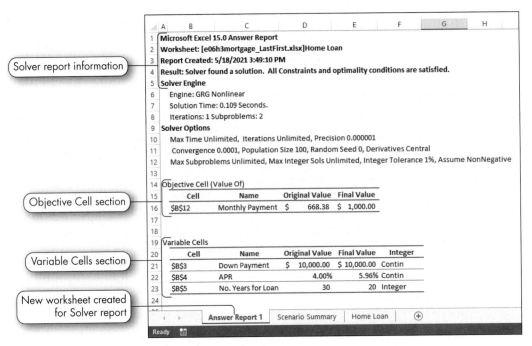

FIGURE 6.38 Solver Answer Report

The remaining sections of the report help you analyze the results. The section displays the objective cell information. Specifically, this section shows the original and final objective cell values. For example, using the original worksheet values, the original total interest paid in cell B14 was $100,617.31. The final minimized total interest paid is $47,064.23.

The third section displays the variable cells. Specifically, it displays the cell references, the variable cell names, original values, and final values. For example, the original down payment was $10,000, and the final value is $8,000.

The final section lists the constraints. It displays the cell reference, description, new cell value, formula, status, and slack for each defined constraint. In this case, the down payment slack ($3,000) is the difference between the lower constraint ($5,000) and the final value ($8,000). The Status column indicates Binding or Not Binding. A **binding constraint** is a rule that Solver has to enforce to reach the objective value. That is, the value hits the maximum allowable value for a less-than-or-equal-to, minimum allowable value for a greater-than-or-equal-to, equal to, or integer constraint. For example, $B$3<=8000 is a binding constraint. That is, the down payment was raised to its maximum limit of $8,000 to identify the optimal least amount of total interest paid. If this constraint had not been set, Solver could have identified a higher down payment to obtain a lower value for the objective cell. A **nonbinding constraint** is one that does not restrict the target value that Solver finds. For example, $B$3>=5000 is nonbinding. Solver did not have to stop at a lowest down payment of $5,000 to reach the optimal total interest paid value.

If you change any of the Solver parameters—objective cell, changing variable cells, or constraints—you need to generate another report. Solver does not update the report automatically. Each time you generate a report, Solver creates another new worksheet with names like Answer Report 1, Answer Report 2, and so on. Delete any reports you no longer need to minimize the file size of your workbook.

Configure Solver

You can closely monitor the trial solutions prior to reaching the final solution. Solver is a mathematical modelling operation, and you can determine solutions using the associated mathematics. However, stepping through Solver enables you to view the steps Solver performs.

To step through trial solutions, complete the following steps:

1. Click Options in the Solver Parameters dialog box to open the Options dialog box.
2. Select the Show Iteration Results check box to see the values of each trial solution and click OK.
3. Click Solve in the Solver Parameters dialog box.
4. Complete one of the following steps when the Show Trial Solution dialog box displays:
   - Click Stop to stop the process and open the Solver Results dialog box.
   - Click Continue to continue the process and display the next trial solution.

You can also use the Options dialog box to customize Solver further. Because Solver uses an iterative approach, you can specify the number of iterations to try, how much time to take to solve the problem, and how precise the answer should be (i.e., accuracy to what number of decimal places), among other settings.

Save and Restore a Solver Model

When you use Solver, Excel keeps track of your settings and saves only the most recent Solver settings. In some cases, you may want to save the parameters of a model so that you can apply them again in the future. Saving a Solver model is helpful if the original data source might change and you want to compare results by generating multiple Solver answer reports. When you save a Solver model, you save the objective value, the changing variable cells, and the constraints.

When you save a Solver model, Excel places the information in a small block of cells on a worksheet. The number of cells required to save the Solver model is dependent on the number of constraints in the model. After creating a Solver model you would like to save, click Load/Save in the Solver Parameters dialog box. Next, click in the worksheet where the first cell is to be placed. Then click Save to return to the Solver Parameters dialog box.

If you want to use an existing Solver model with new or updated data, you must return to a previous Solver model.

To use a Solver model that you saved, complete the following steps:

1. Click Load/Save in the Solver Parameters dialog box.
2. Select the worksheet cells that contain the Solver data. You must select all cells with the Solver data.
3. Click Load to load the model's values and return to the Solver Parameter dialog box.

Quick Concepts

10. Explain the advantage of using Solver over Goal Seek. ***p. 411***

11. Describe a situation in which you would want to define a constraint as an integer. ***pp. 413–414***

12. Describe a situation in which you would use Solver to maximize results. ***pp. 415–416***

Hands-On Exercises

Skills covered: Load the
Solver Add-In • Identify the
Objective Cell and Changing
Cells • Define Constraints •
Create a Solver Report

4 Solver

Although Goal Seek and Scenario Manager were helpful in further analyzing your home purchase, you want
to ensure the spreadsheet model imposes constraints on the situation. Therefore, you will continue your
analysis by using Solver.

STEP 1 — LOAD THE SOLVER ADD-IN

Before you can use Solver to analyze your home loan model, you need to load Solver. If Solver is already loaded, skip
Step 1 and start with Step 2. Refer to Figure 6.39 as you complete Step 1.

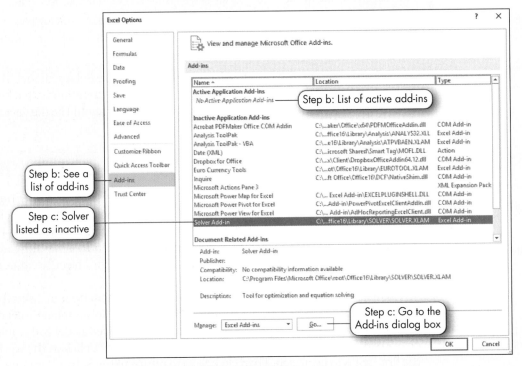

FIGURE 6.39 Excel Options Dialog Box

a. Click the **File tab** and click **Options**.

The Excel Options dialog box opens so that you can customize Excel settings.

b. Click **Add-ins** on the left side of the Excel Options dialog box.

The Excel Options dialog box displays a list of active and inactive application add-ins.

c. Check to see where Solver is listed. If Solver is listed in the Active Application Add-ins list,
click **Cancel**, and then skip Step d. If Solver is listed in the Inactive Application Add-ins
list, click the **Manage arrow**, select **Excel Add-ins,** and then click **Go**.

The Add-ins dialog box opens, containing a list of available add-in applications.

d. Click the **Solver Add-in check box** in the Add-ins available list and click **OK**.

> **MAC TROUBLESHOOTING:** To load the Solver Add-in, click the Tools menu, and select Excel
> Add-ins. Click the Solver Add-in checkbox to select it. Click OK.

Before using Solver, you want to reset the variables to their original values. After entering the original variable values again, you will specify the monthly payment cell as the objective cell and the home cost, down payment, APR, and number of years for the loan as the changing variable cells. Refer to Figure 6.40 as you complete Step 2.

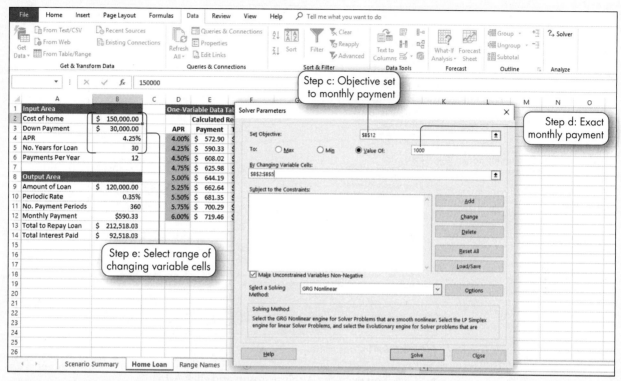

FIGURE 6.40 Objective and Changing Variable Cells

a. Open *e06h3Mortgage_LastFirst* if you closed it at the end of Hands-On Exercise 3, and save it as **e06h4Mortgage_LastFirst**, changing h3 to h4.

b. Click the **Home Loan worksheet tab**, click the **Data tab**, and click **Solver** in the Analyze group.

The Solver Parameters dialog box opens so that you can define the objective and changing variable cells.

c. Click **cell B12** to enter it in the Set Objective box.

You set the objective cell as the monthly payment.

d. Click **Value Of** and type **1000** in the Value Of box.

You specified that you want an exact $1,000 monthly home payment.

e. Click in the **By Changing Variable Cells box** and select the **range B2:B5**. Click **Close**.

TROUBLESHOOTING: Be careful to select the correct range. If you accidentally select cell B6, Solver might produce inaccurate results.

f. Save the workbook.

You define the constraints: $100,000 to $300,000 cost, $5,000 to $10,000 down payment, 4% to 6% APR, and 15- to 30-year loan. In addition, you set an integer constraint for the years so that Solver does not produce a fractional year, such as 5.71. Refer to Figure 6.41 as you complete Step 3.

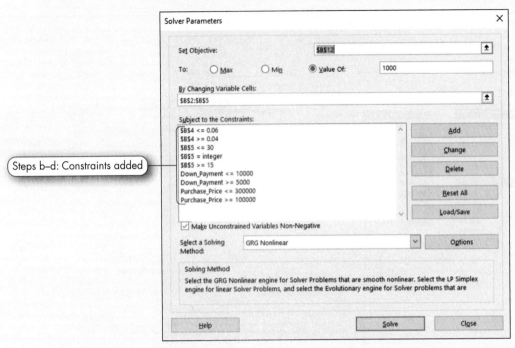

Steps b–d: Constraints added

FIGURE 6.41 Constraints

a. Click **Solver** in the Analyze group and click **Add**.

   The Add Constraint dialog box opens so that you can define the first constraint.

b. Click **cell B2**, make sure **<=** is selected, click in the **Constraint box**, and then type **300000**.

   You defined a constraint that the total home cost cannot exceed $300,000.

c. Click **Add** to define another constraint. Click **cell B2**, click the **operator arrow**, select **>=**, click in the **Constraint box**, and then type **100000**.

   The second constraint specifies that the cost of the home must be at least $100,000.

d. Add the following constraints in a similar manner. After you enter the last constraint, click **OK** in the Add Constraint dialog box.

   • **B3<=10000**
   • **B3>=5000**
   • **B4<=6%**
   • **B4>=4%**
   • **B5<=30**
   • **B5>=15**
   • **B5 int**

   TROUBLESHOOTING: Click Add to complete the current constraint and open an Add Constraint dialog box to enter another constraint. Click OK in the Add Constraint dialog box only when you have completed the last constraint and want to return to the Solver Parameters dialog box to solve the problem.

e. Check the constraints carefully against those shown in Figure 6.41 and Step d. Click **Close**.

f. Save the workbook.

STEP 4 **CREATE A SOLVER REPORT**

Now that you have completed the parameters for restricting the result based on the cost of the home, the down payment, the APR, and the number of years for the loan, you are ready to generate a Solver report. Refer to Figure 6.42 as you complete Step 4.

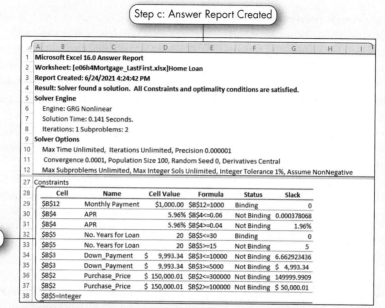

Step c: Answer Report Created

Step d: Constraints Displayed

FIGURE 6.42 Solver Answer Report

a. Click **Solver** in the Analyze group and click **Solve**.

The Solver Results dialog box opens. Look at the worksheet data, the new values display in the changing cells, and the $1000 target monthly payment displays in cell B12.

b. Select **Answer** in the Reports list and click **OK**.

Solver generates a report and displays it in a new worksheet named Answer Report 1.

> **TROUBLESHOOTING:** If you see the error message, *Solver: An unexpected internal error occurred, or available memory was exhausted*, close Solver, click Undo, remove Solver as an add-in, save and close the workbook, open the workbook again, and then enable the Solver add-in again. Then click Solver in the Analyze group, click Solve, select Answer, and then click OK.

c. Click the **Answer Report 1** worksheet tab.

Solver adjusts the values in the changing cells B2:B5 to obtain the exact value of $1000 for the objective cell B12. The report shows the previous and final values of the objective and variable cells. Your final values may vary slightly from those shown in the figure.

d. Scroll down through the worksheet to see the constraints.

In addition, the report displays the constraints—cell references, descriptive labels, current cell values, formulas, status (binding/not binding), and slack. Although not specified, integer constraints are always binding. Had you not constrained the years to a whole number, Solver might have found different values for the variable cells. However, you need to enforce that constraint because the term of the mortgage is a whole year. The 4% APR constraint is Not binding, meaning that Solver found the lowest possible APR to produce its answer. Finally, the 30-year limit is binding, meaning that Solver could not use a larger number of years for the loan to derive its answer.

e. Create a footer on all worksheets with your name on the left side, the sheet name code in the center, and the file name code on the right side.

f. Save and close the file. Based on your instructor's directions, submit e06h4Mortgage_LastFirst.

Chapter Objectives Review

After reading this chapter, you have accomplished the following objectives:

1. Create and maintain range names.

- Define a range name: You can use range names in formulas to make the formulas easier to interpret by using a descriptive name for the value(s) contained in a cell or range.
- Edit or delete a range name: Once created, range names can be added, edited, or deleted.
- Use range names in formulas: Range names can be used in formulas and will replace the traditional cell reference when using autocomplete.
- Insert a list of range names: A list of range names can be inserted into a workbook for documentation purposes.

2. Create a one-variable data table.

- A one-variable data table enables you to compare different values for one variable to compare the effects on one or more results.
- Set up one-variable substitution values: Substitution values replace the original value of a variable in a data table.
- Add formulas to the one-variable data table: After entering a substitution value, a formula must be added to relate mathematically to the substitution values.
- Calculate results for a one-variable data table: Excel uses the substitution values individually to replace the original variables to populate the data table.
- Format a one-variable data table: After completing the data table, all values should be appropriately formatted.

3. Create a two-variable data table.

- A two-variable data table enables you to compare results for two variables at the same time but for only one result.
- Set up two-variable substitution values: Use the top row for one variable's substitution values and the first column for the second variable's substitution values.
- Add a formula to the data table: Enter the required formula in the top-left corner of the data table.
- Calculate results for a two-variable data table: Select the data table boundaries and choose Data Table from the What-If Analysis group.

4. Determine optimal input values using Goal Seek.

- Use Goal Seek to work backward with a problem when you know what you want for the result but you do not know the value of a variable to achieve that goal. If you accept the results, Excel enters the identified input value directly in the variable cell.

5. Use Scenario Manager.

- Use Scenario Manager to create a set of scenarios, each with multiple variables. The Scenario Manager dialog box enables you to add, delete, and change scenarios. For each scenario, you specify a name, the changing cells, and the values for those changing cells.
- The Scenario Manager dialog box enables you to add, delete, and change scenarios.
- For each scenario, you specify a name, the changing cells, and the values for those changing cells.
- Create and add scenarios: Use the Scenario Manager dialog box to create scenarios to help analyze possible outcomes.
- View and edit scenarios: Sometimes analysis environments evolve and existing scenarios must be edited. Scenarios can be viewed and edited from the Scenario Manager dialog box.
- Generate a Scenario Summary report: After you create the scenarios with specific values, you can generate a summary report.
- Excel creates the summary report in a structured format on a new worksheet and displays the values for the changing cells and their effects on the results cells so that you can compare the results easily.

6. Load the Solver add-in.

- Solver is an add-in program for Excel. When you enable Solver, Excel places Solver in the Analyze group on the Data tab.

7. Optimize results with Solver.

- Solver is an optimization tool that enables you to maximize or minimize the value of an objective function, such as profit or cost. Solver uses an iterative process to use different values for variable cells until it finds the optimum objective value within the constraints you set.
- Identify the objective cell and changing cells: The objective cell contains the information that is to be set to value of, minimum, or maximum by Solver.
- Define constraints: Set in the Solver dialog box, constraints are limitations that are imposed on Solver.
- Create a Solver report: In the Solver Results dialog box, choose an option under Reports to have Excel create a report on a new worksheet.
- Configure Solver: Solver's calculation settings can be configured by clicking Options in the Solver Parameters dialog box.
- Save and restore a Solver model: A Solver model can be imported or exported by clicking Load/Save in the Solver Parameters dialog box.

Key Terms Matching

Match the key terms with their definitions. Write the key term letter by the appropriate numbered definition.

a. Add-in
b. Binding constraint
c. Changing variable cell
d. Constraint
e. Goal Seek
f. Nonbinding constraint
g. Objective cell
h. One-variable data table
i. Optimization model

j. Range name
k. Scenario
l. Scenario Manager
m. Scenario Summary report
n. Solver
o. Substitution value
p. Two-variable data table
q. Variable
r. What-if analysis

1. _____ A constraint that Solver must enforce to reach the target value. **p. 416**

2. _____ A cell containing a variable whose value changes until Solver optimizes the value in the objective cell. **p. 412**

3. _____ An add-in application that manipulates variables based on constraints to find the optimal solution to a problem. **p. 411**

4. _____ A data analysis tool that provides various results based on changing a single variable. **p. 390**

5. _____ A set of values that represent a possible situation. **p. 402**

6. _____ The cell that contains the formula-based value that you want to maximize, minimize, or set to a value in Solver. **p. 412**

7. _____ This data analysis technique finds the highest, lowest, or exact value for one particular result by adjusting values for selected variables. **p. 411**

8. _____ A limitation that does not restrict the target value that Solver finds. **p. 416**

9. _____ The process of changing variables to observe how changes affect calculated results. **p. 390**

10. _____ An input value that you can change to see how that change affects other values. **p. 390**

11. _____ A value that replaces the original value of a variable in a data table. **p. 390**

12. _____ A limitation that imposes restrictions on Solver. **p. 413**

13. _____ A program that can be added to Excel to provide enhanced functionality. **p. 411**

14. _____ A worksheet that contains scenario results. **p. 404**

15. _____ A data analysis tool that provides results based on changing two variables. **p. 394**

16. _____ A tool that identifies the necessary input value to obtain a desired goal. **p. 401**

17. _____ A What-If analysis tool that enables you to define and manage scenarios to compare how they affect results. **p. 402**

18. _____ A word or string of characters that represents one or more cells. **p. 382**

Multiple Choice

1. Which what-if analysis tool is the best option for complex calculations requiring constrained optimization?

   (a) Goal Seek
   (b) Scenario Manager
   (c) Data Tables
   (d) Solver

2. What tool is used to view existing range names?

   (a) Name Box
   (b) Scenario Manager
   (c) Name Manager
   (d) Solver

3. Which tool is most effective when comparing the impact of various combinations of production expenses and new customer acquisition on net sales profit?

   (a) Goal Seek
   (b) Solver
   (c) Two-variable data table
   (d) Scenario Manager

4. This tool calculates the value required in a single cell to produce a result within a related cell.

   (a) Goal Seek
   (b) Solver
   (c) One- or two-variable data table
   (d) Scenario Manager

5. This analysis tool can handle multiple adjustable cells while minimizing, maximizing, or meeting goals.

   (a) Goal Seek
   (b) Solver
   (c) One- or two-variable data table
   (d) Scenario Manager

6. Which of the following is an Excel add-in?

   (a) Goal Seek
   (b) Solver
   (c) One- or two-variable data table
   (d) Scenario Manager

7. Which of the following is *not* an acceptable range name?

   (a) Apr
   (b) Rate_2021
   (c) 2021_Rate
   (d) Payment

8. What is the keyboard shortcut to open the Paste Name dialog box?

   (a) F2
   (b) F3
   (c) F4
   (d) F5

9. Which of the following tools can incorporate constraints?

   (a) Goal Seek
   (b) Solver
   (c) Data Tables
   (d) Scenario Manager

10. The Solver add-in displays on this tab in the ribbon.

    (a) Home tab.
    (b) Formulas tab.
    (c) Data tab.
    (d) Analyze tab.

Practice Exercises

1 Monthly Commission

You are a sales rep for Speedway International auto sales, an auto dealership that specializes in online sales. Each month you are paid 2% commission on all sales and you pay 4% income tax based on your current home office. You have decided to create an Excel worksheet and use one- and two-variable data tables to predict your net income due to the variability in monthly sales and tax rate based on the sales location. You will also use Solver to determine the exact amount of sales required to meet your monthly income goal and create range names to make your references easier to understand within your financial calculations. Refer to Figure 6.43 as you complete this exercise.

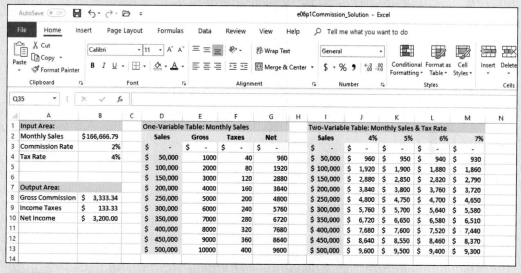

FIGURE 6.43 Monthly Commission

a. Open *e06p1Commission* and save it as **e06p1Commission_LastFirst**.

b. Select the **ranges A2:B4** and **A8:B10**. Click the **Formulas tab**, click **Create from Selection** in the Defined Names group, and then click Left column. Click **OK**.

c. Click **Name Manager**, click **Commission_Rate**, and then click **Edit**. Highlight **Commission_ Rate** and press **Delete**. Type **Commission** and click **OK**.

d. Adapt the technique used in Step c to edit the existing range names as follows and click **Close**.
   - **Gross_Commission = Gross**
   - **Net_Income = Net**
   - **Monthly_Sales = Sales**

e. Click **cell B10**, type **=** and click **cell B8**. Type **-**, click **cell B9**, and then press **Ctrl+Enter**.

f. Ensure the Formulas tab is displayed. Click **Define Name** in the Defined Names group and click **Apply Names**. Select all six names in the Apply names box and click **OK**.

g. Click **cell D3** and complete the following steps to enter a series of substitution values for the bonus percentage:
   - Type **0.00** and press **Ctrl+Enter** to keep **cell D3** active.
   - Click **Fill** in the Editing group on the Home tab and select **Series**.
   - Click **Columns** in the Series in section, type **50000** in the Step value box, type **500000** in the Stop value box, and then click **OK**.
   - Adjust the width of Column D to **11**.

h. Click **cell E2**. Type **=**, press **F3**, and then select **Gross**. Click **OK** and press **Ctrl+Enter**.

i. Press **Tab** and adapt the technique used in Step h to enter a reference in **cell F2** for income tax and **cell G2** for net income.

j. Complete the one-variable data table by doing the following:
- Select the **range D2:G13**.
- Click the **Data tab**, click **What-If Analysis** in the Forecast group, and then select **Data Table**.
- Click in the **Column input cell box**, click **cell B2**, and then click **OK**.
- Select the **range E3:G13**, click the **Home tab**, and then select **Accounting Number Format** with zero decimal places.

k. Create column headings for the data table by doing the following:
- Type **Sales** in **cell D2**.
- Click **cell E2** and click the **Number Dialog Box Launcher** in the Number group.
- Click **Custom** in the Category list, scroll up in the Type list, and then select **General**.
- Select **General** in the Type box, type **"Gross"**, and then click **OK**.
- Adapt the above steps to create a custom number format to display **Taxes** in **cell F2** and **Net** in **cell G2**.
- Center and bold the **range D2:G2**.

l. Set up the variables for the two-variable data table by copying the **range D3:D13** and pasting it in the **range I3:I13**. Type **4%** in **cell J2** and press **Ctrl+Enter**.

m. Click **Fill** in the Editing group on the Home tab and select **Series**. Click **Rows** in the Series in section, type **1%** in the Step value box, type **7%** in the Stop value box, and then click **OK**. Type **=Net** in **cell I2**.

n. Complete the two-variable data table by doing the following:
- Select the **range I2:M13**.
- Click the **Data tab**, click **What-If Analysis** in the Forecast group, and then select **Data Table**.
- Click **cell B4** to enter that reference in the Row input cell box.
- Click in the **Column input cell box**, click **cell B2**, and then click **OK**.

o. Select the **range J3:M13** and apply **Accounting Number Format** with zero decimal places.

p. Click **cell I2** and click the **Number Dialog Box Launcher** in the Number group. Click **Custom** in the Category list, scroll up in the Type list, and then select **General**. Select **General** in the Type box, type **"Sales"**, and then click **OK**. Bold and center data in this cell.

q. Select **cell B10**, click the **Data tab**, click **Solver** in the Analyze group and enter the following parameters:
- Set Objective = **Net**
- To Value of: = **3200**
- By Changing Variable Cells: **Sales, Tax_Rate**

r. Click **Add** and enter the constraint **Tax_Rate <= 7%**.

s. Click **Add**, enter the constraint **Tax_Rate >=4%**, and then click **OK**.

t. Click **Solve**, click **Answer** in the Reports box, and then click **OK**.

u. Create a new worksheet named **Range Names**. Click **cell A1** and click the **Formulas tab**. Click **Use in Formula** in the Defined Name group and click **Paste Names**. Click **Paste List** and resize column A as needed.

v. Create a footer on all worksheets with your name on the left side, the sheet name code in the center, and the file name code on the right side.

w. Save and close the workbook. Based on your instructor's directions, submit e06p1Commission_LastFirst.

2 Burton's Sandwich Shop

Burton has opened an artisan grilled cheese sandwich shop. His budget must account for fixed expenses, such as the facility lease, utilities, and credit card equipment fees. In addition, he accounts for variable costs including cost of goods sold and credit card processing fees. You will use Goal Seek to determine how many sandwiches he must sell to earn a net profit of $3,500. You then will use Scenario Manager to evaluate several possible situations. Refer to Figure 6.44 as you complete this exercise.

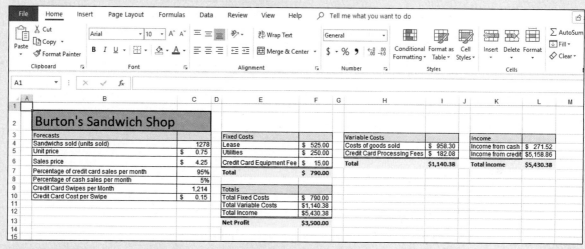

FIGURE 6.44 Burton's Sandwich Shop

a. Open *e06p2Deli* and save it as **e06p2Deli_LastFirst**.

b. Enter the following formulas:
  - **Cell I4**: =**C5*C4** to calculate the projected cost of goods sold.
  - **Cell I5**: =**C9*C10** to calculate the total credit card processing fees.
  - **Cell L4**: =**C4*C6*C8** to calculate the total income from cash sales.
  - **Cell L5**: =**C9*C6** to calculate the total income from credit card sales.

c. Click the **Data tab**, click **What-If Analysis** in the Forecast group, and then select **Goal Seek**.

d. Complete the Goal Seek by doing the following:
  - Click **cell F13** to add the cell reference to the *Set cell* box.
  - Click in the **To value box** and type **3500**.
  - Click in the **By changing cell box** and click **cell C4**.
  - Click **OK** in the Goal Seek dialog box and click **OK** in the Goal Seek Status dialog box. It will take 1,278 sandwiches for Burton to reach a net profit goal of $3,500.

e. Click **What-If Analysis** in the Forecast group and select **Scenario Manager**.

f. Create the first scenario by doing the following:
  - Click **Add** and type **Current Conditions** in the Scenario name box.
  - Click in the **Changing cells box**, and type **C4,C6**. Click in the **Comment box** and edit it to reflect your name, such as "Created by Jason Davidson on 9/4/2021," and then click **OK**.
  - Type **1278** in the $C$4 box, leave the other current value intact, and then click **OK**.

g. Create the following three scenarios, and then click **OK**.

Scenario Name	Ideal Case	Increased Costs	Low Sales
$C$4	1,500	700	500
$C$6	4.25	4.50	4.00

h. Click **Summary**, select and delete the suggested range in the Result cells box, and press and hold **Ctrl** as you click **cells C4**, **C6**, and **F13**. Click **OK**.

i. Make these changes to the summary on the Scenario Summary worksheet:
- Delete the blank column A, the Current Values column, the blank row 1, and the notes in the **range A10:A12**.
- Click **cell A5**, type **Units Sold**, and then press **Enter**.
- Type **Sales Price** in **cell A6** and type **Net Profit** in **cell A10**.
- Increase the width of column A to display the labels.
- Delete column B containing the cell references because these references would have no meaning if you distribute only the Scenario Summary worksheet to others.

j. Create a footer with your name on the left side, the sheet name code in the center, and the file name code on the right side for each worksheet.

k. Save and close the workbook. Based on your instructor's directions, submit e06p2Deli_LastFirst.

Mid-Level Exercises

1 Housing Construction Cost Variables

Your friends, Elijah and Valerie Foglesong, want to build their dream house. They identified tentative costs, but they cannot afford the $414,717 estimated cost. You will use Goal Seek to determine an estimate of the total finished square footage they can afford. You will also use Scenario Manager to help evaluate negotiation price per square foot and the lot fee. To provide more flexibility in their decision making, you will create a data table listing various finished square footages and their effects on the base house cost and total cost. Finally, you will create another data table showing combinations of square footages and lot prices to identify total costs. Although a builder's overall house design specifies the square footage, the Foglesongs can use your data tables to help guide them in their decision.

a. Open *e06m1House* and save it as **e06m1House_LastFirst**.

b. Select the **cells B9, B15, B21, B23,** and assign appropriate range names.

c. Click **cell B25** and use range names to create a formula to calculate the total house cost.

d. Create a new worksheet named **Range Names** and paste a list of the range names starting in **cell A1**.

e. Use Goal Seek to determine the total square footage to meet the total cost goal of $350,000.

f. Enter a series of total square footages ranging from 1,800 to 3,600 in increments of 200 in the **range D6:D15**. Apply **Blue font color** and **Comma Style** with zero decimal places to the series. Enter references to the base cost and total cost in the appropriate cells on row 5.

g. Complete the data table using the appropriate input cell. Apply Custom number formats to give appropriate descriptions to the second and third columns. Apply these formats to the headings: bold, center, and **Blue font color**.

h. Identify the square footage, base price, and total cost that come closest to their goal. Apply **Yellow fill color** to those cells in the data table.

i. Copy the square footage substitution values to the **range H6:H15** and remove the fill color. Enter these lot price substitution values in the **range I5:K5: 90000, 96000,** and **102675**. Format these values with **Accounting Number Format** with zero decimal places and **Blue font color**.

j. Enter the reference to the total cost formula in the appropriate location for the second data table. Complete the data table using the appropriate input cells. Apply a Custom number format to the reference to the formula cell. Apply **Yellow fill color** to the total price in each column that comes closest without going over their goal.

k. Format results in both tables with **Accounting Number Format** with zero decimal places.

l. Use Scenario Manager to create three scenarios based on the information below.

Scenario Name	Ideal Costs	Increased Costs	Low Costs
$B$8	80	100	60
$B$23	102,675	110,000	80,000

m. Create an appropriately formatted Scenario Summary Report based on **cell B25**.

n. Create a footer on all three worksheets with your name on the left side, the sheet name code in the center, and the file name code on the right side. Adjust the orientation, margins, and scaling to fit on one page.

o. Save and close the workbook. Based on your instructor's directions, submit e06m1House_LastFirst.

2 Indy Deck Builders

ANALYSIS
CASE

You are the business manager for Indy Deck Builders, a local construction company that specializes in new deck installation. Your company offers three deck models. Model A, which costs $2,000, model B costs $3,500, and model C costs $5,000. You currently have 45 contracts to build model A, 55 for model B, and 75 for model C. Once the contracts have been completed, you will have a surplus of materials (wood, hardware, and paint) remaining in inventory. After expenses, your company's net profit is $492,031.25. You would like to use Solver to forecast how many additional contracts you can accept to maximize profit while not exceeding the raw materials in inventory.

a. Open *e06m2DeckBuilders* and save it as **e06m2DeckBuilders_LastFirst**.
b. Create range names based on the values in the **range C15:C16**.
c. Apply the **Total_Profit** and **Total_Building_Expense** range names to the worksheet.
d. Load the Solver add-in if it is not available.
e. Set the objective cell to **Max** Net Profit (**cell C17**).
f. Assign Total Contracts (**range C8:E8**) as the Changing Variables Cells.
g. Set a constraint to ensure contracts are whole numbers.
h. Set a constraint to ensure the raw materials used in the range E11:E13 do not exceed the inventory in the range D11:D13.
i. Set a constraint to ensure that the Total Contracts in the range C8:E8 are greater or equal to the existing contracts in the range C7:E7.
j. Create an Answer Report to outline your findings.
k. Create a footer on all worksheets with your name on the left side, the sheet name code in the center, and the file name code on the right side.
l. Save and close the file. Based on your instructor's directions, submit e06m2DeckBuilders_LastFirst.

Running Case

New Castle County Technical Services

New Castle County Technical Services (NCCTS) provides technical support services for a number of companies in New Castle County, Delaware. You previously created charts to depict summary data by service type, customer, and days open; sorted the main dataset for analysis; and prepared it to be printed on two pages. You applied conditional formatting to highlight transactions that took more than nine days to close and displayed data bars for the amount billed to give a quick visual for transaction amounts. You filtered a copy of the dataset and converted the summary sections into tables. Finally, you created a PivotTable and PivotChart to analyze agent performance in resolving disaster recovery support calls. Next you will continue your analysis of disaster recovery services using one- and two-variable data tables as well as Goal Seek.

a. Open *e06r1NCCTS* and save it as **e06r1NCCTS_LastFirst**.
b. Ensure the Disaster Recovery Forecast sheet is active. Create range names based on the values in the **range B15:B16**.
c. Edit the name range Disaster_Recovery to the more appropriate name **Disaster_Recovery_Rate**.
d. Use the formula **Disaster_Recovery_Rate*Hours_Billed** to calculate the Amount Billed in **cell B17**.
e. Create a series of substitution values in the **range D4:D12** based on hours billed. The substitution values should range from five to nine hours in half hour increments.
f. Enter a reference to the Amount Billed in the appropriate location for the first data table. Complete the data table using the appropriate input cells. Apply a Custom number format to the reference to the formula cell.

g. Apply **Comma Style format** to the **range E4:E12**.

h. Copy the substitution values used in the first data table to the **range G4:G12**.

i. Create a series of substitution values in the **range H3:N3** based on hourly rate. The substitution values should range from $65 to $95 in increments of $5.00. Apply **Accounting Number format** to the substitution values.

j. Enter a reference to the Amount Billed in the appropriate location for the second data table. Complete the data table using the appropriate input cells. Apply **Comma Style** format to the results and create a **Custom number format** to the reference to the formula cell.

k. Use Goal Seek to determine the optimal hourly rate (cell B15) to bill $500.00 for a 5.5-hour repair.

l. Insert a footer with your name on the left side, the sheet name in the center, and the file name code on the right side.

m. Save and close the workbook. Based on your instructor's directions, submit e06r1NCCTS_LastFirst.

Disaster Recovery

IT Management

You work as an IT manager for Bower Industries, a Web hosting company that provides off-site Web hosting for online businesses. Your current service level agreement promises customers 24/7 server availability; however, in the unlikely event of a server outage, you need to gauge the economic impact. Based on your current user base, you estimate a cost of $1,500 an hour in customer refunds if an outage were to occur. Your assistant has attempted to create a one-variable data table to further estimate the economic impact of outages between one and five hours in length. Unfortunately, the one-variable data table is not returning the correct results due to an error in the input values. You will correct the error as well as add existing range names to the Total Cost for Outage formula. Finally, you will create a custom number format for cell E3.

Open *e06d1NetworkOutage* and save it as **e06d1NetworkOutage_LastFirst**. Delete the inaccurate values in the **range E4:E12**. Apply the pre-existing range names to the worksheet. Enter a reference to the Total Cost for Outage (cell B6) in **cell E3**. Create a one-variable data table to detail the sensitivity of expense based on an outage range of one to five hours based on half-hour increments. Add a Custom number format to cell E3 to display the word **Cost**. Create a footer with your name, the sheet name code, and the file name code. Save and close the file. Based on your instructor's directions, submit e06d1NetworkOutage_LastFirst.

High West Fashions

You are the digital marketing director for High West Fashions, a regional clothing company that specializes in custom t-shirts. Your company has decided to launch an online advertising campaign that enables customers to purchase heavily discounted products. You have the task of determining the optimal amount of advertising to purchase in order to maximize profit and most effectively utilize resources.

Range Names

Before using Excel's Analysis tools to help complete your forecasts, you will create range names for key input cells to simplify the creation of formulas moving forward.

1. Open *e06c1DirectMarketing* and save it as **e06c1DirectMarketing_LastFirst**.

2. Create appropriate range names for Design Fee (**cell B8**), Cost per Ad (**cell B9**), Total Clicks (**cell B10**), Profit Per Click (**B11**), and Gross Profit (**cell B12**).

3. Edit the existing name range **Design_Fee** to reflect the current year. Example: Design_Fee2021.

4. Use the newly created range names to create a formula to calculate Gross Profit (**cell B12**) and Net Profit (**cell B13**). Gross profit is the product of total clicks and profit per click. Net profit is Gross profit - ad design fee - total clicks * cost per ad design.

5. Create a new worksheet labeled **Range Names**, paste the newly created range name information in **cell A1**, and then resize the columns as needed for proper display.

Goal Seek

Currently, you estimate that if 10000 ads are purchased with a 5% response rate, you will earn $3,125. Your next task is to determine the optimal click response rate to earn a $5,000 net profit.

6. Use Goal Seek to determine the optimal click rate in order to earn a $5,000 net profit.

7. Enter the values in the Q&A worksheet.

One-Variable Data Table

Your initial forecast includes 10000 ads with a 5% response rate. You want to evaluate the change in gross profit and net profit as the click response rate changes. You will create a one-variable data table using substitution values from 2% to 6.5% to complete the task.

8. Start in **cell E4**. Complete the series of substitution values ranging from 2% to 6.5% at increments of .50% vertically down column E. Format the **range E4:E13** with percentage number format and two decimal points.

9. Enter references to the **Gross Profit** and **Net Profit** in the correct location for a one-variable data table.

10. Complete the one-variable data table and format the results with **Accounting Number Format** with no decimal places.

11. Apply Custom number formats to make the formula references display as descriptive column headings. Bold and center the headings and substitution values.

12. Answer question 2 on the Q&A worksheet. Save the workbook.

Two-Variable Data Table

You are considering increasing the number of ads purchased to raise net profit. You are also interested in how net profit will change if the response rate changes as well as the total number of ads purchased. You will create a two-variable data table to complete the task.

13. Copy the response rate substitution values from the one-variable data table and paste the values starting in **cell I4**.

14. Type **10000** in **cell J3**. Complete the series of substitution values from 10000 to 40000 at 5000 increments.

15. Enter the reference to net profit formula in the correct location for a two-variable data table.

16. Complete the two-variable data table and format the results with **Accounting Number Format** with no decimal places.

17. Apply a Custom number format to make the formula reference display as a descriptive column heading. Bold and center the heading and substitution values.

18. Answer questions 3 and 4 on the Q&A worksheet. Save the workbook.

Scenario Manager

Up to this point, you have created forecasts based on static amounts; however, it is important to plan for both positive and negative outcomes. To help you analyze best, worst, and most likely outcomes, you will use Scenario Manager.

19. Create a scenario named **Best Case**, using Number of Ads and Click Rate. Enter these values for the scenario: **40000**, and **6.5%**.

20. Create a second scenario named **Worst Case**, using the same changing cells. Enter these values for the scenario: **10000**, and **1%**.

21. Create a third scenario named **Most Likely**, using the same changing cells. Enter these values for the scenario: **10000**, and **6.83%**.

22. Generate a Scenario Summary report using Gross Profit and Net Profit.

23. Format the summary as discussed in the chapter.

24. Answer question 5 on the Q&A worksheet. Save the workbook.

Use Solver

You realize the best-case scenario may not be realistic. You have decided to continue your analysis by using Solver to determine the perfect production blend to reach an ideal goal of $20,000 net profit.

25. Load the Solver add-in if it is not already loaded.

26. Set the objective to calculate a net profit of **$20,000**.

27. Use **Number of Ads** and **Click Rate** as changing variable cells.

28. Set constraints to ensure Number of Ads purchased is less than or equal to 40,000 and is a whole number.

29. Set constraints to ensure Click Rate is less than or equal to 10%.

30. Solve the problem. Generate the Answer Report. If you get an internal memory error message, remove Solver as an add-in, close the workbook, open the workbook, add Solver in again, and finish using Solver.

31. Answer question 6 on the Q&A worksheet.

32. Create a footer on all five worksheets with your name on the left side, the sheet name code in the center, and the file name code on the right side.

33. Save and close the file. Based on your instructor's directions, submit e06c1DirectMarketing_LastFirst.

Specialized Functions

LEARNING OUTCOME

You will manipulate data using date, logical, statistical, and financial functions.

OBJECTIVES & SKILLS: After you read this chapter, you will be able to:

CASE STUDY | Home Protection, Inc.

You are an assistant accountant in the Human Resources (HR) Department for Home Protection, Inc., a company that sells smart home security systems to residential customers. Home Protection, Inc., with locations in Atlanta, Boston, Chicago, and Cleveland, has a manager at each location who oversees several account representatives. You have an Excel workbook that contains names, locations, titles, hire dates, and salaries for the 20 managers and account representatives. To prepare for your upcoming salary analyses, you downloaded salary data from the corporate database into the workbook.

The HR manager wants you to perform several tasks based on locations and job titles. You will use date functions to identify the year each employee was hired and how many years the employees have worked for the company and logical functions to calculate annual bonus amounts. In addition, you will insert math and statistical functions and a map to help analyze the data. Finally, you will review financial aspects of automobiles purchased for each manager.

Using Date, Logical, Statistical, and Financial Functions

CHAPTER 7

FIGURE 7.1 Home Protection, Inc.

CASE STUDY | Home Protection, Inc.

Starting File	File to be Submitted
e07h1Salary	e07h3Salary_LastFirst

MyLab IT Grader An alternate version of this project is available as a MyLab IT Grader Assessment

Date and Logical Functions

You have learned that dates are stored as serial numbers. This method of storing dates enables you to perform calculations using cells that contain dates. The Date & Time category in the Function Library contains a variety of functions that work with dates. Previously, you used the TODAY function to return the current date and the NOW function to display the current date and time.

Logical functions enable you to test conditions to determine if a condition is true or false. You have used the IF function, which is the most commonly used logical function. Other logical functions, such as SWITCH and IFS, are useful to perform additional conditional tests. Furthermore, you can use two or more functions together to perform complex calculations.

In this section, you will learn how to use date and advanced logical functions. Specifically, you will learn how to use date functions to extract the day, month, and year; calculate the number of days and years between two dates; and identify which day of the week a date falls on. In addition, you will use advanced logical functions to evaluate data with several potential outcomes.

Using Date Functions

The Date & Time category in Excel's Function Library group on the Formulas tab includes a variety of date and time functions. You can use these functions to perform simple and complex date calculations, such as when employees are eligible for certain benefits, what the date is six months from now, or what day of the week a date falls on.

> **TIP: ENTERING FUNCTIONS**
> As you are learning what functions are contained in which categories, it may be easier to use the functions in the Function Library group on the Formulas tab. However, if you know which function you want, you can type the equal sign, the function name, and the opening parenthesis. Then you can click Insert Function to the left of the Formula Bar to open the Function Arguments dialog box (or the Formula Builder pane on a Mac) to enter the arguments for that function.

STEP 1 Use the DAY, MONTH, and YEAR Functions

Recall that dates are stored as serial numbers. For example, 9/1/2021 is stored as 44440 and 10/1/2021 is stored as 44470. As you know, you can calculate the number of days between two dates. Therefore, when you subtract 9/1/2021 from 10/1/2021, the result is 30 days. In addition to calculating the number of days between two dates, you can use Date & Time functions to perform a variety of actions with cells containing dates. Although a cell reflects an exact date, such as 9/1/2021, the cell contains a serial number, such as 44440. If you want to extract just the month, day, or year, you can see the components (9, 1, or 2021). However, for Excel to extract the component from the serial number, specific functions must be used. For example, the owner of a wedding catering business can use date functions to extract the months from dates to identify which month had the most weddings to cater. The *DAY function* displays the day (1–31) within a given date. The *MONTH function* displays the month (1–12), where 1 is January and 12 is December, for a specific date. The *YEAR function* displays the year (such as 2021) for a specific date. Figure 7.2 illustrates two dates and the results of using the DAY, MONTH, and YEAR functions. The serial_number argument refers to the cell containing a date. If you want to enter a date directly in the argument, enclose the date in quotation marks, such as =DAY("6/30/2021").

`=DAY(serial_number)`

`=MONTH(serial_number)`

`=YEAR(serial_number)`

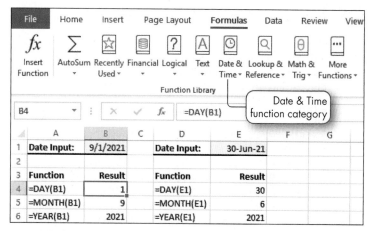

FIGURE 7.2 DAY, MONTH, and YEAR Functions

Use the DAYS and YEARFRAC Functions

A common use of date functions is to calculate the number of days between two dates. For example, a credit card company calculates the number of days from a payment due date and the actual payment date to determine how much interest or fees to charge. The ***DAYS function*** calculates the number of days between two dates using two arguments: end_date for the recent date and start_date for the older date. For example, if the end date is 9/30/2021 and the start date is 9/1/2021, the DAYS function calculates 29 days between those two dates (see the range A1:B5 in Figure 7.3). In cell E5, the DAYS function calculates 1,276 days between 1/1/2018 and 6/30/2021.

	A	B	C	D	E
1	Start Date	9/1/2021		Start Date	1/1/2018
2	End Date	9/30/2021		End Date	6/30/2021
3					
4	Function	Result		Function	Result
5	=DAYS(B2,B1)	29		=DAYS(E2,E1)	1,276
6	=YEARFRAC(B1,B2)	0.08		=YEARFRAC(E1,E2)	3.50

FIGURE 7.3 DAYS and YEARFRAC Functions

Another common use of date functions is to calculate the fraction of a year or years between two dates. The ***YEARFRAC function*** calculates the fraction of a year between two dates based on the number of whole days using the start_date and end_date arguments. In Figure 7.3, the YEARFRAC function in cell B6 calculates 0.08 or 8% of a year exists between 9/1/2021 and 9/30/2021. In cell E6, the YEARFRAC function calculates 3.5 years exist between 1/1/2018 and 6/30/2021. The DAYS and YEARFRAC functions use the same arguments (start_date and end_date), but in reverse order.

=DAYS(end_date,start_date)

=YEARFRAC(start_date,end_date)

TIP: CUSTOM DATE FORMATS

You can customize the date format in the Format Cells dialog box. Select the custom category and build the date using *m* for month, *d* for day, and *y* for year. The number of *d*s, *m*s, and *y*s indicates the resulting format. For example, use *m* for the numeric month, so that 1 represents January, and use *mmm* to display the three-letter month abbreviation, such as Jan. Use *yy* to display the last two digits of the year, such as 21, or *yyyy* to display the complete year, such as 2021.

STEP 2 Use the WEEKDAY Function

Often worksheets will display short dates, such as 11/8/2021. However, the short date format does not indicate the weekday, such as Monday. The **WEEKDAY function** identifies the day of the week and returns an integer, such as 1 for Sunday and 2 for Monday by default. The return_type argument specifies what integer is assigned to which weekday.

=WEEKDAY(serial_number,[return_type])

TIP: WEEKDAY RETURN_TYPE

When you build the WEEKDAY function in the Function Arguments dialog box, the bottom of the dialog box displays the return_type values and their descriptions, such as "for Monday=1 through Sunday=7, use 2." When you type the WEEKDAY function from scratch, a ScreenTip displays the applicable return_type codes so that you can specify what weekday is represented by a return value of 1.

Use Other Date Functions

Excel contains several other date functions that are useful. For example, you can determine that 8/1/2021 is three months from 5/1/2021, identify that 5/1/2021 is the 17th week within 2021, and calculate that there are 20 workdays in May 2021. Table 7.1 lists and describes some of these functions, and Figure 7.4 shows results of date functions.

TABLE 7.1	Date Functions	
Function	**Description**	**Syntax**
DATE function	Displays the date when provided with the numeric year, month, and date arguments; useful to display a complete date that is built from individual cells containing the year, month, and day	=DATE(year,month,day)
DAYS360 function	Calculates the number of days between two dates based on a 360-day year using 30 days per month	=DAYS360(start_date, end_date,[method])
EDATE function	Displays the serial number representing a date X number of months in the future or past from a given date; use a minus sign at the beginning of the months argument to calculate the serial number for a date in the past	=EDATE(start_date, months)
EOMONTH function	Displays the serial number representing the last day of a month that is X number of months from a given date; use a minus sign at the beginning of the months argument to calculate the serial number for a date in the past	=EOMONTH(start_date,months)
ISOWEEKNUM function	Returns the number of the week within the year for the specific date	=ISOWEEKNUM(date)
NETWORKDAYS function	Calculates the number of work days (excluding weekends) between two dates; can optionally exclude federal and state holidays as well as other nonwork days	=NETWORKDAYS(start_date,end_date,[holidays])
WORKDAY function	Calculates a serial number of a date, given a specified number of days before or after a date, excluding specified holidays	=WORKDAY(start_day, days,[holidays])

⊿	A	B	C	D
1	Start Date:	5/1/2021	1/1/2021	
2	End Date:	5/31/2021	1/1/2022	
3	Parts of Date:	5	31	2021
4				
5	Function	Result	Formatted	
6	=DATE(D3,B3,C3)	5/31/2021		
7	=DAYS360(C1,C2)	360		
8	=EDATE(B1,3)	44409	8/1/2021	
9	=EDATE(B1,-3)	44228	2/1/2021	
10	=EOMONTH(B1,3)	44439	8/31/2021	
11	=EOMONTH(B1,-3)	44255	2/28/2021	
12	=ISOWEEKNUM(B1)	17		
13	=NETWORKDAYS(B1,B2,B2)	20		
14	=WEEKDAY(B1)	7		
15	=WORKDAY(B1,90)	44442	9/3/2021	

FIGURE 7.4 Results of Date Functions

Using Advanced Logical Functions

Logical functions evaluate an expression to perform a conditional test and return a result. So far, you have used the IF logical function. Other useful logical functions include SWITCH, IFS, AND, OR, and NOT to evaluate complex conditional situations. Click Logical Functions in the Functions group on the Formulas tab to display an alphabetical list of logical functions.

STEP 3 ## Use the SWITCH Function

As you know, the IF function evaluates a logical test or condition. If the condition is true, the function provides one result; if the condition is false, it provides another result. While the IF function is easy to construct for two results, it can become complex when there are three or more results that can occur. In these situations, consider using other logical functions. The **SWITCH function** is a logical function that evaluates an expression (usually a cell containing a value or text), compares it to a list of values, and returns the first corresponding result. In other words, the SWITCH function enables you to "switch" the display of a value with a value in another cell. The value and result arguments can also contain text or cell references.

=SWITCH(expression, value1, result1, [default or value2, result2])

Note that the value and result arguments are displayed in pairs, such as value1 and result1, and then value2 and result2 to help you track which result pertains to which value. Although the SWITCH function can include up to 126 comparison results, the fewer comparisons, the easier it is to create the function. If no match exists, the function returns a #N/A! error. To prevent this error, you can include an optional default value to return if no match is found. For example, you can include "No Match" after the last result argument to display *No Match* if the expression does not match any of the values in the value arguments.

Figure 7.5 shows the SWITCH function used to switch four states into their respective geographic regions. The function evaluates the state abbreviation in cell D2. If cell D2 contains IL or OH, Midwest (cell A2) is returned. If cell D2 contains MA, Northeast (cell A3) is returned. If cell D2 contains GA, South (cell A4) is returned. If no match is found, the function returns Other Region (cell A5).

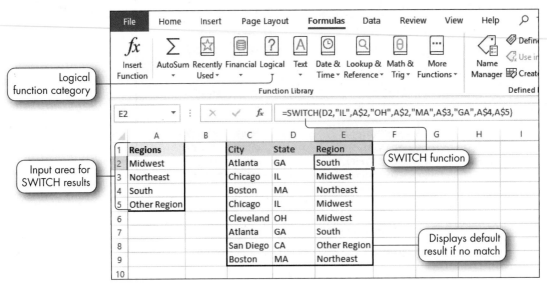

FIGURE 7.5 SWITCH Function Example

TIP: VLOOKUP FUNCTION VS. SWITCH FUNCTION

In some cases, the VLOOKUP function may be more efficient to obtain results. For example, VLOOKUP would be more efficient than SWITCH to look up state abbreviations for all 50 states. However, the SWITCH function is useful when data is not conducive to building a lookup table that is required for the VLOOKUP function.

STEP 4 · Use the IFS Function

While the SWITCH function is useful to testing one condition where multiple results exist, it does not evaluate *multiple* expressions or conditions. Therefore, you can use the ***IFS function*** to evaluate up to 127 conditions and return a result that corresponds to the first true condition. Although you can test up to 127 conditions, you should minimize the number of conditions and results. The more conditions you build into the function, the more complex the logic gets to ensure the logical tests are in the correct sequence to obtain accurate results. It is also important to note that although more than one logical test may be true, Excel executes only the value_if_true argument for the first logical test that is true.

=IFS(logical_test1,value_if_true1,logical_test2,value_if_true2, . . .)

For example, assume you want to calculate bonuses for employees based on hire date. You divided the hire dates into three timelines. If an employee was hired before 1/1/2010, the employee receives a 9% bonus. If an employee was hired between 1/1/2010 and 12/31/2019, the employee receives a 5% bonus. Finally, an employee hired on or after 1/1/2020 receives a 3% bonus

Figure 7.6 illustrates the bonus-calculation process as a flowchart. Diamonds are logical_test arguments, and rectangles are value_if_true arguments. You must include one logical test for each result. Because you have three bonus rates, you include three logical tests. Logical_test1 evaluates if the employee was hired before 1/1/2010 (C7<C$2). If that test is true, the salary is multiplied by 9% (D7*D$2). If that test is false, logical_test2 is evaluated to see if the employee was hired before 1/1/2020 (C7<C$3). If the second test is true, the salary is multiplied by 5% (D7*D$3). If the second test is false, logical_test3 is evaluated to see if the employee was hired on or after 1/1/2020 (C7>=C$4). If that test is true, the salary is multiplied by 3% (D7*D$4). Excel continues performing logical tests until it finds a true statement. If no logical tests evaluate to true, Excel displays #N/A.

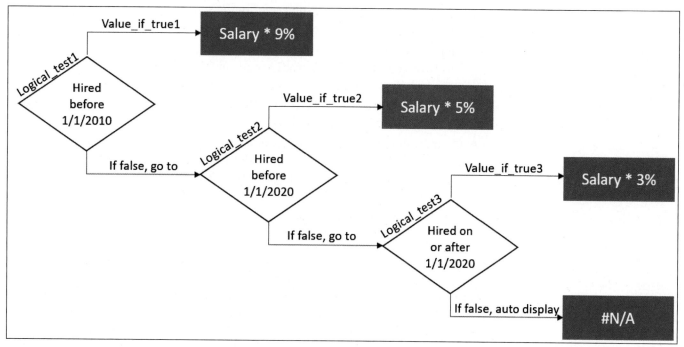

FIGURE 7.6 IFS Function Flowchart

> **TIP: CREATING A RESULT FOR FALSE**
> To avoid the default #N/A result if all logical tests are false, you can create a final logical_test argument with TRUE and a final value_if_true argument to return if all other logical tests are false. For example, you could change the bonus calculation to this to give no bonus if an employee was hired on or after 1/1/2020 using this function:
>
> =IFS(C7<C$2,D7*D$2,C7<C$3,D7*D$3,TRUE,0).

In Figure 7.7, the IFS function uses relative cell references for the hire date (cell C7) so that the cell reference will change to the next hire date when you copy the formula down the column. The formula uses mixed references for the date thresholds (C$2 and C$3) and for the bonus rates (D$2, D$3, and D$4) so that the references will point to the same rows when you copy the formulas down the column.

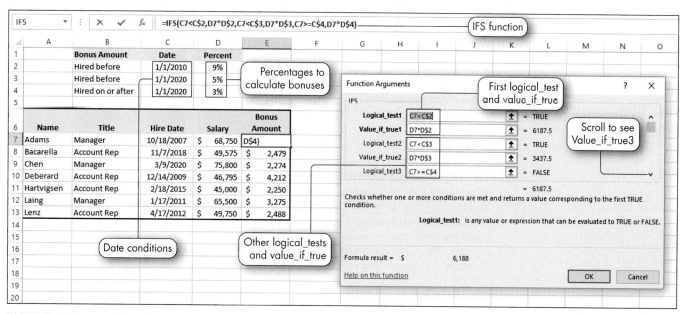

FIGURE 7.7 Results of IFS Function

The following statements explain how the bonus is calculated for the individual representatives using the IFS function (refer to Figure 7.7):

- Adams was hired on 10/18/2007. The first logical test (C7<C$2) is true. This causes Excel to execute the value_if_true1 argument D7*D$2, which is $68,750 * 9%.

- Bacarella was hired on 11/7/2018. The first logical test (C8<C$2) is false, but the second logical test (C8<C$3) is true. Excel executes the value_if_true2 argument D8*D$3, which is $49,575 * 5%.

- Chen was hired on 3/9/2020. The first logical test (C9<C$2) and second logical test (C9<C$3) are false; however, the third logical test (C9>=C$4) is true. Excel executes the value_if_true3 argument D9*D$4, which is $75,800 * 3%.

Nest IF within an IF Function

As an alternative to the IFS function, you can use a nested IF function to evaluate multiple conditions with three or more outcomes. A *nested function* is a function that is embedded or "nested" within an argument of another function. Figure 7.8 shows the bonus example using a nested IF function. The first logical_test and value_if_true arguments are identical to the first two arguments used in the IFS function. However, you must nest another IF function in the value_if_false argument to test another condition and provide multiple results if the value is true or false. With three outcomes, you build two logical tests. If both logical tests are false, the final value_if_false argument is executed. In the Formula Bar, the nested IF statement looks like this:

=IF(C7<C$2,D7*D$2,IF(C7<=C$3,D7*D$3,D7*D$4))

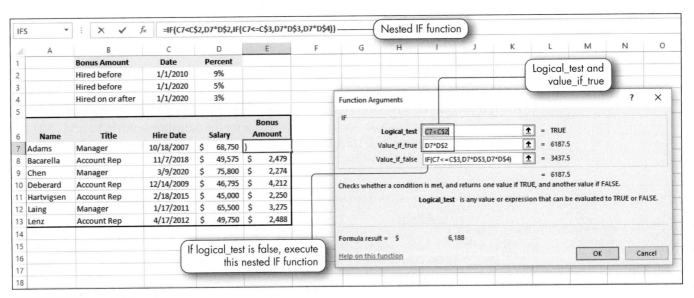

FIGURE 7.8 Nested IF Functions

> **TIP: HOW MANY LOGICAL TESTS?**
> To determine how many logical tests are required in a nested IF function, count the number of possible outcomes and subtract one. For example, if you have three possible outcomes (such as Exceeds Expectations, Meets Expectations, and Below Expectations), you need only two logical tests. The first logical test produces one outcome (Exceeds Expectations). The nested logical test produces a second outcome (Meets Expectations) if true or produces the third outcome (Below Expectations) if false. Therefore, you do not need a third logical test to produce the third outcome.

Use AND, OR, and NOT Functions

Excel contains three logical functions to determine whether certain conditions are true or false. These functions are AND, OR, and NOT. You can use these functions to test a logical condition and display either TRUE or FALSE in the cell.

Sometimes, you want to know whether the combination of two conditions is true or false. For example, you can display TRUE if an employee's title is Manager *and* if that employee earns less than $70,000. The **AND function** accepts two or more logical tests and displays TRUE if all conditions are true or FALSE if any one of the conditions is false.

=AND(logical1,logical2)

Truth tables help analyze the conditions to determine the overall result. A **truth table** is a matrix that provides the results (TRUE or FALSE) for every possible combination for an AND, OR, or NOT criteria combination. Table 7.2 illustrates the AND truth table to determine if both conditions (job title is Manager and salary is less than $70,000) are met. The truth table reveals that the AND function displays TRUE only if both conditions are true. If either condition is false, the AND function displays FALSE. Figure 7.9 shows the results of the AND function.

The results of the AND function apply the rules of the AND truth table:

- Adams is a Manager, so the first logical test B5="Manager" is true. The salary is $68,750, so the second logical test D5<$70,000 is true. Because both logical tests are true, the AND function returns TRUE in cell E5.

- Barcarella is an Account Rep, so the first logical test B6="Manager" is false. The salary is $49,575, so the second logical test D6<$70,000 is true. However, because the first logical test is false, the AND function returns FALSE in cell E6.

- Chen is a Manager so the first logical test B7="Manager" is true. The salary is $75,800, so the second logical test D7<$70,000 is false. Because the second logical test is false, the AND function returns FALSE in cell E7.

Unlike the AND function where *all* conditions must be true, the **OR function** evaluates to TRUE if *any* of the conditions are true. It returns FALSE only if all conditions are false. For example, use the OR function to identify employees who are either managers *or* who earn less than $70,000.

=OR(logical1,logical2)

TABLE 7.2 AND Truth Table

		Logical Test 2 Current Salary < $70,000	
		TRUE	FALSE
Logical Test 1 Job Title = Manager	TRUE	TRUE	FALSE
	FALSE	FALSE	FALSE

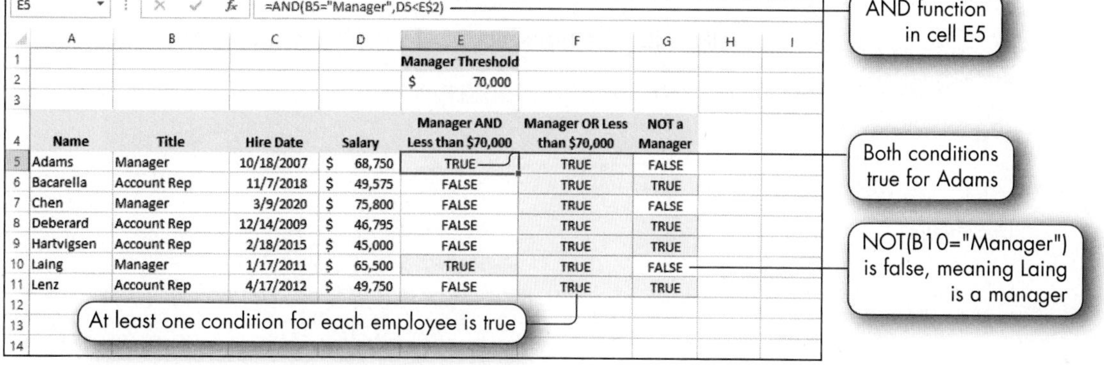

FIGURE 7.9 AND, OR, and NOT Functions

Table 7.3 illustrates the OR truth table to determine if either condition is met. The truth table reveals that the OR function displays TRUE if at least one condition is true. When both conditions are false, the OR function displays FALSE.

TABLE 7.3   OR Truth Table

| | | Logical Test 2 Current Salary < $70,000 | |
		TRUE	**FALSE**
Logical Test 1 Job Title = Manager	**TRUE**	TRUE	TRUE
	FALSE	TRUE	FALSE

In Figure 7.9, column F uses the OR function to determine if employees are either managers or earn less than $70,000. The results indicate that either condition is met for all employees. That is, all employees are either managers or earn less than $70,000. Table 7.4 displays the differences between AND and OR functions.

TABLE 7.4   AND vs. OR

	All conditions are true	At least one condition is true	At least one condition is false	All conditions are false
AND	TRUE	FALSE	FALSE	FALSE
OR	TRUE	TRUE	TRUE	FALSE

The **NOT function** evaluates only one logical test and reverses the truth of the logical test. If the logical argument is true, the NOT function returns FALSE, and if the logical argument is false, the NOT function returns TRUE. For example, in Figure 7.9 cell G5 contains =NOT(B5="Manager"). The result is FALSE because Adams is a manager. Cell G6 displays TRUE because it is true that Bacarella is not a manager.

=NOT(logical)

Nest AND, OR, and NOT Functions within an IF Function

Although you can use the AND, OR, and NOT functions individually, you can nest these functions within the logical_test argument of an IF function to make these functions more useful. For example, you can nest AND(B5="Manager",D5<E$2) in the logical_test argument to determine if an employee is (1) a manager and (2) earns less than $70,000. If both conditions are true, you can use the value_if_true argument to display the message *Due for raise*. If either condition is false, you can use the value_if_false argument to display *N/A*. The quotation marks are required when the result should display text. The complete function looks like this:

=IF(AND(B5="Manager",D5<E$2),"Due for raise","N/A")

TIP: CREATING A NESTED FUNCTION

You can create the nested function first (such as the AND function) as an individual function in a cell. After entering that function, click between the equal sign and the function name in the Formula Bar and type IF(. You can then click within the outer function name and click Insert Function to display the Function Arguments dialog box. The nested function displays as an argument within the main function (see Figure 7.10). To then dissect the arguments for the nested function, click within the nested function name in the Formula Bar and click Insert Function. The Function Arguments dialog box changes to display the arguments for the nested function.

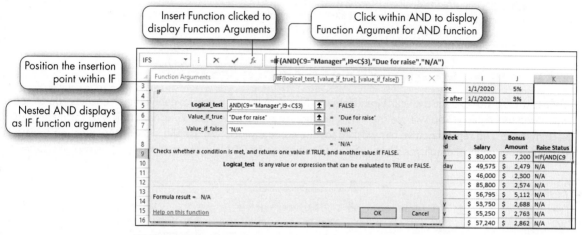

FIGURE 7.10 Toggling Between Function Arguments Dialog Boxes

Quick Concepts

1. Describe situations when you would use the MONTH and YEAR functions. *p. 436*

2. Explain why you would use the SWITCH function in combination with the WEEKDAY function in adjoining columns. *pp. 438–439*

3. Explain when you would use the IFS function instead of the IF function. *p. 440*

Hands-On Exercises

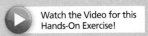

Skills covered: Use the YEAR Function • Use the YEARFRAC Function • Use the WEEKDAY Function • Use the SWITCH Function • Use the IFS Function • Nest an AND Function within an IF Function

1 Date and Logical Functions

As the Home Protection, Inc., accounting assistant, you have been asked to identify underpaid account representatives to bring their salaries up to a new minimum standard within the corporation. In addition, you want to calculate annual bonus amounts based on hire date as well as create a quick search lookup field for instant access to individual information.

STEP 1 USE THE YEAR AND YEARFRAC FUNCTIONS

Your first task is to extract the year hired from the hire date for each employee. Doing so enables you to see the year hired more easily. You will use the YEAR function to extract the year. Your next task is to calculate how long each manager and representative has worked for the company. You will use the YEARFRAC function to calculate the difference between an employee's hire date and December 31, 2021. Refer to Figure 7.11 as you complete Step 1.

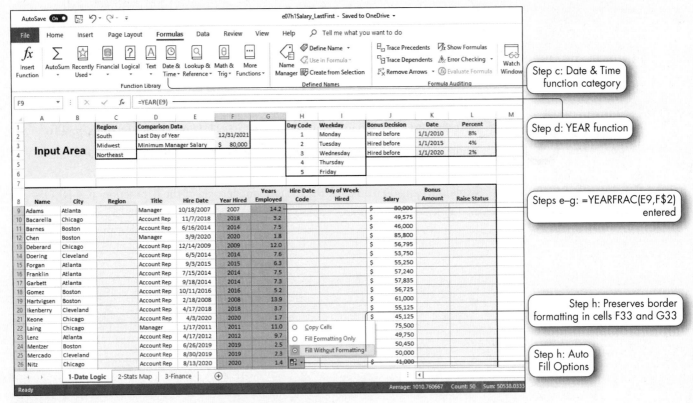

FIGURE 7.11 Years Extracted from Hire Dates and Years Worked

a. Open *e07h1Salary* and save it as **e07h1Salary_LastFirst**.

> **TROUBLESHOOTING:** If you make any major mistakes in this exercise, you can close the file, open *e07h1Salary* again, and then start this exercise over.

b. Click **cell F9** in the 1-Date Logic worksheet.

c. Click the **Formulas tab**, click **Date & Time** in the Function Library group, scroll through the list of functions, and then select **YEAR**.

The Function Arguments dialog box opens for the YEAR function.

d. Click **cell E9** to enter it in the Serial_number box within the Function Arguments dialog box and click **OK**.

MAC TROUBLESHOOTING: In the Formula Builder, you may have to click the plus sign to display additional criteria. After entering the arguments, click Done.

You selected cell E9, which contains the hire date for Adams. Although the year displays, remember that dates are stored as serial numbers. Excel extracts the year 2007 from the serial number stored in cell E9. The Formula Bar displays =YEAR(E9).

e. Click **cell G9**, type **=YEARFRAC(** and click **Insert Function** to the left of the Formula Bar.

The Function Arguments dialog box opens for the YEARFRAC function. The two required arguments are Start_date and End_date.

f. Click **cell E9** to enter it in the Start_date box.

Cell E9 contains the hire (start) date for Adams. Adams started working for the company on 10/18/2007.

g. Click in the **End_date box**, click **cell F2**, press **F4** twice, and then click **OK**.

Cell F2 contains 12/31/2021. The mixed reference F$2 keeps the reference to row 2 absolute so that it does not change when you copy the formula down the column. The formula indicates that Adams has worked at the company 14.2 years.

h. Select the **range F9:G9**, double-click the **cell G9 fill handle**, click **Auto Fill Options**, and then select **Fill Without Formatting**. Save the workbook.

Selecting Fill Without Formatting copies the functions down the columns and preserves existing formatting, such as the bottom borders in cells F33:G33.

Because Adams has the earliest hire date, he has worked at the company the longest (indicated by 14.2 years). Nitz is the newest employee, being hired on 8/13/2020.

TROUBLESHOOTING: If you used other actions instead of the Auto Fill Options after double-clicking the fill handle, you can select the range F33:G33, click the Border arrow in the Font group on the Home tab, and then select Thick Bottom Border.

You want to identify which day of the week each employee was hired. To do this, you will insert a WEEKDAY function to return an integer representing the weekday and then use the VLOOKUP function to lookup the weekday numbers and return the actual days of the week. Refer to Figure 7.12 as you complete Step 2.

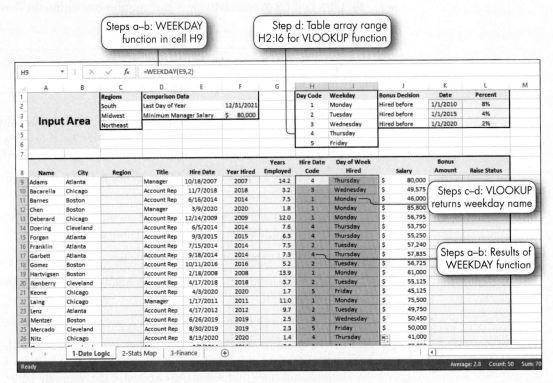

FIGURE 7.12 Weekdays Identified

a. Click **cell H9**, click the **Formulas tab**, click **Date & Time** in the Function Library group, scroll through the list of functions, and then select **WEEKDAY**.

The Function Arguments dialog box opens for the WEEKDAY function.

b. Click **cell E9** to enter it in the Serial_number box, type **2** in the Return_type box, and then click **OK**.

The Formula Bar displays =WEEKDAY(E9,2). You entered 2 as the Return_type, which is the code that designates 1 for Monday, 2 for Tuesday, and so on. The result is 4, which means Adams was hired on a Thursday. However, the function results are not useful until they are converted to the actual weekday names. Therefore, you will use the VLOOKUP function to display the actual weekday names.

c. Click **cell I9**, type **=VLOOKUP(** and then click **Insert Function**.

The Function Arguments dialog box opens so that you can enter the arguments.

d. Type **H9** in the Lookup_value box, type **H$2:I$6** in the Table_array box, type **2** in the Col_index_num box, and then click **OK**.

The Lookup_value arguments looks up the value returned by the WEEKDAY function. The Table_array argument identifies the range containing the lookup table of weekday numbers and their respective weekday names. You used mixed references in the Table_array argument so that the row numbers will not change when you copy the formula. The Col_index_num argument returns the value in the matching value in the second column of the lookup table.

e. Select the **range H9:I9**, double-click the **cell I9 fill handle**, click the **Auto Fill Options**, and then select **Fill Without Formatting**. Save the workbook.

STEP 3 USE THE SWITCH FUNCTION

Column B contains the city for each account rep and manager. However, you want to display the regions. Atlanta is in the Mid-Atlantic, Boston is in New England, and Chicago and Cleveland are both in the Midwest. You will use the SWITCH function to identify which region each city is in. Refer to Figure 7.13 as you complete Step 3.

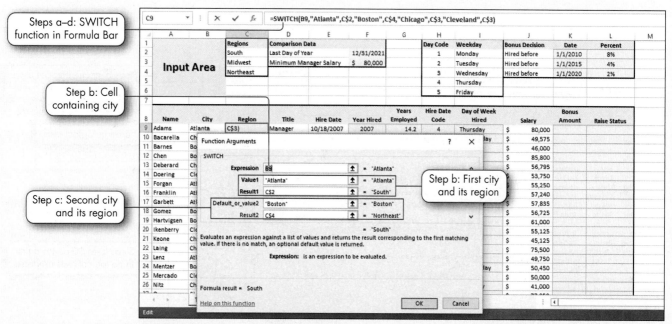

FIGURE 7.13 Regions Returned by SWITCH Function

a. Click **cell C9**, click **Logical** in the Function Library group, and then select **SWITCH**.

The Function Arguments dialog box opens for the SWITCH function.

b. Click **cell B9** to enter B9 in the Expression box, type **Atlanta** in the Value1 box, and then type **C$2** in the Result1 box.

The expression is the cell containing the city. You will switch the text Atlanta for the text Mid-Atlantic. You used a mixed cell reference to cell C2 so that the row number does not change as you copy the function later. The dialog box expands so that you can enter another value and result.

c. Type **Boston** in the Default_or_value2 box and type **C$4** in the Result2 box.

As you enter a cell reference in each Result box, the corresponding region displays on the right side of the dialog box.

d. Press **Tab**, type **Chicago** in the Default_or_value3 box, press **Tab**, and then type **C$3** in the Result3 box. Press **Tab**, type **Cleveland** in the Default_or_value4 box, press **Tab**, and then type **C$3** in the Result4 box. Click **OK**.

The SWITCH function evaluates the Atlanta in cell B9 and returns South in cell C9, indicating that Atlanta is in the South region.

e. Select **cell C9**, click **Copy** on the Home tab, select the **range C10:C33**, click the **Paste arrow**, and then select **Formulas**. Press **Esc**. Save the workbook.

In Steps 1 and 2, you double-clicked the fill handle to copy the functions down the column and selected the Fill Without Formatting option to preserve the bottom borders on row 33. This time, you copied the function and used Paste Formulas to paste only the formulas to preserve the borders. Note that either method copies a function down a column and preserves the existing formatting in the destination cells.

Your next task is to calculate the annual bonus amount for each employee. The company uses a tiered bonus system that awards a specific percentage of salary based on hire date. Employees hired before 1/1/2010 receive 8%. Employees hired before 1/1/2020 receive 4%, and employees that were hired on or after 1/1/2020 receive 2%. You will use the IFS function to calculate each employee's bonus. Refer to Figure 7.14 as you complete Step 4.

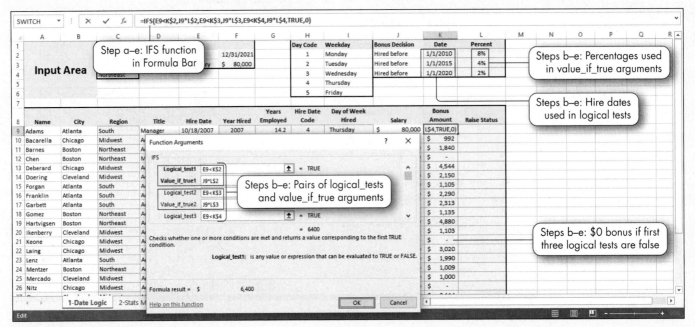

FIGURE 7.14 Bonuses Calculated

a. Click **cell K9**, type **=IFS(** and then click **Insert Function**.

b. Type **E9<K$2** in the Logical_test1 box.

The logical test compares the hire date to the first bonus threshold, 1/1/2010. You used relative cell references for the employee's hire date (cell E9) so that it will change when you copy the function down the column. You used a mixed reference for the threshold date (cell K$2) to ensure the row number does not change as you copy the function.

c. Type **J9*L$2** in the Value_if_true1 box.

If the hire date is before 1/1/2010, Excel will multiply the salary by the 8% bonus rate stored in cell L2. If the logical test is false, the next logical test is evaluated.

d. Type **E9<K$3** in the Logical_test2 box and type **J9*L$3** in the Value_if_true2 box.

If the first logical test is false, Excel will evaluate the second logical test. If the hire date is before 1/1/2015, Excel multiplies the salary by the 4% bonus rate stored in cell L3.

e. Type **E9<K$4** in the Logical_test3 box and type **J9*L$4** in the Value_if_true3 box.

If the second logical test is false, Excel will evaluate the third logical test. If the hire date is before 1/1/2020, Excel multiplies the salary by the 2% bonus rate stored in cell L4.

f. Type **TRUE** in the Logical_test4 box, type **0** in the Value_if_true4 box, and then click **OK**.

Because the IFS function does not have an Else argument, you must create a "catch all" logical test for all other conditions not addressed by the logical_tests. In this case, you type TRUE and give no bonus if the employee was hired on or after 1/1/2020.

The IFS function returns $6,400. Because Adams was hired before 1/1/2010, she qualifies for the 8% bonus rate. This is calculated by multiplying the current salary, $80,000 (cell J9), by the bonus percentage rate of 8% (cell L2).

g. Click **Copy** on the Home tab, select the **range K10:K33**, click the **Paste arrow**, and then select **Formulas**. Press **Esc**. Save the workbook.

The copied functions calculate the respective bonus based on each employee's hire date. Since Keone was hired after 1/1/2020, that employee did not get a bonus, so the Value_if_true4 argument returns 0.

STEP 5 NEST AN AND FUNCTION WITHIN AN IF FUNCTION

The HR Director recommends that the company pay managers at least $80,000. You will nest an AND function inside an IF function to determine which managers should receive pay raises based on their current salary level. The salary threshold is stored in cell F3 in the 1-Date Logic worksheet. Refer to Figure 7.15 as you complete Step 5.

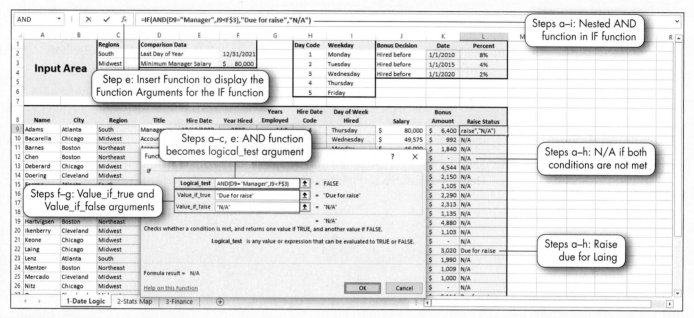

FIGURE 7.15 Weekdays Identified

a. Click **cell L9**, click the **Formulas tab**, click **Logical** in the Function Library group, and then select **AND**.

b. Type **D9="Manager"** in the Logical1 box.

The first logical test is to evaluate if the job title in cell D9 is Manager. You must enclose the text with quotation marks. The logical test evaluates to TRUE, as indicated to the right side of the Logical1 argument box.

c. Type **J9<F$3** in the Logical2 box and click **OK**.

The second logical test evaluates if the salary is less than $80,000. It evaluates to FALSE, as indicated to the right side of the argument box. Because the second logical test is false, the AND function returns FALSE. Both conditions must be true for the AND function to return TRUE. You used a relative reference to cell J9 so that it changes to the next salary and a mixed reference to F$3 so that the row number does not change when you copy the function down the column.

> **TROUBLESHOOTING:** Do not make cells D9 or J9 absolute or mixed. If you do, the function will use the incorrect cell references when you copy the function down the column.

d. Double-click the **cell L9 fill handle**, click **Auto Fill Options**, and then select **Fill Without Formatting**.

Most of the function results display FALSE down the column. The AND function displays TRUE in cells L22 and L27 for Laing and Omweg because both the title is Manager *and* the salary is less than $80,000.

e. Click **cell L9**, click after the equal sign in the Formula Bar, type **IF(** and click between the *I* and *F* in the Formula Bar, and then click **Insert Function**.

The Function Arguments dialog box opens for the IF function. The original AND function becomes the Logical_test argument for the IF function.

f. Type **Due for raise** in the Value_if_true box.

If both conditions specified in the AND function are true, the employee is eligible for a raise.

g. Type **N/A** in the Value_if_false box and click **OK**.

h. Double-click the **cell L9 fill handle**, click **Auto Fill Options**, and then select **Fill Without Formatting**.

The nested IF function evaluates the employee's title and salary. If both arguments in the AND function are true, then *Due for raise* is displayed; if not, *N/A* is displayed. Adams and Chen are managers; however, their salaries are at least $80,000. Laing and Omweg are managers *and* earn less than $80,000, so they are due for a raise.

i. Save the workbook. Keep the workbook open if you plan to continue with the next Hands-On Exercise. If not, close the workbook and exit Excel.

Conditional Math and Statistical Functions

Every day, you rely on statistics to make routine decisions. When you purchase a car, you compare the average miles per gallon (MPG) among several vehicles. The automobile manufacturer conducted multiple test drives, recorded the MPG under various driving conditions, and then calculated the MPG statistic based on average performance. Statistics involve analyzing a collection of data and making inferences to draw conclusions about a dataset.

You have already learned to use the COUNT, SUM, AVERAGE, MAX, and MIN statistical functions. However, at times you will want to calculate a statistic based on a condition. Excel's math and statistical function categories contain functions that perform conditional calculations, such as calculating a total only when a specific circumstance or set of circumstances exists.

In this section, you will use math and statistical functions to perform conditional statistical calculations. In addition, you will learn how to insert a map to represent aggregated data by geographic region.

Using Functions to Evaluate One Condition

When you use COUNT, SUM, and AVERAGE functions, Excel calculates the respective number of values, total, or the mathematical average, respectively, in the specified range. The math and statistical function categories contain related functions—COUNTIF, SUMIF, and AVERAGEIF—that perform similar calculations but use criteria to extract the values to count, total, or average. For example, you can count the number of times a city appears in a customer list or total the salaries for managers. A benefit of using these functions is that you do not have to sort a dataset to perform the calculations based on groups. Using these functions enables you to preserve the organization of the dataset.

Use More Functions in the Function Library and point to Statistical to insert the COUNTIF and AVERAGEIF functions. Use Math & Trig to select the SUMIF function.

When entering criteria that contain text or a date, you must surround the criteria with quotation marks, such as "Account Rep" or "5/10/2021". If you enter criteria using the Function Argument box, Excel automatically adds quotation marks around the text or date. If you type the function directly in the cell or in the Formula Bar, you must type the quotation marks.

Do not use quotation marks for an individual value, such as an exact match for the value 25, in the criteria argument. If you want to build a criterion with a comparison to a value, use quotation marks around the entire comparison, such as "<25". If you want to build a comparison to a value that is stored in a cell, build the comparison like this: "<"&C5. Include the ampersand sign (&) between the quotation mark and the cell reference.

TIP: WILDCARDS IN CONDITIONS

The criteria argument is not case sensitive. Account Rep, account rep, or ACCOUNT REP will produce the same results. You can use wildcards in the criteria argument. Use the question mark to match a single character, such as using the criterion O? to match the state abbreviations that start with the letter O (OH, OK, and OR) or use the criterion ?L to match the state abbreviations that end with the letter L (AL, FL, and IL). Use an asterisk to match any number of characters, such as Account* to match Account Rep, Account Manager, and Accounts Payable. The criterion *Rep will match Senior Rep and Account Rep. The criterion *Account* will match New Accounts Director and Account Manager.

STEP 1 ▶ Use the COUNTIF Function

The ***COUNTIF function*** is a statistical function, similar to the COUNT function except that it counts the number of cells in a range that meet a specified condition. In Figure 7.16, cell G2 contains =COUNTIF(B2:B8,"Account Rep") to count the number of employees with the Account Rep title, which is four.

=COUNTIF(range,criteria)

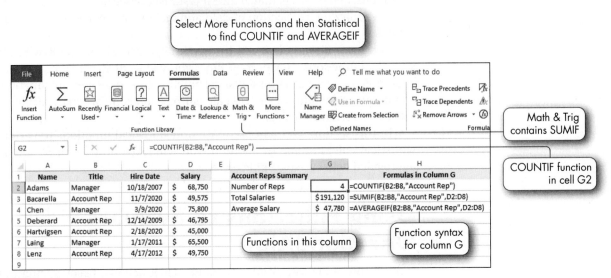

FIGURE 7.16 Functions for One Condition

The COUNTIF function contains two arguments: range and criteria. The range argument specifies the range of cells you want to evaluate to see if the cell contents meet a condition. In Figure 7.16 the range contains the job titles. The criteria argument specifies the condition to be met. In this case, the criteria argument contains the text Account Rep. The function counts only cells in the range that contain Account Rep.

STEP 2 ▶ Use the SUMIF Function

The ***SUMIF function*** is a statistical function similar to the SUM function except that it calculates the total of values in a range that meet a specified condition. For example, use the SUMIF function to calculate the total salaries for all Account Reps.

=SUMIF(range,criteria,sum_range)

Similar to the COUNTIF function, the SUMIF function contains range and criteria arguments, the range of cells that will be evaluated, and the specific condition, respectively. In addition, the SUMIF function contains a third argument, sum_range, which specifies the range containing the values to add if the condition is met. In Figure 7.16, cell G3 contains the function =SUMIF(B2:B8,"Account Rep",D2:D8). The range argument is B2:B8 that contains job titles. The criteria for that range is Account Rep. Within the Title range, Excel identifies cells containing Account Rep and uses the sum_range argument to sum the respective salaries in the range D2:D8. The total value of salaries for Account Reps is $191,120.

STEP 3 ▶ Use the AVERAGEIF Function

The ***AVERAGEIF function*** calculates the average, or arithmetic mean, of all cells in a range that meet a specified condition. For example, use the AVERAGEIF function to calculate the average salary for only the Account Reps.

=AVERAGEIF(range,criteria,average_range)

The AVERAGEIF function contains three required arguments: range, criteria, and average_range. The range and criteria arguments have the same meanings as the same arguments in the COUNTIF and SUMIF functions. The average_range argument specifies the range containing values that you want to average if the condition is met. In Figure 7.16, cell G4 contains the AVERAGEIF function. The function calculates the average salary in the range D2:D8 when the job title in the range B2:B8 is Account Rep.

> **TIP: REFERENCING THE INPUT RANGE**
> When using the SUMIF, AVERAGEIF, and COUNTIF functions, you can create an input range to specify the condition and simply use a cell reference as the criteria argument in the function. This enables the user the flexibility to change the criteria and receive instant calculation updates.

Using Functions to Evaluate Multiple Conditions

Whereas the previously described functions enable you to perform conditional calculations, they can address only a single condition. Similar math and statistical functions enable you to specify more than one condition: COUNTIFS, SUMIFS, AVERAGEIFS, MAXIFS, and MINIFS.

STEP 4 Use the COUNTIFS, SUMIFS, and AVERAGEIFS Functions

The **COUNTIFS function** counts the number of cells in a range that meet multiple criteria. In Figure 7.17, cell G2 contains =COUNTIFS(B2:B8,"Account Rep",C2:C8,">1/1/2020"). This function counts the number of Account Reps hired after 1/1/2020. Two Account Reps were hired after 1/1/2020.

=COUNTIFS(criteria_range1,criteria1,criteria_range2,criteria2 . . .)

The COUNTIFS function contains at least four arguments: two ranges and their respective criteria. Each criteria_range argument specifies a range of cells that is evaluated based on the criteria in the respective criteria argument. For example, criteria_range1 uses criteria1, criteria_range2 uses criteria2, and so on.

The **SUMIFS function** calculates the total value of cells in a range that meet multiple criteria. In Figure 7.17, cell G3 contains =SUMIFS(D2:D8,B2:B8,"Account Rep",C2:C8,">1/1/2020"). This function sums the salaries for Account Reps hired after 1/1/2020. The sum of the salaries for the Account Reps who were hired after 1/1/2020 is $94,575.

=SUMIFS(sum_range,criteria_range1,criteria1,criteria_range2,criteria2 . . .)

G2	COUNTIFS function in cell G2		=COUNTIFS(B2:B8,"Account Rep",C2:C8,">1/1/2020")				
	Name	**Title**	**Hire Date**	**Salary**	**Account Reps Hired After 1/1/2015**	**G**	**Formulas in Column G**
1					**Account Reps Hired After 1/1/2015**		**Formulas in Column G**
2	Adams	Manager	10/18/2007	$ 68,750	Number of Account Reps	2	=COUNTIFS(B2:B8,"Account Rep",C2:C8,">1/1/2020")
3	Bacarella	Account Rep	11/7/2020	$ 49,575	Total Salaries	$ 94,575	=SUMIFS(D2:D8,B2:B8,"Account Rep",C2:C8,">1/1/2020")
4	Chen	Manager	3/9/2020	$ 75,800	Average Salary	$ 47,288	=AVERAGEIFS(D2:D8,B2:B8,"Account Rep",C2:C8,">1/1/2020")
5	Deberard	Account Rep	12/14/2009	$ 46,795	Highest Salary	$ 49,575	=MAXIFS(D2:D8,B2:B8,"Account Rep",C2:C8,">1/1/2020")
6	Hartvigsen	Account Rep	2/18/2020	$ 45,000	Lowest Salary	$ 45,000	=MINIFS(D2:D8,B2:B8,"Account Rep",C2:C8,">1/1/2020")
7	Laing	Manager	1/17/2011	$ 65,500			
8	Lenz	Account Rep	4/17/2012	$ 49,750			
9						Function results in this column	Function syntax for column G
10				Title and Hire Date columns used in the functions			
11							

FIGURE 7.17 Functions for Multiple Conditions

The SUMIFS function contains at least five arguments: sum_range, criteria_range1, criteria1, criteria_range2, and criteria2. The sum_range argument specifies the range containing the values to add when all conditions are met. It is important to note that in the SUMIF function, the sum_range is the last argument, whereas in the SUMIFS function, the sum_range is the first argument.

The ***AVERAGEIFS function*** calculates the average value of cells in a range that meet multiple criteria. In Figure 7.17, cell G4 contains =AVERAGEIFS(D2:D8,B2:B8, "Account Rep",C2:C8,">1/1/2020"). This function calculates the average salary for Account Reps hired after 1/1/2020. The average salary for Account Reps who were hired after 1/1/2020 is $47,288.

=AVERAGEIFS(average_range,criteria_range1,criteria1,criteria_range2,criteria2 . . .)

The AVERAGEIFS function contains at least five arguments. The average_range argument specifies the range of cells containing values that will be averaged when all conditions are met. Similar to the SUMIFS function where the sum_range is the last argument, the average_range is the last argument in the AVERAGEIFS function.

> **TIP: ADDITIONAL CRITERIA**
> Whereas the syntax shows only two criteria for SUMIFS, AVERAGEIFS, and COUNTIFS, you can continue adding criteria ranges and criteria. If you type the function in a cell, separate the criteria ranges and criteria with commas. If you use the Function Arguments dialog box, it expands to display another Criteria box as you enter data in existing boxes, or you can press Tab within the dialog box to see additional criteria ranges and criteria boxes. You can enter up to 127 criteria to be evaluated.

Use the MAXIFS and MINIFS Functions

Similar to the SUMIFS function, the MAXIFS and MINIFS functions are also used when you want to perform a calculation when multiple conditions exist. The ***MAXIFS function*** returns the highest value in a range that meet multiple criteria. In Figure 7.17, cell G5 contains =MAXIFS(D2:D8,B2:B8,"Account Rep",C2:C8,">1/1/2020"). The highest salary for Account Reps hired after 1/1/2020 is $49,575. The MAXIFS function contains at least five arguments. The max_range argument specifies the range of cells containing values to identify the highest value when all conditions are met. The criteria_range and criteria arguments have the same meaning as these arguments for the other IFS functions.

=MAXIFS(max_range,criteria_range1,criteria1,criteria_range2,criteria2 . . .)

The ***MINIFS function*** returns the lowest value in a range that meet multiple criteria. In Figure 7.17, cell G6 contains =MINIFS(D2:D8,B2:B8,"Account Rep",C2:C8,">1/1/2020"). The lowest salary for Account Reps hired after 1/1/2020 is $45,000. The MINIFS function contains at least five arguments. The min_range argument specifies the range of cells containing values to identify the lowest value when all conditions are met. The criteria_range and criteria arguments have the same meaning as these arguments for the other IFS functions.

=MINIFS(min_range,criteria_range1,criteria1,criteria_range2,criteria2 . . .)

STEP 5 Inserting a Map

After inserting conditional functions to aggregate data in a summary range in a worksheet, you can then use that aggregated data for further analysis. For example, you can create different types of charts depending on the data. In addition, if the aggregated data contains geographic regions, you can create a ***map chart*** to compare values across those geographical regions. To use a map chart, the dataset must contain countries, states, counties, or postal codes. In addition, the dataset should contain aggregated data and not multiple data points for the same category. The map chart is useful to plot aggregated data, such as data containing conditional statistical functions. The Insert Map Chart command is in the Charts group on the Insert tab. Figure 7.18 shows a map created from the range A1:B10. Each state abbreviation is listed only once. The map applies fill color to the different states based on the value for each state. The darker the fill color, the higher the value. In this case, California has the darkest fill color, indicating it has the highest sales, whereas Florida has the lightest fill color because it has the lowest sales.

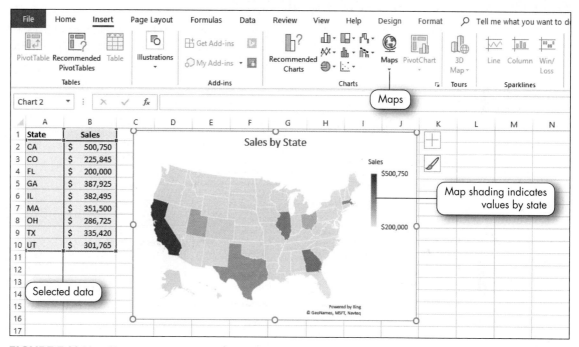

FIGURE 7.18 Map Chart

After you insert a map, you can customize it like a chart. You can change the chart (map) title, adjust the size and width, select the location, and change a data series color. By default, the chart may include a large geographic region, such as the entire United States, even if only a few states have data. You can display the Format Data Series task pane and change the Map area to Only regions with data.

Quick Concepts

4. Explain when you use quotation marks around the criteria argument in the COUNTIF function and how you can avoid using quotation marks. ***p. 453***

5. Explain when you would use SUMIFS instead of SUMIF. ***p. 455***

6. Describe the type of data required to create a map in Excel. ***p. 457***

Hands-On Exercises

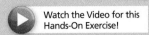

Skills covered: Use the
COUNTIF Function • Use
the SUMIF Function • Use the
AVERAGEIF Function • Use the
COUNTIFS Function • Use
the SUMIFS Function • Use the
AVERAGEIFS Function • Use
the MAXIFS Function • Use the
MINIFS Function • Insert a Map

2 Conditional Math and Statistical Functions

You want to calculate summary statistics for the Home Protection, Inc., employees. You want to identify the number of employees and total payroll by state, and average salaries. Then you will turn your attention to focus on Account Reps who have been with the company the longest. Finally, you will depict summary data in a map.

STEP 1 USE THE COUNTIF FUNCTION

You want to calculate the number of employees in each state. You set up a worksheet with a summary section to calculate statistics by states, indicated by the state abbreviations. This will require the use of the COUNTIF function. Refer to Figure 7.19 as you complete Step 1.

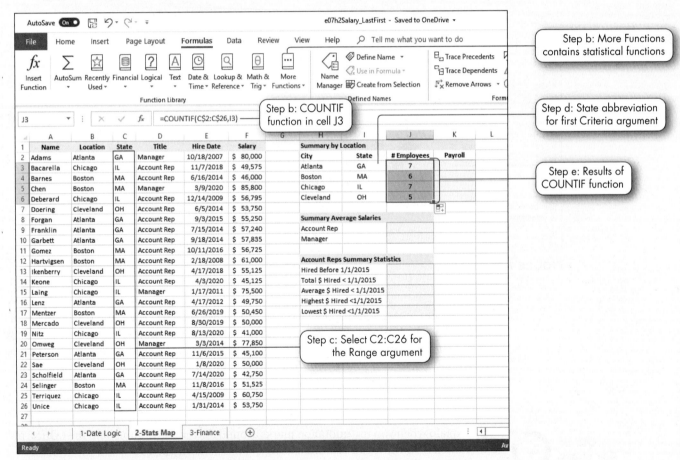

FIGURE 7.19 Number of Employees by State

    a. Open *e07h1Salary_LastFirst* if you closed it at the end of Hands-On Exercise 1 and save it as **e07h2Salary_LastFirst**, changing h1 to h2. Click the **2-Stats Map sheet tab**.

b. Click **cell J3**, click the **Formulas tab**, click **More Functions** in the Function Library group on the Formulas tab, point to **Statistical**, scroll through the list, and then select **COUNTIF**.

Cell J3 is the cell in which you want to calculate the total number of employees in Georgia. The Function Arguments dialog box opens so that you can enter the range and criteria arguments.

c. Select the **range C2:C26** to enter it in the Range box. Press **F4** twice.

The range C$2:C$26 contains the states to be counted. You made the range a mixed reference so that the rows do not change as you copy the function down the column.

d. Click in the **Criteria box**, click **cell I3** to enter it, and then click **OK**.

Because cell I3 contains the state abbreviation, you used the cell reference rather than typing the abbreviation in the Criteria box. Keep the relative reference so that it will change to the correct cell reference as you copy the function down the column. The function results indicate that seven employees work in Georgia.

e. Double-click the **cell J3 fill handle** to copy the function to the **range J4:J6**. Save the workbook.

In the copied functions, the criteria argument reflects the state abbreviation for the respective row. By using the cell reference in the original function instead of text, you do not have to manually type state abbreviations to enter the remaining COUNTIF functions.

STEP 2 USE THE SUMIF FUNCTION

Next, you want to calculate the total payroll by summing employee salaries in each state using the SUMIF function. Refer to Figure 7.20 as you complete Step 2.

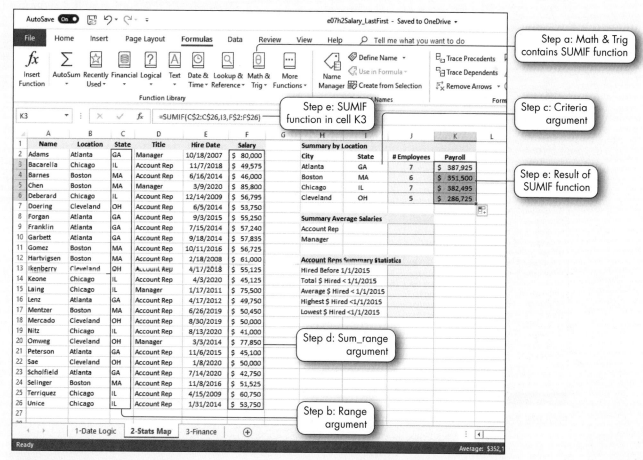

FIGURE 7.20 Total Payroll by State

a. Click **cell K3** in the 2-Stats Map worksheet, click **Math & Trig** in the Function Library group, and then select **SUMIF**.

The Function Arguments dialog box opens so that you can enter the range, criteria, and sum_range arguments.

b. Select the **range C2:C26** to enter it in the Range box. Press **F4** twice.

The range C$2:C$26 contains the states to be used to apply the criterion.

c. Click in the **Criteria box** and click **cell I3**.

Cell I3 contains the criterion for the first state.

d. Click in the **Sum_range box**, select the **range F2:F26**, press **F4** twice, and then click **OK**.

The range F2:F26 contains the salaries to be used to calculate total salaries by state. The total payroll is $387,925 for Georgia employees.

e. Double-click the **cell K3 fill handle** to copy the function to the **range K4:K6**. Save the workbook.

STEP 3 ▸ **USE THE AVERAGEIF FUNCTION**

You now want to focus on average salaries by job title. You will calculate the average account rep salary and the average manager salary using the AVERAGEIF function. Refer to Figure 7.21 as you complete Step 3.

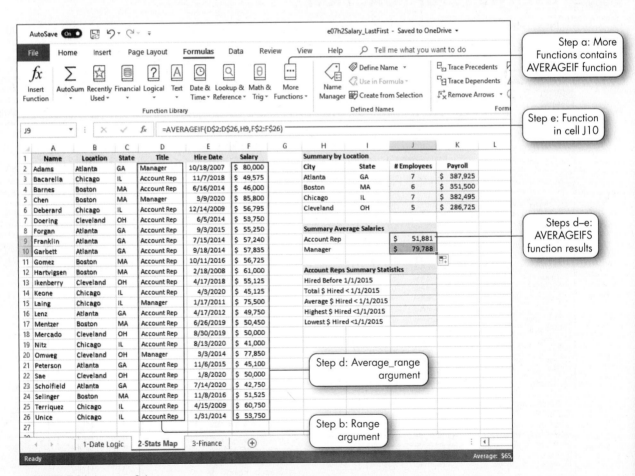

FIGURE 7.21 Average Salaries

a. Click **cell J9** in the 2-Stats Map worksheet, click **More Functions** in the Function Library group, point to **Statistical**, and then select **AVERAGEIF**.

The Function Arguments dialog box opens so that you can enter the range, criteria, and average_range arguments.

b. Select the **range D2:D26** to enter it in the Range box. Press **F4** twice.

The range D$2:D$26 contains the job titles to be used to apply the criterion.

c. Click in the **Criteria box** and click **cell H9**.

Cell H9 contains the criterion, Account Rep.

d. Click in the **Average_range box**, select the **range F2:F26**, press **F4** twice, and then click **OK**.

The average salary for Account Reps is $51,881.

e. Drag the **cell J9 fill handle** to copy the function to **cell J10**. Save the workbook.

STEP 4 USE THE COUNTIFS, SUMIFS, AVERAGEIFS, MAXIFS, AND MINIFS FUNCTIONS

Now you want to focus on the summarizing data for Account Reps hired before 1/1/2015. Specifically, you want to calculate the total number of Account Reps, total salary payroll, average salary, highest salary, and lowest salary. Because each of these calculations requires two criteria, you will use the SUMIFS, AVERAGEIFS, COUNTIFS, MAXIFS, and MINIFS functions. Refer to Figure 7.22 as you complete Step 4.

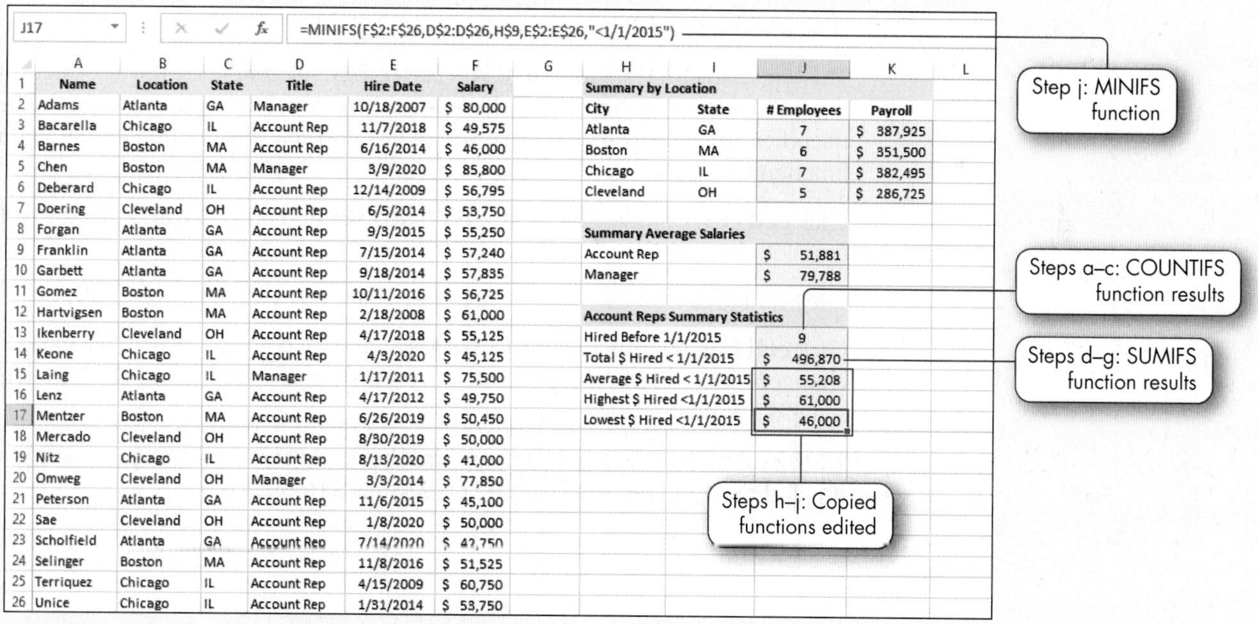

J17 : fx =MINIFS(F$2:F$26,D$2:D$26,H$9,E$2:E$26,"<1/1/2015")

	A	B	C	D	E	F	G	H	I	J	K	L
1	Name	Location	State	Title	Hire Date	Salary		Summary by Location				
2	Adams	Atlanta	GA	Manager	10/18/2007	$ 80,000		City	State	# Employees	Payroll	
3	Bacarella	Chicago	IL	Account Rep	11/7/2018	$ 49,575		Atlanta	GA	7	$ 387,925	
4	Barnes	Boston	MA	Account Rep	6/16/2014	$ 46,000		Boston	MA	6	$ 351,500	
5	Chen	Boston	MA	Manager	3/9/2020	$ 85,800		Chicago	IL	7	$ 382,495	
6	Deberard	Chicago	IL	Account Rep	12/14/2009	$ 56,795		Cleveland	OH	5	$ 286,725	
7	Doering	Cleveland	OH	Account Rep	6/5/2014	$ 53,750						
8	Forgan	Atlanta	GA	Account Rep	9/3/2015	$ 55,250		Summary Average Salaries				
9	Franklin	Atlanta	GA	Account Rep	7/15/2014	$ 57,240		Account Rep		$ 51,881		
10	Garbett	Atlanta	GA	Account Rep	9/18/2014	$ 57,835		Manager		$ 79,788		
11	Gomez	Boston	MA	Account Rep	10/11/2016	$ 56,725						
12	Hartvigsen	Boston	MA	Account Rep	2/18/2008	$ 61,000		Account Reps Summary Statistics				
13	Ikenberry	Cleveland	OH	Account Rep	4/17/2018	$ 55,125		Hired Before 1/1/2015		9		
14	Keone	Chicago	IL	Account Rep	4/3/2020	$ 45,125		Total $ Hired < 1/1/2015		$ 496,870		
15	Laing	Chicago	IL	Manager	1/17/2011	$ 75,500		Average $ Hired < 1/1/2015		$ 55,208		
16	Lenz	Atlanta	GA	Account Rep	4/17/2012	$ 49,750		Highest $ Hired <1/1/2015		$ 61,000		
17	Mentzer	Boston	MA	Account Rep	6/26/2019	$ 50,450		Lowest $ Hired <1/1/2015		$ 46,000		
18	Mercado	Cleveland	OH	Account Rep	8/30/2019	$ 50,000						
19	Nitz	Chicago	IL	Account Rep	8/13/2020	$ 41,000						
20	Omweg	Cleveland	OH	Manager	3/3/2014	$ 77,850						
21	Peterson	Atlanta	GA	Account Rep	11/6/2015	$ 45,100						
22	Sae	Cleveland	OH	Account Rep	1/8/2020	$ 50,000						
23	Scholfield	Atlanta	GA	Account Rep	7/14/2020	$ 42,750						
24	Selinger	Boston	MA	Account Rep	11/8/2016	$ 51,525						
25	Terriquez	Chicago	IL	Account Rep	4/15/2009	$ 60,750						
26	Unice	Chicago	IL	Account Rep	1/31/2014	$ 53,750						

Step j: MINIFS function

Steps a–c: COUNTIFS function results

Steps d–g: SUMIFS function results

Steps h–j: Copied functions edited

FIGURE 7.22 Functions for Multiple Conditions

a. Click **cell J13**, click **More Functions** and point to **Statistical** in the Function Library group, scroll through the list, and then select **COUNTIFS**.

b. Type **D2:D26** in the Criteria_range1 box, click in the **Criteria1 box**, and then click **cell H9**.

Similar to the COUNTIF function, COUNTIFS counts data points in a range that match specified criteria. In this step the first criterion is Account Rep, which is stored in cell H9.

c. Click in the **Criteria_range2 box** and type **E2:E26**. Type **<1/1/2015** in the Criteria2 box and click **OK**.

The function returns 9, the total number of Account Reps hired before 1/1/2015, by using the criteria Account Rep and <1/1/2015 to filter the data ranges D2:D26 and E2:E26.

d. Click **cell J14**, click **Math & Trig** in the Function Library group, and then select **SUMIFS**.

e. Type **F$2:F$26** in the Sum_range box.

The range F2:F26 is the range containing the salaries that you want to sum. Use mixed references in the Sum_range argument so that you can copy the function.

f. Type **D$2:D$26** in the Criteria_range1 box, type **H$9** in the Criteria1 box.

The range D2:D26 is the first criteria range, and Account Rep is the text you want to use as a filter for that range. Use mixed references in the Criteria_range1 and Criteria1 arguments so that you can copy the function.

g. Type **E$2:E$26** in the Criteria_range2 box, type **<1/1/2015** in the Criteria2 box, and then click **OK**.

The range E2:E26 is the second criteria range to apply the condition of hire dates before 1/1/2015. The total payroll for Account Reps hired before 1/1/2015 is $496,870.

TROUBLESHOOTING: If you misspell criterion text, the results will display 0. Always check the criterion text to make sure it matches text in the respective column.

h. Drag the **cell J14 fill handle** to the **range J15:J17**.

This copies the SUMIFS function. You used mixed references for the arguments in the original function so that you could copy the function. The arguments are the same for the other functions you want, so it will be faster to edit the function names in the copied functions.

i. Click **cell J15**. Change SUMIFS to **AVERAGEIFS** and press **Enter**. Keep the rest of the function the same.

The average payroll for Account Reps hired before 1/1/2015 is $55,208.

j. Click **cell J16**, change SUMIFS to **MAXIFS**, and then press **Enter**. Click **cell J17**, and change SUMIFS to **MINIFS**, and then press **Enter**. Keep the rest of the function the same. Save the workbook.

The highest salary for Account Reps hired before 1/1/2015 is $61,000. The lowest salary for Account Reps hired before 1/1/2015 is $46,000.

STEP 5 INSERT A MAP

Finally, you want to insert a map to indicate the total payroll by state. You will use the summary information generated from the SUMIF functions in the range K2:K6. Refer to Figure 7.23 as you complete Step 5.

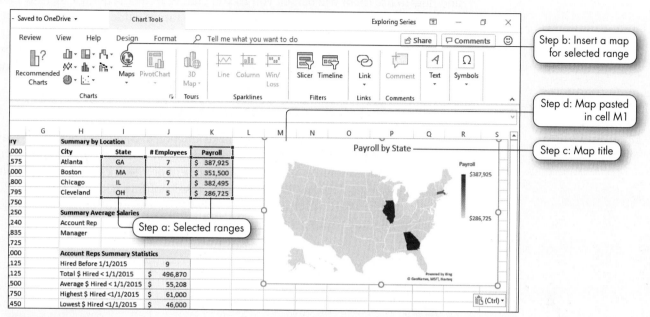

FIGURE 7.23 Map

a. Use **Ctrl** to select the non-adjacent **ranges I2:I6** and **K2:K6** in the 2-Stats Map worksheet.

b. Click the **Insert tab**, click **Maps** in the Charts group, and then select **Filled Map**.

A map is inserted in the worksheet. The fill colors range from dark (highest salary) to light blue (lowest salary) for the four states.

c. Click the **chart title**, type **Payroll by State**, and then click the **chart area**.

d. Cut the map chart, click **cell M1**, and then click **Paste**.

e. Save the workbook. Keep the workbook open if you plan to continue with the next Hands-On Exercise. If not, close the workbook, and exit Excel.

Financial Functions

Excel's financial functions are helpful for business financial analysts and for you in your personal financial management. Knowing what different financial functions can calculate and how to use them will benefit you as you plan retirement savings, identify best rates to obtain your financial goals, and evaluate how future values of different investments compare with today's values.

In this section, you will learn how to prepare a loan amortization table using financial functions. In addition, you will use other financial functions to complete investment analyses.

Using Financial Functions

Previously, you worked with the PMT financial function to calculate the monthly payment of a loan. The Financial category includes a variety of functions to calculate details for investments. For example, you can calculate present or future values, rates, and number of payment periods. Figure 7.24 displays the results of financial functions in column B and shows the function syntax in column C. Click Financial in the Function Library group on the Formulas tab to display a list of financial functions.

	A	B	C	D
1		**Present Value**		
2	Lump Sum	$1,000,000.00		
3	Present Value	$1,246,221.03	=PV(B6,B5,-B4)	
4	Per Year	$100,000.00		
5	No. of Years	20		
6	Rate	5%		
7				
8		**Future Value**		
9	Yearly Contribution	$3,000.00		
10	No. of Years	40		
11	APR	7%		
12	Future Value	$598,905.34	=FV(B11,B10,-B9)	
13	Total Contributed	$120,000.00	=B9*B10	
14	Interest	$478,905.34	=B12-B13	
15				
16		**Net Present Value**		
17	Invest End of Year	$3,000.00		
18	Yearly Income	$1,200.00		
19	Rate	3%		
20	Net Present Value	$382.85	=NPV(B19,-B17,B18,B18,B18)	
21				

FIGURE 7.24 Financial Functions

Recall that the PMT function uses the rate, nper, and pv arguments. These arguments are also used in many other financial functions that will be discussed in this section. In addition, the PMT function includes the optional arguments fv and type. These arguments are also common to many financial functions. For your review, these arguments are described as follows:

- **Rate.** The rate argument is the interest rate for one period. It is also called the rate of return or the percentage return on an investment. If an investment pays 12% per year and each period is one month, the rate is 1%.

- **Nper.** The nper argument represents the total number of payment or investment periods. With a four-year loan consisting of monthly payments, the number of payment periods is 48. You should perform the calculation using the input cells, such as B$4*B$5, in the nper argument instead of typing 48 in case the number of years or number of payments per year changes.

- **Pmt.** The pmt argument is the fixed periodic payment for a loan or investment.

- **Pv.** The pv argument represents the present value of the loan or investment.
- **Fv.** The fv argument represents the future value of the loan or investment. If you omit this argument, Excel defaults to 0.
- **Type.** The type argument represents the timing of the payments. Enter 0 if the payments are made at the end of the period, or enter 1 if the payments are made at the beginning of the period. If you omit this argument, Excel assumes a default of 0.

STEP 1 ▶ Use the PV, FV, and NPV Functions

Suppose you win the lottery and have a choice of receiving $100,000 per year for the next 20 years or take $1 million today. Which would you choose? The PV function will help you determine the better choice. The *PV function* calculates the total present (current) value of an investment with a fixed rate, a specified number of payment periods, and a series of identical payments that will be made in the future. This function illustrates the time value of money in which the value of $1 today is worth more than the value of $1 received at some time in the future, given that you can invest today's $1 to earn interest.

The PV function has three required arguments (rate, nper, and pmt) and two optional arguments (fv and type). If you do not know the payment value (pmt), you must enter a value for the fv argument. In Figure 7.24, cell B3 contains the PV function. The yearly payments of $100,000 invested at 5% yield a higher present value ($1,246,221.03) than the $1 million lump-sum payment. The PV function results indicate that it would be better to take the 20 yearly payments than the $1 million today.

`=PV(rate,nper,pmt,[fv],[type])`

> **TIP: NEGATIVE SIGN IN FUNCTION**
> For many financial functions, the calculated results display as a negative value. The negative result occurs because Excel interprets these calculations as a negative cash flow (money leaving your account). To make the results easier to work with, a negative sign is placed after the equal sign or before an argument so that the results display as a positive result.

The *FV function* calculates the future value of an investment, given a fixed interest rate, term, and identical periodic payments. For example, you can use the FV function to determine how much an individual retirement account (IRA) would be worth at a future date. The FV function has three required arguments (rate, nper, and pmt) and two optional arguments (pv and type). If you omit the pmt argument, you must enter a value for the pv argument.

`=FV(rate,nper,pmt,[pv],[type])`

In Figure 7.24, cell B12 contains the FV function. Assume that you plan to contribute $3,000 a year to an IRA for 40 years and that you expect the IRA to earn 7% interest annually. The future value of that investment—the amount you will have 40 years later—would be $598,905.34. You would have contributed $120,000 ($3,000 a year for 40 years). The extra $478,905.34 results from compound interest you will earn over the life of your $120,000 investment.

Suppose your company is purchasing new equipment, and you want to determine if the predicted cash flows generated by the new equipment will cover the initial expense within a certain time frame. You would use the NPV function to evaluate this situation. The *NPV function* calculates the net present value of an investment, given a fixed rate (rate of return) and future payments (negative values) or income (positive values) that may be identical or different. The NPV and PV functions are very similar in concept. The difference is that the PV function requires equal payments at the end of a payment period, whereas the NPV function can have unequal but constant payments or income. The NPV function contains two required arguments (rate and value1) and additional optional arguments (such as value2). If an investment returns a positive net present value, the investment is profitable. If an investment returns a negative net present value, the investment will lose money.

=NPV(rate,value1,[value2],...)

The value arguments represent a sequence of payments and income during the investment period. To provide an accurate net present value, the cash flows must occur at equally spaced-out time periods and must occur at the end of each period.

In Figure 7.24, cell B20 contains the NPV function. Assume the new equipment your company is purchasing costs $3,000. The equipment is expected to generate an additional $1,200 during the second, third, and fourth years. You want to determine what the net present value is to decide if the new equipment is worth the cost to obtain the additional revenue. The 3% rate is the first argument, and the cell reference to B17 is negative because the equipment cost is a negative on cash flow. The cell reference to $1,200 is entered for value2, value3, and value4 arguments. With a 3% rate, the net present value is $382.85. The positive NPV is a good indication that purchasing the equipment may be a good investment for the company.

TIP: BEGINNING OR END OF INVESTMENT PERIOD PAYMENT

Net present value is impacted by the timing of the payments—whether the payments are made in the beginning or end of the payment period. For example, if you pay the $3,000 at the beginning of the first year instead of the end of the first year, you cannot discount the $3,000 since it is already in today's value. You would subtract the initial investment after the function: =NPV(B19,B18,B18,B18)–B17. By investing $3,000 immediately, the net present value is higher at $394.33.

Use the NPER and RATE Functions

In some situations, you have a payment goal and know the stated interest rate, but you want to calculate how many payments you will make. In other situations, you know the payment and number of payments, but you want to calculate the rate. The NPER and RATE functions are useful in these situations.

The **NPER function** calculates the number of payment periods for an investment or loan given a fixed interest rate, periodic payment, and present value. You can use NPER to calculate the number of monthly payments required to make over the course of the car loan, given a loan of $30,000, an APR of 5.25%, and a monthly payment of $694.28. In Figure 7.25, cell B6 contains the NPER function. The NPER would be 48.0001, or about 48 payments. The NPER function contains three required arguments (rate, pmt, and pv) and two optional arguments (fv and type).

=NPER(rate,pmt,pv,[fv],[type])

⊿	A	B	C	D
1		**Number of Periods**		
2	Loan	$ 30,000.00		
3	APR	5.25%		
4	No. of Payment Periods in Year	12		
5	Monthly Payment	$ 694.28		
6	Number of Periods	48	=NPER(B3/B4,-B5,B2)	
7				
8		**Rate**		
9	Loan	$ 30,000.00		
10	Monthly Payment	$ 694.28		
11	No. of Periods in Year	12		
12	Years	4		
13	Periodic Rate	0.44%	=RATE(B11*B12,-B10,B9)	
14	APR	5.25%	=B11*B13	
15				

FIGURE 7.25 Financial Functions

Assume you are buying a car, and the dealer is offering you company financing for a $30,000 loan with a $694.28 monthly payment. You want to determine if the rate the dealer is offering is better or worse than the rate you can obtain from the bank. You can use the **RATE function** to calculate the periodic rate for an investment or loan given the number of payment periods, a fixed periodic payment, and present value. Using the car dealer financing example in Figure 7.25, cell B9 contains the $30,000 loan, cell B10 contains the monthly payment, cell B11 contains the number of months in 1 year, cell B12 contains the number of years to pay off the loan, and cell B13 contains the RATE function. Given the input data, the periodic (monthly) rate is 0.44%. The APR (5.25%) is found by multiplying the periodic rate by 12. The RATE function contains three required arguments (nper, pmt, and pv) and two optional arguments (fv and type).

=RATE(nper,pmt,pv,[fv],[type])

Creating a Loan Amortization Table

You used the PMT function to calculate the monthly payment for an automobile or house loan with a fixed interest rate (such as 5.75% APR) for a specified period of time (such as 30 years). Recall that a portion of the monthly payment covers the interest you owe and a portion of the monthly payment pays down your principal (the amount you borrowed from the bank).

At the beginning of the loan, the monthly payment includes a large interest payment and a smaller principal payment. With each succeeding payment, the interest portion of the monthly payment decreases, and the principal portion of the monthly payment increases. At the end of the loan, most of the monthly payment consists of a large principal portion and a smaller interest portion.

To see the interest and principal portions of each monthly payment and the reduction in the loan amount, you can create a **loan amortization table**, which is a schedule that calculates the interest per payment period, principal repayment for each payment, and remaining loan balance after each payment is made. Figure 7.26 shows the top and bottom portions of an amortization schedule (rows 18:46 are hidden) for an automobile loan of $20,000 with an APR of 2.5% for a four-year loan with a monthly payment of $438.28, rounded to the nearest penny. The borrower pays a total of $21,037.47 (48 payments of $438.28, which includes $1,037.47 in interest) over the life of the loan.

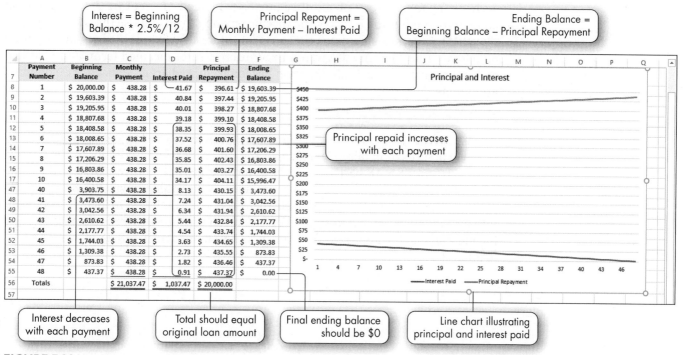

FIGURE 7.26 Loan Amortization Table

The body of the worksheet reflected in Figure 7.26 shows how principal and interest comprise each payment. The balance of the loan at the beginning of the first period is $20,000. The monthly payment includes interest and principal repayment. The interest for the first month ($41.67) is calculated by multiplying the beginning loan balance for the period, which is the original loan amount ($20,000) by the monthly interest rate (2.5% divided by 12).

The principal repayment is the amount of the monthly payment that is left over after deducting the monthly interest. For the first payment, the principal repayment is $396.61 ($438.28 – $41.67).

The remaining balance is the difference between the beginning balance and the principal repayment. For the first month, subtract the principal repayment from the original loan amount ($20,000 – $396.61).

The interest for the second month ($40.84) is less than interest for the previous period. This is because the balance to start the second period ($19,603.39) is less than the loan balance for the first period ($20,000) because $396.61 was paid in principal with the first payment. For each month, the principal and interest always equal the monthly payment.

TIP: EXTRA PRINCIPAL PAYMENT

Many homebuyers choose a 30-year mortgage to keep the monthly payment low but opt to pay extra toward the principal each month to reduce the length of the mortgage and the total interest paid. This reduction in interest can be substantial. For example, paying an extra $50 a month on a 30-year, $350,000 mortgage with an interest rate of 4.5% APR can save more than $18,000 in interest over the life of the mortgage and pay off the mortgage about 1.5 years before its original payoff date.

Calculate Interest and Principal Payments with IPMT and PPMT Functions

Sometimes you want to know just the interest paid for a specific loan payment, perhaps for tax reasons or another purpose. Instead of creating a complete loan amortization table and locating the specific payment, you can use the IPMT function. The *IPMT function* calculates the periodic interest for a specified payment period on a loan or an investment given a fixed interest rate, specified term, and identical periodic payments. The IPMT function has four required arguments and two optional arguments.

=IPMT(rate,per,nper,pv,[fv],[type])

As Figure 7.27 shows, the IPMT function calculates interest for each payment period in a loan amortization table. For example, the calculation for interest for the first period is =IPMT(B$3/B$5,A8,B$4*B$5,-B$2). You can type the negative sign after the equal sign or before the pv argument. The per argument is the specific payment period to use to calculate the interest where the first payment period is 1. It is best to include a payment number column as shown in Figure 7.27. You can use a relative cell reference to avoid having values in the argument. The first monthly payment of $438.28 includes $41.67 in interest.

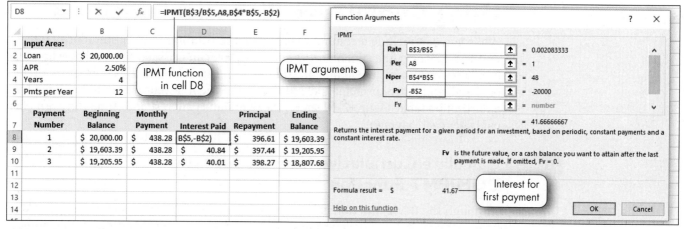

FIGURE 7.27 Interest Calculated

Sometimes you want to know just the principal paid for a specific loan payment. Similar to using the IPMT function without creating a loan amortization table, you can use the PPMT function by itself. The ***PPMT function*** calculates the principal payment for a specified payment period on a loan given a fixed interest rate, specified term, and identical periodic payments. The PPMT function has the same four required arguments and two optional arguments as the IPMT function.

=PPMT(rate,per,nper,pv,[fv],[type])

As Figure 7.28 shows, the PPMT function calculates the principal repayment in column E. For example, cell E8 contains =PPMT(B$3/B$5,A8,B$4*B$5,-B$2). You can type the negative sign after the equal sign or before the pv argument. The first monthly payment of $438.28 includes $396.61 in principal repayment.

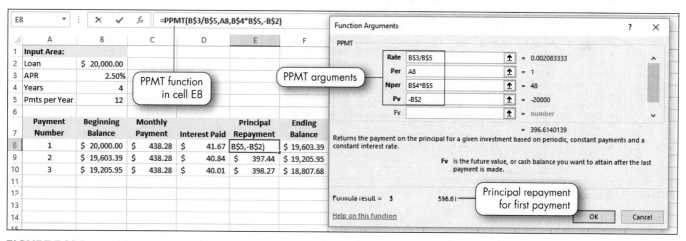

FIGURE 7.28 Principal Repayment Calculated

Using Cumulative Financial Functions

While you can include a column to calculate the running total or cumulative interest and principal paid in a loan amortization table, you can use special cumulative financial functions for a point in a loan. For example, you can calculate the cumulative interest paid and cumulative principal paid at the end of the first year without creating a loan amortization table. Figure 7.29 shows the cumulative interest and cumulative principal paid after each payment.

STEP 3 ▶ Calculate Cumulative Interest with the CUMIPMT Function

Although the IPMT function calculates the amount of interest paid in one particular loan payment, it does not determine the amount of interest paid over a specific number of payments. You can use the **CUMIPMT function** to calculate the cumulative interest through a specified payment period. This function accumulates the interest paid between selected payments or throughout the entire loan. For the first payment, the cumulative interest is the same as the periodic interest. From that point on, you can calculate the cumulative interest, such as the sum of the interest paid for the first two periods, as shown in cell H9 in Figure 7.29.

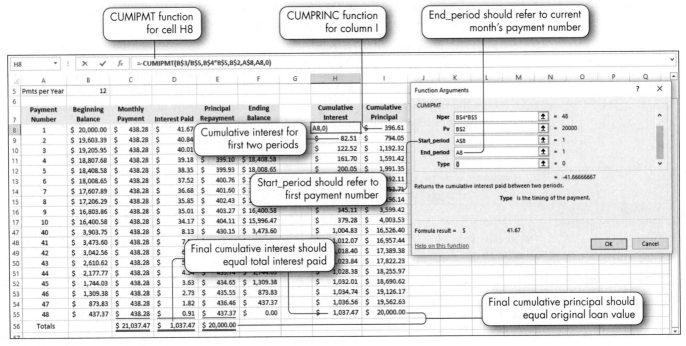

FIGURE 7.29 Cumulative Functions

The CUMIPMT contains six arguments. The rate, nper, pv, and type arguments are the same arguments that you use in any financial function. The start_period argument specifies the first period you want to start accumulating the interest, and the end_period argument specifies the last payment period you want to include. Unlike some financial functions where you can type the minus sign either after the equal sign or before the pv argument, you must enter the minus sign after the equal sign for the CUMIPMT function.

=CUMIPMT(rate,nper,pv,start_period,end_period,type)

In Figure 7.29, the first cumulative interest payment formula in cell H8 uses 1 for both the start_period and end_period arguments. From that point on, the start_period is still 1, but the end_period changes to reflect each payment period, using the payment numbers in column A. The final cumulative interest should equal the total of the Interest Repayment column in the loan amortization table.

STEP 4 ▶ Calculate Cumulative Principal Payments with the CUMPRINC Function

You can use the **CUMPRINC function** to calculate the cumulative principal through a specified payment period. This function accumulates the principal repayment between selected payments or throughout the entire loan. For the first payment, the cumulative principal paid is the same as the first principal repayment. From that point on, you can calculate the cumulative principal payment, such as the sum of the principal repayment paid for the first two periods, as shown in cell I9 in Figure 7.29. The final cumulative principal should equal the original loan amount and the total of the Principal Repayment column in the loan amortization table.

The CUMPRINC contains six arguments. The rate, nper, pv, start_period, end_period, and type arguments are the same arguments that you use in the CUMIPMT function. Like the CUMIPMT function, you must enter the minus sign after the equal sign for the CUMIPMT function to display positive results.

=CUMPRINC(rate,nper,pv,start_period,end_period,type)

TIP: CALCULATING CUMULATIVE INTEREST OR PAYMENT BETWEEN TWO PERIODS

If you do not want to calculate a running total for the entire loan, you can specify the interest or principal payment between two periods, such as between payment periods 13 and 24, to calculate the total interest or total principal paid for the second year of the loan.

Quick Concepts

7. Explain the difference between PV and NPV functions. ***p. 465***

8. Explain why you would create a loan amortization table. ***p. 467***

9. Describe the purpose of the CUMIPMT and CUMPRINC functions. ***pp. 470–471***

Hands-On Exercises

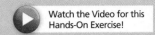
Skills covered: Use the
PV Function • Insert Formulas in a
Loan Amortization Table • Use
the IPMT Function • Use the
PPMT Function • Use the CUMIPMT
Function • Use the CUMPRINC
Function

3 Financial Functions

The location managers want new company cars. Angela Khazen, the chief financial officer, has determined that the company can afford $450 monthly payments based on a 5.25% APR for four-year loans. She wants you to prepare a loan amortization table and running totals for interest and principal repayment.

STEP 1 USE THE PV FUNCTION

Because Angela determined the monthly payment for an automobile, you will use the PV function to calculate the loan amount. Other variables, such as trade-in value of the current vehicle, are usually considered, but you will exclude those variables. Refer to Figure 7.30 as you complete Step 1.

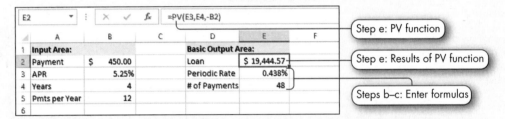

FIGURE 7.30 PV Function

a. Open *e07h2Salary_LastFirst* if you closed it at the end of Hands-On Exercise 2, and save it as **e07h3Salary_LastFirst**, changing h2 to h3. Click the **3-Finance sheet tab**.

You will calculate the periodic interest rate and number of payment periods before you can calculate the present value of the loan.

b. Click **cell E3**, type **=B3/B5**, and then press **Enter**.

The periodic rate, 0.438%, is the result of dividing the APR by the number of payments per year.

c. Type **=B4*B5** in **cell E4** and press **Enter**.

The total number of monthly payments, 48, is the product of the number of years the loan is outstanding and the number of payments per year.

d. Click **cell E2**, click **Financial** in the Function Library group on the Formulas tab, scroll through the list, and then select **PV**.

e. Click **cell E3** to enter that cell reference in the Rate box, click in the **Nper box**, and then click **cell E4**. Click in the **Pmt box**, type -B2, and then click **OK**.

The result is $19,444.57 based on four years of $450 monthly payments with an APR of 5.25%. You entered a negative sign before the Pmt argument to display the result as a positive value. If you do not enter a negative sign, Excel will display the loan as a negative value.

f. Apply **Accounting Number Format** to **cell E2**. Save the workbook.

Angela wants you to create an amortization table. The column labels and payment numbers have already been entered into the worksheet. Now you will enter formulas to show the beginning loan balance for each payment, the monthly payment, interest paid, and principal repayment. Refer to Figure 7.31 as you complete Step 2.

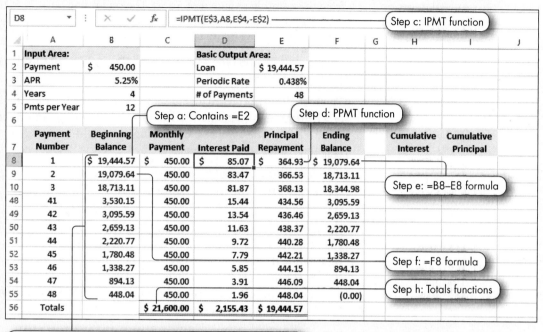

FIGURE 7.31 Loan Amortization Table

a. Click **cell B8**, type **=E2**, and then press **Tab**.

You entered a reference to the original loan amount because that is the beginning balance for the first payment. Referencing the original cell is recommended instead of typing the value directly in the cell due to internal rounding. Furthermore, if you change the original input values, the calculated loan amount will change in both cells B8 and E2.

b. Type **=B$2** in **cell C8** and press **Ctrl+Enter**. Drag the **cell C8 fill handle** to copy the payment to the **range C9:C55**.

The monthly payment is $450.00. You entered a reference to the original monthly payment so that if you change it in cell B2, Excel will update the values in the Monthly Payment column automatically. The cell reference must be a mixed (B$2) or absolute ($B$2) reference to prevent the row number from changing when you copy the formula down the column later.

c. Click **cell D8**, click **Financial** in the Function Library on the Formulas tab, select **IPMT** to open the Function Arguments dialog box, type **E$3** in the Rate box, type **A8** in the Per box, type **E$4** in the Nper box, type **-E$2** in the PV box, and then click **OK**. Drag the **cell D8 fill handle** to copy the IPMT function to the **range D9:D55**.

The IPMT function calculates the interest of a specific payment based on the starting balance of $19,444.57 with a periodic interest of .438% over 48 payments. By keeping cell A8 as a relative cell address, the function adjusts the period to match the specific period of evaluation.

d. Click **cell E8**, click **Financial** in the Function Library, select **PPMT** to open the Function Arguments dialog box, type **E$3** in the Rate box, type **A8** in the Per box, type **E$4** in the Nper box, type **-E$2** in the PV box, and then click **OK**. Drag the **cell E8 fill handle** to copy the PPMT function to the **range E9:E55**.

To calculate the principal repayment, subtract the interest of the first payment $85.07 from the monthly payment of $450. The remaining portion of the payment $364.93 goes toward paying down the principal owed. Using the PPMT function automatically completed these calculations.

e. Click in **cell F8** and type **=B8-E8**. Drag the **cell F8 fill handle** to copy the formula to the **range F9:F55**

This calculates the ending balance after the first payment is made. The ending balance of $19,079.64 is calculated by subtracting the amount of principal in the payment $364.93 from the balance currently owed $19,444.57. The copied formulas show negative results until you complete the Beginning Balance column next.

f. Click in **cell B9**, type **=F8**, and then press **Ctrl+Enter**. Drag the **cell B9 fill handle** to copy the cell reference to the **range B10:B55.**

The beginning balance of the second payment is also the ending balance of the first payment. The easiest method to populate the column is by referencing the ending balance from the prior month (cell F8). However, this can also be calculated by subtracting the previous principal repayment value (such as $364.93) from the previous month's beginning balance (such as $19,444.57). The formula results in column F are now positive numbers. The ending balance in cell F55 should be $0, indicating that the loan has been completely paid off.

g. Select the **range B8:F8** and apply **Accounting Number Format**. Select the **range B9:F55** and apply **Comma Style**.

h. Enter SUM functions in **cells C56, D56,** and **E56**.

i. Select the **range C56:E56,** click the **Home tab,** click **Cell Styles** in the Styles group, and then select **Total**. Save the workbook.

You calculated totals for the appropriate columns, noting that column B is a running balance and cannot be logically totaled. Figure 7.31 shows the top and bottom portions of the amortization table with rows 11 through 47 hidden.

STEP 3 CALCULATE CUMULATIVE INTEREST WITH THE CUMIPMT FUNCTION

The loan amortization table shows how much of each payment is interest and how much pays down the principal. However, Angela wants you to include a column to show the cumulative interest after each payment. Refer to Figure 7.32 as you complete Step 3.

H8		✕ ✓	fx	=-CUMIPMT(E$3,E$4,E$2,A$8,A8,0)						
	A	B	C	D	E	F	G	H	I	J
1	Input Area:			Basic Output Area:						
2	Payment	$ 450.00		Loan	$ 19,444.57			Steps a–e: CUMIPMT function		
3	APR	5.25%		Periodic Rate	0.438%					
4	Years	4		# of Payments	48					
5	Pmts per Year	12						Step f: Last result should match cell D56 total		
6										
7	Payment Number	Beginning Balance	Monthly Payment	Interest Paid	Principal Repayment	Ending Balance		Cumulative Interest	Cumulative Principal	
8	1	$ 19,444.57	$ 450.00	$ 85.07	$ 364.93	$ 19,079.64		$ 85.07		
9	2	19,079.64	450.00	83.47	366.53	18,713.11		$ 168.54		
10	3	18,713.11	450.00	81.87	368.13	18,344.98		$ 250.41		
48	41	3,530.15	450.00	15.44	434.56	3,095.59		$ 2,101.02		
49	42	3,095.59	450.00	13.54	436.46	2,659.13		$ 2,114.57		
50	43	2,659.13	450.00	11.63	438.37	2,220.77		$ 2,126.20		
51	44	2,220.77	450.00	9.72	440.28	1,780.48		$ 2,135.92		
52	45	1,780.48	450.00	7.79	442.21	1,338.27		$ 2,143.71		
53	46	1,338.27	450.00	5.85	444.15	894.13		$ 2,149.56		
54	47	894.13	450.00	3.91	446.09	448.04		$ 2,153.47		
55	48	448.04	450.00	1.96	448.04	(0.00)		$ 2,155.43		
56	Totals		$ 21,600.00	$ 2,155.43	$ 19,444.57					
57										

FIGURE 7.32 Cumulative Interest

a. Click **cell H8**, click **Financial** in the Function Library group on the Formulas tab, and then select **CUMIPMT**.

   The Function Arguments dialog box displays so that you can enter the arguments for the CUMIPMT function.

b. Type the following arguments: **E$3** in the Rate box, **E$4** in the Nper box, **E$2** in the Pv box, and **A$8** in the Start_period box.

   Make sure the cell references you enter in the Rate, Nper, Pv, and Start_period boxes are mixed as shown to prevent the row number from changing as you copy the formula down the column.

c. Type **A8** in the End_period box.

   This reference should be relative so that it reflects the current month's payment number as you copy the formula down the column.

d. Press **Tab**, type **0** in the Type box, and then click **OK**.

   The cumulative interest for the first payment is the same as the first payment's interest. However, the formula displays a negative result, as indicated by the parentheses.

e. Edit the function by typing **-** between = and CUMIPMT to convert the results to a positive value. Press **Enter**.

   The cumulative interest at the end of the first payment is identical to the interest on the first payment.

f. Copy the function through **cell H55**. Save the workbook.

   The cumulative interest in cell H55 should match the total interest paid calculated in cell D56: $2,155.43.

STEP 4 CALCULATE CUMULATIVE PRINCIPAL WITH THE CUMPRINC FUNCTION

Angela wants to see the cumulative principal paid after making each loan payment. You will use the CUMPRINC function to calculate the cumulative principal paid. Refer to Figure 7.33 as you complete Step 4.

I8 | =-CUMPRINC(E$3,E$4,E$2,A$8,A8,0)

Steps a–c: CUMPRINC function

Step d: Last result should match cell E56 total

	A	B	C	D	E	F	G	H	I	J
1	Input Area:			Basic Output Area:						
2	Payment	$ 450.00		Loan	$ 19,444.57					
3	APR	5.25%		Periodic Rate	0.438%					
4	Years	4		# of Payments	48					
5	Pmts per Year	12								
6										
7	Payment Number	Beginning Balance	Monthly Payment	Interest Paid	Principal Repayment	Ending Balance		Cumulative Interest	Cumulative Principal	
8	1	$ 19,444.57	$ 450.00	$ 85.07	$ 364.93	$ 19,079.64		$ 85.07	$ 364.93	
9	2	19,079.64	450.00	83.47	366.53	18,713.11		$ 168.54	$ 731.46	
10	3	18,713.11	450.00	81.87	368.13	18,344.98		$ 250.41	$ 1,099.59	
48	41	3,530.15	450.00	15.44	434.56	3,095.59		$ 2,101.02	$ 16,348.98	
49	42	3,095.59	450.00	13.54	436.46	2,659.13		$ 2,114.57	$ 16,785.43	
50	43	2,659.13	450.00	11.63	438.37	2,220.77		$ 2,126.20	$ 17,223.80	
51	44	2,220.77	450.00	9.72	440.28	1,780.48		$ 2,135.92	$ 17,664.08	
52	45	1,780.48	450.00	7.79	442.21	1,338.27		$ 2,143.71	$ 18,106.29	
53	46	1,338.27	450.00	5.85	444.15	894.13		$ 2,149.56	$ 18,550.44	
54	47	894.13	450.00	3.91	446.09	448.04		$ 2,153.47	$ 18,996.53	
55	48	448.04	450.00	1.96	448.04	(0.00)		$ 2,155.43	$ 19,444.57	
56	Totals		$ 21,600.00	$ 2,155.43	$ 19,444.57					

FIGURE 7.33 Cumulative Principal

a. Click **cell I8**, click **Financial** in the Function Library group on the Formulas tab, and then select **CUMPRINC**.

The Function Arguments dialog box displays so that you can enter the arguments for the CUMPRINC function.

b. Type **E$3** in the Rate box, **E$4** in the Nper box, **E$2** in the Pv box, **A$8** in the Start_period box, **A8** in the End_period box, press **Tab**, and then type **0** in the Type box.

c. Click **OK** and edit the function by typing - between = and CUMPRINC. Press **Ctrl+Enter**.

d. Copy the function from **cell I8** to the **range I9:I55**.

The cumulative principal in cell I55 should match the total principal repayment calculated in cell E56: $19,444.57.

e. Save and close the file. Exit Excel. Based on your instructor's directions, submit e07h3Salary_LastFirst.

Chapter Objectives Review

After reading this chapter, you have accomplished the following objectives:

I. Use date functions.

- Use the DAY, MONTH, and YEAR functions: The DAY function displays the day (1–31) within a month. The MONTH function displays the month (1–12) where 1 is January and 12 is December for a date. The YEAR function displays the year such as 2021 for a specific date.
- Use the DAYS and YEARFRAC functions: The DAYS function calculates the number of days between two dates, and the YEARFRAC function calculates the fraction of a year between two dates.
- Use the WEEKDAY function: The WEEKDAY function returns a serial number representing the weekday where 1 is Sunday and 7 is Saturday. The optional return_type argument enables you to change which day of the week equals 1.
- Use other date functions: Other helpful date functions include DATE, DAYS360, EDATE, EOMONTH, ISOWEEKNUM, NETWORKDAYS, and WORKDAY.

2. Use advanced logical functions.

- Use the SWITCH function: The function evaluates an expression, such as OH, and returns a result, such as Ohio.
- Use the IFS function: The function evaluates multiple conditions to return a result that corresponds with the first true condition.
- Nest IF within an IF function: When more than two outcomes are possible, you can nest an additional IF function within the value_if_true argument and/or value_if_false argument in an IF function.
- Use AND, OR, and NOT functions: Use AND, OR, and NOT statements to evaluate multiple conditions at the same time. The AND function returns TRUE if all conditions are true. The OR function returns TRUE if any condition is true. The NOT function returns TRUE if the statement is false and FALSE if the statement is true.
- Nest AND, OR, and NOT Functions within an IF function: Nesting these functions within an IF function enables you to make the results more useful for complex logical tests. You can test two conditions at one time to determine if the combined test is true or false.

3. Use functions to evaluate one condition.

- Use the COUNTIF function: This statistical function counts the number of cells that meet a specified condition in a range. For example, COUNTIF can return the number of Account Reps in a dataset.
- Use the SUMIF function: This statistical function calculates the total in a range based on a condition being met in another range. For example, SUMIF can calculate the total salaries for only Account Reps in a dataset.
- Use the AVERAGEIF function: This statistical function calculates the average in a range based on a condition being met in another range. For example, AVERAGEIF can calculate the average salary for only Account Reps in a dataset.

4. Use functions to evaluate multiple conditions.

- Use the COUNTIFS, SUMIFS, and AVERAGEIFS functions: These functions return a count, sum, and average, respectively, when multiple conditions exist. For example, these functions can provide calculations for Account Reps who were hired after 1/1/2020.
- Use the MAXIFS and MINIFS functions: These functions return the highest and lowest values, respectively, from a range when multiple conditions exist.

5. Insert a map.

- A map chart can compare values across geographic regions by displaying light to dark fill colors to indicate the highest and lowest numbers. The dataset must include countries, states, or other geographic data to plot data in a map.

6. Use financial functions.

- Use the PV, FV, and NPV functions: The PV function calculates the present value of an investment. The FV function calculates the future value of an investment. These functions require a fixed rate, specified term, and identical periodic payments. The NPV function calculates net present value for an investment with a fixed rate where future payments may be identical or different.
- Use the NPER and RATE functions: The NPER function calculates the number of payment periods for a loan or an investment with a fixed rate, present value, and identical periodic payments. The RATE function calculates the periodic interest rate for an investment or loan with a given number of payment periods, a fixed period payment, and present value.

7. Create a loan amortization table.

- A loan amortization table is a schedule of monthly payments, interest per period, principal repayment per period, and balances.
- Insert formulas in a loan amortization table: The beginning balance for the first period is the amount of the loan. The formula to calculate each period's interest is calculated using the beginning balance for that loan period and the monthly interest rate. The principal prepayment is the difference between the monthly payment and the interest paid. The interest payment decreases throughout the loan.
- Calculate interest and principal payments with IPMT and PPMT functions: The IPMT function calculates the periodic interest for a specified payment period on a loan or investment. The PPMT function calculates the principal payment for a specified payment period on a loan or investment.

8. Use cumulative financial functions.

- Calculate cumulative interest with the CUMIPMT function: The CUMIPMT function calculates the cumulative interest for a specific period on a loan or investment.
- Calculate cumulative principal payments with the CUMPRINC function: The CUMPRINC function calculates the cumulative principal for a specific payment period.

Key Terms Matching

Match the key terms with their definitions. Write the key term letter by the appropriate numbered definition.

a. AND function
b. AVERAGEIFS function
c. COUNTIF function
d. CUMIPMT function
e. CUMPRINC function
f. FV function
g. IFS function
h. IPMT function
i. Loan amortization table
j. Map chart

k. NPER function
l. NPV function
m. OR function
n. PPMT function
o. PV function
p. SUMIF function
q. SUMIFS function
r. WEEKDAY function
s. YEAR function
t. YEARFRAC function

1. _____ Calculates the number of periods for an investment or loan given a fixed rate, period payment, and present value. **p. 466**

2. _____ Calculates the future value of an investment given a fixed rate, a term, and identical periodic payments. **p. 465**

3. _____ Calculates the net present value of an investment with a fixed rate and periodic payments that may be identical or different. **p. 465**

4. _____ Calculates cumulative principal for a specified payment period. **p. 471**

5. _____ Calculates the present value of an investment with a fixed rate, specified number of periods, and identical periodic payments that will be made in the future. **p. 465**

6. _____ Calculates cumulative interest for a specified payment period. **p. 470**

7. _____ A schedule showing monthly payments, interest per payment, amount toward paying off the loan, and the remaining balance for each payment. **p. 467**

8. _____ Calculates the principal payment for a specified payment period on a loan or an investment given a fixed rate, a specified term, and identical periodic payments. **p. 469**

9. _____ Calculates periodic interest for a specific payment period on a loan or investment with a fixed rate, a specified term, and identical periodic payments. **p. 468**

10. _____ Returns the average of all cells that meet multiple criteria. **p. 456**

11. _____ A type of chart that displays a visual representation of geographic regions to illustrate relative values. **p. 457**

12. _____ Returns a number representing the day of the week where 1 represents Sunday and 7 represents Saturday by default. **p. 438**

13. _____ Calculates the total of a range of values when a specified condition is met. **p. 454**

14. _____ A logical function that evaluates multiple conditions and returns a result that corresponds with the first true condition. **p. 440**

15. _____ Calculates the fraction of a year between two dates based on the number of whole days. **p. 437**

16. _____ Returns the number of cells that meet a condition. **p. 454**

17. _____ Extracts the year from a date. **p. 436**

18. _____ Calculates the total of a range of values when multiple conditions are met. **p. 455**

19. _____ Returns TRUE if any argument is true and returns FALSE if all arguments are false. **p. 443**

20. _____ Returns TRUE when all arguments are true and FALSE when at least one argument is false. **p. 443**

Multiple Choice

1. The date 8/3/2021 is stored in cell C1. What function is used to extract just 3?

   (a) =YEAR(C1)

   (b) =MONTH(C1)

   (c) =DAYS(B1,C1)

   (d) =DAY(C1)

2. The date February 16, 2021 is stored in cell B1. The last day of the semester (May 7, 2021) is stored in cell B2. Which function calculates the number days until the end of the semester?

   (a) =DAYS(B1,B2)

   (b) =DAYS(B2,B1)

   (c) =YEARFRAC(B1,B2)

   (d) =DAY(B1)

3. For which situation would you use the SWITCH function?

   (a) You want to display a bonus if an employee earned a 5 on a performance evaluation and was hired before 1/1/2021.

   (b) You want to calculate a three-tier bonus based on salaries for employees: 5% bonus for employees who exceeded their goals, 3% bonus for employees who met their goals, and 0% for employees who did not meet their goals.

   (c) You have a spreadsheet with a list of articles and a column containing authors' initials (JD, KM, MP, RG). You want to create another column that evaluates the initials and returns their respective names.

   (d) You have a list of graduating students. You want to calculate the average GPA for only students graduating with a marketing degree

4. A workbook contains a list of houses and the months that they were sold in Florida. You are interested in determining the average price of sold houses in June in Ft. Lauderdale. What function is best suited for this calculation?

   (a) AVERAGEIFS

   (b) AVERAGEIF

   (c) SUMIF

   (d) MAXIFS

5. You want to create a spreadsheet with populations. Which of the following could *not* be used to produce a map chart in Excel?

   (a) State names, such as Ohio, Oklahoma, Oregon

   (b) City names, such as Boston, Denver, Los Angeles

   (c) Postal codes, such as 73085, 73701, 74074

   (d) State abbreviations, such as TX, CO, CA, MA

6. What function would you use to calculate the total interest paid for the first year of a mortgage?

   (a) CUMIPMT

   (b) PMT

   (c) PPMT

   (d) CUMPRINC

7. A dataset contains a list of U.S. Representatives, the states they represent, the years they were elected, and their salaries. You want to identify the highest-paid representative who was elected before 1/1/2020. What is the best function to use?

   (a) MAX

   (b) IFS

   (c) MAXIFS

   (d) YEARFRAC

8. You constructed a loan amortization table with beginning balance, monthly payment, interest paid, principal repayment, and ending balance columns. If all the formulas are correct, which is the only column that shows an increase in value throughout the term of the loan?

   (a) Beginning Balance

   (b) Monthly Payment

   (c) Interest Paid

   (d) Principal Repayment

9. A local police chief wants to create a rule that a person will be ticketed if an officer pulls over a person for exceeding the speed limit by at least five miles per hour or if that person has two or more speeding violations on record. Which function should be used?

   (a) AND

   (b) MAXIFS

   (c) OR

   (d) SWITCH

10. What function would you use to calculate the total number of periods in a loan or investment?

    (a) NPER

    (b) RATE

    (c) PV

    (d) FV

Practice Exercises

1 Furniture Sales

As the manager of Reid's Furniture Store, you track sales transactions by salesperson, department, amount, and payment type. Customers either finance their purchase through your store or pay in full at the time of purchase. You will calculate down payments and balances for all transactions. If a transaction is paid in full, the balance is zero. Customers who finance their transactions must pay off the balance within four years from the transaction date. You want to complete the March transaction log and use conditional functions to summarize key paid-in-full transactions. Next, you will insert financial functions and formulas to complete a loan amortization table and to calculate cumulative summaries. Finally, you will insert a map to indicate sales by postal code. Refer to Figure 7.34 as you complete this exercise.

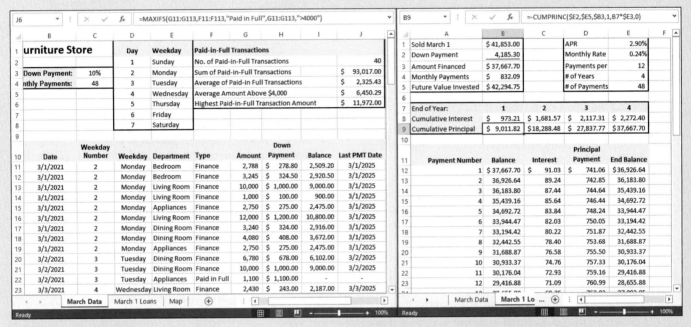

FIGURE 7.34 Furniture Store

a. Open *e07p1Furniture* and save it as **e07p1Furniture_LastFirst**.

b. Click **cell C11** and extract the weekday by serial number by completing the following steps:
   - Click the **Formulas tab**, click **Date & Time** in the Function Library group, and then select **WEEKDAY**.
   - Type **B11** in the Serial_number box, type **1** in the Return_type box, and then click **OK**.
   - Copy the function from **cell C11** to the **range C12:C113**.

c. Click **cell D11** and switch the weekday numbers for weekday names by completing the following steps:
   - Click **Logical** in the Function Library group and select **SWITCH**.
   - Type **C11** in the Expression box.
   - Type **1** in the Value1 box and type **E$2** in the Result1 box.
   - Type **2** in the Default_or_value2 box and type **E$3** in the Results 2 box.
   - Continue typing numbers **3** through **7** in the respective Default_or_value boxes and type **E$4** through **E$8** in the respective Result boxes. Click **OK**.
   - Copy the function from **cell D11** to the range **D12:D113**.

d. Click **cell H11** and calculate the down payment for all sales. If a transaction is not financed, the down payment is identical to the amount. If the transaction is financed, the down payment is 10% of the amount purchased. Complete the following steps:

- Click **Logical** in the Function Library and select **IF**.
- Type **NOT(F11="Finance")** in the Logical_test box in the Function Arguments dialog box.
- Press **Tab** and type **G11** in the Value_if_true box.
- Press **Tab** and type **G11*C$3** to multiply the amount purchased by the down payment percentage rate in cell C3. Click **OK**.
- Double-click the **cell H11 fill handle** to copy the formula to the **range H12:H113**.

e. Click **cell I11**, type **=G11-H11**, and press **Ctrl+Enter**. Copy the formula to the **range I12:I113**. Notice that paid-in-full transactions show a negative sign (–) instead of a value.

f. Click **cell J11** and calculate the date the payment is due by completing the following steps:

- Click **Logical** in the Function Library and select **IF**.
- Type **I11** in the Logical_test box in the Function Arguments dialog box.
- Click in the **Value_if_true box**, click the **Name Box arrow**, select **More Functions**, type **EDATE**, click **Go**, and then click **OK**.
- Type **B11** in the Start_date box.
- Click in the **Months box**, type **C$4**, and then click **OK**.
- Edit the function to look like this: **=IF(I11>0,EDATE(B11,C$4),"-")**
- Double-click the **cell J11 fill handle** to copy the formula to the **range J12:I113**.

g. Click **cell J2** and calculate the number of paid-in-full transactions by completing the following steps:

- Click **More Functions** in the Function Library group, point to **Statistical**, scroll down, and then select **COUNTIF**.
- Type **F11:F113** in the Range box, type **"Paid in Full"** in the Criteria box, and then click **OK**. The function indicates that 40 transactions were paid in full.

h. Click **cell J3** and calculate the total dollar amount of the paid-in-full transactions by completing the following steps:

- Click **Math & Trig** in the Function Library group, scroll down, and then select **SUMIF**.
- Type **F11:F113** in the Range box, type **"Paid in Full"** in the Criteria box, type **G11:G113** in the Sum_range box, and then click **OK**. The function indicates that the total amount of paid-in-full transactions is $93,017.

i. Click **cell J4** and calculate the average transaction amount for the paid-in-full transactions by completing the following steps:

- Click **More Functions** in the Function Library group, point to **Statistical**, and then select **AVERAGEIF**.
- Type **F11:F113** in the Range box, type **"Paid in Full"** in the Criteria box, type **G11:G113** in the Average_range box, and then click **OK**. The function indicates that the average transaction for paid-in-full transactions is $2,325.43.

j. Click **cell J5** and calculate the average transaction amount for transactions over $4,000 by completing the following steps:

- Click **More Functions** in the Function Library group, point to **Statistical**, and then select **AVERAGEIFS**.
- Type **G11:G113** in the Average_range box, type **F11:F113** in the Criteria1_range box, type **"Paid in Full"** in the Criteria1 box, type **G11:G113** in the Criteria_range2 box, type **">4000"** in the Criteria2 box, and then click **OK**. The function indicates that the average transaction for paid-in-full transactions over $4,000 is $6,450.29.

k. Click **cell J6**. Adapt Step j to use the **MAXIFS** function. The function returns $11,972.00.

l. Click the **March 1 Loans sheet tab**, click **cell B5**, and calculate the future value of the loan payments given compound interest by completing the following steps:

- Click **Financial** in the Function Library group, scroll through the list, and then select **FV**.
- Type **E2** in the Rate box, **E5** in the Nper box, **-B4** in the Pmt box, and then click **OK**.
- Format **cell B5** with **Accounting Number Format**.

m. Click **cell B8**, click **Financial** in the Function Library group on the Formulas tab, and then select **CUMIPMT**. Complete the following steps to calculate cumulative interest at the end of each year:

- Type **$E2** in the Rate box, **$E5** in the Nper box, **$B3** in the Pv box, **1** in the Start_period box, **B7*$E3** in the End_period box, **0** in the Type box, and then click **OK**. Edit the function by typing – after equal sign. The cumulative interest at the end of the first year is $973.21.
- Click the **Home tab**, click **Copy**, select the **range C8:E8**, click the **Paste arrow**, and then click **Formulas**.
- Enter the CUMPRINC function in **cell B9** using the same arguments you used for the CUMIPMT function. Include the – sign after the equal sign and copy the formulas to the **range C9:E9**.

n. Enter functions and formulas in the amortization table by completing the following steps:

- Click **cell C12**, click **Financial** in the Function Library group on the Formulas tab, scroll through the list, and then select **IPMT**. Type **E$2** in the Rate box, **A12** in the Per box, **E$5** in the Nper box, **-B$3** in the Pv box, and then click **OK**. The first payment includes $91.03 in interest.
- Click **cell D12**, click **Financial** in the Function Library group, scroll through the list, and then select **PPMT**. Type **E$2** in the Rate box, **A12** in the Per box, **E$5** in the Nper box, **-B$3** in the Pv box, and then click **OK**. The first payment includes $741.06 in principal payment.
- Type **=B12-D12** in **cell E12**.
- Type **=E12** in **cell B13**. Copy the formula in **cell B13** to the **range B14:B59**.
- Select the **range C12:E12** and copy the functions and formula to the **range C13:E59**.
- Enter the SUM function in **cells C60** and **D60**. Double underlines should display.
- Apply **Accounting Number Format** to the **ranges B12:E12** and **C60:D60**.
- Apply **Comma Style** to the **range B13:E59**.
- Apply **Underline** to the **range C59:D59**.

o. Click the **Map sheet tab** and insert a map by completing the following steps:

- Select the **range B2:C6**, click the **Insert tab**, click **Maps** in the Charts group, and then click **Filled Map**.
- Cut the map chart and paste it in **cell A9**.
- Select the *Chart Title* and type **March Sales by Zip Code**.

p. Create a footer with your name on the left side, the sheet name code in the center, and the file name code on the right side on all sheets.

q. Save and close the file. Exit Excel. Based on your instructor's directions, submit e07p1Furniture_LastFirst.

As a loan officer at Tri-State Mortgage Company, you want to analyze loans that were managed by another officer who just retired. You will review the number of years to date for loans, identify pay-off years, and rates. In addition, you want to calculate summary statistics by 30- and 15-year loans. Furthermore, you want to calculate the cumulative interest and principal paid to date as well as the interest and principal payment for the current month, December 2021. Finally, you will analyze each loan to make a recommendation. To perform these calculations, you will use date, financial, conditional, and logical functions. Refer to Figure 7.35 as you complete this exercise.

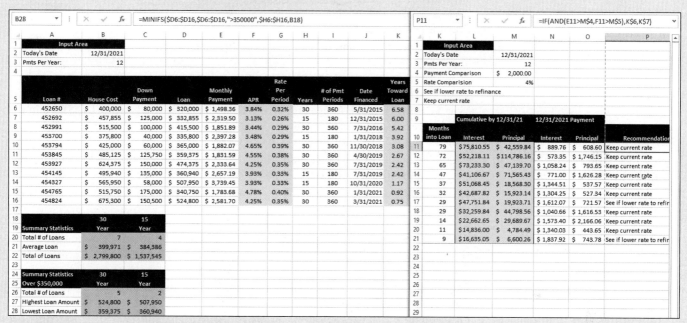

FIGURE 7.35 Tri-State Mortgage Company

a. Open *e07p2Loans* and save it as **e07p2Loans_LastFirst**.

b. Calculate the number of years since each loan was created by completing the following steps:
  - Click **cell K6** in the Summary sheet, click the **Formulas tab**, click **Date & Time** in the Function Library group, and then select **YEARFRAC**.
  - Type **J6** in the Start_date box, type **B$2** in the End_date box, and then click **OK**.
  - Double-click the **cell K6 fill handle** to copy the function to the **range K7:K16**.

c. Calculate the year in which each loan matures by completing the following steps:
  - Click **cell L6**, click **Date & Time**, and then select **YEAR**.
  - Type **J6** in the Serial_number box and click **OK**.
  - Edit the function by typing **+H6** after the closing parenthesis.
  - Double-click the **cell L6 fill handle** to copy the function to the **range L7:L16**.

d. Calculate the periodic rate and APR for each loan by completing the following steps:
  - Click **cell G6**, click **Financial** in the Function Library group, scroll down, and then select **RATE**.
  - Type **I6** in the Nper box, type **-E6** in the Pmt box, type **D6** in the Pv box, and then click **OK**.
  - Double-click the **cell G6 fill handle** to copy the function to the **range G7:G16**.
  - Click **cell F6**, type **=G6*B$3**, and then press **Ctrl+Enter**.
  - Double-click the **cell F6 fill handle** to copy the formula to the **range F7:F16**.

e. Calculate the number of 30-year loans and the number of 15-year loans by completing the following steps:
- Click **cell B20**, click **More Functions** in the Function Library group, point to **Statistical**, scroll down, and then select **COUNTIF**.
- Type **$H6:$H16** in the Range box, type **B18** in the Criteria box, and then click **OK**.
- Drag the **cell B20 fill handle** across to **cell C20**.

f. Calculate the average loan amount for 30-year loans and for 15-year loans by completing the following steps:
- Click **cell B21**, click **More Functions**, point to **Statistical**, and then select **AVERAGEIF**.
- Type **$H6:$H16** in the Range box, type **B18** in the Criteria box, type **$D6:$D16** in the Average_range box, and then click **OK**.
- Drag the **cell B21 fill handle** across to **cell C21**.

g. Calculate the total loan amount for 30-year loans and for 15-year loans by completing the following steps:
- Click **cell B22**, click **Math & Trig** in the Function Library group, scroll down, and then select **SUMIF**.
- Type **$H6:$H16** in the Range box, type **B18** in the Criteria box, type **$D6:$D16** in the Sum_range box, and then click **OK**.
- Drag the **cell B22 fill handle** across to **cell C22**.

h. Calculate the number of 30-year loans that are more than $350,000 and the number of 15-year loans that are more than $350,000 by completing the following steps:
- Click **cell B26**, click **More Functions**, point to **Statistical**, scroll down, and then select **COUNTIFS**.
- Type **$D6:$D16** in the Criteria_range1 box, type **">350000"** in the Criteria1 box, type **$H6:$H16** in the Criteria_range2 box, type, type **B18** in the Criteria2 box, and then click **OK**.
- Drag the **cell B26 fill handle** across to **cell C26**.

i. Identify the highest 30-year loan that is more than $350,000 and the highest 15-year loan that is more than $350,000 by completing the following steps:
- Click **cell B27**, click **More Functions**, point to **Statistical**, and then select **MAXIFS**.
- Type **$D6:$D16** in the Criteria_range1 box, type **">350000"** in the Criteria1 box, type **$H6:$H16** in the Criteria_range2 box, type **B18** in the Criteria2 box, and then click **OK**.
- Drag the **cell B27 fill handle** across to **cell C27**.

j. Adapt Step i to enter the MINIFS function in **cell B28** and copy it to **cell C28**.

k. Calculate the number of months that have transpired between their start dates and December 31, 2021, by subtracting the number of years from 2021, multiplying it by 12 months, and then adding the difference in months from the loan date and December 31, 2021, by completing the following steps:
- Click the **Cumulative sheet tab** and click **K11**.
- Type **=(YEAR(M$2)-YEAR(J11))*12+MONTH(M$2)-MONTH(J11)** and press **Ctrl+Enter**.
- Double-click the **cell K11 fill handle** to copy the formula to the **range K12:K21**.

l. Calculate the cumulative interest paid by each customer for the duration of the loan to date (December 31, 2021) by completing the following steps:
- Click **cell L11**, click **Financial** in the Function Library group, and then select **CUMIPMT**.
- Type **G11** in the Rate box, type **I11** in the Nper box, type **D11** in the PV box, type **1** in the Start_period box, type **K11** in the End_period box, press **Tab**, type **0** in the Type box, and then click **OK**. Edit the function by typing – to the right of the equal sign.
- Double-click the **cell L11 fill handle** to copy the formula to the **range L12:L21**.

m. Calculate the cumulative principal paid by each customer for the duration of the loan to date (December 31, 2021) by completing the following steps:

- Click **cell M11**, click **Financial** in the Function Library group, and then select **CUMPRINC**.
- Type **G11** in the Rate box, type **I11** in the Nper box, type **D11** in the PV box, type **1** in the Start_period box, type **K11** in the End_period box, press **Tab**, type **0** in the Type box, and then click **OK**. Edit the function by typing – to the right of the equal sign.
- Double-click the **cell M11 fill handle** to copy the formula to the **range M12:M21**.

n. Calculate the interest paid in the December 31, 2021, payment for each loan by completing the following steps:

- Click **cell N11**, click **Financial** in the Function Library group, and then select **IPMT**.
- Type **G11** in the Rate box, type **K11** in the Per box, type **I11** in the Nper box, type **-D11** in the PV box, and then click **OK**.
- Double-click the **cell N11 fill handle** to copy the formula to the **range N12:N21**.

o. Calculate the principal paid in the December 31, 2021, payment for each loan by completing the following steps:

- Click **cell O11**, click **Financial** in the Function Library group, and then select **PPMT**.
- Type **G11** in the Rate box, type **K11** in the Per box, type **I11** in the Nper box, type **-D11** in the PV box, and then click **OK**.
- Double-click the **cell O11 fill handle** to copy the formula to the **range O12:O21**.

p. Select the **range L11:O21** and apply **Accounting Number Format**.

q. Display a message of either *Keep the current rate* or *See if lower rate to refinance* by completing the following steps:

- Click **cell P11**, click **Logical** in the Function Library group on the Formulas tab, and then select **IF**.
- Type **AND(E11>M$4,F11>M$5)** in the Logical_test box, type **K$6** in the Value_if_true box, type **K$7** in the Value_if_false box, and then click **OK**.
- Double-click the **cell P11 fill handle** to copy the formula to the **range P12:P21**.

r. Create a footer with your name on the left side, the sheet name code in the center, and the file name code on the right side on all sheets.

s. Save and close the file. Exit Excel. Based on your instructor's directions, submit e07p2Loans_LastFirst.

Mid-Level Exercises

1 University Admissions Office

MyLab IT Grader

You work in the Admissions Office for a small regional university in Massachusetts. Your assistant entered a list of college applicants for the Fall 2021 semester. You determine if a student qualifies for early admission or early rejection based on SAT and GPA. After determining the immediate admissions and rejections, you calculate a total score based on SAT and GPA to determine regular admissions and rejections.

a. Open *e07m1Admissions* and save it as **e07m1Admissions_LastFirst**.

b. Insert the DAYS function in **cell D11** that calculates the number of days between the Initial Deadline stored in cell B8 and the Date Received stored in cell C11. Use mixed and relative references correctly. Copy the function to the **range D12:D67**. A negative value indicates the application was received after the initial deadline.

c. Insert an IF function with a nested AND function in **cell G11** to display either **Yes** or **No** in the Admit Early column. The university admits a student early if that student meets both the Early Admission criteria for the SAT (cell B3) and GPA (cell B4). That is, the student's SAT score must be 1400 or higher, and the GPA must be 3.80 or higher. Use relative and mixed references to the cells in the Admission Criteria range. Based on the requirements, the first student *2020005* will be admitted early. Copy the function to the **range G12:G67**.

d. Insert an IF function with a nested OR in **cell H11** to display either **Yes** or **No** in the Reject Early column. The university rejects a student early if that student has either an SAT score less than 800 (cell C3) or a GPA below 1.80 (cell C4). Use relative and mixed references to the cells in the Admission Criteria range. Copy the function to the **range H12:H67**.

e. Enter a formula in **cell I11** to calculate an applicant's score. Multiply the GPA (cell F11) by the multiplier (cell B7) and then add that result to the SAT score (cell E11). The first score is 3925. Copy the formula to the **range I12:I67**.

f. Insert an IFS function in **cell J11**. If Admit Early (cell G11) is Yes, display the text **Early Admission**. If Reject Early (cell H11) is Yes, display the text **Early Rejection**. If the score (cell I11) is greater than the threshold score (cell B6), display **Admit**. If the score (cell I11) is less than or equal to the threshold score (cell B6), display **Reject**. Use mixed reference to cell B6. Copy the function to the **range J12:J67**.

g. Insert the COUNTIF function in **cell H3** to count the number of Early Admissions in the range J11:J67. Use mixed reference for the Range argument and use cell E3 as the condition. Copy the function to the **cell H4**. It should adjust automatically to count the number of Admit in the range J11:J67.

h. Insert the AVERAGEIF function in **cell I3** to calculate the average SAT score in the range E11:E67 where Final Decisions in the range J11:J67 are Early Admission. Use mixed references so that the row numbers in the ranges do not change when copied down. Use a relative reference to **cell E3** for the condition. Apply Number format with zero decimal places. Copy the function to **cell I4**. The copied formula should calculate the average SAT score where Final Decisions are Admit.

i. Insert the AVERAGEIF function in **cell J3** to calculate the average GPA score in the range F11:F67 where Final Decisions in the range J11:J67 are Early Admission. Use mixed references so that the row numbers in the ranges do not change when copied down. Use a relative reference to **cell E3** for the condition. Copy the function to **cell J4**. The copied formula should calculate the average GPA score where Final Decisions are Admit.

j. Insert the COUNTIFS function in **cell H5** to count the number of applications that meet two conditions: Scores in the range I11:I67 are greater than or equal to 3500 and Final Decisions in the range J11:J67 are Early Admissions (cell E3).

k. Insert the COUNTIFS function in **cell H6** to count the number of applications that meet two conditions: Residences in the range B11:B67 are In State and Final Decisions in the range J11:J67 are Early Admissions (cell E3).

l. Insert the MAXIFS function in **cell H7** to identify the highest score in the range I11:I67 that meets two conditions: Residences in the range B11:B67 are In State and Final Decisions in the range J11:J67 are Early Admissions (E3).

m. Insert the AVERAGEIFS function in **cell H8** to calculate the average score in the range I11:I67 that meets two conditions: Residences in the range B11:B67 are In State and Final Decisions in the range J11:J67 are *Adm*. Use the asterisks as wildcards so that it includes both Early Admission and Admit.

n. Insert the AVERAGEIFS function in **cell I5** to calculate the average SAT score that meets two conditions: Scores in the range I11:I67 are greater than or equal to 3500 and Final Decisions in the range J11:J67 are Early Admissions (cell E3). Use mixed references appropriately and copy the function to **cell J5**. The copied function should calculate the average GPA score that meets both conditions.

o. Insert the AVERAGEIFS function in **cell I6** to calculate the average SAT score that meets two conditions: Residences in the range B11:B67 are In State and Final Decisions in the range J11:J67 are Early Admissions (cell E3). Use mixed references appropriately and copy the function to **cell J6**. The copied function should calculate the average GPA score that meets both conditions.

p. Display the Map worksheet and create a map chart from the **range A1:B5**. Change the chart title to **Admissions by State**. Display the Format Data Series task pane and select **Only regions with data** as the map area.

q. Cut the map and paste it in **cell C1**. Set **3.12"** height and **3.26"** width for the map.

r. Create a footer with your name on the left side, the sheet name code in the center, and the file name code on the right side on all sheets.

s. Save and close the file. Exit Excel. Based on your instructor's directions, submit e07m1Admissions_LastFirst.

---

2 Personal Financial Management

Your family is considering purchasing a house and investing in a business venture. You started the structure for a loan amortization table and the investment table. You will complete the first five years of the 20-year loan amortization table. To complete the table, you will enter formulas to calculate the beginning balance, monthly payment, and ending balance. You will use financial functions to calculate the interest and principal paid for each monthly payment. In addition, you want to calculate cumulative interest after the first year, total interest over the life of the loan, and the amount of principal paid after the first year. You also want to see how many months half or more of the payment is for interest. You will then focus your attention on completing an investment table using date functions, formulas, and a financial function to calculate the future value of the investment.

a. Open *e07m2Finances* and save it as **e07m2Finances_LastFirst**.

b. Enter **=D2** in **cell B9** to reference the loan amount for the beginning balance it the Loan worksheet.

c. Enter a formula in **cell C9** to reference the monthly payment in cell D3. Use a mixed reference and copy the formula to the **range C10:C68**.

d. Insert the IPMT function in **cell D9** to calculate the interest paid for the first month using mixed cell references to the input area for the Rate, Nper, and PV arguments and using cell A9 for the Per argument. Make sure the result is a positive value and copy the function to the **range D10:D68**.

e. Insert the PPMT function in **cell E9** to calculate the principal paid for the first month using mixed cell references to the input area for the Rate, Nper, and PV arguments and using cell A9 for the Per argument. Make sure the result is a positive value and copy the function to the **range E10:E68**.

f. Calculate the ending balance in **cell F9** by subtracting the Principal Repayment from the Beginning Balance. Copy the formula to the **range F10:F68**.

g. Enter a formula in **cell B10** to reference the first month's ending balance in cell F9. Copy the formula to the **range B11:B68**.

h. Format the **range B9:F68** with **Accounting Number Format**.

i. Calculate cumulative values by completing the following steps:

- Insert the CUMIPMT function in **cell F2** that calculates the cumulative interest paid for the first year. Use **A9** for the Start_period and **B6** for the End_period arguments. Make sure the result is a positive value.
- Insert the CUMIPMT function in **cell F3** that calculates the total cumulative interest paid for the entire loan. Use **A9** for the Start_period and **D6** for the End_period arguments. Make sure the result is a positive value.
- Insert the CUMPRINC function in **cell F4** that calculates the cumulative principal paid for the first year. Use **A9** for the Start_period and **B6** for the End_period arguments. Make sure the result is a positive value.

j. Insert the COUNTIF function in **cell F5** that counts the number of payment periods in which the interest in the loan amortization table is higher than one-half of the monthly payment (cell D4). Apply **General number format** to the cell.

k. Display the Investment sheet and insert the YEAR function in **cell D4** that extracts the year from cell D3 and adds the number of years (cell B3) to identify the payoff year. Apply **General number format**.

l. Type =**D3** in **cell A7** to refer to the start date. Type **0** in **cell B7**, type =**E7** in **cell B8**, and then copy the formula from **cell B8** to the **range B9:B54**. Type a mixed reference to cell D2 in **cell D7** and copy the formula from **cell D7** to the **range D8:D54**.

m. Enter a formula in **cell C7** that multiplies the beginning balance in cell B7 to the result of dividing the APR by the No. of Pmts per Year. Use mixed and relative cell references correctly. Copy the formula to the **range C8:C54**.

n. Type a formula in **cell E7** to calculate the ending balance by adding the Beginning Balance, Interest Earned, and End-of-Period Investment for row 7. Copy the formula to the **range E8:E54**.

o. Insert the DATE function in **cell A8** with a nested YEAR function, MONTH function, and DAY function in the respective arguments. Within the Month argument, add **1** to the result of the MONTH function to display one month from the date in cell A7. Use cell A7 in the nested arguments. Copy the function to the **range A9:A54** but preserve the fill color in those cells.

p. Insert a financial function in **cell E56** to calculate the future value of the investment. Use references to the respective cells in the input area for the arguments.

q. Create a footer with your name on the left side, the sheet name code in the center, and the file name code on the right side on all sheets.

r. Save and close the file. Exit Excel. Based on your instructor's directions, submit e07m2Finances_LastFirst.

New Castle County Technical Services

New Castle County Technical Services (NCCTS) provides technical support services for a number of companies in New Castle County, Delaware. You previously used What-If Analysis tools to create one- and two-variable data tables to analyze the impact of various changes in the hourly rate and the hours billed. You also used Goal Seek to determine the optimum billing rate to earn $500 for a 5.5-hour repair. Moving forward, NCCTS would like to expand and upgrade its network operation center. It is estimated this will cost $65,000, which your company would like to finance over a four-year span. Your next task is to utilize the WEEKDAY and SWITCH functions to add functionality to the March Hours worksheet. You will then complete an Amortization schedule to detail payment and interest information for the $65,000 investment financed over four years (48 months) paid monthly with a 5.25% annual percentage rate (APR).

a. Open *e07r1NCCTS* and save it as **e07r1NCCTS_LastFirst**.

b. Display the March Hours worksheet, create a nested function in **cell I5** using the SWITCH function and WEEKDAY function to calculate the day of the week that the technical support issue was resolved based on the date in cell H5. In the nested WEEKDAY function, use 1 as the return_type. In the SWITCH function, the value1 argument should be 1, and the Result1 should be Sunday.

c. Copy the function from **cell I5** to the **range I6:I39**.

d. Insert the AVERAGEIF function in **cell O5** to determine the average hours logged on Hardware Support.

e. Insert the MAXIFS function in **cell O6** to determine the max hours logged on Hardware Support.

f. Insert the SUMIF function in **cell O7** to determine the total hours logged on Hardware Support.

g. Display the Amortization worksheet and enter a formula in **cell E3** that calculates the periodic interest rate. Note payments will be made on a monthly basis.

h. Enter a formula in **cell E4** the calculates the total number of payments.

i. Insert the PV in **cell E2** to determine present value of the loan amount.

j. Enter a reference to the beginning balance of the loan in **cell B8**.

k. Enter a reference to the monthly payment in **cell C8**. Use a mixed reference.

l. Insert the IPMT function in **cell D8** to calculate the interest paid for the first payment. Use appropriate mixed and relative cell references.

m. Insert the PPMT function in **cell E8** to calculate the principal repayment for the first payment. Use appropriate mixed and relative cell references.

n. Enter a formula in **cell F8** to calculate the ending balance of the loan after the first payment.

o. Enter a reference to the ending balance of payment 1 (F8) in **cell B9**. Copy the formula to the **range B10:B55**.

p. Select the **range C8:F8** and copy the functions and formulas to the **range C9:F55**.

q. Insert the CUMIPMT function in **cell H8** to calculate the total interest due on the first payment. Use appropriate mixed and relative cell references. Copy the function from cell H8 to the **range H9:H55**.

r. Insert the CUMPRINC function in **cell I8** to calculate the total principal repayment after the first payment. Use appropriate mixed and relative cell references. Copy the function from **cell I8** to the **range I9:I55**.

s. Insert the SUM function in **cell D56** and **cell E56**.

t. Insert a footer with your name on the left side, the sheet name in the center, and the file name code on the right side on all sheets.

u. Save and close the workbook. Based on your instructor's directions, submit e07r1NCCTS_LastFirst.

Home Studio Recording Equipment

Your friend Chris owns a home studio with recording equipment. He created a workbook with three sheets: an equipment inventory, a loan amortization table, and an investment worksheet. However, each sheet contains errors that need to be identified and corrected. Open *e07d1Equipment* and save it as **e07d1Equipment_LastFirst.**

Review the Equipment sheet. The function in cell B3 should count the number of items where the date is older than 1/1/2017 (cell B2). Insert a comment in cell B3 that states the error, and then correct the error in the function. The function in cell B4 should total the cost where the date is older than 1/1/2017. However, it is not providing a correct monetary total, and the result is not formatted correctly. Insert a comment in cell B4 that states the error, and then correct the error in the function. The IF function in cell D7 should test that two conditions are met: the date is before 1/1/2017 and the cost is less than $300. If both conditions are true, display *Consider replacing*. If not, display *Keep using*. Correct the errors in the function and copy the function to the range D8:D29. Then insert a comment in cell D7 that explains what the error was.

Review the Loan sheet. Insert a comment in cell B8 that identifies the error and correct the error. Review the functions in cells D8, E8, and G8. Correct the errors and copy the functions down their respective columns. Insert comments in cells D8, E8, and G8 that explain the errors. Insert a comment in cell H19 to explain the error after comparing the function to the function in cell H31. Correct the error in cell H19. Review the EDATE function in cell H3. The last payment date should be 8/1/2026. Insert a comment in cell H3 and correct the error. Review the function in cell H4. The wrong date function was used, and the number format is not correct. Insert the correct date function and insert a comment in cell H4 to explain the errors.

Review the PV and NPV sheet. The investment period is on an annual basis rather than a monthly basis. Insert a comment in cell H6 that identifies the error and correct the error. Review the NPV function and formula in cell I9. Review the NPV information covered earlier in this chapter. Insert a comment in cell I9 that identifies the error and correct the error.

Create a footer with your name on the left side, the sheet name in the center, and the file name code on the right side on all sheets. Save and close the file. Exit Excel. Based on your instructor's directions, submit e07d1Equipment_LastFirst.

Real Estate Company

You are the office manager for a real estate company in northern Utah County. You tracked real estate listings, including city, agent, listing price, sold price, etc. Agents can represent a seller, a buyer, or both (known as dual agents). Your assistant prepared the spreadsheet structure with agent names, agent types, the listing and sold prices, and the listing and sold dates. You want to complete the spreadsheet by calculating the number of days each house was on the market before being sold, agent commissions, and bonuses. In addition, you will use conditional functions to calculate summary statistics.

For further analysis, you will insert a map chart to indicate the average house selling price by city. Finally, you will create a partial loan amortization table and calculate cumulative interest and principal to show a potential buyer to help the buyer make decisions.

Perform Calculations

The spreadsheet contains codes (BA, DA, SA) to represent agent roles (Buyer's Agent, Dual Agent, Seller's Agent). You want to switch the codes for the actual descriptions. In addition, you want to calculate the number of dates between the list date and sale date. Furthermore, you will calculate agent commissions based on their role and then calculate a bonus if the agent was a Dual Agent and if the house sold within 30 days after being listed.

1. Open *e07c1RealEstate* and save as **e07c1RealEstate_LastFirst**. Make sure the Details sheet tab is active.

2. Insert the SWITCH function in **cell E12** to evaluate the agent code in cell D12. Include mixed cell references to the codes and roles in the range J2:K4 for the values and results arguments. Copy the function to the **range E13:E39**.

3. Insert the DAYS function in **cell J12** to calculate the number of days between the Listing Date and the Sale Date. Copy the function to the **range J13:J39**.

4. Insert the IFS function in **cell K12** to calculate the agent's commission based on the agent code and the applicable rates in the range L2:L4. Use relative and mixed references correctly. Copy the function to the **range K13:K39**.

5. Insert an IF function with a nested AND function in **cell L12** to calculate a bonus. The AND function should ensure both conditions are met: Sold Price divided by the Listing Price is greater than or equal to 100% (cell L7) *and* the Days on Market are less than or equal to 30 (cell L8). If both conditions are met, the bonus is $1,000 (cell L9). Otherwise, the bonus is $0. Use mixed cell references to the input values in the range L7:L9. Copy the function to the **range L12:L39**.

Calculate Cumulative Statistics for One Condition

The top-left section of the spreadsheet is designed for summary statistics for one condition. You will calculate average selling prices and the number of houses sold in each city (the condition). Then you will calculate the total commissions for each agent (the condition).

6. Insert the AVERAGEIF function in **cell B2** to calculate the average Sold Price for houses in the city of Alpine. Use mixed references for the range; use a relative reference to cell A2. Copy the function and use the Paste Formulas option to paste the function in the **range B3:B5** so that the bottom border in cell B5 is preserved.

7. Insert the COUNTIF function in **cell C2** to count the number of houses in the city of Alpine. Use mixed references for the range; and use a relative reference to cell A2. Copy the function and use the Paste Formulas option to paste the function in the **range C3:C5** so that the border in cell C5 is preserved.

8. Insert the SUMIF function in **cell B7** to total the commissions by agent. Use mixed references for the ranges; and use a relative reference to cell A7. Copy the function and use the Paste Formulas option to paste the function in the **range B8:B9** so that the borders are preserved.

Calculate Cumulative Statistics for Two Conditions

The top-middle section of the spreadsheet is designed for summary statistics for multiple conditions. You will calculate the number of houses sold, the total value of those houses, and the highest-price house sold for each agent when he or she served as a Dual Agent (DA). Use mixed references for ranges and the agent code condition in cell J3. Use relative cell references to the agent condition in cell E2. When you copy the formulas, use the paste Formulas options to preserve border formatting.

9. Insert the COUNTIFS function in **cell F2** to count the number of houses sold by the first agent (cell E2) who was a Dual Agent (DA) (J3) for that house. Copy the function to the **range F3:F4** and preserve the bottom border for **cell F4**.

10. Insert the SUMIFS function in **cell G2** to sum the selling prices of the houses sold by the first agent (cell E2) who was a Dual Agent (DA) (J3) for that house. Copy the function to the **range G3:G4** and preserve the bottom border for **cell G4**.

11. Insert the MAXIFS function in **cell H2** to display the highest-price house sold by the first agent (cell E2) who was a Dual Agent (DA) (J3) for that house. Copy the function to the **range H3:H4** and preserve the borders in the **range H3:H4**.

Insert a Map

The Map worksheet contains a list of cities, postal codes, and average house sales. You will insert a map chart to depict the averages visually using the default gradient fill colors.

12. Display the Map worksheet, select the **range B1:C5** and insert a map chart.

13. Cut the map chart and paste it in **cell A7**. Set a **2.31"** height and **3.62"** width.

14. Change the map title to **Average Selling Price by Zip Code**.

15. Display the Format Data Series task pane, select the option to display only regions with data, and show all labels. Close the task pane.

> **MAC TROUBLESHOOTING:** Press Ctrl+click the map and select from the list to access the Format Data Series pane.

Loan Amortization

Your assistant set up the structure for inputs and a partial loan amortization table. You will insert formulas and functions to complete the table using appropriate mixed and relative cell references. In addition, you will calculate the cumulative interest and cumulative principal for the first year. Finally, you will calculate the monthly rate and APR that would result in a lower monthly payment. Make sure all results are positive.

16. Display the Loan worksheet. In **cell B8**, type a reference formula to cell B1. The balance before the first payment is identical to the loan amount. Do not type the value; use the cell reference instead. In **cell B9**, subtract the principal from the beginning balance on the previous row. Copy the formula to the **range B10:B19**.

17. Calculate the interest for the first payment using the IPMT function in **cell C8**. Copy the function to the **range C9:C19**.

18. Calculate the principal paid for the first payment using the PPMT function in **cell D8**. Copy the function to the **range D9:D19**.

19. Insert the CUMIPMT function in **cell B22** that calculates the cumulative interest after the first year. Use references to cells A8 and A19 for the period arguments.

20. Insert the CUMPRINC function in **cell B23** that calculates the cumulative principal paid after the first year. Use references to cells A8 and A19 for the period arguments.

21. Use the RATE financial function in **cell B27** to calculate the periodic rate using $1,400 as the monthly payment (cell B26), the NPER, and loan amount in the original input section.

22. Calculate the APR in **cell B28** by multiplying the monthly rate (cell B27) by 12.

Workbook Completion

You are ready to complete the workbook by adding a footer with identifying information.

23. Create a footer with your name on the left side, the sheet name code in the center, and the file name code on the right side of each worksheet.

24. Save and close the file. Exit Excel. Based on your instructor's directions, submit e07c1RealEstate_LastFirst.

Excel

Statistical Functions

LEARNING OUTCOME You will employ statistical functions to analyze data for decision making.

OBJECTIVES & SKILLS: After you read this chapter, you will be able to:

CASE STUDY | Education Evaluation

You are the superintendent of schools for Banton School System, a K–12 school district in Erie, Pennsylvania. You and your team have the task of evaluating student and teacher performance across schools in your district. As part of your evaluation, you want to perform several statistical calculations based on location, age, and test scores.

First, you will assess middle school students' standardized testing performance. As part of this analysis, you will perform basic descriptive statistical calculations. You will also compare performance to attendance and test the correlation between test scores and daily turnout. You will perform a more advanced evaluation of high school students' performance using the Analysis ToolPak. Finally, you will perform trend analysis to evaluate teachers' salaries based on years of service.

CHAPTER 8

Analyzing Statistics

YanLev/Shutterstock

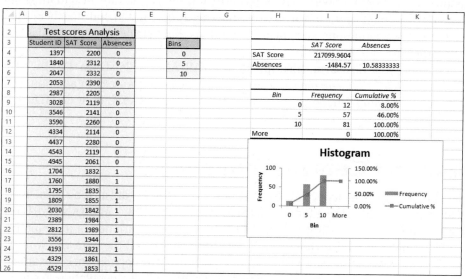

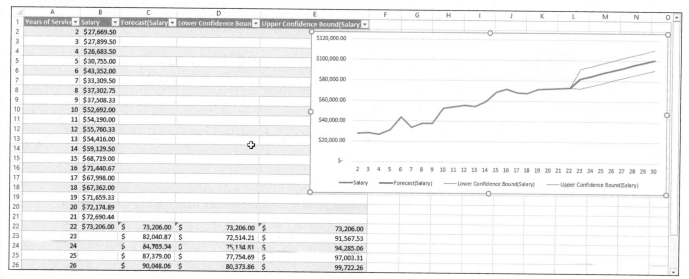

FIGURE 8.1 Educational Evaluation Math and Statistical Functions

CASE STUDY | Education Evaluation

Starting File	File to be Submitted
e08h1Assessment	e08h3Assessment_LastFirst

MyLab IT Grader An alternate version of this project is available as a MyLab IT Grader Assessment

Descriptive Statistical Functions

Attempting to make decisions based on datasets with hundreds—if not thousands—of entries can be a daunting task. Analyzing, summarizing, and describing a large dataset would be close to impossible without the right set of tools. Descriptive statistics provide the tools that help analyze and describe large datasets in pockets of manageable and usable information. While descriptive statistics like average and median are useful in defining the characteristics of a specific dataset, they are only calculations that describe the data and do not provide insight that is applicable into data outside the dataset. For example, a job satisfaction survey of high school teachers in Ohio would not provide any insight into high school teachers' opinions in Arkansas because the survey does not include teachers from other states. In these situations, statistical calculations that help describe the tendencies or trends in the data can be helpful.

In this section, you will use statistical functions—VARIANCE, STANDARD DEVIATION, CORREL, and FREQUENCY—to measure central tendencies of datasets. In addition, you will use relative-standing functions, such as RANK, PERCENTRANK, PERCENTILE, and QUARTILE.

Measuring Central Tendency

In earlier chapters, you learned AVERAGEIF, SUMIF, and COUNTIF are all tools to measure central tendency. To add to these functions, Excel offers FREQUENCY, VARIANCE, STDEV (standard deviation), and CORREL to help define the shape and variation of a population or a sample of data. A *population* is a dataset that contains all the data you want to evaluate. A *sample* is a smaller, more manageable portion of the population. For example, all educators in the state of Pennsylvania constitute an example of a population. A survey of 10% of the educators of each city in Pennsylvania is a sample.

STEP 1 ▶ Use the Standard Deviation and Variance Functions

Variance is a measure of a dataset's dispersion, such as the difference between the highest and lowest test scores in a class. *Standard deviation* is the measure of how far the data sample is spread around the mean. In statistics, mean is also referred to as μ. If calculated manually, the standard deviation is the square root of the variance.

> **TIP: μ (MU)**
> When working in formal statistical applications the Greek letter μ often appears. The symbol μ, pronounced "mu," is another method of describing the average or mean of a range of numbers.

Standard deviation and variance are two of the most popular tools to measure variations within a dataset. Recall that when working in descriptive statistics, the statistician can utilize data from the entire population or from a sample of the population. Excel offers a variety of functions for these calculations based on the use of a sample or a population. Table 8.1 details the options available in Excel.

TABLE 8.1 Standard Deviation and Variance

Statistical Measures	Function	Description
Standard Deviation	STDEVA	Standard deviation of a sample, including logical values and text
	STDEVPA	Standard deviation of a population, including logical values and text
	STDEV.P	Standard deviation of a population
	STDEV.S	Standard deviation of a sample
Variance	VARA	Variance of a sample, including logical values and text
	VARPA	Variance of a population, including logical values and text
	VAR.P	Variance of a population
	VAR.S	Variance of a sample

The variance of a sample is the summation of the squared deviations divided by the sample size $(n - 1)$, in which n is the number of data points. The variance describes how the data points compare to the mean. For example, a large variance indicates the data points are spread farther from the average, while a small variance indicates the data points are very close to the average. The standard deviation also describes the same data spread as the variance; however, the advantage is the standard deviation uses the same units of measure as the original data points and is easier to understand. This value is calculated mathematically by determining the square root of the variance. While calculating standard deviation and variance mathematically may seem daunting, in Excel the functions are no more complicated than using a SUM function.

=STDEV.P(number1,number2,...)

=VAR.P(number1,number2,...)

The STDEV.P and VAR.P functions return values for an entire population. Recall that a population is the entire dataset that is possible. While it would be ideal to have access to 100% of all data that involves your study, it is often not realistic and in many cases sample data must be used. Excel functions calculate sample variations as well, as described in Table 8.1 and as displayed in syntax below.

=STDEV.S(number1,number2,...)

=VAR.S(number1,number2,...)

STEP 2 ▶ **Use the CORREL Function**

The **CORREL function**, short for "correlation coefficient," determines the strength of a relationship between two variables. When used to compare datasets, the function will return a value between –1 and 1. The closer the value is to 1, the stronger the relationship. For example, Figure 8.2 depicts the strength of the relationship between salary and credit score. Cell D3 contains a calculated correlation of .91313591. In other words, this suggests a strong correlation that people with high salaries are more likely to have better credit scores.

In Figure 8.2, the input variables for the CORREL function are entered in arrays. For example, the ranges B2:B15, C7:C10, and D16:D27 are all arrays.

=CORREL(array1,array2)

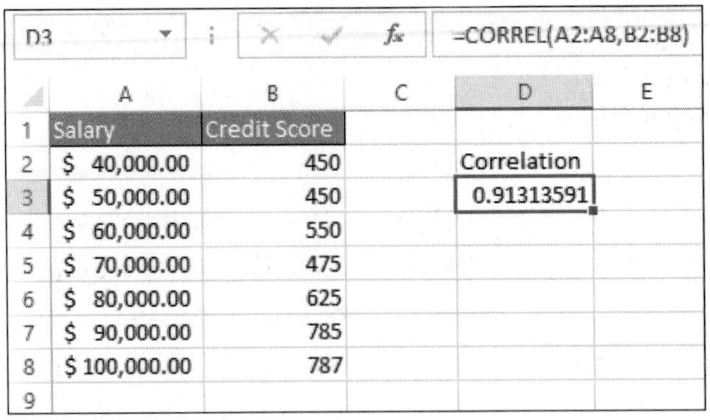
D3 =CORREL(A2:A8,B2:B8)

	A	B	C	D	E
1	Salary	Credit Score			
2	$ 40,000.00	450		Correlation	
3	$ 50,000.00	450		0.91313591	
4	$ 60,000.00	550			
5	$ 70,000.00	475			
6	$ 80,000.00	625			
7	$ 90,000.00	785			
8	$ 100,000.00	787			
9					

FIGURE 8.2 CORREL Function

STEP 3 Use the FREQUENCY Function

The ***FREQUENCY function*** is a descriptive statistical function in Excel that determines the frequency distribution of a dataset. Frequency distribution is a meaningful descriptive tool because it determines how often a set of numbers appears within a dataset. For example, you may want to determine how many student grades fall within the specific range of 100% to 90%, 89% to 80%, and 79% to 70%. This can be accomplished using FREQUENCY. Using the FREQUENCY function is somewhat unique, because it returns the frequency of numeric occurrence in bins. ***Bins*** are data ranges in which values can be categorized and counted. For example, when evaluating grades, bin 100%–90% would contain the number of students who received an A.

In Figure 8.3, the FREQUENCY function returns the number of occurrences of each salary in the dataset as determined by bins in the range H3:H5. In this scenario, there are 12 occurrences of salaries that are less than or equal to $39,203.50 that fall within the first quartile.

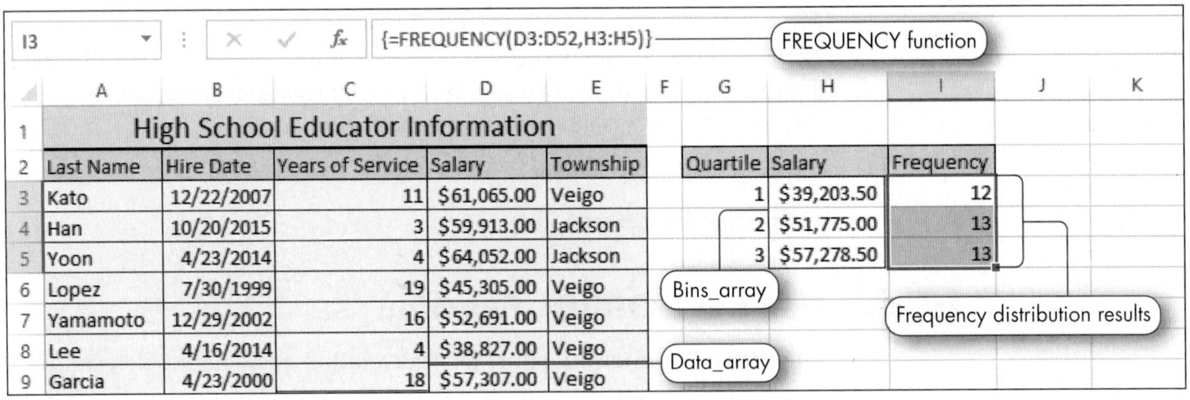
I3 {=FREQUENCY(D3:D52,H3:H5)}

	A	B	C	D	E	F	G	H	I
1	High School Educator Information								
2	Last Name	Hire Date	Years of Service	Salary	Township		Quartile	Salary	Frequency
3	Kato	12/22/2007	11	$61,065.00	Veigo		1	$39,203.50	12
4	Han	10/20/2015	3	$59,913.00	Jackson		2	$51,775.00	13
5	Yoon	4/23/2014	4	$64,052.00	Jackson		3	$57,278.50	13
6	Lopez	7/30/1999	19	$45,305.00	Veigo				
7	Yamamoto	12/29/2002	16	$52,691.00	Veigo				
8	Lee	4/16/2014	4	$38,827.00	Veigo				
9	Garcia	4/23/2000	18	$57,307.00	Veigo				

FIGURE 8.3 FREQUENCY Function

The FREQUENCY function requires two input variables: the data_array and the bins_array.

```
=FREQUENCY(data_array,bins_array)
```

- **data_array.** The data_array is the range of cells that contains the values that are being evaluated for frequency of occurrence. In Figure 8.4, the data_array in column D (D3:D52) is being evaluated to determine how many salaries fall within the first, second, or third quartile.

- **bins_array.** The bins_array is the range of numbers that specifies the bins in which the data should be counted. Similar to a VLOOKUP table, data bins must be defined in the worksheet prior to using the FREQUENCY function. Furthermore, the data must be expressed in breakpoints and cannot be summarized in ranges. For example, in Table 8.2, the breakpoints are single percentages instead of ranges. In Figure 8.4, the range H3:H5 displays the quartile values that will be used as bins to determine frequency of occurrence within the data array.

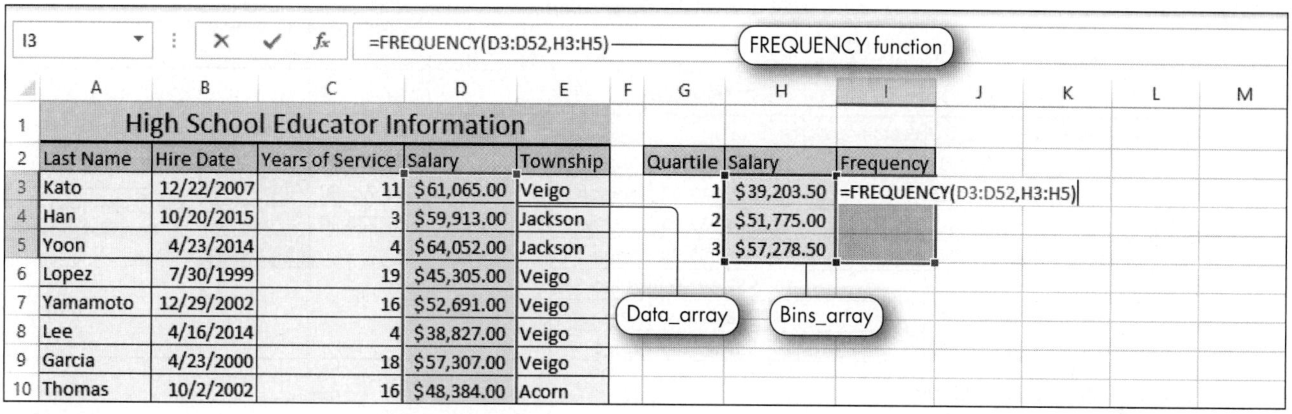

FIGURE 8.4 Frequency Function Input Variables

TABLE 8.2   Bins_array Examples

Correct – Breakpoints	Incorrect – Ranges
59%	0%–59%
60%	60%–69%
70%	70%–79%
80%	80%–89%
90%	90%–100%
100%	

The benefit of FREQUENCY over COUNTIF, which could perform a similar calculation, is that FREQUENCY evaluates an entire dataset in one calculation. Unlike other Excel functions, you do not simply type the FREQUENCY function in a cell and press Enter. Instead, you must first select the cells in which you want to put the FREQUENCY function, type the formula, and then press Ctrl+Shift+Enter. This will return calculation results for all bins defined in the function. If you simply press Enter, the FREQUENCY function will only calculate the frequency of the data that fall in the first cell of bins_array.

To use the FREQUENCY function, complete the following steps:

1. Select a blank range of cells equal to the number of bins to output results.
2. Type =FREQUENCY in the first cell of the output range and press Tab.
3. Select the data_array and type a comma.
4. Select the bins_array and type the right parenthesis.
5. Press Ctrl+Shift+Enter.

	A	B	C	D	E	F	G	H	I	J	K	L
I3			fx	{=FREQUENCY(D3:D52,H3:H5)}				FREQUENCY function				
1	High School Educator Information											
2	Last Name	Hire Date	Years of Service	Salary	Township		Quartile	Salary	Frequency			
3	Kato	12/22/2007	11	$61,065.00	Veigo		1	$39,203.50	12			
4	Han	10/20/2015	3	$59,913.00	Jackson		2	$51,775.00	13			
5	Yoon	4/23/2014	4	$64,052.00	Jackson		3	$57,278.50	13	Outlier return value		
6	Lopez	7/30/1999	19	$45,305.00	Veigo				12			
7	Yamamoto	12/29/2002	16	$52,691.00	Veigo							
8	Lee	4/16/2014	4	$38,827.00	Veigo							
9	Garcia	4/23/2000	18	$57,307.00	Veigo							

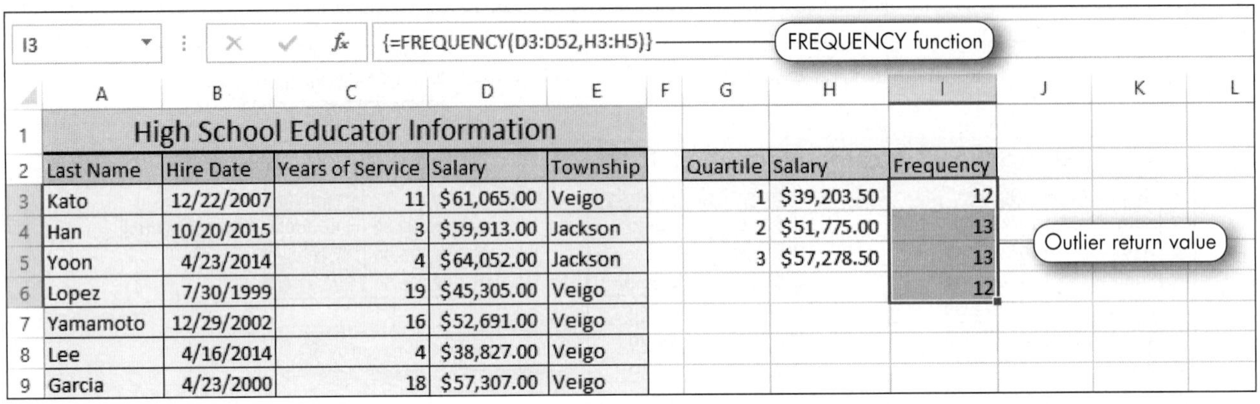

FIGURE 8.5 Numeric Outliers

	A	B	C	D	E	F	G	H	I	J	K	L
1	High School Educator Information											
2	Last Name	Hire Date	Years of Service	Salary	Township		Quartile	Salary	Frequency			
3	Kato	12/22/2007	11	$61,065.00	Veigo		1	$39,203.50	12			
4	Han	10/20/2015	3	$59,913.00	Jackson		2	$51,775.00	13			
5	Yoon	4/23/2014	4	$64,052.00	Jackson		3	$57,278.50	13			
6	Lopez	7/30/1999	19	$45,305.00	Veigo		Edit warning		12			
7	Yamamoto	12/29/2002	16	$52,691.00	Veigo							
8	Lee	4/16/2014	4	$38,827.00	Veigo		Microsoft Excel		×			
9	Garcia	4/23/2000	18	$57,307.00	Veigo							
10	Thomas	10/2/2002	16	$48,384.00	Acorn		⚠ You can't change part of an array.					
11	Gao	7/16/2006	12	$37,575.00	Jackson							
12	Cruz	8/6/2011	7	$60,913.00	Veigo		OK					
13	Cruz	9/11/2006	12	$58,134.00	Acorn							

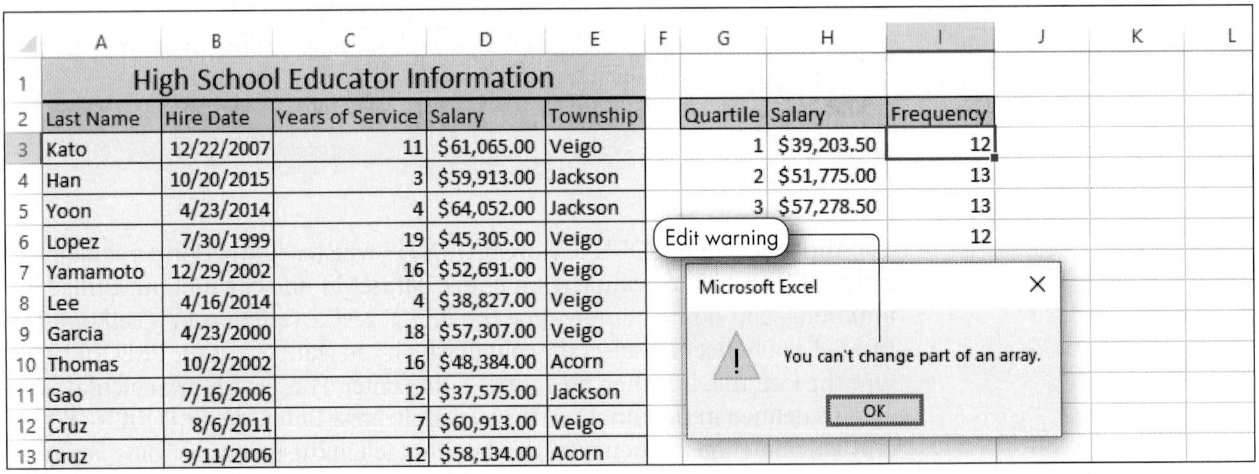

FIGURE 8.6 Changing an Array

Use the LARGE and SMALL Functions

In an earlier chapter, you learned the benefits of examining the high points and low points of your data using the MAX and MIN functions. Moving forward, you may want to extend this analysis by exploring various high or low points within the data. For example, you may be interested in the three students with the worst attendance, or the three students with the best attendance. In these situations, the LARGE and SMALL functions can be beneficial. The *LARGE function* returns the *k*th largest value in a dataset. For example, as shown in Figure 8.7, you could determine third most absences using the LARGE function. In contrast, the ***SMALL function*** returns the *k*th smallest value in a dataset. As shown also in Figure 8.7, the SMALL function could be used to determine the top three best attendance records. It is important to note that the SMALL and LARGE functions can return a value at any position within a range of data. For example, out of 50 students surveyed, you could return the value of the student with the 25th ranked attendance. Figure 8.7 displays the syntax for both the LARGE and SMALL functions.

=LARGE(array, k)

- **array.** The array is an array or range of numeric data for which you want to determine the *k*th largest value.
- **k.** This argument is the position (from the largest) in the array or range of the value to return.

=SMALL(array, k)

- **array.** The array is an array or range of numeric data for which you want to determine the *k*th smallest value.
- **k.** This argument is the position (from the smallest) in the array or range of the value to return.

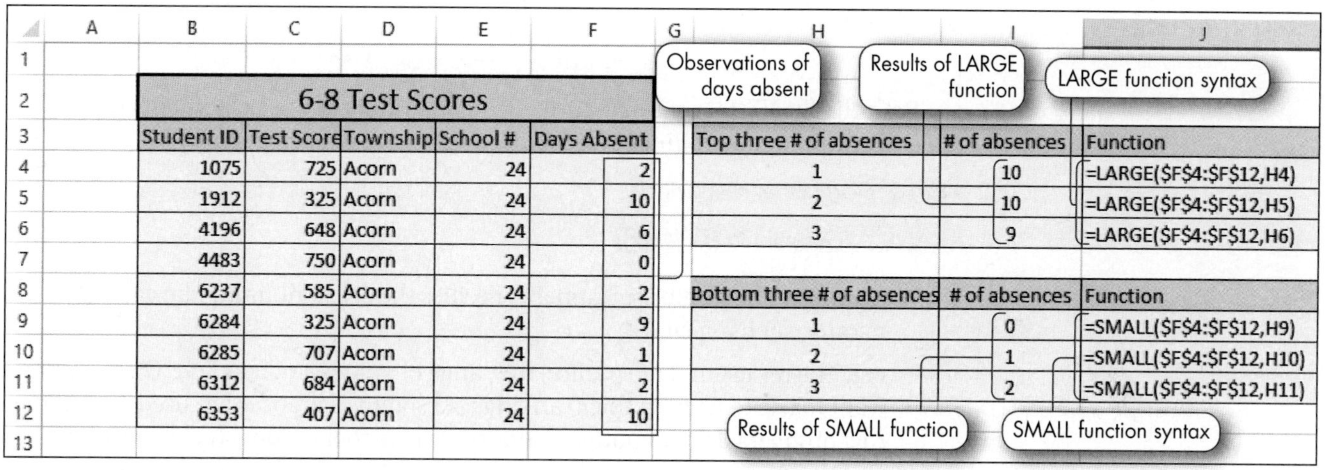

6-8 Test Scores

Student ID	Test Score	Township	School #	Days Absent
1075	725	Acorn	24	2
1912	325	Acorn	24	10
4196	648	Acorn	24	6
4483	750	Acorn	24	0
6237	585	Acorn	24	2
6284	325	Acorn	24	9
6285	707	Acorn	24	1
6312	684	Acorn	24	2
6353	407	Acorn	24	10

Top three # of absences	# of absences	Function
1	10	=LARGE($F$4:$F$12,H4)
2	10	=LARGE($F$4:$F$12,H5)
3	9	=LARGE($F$4:$F$12,H6)

Bottom three # of absences	# of absences	Function
1	0	=SMALL($F$4:$F$12,H9)
2	1	=SMALL($F$4:$F$12,H10)
3	2	=SMALL($F$4:$F$12,H11)

FIGURE 8.7 LARGE and SMALL Functions

Use the RANK and PERCENTRANK Functions

Excel contains two rank functions: RANK.EQ and RANK.AVG. As shown in Figure 8.8, the ***RANK.EQ function*** identifies a value's rank within a list of values, omitting the next rank when tie values exist. For example, the rank of 1 appears in E13. Figure 8.8 indicates that the $57,912.00 salary is the highest-ranking salary in the list, $55,452.00 is the second-highest-ranking salary, and so on. If the range of values contains duplicate numbers (such as $44,966.00 in cells D5 and D6), both values receive the same rank (8), the next ranking (9) is skipped, and the next value ($40,590) is assigned the ranking of 10.

The ***RANK.AVG function*** identifies the rank of a value but assigns an average rank when identical values exist. In Figure 8.8, column F shows the results of the RANK.AVG function in which both $44,966 values have a ranking of 8.5—the average of rankings 8 and 9—instead of a rank of 8. Some statisticians consider the RANK.AVG function results to be more accurate than the RANK.EQ function results.

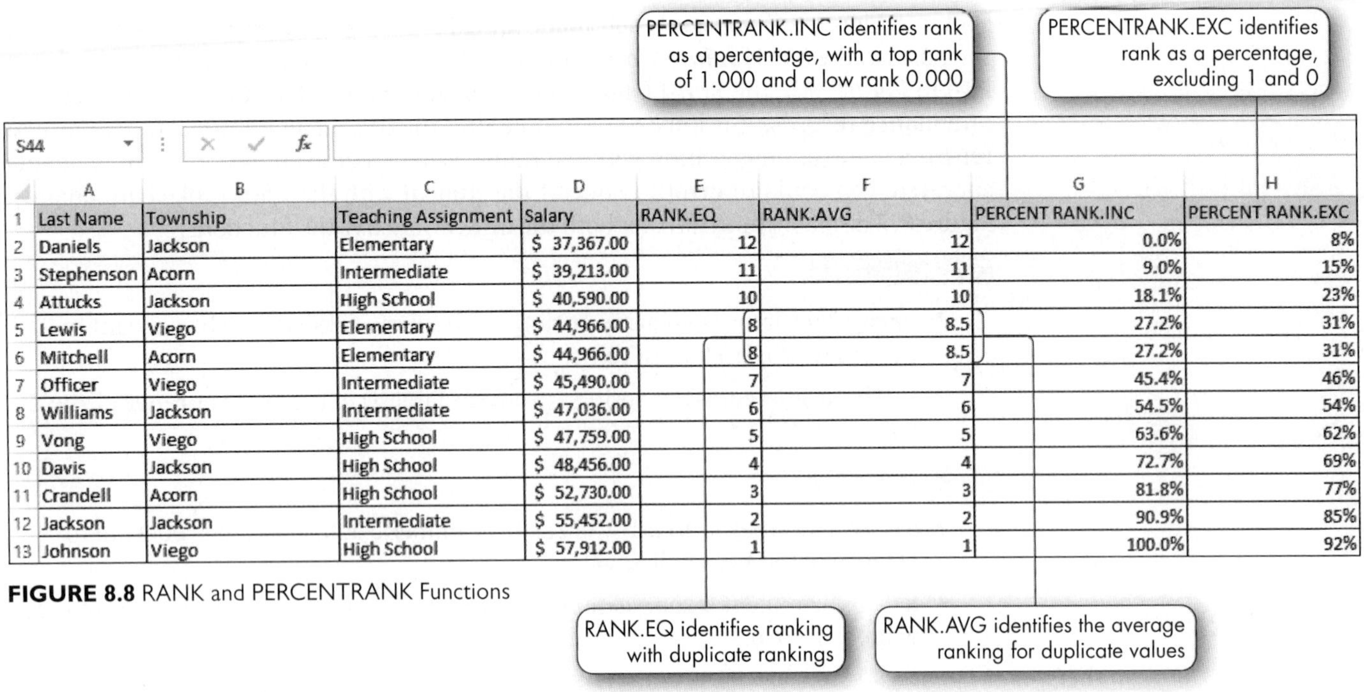

	A	B	C	D	E	F	G	H
1	Last Name	Township	Teaching Assignment	Salary	RANK.EQ	RANK.AVG	PERCENT RANK.INC	PERCENT RANK.EXC
2	Daniels	Jackson	Elementary	$ 37,367.00	12	12	0.0%	8%
3	Stephenson	Acorn	Intermediate	$ 39,213.00	11	11	9.0%	15%
4	Attucks	Jackson	High School	$ 40,590.00	10	10	18.1%	23%
5	Lewis	Viego	Elementary	$ 44,966.00	8	8.5	27.2%	31%
6	Mitchell	Acorn	Elementary	$ 44,966.00	8	8.5	27.2%	31%
7	Officer	Viego	Intermediate	$ 45,490.00	7	7	45.4%	46%
8	Williams	Jackson	Intermediate	$ 47,036.00	6	6	54.5%	54%
9	Vong	Viego	High School	$ 47,759.00	5	5	63.6%	62%
10	Davis	Jackson	High School	$ 48,456.00	4	4	72.7%	69%
11	Crandell	Acorn	High School	$ 52,730.00	3	3	81.8%	77%
12	Jackson	Jackson	Intermediate	$ 55,452.00	2	2	90.9%	85%
13	Johnson	Viego	High School	$ 57,912.00	1	1	100.0%	92%

FIGURE 8.8 RANK and PERCENTRANK Functions

Both the RANK.EQ and RANK.AVG functions contain two arguments (number and ref) and one optional argument (order).

=RANK.EQ(number,ref,[order])

=RANK.AVG(number,ref,[order])

- **number.** The number argument specifies the cell containing the value you want to rank, such as cell D2.
- **ref.** The ref argument specifies the range of values, such as D$2:D$13, that you want to use to identify their rankings. Absolute references are used so that the row numbers do not change as the formula is copied down the column.
- **order.** The optional order argument enables you to specify how you want to rank the values. The implied default is 0, which ranks the values in descending order. Because the order argument was omitted in Figure 8.8, the first-rank salary is the highest salary value of $57,912. If you enter any nonzero value for the order argument, Excel ranks the values in ascending order (i.e., low to high). If the order argument were 2, the first-ranked salary would be the lowest value, which is $37,367.

Some functions have a descriptor added to the function name to further clarify the function's purpose and to distinguish functions that perform similar tasks but have subtle differences. The .INC descriptor indicates *inclusive* functions, that is, the functions *include* particular parameters. The .EXC descriptor indicates *exclusive* functions, that is, functions that *exclude* particular parameters.

The ***PERCENTRANK.INC function*** displays a value's rank as a percentile of the range of data in the dataset. In other words, you can use this function to identify a value's relative standing compared to other values in the dataset. Excel displays ranks as decimal values between 0 and 1, but you can format the results with Percent Style. The first rank is 1.000, and the lowest percent rank is 0.000, because the .INC descriptor *includes* 0 and 1. The percent rank correlates with the rank of a value. For example, in Figure 8.8, the $57,912 salary is the highest-ranking salary; its percent rank is 1.00, or 100% percentile. The

$55,452 value is the second-highest-ranking salary; its percent rank is 0.909, indicating that this salary is in the 90.9% percentile.

The ***PERCENTRANK.EXC function*** is similar to PERCENTRANK.INC in that it returns a value's rank as a percent. This function adheres to best practices in that a percent rank is between 0 and 1 because the EXC descriptor *excludes* the 0 and 1. For this function, the $57,912 salary has a percent rank of 0.923 or is in the 92.3% percentile.

Both the PERCENTRANK.INC and PERCENTRANK.EXC functions contain two required arguments (array and *x*) and one optional argument (significance).

=PERCENTRANK.INC(array,x,[significance])

=PERCENTRANK.EXC(array,x,[significance])

- **array.** The array argument specifies the range that contains the values to compare, such as D$2:D$13.

- **x.** The x argument specifies an individual's salary, such as cell D2.

- **significance.** The optional significance argument designates the number of significant digits for precision. If you omit the significance argument, Excel displays three significant digits.

Use the QUARTILE and PERCENTILE Functions

A ***quartile*** is a value used to divide a range of numbers into four equal groups. The ***QUARTILE.INC function*** identifies the value at a specific quartile for a dataset, *including* quartile 0 for the lowest value and quartile 4 for the highest value in the dataset. The ***QUARTILE.EXC function*** is similar in that it returns the value at a specific quartile, but *excludes* quartiles 0 and 4. These functions contain two required arguments: array and quart. The array argument specifies the range of values. The quart argument is a number that represents a specific quartile (see Table 8.3).

=QUARTILE.INC(array,quart)

=QUARTILE.EXC(array,quart)

TABLE 8.3 Quart Argument

Argument Value	Description
0	Lowest value in the dataset. Identical to using the MIN function. Allowed in QUARTILE.INC only.
1	First quartile of the dataset. Identifies the value at the 25th percentile.
2	Second quartile or median value within the dataset. Identifies the value at the 50th percentile.
3	Third quartile of the dataset. Identifies the value at the 75th percentile
4	Fourth quartile or highest value within the dataset. Identical to using the MAX function. Allowed in QUARTILE.INC only.

In Figure 8.9, cell B24 contains =QUARTILE.INC(D$2:D$13,A24), where cell A24 contains the quartile of Salary. The function returns $37,367, which is the lowest salary in the range. Cell B25 contains =QUARTILE.INC(D$2:D$13,A25) to identify the top salary in the first quartile, which is $43,872. Column G contains the PERCENTRANK.INC function and column H contains the PERCENTRANK.EXC function. Any salaries with 25% or less fall in the first quartile, salaries above 25% and up to 50% fall in the second quartile, salaries above 50% and up to 75% fall in the third quartile, and salaries above 75% fall in the fourth (or top) quartile. The dataset is sorted in ascending order by salary, and the data in columns D and H are color coded to help you identify values within each quartile.

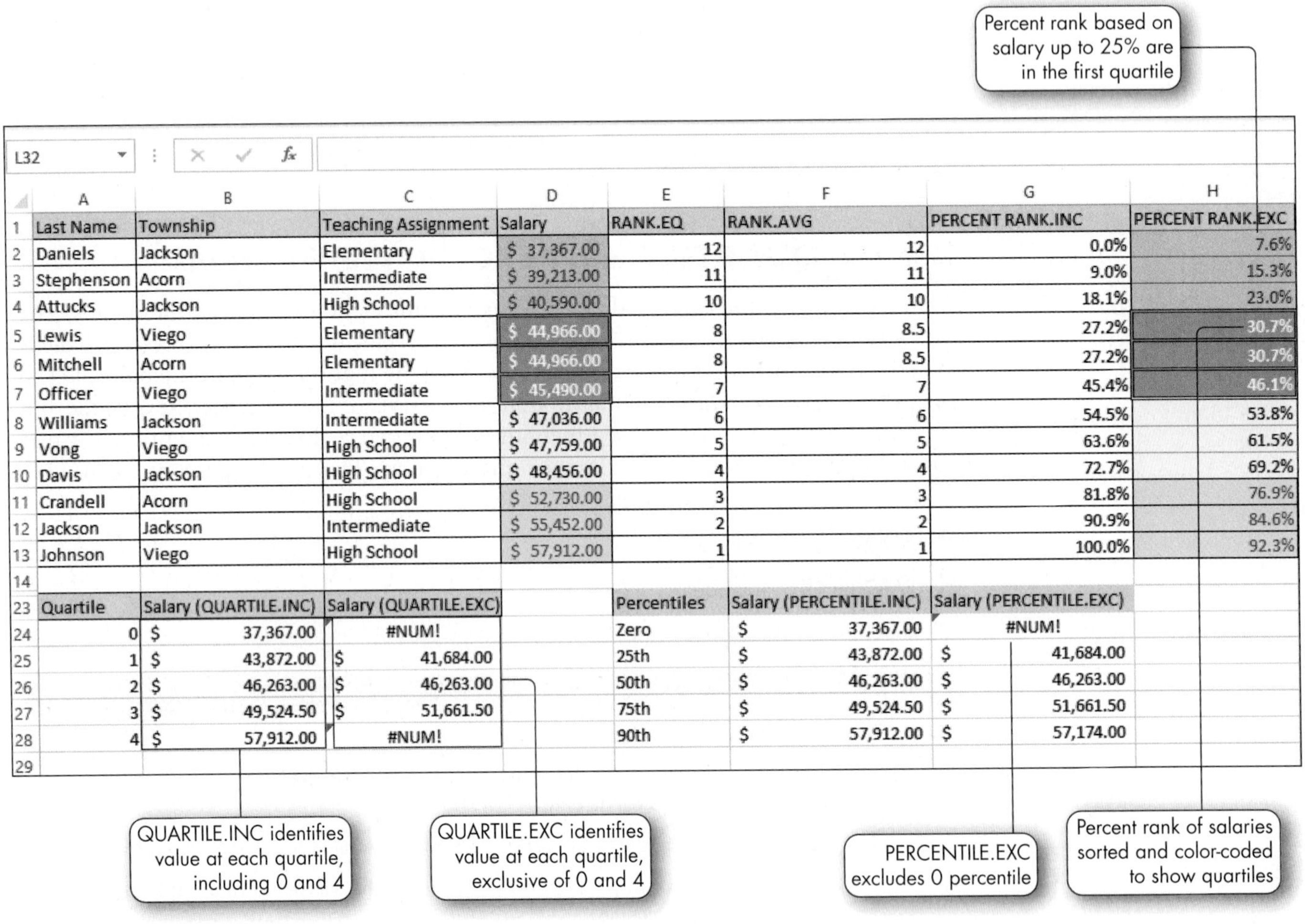

Percent rank based on salary up to 25% are in the first quartile

L32

	A	B	C	D	E	F	G	H
1	Last Name	Township	Teaching Assignment	Salary	RANK.EQ	RANK.AVG	PERCENT RANK.INC	PERCENT RANK.EXC
2	Daniels	Jackson	Elementary	$ 37,367.00	12	12	0.0%	7.6%
3	Stephenson	Acorn	Intermediate	$ 39,213.00	11	11	9.0%	15.3%
4	Attucks	Jackson	High School	$ 40,590.00	10	10	18.1%	23.0%
5	Lewis	Viego	Elementary	$ 44,966.00	8	8.5	27.2%	30.7%
6	Mitchell	Acorn	Elementary	$ 44,966.00	8	8.5	27.2%	30.7%
7	Officer	Viego	Intermediate	$ 45,490.00	7	7	45.4%	46.1%
8	Williams	Jackson	Intermediate	$ 47,036.00	6	6	54.5%	53.8%
9	Vong	Viego	High School	$ 47,759.00	5	5	63.6%	61.5%
10	Davis	Jackson	High School	$ 48,456.00	4	4	72.7%	69.2%
11	Crandell	Acorn	High School	$ 52,730.00	3	3	81.8%	76.9%
12	Jackson	Jackson	Intermediate	$ 55,452.00	2	2	90.9%	84.6%
13	Johnson	Viego	High School	$ 57,912.00	1	1	100.0%	92.3%
14								
23	Quartile	Salary (QUARTILE.INC)	Salary (QUARTILE.EXC)		Percentiles	Salary (PERCENTILE.INC)	Salary (PERCENTILE.EXC)	
24	0	$ 37,367.00	#NUM!		Zero	$ 37,367.00	#NUM!	
25	1	$ 43,872.00	$ 41,684.00		25th	$ 43,872.00	$ 41,684.00	
26	2	$ 46,263.00	$ 46,263.00		50th	$ 46,263.00	$ 46,263.00	
27	3	$ 49,524.50	$ 51,661.50		75th	$ 49,524.50	$ 51,661.50	
28	4	$ 57,912.00	#NUM!		90th	$ 57,912.00	$ 57,174.00	
29								

QUARTILE.INC identifies value at each quartile, including 0 and 4

QUARTILE.EXC identifies value at each quartile, exclusive of 0 and 4

PERCENTILE.EXC excludes 0 percentile

Percent rank of salaries sorted and color-coded to show quartiles

FIGURE 8.9 QUARTILE and PERCENTILE Functions

Range C24:C28 contains the QUARTILE.EXC function. For example, cell C24 contains =QUARTILE.EXC(D$2:D$13,A24). Because QUARTILE.EXC excludes 0 and 4, the function returns #NUM! error values when 0 and 4 are used as the quart argument in cells C24 and C28. The salaries at the second quartiles are identical for either QUARTILE function; however, the salaries for the third quartiles differ based on which function you use. Table 8.4 summarizes the findings from the QUARTILE.INC functions.

TABLE 8.4 Quartile Grouping		
Quartile	**Salary at Top of Quartile**	**Salaries**
1 (0.25 or lower)	$43,872.00	$37,367 $39,213 $40,590
2 (between 0.251 and 0.5)	$46,263.50	$44,966 $44,966 $45,490
3 (between 0.501 and 0.75)	$49,524.50	$47,036 $47,759 $48,456
4 (above 0.75)	$57,912.00	$52,730 $55,452 $57,912

The **PERCENTILE.INC function** identifies the kth percentile of a specified value within a list of values, including the 0th and 100th percentiles. College admissions offices find this function helpful when identifying college applicants' percentiles to determine which candidates to admit to their college. For example, a college might have a policy to admit only candidates who fall within the 80th percentile. The **PERCENTILE.EXC function** also identifies a value at a specified percentile; however, the .EXC *excludes* 0th and 100th percentiles.

The PERCENTILE functions contain two required arguments: array and k. The array argument specifies the range containing values to determine individual standing. For the PERCENTILE.INC function, the k argument specifies the percentile value from 0 to 1. For the PERCENTILE.EXC function, the k argument *excludes* values 0 and 1. For example, 0.25 represents the 25th percentile. In Figure 8.9, cell F25 contains =PERCENTILE.INC(D$2:D$13,0.25) to identify the value at the 25th percentile. Note that this salary ($43,872) is the same as the value returned by =QUARTILE.INC(D$2:D$13,A25). However, unlike the QUARTILE.INC function that has distinct quartiles (0, 1, 2, 3, 4), you can specify any decimal value for the k argument in the PERCENTILE functions, such as =PERCENTILE.INC(D$2:D$13,0.9) to find the value at the 90th percentile. The PERCENTILE.EXC returns different values than PERCENTILE.INC at the higher percentiles. Also, =PERCENTILE.EXC(D$2:D$13,0) returns an error because the .EXC descriptor excludes 0 as a legitimate parameter.

=PERCENTILE.INC(array,k)

=PERCENTILE.EXC(array,k)

Quick Concepts

1. Describe when you would use STDEV.S instead of STDEV.P. ***p. 496***

2. Explain what a value of 0.98 indicates when using the CORREL function. ***p. 497***

3. Explain the benefit of using FREQUENCY instead of COUNTIF. ***p. 498***

Hands-On Exercises

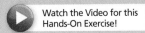

MyLab IT HOE1 Sim Training

Watch the Video for this
Hands-On Exercise!

Skills covered: Use the
Standard Deviation Function •
Use the Variance Function • Use
the CORREL Function • Use the
FREQUENCY Function

1 Descriptive Statistical Functions

As the superintendent, you have been tasked with evaluating student performance. You have decided to base your assessment on standardized test scores and total attendance. You will also test the correlation between test scores and attendance. You plan to base your calculations on a sample of 50 students from the district.

STEP 1 CALCULATE STANDARD DEVIATION AND VARIANCE

The sample you have collected contains test scores as well as attendance information of sixth-grade through eighth-grade students across the district. You will calculate the standard deviation of the test scores within the sample. Refer to Figure 8.10 as you complete Step 1.

| | I9 | | | f_x | =VAR.S(C4:C53) | | | | | |

	A	B	C	D	E	F	G	H	I	J
1										
2		**6-8 Test Scores**								
3		Student ID	Test Score	Township	School #	Days Absent				
4		4483	750	Acorn	24	0		Max Test Score	Sample Size	Average
5		7486	621	Acorn	26	0		800	50	517
6		8843	650	Acorn	26	0				
7		9849	550	Acorn	26	0				
8		7825	715	Jackson	56	0		Standard Deviation	Variance	Correlation
9		8049	799	Jackson	56	0		181	32803	
10		3817	400	Veigo	83	0				
11		6285	707	Acorn	24	1		Days Absent	Frequency	
12		7717	600	Acorn	26	1			0	
13		4562	321	Veigo	83	1			5	
14		1075	725	Acorn	24	2			10	
15		6237	585	Acorn	24	2		Steps b–c: Standard deviation of test scores	Steps d–e: Variance of test scores	
16		6312	684	Acorn	24	2				
17		7025	596	Acorn	26	2				

FIGURE 8.10 Calculate Standard Deviation and Variance

a. Open *e08h1Assessment* and save it as **e08h1Assessment_LastFirst**.

b. Click the **Test Scores worksheet tab**. Click **cell H9**, click the **Formulas tab**, click **More Functions** in the Function Library group, point to **Statistical**, and then select **STDEV.S**.

STDEV.S is being used because the data is a random sample of 50 test scores. If every test score in the population were included in the dataset, STDEV.P would be used.

c. Select the **range C4:C53** and click **OK**. (On a Mac, click Done.) With **cell H9** still selected, click **Decrease Decimal** in the Number group on the Home tab until no decimal points are displayed.

The standard deviation for the sample is 181; therefore, assuming the distribution is normal, about 66% of students will receive a test score between 336 and 698. This is calculated by adding the standard deviation, 181, to the average test score of 517 to determine the high end of the range, and subtracting 181 from 517 to determine the low end of the range.

d. Tab to **cell I9**, click the **Formulas tab**, click **More Functions** in the Function Library group, point to **Statistical**, and then select **VAR.S**.

e. Select the range **C4:C53** and click **OK**. With **cell I9** still selected, click **Decrease Decimal** located in the Number group on the Home tab until no decimal points are displayed.

The results of the VAR.S function (32803) would indicate a large dispersion. The larger the variance, the greater the dispersion of data around the mean test score. This means the data observations are somewhat spread out from the average and from each other.

f. Save the workbook.

STEP 2 ▶ USE THE CORREL FUNCTION

After calculating the standard deviation and variance to help determine the data points' distance from the mean, you theorize that there is a direct relationship between attendance and test scores. You will use the CORREL function to test the strength of the relationship. Refer to Figure 8.11 as you complete Step 2.

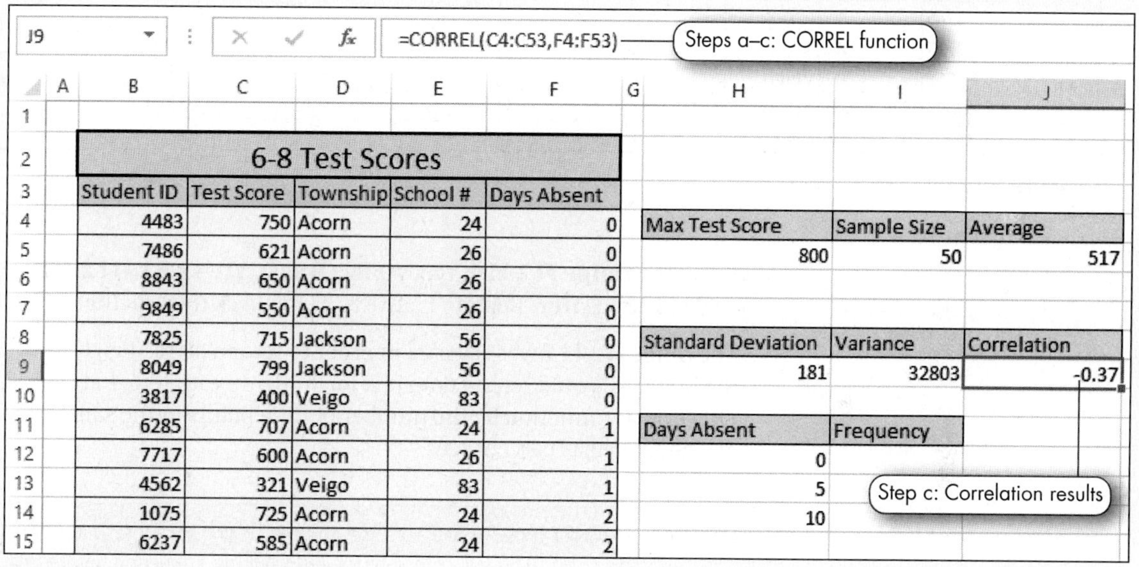

| J9 | ▼ : × ✓ fx | =CORREL(C4:C53,F4:F53) ──── Steps a–c: CORREL function |

	A	B	C	D	E	F	G	H	I	J
1										
2			**6-8 Test Scores**							
3		Student ID	Test Score	Township	School #	Days Absent				
4		4483	750	Acorn	24	0		Max Test Score	Sample Size	Average
5		7486	621	Acorn	26	0		800	50	517
6		8843	650	Acorn	26	0				
7		9849	550	Acorn	26	0				
8		7825	715	Jackson	56	0		Standard Deviation	Variance	Correlation
9		8049	799	Jackson	56	0		181	32803	-0.37
10		3817	400	Veigo	83	0				
11		6285	707	Acorn	24	1		Days Absent	Frequency	
12		7717	600	Acorn	26	1		0		
13		4562	321	Veigo	83	1		5	Step c: Correlation results	
14		1075	725	Acorn	24	2		10		
15		6237	585	Acorn	24	2				

FIGURE 8.11 Use the CORREL Function

a. Click **cell J9**, click the **Formulas tab**, click **More Functions** in the Function Library group, point to **Statistical**, and then select **CORREL**.

b. Click the **Array1 box** and select **C4:C53**, click in the **Array2 box** and select **F4:F53**, and then click **OK**. (On a Mac, click Done.)

c. Ensure **cell J9** is selected and click **Decrease Decimal** in the Number group on the Home tab until two decimal positions are displayed.

The result is –0.37. This means that there is a slightly negative correlation between attendance and test scores. Thus, the more days a student is absent, the lower the test scores received.

d. Save the workbook.

You want to determine the frequency of student absences based on the criteria of perfect attendance. Attendance is divided into the following bins: 0 days absent, 1 to 5 days absent, and 6 to 10 days absent. To do this, you will use the FREQUENCY function. Refer to Figure 8.12 as you complete Step 3.

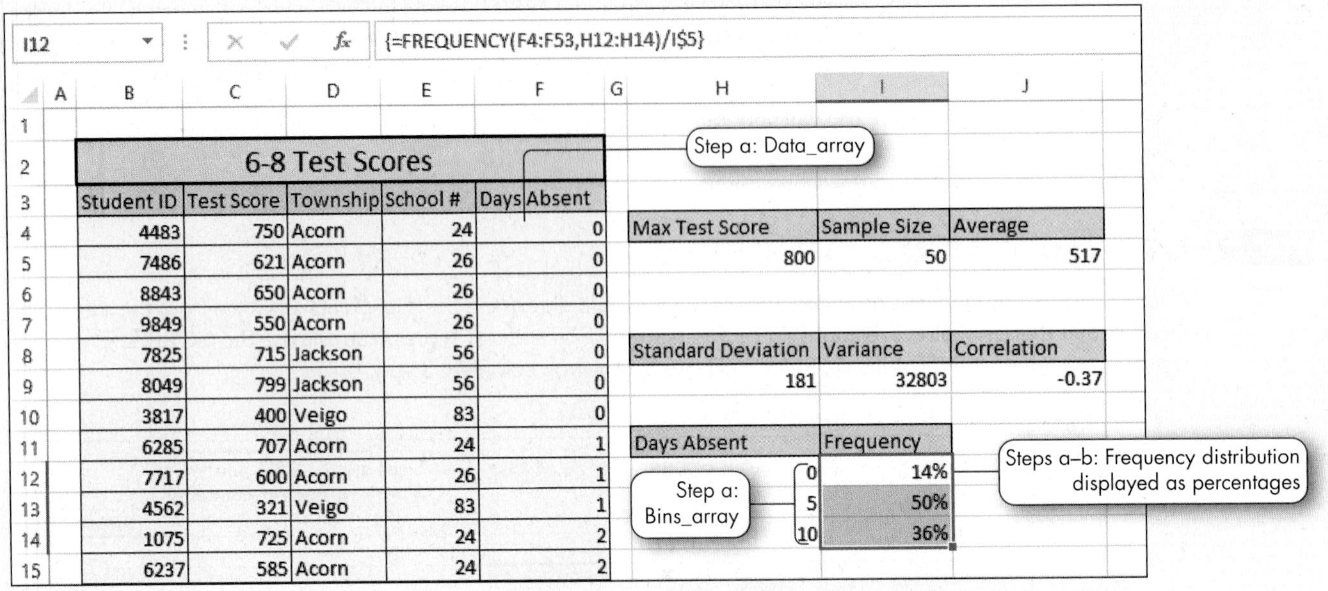

FIGURE 8.12 Frequency Distribution

a. Select the **range I12:I14**, type **=FREQUENCY(F4:F53,H12:H14)/I$5**, and then press **Ctrl+Shift+Enter**. Refer to Figure 8.12 to check the function.

The range I12:I14 was selected in order to return all results. If only I12 were selected, the function would return data just for students with 0 to 4 absences. You divided the FREQUENCY function by the number of data points in the sample (50) so that the results are calculated as percentages.

> **TROUBLESHOOTING:** Make sure you add the closing parenthesis after the bins_array argument, but before adding /I$5. This will complete the FREQUENCY function before dividing the results by 50 to calculate the percentage.

b. Ensure the **range I12:I14** is still selected and apply the **Percentage Number Format** in the Number group on the Home tab.

From the results, you can determine that 14% of the students had perfect attendance, 50% missed between 1 to 5 days, and 36% missed between 6 and 10 days.

c. Save the workbook. Keep the workbook open if you plan to continue with the next Hands-On Exercise. If not, close the workbook, and exit Excel.

Inferential Statistics

Descriptive statistics help define characteristics of a population such as mean, standard deviation, and variance. However, in many situations, you may want to research a population that you may not have the time or resources to evaluate—for example, evaluating test scores for every student in the state of Pennsylvania. In situations in which the population is too large to acquire every point of data needed, samples must be used. The limitation of dealing with samples is that they do not contain all the information available. Depending on the sample set selected, the relationship between the sample set and the entire population may or may not be very strong. Inferential statistics analyze differences between groups and relationships within groups of data. They can be applied to samples to enable you to make more informed statements about a population within a certain margin of error.

In this section, you will use the Excel add-in Analysis ToolPak to calculate inferential statistics on the school system's high school students. You will be required to load the Analysis ToolPak prior to performing calculations.

STEP 1 ▶ Loading the Analysis ToolPak

The **Analysis ToolPak** is an add-in program that provides statistical analysis tools. Much like the Solver add-in, the Analysis ToolPak must be enabled before use (see Figure 8.13). You can use the Analysis ToolPak to perform various calculations such as ANOVA, Correlation, F-Tests, T-Tests, Z-Tests, and more.

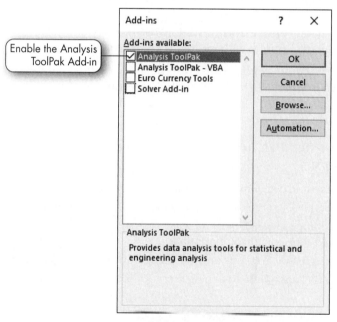

Enable the Analysis ToolPak Add-in

FIGURE 8.13 Analysis ToolPak

> **To enable the Analysis ToolPak Add-in, complete the following steps:**
>
> 1. Click the File tab and click Options.
> 2. Select Add-ins from the list on the left side.
> 3. Ensure that Excel Add-ins is selected in the Manage box and click Go.
> 4. Click the Analysis ToolPak check box to select it and click OK.

> **On a Mac, to enable the Analysis ToolPak Add-in, complete the following steps:**
>
> 1. Click the Tools menu and select Excel Add-ins.
> 2. Click the Analysis ToolPak checkbox to select it.
> 3. Click OK.

Performing Analysis Using the Analysis ToolPak

The Analysis ToolPak offers 19 tools that fit a variety of needs across all professions. In Excel, there are alternate options to many of these tools, such as the FREQUENCY function versus the Histogram summary in the ToolPak. The benefit of using the Analysis ToolPak versus the corresponding Excel function is that the ToolPak will generate reports, while the function equivalents only return values.

STEP 2 ⟩ **Perform Analysis of Variance (ANOVA)**

In statistics, it is common to compare the means between two or more sample groups of data—for example, comparing test scores from a cross-section sample of multiple high schools in the same district or comparing test scores in a time-series sample over a period of years from the same high school. A common tool to compare these samples is analysis of variance, also abbreviated as ANOVA.

ANOVA is a statistical hypothesis test that determines if samples of data were taken from the same population. In practical use, it can be used to accept or reject a hypothesis. There is no one function to calculate ANOVA in Excel; however, you can create an ANOVA report using the Analysis ToolPak.

Three types of ANOVA calculations can be performed:

- **Single factor.** Tests how two or more datasets change based on one independent variable.

- **Two factor with replication.** Tests how two or more datasets change based on two independent variables with multiple combinations of each data observation.

- **Two factor without replication.** Tests how two or more datasets change based on two independent variables without multiple combinations of each data observation.

> **To use the Analysis ToolPak to create a single factor ANOVA report, complete the following steps:**
>
> 1. Click the Data tab and click Data Analysis in the Analysis group.
> 2. Select Anova: Single Factor in the Data Analysis dialog box and click OK.
> 3. Click the Input Range selection box and select the range of data you want to analyze. (Note this should contain only numeric data.)
> 4. Select either Grouped By Columns or Grouped By Rows based on your data layout.
> 5. Choose the default Alpha 0.05 (meaning there is a 5% chance of rejecting the null hypothesis).
> 6. Select an output option.
> 7. Click OK.

Excel reports the results on a new worksheet in the same workbook if the *New Worksheet Ply* option is selected. The results of the sample test scores can be viewed in Figure 8.14. The summary portion of the report provides basic descriptive statistics of each group analyzed. The ANOVA portion of the report breaks the data into two sets: between groups and within groups. ANOVA analysis within groups measures random variation. ANOVA analysis between groups measures variation due to differences within the group. Table 8.5 provides further detail on the ANOVA summary information.

	A	B	C	D	E	F	G
1	Anova: Single Factor						
2							
3	SUMMARY						
4	*Groups*	*Count*	*Sum*	*Average*	*Variance*		
5	High School 1	50	64632	1292.64	250915.7		
6	High School 2	50	61331	1226.62	220865.5		
7	High School 3	50	66208	1324.16	187754.1		
8							
9							
10	ANOVA						
11	*Source of Variation*	*SS*	*df*	*MS*	*F*	*P-value*	*F crit*
12	Between Groups	247770	2	123885	0.563511	0.570432	3.057621
13	Within Groups	32317224	147	219845.1			
14							
15	Total	32564994	149				
16							

FIGURE 8.14 ANOVA Results

TABLE 8.5 ANOVA Summary Report

Abbreviation	Full name	Explanation
SS	Sum of squares	Sum of the squares of the data points in the sample. This is a measure of how far the data observations are from the mean.
df	Degrees of freedom	The number of data points in the sample – 1 ($N - 1$). The larger the degrees of freedom, the more data observations are included in the calculations. This can lead to a higher probability that the data accurately represents the population.
MS	Mean square	The mean of the sample squared. This is an estimate of variance across the data.
F	F ratio	Equal to the mean square between groups of data divided by the mean square within groups of data
P-value	Probability	Probability of population being similar to the sample
F crit	Critical value of F	Used to determine if the F-Test is significant

STEP 3 Calculate COVARIANCE

Covariance is similar to correlation. It is a measure of how two sets of data vary simultaneously. It is calculated by taking the average of the products of the deviations of a data point pair in two datasets. In Excel, there are COVARIANCE.P and COVARIANCE.S functions that can calculate covariance of population or sample data. The data used to manually calculate COVARIANCE using functions can also be used to calculate COVARIANCE in the Analysis ToolPak. While both the Analysis ToolPak and COVARIANCE functions will return the covariance, the COVARIANCE function is limited to two sets of data.

For example, you may hypothesize that the more days of school missed by a student, the lower the student's SAT scores (which would produce a negative covariance). The CORREL function would return a numerical value that analyzes the strength of the relation. The covariance analysis will produce a matrix that shows how the datasets change together (see Figure 8.15). A positive covariance indicates a positive relationship, a negative value indicates an inverse relationship, and a 0 value indicates no relationship. For example, –1484.57 indicates a negative relationship between test scores and attendance, confirming the hypothesis.

⊿	A	B	C	D	E	F	G	H
1								
2		Test scores Analysis						
3		Student ID	SAT Score	Absences				
4		1003	485	10				
5		1016	1749	2				
6		1017	1586	3				
7		1030	1016	8				
8		1114	1761	2				
9		1129	868	9			SAT Score	Absences
10		1169	1328	5		SAT Score	217099.9604	
11		1234	1226	6		Absences	-1484.57	10.58333333
12		1236	761	10				
13		1246	1038	7				

Negative covariance indicates negative relationship

Variance within data

FIGURE 8.15 COVARIANCE Results

To create a covariance report, complete the following steps:

1. Click the Data tab and click Data Analysis in the Analysis group.
2. Select Covariance and click OK.
3. Click the Input Range selection box and select the range of the data you want to analyze.
4. Select Grouped By Columns or Grouped By Rows depending on the organization of the datasets.
5. Click the Labels in First Row check box, if the first row contains labels, to select it.
6. Choose the Output Range or choose to place the output in a new workbook or worksheet and click OK.

STEP 4 ▶ Create a Histogram

A *histogram* is a visual display of tabulated frequencies (see Figure 8.16). This is a useful tool to help visualize the data calculated using the FREQUENCY function. A histogram displays data in a similar fashion to a column chart, however, the data displayed depicts a series of data observations that could span multiple groups compared to a single series of data in a column chart. There are several ways to create a histogram in Excel; however, one of the simplest methods is by using the Analysis ToolPak. Creating a histogram is somewhat similar to using the FREQUENCY function in that it requires bins to tabulate the data and will return a frequency distribution table. Each bin will appear as a column in the histogram, and like the FREQUENCY function, the bin size must be predefined. Figure 8.16 depicts a completed histogram of days absent based on the bins in column A. Furthermore, you have the option of creating a Pareto (sorted histogram) or cumulative percentage histogram along with the chart output.

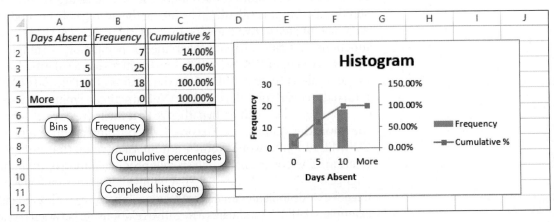

FIGURE 8.16 Histogram Results

To create a histogram, complete the following steps:

1. Click the Data tab, click Data Analysis, select Histogram, and click OK.
2. Enter the Input Range in the Input Range box.
3. Enter the Bin Range in the Bin Range box.
4. Click the Labels box (clicking this option will include column headings in the histogram).
5. Select the output options.
6. Select Chart Output to display the visual histogram in the output.
7. Click OK.

TIP: MANUALLY CREATE A HISTOGRAM

While the Analysis ToolPak can quickly create a histogram, it is not the only option in Excel. You can manually create a histogram by clicking the Insert tab, clicking Insert Statistic Chart, and selecting Histogram. It is important to note that the frequency table is automatically created only when using the Analysis ToolPak.

STEP 5 # Creating a Forecast Sheet

A *Forecast Sheet* is a business intelligence feature that creates a forecast worksheet to detail trends based on historical data. This feature extrapolates information based on given data and generates a worksheet that details the predictions. For example, suppose you track average SAT test scores over the years as they compare to average teacher salaries. As shown in Figure 8.17, the Forecast Sheet feature will generate a chart and corresponding table to provide a forecast based on given data. The results will provide information with a default confidence level of 95% and gives the user the option of setting start values, end values, and chart type within the forecast. Forecast Sheet can create either a line chart or column chart to visualize the data. (On a Mac, the Forecast Sheet feature is not available.)

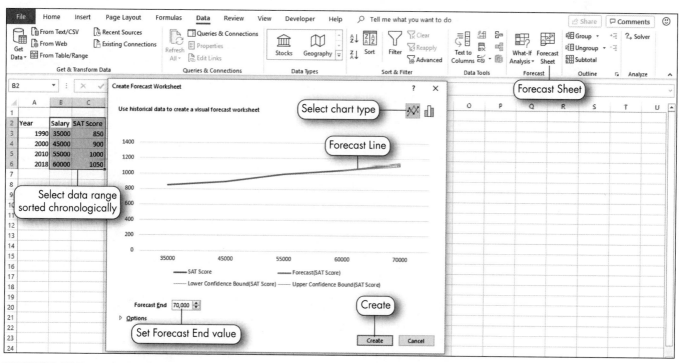

FIGURE 8.17 Forecast Worksheet

To create a Forecast worksheet, complete the following steps:

1. Sort the data in chronological order.
2. Select the sorted data range for the forecast.
3. Click the Data tab and click Forecast Sheet.
4. Set the value for the Forecast End.
5. Click Create.

Quick Concepts

4. Explain the difference between inferential statistics and descriptive statistics. *p. 509*
5. Describe the benefit of using the Analysis ToolPak to calculate COVARIANCE over the COVARIANCE.P or COVARIANCE.S functions. *p. 511*
6. Explain how data bins are depicted in histograms. *p. 512*

Hands-On Exercises

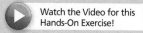
Skills covered: Load the Analysis ToolPak • Perform Analysis of Variance (ANOVA) • Calculate COVARIANCE • Create a Histogram • Create a Forecast Sheet

2 Inferential Statistics

For the next portion of your educational assessment, you will analyze SAT data across multiple high schools in the district. As part of the analysis, you use the Analysis ToolPak to calculate an ANOVA report as well as test the variation of test scores and SAT results using covariance. You will create a histogram of all SAT scores in the sample, and finally you will use the Forecast Sheet feature to forecast the outcomes of absences on test scores.

STEP 1 LOAD THE ANALYSIS TOOLPAK

Before you begin your calculations, you need to enable the Analysis ToolPak add-in. If the ToolPak is already loaded, Data Analysis will appear in the Analysis group on the Data tab. Refer to Figure 8.18 as you complete Step 1.

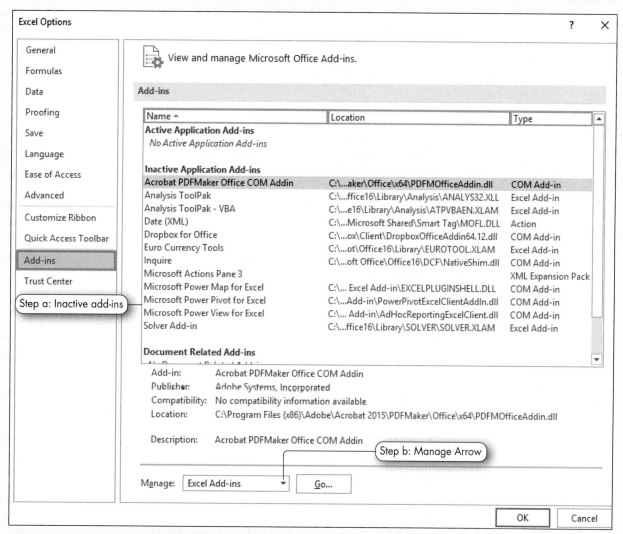

FIGURE 8.18 Excel Options Dialog Box

TROUBLESHOOTING: If the Analysis ToolPak add-in is already enabled, skip to Step 2.

a. Click the **File tab**, click **Options**, and then click **Add-ins** on the left pane.

The Excel Options dialog box displays a list of active and inactive application add-ins.

b. Click the **Manage arrow**, ensure **Excel Add-ins** is selected, and then click **Go**.

The Add-ins dialog box opens, containing a list of available add-in applications.

c. Click the **Analysis ToolPak check box** in the Add-ins available list to select it and click **OK**.

d. Save the workbook.

MAC TROUBLESHOOTING: Click the Tools menu and select Excel Add-ins. Click the Analysis ToolPak checkbox to select it. Click OK. Save the workbook.

STEP 2 PERFORM ANALYSIS OF VARIANCE (ANOVA)

You are ready to create an analysis of variance using the Analysis ToolPak. You will analyze a cross-section data sample of SAT scores from three high schools in the school district to explore variance based on location. Refer to Figure 8.19 as you complete Step 2.

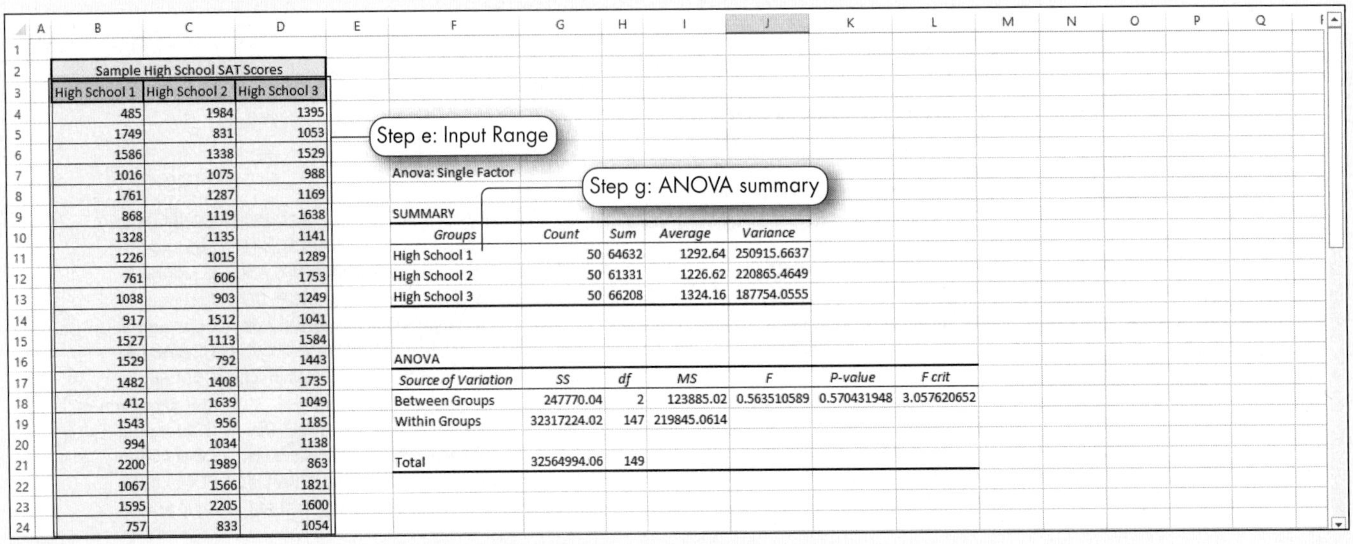

FIGURE 8.19 ANOVA Summary

a. Open *e08h1Assessment_LastFirst* if you closed it at the end of Hands-On Exercise 1, and save it as **e08h2Assessment_LastFirst,** changing h1 to h2.

b. Click the **High School Samples worksheet tab**.

c. Click the **Data tab** and click **Data Analysis** in the Analysis group.

d. Select **Anova: Single Factor** from the Analysis Tools list box and click **OK**.

e. Click the Input Range box and select **B3:D53**.

This selects the dataset to be utilized for the ANOVA.

f. Click the **Labels in first row check box** (on a Mac, click First Row) to select it and leave the Alpha setting at the default 0.05.

The data used for the ANOVA contains three sets of data observations with labels. These values will be used as descriptive labels in the output.

g. Click **Output Range** in the Output options section and type **F7** in the output range box. Click **OK**.

This embeds the ANOVA output on the current worksheet. Notice the P-value of .57: this indicates that there is natural variation in the test scores and there is no relationship between test scores and location.

h. Ensure the **range F7:L21** is selected, click the **Home tab**, and then select **AutoFit Column Width** from the Format menu in the Cells group.

i. Save the workbook.

STEP 3 ▸ CALCULATE COVARIANCE

You hypothesize that there is a negative relationship between attendance and test scores. Your next assessment is an analysis of trends between SAT scores and attendance. To complete this task, you will create a covariance summary. Refer to Figure 8.20 as you complete Step 3.

	A	B	C	D	E	F	G	H	I	J	K
2		Test scores Analysis					*Step e: Labels in first row selected*				
3		Student ID	SAT Score	Absences		Bins	Covariance				? ✕
4		1003	485	10		0	Input				
5		1016	1749	2		5	Input Range: $C$3:$D$153				OK
6		1017	1586	3		10	Grouped By: ● Columns				Cancel
7		1030	1016	8			○ Rows				Help
8		1114	1761	2			☑ Labels in first row				
9		1129	868	9			*Step d: Input Range*				
10		1169	1328	5			Output options				
11		1234	1226	6			● Output Range: $H$3				
12		1236	761	10			○ New Worksheet Ply:				
13		1246	1038	7			○ New Workbook				
14		1251	917	9			*Step f: Output Range*				
15		1286	1527	3							

FIGURE 8.20 COVARIANCE Summary

a. Make the **Combined Score Samples worksheet** active.

b. Click the **Data tab** and click **Data Analysis** in the Analysis group.

c. Select **Covariance** from the Analysis Tools list box and click **OK**.

d. Click in the **Input Range box** and type **C3:D153**.

This selects the dataset to be utilized for the covariance summary.

e. Ensure **Columns** and **Labels in first row** are selected.

f. Click **Output Range** in the Output options section, type **H3** in the Output Range box, and click **OK**.

By selecting cell H3 for the output range, you place the summary starting in cell H3 on the worksheet. The covariance of −1484.57 indicates a negative relationship between attendance and test scores. This means that based on the results, as the days absent increase, test scores decrease.

g. Resize **columns I:J** to a width of **13**.

h. Save the workbook.

Your next task is to create a histogram to document the frequency of absences in the high school. To complete the task, you will organize the data into bins for perfect attendance, 1 to 5 absences, and 6 to 10 absences. Refer to Figure 8.21 as you complete Step 4.

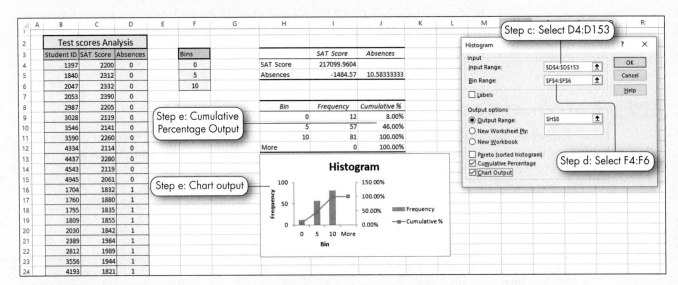

FIGURE 8.21 Complete Histogram

a. Ensure the Combined Score Samples worksheet is still active and click **Data Analysis** in the Analysis group on the Data tab.

b. Select **Histogram** from the Analysis Tools list box and click **OK**.

c. Click the **Input Range box** and select the **range D4:D153**.

d. Click the **Bin Range box** and select the **range F4:F6**.

e. Click **Output Range** in the Output options section, type **H8** in the Output Range box, click **Cumulative Percentage**, click **Chart Output**, and then click **OK**.

The Data Analysis ToolPak places the frequency information and histogram starting in cell H8.

f. Move the newly created histogram chart so that the upper-left corner is in cell H13 directly under the data.

g. Save the workbook.

Your data only contains data from students with up to 10 absences; however, you want to predict the impact on test scores of students with more than 10 absences. Your last task is creating a forecast sheet to predict the impact of up to 15 absences on SAT scores. To complete the task, you will sort the data and create a forecast sheet ending with a forecast of 15 absences. Refer to Figure 8.22 as you complete Step 5.

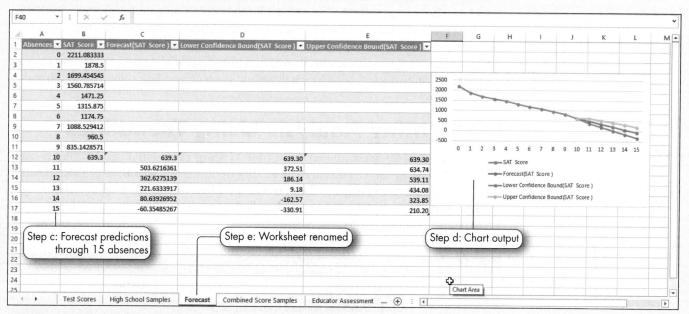

FIGURE 8.22 Create Forecast Sheet

> **MAC TROUBLESHOOTING:** The Forecast Sheet feature is not available on Excel for Mac.

a. Ensure the Combined Score Samples worksheet is active. Click **cell D4**. Click **Sort Smallest to Largest** in the Sort & Filter group on the Data tab.

Before creating the Forecast sheet, the data must be sorted. The data is now sorted in ascending order based on absences.

b. Select the **range C3:D153** and click **Forecast Sheet** in the Forecast group.

c. Type **15** in the Forecast End box and click **Create**.

d. Click the newly created chart, click the **Design tab** and select **Style 12** in the Chart Styles group. Position the chart so the upper-left corner is in **cell F4** and resize so it fills the **range F4:L16**.

e. Rename the worksheet **Forecast**.

f. Save the workbook. Keep the workbook open if you plan to continue with the next Hands-On Exercise. If not, close the workbook, and exit Excel.

Trend Analysis

When tracking data over time, patterns can emerge that provide insight into the nature of the information. For example, tracking the starting salaries of recent college graduates shows a steady increase year over year. While there is a possibility some of the data observations collected happened due to random chance, trend analysis can be performed to help predict within a reasonable level of confidence how the data will change over time. *Trend Analysis* is a method of analyzing historical data to gain insight into predicting potential future outcomes. The information gained from this analysis can then be used to make more informed decisions.

In this section, you will use statistical functions to perform trend analysis to forecast results based on historical data. You will also create a chart to visualize the data trends.

Performing Analysis Using Trendlines

In an earlier chapter you explored the various types of charts that can be created using Excel. Some charts can be enhanced by adding trendlines. A *trendline* is a visualization that shows patterns in data. Excel can create six different variations of trendlines based on the nature of your data. Table 8.6 details the trendline capabilities of Excel and the underlying equations used.

TABLE 8.6	Trendline Descriptions	
Name	**Description**	**Equation**
Linear	Linear trendlines create a least squares line to best fit simple linear datasets.	$Y = mx + b$
Logarithmic	Logarithmic trendlines are best used to track rate of change when the data observation decreases or increases quickly.	$Y = c \ln(x) + b$
Polynomial	Polynomial trendlines are best used to visualize data that has large variations in observations.	$Y = b + c_1x + c_2x^2 + c_3x^3 \ldots$
Power	Power curve trendlines are best used for data observations that increase at a specific rate over time.	$Y = cx^b$
Exponential	Exponential trendlines are best used when date values increase or decrease at a specific rate.	$Y = ce^{bx}$
Moving Average	Moving Average trendlines are best utilized to evenly visualize data that fluctuates over time.	$F_t = A_t + A_{t-1} + \ldots A_{t-n+1}/n$

STEP 1 ▶ Add a Linear Trendline to a Chart

A *linear trendline* is a chart element that is drawn through the center of the data observations on a chart—in other words, it creates a least squares line to best fit simple linear datasets. As shown in Figure 8.23, the linear trendline visualizes the increase of educator's salaries over time. The linear equation $y = 2967.3x + 16304$ is the algorithm used to draw the line. This equation can also be used as an instrument for forecasting. Simply replace the x with the educator's years of service and solve for y. The result is the predicted salary based on years of service plus or minus the standard error. For example, if an educator worked for 25 years, his or her predicted salary is $y = 2967.3(25) + 16304$. Based on this linear equation, the predicted salary is \$90,486.50. The *standard error* is the level of accuracy of the forecast. In this example, the standard error is \$5,557.87. Therefore, the predicted salary for an educator at 25 years of service is \$90,486.50 with a predicted standard error of \$5,557.87. You will explore the standard error function (STEYX) later in the chapter.

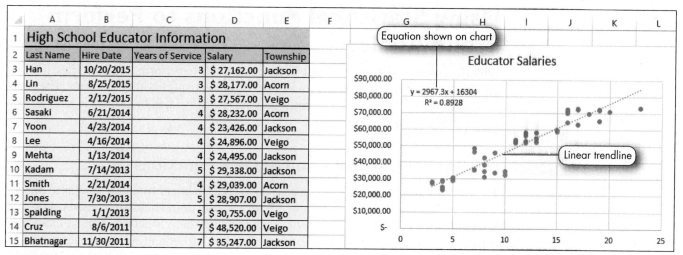

FIGURE 8.23 Linear Trendline

In Excel, trendlines are considered Chart Elements and can be added from the Chart Elements pane. To add a linear trendline to a chart, select the chart and click Chart Elements. Select the trendline and trendline options. Two commonly used trendline options are Display Equation on chart and Display R-squared value on chart (see Figure 8.24). The R-squared value indicates how closely the linear trendline represents the actual data. Think of the R-squared value as a percentage; the higher the value, the more accurately the trendline represents the data observations. Display equation on chart places the linear equation used to extrapolate the line on the chart.

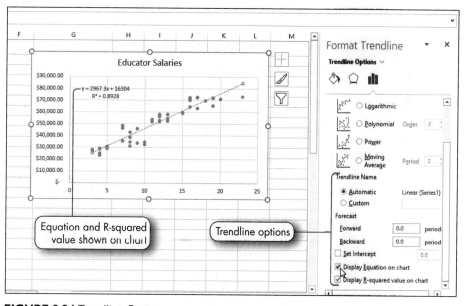

FIGURE 8.24 Trendline Options

TIP: TRENDLINE FORMATTING

When formatting a trendline to display the linear equation on a chart, it is important to note that equation values will round up. If manually calculating the equation values (as shown later in the chapter) the manual calculations will vary if the values are not rounded in the same manner.

Using Statistical Functions to Perform Trend Analysis

While it is useful to use Excel's built-in chart elements to perform trend analysis, it is also possible to determine the variables of a linear equation using existing functions. The linear equation created using chart elements can also by calculated by using the INTERCEPT, SLOPE, RSQ, and STEYX functions.

STEP 2 Use the INTERCEPT and SLOPE Functions

The Forecast Sheet tool in Excel can be used to create a linear trendline similar to the one shown in figure 8.24; however, there are several functions that can be used collectively to perform the same task numerically. While using these functions can be more time consuming, the benefit is accuracy. As noted earlier, a trendline automatically created by Excel rounds the values in the linear equation up. Using the following statistical functions will not round values and will produce more accurate results. The **INTERCEPT function** calculates the point at which a line will intersect the y-axis by using a best-fit regression line plotted through the known x-values and y-values. In the linear equation $y = mx + b$, the intercept is represented by the letter b. The intercept could also be interpreted as a base value that is added to the variable multiplied by the slope to determine the forecasted value.

=INTERCEPT(known_ys, known_xs)

The **SLOPE function** returns the slope of the linear regression line through the given data points. In the linear equation $y = mx + b$, the slope is represented by the letter m. The slope of the line depicts the nature of the data (trending upward or downward).

=SLOPE(known_ys, known_xs)

STEP 3 Use the RSQ and STEYX Functions

The **RSQ function** returns the square of the Pearson product moment correlation coefficient through the given data points. In other words, the RSQ function returns the R-squared value, which denotes how closely the trendline represents the data.

=RSQ(known_ys, known_xs)

The **STEYX function** returns the standard error of the predicted y-value for each x in a regression. Short for *standard error*, the STEYX function provides a numeric value that enables you to adjust for inaccuracy in your data. This number should be used to calculate a numeric range for a forecast. For example, the estimated salary for a teacher of 25 years is $90,486.50. With a standard error of $5,557.87, a teacher who has worked for 25 years could expect to earn a salary between $84,928.63 ($90,486.50 – $5,557.87) and $96,044.37 ($90,486.50 + $5,557.87).

=STEYX(known_ys, known_xs)

STEP 4 Use the FORECAST Function

While many statisticians and data analysts opt to manually calculate trends, Excel offers several functions that can quickly create a forecast with very minimal mathematic requirements. The ***FORECAST.LINEAR function*** calculates, or predicts, a future value along a linear trend by using existing values. This function uses the same linear formula $y = mx + b$ to perform the calculation, which is also the same formula used to create the forecast sheet in the prior section. As shown in figure 8.25 the forecast values calculated using the FORECAST.LINEAR function are more accurate because the SLOPE and INTERCEPT values are not rounded. This results in the more accurate forecast $90,485.30.

```
=FORECAST.LINEAR(x, known_ys, known_xs)
```

The FORECAST.LINEAR function has three required arguments.

- **x.** The x argument is the data point for which you want to predict a value. This must be a numeric value.
- **known_ys.** The known_ys is the dependent array or range of numeric data.
- **known_xs.** The known_xs is the independent array or range of numeric data.

Figure 8.25 displays the results of the FORECAST.LINEAR function compared to the manual linear equation formula.

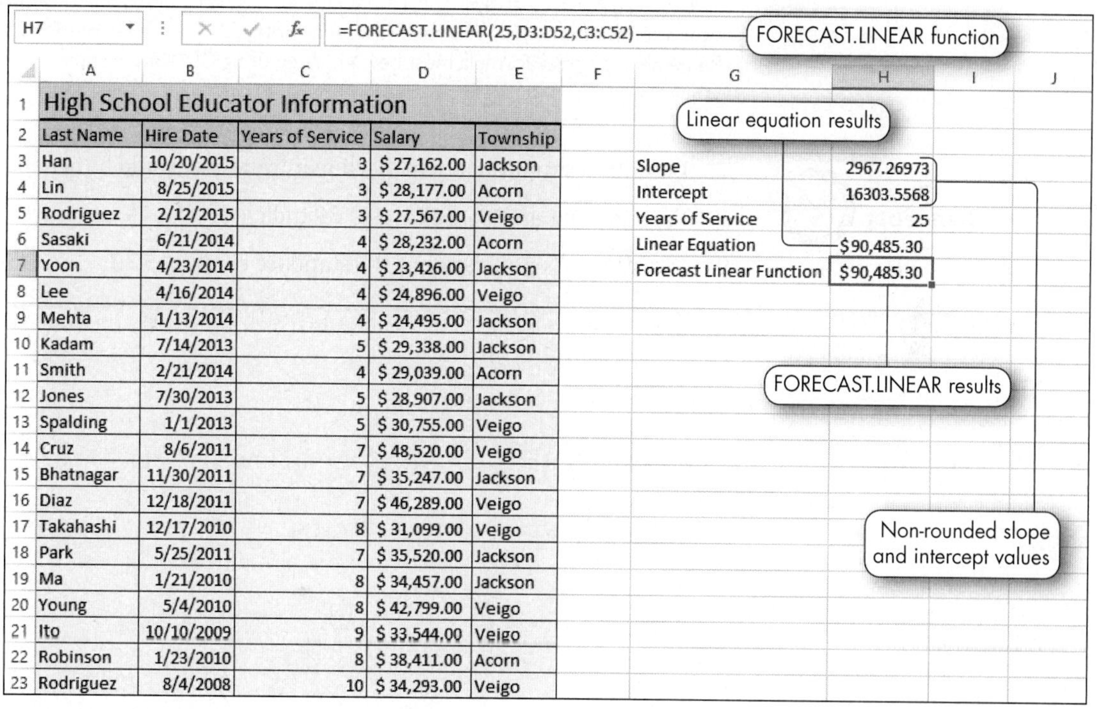

	A	B	C	D	E	F	G	H
1	High School Educator Information							
2	Last Name	Hire Date	Years of Service	Salary	Township			
3	Han	10/20/2015	3	$ 27,162.00	Jackson		Slope	2967.26973
4	Lin	8/25/2015	3	$ 28,177.00	Acorn		Intercept	16303.5568
5	Rodriguez	2/12/2015	3	$ 27,567.00	Veigo		Years of Service	25
6	Sasaki	6/21/2014	4	$ 28,232.00	Acorn		Linear Equation	$90,485.30
7	Yoon	4/23/2014	4	$ 23,426.00	Jackson		Forecast Linear Function	$90,485.30
8	Lee	4/16/2014	4	$ 24,896.00	Veigo			
9	Mehta	1/13/2014	4	$ 24,495.00	Jackson			
10	Kadam	7/14/2013	5	$ 29,338.00	Jackson			
11	Smith	2/21/2014	4	$ 29,039.00	Acorn			
12	Jones	7/30/2013	5	$ 28,907.00	Jackson			
13	Spalding	1/1/2013	5	$ 30,755.00	Veigo			
14	Cruz	8/6/2011	7	$ 48,520.00	Veigo			
15	Bhatnagar	11/30/2011	7	$ 35,247.00	Jackson			
16	Diaz	12/18/2011	7	$ 46,289.00	Veigo			
17	Takahashi	12/17/2010	8	$ 31,099.00	Veigo			
18	Park	5/25/2011	7	$ 35,520.00	Jackson			
19	Ma	1/21/2010	8	$ 34,457.00	Jackson			
20	Young	5/4/2010	8	$ 42,799.00	Veigo			
21	Ito	10/10/2009	9	$ 33,544.00	Veigo			
22	Robinson	1/23/2010	8	$ 38,411.00	Acorn			
23	Rodriguez	8/4/2008	10	$ 34,293.00	Veigo			

FIGURE 8.25 FORECAST.LINEAR function

Along with FORECAST.LINEAR, Excel has four additional forecast functions that utilize a variety of algorithms to calculate results. Details about Excel's forecast functions are shown in Table 8.7.

TABLE 8.7 Forecasting Functions in Excel	
Name	**Description**
FORECAST.ETS	Returns the forecasted values for a specific future target date using exponential smoothing method.
FORECAST.ETS.CONFINT	Returns a confidence interval for the forecast value at the specified target date.
FORECAST.ETS.SEASONALITY	Returns the length of the repetitive pattern Excel detects for the specified time series.
FORECAST.ETS.STAT	Returns the requested statistic for the forecast.
FORECAST.LINEAR	Calculates, or predicts, a future value along a linear trend by using existing values.

> **TIP: FORECAST VS. TREND FUNCTION**
> The TREND function is an alternative to the FORECAST function. The TREND function performs the same calculations as the FORECAST.LINEAR function; however, like the FREQUENCY function, TREND can calculate arrays. The TREND function is best utilized when calculating multiple forecasts over a series of time. For example, calculating potential teacher salaries for 25 to 35 years of service. Remember, an array formula must be completed using Ctrl+Shift+Enter.

Quick Concepts

7. Describe a situation in which a linear trendline would be beneficial. *p. 520*

8. Explain what an RSQ value of 0.89 indicates about a linear trendline. *p. 522*

9. Describe the significance of the standard error. *p. 522*

Hands-On Exercises

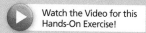
Skills covered: Add a Trendline to a Chart • Use the INTERCEPT and SLOPE Functions • Use the RSQ and STEYX Functions • Use the FORECAST Function

3 Trend Analysis

For your next task, you will create a linear trendline visualizing the changes in teachers' salaries as their careers progress. You will then use the INTERCEPT and SLOPE functions to verify the trendline equation. Next, you will use the STEYX and RSQ functions to verify the accuracy of your findings. Finally, you will finalize the project by using the FORECAST.LINEAR function to forecast the salary of a teacher who works for 30 years.

STEP 1 ADD A TRENDLINE TO A CHART

You have collected a sample set of data that includes the years of service and salaries of 50 teachers from the Banton school system. You want to use this data to create a trendline that can be used for forecasting. You will create a scatter plot chart of the data and add a linear trendline with equation and R-squared. Refer to Figure 8.26 as you complete Step 1.

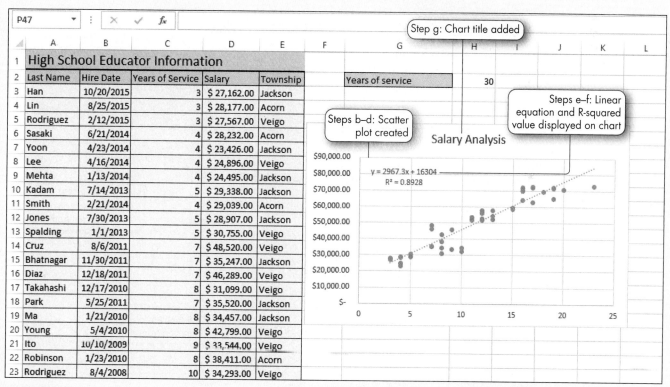

FIGURE 8.26 Add a Trendline to a Chart

a. Open *e08h2Assessment_LastFirst* if you closed it at the end of Hands-On Exercise 2, and save it as **e08h3Assessment_LastFirst,** changing h2 to h3.

b. Make the **Educator Assessment worksheet** active and click **cell G4**. Click the **Insert tab,** click **Insert Scatter (X,Y) or Bubble chart** in the Charts group, and select **Scatter**.

This creates a blank scatter plot. You will manually add *X,Y* data in the next step.

c. Click **Select Data** in the Data group on the Design tab. Click **Add** (on a Mac, click the plus sign) in the Legend Entries section of the Select Data Source dialog box.

The Edit Series dialog box displays for manual input of *X,Y* values.

d. Click in the **Series X values box** and select the **range C3:C52**. Click the **Series Y values box**, delete the current value (={1}), and then select the **range D3:D52**. Click **OK** and click **OK** again to complete the chart.

e. Click **Chart Elements**, click the **Trendline arrow,** and select **More Options**. In the Format Trendline task pane, scroll down and click **Display Equation on chart** and **Display R-squared value on chart**. Accept all additional default options and close the Format Trendline pane.

> **MAC TROUBLESHOOTING:** Click Add Chart Elements on the Chart Design tab.

By adding these options, you now display the R-squared value and linear equation directly on the chart.

f. Move the Linear equation and R-squared values to the upper-left corner of the chart Plot Area.

g. Add the chart title **Salary Analysis** and reposition the chart so the upper-left corner is in cell F6.

h. Save the workbook.

STEP 2 ▶ USE THE INTERCEPT AND SLOPE FUNCTIONS

Excel automatically created the linear equation $y = 2967.3x + 16304$ however, you can calculate this equation manually using functions in Excel. You will use this method to verify the accuracy of the chart. Next, you will use the INTERCEPT and SLOPE functions to verify the results. Refer to Figure 8.27 as you complete Step 2.

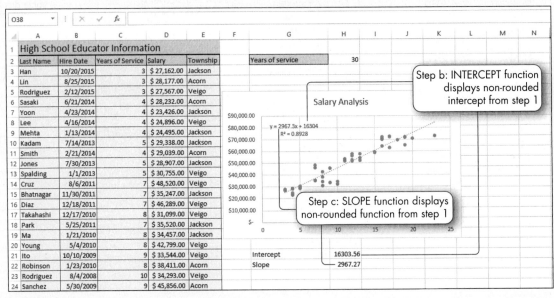

FIGURE 8.27 INTERCEPT and SLOPE functions

a. Click **cell G21** and type **Intercept**. Click **cell G22** and type **Slope**.

b. Click **cell H21**, type **=INTERCEPT(** and click **Insert Function** on the Formula Bar. Click **Known_ys**, select **range D3:D52**, and press **Tab** so the insertion point is in the **Known_xs box**. Select **range C3:C52** and click **OK** (on a Mac, click **Done**).

The INTERCEPT function returns the value 16303.55681, which matches the intercept created as part of the linear equation in the prior step. This indicates the intercept was calculated correctly.

c. Click **cell H22**, type **=SLOPE(D3:D52, C3:C52)**, and press **Ctrl+Enter**.

The SLOPE function returns the value 2967.269728. This matches the slope created as part of the linear equation in the prior step. This indicates the slope was calculated correctly.

d. Save the workbook.

STEP 3 > USE THE RSQ AND STEYX FUNCTIONS

Your next step is to test the accuracy of your trendline by using the RSQ and STEYX functions. Refer to Figure 8.28 as you complete Step 3.

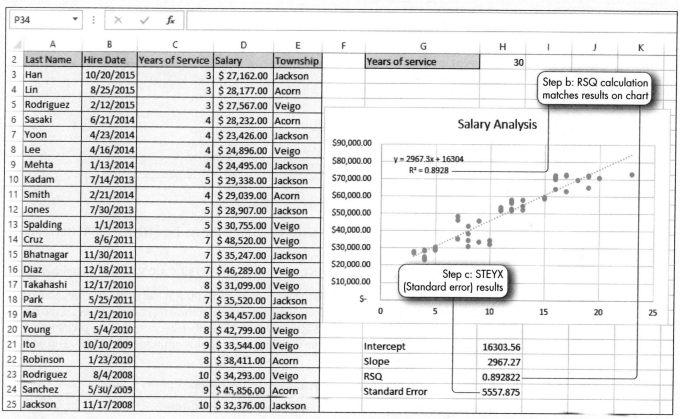

FIGURE 8.28 R-squared value and Standard Error

a. Click **cell G23** and type **RSQ**. Click **cell G24** and type **Standard Error**.

b. Click **cell H23**, type **=RSQ(D3:D52, C3:C52)**, and then press **Enter**.

The RSQ function uses the same Known_ys and Known_xs as used to calculate the SLOPE and INTERCEPT. The RSQ function returns the value 0.892822. This indicates that the linear trendline accurately represents 89% of your data observations.

c. Click **cell H24**, type **=STEYX(D3:D52, C3:C52)**, and then press **Ctrl+Enter**.

The STEYX function returns the standard error 5557.874553. This means that if the trendline or rounded linear equation $y = 2967.3x + 16304$ is used to forecast a potential salary, it will be accurate plus or minus $5557.87.

d. Save the workbook.

For your final task, you will use the FORECAST.LINEAR function to predict the salary of a teacher who has worked for 30 years. You will then manually check the results using the linear equation $y = mx + b$ in which m and b represent intercept and slope, respectively. Refer to Figure 8.29 as you complete Step 4.

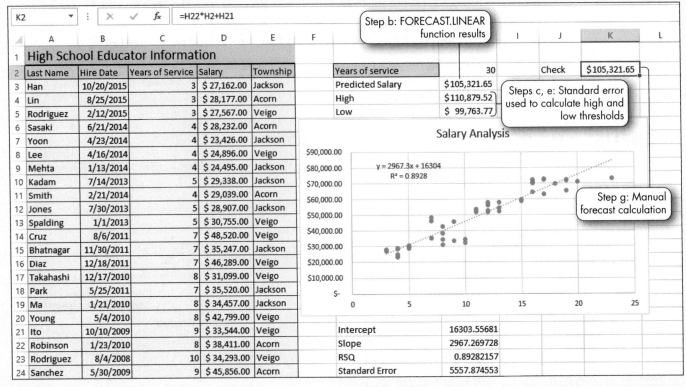

FIGURE 8.29 FORECAST.LINEAR function

a. Click **cell G3** and type **Predicted Salary**, press **Enter**. Type **High**, press **Enter**, and type **Low**.

b. Click **cell H3**, type **=FORECAST.LINEAR(H2,D3:D52,C3:C52)**, and then press **Enter**.

Cell H2 contains a reference to the years of service you will use as the starting point for the forecast. Based on the historical data, you determine a teacher who has served for 30 years will earn a salary of $105,321.65. Remember, because this is a prediction, you must take into consideration the standard error of plus or minus $5557.87. You add this into your final prediction.

c. Click **cell H4**, type **=H3+H24**, and then press **Enter**.

d. Click **cell H5**, type **=H3-H24**, and then press **Ctrl+Enter**.

e. Select the **range H3:H5** and apply **Accounting Number Format**.

f. Click **cell J2** and type **Check**.

g. Click **cell K2**, type **=H22*H2+H21**, and then press **Ctrl+Enter**.

The FORECAST.LINEAR function uses the equation $y = mx + b$. In this step, you verified the accuracy of the function by manually calculating the forecast in which m equals the intercept and b equals the slope. The manual calculation returns the value $105,321.65, which matches the calculation created by the FORECAST.LINEAR function, verifying your calculations are correct.

h. Ensure that cell K2 is still selected and apply **Accounting Number Format**.

i. Save and close the file. Based on your instructor's directions, submit e08h3Assessment_LastFirst.

Chapter Objectives Review

After reading this chapter, you have accomplished the following objectives:

1. Measure central tendency.

- Measures of central tendency define basic characteristics of a population or sample of data.
- Use the standard deviation and variance functions: The STDEV.S and STDEV.P functions help determine variations in a data series, specifically how far the sample or population is spread around the mean. The VAR.S and VAR.P functions determine the summation of the squared deviations divided by the amount of the sample – 1 or the total population.
- Use the CORREL function: The CORREL function determines the correlation coefficient. The value returned will be between –1 and 1. The closer the value is to 1, the stronger the positive relationship between datasets.
- Use the FREQUENCY function: The FREQUENCY function is an array function that calculates the number of occurrences of specific values of data that appear in a data series.
- Use the LARGE and SMALL functions: The LARGE function returns the kth largest value in a dataset. The SMALL function returns the kth smallest value in a dataset.
- Use the RANK and PERCENTRANK functions: The RANK.EQ and RANK.AVG functions calculate ranking for individual values within a list. PERCENTRANK.INC and PERCENTRANK.EXC calculate rank as a percentage for each value in a list.
- Use the QUARTILE and PERCENTILE functions: The QUARTILE.INC and QUARTILE.EXC functions identify the value at a specific quartile. PERCENTILE.INC and PERCENTILE.EXC identify the kth percentile of a value.

2. Load the Analysis ToolPak.

- The Analysis ToolPak is an Excel add-in that must be loaded before use. You can use the Analysis ToolPak to perform various calculations such as ANOVA, Correlation, F-Tests, T-Tests, Z-Tests, and more.

3. Perform analysis using the Analysis ToolPak.

- There are 19 tools available within the Analysis ToolPak. Many of the tools have function counterparts that can be used. The benefit of using the ToolPak over the functions is the final summary report options in the ToolPak.
- Perform analysis of variance (ANOVA): ANOVA is an abbreviation of analysis of variance. This statistical tool compares the means between two data samples to determine if they were derived from the same population.

- Calculate COVARIANCE: COVARIANCE is a measure of how two sample sets of data vary simultaneously. COVARIANCE.P can be used to calculate the COVARIANCE of a dataset that encompasses the entire population. COVARIANCE.S calculates the COVARIANCE of a sample dataset.
- Create a histogram: A histogram is a tabular display of data frequencies organized into bins. The histogram feature of the Analysis ToolPak is comparable to the FREQUENCY function. It will return the number of occurrences of data points based on predefined bins. It also has charting capabilities.

4. Create a forecast sheet.

- Excel offers a business intelligence feature that creates a numeric and visual forecast based on the seasonality of historical data. This feature can be used as a stand-alone tool or in conjunction with new time-series forecasting functions.

5. Perform analysis using trendlines.

- Add a linear trendline to a chart: A trendline is a visualization that shows patterns in the data. Excel can create six different variations of trendlines based on the nature of your data.

6. Use statistical functions to perform trend analysis.

- Use the INTERCEPT and SLOPE functions: The INTERCEPT function calculates the point at which a line will intersect the y-axis by using a best-fit regression line plotted through the known x-values and y-values. In the linear equations $y = mx + b$, the intercept is represented by the letter b. The SLOPE function returns the slope of the linear regression line through the given data points. In the linear equation $y = mx + b$, the slope is represented by the letter m.
- Use the RSQ and STEYX functions: The RSQ function returns the square of the Pearson product moment correlation coefficient through the given data points. The STEYX function returns the standard error of the predicted y-value for each x in a regression. Short for standard error, the STEYX function will provide a numeric value that allows you to adjust for inaccuracy in your data.
- Use the FORECAST function: The FORECAST.LINEAR function calculates, or predicts, a future value along a linear trend by using existing values. This function uses the same linear formula $y = mx + b$ to perform the calculation.

Key Terms Matching

Match the key terms with their definitions. Write the key term letter by the appropriate numbered definition.

a. Analysis ToolPak
b. ANOVA
c. Bins
d. CORREL function
e. Forecast Sheet
f. FORECAST.LINEAR function
g. FREQUENCY function
h. Histogram
i. INTERCEPT function
j. LARGE function

k. Population
l. RSQ function
m. Sample
n. SLOPE function
o. SMALL function
p. Standard Deviation
q. Standard Error
r. STEYX function
s. Trendline
t. Variance

1. _____ A statistical tool that compares the means between two data samples to determine if they were derived from the same population. **p. 510**

2. _____ The level of accuracy of the forecast. **p. 520**

3. _____ A statistical function that returns the square of the Pearson product moment correlation coefficient through the given data points. **p. 522**

4. _____ An add-in program that contains tools for performing complex statistical analysis. **p. 509**

5. _____ A measure of a dataset's dispersion, such as the difference between the highest and lowest points in the data. **p. 496**

6. _____ A measure of a how far the data sample is spread around the mean. **p. 496**

7. _____ A calculation of the number of occurrences of numeric values in a dataset based on predetermined bins. **p. 498**

8. _____ A statistical function that determines the strength of a relationship between two variables. **p. 497**

9. _____ A visualization that shows patterns in the data. **p. 520**

10. _____ A statistical function that returns the kth smallest value in a dataset. **p. 501**

11. _____ A statistical function that returns the standard error of the predicted y-value for each x in a regression. **p. 520**

12. _____ A dataset that contains all the information you would like to evaluate. **p. 496**

13. _____ A statistical function that returns the slope of the linear regression line through the given data points. **p. 522**

14. _____ A statistical function that returns the kth largest value in a dataset. **p. 501**

15. _____ A statistical function that calculates the point at which a line will intersect the y-axis by using a best-fit regression line plotted through the known x-values and y-values. **p. 522**

16. _____ A smaller portion of the population that is easier to evaluate. **p. 496**

17. _____ A visual display of tabulated frequencies. **p. 512**

18. _____ A statistical function that calculates, or predicts, a future value along a linear trend by using existing values. **p. 523**

19. _____ A business intelligence feature that creates a forecast worksheet to detail trends based on historical data. **p. 513**

20. _____ Data ranges in which values can be categorized and counted. **p. 498**

Multiple Choice

1. Which of the following functions should be used to determine how far the sample data is spread around the mean?
   - (a) COVARIANCE.P
   - (b) STDEV.S
   - (c) CORREL
   - (d) FREQUENCY

2. In the linear equation $y = mx + b$, which function would you use to calculate b?
   - (a) SLOPE
   - (b) STYEX
   - (c) INTERCEPT
   - (d) RSQ

3. What does a negative COVARIANCE indicate?
   - (a) No relationship between datasets
   - (b) A positive relationship between datasets
   - (c) An inverse relationship between datasets
   - (d) A statistically insignificant dataset

4. A worksheet contains sales dollars for agents with your company. The values are $1,250, $1,090, $985, $985, $880, $756, $675, $650, and $600. What function could be used to return the third largest value?
   - (a) FREQUENCY
   - (b) STEYX
   - (c) LARGE
   - (d) SLOPE

5. What function would you use to calculate the strength of a relationship between two or more variables?
   - (a) STDEV.S
   - (b) CORREL
   - (c) STDEV.P
   - (d) FREQUENCY

6. You hypothesize that there is a relationship between lack of regular exercise and illness. To research this theory, you have compiled a sample set of data that contains numbers of days in which an hour or more of exercise is completed as well as numbers of days sick within a calendar year. What tool in Excel could you use to investigate the relationships between the data?
   - (a) CORREL
   - (b) PERCENTRANK.INC
   - (c) VAR.S
   - (d) RSQ

7. Which of the following functions should be used to determine how closely a linear trendline represents the data being evaluated?
   - (a) STEYX
   - (b) RSQ
   - (c) SLOPE
   - (d) INTERCEPT

8. What is the difference between STDEV.S and STDEV.P?
   - (a) STDEV.S calculates the standard deviation of a sample; STDEV.P calculates the standard deviation of a population.
   - (b) STDEV.P calculates the standard deviation of a population; STDEV.S calculates average variation.
   - (c) STDEV.P calculates the standard deviation of a population; STDEV.S calculates variance.
   - (d) There is no difference.

9. What is the difference between a sample and a population?
   - (a) A sample contains all data you want to evaluate, while a population contains a portion of data available.
   - (b) A population contains all data you want to evaluate, while a sample contains a portion of the data.
   - (c) A sample contains all data from the population except statistical outliers.
   - (d) There is no difference.

10. What keystroke combination is required to calculate a Frequency data array?
    - (a) Ctrl+Enter
    - (b) Alt+Enter
    - (c) Ctrl+Shift+Enter
    - (d) Ctrl+Shift+Delete

Practice Exercises

1 | Grind Stone Coffee

You are a business analyst for Grind Stone Coffee Company, a local supplier of organic coffee beans. You have been given a worksheet containing data that documents units produced and corresponding profit. You will use the data to forecast the profit if 25,000 units of coffee are sold. To complete the task you will use the FORECAST.LINEAR function as well as manually calculate the forecast by adding a trendline to a scatter plot chart. Refer to Figure 8.30 as you complete this exercise.

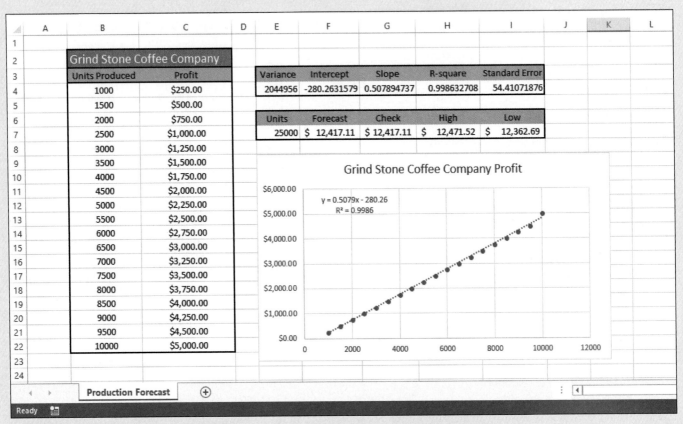

FIGURE 8.30 Grind Stone Coffee Company

a. Open *e08p1CoffeeProduction* and save it as **e08p1CoffeeProduction_LastFirst**.

b. Click **cell C3**. Click the **Insert tab**, click **Insert Scatter (X, Y) or Bubble Chart** in the Charts group, and then click **Scatter**.

c. Move the newly created chart so the upper-left corner begins in **cell E9**.

d. Click **Chart Elements**, click the arrow to the right of **Trendline**, and then select **More Options**.

> **MAC TROUBLESHOOTING:** Click the Chart Design tab and click Add Chart Element.

e. Ensure that **Linear, Display Equation on chart** and **Display R-squared value on chart** are selected in the Format Trendline pane.

f. Close the Format Trendline pane and move the newly created Chart Element to the upper-left corner of the Plot Area.

g. Click **cell E4** and type **=VAR.S(C4:C22)**.

h. Click **cell F4** and type **=INTERCEPT(C4:C22,B4:B22)**.

i. Adapt the prior step to enter functions to calculate SLOPE, RSQ, and STEYX in the **range G4:I4**.

j. Click **cell F7**. Click the **Formulas tab** and click **More Functions** in the Function Library group. Point to **Statistical** and select **FORECAST.LINEAR**. Do the following:

- Click **cell E7** to enter a reference for the units of coffee produced in the forecast and press **Tab**.
- Select the **range C4:C22** and press **Tab** to enter a reference to the profit based on units produced.
- Select the **range B4:B22** and click **OK** to enter a reference to the units produced.

k. Click **cell G7**, type **=G4*E7+F4**, and then press **Ctrl+Enter**.

l. Click **cell H7** and type **=F7+I4**.

m. Click **cell I7** and type **=F7-I4**.

n. Format the **range F7:I7** with **Accounting Number Format**.

o. Create a footer with your name on the left side, the sheet name code in the center, and the file name code on the right side.

p. Save and close the workbook. Based on your instructor's directions, submit e08p1CoffeeProduction_LastFirst.

2 Indy Car

You have been hired to analyze the effectiveness of carbon-hardening additives to Indy car tires. The added carbon increases the puncture strength, and you will analyze its impact on burn temperature and weight. You will use Excel's statistical functions and the Analysis ToolPak to complete the next steps. Refer to Figure 8.31 as you complete this exercise.

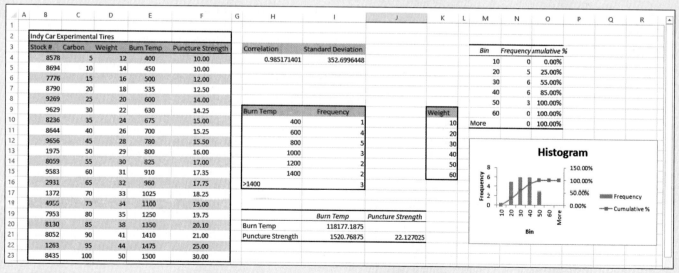

FIGURE 8.31 Indy Car

a. Open *e08p2IndyCar* and save it as **e08p2IndyCar_LastFirst**.

b. Click **cell H4** in the Tires worksheet. Type **=CORREL** and press **Tab**. Select the **range C4:C23** for the first argument, type **comma**, and then select the **range E4:E23** for the second argument. Press **Ctrl+Enter**.

c. Click **cell I4**. Type **=STDEV.S** and press **Tab**. Select the **range E4:E23** and press **Ctrl+Enter**.

d. Select the **range I10:I16**. Type **=FREQUENCY** and press **Tab**. Select the **range E4:E23** and type **comma**. Select the **range H10:H15** and press **Ctrl+Shift+Enter.**

e. Load the Analysis ToolPak by completing the following steps, or if it is already available, skip to Step f.

- Click the **File tab**.
- Click **Options** and select **Add-ins** on the left side of the Excel Options dialog box.
- Select **Excel Add-ins** in the Manage box and click **Go**.
- Click **Analysis ToolPak** in the Add-ins dialog box and click **OK**.

> **MAC TROUBLESHOOTING:** Click the Tools menu and select Excel Add-ins. Click the Analysis ToolPak checkbox to select it. Click OK.

f. Click the **Data tab** and click **Data Analysis** in the Analysis group. Select **Histogram**, click **OK**, and then complete the following steps:

- Type **D4:D23** in the Input Range box.
- Type **K10:K15** in the Bin Range box.
- Click Output range and type **M3** in the Output Range box.
- Click **Cumulative Percentage** to select the option.
- Click **Chart Output** to select the option.
- Click **OK**.
- Position the chart so the upper-left corner starts in **cell M12** and resize it so the chart fills the **range M12:R20**.

g. Click **Data Analysis** in the Analysis group, select **Covariance**, and then click **OK**. Complete the following steps:

- Type **E3:F23** in the Input Range box.
- Click **Columns**.
- Click **Labels in first row**.
- Click Output Range and type **H19** in the Output Range box.
- Click **OK**.
- Resize **columns H:J** and **M:O** so all the contents are visible.

h. Click the **Test Drive worksheet**. Click the **Data tab**. Click **Data Analysis** in the Analysis group, select **Anova: Single Factor** and click **OK**. Then complete the following steps:

- Type **C2:E21** in the Input Range box.
- Click **Columns**.
- Click **Labels in first row**.
- Click Output Range and type **G2** in the Output Range box.
- Click **OK**.
- Resize **Columns G:M** so all the contents are visible.

i. Select the **range B2:C21**, click the **Data tab**, click **Forecast Sheet** in the Forecast group, and then click **Create**.

> **MAC TROUBLESHOOTING:** The Forecast Sheet feature is not available in Excel for Mac.

j. Rename the newly created worksheet **Forecast** and reposition the chart so all the data points are visible.

k. Create a footer on all worksheets with your name on the left side, the sheet name code in the center, and the file name code on the right side.

l. Save and close the workbook. Based on your instructor's directions, submit e08p2IndyCar_LastFirst.

Mid-Level Exercises

1 Portfolio Analysis

MyLab IT Grader

You are a financial advisor, and a client wants you to complete an analysis of his portfolio. As part of the analysis, you will calculate basic descriptive statistics with the Analysis ToolPak, calculate standard deviation and variance in value, calculate correlation between asset age and value, and create a stock forecast sheet.

a. Open *e08m1Portfolio* and save it as **e08m1Portfolio_LastFirst**.

b. Use the **STDEV.S function** to calculate the standard deviation between the current values of all commodities in **cell G6**.

c. Use the **VAR.S function** to calculate the variance between the current values of all commodities in **cell G9**.

d. Ensure the Analysis ToolPak is loaded.

e. Create a descriptive statistics summary based on the current value of investments in **column E**. Ensure labels and summary statistics are included. Display the output in **cell G12**.

f. Format the mean, median, mode, minimum, maximum, and sum in the report as **Accounting Number Format**. Resize the column as needed.

g. Use the **FREQUENCY function** to calculate the frequency distribution of commodity values in the **range J6:J11** based on the values located in the **range I6:I10** and be sure to include outliers.

h. Click the **Trend worksheet** and use the **CORREL function** to calculate the correlation of purchase price and current value listed in the **range C3:D10**.

i. Create a **Forecast Sheet** displaying a forecast of purchase price through 1/1/2025.

> **MAC TROUBLESHOOTING:** The Forecast Sheet feature is not available in Excel for Mac.

j. Name the newly created worksheet **Forecast_2025**.

k. Create a footer on all worksheets with your name on the left side, the sheet name code in the center, and the file name code on the right side.

l. Save and close the workbook. Based on your instructor's directions, submit e08m1Portfolio_LastFirst.

2 Reading Comprehension Scores

MyLab IT Grader

ANALYSIS CASE

As an elementary school principal, you are concerned about students' reading comprehension. You brought in a reading consultant to help design an experimental study to compare the current teaching method (the control group), a stand-alone computer-based training (CBT) program, and a combination of the traditional teaching method and CBT (hybrid). The consultant randomly assigned 72 third-grade students into three groups of 24 each. During the two-week study, students were taught reading comprehension skills based on the respective methodology. At the end of the two-week period, students completed a standardized reading comprehension test. The consultant prepared a worksheet listing the test scores for each group. No student names or IDs were reported to you.

Now you want to calculate some general statistics and conduct a one-way analysis of variance (ANOVA). Doing so will enable you to compare the three sample group means and evaluate the variances within each group compared to the variances among the three groups.

a. Open *e08m2Stats* and save it as **e08m2Stats_LastFirst**.

b. Calculate the descriptive statistics in the **range F2:H8**. For the variance and standard deviation, use the functions that include the *.S* descriptor. Format the values with **Comma Style** with three decimal places.

c. Check the Data tab to see if it contains the Data Analysis command. If not, load the Analysis ToolPak add-in program as directed in the chapter.

d. Use the Analysis ToolPak and select the **Anova: Single Factor**. Use the following specifications:

- Select the range **A1:C25** as the Input Range.
- Select the **Labels in first row check box**.
- Confirm the alpha value is **0.05**.
- Place the **Output Range** starting in **cell E11**.

e. Apply **Comma Style** with three decimal places to the averages and variances in the ANOVA table. Verify that the averages and variances in the ANOVA table match those you calculated in the General Stats section. If they do not match, correct the functions in the General Stats section. If needed, format the P-value (cell J22) with **Comma Style** and six decimal places.

f. Answer the questions on the Q&A worksheet.

g. Apply **Landscape orientation** to the Reading Performance Scores worksheet.

h. Create a footer on all worksheets with your name on the left side, the sheet name code in the center, and the file name code on the right side.

i. Save and close the workbook. Based on your instructor's directions, submit e08m2Stats_LastFirst.

Running Case

New Castle County Technical Services

New Castle County Technical Services (NCCTS) provides technical support services for a number of companies in New Castle County, Delaware. Previously, you created an amortization schedule to detail payment and interest information on a $65,000 facility upgrade. NCCTS has kept the historical financial data regarding their past facility upgrades and you want to use this information to predict the cost of the next upgrade in five years. You will add a linear trendline to a scatter plot chart, as well as use the FORECAST function to complete your calculations. You will also use statistical functions to verify the results of the linear trendline.

a. Open *e08r1NCCTS* and save it as **e08r1NCCTS_LastFirst**.

b. Create a Scatter Plot on the Historical_Data worksheet that displays the purchase date on the X axis and the Cost on the Y axis.

c. Add a linear trendline to the chart, display the R-squared value and equation.

d. Add an appropriate chart title.

e. Insert a function in **cell E5** to calculate the INTERCEPT of the trendline.

f. Insert a function in **cell F5** to calculate the SLOPE of the trendline.

g. Insert a function in **cell G5** to calculate the R-squared value of the trendline.

h. Insert a function in **cell H5** to calculate the Standard Error.

i. Use the FORECAST.LINEAR function to calculate the estimated cost of equipment upgrades in **cell F8**. The prediction should be based on the year 2025. Format the results as currency.

j. Use the standard error calculated in **cell H5** to determine the high and low thresholds in the **range G8:H8**. Ensure the results are displayed as currency.

k. Use the linear equation ($y = mx + b$) in **cell E11** to manually check your work. Ensure the results are displayed as currency.

l. Create a footer on all worksheets with your name on the left side, the sheet name code in the center, and the file name code on the right side.

m. Save and close the workbook. Based on your instructor's directions, submit e08r1NCCTS_LastFirst.

Disaster Recovery

College Admissions

You are working as a summer intern for the office of admissions at your local university. You have been given historical enrollment information and you want to forecast potential student enrollment in 2025. After using the FORECAST.LINEAR function to complete the forecast, you decide to manually check your work. Unfortunately, you determine there is an error in the worksheet. To locate the error and complete the forecast do the following: Open *e08d1StudentEnrollment* and save it as **e08d1StudentEnrollment_LastFirst**. Locate the FORECAST.LINEAR function used in cell E6. Note the known_x's and known_y's arguments are reversed. Edit the function's arguments to the correct known_x's and known_y's. If this step is done correctly, the Check cell will match and a green fill color will automatically be added. Next, complete the High and Low threshold calculations in the range F6:G6. Create a footer with your name, the sheet name, and the file name on each worksheet. Save and close the workbook. Based on your instructor's directions, submit e08d1StudentEnrollment_LastFirst.

Capstone Exercise

Golden State 5k

You are an organizer for the Golden State 5k, an annual 5k held across several cities in California to raise money for at risk youth. As part of your duties, you track donations, volunteer information, and race results. This year, you have decided to use Excel to calculate frequency distribution by age and time, calculate various descriptive statistics, and forecast participation rate as well as donation rate for 2025.

Measure Central Tendency

You want to calculate the frequency distribution of the recorded race times as well as explore the potential relationship between completion time and age. Note that the data used for this exercise is sample data of the larger population.

1. Open *e08c1GoldenState5k* and save it as **e08c1GoldenState5k_LastFirst**.

2. Ensure the RaceResults worksheet is active, then use the FREQUENCY function to calculate the frequency distribution of the race results in column D. Place your results in the **range G4:G10**.

3. Enter a function in **cell F22** to calculate the correlation between age (Column C) and race time (Column D).

4. Enter a function in **cell G22** to calculate the covariance between age and race time.

5. Enter a function in **cell H22** to calculate the variance of the ages in the dataset.

6. Enter a function in **cell I22** to calculate the standard deviation of the ages in the dataset.

Use the Analysis ToolPak and Forecast Sheet

You will use the Analysis ToolPak to create a histogram to visualize the ages of the runners observed. You want to use the Analysis ToolPak to complete a single factor ANOVA on volunteer information by city.

7. Ensure the Analysis ToolPak add-in is active.

8. Use the Analysis ToolPak to create a histogram based on the ages of the runners surveyed. Use the **range C3:C53** as the Input Range and **F12:F18** as the Bin Range. Ensure that labels, cumulative percentage and chart output are included in the results. Use **cell H12** as the Output Range.

9. Make the VolunteerInfo worksheet active.

10. Use the Analysis ToolPak to perform a single factor ANOVA including labels on the **range C5:E21**. Place the results starting in **cell G5**. Resize columns G:M as needed.

Perform Trend Analysis

For your last steps, you will create a Forecast Sheet to visualize participation trend and you will add a linear trendline to a scatter plot to visualize growth in donations. You will use the FORECAST.LINEAR function to forecast donations if the goal of 20,000 participants is reached.

11. Create a Forecast Sheet that depicts year over year growth in participation. Set the Forecast end year as 2025, and place the results on a new worksheet named **2025Forecast**. Resize and reposition the chart to fill the **range G2:P22**. (On a Mac, the Forecast Sheet feature is not available.)

12. Make the Participants worksheet active and create a scatter plot chart that places the Participant observations on the X axis and the Donation dollars on the Y axis. Be sure to add an appropriate chart title.

13. Add a linear trendline to the chart that also shows the Equation and the R-squared value.

14. Enter a function in **cell F6** to calculate the intercept of the linear trendline created in the prior step.

15. Enter a function in **cell G6** to calculate the Slope of the linear trendline.

16. Enter a function in **cell H6** to calculate the RSQ of the linear trendline.

17. Enter a function in **cell I6** to calculate the Standard Error.

18. Use the FORECAST.LINEAR function in **cell F9** to forecast potential donations once the goal of 20,000 participants is reached. Format the results as Currency.

19. Complete your analysis by adding formulas in the **range G9:H9** to calculate the high and low thresholds of the forecast. Apply **Accounting Number Format** to the results in the **range F9:H9**.

20. Create a footer on all worksheets with your name on the left side, the sheet name code in the center, and the file name code on the right side.

21. Save and close the workbook. Based on your instructor's directions, submit e08c1GoldenState5k_LastFirst.

CHAPTER 8 • Capstone Exercise

Multiple-Sheet Workbook Management

LEARNING OUTCOME You will demonstrate data management and error control within workbooks containing links and 3-D formulas.

OBJECTIVES & SKILLS: After you read this chapter, you will be able to:

CASE STUDY | Circle City Sporting Goods

You are the regional manager of Circle City Sporting Goods (CCSG), a comprehensive retailer that has locations in Indianapolis, Bloomington, and South Bend. Each store manager gathers monthly data for every department and prepares a quarterly worksheet. The worksheets are identical to help you consolidate sales data for all three locations.

You want to review sales data for the past fiscal year. Before consolidating data, you will format the worksheets, copy data to a summary sheet, and insert hyperlinks to the individual quarterly sheets. Later, you will consolidate each store's data into a regional workbook. You will use auditing tools to identify errors and add validation to ensure accurate data entry. Finally, you will use tools to protect data, worksheets, and workbooks against unauthorized access, and then mark the workbook as final.

YanLev/Shutterstock

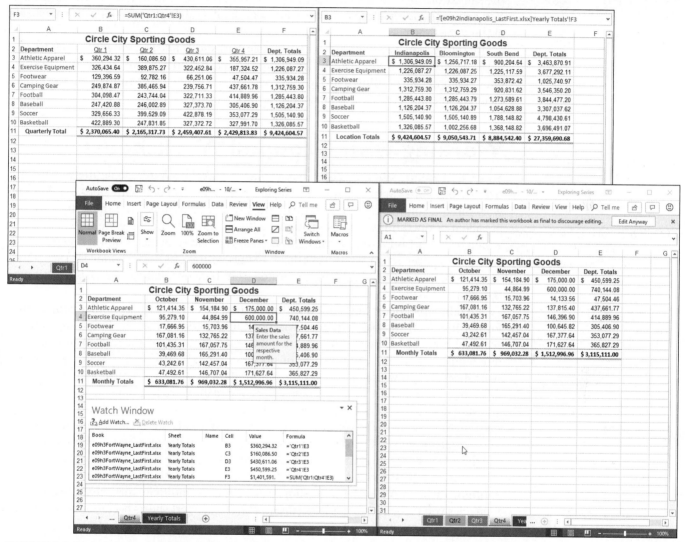

CHAPTER 9

FIGURE 9.1 Circle City Sporting Goods Workbook

CASE STUDY | Circle City Sporting Goods

Starting Files	Files to be Submitted
e09h1Indianapolis	**e09h2IndianaFiles_LastFirst.zip**
e09h2Bloomington	**e09h4FortWayne_LastFirst**
e09h2SouthBend	
e09h2Indiana	
e09h3FortWayne	

MyLab IT Grader An alternate version of this project is available as a MyLab IT Grader Assessment

Multiple Worksheets

A workbook can contain one or more worksheets of related data. Deciding how to structure data into multiple worksheets and how to manage these worksheets is important. You should determine how much data to enter on each worksheet, when to divide data among several worksheets, and how to format worksheets efficiently. In addition, you can create links among the worksheets to enable effective navigation. For example, you can create a documentation worksheet and then insert links to each worksheet.

When you are working with a large dataset, you often want to see multiple sections of the same worksheet or see different worksheets in the same workbook at the same time. You can open multiple copies of the same workbook and display portions of worksheets at the same time.

In this section, you will work with multiple worksheets and insert hyperlinks from one worksheet to other worksheets. In addition, you will group worksheets together to enter data and apply formatting. Finally, you will manage windows by controlling worksheet visibility, opening and arranging windows, and splitting a window.

Working with Grouped Worksheets

You will encounter situations that require data in a workbook to be separated into several worksheets. For example, a sales manager creates a workbook with sales data on one worksheet, a column chart on another sheet, and a PivotTable on a third sheet. A vice president of operations creates scenarios with Scenario Manager, generates a scenario summary report on a new worksheet or creates a Solver model, and then generates a Solver answer report on a new worksheet. In these situations, the original data are stored in individual worksheets that are separated from the consolidated analysis to organize the data.

In other instances, worksheets within a workbook may contain similar content and formatting. For example, a budget workbook might contain detailed monthly data on separate worksheets. By placing monthly data on separate worksheets, you can focus on one month's data at a time instead of presenting data for an entire year on only one worksheet. When worksheets contain similar data but for different time periods (such as months) or different locations (such as department store locations in several states), you should structure and format the data the same on all worksheets. For example, each monthly worksheet in the yearly budget workbook should contain an identical structure and format for the list of income and expenses. The only differences among the worksheets are the actual values and the column labels that identify the respective months.

Creating worksheets with identical structure and formatting provides consistency and continuity when working with the same type of data on multiple worksheets. In addition, it enables you to locate particular items quickly on all worksheets because you know the structure is identical.

STEP 1 Group and Ungroup Worksheets

Although you can design and format worksheets individually, you can improve your productivity by designing and formatting the worksheets as a group. **Grouping** is the process of selecting two or more worksheets so that you can perform the same action at the same time on all selected worksheets. Table 9.1 describes how to group worksheets. When you group worksheets, the grouped worksheet tabs display as active worksheets. That is, the bottom of all active grouped sheet tabs contains a green horizontal bar. The word Group displays to the right of the filename in the title bar.

TABLE 9.1	Grouping Worksheets
To Group	**Do This**
All worksheets	Right-click a sheet tab and select Select All Sheets.
Adjacent worksheets	Click the first sheet tab, press and hold Shift, and then click the last sheet tab.
Nonadjacent worksheet tabs	Click the first sheet tab, press and hold Ctrl, and then click each additional sheet tab.

When you are finished working on grouped worksheets, you should ungroup them. *Ungrouping* is the process of deselecting grouped worksheets so that actions performed on one sheet do not affect other worksheets. You can ungroup sheets by clicking a sheet tab that is not grouped or right-clicking a sheet tab and selecting Ungroup Sheets.

> **TIP: CAUTION WITH GROUPING!**
> Make sure that you ungroup worksheets before you perform a task on only one worksheet. If you forget to ungroup sheets, you could potentially ruin several worksheets by overwriting data on all worksheets instead of just one worksheet. Before making changes with grouped worksheets, consider saving the workbook with another filename. That way, if you accidentally overwrite data on grouped worksheets, you can revert to the data on the original worksheets.

Fill Across Worksheets

After you create one worksheet, you can create additional worksheets that have the same headings and formats used on the original worksheet. For example, assume you created a worksheet showing quarterly sales by department for Indianapolis and want to use the same structure to create quarterly sales worksheets for Bloomington, South Bend, and Fort Wayne. If the other worksheets have not been created yet, you can use the Move or Copy dialog box to copy an entire worksheet and change the data in the duplicate worksheets for the unique cities. However, if other worksheets exist but are missing some headings or have not been formatted, you can use the Fill command to copy the headings or formatting from one worksheet to the other worksheets.

> **To fill data and/or formats from one worksheet to other existing worksheets, complete the following steps:**
>
> 1. Click the sheet tab that contains the data and/or formats you want to copy. Select the range that you want to fill across the worksheets.
> 2. Press Ctrl while you click the destination sheet tabs—the worksheets to which you want to copy the data and/or formats.
> 3. Click the Home tab, click Fill in the Editing group, and then select Across Worksheets to open the Fill Across Worksheets dialog box (see Figure 9.2).
> 4. Select one option in the dialog box:
>   - Click All to copy data and formatting from the current worksheet to the grouped worksheets.
>   - Click Contents to copy the data only from the current worksheet to the grouped worksheets without copying the formatting to the other worksheets.
>   - Click Formats to copy only the formatting from the current worksheet to the grouped worksheets. The data is not copied to the grouped worksheets.
> 5. Click OK.

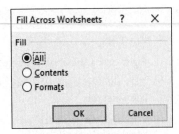

FIGURE 9.2 Fill Across Worksheets Dialog Box

Excel copies the data and/or formatting to the same cells in the other worksheets. For example, cell A1 contains the text Circle City Sporting Goods bold, centered, and in 14-pt font. When you select All in the Fill Across Worksheets dialog box, Excel copies text and formatting from the active cell or selected range in the current worksheet to the same cell or range in the grouped worksheets.

> **TIP: CONDITIONAL FORMATTING**
> Excel disables the Conditional Formatting feature when you group worksheets. You cannot group worksheets and then create and manage conditional formats. However, you can create a conditional formatting rule on one worksheet, group the worksheets, click Fill, select Fill Across Worksheets, and then select Formats to replicate the conditional formatting rule to a range on other worksheets.

STEP 2 ## Enter and Format Data on Grouped Worksheets

The previous discussion assumes you used data on an existing worksheet to fill in data on other worksheets. However, if you want to create several worksheets with the same structure at the same time, you can group the worksheets and enter data as you create the worksheets. You can enter labels, values, dates, and formulas efficiently on grouped worksheets, saving you from entering the same data on each worksheet individually. For example, if you enter row labels in the range A5:A10 to describe the different types of monthly income and expenses, Excel enters the same row labels in the same location (the range A5:A10) on the other grouped worksheets. When you enter a formula on grouped worksheets, Excel enters the formula in the same cell address on all grouped worksheets. For example, if you enter =A4-B4 in cell C4 on the active worksheet, Excel enters =A4-B4 in cell C4 on all grouped worksheets. The formulas use the values on the respective worksheets.

When you group similar worksheets, you can make structural changes for all worksheets at the same time. For example, if you insert a row between rows 4 and 5 and widen column B on the displayed worksheet, Excel inserts a row between rows 4 and 5 and widens column B on all grouped worksheets. You can cut, copy, and paste data to the same locations, and delete cell contents, rows, and columns on grouped worksheets.

You can apply text formatting, alignment settings, and number formats in the same cells on grouped worksheets. Figure 9.3 shows worksheets that were grouped to enter and format data. The top image shows the Qtr1 worksheet data with the original formatting, and the bottom image shows the Qtr4 worksheet after copying the formats from the Qtr1 worksheet.

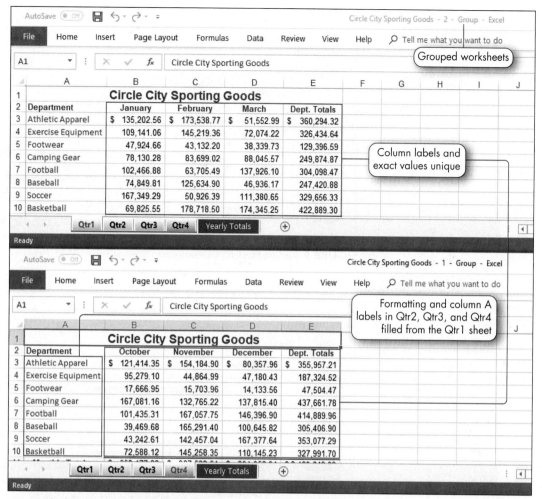

FIGURE 9.3 Multiple Worksheets Grouped

You can select Page Setup options for grouped worksheets. You can insert identical headers and footers, set the page orientation, set the print areas, and adjust the scaling all at one time instead of applying these page layouts individually to each worksheet. After grouping worksheets, you can display them in Print Preview, select print settings, and then finally print the grouped worksheets.

TIP: UNAVAILABLE TASKS

Some tasks are not available on grouped worksheets. These tasks are grayed out on the ribbon or in menus. For example, you cannot apply conditional formatting or format data as a table on grouped worksheets. Most commands on the Insert and Data tabs are unavailable for grouped worksheets.

STEP 3 **Inserting Hyperlinks**

When you create a workbook that has multiple worksheets, it is a good practice to include a documentation worksheet designed like a table of contents. On the documentation worksheet, enter labels to describe each worksheet and create hyperlinks to the respective worksheets. A **hyperlink** is an electronic link that, when clicked, opens an existing file, opens a browser and goes to a webpage (see Figure 9.4), goes to a specific cell or named range in the same workbook (see Figure 9.5), or opens an email client and inserts an email address into the To box. You can add hyperlinks to link to charts, images, and objects contained in a worksheet. For example, you can link the chart to another worksheet that contains the data source or link a text box to a webpage containing statistics related to the data in the worksheet.

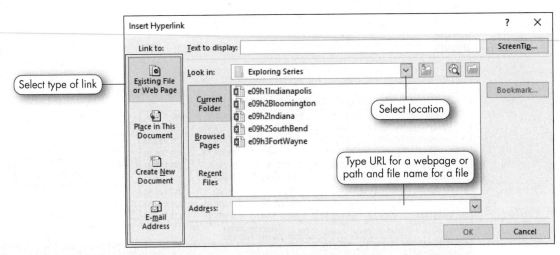

FIGURE 9.4 Insert Hyperlink Dialog Box (Existing File or Web Page)

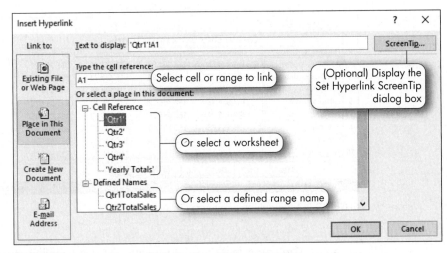

FIGURE 9.5 Insert Hyperlink Dialog Box (Place in This Document)

To create a hyperlink, complete the following steps:

1. Click the cell that will contain the hyperlink or select an object, such as a chart, that you want to use as the hyperlink.
2. Click the Insert tab, click Link in the Links group, and then click Insert Link to open the Insert Hyperlink dialog box. (On a Mac, click Insert on the menu bar and then select Hyperlink.)
3. Select the type of target in the *Link to* section on the left side of the dialog box: Existing File or Web Page, Place in This Document, Create New Document, or E-mail Address. The options in middle section of the dialog box change based on the target you select.
4. Select specific location options in the middle section of the dialog box. If you selected Existing File or Web Page in Step 2, select Current Folder, Browsed Pages, or Recent Files and then select the specific file or enter the URL in the Address box for a webpage. If you selected Place in This Document type, specify a target location, such as a cell reference, worksheet, or range name.
5. (Optional) Click ScreenTip (refer to Figure 9.5) to open the Set Hyperlink ScreenTip dialog box, type the text you want to display when the user positions the pointer over the hyperlink in the ScreenTip text box (see Figure 9.6), and then click OK.
6. Click OK in the Insert Hyperlink dialog box.

FIGURE 9.6 Set Hyperlink ScreenTip Dialog Box

TIP: OTHER WAYS TO CREATE A HYPERLINK
Two other methods exist to create hyperlinks. You can right-click the cell or object and select Link; alternatively, make the cell where you want the hyperlink to be the active cell and press Ctrl+K.

To modify a hyperlink, click Link in the Links group on the Insert tab and select Insert Link (or right-click the link and select Edit Hyperlink) to open the Edit Hyperlink dialog box, which is similar to the Insert Hyperlink dialog box. Make the changes and click OK.

To remove a hyperlink, right-click it and select Remove Hyperlink. Alternatively, display the Edit Hyperlink dialog box and click Remove Link. This action removes the hyperlink but does not delete the cell contents or object.

Workbook hyperlinks are similar to hyperlinks on a webpage. Text hyperlinks are blue with a blue underline until you click the hyperlink. When you point to a hyperlink, the pointer looks like a hand, and Excel displays a ScreenTip. If you did not create a custom ScreenTip, the default ScreenTip indicates the link's destination. If a custom ScreenTip was created in the Set Hyperlink ScreenTip dialog box, the custom ScreenTip displays instead of the link's destination. Click the hyperlink to visit the link's destination. After you click a text hyperlink, the color changes to purple to distinguish between links you have clicked and links you have not clicked. The hyperlink color changes back to blue if you edit the hyperlink or close the workbook and open it again. If you change the default workbook theme, the hyperlink colors will change.

Managing Windows

Because a workbook may contain several worksheets, you can manage the worksheets onscreen to enable you to focus on a specific worksheet and reduce information overload. You can control worksheet visibility, open and arrange windows for ease of use, split a window to see different parts of a worksheet, and save the layout of the worksheet windows.

Hide and Unhide Worksheets

If a workbook contains so many worksheets that each sheet tab is not visible, use the worksheet scroll buttons on the left side of the worksheet tabs to find the worksheet you want to review. If you do not need to view a worksheet, you can hide it. Hiding worksheets minimizes scrolling through worksheet tabs. Hiding worksheets is also useful when you want to display a worksheet on a projector in a meeting, but you do not want to accidently click a worksheet containing confidential data. Use Format in the Cells group on the Home tab and select Hide & Unhide to hide or unhide sheets. You can also right-click a sheet tab and select Hide. To unhide a worksheet, you can right-click any visible tab, select Unhide, and then select the worksheet to unhide. When you select Unhide Sheet, the Unhide dialog box opens (see Figure 9.7) so that you can select which sheet to display again.

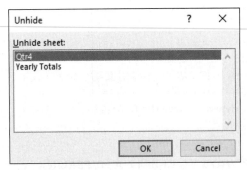

FIGURE 9.7 Unhide Dialog Box

STEP 4 **Open and Arrange Windows**

When you work with a workbook with multiple worksheets, sometimes you want to see the contents of two worksheets at the same time. For example, you want to compare the Qtr1 and Qtr2 worksheets simultaneously. Instead of clicking back and forth between worksheet tabs, you can open an additional window of the same workbook and display different worksheets within each window. To open another window of the current workbook, click New Window in the Window group on the View tab. Excel opens another window of the current workbook. The title bar adds *:1* to the original workbook view and *:2* to the second window. Although only one window appears maximized, both windows are open. Once multiple windows of the same workbook are open, you can display a different worksheet in each window, and then arrange and display all windows onscreen at the same time.

> **To see all windows of the same workbook, complete the following steps:**
>
> 1. Click Arrange All in the Window group on the View tab. (On a Mac, click Window in the menu bar and select Arrange.)
> 2. Select one of the options from the Arrange Windows dialog box (see Figure 9.8). You can display windows in a tiled arrangement, horizontally, vertically, or in a cascaded view. Tiled windows are arranged in rows and columns like ceiling tiles. Horizontal windows are arranged horizontally in rows; vertical windows are arranged side-by-side vertically. Cascaded windows are arranged overlapping each other with only the title bars displaying for the windows behind the front window. If you have other workbooks open when you click Arrange All, Excel includes those workbook windows.
> 3. Click the *Windows of active workbook* check box to select it to display windows for the current workbook only.

FIGURE 9.8 Arrange Windows Dialog Box

Split a Window

When you work with data that does not fit onscreen at the same time, you may want to view different sections at the same time. For example, you may need to look at input data on rows 5 and 6 and see how changing the data affects overall results on row 361. To see different worksheet sections at the same time, split the worksheet window. *Splitting* is the process of dividing a worksheet window into two or four resizable panes so that you can view separate parts of a worksheet at the same time. Figure 9.9 shows the worksheet split between rows 13 and 361 to display the input area, first four payments, last nine payments, and the totals. To split a worksheet into panes, position the active cell where you want the worksheet window to split and click Split in the Window group on the View tab. All panes are part of the same worksheet; any changes you make to one pane affect the entire worksheet.

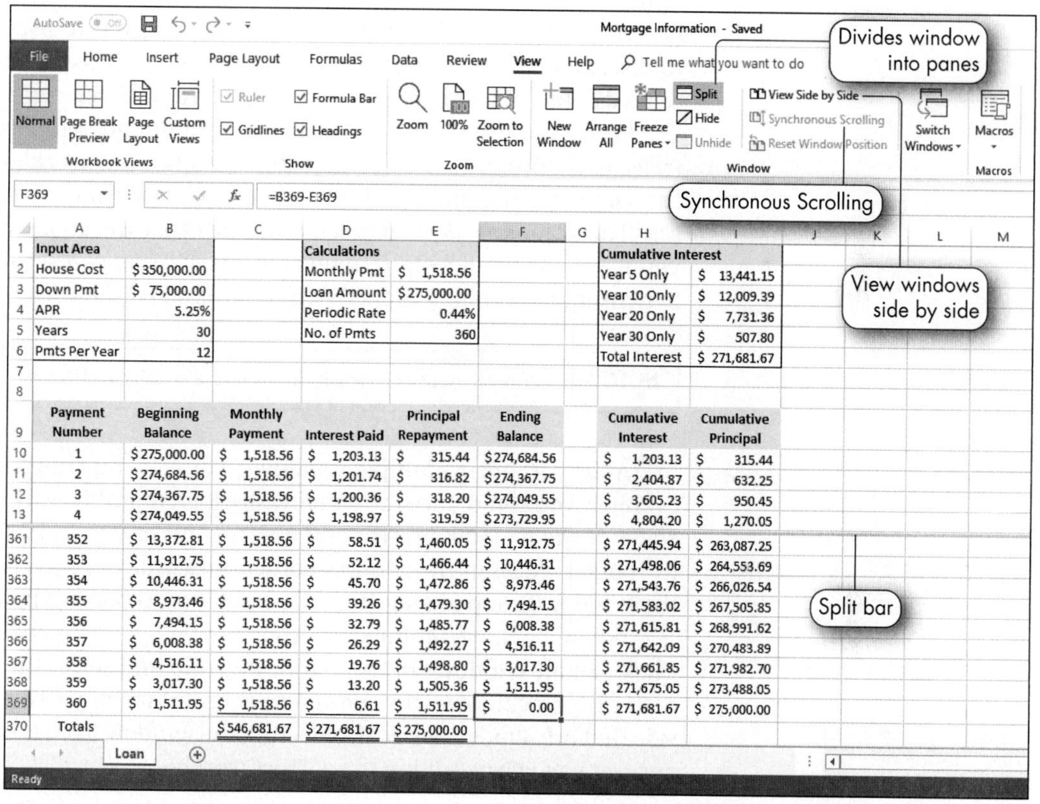

FIGURE 9.9 Split Panes

Depending on which cell is the active cell, Excel splits the worksheet into two or four panes with *split bars*—vertical and horizontal lines that frame the panes—above and to the left of the active cell. If the active cell is in row 1 (except cell A1), the worksheet displays in two vertical panes. A vertical split bar displays between the active cell and the column to its left. For example, if the active cell is D1, the split bar displays between columns C and D. If the active cell is in column A (except cell A1), the worksheet displays in two horizontal panes. A horizontal split bar displays between the active cell and the row above it. For example, if the active cell is A10, the split bar displays between rows 9 and 10. If the active cell is cell A1 or any cell other than the first row or first column, the worksheet displays vertical and horizontal split bars to split the worksheet into four panes.

Once the window is split, you can further customize the display by dragging a split bar between the panes. Drag the vertical split bar to divide the worksheet into left and right (vertical) panes. Drag the horizontal split bar to divide the worksheet into upper and lower (horizontal) panes. Initially, the active cell will be mirrored across all split panes; however, you can scroll each pane to the range you want to see.

To remove panes, click Split in the Window group on the View tab or double-click the split bar. You can also remove panes by dragging the vertical split bar to the left or right edge of the window or a horizontal split bar to the top or bottom of the window.

> **TIP: FREEZE PANES OR SPLIT BARS**
> You cannot use the Freeze Panes settings and split bars at the same time. Freezing panes is useful when you want to keep the first row and column labels onscreen as you scroll through a large dataset. Splitting a window is helpful when you want to see different sections of a worksheet but not necessarily the first row or column.

Apply Other Window Settings

The Window group on the View tab contains additional commands to arrange worksheets or workbooks onscreen. If you have two or more workbooks open, you can click View Side by Side to display the Compare Side by Side dialog box to select which workbook you want to display side by side with the active workbook. This view is helpful when comparing related data, such as budgets from two different years.

When you use the View Side by Side command, Synchronous Scrolling is activated (refer to Figure 9.9). When you scroll through one workbook window, Excel scrolls in the same direction in the other workbook window at the same time. For example, if you scroll down in one workbook window, the other workbook window also scrolls down. If you want one window to remain stationary while you scroll in the other window, click Synchronous Scrolling in the Window group to disable it.

> **MAC TIP:** Synchronous Scrolling is not available on Mac for Excel.

After you open multiple windows, you can rearrange or resize the windows. For example, you can reduce the window size for a monthly workbook by dragging the outside edges of the window inward and enlarge the size of a quarterly workbook by dragging the outside edges of the window border outward. You can click Reset Window Position in the Window group to make the side-by-side workbooks windows equal size again.

When you have multiple workbooks open, you can change which window is active. Click Switch Windows in the Window group and select the window you want to be the active Excel window. This command is useful when you display two workbooks side by side that are almost identical. Selecting the window from the Switch Windows command ensures you will be editing the correct workbook.

Quick Concepts

1. Describe the benefits of grouping worksheets and explain what precautions should be taken when using grouped worksheets. *p. 542*

2. Explain when you would insert hyperlinks in a worksheet. *p. 545*

3. Explain the benefits of using split windows. *p. 549*

Hands-On Exercises

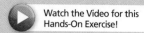

Skills covered: Group Worksheets • Fill Across Worksheets • Enter and Format Data on Grouped Worksheets • Insert Hyperlinks • Open and Arrange Windows

1 Multiple Worksheets

After reviewing last year's fiscal data, you want to improve the appearance of the worksheets for Circle City Sporting Goods. You want to enter a missing heading on the summary worksheet and enter formulas across the quarterly worksheets. To save time, you will group the worksheets to perform tasks on all grouped worksheets at the same time. After you complete the quarterly worksheets, you will insert hyperlinks from the yearly worksheet to the quarterly worksheets.

STEP 1 GROUP AND FILL ACROSS WORKSHEETS

You noticed that the main title and the row headings are displayed only in the Qtr1 worksheet in the Indianapolis workbook. You will fill in the title and row headings for the other three quarterly worksheets as well as the yearly worksheet. Refer to Figure 9.10 as you complete Step 1.

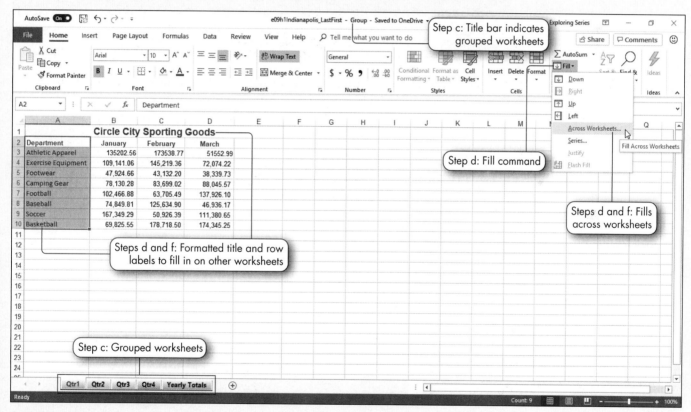

FIGURE 9.10 Formatted Title and Row Headings

a. Open *e09h1Indianapolis* and save it as **e09h1Indianapolis_LastFirst**.

> **TROUBLESHOOTING:** If you make any major mistakes in this exercise, you can close the file, open *e09h1Indianapolis* again, and then start this exercise over.

b. Click the **Qtr1 sheet tab** and click each worksheet tab to see the differences.

The Qtr1 worksheet contains a title and row labels, whereas the Qtr2, Qtr3, and Qtr4 worksheets are missing the title and the row labels. The Yearly Totals worksheet is empty.

c. Click the **Qtr1 sheet tab**, press and hold **Shift**, and then click the **Yearly Totals sheet tab**.

You grouped all worksheets together. Anything you do to the active worksheet affects all grouped worksheets. The title bar displays Group after the file name.

d. Click **cell A1** in the Qtr1 worksheet to select it, click **Fill** in the Editing group on the Home tab, and then select **Across Worksheets**.

The Fill Across Worksheets dialog box opens so that you can select what to fill from the active worksheet to the other grouped worksheets. The default option is All, which will fill in both the content and the formatting.

e. Click **OK**. Keep the worksheets grouped.

Excel fills in the formatted title from the Qtr1 worksheet to the other worksheets.

f. Select the **range A2:A10** on the Qtr1 worksheet, click **Fill** in the Editing group on the Home tab, select **Across Worksheets**, and then click **OK**.

> **TROUBLESHOOTING:** Do not select the range A1:D10 to fill across worksheets. If you do, you will overwrite the other worksheet data with the January, February, and March labels and data. If this happens, click Undo to restore data in the other worksheets and complete Step f again.

g. Right-click the **Yearly Totals sheet tab** and select **Ungroup Sheets**. Click each worksheet to review the results. Save the workbook once your review is complete.

You ungrouped the worksheets. All worksheets that were grouped contain the formatted title and row labels that were copied across worksheets.

> **MAC TROUBLESHOOTING:** Press Control and click the sheet tab. Select Ungroup Sheets.

STEP 2 ENTER AND FORMAT DATA ON GROUPED WORKSHEETS

You will regroup the worksheets so that you can increase the width of column A in all worksheets at the same time. In addition, you want to insert monthly and department totals for the quarterly worksheets. Refer to Figure 9.11 as you complete Step 2.

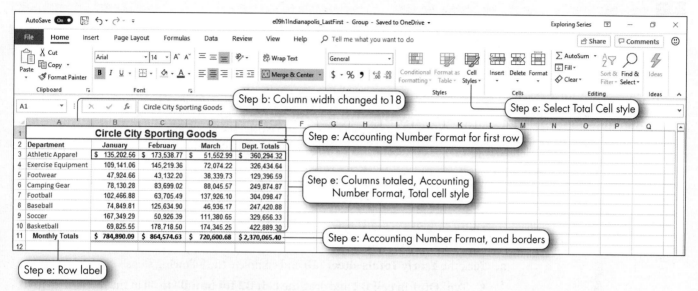

FIGURE 9.11 Data and Formatting Filled in Qtr4 Worksheet

a. Right-click the **Yearly Totals sheet tab** and select **Select All Sheets**.

b. Click **cell A2**, click **Format** in the Cells group on the Home tab, select **Column Width**, type **18** in the Column width box, and then click **OK**.

You changed the column width of column A in all grouped worksheets to 18.

c. Click the **Qtr1 sheet tab** to ungroup the sheets.

d. Press and hold **Shift** and click the **Qtr4 sheet tab**.

You ungrouped all the sheets and regrouped only the four quarterly worksheets because you want to add functions and formatting to the quarterly worksheets only.

e. Do the following to the grouped quarterly worksheets:

- Select the **range B3:E11** and click **AutoSum** in the Editing group on the Home tab to insert department totals in column E and monthly totals in row 11.
- Apply **Accounting Number Format** to the **ranges B3:E3** and **B11:E11**.
- Type **Monthly Totals** in **cell A11**. Keep **cell A11** as the active cell, click **Bold** in the Font group, and then click **Increase Indent** in the Alignment group on the Home tab.
- Type **Dept. Totals** in **cell E2**.
- Select the **range B11:E11**, click **Cell Styles** in the Styles group, and then select **Total**.
  You applied the Total cell style to the monthly totals to conform to standard accounting formatting practices that displays a single line immediately above the totals and a double line immediately below the totals.

f. Click **cell A1**, right-click the **Qtr4 sheet tab**, and then select **Ungroup Sheets**. Click each quarterly sheet tab to ensure the formats were applied to each worksheet and save the workbook.

You want to insert hyperlinks on the Yearly Totals worksheet so that you can jump back to the respective quarterly worksheet quickly. Refer to Figure 9.12 as you complete Step 3.

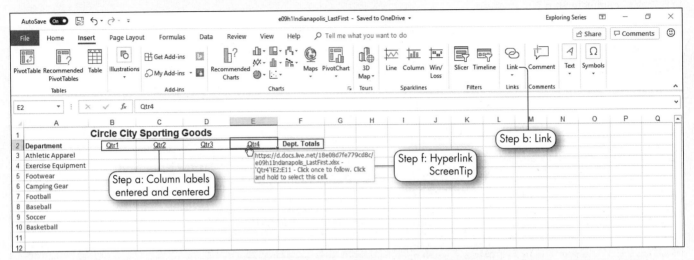

FIGURE 9.12 Hyperlinks

a. Click the **Yearly Totals sheet tab** and complete the following steps:

- Type **Qtr1** in **cell B2** and drag the **cell B2 fill handle** to fill in the remaining quarter labels in the **range C2:E2**.
- Select the **range B2:F2** and click **Center** in the Alignment group on the Home tab.
- Type **Dept. Totals** in **cell F2**. Apply **bold** and **Purple font color** to **cell F2**.

b. Click **cell B2**, click the **Insert tab**, click **Link** in the Links group, and then select **Insert Link**.

> **MAC TROUBLESHOOTING:** Click the Insert menu and select Hyperlink.

The Insert Hyperlink dialog box opens so that you can specify the destination when the user clicks the hyperlink.

c. Click **Place in This Document** in the *Link to* section on the left side of the dialog box.

d. Click in the **Type the cell reference box**, delete **A1**, type **E2:E11**, click **'Qtr1'** in the *Or select a place in this document* list, and then click **OK**.

You created a hyperlink to the range E2:E11 in the Qtr1 worksheet. Note that if you do not specify a reference cell for the link, it will default to cell A1.

e. Create the following hyperlinks by adapting Steps b through d:

- **Cell C2**: Create a hyperlink to the **range E2:E11** in the Qtr2 worksheet.
- **Cell D2**: Create a hyperlink to the **range E2:E11** in the Qtr3 worksheet.
- **Cell E2**: Create a hyperlink to the **range E2:E11** in the Qtr4 worksheet.

f. Point to **cell E2** to display the ScreenTip.

The ScreenTip displays the hyperlink's destination. The path and file name shown on your screen will differ from those shown in the figure. If you created a ScreenTip in the Insert Hyperlink dialog box, that text would display instead of the destination.

g. Click **cell E2**.

The hyperlink jumps to the destination: the range E2:E11 in the Qtr4 worksheet.

h. Click the **Yearly Totals sheet tab** and click the other hyperlinks to ensure they work. When you are finished, click the **Yearly Totals sheet tab** and save the workbook.

> **TROUBLESHOOTING:** If a hyperlink does not display the correct range and worksheet, right-click the cell containing the incorrect hyperlink, select Edit Hyperlink, and then edit the hyperlink in the Edit Hyperlink dialog box.

You want to see the four quarterly sales data worksheets at the same time. To do this, you will open additional windows of the workbook and arrange them. Refer to Figure 9.13 as you complete Step 4.

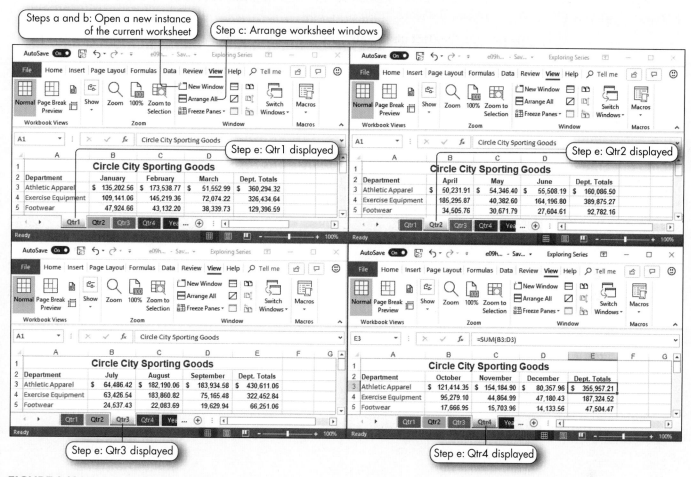

FIGURE 9.13 Worksheet Windows

a. Click the **View tab** and click **New Window** in the Window group.

> **MAC TROUBLESHOOTING:** Click the Window menu and select New Window.

You opened another window of the same workbook. The title bar displays the same file name with – 2. The Home tab displays in the new window.

b. Repeat Step a two times.

Two new windows open with – 3 and – 4 at the end of each file name. You now have four windows open of the same workbook. The active window should be the fourth window.

c. Click the **View tab** and click **Arrange All** in the Window group.

> **MAC TROUBLESHOOTING:** Click the Windows menu and select Arrange.

The Arrange Windows dialog box opens so you can specify how you want to arrange the open worksheet windows.

d. Ensure Tiled is selected, click the **Windows of active workbook check box** to select it, and then click **OK**.

Clicking the *Windows of active workbook* check box ensures that the windows display for the active workbook. If other workbooks are open, those windows do not display. Excel arranges the four windows of the same workbook. Currently, all the Excel windows display the Yearly Totals worksheet.

e. Click the **Qtr1 sheet tab** twice in the top-left window, click the **Qtr2 sheet tab** twice in the top-right window, click the **Qtr3 sheet tab** twice in the bottom-left window, and click the **Qtr4 sheet tab** twice in the bottom-right window.

Each window displays a different quarterly worksheet.

f. Close three of the open windows so that you have one window of the workbook. Maximize the Excel window.

g. Save the workbook. Keep the workbook open if you plan to continue with the next Hands-On Exercise . If not, close the workbook and exit Excel.

3-D Formulas and Linked Workbooks

Excel workbooks often contain data on different worksheets or in different workbooks for different time periods, geographic regions, or products. For example, a workbook might contain a worksheet to store data for each week in a month, data for each location of a chain of department stores, or data for sales of each type of automobile produced by one manufacturer. While you have experience creating formulas and functions to perform calculations within one worksheet, you can apply that knowledge to consolidate, or combine, data from multiple worksheets into one. For example, you can consolidate sales data from all department store locations into one worksheet for the year.

Additional data analysis occurs over time. To avoid overloading a workbook with detailed sales data for several years, create individual worksheets with detailed annual sales data in one workbook. After creating individual worksheets, you can create a summary worksheet to consolidate the data and compute the average yearly sales for the past 10 years on that new sheet.

In this section, you will create a formula with a 3-D reference to consolidate data from several worksheets. In addition, you will learn how to link data from several workbooks to one workbook.

Inserting Formulas and Functions with 3-D References

So far, you have created formulas that reference cells in the same worksheet to make it easier to update or apply changes automatically when performing what-if analyses. For example, when you created a one-variable data table, you entered a reference, such as =B12, to display the contents of a formula in cell B12 instead of performing the calculation again in the one-variable data table. The reference to cell B12 is a two-dimensional reference, where the column is one dimension and the row number is the second dimension. At times, you may want to refer to data from another worksheet as you create a formula on the current worksheet.

STEP 1 ▶ Insert a Formula with a 3-D Reference

When a workbook contains multiple worksheets, you can create a *3-D reference*, which is a reference within a formula or function on one worksheet that includes the name of another worksheet, column letter, and row number located within the workbook. The term *3-D reference* comes from having a reference with three dimensions: worksheet name, column letter, and row number. For example, cell B4 in the October worksheet contains a value that you want to use in another worksheet. Instead of retyping the value in the other worksheet, you can create a 3-D reference, such as =October!B4. Doing so is efficient because if the value in cell B4 in the October worksheet changes, you do not have to edit the value in the other worksheet; the reference does that for you automatically.

If worksheet names include spaces, the 3-D reference includes single quotation marks before and after the worksheet name, such as 'October Sales'. The 3-D reference includes an exclamation point to separate the worksheet name and the cell reference.

='Worksheet Name'!RangeOfCells

To insert a 3-D reference, complete the following steps:

1. Click the cell on the worksheet where you want to enter a formula and type an equal sign.
2. Click the sheet tab that contains the cell you want to reference.
3. Click the target cell that contains the value, label, or formula you want.
4. Press Enter.

What you have learned in previous chapters about using cell references in formulas applies to 3-D references. You can use a 3-D reference to build formulas using data from multiple worksheets, such as adding values from two different worksheets. For example, the formula =October!B4+November!B4 adds the values stored in cells B4 on both worksheets.

You can also create a formula that references a value on another worksheet and performs a calculation using a value on the current worksheet. For example, you can set a goal to increase sales by 3% over last month's sales. Figure 9.14 shows the formula with the 3-D reference. The sales goal of 103% is entered in cell B2 in the November sheet. The formula to calculate the sales goal for the Athletic Department in cell B4 is =October!B4*November!B$2. The value stored in cell B4 in the October worksheet is multiplied by the value stored in cell B2 in the November sheet.

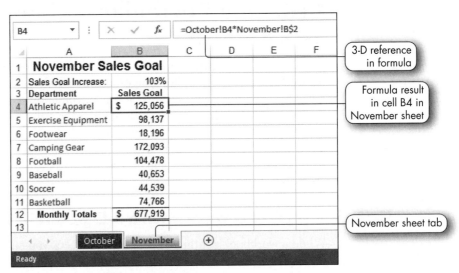

FIGURE 9.14 3-D Reference in a Formula

STEP 2 Insert a Function with a 3-D Reference

An advantage of including several related worksheets in one workbook is that you can consolidate data from the worksheets into a summary worksheet. For example, with the Circle City Sporting Goods workbook, you will generate the fourth quarter totals from three monthly totals.

When individual worksheets have an identical structure (i.e., totals for the Athletic Apparel department are in cell B4 in each monthly worksheet), you can use a 3-D reference in the SUM function that refers to the same cell or range in the October, November, and December worksheets. As you know, using functions improves efficiency in performing calculations. Instead of entering =October!B4+November!B4+December!B4, you can use the SUM function with 3-D references to the same cells in the other worksheets. In Figure 9.15, the SUM function with 3-D references in cell B4 in the Qtr4 worksheet is =SUM(October:December!B4).

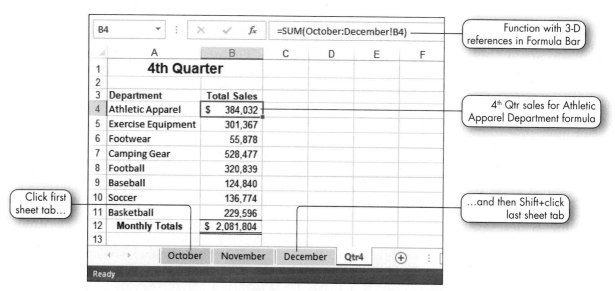

FIGURE 9.15 SUM Function with 3-D References

The function =SUM(October:December!B4) includes 3-D references that add the values in cell B4 in each worksheet, starting in the October worksheet and ending in the December worksheet, including any worksheets between those two worksheets. You can type a function with 3-D references directly into a cell, but the semi-selection method is more efficient.

=SUM('First Worksheet:Last Worksheet'!RangeOfCells)

To build a function using 3-D references, complete the following steps:

1. Click the cell in which you will enter a function with 3-D references.
2. Type an equal sign, type the name of the function, such as SUM, and then type an opening parenthesis.
3. Click the first sheet tab, such as October.
4. Press and hold Shift as you click the last sheet tab for adjacent worksheets, or press and hold Ctrl as you click nonadjacent sheet tabs.
5. Click the cell or select the range that contains the value(s) you want to use in the function argument and press Enter.

You can use a variety of functions with 3-D references. Some of these functions include SUM, AVERAGE, COUNT, MAX, MIN, PRODUCT, and some standard deviation and variance functions. Other functions, such as PMT, VLOOKUP, and COUNTIF, do not work with 3-D references.

When you have a function such as =SUM(B1:B5) and insert a new fourth row, Excel modifies the SUM function to include the new row: =SUM(B1:B6). Similarly, if you insert or copy a worksheet between the beginning and ending worksheet references, the function containing the 3-D references automatically includes the worksheet data points in the calculation. If you move a worksheet out of the range, Excel excludes that worksheet's values from the formula containing the 3-D references. Finally, if you move or delete the last worksheet that is referenced in a 3-D formula, Excel adjusts the worksheet references in the formula for you.

Linking Workbooks

Workbook linking is another way of consolidating data. When you link workbooks, you consolidate the data from several workbooks into another workbook. **Linking** is the process of creating external cell references from worksheets in one workbook to cells on a worksheet in another workbook. For example, you created three workbooks—Indianapolis,

Bloomington, and South Bend—one for each store location. Each store manager maintains a workbook to record sales by department (such as exercise equipment, footwear, and camping gear) for a particular time period. As district manager, you want to consolidate the data from each store workbook into one regional workbook. Including all the city data in the regional workbook would add unnecessary details in the regional workbook and dramatically increase the file size of that workbook. Therefore, you will create links from specific cells of data in the individual workbooks to your active workbook.

Before creating links, identify the source and destination files. A **source file** is one that contains original data that you want to use in another file. For example, the individual department store workbooks—Indianapolis, Bloomington, and South Bend—are source files. The **destination file** is a file containing a link to receive data from the source files—that is, the target file that needs the data. In this case, the regional workbook is the destination file. When you link workbooks, you create a connection between the source and destination files. If data change in the source file, the data in the destination file is updated also. Another benefit of linking files is that the destination file always contains the most up-to-date data.

STEP 3 Create a Link to Another Workbook

When you create a link between source and destination files, you establish an external reference or pointer to one or more cells in another workbook. The external reference is similar to the worksheet reference that you created for 3-D formulas. However, an external reference must include the workbook name to identify which workbook contains the linked worksheet and cell reference. For example, =[Indianapolis.xlsx]Qtr3!E3 creates a link to cell E3 in the Qtr3 worksheet in the Indianapolis workbook. The link includes the workbook name and file name extension between brackets, the worksheet name, exclamation mark, and cell reference. Because of the complexity of building this type of formula, it is best to use the semi-selection process to create the external reference. Table 9.2 lists additional rules to follow when entering external references.

=[WorkbookName]WorksheetName!RangeOfCells

TABLE 9.2 External References

Situation	Rule	Example
Workbook and worksheet names do not contain spaces; source and destination files are in the same folder.	Type brackets around the workbook name and an exclamation mark between the worksheet name and range.	[Indianapolis.xlsx]Qtr3!A1
Workbook or worksheet name contains spaces; source and destination files are in the same folder.	Type single quotation marks on the left side of the opening bracket and the right side of the worksheet name.	'[South Bend.xlsx]Qtr3'!A1
Worksheet name contains spaces; source and destination files are in the same folder.	Type single quotation marks on the left side of the opening bracket and the right side of the worksheet name.	'[Bloomington.xlsx]Qtr 3 Sales'!A1
Source workbook is in a different folder from the destination workbook.	Type a single quotation mark, and the full path—drive letter and folder name—before the opening bracket and a single quotation mark after the worksheet name.	'C:\Data[Indianapolis.xlsx]Sheet1'!A1

Excel displays formulas with external references in two ways, depending on whether the source workbook is open or closed. When the source is open, the external reference shows the file name, worksheet, and cell reference. When the source workbook is closed, the external reference shows the full path name in the Formula Bar. By default, Excel creates absolute cell references in the external reference. However, you can edit the external reference to create a relative or mixed cell reference.

> **To create a link to cells in another workbook, complete the following steps:**
>
> 1. Open the destination workbook and all source workbooks.
> 2. Select the cell to hold the external reference.
> 3. Type the equal sign. If you want to perform calculations or functions on the external references, type the expression or function.
> 4. Switch to the source workbook and click the sheet tab for the worksheet that contains the cells to which you want to link.
> 5. Select the cells to which you want to link and press Enter.

TIP: DRIVE AND FOLDER REFERENCE

Excel updates an external reference regardless of whether the source workbook is open. The source workbooks must be in the same folder location as when you created the link to update the destination workbook. If the location of the workbooks changes, as may happen if you copy the workbooks to a different folder, click Edit Links in the Connections group on the Data tab.

Manage and Update Linked Workbooks

If you create an external reference when both the source and destination files are open, changes you make to the source file occur in the destination file as well. However, if the destination file is closed when you change data in the source file, the destination file is not automatically updated to match the source file. Excel does not update linked data in a destination workbook automatically to protect the workbook against malicious activity, such as viruses.

When you open the destination file the first time, Excel displays the Security Warning Message Bar between the ribbon and Formula Bar with the message *Automatic updates of links has been disabled*. If you are confident that the source files contain safe data, enable the links in the destination file. Click Enable Content to update the links and save the workbook (see Figure 9.16). The next time you open the destination file, Excel displays a message box that prompts the user to update, do not update, or select help. Click Update to update the links.

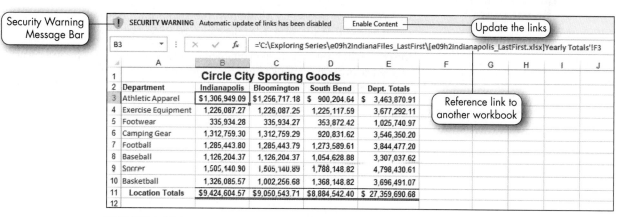

FIGURE 9.16 Security Warning to Update Links

If you rename the source workbook, you must edit the reference in the destination file to match the name of the source workbook. Otherwise, when you open the destination file, Excel displays an error message: *This workbook contains one or more links that cannot be updated.*

To edit a link to a source file, complete the following steps:

1. Click Edit Links to display the Edit Links dialog box (see Figure 9.17). (On a Mac, click the Data tab and select Edit Links.)
2. Select the source where the Status column indicates an error.
3. Click Change Source to open the Change Source dialog box.
4. Navigate through your folders to find the source file, select the source file, and then click OK.
5. Click Close in the Edit Links dialog box.

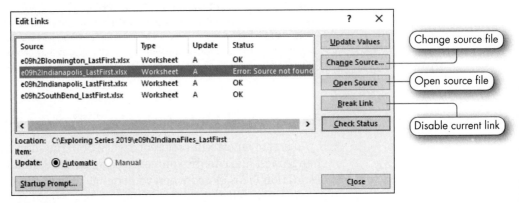

FIGURE 9.17 Edit Links Dialog Box

In the Edit Links dialog box, the Status column displays OK if the external reference link to the source file still works. If a problem exists, the Status column indicates the type of error, such as *Error: Source not found.*

Quick Concepts

4. Explain why you would create a 3-D reference in one worksheet that refers to a cell in another worksheet instead of just typing a value in the second worksheet. *p. 557*

5. Describe how worksheets within a workbook should be structured to build a function (such as AVERAGE) using 3-D references. *p. 558*

6. Describe what happens when you open a workbook with links to other workbooks where the other workbooks have been moved to a different folder on your computer. *p. 561*

Hands-On Exercises

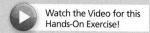
Skills covered: Insert a Formula with a 3-D Reference • Insert a Function with a 3-D Reference • Create a Link to Another Workbook • Complete the Linked Workbook

2 3-D Formulas and Linked Workbooks

Previously, you set up the four quarterly worksheets and the yearly total worksheet for Circle City Sporting Goods. Next, you want to calculate total yearly sales for each department as well as the overall total sales. In addition, you want to link sales data from all three locations into one workbook.

STEP 1 INSERT A FORMULA WITH A 3-D REFERENCE

Each quarterly worksheet calculates the sales totals for a three-month period for each department. You want to insert 3-D references to each worksheet to consolidate the quarterly sales on the Yearly Totals worksheet. Refer to Figure 9.18 as you complete Step 1.

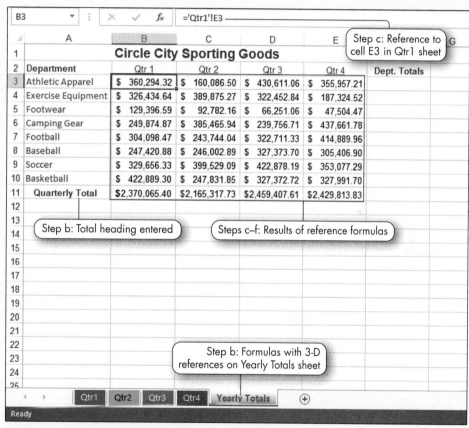

FIGURE 9.18 Worksheet References

a. Open *e09h1Indianapolis_LastFirst* if you closed it at the end of Hands-On Exercise 1, and save it as **e09h2Indianapolis_LastFirst**, changing h1 to h2.

b. Click the **Yearly Totals sheet tab**. Type **Quarterly Total** in **cell A11**. Apply **bold**, change the font color to **Purple**, and then click **Increase Indent** in cell B3.

c. Click **cell B3**, type = and click the **Qtr1 sheet tab**, click **cell E3** in that worksheet, and then press **Ctrl+Enter**.

Look at the Formula Bar. The formula is ='Qtr1'!E3, where Qtr1 refers to the worksheet, and E3 refers to the cell within that worksheet.

d. Double-click the **cell B3 fill handle** to copy the formula to the **range B4:B11**.

The formula's cell reference is relative, so it changes as you copy the formula down the column. The formula in cell B4 is ='Qtr1'!E4.

e. Click **cell C3** in the Yearly Totals worksheet, type **=** and click the **Qtr2 sheet tab**, click **cell E3** in that worksheet, and then press **Ctrl+Enter**. Double-click the **cell C3 fill handle** to copy the formula to the **range C4:C11**.

Look at the Formula Bar. The formula is ='Qtr2'!E3, where Qtr2 refers to the worksheet and E3 refers to the cell within that worksheet.

f. Adapt Step e to enter references to the appropriate totals in the Qtr3 and Qtr4 worksheets. Save the workbook.

STEP 2 INSERT A FUNCTION WITH A 3-D REFERENCE

You want to calculate the total annual sales by department. Although you could simply sum the values in the Yearly Totals worksheet, you want to build a function with 3-D references to provide a cross-check that the totals are correct. Refer to Figure 9.19 as you complete Step 2.

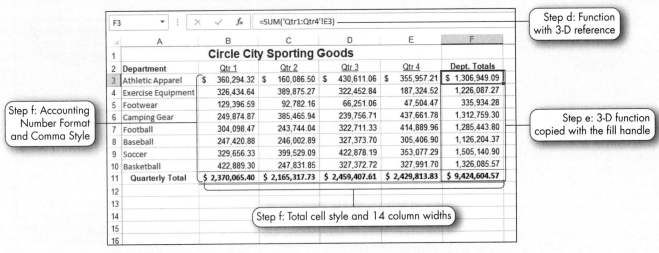

FIGURE 9.19 3-D Formulas

a. Click **cell F3** in the Yearly Totals worksheet.

b. Type **=SUM(**

You start the 3-D formula with =, the function name, and the opening parenthesis.

c. Click the **Qtr1 sheet tab**, press and hold **Shift**, and then click the **Qtr4 sheet tab**.

You grouped the worksheets together so that you can use a common cell reference for the range of cells to sum.

d. Click **cell E3**, the cell containing the quarterly sales, and press **Ctrl+Enter**.

Look at the Formula Bar. The function is =SUM('Qtr1:Qtr4'!E3). If you select the range B3:E3 in the Yearly Totals worksheet, the status bar shows that the sum is $1,306,949.09, the same unformatted value that displays when you inserted the 3-D formula.

e. Double-click the **cell F3 fill handle** to copy the formula to the **range F4:F11**.

f. Apply **Accounting Number Format** to the **ranges B3:F3** and **B11:F11**. Apply **Comma Style** to the **range B4:F10**. Apply the **Total cell style** to the **range B11:F11**. With the range B11:F11 still selected, change the column width to **14**. Save the workbook.

You want to link the Indianapolis, Bloomington, and South Bend workbooks to display their totals in the Indiana workbook. The South Bend and Bloomington workbooks have the same structure as the Indianapolis workbook on which you have been working. Refer to Figure 9.20 as you complete Step 3.

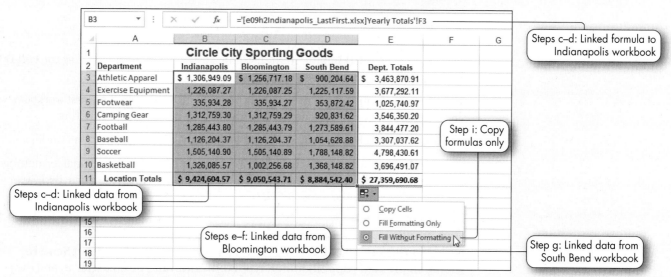

FIGURE 9.20 Linked Workbooks

a. Open *e09h2Bloomington* and save it as **e09h2Bloomington_LastFirst**; open *e09h2SouthBend* and save it as **e09h2SouthBend_LastFirst**; and then open *e09h2Indiana* and save it as **e09h2Indiana_LastFirst**, making sure you save the workbooks in the same folder as your e09h2Indianapolis_LastFirst workbook.

b. Make sure e09h2Indiana_LastFirst is the active workbook.

   This workbook will contain the links to the three location workbooks.

c. Click **cell B3**, type **=**, click the **View tab**, click **Switch Windows** in the Windows group, select **e09h2Indianapolis_LastFirst**, click the **Yearly Totals sheet tab**, click **cell F3** containing the yearly department totals, and then press **Ctrl+Enter**.

MAC TROUBLESHOOTING: Click the Window menu and select e09h2Indianapolis_LastFirst.

   The formula ='[e09h2Indianapolis_LastFirst.xlsx]Yearly Totals'!$F$3 creates a link to the Indianapolis workbook.

d. Edit the cell reference in the formula to make the cell F3 reference relative and press **Ctrl+Enter**.

   You must make this cell reference relative before copying it down the column in Step f. Otherwise, the results will show the value for cell F3 for the other Indianapolis departments.

e. Click **cell C3**, type **=**, click the **View tab**, click **Switch Windows**, select **e09h2Bloomington_LastFirst**, click the **Yearly Totals sheet tab**, click **cell F3**, and then press **Ctrl+Enter**.

MAC TROUBLESHOOTING: Click the Window menu.

   You created a link to the Bloomington workbook. The formula looks like ='[e09h2Bloomington_LastFirst.xlsx]Yearly Totals'!$F$3.

f. Edit the cell reference in the formula to make the cell F3 reference relative.

g. Click **cell D3**, type **=**, click the **View tab**, click **Switch Windows**, select **e09h2SouthBend_LastFirst**, click the **Yearly Totals sheet tab**, click **cell F3**, and then press **Ctrl+Enter**. Edit the cell reference in the formula to make cell F3 reference relative.

You created a link to the South Bend workbook. The formula looks like ='[e09h2SouthBend_LastFirst.xlsx]Yearly Totals'!F3.

h. Select the **range B3:D3** in the e09h2Indiana_LastFirst workbook and drag the **cell D3 fill handle** down to **cell D11**.

You copied the formulas down the columns in the e09h2Indiana_LastFirst workbook. The formulas and formatting are copied, overwriting the original formatting.

i. Click the **Auto Fill button** and select **Fill Without Formatting**. Save the workbook.

Fill Without Formatting copies only the formulas and preserves the original formatting: Accounting Number Format for rows 3 and 11, Comma Style for the range B4:E10, and the Total cell style for the range B11:D11.

j. Save and close all files. Open File Explorer. Select **e09h2Bloomington_LastFirst**, **e09h2Indiana_LastFirst**, **e09h2Indianapolis_LastFirst**, and **e09h2SouthBend_LastFirst**. Right-click one of the selected files, select **Send to**, select **Compressed (zipped) folder**, type **e09h2IndianaFiles_LastFirst**, and then press **Enter**. You will submit this file to your instructor at the end of the last Hands-On Exercise.

MAC TROUBLESHOOTING: Open Finder and select the files. Click the File menu and select Compress.

---

k. Keep Excel open if you plan to continue with the next Hands-On Exercise. If not, exit Excel.

Formula Audits and Data Validation

Errors can occur in a worksheet in several ways. Sometimes, an error may occur with a function name, such as =AVG(B1:E1) when the formula should be =AVERAGE(B1:E1). A **syntax error** is an error that occurs because a formula or function violates construction rules. If you misspell a function name, Excel displays #NAME? Another common type of error is a **run-time error**, which occurs while Excel tries to execute a syntactically correct formula or function, but the formula or function contains a cell reference with invalid or missing data. For example, if you create a formula that divides a value stored in a cell by a cell that does not contain a value, a divide-by-zero error occurs, and Excel displays #DIV/0! in the cell containing the formula. If you add a cell containing a value to a cell containing text, Excel displays #VALUE!

Excel helps you detect and correct syntax and run-time errors. Table 9.3 lists some common syntax and run-time errors and the reasons for those errors.

TABLE 9.3	Syntax and Run-Time Errors Explained
Error	**Reasons**
#DIV/0!	Formula attempts to divide a value by zero or an empty cell
#NAME?	Misspelled or invalid range name Misspelled or invalid function name, such as VLOKUP instead of VLOOKUP Parentheses missing for function, such as =TODAY instead of =TODAY( ) Omitted quotation marks around text, such as using *text* instead of "*text*" in the function =IF(A4="text",A5,A6) Missing colon in a range reference, such as =SUM(A1A8)
#N/A	Function is missing one or more required arguments VLOOKUP, HLOOKUP, or MATCH functions do not return a match when trying to find an exact match in an unsorted list
#NULL!	Incorrect range separator, such as using a semicolon instead of a colon within a reference to a range Formula requires cell ranges to intersect and they do not
#NUM!	Invalid numeric value contained in a formula or a function Invalid arguments used in a function
#REF!	Formula contains a reference to a cell that was deleted or replaced with other data
#VALUE!	Incorrect type of data used in an argument, such as referring to a cell that contains text instead of a value

Results that appear to be correct but are not create an error that is more difficult to detect. For example, entering an incorrect range, such as =AVERAGE(B1:D1) when the range should be =AVERAGE(B1:E1), is more challenging to detect. **Logic errors** are the result of a syntactically correct formula but logically incorrect construction, which produces inaccurate results. Logic errors occur when a formula contains a wrong cell reference or wrong operator (such as dividing instead of multiplying). Another type of error is a **circular reference**, which occurs when a formula contains a direct or an indirect reference to the cell containing the formula. For example, in Figure 9.21, the formula in cell A4 contains a circular reference because A4 is in the formula =SUM(A1:A4). A formula should not contain a reference in the cell containing that formula.

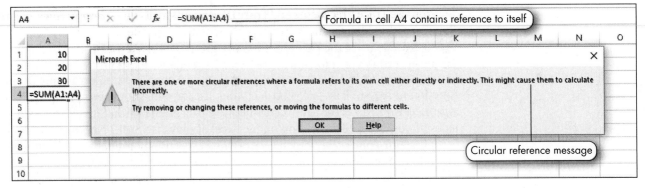

FIGURE 9.21 Circular Reference

Excel displays a warning message when you enter a formula containing a circular reference or when you open an Excel workbook that contains an existing circular reference. Click Help to display the *Find and fix a circular reference* topic or click OK to accept the circular reference. Until you resolve a circular reference, the status bar indicates the location of a circular reference, such as *Circular References: A4*.

You can design worksheets to help facilitate correct data entry, such as ensuring that a user enters a value, not text. Doing so helps prevent formula errors because the user must enter valid data. Although you can design workbooks to require valid data, sometimes you will work with workbooks that other people created that contain errors in the formulas.

In this section, you will learn how to use formula auditing tools to detect errors. You will also apply data validation rules to make sure users enter correct data into input cells.

Auditing Formulas

Recall that you can press Ctrl+ the grave accent key (`) or click Show Formulas in the Formula Auditing group on the Formulas tab to display cell formulas. Displaying the formulas enables you to identify some errors, but you might not be able to detect all errors immediately.

Excel detects potential logic errors even if the formula does not contain a syntax error. For example, Excel might detect that =SUM(B2:B5) contains a potential error if cell B1 contains a value, assuming the possibility that the function might need to include B1 in the range of values to add. When this occurs, Excel displays a green triangle in the top-left corner of the cell. Click the cell containing the green triangle and click the error icon, the yellow diamond with the exclamation mark, to see a list of options to correct the error.

You can use *formula auditing*, a set of tools that enable you to display or trace relationships for formula cells, show formulas, check for errors, and evaluate formulas to detect and correct errors in formulas. The Formula Auditing group on the Formulas tab contains commands to enable you to audit a workbook.

STEP 1 Trace Precedents and Dependents

Although Excel displays error messages, identifying which cell is causing the error could be challenging. Even if your worksheet does not contain errors, you can use formula auditing tools to identify which cells are used in formulas. This is especially helpful when you want to check the accuracy of formulas or see what values are used in the formula calculations. Using formula auditing tools visually indicates the values being used in the formula. Formulas involve both precedent and dependent cells. *Precedent cells* are cells that are referenced by a formula in another cell. For example, assume an hourly pay rate ($10.25) is stored in cell A1, hours worked (40) is stored in cell A2, and the formula =A1*A2 is stored in cell A3 to calculate the gross pay. Cells A1 and A2 are precedent cells to the formula in cell A3. *Dependent cells* contain formulas that depend on other cells to generate their values. For example, if cell A3 contains the formula =A1*A2, cell A3 is a dependent of cells A1 and A2.

You use Trace Precedents and Trace Dependents to display **tracer arrows**, colored lines that show the relationship between precedent and dependent cells (see Figure 9.22). Use Trace Precedents in the Formula Auditing group on the Formula tab to trace precedents for a cell containing a formula. Use Trace Dependents to trace dependent cells for a cell containing a value, date, or text that may be used in a formula. The tracer starts in a precedent cell with the arrowhead ending in the dependent cell. The tracer arrows enable you to identify cells that cause errors. Blue arrows show cells with no errors; red arrows show cells that cause errors.

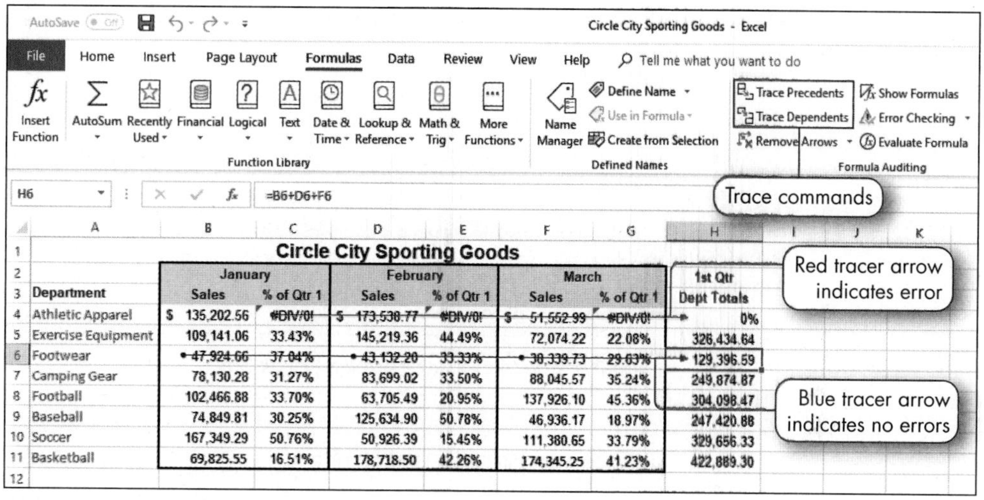

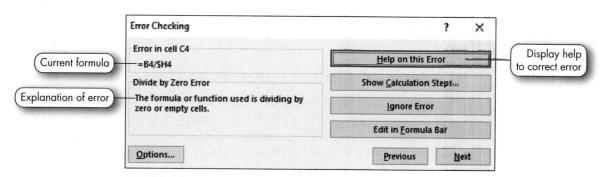

FIGURE 9.22 Trace Precedents

When you are finished using the tracer arrows, you can remove them. Click Remove Arrows in the Formula Auditing group on the Formulas tab to remove all tracer arrows, or click the Remove Arrows arrow and select Remove Arrows, Remove Precedent Arrows, or Remove Dependent Arrows.

STEP 2 ► **Check for and Repair Errors**

When the tracing of precedents or dependents shows errors in formulas, or if you want to check for errors that have occurred in formulas anywhere in a worksheet, you can click Error Checking in the Formula Auditing group on the Formulas tab. The Error Checking dialog box opens (see Figure 9.23), identifies the first cell containing an error, and describes the error.

FIGURE 9.23 Error Checking Dialog Box

Click *Help on this error* to see a description of the error. Click Show Calculation Steps to open the Evaluate Formula dialog box (see Figure 9.24), which provides an evaluation of the formula and shows which part of the evaluation will result in an error. The Evaluation box displays values rather than cell references so that you can evaluate the formula. Clicking Ignore Error either moves to the next error or indicates that error checking is complete.

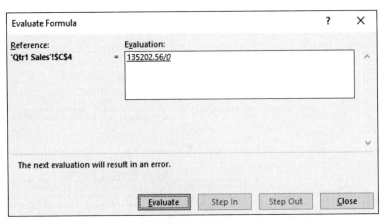

FIGURE 9.24 Evaluate Formula Dialog Box

Evaluate a Formula

Understanding how a nested formula is calculated is difficult because intermediate calculations and logic tests exist. You can use the Evaluate Formula dialog box to view different parts of a nested formula and evaluate each part.

To evaluate a formula for errors, complete the following steps:

1. Select the cell you want to evaluate.
2. Click Evaluate Formula in the Formula Auditing group on the Formulas tab to display the Evaluate Formula dialog box (refer to Figure 9.24).
3. Click Evaluate to examine the value of the reference that is underlined.
4. Click Step In to display the other formula in the Evaluation box if the underlined part of the formula is a reference to another formula.
5. Click Step Out to return to the previous cell and formula.
6. Continue clicking Step In and Step Out until you have evaluated the entire formula and click Close.

> **MAC TIP:** Evaluate Formula is not available in Excel for Mac.

Use the IFERROR Function to Detect Errors

If you create a workbook for others to use, you should anticipate errors the users will introduce so that you can provide a way to identify and correct those errors. The **IFERROR function** is a logic function that checks a cell to determine if that cell contains an error or if a formula will result in an error. If no error exists, the IFERROR function returns the value of the formula. The Value argument contains the value being checked for an error, and the Value_if_error argument is the value to return if the formula evaluates to an error. IFERROR detects the following types of errors: #N/A, #VALUE!, #REF!, #DIV/0!, #NUM!, #NAME?, and #NULL, although the output does not indicate the type of error.

Typically, you use a text string enclosed in quotation marks to return an error message. For example, if you divide the contents of cells in row 2 by cell B1 and anticipate that a #DIV/0! error might occur, you can use =IFERROR(A2/B1,"You cannot divide by zero. Change the value of cell B1 to a value higher than 0.").

=IFERROR(value,value_if_error)

TIP: INFORMATION FUNCTIONS

The Information functions contain additional functions you can use for error checking. Of particular interest are the ERROR.TYPE and ISERROR functions. Use Help to learn how to incorporate these functions in error-checking tasks.

STEP 3 ▶ Setting Up a Watch Window

When you work with a worksheet containing a large dataset, the input area may be on one sheet and formulas on another sheet. For example, in the Circle City Sporting Goods workbook, the department quarterly sales are on four individual worksheets, and the yearly totals are on a different worksheet. Although you can create and arrange windows of the same workbook to view quarterly sales and the yearly worksheet at the same time, the individual windows are small. Alternatively, you can set up a Watch Window to check how changes in the quarterly worksheet affect formula results in the yearly worksheet. A *Watch Window* is a separate window that displays the workbook name, worksheet name, cell addresses, values, and formulas so you can monitor and examine formula calculations involving cells not immediately visible on the screen. The Watch Window adds a watch for every cell in the selected range. Any time you make a change to the watched cell(s), the Watch Window displays the current value of the watched cell(s). You can double-click a cell in the Watch Window to jump to that cell quickly.

MAC TIP: Watch Window is not available in Excel for Mac.

To add cells to the Watch Window, complete the following steps:

1. Click Watch Window in the Formula Auditing group on the Formulas tab. The Watch Window dialog box opens.
2. Click Add Watch in the Watch Window to open the Add Watch dialog box.
3. Select the cells to watch in the Add Watch dialog box. If you have applied a filter to a dataset, consider using Ctrl+click to select cells. Otherwise, the cells on hidden rows will also be added to the Watch Window.
4. Click Add. The Add Watch dialog box closes, and the Watch Window shows the cells and formulas you selected to watch (see Figure 9.25).

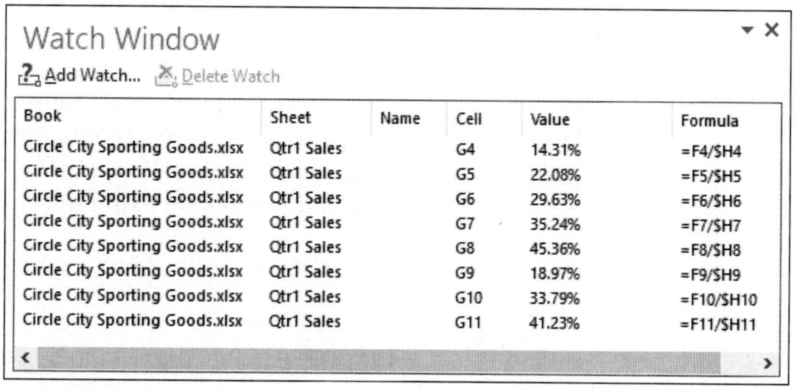

Watch Window ▾ ✕

Add Watch... Delete Watch

Book	Sheet	Name	Cell	Value	Formula
Circle City Sporting Goods.xlsx	Qtr1 Sales		G4	14.31%	=F4/$H4
Circle City Sporting Goods.xlsx	Qtr1 Sales		G5	22.08%	=F5/$H5
Circle City Sporting Goods.xlsx	Qtr1 Sales		G6	29.63%	=F6/$H6
Circle City Sporting Goods.xlsx	Qtr1 Sales		G7	35.24%	=F7/$H7
Circle City Sporting Goods.xlsx	Qtr1 Sales		G8	45.36%	=F8/$H8
Circle City Sporting Goods.xlsx	Qtr1 Sales		G9	18.97%	=F9/$H9
Circle City Sporting Goods.xlsx	Qtr1 Sales		G10	33.79%	=F10/$H10
Circle City Sporting Goods.xlsx	Qtr1 Sales		G11	41.23%	=F11/$H11

FIGURE 9.25 Watch Window

STEP 4 ▶ Creating a Data Validation Rule

When you distribute a workbook to other people, they do not always enter the correct type of data. For example, a user might enter $900 for an expense that should be less than $500, or a user might enter 7/21/2030 instead of a date between 1/1/2021 and 12/31/2021. To prevent users from entering incorrect data, you can set up data validation rules. A **data validation rule** defines what type of data can be entered in a cell, therefore preventing people from entering "wrong" data in a cell. Data validation rules enable you to specify and correct the kind of data that can be entered, display an input message that alerts users when they click a cell that only specific types of data can be entered in that cell, and display error messages when others attempt to enter incorrect data.

> **To set up a data validation rule, complete the following steps:**
> 1. Click the input cell for which the rule will be applied.
> 2. Click the Data tab and click Data Validation in the Data Tools group.
> 3. Specify the data validation criteria on the Settings tab.
> 4. Click the Input Message tab and enter the input title and message.
> 5. Click the Error Alert tab, enter the error alert specifications, and then click OK.

Specify Data Validation Criteria

In the Data Validation dialog box, use the Settings tab to specify the **validation criteria**— the rules that dictate the type of data that can be entered in a cell. Use the Allow setting to specify what type of data the user can enter, such as a whole number. For example, if you specify whole number and the user attempts to enter a decimal, Excel can prevent the user from entering the decimal value and display an error message. Table 9.4 lists the types of data-entry validations.

TABLE 9.4	Validation Allowances
Option	**Description**
Any value	Allows any type of data to be entered
Whole number	Restricts data entry by accepting whole numbers only
Decimal	Restricts data entry by accepting only decimal numbers
List	Displays a list to select data to enter in a cell
Date	Restricts data entry by accepting only a date
Time	Restricts data entry by accepting only a time
Text length	Restricts data entry to a specific number of characters
Custom	Used for creating a custom formula

After you select the type of allowance in the Data Validation dialog box, click Data to select a condition. For example, you can select *between* to restrict a date to be between two dates or restrict an expense to a decimal that is less than or equal to a value such as $100. Figure 9.26 shows a validation rule in which the cell contents must be (a) a whole number and (b) within a minimum and maximum value, which are stored respectively in cells G5 and G6.

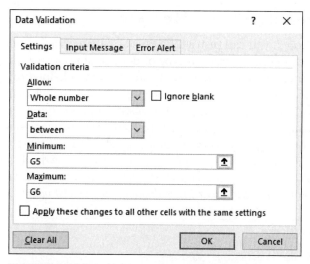

FIGURE 9.26 Data Validation Settings Tab: Criteria

To make data entry easier or to limit items to certain defined items and thereby be more accurate, you can create a list of valid entries from data contained in cells. Enter the list of valid entries in a single column or row without blank cells in a worksheet. Then, within the Data Validation dialog box, select List from the Allow menu, click in the Source box and select the range that contains the list you created (see Figure 9.27). Ensure that the *In-cell dropdown* check box is selected and that the *Ignore blank* check box is not selected. After you complete the validation settings, Excel displays an arrow in the cell containing the data validation rule. The user clicks the arrow and selects data from the list.

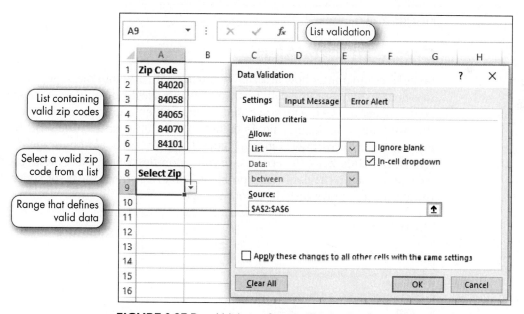

FIGURE 9.27 Data Validation Settings Tab: In-Cell Dropdown

Create an Input Message

Although you can restrict the type of data a person enters in a cell, you should consider informing the user what type of data is allowed. For example, you can inform the user to enter a whole number or a value within a defined range. Within the Data Validation dialog box, you can create an ***input message***, which is descriptive text or an instruction that informs a user about the restrictions for entering data in a cell. You add input messages to cells, and Excel displays these messages when a user moves to a cell that has a data-entry restriction. Input messages consist of two parts: a title and an input message (see Figure 9.28). These messages should describe the data validation and explain or show how to enter data correctly. For example, an input message might be *Enter hire date in the format: mm/dd/yyyy* or *Enter Employee name: last name, first name.*

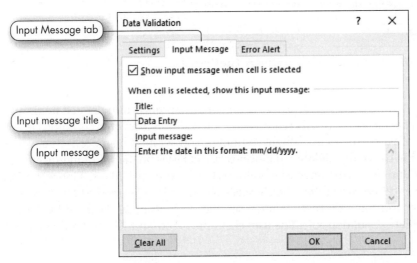

FIGURE 9.28 Data Validation Input Message Tab

Create an Error Alert

Sometimes, no matter how descriptive you are with an input message, users will attempt to enter invalid data in a cell. Instead of using Excel's default error message, you can create an ***error alert***, a message that displays when a user enters invalid data in a cell that contains a validation rule. To create an error alert, specify the style, title, and error message on the Error Alert tab (see Figure 9.29). The error alert message should be polite and clearly state what the error is. Cryptic, non-descriptive alert messages do not help users understand the data-entry problem. Table 9.5 shows the error styles that control the icon that displays with the error message.

FIGURE 9.29 Data Validation Error Tab

TABLE 9.5	Error Styles	
Icon	**Style**	**Description**
⊗	Stop	Prevents the user from entering invalid data
⚠	Warning	Accepts invalid data but warns user that data are invalid
ⓘ	Information	Accepts invalid data but provides information to the user

> **TIP: DATA VALIDATION ON MULTIPLE SHEETS**
> Although you may have several identical worksheets where you want to apply the data validation rule, you cannot group the worksheets and create the data validation rule. You must create the data validation rule on one worksheet. Then you can select and copy the range containing the data validation. Display the other worksheet that is identical in structure, click the Paste arrow on the Home tab, select Paste Special, click Validation in the Paste Special dialog box, and then click OK.

STEP 5 **Test the Data Validation Rule**

After you create a data validation rule, you should test it with sample data. Enter valid data to ensure no message displays. Enter invalid data to determine if the rule works. If you selected the Stop error alert style, the invalid data should not be entered. Make sure the error message box displays and check that the wording is clear. If you applied the Warning or Information error alert style, the message displays but you should be able to enter the data. Click Yes to accept the data entry, click No to reject the data entry and try again, click Cancel to cancel the data entry and revert to the previous data entered, or click Help to display a Help window. If the data validation does not produce the results you expect, you should edit the data validation rule to correct it.

Some data does not go through data validation checks, particularly if the data is entered by copying or using the Auto Fill command. Furthermore, a colleague may send you a workbook that does not contain data validation checks. You can then set up data validation rules for the existing data. After defining data validation rules, you can display circles around invalid text. To display circles for invalid data, click the Data Validation arrow in the Data Tools group and select Circle Invalid Data. When the user corrects the invalid data, the circles are removed.

Quick Concepts

7. Describe the difference between precedent and dependent cells. ***p. 568***

8. Explain when you would set up a Watch Window. ***p. 571***

9. Describe the benefit of creating a data validation rule. ***p. 572***

Hands-On Exercises

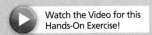

Skills covered: Trace
Precedents and Dependents •
Check for and Repair Errors • Set
Up a Watch Window • Create
a Data Validation Rule • Test the
Data Validation Rule

3 Formula Audits and Data Validation

A colleague prepared a worksheet based on projected data if the company opened a store in Fort Wayne. Unfortunately, your colleague introduced several errors in the worksheet. You will use auditing tools to identify and correct the errors. In addition, you will insert validation rules to ensure only valid data are entered in the future.

STEP 1 TRACE PRECEDENTS AND DEPENDENTS

You want to display precedent and dependent arrows to identify sources and destinations for cells being used in formulas in the Fort Wayne workbook. Refer to Figure 9.30 as you complete Step 1.

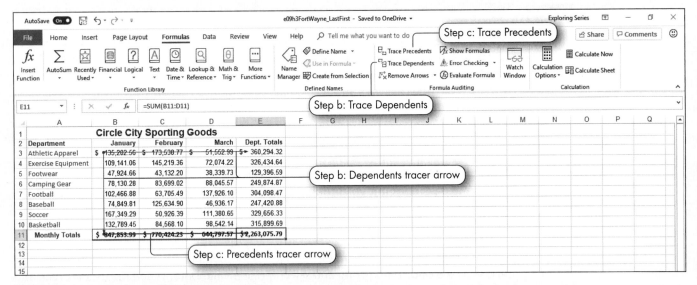

FIGURE 9.30 Dependent and Precedent Arrows

a. Open *e09h3FortWayne*, click **OK** when prompted to fix a circular error, and then save it as **e09h3FortWayne_LastFirst**.

b. Ensure that the Qtr1 worksheet is active, click **cell B3**, click the **Formulas tab**, and then click **Trace Dependents** in the Formula Auditing group.

Excel displays tracer arrows from cell B3 to cells E3 and B11, indicating that value in cell B3 is used in formulas in cells E3 and B11.

c. Click **cell E11** and click **Trace Precedents** in the Formula Auditing group.

Excel displays a tracer arrow, showing that the values in the range B11:D11 are used within the current cell's formula.

d. Click **Remove Arrows** in the Formula Auditing group. Save the workbook.

CHECK FOR AND REPAIR ERRORS

The Qtr2 worksheet contains errors. You will use the Error Checking dialog box and trace precedents to identify the errors. Refer to Figure 9.31 as you complete Step 2.

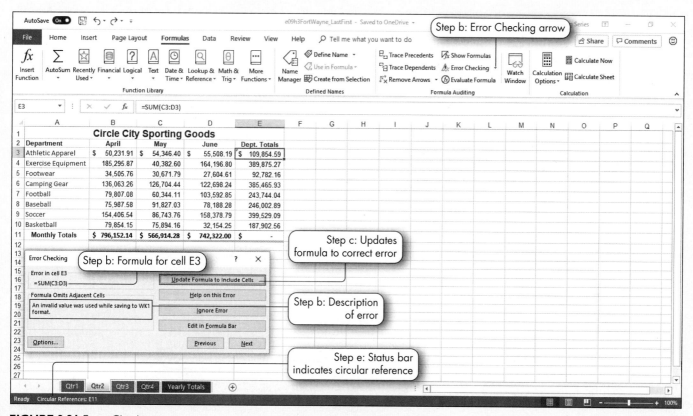

FIGURE 9.31 Error Checking

a. Click the **Qtr2 sheet tab**, look for the green error checking indicator in cell E3, and then click **cell A1**.

b. Click the **Error Checking arrow** in the Formula Auditing group and select **Error Checking**.

The Error Checking dialog box opens, indicating an error exists in cell E3. Excel detects that the formula in cell E3 does include a cell in the range.

c. Click **Update Formula to Include Cells**.

Excel modifies the formula from =SUM(C3:D3) to =SUM(B3:D3) to include the April sales.

d. Click **OK** in the message box that informs you that error checking is complete.

When you opened the workbook, an error message stated that the workbook contains a circular reference. The status bar still indicates that a circular reference exists.

e. Click the **Error Checking arrow** in the Formula Auditing group, point to **Circular References**, and then select **$E$11**.

The formula in cell E11 includes a reference to E11 in the function argument.

f. Change the formula to **=SUM(B11:D11)**. Save the workbook.

The status bar no longer indicates that a circular reference exists.

You want to set up a Watch Window to watch the results of formulas in the Yearly Totals worksheet when you change values in another worksheet. Refer to Figure 9.32 as you complete Step 3.

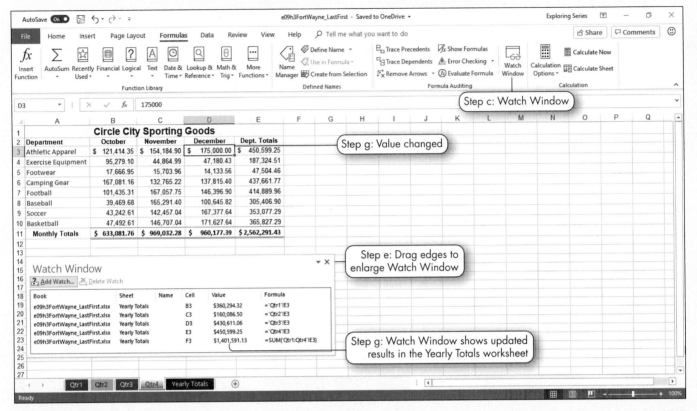

FIGURE 9.32 Watch Window

MAC TROUBLESHOOTING: Watch Window is not available in Excel for Mac.

---

a. Click the **Yearly Totals sheet tab**.

b. Select the **range B3:F3**.

You selected the range you want to watch to ensure formulas work correctly.

c. Click the **Formulas tab**, click the **Watch Window** in the Formula Auditing group, and click **Add Watch** in the Watch Window.

The Add Watch dialog box opens, indicating the worksheet and cells you selected.

d. Click **Add** in the Add Watch dialog box.

The Watch Window adds a watch for every cell in the selected range. It shows the workbook name, worksheet name, cell address, current value, and formula. The Watch Window command on the ribbon displays with a green background to indicate that the Watch Window is active.

e. Move the Watch Window below the dataset, with the top-left corner in cell A14. Drag the outer edges of the Watch Window to enlarge the height and width to fully display the information within the dialog box. Drag the column widths within the Watch Window to display the entire book name and sheet.

f. Click the **Qtr4 sheet tab**.

The Watch Window remains onscreen. The current Athletic apparel total is $355,957.21, shown in cell E3 and in the Watch Window. The Watch Window also shows the Athletic Apparel Yearly Total to be $1,306,949.08.

g. Click **cell D3**, type **175000**, and then press **Ctrl+Enter**.

The Qtr4 Athletic Apparel total changed to $450,599.25 in cell E3 and in the Watch Window. The Watch Window also shows that the total Athletic Apparel sales are now $1,401,591.13.

h. Click **Watch Window** in the Formula Auditing group to hide the Watch Window. Save the workbook.

STEP 4 CREATE A DATA VALIDATION RULE

You want to insert a validation rule for the Exercise Equipment, Footwear, and Camping Gear values on the Qtr4 worksheet. Based on projections, you believe the maximum revenue would be no more than $500,000. You will specify the input message and an alert if the user enters more than 500,000; however, you will let the incorrect value be entered. Refer to Figure 9.33 as you complete Step 4.

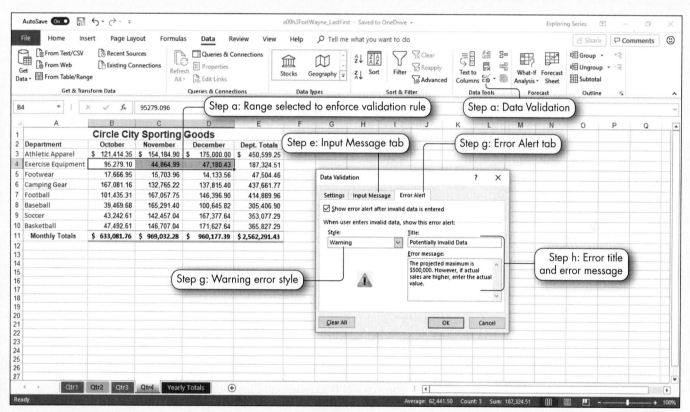

FIGURE 9.33 Data Validation

a. Select the **range B4:D4** on the Qtr4 worksheet, click the **Data tab**, and then click **Data Validation** in the Data Tools group.

The Data Validation dialog box opens.

b. Click the **Allow arrow** and select **Decimal** to allow for dollar-and-cents entries.

The dialog box displays Data, Minimum, and Maximum options.

c. Click the **Data arrow** and select **less than or equal to**.

d. Click in the **Maximum box** and type **500000**.

You are restricting the data entry to values less than or equal to $500,000.

e. Click the **Input Message tab** in the Data Validation dialog box.

The dialog box displays the options for entering the input message.

f. Click in the **Title box** and type **Sales Data**. Click in the **Input message box** and type **Enter the sales amount for the respective month.** (including the period).

g. Click the **Error Alert tab** in the Data Validation dialog box, click the **Style arrow**, and then select **Warning**.

The stop style would prevent values outside the acceptable maximum from being entered. However, your sales projections might be wrong, so you want to allow values over the maximum.

h. Click in the **Title box** and type **Potentially Invalid Data**. Click in the **Error message box** and type **The projected maximum is $500,000. However, if actual sales are higher, enter the actual value.** (including the period). Click **OK**. Save the workbook.

STEP 5 **TEST THE DATA VALIDATION RULE**

You want to test the data validation rule to make sure the error displays correctly if invalid data is entered. Refer to Figure 9.34 as you complete Step 5.

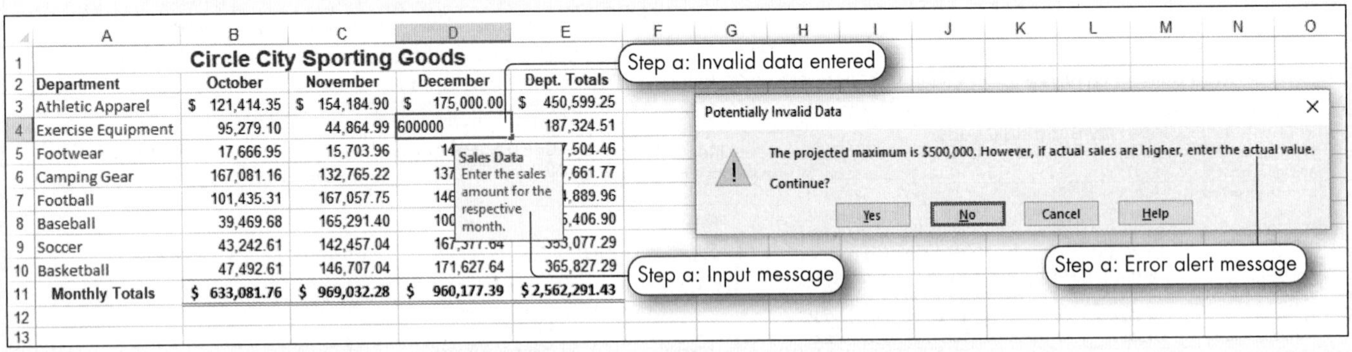

FIGURE 9.34 Error Alert Message

a. Click cell **D4**, notice the input message you created from Step 4g, type **600000**, and then press **Enter**.

The error message you created displays (refer to Figure 9.34).

b. Click **Yes**. Change the width of column D to **14** to display the column total.

Note that even though 600000 is beyond the validation limit, the user is still able to enter the number by clicking Yes.

c. Click the **Data tab**, click the **Data Validation arrow** in the Data Tools group, and then select **Circle Invalid Data**.

Excel circles the value in cell D4, indicating that the value violates the validation rule.

d. Save the workbook. Keep the workbook open if you plan to continue with the next Hands-On Exercise. If not, close the workbook and exit Excel.

Workbook Protection

When you distribute workbooks to other people, you can protect cells or worksheets from unauthorized or accidental changes. For example, you can protect cells containing formulas and enable a user to change only cells containing values. Protecting a worksheet ensures that people do not delete or modify formulas, change formatting, or alter the worksheet structure. In addition to protecting worksheet data, you can protect the workbook from unauthorized access and designate that you have finalized a workbook.

In this section, you will learn how to lock and unlock cells and protect a worksheet. In addition, you will learn how to protect the structure of a workbook from being altered. Finally, you will learn how to password-protect a workbook and mark it as final.

Protecting Cells and Worksheets

You can save a workbook as a template and use it to create new workbooks that have identical structure and formatting to use to enter data for similar purposes. For example, you can create a template of the quarterly sales workbook so that managers can enter department data for their respective stores. Before distributing templates to users to enter data, you can protect cells that you do not want to be changed and specify in which cells the users can enter or change data. This process requires that you keep protected cells locked, unlock cells for data entry, and then protect the worksheet.

STEP 1 ### Lock and Unlock Cells

A *locked cell* is one that prevents users from editing the contents or formatting of that cell in a worksheet in which protection is turned on. By default, all cells in a workbook are locked, but the locked cells are not enforced until you protect the worksheet. To enable the contents of certain cells to be modified in a protected worksheet, you must first unlock those cells before protecting the worksheet. When the active cell is locked, a border displays around the padlock icon for the Lock Cell option on the Format menu in the Cells group on the Home tab (see Figure 9.35). When the active cell is unlocked, no border displays around the Lock Cell option. In addition, the Locked check box is selected by default in the Protection tab in the Format Cells dialog box.

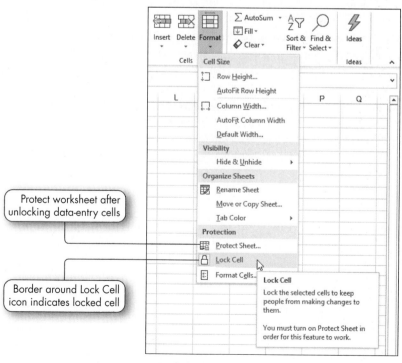

Protect worksheet after unlocking data-entry cells

Border around Lock Cell icon indicates locked cell

FIGURE 9.35 Locked Cells

Before protecting the worksheet, you should unlock the cells that you want users to be able to edit. For example, you can unlock the monthly sales values so that managers can enter the values; however, you will keep the column and row labels and the formulas locked to prevent users from changing these cells.

To unlock cells, complete the following steps:

1. Select the cells in which you want users to be able to enter or edit data.
2. Click the Home tab and click Format in the Cells group.
3. Select Lock Cell in the Protection section.
4. Click OK.

If you accidentally unlock cells or decide you no longer want cells to be unlocked, you can lock the cells again. To relock cells, repeat the above process.

> **TIP: USING THE FORMAT CELLS DIALOG BOX**
> Alternatively, after selecting a cell or range of cells to unlock, you can open the Format Cells dialog box, click the Protection tab, deselect the Locked check box, and then click OK.

STEP 2 ▶ Protect a Worksheet

After unlocking cells that you want the users to be able to modify, you are ready to protect the worksheet. When you protect a worksheet, you prevent users from altering the content of the locked cells. During the process of protecting a worksheet, you have the option to add a password to ensure that only those who know the password can unprotect the worksheet. If you enter a password to protect the worksheet, select a password that you can remember. If you forget the password, you will not be able to unprotect the worksheet. There is no way to reset or remove a password if you forget it.

To protect a worksheet, complete the following steps:

1. Click the Home tab and click Format in the Cells group.
2. Select Protect Sheet in the Protection section (or click Protect Sheet in the Protection group on the Review tab) to open the Protect Sheet dialog box (see Figure 9.36).
3. Select the check boxes for actions you want users to be able to do in the *Allow all users of this worksheet to* list. Usually, you will let users select locked and unlocked cells, but you do not let users change the format or structure of the protected worksheet.
4. Type a password in the *Password to unprotect sheet* box (optional) and click OK. If you entered a password, the Confirm Password dialog box opens (see Figure 9.37). Type the same password in the *Reenter password to proceed* box.
5. Read the caution statement and click OK.

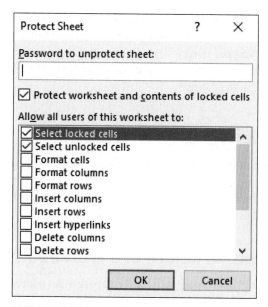

FIGURE 9.36 Protect Sheet Dialog Box

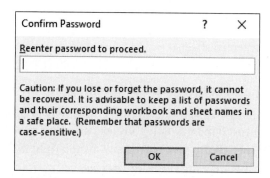

FIGURE 9.37 Confirm Password Dialog Box

> **TIP: PASSWORDS**
> Passwords can be up to 255 characters, including letters, numbers, and symbols. Passwords are case sensitive, so *passWORD* is not the same as *Password*. Typically, you should use a combination of uppercase and lowercase letters, as well as numbers and symbols. Choose passwords carefully, using characters you can easily remember but that other people cannot easily guess.

After you protect a worksheet, most commands on the ribbon are dimmed, indicating that they are not available. If someone tries to enter or change data in a locked cell on a protected worksheet, Excel displays the warning message and instructs the user how to remove the protection (see Figure 9.38).

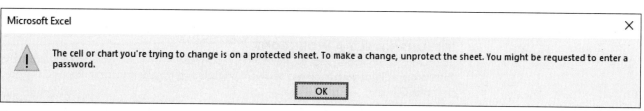

FIGURE 9.38 Warning Message

To unprotect a worksheet, click Unprotect Sheet in the Protect group on the Review tab or click Format in the Cells group on the Home tab, and select Unprotect Sheet. When the Unprotect Sheet dialog box opens, type the password in the Password box (if the worksheet was password protected) and click OK. The worksheet is then unprotected so that you can make changes.

Protecting a Workbook

In addition to protecting a worksheet, you can protect an entire workbook to ensure the integrity of its contents. Workbook protection includes marking the workbook as final with an easy-to-remove Read-Only mode. In addition, you can protect the workbook from unauthorized access by using a password.

Protect the Structure of a Workbook

Although locking cells and protecting a worksheet prevents unauthorized modifications, users might make unwanted changes to other parts of the workbook. You can prevent users from inserting, deleting, renaming, moving, copying, and hiding worksheets within the workbook by protecting the workbook with a password. Protecting an entire workbook does not affect locked or unlocked cells within a workbook; it merely prevents worksheet manipulation from occurring. That is, to protect certain cells from being changed, you must still protect a worksheet and ensure cells are locked. Note that you can display the contents of protected sheets.

To protect the structure of a workbook, complete the following steps:

1. Click the Review tab and click Protect Workbook in the Protect group. The Protect Structure and Windows dialog box opens (see Figure 9.39).
2. Click the check boxes to select the actions you want in the *Protect workbook for* section.
3. Type a password in the *Password (optional)* box and click OK. The Confirm Password dialog box opens.
4. Type the same password in the *Reenter password to proceed* box and click OK.

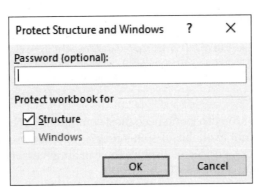

FIGURE 9.39 Protect Structure and Windows Dialog Box

TIP: UNPROTECT A WORKBOOK
To unprotect a workbook, click the Review tab, click Protect Workbook, type the password in the Password box (if the workbook was password protected) in the Unprotect Workbook dialog box, and then click OK.

STEP 3 ▶ Encrypt a Workbook File with a Password

While it is useful to lock cells and protect worksheets against changes, you can add further protection by restricting its access to authorized people only. To do this, you can encrypt the file with a password the user is required to enter in order to open the workbook. Encrypting a file with a password is a best practice in case a file is accidentally distributed to unauthorized people, or if someone else obtains your computer or external storage device.

To encrypt a workbook with a password, complete the following steps:

1. Click the File tab.
2. Click Protect Workbook and select Encrypt with Password. The Encrypt Document dialog box opens (similar to the Confirm Password dialog box).
3. Type a password in the Password box and click OK. The confirm Password dialog box opens.
4. Type the same password in the *Reenter password* box and click OK. The Permissions area displays *A password is required to open this workbook.*

On a Mac to encrypt a workbook with a password, complete the following steps:

1. Click File on the menu bar and select Save As.
2. Click Password to open and type a password.
3. Click Password to modify and type a password.
4. Click OK.

To delete a password for an open workbook, display the Encrypt with Password dialog box, delete the password symbols, and click OK. Then save the file again.

STEP 4 ▶ Mark a Workbook as Final

After completing a workbook, you may want to communicate that it is a final version of the workbook. The *Mark as Final* command communicates that it is a final version and makes the file read-only. Excel prevents users from typing in and editing the workbook, displays a *Marked as Final* icon to the right of Ready on the status bar, and sets the Status document property as Final. If a workbook is shared, you cannot mark it as final; you must first remove the sharing attribute.

To mark a workbook as final, complete the following steps:

1. Click the File tab.
2. Click Protect Workbook and select *Mark as Final*. A warning message box displays, stating *This workbook will be marked as final and then saved.*
3. Click OK. If you have not saved the file, you will be prompted to do so. Excel then displays an information message box (see Figure 9.40).
4. Click OK. When you click the File tab, the Permissions area displays *This workbook has been marked as final to discourage editing.*

> **MAC TIP:** On a Mac, click the Review tab and click Always Open Read-Only.

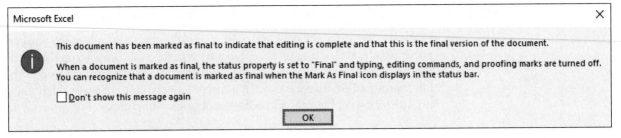

FIGURE 9.40 Mark as Final Verification Box

The MARKED AS FINAL Message Bar displays below the ribbon, stating that *An author has marked this workbook as final* to discourage editing. A user can click Edit Anyway to remove the marked-as-final indication and begin editing the workbook. The ribbon tabs are visible, but the commands are hidden. The title bar displays Read-Only after the file name (see Figure 9.41).

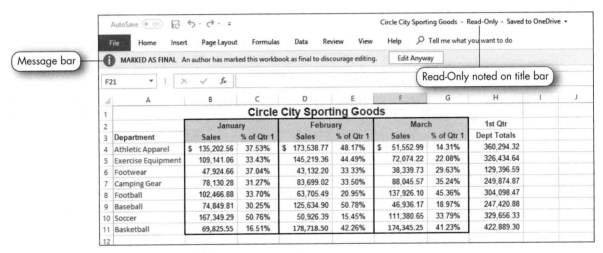

FIGURE 9.41 Workbook Marked as Final

TIP: ENCRYPTING WITH PASSWORD AND MARKING AS FINAL

If you want to encrypt a file with a password and mark it as final, you must encrypt it with a password before marking it as final.

Quick Concepts

10. Explain when you would lock cells and protect a worksheet. ***p. 581***

11. Explain why you would use the Protect Workbook option even though you had previously locked cells and protected a worksheet. ***p. 584***

12. Describe the importance of selecting passwords to protect a workbook. ***p. 583***

Hands-On Exercises

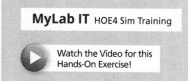
Skills covered: Unlock Cells • Protect a Worksheet • Encrypt a Workbook File with a Password • Mark a Workbook as Final

4 Workbook Protection

You want to add protections to the Fort Wayne workbook before distributing the workbook to others.

STEP 1 UNLOCK CELLS

Before protecting the quarterly worksheets, you will unlock cells containing the monthly department sales amounts. Unlocking the cells will enable the user to enter values into designated ranges in the worksheets. Refer to Figure 9.42 as you complete Step 1.

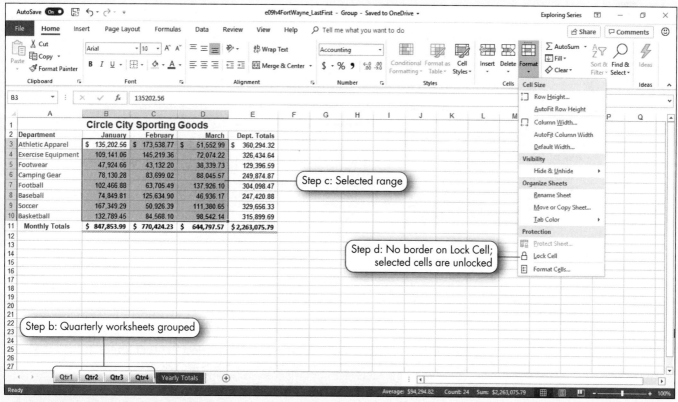

FIGURE 9.42 Unlock Input Cells

a. Open *e09h3FortWayne_LastFirst* if you closed it at the end of Hands-On Exercise 3, and save it as **e09h4FortWayne_LastFirst**, changing h3 to h4.

b. Click the **Qtr1 sheet tab**, press and hold **Shift**, and click the **Qtr4 sheet tab**.

You want to unlock the same cells in the quarterly worksheets.

c. Select the **range B3:D10**.

You selected the range containing values for the monthly department sales values.

d. Click the **Home tab**, click **Format** in the Cells group, and then select **Lock Cell**. Click **Format** to display the menu again.

The Lock Cell option does not change to Unlock Cell. However, when you unlock a cell, the Lock Cell command does not have a border around the padlock icon on the menu. The selected cells are unlocked and will remain unlocked when you protect the worksheet later.

e. Click **Format** to close the menu, right-click the **Qtr1 sheet tab**, and then select **Ungroup Sheets**. Save the workbook.

STEP 2 ▶ PROTECT A WORKSHEET

Now that you have unlocked the input cells, you are ready to protect the quarterly worksheets. The other cells in the worksheets still have the Lock Cell property enabled. After you protect the worksheets, users will not be able to modify those cells. Refer to Figure 9.43 as you complete Step 2.

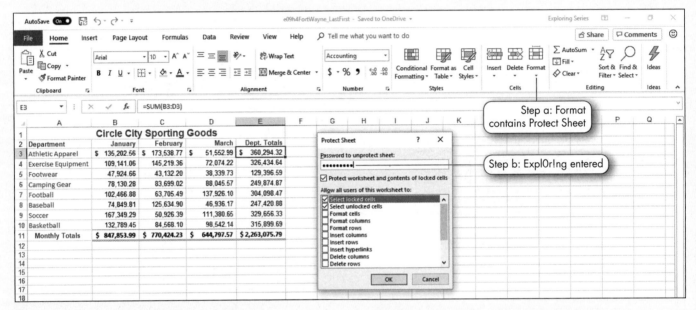

FIGURE 9.43 Protect the Worksheets

a. Click **Format** in Cells group on the Home tab and select **Protect Sheet**. Ensure the *Select locked cells* and *Select unlocked cells* check boxes are selected.

The Protect Sheet dialog box opens. The *Protect worksheet and contents of locked cells* check box is selected by default. In addition, the users can *Select locked cells* and *Select unlocked cells*. Although they can select locked cells, they will not be able to change those cells. Notice that users cannot format data, insert columns or rows, or delete columns or rows.

b. Type **Expl0r!ng** (using a zero, not the letter O) in the *Password to unprotect sheet* box and click **OK**.

Remember that passwords are case sensitive and that you must remember the password. If you forget the password, you will not able to unprotect the sheet.

c. Read the caution, type **Expl0r!ng** in the *Reenter password to proceed* box, and then click **OK**.

You password-protected the Qtr1 worksheet.

d. Click **cell E3** and try to type **100**. Click **OK** to close the warning box.

> **TROUBLESHOOTING:** If you can enter the new value without the warning box, the cell is not locked. Click Undo to restore the formula, review Steps 1 and 2a-d and then click the cell.

e. Adapt and repeat Steps a–d to set the same password on the Qtr2, Qtr3, and Qtr4 worksheets. Save the workbook.

The Protect Sheet option is unavailable for grouped sheets. You must protect each sheet individually.

STEP 3 ▶ ENCRYPT A WORKBOOK FILE WITH A PASSWORD

You want to protect the workbook so that unauthorized people cannot open the file. Therefore, you will encrypt the workbook with a password. Refer to Figure 9.44 as you complete Step 4.

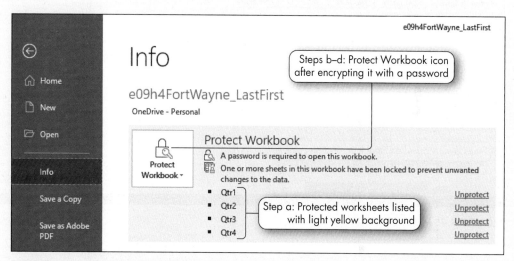

FIGURE 9.44 Protect the Workbook

> **MAC TROUBLESHOOTING:** Complete Step 3 with these steps: Click the File menu, click Save As, and click Options. Type the password to open. Type the password to modify. Click OK. Click Save.

a. Click the **File tab**.

Protect Workbook has a light yellow background with a note *One or more worksheets in this workbook have been locked to prevent unwanted changes to the data.* The four quarterly worksheets are listed with links to unprotect them.

b. Click Protect Workbook and select Encrypt with Password.

The Encrypt Document dialog box opens.

c. Type **Expl0r!ng** in the Password box and click **OK**.

The Confirm Password dialog box opens.

d. Type **Expl0r!ng** in the Reenter password box and click **OK**.

e. Click **Protect Workbook** and select **Encrypt with Password**, delete the password in the Password box.

You deleted the password for this Hands-On Exercise file so that you can access the workbook without having to enter a password.

f. Click **OK** and click the **Back arrow**. Save the workbook.

You want the recipients of the Fort Wayne workbook to know that it is final. Refer to Figure 9.45 as you complete Step 4.

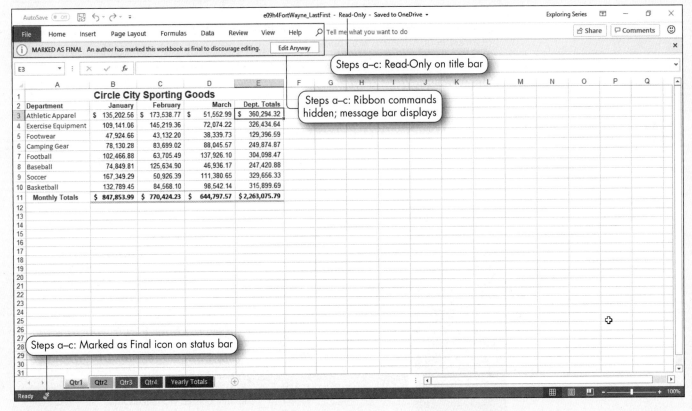

FIGURE 9.45 Marked as Final

> **MAC TROUBLESHOOTING:** Mark as Final is not available in Excel for Mac. Instead, use Always Open Read-Only on the Review tab.

a. Click the **File tab**, click **Protect Workbook**, and then select **Mark as Final**.

A message box displays, indicating that *This workbook will be marked as final and then saved.*

b. Click **OK**.

The workbook is saved. Another message box displays *This document has been marked as final to indicate that editing is complete and that this is the final version of the document.*

c. Click **OK**.

Read-Only displays on the title bar, the ribbon commands are hidden, the MARKED AS FINAL message bar displays, and a Marked as Final icon displays on the status bar.

d. Close the file. Exit Excel. Based on your instructor's directions, submit the following:

e09h2IndianaFiles_LastFirst.zip

e09h4FortWayne_LastFirst

Chapter Objectives Review

After reading this chapter, you have accomplished the following objectives:

1. Work with grouped worksheets.

- Group and ungroup worksheets: Group worksheets to perform the same action simultaneously to those worksheets. When you group worksheets, [Group] displays after the file name on the title bar. After performing actions on grouped worksheets, ungroup the worksheets before performing an action on an individual worksheet.
- Fill across worksheets: If you have already entered or formatted data on one sheet, you can copy that data or formatting to other sheets. Group the worksheets, select the range that contains the data or format you want to copy, and select Fill Across Worksheets to copy data and formatting across the grouped worksheets.
- Enter and format data on grouped worksheets: Any changes you make while worksheets are grouped will affect all grouped worksheets. Grouping worksheets enables you to quickly enter data, make structural changes such as changing column width, adjusting formatting such as applying borders, and changing page layouts. Backup your file before making changes on grouped worksheets. That way, if you accidentally overwrite data, you have a backup to use.

2. Insert hyperlinks.

- Hyperlinks are electronic links that, when clicked, connect one cell to another cell in the same worksheet, a different worksheet, or a different worksheet in another workbook. You can also create hyperlinks to link to webpages or email addresses.

3. Manage windows.

- Hide and unhide worksheets: You hide worksheets so that the sheet tabs are not visible. It is beneficial to hide worksheets containing confidential information. When you want to display the worksheet again, you can unhide it.
- Open and arrange windows: Use the Arrange Window dialog box to display multiple windows as tiled, horizontal, vertical, or cascade. You can select an option to display multiple windows of the same workbook.
- Split a window: When you work with large worksheets, you can split the worksheet window into resizable panes. Horizontal and vertical split bars display so that you can move them to show more of one part of the window. You can double-click a split bar to remove it.
- Apply other window settings: You can view two or more workbooks side by side to compare related data. If you adjust window sizes, you can reset the window position. Finally, you can use Switch Windows to select which window will be the active Excel workbook.

4. Insert formulas and functions with 3-D references.

- Insert a formula with a 3-D reference: A 3-D reference includes the worksheet name, the column letter, and the row number. A formula with a 3-D reference is useful to obtain the value from a cell or range in another worksheet. The formula contains the worksheet name, an exclamation point, and the cell reference, such as ='October Sales'!E15. Single quotation marks enclose the sheet name when the sheet name contains a space.
- Insert a function with a 3-D reference: A function may contain 3-D references to consolidate data from two or more worksheets. If the data are structured in identical cells on all worksheets, you can use a function such as SUM to total the values in the same cell on all worksheets. A function with a 3-D reference looks something like this: =SUM('Qtr1:Qtr4'!E3) where cell E3 in all sheets from Qtr1 to Qtr4 are included the range.

5. Link workbooks.

- Create a link to another workbook: You can establish an external reference or pointer to one or more cells in an external worksheet. If the source data are changed, the destination data are also changed.
- Manage and update linked workbooks: When a destination file is first opened, you will be prompted to enable automatic link updates. You can edit links if you have moved source files and the destination file does not recognize the change in location.

6. Audit formulas.

- Trace precedent and dependents: You can display arrows that depict the relationships between precedent and dependent cells so that you can identify cells used in formulas. Precedent cells are cells referenced in a formula; dependent cells contain formulas that refer to other cells.
- Check for and repair errors: Check and repair errors by selecting *Error checking* in the Formula Auditing group on the Formulas tab. The dialog box enables you to obtain help on the error, show calculation steps, ignore the error, or edit the error in the Formula Bar.
- Evaluate a formula: Use the Evaluate Formula command to provide an evaluation of a formula that shows the portion that returns an error.
- Use the IFERROR function to detect errors: The IFERROR function checks a value and returns the results, if possible, or an error message.

7. Set up a Watch Window.

- When you work with large datasets, you can watch formulas in cells that are not visible by using the Watch Window feature. The Watch Window displays the worksheet and cells containing formulas that you set to watch. When changes are made to precedent cells, the Watch Window indicates how that affects the results of formulas in the cells that are being watched.

8. Create a data validation rule.

- Specify data validation criteria: To specify criteria, use the Settings tab in the Data Validation dialog box. Select the type of data allowed: whole number, decimal, list, date, time, or custom formula. Then select the condition, such as before or greater than or equal to.
- Create an input message: An input message is descriptive text or instructions for data entry. The Data Validation dialog box enables you to enter a title and an input message to display when a user clicks the cells that contains the input message.
- Create an error alert: An error alert is a message that displays when a user enters invalid data. An error alert displays a style (Stop, Warning, or Information), a title, and the error message.
- Test the data validation rule: After you create a data validation rule, you should test it with sample data to ensure that only valid data can be entered and the correct messages display.

9. Protect cells and worksheets.

- Lock and unlock cells: By default, the Locked property is selected for all cells in new workbooks you create. However, this property has no effect until you protect the worksheet. You can unlock cells to enable data entry for a protected worksheet.
- Protect a worksheet: After unlocking data-entry cells, you should password-protect the worksheet. Doing so ensures that users cannot change data in locked cells.

10. Protect a workbook.

- Protect the structure of a workbook: For additional protection, you can protect a workbook to prevent users from inserting, deleting, renaming, or moving worksheets. Users can still view the contents of worksheets, however.
- Encrypt a workbook file with a password: For enhanced protection, password-protect a file. If a person does not enter the correct password, he or she cannot open the workbook.
- Mark a workbook as final: You can mark a workbook as final to indicate that you approve that particular version of the workbook. Marking a workbook as final makes it a read-only file. However, a user can enable editing in the file and make changes, removing the marked-as-final designation.

Key Terms Matching

Match the key terms with their definitions. Write the key term letter by the appropriate numbered definition.

a. 3-D reference

b. Circular reference

c. Data validation rule

d. Dependent cell

e. Destination file

f. Error alert

g. Formula auditing

h. Grouping

i. Hyperlink

j. Input message

k. Linking

l. Locked cell

m. Logic error

n. Precedent cell

o. Source file

p. Split bar

q. Syntax error

r. Tracer arrow

s. Watch Window

t. Validation criteria

1. _____ Occurs when a formula or function violates construction rules. **p. 567**

2. _____ An electronic link that, when clicked, goes to another location in the same or a different worksheet, opens another file, opens a webpage in a Web browser, or opens an email client and inserts an email address into the To box. **p. 545**

3. _____ Conditions that dictate the type of data that can be entered in a cell. **p. 572**

4. _____ An area that displays the workbook name, worksheet name, cell addresses, values, and formulas so you can monitor and examine formula calculations involving cells not immediately visible on the screen. **p. 571**

5. _____ A file that contains a link to retrieve data from a source file. **p. 560**

6. _____ Specified rules that must be followed to allow data to be entered in a cell. **p. 572**

7. _____ Tools to enable you to detect and correct errors in formulas by identifying relationships among cells. **p. 568**

8. _____ A colored line that shows relationships between precedent and dependent cells. **p. 569**

9. _____ The process of creating external cell references from worksheets in one workbook to cells on a worksheet in another workbook. **p. 559**

10. _____ The process of selecting two or more worksheets so that you can perform the same action at the same time on all selected worksheets. **p. 542**

11. _____ A cell in a worksheet that prevents a user from entering data if the worksheet is protected. **p. 581**

12. _____ Occurs when a formula contains a direct or an indirect reference to the cell containing the formula. **p. 567**

13. _____ A vertical or horizontal line that frames panes in a worksheet and enables the user to resize the panes. **p. 519**

14. _____ A cell containing a formula that relies on other cells to obtain its value. **p. 568**

15. _____ Occurs when a formula uses incorrect cell references or incorrect operator that produces inaccurate results. **p. 567**

16. _____ A reference within a formula or function on one worksheet that includes the name of another worksheet, column letter, and row number located within a workbook. **p. 557**

17. _____ A file that contains original data that you want to use in another file. **p. 560**

18. _____ A cell that is referenced by a formula in another cell. **p. 568**

19. _____ A message that displays when the user enters invalid data in a cell containing a validation rule. **p. 574**

20. _____ Descriptive text or instructions that inform a user about the restrictions for entering data in a cell. **p. 574**

Multiple Choice

1. You have a workbook that contains sales data where each sales rep's data is stored on a separate worksheet. Which task is the *least likely* to be done while the worksheets are grouped?

   (a) Fill the sales categories across the worksheets.

   (b) Format the column and row labels at the same time.

   (c) Enter specific values for the first sales rep.

   (d) Format the values with an appropriate number style.

2. You want to create a hyperlink to an online dataset from the United States Census Bureau. Which type of link do you create?

   (a) Existing File or Web Page

   (b) Place in This Document

   (c) Create New Document

   (d) E-mail Address

3. A worksheet contains over 400 rows. The first 10 rows contain input data, and functions containing summary statistics are in the last 10 rows. What is the most efficient method to see the input area and summary statistics at the same time without having to scroll back and forth between sections?

   (a) Open multiple windows of the same workbook and use the Arrange Windows command to tile the windows.

   (b) Display a Watch Window for the input section as you view the summary statistics section.

   (c) Select the summary statistics and use the Freeze Panes option.

   (d) Use the Split command and adjust one pane to see the input section and another pane to see the summary statistics.

4. Which function correctly adds data in cell D25 across multiple worksheets?

   (a) =SUM(Monday,Friday:D25)

   (b) =SUM(Monday:Friday!D25)

   (c) =COUNT(Mon:D25,Tues:D25,Wed:D25,Thurs:D25, Fri:D25)

   (d) =Monday:D25+Friday:D25

5. The SalesQtr2 workbook contains links to data in the April, May, and June workbooks. Which workbook is the destination file?

   (a) June

   (b) April

   (c) May

   (d) SalesQtr2

6. You use Trace Precedents for a cell containing a formula. What indicates an error in the precedents used?

   (a) A red tracer arrow displays between the dependent and precedent cells.

   (b) A warning message box displays onscreen.

   (c) A blue tracer arrow points to the cell containing the error.

   (d) A Watch Window displays on the right side of the screen.

7. You want to monitor the results of cell formulas on a different worksheet as you change data on another worksheet. You should create a:

   (a) data validation window.

   (b) hyperlink between worksheets.

   (c) Watch Window.

   (d) Circular Reference Window.

8. Which data validation alert style should you use to prevent the user from entering invalid data?

   (a) Information

   (b) Stop

   (c) Warning

   (d) Failure

9. You want to make sure employees enter data only in particular cells and not change or delete other data. What is the first step?

   (a) Lock cells that you do not want the users to change.

   (b) Protect the worksheet with a password.

   (c) Use the Mark as Final option.

   (d) Unlock cells that will be used for data entry.

10. If you forget the password you used to protect a workbook, how do you reset it?

   (a) You cannot reset the password.

   (b) You can reset it in Excel Options.

   (c) You can email the workbook to Office.com for reset.

   (d) Use the password reset option in the Properties pane for the workbook.

Practice Exercises

1 Organic Foods Corporation

The Organic Foods Corporation operates three stores in different areas of Portland. The manager of each store prepared a workbook that summarizes the first-quarter results. As the assistant to the general manager, you will complete the Downtown workbook and link data from the three workbooks to a consolidated workbook. Refer to Figure 9.46 as you complete this exercise.

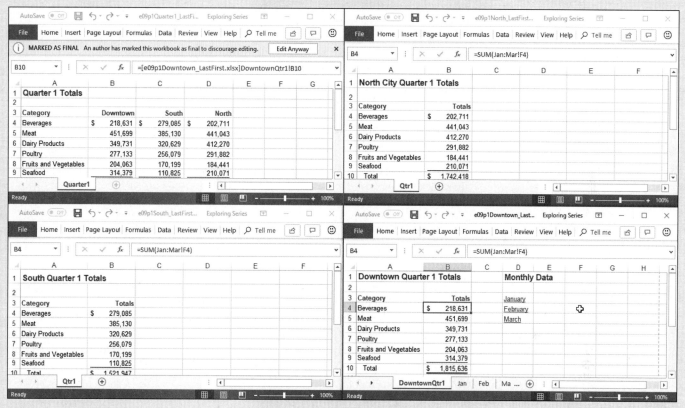

FIGURE 9.46 Organic Foods Corporation

a. Open *e09p1Downtown* and save it as **e09p1Downtown_LastFirst**. Click each sheet tab to see what work has been done and what work you will do.

b. Click the **Jan sheet tab**, press and hold **Shift**, click the **Mar sheet tab**, and then complete the following steps:
   - Click **cell A1**, click **Fill** in the Editing group on the Home tab, and then select **Across Worksheets**. Click **Formats** in the Fill Across Worksheets dialog box and click **OK**.
   - Select the **range B10:F10**, click **Fill** in the Editing group, and then select **Across Worksheets**. Click **Formats** in the Fill Across Worksheets dialog box and click **OK**.
   - Select the **range F3:F9**, click **Fill** in the Editing group, and then select **Across Worksheets**. Click **Formats** in the Fill Across Worksheets dialog box and click **OK**.
   - Select the **range B4:F10** and click **AutoSum** in the Editing group.
   - Select the **range B4:E9**, click **Format** in the Cells group, and then select **Lock Cell** (to unlock the cells).
   - Select **rows 1:10**, click **Format** in the Cells group, select **Row Height**, type **15** in the Row height box, and then click **OK**. Click **cell A1**.

c. Right-click the **Jan sheet** and select **Ungroup Sheets**. Click the **DowntownQtr1 sheet tab**, click **cell B4**, and then insert a function with a 3-D reference by completing the following steps:

- Type **=SUM(**
- Click the **Jan sheet tab**, press and hold **Shift**, and then click the **Mar sheet tab**.
- Click **cell F4** and press **Ctrl+Enter**.
- Double-click the **cell B4 fill handle** to copy the formula to the **range B5:B10**.

d. Format the data by doing the following:

- Select the **range B5:B9**, click **Comma Style** in the Number group, and then click **Decrease Decimal** twice in the Number group.
- Click **cell B9**, click **Underline** in the Font group, click **cell B10**, click the **Underline arrow** in the Font group, and then select **Double Underline**.

e. Insert hyperlinks on the DowntownQtr1 sheet by completing the following:

- Click **cell D3**, click the **Insert tab**, click **Link**, and then select **Insert Link** in the Links group.

> **MAC TROUBLESHOOTING:** Click the Insert menu and click Hyperlink.

- Click **Place in This Document**, click **Jan** in the *Or select a place in this document* list, and then click **OK**.
- Create hyperlinks in **cells D4** and **D5** of the DowntownQtr1 sheet to the Feb and Mar sheets, respectively.

f. Create a footer with your name on the left side, the sheet name code in the center, and the file name code on the right side of all sheets.

g. Protect the worksheets (without a password) by doing the following:

- Click the **DowntownQtr1 sheet tab**, click the **Home tab**, click **Format** in the Cells group, select **Protect Sheet**, and then click **OK** in the Protect Sheet dialog box.
- Use the same process to protect the other sheets in the workbook and then save the workbook.

h. Open *e09p1South* and save it as **e09p1South_LastFirst**, open *e09p1North* and save it as **e09p1North_LastFirst**, and then open *e09p1Quarter1* and save it as **e09p1Quarter1_LastFirst**.

i. Click the **View tab**, click **Switch Windows** in the Window group, and then select **e09p1North_LastFirst**.

> **MAC TROUBLESHOOTING:** Click the Window menu.

j. Click the **Jan sheet tab**, press and hold **Shift**, and then click the **Mar sheet tab** to group the worksheets. Right-click the **Jan sheet tab** and select **Hide** to hide the grouped worksheets.

k. Adapt Steps i and j to switch to the e09p1South_LastFirst workbook and hide the Jan, Feb, and Mar worksheets in that workbook.

l. Click the **View tab**, click **Switch Windows** in the Window group, and then select **e09p1Quarter1_LastFirst**.

m. Click **Arrange All** in the Window group, ensure that the *Windows of active workbook* check box is not selected, and then click **OK** in the dialog box. Click within each window and double-click the **View tab** in each window to collapse the ribbon.

> **MAC TROUBLESHOOTING:** Click the Window menu and select Arrange.

n. Add links by completing the following steps in the e09p1Quarter1_LastFirst workbook:

- Click **cell B4** in the Quarter1 worksheet. Type **=**, click **cell B4** in the DowntownQtr1 worksheet in the e09p1Downtown_LastFirst file, and then press **Ctrl+Enter**. Edit the formula to change $B$4 to **B4**. Copy the formula down the Downtown column to the **range B5:B10**.
- Click **cell C4** in the Quarter1 worksheet. Type **=**, display e09p1South_LastFirst, click **cell B4** in the Qtr1 worksheet, and then press **Ctrl+Enter**. Edit the formula to change $B$4 to **B4**. Copy the formula down the South column to the **range C5:C10**.
- Click **cell D4** in the Quarter1 worksheet. Type **=**, display e09p1North_LastFirst, click **cell B4** in the Qtr1 worksheet, and then press **Ctrl+Enter**. Edit the formula to change $B$4 to **B4**. Copy the formula down the North column to the **range D5:D10**.
- Maximize the e09p1Quarter1_LastFirst workbook. Select the **ranges B4:D4** and **B10:D10** in the Quarter1 worksheet and apply **Accounting Number Format** with zero decimal places. Select the **range B5:D9** and apply **Comma Style** with zero decimal places.
- Select the **range B9:D9** and click **Underline**. Select the **range B10:D10**, click the **Underline arrow**, and then select **Double Underline**.

o. Create a footer with your name on the left side, the sheet name code in the center, and the file name code on the right side of the Quarter1 worksheet in the e09p1Quarter1_LastFirst workbook.

p. Make sure the e09Quarter1_LastFirst workbook is active, click the **File tab**, click **Protect Workbook**, and then select **Mark as Final**. Click **OK** in each dialog box that displays. Close e09Quarter1_LastFirst.

MAC TROUBLESHOOTING: Click the File menu click Save As, and then click Options to protect the workbook with a password. Mark as Final is not available in Excel for Mac. Instead, use Always Open Read-Only on the Review tab.

---

q. Save and close the other three files. Open File Explorer and complete the following steps:

- Select **e09p1Downtown_LastFirst**, **e09p1North_LastFirst**, **e09p1Quarter1_LastFirst**, and **e09p1South_LastFirst**.
- Right-click a selected file.
- Select **Send to**, select **Compressed (zipped) Folder**, type **e09p1OrganicFiles_LastFirst**, and then press **Enter**.

MAC TROUBLESHOOTING: Open Finder, select the files, click the File menu, and then click Compress.

---

r. Based on your instructor's directions, submit e09p1OrganicFiles_LastFirst.zip.

2 Retirement Planning

An associate created a workbook to help people plan for retirement based on a set of annual contributions to a retirement account. A user indicates the age to start contributions, projected retirement age, the number of years in retirement, and the rate of return expected to earn on the money when the user retires. The worksheet determines the total amount the user will have contributed, the amount the user will have accumulated, and the value of the monthly retirement amount. You will fill a title across worksheets and enter formulas with 3-D references. However, other formulas in the worksheet contain errors. You will use the auditing tools to identify and correct the errors. You will specify validation rules to ensure users enter valid data. Refer to Figure 9.47 as you complete this exercise.

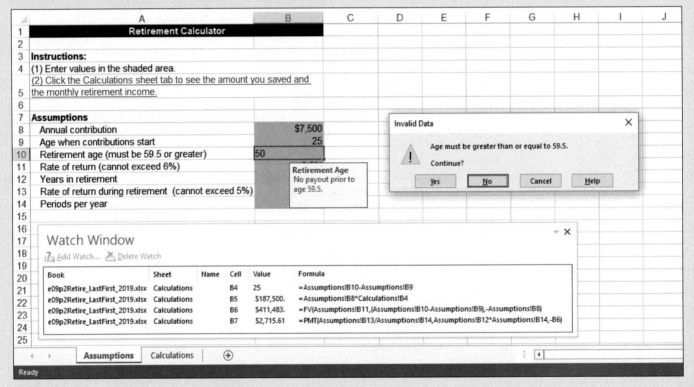

FIGURE 9.47 Retirement Planning

a. Open *e09p2Retire* and save it as **e09p2Retire_LastFirst**.

b. Click **cell A1** in the Assumptions worksheet. Complete the following steps to fill the title and formats from the Assumptions sheet to the Calculations worksheet:
- Press **Ctrl** and click the **Calculations sheet tab**.
- Click **Fill** in the Editing group on the Home tab and select **Across Worksheets**.
- Click **OK** in the Fill Across Worksheets dialog box.
- Right-click the **Calculations sheet tab** and select **Ungroup Sheets**. Notice the formatted title in cell A1.

c. Click **cell B4** in the Calculations sheet and insert a formula with 3-D references by completing the following steps:
- Type **=**
- Click the **Assumptions sheet tab** and click **cell B10**.
- Type **–**, click **cell B9** in the Assumptions worksheet, and then press **Enter** to calculate the number of years until retirement.

d. Click **cell B5** in the Calculations sheet and insert a formula with 3-D references by completing the following steps:

- Type **=**
- Click the **Assumptions sheet tab** and click **cell B8**.
- Type *****, click the **Calculations sheet tab**, click **cell B4**, and then press **Enter** to calculate the total amount contributed into your retirement account.

e. Click **cell B7** in the Calculations sheet, click the **Formulas tab**, and then click **Trace Precedents** in the Formula Auditing group. Excel displays a worksheet icon with the tracer line to indicate the precedents are on another worksheet.

f. Click the **Error Checking arrow** in the Formula Auditing group and select **Error Checking**.

g. Click **Show Calculation Steps** in the Error Checking dialog box. The Evaluate Formula dialog box opens, showing the formula and stating that the next evaluation will result in an error. Complete the following steps:

- Click **Evaluate** to see the error replace the argument in the function: #DIV/0!.
- Click **Step In** to see the value and click **Step Out** to return to the evaluation.
- Repeat the Step In and Step Out process and click **Close**.
- Click **Next** in the Error Checking dialog box and click **OK** in the message box.
- Click the **Assumptions sheet tab**, click **cell B14**, type **12**, and then press **Enter**.

h. Click the **Calculations Sheet tab** to notice that the function now calculates the monthly retirement income in cell B7.

i. Click **Remove Arrows** in the Formula Auditing group to remove the precedents arrow.

j. Click **Watch Window** in the Formula Auditing group and complete the following steps:

- Click **Add Watch**.
- Move the dialog boxes so that you can see the data.
- Select the **range B4:B7** in the Calculations worksheet and click **Add**.
- Resize the Watch Window so that you can see most of the details.
- Click the **Assumptions sheet tab** and move the Watch Window below the input area.

MAC TROUBLESHOOTING: Watch Window is not available in Excel for Mac.

---

k. Create a data validation rule to ensure the retirement age is greater than or equal to 59.5 by completing the following steps:

- Click **cell B10**, click the **Data tab**, and then click **Data Validation** in the Data Tools group.
- Click the **Settings tab**, click the **Allow arrow**, and then select **Decimal**.
- Click the **Data arrow** and select **greater than or equal to**.
- Click in the **Minimum box** and type **59.5**.
- Click the **Input Message tab**, click in the **Title box**, and then type **Retirement Age**.
- Click in the **Input message box** and type **No payout prior to age 59.5.** (including the period).
- Click the **Error Alert tab**, click the **Style arrow**, and then select **Warning**.
- Click in the **Title box** and type **Invalid Data**.
- Click in the **Error message box** and type **Age must be greater than or equal to 59.5.** (including the period), and then click **OK**.

l. Create a data validation rule to ensure the rate of return cannot exceed 6% by completing the following steps:

- Click **cell B11**, click the **Data tab**, and then click **Data Validation** in the Data Tools group.
- Click the **Settings tab**, click the **Allow arrow**, and then select **Decimal**.
- Click the **Data arrow** and select **less than or equal to**.
- Click in the **Maximum box** and type **0.06**.
- Click the **Input Message tab**, click in the **Title box**, and then type **Rate of Return**.
- Click in the **Input message box** and type **The rate of return cannot exceed 6%.** (including the period).

- Click the **Error Alert tab**, click the **Style arrow**, and then select **Warning**.
- Click in the **Title box** and type **Invalid Data**. Click in the **Error message box**, type **Rate must be less than or equal to 6%.** (including the period), and then click **OK**.

m. Type **50** in **cell B10** and press **Enter**. Click **No** when the error message displays, change the value to **60**, and then press **Enter**.

n. Type **8.5%** in **cell B11**. Click **No** when the error message displays, change the value to **6%**, and then press **Enter**.

o. Create a hyperlink by completing these steps:
- Click **cell A5** in the Assumptions sheet, click the **Insert tab**, click **Link**, and then select **Insert Link**.

> **MAC TROUBLESHOOTING:** Click the Insert menu and click Hyperlink.

- Click **Place in This Document**, click **Calculations** in the *Or select a place in this document* list, and then click **OK**.

p. Delete the 20 in **cell B12** in the Assumptions sheet, look at cell B7 in the Calculations sheet to see the #NUM! error. Click **Undo** on the Quick Access Toolbar to restore the value in cell B12. Delete the 12 in **cell B14** in the Assumptions sheet, look at cell B7 in the Calculations sheet to see the #DIV/0! Error. Click **Undo** on the Quick Access Toolbar to restore the value in cell B14. Prevent errors by completing these steps:
- Click the **Calculations sheet tab**, click **cell C7**, click between the equal sign and PMT in the Formula Bar, and then type **=IFERROR(**
- Click within IFERROR and click **Insert Function** to open the Function Arguments dialog box for the IFERROR function.
- Click in the **Value_if_error box**, type **Missing a value in cell B12 or B14 in the Assumptions worksheet.** (including the period), and then click **OK**.
- Delete the 12 in **cell B14** in the Assumptions sheet and click the **Calculations sheet tab** to see the result in cell B7.
- Click **Undo** to restore the 20 in cell B14 in the Assumptions sheet.

q. Right-click the **Calculations sheet tab**, select **Protect Sheet**, and then click **OK**.

r. Create a footer with your name on the left side, the sheet name code in the center, and the file name code on the right side of both worksheets.

s. Save and close the file. Based on your instructor's directions, submit e09p2Retire_LastFirst.

ANALYSIS CASE

You carefully tracked your income and expenses for three months using one worksheet per month. The worksheets contain the same expense categories. You used the Miscellaneous category to include a variety of expenses, including a vacation in June. For each month, you calculated the difference between your income and expenses as you were saving for your vacation in June. Now you want to create a three-month summary to analyze your spending habits.

a. Open *e09m1Expenses* and save it as **e09m1Expenses_LastFirst**.

b. Group the April, May, and June worksheets and complete the following steps:
- Type **Savings, Income, & Expenses** in cell A1.
- Select the range A1:C1 and apply the Heading 1 cell style.
- Click **cell C6** and add the Beginning Saving Balance to the Monthly Savings Added amount.
- Unlock **cell C9** and the **range B12:B20** in the grouped worksheets.
- Ungroup the worksheets.

c. Create formulas with 3-D references by completing the following steps:
- Display the May worksheet. In **cell C4**, create a formula with a 3-D reference to **cell C6** (the Ending Savings Balance) in the April worksheet.
- Display the June worksheet. In **cell C4**, create a formula with a 3-D reference to **cell C6** (the Ending Savings Balance) in the May worksheet.
- Display the Qtr 2 worksheet. In **cell C4**, create a formula with a 3-D reference to **cell C6** (the Ending Savings Balance) in the June worksheet.

d. Build functions with 3-D references in the Qtr 2 worksheet by completing the following steps:
- Click **cell C9** and insert the SUM function with a 3-D reference to total the salary amounts for all three months.
- Click **cell B12** and insert the SUM function with a 3-D reference to total the rent amount for all three months.
- Copy the function in **cell B12** to the **range B13:B20**.
- Copy the function in **cell C9** to **cells C21** and **C23**.

e. Display the April worksheet, group all four worksheets, and complete the following steps:
- Select the **range A8:C23**.
- Fill the formats only across the grouped worksheets to copy the font formatting, indents, and number formatting.
- Ungroup the worksheets.

f. Create hyperlinks on the shapes on the Qtr 2 worksheet by completing these steps:
- Select the **April shape**, insert a hyperlink to **cell C23** in the April worksheet, and include the ScreenTip with the text **April balance**.
- Select the **May shape**, insert a hyperlink to **cell C23** in the May worksheet, and include the ScreenTip with the text **May balance**.
- Select the **June shape**, insert a hyperlink to **cell C23** in the June worksheet, and include the ScreenTip with the text **June balance**.
- Click each shape to test the hyperlinks and correct any errors.

g. Display the April worksheet, click **cell C23**, and then trace precedents. Click **cell B14** and trace dependents.

h. Display the Qtr 2 worksheet. Select **cells C4, C9, C21**, and **C23**. Set a Watch Window to watch the formulas. Adjust the size and move the Watch Window to cover the **range E14:G21**.

i. Use the data in the four worksheets to enter data in the **range E7:E12** in the Analysis section to provide either a text or a number that relates to the labels in the range F7:F12.

j. Display the April worksheet and create a data validation rule in **cell B20** by completing these steps:
- Allow decimal values that are less than or equal to **$100**.
- Create the input message title **Miscellaneous Expense** and input message **The maximum miscellaneous expense is $100.** (including the period).

- Create an error alert with the Stop style, error title **Invalid Data**, and error message **You must enter a value less than or equal to $100.** (including the period).
- Test the rule by trying to enter **500**. The rule should prevent you from entering that value. Click **Cancel** to revert to the original $100 value.

k. Create a footer with your name on the left side, the sheet name code in the center, and the file name code on the right side of all worksheets.

l. Protect all four worksheets without a password to enforce the locked cells.

m. Mark the workbook as final.

n. Save and close the file. Based on your instructor's directions, submit e09m1Expenses_LastFirst.

---

2   Pizza Sales

You manage a chain of pizza restaurants in Augusta, Lewiston, and Portland, Maine. Each store manager created a workbook containing the quarterly sales for each type of sale (dine-in, carry-out, and delivery). You want to create links to a summary workbook for the yearly totals.

a. Open *e09m2Augusta* and save it as **e09m2Augusta_LastFirst**, open *e09m2Lewiston* and save it as **e09m2Lewiston_LastFirst**, and open *e09m2Portland* and save it as **e09m2Portland_LastFirst**.

b. Calculate totals in the **ranges F4:F6** and **B7:F7** in all three workbooks.

c. Open *e09m2Pizza* and save it as **e09m2Pizza_LastFirst**. Continue working in this workbook.

d. Display the Augusta worksheet; in **cell B4** insert a link to the Dine-In total in **cell F4** in the *e09m2Augusta_LastFirst* workbook. Edit the formula to make the cell reference relative, use AutoFill to copy the formula to the **range B5:B7**, and then select the Fill Without Formatting

e. Display the Portland worksheet; in **cell B4** insert a link to the Dine-In total in **cell F4** in the *e09m2Portland_LastFirst* workbook. Edit the formula to make the cell reference relative, copy the formula, and use the paste option to paste the Formula to the **range B5:B7** to preserve the existing formatting.

f. Display the Lewiston worksheet; in **cell B4** insert a link to the Dine-In total in **cell F4** in the *e09m2Lewiston_LastFirst* workbook. Edit the formula to make the cell reference relative, copy the formula, and then use the paste option to paste the Formula to the **range B5:B7** to preserve the existing formatting.

g. Close the Augusta, Portland, and Lewiston workbooks.

h. Select the **range A1:B7** in the Lewiston worksheet. Group the Lewiston and Summary worksheets. Fill formatting only across the grouped worksheets. Ungroup the worksheets and change the width of column B to **16** in the Summary worksheet.

i. Insert functions with 3-D references in the Summary worksheet by completing the following steps:
- Insert a SUM function in **cell B4** that calculates the total Dine-In sales for the three cities.
- Copy the formula in **cell B4** and use the Paste Formulas option in the **range B5:B7** to preserve the formatting.

j. Display the Contents worksheet and insert the following hyperlinks:
- Insert a hyperlink in **cell A3** that links to **cell B7** in the Augusta sheet. Include the ScreenTip text: **Augusta total sales** (no period).
- Insert a hyperlink in **cell A4** that links to **cell B7** in the Portland sheet. Include the ScreenTip text: **Portland total sales** (no period).
- Insert a hyperlink in **cell A5** that links to **cell B7** in the Lewiston sheet. Include the ScreenTip text: **Lewiston total sales** (no period).
- Insert a hyperlink in **cell A6** that links to **cell B7** in the Summary sheet. Include the ScreenTip text: **Total sales for all locations** (no period).

602   CHAPTER 9 • Mid-Level Exercises

k. Select the **range B3:B5** on the Future worksheet and add the following data validation rule:
  - Allow **Date** between **3/1/2021** and **10/1/2021**.
  - Enter the input message title: **Proposed Date**.
  - Enter the input message: **Enter the proposed opening date for this location.** (including the period).
  - Select the Information error alert style.
  - Enter the error alert title: **Confirm Date**.
  - Enter the error message: **Confirm the date with the VP.** (including the period).
  - Enter **10/5/2021** in **cell B5** and click **OK** in the Confirm Date message box.

l. Make these changes to the Future worksheet:
  - Unlock the **range B3:B5**.
  - Protect the worksheet by adding the password **Expl0r!ng**.
  - Hide the Future worksheet.

m. Create a footer with your name on the left side, the sheet name code in the center, and the file name code on the right side of the five visible worksheets.

n. Mark the workbook as final. (On a Mac, use Always Open Read-Only).

o. Close the file and exit Excel. Open File Explorer, select the four e09m2 files, and create a compressed (zipped) folder named **e09m2PizzaFiles_LastFirst**.

p. Based on your instructor's directions, submit e09m2PizzaFiles_LastFirst.zip.

Running Case

New Castle County Technical Services

New Castle County Technical Services (NCCTS) provides technical support services for a number of companies in New Castle County, Delaware. Previously, you analyzed support calls for March. Now, you will focus on the second-quarter (April, May, and June) support calls. In particular, you will format the data sets consistently and duplicate April's monthly summary section for May and June. In addition, you will create a quarterly summary sheet to consolidate data for the three months. Although data has been entered, you want to create a data validation rule and test it before implementing it for the third quarter. Finally, you will protect the worksheets and encrypt the workbook with a password.

a. Open *e09r1NCCTS* and save it as **e09r1NCCTS_LastFirst**.

b. Group the April, May, and June worksheets with the April data displayed. Complete the following steps:
  - Select the **range A1:H1** and fill formats and content across worksheets.
  - Select the **range A2:H35** and fill only the formats across the worksheets.
  - Select **column B** and change the width to **10**.
  - Select **columns C:E** and change the width to **9**.
  - Select **columns F:G** and change the width to **11**.
  - Select **column H** and change the width to **13**.
  - Select **column J** and change the width to **9**.
  - Select **columns K:L** and change the width to **12**.
  - Select the **range A2:H35** and unlock cells.

c. Keep the worksheets grouped, select the **range J1:L13**, and then fill content and formatting across the worksheets. Ungroup the worksheets.

d. Create a data validation rule for the Customer Satisfaction column (range H2:H35) in the April sheet by completing these steps:
- Allow **Whole numbers** between **1** and **5**.
- Enter the input message title: **Customer Satisfaction**.
- Enter the input message: **Enter a number between 1 and 5.** (including the period).
- Select the **Stop** error alert style.
- Enter the error alert title: **Incorrect Number**.
- Enter the error message: **You entered an incorrect number. Please enter a whole number between 1 and 5.** (including the period).

e. Copy the selected range, select the **range H2:H35** in the May worksheet, and use Paste Special to paste the validation rule. Repeat the process to paste the validation rule to the **range H2:H35** in the June worksheet.

f. Display the Quarter worksheet and insert the following hyperlinks:
- Insert a hyperlink in **cell A4** that links to **cell K13** in the April sheet. Include the ScreenTip text: **April Summary** (no period).
- Insert a hyperlink in **cell A5** that links to **cell K13** in the May sheet. Include the ScreenTip text: **May Summary** (no period).
- Insert a hyperlink in **cell A6** that links to **cell K13** in the June sheet. Include the ScreenTip text: **June Summary** (no period).

g. Insert formulas with 3-D references in the Quarter sheet by completing these steps:
- **Cell B4:** Enter a formula with a 3-D reference to cell K13 in the April sheet.
- **Cell B5:** Enter a formula with a 3-D reference to cell K13 in the May sheet.
- **Cell B6:** Enter a formula with a 3-D reference to cell K13 in the June sheet.
- Select the **range B4:B6**, use the fill handle to copy the formulas to the **range C4:C7**, and then select **Fill Without Formatting** to preserve the borders.
- Apply Accounting Number Format to the range C4:C6.

h. Insert functions with 3-D references to calculate averages and totals for the different call types in the Quarter sheet by completing these steps:
- **Cell B9:** Insert an IFERROR function with a nested AVERAGE function that averages the hours in cell K3 in the April, May, and June sheets. The second argument of the IFERROR function should be **Missing values for all three months**. This will prevent #DIV/0! Errors if all three months do not have data for a specific category.
- **Cell C9:** Insert a SUM function that totals the amounts in cell L3 in the April, May, and June sheets.
- Select the **range B9:C9**, use the fill handle to copy the functions to the **range B10:C18**, and select **Fill Without Formatting** to preserve the borders.

i. Protect each worksheet using the default settings in the Protect Sheet dialog box.

j. Create a footer with your name on the left side, the sheet name code in the center, and the file name code on the right side on all worksheets.

k. Encrypt the workbook with the password **Expl0r!ng**. After you verify that the password works, display the Encrypt Document dialog box and remove the password.

l. Save and close the file. Based on your instructor's directions, submit e09r1NCCTS_LastFirst.

Disaster Recovery

Gradebook Errors

You are taking a teaching methods course at your college to prepare you to be a secondary education teacher. One course module teaches students about gradebook preparation, in which you learn how to create formulas to assign grades based on course assessment instruments. Your methods professor assigned a flawed gradebook to see how well you and the other future teachers will do in identifying and correcting the errors. Open *e09d1Grades* and save it as **e09d1Grades_LastFirst**.

Set validation rules for the range of quiz and final exam scores to accept whole number scores between 0 and 100 only. Create appropriate input and error messages. Use the feature to circle invalid data. Use the Windows Snipping Tool to capture a screenshot of the Excel window, copy it, and paste it in **cell N2**. Crop the image to show just column letters, row numbers, and spreadsheet data through column M. Adjust the height of the screenshot to 3".

Insert a comment in each cell containing invalid data describing what is wrong with the data and how to fix it. Then fix the data-entry errors.

Use the auditing tools to find errors and display precedents and dependents to identify errors. The auditing tools will not find the errors. They will help you trace formulas so that you can identify logic errors in formulas and functions. Use the Windows Snipping Tool to capture a screenshot of the Excel window, copy it, and paste it in cell N21. Crop the image to show just column letters, row numbers, and spreadsheet data through column M. Adjust the height of the screenshot to 3". Correct the errors in the formulas. Insert comments indicating the errors found and how you corrected the formulas.

Delete the data in the **range E3:G3** and notice the #DIV/0! Error in cells H3, K3, and L3. Click **Undo** to restore the quiz values. Edit the quiz average function in **cell H3** by enclosing it as the first argument in an IFERROR function. Type **Missing all three quiz scores** in the Value_if_errors argument. Save the workbook. Delete the range E3:G3 again. Notice the message in cell H3. Click **Undo** to restore the quiz values. Copy the IFERROR function with the nested AVERAGE function from **cell H3** to the **range H4:H12**.

Create a footer with your name on the left side, the sheet name code in the center, and the file name code on the right side of the worksheet. Save and close the file. Based on your instructor's directions, submit e09d1Grades_LastFirst.

Capstone Exercise

Housecleaning Service

You manage a housecleaning service. As manager, you schedule the cleaners with clients, provide cleaning supplies, and insure the cleaners. You pay the cleaners for their time and mileage reimbursement. You set up a monthly workbook with one worksheet per week to enter the dates, mileage to each house, and start and stop times. You then calculate the hours worked. You are ready to calculate weekly totals and the monthly totals.

Group Worksheets

The title and column labels in the Week 1 worksheet are formatted with cell styles. You want to apply this formatting and add column labels to the other weekly worksheets. In addition, you want to unlock the data-entry cells on the weekly worksheets. Although the current data does not extend to row 40, you want to unlock cells through row 40 in case data entry is required in the future.

1. Open *e09c1HouseCleaners* and save it as **e09c1HouseCleaners_LastFirst**.

2. Group the Week 1, Week 2, Week 3, and Week 4 worksheets and do the following:
   - Select the **range A1:B1** on Week 1 and fill formats only across the other weekly worksheets.
   - Select the **range A11:E11** and fill both content and formatting across the other weekly worksheets.
   - Select the **range A12:D40** and unlock the cells.

3. Ungroup the weekly sheets, select the **range D12:D40** in the Week 1 sheet, and then create a data validation rule with these specifications:
   - Allow **Time** greater than **cell C12**.
   - Enter the input message title: **End Time**.
   - Enter the input message: **Enter the end time.** (including the period).
   - Select the **Stop error alert style**.
   - Enter the error alert title: **Incorrect End Time**.
   - Enter the error message: **The end time must be later than the start time.** (including the period).

4. Select the **range D12:D40** (if needed) and click **Copy**. Click the **Week 2 sheet tab** and group Week 2, Week 3, and Week 4 sheets.

5. Select the **range D12:D40**, click the **Paste arrow** on the Home tab, select **Paste Special**, click **Validation** in the Paste Special dialog box, and then click **OK**. Ungroup the sheets.

6. Display the Week 2 sheet and insert a split bar between rows 22 and 23.

Check for and Repair Errors

Although the data validation will prevent future errors in data entry, it did not correct errors in the existing data.

7. Display the Week 1 sheet.

8. Circle invalid data to identify cells containing invalid end times. Display the Month sheet. In **cells H4** and **H5**, enter the cell references (e.g., A1) that contained errors.

9. Display the Week 1 sheet again. Change the first incorrect end time to **11:00 AM**. Change the second end time to **4:15 PM**.

Link Workbooks

The hourly rate you charge clients, the hourly wage you pay your housecleaners, and the mileage allowance are stored in a separate workbook. You will create links to those inputs to perform calculations in the weekly worksheets.

10. Open *e09c1HouseInput* and save it as **e09c1HouseInput_LastFirst**. Arrange the two open workbooks vertically to display both workbooks at the same time.

11. Display the e09c1HouseCleaners_LastFirst workbook and group the four weekly worksheets.

12. Click **cell B5**. Multiply the Total Hours in **cell B4** by the Customer Cost per Hour in **cell B3** in the e09c1HouseInput_LastFirst workbook.

13. Click **cell B6**. Multiply the Total Hours in **cell B4** by the Cleaner's Pay per Hour in **cell B4** in the e09c1HouseInput_LastFirst workbook.

14. Click **cell B7**. Multiply the Mileage in **cell B3** by the Cleaner's Mileage Reimbursement in the e09c1HouseInput_LastFirst workbook.

15. Ungroup the worksheets, close e09c1HouseInput_LastFirst, and maximize e09c1HouseCleaners_LastFirst.

Create 3-D References

The Month worksheet was created to calculate the totals for the month. You will insert functions with 3-D references to add data from each worksheet. In addition, you will insert formulas with 3-D references to obtain the total weekly client charge from each worksheet.

16. Display the Month worksheet and insert a SUM function in **cell B3** that uses a 3-D reference to add the mileage from the four weekly worksheets.

17. Copy the function from **cell B3** to the **range B4:B8**.

18. Use the Auto Fill button to Fill Without Formatting to preserve the original formatting in the range.

19. Click **cell E3** in the Month worksheet and create a formula with a 3-D reference to display the contents of **cell B5** from the Week 1 worksheet.

20. Adapt Step 19 to create formulas with 3-D references in the **range E4:E6** to display the contents of **cell B5** from the Week 2, Week 3, and Week 4 worksheets, respectively.

Create Hyperlinks

You want to create hyperlinks from the Month sheet to the cells containing the total weekly client charge for each week.

21. Insert a hyperlink in **cell D3** that links to **cell B5** in the Week 1 sheet. Include the ScreenTip text: **Total client charges for Week 1** (no period).

22. Insert a hyperlink in **cell D4** that links to **cell B5** in the Week 2 sheet. Include the ScreenTip text: **Total client charges for Week 2** (no period).

23. Insert a hyperlink in **cell D5** that links to **cell B5** in the Week 3 sheet. Include the ScreenTip text: **Total client charges for Week 3** (no period).

24. Insert a hyperlink in **cell D6** that links to **cell B5** in the Week 1 sheet. Include the ScreenTip text: **Total client charges for Week 4** (no period).

Finalize the Workbook

You are ready to finalize the workbooks by adding a footer and protecting the worksheets. In addition, you will mark the workbook final. Finally, you will compress the files into one zip folder.

25. Create a footer on all worksheets with your name on the left side, the sheet name code in the center, and the file name code on the right side. Save and close the workbooks.

26. Protect each worksheet so that others can select the default cells but not make any changes.

27. Mark the Workbook as Final. Close the workbook and exit Excel.

28. Open File Explorer, select **e09c1HouseCleaners_LastFirst** and **e09c1HouseInput_LastFirst** and compress them into a folder named **e09c1HouseCleaners_LastFirst**. Based on your instructor's directions, submit e09c1HouseCleaners_LastFirst.zip.

Power Add-Ins

LEARNING OUTCOME   You will import, format, and manipulate data from external sources.

OBJECTIVES & SKILLS: After you read this chapter, you will be able to:

CASE STUDY | Stock Analysis

You are a financial analyst for a brokerage firm. Your manager wants you to analyze commodity sales patterns of his top five brokers for the first quarter. Unfortunately, the data required to complete the analysis are distributed among several key data sources. You received basic broker information through an email and transaction information from an Access database, and you will need to retrieve real-time NASDAQ trading information from the Web. You do not want to simply copy and paste the data into the worksheet; you want to connect and transform data in Excel so that the constantly changing values are always up to date.

You also want to create data visualizations to provide geospatial information and a business dashboard.

CHAPTER 10

Managing Data

YanLev/Shutterstock

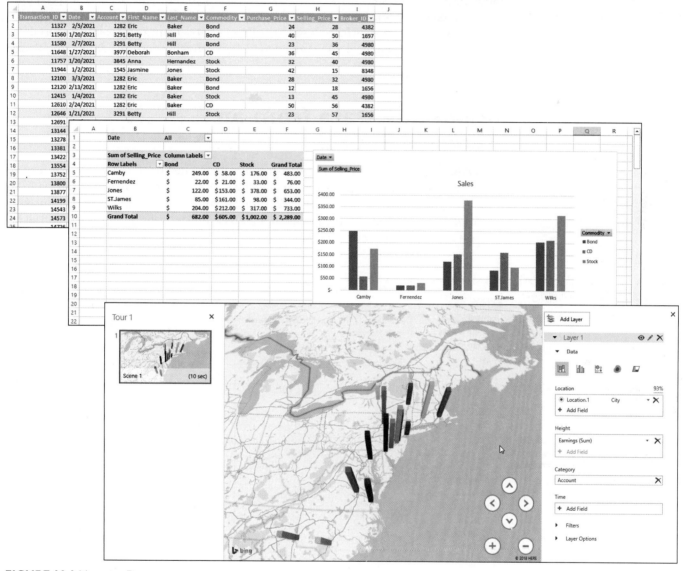

FIGURE 10.1 Managing Data

CASE STUDY | Stock Analysis

Starting Files	Files to be Submitted
Blank Excel Workbook e10h1Broker_Info.txt e10h1Client_Info.csv e10h1Transactions.accdb	e10h1Broker_Info_LastFirst.txt e10h1Client_Info_LastFirst.csv e10h1Transactions_LastFirst.accdb e10h3Commodities_LastFirst

MyLab IT Grader An alternate version of this project is available as a MyLab IT Grader Assessment

Get and Transform Data

Data originate from and are stored in a variety of locations and formats. When you use Excel to manipulate data and perform quantitative analyses, you might obtain data that originate in an external source—somewhere other than an Excel workbook. For example, you might download customer data from a large database stored on your organization's server, or you might receive a text file containing data you need to manipulate in Excel.

External data may not be properly formatted for your Excel worksheet, but connecting to external data and formatting it in Excel maintains greater accuracy than if you manually enter the data. Furthermore, connecting to external data in a worksheet enables you to update the worksheet data based on changes from the external source.

In this section, you will learn how to use Excel's Get & Transform tools to import data, as well as how to manage data connections. Then you will shape the data using Power Query Editor.

Importing Data from an External Source

Importing is the process of inserting external data created or stored in another format into the current application. As shown in Figure 10.2, Excel enables you to import from a variety of data formats using the Get & Transform tools. Get & Transform can be used to import data to Excel from sources such as database tables, websites, text files, and so on by creating a link to the external file.

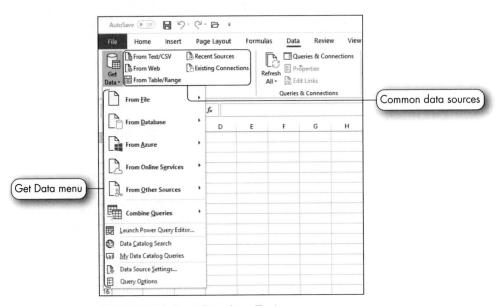

FIGURE 10.2 Get & Transform Tools

When you import external data using Get & Transform tools, the data is placed in a table and a link to the original data source is automatically created. You can refresh the Excel worksheet so that the imported data are updated if any changes are made to the original data source. Before connecting data to an Excel document, decide whether you need to manage the data as a separate dataset in Excel or if you want to maintain a connection to the original data source. If you choose to to manage the data as a separate dataset in can be embedded in the document. When you add external data into Excel without creating a link to the original data source, you *embed* the data within the Excel worksheet. That means you edit the data directly within Excel because there is no connection to the original data source. Changes in the original data source or the embedded data in Excel do not change the other data; they are two separate datasets.

> **MAC TIP:** Power Query and other Get and Transform tools are unavailable on Mac. As an alternative, click the Data tab and select the file type. Furthermore, when importing a database using a Mac, the corresponding ODBC (Open Database Connectivity) drivers must be installed during Office setup. For more information, search importing a database into Excel for Mac on Microsoft's website.

STEP 1 ## Get Data from a Text/CSV File

One of the most common file types imported into Excel is text files. A *text file* (indicated by the .txt file extension) is a data file that contains characters, such as letters, numbers, and symbols, including punctuation and spaces. However, a text file does not contain formatting, sound, images, or video. You can use a text editor, such as Notepad, to create a text file, or you can download data from an organization's database or server as a text file. The benefit of a text file is that you can import a text file easily into a variety of programs, such as Excel or Access. After importing data from a text file, you can format the data within Excel.

Text files can contain *delimiters*, special characters (such as a tab) that separate data. A *tab-delimited file* uses tabs to separate data into columns. Figure 10.3 shows a tab-delimited file in Notepad and the imported data in Excel. In the tab-delimited file, the columns do not align; only one tab separates columns. If the user pressed Tab multiple times to align the data, the data would not have been imported correctly into Excel because Excel counts the number of tabs to determine the column into which the data is imported. An extra tab in a text file imports as a blank cell in Excel.

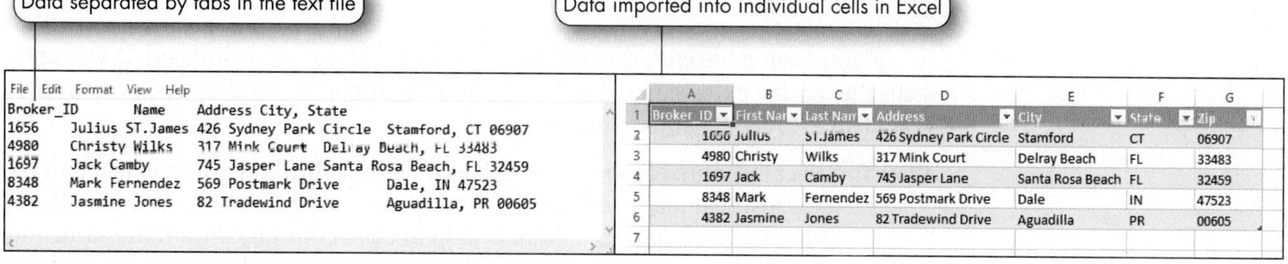

FIGURE 10.3 Tab-Delimited Text File and Data Connected in Excel

The ***comma-separated values (CSV) file*** uses commas to separate data into columns and a newline character to separate data into rows. A ***newline character*** is a special character that designates the end of a line and separates data for the next line or row. Many websites, such as census.gov, contain links to download a delimited text file that can be imported to or embedded in Excel. Figure 10.4 shows a CSV file in Notepad and the connected data in Excel. In the CSV file, commas are used only to separate data; commas are *not* used as the thousands separators in values or as punctuation marks. Otherwise, Excel would separate data at the commas used for punctuation or in values.

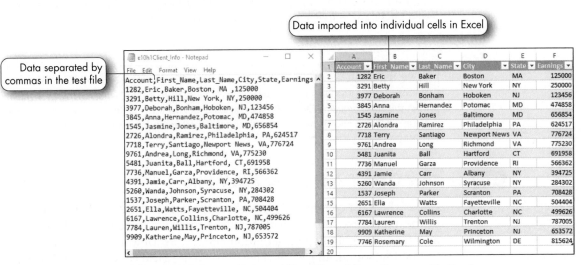

FIGURE 10.4 Comma Delimited Text File and Data Connected in Excel

Get & Transform import tools are located on the Data tab in the Get & Transform Data group. To import text or CSV data, click From Text/CSV on the Data tab. Then choose the corresponding file's origin, delimiter, and data type detection. Excel previews the data based on the default language and location settings of the host computer. If the default language is not the required language, the file origin can be changed during the import process. After the file origin, delimiter, and data type detection has been reviewed in the preview window, click Load to import the data into a table.

If you open a file with the .csv file extension from File Explorer instead of using Get & Transform, Excel opens the file directly without emending the information in a workbook. Because commas are used to delimit the data, data between commas in the CSV file are imported into individual cells in Excel. Each line within the CSV file becomes a row within Excel.

If you open a file with the .txt file in Windows, it opens in Notepad. If you open a file with the .txt file extension using Excel, the Text Import Wizard opens, prompting you to complete a three-step importing process.

Step 1: Select Delimited or Fixed width based on how the data are structured in the text file. Most text files use delimiters to separate data; therefore, you usually select Delimited to import text data. If data in each column contain the same number of characters and spaces are used only to separate columns, you can choose Fixed width. A ***fixed-width text file*** is a file in which each column contains a specific number of characters, such as five characters for the first column, 20 for the second column, and so on, to separate the fields.

Set the *Start import at row* value to where you want the data to begin (see Figure 10.5). Look at the *Preview of file* section to see the data in the text file and how they will be imported based on the *Start import at row* setting. If the text file contains a title or extraneous data extending across multiple columns, do not import from row 1; start importing from the row that contains the actual data. Click the *My data has headers* check box to select it, if the text file contains column headings that describe the contents of each column.

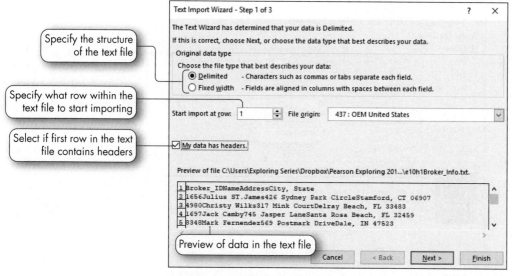

FIGURE 10.5 Step 1 Importing Delimited Files

Step 2: The Text Import Wizard displays two options for importing data.

- Click the appropriate delimiter check box, such as Tab, if the text file is delimited. Click the *Other* check box and type the specific character in the box if the text file contains a different delimiter (see Figure 10.6).
- Move the column break lines to where the columns begin and end if the text file contains fixed-width columns.

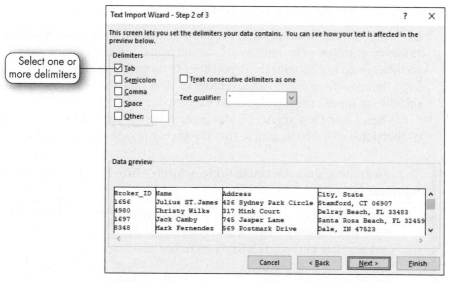

FIGURE 10.6 Step 2 Choosing Delimiter

Step 3: Select an option in the *Column data format* section for each column you want to import in the Text Import Wizard (see Figure 10.7).

Click the column heading in the Data preview window and select an option in the *Column data format* section. If you do not want to import a column, select the column and click *Do not import column (skip)*. The default column data format is General, but you can apply a different format. For example, you might want a column of dates to have the Date format.

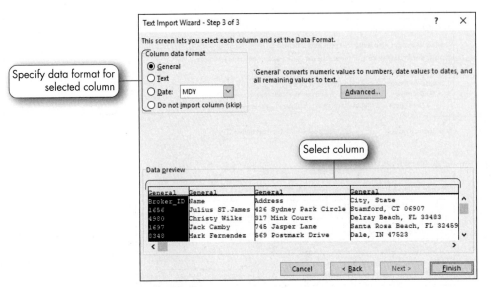

FIGURE 10.7 Step 3 of the Text Import Wizard

After you import data from a text file, review the data in Excel. Unlike Get & Transform, the data will not be formatted as a table. Typically, you need to adjust column widths and format the data, such as centering column labels and applying the Accounting Number Format to monetary data. Check for and correct any data errors that may have occurred at import. It is important to note that data imported into Excel using the Text Import Wizard does not maintain a connection to the external file; therefore, any changes made to the original text file will not be reflected in the workbook.

STEP 2 ▶ ## Import an Access Database Table or Query

Large amounts of data are often stored in databases, such as an Access database table. However, database programs are not intuitive about manipulating data for quantitative analyses or do not contain the capabilities to do so. For example, a car dealership might use a database to maintain an inventory of new cars on the lot, but to analyze monthly sales by car model, the manager uses Excel and creates a PivotTable.

When importing an Access database table or query into Excel, you maintain a connection to the Access data so that the Excel worksheet data are always current.

> **To import an Access database table or query into Excel, complete the following steps:**
>
> 1. Start Excel, start a new workbook or open an existing workbook, and then click the worksheet tab to which you want to import the data.
> 2. Click the Data tab and click Get Data in the Get & Transform Data group. Select From Database and select From Microsoft Access Database. Browse to the database and click Import.
> 3. Choose a table or query from the list in the Navigator Pane (see Figure 10.8) and click Load to directly import the database object or Edit to open the Power Query Editor.

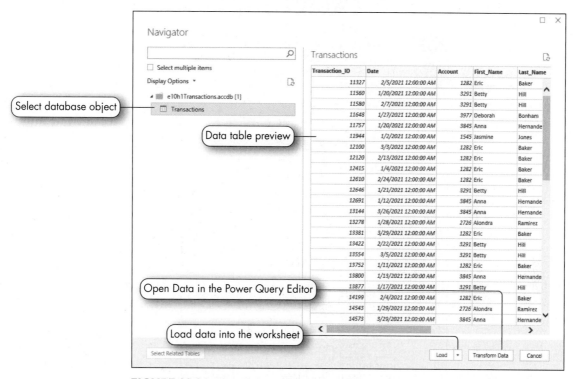

FIGURE 10.8 Import an Access Database Table

If you import the data as a table, Excel formats the data using a default Excel table style. In addition, Excel displays the Table Tools Design tab as well as the filter arrows so that you can sort and filter data (see Figure 10.9).

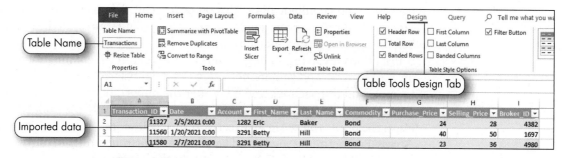

FIGURE 10.9 Imported Access Table

TIP: COPYING DATA FROM AN ACCESS TABLE

If you do not want to create a link to the Access database table, you can open the table in Access, select the table including field names, copy it, and then paste the data in Excel.

Import Data from Other Sources

You can import data from sources other than text files and Access databases. Click Get Data in the Get & Transform Data group and click From Other Sources to display a list of additional sources, as shown in Figure 10.10. Use Help to learn about each source and the type of data you can import. Some services require a username and password. Some marketplace datasets require a fee to obtain.

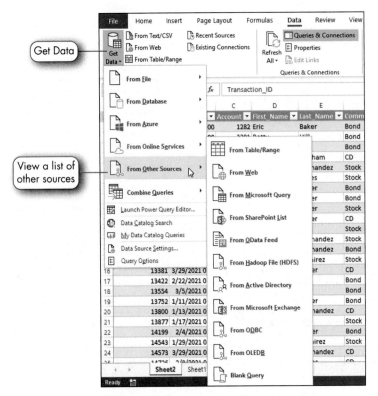

FIGURE 10.10 Import Data from Other Sources

STEP 3 Transform Data

The true benefit of importing data using Get & Transform is the ability to connect, transform, and combine data. This process is called data shaping. **Data shaping** is the process of editing information from one or more data sources to the required parameters before importing the data into an application. For example, you want to import all transactions involving savings bonds for the year. If all commodity sales are stored in an Access table, and you are not using Get & Transform, you would have no choice but to import all transactions and filter after the import, or create a query in Access before importing. In contrast, Excel enables you to select exactly the information you want to import before it is placed in an Excel worksheet without the need to first restrict the data in Access. Furthermore, you can add additional data from multiple sources, edit formatting, and add calculated fields before completing the import.

When using Get & Transform, data is shaped using the Power Query Editor. The **Power Query Editor** is a Business Intelligence tool that can connect and shape data from multiple data sources. When working with traditional relational databases, queries are used to pull subsets of data from larger data sources. These portions of data can be combined and shaped for analysis. In Excel, when data is imported it is considered a query. Once a query is created in Excel, the Power Query Editor can be used to make adjustments. As shown in Figure 10.11, these tools are organized into groups that are located on the Power Query ribbon. (On a Mac, Get & Transform is not available.)

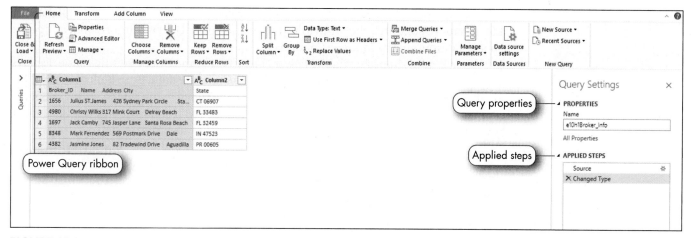

FIGURE 10.11 Power Query Editor Window

To access the Power Query Editor, click Transform Data after previewing the data during the import process. As shown in Figure 10.12, when the Power Query Editor is active, if there are multiple queries used in the workbook, you can expand and collapse views using the Navigator Pane.

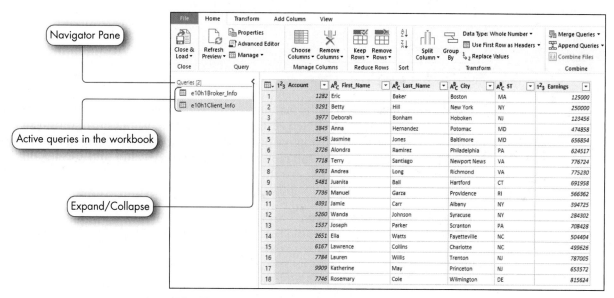

FIGURE 10.12 Query Navigator Pane

When data is loaded into the Power Query Editor, it displays in a table. Each column and row of the table can be formatted, appended, removed, or split. You can also add data by adding a custom calculated field. To format data, click the Home tab on the Power Query Editor ribbon and select options in the Transform group. Table 10.1 describes the formatting features for each Transform tool.

TABLE 10.1	Transform Tools
Tool	**Description**
Split Column	Separate elements of a column into multiple columns based on a delimiter
Group by	Group rows in a table based on the values in the currently selected columns
Data Type	Change the data type for a column
Use First Row as Headers	Promote the first row of a table into column headers
Replace Values	Replace existing values in the current column with a specified new value

You can add columns or remove them as needed to accommodate additional data. To add or remove columns, click the Home tab on the Power Query Editor ribbon, and select Choose Columns in the Manage Columns group.

When data is shaped using the Power Query Editor, the Query Settings pane displays with the name of the query and the steps taken to shape the data. By default the source file name is used as the query name, however, this can be edited in the Query Settings pane. If at any point an edit is made that does not have the desired results, the step can be undone by clicking the X next to the step in the Applied steps box (see Figure 10.13).

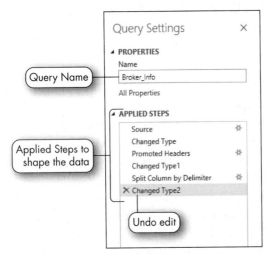

FIGURE 10.13 Query Settings Pane

Once the data is edited to the parameters you want, click Close & Load to import the data into the worksheet. As noted earlier, data imported using Get & Transform tools maintain a connection to the original data source and update if the original data source is changed. Furthermore, you can reopen the Power Query Editor and reshape the data as needed.

> **TIP: EDITING SHAPED DATA**
> Even after data is shaped and loaded into Excel using the Power Query Editor, steps can be undone. Because the data imported into Excel is a connection that is viewed as a query, the steps taken to shape the data can be edited or undone in the Query Settings pane.

Managing Queries and Connections

When you import data using the Get & Transform tools (Power Query), Excel creates a link to the original data source so that you can update the data quickly when the original source is modified. After you create the initial query using the Power Query Editor, you can view or modify the link. The Queries & Connections group on the Data tab contains options to manage the external data connections. To review active queries or external program connections, click the Data tab, and click Queries & Connections in the Queries & Connections group. This opens the Queries & Connections pane that displays active queries and external program connections (see Figure 10.14).

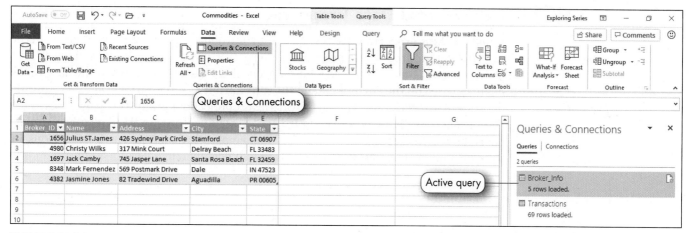

FIGURE 10.14 View Current Queries

You can remove a connection if you no longer want to link the data to the external data source. To remove a connection, select the table containing the imported data and click the Design tab. Next, click Unlink, and click OK in the warning message box. After you disconnect the data in Excel from the external data source, you will not be able to refresh the data.

You also can edit or change the original data source. For example, the file location containing the linked document has been modified or the URL for a website that contains imported data has been updated.

To edit the query data source, complete the following steps:

1. Double-click the query (or right-click the query) in the Queries & Connections pane and select Edit to open the Power Query Editor.
2. Click Data source settings in the Data Sources group and select Change Source.
3. Browse to the location of the file, set the preferences as shown in Figure 10.15, and then click OK.

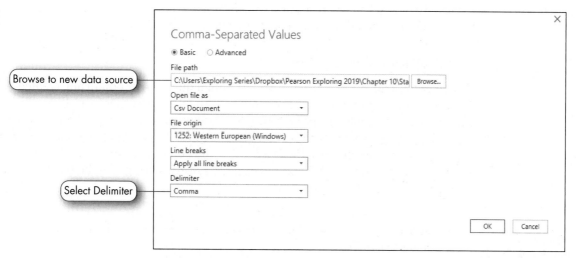

FIGURE 10.15 Edit Data Source Settings

External Data properties are settings that control how imported data connects to the external data source. These properties also specify how the data displays in Excel, how often the data is refreshed, and what happens if the number of rows in the data range changes based on the current data in the external data source. To view and edit external data properties, click Properties in the Queries & Connections group to display the External Data Properties dialog box (see Figure 10.16). The features in the dialog box change depending on the type of external data. For example, the dialog box has fewer options for a connection to an Access database table than it does for a text file.

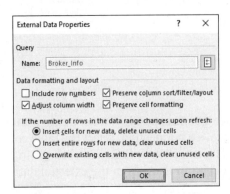

FIGURE 10.16 External Data Properties for a Text File

Data in a database or in an external text file may be updated periodically. Although you created a connection to the external data when it was imported into Excel, it will not be automatically updated when the source data changes. For example, if you created a connection to a database containing sales information, if a new sale is recorded, it will not automatically display in the Excel workbook. To ensure that the Excel data is current, you need to ***refresh*** the connections to the original external data source periodically. Refreshing the connection updates the linked data in an Excel workbook with the most up-to-date information.

There are several methods to refresh external data, depending on which data sources are being updated. To refresh all data in a workbook, click Refresh All in the Queries & Connections group. To update a single data source, select the range containing the external data, click the Refresh All arrow, and then select Refresh. Alternatively, right-click in a range of data and select Refresh to update only that data.

Edit Query Properties

When Get & Transform is used to import data a query is automatically created. Query properties determine the frequency in which the data refreshes as well as a variety of advanced online analytical processing (OLAP) settings. Query properties can be accessed by clicking the Query Properties in the External Data Properties dialog box. Alternatively, right-click the active query in the Queries & Connections pane and select Properties. Once the Query Properties dialog box is active, the refresh settings can be set in the Refresh Control area of the Usage tab.

Quick Concepts

1. Describe the purpose of delimiters in a text file. Name two common text file delimiters. ***p. 611***

2. Explain the difference between opening a text file directly in Excel and using Get & Transform to import text file data. ***p. 611***

3. Outline a situation in which you would want to refresh a connection to external data. ***p. 610***

Hands-On Exercises

Skills covered: Get Data from a Text File • Get Data from an Access Database Table or Query • Transform Data • Set Connection Properties

1 Get and Transform Data

To begin your analysis report, you will import client information stored in a CSV file. Then you will import and shape a text file of broker information you received via email. You will also add transaction information that is stored in an Access database table. Your last step is to configure the data connection, as you will need to refresh the connection to import the most up-to-date data into your worksheet when the workbook is opened.

STEP 1 IMPORT A TEXT FILE

You have a list of client information stored as a CSV file. You want to use Get & Transform Data (Power Query) to import the file, so the information will update as new clients are added. Refer to Figure 10.17 as you complete Step 1.

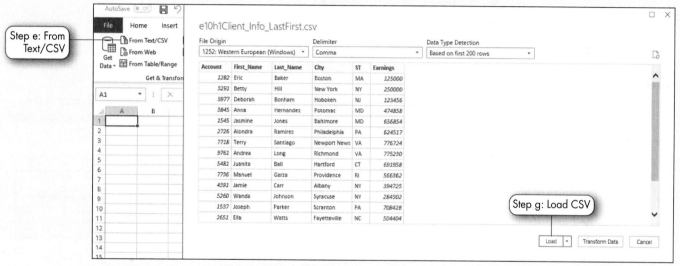

FIGURE 10.17 Import Data from a Text File

a. Start Excel, click **Open**, and open the file *e10h1Client_Info.csv*.

   Excel opens the CSV file.

> **TROUBLESHOOTING:** When browsing to open a file, by default, only Excel files will be displayed. To view other available files, such as .txt or .csv files, select All Files in the Open window.

b. Click **File**, click **Save As**, and navigate to the solutions folder on your computer. Rename the file **e10h1Client_Info_LastFirst.csv**, click **Save**, and then close the workbook.

   You saved the required CSV file in the solutions folder.

c. Click the **File tab**, click **New**, and then click **Blank workbook.** Save the file with the name **e10h1Commodities_LastFirst.**

d. Click the **Data tab** and click **From Text/CSV** in the Get & Transform Data group.

e. Browse to the location of the file *e10h1Client_Info_LastFirst.csv*, select the file, and click **Import**.

A window opens displaying File Origin, Delimiter, Data Type, and a data preview.

f. Review the data for accuracy and click **Load**.

You used Get & Transform to import the file e10h1Client_Info_LastFirst.csv into a new worksheet while maintaining a connection to the external data source.

g. Rename the worksheet **Clients**.

h. Save the workbook.

STEP 2 **GET DATA FROM AN ACCESS DATABASE**

All commodity transactions are stored in an Access database. You will use the Get & Transform tools to import this data while maintaining a connection to the database. You want to use the Power Query Editor to shape the data. Refer to Figure 10.18 as you complete Step 2.

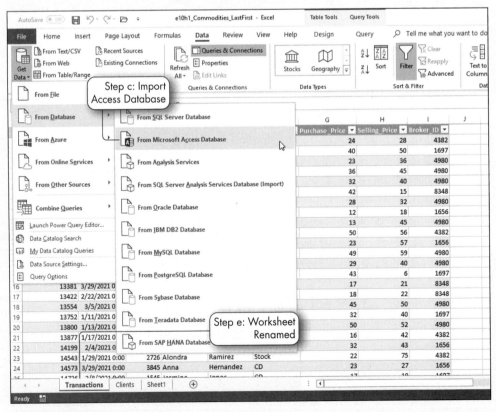

FIGURE 10.18 Import Access Table

a. Minimize Excel and use File Explorer to locate the file *e10h1Transactions.accdb*.

b. Right-click the file **e10h1Transactions.accdb**, click **Rename**, and rename the file **e10h1Transactions_LastFirst.accdb.** Move the file to your solutions folder and maximize Excel.

c. Click the **Data tab** and click **Get Data**. Point at **From Database**, select **From Microsoft Access Database**, and browse to the file *e10h1Transactions_LastFirst.accdb*. Click **Import**.

d. Select the **Transactions table** in the Navigator Pane and click **Load**.

   The Access database table *Transactions* was imported as an Excel table.

e. Rename the worksheet **Transactions**.

f. Save the workbook.

STEP 3 TRANSFORM DATA

The database table you imported in the previous step contains data that was incorrectly formatted. You will use the Power Query Editor to reformat the data. In addition, a coworker created a list of broker contact information as a tab-delimited file in Notepad. You will use the Power Query Editor to shape the data by splitting the columns and providing unique data labels before importing it to Excel. Refer to Figure 10.19 as you complete Step 3.

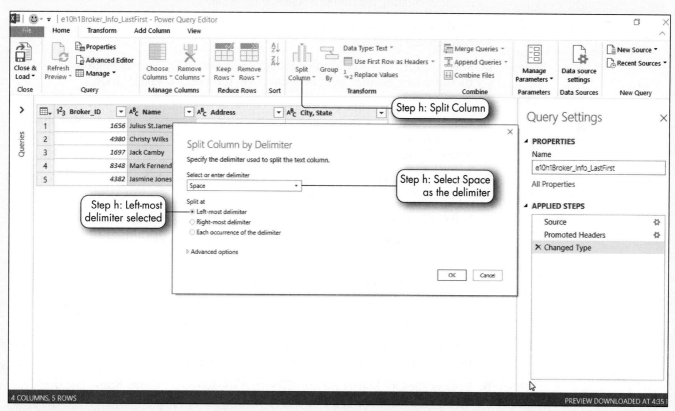

FIGURE 10.19 Transform Data

a. Click any cell in the Transactions table, click the **Query tab**, and then click **Edit** in the Edit group.

The Power Query Editor opens.

b. Click the **Date column**, click **Data Type** in the Transform group, and then select **Date**.

You used the Power Query Editor to change the date/time format to date format.

c. Adapt the previous step to apply **Currency** to the Purchase_Price and Selling_Price columns.

d. Click **Close & Load** in the Close group to exit the Power Query Editor.

e. Minimize Excel. Use File Explorer to locate the file *e10h1Broker_Info.txt*. Rename the file **e10h1Broker_Info_LastFirst.txt** and move the file to your solutions folder.

f. Maximize Excel. Click the **Data tab**. Click **From Text/CSV** in the Get & Transform Data group, browse to the file *e10h1Broker_Info_LastFirst.txt*, and click **Import**.

g. Click the **Delimiter arrow**, select **Tab**, and then click **Transform Data**.

Although the file is tab delimited, the broker names and addresses are not separated in meaningful ways. You will use the Power Query Editor to split the columns before finishing the Import process. The Power Query Editor opens displaying the data to import.

h. Select the **Name column**, click **Split Column** in the Transform group, and then select **By Delimiter**. Ensure Space is selected from the Select or enter delimiter list, click **Left-most delimiter**, and then click **OK**.

This splits the first and last names in the Name column using the first space as the delimiter creating the columns Name.1 and Name.2.

i. Double-click the **Name.1 column** and type **First**. Next double-click the **Name.2 column** and type **Last**.

j. Select the **City, State column**, click **Split Column** in the Transform group, and select **By Delimiter**. Ensure **Comma** is selected as the delimiter and click **OK**.

The Power Query Editor identifies the comma as a delimiter and splits the data into two columns. One with City data and the other with State and Zip Code data. Note that the space before the state abbreviation was included in the City, State.2 column. This will be removed in the next step.

k. Click the **City, State.2 column** and click the **Transform tab**. Click **Format** in the Text Column group and select **Trim**.

You used the Trim feature to remove the space at the beginning of the column field.

l. Click **Split Column** and select **By Delimiter**. Ensure Space is selected as the delimiter and click **OK**.

You split the column using a space as the delimiter.

m. Click the **X** located to the left of the step *Changed Type3* in the Applied Steps box located in the Query Settings pane and click Delete in the message box.

When splitting the column, Excel auto formatted the zip codes as numbers. You removed the number formatting so the zip codes are displayed correctly.

n. Rename the City, State.1 column **City**, the City, State.2.1 column **State**, and the City, State.2.2 column **Zip Code**.

o. Click the **Home tab** and click **Close & Load**.

p. Rename the worksheet **Brokers**.

q. Save the workbook.

SET EXTERNAL DATA PROPERTIES

You want to change the refresh property so that it will refresh the data from the Access database when the workbook is opened. This change will enable you to monitor stock price changes throughout the day. Refer to Figure 10.20 as you complete Step 4.

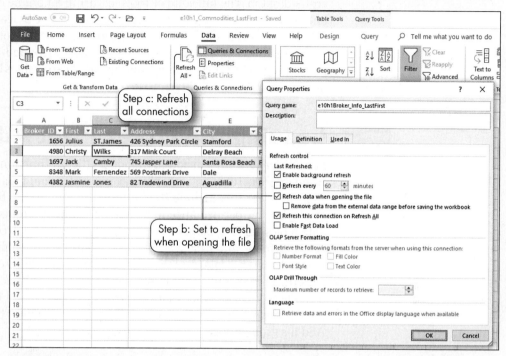

FIGURE 10.20 Maintain Connections

a. Click **cell A1** on the Transactions sheet tab. Click the **Data tab**, click **Properties** in the Queries & Connections group, and then click the **Query Properties icon** to the right of the Name box.

The Query Properties dialog box opens so that you can modify the properties.

b. Click to select **Refresh data when opening the file**, click **OK** to exit the Query Properties dialog box, and then click **OK** again to exit the External Data Properties dialog box.

The table imported from the database will update every time the workbook is opened.

c. Click **Refresh All** in the Queries & Connections group.

The status bar displays *Running background query* and the connected data is updated.

d. Save the workbook. Keep the workbook open if you plan to continue with the next Hands-On Exercise. If not, close the workbook, and exit Excel.

Power Pivot

Microsoft's ***Power BI*** (Business Intelligence) is an online application suite designed to enable users to manage, supplement, visualize, and analyze data. A free visualization application, Power BI desktop is available for download at https://powerbi.microsoft.com/en-us/desktop. The full suite of tools featuring an online data repository is available via online subscription; however, several popular Power BI features such as Power Pivot and 3D Maps are available as Excel add-ins for Office Professional Plus users.

In this section, you will explore the Power Pivot add-in. You will learn how to load Power Pivot, add data to a data model, create relationships between multiple data sources, and create a PivotTable.

STEP 1 Loading the Power Pivot Add-In

Power Pivot is a built-in add-in that offers the key functionality that is included in Excel's standard PivotTable options, plus a variety of useful features for the advanced business user. Key features include handling and compressing big data files, identifying and displaying key performance indicators, creating relationships between multiple related data tables, and importing data from a vast array of sources.

By default, Power Pivot is not enabled and must be enabled before use. Once enabled, a Power Pivot tab displays on the ribbon. As shown in Figure 10.21, to enable Power Pivot, click the File tab and click Options. Select Add-ins and click COM Add-ins in the Manage box. Click Go, select Microsoft Power Pivot for Excel, and then click OK. Alternatively, if the Developer tab is enabled, Power Pivot can be enabled by clicking Com Add-ins in the Add-ins group.

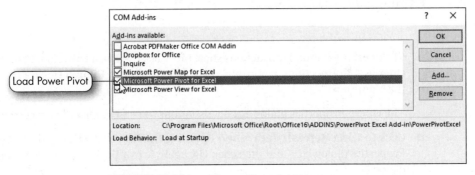

FIGURE 10.21 Load Power Pivot Add-In

> **MAC TROUBLESHOOTING:** Currently, the Power Pivot and Power Map Add-ins are not available in Excel for Mac.

STEP 2 Adding Data to a Data Model

PivotTables can visualize data from different angles, enabling you to gain insight and perspective. While PivotTables are an incredibly useful tool, they are limited to working with flat data, which is data located within the current workbook. For example, without the Power Pivot add-in, a PivotTable cannot be created using external files. Power Pivot offers the same ability to visualize and "pivot" data from diverse perspectives; however, it also can aggregate multiple related data sources using a data model. A ***data model*** enables you to integrate data from multiple sources within an Excel workbook. The data compiled in a data model can then be aggregated into a PivotTable using Power Pivot. As shown in Figure 10.22, external data can be added to a data model during the import process.

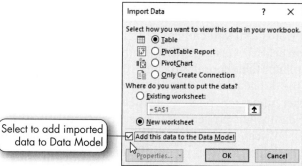

Select to add imported data to Data Model

FIGURE 10.22 Add Data to a Data Model

When using Get & Transform tools to import data to a data model, click the Load arrow and select Load To, which opens the Import Data dialog box. Check *Add this data to the Data Model* and click OK. This imports the data into the workbook and adds the connection to the existing data model. If no data model exists, a new data model will be created with the active connection (refer to Figure 10.22). If you want to add data that has already been imported into a worksheet to a data model, select the data, click the Power Pivot tab, and then click Add to Data Model in the Tables group (see Figure 10.23).

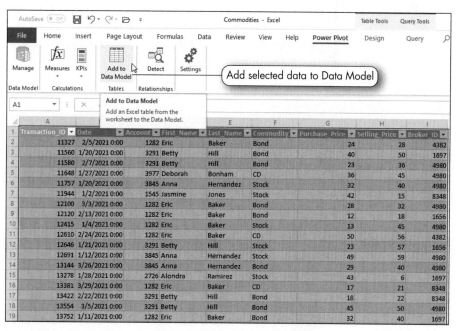

Add selected data to Data Model

FIGURE 10.23 Add Data from a Worksheet to a Data Model

Create Relationships with Power Pivot

A key feature of Power Pivot is that you can create relationships among multiple data sources that share common fields. For example, suppose that one table contains commodity broker names and IDs. A related table contains the sales dates and sales amounts, but only the brokers' IDs to avoid the duplication of data. If you want to create a separate dataset that includes just the broker names and related sales data, you need to pull the data from two tables. To ensure the data aligns properly, you must create a relationship based on a common field (such as ID) between the tables. A ***relationship*** is an association between two related tables where both tables contain a common field of data, such as IDs. After you create a relationship between tables, you can use Power Pivot to create a PivotTable to display the brokers' names instead of their IDs in the final data table.

> **To create a Power Pivot relationship, complete the following steps:**
>
> 1. Click the Power Pivot tab and click Manage.
> 2. Click the Design tab and click Create Relationship (see Figure 10.24).
> 3. Click the Table 1 arrow and select the name of the primary table. The primary table in this example is Transactions.
> 4. Select the name of the column that contains a relationship to the related or lookup table in the Table 1 Columns box. For example, the column that relates to the other table is Account (see Figure 10.24).
> 5. Click the Table 2 arrow and select the name of the related or lookup table. For example, the related table is ClientNames.
> 6. Click the Table 2 Columns box, select the name of the column that is related to the primary table, and then click OK.

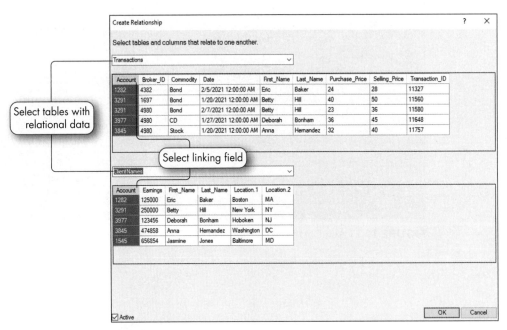

FIGURE 10.24 Create Relationships

STEP 4 # Creating a PivotTable and PivotChart Using Power Pivot

After you create a relationship between the tables, you can use Power Pivot to create a PivotTable or PivotChart. A PivotTable or PivotChart created with Power Pivot has the same functionality as if it were created from one set of data.

To create a PivotTable using related tables, complete the following steps:

1. Click the Power Pivot tab and click Manage.
2. Click PivotTable on the Power Pivot Home tab and select the PivotTable or PivotChart option (see Figure 10.25).
3. Select an option to either create the PivotTable or PivotChart on a new worksheet or an existing worksheet.
4. Click OK.

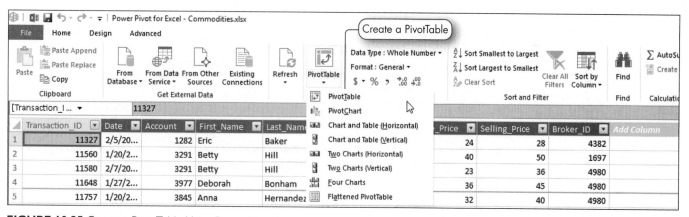

FIGURE 10.25 Create a PivotTable Using Power Pivot

Quick Concepts

4. Explain the benefit of using Power Pivot. *p. 626*
5. Explain the significance of adding data to a data model. *pp. 626–627*
6. Describe a situation in which you would define relationships within your data. *p. 628*

Hands-On Exercises

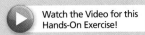

Skills covered: Load the Power Pivot Add-In • Add Data to a Data Model • Create Relationships • Create a PivotTable and PivotChart Using Power Pivot

2 Power Pivot

For your next task, you have decided to enhance your report by using Power Pivot to create a PivotTable and PivotChart. You will first load the Power Pivot add-in, add the existing data to a data model, and then create relationships.

STEP 1 ▶ LOAD THE POWER PIVOT ADD-IN

Your business computer does not currently have any of Microsoft's Power Add-Ins enabled. Your first step is to enable the Power Pivot add-in. Refer to Figure 10.26 as you complete Step 1.

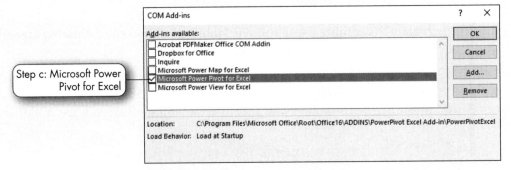

FIGURE 10.26 Enable Power Pivot Add-In

> **MAC TROUBLESHOOTING:** The Power Pivot Add-in is not available with Excel for Mac. Carefully review the following exercise and continue to the next section.

a. Open *e10h1Commodities_LastFirst* if you closed it at the end of Hands-On Exercise 1, and save it as **e10h2Commodities_LastFirst**, changing h1 to h2.

b. Click the **Insert tab**, click the **My Add-ins arrow** in the Add-ins group, and then select **Manage Other Add-ins**. Click the Manage box arrow, select **COM Add-ins** from the Manage box, and then click **Go**.

c. Select **Microsoft Power Pivot for Excel** and click **OK**.

The Power Pivot tab displays on the ribbon.

d. Save the workbook.

STEP 2 · ADD DATA TO A DATA MODEL

You want to use Power Pivot to analyze the data that was imported using Get & Transform. Because the data has already been imported, you will add the existing data to a data model. Refer to Figure 10.27 as you complete Step 2.

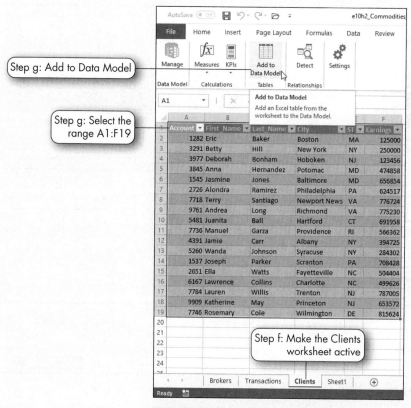

FIGURE 10.27 Add Data to a Data Model

a. Ensure the Transactions worksheet is active.

b. Select the **range A1:I70**, click the **Power Pivot tab**, and then click **Add to Data Model** in the Tables group.

The Transactions table is added to a new data model in the Power Pivot for Excel window.

c. Click the **File tab** on the Power Pivot ribbon and click **Close**.

d. Click the **Brokers worksheet.**

e. Select the **range A1:G6**, and click **Add to Data Model** in the Tables group. Click the **File tab** on the Power Pivot ribbon and click **Close**.

f. Ensure the Clients worksheet is active.

g. Select the **range A1:G6**, and click **Add to Data Model** in the Tables group. Click the **File tab** on the Power Pivot ribbon and click **Close**.

h. Save the workbook.

After adding all imported data to the data model, you will define the relationships between the transactions database table, the broker information, and client information. Refer to Figure 10.28 as you complete Step 3.

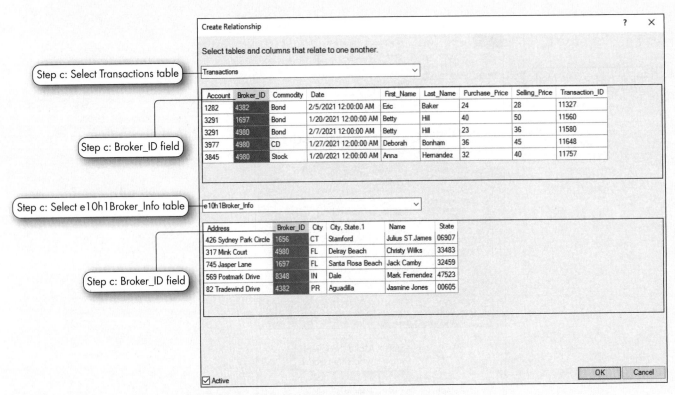

FIGURE 10.28 Create Relationships

a. Click the **Power Pivot tab**. Click **Manage** in the Data Model group, click the **Design tab**, and then click **Create Relationship** in the Relationships group.

The Create Relationship window opens.

b. Select the **Transactions table** from the first list and ensure the Account field is selected in the preview pane. Select **e10h1Client_Info_LastFirst** from the second list, ensure the Account field is selected, and then click **OK**.

You created a one-to-many relationship between the two tables using the Account field as the common field.

c. Click **Create Relationship** in the Relationships group, select **Transactions** from the first list, and then click the **Broker_ID** field in the preview pane. Select **e10h1Broker_Info _LastFirst** from the second list, ensure the Broker_ID field is selected, and then click **OK**.

You created a relationship between the two tables using the Broker_ID field as the common field.

d. Save the workbook.

STEP 4 CREATE A PIVOTTABLE USING POWER PIVOT

You want to summarize the sales of each agent in a PivotTable based on commodity. As your last step, you will use the relational data in the data model to create a PivotTable and PivotChart. Refer to Figure 10.29 as you complete Step 4.

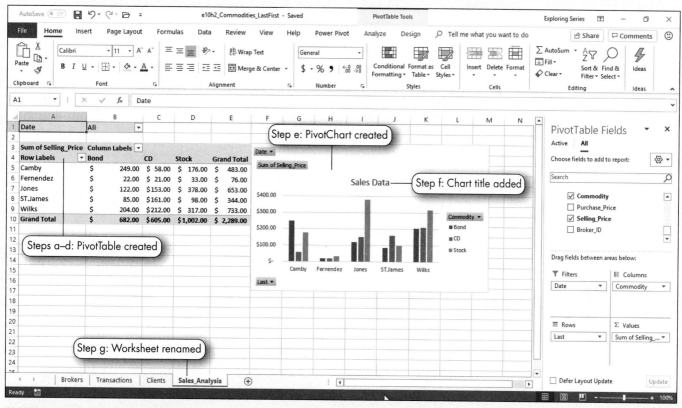

FIGURE 10.29 Create a PivotTable

a. Close the Queries & Connections pane. Click the **Home tab** in the Power Pivot for Excel window and click **PivotTable**. Click **Existing Worksheet** in the Create PivotTable dialog box, click the **Collapse icon,** and click the worksheet named **Sheet1**. Click **cell A1**, click **OK**, and click **OK** again.

You created a blank PivotTable based on the data model in the Sheet1 worksheet starting in cell A1.

b. Click the **Expand arrow** to the left of the e10h1Broker_Info_LastFirst table in the PivotTable Fields pane and drag the **Last field** to the Rows box.

You added the last names of the brokers as rows of the PivotTable to track their sales.

c. Scroll down and click the **Expand arrow** to the left of the Transactions table in the PivotTable Fields pane. Drag the **Date field** to the Filters box, and then drag the **Commodity field** to the Columns box.

You added the commodity to the columns to display the different types of commodities the brokers have traded.

d. Drag the **Selling_Price field** to the Values box, select the **range B5:E10**, and then apply **Accounting Number Format**.

You completed the PivotTable by adding the Selling_Price values and formatted the results with Accounting Number Format.

Hands-On Exercise 2   633

e. Click the **Analyze tab** and click **PivotChart** in the Tools group. Select **Clustered Column chart** in the Insert Chart dialog box and click **OK**.

You added a Clustered Column PivotChart to the worksheet.

f. Reposition the PivotChart so the upper left corner starts in cell F3. Click the **Design tab** and click **Add Chart Element**. Point to Chart Title and select **Above Chart**. Double-click the chart title and type **Sales Data**.

You added a PivotChart to visualize the data in the PivotTable graphically. Based on the PivotChart, Stocks were the most lucrative of the commodities sold for most brokers.

g. Rename the worksheet **Sales_Analysis** and click **cell A1**.

h. Save the workbook. Keep the workbook open if you plan to continue with the next Hands-On Exercise. If not, close the workbook, and exit Excel.

3D Maps

While Power Pivot can create tabular data that can be viewed from diverse angles, some may find visual representations of data more helpful to grasp large volumes of data. **Data visualization** is a method of summarizing data graphically to better understand the significance of the information. Microsoft 3D Maps is a business intelligence visualization tool that creates three-dimensional geospatial maps based on a single set or a relational set of data. These visualizations can contain layers of data and can be animated based on a time dimension.

In this section, you will learn to visualize data using 3D Maps. You will add dimensions to maps, and further segregate information using categories.

STEP 1 ▶ Using 3D Maps

Similar to Power Pivot, by default, the Power Map add-in is not enabled. Before creating a 3D Map, you must first load the add-in. As shown in Figure 10.30, to enable Power Map, click the File tab and click Options. Select Add-ins and click COM Add-ins in the Manage box. (On a Mac, Power Map is not available.)

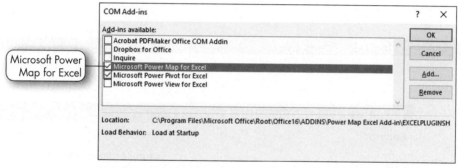

FIGURE 10.30 Load Power Map Add-in

If your data contains geographic information, it can be visualized using 3D Maps. As shown in Figure 10.31, 3D Maps can overlay your geographic data on a custom map or general world map provided by Bing. Table 10.2 details the types of geographic information that can be visualized using 3D Maps.

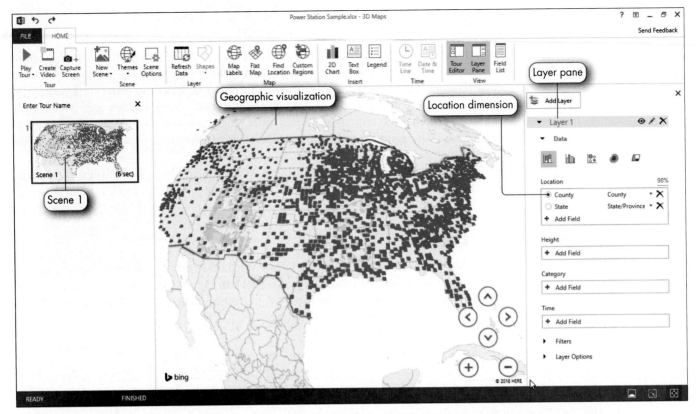

FIGURE 10.31 3D Map

TABLE 10.2	**Geographic Formats**
Format	**Example**
Latitude/Longitude	Latitude Longitude 32.312212 -86.45364
Street Address	1057 West 58th Street
City	Indianapolis
County	Hamilton County
State/Province	Indiana or IN
Zip Code/Postal Code	46038
Country/Region	United States

To create a 3D Map based on geographic information, first decide how you want to visualize the data. For example, if you want to map a flight plan, organize each stop of the flight in a table based on longitude and latitude or city and state (see Figure 10.32). Once data is organized based on geographic information, it can be visualized on a 3D Map by selecting the data and clicking 3D Maps on the Insert tab.

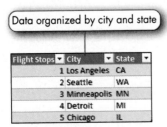

FIGURE 10.32 Geospatial Data Organization

An Excel workbook can support multiple 3D Maps; each map added to the worksheet is called a *tour*. Each tour contains scenes of geographic visualizations that are organized by layer. When a 3D Map is created, it is loaded into a default tour with a 10-second animated scene. To play a tour, click the Home tab on the 3D Maps ribbon and click Play Tour in the Tour group.

STEP 2 ▷ Add Dimensions

Visualizations are added to 3D Maps in layers of which there are four categories, known as dimensions. **Dimensions** are attributes that contribute to the visualization of data. The possible dimensions of 3D Maps are location, height, category, and time. For example, a dataset that contains warehouse information may contain locations of each warehouse, as well as total inventory and type of inventory at each site. In this example, location and inventory are dimensions. 3D Maps would use the location information as the location dimension, total inventory as the height dimension, and types of inventory as the category dimension. This would create a geographic visualization, displaying each warehouse based on inventory level. This visualization could be expanded by adding a category dimension. For example, within each warehouse, the inventory could be organized into electronics, clothing, and home goods. As shown in Figure 10.33, not only could this visually depict inventory in 3D columns, it can also be color-coded based on the category dimension.

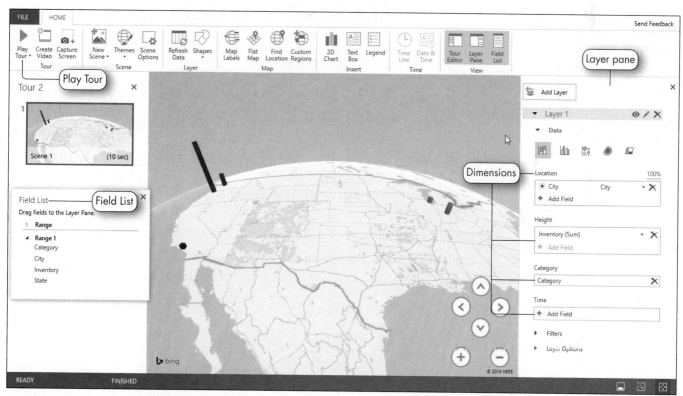

FIGURE 10.33 3D Map Dimensions

To add dimensions to a 3D Map, drag the field from the Field List to the appropriate dimension box within the layer. To add an additional layer, click Add Layer at the top of the Layer pane. Each layer contains independent dimensions that can be visualized simultaneously or revealed as part of an animated tour.

STEP 3 **Create a Tour**

As previously noted, 3D Maps are created in tours. A *tour* is a time-based animation that can display a 3D Map from different perspectives. Tours are broken down into animated segments called *scenes*. By default, a 3D Map contains one scene. Scenes can be added by clicking New Scene in the Scene group on the 3D Maps ribbon.

When a new scene is created, it copies the layer information from the previous scene by default. Similar to a PivotTable, this new scene can be edited and repositioned to display the data from a different perspective based on visual orientation or time. When a tour is played, 3D Maps displays each scene sequentially, with animated transitions as defined by the scene options (see Figure 10.34). There is no limit to the number of scenes that can be added to a tour; however, a large number of scenes will increase the workbook file size. After adding scenes to the tour, click Play Tour in the Tour group to view the animation.

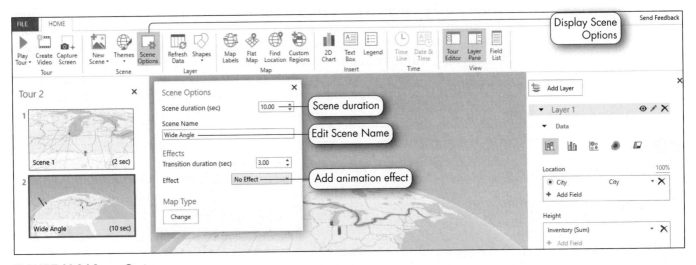

FIGURE 10.34 Scene Options

7. Describe when you would use 3D Maps (Power Map) instead of Excel's basic map feature. *p. 635*

8. Describe the significance of adding dimensions to a 3D Map. *p. 637*

9. Explain the benefit of creating a 3D Map tour. *p. 638*

Hands-On Exercises

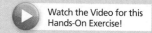
Skills covered: Create a 3D Map • Add Dimensions • Create a Tour

3 3D Maps

You want to use 3D Maps to create a 3D Map tour that displays your current client locations. You want to visualize locations and client salaries. You will first need to load the Power Map add-in and add the existing client information to the 3D Map.

STEP 1 CREATE A 3D MAP

Your business computer does not currently have the Power Map add-in enabled. Your first step is to enable the Power Map add-in. Refer to Figure 10.35 as you complete Step 1.

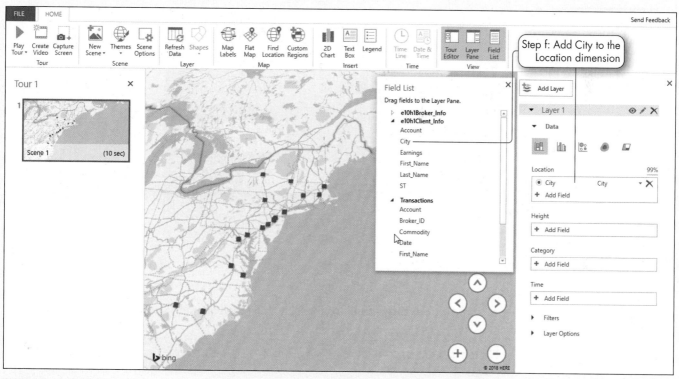

FIGURE 10.35 Create a 3D Map

> **MAC TROUBLESHOOTING:** The Power Map Add-in is not available in Excel for Mac.

---

a. Open *e10h2Commodities_LastFirst* if you closed it at the end of Hands-On Exercise 2, and save it as **e10h3Commodities_LastFirst**, changing h2 to h3.

b. Click the **Insert tab**, click the **My Add-ins arrow** in the Add-ins group, and then select **Manage Other Add-ins**. Select **COM Add-ins** from the Manage box and click **Go**.

c. Select **Microsoft Power Map for Excel** and click **OK**.

The Power Map add-in is now enabled.

d. Click the **Clients worksheet** and select the **range A1:F19**.

e. Click the **Insert tab**, click **3D Map** in the Tours group, and then select **Open 3D Maps**.

3D Maps opens with the field list displaying available data fields.

f. Drag the **City field** from the e10h1Client_Info_LastFirst Field List to the Location box in the Layer pane and ensure City is selected as the geographical data type.

STEP 2 ▸ **ADD DIMENSIONS**

You want to add earnings and account numbers as dimensions to enhance the visualizations on the 3D Map. Refer to Figure 10.36 as you complete Step 2.

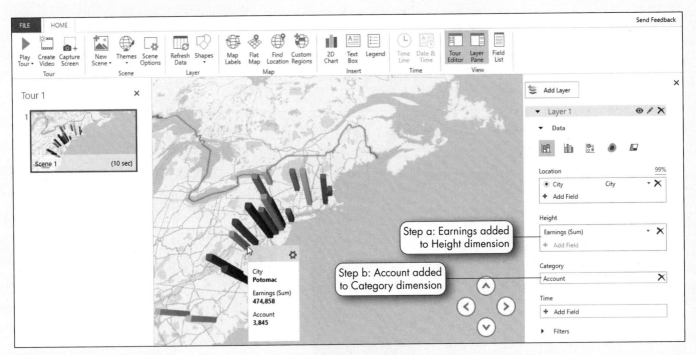

FIGURE 10.36 Add Dimensions

a. Drag the **Earnings field** from the Field List to the **Height** dimension in the Layer pane.

> **TROUBLESHOOTING:** If the field list is not displayed, click Field List in the View group on the 3D Maps ribbon.

b. Drag the **Account field** to the **Category dimension** in the Layer pane.

By adding the Account number to the category dimension, 3D Maps color codes the visualizations based on account number.

c. Close the Field List. Right-click the **Layer 1 Legend**, and click **Remove**.

STEP 3 ▸ CREATE A TOUR

After adding the dimensional visualizations to the 3D Map, you want to create a tour to better view the data from different angles. Refer to Figure 10.37 as you complete Step 3.

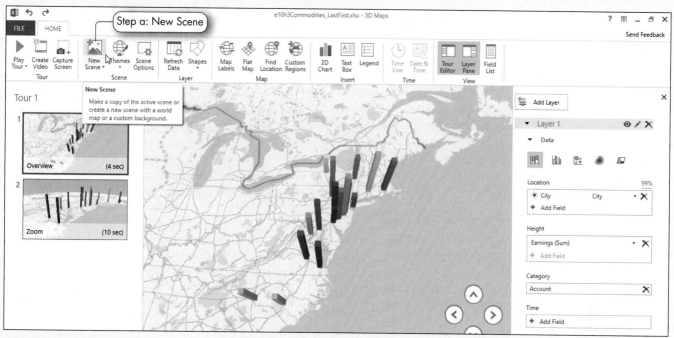

FIGURE 10.37 Create a Tour

a. Click and drag the 3D Map so Kansas is in the middle of the map area. Zoom out until the entire United States map can be viewed and click **New Scene** in the Scene group.

You added a second scene to Tour 1.

b. Click **New Scene** in the Scene group. Click **Zoom in**, **Tilt down**, and **Rotate Right** until the entire Eastern seaboard fills the map area.

> **TROUBLESHOOTING:** The 3D Map used in this exercise was designed using the screen resolution 1360 x 768. If using a different screen resolution the 3D Map may display differently from Figure 10.37. If you are not using 1360 x 768 screen resolution modify the zoom and tilt position to best match the image.

c. Click **Scene 1** in the Tour 1 pane, click **Scene options** in the Scene group, and type **Overview** in the Scene Name box.

d. Change the Scene Duration to **4.00** and the Effect to **Fly Over**. Close the Scene Options dialog box.

You changed the animation from the default time to 4 seconds and added the Fly Over animation.

e. Click **Scene 2** in the Tour 1 pane, click **Scene Options**, and type **Zoom** in the Scene Name box. Close the Scene Options dialog box.

f. Click **Play Tour** in the Tour group to check your work.

g. Press **Esc** to exit the Tour. Close 3D Maps. Save and close the file.

h. Use Windows Explorer to locate the solutions folder. Right-click the folder, click **Send To**, and select **Compressed (zipped) folder**. Rename the folder **e10h3Commodities_LastFirst**. Based on your instructor's directions, submit the compressed solutions folder.

> **TROUBLESHOOTING:** Be sure to submit the compressed solution folder and all corresponding files without changing the file names. It is important to keep all files that are linked in the final document in the solutions folder to maintain the connection when the file is opened by your instructor.

Chapter Objectives Review

After reading this chapter, you have accomplished the following objectives:

1. Import data from an external source.

- Get data from a text/CSV file: Text files contain delimiters to separate data. A tab-delimited file is a text file that uses tabs to separate data, and a comma-separated values file is a text file that uses commas to separate data. The Text Import Wizard guides you through importing data and selecting the delimiter.

- Import an Access database table or query: You can copy data from an Access table into Excel. If you want to maintain a connection to the Access table, import it using the Get & Transform tools. You can then select the table or query, how to view the data, and where to place it.

- Import data from other sources: You can import data from other sources, such as an SQL database or from a website.

- Transform data: Power Query Editor enables you to edit information from one or more data sources to specific parameters before importing the data into an application.

2. Manage queries and connections.

- Set External Data properties: External Data properties are settings that control how imported data connects to the external data source. These properties also specify how the data displays in Excel, how often the data is refreshed, and what happens if the number of rows in the data range changes based upon the current data in the external data source. Click Refresh All to refresh all connections or click the Refresh All arrow to select a specific refresh option.

- Edit query properties: When Get & Transform tools are used to import data a Query is automatically created. Query properties determine the frequency in which the data refreshes as well as a variety of advanced online analytical processing (OLAP) settings.

3. Load the Power Pivot add-in.

- Power Pivot is not loaded as part of the default installation of Excel. In order to access the add-in, it must first be loaded.

4. Add data to a data model.

- A data model enables you to integrate data from multiple sources within an Excel workbook. When using Power Pivot, multiple data sources can be combined, edited, and visualized if added to the data model.

- Create relationships with Power Pivot: Power Pivot enables you to create relationships between multiple data sources that share common fields. You can then build PivotTables based on linked data without needing to combine the data sources.

- Create a PivotTable and PivotChart using Power Pivot: Power Pivot creates PivotTables and PivotCharts that utilize multiple data sources linked through relationships with common fields.

5. Use 3D Maps.

- 3D Map (Power Map) is an Excel add-in that enables you to visualize geospatial data.

- Add dimensions: 3D Map visualizations are based on data categories called dimensions. The four dimensions are location, height, category, and time.

- Create a tour: A tour is an animation that enables you to view a 3D Map from different angles over time. Tours are comprised of scenes. There is no limit to the number of scenes in a tour and scene options can be edited to modify display time, name, and animation transition.

Key Terms Matching

Match the key terms with their definitions. Write the key term letter by the appropriate numbered definition.

a. Comma-separated values (CSV) file

b. Data model

c. Data shaping

d. Data visualization

e. Delimiter

f. Dimension

g. Embed

h. External Data properties

i. Fixed-width text file

j. Importing

k. Newline character

l. Power BI

m. Power Pivot

n. Power Query Editor

o. Refresh

p. Relationship

q. Scene

r. Tab-delimited file

s. Text file

t. Tour

1. _____ An animated segment within a Tour. **p. 638**

2. _____ An association between two related tables where both tables contain a related field of data, such as IDs. **p. 628**

3. _____ A business intelligence tool that can connect and shape data from multiple sources. **p. 616**

4. _____ A feature that enables you to integrate data from multiple sources within a workbook. **p. 626**

5. _____ A file type that uses commas to separate data into columns and a newline character to separate data into rows. **p. 612**

6. _____ A special character (such as a tab or space) that separates data. **p. 611**

7. _____ A method of importing external data into Excel but not maintaining a link to the original data source. **p. 611**

8. _____ A special character that designates the end of a line and separates data for the next line or row. **p. 612**

9. _____ A built-in add-in that offers the key functionality that is included in Excel's stock PivotTable options, plus a variety of useful features for the power user. **p. 626**

10. _____ A process that updates the linked data in an Excel workbook with the most up-to-date information. **p. 620**

11. _____ The process of inserting external data—data created or stored in another format—into the current application. **p. 610**

12. _____ The settings that control how imported data in cells connect to their source data. **p. 620**

13. _____ The process of editing information from one or more data sources to desired parameters before importing into an application. **p. 616**

14. _____ An online application suite designed to help users manage, supplement, visualize, and analyze data. **p. 626**

15. _____ A time-based animation that can display a 3D Map from different perspectives. **p. 637**

16. _____ A file type that uses tabs to separate data into columns. **p. 611**

17. _____ A data file that contains characters, such as letters, numbers, and symbols, including punctuation and spaces. **p. 611**

18. _____ A method of summarizing data visually to better understand the significance of the information. **p. 635**

19. _____ Attributes that contribute to the visualization of data. **p. 637**

20. _____ A file in which each column contains a specific number of characters. **p. 612**

Multiple Choice

1. A special character that is used to separate a text file is called a:

   (a) position holder.

   (b) delimiter.

   (c) column spacer.

   (d) start tag.

2. Which of the following file formats *cannot* be imported using Get & Transform?

   (a) Access Data Table

   (b) HTML

   (c) CSV

   (d) MP3

3. Which of the following Power BI tools is best suited for editing data before import?

   (a) Power Pivot

   (b) 3D Maps (Power Map)

   (c) Power Query Editor

   (d) PivotTables

4. In which of the following scenarios would you choose to embed versus import data?

   (a) You want to maintain connections with external files.

   (b) You want the data to update automatically when the external source is updated.

   (c) You want to reduce file size.

   (d) You do not want to save the original data sources.

5. When creating a 3D Map, what is the best way to view your data from different perspectives over time?

   (a) Add a layer

   (b) Add scenes

   (c) Add dimensions

   (d) Create a custom map

6. What tool should be used to remove fields and format data when importing?

   (a) Power Pivot

   (b) Power Query Editor

   (c) 3D Maps (Power Map)

   (d) Relationship builder

7. What Power Add-In is best for visualizing geospatial data?

   (a) Get & Transform

   (b) Power Pivot

   (c) Power View

   (d) 3D Maps (Power Map)

8. Which of the following is *not* a dimension of a 3D Map layer?

   (a) Columns

   (b) Time

   (c) Location

   (d) Height

9. Which of the following tools can be used to aggregate relational data from multiple sources?

   (a) Power Pivot

   (b) 3D Maps (Power Map)

   (c) Get & Transform

   (d) PivotTables

10. Which of the following is *not* a benefit of shaping data with the Power Query Editor?

    (a) All changes can be undone.

    (b) Data can be merged from multiple sources.

    (c) Shaped data can be added to a data model.

    (d) Shaped data does not retain links to external file sources.

Practice Exercises

1 Earline's Bakery

FROM SCRATCH You are the finance manager for Earline's bakery, a local bakery that has six stores in the greater Indianapolis area. Your stores ran a fall promotion and you would like to use Power Add-Ins in Excel to analyze the results by store. You will import data from various sources into an Excel workbook and use 3D Maps to visualize the data. Refer to Figure 10.38 as you complete this exercise.

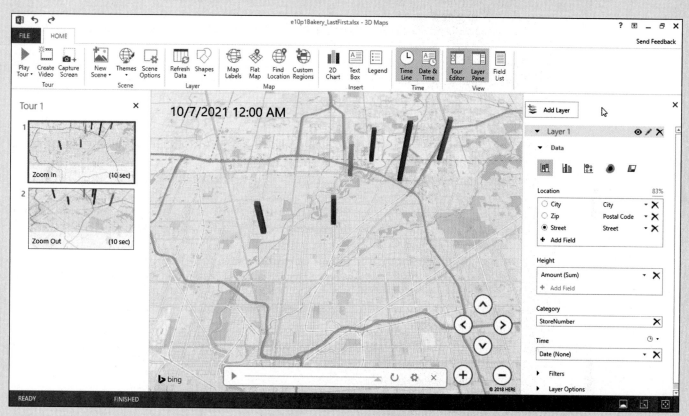

FIGURE 10.38 Earline's Bakery

MAC TROUBLESHOOTING: Excel Power Add-ins are currently unavailable for Excel for Mac.

a. Start a new blank workbook and save it as **e10p1Bakery_LastFirst**.

b. Click the **File tab**, click **Options**, and click **Add-ins**.

c. Select **COM Add-ins** in the Manage box and click **Go**.

d. Select **Microsoft Power Map for Excel** and click **OK**.

e. Minimize Excel and use File Explorer to locate the file *e10p1Bakery_Stores.txt*. Move the file to your solutions folder and rename it **e10p1Bakery_Stores_LastFirst.txt**.

f. Use File Explorer to locate the database *e10p1Bakery_Transactions.accdb*. Move the file to the your solutions folder and rename it **e10p1Bakery_Transactions_LastFirst.accdb**.

g. Maximize Excel. Click the **Data tab** and click **From Text/CSV** in the Get & Transform Data group. Browse to the file *e10p1Bakery_Stores_LastFirst.txt*, click **Import**, and click **Transform Data**.

h. Select the **State Zip column** in the Power Query Editor and click **Remove Columns** in the Manage Columns group..

i. Click **Close & Load** in the Close group.

j. Rename the worksheet **Stores**.

k. Click the **Data tab**. Click **Get Data**, select **From Database**, and then select **From Microsoft Access Database**. Browse to the file *e10p1Bakery_Transactions_LastFirst.accdb* and click **Import**. Select the **Transactions table** and click **Transform Data**.

l. Select the **Date field**. Click **Data Type** in the Transform group and select **Date**. Click **Close & Load** in the Close group and click **Close & Load**.

m. Rename the worksheet **Transactions**.

n. Click the **Data tab** and click **Relationships** in the Data Tools group. Click **New**, select **Transactions** in the Table box and **StoreNumber** in the Column (Foreign) box. Select **e10p1Bakery_Stores _LastFirst** in the Related Table box, select **StoreNumber** in the Related Column (Primary) box Click **OK** and click **Close**.

o. Click **Cell A1**, click the **Insert tab**, and then click **3D Map**. Select **Open 3D Maps**. Drag the fields **Street**, **City**, and **Zip** to the Location dimension in the Layer pane. Drag **Amount** to the Height dimension, **StoreNumber** from the Transactions table to the Category dimension, and **Date** to the Time dimension in the Layer pane.

p. Right-click the legend and select **Remove**.

q. Close the Field List and click **Zoom In** until the North East portion of the city of Indianapolis fills the map area.

r. Click **New Scene** in the Scene group. Zoom Out until the entire city outline can be viewed and click **Rotate Right** 4 times.

s. Click **Scene 1** and click **Scene Options** in the Scene group. Set the Scene duration to **4 seconds**, add the Scene Name **Zoom In**, and then add the **Fly Over Effect**. Close the Scene Options window.

t. Click **Scene 2** and click **Scene Options** in the Scene group. Set the Scene duration to **4 seconds** and add the **Fly Over Effect**. Add the Scene Name **Zoom Out** and close the Scene Options window.

u. Click **Play Tour** in the Tour group to view the animation, press **Esc**, and then close 3D Maps.

v. Right-click **Sheet 1** and select **Delete**.

w. Save and close the workbook. Use Windows Explorer to browse to your solutions folder. Ensure the following files are in the folder:

e10p1Bakery_LastFirst

e10p1Bakery_Stores_LastFirst.txt

e10p1BakeryTransactions_LastFirst.accdb

x. Right-click the folder, click **Send To**, and select **Compressed (zipped) folder**. Rename the compressed folder **e10p1Bakery_LastFirst**. Based on your instructor's directions, submit the compressed solutions file.

TROUBLESHOOTING: Be sure to submit the compressed solution folder and all corresponding files without changing the file names. It is important to keep all files that are linked in the final document in the solutions folder to maintain the connection when the file is opened by your instructor.

You own a local convenience store and you recently installed an automated movie rental kiosk. You are interested in analyzing the usage of the kiosk as well as the most popular movies. You have compiled an Access database with earning information and a CSV text file with the current inventory. You plan to use the Get & Transform tools to import the data into Excel and Power Pivot to complete the analysis. Refer to Figure 10.39 as you complete this exercise.

FIGURE 10.39 Movie Rental

MAC TROUBLESHOOTING: Excel Power Add-ins are currently unavailable for Excel for Mac.

---

a. Start a new blank workbook and save it as **e10p2MovieRentals_LastFirst**.

b. Click the **File tab**, click **Options**, and click **Add-ins**.

c. Select **COM Add-ins** in the Manage box and click **Go**.

d. Select **Microsoft Power Pivot for Excel** and click **OK**.

e. Minimize Excel and use File Explorer to locate the file *e10p2Inventory.csv*. Move the file to your solutions folder and rename it **e10p2Inventory_LastFirst.csv**.

f. Use File Explorer to locate the database *e10p2MovieRentals.accdb*. Move the file to your solutions folder and rename it **e10p2MovieRentals_LastFirst.accdb**.

g. Maximize Excel. Click the **Data tab** and click **From Text/CSV** in the Get & Transform Data group. Browse to the file *e10p2Inventory_LastFirst.csv*, click **Import**, and click **Load**.

h. Rename Sheet2 as **Inventory**.

i. Click the **Data tab**. Click **Get Data**, select **From Database**, and select **From Microsoft Access Database**. Browse to the file *e10p2MovieRentals_LastFirst.accdb* and select **Import**. Select the **Earnings query** and click **Transform Data**.

j. Ensure the Date field is selected. Click **Data Type** in the Transform group and select **Date**. Click **Close & Load** in the Close group.

k. Rename Sheet3 as **Transactions** and close the Queries & Connections pane.

l. Select the **range A1:D50**, click the **Power Pivot tab**, and click **Add to Data Model** in the Tables group.

m. Close Power Pivot for Excel and make the Inventory worksheet active. Select the **range A1:C30** and click **Add to Data Model** in the Tables group.

n. Click **PivotTable**, click **New Worksheet**, and then click **OK**.

o. Click the **Power Pivot tab**, click **Manage** in the Data Model group, and then click the **Design tab**. Click **Create Relationship** in the Relationships group. Select the **Earnings Table** in the first relationship box and click the **Serial # field**. Select the **e10p2Inventory_LastFirst table** in the second relationship box, click **Serial #**, and then click **OK**. Once the relationship is created, close the Power Pivot for Excel window.

p. Click **e10p2Inventory_LastFirst** and **Earnings** in the Pivot Table Fields pane to view the fields. Drag **Movie Title** to the Rows area and Price to the Values area.

q. Select the range **C4:C33** and apply **Accounting Number Format**.

r. Click the **Analyze tab** and click **PivotChart** in the Tools group. Select **Clustered Column Chart** and click **OK**.

s. Reposition and resize the chart so the chart spans the **range E3:L17**.

t. Rename the worksheet as **Earnings_Breakdown**.

u. Right-click **Sheet1** and select **Delete**.

v. Click the **Transactions worksheet**. Click the **Data tab**, click **Properties** in the Queries & Connections group, and click the **Query Properties** icon. Select **Refresh data when opening the file**, click **OK**, and then click **OK** again to close the External Data Properties dialog box.

w. Save and close the file. Use Windows Explorer to browse to your solutions folder. Ensure the following files are in the folder:

e10p2MovieRentals_LastFirst

e10p2Inventory_LastFirst.csv

e10p2MovieRentals_LastFirst.accdb

x. Right-click the folder, click **Send To**, and select **Compressed (zipped) folder**. Rename the compressed folder **e10p2MovieRentals_LastFirst**. Based on your instructor's directions, submit the e10p2MovieRentals_LastFirst compressed solutions file.

Mid-Level Exercises

1 Dow Jones Industrial Average

FROM SCRATCH You are an intern for Hicks Financial, a small trading company located in Toledo, Ohio. Your intern supervisor wants you to create a report that details all trades made in February using current pricing information from the Dow Jones Industrial Average. To complete the task, you will import and shape data using Get & Transform. Then you will summarize your findings using Power Pivot.

> **MAC TROUBLESHOOTING:** Excel Power Add-ins are currently unavailable for Excel for Mac.

a. Open Excel and create a new blank workbook.

b. Save the workbook as **e10m1Dow_LastFirst**.

c. Minimize Excel. Use File Explorer to locate the file *e10m1TradeInfo.csv*. Move the file to your solutions folder and rename it **e10m1TradeInfo_LastFirst.csv**.

d. Maximize Excel. Click the **Data tab** and click **From Web** in the Get & Transform Data group. Type **https://money.cnn.com/data/markets/dow** in the URL box and click **OK**. Click **Table 2** in the Navigator window and click **Transform Data**.

e. Use the Power Query Editor to remove the columns **P/E**, **Volume**, and **YTD change**. Name the query **Dow** and load the data.

f. Name the worksheet **Current_Price**.

g. Use Get & Transform tools to import and transform trade data located in the file *e10m1TradeInfo_LastFirst.csv*.

h. Use the Power Query Editor to remove the NULL value columns.

i. Load the data and rename the worksheet **Trades**.

j. Add the Dow table and the e10m1TradeInfo_LastFirst.csv table to the Data Model.

k. Use Power Pivot to create the following relationship:

Table	Field
e10m1TradeInfo_LastFirst	Company
Table	**Field**
Dow	Company

l. Create a PivotTable on a new worksheet with **Date** as a Filter, the **Company** field from the Dow table as the Rows and **Price** as the Values.

> **TROUBLESHOOTING:** Excel can Auto-Detect relational data. If a warning appears suggesting the use of the Auto-Detect feature, click the X to close and continue to the next step.

m. Create a Clustered Column PivotChart based on the PivotTable that compares the trading price of Apple and Coca-Cola stocks.

n. Add the chart title **Trading Comparison**, remove the Legend, and apply **Accounting Number Format** to the range C4:C6. Name the worksheet **Price_Comparison**.

o. Delete Sheet1.

p. Edit the connection properties to Refresh data when opening the file.

q. Save and close the workbook. Use Windows Explorer to browse to your solutions folder. Ensure the following files are in the folder:

e10m1Dow_LastFirst

e10m1TradeInfo_LastFirst.csv

r. Right-click the folder, click **Send To**, and select **Compressed (zipped) folder**. Name the compressed folder **e10m1Dow_LastFirst**. Based on your instructor's directions, submit the e10m1Dow_LastFirst compressed solutions file.

> **TROUBLESHOOTING:** Be sure to submit the compressed solution folder and all corresponding files without changing the file names. It is important to keep all files that are linked in the final document in the solutions folder to maintain the connection when the file is opened by your instructor.

2 Flight Plan

FROM SCRATCH

You are a student at the Aviation Experts flight school in New York City, and as part of your training, you are required to create a flight plan for a cross country trip. You have decided to import your destination information into Excel and use 3D Maps to create an animated tour of the cities you will fly over.

> **MAC TROUBLESHOOTING:** The Power Map Add-in is not available in Excel for Mac.

a. Open Excel and create a new blank workbook.

b. Save the workbook as **e10m2FlightPlan_LastFirst**.

c. Minimize Excel. Use File Explorer to locate the text file *e10m2FlightPlan.txt*. Move the file to the solutions folder and rename it **e10m2FlightPlan_LastFirst.txt**.

d. Maximize Excel and use the Get & Transform tools to import the text file *e10m2FlightPlan_LastFirst.txt*. Rename the worksheet **Flights**.

e. Edit the connection properties to refresh when the file is opened.

f. Insert a 3D Map that uses Latitude and Longitude as Location dimensions.

g. Zoom in until New York City fills the screen. Rename Scene1 as **New York**, set the Scene duration to **4 seconds**, and the effect **Dolly**.

h. Add a new Scene named **Chicago** and reposition the map so Chicago fills the screen.

i. Add a new Scene named **Denver** and reposition the map so Denver fills the screen.

j. Add a new Scene named **Los Angeles** and reposition the map so Los Angeles fills the screen.

k. Play the tour to preview your flight plan then exit 3D Maps.

l. Save and close the workbook. Use Windows Explorer to browse to your solutions folder. Ensure the following files are in the folder:

  e10m2FlightPlan_LastFirst

  e10m2FlightPlan_LastFirst.txt

m. Right-click the folder, click **Send To**, and select **Compressed (zipped) folder**. Name the compressed file **e10m2FlightPlan_LastFirst**. Based on your instructor's directions, submit the compressed solutions file.

> **TROUBLESHOOTING:** Be sure to submit the compressed solution folder and all corresponding files without changing the file names. It is important to keep all files that are linked in the final document in the solutions folder to maintain the connection when the file is opened by your instructor.

Running Case

New Castle County Technical Services

New Castle County Technical Services (NCCTS) provides technical support services for a number of companies in New Castle County, Delaware. Previously, you analyzed support calls for the second quarter (April, May, June). You would like to continue analyzing the data by importing a text file of customers and summarizing the relational data using Power Pivot.

a. Use File Explorer to locate the text file *e10r1NCCTS_Customers.csv*. Move the file to your solution folder and rename it **e10r1NCCTS_Customers_LastFirst.csv**.

b. Open the file *e10r1NCCTS* and save it as **e10r1NCCTS_LastFirst**.

c. Import the file *e10r1NCCTS_Customers_LastFirst.csv* and use the Power Query Editor to ensure the First Row is used as Headers.

d. Name the newly created worksheet **Customers** and add the e10rsNCCTS_Customers table to the Data Model.

e. Make the April worksheet active, convert the **range A1:H28** to a table named **April**, and add the table to the Data Model.

f. Make the May worksheet active, convert the **range A1:H31** to a table named **May**, and add the table to the Data Model.

g. Make the June worksheet active, convert the **range A1:H30** to a table named **June**, and add the table to the Data Model.

h. Create the following relationships:

Table	Column (Foreign)
Data Model Table: April	Customer ID
Table	**Column (Primary)**
e10r1NCCTS_Customers_LastFirst	Customer ID

Table	Column (Foreign)
Data Model Table: May	Customer ID
Table	**Column (Primary)**
e10r1NCCTS_Customers_LastFirst	Customer ID

Table	Column (Foreign)
Data Model Table: June	Customer ID
Table	**Column (Primary)**
e10r1NCCTS_Customers_LastFirst	Customer ID

i. Create a PivotTable with the **Customer ID** in the Rows area and **Hours Logged** from April, May, and June in the Values area.

j. Insert a Stacked Column PivotChart with the title **Hours Logged By Customer**. Reposition the PivotChart so the upper right corner is in cell F3.

k. Rename the worksheet **Hours Logged**.

l. Edit the connection properties of the e10r1NCCTS_Customers_LastFirst file to refresh the data when opening the file.

m. Save the workbook. Use Windows Explorer to browse to your solutions folder. Ensure the following files are in the folder:

e10r1NCCTS_Customers_LastFirst.csv

e10r1NCCTS_LastFirst

n. Right-click the folder, click **Send To**, and select **Compressed (zipped) folder**. Name the compressed file **e10r1NCCTS_LastFirst**. Based on your instructor's directions, submit the compressed solutions file.

> **TROUBLESHOOTING:** Be sure to submit the compressed solution folder and all corresponding files without changing the file names. It is important to keep all files that are linked in the final document in the solutions folder to maintain the connection when the file is opened by your instructor.

Disaster Recovery

Personal Book Library

You have a pre-existing Excel workbook that contains data imported from a database. The imported data's source file is e10d1MovieRentals. The file is set to refresh when opened; however, you receive the error message *[Data.Format.Error] Could not find the file 'e10d1MovieRentals.accdb'*. You have been asked to identify the cause of the error and repair the file. Locate the file e10d1MovieRentals.accdb in Windows Explorer, movie it to your solutions folder, and rename it e10d1MovieRentals_LastFirst.accdb. Open the workbook *e10d1MovieRentals* and save the file in the solutions folder as **e10d1MovieRentals_LastFirst**. Make the Transactions worksheet active, and open the Earnings table located in the e10d1MovieRentals database in the Power Query Editor. Click **Data source settings** and connect to the file *e10d1MovieRentals_LastFirst.accdb*. Refresh the data and close the Power Query Editor. Close Excel. Use Windows Explorer to browse to your solutions folder. Ensure the following files are in the folder:

e10d1MovieRentals_LastFirst

e10d1MovieRentals.accdb

Right-click the folder, click Send To, and select Compressed (zipped) folder. Rename the compressed file **e10d1MovieRentals_LastFirst**. Based on your instructor's directions, submit the compressed solutions file.

> **MAC TROUBLESHOOTING:** The Power Query Editor is unavailable in Excel for Mac.

You are the sales manager for Oxford Auto Sales, a Web-based auto dealer that specializes in online transactions. As part of your duties, you generate weekly reports that detail new customer contacts, online sales rep information, and sales. This week, you have decided to overhaul your report by updating agent contact information, importing customer data stored in a text file, implementing a PivotTable using Power Pivot, and utilizing 3D Maps to track sales.

Get and Transform Data

You plan to start creating your new report by importing the agent contact information that is stored in a CSV file and vehicle information stored in an Access Database.

1. Use File Explorer to locate the text file *e10c1Agents. csv*. Move the file to your solutions folder and rename it **e10c1Agents _LastFirst.csv**.

    Locate the database file *e10c1Vehicles.accdb*. Move the file to your solutions folder and rename it **e10c1Vehicles_LastFirst.accdb**.

    Locate the text file *e10c1Customer_Leads.txt*. Move the file to your solutions folder and rename it **e10c1Customer_Leads_LastFirst.txt**.

    Open Excel and create a new workbook; save the workbook as **e10c1AutoSales_LastFirst**.

2. Import the file *e10c1Agents_LastFirst.csv*.

3. Rename the worksheet **Agents**.

4. Import the file *Vehicles* table located in the database *e10c1Vehicles_LastFirst.accdb*.

5. Rename the worksheet **Sales**.

Transform Data

You want to import a list of customer contact information acquired through a Web information form. The data is stored as a tab delimited text file and requires data shaping before usage.

6. Load the file *e10c1Customer_Leads_LastFirst.txt* in the Power Query Editor.

7. Use the Power Query Editor to ensure the first row is used as Headers.

8. Close and load the table.

9. Rename the worksheet **Customer_Leads**.

Add Data to a Data Model

You want to use Power Pivot to summarize the relational data that has imported into Excel. First, you will add the data tables to a Data Model.

10. Load the Power Pivot Add-In.

11. Add the **Vehicles**, **e10c1Agents_LastFirst**, and **e10c1Customer_Leads_LastFirst** tables to the Data Model.

Create Relationships

After adding the imported data to the data model, you will create a relationship between the AgentID fields in the Vehicles and Agents tables.

12. Define the following relationship:

Table	Field
E10c1Agents	AgentID
Vehicles	AgentID

Create a PivotTable Using Power Pivot

After importing the data, creating a data model, and defining relationships, you will summarize the sales data in a PivotTable using Power Pivot.

13. Use Power Pivot to create a PivotTable on Sheet1 starting in **cell A1**.

14. Rename the worksheet **SalesAnalysis**.

15. Add **Last** from the e10c1Agents_LastFirst table to the Rows area and **Price** to the Values area.

16. Format the **range B2:B18** with **Accounting Number Format** with zero decimals.

17. Insert a Clustered Column Pivot Chart.

18. Add the Chart Title **Sales**.

Create a 3D Map

For your last step, you want to use 3D Maps to create a geospatial visualization of your sales data.

19. Load the Power Map add-in.

20. Create a 3D Map based on the Vehicles table in the Sales worksheet.

21. Add **City** and **State** to the Location dimension.

22. Zoom in so Los Angeles fills the entire map.

23. Edit Scene 1 by changing the name to **West Coast**, setting the Scene duration to **6 seconds**, and then setting the Effect to **Dolly**.

24. Add a new scene called **East Coast**. Zoom out and reposition the map to view the Eastern seaboard.

25. Set the Scene duration to **6 seconds** and set the Transition Effect to **Dolly**.

26. Preview the tour to test your work and close 3D Maps.

27. Edit the connection properties of e10c1Agents _LastFirst.csv, e10c1Vehicles_LastFirst.accdb, and e10c1Customer_Leads_LastFirst.txt to refresh when opening the file.

28. Save and close the file. Use Windows Explorer to browse to your solutions folder. Ensure the following files are in the folder:

e10c1AutoSales_LastFirst

e10c1Agents_LastFirst.csv

e10c1Customer_Leads_LastFirst.txt

e10c1Vehicles_LastFirst.accdb

29. Right-click the folder, click **Send To**, and select **Compressed (zipped) folder**. Rename the compressed file **e10c1AutoSales_LastFirst**. Based on your instructor's directions, submit the e10c1AutoSales_LastFirst compressed solutions file.

Excel

Additional Specialized Functions

LEARNING OUTCOME — You will manipulate data using text, database, and lookup functions.

OBJECTIVES & SKILLS: After you read this chapter, you will be able to:

CASE STUDY | Halloween Center

Halloween Center is a supercenter corporation that opens stores around the country in September and October. The stores sell high-quality costumes and accessories. In addition, each location has a haunted house that generates revenue through admissions fees. You are the regional manager over Utah, Colorado, New Mexico, and Arizona, where stores are located in 10 major cities.

You created a workbook with three worksheets. The first worksheet stores a list of manager and assistant manager information. Your first task will be to manipulate the text to make the lists easier to read. The second worksheet contains a list of gross sales by store at the end of each week. You will use advanced filtering and database functions to analyze the sales. Finally, the last worksheet contains a consolidated list of the weekly sales in an easy-to-read format. You will use lookup functions to search for and find data within the dataset.

Using Text, Database, and Lookup Functions

YanLev/Shutterstock

	A	B	C	D	E	F	G
1	Names	Last, First	Address	City	State	Zip	
2	Alice Freeman	Freeman, Alice	132 W Grand Avenue	Phoenix	AZ	85001	
3	Derek Montgomery	Montgomery, Derek	205 E Grant Road	Tucson	AZ	85705	
4	Kyle Garrett	Garrett, Kyle	1625 N Foothills Parkway	Boulder	CO	80301	
5	Jennifer Monroe	Monroe, Jennifer	931 W Colfax Avenue	Denver	CO	80204	
6	Kirby Patterson	Patterson, Kirby	160 N Main Street	Pueblo	CO	81003	
7	Marco Chavez	Chavez, Marco	567 N University Blvd	Albuquerque	NM	87196	
8	Amarante Beaufort	Beaufort, Amarante	1506 S Main Street	Las Cruces	NM	88005	
9	Arturo Soriano	Soriano, Arturo	25 N Main Street	Ogden	UT	84401	
10	Paulino Torres						
11	Eleonore Krause						

	A	B	C	D	E	F	G	H
1	FIRST	MIDDLE	LAST	COMBINED NAME	STATE MANAGER NAMES	STATE	PHONE	AREA CODE
2	JENNIFER		RAMIREZ	JENNIFER RAMIREZ	Jennifer Ramirez	NM	505.555.2528	505
3	BASIL	L.	MOMANI	BASIL L. MOMANI	Basil L. Momani	UT	801.555.8824	801
4	ALEXIS		BALDWIN	ALEXIS BALDWIN	Alexis Baldwin	CO	720.555.3368	720
5	DIMITRIUS	E.						602

Criteria Range

Store Num	City	State	Week Ending	Gross Sales		Summary Statistics		
		UT	10/31/2021			Total Sales	$	165,837
						Average Sales	$	55,279
						Highest Sales	$	70,925
						Lowest Sales	$	35,987
						Number of Stores		3

Output Range

Store Num	City	State	Week Ending	Gross Sales
150	Ogden	UT	10/31/2021	35,987
120	Orem			
101	Salt L			

	A	B	C	D	E	F	G	H	I	J	K
1	Store Num	440	Week End:	10/31/2021		Gross Sales	$ 29,615		Cell B2	=MATCH(B1,A5:A14,0)	
2	Index Num	4		7					Cell D2	=MATCH(D1,A4:G4,0)	
3									Cell G1	=INDEX(A5:G14,B2,D2)	
4	Store Num	City	10/3/2021	10/10/2021	10/17/2021	10/24/2021	10/31/2021				
5	430	Albuquerque	25,971	28,800	35,974	40,818	43,105				
6	235	Boulder	25,600	27,982	31,948	35,464	41,628				
7	215	Denver	31,640	35,785	58,925	67,945	75,900				
8	440	Las Cruces	17,500	20,645	24,105	26,000	29,615				
9	150	Ogden	12,642	20,675	25,781	30,102	35,987				
10	120	Orem	18,655	25,462	41,925	45,720	58,925				
11	310	Phoenix	27,610	31,010	34,725	37,097	40,105				
12	265	Pueblo	15,682	20,367	24,618	30,672	35,105				
13	101	Salt Lake City	25,725	31,650	55,875	73,841	70,925				
14	315	Tucson	18,765	22,417	29,648	33,417	35,975				
15											
16											
17	Store Num	430	235	215	440	150	120	310	265	101	315
18	City	Albuquerque	Boulder	Denver	Las Cruces	Ogden	Orem	Phoenix	Pueblo	Salt Lake City	Tucson
19	10/3/2021	$ 25,971	$ 25,600	$ 31,640	$ 17,500	$ 12,642	$ 18,655	$ 27,610	$ 15,682	$ 25,725	$ 18,765
20	10/10/2021	$ 28,800	$ 27,982	$ 35,785	$ 20,645	$ 20,675	$ 25,462	$ 31,010	$ 20,367	$ 31,650	$ 22,417
21	10/17/2021	$ 35,974	$ 31,948	$ 58,925	$ 24,105	$ 25,781	$ 41,925	$ 34,725	$ 24,618	$ 55,875	$ 29,648
22	10/24/2021	$ 40,818	$ 35,464	$ 67,945	$ 26,000	$ 30,102	$ 45,720	$ 37,097	$ 30,672	$ 73,841	$ 33,417
23	10/31/2021	$ 43,105	$ 41,628	$ 75,900	$ 29,615	$ 35,987	$ 58,925	$ 40,105	$ 35,105	$ 70,925	$ 35,975

FIGURE 11.1 Halloween Center

CASE STUDY | Halloween Center

Starting File	File to be Submitted
e11h1Halloween	e11h3Halloween_LastFirst

MyLab IT Grader An alternate version of this project is available as a MyLab IT Grader Assessment

Text Manipulation

When you import data from external sources or want to modify a workbook created by someone else, the data may not be structured in a way that meets your needs. For example, data that was in multiple columns in a data source might import into only one column in Excel. However, structuring data in multiple columns would facilitate sorting and filtering at deeper levels. Furthermore, external data might be in all capital letters, and you want to display the data in upper- and lowercase so that the data are easier to read. Excel contains features to help you manipulate text to fit your needs.

In this section, you will learn how to separate text stored in one column into multiple columns and use Flash Fill to fill a column of data based on a pattern of data entered. In addition, you will use some text functions to manipulate text in a worksheet.

Filling and Separating Text in Columns

Whether you use someone else's workbook or import data from external sources, it is likely that you will want to separate data into multiple columns or consolidate data into a single column to manipulate the data in a specific way. Other times, you want to create different data patterns from existing text. You can use Flash Fill and Convert Text to Columns to manipulate text in a worksheet.

STEP 1 ▸ Use Flash Fill

A dataset containing too much data in one column can be hard to read and difficult to manipulate the data. For example, a dataset where City, State, and Zip Code data are contained in one column is challenging to sort data by state abbreviations given that the sort order is determined by the first letter of data. In this case the sort order would be by City. You can use Flash Fill, an Excel command that is used for data manipulation. As a new pattern is created from existing data (such as breaking a component of data in one column into a separate column, or combining data from multiple columns into a single column), Flash Fill recognizes that pattern for the remaining rows and completes the data manipulation automatically.

In Figure 11.2, column J contains City, State, and Zip Code data for several locations. To sort the data by state, the data must be separated into its own column. To use Flash Fill to fill in state abbreviations in column K, type the first state abbreviation (GA) in cell K2, keep cell K2 as the active cell, click Fill in the Editing group on the Home tab, and then select Flash Fill. Excel detects the pattern you created in the first cell and uses data in column J to fill in just the state abbreviations in column K. Column K shows the results after using Flash Fill.

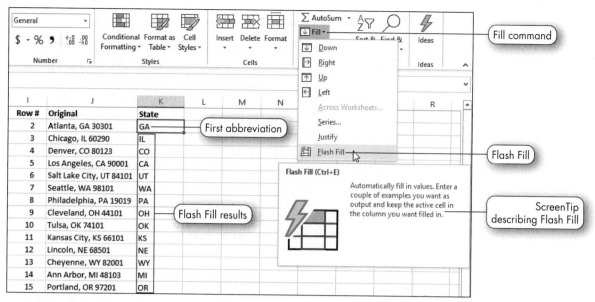

FIGURE 11.2 Results of Flash Fill

> **TIP: CREATING OTHER FILL PATTERNS**
> In addition to using Flash Fill to extract data from one column, you can use Flash Fill to create a pattern of text. For example, assume a column contains first and last names, such as *Ian Bacarella*. In an adjoining column, you can enter *Bacarella, Ian* to create a pattern of last name, comma, and first name using Flash Fill. You can also use Flash Fill with numbers and dates. For example, if one column contains dates such as 11/5/2021, you can enter 11 in an adjoining column and use Flash Fill to fill in the month numbers.

STEP 2 ## Convert Text to Columns

Although Flash Fill is very useful, it can only manipulate data one column at a time. For example, if you want to extract City, State, and Zip Code information from a single column into three separate columns, you would have to use Flash Fill three times for each data component. Another way to convert text in one column into multiple columns is using Text to Columns. Excel separates the selected range into multiple columns, breaking apart the text at delimiters such as a comma or space. Unlike Flash Fill, which preserves the original column of data, after you use Text to Columns, the original column contains the left portion of the text, and the other portions of text are separated into one or more columns to the right of the original column.

Before using Text to Columns, review the dataset to ensure the data in the column is structured identically and contains a common delimiter, such as a comma or a space in the same location throughout the column. Insert enough empty columns to the right of the column containing text to separate to avoid overwriting data. Excel does not insert new columns automatically. It separates text by placing data into adjoining columns. If cities, state abbreviations, and zip codes are stored in one column and you separate the data into three columns, you must have two empty columns: one for the state abbreviations and one for the zip codes.

To use Text to Columns, complete the following steps:

1. Select the range in a column that contains the text to separate.
2. Click the Data tab and click Text to Columns in the Data Tools group. The Convert Text to Columns Wizard displays.
3. Specify the file type (Delimited or Fixed width) and click Next.
4. Specify one or more delimiters, such as a Comma or Space, that will be used to separate the data (see Figure 11.3). Click Next.
5. Select the column data format (such as Text) or select the option to skip a column, select the destination, and then click Finish.

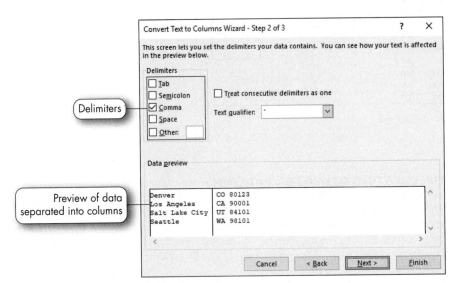

FIGURE 11.3 Convert Text to Columns – Step 2 of 3

One caution about converting text to columns is when some data do not have the same structure within the column. Figure 11.4 shows three different worksheets, with each worksheet at a different stage of converting text to columns. In the worksheet on the left side, column A contains city names, state abbreviations, and zip codes. Commas separate the cities from the state abbreviations, and spaces separate the state abbreviations from the zip codes. However, you cannot use both the comma and space in the same conversion process with this dataset because Denver and Seattle are one-word city names, and Los Angeles and Salt Lake City are multiple-word city names. Using the space delimiter would separate Los Angeles into two cells and Salt Lake City into three cells.

Therefore, you should use the Convert Text command twice. During the first process, use the comma to separate the data after the cities. In Figure 11.4, the middle worksheet shows the results. The cities remain in column A, and the state abbreviations and zip codes are separated into column B. Note that a space exists before the state abbreviations in column B because the original data had a space after the comma. After the comma delimiter was removed, the space remains.

To further separate State from Zip Code, use the space as the delimiter. In Step 3 of the Wizard, select the blank column in the *Data preview* window and click the *Do not import column (skip)* to eliminate the column of spaces before clicking Finish. In Figure 11.4, the worksheet on the right side shows the final results after using Text to Columns twice.

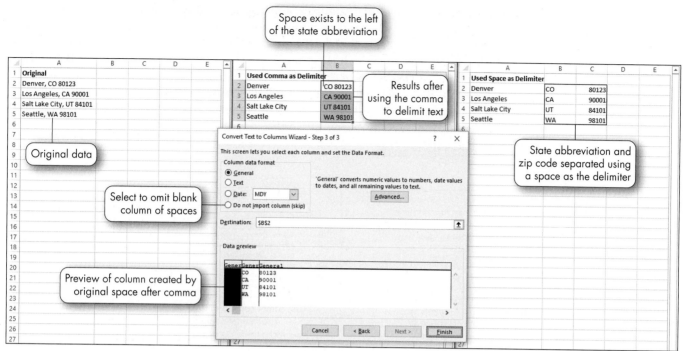

FIGURE 11.4 Text to Columns Results

Manipulating Text with Functions

Excel has 28 functions that are specifically designed to change or manipulate text. The Function Library group on the Formulas tab contains a Text Library command that, when clicked, displays a list of text functions. You can also access text functions from the Insert Function dialog box. Some of the most commonly used text functions are CONCAT, TEXTJOIN, PROPER, UPPER, LOWER, LEFT, RIGHT, and MID.

STEP 3 ▷ ## Use the **CONCAT** and **TEXTJOIN** Functions

Sometimes worksheets will contain text in multiple cells that you want to combine in one cell. For example, a worksheet could contain a column for first names (Kayla), a column for middle names (Anne), and a column for last names (Coleman). You can combine a person's complete name in one cell, such as *Kayla Anne Coleman*, or combine names with last and first names such as *Coleman, Kayla*. The second example illustrates the inclusion of a comma and space inserted between the combined last and first names. The ***CONCAT function*** joins up to 253 text strings into one text string up to 32,767 characters, but the function requires that you enter delimiter characters as needed between each text argument.

Figure 11.5 shows two examples of using the CONCAT function to concatenate data. The example on the left side displays first name and last name together in column C. The example on the right side displays the names in this sequence Last, First in column C. On the left side of Figure 11.5, the first name is in cell A2, the last name is in cell B2, and cell C2 contains =CONCAT(A2," ",B2). The comma included inside quotes inserts a space between the first and last name, such as *Elizabeth Adams*. On the right side of Figure 11.5, cell C2 contains =CONCAT(B2,", ",A2) to include the comma and space between the last and first names, such as *Adams, Elizabeth*.

=CONCAT(text1,text2)

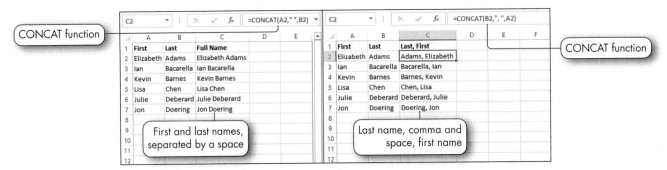

FIGURE 11.5 CONCAT Function Results

When constructing a CONCAT function, include any delimiters (such as commas and spaces) correctly within quotation marks so that you get the correct result. If you do not include delimiters between text strings, the combined text may not display as you expect.

> **TIP: OTHER WAYS TO CONCATENATE**
> Instead of using the CONCAT function to combine text, you can use the ampersand (&) operator. For example, =A4&B4 returns the same value as =CONCAT(A4,B4). The CONCAT function replaces the CONCATENATE function; however, you can still use the CONCATENATE function.

Another similar function to CONCAT is the **TEXTJOIN function** that combines up to 252 text strings to produce a result of up to 32,767 characters. The TEXTJOIN function contains an argument specifically to include the delimiter that you want to use to separate each text argument in the combined text.

=TEXTJOIN(delimiter,ignore_empty,text1,text2)

You enter the delimiter character, such as a space or comma, directly in the delimiter argument, or you can specify a cell that contains the delimiter character. For example, =TEXTJOIN(" ",A2,B2,C2) combines the contents of cells A2, B2, and C2 and separates the combined data with a space between each text being combined.

Although you can include individual cells for the text arguments, an advantage of using TEXTJOIN is that you can include a range of text cells without having to include separate arguments for a delimiter between each text string that is combined. The delimiter argument will automatically insert the delimiter between the contents of each cell being combined. For example, you can use the range A2:C2 in =TEXTJOIN(" ",A2:C2) instead of individual cells used in =TEXTJOIN(" ",A2,B2,C2) to produce the same results.

Another benefit the TEXTJOIN function has over the CONCAT function is the ignore_empty argument, which can be used to ignore empty cells when combining text. The default is set to TRUE so that empty cells are ignored in the result. In Figure 11.6, column A contains first names, column B contains middle initials, and column C contains last names. However, the middle initial cell is empty for some people. To avoid having an extra space instead of a middle name, make sure the ignore_empty is TRUE. Enter FALSE for the ignore_empty argument if you want to include the empty cell in the result.

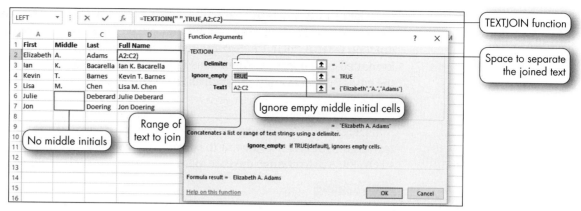

FIGURE 11.6 TEXTJOIN Function Results

TIP: INTERPRETING ERRORS

If the CONCAT or TEXTJOIN function tries to return text that contains more than 32,767 characters, it will return the #VALUE! error. If you use these functions in Excel 2016 or an older version of Excel that does not support these functions, the function will return the #NAME? error.

STEP 4 Use the **PROPER, UPPER,** and **LOWER** Functions

You obtain data from a variety of sources: workbooks distributed to you by other people, data downloaded from a server, and data copied and pasted from a table on a webpage. When you obtain data from these sources, text may display in a variety of case or capitalization styles, such as ALL CAPS, Title Case, and lowercase. Depending on your usage of data, you may need to change the case of text in a worksheet. Excel contains three functions to change the case or capitalization of text: PROPER, UPPER, and LOWER. Figure 11.7 illustrates the results of these three functions. Column A contains names in irregular capitalization style, and the other columns contain text functions to display the text differently.

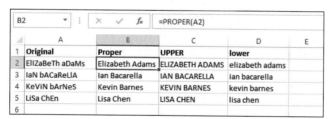

FIGURE 11.7 PROPER, UPPER, and LOWER Functions

Use the **PROPER function** to capitalize the first letter of each word in a text string, including the first letter of prepositions (such as *of*) and articles (such as *a*). The PROPER function converts all other letters to lowercase. The text argument is a text string that must be enclosed in quotation marks, a formula that returns text, or a reference to a cell that contains text that you want to partially capitalize. In Figure 11.7, cell B2 contains =PROPER(A2) to change the case to proper case, such as *Elizabeth Adams*.

=PROPER(text)

The **UPPER function** converts text strings to uppercase letters. The text argument is the text to be converted to all capitals and can be a cell reference or a text string. Use this function when a cell or range contains text in lowercase letters and you want the text to be formatted in all uppercase letters. In Figure 11.7, cell C2 contains =UPPER(A2) to change the case to uppercase letters, such as *ELIZABETH ADAMS*.

=UPPER(text)

The **LOWER function** converts all uppercase letters in a text string to lowercase. The text argument is text you want to convert to lowercase. In Figure 11.7, cell D2 contains =LOWER(A2) to change the case to lowercase letters, such as *elizabeth adams*.

=LOWER(text)

TIP: NESTED TEXT FUNCTIONS

Text functions are often used in nested functions. You can nest text functions, such as nesting the CONCAT function inside an UPPER function argument. For example, =UPPER((CONCAT (A2,", ",A3)) concatenates the contents of cells A2, a comma and a space, and the contents of cell A3. The concatenated result is then converted to uppercase.

Use the LEFT, RIGHT, and MID Functions

You can extract text from the left, right, or middle of a text string. Extracting a portion of the text is useful when you want to isolate or identify a particular text string. For example, a column contains phone numbers, such as 801-555-1234. You can use the LEFT, MID, and RIGHT text functions in three separate columns to extract the area code, the prefix, and the last four digits components from one column. These three functions include the required argument *text*, which is the cell containing the text for which you want to extract a portion of the text string. Figure 11.8 shows examples of these three functions.

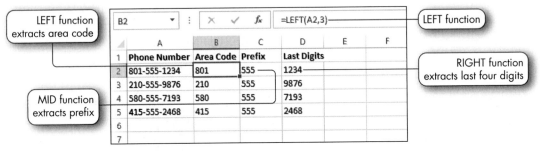

FIGURE 11.8 LEFT, RIGHT, and MID Functions

The **LEFT function** extracts the specified number of characters from the left side of a text string. For example, =LEFT(A2,3) in cell B2 extracts the first three characters from the left side of the text string stored in cell A2. The result is 801.

=LEFT(text,num_chars)

The **RIGHT function** extracts the specified number of characters from the right side of a text string. For example, =RIGHT(A2,4) in cell D2 extracts the first four characters from the right side of the text string stored in cell A2. The result is 1234.

=RIGHT(text,num_chars)

The **MID function** extracts the characters from the middle of a text string, given a starting position and length. For example, =MID(A2,5,3) in cell C2 starts at the fifth character and extracts the first three characters at that point in the text string stored in cell A2. The result is 555.

`=MID(text,start_num,num_chars)`

Use Other Text Functions

Other text functions enable you to achieve a variety of text manipulations. Table 11.1 lists a few other common text functions and their descriptions.

TABLE 11.1	Date Functions	
Function	**Description**	**Syntax**
FIND *function*	Identifies the starting position of one text string within another text string	=FIND(text_text,within_ text,*start_num*)
LEN *function*	Identifies the number of characters in a text string	=LEN(text)
SUBSTITUTE *function*	Substitutes an old text string with new text string. Instance_num specifies which occurrence of old_text you want to replace with new_text. When instance_num is specified, only that instance is changed. If you do not include instance_num, all occurrences are changed.	=SUBSTITUTE(text,old_ text,new_text,*instance_num*)
TRIM *function*	Removes leading and trailing spaces in a text string and extra spaces between words but maintains one space between words in a text string.	=TRIM(text)

TIP: TEXT FUNCTIONS VERSUS FLASH FILL

For many situations, you can use Flash Fill to accomplish the same result as text functions. Both Flash Fill and text functions can be used within a dataset on the same worksheet. However, text functions are required when manipulating text stored in other locations on the worksheet outside of the dataset or on another worksheet.

Quick Concepts

1. Describe the difference between the Text to Columns and Flash Fill capabilities. *p. 659*

2. Describe the benefits of using the TEXTJOIN function over the CONCAT function. *p. 662*

3. Explain the difference among the PROPER, UPPER, and LOWER functions. *p. 663*

Hands-On Exercises

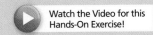
Skills covered: Use Flash Fill • Convert Text to Columns • Use the TEXTJOIN Function • Use the PROPER Function • Use the LEFT Function

1 Text Manipulation

After obtaining a workbook containing information about individual store managers and the state managers for Halloween Center, you want to manipulate the text within the worksheet. You want to make the data easier to access and display in multiple formats for future use.

STEP 1 USE FLASH FILL

The first column contains first and last names of the store managers. To facilitate future sorting by last name, you want to display last names and then first names in the second column. You will enter the text pattern for the first store manager and the use Flash Fill to fill in the rest of the text. Refer to Figure 11.9 as you complete Step 1.

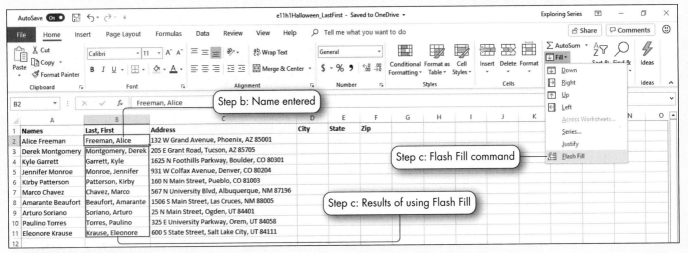

FIGURE 11.9 Flash Fill Names

a. Open *e11h1Halloween* and save it as **e11h1Halloween_LastFirst**.

> **TROUBLESHOOTING:** If you make any major mistakes in this exercise, you can close the file, open *e11h1Halloween* again, and then start this exercise over.

b. Make sure that the Store Managers worksheet is active. Click **cell B2**, type **Freeman, Alice** and then press **Ctrl+Enter**.

You entered the last name, followed by the first name to set the pattern.

c. Click **Fill** in the Editing group and select **Flash Fill**. Save the workbook.

Excel identified the text pattern you entered in cell B2 based on the data in cell A2 and used that to fill in the rest of the names in column B.

STEP 2 **CONVERT TEXT TO COLUMNS**

Currently, the Store Managers worksheet contains the complete addresses in the third column. At some point, you may want to sort the addresses by city or state. However, the dataset cannot be sorted easily in its current state. Therefore, you will separate the street addresses, cities, states, and postal codes into separate columns. You will separate the addresses using Text to Columns. Refer to Figure 11.10 as you complete Step 2.

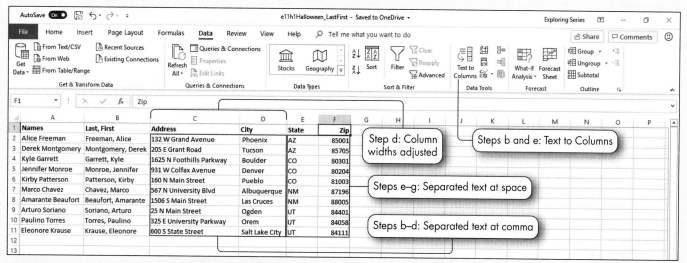

FIGURE 11.10 Address Data Separated into Columns

a. Select the **range C2:C11**.

b. Click the **Data tab** and click **Text to Columns** in the Data Tools group.

The Convert Text to Columns Wizard dialog box opens so that you can select the file type. The default is Delimited.

c. Ensure Delimited is selected and click **Next**.

Commas separate the addresses, cities, and states.

d. Click the **Comma check box** to select it, deselect any other check boxes, click **Next**, and then click **Finish**. Change the width of column C to **25**. Change the width of column D to **13**.

Excel separated the addresses into three columns: street addresses in the original address column, cities in column D, and state abbreviations and zip codes in column E. Now you want to separate the state abbreviations and zip codes.

e. Select the **range E2:E11**, click the **Data tab**, and then click **Text to Columns** in the Data Tools group.

f. Ensure Delimited is selected, click **Next**, click the **Comma check box** to deselect it, click the **Space check box** to select it.

The Data preview window shows a blank column created by the space after the original comma. You will omit the blank column when converting the text to columns.

g. Click **Next**, click **Do not import column (skip)** option to select it, and then click **Finish**. Click **cell F1** and apply **Align Right**. Save the workbook.

You excluded the blank column. Excel separates the cities and zip codes into two columns. You applied Align Right for the label in cell F1 to align over the Zip Codes.

> **TROUBLESHOOTING:** If a blank column is inserted, click Undo, repeat Steps a–g and make sure you select *Do not import column (skip)*.

The State Managers sheet contains a list of the four state managers. The first column contains first names, the second column contains middle initials for some managers, and the third column contains last names. You will use the TEXTJOIN function to combine the names into one column. Refer to Figure 11.11 as you complete Step 3.

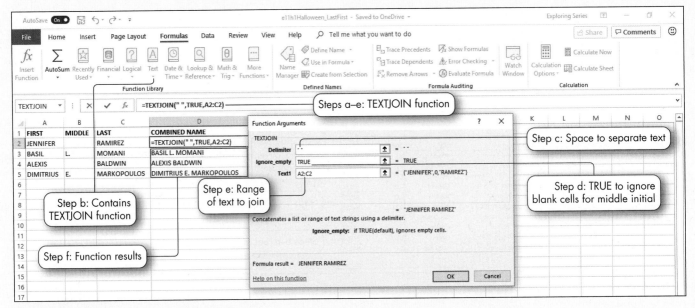

FIGURE 11.11 Names Combined with TEXTJOIN

a. Click the **State Managers sheet tab** and click **cell D2**.

You want to display the managers' full names in the COMBINED NAME column.

b. Click the **Formulas tab**, click **Text** in the Function Library group, scroll through the list, and then select **TEXTJOIN**.

The Function Arguments dialog box opens so that you can enter the arguments for the TEXTJOIN function.

c. Press **Spacebar** in the Delimiter box.

When you combine the first name, middle initial, and last name, you want to separate the text with a space. When you press Spacebar within the Delimiter box, Excel will add the quotation marks automatically when you press Tab or click OK.

d. Press **Tab** and type **TRUE** in the Ignore_empty box.

Column B contains middle initials for two managers; however, middle initials are not listed for the other two managers. Therefore, you need to ignore the blank cells to avoid inserting extra space delimiters when combining the text.

e. Press **Tab**, select the **range A2:C2** to enter it in the Text1 box, and then click **OK**.

Excel combined the first and last names; however, it ignored cell B2 because it is empty.

f. Double-click the **cell D2 fill handle** to copy the function to the **range D3:D5**. Save the workbook.

To improve the readability of the managers' names, you will use the PROPER function to convert the text to upper and lowercase. In addition, you will use the LEFT function to extract the area code from the phone numbers. Refer to Figure 11.12 as you complete Step 4.

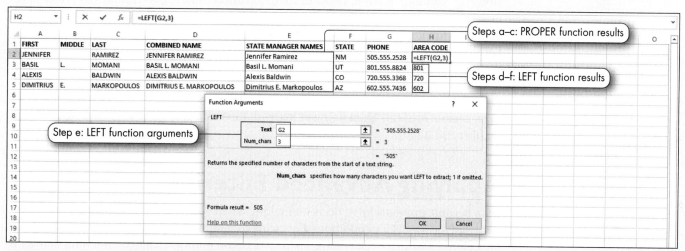

FIGURE 11.12 List after Using the PROPER and LEFT Functions

a. Click **cell E2**, click **Text** in the Function Library group, and then select **PROPER**.

The Function Arguments dialog box opens so that you can enter the arguments for the PROPER function.

b. Click **cell D2** to enter D2 in the Text argument and click **OK**.

Excel converts the text in cell D2 to proper case so that only the first letter of each word is capitalized.

c. Double-click the **cell E2 fill handle** to copy the function to the **range E3:E5**.

d. Click **cell H2**, click **Text** in the Function Library group, and then select **LEFT**.

The Function Arguments dialog box opens so that you can enter the arguments for the LEFT function.

e. Select **cell G2** to enter G2 in the Text box, press **Tab**, type **3** in the Num_chars box, and then click **OK**.

Excel extracts the first three characters (the area code) from the phone number in cell G2.

f. Double-click the **cell H2 fill handle** to copy the function to the **range H3:H5**.

g. Save the workbook. Keep the workbook open if you plan to continue with the next Hands-On Exercise. If not, close the workbook and exit Excel.

Database Filtering and Functions

Databases store and manipulate data, such as inventory details about automobiles at a dealership or financial transaction details for your credit card. You have some experience in using Excel tables to perform basic database tasks, such as sorting and filtering data. However, you may want to perform more advanced filtering techniques to preserve the original dataset and display filtered results in another location of the worksheet. In addition, you can use database functions to calculate general statistics for filtered data. For example, after you filter a dataset to show sales data for the week ending October 3, you can use database functions to calculate the total sales for that week only.

In this section, you will learn how to use advanced filtering techniques and insert database functions. Specifically, you will define a criteria range and extract data that meet certain criteria. Then you will insert database functions to calculate results based on filtered data.

Applying Advanced Filtering

Data become more useful in decision making when you reduce the records to a subset of data that meets specific conditions. For example, a manager might want to identify records for Colorado for the week ending 10/3/2021. The manager can use the filter arrows to filter the table data by job title, salary, location, and date, and Excel will filter the original dataset by hiding records that do not meet the conditions. Sometimes, however, it may be important to keep the original dataset visible and create a copy of only those records that meet these conditions in another location of the worksheet. To do so, the manager can use advanced filtering techniques.

STEP 1 ▶ Define the Criteria and Output Ranges

Before you apply advanced filtering techniques, you must define a criteria range. A *criteria range* is a range of two or more adjacent cells that specifies the conditions used to control the results of a filter. The criteria row is often located below the dataset or on another worksheet. A criteria range must contain at least two rows and one column. The first row contains the column labels as they display in the dataset, and the second row contains the conditions (e.g., values) for filtering the dataset. The *output range* is a range of cells that contains the list of records from a dataset that meets the conditions specified in the criteria range. Figure 11.13 shows the original dataset, criteria range, and the output range in the same worksheet.

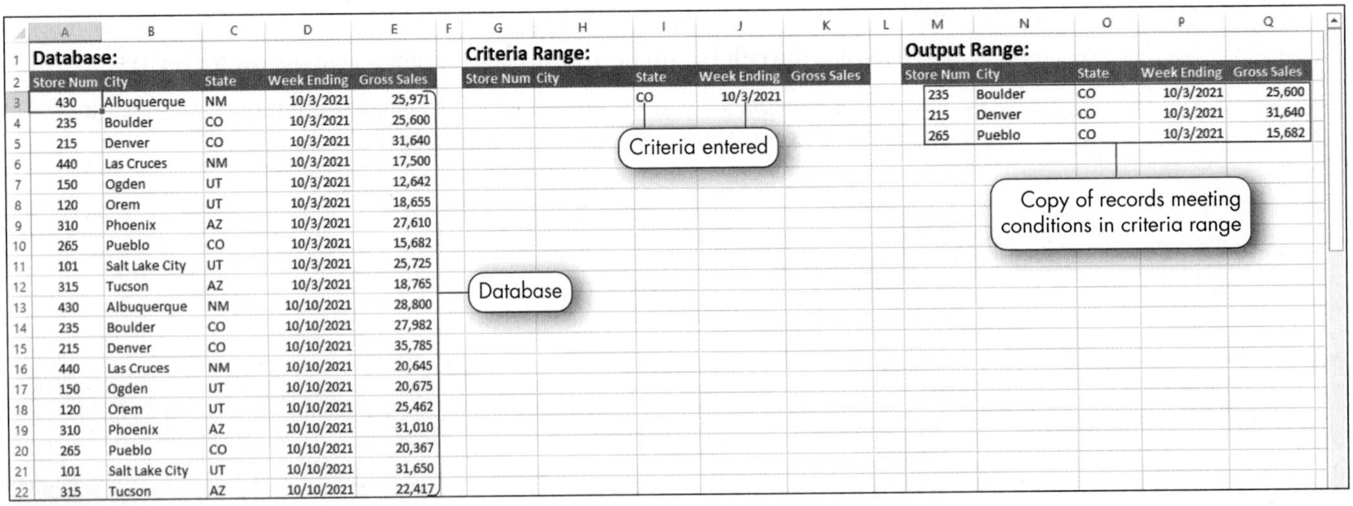

FIGURE 11.13 Data, Criteria Range, and Output Range

In Figure 11.13, the criteria range is located in the range G2:K3. When you want to specify one or more conditions that must be met, you enter the conditions on one row. In this case, the conditions are located immediately below their respective labels: CO below State and 10/3/2021 below Week Ending. Each row of conditions sets an AND condition; that is, both conditions (state abbreviation and date) must be met.

> **TIP: CRITERIA RANGE**
> In Figure 11.13, the criteria range could be defined as I2:J3 because those cells contain the column heading and criterion. However, it is a good practice to include all of the column headings in the criteria range so that you can change criteria on row 3 without having to edit the criteria range when you perform the advanced filter.

By default, Excel looks for an exact match. For example, the State column in the database contains two-letter state abbreviations, such as CO. You must enter the criteria exactly as it is contained in the dataset. If you enter Colorado in the criteria range, Excel would not find a match, and no records would display in the Output range.

If you want to avoid an exact match for values, enter relational operators. For example, entering <10/3/2021 sets the condition for weeks ending before 10/3/2021. You can use <, >, <=, >=, and <> relational operators, similar to using relational operators in the logical_test argument of an IF function.

The output range M2:Q5 displays a copy of only the records that meet both conditions. Therefore, only records for CO for the week ending 10/3/2021 are included. The records for other states for the week ending 10/3/2021 are excluded. The other weeks for CO are also excluded.

You can set an OR condition in the criteria range. For example, you want to display (a) records for CO where gross sales were greater than $50,000 or (b) for UT where gross sales were greater than $50,000. Figure 11.14 shows the conditions in the criteria range G2:K4. Notice that this criteria range contains three rows: column labels on the first row, the first set of conditions on the second row, and the second set of conditions on the third row. Recall that each row of conditions sets an AND condition. Each additional row sets an OR condition.

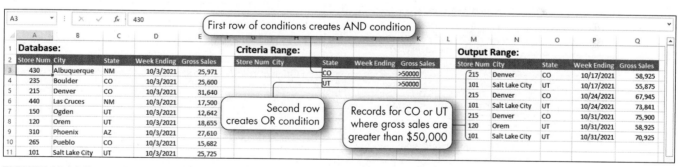

FIGURE 11.14 Criteria Range with AND and OR Conditions

> **TIP: DISPLAYING EMPTY AND NONEMPTY FIELDS**
> Using equal (=) and not equal (<>) symbols with the criteria values selects records with empty and nonempty fields, respectively. An equal with nothing after it will return all records with no entry in the designated column. An unequal (<>) with nothing after it will select all records with an entry in the column. An empty cell in the criteria range returns every record in the list.

STEP 2 ▶ **Apply an Advanced Filter**

After you create the criteria and output ranges, you are ready to apply the advanced filter using the Advanced Filter dialog box. This dialog box enables you to filter the table in place or copy the selected records to another area in the worksheet, specify the list range, specify the criteria range, or display unique records only.

To apply the advanced filter, complete the following steps:

1. Click a cell in the dataset if the dataset, criteria range, and output range are on the same worksheet. If the criteria and output ranges are on a different sheet from the dataset, click within the criteria range.
2. Click the Data tab and click Advanced in the Sort & Filter group.
3. Click the action:
   - *Filter the list, in-place* to filter the range by hiding rows that do not match your criteria.
   - *Copy to another location* if you want to copy the rows that match your criteria instead of filtering the original dataset.
4. Ensure the List range displays the range containing the original dataset, including the column headings. If the criteria and output ranges are on a separate sheet from the dataset, click the sheet containing the dataset and select the dataset to enter the range.
5. Enter the criteria range, including the criteria labels, in the Criteria range box.
6. Specify the *Copy to range* if you selected *Copy to another location* in Step 3. Enter only the starting row. Excel will fill in the rows below the column labels with the records that meet the conditions you set. Make sure the *Copy to range* contains sufficient empty rows to accommodate the copied records. If the worksheet does not contain enough empty rows below the column labels in the output range, Excel will replace existing data with the copied records. Click OK.

Figure 11.15 shows the Advanced Filter dialog box with settings to produce the advanced filter shown in Figure 11.14. The List range box contains all the Database data including the headings in row 2. The Criteria range includes both rows of criteria plus the header row. The Copy to box contains cell references to the header row of the output range area.

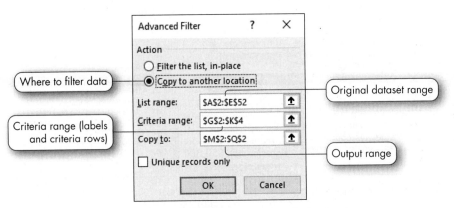

FIGURE 11.15 Advanced Filter Dialog Box

TIP: AUTO RANGE NAME
When you use the Advanced Filter dialog box, Excel assigns the range name Criteria to the criteria range and Extract to the output range. If you enter the criteria range in a database function, Excel will change the exact range to Criteria in the database function argument.

Manipulating Data with Database Functions

Previously, you used statistical functions such as SUMIF and SUMIFS to perform calculations based on conditions. Although you can use those functions on datasets, the **database functions** analyze data for selected records in a dataset using the defined criteria range to set conditions for records in a dataset. Database functions are similar to statistical functions (SUM, AVERAGE, MAX, MIN, COUNT) except that database functions restrict the results to data that meets specific criteria. Data not meeting the specified criteria are filtered out. All database functions use a criteria range that defines the conditions for filtering the data to be used in the calculations. Database functions have three arguments: database, field, and criteria.

- **Database.** The database argument is the entire dataset, including column labels and all data, on which the function operates. The database reference may be represented by a range name. In Figure 11.16, the database argument is A2:E52.

- **Field.** The field argument is the column that contains the values operated on by the function. You can enter either the name of the column label in quotation marks, such as "Gross Sales" or the number that represents the location of that column within the table. For example, if the Gross Sales column is the fifth column in the table, you can enter a 5 for the field argument. You can also enter a cell reference containing the column label, for example, E2, as shown in Figure 11.16.

- **Criteria.** The criteria argument defines the conditions to be met by the function. This range must contain at least one column label and a cell below the label that specifies the condition. The criteria argument may include more than one column with conditions for each column label, indicated by a range such as G2:K3 or a range name. In Figure 11.16, the criteria range specifies 10/3/2021 as the Week Ending condition. Although the date is the only criterion, you use the entire criteria range so that you can change or add criteria on row 3 without having to change the criteria range in the function.

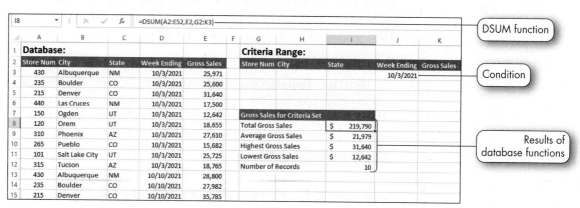

FIGURE 11.16 Database Functions

To insert a database function, complete the following steps:

1. Click Insert Function in the Function Library group or click Insert Function between the Name Box and Formula Bar to open the Insert Function dialog box.
2. Click the *Or select a category* arrow and select Database.
3. Choose the database function in the *Select a function* list and click OK.
4. Enter the Database, Field, and Criteria arguments in the Function Arguments dialog box and click OK.

STEP 3 Use the DSUM and DAVERAGE Functions

In Figure 11.16, a criteria range is used in the range G2:K3 to filter results of the weekly sales to those sales occurring in the week ending 10/3/2021. Database functions are then used in the range I8:I12 to calculate summary statistics for the records meeting the criteria. The **DSUM function** is a database function that adds the values in a column that match conditions specified in a criteria range. In Figure 11.16, cell I8 contains =DSUM(A2:E52,E2,G2:K3) to calculate the total gross sales for the week ending 10/3/2021. The total gross sales are $219,790.

=DSUM(database,field,criteria)

The **DAVERAGE function** is a database function that determines the arithmetic mean, or average, of values in a column that match conditions specified in a criteria range. In Figure 11.16, cell I9 contains =DAVERAGE(A2:E52,E2,G2:K3) to calculate the average gross sales for the week ending 10/3/2021. The average gross sales are $21,979.

=DAVERAGE(database,field,criteria)

STEP 4 Use the DMAX and DMIN Functions

The **DMAX function** is a database function that identifies the highest value in a column that matches specified conditions in a criteria range. In Figure 11.16, cell I10 contains =DMAX(A2:E52,E2,G2:K3) to calculate the highest gross sales for the week ending 10/3/2021. The highest gross sales are $31,640.

=DMAX(database,field,criteria)

The **DMIN function** is a database function that identifies the lowest value in a column that matches specified conditions in a criteria range. In Figure 11.16, cell I11 contains =DMIN(A2:E52,E2,G2:K3) to calculate the lowest gross sales for the week ending 10/3/2021. The lowest gross sales are $12,642.

=DMIN(database,field,criteria)

Use the DCOUNT and DCOUNTA Functions

The **DCOUNT function** is a database function that counts the cells that contain numbers in a column that match specified conditions in a criteria range. In Figure 11.16, cell I12 contains =DCOUNT(A2:E52,E2,G2:K3) to count the number of records for the week ending 10/3/2021, which is 10. However, if one of the records is missing a value, DCOUNT excludes that record from being counted. If after completing the DCOUNT, you decide you want to change the match conditions, you can do so by altering the information entered in the criteria area. To count records containing an empty cell or non-numeric data, use DCOUNTA instead.

=DCOUNT(database,field,criteria)

=DCOUNTA(database,field,criteria)

Use the DGET Function

The **DGET function** is a database function that extracts a single value from a field or column within a dataset that matches specified conditions. Using the dataset in Figure 11.16 as an example, if the criteria range specified store 235 for the week ending 10/3/2021, the DGET function would return $25,600 for the Gross Sales.

Note that the DGET function can return only one result. If the criteria range did not include the week ending criteria and only included store 235, the function would return #NUM because the dataset contains multiple records that meet the condition for store 235. Usually, you need to specify two or more conditions to obtain a single result. On the other hand, if no records match the condition, the DGET function returns #VALUE!

=DGET(database,field,criteria)

TIP: ADDITIONAL DATABASE FUNCTIONS

Excel contains additional database functions, such as DSTDEV to calculate the sample population standard deviation for values in a column and DVAR to estimate the sample population variance for values in a column when specified conditions are met.

Quick Concepts

4. Explain why you would use advanced filtering instead of basic filtering. **p. 670**

5. Describe the benefits of using database functions. **p. 673**

6. Describe the purpose of the Field argument in a database function. **p. 673**

Hands-On Exercises

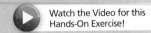

Skills covered: Define the Criteria and Output Ranges • Apply an Advanced Filter • Use the DSUM Function • Use the DAVERAGE Function • Use DMIN Function • Use the DMAX Function • Use the DCOUNT Function • Use the DGET Function

2 Database Filtering and Functions

You want to set specific criteria to analyze the gross sales for Halloween Center. In addition, you want to calculate summary statistics based on the filtered results.

STEP 1 DEFINE THE CRITERIA AND OUTPUT RANGES

Before filtering data to meet conditions, you will set up the criteria and output ranges. You will create these ranges by copying the original column labels for the database and pasting the labels in other areas of the worksheet. Refer to Figure 11.17 as you complete Step 1.

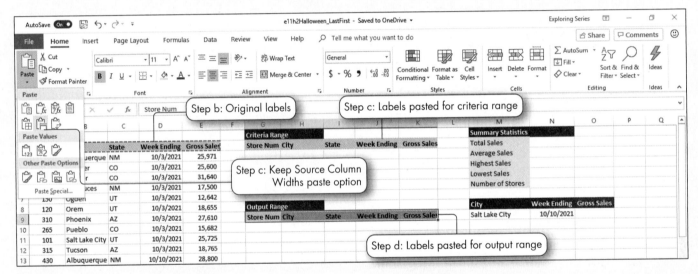

FIGURE 11.17 Criteria and Output Ranges

a. Open *e11h1Halloween_LastFirst* if you closed it at the end of Hands-On Exercise 1, and save it as **e11h2Halloween_LastFirst**, changing h1 to h2. Click the **Database sheet tab**.

b. Select the **range A2:E2** and click **Copy** in the Clipboard group on the Home tab.

You copied the range containing the column labels.

c. Click **cell G2**, click the **Paste arrow** in the Clipboard group on the Home tab, and then select **Keep Source Column Widths**.

> **TROUBLESHOOTING:** If you click Paste, the data pastes in the cells without copying the column widths of the original data. If this happens, click Undo and repeat Steps a–c, ensuring you select the Keep Source Column Widths paste option.

You pasted the range containing the column labels for the criteria range.

d. Click **cell G9**, click **Paste**, and then press **Esc**. Save the workbook.

You pasted another copy of the column labels for the output range in cells G9:K9.

You are ready to enter conditions in the criteria range. You want to display records for Utah stores for the week ending 10/31/2021. Refer to Figure 11.18 as you complete Step 2.

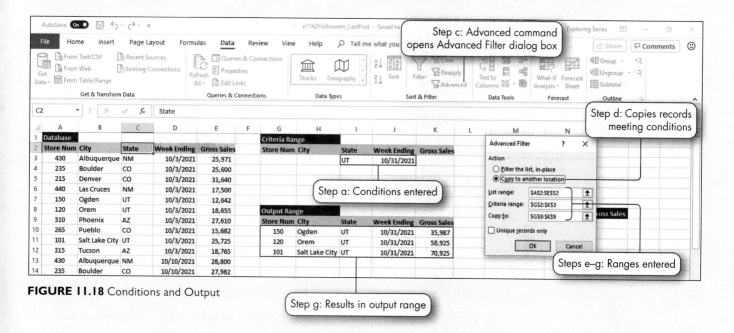

FIGURE 11.18 Conditions and Output

a. Type **UT** in **cell I3** and type **10/31/2021** in **cell J3**.

You entered the conditions on the first row below the labels in the criteria range. UT exactly matches the state data in the dataset. You create an AND condition so that sales from UT in the week ending 10/31/2021 display.

b. Click **cell C2**.

c. Click the **Data tab** and click **Advanced** in the Sort & Filter group.

The Advanced Filter dialog box opens so that you can specify the desired filter action, the list, the criteria range, and other details.

d. Click **Copy to another location**.

This action will copy the records that meet the conditions to a new location instead of filtering the original dataset.

e. Ensure that the List range box contains $A$2:$E$52.

This range contains the original dataset. The List range box may display the sheet name along with the range, such as 'Database'!$A$2:$E$52.

f. Click in the **Criteria range box** and select the **range G2:K3**.

You selected the labels and the row containing the conditions for the criteria range. The Criteria range box may display the sheet name along with the range, such as 'Database'!$G$2:$K$3.

g. Click in the **Copy to box**, select the **range G9:K9**, and then click **OK**. Save the workbook.

Make sure you select only the labels for the output range. The Copy to box may display the sheet name along with the range, such as 'Database'!$G$9:$K$9. Excel copies the records that meet the condition below the output range labels.

Now you want to calculate summary statistics for the Utah stores for the week ending 10/31/2021. You will enter database functions to calculate total gross sales and average gross sales for that week. Refer to Figure 11.19 as you complete Step 3.

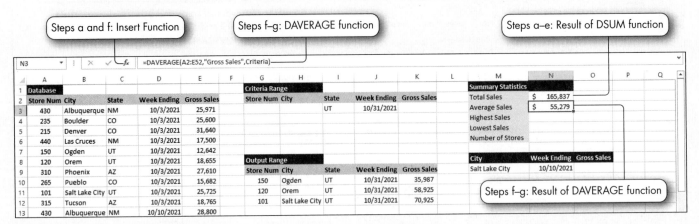

FIGURE 11.19 Total and Average Gross Sales

a. Click **cell N2** and click **Insert Function** between the Name Box and the Formula Bar.

The Insert Function dialog box opens so that you can select a function category and function.

b. Click the **Or select a category arrow**, select **Database**, scroll through the *Select a function* list, scroll through the list, select **DSUM**, and then click **OK**.

The Function Arguments dialog box opens so that you can specify the arguments for the DSUM function.

c. Select **A2:E52** to enter the range in the Database box and press **Tab**.

The Database argument must include the column labels and original dataset.

d. Type **Gross Sales** in the Field box and press **Tab**.

Excel enters the quotation marks around Gross Sales for you. Alternatively, you can enter 5 to represent the Gross Sales column position in the dataset.

> **TROUBLESHOOTING:** If you type the function instead of using the dialog box, make sure you type the double quotation marks (") around text. Otherwise, Excel will display an error message.

e. Select the **range G2:K3** to enter in the Criteria box and click **OK**.

The Insert Function dialog box may display the range name Criteria instead of G2:K3 and #VALUE on the right side of the Criteria box. However, the function result is correct. For the week ending 10/31/2021, the total gross sales for Utah stores is $165,837.

f. Click **cell N3**, click **Insert Function**, make sure DAVERAGE is selected, and then click **OK**.

In the Insert Function dialog box, the Database category was active, and DAVERAGE was selected. The Function Arguments dialog box opens.

g. Select the **range A2:E52** to enter the range in the Database box, type **Gross Sales** in the Field box, select the **range G2:K3** in the Criteria box, and then click **OK**. Save the workbook.

The average gross sales for Utah stores is $55,279.

You want to identify the highest and lowest gross sales for Utah stores for the week ending in 10/31/2021. In addition, you want to count the records to ensure all three stores are being included in the summary. Finally, you want to display the gross sales for Salt Lake City for the week ending 10/3/2021. Refer to Figure 11.20 as you complete Step 4.

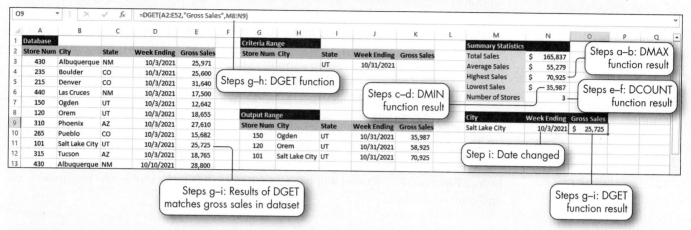

FIGURE 11.20 Results for DMAX, DMIN, DCOUNT, and DGET Functions

a. Click **cell N4**, click **Insert Function**, select **DMAX** in the *Select a function* list, and then click **OK**.

The Function Arguments dialog box opens so that you can specify the arguments for the DMAX function.

b. Select the **range A2:E52** to enter it in the Database box, type **Gross Sales** in the Field box, select the **range G2:K3** to enter it in the Criteria box, and then click **OK**.

The highest sales for Utah stores for the week ending 10/31/2021 is $70,925. Compare this to the gross sales in the range K10:K12 to verify the accuracy.

c. Click **cell N5**, click **Insert Function**, select **DMIN** in the *Select a function* list, and then click **OK**.

d. Select the **range A2:E52** to enter it in the Database box, type **Gross Sales** in the Field box, select the **range G2:K3** to enter it in the Criteria box, and then click **OK**.

The lowest sales for Utah stores for the week ending 10/31/2021 is $35,987. Compare this to the gross sales in the range K10:K12 to verify the accuracy.

e. Click **cell N6**, click **Insert Function**, select **DCOUNT** in the *Select a function* list, and then click **OK**.

f. Type **A2:E52** in the Database box, type **Gross Sales** in the Field box, type **G2:K3** in the Criteria box, and then click **OK**.

The number of Utah stores with data for the week ending 10/31/2021 is three. Compare this to the number of records in the output range G9:K12 to verify the accuracy.

g. Click **cell O9**, click **Insert Function**, select **DGET** in the *Select a function* list, and then click **OK**.

h. Type **A2:E52** in the Database box, type **Gross Sales** in the Field box, select the **range M8:N9** to enter it in the Criteria box, and then click **OK**.

The gross sales for the Salt Lake City store for the week ending 10/10/2021 are $31,650.

i. Click **cell N9**, type **10/3/2021**, and then press **Enter**. Click **cell O9**.

When you change the criteria, the result of the database function changes. Using 10/3/2021 as the criterion, the gross sales for the Salt Lake City store for the week ending 10/3/2021 are $25,725.

j. Save the workbook. Keep the workbook open if you plan to continue with the next Hands-On Exercise. If not, close the workbook and exit Excel.

Lookup Functions

Previously, you used the VLOOKUP and HLOOKUP functions to look up a value, compare it to a lookup table, and then return a result from the lookup table. Recall you can look up an exact value, such as number of years for a loan (such as 15, 25, or 30) and return the applicable interest rate. You also used these functions to look up a value within a range, such as looking up 85 on a test, and return the appropriate letter grade, such as B for scores between 80 and 89. Recall that the VLOOKUP and HLOOKUP functions require that the lookup table is arranged in a specific sequence. Furthermore, if a column is added to the table array, the VLOOKUP function will not return the correct result. Therefore, the INDEX and MATCH functions can be used if the table array might change. Excel contains 29 lookup and reference functions to enable you to look up a variety of data.

In this section, you use advanced lookup and reference functions. You will identify the location of specific data and return related data based on that position number. In addition, you will use a lookup and reference function to check the accuracy of another lookup function. Finally, you will use a function to display formulas and transpose rows and columns of data.

Using Advanced Lookup Functions

As you develop more complex datasets, you often will want to be able to quickly locate data that meets certain conditions. At a basic level, you could use the Find feature to find data that contains particular data within a dataset. However, to assist others who use your workbooks, it is helpful to include input cells for users to input data for the conditions they are looking for and then display the results in output cells. The MATCH, INDEX, and CHOOSE functions enable you to build these input and output sections. Other useful lookup and reference functions include FORMULATEXT and TRANSPOSE. You can select these functions by clicking the Lookup & Reference command in the Function Library on the Formulas tab or by using the Insert Function dialog box.

STEP 1 ▶ Use the MATCH Function

Identifying the location of specific data within a range can be helpful when the sequence within the dataset may seem random. For example, assume that a dataset contains a list of people who completed a puzzle in sequential order by time and you want to find the location for a certain contestant, but you do not know where that person's name is positioned in the dataset. You can use the MATCH function to identify the position of the data you want. The **MATCH function** searches through a range for a specific value and returns the relative position of that value within the range. The following list explains the arguments of the MATCH function.

=MATCH(lookup_value,lookup_array,[match_type])

- **Lookup_value.** This argument is the specific data that you want to find in the array or list. It can be a value, label, logical value, or cell reference that contains one of these items.
- **Lookup_array.** This argument is a range that contains a list of lookup values. It is usually a range for a column heading or row heading; it does not usually include the entire dataset.
- **Match_type.** This argument is 1, 0, or -1 to indicate which value to return. Use 1 to find the largest value that is less than or equal to the lookup_value when the values in the lookup_array are arranged in ascending order. Use -1 to find the smallest value that is greater than or equal to the lookup_value when the values in the lookup_array are in descending order. Use 0 to find the first value that is identical to the lookup_value when the values in the lookup_array have no logical order.

In Figure 11.21, cell B2 contains a MATCH function. The lookup_value refers to cell B1 that contains the store number to look up. In this case, you want to look up store number 440. The lookup_array argument is the range containing the store numbers used as row labels in the range A5:A8. The match_type is 0 to find an exact match for 440. In this case, 440 is in the fourth position within the range.

Cell D2 contains =MATCH(D1,A4:G4,0). Cell D1 contains the value to look up, which is 10/31/2021. The range A4:G4 that contains the column labels is the lookup_array, and 0 is the match_type. In this case, 10/31/2021 is in the seventh position in the range.

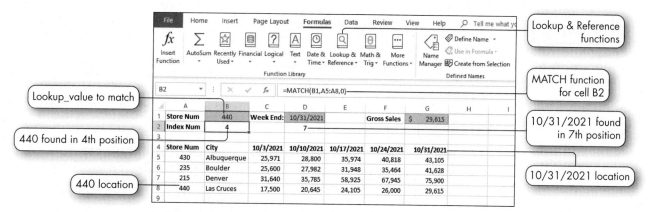

FIGURE 11.21 MATCH Functions

STEP 2 ▸ Use the INDEX Function

In isolation, the MATCH function may seem limited in usage. However, the result (position of a value) from the MATCH function is most often used as an argument within the INDEX function to produce more meaningful results. For example, you can use the MATCH function to identify the position for a specific store number in the first column and use another MATCH function to identify the position number of a date on the first row. You can then use the INDEX function to return the gross sales for that store for that date. Specifically, the **INDEX function** returns the value at the intersection of a specific row and column within a given range. The INDEX and MATCH functions are most often used together to identify positions of particular data and then those positions are used to return a value. Unlike the VLOOKUP or HLOOKUP function that identifies either the column or row number containing the value to return, the INDEX function can look up data based on a row and a column at the same time. Using the INDEX and MATCH functions together may be better if you think the table array data for a VLOOKUP or HLOOKUP function may change. If a change in the table array happens, the VLOOKUP and HLOOKUP functions will display an error. However, the INDEX and MATCH combination would be unaffected by a change in the table array.

=INDEX(array,row_num,[column_num])

- **Array.** This argument is one or more ranges.
- **Row_num.** This argument identifies the row number within the array range.
- **Column_num.** This argument identifies the column within the reference that contains the value you want.

In Figure 11.22, cell G1 contains an INDEX function. The array argument is A5:G8. The row_num argument is the result of the MATCH function in cell B2, which is 4. The column_num is the result of the MATCH function in cell D2, which is 7. Therefore, the intersection of the fourth row and seventh column is $29,615, which is the sales amount for store 440 for the week ending 10/31/2021.

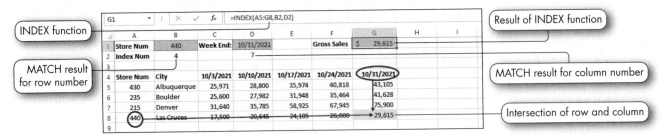

FIGURE 11.22 INDEX Function Result

> **TIP: NEST MATCH FUNCTIONS WITHIN AN INDEX FUNCTION**
> Instead of using separate cells for the MATCH and INDEX functions, you can nest the MATCH functions in the row_num and column_num arguments within the INDEX function. Using the above example, the function in cell G1 would be =INDEX(A5:G8,MATCH(B1,A5:A8,0),MATCH(D1,A4:G4,0)).

Use the CHOOSE Function

After using the MATCH and INDEX functions, you should double-check the accuracy of the results. One way to do this is to use the **CHOOSE function**, which returns a value from a list using an index number between 1 and 254. Instead of entering the actual value for the index_num argument, you can refer to a cell containing the MATCH function to obtain the index number. That index number is then used to identify the related search value. The CHOOSE function can also be used to return the day of a week given the integer returned from the WEEKDAY function.

`=CHOOSE(index_num,value1,[value2])`

In Figure 11.23, the CHOOSE function in cell D3 is used to double-check the accuracy of the MATCH function in cell D2. The index_num argument is D2-2, which is a calculation to determine a position number. The index_num argument subtracted 2 because cells A5 and B5 were not included in the value arguments; 7 minus 2 equals 5, which is the position of 10/31/2021. The value1 through value5 arguments contain references to the range C5:F5. Note that you must enter each cell reference as a separate argument instead of the entire range.

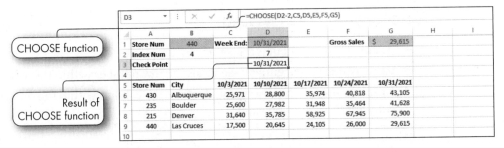

FIGURE 11.23 CHOOSE Function Result

STEP 3 ▸ Use the FORMULATEXT Function

You have used the Show Formulas command in the Formula Auditing group on the Formulas tab to display formulas instead of formula results in a worksheet. While this command is helpful to review formulas, it does not show both formula results and formulas at the same time. However, you can insert the ***FORMULATEXT function*** in a cell to return the formula as a string that is stored in another cell. This enables you to review formula results and formulas at the same time. While the FORMULATEXT function is especially useful to insert on the same sheet that contains the formula or function, you can use this function to return the formula or function located on another sheet or another workbook. Reference is the only argument, and it is a reference to a cell containing a formula. In Figure 11.24, the range J1:J4 contains FORMULATEXT functions for cells B2, cell D2, D3, and G1, respectively.

`=FORMULATEXT(reference)`

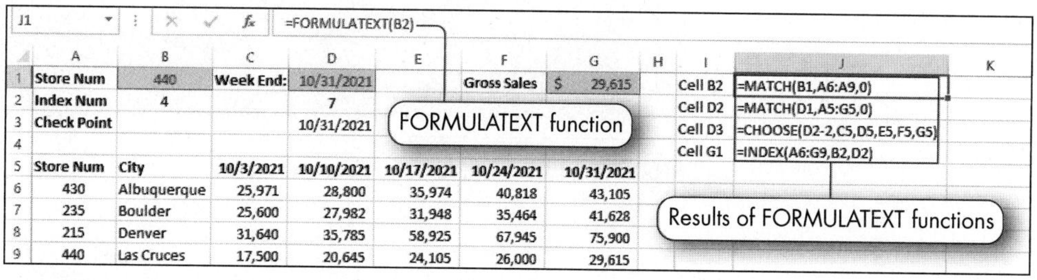

FIGURE 11.24 FORMULATEXT Function Result

TIP: RETURNING #N/A
The FORMULATEXT function returns #N/A when any of these conditions exist: the workbook containing the formula being referenced is not open, the cell being referenced does not contain a formula, the formula cannot be displayed because the worksheet being referenced is protected, or the formula being referenced is longer than 8,192 characters.

STEP 4 ▸ Use the TRANSPOSE Function

Assume a colleague gave you a worksheet containing a dataset. However, you want to rearrange the data by transposing the columns and rows. Previously, you learned how to copy data and use the Transpose paste option to rearrange the rows and columns of data. Another option is to use the ***TRANSPOSE function*** to transpose or rearrange the data from columns to rows and rows to columns. The benefit of using TRANSPOSE is that if a value changes in the original dataset, it will also change in the transposed data. If you used the copy and Transpose paste option, the pasted data will not be updated.

`=TRANSPOSE(array)`

To use the TRANSPOSE function, complete the following steps:

1. Select a range of blank cells that contains the same number of cells in the data that you want to transpose, but reversing the size. For example, if the original dataset is 11 rows by 7 columns, select a blank range of 7 rows by 11 columns.
2. Type =TRANSPOSE(while keeping the blank cells selected.
3. Select or type the range containing the original dataset.
4. Press Ctrl+Shift+Enter.

Figure 11.25 shows the original dataset in the range A1:G11. The range A13:K19 was originally blank while entering the TRANSPOSE function. After the function was entered, the dataset is transposed: Columns of dates became rows, and rows of store sales become columns. Excel displays {=TRANSPOSE(A1:G11)} in the Formula Bar.

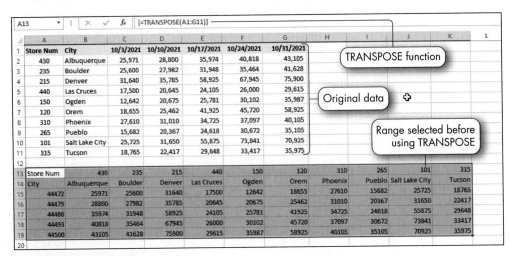

FIGURE 11.25 TRANSPOSE Function Result

TIP: FORMATTING AFTER USING TRANSPOSE

Note that the TRANSPOSE function does not preserve font and number formatting. After using the TRANSPOSE function, you should format data appropriately.

Quick
Concepts

7. Explain how the MATCH and INDEX functions can be used together. ***p. 681***

8. Explain when the FORMULATEXT function would be useful. ***p. 683***

9. Describe what tasks should be completed before using the TRANSPOSE function. ***p. 683***

Hands-On Exercises

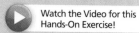
Skills covered: Use the MATCH Function • Use the INDEX Function • Use the FORMULATEXT Function • Use the TRANSPOSE Function

3 Lookup Functions

You created the structure for the Lookup worksheet. The purpose of this worksheet is to look up gross sales for a store for a particular end of week. You will use lookup functions to complete the worksheet.

STEP 1 USE THE MATCH FUNCTION

Your first step is to identify the positions for cells containing 440, a specific store number, and 10/31/2021, a specific date. You will use the MATCH function to identify those positions. Refer to Figure 11.26 as you complete Step 1.

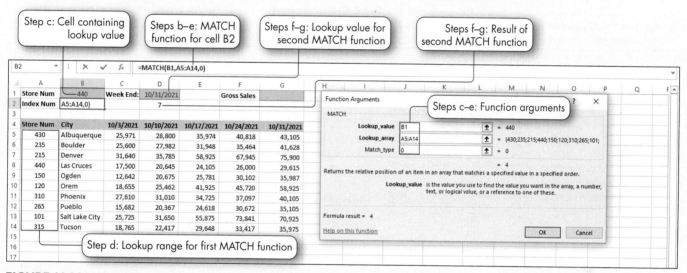

FIGURE 11.26 MATCH Function

a. Open *e11h2Halloween_LastFirst* if you closed it at the end of Hands-On Exercise 2, and save it as **e11h3Halloween_LastFirst**, changing h2 to h3. Click the **Lookup sheet tab**.

b. Click **cell B2**, click the **Formulas tab**, click **Lookup & Reference** in the Function Library group, and then select **MATCH**.

The Function Arguments dialog box opens so that you can enter the Lookup_value, Lookup_array, and Match_type arguments.

c. Select **cell B1** to enter B1 in the Lookup_value argument.

Cell B1 contains the store number to look up.

d. Press **Tab** and select the **range A5:A14** to enter it in the Lookup_array argument.

The range A5:A14 contains the list of store numbers.

e. Press **Tab**, type **0** in the Match_type argument, and then click **OK**.

The MATCH function returns 4, indicating that store 440 is the fourth store.

f. Click **cell D2**, click the **Formulas tab**, click **Lookup & Reference** in the Function Library group, and then select **MATCH**.

g. Select **cell D1** to enter D1 in the Lookup_value argument, press **Tab**, and select the **range A4:G4** to enter it in the Lookup_array argument, press **Tab**, type **0** in the Match_type argument, and then click **OK**. Save the workbook.

The MATCH function looks up the value in cell D1, which is 10/31/2021, compares it to the range A5:G5, and returns 7. The date 10/31/2021 is in the seventh position in the list.

STEP 2 USE THE INDEX FUNCTION

In the last step, you entered the MATCH function to identify the positions of the store number and date. Now you will use the results of those two functions to return the respective sales amount. Refer to Figure 11.27 as you complete Step 2.

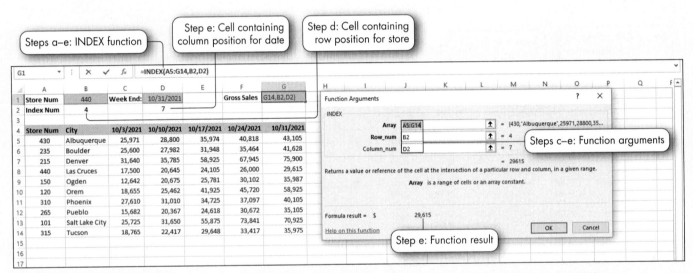

FIGURE 11.27 Index Function

a. Click **cell G1**, click **Lookup & Reference** in the Function Library on the Formulas tab, and then select **INDEX**.

The Select Arguments dialog box opens so that you can select the type of arguments to build the function.

b. Click **OK** with array,row_num,column_num selected.

This argument specifies the array or range to evaluate first, followed by identifying the row number and column number to index. The Function Arguments dialog box opens so that you can enter the required arguments for the INDEX function.

c. Select the **range A5:G14** to enter it in the Array box.

This range defines the location from which Excel will extract information.

d. Press **Tab** and type **B2** in the Row_num box.

Cell B2 contains the result of the MATCH function to identify the position of the store number.

e. Press **Tab**, type **D2** in the Column_num box, and then click **OK**. Save the workbook.

Cell D2 contains the result of the MATCH function to identify the position of the date. The INDEX function returns $29,615, the sales for store 440 for 10/31/2021.

STEP 3 › USE THE FORMULATEXT FUNCTION

Although the MATCH and INDEX functions are correctly identifying the position of a store number and date, you want to list the functions used in the worksheet for easy reference. Refer to Figure 11.28 as you complete Step 3.

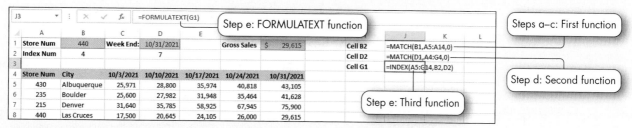

FIGURE 11.28 FORMULATEXT Function

a. Click **cell J1**.

b. Click **Lookup & Reference** in the Function Library group and select **FORMULATEXT**.

c. Select **cell B2** to enter it in the Reference box and click **OK**.

   The FORMULATEXT function returns the MATCH function stored in cell B2.

d. Click **cell J2**, type **=FORM**, double-click **FORMULATEXT** from the function ScreenTip, select **cell D2**, and then press **Ctrl+Enter**.

   The FORMULATEXT function returns the MATCH function stored in cell D2.

e. Click **cell J3**, type **=FORM**, double-click **FORMULATEXT** from the function ScreenTip, type **G1**, and then press **Ctrl+Enter**.

   The FORMULATEXT function displays the INDEX function stored in cell D2. Save the workbook.

STEP 4 › USE THE TRANSPOSE FUNCTION

You want to display the data to show weekly sales in rows with the cities in columns. You will use the TRANSPOSE function to do this. Finally, you will format the transposed data. Refer to Figure 11.29 as you complete Step 4.

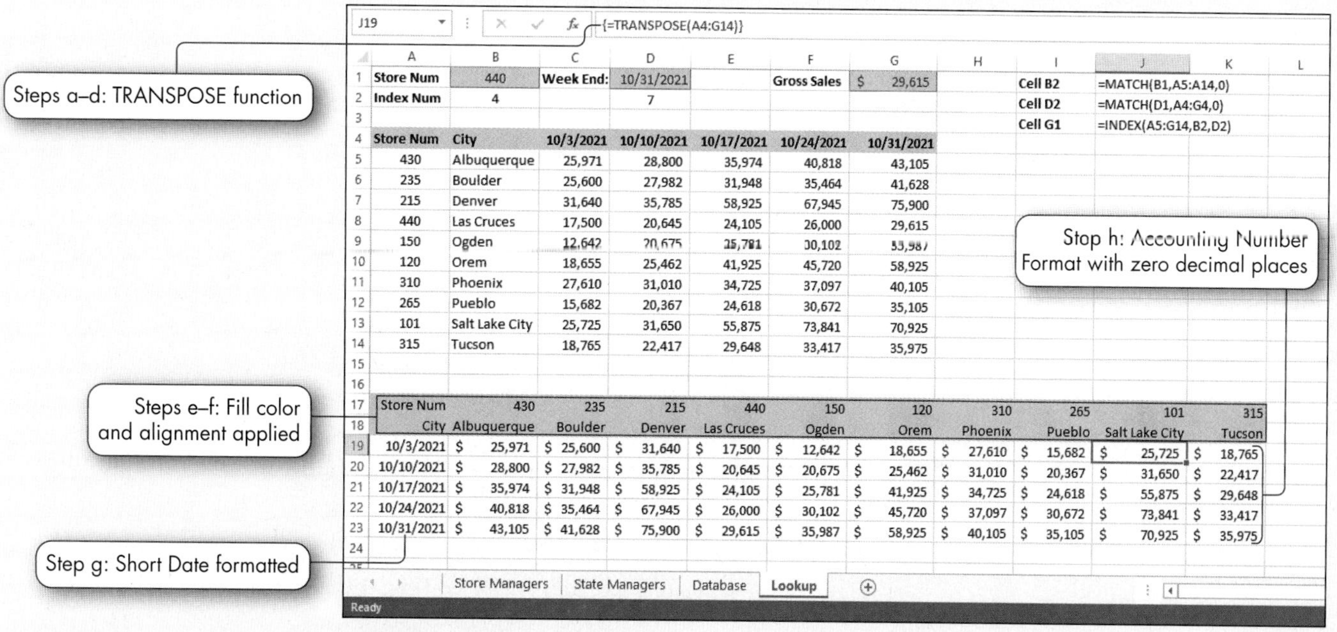

FIGURE 11.29 Transposed Data

a. Select the **range A17:K23**.

Before using the TRANSPOSE function, you must select the same number of cells as the original dataset, but transposing the number of columns and rows.

b. Type **=TRANSPOSE(**. (Do not type the period.)

c. Select the **range A4:G14** to enter that range in the function.

d. Press **Ctrl+Shift+Enter**.

Excel transposes the data in the selected range; however, the font and number formatting did not copy.

> **TROUBLESHOOTING:** If Excel does not copy and transpose the data, you probably pressed only Enter. Click Undo and repeat Steps a–d, ensuring you press Ctrl+Shift+Enter.

e. Select the **range A17:K18**, click the **Home tab**, click the **Fill Color arrow** in the Font group, and then select **Orange, Accent 2, Lighter 60%**.

f. Click **Align Right** in the Alignment group on the Home tab.

g. Select the **range A19:A23**, click the **Number Format arrow** in the Number group, and then select **Short Date**.

h. Select the **range B19:K23** and click **Accounting Number Format** in the Number group. Click **Decrease Decimal** twice.

i. Change the width of **column J** to **13**.

j. Save and close the file. Exit Excel. Based on your instructor's directions, submit e11h3Halloween_LastFirst.

Chapter Objectives Review

After reading this chapter, you have accomplished the following objectives:

1. Fill and separate text in columns.

- Use Flash Fill: Flash Fill enables you to enter data into a cell that uses part of the data in a previous column. The data in the previous column must be similarly structured. The Flash Fill command can then be used to quickly fill the new column with the same type of data typed in the first cell.
- Convert text to columns: The Text to Columns command is used to separate text into two or more columns, dividing the data at delimiters. Common delimiters include commas and spaces.

2. Manipulate text with functions.

- Use the CONCAT and TEXTJOIN functions: The CONCAT function concatenates two or more text strings. To avoid the combined text running together, you include delimiters as arguments. The TEXTJOIN function also joins text strings together. A benefit of this function is that the first argument specifies the delimiter.
- Use the PROPER, UPPER, and LOWER functions: These functions control the capitalization style of text. The PROPER function returns text in which the first letter of each word is capitalized. The UPPER function returns text in all capitals. The LOWER function returns text in lowercase letters.
- Use the LEFT, RIGHT, and MID functions: These functions extract characters from a text string. The LEFT function extracts specified number of characters from the left side. The RIGHT function extracts specified number of characters from the right side. The MID function extracts specified number of characters starting at a particular position in the text string.
- Use other text functions: Excel contains other useful text functions to manipulate text. The FIND function identifies the starting position of a text string within a text string. The LEN function identifies the number of characters in a text string. The SUBSTITUTE function substitutes an old text string with a new text string. The TRIM function removes leading and trailing spaces in a text string but maintains one space between words within the text string.

3. Apply advanced filtering.

- Define the criteria and output ranges: To create the criteria range, copy the column labels for the database and paste the labels in another range. Include the criteria below the respective labels in the row or rows below the labels. Each row creates criteria that all conditions must be met. Entering conditions on a second row creates an or condition. Copy the column labels and paste the labels in another range as the first row of the output range.
- Apply an advanced filter: The advanced filter displays records that meet the criteria specified in the criteria range.

4. Manipulate data with database functions.

- Database functions have three arguments: database, field, and criteria. The database argument is the entire dataset. The field argument is the column that contains the values operated on by the function. The criteria argument defines the conditions to be met.
- Use the DSUM and DAVERAGE functions: The DSUM function adds the values in a database column based on specified conditions. The DAVERAGE function averages the values in a database column based on specified conditions.
- Use the DMAX and DMIN functions: The DMAX function returns the highest value in a database column that matches specified criteria. In contrast, the DMIN function returns the lowest value in a database column that matches specified conditions.
- Use the DCOUNT and DCOUNTA functions: The DCOUNT function counts the cells that contain numbers in a database column that match specified criteria. The DCOUNTA function counts nonblank cells within the database that matches the specified criteria.
- Use the DGET function: The DGET function retrieves a value from the database based on specified criteria. An error is returned if more than one record meets the condition or if no record meets the condition.

5. Use advanced lookup functions.

- Use the MATCH function: The MATCH function returns the position of a value in a list.
- Use the INDEX function: The INDEX function returns data at the intersection of a row and a column in an array.
- Use the CHOOSE function: The CHOOSE function returns a value from a list of 1 to 254 values based on an index value.
- Use the FORMULATEXT function: The FORMULATEXT function returns the formula that is stored in another cell as a string.
- Use the TRANSPOSE function: The TRANSPOSE function transposes or rearranges data from columns to rows and rows to columns in an array.

Key Terms Matching

Match the key terms with their definitions. Write the key term letter by the appropriate numbered definition.

a. CONCAT function
b. Criteria range
c. Database functions
d. DAVERAGE function
e. DCOUNT function
f. DMAX function
g. DMIN function
h. DSUM function
i. FORMULATEXT function
j. INDEX function

k. LEFT function
l. LOWER function
m. MATCH function
n. MID function
o. Output range
p. PROPER function
q. RIGHT function
r. TEXTJOIN function
s. TRANSPOSE function
t. UPPER function

1. _____ A text function that combines text strings and requires a separate argument for each delimiter to include in the combined text. **p. 661**

2. _____ A text function that combines text strings and inserts a delimiter you specify in the first argument. **p. 662**

3. _____ A text function that capitalizes the first letter of each word in a text string. **p. 663**

4. _____ A text function that extracts a specified number of characters from the left side of a text string. **p. 664**

5. _____ A range of cells that contains the list of records from a dataset that meets the specified conditions. **p. 670**

6. _____ A database function that identifies the lowest value in a column that matches specified conditions in a criteria range. **p. 674**

7. _____ A function that searches through a range for a specific value and returns the relative position of that value within the range. **p. 680**

8. _____ A text function that converts text strings to all capital letters. **p. 664**

9. _____ A database function that adds the values in a column that matches conditions specified in a criteria range. **p. 674**

10. _____ A function that returns a value at the intersection of a specified row and column within a given range. **p. 681**

11. _____ A database function that counts the cells that contain numbers in a column that matches specified conditions in a criteria range. **p. 674**

12. _____ A text function that extracts the characters from the middle of a text string, given a starting position and length. **p. 664**

13. _____ A text function that converts a text string to all lowercase letters. **p. 664**

14. _____ A set of functions that provide statistical calculations for a database. **p. 673**

15. _____ A database function that determines the average of values in a column that matches conditions specified in a criteria range. **p. 674**

16. _____ A function that returns the text version of a formula stored in another cell. **p. 683**

17. _____ A function that rearranges data from columns to rows and rows to columns. **p. 683**

18. _____ A database function that identifies the highest values in a column that matches specified conditions in a criteria range. **p. 674**

19. _____ A range of two or more adjacent cells that specifies the conditions used to control the results of a filter. **p. 670**

20. _____ A text function that extracts the specified number of characters from the right side of a text string. **p. 664**

Multiple Choice

1. When you are performing an advanced filter, in which argument box do you enter the range for the dataset?

   (a) Criteria range
   (b) List range
   (c) Copy to
   (d) Database

2. You are entering the conditions in a criteria range to perform an advanced filter. You want to find records in which the state abbreviation is CA or WA. Where do you enter these conditions?

   (a) As *CA or WA* in the cell immediately below the STATE label
   (b) As *CA and WA* in the cell immediately below the STATE label
   (c) In two cells on the same row with *CA* below the STATE label and *WA* below another label
   (d) *CA* below the STATE label and *WA* below the CA condition

3. Which function identifies the lowest value in a database column based on specified criteria located in a criteria range?

   (a) DMIN
   (b) DMAX
   (c) MINIFS
   (d) MIN

4. Which function identifies and returns the position of a value within an array?

   (a) ARRAY
   (b) INDEX
   (c) MATCH
   (d) CHOOSE

5. What function should you use to look up a specified value within a database at the intersection of a specific row and column position?

   (a) CHOOSE
   (b) INDEX
   (c) MATCH
   (d) TRANSPOSE

6. Column A contains numbers such as 2021001. You enter 2021-001 in the adjoining cell in column B. What feature can you use to quickly complete the text pattern down column B?

   (a) Transpose
   (b) Text to Columns
   (c) Paste Special
   (d) Flash Fill

7. A column contains phone numbers such as (801)-555-1234. What function should you use to extract the last four digits?

   (a) LEFT
   (b) RIGHT
   (c) MID
   (d) LEN

8. A column contains names in uppercase, which is hard to read. Which function displays the names where the first letter of each word is capitalized?

   (a) INITIALCAPS
   (b) LOWER
   (c) PROPER
   (d) TITLECASE

9. A worksheet contains addresses in column C. The addresses use commas after the street, city, and state, such as 129 Elm Street, Burlington, NC, 27215. Column D contains the phone number. You use Text to Columns to divide the addresses into multiple columns using comma delimiters. You successfully divide the addresses into four columns. What happens to the phone numbers in column D?

   (a) The phone numbers are overwritten with city names.
   (b) The phone numbers are converted to commas.
   (c) Excel phone number column is moved to the right side of all the columns containing the parts of the addresses.
   (d) The phone number column is moved to the left of the original address column.

10. Database functions such as DSUM contain all of the following arguments except:

    (a) Database.
    (b) Criteria.
    (c) Field.
    (d) Output.

Practice Exercises

1   Home Protection, Inc. Employees

You are an assistant accountant in the Human Resources (HR) Department for Home Protection, Inc., a company that sells smart home security systems to residential customers. Home Protection, Inc., with locations in Atlanta, Boston, Chicago, and Cleveland, has a manager at each location who oversees several account representatives. You want to use text functions to format text and apply a filter to copy records for account representatives at Boston and Chicago. Finally, you want to be able to enter an employee's name and display that person's salary. Refer to Figure 11.30 as you complete this exercise.

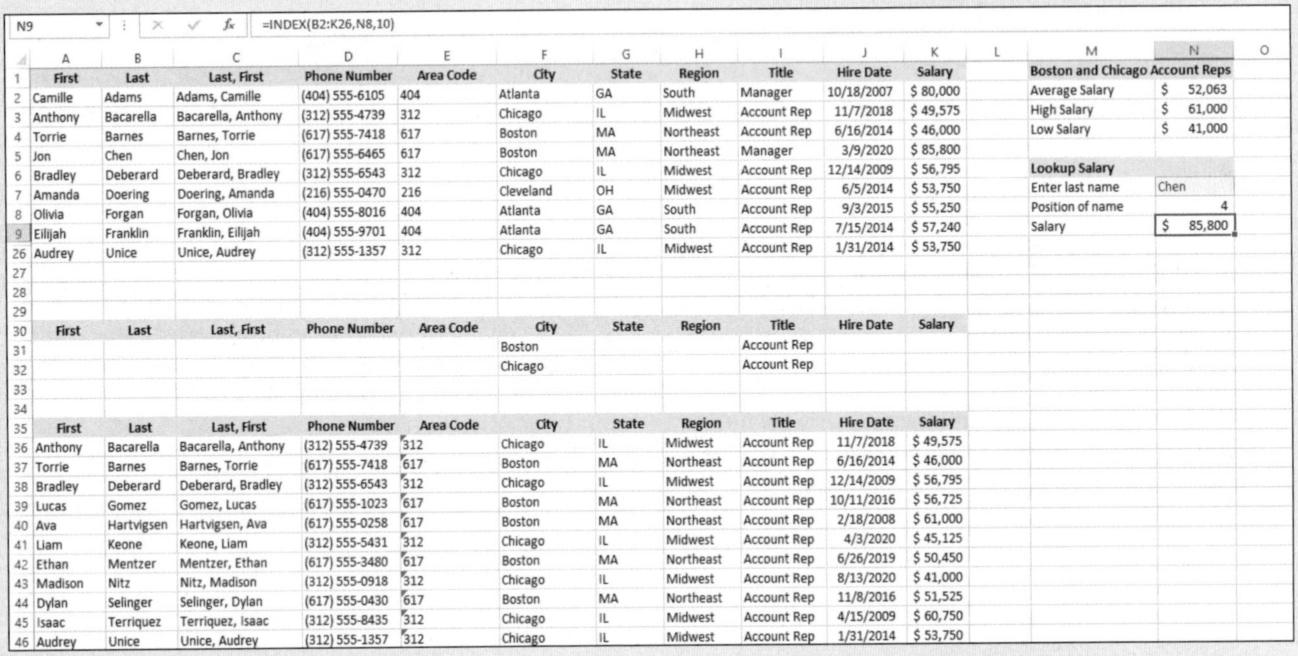

	A	B	C	D	E	F	G	H	I	J	K	L	M	N	O
	First	Last	Last, First	Phone Number	Area Code	City	State	Region	Title	Hire Date	Salary		Boston and Chicago Account Reps		
1	First	Last	Last, First	Phone Number	Area Code	City	State	Region	Title	Hire Date	Salary				
2	Camille	Adams	Adams, Camille	(404) 555-6105	404	Atlanta	GA	South	Manager	10/18/2007	$ 80,000		Average Salary	$ 52,063	
3	Anthony	Bacarella	Bacarella, Anthony	(312) 555-4739	312	Chicago	IL	Midwest	Account Rep	11/7/2018	$ 49,575		High Salary	$ 61,000	
4	Torrie	Barnes	Barnes, Torrie	(617) 555-7418	617	Boston	MA	Northeast	Account Rep	6/16/2014	$ 46,000		Low Salary	$ 41,000	
5	Jon	Chen	Chen, Jon	(617) 555-6465	617	Boston	MA	Northeast	Manager	3/9/2020	$ 85,800				
6	Bradley	Deberard	Deberard, Bradley	(312) 555-6543	312	Chicago	IL	Midwest	Account Rep	12/14/2009	$ 56,795		Lookup Salary		
7	Amanda	Doering	Doering, Amanda	(216) 555-0470	216	Cleveland	OH	Midwest	Account Rep	6/5/2014	$ 53,750		Enter last name	Chen	
8	Olivia	Forgan	Forgan, Olivia	(404) 555-8016	404	Atlanta	GA	South	Account Rep	9/3/2015	$ 55,250		Position of name	4	
9	Eilijah	Franklin	Franklin, Eilijah	(404) 555-9701	404	Atlanta	GA	South	Account Rep	7/15/2014	$ 57,240		Salary	$ 85,800	
26	Audrey	Unice	Unice, Audrey	(312) 555-1357	312	Chicago	IL	Midwest	Account Rep	1/31/2014	$ 53,750				
27															
28															
29															
30	First	Last	Last, First	Phone Number	Area Code	City	State	Region	Title	Hire Date	Salary				
31						Boston			Account Rep						
32						Chicago			Account Rep						
33															
34															
35	First	Last	Last, First	Phone Number	Area Code	City	State	Region	Title	Hire Date	Salary				
36	Anthony	Bacarella	Bacarella, Anthony	(312) 555-4739	312	Chicago	IL	Midwest	Account Rep	11/7/2018	$ 49,575				
37	Torrie	Barnes	Barnes, Torrie	(617) 555-7418	617	Boston	MA	Northeast	Account Rep	6/16/2014	$ 46,000				
38	Bradley	Deberard	Deberard, Bradley	(312) 555-6543	312	Chicago	IL	Midwest	Account Rep	12/14/2009	$ 56,795				
39	Lucas	Gomez	Gomez, Lucas	(617) 555-1023	617	Boston	MA	Northeast	Account Rep	10/11/2016	$ 56,725				
40	Ava	Hartvigsen	Hartvigsen, Ava	(617) 555-0258	617	Boston	MA	Northeast	Account Rep	2/18/2008	$ 61,000				
41	Liam	Keone	Keone, Liam	(312) 555-5431	312	Chicago	IL	Midwest	Account Rep	4/3/2020	$ 45,125				
42	Ethan	Mentzer	Mentzer, Ethan	(617) 555-3480	617	Boston	MA	Northeast	Account Rep	6/26/2019	$ 50,450				
43	Madison	Nitz	Nitz, Madison	(312) 555-0918	312	Chicago	IL	Midwest	Account Rep	8/13/2020	$ 41,000				
44	Dylan	Selinger	Selinger, Dylan	(617) 555-0430	617	Boston	MA	Northeast	Account Rep	11/8/2016	$ 51,525				
45	Isaac	Terriquez	Terriquez, Isaac	(312) 555-8435	312	Chicago	IL	Midwest	Account Rep	4/15/2009	$ 60,750				
46	Audrey	Unice	Unice, Audrey	(312) 555-1357	312	Chicago	IL	Midwest	Account Rep	1/31/2014	$ 53,750				

Cell N9: =INDEX(B2:K26,N8,10)

FIGURE 11.30 Home Protection, Inc., Employee Database

a. Open *e11p1Employees* and save it as **e11p1Employees_LastFirst**.

b. Click **cell C2**, click the **Formulas tab**, click **Text** in the Function Library, scroll down, and then select **TEXTJOIN**. Finish the function by completing the following steps:

- Type **,** (a comma) and press **Spacebar** in the Delimiter box.
- Press **Tab** and type **TRUE** in the Ignore_empty box.
- Press **Tab** and select **cell B2** to enter it in the Text1 box.
- Press **Tab**, select **cell A2** to enter it in the Text2 box, and then click **OK**.
- Copy the function from **cell C2** to the **range C3:C26**.

c. Click **cell E2** and extract the area code by completing the following steps:

- Click **Text** in the Function Library group and select **LEFT**.
- Type **D2** in the Text box.
- Type **4** in the Num_chars box and click **OK**. This extracts (404. You will embed this function within another function to exclude the parenthesis.
- Click between the equal sign and LEFT in the Formula Bar.
- Type **RIGHT(** and click after the closing parenthesis. Type **,3)** and click **Enter**.
- Copy the function from **cell E2** to the **range E3:E26**.

d. Separate the cities and states by completing the following steps:

- Select the **range F2:F26**.
- Click the **Data tab** and click **Text to Columns** in the Data Tools group.
- Click **Next**. Click the **Comma** and **Space check boxes** to select them. Deselect other check boxes.
- Click **Next** and click **Finish**.

e. Create a criteria range by completing the following steps:
- Copy the **range A1:K1**, click **cell A30**, and then click **Paste**.
- Type **Boston** in **cell F31** and type **Account Rep** in **cell I31**.
- Type **Chicago** in **cell F32** and type **Account Rep** in **cell I32**.

f. Copy the **range A30:K30**, click **cell A35**, and then click **Paste** to create the output area.

g. Click **cell A26** and apply the advanced filter by completing the following steps:
- Click the **Data tab** and click **Advanced** in the Sort & Filter group.
- Click **Copy to another location**.
- Make sure the List range is $A$1:$K$26.
- Type **A30:K32** in the Criteria box.
- Type **A35:K35** in the Copy to box and click **OK**.

h. Click **cell N2**, click the **Formulas tab**, click **Insert Function**, click the **Or select a category**, select **Database**, make sure DAVERAGE is selected, and then click **OK**. Finish the DAVERAGE function by completing the following steps:
- Select the **range A1:K26** to enter it in the Database box.
- Type **Salary** in the Field box.
- Select the **range A30:K32** to enter it in the Criteria box and click **OK**.

i. Click **cell N3** and adapt Step h to select the **DMAX** function and enter the arguments.

j. Click **cell N4** and adapt Step h to select the **DMIN** function and enter the arguments.

k. Type **Lenz** in **cell N7**, click **cell N8**, and complete the following steps:
- Click the **Formulas tab**, click **Lookup & Reference** in the Function Library group, and then select **MATCH**.
- Click **cell N7** to enter it in the Lookup_value box.
- Select the **range B2:B26** to enter it in the Lookup_array box.
- Type **0** in the Match_type box and click **OK**. The function returns 15, that Lenz is in the 15th position.

l. Click **cell N9** and complete the following steps:
- Click **Lookup & Reference** in the Function Library group, select **INDEX**, and then click **OK** in the Select Arguments dialog box.
- Select the **range B2:K26** to enter it in the Array box.
- Click **cell N8** to enter it in the Row_num box.
- Type **10** in the Column_num box and click **OK**. Lenz's salary is $49,750, which matches the salary in cell K16.
- Type **Chen** in **cell N7** and notice that the position number in cell N8 and the salary in cell N9 change.

m. Create a footer with your name on the left side, the sheet name code in the center, and the file name code on the right side on all sheets.

n. Save and close the file. Exit Excel. Based on your instructor's directions, submit e11p1Employees_LastFirst.

2 Tech Support Calls

You are the IT Tech Support Manager at a university. Your tech support staff log each call to document dates, computer numbers, descriptions of the issues, and other details. You downloaded a report into a spreadsheet and noticed some data should be formatted better. In addition to formatting data, you are interested in one technical support staff's records for solving a particular problem. You will use advanced database filtering and database functions to analyze the data. Furthermore, you want to be able to enter a computer number and find the description using lookup functions. Refer to Figure 11.31 as you complete this exercise.

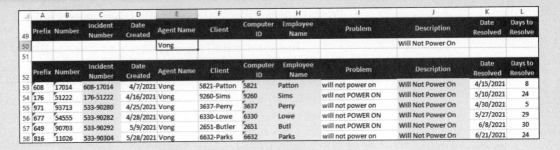

	Prefix	Number	Incident Number	Date Created	Agent Name	Client	Computer ID	Employee Name	Problem	Description	Date Resolved	Days to Resolve
49	Prefix	Number	Incident Number	Date Created	Agent Name	Client	Computer ID	Employee Name	Problem	Description	Date Resolved	Days to Resolve
50					Vong					Will Not Power On		
51												
52	Prefix	Number	Incident Number	Date Created	Agent Name	Client	Computer ID	Employee Name	Problem	Description	Date Resolved	Days to Resolve
53	608	17014	608-17014	4/7/2021	Vong	5821-Patton	5821	Patton	will not power on	Will Not Power On	4/15/2021	8
54	176	51222	176-51222	4/16/2021	Vong	9260-Sims	9260	Sims	will not POWER ON	Will Not Power On	5/10/2021	24
55	971	93713	533-90280	4/25/2021	Vong	3637-Perry	3637	Perry	will not power on	Will Not Power On	4/30/2021	5
56	677	54555	533-90282	4/28/2021	Vong	6330-Lowe	6330	Lowe	will not POWER ON	Will Not Power On	5/27/2021	29
57	649	90703	533-90292	5/9/2021	Vong	2651-Butler	2651	Butl	will not POWER ON	Will Not Power On	6/8/2021	30
58	816	11026	533-90304	5/28/2021	Vong	6632-Parks	6632	Parks	will not power on	Will Not Power On	6/21/2021	24

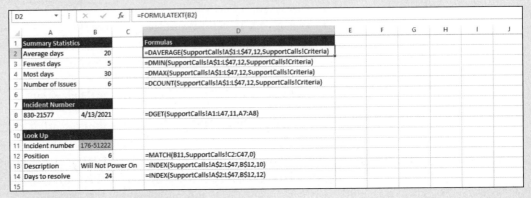

D2   fx   =FORMULATEXT(B2)

	A	B	C	D	E	F	G	H	I	J
1	Summary Statistics			Formulas						
2	Average days	20		=DAVERAGE(SupportCalls!A$1:L$47,12,SupportCalls!Criteria)						
3	Fewest days	5		=DMIN(SupportCalls!A$1:L$47,12,SupportCalls!Criteria)						
4	Most days	30		=DMAX(SupportCalls!A$1:L$47,12,SupportCalls!Criteria)						
5	Number of Issues	6		=DCOUNT(SupportCalls!A$1:L$47,12,SupportCalls!Criteria)						
6										
7	Incident Number									
8	830-21577	4/13/2021		=DGET(SupportCalls!A1:L47,11,A7:A8)						
9										
10	Look Up									
11	Incident number	176-51222								
12	Position	6		=MATCH(B11,SupportCalls!C2:C47,0)						
13	Description	Will Not Power On	=INDEX(SupportCalls!A$2:L$47,B$12,10)							
14	Days to resolve	24		=INDEX(SupportCalls!A$2:L$47,B$12,12)						
15										

FIGURE 11.31 University Tech Support

a. Open *e11p2TechSupport* and save it as **e11p2TechSupport_LastFirst**.

b. Click **cell C2**, type **831-91089**, and then press **Ctrl+Enter**. Click **Fill** in the Editing group and select **Flash Fill** to fill the **range C3:C47** with the combination of prefixes and numbers.

c. Click **cell G2** and extract the Computer ID from the Client column by completing these steps:
  - Click **Insert Function**, type **Left** in the *Search for a function* box, click **Go**, and then click **OK**.
  - Click **cell F2** to enter it in the Text box, type **4** in the Num_chars box, and then click **OK**.
  - Double-click the **cell G2 fill handle** to copy the function to the **range G3:G47**.

d. Click **cell H2** and extract the client name from the Client column by completing these steps:
  - Click **Insert Function**, type **LEN** in the *Search for a function* box, click **Go**, and then click **OK**. Click **cell F2** to enter it in the Text box and click **OK**. You used the LEN function to identify the length of the characters in cell F2.
  - Edit the function by typing **-5** after the closing parenthesis and press **Ctrl+Enter**. Because the last names are not all the same length, you subtracted 5 from the LEN function result to obtain the number of characters in the last name.
  - Click between the equal sign and LEN in the Formula Bar, type **RIGHT(F2,** (including the comma), click after -5, and then type **)** (a closing parenthesis). Press **Ctrl+Enter**. The RIGHT function extracts the number of characters minus 5 from the right side of the text in cell F2.
  - Double-click the **cell H2 fill handle** to copy the function to the **range H3:H47**.

e. Click **cell J2**, type **=PROPER(I2)**, and then press **Ctrl+Enter**. Double-click the **cell J2 fill handle** to copy the function to the **range J3:J47**. The original text in the Problem column was in different capitalization style, making it difficult to read. Using the PROPER function ensures all descriptions are formatted the same.

f. Create criteria and output ranges by completing the following steps:
  - Copy the **range A1:L1**, click **cell A49**, and then click **Paste** to create the first row of the criteria range.
  - Type **Vong** in **cell E50** and type **Will Not Power On** in **cell J50**.

g. Click **cell A47** and apply the advanced filter by completing the following steps:
- Click the **Data tab** and click **Advanced** in the Sort & Filter group.
- Click **Copy to another location**.
- Make sure the List range is $A$1:$L$47.
- Select the **range A49:L50** to enter it in the Criteria box.
- Select the **range A52:L52** to enter it in the Copy to box and click **OK**.

h. Click the **Info sheet tab** and enter a database function in cell B2 to calculate the average number of days to resolve a case for the output range by completing these steps:
- Click **cell B2**, click the **Formulas tab**, click **Insert Function**, type **DAVERAGE** in the *Search for a function* box, click **Go**, and then click **OK**.
- Click the **SupportCalls sheet tab**, select the **range A1:L47** to enter SupportCalls!A1:L47 in the Database box.
- Type **12** in the Field box because the Days to Resolve is in the 12th column.
- Press **Tab** and type **SupportCalls!Criteria** in the Criteria box, and then press **Ctrl+Enter**.
- Edit the function by changing A1:L47 to **A$1:L$47**. You changed to mixed references so that you can copy and edit the function.

i. Drag the **cell B2 fill handle** down to the **range B3:B5** and change the database function names by completing the following:
- Edit **cell B3** by changing DAVERAGE to **DMIN**.
- Edit **cell B4** by changing DAVERAGE to **DMAX**.
- Edit **cell B5** by changing DAVERAGE to **DCOUNT**.

j. Click **cell B8** and use the DGET function to get the date resolved for incident 830-21577 by completing the following steps:
- Click **Insert Function**, type **DGET** in the *Search for a function* box, click **Go**, and then click **OK**.
- Click the **SupportCalls sheet tab**, select the **range A1:L47** to enter SupportCalls!A1:L47 in the Database box.
- Type **11** in the Field box because the Date Resolved is in the eleventh column.
- Press **Tab**, select the **range A7:A8** in the Info sheet to enter it in the Criteria box, and then press **Ctrl+Enter**.

k. Click **cell B12** and insert a MATCH function to identify the position of the incident number stored in cell B8 by completing the following steps:
- Click the **Formulas tab**, click **Lookup & Reference** in the Function Library group, and then select **MATCH**.
- Click **cell B11** to enter it in the Lookup_value box, type **SupportCalls!C2:C47** in the Lookup_array box, type **0** in the Match_type box, and then click **OK**. 176-51222 is the sixth incident in the database.

l. Click **cell B13** and insert an INDEX function that uses the result from the MATCH function as a row argument with other arguments to return the description for that incident by completing the following steps:
- Click **Lookup & Reference** in the Function Library group, select **INDEX**, and then click **OK** in the Select Arguments dialog box.
- Type **SupportCalls!A$2:L$47** in the Array box.
- Type **B$12** in the Row_num box.
- Type **10** in the Column_num box and click **OK**. The incident is *Will Not Power On*.
- Copy the function from **cell B13** to **cell B14**. Edit the function in **cell B14** by changing 10 to **12** for the last argument. It took 24 days to resolve that incident.

m. Click **cell D2**, click **Lookup & Reference** in the Function Library group, and then select **FORMULATEXT**. Click **cell B2** to enter it in the Reference box and click **OK**.

n. Copy the function in **cell D2** to the **ranges D3:D5**, **D8**, and **D12:D14**.

o. Add your name to the left side of the footer on both sheets.

p. Save and close the file. Exit Excel. Based on your instructor's directions, submit e11p2TechSupport_LastFirst.

1 Student Internship Program

As the Internship Director for a regional university, you created a list of students who are currently in this semester's internship program. You have some final touches to complete the worksheet, particularly in formatting text. In addition, you want to create an advanced filter to copy a list of senior accounting students. Finally, you want to insert summary statistics and create an input area to look up a student by ID to display his or her name and major.

a. Open *e11m1Internships* and save it as **e11m1Internships_LastFirst**.

b. Extract the last four digits of the first student's ID in **cell B2** using the RIGHT function. Copy the function from **cell B2** to the **range B3:B42**. Apply center horizontal alignment to the **range B2:B42**.

c. Convert the text in the **range C2:C42** into two columns using a space as the delimiter.

d. Use a text function in **cell G2** to convert the text in cell F2 into upper and lowercase letters. Copy the function to the **range G3:G42**. Hide column F.

e. Create a criteria range by copying the **range A1:I1** and pasting it in **cell A44**. Create conditions for **Senior Accounting** majors on row 45 and an OR condition for **Junior Accounting** majors in the respective cells on row 46.

f. Create an output range by copying the **range A44:I44** to **cell A48**.

g. Perform the advanced filter by copying data to the output range. Use the appropriate ranges for list range, criteria range, and output range.

h. Display the Info worksheet and insert the DSUM function in **cell B2** to calculate the total tuition for junior and senior accounting students. Use the **range A1:I42** for the database, **Tuition** for the field, and the criteria range.

i. Insert database functions by completing these steps:
- **Cell B3:** Insert the DAVERAGE function to calculate the average GPA for junior and senior accounting students on the Students worksheet. Use mixed references in the ranges.
- **Cell B4:** Insert the DMAX function to identify the highest GPA for junior and senior accounting students on the Students worksheet. Use mixed references in the ranges.
- **Cell B5:** Insert the DMIN function to identify the lowest GPA for junior and senior accounting students on the Students worksheet. Use mixed references in the ranges.
- **Cell B6:** Insert the DCOUNT function to count the number of junior and senior accounting students on the Students worksheet. Use mixed references in the ranges.
- **Cell B9:** Insert the DGET function to retrieve the last name of the student who has the ID listed in cell A9. Use the column number representing the Last Name column for the field argument and use the criteria range A8:A9. Edit the function to make the column letters absolute.
- Copy the DGET function from **cell B9** to **cell C9**. Edit the field number to represent the GPA column.

j. Format the **range B3:B6** with **Comma Style**. Decrease the number of decimal places to zero for **cell B6**.

k. Insert the MATCH function in **cell B13** to identify the position of the ID stored in cell B12. Use the range A2:A42 in the Students worksheet as the lookup_array argument and look for exact matches only.

l. Insert the INDEX function in **cell B14** with **Students!A$2:I$42** as the array, **B$13** that contains the MATCH function as the row number, and **4** as the column number.

m. Copy the function from **cell B14** to **cell B15**. Edit the function to change the column number to **7**.

n. Change the ID in **cell B12** to **11282378**. The results of the MATCH and INDEX functions should change.

o. Insert the FORMULATEXT function in **cell D2** to display the formula that is stored in cell B2. Copy the function to the **range D3:D6** and to the **range D13:D15**. In **cell D8**, insert the FORMULATEXT function to display the function that is stored in cell B9, and in **cell D9**, insert the FORMULATEXT function to display the function that is stored in cell C9. Increase the width of column D to **50**.

p. Create a footer with your name on the left side, the sheet name code in the center, and the file name code on the right side on all sheets.

q. Save and close the file. Exit Excel. Based on your instructor's directions, submit e11m1Internships_LastFirst.

2 | Innovations Game Studio

Innovations Game Studio has locations in Portland, Seattle, and Salt Lake City. Each location has game-development teams to produce video games for various consoles. You will use text functions to format the list and copy records of programmers in one location. In addition, you will insert database functions to calculate summary statistics and create a lookup area to look up an employee's ID to retrieve that person's name, job title, and salary.

a. Open *e11m2GameStudio* and save it as **e11m2GameStudio_LastFirst**.

b. Display the **Salary Data** worksheet. Insert the TEXTJOIN function in **cell E2** to join the **range B2:D2**, using a space delimiter and ignoring blank cells. Copy the function to the **range E3:E49**.

c. Select the **range F2:F49** and convert text to columns using the comma delimiter to separate the department names from the job titles. Click **OK** when prompted with *There's already data here. Do you want to replace it?*

d. Insert a LEN function in **cell I2** that identifies the number of characters in cell H2. Edit the function by subtracting 4 after the closing parenthesis. The result subtracts the two-letter state abbreviation, space, and comma, leaving the number of characters in the city. Edit the cell contents to nest the LEN function as the num_chars argument for a LEFT function. Use cell H2 as the text argument. The nested function result should display the city name only. Copy the function to the **range I3:I49**.

e. Insert an UPPER function in **cell J2** that nests the RIGHT function with cell H2 as the text function and the correct number of characters to extract just the state abbreviation. Copy the function to the **range J3:J49**.

f. Create a criteria range by copying the **range A1:K1** and pasting it in **cell A51**. Create conditions using **Programming** as the department and **Salt Lake City** as the city in the respective cells on row 52.

g. Create an output range by copying the **range A51:K51** to **cell A54**.

h. Perform the advanced filter by copying data to the output range. Use the appropriate ranges for list range, criteria range, and output range.

i. Hide columns B, C, D, and H in the Salary Data worksheet. Change the width of column F to **21**.

j. Insert database functions by completing these steps on the Information worksheet:
   - **Cell B2:** Insert the DSUM function to calculate the total salary for programmers in Salt Lake City. Use the range A$1:K$49 in the Salary Data worksheet for the database, Salary for the field, and the criteria range.
   - **Cell B3:** Insert the DAVERAGE function to calculate the average salary for programmers in Salt Lake City.
   - **Cell B4:** Insert the DMAX function to identify the highest salary for programmers in Salt Lake City.
   - **Cell B5:** Insert the DMIN function to identify the lowest salary for programmers in Salt Lake City.
   - **Cell B6:** Insert the DCOUNT function to count the number of programmers in Salt Lake City.

k. Format the **range B2:B5** with **Accounting Number Format** with zero decimal places. Format **cell B6** with **Comma Style** with zero decimal places.

l. Insert a CONCAT function in **cell B1** that concatenates the text in 'Salary Data'!F52 and 'Salary Data'!I52 separated by a space, the word **in**, and another space. The result should look like this: Programming in Salt Lake City.

m. Insert the MATCH function in **cell E3** to identify the position of the ID stored in cell E2. Use the range A2:A49 in the Salary Data worksheet for the lookup_array argument and look for exact matches only.

n. Insert the INDEX function in **cell E4** with **Salary Data!A$2:K$49** as the array, **E$3** that contains the MATCH function as the row number, and **4** as the column number to retrieve the last name corresponding to the ID in cell E3.

o. Copy the INDEX function to the **range E5:E6**. Edit the function in **cell E5** by changing 4 to **7**. Edit the function in **cell E6** by changing 4 to **11**. Format **cell E6** with **Accounting Number Format** with zero decimal places. Change the ID in **cell E2** to **17604** to test the results of the MATCH and INDEX functions.

p. Insert FORMULATEXT functions by completing these steps:
- **Cell H2:** Insert the function to display the formula that is stored in cell B2.
- **Cell H3:** Insert the function to display the formula that is stored in cell E3.
- **Cell H4:** Insert the function to display the formula that is stored in cell E4.
- **Cell H5:** Insert the function to display the formula that is stored in cell B5.
- **Cell H6:** Insert the function to display the formula that is stored in cell B6.

q. Change the width for column H to **57**.

r. Create a footer with your name on the left side, the sheet name code in the center, and the file name code on the right side on all sheets.

s. Save and close the file. Exit Excel. Based on your instructor's directions, submit e11m2GameStudio_LastFirst.

Running Case

New Castle County Technical Services

New Castle County Technical Services (NCCTS) provides technical support services for a number of companies in New Castle County, Delaware. Previously, you imported a text file into the workbook and analyzed data by using Power Pivot. Now you will manipulate text with text functions and use Flash Fill to complete a column. Then you will create criteria and output ranges to perform an advanced filter and use database functions to provide summary statistics. Finally, you will use lookup functions to lookup a call and display the hours logged.

a. Open *e11r1NCCTS* and save it as **e11r1NCCTS_LastFirst**.

b. Click **cell D2** on the Customers sheet and insert the TEXTJOIN function to combine the Customer ID and uppercase Last name with a hyphen as the delimiter. Nest the UPPER function within the TEXTJOIN function.

c. Insert the LEN function in **cell E2** to identify the length of the new Customer Code in cell D2. You want to ensure the newly created Customer Code contains no more than 15 characters for each customer.

d. Display the April worksheet, type **4-080** in **cell B2** to create a new Call ID based on the month number 4 for April. Use Flash Fill to complete the **range B3:B28**.

e. Create criteria and output ranges by completing the following steps:
- Copy the **range A1:I1** and paste it in **cell A31** and **cell A35**.
- Enter the call type IDs **3** and **4** in the respective cells within the criteria range.

f. Perform an advanced filter by copying the data to the **range A35:I35**.

g. Insert the database function in **cell L32** to calculate the total hours logged for the criteria Call Type ID 3 and 4.

h. Insert the database function in **cell L33** to calculate the average hours logged for the criteria Call Type ID 3 and 4.

i. Insert the DGET function in **cell L36** to get the hours logged for the Call ID stored in cell K36. Click **cell K36** and change the value to **4-099**.

j. Insert the INDEX function with a nested MATCH function in **cell L17**. Use the range B2:I28 as the array. The nested MATCH function should identify the position of the Call ID that is stored in cell L16 compared to the range B2:B28. Use 5 for the column_num argument.

k. Insert a footer with your name on the left side, the sheet name in the center, and the file name code on the right side on Customers and April worksheets.

l. Save and close the workbook. Based on your instructor's directions, submit e11r1NCCTS_LastFirst.

Disaster Recovery

Houses Sold

You are the manager for a real estate agency. Your assistant created a list of houses that were put on the market in April. However, the list contains several issues and errors that you will fix. Open *e11d1Houses* and save it as **e11d1Houses_LastFirst.**

First, the CONCAT function in the Code-Num column concatenates the Code and Num data in columns A and B. However, the concatenated result should have a hyphen, such as CH-1. Correct the function in cell C5 and copy the corrected function down the column. Next, your assistant combined the street address with the cities. Luckily, a comma separates the data. Convert the text to columns to separate the addresses from the cities.

Your assistant created criteria and output ranges. However, the conditions in the criteria range are not correctly entered. You want to identify houses in American Fork that were represented by Goodrich or Carey. Correct the criteria range and run the advanced filter to copy the records to the output range. Six records should be copied.

The database function in cell E2 does not correctly identify the number of records for houses in American Fork. Correct the function name and the field argument. The INDEX function in cell H2 is incorrect. It should use the position in cell I1 as the row number and the correct column for the selling price. Correct the function's arguments and format the result with Accounting Number Format with zero decimal places. Change the number in **cell H1** to **CH-1** to see if the results update correctly.

Create a footer with your name on the left side, the sheet name in the center, and the file name code on the right side on all sheets. Save and close the file. Exit Excel. Based on your instructor's directions, submit e11d1Houses_LastFirst.

Capstone Exercise

University Donors List

You are a development officer for a state university. As an officer, you manage a portfolio of important donors who contribute financially to different areas within the university. You categorize the donors based on the college or school for which they want their donations associated.

You recently downloaded the portfolio to an Excel workbook. Based on the way the data downloads from the main database, you want to format the text for readability and to make it easier for you to analyze. In addition, you will create an advanced filter to review a list of donors for a particular college or school. Finally, you want to create a look up area to look up data for a specific donor and create a summary section.

Extract and Join Test

The first column displays the name of the college or school (such as ART or BUSINESS) associated with each. You want to assign a three-character code for each college and use that code to attach to existing donor IDs to create a unique field. Because the data may be used to create mailings, you want to display the college/school names in upper and lowercase.

1. Open *e11c1Donors* save as **e11c1Donors_LastFirst**.
2. Insert the LEFT function in **cell B8** that extracts the first three characters from the college name in cell A8. Copy the function to the **range B9:B35**.
3. Insert the CONCAT function in **cell D8** that combines the college ID in cell B8 with the donor ID in cell C8 with a hyphen between the two text strings. Copy the function to the **range D9:D35**.
4. Insert a text function in **cell J8** that displays the college name from cell A8 with just the first letter capitalized, such as Engineering. Copy the function to the **range J9:J35**.

Fill in Columns

The Full Name column displays last and first names of the donors. You want to display last names only in a separate column. The Address column contains street addresses, city names, and state abbreviations. To manage the address list better, you will separate the data into three columns.

5. Type **Schneider** in **cell F8** and use Flash Fill to fill in the last names for the donors in the **range F9:F35**.
6. Select the addresses in the **range G8:G35** and convert the text to columns, separating the data at commas.

Look Up Area

The top-left section of the spreadsheet is designed to be able to enter a donor's ID, such as ENG-15, and look up that person's position in the list, display the donor's full name, and display the amount donated this year.

7. Insert the MATCH function in **cell B3** to look up the donor ID in cell B2, compare it to the list in the range D8:D35, and then return the donor's position within the list.
8. Insert an INDEX function in **cell B4** that uses the range D8:K35, looks up the row position number from the MATCH function result, and then uses the column position number for Full Name.
9. Insert an INDEX function in **cell B5** that uses the range D8:K35, looks up the row position number from the MATCH function result, and then uses the column position number for Donation. Format the value as **Accounting Number Format** with zero decimal places.

Advanced Database Filtering

To analyze the donor records, you are ready to create criteria and output ranges. You will enter conditions to find records for donors to the College of Business who donated $1,000 or more.

10. Copy the **range A7:K7** to **cell A38** to create the column labels for the criteria range.
11. Copy the column labels to **cell A42**.
12. Type **Business** in **cell J39** and >=**1000** in **cell K39**.
13. Perform the advanced filter by copying the records to the output area.

Insert Database Functions

Now that you created a copy of the records meeting the conditions, you are ready to enter database functions in the Summary area.

14. Insert the database function in **cell K2** to total the value of the donations for the records that meet the conditions in the criteria range.
15. Insert the database function in **cell K3** to calculate the average donation for the records that meet the conditions in the criteria range.
16. Insert the database function in **cell K4** to count the number of records that meet the conditions in the criteria range.
17. Format the **range K2:K3** with **Accounting Number Format** with zero decimal places. Format **cell K4** with **Comma Style** with zero decimal places.

Workbook Completion

You are ready to complete the workbook by entering a function to display formulas as text and adding a footer with identifying information.

18. Insert the FORMULATEXT function in **cell G2** to display the formula stored in cell B3. Insert the FORMULATEXT function in **cell G3** to display the formula stored in cell B4. Insert the FORMULATEXT function in **cell G4** to display the formula stored in cell D8. Insert the FORMULATEXT function in **cell G5** to display the formula stored in cell K2.

19. Create a footer with your name on the left side, the sheet name code in the center, and the file name code on the right side of each worksheet.

20. Save and close the file. Exit Excel. Based on your instructor's directions, submit e11c1Donors_LastFirst.

Templates, Workbook Inspection, and Macros

LEARNING OUTCOME You will demonstrate how to design templates, inspect workbooks, and create macros.

OBJECTIVES & SKILLS: After you read this chapter, you will be able to:

CASE STUDY | Wilhelmina's Total Lawn Care

Recently, you took a position as the senior account manager at Wilhelmina's Total Lawn Care (WTLC), a lawn care company located in Leland, Michigan. WTLC specializes in full service lawn care ranging from landscaping to weekly maintenance. The previous manager used a paper-based system to prepare expense reports, invoices, and payroll statements. However, this was a time-consuming process and required manual recalculation when any values changed.

You want to start automating tasks using your extensive experience with Excel. You decide to start with the client invoice report form. Because each of the company's billing representatives utilizes the same procedures, you will adapt an Excel template to use as a model for creating invoices. The template needs to be generic enough to accommodate a range of options, but it also needs to maintain a standard design to facilitate easy data entry.

You will download an existing Excel invoice template, customize the template for your business needs, and inspect the worksheet for accessibility. Finally, you will create macros to perform a series of tasks, such as clearing the values to reset the form and finalizing the invoice for management approval.

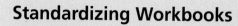

Standardizing Workbooks

CHAPTER 12

YanLev/Shutterstock

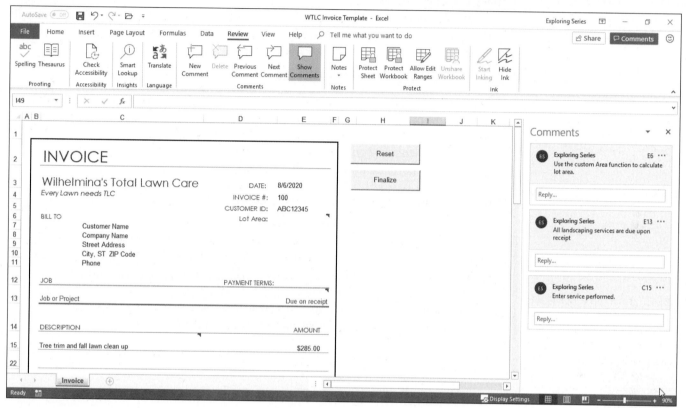

FIGURE 12.1 WTLC Invoice Template

CASE STUDY | Wilhelmina's Total Lawn Care

Starting File	File to be Submitted
e12h1Invoice	e12h4Invoice_LastFirst

MyLab IT Grader An alternate version of this project is available as a MyLab IT Grader Assessment

Templates

Designing the perfect workbook can be time consuming. By now, you know you must plan the layout before you enter data to minimize data-entry changes later. You determine what column and row labels are needed to describe the data, where to place the labels, and how to format the labels. In addition, you enter and format quantitative data. The longer you work for the same department or organization, the more you will notice that you create the same types of workbooks. Excel has the right tools to improve your productivity in developing consistently formatted workbooks. Some of these tools include templates, themes, backgrounds, and styles.

In this section, you will select an Excel template. After opening the template, you will edit the design, save the template for distribution, and test the final template.

STEP 1 Selecting a Template

A *template* is a partially completed document that you use as a model to create other documents that have the same structure and purpose. A template typically contains standard labels, formulas, and formatting but may contain little or no quantitative data. Templates help ensure consistency and standardization for similar workbooks, such as detailed sales reports for all 12 months of a year.

To open a template, complete the following steps:

1. Start Excel, or if you are already working within a workbook, click the File tab and click New. (On a Mac, click the File menu and select New from Template.) Backstage view displays a gallery of featured templates (see Figure 12.2).
2. Select a template from templates you have recently used, sample templates that were installed with the software, or download new templates to meet the business need from Office.com. A window will display a sample of the selected template (see Figure 12.3).
3. Click Create to load the template data as a new workbook.

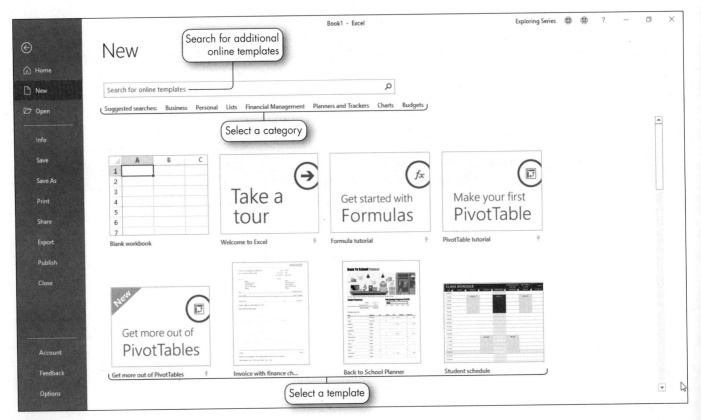

FIGURE 12.2 Template Gallery

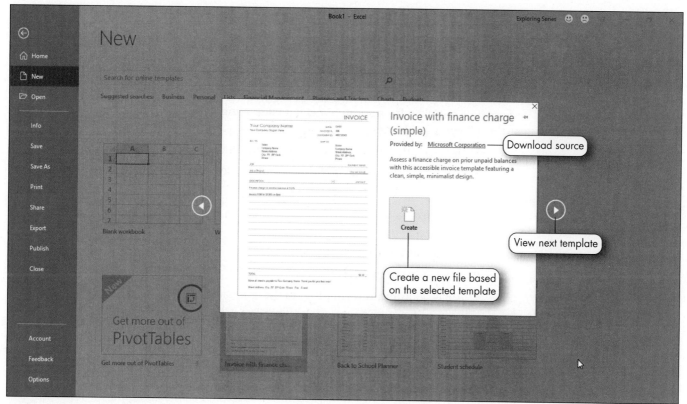

FIGURE 12.3 Preview of Template

The *Search for online templates* box enables you to search Office.com for a template by entering your search conditions. Alternatively, you can select a template from a category, such as Business. These templates are created by Microsoft, a Microsoft partner, or a member of the Microsoft community.

STEP 2 ## Edit an Existing Template

While downloading an existing template can be a time saving technique, it is important to note that it may not perfectly fit your business needs. Workbooks available for download in the template gallery are created as a generic starting point and they may not contain the look and feel of your company's brand image, required calculations, and appropriate labelling. It is important to carefully review files downloaded from the template gallery and edit the content for your use. You can apply a theme or add a background or logo to ensure a consistent look and feel. You may also want to add custom calculations and add or remove columns or rows. Once the changes have been made, the template can either be saved as a normal workbook, an Excel Template, a macro-enabled workbook, or a Macro Enabled Template.

STEP 3 Creating a Template

Using Excel templates saves time when designing workbooks, but the template gallery may not always have options that meet your exact needs. When this is the case, you can create a workbook with the specifications you need and save it as a template, so it can be used as a model to create identically structured workbooks for unique data. When you create a template from scratch instead of starting with an existing template, adhere to the following guidelines:

- Use formatted, descriptive labels and formulas.
- Avoid values when possible in formulas; use cell references instead.
- Use appropriate functions to trap errors.
- Include data-validation settings (valid data rules, warning messages, input messages).
- Include instructions for the template.
- Turn off worksheet gridlines for clarity.
- Apply appropriate formatting to the template.
- Give worksheets meaningful names and delete worksheets that are not used.

After finalizing your workbook, the file type must be changed to an Excel Template (.xltx) or Macro-Enabled Template (.xltm) in order for it to display in the template gallery. This can be done by either exporting the file or using the Save As dialog box.

TIP: EXPORT VS. SAVE AS

When exporting a file in Excel, a new copy of the file is created with the properties designated in Backstage view, i.e., Excel Template or Macro-Enabled Template. While using the Save As feature can yield the same results, it is important to note that using Save As can overwrite the current file if the file name and type is not changed.

To save a workbook as a template, complete the following steps:

1. Click the File tab and click Export. (On a Mac, click the File menu and select Save as Template.)
2. Click Change File Type.
3. Click Template in the Change File Type list and click Save As to open the Save As dialog box. Notice that the *Save as type* is set to Excel Template.
4. Select the storage location, type a name in the File name box, and then click Save.

TIP: TRAP ERRORS WITH THE IFERROR FUNCTION AND SET DATA VALIDATION

Formulas used in workbooks display zeros or error messages when you remove values in reference cells to create a template. You can use the IFERROR function to check a cell to see if it contains errors or if a formula will result in an error. If no error exists, the IFERROR function returns the value of the formula. If an error does occur, you can enter an argument in the function to display a customized error message instead of a default error, such as #DIV/0!. In addition, you can set validation rules so template users will enter correct data.

In order for your template to display in the template gallery in Backstage view, it must be saved in the custom office template folder. The default folder location is C:\Users\Username\Documents\Custom Office Templates in Windows 10. (On a Mac, use the folder /Users/<username>/Library/GroupContainers/UBF8T346G9.Office/User Content/Templates). If you use File Explorer to find the Custom Office Templates folder, you will need to display hidden folders to do so. This default location can be changed by editing save options. To access save options click the File tab, click Options, and click Save. If you save your custom templates in the correct location, you can access them to create new workbooks by clicking the File tab, clicking New, and then clicking Personal in the template gallery of Backstage view. The New page displays thumbnails and names for the templates you created.

Quick Concepts

1. Describe the benefits of downloading templates from the template gallery. *pp. 704–705*

2. Describe changes you may make to a template downloaded from the template gallery. *p. 705*

3. Describe a situation in which you would create a custom template. *pp. 706–707*

Hands-On Exercises

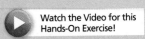
Skills covered: Select a Template • Edit an Existing Template • Create a Template

1 Templates

You need to get up and running quickly as the new senior account manager at WTLC. You decide to use the Invoice with finance charge (simple) template that is part of the Office template downloads. After opening the template, you will modify it by changing cell colors, removing sample text, and adding the company information. As your last step, you will save the document as a template that will be distributed to your sales reps.

STEP 1 SELECT A TEMPLATE

To save time, you will create a new report using a template. After reviewing the templates available in the template gallery, you decide the Invoice with finance charge (simple) template shown in Figure 12.4 is sufficient to build your company's invoice form. Your first step is to review and download the template. Refer to Figure 12.4 as you complete Step 1.

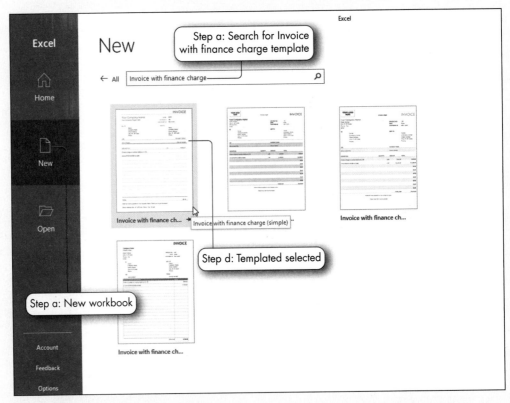

FIGURE 12.4 Invoice Template

a. Open Excel, click **New**, and then search for the **Invoice with finance charge (simple) template** in the template gallery. (On Mac click File and click New from Template.)

> **TROUBLESHOOTING:** Microsoft Office templates are frequently added, removed, or edited. When searching online templates, it is a good practice to make a backup copy of the original template, because it may not always be available. If the template is not available in the Office Gallery, you can use the template file e12h1Invoice from the student data files. Figure 12.4 shows the Invoice template as it appears in the template gallery.

The Invoice template provides the basic design you need, but you want to add your company's contact information. You also want to delete the sample data and remove the developer's data validation comments. Refer to Figure 12.5 as you complete Step 2.

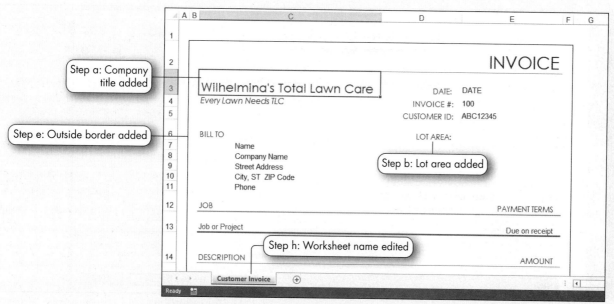

FIGURE 12.5 Edit the Invoice Template

a. Click **cell B2** and type **Wilhelmina's Total Lawn Care**. Click **cell B3**, click **Italic** in the Font group, and type **Every Lawn Needs TLC**.

b. Select **cell C5**, type **LOT AREA:**, and then delete the values in the **range D6:D10** and **B14:B15**.

c. Click **cell B27** and type **1234 Caesar Parkway, Leland, MI 49654**.

d. Right-click **Row 1** and select **Insert**. Right-click **Column A** and select **Insert**. Select **column A**, click **Format** in the Cells group, and then select **Column Width**. Type **2** and click **OK**.

   You added a new row and column to provide more space between the start of the text and the edge of the document.

e. Select the **range B2:F29**, click the **border arrow** in the Font group, and then select **Outside Borders**.

   You added a border around the text in the template to make the document easier to read.

f. Select the **range B2:F25** and **range C27:D28**. Click the **Data tab**, click the **Data Validation arrow** in the Data Tools group, and then select **Data Validation**. Click **OK** when the warning message appears.

g. Click the **Input Message tab**, click **Clear All**, and then click **OK**.

   You removed generic notes in the template that were added by the document creator and saved as Data Validation Input Messages.

h. Double-click the **worksheet tab** and type **Customer Invoice**. Save the workbook.

After a file is downloaded Into the template gallery, it will open as a normal Excel workbook (.xlsx) by default. You want to save your edited file as a template so it can be shared with your employees. Refer to Figure 12.6 as you complete Step 3.

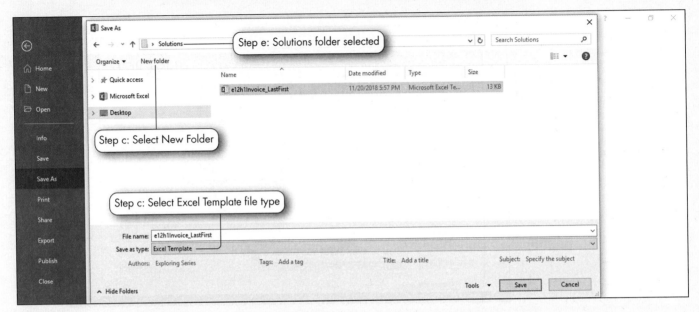

FIGURE 12.6 Save as a Template

a. Click the **File tab**.

b. Click **Export**, click **Change File Type**, and click **Template**.

c. Click **Save As**, navigate to the location of your student data files, and click **New Folder**. (On Mac, click File and click Save as template.)

d. Name the folder Solutions.

e. Save the file in the Solutions folder with the name **e12h1Invoice_LastFirst**.

When a workbook is saved as a template, by default it is automatically placed in the Custom Office Templates directory. Exporting the file placed the template in your student data file solutions folder.

Checking for Issues and Workbook Documentation

When you prepare to share an electronic copy of a workbook with others, you should run some checking tools to review your workbook for issues that might reveal personal information or create problems with other users. For example, if you are conducting a confidential analysis for a client or if you have a confidentiality agreement with a client, that client probably does not want to reveal that you did some analyses. You should remove any properties or identifying attributes that indicate you worked on the workbook. After reviewing and updating a workbook, you can protect the integrity of the workbook. For example, you can save the workbook with a password, or restrict who is able to edit or print the workbook.

In this section, you will prepare a workbook for sharing and protect a workbook. You will use tools to check for issues and mark a workbook as final.

Checking for Issues

Often, people prepare and distribute workbooks to others inside and outside their organizations. For example, you might distribute the customer invoice template during new hire training. Excel contains three tools—Document Inspector, Accessibility Checker, and Compatibility Checker—that check the workbook for issues and alert you so that you can make any necessary changes before distributing the workbook.

STEP 1 Use Document Inspector

Recall that document properties contain details about a workbook, such as the author and organization that are added automatically, which you may not want publicized. Furthermore, it may contain documentation such as comments, header/footer information, XML data, and hyperlinks that are manually added to the workbook for internal use only. The **Document Inspector** is a tool that reviews a workbook for hidden or personal data stored in the document. The Document Inspector then informs you of these details so that you can select what data to remove. However, you cannot remove these elements if the file is a shared workbook. If the workbook is shared, you must first save a copy and turn off sharing in order to use the Document Inspector. Table 12.1 lists the information evaluated by the Document Inspector. The Document Inspector is not available on Excel for Mac.

TABLE 12.1 Data Evaluated by the Document Inspector	
Data Type	**Description**
Comments and Ink Annotations	If you collaborated with colleagues to create the document, comments or ink annotations can contain personal information.
Document Properties and Personal Information	Metadata that is created automatically, such as the author property, document creation date, and edit dates.
Headers and Footers	Information located in headers and footers not intended to be publicly shared.
Hidden Rows, Columns, and Worksheets	Hidden worksheets or workbooks can contain private information not intended to be publicly shared.
Document Server Properties	The document could contain the location and name of private file servers.

TABLE 12.1   Data Evaluated by the Document Inspector (continued)

Data Type	Description
Custom XML Data	The document could contain XML that provides names and file locations of linked documents.
Invisible Content	Items formatted as invisible can contain private content that can be discovered if the item is unhidden.
External Links	External links can contain path information to other files or servers.
Embedded Files or Objects	Embedded files and objects can contain hidden metadata with private information.
Macros of VBA Code	Macros and VBA modules can contain comments and file paths to private information and servers.
Items That May Have Cached Data	PivotTables, PivotCharts, Slicers, and timelines can contain invisible private cached data.
Excel Surveys	Excel surveys created using Office online can contain private data hidden in a workbook.
Scenario Manager Scenarios	Scenarios created using scenario manager can contain authoring information and edit dates not intended for distribution.
Filters	Active Autofilters and table filters can contain cached private data.
Hidden Names	Hidden names and data in a workbook can contain private information not intended to be shared.

TIP: MAKE A BACKUP!
Before using Document Inspector, you should save a copy of the workbook, and then run Document Inspector on the duplicate workbook, because you cannot always restore all data that Document Inspector removes.

To use Document Inspector, complete the following steps:

1. Click the File tab and click Info.
2. Click Check for Issues and select Inspect Document to open the Document Inspector dialog box (see Figure 12.7). Excel will prompt you to save the workbook if you have made any changes that have not been saved yet.
3. Select the check boxes for the types of document content you want to inspect.
4. Click Inspect to display the inspection results.
5. Click Remove All for the types of content that you want to remove. Keep in mind that you might not be able to undo the changes. Use Help to learn more about hidden data and personal information that can be contained in a workbook.

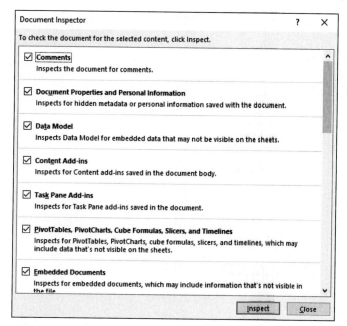

FIGURE 12.7 Document Inspector

Check Accessibility

With a diverse audience of people using technology today, you should ensure your documents are accessible by everyone. The ***Accessibility Checker*** is a tool that reviews a workbook to detect potential issues that could hinder users who access your files and alerts you to these issues so that you can address them. The Accessibility Checker identifies the following types of issues, among others:

- Objects (such as charts and tables) that do not contain alternative (alt) text that make files more accessible to users who use screen readers
- Tables containing header rows
- Tables containing merged cells
- Hyperlinks that do not have ScreenTips

Accessibility Checker provides three types of feedback for each issue:

- **Error.** Content that creates extreme difficulty or impossibility for persons with disabilities to view correctly.
- **Warning.** Content that is difficult for users to comprehend.
- **Tip.** Content that is understandable but could be presented or organized differently to maximize comprehension.

To use the Accessibility Checker, complete the following steps:

1. Click the Review tab.
2. Click Check Accessibility in the Accessibility group. The Accessibility Checker task pane opens on the right side of the worksheet window, showing the results (see Figure 12.8).
3. Click a listed issue to see feedback in the Additional Information window. This window tells you why you should fix the problem and how to fix it.

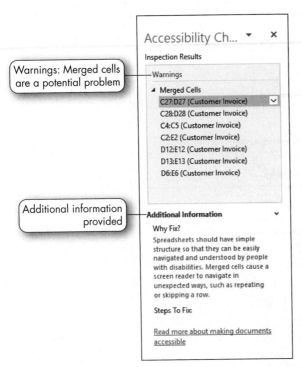

Warnings: Merged cells are a potential problem

Additional information provided

FIGURE 12.8 Accessibility Checker

STEP 3 ## Check Compatibility

When you provide an Excel workbook for others to use, be aware that the recipients may have an older version of Excel installed on their computers. Because each version of Excel contains new features, you may be using features that are not compatible with previous versions. For example, you may be using a chart style or PivotTable feature that was not available in previous versions of Excel. The *Compatibility Checker* is a tool that evaluates the workbook's contents to identify what data and features are not compatible with previous versions. By default, Compatibility Checker selects all Excel versions 97 through the current version. However, you can select a specific version to review for your workbook. The Compatibility Checker summarizes the issues that it finds within the dialog box and can create a worksheet that contains a list of issues. The Compatibility Checker is not available in Excel for Mac.

To use Compatibility Checker, complete the following steps:

1. Click the File tab and click Info.
2. Click Check for Issues and select Check Compatibility. The Microsoft Excel - Compatibility Checker dialog box opens, showing a list of issues (see Figure 12.9).
3. Click the *Check compatibility when saving this workbook* check box if you want to check compatibility every time you save the workbook. Deselect the check box if you do not want to check the workbook automatically when saving.
4. Click Copy to New Sheet to create a report that lists the issues on a separate worksheet.
5. Click OK after reviewing the issues so that you can address them in the workbook.

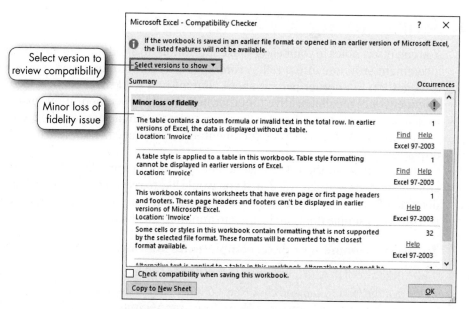

FIGURE 12.9 Compatibility Checker

It is helpful to select the option to copy a list of compatibility issues to a new worksheet named Compatibility Report. The worksheet organizes issues into groups, such as *Significant loss of functionality* and *Minor loss of fidelity* (see Figure 12.10). The worksheet indicates the number of occurrences per issue type and the worksheet and cell reference containing the issue. The last column indicates which version(s) of Excel are not compatible with that issue.

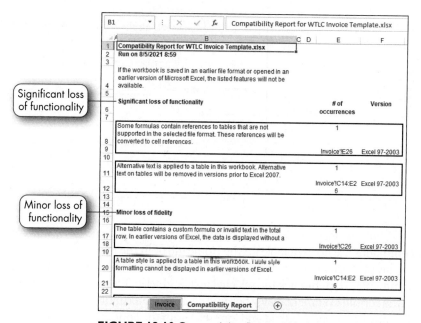

FIGURE 12.10 Compatibility Report Worksheet

> ### TIP: UNSUPPORTED FEATURES
> Type *Check file compatibility with earlier versions* in the Tell Me box to find out about Excel features that are not supported in earlier versions. This help topic provides details about significant loss of functionality, what it means, and what to do to solve the problem.

STEP 4 ▶ Annotating a Worksheet

You can insert notes to yourself or make suggestions to another team member by inserting a comment or a note into a cell. A **comment** is an annotation to ask a question or offer a suggestion to another person about content in a worksheet cell (see Figure 12.11). Comments are a collaborative tool that help provide documentation, instruction, and feedback in a workbook. If no feedback is required, a simple note can be used to annotate the document. A **note** is a basic documentation tool that can annotate a cell but does not display as a discussion thread.

For example, in the Invoice workbook, you want to provide information on how to enter details on services provided. If you would like to receive questions or feedback on the document, a comment should be used. If no feedback or interaction with the collaborator is required, a simple note can be used to annotate the document.

> **To insert a comment or note, complete the following steps:**
>
> 1. Click the cell in which you want to insert the comment.
> 2. Click the Review tab and click New Comment in the Comments group, or click **Notes** in the Notes group and select **New Note**. Alternatively, right-click the cell and select **New Comment** or **New Note**.
> 3. Type the text that you want to display in the comment or note and click any cell outside the annotation.

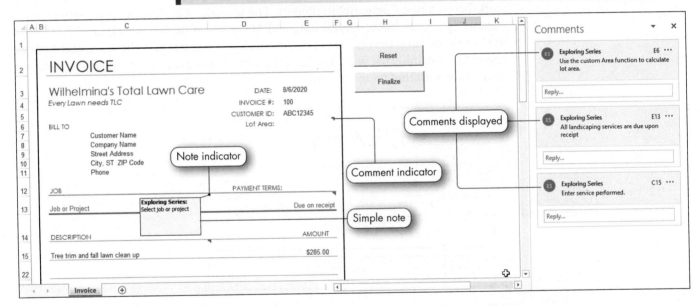

FIGURE 12.11 Comment

You can format comment text similar to other text, however, certain formatting commands are not available on the Home tab or in the Font dialog box. Instead, you need to display the Format Comment dialog box. To display the Format Comment dialog box, select the comment text, right-click the selected text, and select Format Comment. Next, select formats in the Format Comment dialog box and click OK. Alternatively, select comment text and apply font attributes, such as bold and font size, from the Font group on the Home tab.

Once a comment is created it appears as a discussion thread when displayed. This thread features a reply box that allows collaborators to provide direct feedback. The comment thread is then stored in the comment and is available for review.

STEP 5 ▶ Edit and Delete Annotations

You may need to edit a comment or simple note in the event of a clerical error or if information changes. For example, you might have originally inserted a general comment such as *payment due upon receipt*. Later, you may decide to give customers 30 days to pay the invoice therefore the comment should be edited to say *Payment due within 30 days*.

To edit a comment, complete the following steps:

1. Point to the cell containing the comment to be edited.
2. Point to the comment and click Edit.
3. Edit the comment text and click Save.

To edit a note, complete the following steps:

1. Click the cell that contains the note you want to edit.
2. Click the Review tab, click Notes in the Notes group, and select Edit Note. Alternatively right-click the cell and select Edit Note.
3. Edit the note text.
4. Click outside the note box after you edit the note.

After you read a comment or note if you no longer need the annotation, it can be deleted. To delete a comment, select the cell that contains the comment, and click Delete in the Comments group on the Review tab. Alternatively, you can right-click the cell and select Delete Comment. Excel immediately deletes the comment without providing a warning. If you want to restore the comment, immediately click Undo on the Quick Access Toolbar. To delete a note, right-click the cell that contains the note and select Delete Note.

> **TIP: REMOVING ALL COMMENTS**
> To remove all comments at the same time, press Ctrl+G to display the Go To dialog box, click Special, ensure that Comments is selected, and then click OK. This selects all cells containing comments in the current worksheet. Click the Home tab, click Clear in the Editing group, and then select Clear Comments.

Print Annotations

When you print a worksheet, comments and notes do not print by default. The Sheet tab in the Page Setup dialog box contains options for printing comments and notes. The default Comments setting is None. If you choose *As displayed on sheet* (legacy), the visible note boxes display where they are located onscreen. Hidden notes do not print. Choose *At end of sheet* to print threaded comments comments on a separate page (see Figure 12.12). This printout includes the cell reference and the comment text for each comment on the active worksheet, even if the comments are hidden.

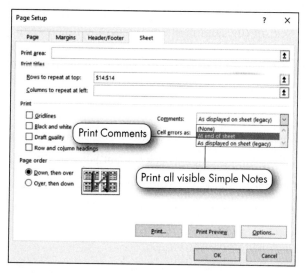

FIGURE 12.12 Page Setup Dialog Box with Comments Options

STEP 6 ▶ Show and Hide Annotations

A purple indicator, known as a *comment indicator*, displays in the top-right corner of a cell containing a comment. A red triangle indicates a simple note. When you point to a cell with a comment, a comment box displays the user name in bold along with the comment. When a comment is displayed, you can add a response using the reply box. When a response is added, the comment box will display the original comment and response as a thread. When you click outside the comment box, it closes, but the comment indicator remains in the cell. Point to that cell to display the comment again. Other comments remain hidden unless you show them. Table 12.2 lists steps to show and hide comments onscreen.

TIP: DISABLE COMMENT INDICATOR

By default, the comment indicator displays as a purple marker in the top-right of a cell. This can be disabled by selecting No Comment or Indicators in the Advanced Display settings in Backstage view.

TABLE 12.2 Show and Hide Comments

Action	Ribbon Method	Shortcut Method
Show a comment	Click the cell containing the comment. Click Show/Hide Comment in the Comments group on the Review tab.	Right-click the cell containing the comment. Select Show/Hide Comments. Point to a cell containing a comment.
Hide a comment	Click the cell containing the comment. Click Show/Hide Comment in the Comments group.	Right-click the cell containing the comment. Select Hide Comment.
Display or hide all comments in the entire workbook	Click Show All Comments in the Comments group. Click Comments on the upper-right corner of the ribbon.	Not applicable

To advance through a series of comments without clicking each cell individually, click Next in the Comments group on the Review tab to go to the cell containing the next comment, or click Previous to go to the cell containing the previous comment. All comments can also be displayed in the Comments pane by clicking the Comments button on the upper-right corner of the ribbon.

Quick Concepts

4. Describe the significance of the Document Inspector. *p. 711*

5. Why is it important to check compatibility? *p. 714–715*

6. Describe a situation in which you would add comments to a workbook. *p. 716*

Hands-On Exercises

Skills covered: Use the Document Inspector • Check Accessibility • Check Compatibility • Annotate a Workbook • Edit and Delete Comments • Show and Hide Comments

2 Checking for Issues and Workbook Documentation

After customizing the Invoice template, you want to inspect the document for personal information and hidden properties, accessibility, and compatibility. You also want to add comments to provide instruction to your sales representatives.

STEP 1 ## USE THE DOCUMENT INSPECTOR

Prior to distributing your template, you want to remove all personal information. You will use the Document Inspector to complete the task. Refer to Figure 12.13 as you complete Step 1.

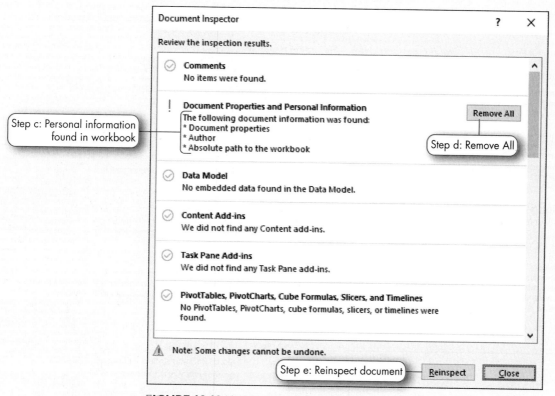

FIGURE 12.13 Use the Document Inspector

a. Open *e12h1Invoice_LastFirst* if you closed it at the end of Hands-On Exercise 1, and save it as **e12h2Invoice_LastFirst**, changing h1 to h2.

> **TROUBLESHOOTING:** If you have trouble locating the file, search for the Custom Office Templates folder on your computer.

b. Click the **File tab**. Click **Info**, click **Check for Issues** in the Info section and then select **Inspect Document**. Click **Yes** when prompted to save changes and then click **Inspect Document**.

The Document Inspector dialog box opens.

c. Ensure all the check boxes are selected and click **Inspect**.

The Document Inspector discovers personal information and header and footer information that should be removed.

d. Click **Remove All** in the Document Properties and Personal Information section. Click **Remove All** in the Headers and Footers section.

e. Click **Reinspect** and click **Reinspect all** to ensure the issues have been resolved. Click **Close** and save the workbook.

STEP 2 CHECK ACCESSIBILITY

The invoice will be sent electronically, and you want to make sure the Invoice template does not contain content that might cause difficulties for users. To ensure this document is compliant with accessibility standards, you will check accessibility. If any issues are discovered, you will make the necessary changes. Refer to Figure 12.14 as you complete Step 2.

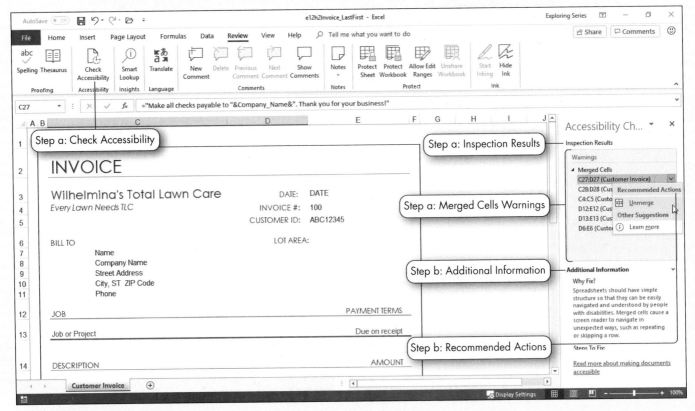

FIGURE 12.14 Check Accessibility

a. Click the **Review tab** and click **Check Accessibility** in the Accessibility group.

The Accessibility Checker task pane displays on the right side. The inspection results display a warning due to merged cells.

b. Select **C27:D27** in the Inspection Results section of the Accessibility Checker pane. Review the *Why Fix* description. Click the arrow to the right of C27:D27 in the Accessibility pane and select **Unmerge**.

You unmerged the range C27:D27 correcting the first accessibility issue. Notice the Merged Cells warning for the range C27:D27 has been removed from the Inspection Results.

c. Adapt the previous step to accept the recommended actions for **C28:D28, C4:C5, C2:E2, D12:E12, D13:E13, D6:E6**.

d. Select **cell C2** and click **Align Left** in the Alignment group.

In the prior step, you unmerged the range C2:E2. When this was completed, the Invoice title was moved to cell C2. You changed the alignment of the text in cell C2 so the title is left justified.

e. Click **cell D13**, type **Due on:** and then press **Ctrl+Enter**.

f. Close the Accessibility Checker pane and save the workbook.

STEP 3 ▶ CHECK COMPATIBILITY

You know that some of remote staff members are using Excel 2010. You want to make sure the workbook does not have critical features that might not display when opened with the older version of the software. Refer to Figure 12.15 as you complete Step 3.

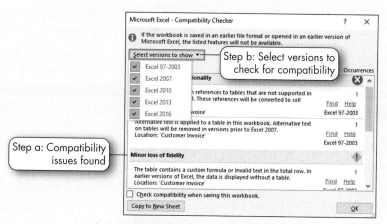

FIGURE 12.15 Check Compatibility

a. Click the **File tab**. Click **Info**, click **Check for Issues**, and select **Check Compatibility**.

The Microsoft Excel – Compatibility Checker dialog box opens. It reports several compatibility issues with Excel 97-2003.

> **MAC TROUBLESHOOTING:** The Compatibility Checker is not available with Excel for Mac.

b. Click **Select versions to show**. Deselect Excel 97-2003. Click **Select versions to show** and deselect Excel 2007.

Because no staff member is using software older than 2010, you modified the compatibility check to display issues with Excel 2010-2016. No issues were found.

c. Click **OK** and save the workbook.

STEP 4 › ANNOTATE A WORKSHEET

You want to add notes to the template to provide instruction to your staff. To do this you will annotate the workbook using comments. Refer to Figure 12.16 as you complete Step 4.

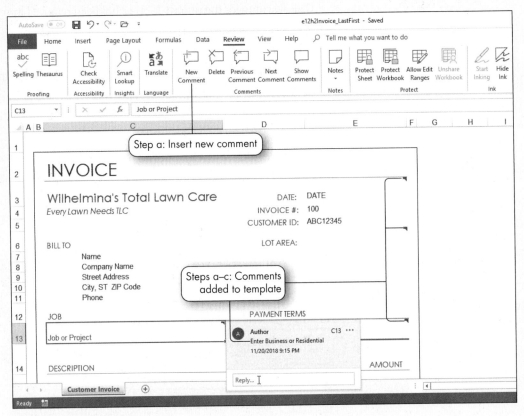

FIGURE 12.16 Insert Comments

a. Click **cell C13** and press **Delete**. Click the **Review tab**, click **New Comment**, and then type **Enter Business or Residential**.

Excel displays a comment indicator in the top-right corner of cell C13 and the newly created comment.

b. Click **cell E3**, click **New Comment**, and then type **Insert date**.

c. Click **cell E6**, click **New Comment**, and then type **Use the custom area function to calculate lot area**.

d. Click **cell E13**, click **New Comment**, and then type **Business jobs are due in 30 days, all others due upon receipt**.

e. Click **Save**.

STEP 5 ▶ EDIT AND DELETE COMMENTS

After inserting comments, you decide you will automate the insertion of the date in a later step. Therefore, you will remove the comment from cell E3. You also want to edit the comment in cell E13 to make a small grammatical change. Refer to Figure 12.17 as you complete Step 5.

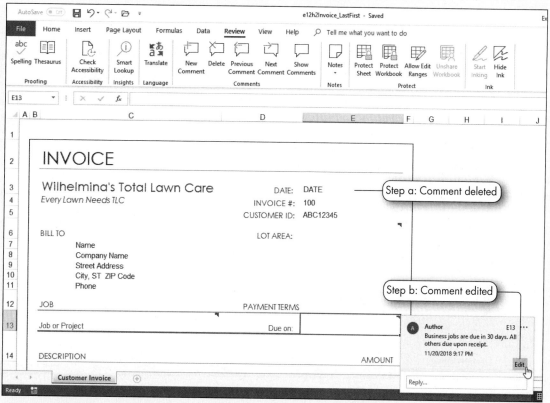

FIGURE 12.17 Edit Comments

a. Click **cell E3**, click the **Review tab**, and then click **Delete** in the Comments group.

b. Click **cell E13** and click **Edit** in the Comment box. Select the text and type **Business jobs are due in 30 days. All others due upon receipt**.

c. Click **Save**.

For your last step, you want to hide the comments to reduce screen clutter. Once the comments are hidden, the comment indicators will still be visible. Refer to Figure 12.18 as you complete Step 6.

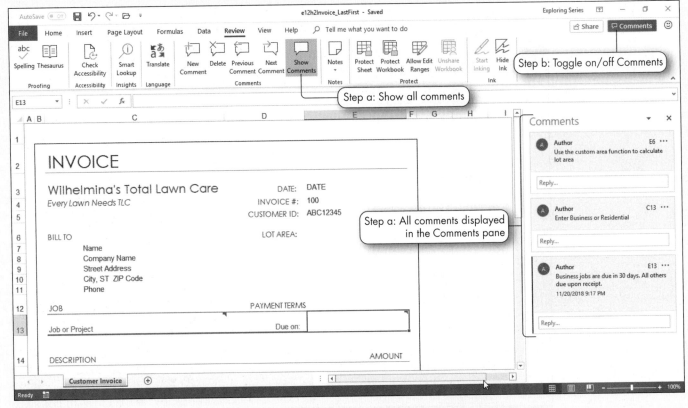

FIGURE 12.18 Hide Comments

a. Click **Show Comments** in the Comments group.

All comments are displayed in the Comments pane.

b. Click the **Comments button** located in the upper-right corner of the ribbon to toggle off the Comments pane.

c. Save the workbook. Keep the workbook open if you plan to continue with the next Hands-On Exercise. If not, close the workbook and exit Excel.

Macros

By now, you have used most of the commands on the ribbon to perform a variety of tasks. Often, you repeat the execution of the same commands as you develop and modify workbooks. Although the sequence to execute commands is easy, you lose productivity when you perform the same procedures repeatedly. Previously, you learned how to create and use templates as models to develop similar workbooks. In addition, you can automate other routine tasks to increase your productivity. For example, think about how often you set a print range, adjust scaling, set margins, insert a standard header or footer, and specify other page setup options prior to printing.

You can automate a series of routine, simple, or even complex tasks by creating a macro. A **macro** is a set of instructions that executes a sequence of commands to automate repetitive or routine tasks. While the term *macro* often intimidates people, you should view macros as your personal assistants that do tasks for you! After you create a macro, you can execute the macro to perform the task with minimal work on your part. As an additional benefit, macros can be saved in templates to automate tasks that may be time consuming or difficult for users without significant experience in Excel. When you run a macro, the macro executes the task the same way each time, and faster than you could execute the commands yourself, thus reducing errors while increasing efficiency.

In this section, you will learn how to use the Macro Recorder to record a macro. You will also learn how to run a macro, edit a macro, create macro buttons, and review macro security issues.

Creating a Macro

Excel provides two methods for creating macros. You can either use the Macro Recorder or type instructions using **Visual Basic for Applications (VBA)**. VBA is a robust programming language that can be used within various software packages to enhance and automate functionality. While programmers use VBA to write macros, you do not need to be a programmer to create macros. It is relatively easy to use the **Macro Recorder** to record your commands, keystrokes, and mouse clicks to store Excel commands as VBA code within a workbook. Before you record a macro, keep the following points in mind:

- Practice the steps before you start recording the macro so that you will know the sequence in which to perform the steps when you record the macro.

- Once you begin recording a macro, most actions you take are recorded in the macro. If you click something in error, you will have to edit the code or rerecord the macro. While you can undo the step, note that undoing an action will also be recorded and the best practice is to rerecord the macro.

- Ensure your macros are broad enough to apply to a variety of situations or actions you perform often for the workbook.

- Determine whether cell references should be relative, absolute, or mixed if you include cell references in the macro.

The default Excel Workbook file format (.xlsx) and template file format (.xltx) cannot store macros. When you save a workbook containing macros, click the *Save as type* arrow in the Save As dialog box, and select one of the following file formats that support macros:

- Excel Macro-Enabled Workbook (.xlsm)

- Excel Binary Workbook (.xlsb)

- Excel Macro-Enabled Template (.xltm)

STEP 1 Use the Macro Recorder

You can access the Macro Recorder in a variety of ways: from the View tab, from the Developer tab, from the status bar, or from the Tools menu if using a Mac. The following list briefly describes what each method includes:

- The View tab contains the Macros group with the Macros command. You can click the Macros arrow to view macros, record a macro, or use relative references.
- The Developer tab, when displayed, provides more in-depth tools that workbook developers use.
- The status bar displays the Macro Recording button so that you can quickly click it to start and stop recording macros.
- The Developer tab includes options that enable you to record a macro as well as open the Visual Basic Editor and set macro security. In addition, it also includes other tools that workbook developers use. The Developer tab does not display by default on the ribbon, so you must customize the ribbon to include it.

> **To display the Developer tab on the ribbon, complete the following steps:**
>
> 1. Click the File tab and click Options to open the Excel Options dialog box.
> 2. Click Customize Ribbon on the left side to display the Customize the Ribbon options.
> 3. Click the Developer check box in the Main Tabs list to select it and click OK. Figure 12.19 shows the Developer tab.

> **On a Mac, to display the Developer tab on the Mac ribbon, complete the following steps:**
>
> 1. Click Excel, click Preferences, and then select Ribbons & Toolbars.
> 2. Select All tabs under Choose commands from, click Developer, and then click Add.
> 3. Click Save.

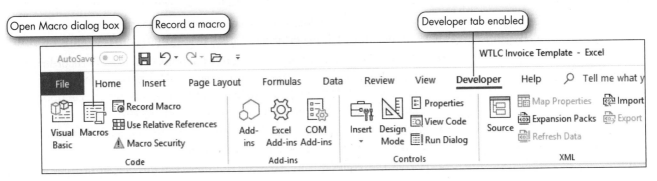

FIGURE 12.19 Developer Tab

Recording a macro is relatively straightforward: You initiate the macro recording, perform a series of commands as you normally do, then stop the macro recording. Be careful and thorough when recording a macro to ensure that it performs the tasks it is designed to do and to avoid the need to edit the macro in the VBA Editor. Before recording a macro, you should practice it first and make sure you know the sequence of tasks you want to perform. After planning and practicing a macro, you are ready to record it. In the event that a mistake is made while recording the macro, it is best practice to stop, delete the macro, and restart the recording. Use the Macro dialog box to select the macro and click Delete. Excel will prompt you with a message box asking if you want to delete the selected macro. Click Yes to confirm the deletion.

The default *Store macro in* setting is This Workbook. If you want to create a macro that is available in any Excel workbook, click the *Store macro in* arrow and select Personal Macro Workbook. This option creates Personal.xlsb, a hidden **_Personal Macro Workbook_** containing the macro in the C:\Users\Your Username\AppData\Roaming\Microsoft\Excel\XLSTART folder within Windows 10. Workbooks stored in the XLSTART folder open automatically when you start Excel. When the Personal Macro workbook opens, the macros in it are available to any other open workbook.

To record a macro, complete the following steps:

1. Click Record Macro using one of the methods described above. The Record Macro dialog box opens (see Figure 12.20 and Figure 12.21). (On a Mac, click the Tools menu, click Macro, and then click Record New Macro.)

2. Type a name for the macro in the Macro name box. Macro names cannot include spaces or special characters and must start with a letter. Use Pascal Case (capitalize the first letter of each word but without a space), a programming naming convention, to increase readability of the macro name.

3. Assign a keyboard shortcut for the macro in the Shortcut key box as necessary. It is best to use Ctrl+Shift+[keyboard letter], such as Ctrl+Shift+C instead of Ctrl+C, because many Ctrl+ shortcuts are already assigned in Excel. (On a Mac, press Option +Command+Shift+[keyboard letter].)

4. Click the *Store macro in* arrow and select a storage location, such as This Workbook.

5. Type a description of the macro and its purpose in the Description box and click OK to start recording the macro.

6. Perform the commands that you want to record.

7. Click the View tab, click Macros in the Macros group, and then select Stop Recording; or click the Developer tab and click Stop Recording in the Code group; or click Stop Recording on the status bar. (On a Mac, click the Tools menu, select Macros, and click Stop Recording.)

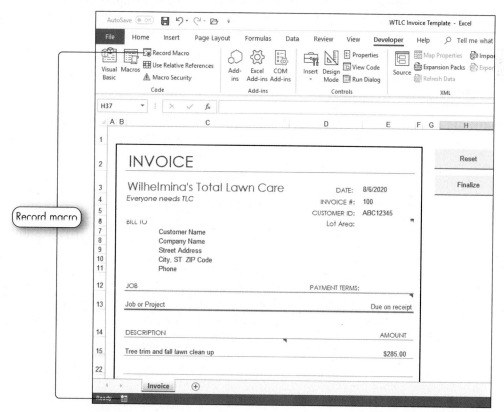

FIGURE 12.20 Record Macro

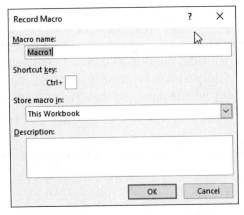

FIGURE 12.21 Record Macro Dialog Box

TIP: ADDING TO AN EXISTING MACRO
You cannot add additional steps to a macro using the Macro Recorder. Additional steps can only be added using the VBA Editor; however, writing new programming code takes time to learn. Until you are comfortable adding a lot of commands to a macro, you can create a temporary macro, record the commands you need, and then copy the code in the VBA Editor and paste it in the appropriate location in the primary macro code.

Use Relative References

It is important to determine if your macro should use relative, absolute, or mixed references before you record the macro. By default, as you select cells when recording a macro, the macro records the cells as absolute references. When you run the macro, the macro executes commands on the absolute cells, regardless of which cell is the active cell when you run the macro. For example, say you want to apply a macro that formats cells that are selected. To increase the flexibility of the macro so that relative references are used when it is run, click the Macros arrow in the Macros group on the View tab and select Use Relative References *before* you perform the commands. Be sure to turn relative references off when the feature is no longer needed.

STEP 2 ▶ ## Run a Macro

After you record a macro, you should run a test to see if it performs the commands as you had anticipated. When you run a macro, Excel performs the tasks in the sequence in which you recorded the steps.

To run a macro, complete the following steps:

1. Select the location where you will test the macro. It is recommended to test a macro in a new, blank workbook if you recorded it so that it is available for multiple workbooks. If you saved it to the current workbook only, insert a new worksheet to test the macro. Be sure to back up the workbook, because macros cannot be undone.

2. Click the View tab, click the Macros arrow in the Macros group, and then select View Macros; or click the Developer tab and click Macros in the Code group. The Macro dialog box opens (see Figure 12.22).

3. Select the macro from the Macro name list and click Run.

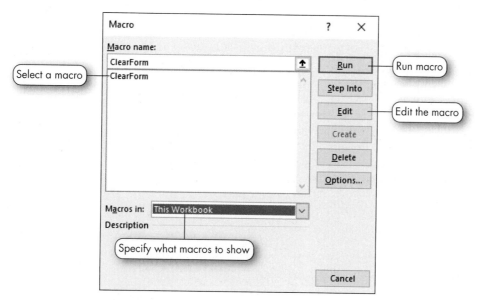

FIGURE 12.22 Macro Dialog Box

Set Macro Security

Macro security is a concern for anyone who uses files containing macros. A macro virus is nothing more than actions written in VBA set to perform malicious actions when run. The proliferation of macro viruses has made people more cautious about opening workbooks that contain macros. By default, Excel automatically disables the macros and displays a security warning that macros have been disabled (see Figure 12.23). Click Enable Content to allow the use of macros.

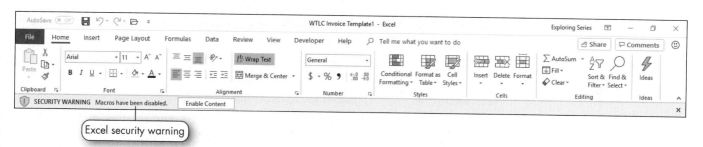

FIGURE 12.23 Security Message Bar

You can use the Trust Center dialog box to change settings to make it easier to work with macros. The Trust Center can direct Excel to trust the files in certain folders, as well as workbooks created by a trusted publisher, and lower the security settings to allow macros. To open the Trust Center, click the File tab to access Backstage view. Click Options, click Trust Center, and then click Trust Center Settings. The Trust Center dialog box displays the sections described in Table 12.3 on the left side of the dialog box (see Figure 12.24). The Trust Center is not available in Excel for Mac.

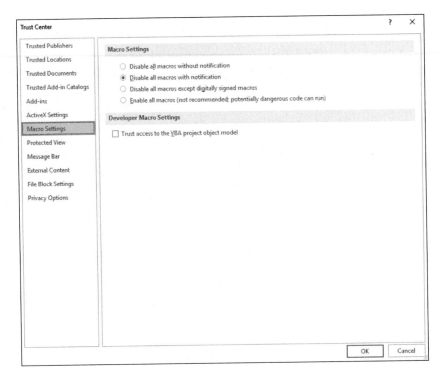

FIGURE 12.24 Trust Center Settings

TABLE 12.3	Trust Center Options
Item	**Description**
Trusted Publishers	Directs Excel to trust digitally signed workbooks by certain creators.
Trusted Locations	Enables you to designate a folder of files from trusted sources. Once a file is stored in a trusted location, it will not open in protected view when accessed.
Trusted Documents	Enables you to trust documents shared over a network to open without Excel displaying any security warnings.
Macro Settings	Enables you to specify how Excel deals with macros.
Protected View	Opens potentially dangerous files in a restricted mode but without any security warnings.
Message Bar	Enables you to specify when Excel shows the message bar when it blocks macros.
File Block Settings	Enables you to select which types of files, such as macros, to open in Protected View or which file type to prevent saving a file in.

STEP 3 Creating a Macro Button

Macros are often created to make worksheets easier to use for people with limited Excel experience. To further ease the process of working with macros, you may want to assign the macro to a button on a worksheet. That way, when you or other people use the workbook, it is easy to click the button to run the macro. Macros can also be assigned to objects within Excel such as shapes, text boxes, or images.

To add a macro button to a worksheet, complete the following steps:

1. Click the Developer tab, click Insert in the Controls group, and then click Button (Form Control) in the Form Controls section of the Insert gallery (see Figure 12.25).
2. Drag the crosshair pointer to draw the button on the worksheet. When you release the mouse button, the Assign Macro dialog box opens (see Figure 12.26).
3. Select the macro to assign to the button and click OK.
4. Right-click the button, select Edit Text, delete the default text, and then type a more descriptive name for the button.
5. Click the worksheet to complete the button.
6. Click the cell that should be the active cell when the macro runs and click the button to execute the macro assigned to the button.

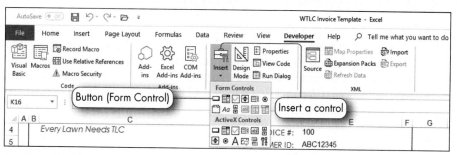

FIGURE 12.25 Form Controls

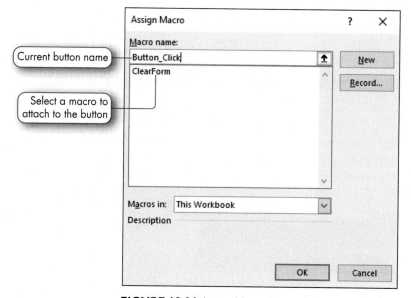

FIGURE 12.26 Assign Macro Dialog Box

> **TIP: OTHER CONTROLS**
> You can insert other controls in a worksheet, such as images and artwork, and assign macros to them. For example, you can insert combo boxes, check boxes, and option buttons by clicking Insert in the Controls group on the Developer tab and selecting the control. Drag an area on the worksheet to draw the control, right-click the object, and then select Assign Macro to assign a macro action for that control.

7. Describe a situation in which a macro would be beneficial. *p. 725*
8. Explain the benefit of using the Macro Recorder. *p. 726*
9. What potential risks are associated with macros? *p. 729*

Hands-On Exercises

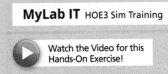
Skills covered: Use the
Macro Recorder • Run a Macro •
Create a Macro Button

3 Macros

Because you want all employees to use the Invoice template, you want to create a macro to clear the form. In addition, you want to create a button to run the macro so that other users can easily clear the form if they do not know what a macro is or how to run it.

STEP 1 USE THE MACRO RECORDER

You do not want to assume the level of Excel expertise throughout your company; therefore, you want to craft a macro that will automate as much as possible. The macro you will create automatically clears existing values in the workbook. Although the template is empty to start, users might open the template, save a workbook, and then want to use that workbook to prepare more invoices. Therefore, you need the macro to clear cells even though the original template has no values. You will first display the Developer tab and use the Macro Recorder to automate the template. Refer to Figure 12.27 as you complete Step 1.

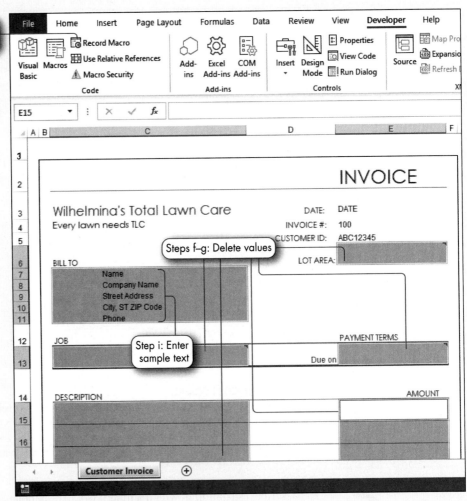

FIGURE 12.27 Record Macro

a. Open *e12h2Invoice_LastFirst.xltx* if you closed it at the end of Hands-On Exercise 2, and save it as **e12h3Invoice_LastFirst**, changing h2 to h3.

TROUBLESHOOTING: If you do not see Templates in Recent Places, click Open and navigate to the local directory that contains your solution files.

b. Click the **File tab** and click **Options** to open the Excel Options dialog box.

c. Click **Customize Ribbon**, click the **Developer check box** in the Main Tabs list to select it, and then click **OK**.

The Developer tab is added to the Ribbon.

MAC TROUBLESHOOTING: Click Excel, click Preferences, and then select Ribbons & Toolbars. Under Choose commands from, select All Tabs, click Developer, and then click Add. Click Save.

d. Click the **Developer tab** and click **Record Macro** in the Code group. (On a Mac, click Tools, click Macro, and then click Record New Macro.)

The Record Macro dialog box opens so that you can name and describe the macro.

e. Type **ClearInvoice** in the Macro name box, click in the **Description box**, type **This macro clears existing values in the current invoice**, and then click **OK**.

TROUBLESHOOTING: Read through Steps f–k in advance before you proceed. Remember, most actions taken in Excel are recorded by the Macro Recorder. Practice the steps below before activating the recorder. If you make a major mistake, delete the macro and repeat Steps d–l.

f. Select the **range C7:C11** and press **Delete**.

Even though the cells contain sample values, they will contain customer information at some point. You want the macro to delete any values that might exist in this range.

g. Adapt Step f for the following cells and ranges:

- **Cell E6**
- **Cell C13**
- **Cell E13**
- **Range C15:E25**

You deleted ranges that might contain values after the user enters data into any workbooks created from the template. It is always good to plan for various possibilities in which data might be entered, even if those ranges do not contain values now.

h. Press **Ctrl+G**, type **C7** in the Reference box of the Go To dialog box, and then click **OK**.

i. Type **Name** in **cell C7** and press **Enter**.

Adapt Step h to enter the following values in the corresponding cells:

Cell	Value
C8	Company Name
C9	Street Address
C10	City, ST ZIP Code
C11	Phone

j. Click **Stop Recording** in the Code group on the Developer tab. (On a Mac, click Tools, click Macro, and then click Stop Recording.)

You stopped the macro recorder from recording your actions.

k. Save the template, and click **No** when prompted that the workbook cannot be saved with the macro in it.

Excel opens the Save As dialog box so that you can select the file type.

l. Click the **Save as type arrow** and select **Excel Macro-Enabled Template**. Click **Save** and click **OK**.

> **TROUBLESHOOTING:** Make sure you select Excel Macro-Enabled Template, not Excel Macro-Enabled Workbook, because you want the file saved as a template, not a workbook. Because the template contains macros, you must save it as an Excel Macro-Enabled Template, not just a template.

STEP 2 ▶ **RUN A MACRO**

You want to make sure the ClearInvoice macro does what you want it to do. You will add some sample data and run the macro. Refer to Figure 12.28 as you complete Step 2.

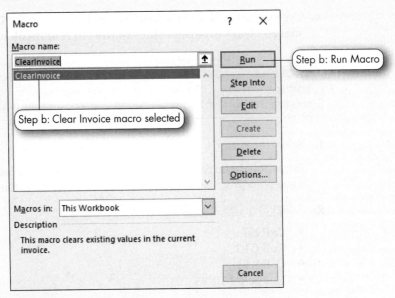

FIGURE 12.28 Run a Macro

a. Click **cell C7**, type **John Doe**, and press **Enter**.

Enter the following values in the corresponding cells:

Cell	Value
C8	John Doe Inc.
C9	123 Sample Street
C10	Leland, MI 49654
C11	(231) 444-4444

b. Click **Macros** in the Code group, select **ClearInvoice**, and click **Run**.

The ClearInvoice macro quickly goes through the worksheet, erasing the values in the specified ranges, goes to the range C7:C11, enters descriptive labels, and then stops.

> **TROUBLESHOOTING:** If the macro does not delete the sample values, delete the macro and repeat Step 1.

c. Save the workbook and click **OK** when prompted that parts of the document may have personal information that cannot be removed by the Document Inspector.

STEP 3 ADD A MACRO BUTTON

Your sales reps may not be Excel experts and not know how to run a macro. To make it easier to clear values from the form, you want to assign the ClearInvoice macro to a button. The users can click the button to clear the form to use it for another customer. You will also add a button to be utilized later in the project. Refer to Figure 12.29 as you complete Step 3.

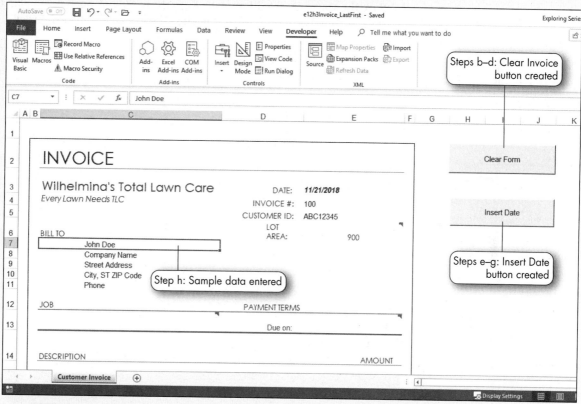

FIGURE 12.29 Macro Button

a. Click the **Developer tab**, click **Insert** in the Controls group, and then click **Button (Form Control)** in the Form Controls section of the gallery.

b. Click the top of **cell H2** and drag down and to the right to the bottom of **cell J2** to create the area where the button will be placed.

The Assign Macro dialog box opens.

c. Select **ClearInvoice** in the Macro name list and click **OK**.

This action assigns the ClearInvoice macro to the button. The button displays in the range H2:J2, is selected, and contains the text *Button 1*. You will provide descriptive text to display on the button.

d. Right-click **Button 1** and select **Edit Text**. Select the **Button 1 text**, type **Clear Form**, and then click any cell on the worksheet outside the button.

The button now shows *Clear Form*, which is more descriptive of the button's purpose than *Button 1*.

e. Click **Insert** in the Controls group and click **Button (Form Control)** in the Form Controls section of the gallery.

f. Click the top of **cell H4** and drag down and to the right to the bottom of **cell J5** to create the area where the button will be placed. Click **Cancel** in the Assign Macro dialog box.

The Assign Macro dialog box is closed because this button will be used in the next portion of the project.

g. Right-click **Button 2** and select **Edit Text**. Select the **Button 2 text**, type **Insert Date**, and then click any cell on the worksheet outside the button.

h. Click **cell C7** and type **John Doe** to enter sample data.

i. Click the **Clear Form button** in the worksheet.

When you click Clear Form, Excel runs the ClearInvoice macro.

j. Save the Macro-Enabled Template. Keep the workbook open if you plan to continue with the next Hands-On Exercise. If not, close the workbook and exit Excel.

Visual Basic for Applications

As you perform commands while recording a macro, those commands are translated into Visual Basic for Applications (VBA). While many casual users will be able to complete required tasks using just the Macro Recorder, more advanced VBA macros can be created by authoring code directly into modules within the Visual Basic Editor. A *module* is a container in which VBA code is stored. The *Visual Basic Editor* is an application used to create, edit, execute, and debug Office application macros using programming code. These macros can then be used within a Macro-Enabled Workbook or Macro-Enabled Template.

The two types of VBA macros are procedures and custom functions. *Sub procedures*, which are also created when using the Macro Recorder, perform actions on a workbook but do not return specific values, such as the ClearInvoice example earlier in the chapter. For example, you can create a sub procedure to insert the current date in a worksheet. Similar to the hundreds of built-in functions in Excel, custom functions can manipulate input variables and return a value.

In this section, you will learn to use VBA to create and edit a sub procedure. You will also learn to create a custom function.

STEP 1 Creating a Sub Procedure

The first step to creating a sub procedure is inserting a new module or editing data in an existing module within the VBA Editor. To access the VBA Editor, press Alt+F11. (On a Mac, Option+F11.) The left side of the VBA window contains the Project Explorer, which is similar in concept and appearance to the File Explorer except that it displays only open workbooks and/or other Visual Basic projects (see Figure 12.30).

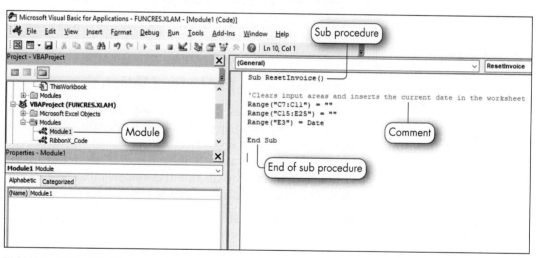

FIGURE 12.30 VBA Editor

The Visual Basic statements display in the Text Editor window on the right side. In Excel, a Visual Basic module consists of at least one *procedure*, which is a named sequence of statements stored in a macro. In Figure 12.30, Module1 contains the ResetInvoice procedure, which is also the name of the macro created in Excel. Module1 is stored in the Invoice workbook.

A procedure or macro always begins and ends with the Sub and End Sub statements. The Sub statement contains the name of the macro, such as Sub ResetInvoice() in Figure 12.30. The End Sub statement is the last statement and indicates the end of the macro. Sub and End Sub are Visual Basic keywords and display in blue. *Keywords* are words or symbols reserved within a programming language for specific purposes.

VBA comments, which are indicated by an apostrophe and display in green, provide information about the macro but do not affect its execution and are used for documentation. Comments can be entered manually or are inserted automatically by the Macro Recorder to document the macro name, its author, and shortcut key (if any). You can add, delete, or modify comments.

> **To create a basic sub procedure that enters a date into a cell, complete the following steps:**
>
> 1. Open the VBA Editor and select Module from the Insert menu. (On a Mac, click the Insert Module icon.)
> 2. Type *Sub CurrentDate()* and press Enter.
> 3. Type ' and add a descriptive comment. Press Enter.
> 4. Type *range("H7") = Date* (replace *H7* with the cell address of the place where the date will display) and press Enter.
> 5. Save and exit the Visual Basic Editor.

Table 12.4 explains some of the lines of code used to create the previous sub procedure. The first word, *range*, refers to an object. An ***object*** contains both data and code and represents an element of Excel such as Range or Selection. A period follows the object name, and the next word is often a method, such as Select or ClearContents, that describes a behavior or action performed on the object.

TABLE 12.4	VBA Editor Code
Explanation	**Code**
Identifies the range H7	Range("H7")
Applies the current date to the cell = Date	= Date
Applies object property, setting the font to bold. To disable, change *true* to *false*.	Font.Bold = true

Use VBA with Protected Worksheets

When working in Excel, it is common to protect the workbook or a portion of the workbook when it is finalized to prevent editing. By default, all cells in a workbook are locked and when a workbook is protected they cannot be edited. It is important to document the workbook password as there is no reset password feature in Excel. Worksheets can be manually protected by clicking the Review tab, and clicking Protect Worksheet, or as shown in Figure 12.31, VBA can be used to protect a worksheet using the statement:

Worksheets("[worksheet name]").Protect Password:= "[password]".

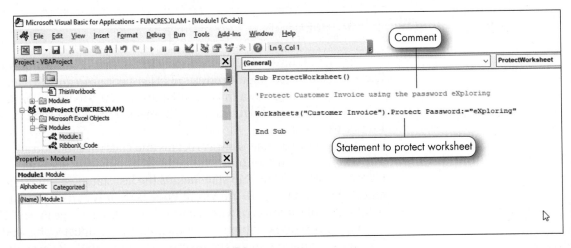

FIGURE 12.31 Protect a Worksheet Using VBA

When using VBA, run-time errors will occur when running VBA scripts that modify locked cells on protected worksheets. A ***run-time error*** is a software or hardware problem that prevents a program from working correctly during execution. This is most commonly due to a procedure such as *Range("E3").Font.Bold = true*, attempting to alter a locked cell. In the example, cell E3 is formatted. However, this will create a run-time error because the worksheet is protected. There are several methods to correct this issue. The simplest, as shown in Figure 12.32, is to encase the current VBA script with a statement that will unprotect the worksheet, run the current script, and then protect the worksheet again before ending the procedure.

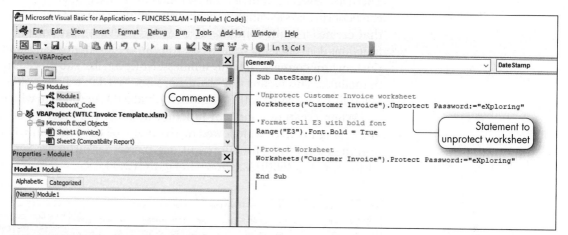

FIGURE 12.32 Unprotect a Worksheet Using VBA

The statement *Worksheets("Customer Invoice").Unprotect Password:= "eXploring"* unprotects the worksheet to enable the format changes to occur. The statement *Worksheets ("Customer Invoice").Protect Password:= "eXploring"* then protects the worksheet again.

STEP 2 ## Edit a Macro in the Visual Basic Editor

If a workbook has macros that were created using the Macro Recorder, you can edit the existing macro using the Visual Basic Editor. For example, if you record a macro to apply bold, Arial font, 12-pt size, and Red font color, each command displays in a separate statement (see Figure 12.33). The two statements to apply bold and italic start with *Selection.Font*, indicating that a font attribute will be applied to the current selection. The statement continues with a period and behavior, such as *Bold = True*, indicating that bold is activated. If the sub procedure is turning off bold, the statement looks like this:

Selection.Font.Bold = False

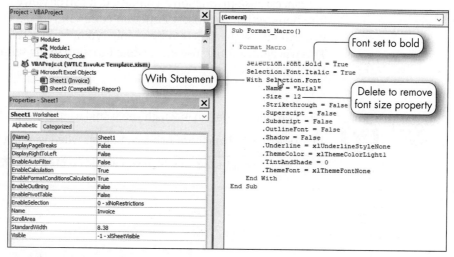

FIGURE 12.33 Edit Macro in VBA Editor

The With statement enables you to perform multiple actions on the same object. All commands between the *With* and the corresponding *End With* statement are executed consecutively. Although the font and font size were changed in the macro, the macro also indicates that other attributes, such as superscript and subscript, are turned off. Those lines of code can be deleted if they are not needed.

STEP 3 ▶ Creating a Custom Function

There are several hundred built-in functions in Excel such as the PROPER function that can perform tasks as simple as capitalizing the first letter of a word, or the SUMIFS function that creates a multi-conditional sum. In the event that one of the numerous built-in functions does not meet your needs, you can create your own custom function using VBA. Custom functions are virtually limitless. However, like sub procedures, they are still saved in modules. This means that if they are not saved to a Personal Macro Workbook, they will only be available within the Macro-Enabled Workbook in which they were created.

When creating a custom function in VBA, you start by creating a new module and typing FUNCTION followed by the name of the function you are creating and the arguments that the function will use inside parentheses. For example, FUNCTION AREA(Length, Width), as shown in Figure 12.34.

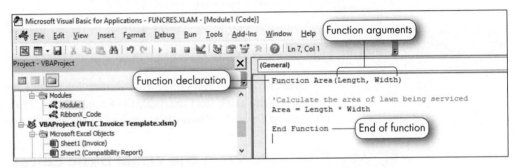

FIGURE 12.34 Create a VBA function

After entering arguments, on the next line you add comments in the same manner they were added to sub procedures. The last step is to enter the statement that defines the function such as:

Area = Length * Width

After completing the statement, check to make sure End Function has been added by the VBA Editor. If not, you must add it manually.

Once a custom function is completed, it can be viewed within Excel under User Defined functions within the Insert Function command in the Function Library. Furthermore, you can access the function by simply typing = in a cell and the name of the function. This will enable you to use the custom function in the same manner as any of the built-in Excel functions.

Quick Concepts

10. Describe a situation in which you would want to access the VBA Editor. ***p. 737***

11. Describe the benefits of using comments when working in VBA. ***pp. 737–738***

12. Describe a situation in which you would create a custom function. ***p. 740***

Hands-On Exercises

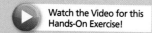

Skills covered: Create a Sub Procedure • Use VBA to Protect a Worksheet • Edit a Macro in the Visual Basic Editor • Create a Custom Function

4 Visual Basic for Applications

You want to automate as much of the invoice template as possible. Therefore, you will create a sub procedure assigned to a macro button to automatically insert the current date into the worksheet. You also want to add a custom function that enables the user to estimate the area of the lawn being serviced.

STEP 1 CREATE A SUB PROCEDURE

In order to use VBA to automatically insert and format the date, you will first create a new module. You will then use the range object to insert the current date and adjust the font property to bold the current date. Refer to Figure 12.35 as you complete Step 1.

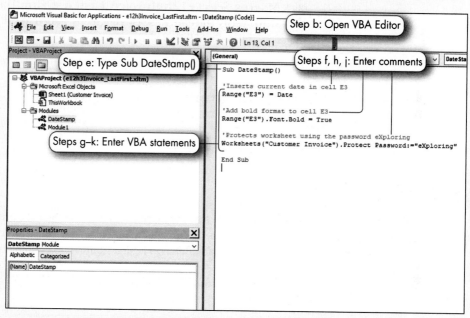

FIGURE 12.35 Create a Sub Procedure

a. Open the Macro-Enabled Template *e12h3Invoice_LastFirst.xltm*, click **Enable Content** to activate the prior macro, and save it as **e12h4Invoice_LastFirst**, changing h3 to h4.

When you use Open or Recent to open a template, you open it as a template to edit. When you use New, you make a copy of the template as a workbook.

b. Click the **Developer tab** and click **Visual Basic** in the Code group.

c. Click the **Insert menu** and select **Module**. (On a Mac, click the Insert Module icon.)

This creates a new module in the Visual Basic Editor.

d. Type **DateStamp** in the name field of the properties window.

e. Type **Sub DateStamp()** on the first line of the newly created module and press **Enter** twice.

Using the keyword *Sub* indicates the beginning of a procedure: the VBA Editor will automatically add the *End Sub* statement.

f. Type **'Unprotects worksheet for editing** and press **Enter**.

This adds a comment making it easier for the future user to understand your work.

g. Type **Worksheets("Customer Invoice").Unprotect Password:="eXploring"** and press **Enter** twice.

h. Type **'Inserts current date in cell E3** and press **Enter**.

i. Type **Range("E3") = Date** and press **Enter** twice.

This enters the current date into cell E3 during run time.

j. Press **Enter**, type **'Adds bold format to cell E3**, and then press **Enter**.

k. Type **Range("E3").Font.Bold = True** and press **Enter** twice.

This sets the entered date to bold.

l. Type **'Protects worksheet using the password eXploring** and press **Enter**.

m. Type **Worksheets("Customer Invoice").Protect Password:="eXploring"** and press **Enter**.

This statement protects the worksheet using the password *eXploring*.

n. Click **File** and select **Close** and return to Microsoft Excel. Click the Developer tab and click **Macros**. Select **e12h4Invoice_LastFirst.xltm!DateStamp.DateStamp** and click **Run**. Verify the date has been correctly added to cell E3 and click **Visual Basic** in the code group. Save the macro.

The procedure adds and formats the current date and protects the document.

> **TROUBLESHOOTING:** If a run-time error occurs, compare your code to Figure 12.35 and correct any mistakes.

o. Save the workbook.

STEP 2 EDIT A MACRO

After running the sub procedure, you decide that the inserted date should be italic instead of bold. You will make this change in the VBA Editor by changing the Italic property. You also add a statement to the ClearInvoice Macro to unprotect the worksheet when clearing its data. Refer to Figure 12.36 as you complete Step 2.

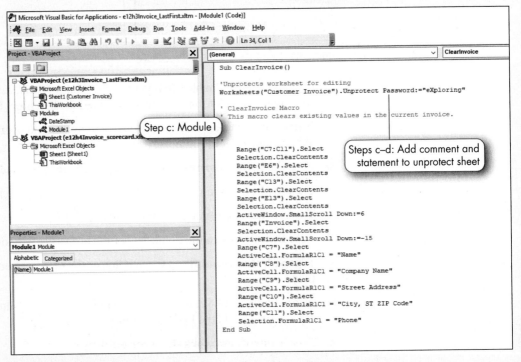

FIGURE 12.36 Edit a Macro

a. Ensure the VBA Editor is displayed. If not, click **Visual Basic** in the Code group.

Excel opens the VBA Editor so that you can edit the macro programming language.

b. Ensure the DateStamp module is selected to display the DateStamp sub procedure created in the previous step. Locate the code *Range("E3").Font.Bold = True* and replace the word *Bold* with **Italic**. Edit the corresponding comment by replacing the word bold with **italic**.

This edits the command to set the inserted date to italic instead of bold.

c. Double click **Module1** in the Project pane to access the ClearInvoice code. Place the insertion point at the end of the first line of code *(Ln1, Col9)*, Press **Enter**, twice type **'Unprotects worksheet for editing**, and then press **Enter**.

d. Type **Worksheets("Customer Invoice").Unprotect password:= "eXploring"** and press **Enter** twice.

The DateStamp procedure protects the workbook. You added a statement to unprotect the workbook to the ClearInvoice Macro or a run time error will occur because a protected workbook cannot be edited.

e. Press Run Sub/UserForm or alternatively press F5 to test the code. Save and exit the VBA Editor.

f. Right-click **Button 2** (labeled *Insert Date*). Select **Assign Macro**, select **DateStamp**, and then click **OK**.

This assigns the DateStamp macro to the Insert Date button created earlier in the exercise.

g. Click **Button 2** to verify the current date is italicized. Once the date is verified, click **Clear Form**.

h. Save the workbook.

STEP 3 ▶ CREATE A CUSTOM FUNCTION

You decide to create a custom function to enable users to manually calculate the area of a yard being serviced. Refer to Figure 12.37 as you complete Step 3.

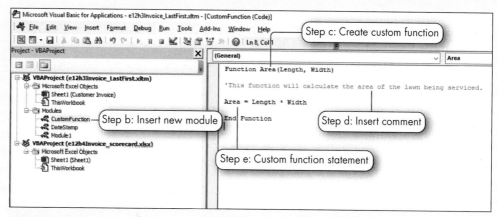

FIGURE 12.37 Create a Custom Function

a. Press **Alt+F11** to open the VBA Editor.

b. Click the **Insert menu** and select **Module**. Type **CustomFunction** in the name field of the properties window.

c. Type **Function Area(Length,Width)** on the first line of the module and press **Enter** twice.

d. Type '**This function will calculate the area of the lawn being serviced**. Press **Enter**.

This will display as a comment in the module. However, it will not impact the calculation of the function.

e. Type the statement **Area = Length * Width** and press **Enter**.

f. Save and exit the VBA Editor.

This creates a custom function that can be used in a similar fashion to any built-in function within Excel.

g. Click **cell E6** and type **=area(20,45)**.

This returns the value 900. You entered a 20ft by 45ft yard to test the newly created function.

h. Save and close all files. Based on your instructor's directions, submit e12h4Invoice_LastFirst.xltm.

Chapter Objectives Review

After reading this chapter, you have accomplished the following objectives:

1. Select a template.

- A template is a partially created workbook that you can use as a model to create a workbook. You can create a workbook based on sample templates stored on your computer, or you can download a template from Office.com to create a new workbook.
- Edit an existing template: Once a template is downloaded it can be edited to fit your specific needs.

2. Create a template.

- You can save a workbook as a template when existing templates do not provide the structure you need. When you save a template, Excel saves it in the C:\Users\Username\Documents\Custom Office Templates folder so that the templates are available when you click the File tab and click New. Templates have an .xltx file name extension.

3. Check for issues.

- Use Document Inspector: The Document Inspector detects personal and hidden data in a workbook and removes the data based on your specifications.
- Check accessibility: The Accessibility Checker detects issues that could hinder a user's ability to use a workbook.
- Check compatibility: The Compatibility Checker detects data and features that are not compatible with previous versions of Excel.

4. Annotate a worksheet.

- Edit and delete comments: If you need to change the text in a comment, you can edit it. If you no longer need a comment, you can delete it from the cell.
- Print comments: By default, comments do not print with a worksheet. However, you can select an option in the Page Setup dialog box to print comments in a worksheet.
- Show and hide comments: A comment indicator displays in the top-right corner of a cell that contains a comment. You can use the ribbon or the shortcut menu to display or hide a comment.

5. Create a macro.

- A macro is a stored procedure that performs multiple, routine, or complex tasks.
- Use the Macro Recorder: The Macro Recorder translates user actions into VBA.
- The Developer tab contains commands to record, run, and edit macros.
- When recording a macro, all user actions will be recorded by the Macro Recorder and stored in VBA.
- Use relative references: By default, when you select cells when recording a macro, the macro records the cells as absolute references. By recording the macro using relative references, you apply the macro to the cells you choose on execution.
- Run a macro: After macros are created, they can be run from the assigned keyboard shortcut, a macro button, or from the Macro dialog box.
- Set macro security: The proliferation of Excel macro viruses has made it dangerous to open workbooks that contain macros. To counter this threat, Excel automatically disables the macros and displays a security warning message that macros have been disabled.

6. Create a macro button.

- To facilitate the running of a macro, you can assign a macro to a button. The Developer tab contains controls, such as buttons, you can insert in a worksheet.

7. Create a sub procedure.

- Sub procedures can be created using the Macro Recorder or entered manually in the VBA Editor. Sub procedures only perform actions and cannot return values.
- Use VBA with protected worksheets: VBA can be used to protect and unprotect worksheets.
- Edit a macro in the Visual Basic Editor: After a sub procedure has been created, it can be edited in the VBA Editor.

8. Create a custom function.

- If the built-in Excel functions do not meet your needs, you can create a custom function using VBA.

Key Terms Matching

Match the key terms with their definitions. Write the key term letter by the appropriate numbered definition.

a. Accessibility Checker

b. Comment

c. Compatibility Checker

d. Document Inspector

e. Keyword

f. Macro

g. Macro Recorder

h. Module

i. Note

j. Object

k. Personal Macro Workbook

l. Procedure

m. Run-time Error

n. Sub Procedure

o. Template

p. Visual Basic for Applications (VBA)

q. Visual Basic Editor

1. _____ A special workbook file used as a model to create similarly structured workbooks. **p. 704**

2. _____ A tool that reviews a workbook to detect potential issues that could hinder users who access your public files and alerts you to these issues so that you can address them. **p. 713**

3. _____ A tool that evaluates the workbook's contents to identify what data and features are not compatible with previous versions. **p. 714**

4. _____ A tool that reviews a workbook for hidden or personal data stored in the workbook or personal document properties, such as author, and informs you of these details so that you can select what data to remove. **p. 711**

5. _____ A note or annotation to ask a question or provide a suggestion to another person about content in a worksheet cell. **p. 716**

6. _____ A set of instructions that executes a sequence of commands to automate repetitive or routine tasks. **p. 725**

7. _____ A tool that records a series of commands in the sequence performed by a user and converts the commands into programming syntax. **p. 725**

8. _____ A hidden workbook stored in the XLSTART folder that contains macros and opens automatically when you start Excel. **p. 727**

9. _____ An application used to create, edit, execute, and debug Office application macros using programming code. **p. 737**

10. _____ A named sequence of statements executed as a unit. **p. 737**

11. _____ A word or symbol reserved within a programming language for specific purposes. **p. 737**

12. _____ A group of Visual Basic statements that performs actions on a workbook but do not return specific values. **p. 737**

13. _____ An object that stores sub procedures and functions. **p. 737**

14. _____ An element that holds both data and code and represents an element of Excel. **p. 738**

15. _____ A software or hardware problem that prevents a program from working correctly. **p. 739**

16. _____ A robust programming language that can be used within various software packages to enhance and automate functionality. **p. 725**

17. _____ A basic documentation tool that annotates a cell but does not display as a discussion thread. **p. 716**

Multiple Choice

1. What does a red triangle in the upper-right corner of a cell indicate?

   (a) A circular reference
   (b) A hidden comment
   (c) A locked cell
   (d) A Data Validation list

2. In Windows 10, where would you save the template so it is available in the available templates list in Backstage view?

   (a) C:\Users\User_name\Libraries\Documents
   (b) Submit it to Office.com
   (c) C:\Users\Username\Documents\Custom Office Templates
   (d) C:\Users\Downloads

3. Where can you search and download Office templates?

   (a) Template gallery
   (b) Excel Options
   (c) Design tab
   (d) Insert tab

4. Which of the following would cause a run-time error?

   (a) Closing a template without saving.
   (b) Running a macro on a protected worksheet.
   (c) Saving with the incorrect file type.
   (d) Adding a comment to a procedure.

5. Which tool should be used to locate and remove private metadata?

   (a) Compatibility Checker
   (b) Accessibility Checker
   (c) Document Inspector
   (d) Document Manager

6. Which of the following is *not* a benefit of using macros?

   (a) Macros can be used for repetitive tasks.
   (b) Macros perform tasks quickly.
   (c) Macros can be saved and reused in different worksheets.
   (d) Macros cannot contain viruses.

7. In which programming language are Excel macros written?

   (a) Java
   (b) C++
   (c) VBA
   (d) SQL

8. Which of the following is *not* true about macros?

   (a) Macros are created using VBA.
   (b) Macros can be saved in XLSM workbooks.
   (c) Macros can use absolute or relative cell referencing.
   (d) Templates cannot contain macros.

9. Which of the following statements is *true* about macro security?

   (a) When you add a Macro-Enabled Workbook to the Trust Center, you must enable the content of that file each time you open it.
   (b) Setting your Trust Center options to include files in a specific folder and then saving macro-enabled files in that folder allows you to open those files with the content enabled.
   (c) Set macro security options on the Developer tab to Secured.
   (d) Macro-enabled files cannot contain viruses.

10. Which of the following is the file extension for a macro enabled template?

    (a) .xlsm
    (b) .xlsb
    (c) .xltm
    (d) .xlsx

Practice Exercises

1 Time Card

You have been hired as an HR intern for Norma's Custard, a local dessert shop in Atlanta, Georgia. You have been asked to create a time card template that can be shared with the company's employees that is clear, concise, and simple to use. You have decided to download and customize an existing time card template from Office.com. To fit your business needs, you will add comments, use the macro recorder to clear the form for a new work week, and inspect the document for issues. Refer to Figure 12.38 as you complete this exercise.

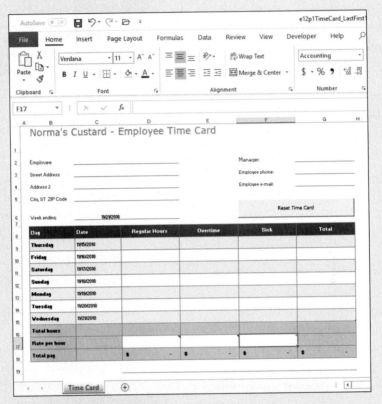

FIGURE 12.38 Time Card Template

a. Start Excel, search and download the **Time card template** as shown in Figure 12.38, and then click **Create**.

b. Save the workbook as an **Excel Macro-Enabled Template** with the file name **e12p1TimeCard_LastFirst**.

c. Click **cell B1** and type **Norma's Custard – Employee Time Card**.

d. Select the **range A1:H22**, click the **Data tab**, and then click the **Data Validation arrow**. Click **Data Validation** in the Data Tools group. Select **Data Validation** and click **OK**. Click the **Input Message tab** in the Data Validation dialog box, click **Clear All**, and click **OK**.

e. Right-click **column G** and select **Delete**.

f. Click **Record Macro** (located in the lower-left corner of the status bar), type **ClearTimeCard** in the macro name box, and then click **OK**.

g. Select the **range D9:F15**, press **Delete**, and then click **cell D9**. Click **Stop** on the status bar to stop the Macro Recorder. (On a Mac, click Tools, select Macro, and click Stop Recording.)

h. Click the **Developer tab**, click **Insert** in the Controls group, and then select **Button (Form Control)**.

i. Click the **Developer tab**, click **Insert** in the Controls group, and then select **Button (Form Control)**. Create a Form Control button that fills the **range F6:G6**. Right-click the button and click **Assign Macro**. Select the **ClearTimeCard macro** and click **OK**.

j. Right-click the **Form Control button**, select **Edit Text**, and then rename the button **Reset Time Card**.

k. Click **cell D17**, click the **Review Tab**, and then click **New Comment** in the Comments group. Type **Enter hourly rate**.

l. Adapt Step k to enter the comments below:

Cell	Comment
E17	**Enter overtime rate**
F17	**Enter sick time rate**

m. Click the **File Tab** and click **Info**. Click **Check for Issues** and then select **Inspect Document**. Click **Yes** and click **Inspect**.

n. Click **Remove All** in the Document Properties and Personal Information section and Headers and Footers section in the Document Inspector dialog box. Click **Close**.

o. Click **Check for Issues** and select **Check Accessibility**.

p. Click **cell B1**, click the **Home tab**, and then click **Merge & Center** in the Alignment group.

q. Adapt Step p to unmerge the remaining merged cells that are listed in the Accessibility pane. Once all issues are resolved, close the Accessibility pane.

r. Click the **File tab** and Click **Info**. **Check for Issues** and select **Check Compatibility**. (On a Mac, the Compatibility Checker is not available.)

s. Click **Select versions to show** and deselect **Excel 97-2003** and **Excel 2007**. Click **OK**.

t. Save the workbook, click **OK** when warned that some personal information cannot be removed by the Document Inspector, and then close the workbook. Based on your instructor's directions, submit e12p1TimeCard_LastFirst.

2 Sales Management

You are the sales manager for Home Sites, Inc., a regional construction company that specializes in building homes for first-time homeowners. You have decided to update a sales worksheet template to more efficiently manage your daily transactions. To accomplish this task, you will use the Macro Recorder and VBA to automate clearing and protecting the workbook. You will assign the macros to buttons and check the worksheet for issues. Refer to Figure 12.39 as you complete this exercise.

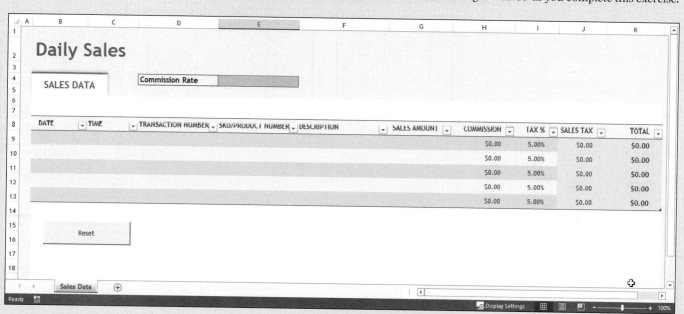

FIGURE 12.39 Daily Sales Template

a. Start Excel. Open *e12p2SalesTemplate* and save it as a Macro-enabled template with the file name **e12p2SalesTemplate_LastFirst**.

b. Click the **Developer tab** and click **Visual Basic** in the code group. Click **Insert** in the Visual Basic Editor and select **Module**. Enter the following text to create a custom function:

- Type **Function Commission (Sales, Rate)** in the Code window and press **Enter** twice.
- Type **Commission = Sales* Rate** and press **Enter**.

c. Click **Insert**, select **Module**, and then enter the following text to create a sub procedure to reset the worksheet:

- Type **Sub Reset()** and press **Enter** twice.
- Type **'Unprotect worksheet** and press **Enter**.
- Type **Sheet1.Unprotect Password:="eXploring"** and press **Enter** twice.
- Type **'Clear contents** and press **Enter**.
- Type **Range("B9:G13").ClearContents** and press **Enter** twice.
- Type **'Protect worksheet** and press **Enter**.
- Type **Sheet1.Protect Password:= "eXploring"**.

d. Click **Save** and exit the Visual Basic Editor.

e. Click **cell H9** and type **=COMMISSION(G9,$E$4)**.

f. Click the **Developer tab**, click **Insert** in the Controls group, and then select **Button (Form Control)**. Create a Form Control button that fills the **range B15:C16**. Select the **Reset macro** and click **OK**. Right-click the **Form Control button**, select **Edit Text**, and then rename the button **Reset**.

g. Click the **File Tab** and click **Info**. Click **Check for Issues** and then select **Inspect Document**. Click **Yes** and click Inspect. Click **Remove All** in the Document Properties and Personal Information section and in the Custom XML Data section. Click **Close**.

h. Click the **Review tab**, and click **Check Accessibility** in the Accessibility group.

i. Click on **Sales Data (Sales Date)** in the Missing Alternate text section of the Accessibility Checker pane. Click on the arrow and select **Mark as decorative**.

j. Click the arrow located to the right of tblSalesData (Sales Data) in the Accessibility pane, select **Quick Styles**, and then select **Ice Blue, Table Style Light 2** (located in the third column of the first row). Close the Accessibility Checker pane and the Alt Text pane.

k. Click the **File tab**, click **Options**, and then click **Trust Center**. Click **Trust Center Settings**, click **Trusted Locations**, and then click **Add new location**. Select the path where the workbook is saved and click **OK** on both windows to return to the workbook.

l. Save and close the workbook. Based on your instructor's directions, submit e12p2SalesTemplate_LastFirst.

Mid-Level Exercises

1 Sorority Dues

You are the outgoing treasurer of your sorority and as your last task, you want to create a membership template to enable future treasurers to track memberships, dues, and activities. To reach your goal you will download and customize an Excel template. As part of the customization process, you will create a macro to format text, use VBA to protect the workbook, and inspect the workbook for issues.

a. Open Excel, search and download the template **Membership list**, and then click **Create**.

b. Save the file as a **Macro-Enabled Template** named **e12m1MembershipDues_LastFirst**.

c. Click **cell A1** and type **Membership Dues**.

d. Delete **Column L**.

e. Select the **range A1:L7** and clear all data validation that was included in the template.

f. Add a comment in **cell A1** that says **Unprotect the worksheet before editing**.

g. Edit the comment to include the password required to unprotect the worksheet as follows: **Unprotect the worksheet using the password eXploring before editing**.

h. Use the Macro Recorder to record a macro named **Sort**. The macro should use relative references and when run will sort the records in ascending order by member name.

i. Ensure the Developer Tab is enabled, create a Form Control Button named **Sort** spanning the cell **range C1:D1**, and then assign the **Sort macro**.

j. Use the VBA Editor to insert a new module named **UnprotectWorkSheet**. Type the following to complete the procedure:
   - **Sub UnProtectWorksheet()**
   - **'Unprotect Sheet**
   - **Worksheets("Member List").Unprotect Password:= "eXploring"**

k. Insert a new module named **ProtectWorksheet**. Type the following to complete the procedure:
   - **Sub ProtectWorksheet()**
   - **'Protect Sheet**
   - **Worksheets("Member List").protect Password:= "eXploring"**

l. Exit the VBA Editor and create a Form Control Button named **Unprotect** spanning the cell B1. Assign the **Unprotect** macro.

m. Create a Form Control Button named **Protect** spanning the **cell E1**. Assign the **Protect macro**.

n. Use the Document Inspector to check the document for issues. Remove the Documents and Properties information and the Headers and Footers information. Do not remove Comments and Macro information.

o. Check the document for Accessibility and compatibility with Excel 2010, 2013, and 2016.

p. Click the **Protect macro button**.

q. Save the workbook. Based on your instructor's directions, submit e12m1MembershipDues_LastFirst.

2 Travel Expense Template

You are a financial analyst for VJD Financial, a wealth management company with 10 offices located across the United States. Currently, your traveling account executives send receipts through interoffice mail to document their travel expenses. You want to create a template to standardize the documentation process. To minimize the amount of development time required, you will download and edit an existing template from Office.com. You will customize the template by editing fields, adding comments, and creating a custom function using VBA.

a. Open Excel, search and download the template **Travel expense log**, and then click **Create**.

b. Save the file as a Macro-Enabled Template named **e12m2TravelExpenseReport_LastFirst**.

c. Select the **range A1:J16** and clear all data validation that was included in the template.

d. Click **cell B7**, type **Mileage Rate**, and apply **Yellow** fill color.

e. Click **cell C7**, click **Align Left** in the Alignment group, and type **.25**, and then apply **Blue, Accent 1, Lighter 80%** fill color.

f. Insert a column after column D. Name the column **Miles**.

g. Use the VBA Editor to create a custom function named **Mileage**. Type the following code to create the custom function:

- **Function Mileage (Miles,Rate)**
- **'Creates custom Mileage function**
- **Mileage = Miles * Rate**

h. Exit the VBA Editor and click **cell F11**. Type **=IFERROR(Mileage(E11,$C$7),0)..** Press **Enter** to complete the function. Hint: The completed function is =IFERROR(Mileage(E11,$C$7),0).

i. Click **cell E10** and add the comment **Enter miles driven**.

j. Save and close the workbook. Based on your instructor's directions, submit e12m2TravelExpenseReport_LastFirst.

Running Case

New Castle County Technical Services

New Castle County Technical Services (NCCTS) provides technical support services for a number of companies in New Castle County, Delaware. Previously, you created an amortization schedule to detail payment and interest information on a $65,000 facility upgrade. Now that the facility upgrade has been approved, you want to receive design proposals from architectural companies. To standardize the proposals you receive, you will create a template that can be used by architects when submitting the design bids. You also want to add comments to the template to provide instruction to the architects, create a macro to clear the template, and inspect the document for issues.

a. Open Excel and search the template gallery for the **Construction proposal template**. Download the template and save it as **e12r12NCCTS_LastFirst.xltm**.

b. Clear all Data Validation in the **range A1:H30** that was included with the template.

c. Delete the logo in the range B1:B2. Delete the contents of the following cells: B6, B8, B10, B12, B14, B16, B18, B20, B21:B30, D33.

d. Enter the following content in the corresponding cells:

Cell	Content
D2	NCCTS
E2	3130 Constitutional Dr. Wilmington, DE 19806
E3	(301) 554-1243
B5	COMPANY NAME

e. Enter the following comments in the corresponding cells:

Cell	Comment
B6	Enter company name.
B8	Enter estimate number.
B12	Enter address.
B16	Enter phone number.
B18	Enter EMAIL address.
B20	Enter sales rep name.
D33	Enter additional comments.

f. Record a macro named **Reset** that when activated deletes the content in the **range D5:F30** and the cells **B6, B8, B12, B14, B16, B18, B20, D33**.

g. Use the VBA editor to insert a module named **Finalize**. Type the following code to create the procedure.
- **Sub Finalize()**
- **'Enter date**
- **[B10]=Date**
- **'Protect worksheet**
- **Worksheets("Proposal").Protect Password:= "eXploring"**

h. Open Module1 in the VBA Editor and type the following code after comment *'Reset Macro*.
- **'Unprotect worksheet**
- **Worksheets("Proposal").Unprotect Password:="eXploring"**

i. Create a form control button named **Reset** spanning the **range I1:J2** and assign the **Reset** macro.

j. Create a form control button named **Finalize** spanning the **range I3:J4** and assign the **Finalize** macro.

k. Use the Document Inspector to remove Document Properties and Personal Information.

l. Inspect the document for accessibility and perform the recommended actions.

m. Use the Compatibility Checker to review compatibility for Excel 2010, 2013, and 2016.

n. Test the Reset and Finalize macros. Save and close the workbook. Based on your instructor's directions, submit e12r12NCCTS_LastFirst.xltm.

Disaster Recovery

Real Estate Listings

You are a real estate analyst who works for Mountain View Realty in the North Utah County area. Your assistant, Joey, compiled a list of houses sold during the past few months in a macro-enabled workbook. Joey created three macros: (1) a Clear macro to clear the existing Criteria Range and run the filter to empty the Output Range, (2) a CedarHills macro to set a criterion in the Criteria Range to filter the list for Cedar Hills only, and (3) a CityAgentCombo interactive macro with input boxes to prompt the user for the city and agent, enter those in respective cells, and run the advanced filter. In addition, Joey created three macro buttons, one to run each macro. However, the macros and buttons have errors. Open e12d1RealEstate and save it as a Macro-Enabled Workbook named **e12d1RealEstate_LastFirst.xltm**. Find the errors in the macros, document the problems in the macro code using programming comments, and then fix the errors. Find and correct the macro button errors. Create a footer with your name on the left side, the sheet name code in the center, and the file name code on the right side of the Input-Output worksheet. Save and close the workbook. Based on your instructor's directions, submit e12d1RealEstate_LastFirst.

Capstone Exercise

Bulldog Collectables

You are the operations manager for Bulldog Collectables, a small start-up company that deals with sports memorabilia. As you prepare to document your inventory, you decide to utilize a template to save time. To complete this task, you will create a worksheet based on an Office.com template; you will also use the Macro Recorder and Visual Basic for Application to automate sorting and calculations within the workbook.

Select and Edit a Template

You want to download a warehouse inventory template. Once downloaded, you will edit the content to fit your business needs.

1. Open Excel and search the template gallery for the **Warehouse inventory** template.
2. Create a new document based on the template and save it as a Macro-Enabled Template named **e12c1Inventory_LastFirst.xltm**.
3. Delete the Inventory Pick List and BIN Lookup worksheets.
4. Delete the Inventory Pick List and BIN Lookup icons located respectively in **cells E2** and **F2**. Select the **range E2:F2** and press **Delete**.
5. Clear all existing Data Validation in the **range A1:K15**.
6. Delete the values in the **range B5:K15**
7. Save the template.

Create the Sort Macro

You want to create a macro that will sort the desired data in one click. To complete this task, you will use the Macro Recorder and assign the macro to a Button Form Control.

8. Record a macro named **Sort**, be sure to use relative references.
9. Ensure the macro sorts by sku (column A) in ascending order.
10. Create a Form Control Button that spans the **range E2:E3**.
11. Assign the Sort macro and edit the button text to **Sort**.

Create a Custom Function

You want to create a custom function to calculate the value of items in your inventory. To complete the task, you will use VBA. The total value of the warehouse inventory is the QTY listed in column G multiplied by the COST in column I.

12. Use the VBA Editor to create a new module.

13. Type the following VBA code to create a custom Inventory Value function:
    - **Function InventoryValue (QTY, COST)**
    - **InventoryValue = QTY * COST**
14. Save and exit the VBA Editor.
15. Click **cell J5** and use the newly created Inventory Value function to calculate the value of the inventory for each item in column I.

Protect the Workbook

You want to use VBA to protect and unprotect the template for editing. Once the modules have been created, you will assign the macros to buttons.

16. Use the VBA Editor to create a new module named **ProtectWorkbook**.
17. Type the following VBA statements to create the sub procedure.
    - **Sub ProtectWorkbook**
    - **'Protect workbook using the password eXploring**
    - **Worksheets("Inventory List").Protect Password:="eXploring"**
18. Insert a new module named **UnprotectWorkbook**.
19. Type the following VBA statements to create the sub procedure.
    - **Sub UnprotectWorkbook**
    - **'Unprotect workbook using the password eXploring**
    - **Worksheets("Inventory List").Unprotect Password:= "eXploring"**
20. Insert a Form Control Button spanning **cell F2:F3** named **Unprotect**. Assign the macro **UnprotectWorkbook**.
21. Insert a Form Control Button spanning the **range G2:H3** named **Protect**. Assign the macro **ProtectWorkbook**.

Add Comments

Because you are not the only person that will use the template, you will add comments to provide instruction.

22. Insert the comment **Inventory based on values in column J** in **cell B3**.
23. Insert the comment **Count of items in column C** in **cell C3**.

Check for Issues

Before completing the template, you will check for issues. You will use the Document Inspector, Compatibility Checker, and Accessibility Checker to complete the task.

24. Inspect the document for private information and hidden properties. Remove Document Properties and Personal Information, and Headers and Footers.

25. Check the document for accessibility issues. Use the Accessibility Checker pane to change the cell styles to repair the issue.

26. Check the document for compatibility with Excel 2010, 2013, and 2016.

Test and Finalize Template

27. Type **2000** in **cell B5** and **1000** in **cell B6**.

28. Click the **Sort Form Control Button**.

29. Click the **Protect Form Control Button** and attempt to delete the valued in the **range B5:B6**.

30. Click the **Unprotect** Form Control Button and delete the values in the **range B5:B6**.

31. Type **2000** in **cell B5** and **1000** in **cell B6**.

32. Save the file as an Excel Macro-Enabled Template.

33. Close the template. Based on your instructor's directions, submit e12c1Inventory_LastFirst.xltm..

Excel Application Capstone Exercise (Chs. 1–4)

You are the financial manager for Judi's Art Gallery. One of your clients, Raymond Chancellor, has a large collection of limited edition signed art by James C. Christensen (1942–2017). Over the years, you have helped Raymond maintain a list of his collection, including the title of the art, medium, issue date, issue price, the price he paid, and current market value. Most of the art is sold out from the publisher, which increases the value of the art. Other art is still readily available or is available in limited quantities. You want to update the list so that he can properly insure his collection.

Format the Worksheet

The first tasks are to improve the formatting of the worksheet by centering the main title over cells, changing vertical alignment, increasing the width of a column so the labels display properly, adding a border, and replacing a word with a different term.

1. Open *eApp_Cap1_Collection* and save it as **eApp_Cap1_Collection_LastFirst**.
2. Select the **range A1:A6** on the Christensen worksheet, merge the cells, and then apply **Middle Align**.
3. Change the width of column K to **17.00**, select the **range K1:K3**, and then apply **Thick Outside Borders**.
4. Click **cell C9** and freeze panes so that rows 1 through 8 and columns A and B are frozen.
5. Select the **range E9:E54** and apply the **Mar-12 date format**.
6. Find all occurrences of **Retired** and replace them with **Sold Out**.

Insert Formulas and Basic Functions

The worksheet contains the Issue Price (the original price when the art was published), Paid (the amount Raymond paid for the art), and the Current Value (the value that the art is worth today). You will calculate what percentage Raymond paid of the issue price and the percentage change in value of the Current Value from the Issue Price. In addition, you will calculate the total, average, lowest, and highest current values for the output area to get a better understanding of the current values for insurance purposes. Use appropriate relative, absolute, and mixed references correctly in your formulas.

7. Click **cell H9** on the Christensen worksheet and insert a formula that calculates the percentage Raymond paid of the issue price by dividing the amount Paid by the Issue Price. Copy the formula from cell H9 to the **range H10:H54**.
8. Click **cell J9** and insert a formula that calculates the percentage change in value by subtracting the Issue Price from the Current Value and then dividing that result by the Issue Price. Copy the formula from cell J9 to the **range J10:J54**.
9. Apply **Percent Style** with one decimal place to the **ranges H9:H54** and **J9:J54**.
10. Insert summary functions in the Current Values section at the top of the worksheet that use the **range I9:I54**:
    - **Cell I2:** Calculate the total current value.
    - **Cell I3:** Calculate the average current value.
    - **Cell I4:** Calculate the lowest current value.
    - **Cell I5:** Calculate the highest current value.

Insert Lookup, Conditional, and Payment Functions

You are ready to insert a function to look up the art codes in a lookup table and display the respective types of art within the dataset. Next, you will insert a function that compares the issue price to the current market value to see if the art has increased in value. Finally, you will insert a financial function to calculate the monthly payment for a piece of art that Raymond is considering purchasing by taking out a loan. Use relative, absolute, and mixed references correctly in your functions.

11. Click **cell C9** and insert a VLOOKUP function that looks up the code in cell B9, compares it to the codes and types of art in the range B2:C6, and then returns the type of art. Copy the function in cell C9 to the **range C9:C54**. Hide column B that contains the codes.

12. Click **cell K9** and insert an IF function that determines if the Issue Price is equal to the Current Value. If the values are the same, display **Same as Issue** (using the cell reference K2); otherwise, display **Increased in Value** (using the cell reference K3). Copy the function from cell K9 to the **range K10:K54**.

13. Display the Purchase worksheet and insert a row above Monthly Payment. Type **Payments in 1 Year** in **cell A5** and type **12** in **cell B5**.

14. Click **cell B6** and insert the PMT function to calculate the monthly payment using cell references, not numbers, in the function, and make sure the function displays a positive result. Apply **Accounting Number Format** and the **Output cell style** to **cell B6**.

Create a Column Chart

The Types of Art input section on the Christensen worksheet displays the total of the issue prices and the total current values of each type of art that Raymond owns. You will create a chart so that Raymond can compare the purchase price to the current value of each type of art.

15. Display the Christensen worksheet, select the **range C1:E6**, and create a clustered column chart.

16. Cut the chart and paste it in **cell C57**, change the height to **4"**, and change the width to **7"**.

17. Customize the chart by doing the following:

- Type **Raymond's Art Collection** for the chart title, apply **bold**, and then apply **Black, Text 1 font color**.
- Place the legend at the top of the chart.
- Add **Primary Minor Horizontal gridlines**.
- Add Alt Text **The column chart compares total issue prices to total current values by type of art. Most of the art value comes from the Limited Edition Canvas category.** (including the period).

Create a Pie Chart

To further analyze the data for Raymond, you will create a pie chart that shows the proportion each type of art contributes to the total current value.

18. Create a pie chart using the **ranges C2:C6** and **E2:E6** and move the chart to a new chart sheet named **Current Values**. Move the Current Values sheet to the right of the Purchase sheet.

19. Customize the chart by doing the following:

- Type **Percentage of Total Current Value** as the chart title and change the font size to **18 pt**.
- Remove the legend.

- Add data labels for categories and percentages; remove value data labels. Change the font size to **16 pt**, **bold**, and **Black, Text 1 font color** for the data labels.
- Choose **Colorful Palette 3** for the chart colors.
- Explode the Masterwork Anniversary Edition slice by **15%** and change the fill color to **Light Blue**.
- Add the Alt Text **Masterwork Anniversary Editions account for 17% of the total value. Other canvas editions account for 58% of the total value.** (including the period).

Insert a Table, Sort and Filter Data, and Apply Conditional Formatting

You will format the main dataset as a table and apply a table style. Then you will apply conditional formatting to highlight art that has increased in value, sort the data so that it is more easily reviewed, and set a filter to focus on a specific art category. Finally, you will add a total row to display summary totals.

20. Display the Christensen worksheet, click in any cell within the dataset, convert the data to a table, assign a table name **Collection**, and then apply **Green, Table Style Light 14.**

21. Apply a conditional format to the **range J9:J54** that highlights cells where the value is greater than 200% with **Green Fill with Dark Green Text**.

22. Sort the dataset by Type of Art and then within Type of Art, sort by Current Value from largest to smallest.

23. Set a filter to display art that has a **Sold Out** status.

24. Add a total row to display the sum of the Issue Price, Paid, and Current Values columns. Remove the total for the Note column.

Select Page Setup Options

You are ready to finalize the workbook so that you can show it to Raymond.

25. Select the Purchase sheet, set **2"** top margin, and then center horizontally on page.

26. Select the Christensen sheet, select **Landscape orientation**, **Legal paper size**, set **0.2"** left and right margins, **0.5"** top and bottom margins, and then set row 8 to repeat at the top of pages.

27. Change the width of **column A** to **27**, the width of **column D** to **11**, and the width of **column J** to **12**. Wrap text in **cell A1** and **cell J8**.

28. Create a footer with your name on the left side, the sheet tab code in the center, and file name code on the right side on all sheets.

29. Display the workbook in Normal View.

30. Save and close the file. Based on your instructor's directions, submit eApp_Cap1_Collection_LastFirst.

Excel Comprehensive Capstone Exercise (Chs. 5–12)

After graduating from college, you and three of your peers founded the software company Tech Store Unlimited (TSU). TSU provides an online market place that fosters business-to-business (B2B), business-to-consumer (B2C), and consumer-to-consumer (C2C) sales. As one of the company's principal owners, you have decided to compile a report that details warehouse information, orders, inventory, and facility management. To complete the task, you will duplicate existing formatting, utilize various conditional logic functions, complete an amortization table, visualize data with PivotTables and 3D Maps, connect and transform several external data sources; finally, you will inspect the workbook for issues.

Format the Workbook

To start your report, you want to ensure formatting is consistent between worksheets. You also want to define range names for later use in what-if analysis.

1. Open the file name *eApp_Cap2_TechStore* and save it as **eApp_Cap2_TechStore_LastFirst**.
2. Group the Employee_Info and New_Construction worksheets in the workbook and fill the **range A1:E1** from the Employee_Info worksheet across all worksheets including the formatting.
3. Make the New_Construction worksheet active and create range names based on each item in the **range A6:B9**.
4. Save the workbook.

Use Conditional Logic and Conditional Formatting

You want to calculate employee 401K eligibility. Any FT employee hired before 1/1/19 is eligible. You will also add formatting to visually indicate eligible employees. To complete the task, you will use conditional logic and conditional formatting.

5. Ensure the Employee_Info worksheet is active.
6. Click **cell G6** and enter a nested logical function that calculates employee 401K eligibility. If the employee is full time (FT) and was hired before the 401k cutoff date of 1/1/19 (cell H3), then he or she is eligible and **Y** should be displayed; non-eligible employees should be indicated with an **N**.
7. Use the fill handle to copy the function down without formatting, completing the **range G6:G25**.
8. Apply conditional formatting to the **range G6:G25** that highlights eligible employees with **Green Fill with Dark Green Text color**.
9. Save the workbook.

Enter Specialized Functions and Data Validation

You want to create a custom lookup function that enables you to locate employee information based on user-defined criteria and employee number. You also want to use conditional math to analyze part-time (PT) salaries. To complete these tasks, you will use data validation; a nested INDEX/MATCH function; and the conditional match functions MAXIFS, SUMIF, COUNTIF, and AVERAGEIF.

10. Create a Data Validation list in **cell J7** based on the employee ID's located in the **range A6:A25**. Add the input message **Select Employee ID** and use the **Stop Style Error Alert**.
11. Use the Data Validation list in **cell J7** to select **Employee_ID 31461** and select **Salary** in **cell K6** to test the function.

12. Enter a nested INDEX and MATCH function in **cell K7** that examines the **range B6:H25** and returns the corresponding employee information based on the match values in **cell J7** and **cell K6**.

13. Enter a conditional math function in **cell K14** that calculates the total number of PT employees.

14. Enter a conditional math function in **cell K15** that calculates the total value of PT employee salaries.

15. Enter a conditional math function in **cell K16** that calculates the average value of PT employee salaries.

16. Enter a conditional math function in **cell K17** that calculates the highest PT employee salary.

17. Apply **Currency Number Format** to the **range K15:K17**.

18. Save the workbook.

Perform Advanced Filtering and Database Functions

You want to determine additional statistical information about your full-time (FT) employees. You plan to use advanced filtering to create an isolated table of full time employees. You also will use Database functions to calculate total number of FT employees and additional summary statistics.

19. Click **cell K11** and type **FT**.

20. Click **cell A28** and type **Full Time Employees**.

21. Use the Format Painter to apply the formatting from the **cell A3** to the **range A28:B28**.

22. Use advanced filtering to restrict the data to display only FT employees based on the criteria in the **range K10:K11**. Place the results in **cell A29**.

23. Enter a database function in **cell K18** to determine the total number of FT employees.

24. Enter a database function in **cell K19** to determine the total value of FT employee salaries.

25. Enter a database function in **cell K20** to determine the average FT employee salary.

26. Enter a database function in **cell K21** to determine the highest FT salary.

27. Format the **range K19:K21** with **Currency Number Format**.

28. Save the workbook.

Use What-If Analysis

As part of your analysis, you will evaluate the cost of adding a new facility. You will use what-if analysis tools to aid in your assessments.

29. Ensure that the New_Construction worksheet is active.

30. Use Goal Seek to reduce the monthly payment in **cell B6** to the optimal value of $8000. Complete this task by changing the Loan amount in **cell E6**.

31. Create the following three scenarios using Scenario Manager. The scenarios should change the **cells B7** and **B8**.

Good	Most Likely	Bad
B7 = 0.0312	B7 = 0.0575	B7 = 0.0625
B8 = 5	B8 = 5	B8 = 3

32. Create a Scenario Summary Report based on the value in **cell B6**.

33. Format the new report appropriately and reorder the worksheets so the Scenario Summary worksheet appears as the last worksheet in the workbook.

34. Save the workbook.

Complete an Amortization Schedule

To continue your analysis of facility expenditures, you want to complete an amortization table detailing payment, principal, interest, cumulative principal, and cumulative interest.

35. Ensure that the New_Construction worksheet is active

36. Enter a reference in **cell B12** to the beginning loan balance.

37. Enter a reference in **cell C12** to the payment amount.

38. Enter a function in **cell D12** based on the payment and loan details that calculates the amount of interest paid on the first payment. Be sure to use the appropriate absolute, relative, or mixed cell references. All results should be formatted as positive numbers.

39. Enter a function in **cell E12** based on the payment and loan details that calculates the amount of principal paid on the first payment. Be sure to use the appropriate absolute, relative, or mixed cell references and ensure the results are positive.

40. Enter a formula in **cell F12** to calculate the remaining balance after the current payment. The remaining balance is calculated by subtracting the principal payment from the balance in column B.

41. Enter a function in **cell G12** based on the payment and loan details that calculates the amount of cumulative interest paid on the first payment. Be sure to use the appropriate absolute, relative, or mixed cell references and ensure the results are positive.

42. Enter a function in **cell H12** based on the payment and loan details that calculates the amount of cumulative principal paid on the first payment. Be sure to use the appropriate absolute, relative, or mixed cell references. All results should be formatted as positive numbers.

43. Enter a reference to the remaining balance of payment 1 in **cell B13**.

44. Use the fill handle to copy the functions created in the prior steps down to complete the amortization table. Expand the width of **columns D:H** as needed.

45. Save the workbook.

Use Get & Transform, PowerPivot, and 3D Maps

You want to create a PivotTable to analyze sales information. To complete this task, you will use Get & Transform to connect and transform the data. Then you will use 3D Maps to create a geographic visualization of warehouse information.

> **MAC TROUBLESHOOTING:** The standard installation of Excel for Mac does include drivers for importing SQL databases but does not include drivers to import data from Access. To import data from Access, third-party ODBC drivers must be purchased and installed. The required drivers can be downloaded. For more information search ODBC drivers that are compatible with Excel for Mac on https://support.office.com.

46. Use Get & Transform to connect and open the **Orders table** in the eApp_Cap2_Orders.accdb database. Use the Power Query editor to format column A with **Date number format** and load the table.

47. Rename the worksheet **Orders** and move the worksheet to the right of the Scenario Summary worksheet.

48. Adapt Steps 46 and 47 to connect and load the **Warehouse table**.

49. Use PowerPivot to create a PivotTable based on the **Inventory table** in the eApp_Cap2_Orders.accdb database. Place the PivotTable on a new worksheet.

50. Create the following relationships:

Relationship 1

Table	Column (Foreign)
Inventory	Warehouse
Table	Column (Primary)
Warehouse	Warehouse

Relationship 2

Table	Column (Foreign)
Orders	Item_Number
Table	**Column (Primary)**
Inventory	Item_Number

51. Add the following fields to the PivotTable:

Rows	Values
Warehouse:Location	Inventory:Current_Inventory
Warehouse:Warehouse	Inventory:Total_Value
Inventory:Item_Number	

52. Insert a Slicer based on Location. Place the upper left corner of the Slicer in **cell F3**.

53. Create a 3D Map that displays the location of all warehouses. (On a Mac, 3D Maps is not available.)

54. Rename the worksheet **Inventory** and move the worksheet to the right of the Orders worksheet.

55. Save the workbook.

Use the Data Analysis ToolPak

After connecting the external sources using Get & Transform, you want to use the Data Analysis ToolPak to calculate summary statistics on the Orders worksheet.

56. Make the **Orders** worksheet active.

57. Load the Data Analysis ToolPak Add-In, if necessary.

58. Use the Data Analysis ToolPak to output Descriptive Statistics including Summary statistics starting in cell G3. The statistics should be based on the quantity of orders located in the **range E1:E50**. Be sure to include column headings in the output. Resize columns G:H as needed.

59. Save the workbook.

Use the Macro Recorder and Insert a Form Control

Since you imported the order information using Get & Transform, the table will update when refreshed. You want to use the Macro Recorder to create a macro to sort the table by date after the workbook has been refreshed.

60. Enable the Developer tab, if necessary.

61. Use the Macro Recorder to record a macro named **Sort**. When activated, the macro should sort the Orders table in ascending order by date.

62. Insert a **Form Control button** in the **range G21:I24**.

63. Add the label **Sort** and assign the **Sort** macro.

64. Save the workbook as a Macro Enabled workbook.

Check Workbook for Issues

For your final step, you want to inspect the document for accessibility issues.

65. Use the Accessibility checker to inspect for issues. Once located, take the recommended actions to alleviate the issues.

66. Create a footer with your name on the left, the sheet code in the center, and the file name on the right for each worksheet.

67. Save and close the file. Based on your instructor's directions, submit eApp_Cap2_TechStore_LastFirst.xlsm.

Microsoft Office 2019 Specialist Excel

Online Appendix materials can be found in the Student Resources located at **www.pearsonhighered.com/exploring.**

MOS Obj #	MOS Objective	Exploring Chapter	Exploring Section Heading
I. **Manage Worksheets and Workbooks**			
1.1 **Import data into workbooks**			
1.1.1	Import data from .txt files	**Chapter 10**: Power Add-ins	Get Data from a Text File
1.1.2	Import data from .csv files	**Chapter 10**: Power Add-ins	Get Data from a Text File
1.2 **Navigate within workbooks**			
1.2.1	Search for data within a workbook	**Chapter 1**: Introduction to Excel	Find and Replace Data
1.2.2	Navigate to named cells, ranges, or workbook elements	**Chapter 1**: Introduction to Excel	Navigate in and Among Worksheets
1.2.3	Insert and remove hyperlinks	**Chapter 9**: Multiple-Sheet Workbook Management	Inserting Hyperlinks
1.3 **Format worksheets and workbooks**			
1.3.1	Modify page setup	**Chapter 1**: Introduction to Excel	Selecting Page Setup Options
1.3.2	Adjust row height and column width	**Chapter 1**: Introduction to Excel	Adjust Column Width, Adjust Row Height
1.3.3	Customize headers and footers	**Chapter 1**: Introduction to Excel	Create a Header or Footer
1.4 **Customize options and views**			
1.4.1	Customize the Quick Access Toolbar	Common Features	Use Common Interface Components
1.4.2	Display and modify workbook content in different views	**Chapter 1**: Introduction to Excel	Identify Excel Window Elements Create a Header or Footer
1.4.3	Freeze worksheet rows and columns	**Chapter 4**: Datasets and Tables	Freezing Rows and Columns
1.4.4	Change window views	**Chapter 9**: Multiple-Sheet Workbook Management	Manage Windows
1.4.5	Modify basic workbook properties	Common Features	Configure Document Properties
1.4.6	Display formulas	**Chapter 1**: Introduction to Excel	Display Cell Formulas
1.5 **Configure content for collaboration**			
1.5.1	Set a print area	**Chapter 4**: Datasets and Tables	Printing Large Datasets
1.5.2	Save workbooks in alternative file formats	**Chapter 12**: Templates, Workbook Inspection, and Macros	Create a Template
1.5.3	Configure print settings	**Chapter 1**: Introduction to Excel	Selecting Page Setup Options Previewing and Printing a Worksheet
1.5.4	Inspect workbooks for issues	**Chapter 12**: Templates, Workbook Inspection, and Macros	Check for Issues

MOS Obj #	MOS Objective	Exploring Chapter	Exploring Section Heading
2. Manage Data Cells and Ranges			
2.1 Manipulate data in worksheets			
2.1.1	Paste data by using special paste options	**Chapter 1**: Introduction to Excel **Chapter 7**: Specialized Functions **Chapter 9**: Multiple-Sheet Workbook Management	Use Paste Options HOE 1 Step 3: Use the Switch Function Data Validation on Multiple Sheets tip
2.1.2	Fill cells by using Auto Fill	**Chapter 1**: Introduction to Excel	Use Auto Fill to Complete a Sequence
2.1.3	Insert and delete multiple columns or rows	**Chapter 1**: Introduction to Excel	Insert Cells, Columns, and Rows Delete Cells, Columns, and Rows
2.1.4	Insert and delete cells	**Chapter 1**: Introduction to Excel	Insert Cells, Columns, and Rows Delete Cells, Columns, and Rows
2.2 Format cells and ranges			
2.2.1	Merge and unmerge cells	**Chapter 1**: Introduction to Excel	Merge Cells
2.2.2	Modify cell alignment, orientation, and indentation	**Chapter 1**: Introduction to Excel	Change Cell Alignment Increase and Decrease Indent TIP: Change Text Orientation
2.2.3	Format cells by using Format Painter	Common Features	Modify Text
2.2.4	Wrap text within cells	**Chapter 1**: Introduction to Excel	Wrap Text
2.2.5	Apply number formats	**Chapter 1**: Introduction to Excel	Applying Number Formats
2.2.6	Apply cell formats from the Format Cells dialog box	Common Features **Chapter 1**: Introduction to Excel	Modify Text Apply Borders and Fill Color Chapter 1 TIP: Format Cells Dialog Box
2.2.7	Apply cell styles	**Chapter 1**: Introduction to Excel	Apply Cell Styles
2.2.8	Clear cell formatting	**Chapter 1**: Introduction to Excel	Edit and Clear Cell Contents
2.3 Define and reference named ranges			
2.3.1	Define a named range	**Chapter 1**: Introduction to Excel	Create and Maintain Range Names
2.3.2	Name a table	**Chapter 1**: Introduction to Excel	Create and Maintain Range Names
2.4 Summarize data visually			
2.4.1	Insert Sparklines	**Chapter 3**: Charts	Create and Customize Sparklines
2.4.2	Apply built-in conditional formatting	**Chapter 4**: Datasets and Tables	Applying Conditional Formatting
2.4.3	Remove conditional formatting	**Chapter 4**: Datasets and Tables	Applying Conditional Formatting
3. Manage Tables and Table Data			
3.1 Create and format tables			
3.1.1	Create Excel tables from cell ranges	**Chapter 4**: Datasets and Tables	Designing and Creating Tables
3.1.2	Apply table styles	**Chapter 4**: Datasets and Tables	Applying a Table Style
3.1.3	Convert tables to cell ranges	**Chapter 4**: Datasets and Tables	Designing and Creating Tables
3.2 Modify tables			
3.2.1	Add or remove table rows and columns	**Chapter 4**: Datasets and Tables	Add and Delete Fields
3.2.2	Configure table style options	**Chapter 4**: Datasets and Tables	Applying a Table Style
3.2.3	Insert and configure total rows	**Chapter 4**: Datasets and Tables	Adding a Total Row

MOS Obj #	MOS Objective	Exploring Chapter	Exploring Section Heading
3.3	**Filter and sort table data**		
3.3.1	Filter records	**Chapter 4**: Datasets and Tables	Filtering Data
3.3.2	Sort data by multiple columns	**Chapter 4**: Datasets and Tables	Sorting Data

4. Perform Operations by using Formulas and Functions

MOS Obj #	MOS Objective	Exploring Chapter	Exploring Section Heading
4.1	**Insert references**		
4.1.1	Insert relative, absolute, and mixed references	**Chapter 2**: Formulas and Functions	Using Relative, Absolute, and Mixed References in Formulas
4.1.2	Reference named ranges and named tables in formulas	**Chapter 6**: What If Analysis	Use Range Names in Formulas
4.2	**Calculate and transform data**		
4.2.1	Perform calculations by using the AVERAGE(), MAX(), MIN(), and SUM() functions	**Chapter 2**: Formulas and Functions	Inserting Basic Math and Statistics Functions
4.2.2	Count cells by using the COUNT(), COUNTA(), and COUNTBLANK() functions	**Chapter 2**: Formulas and Functions	Inserting Basic Math and Statistics Functions
4.2.3	Perform conditional operations by using the IF() function	**Chapter 2**: Formulas and Functions	Using the IF Function
4.3	**Format and modify text**		
4.3.1	Format text by using RIGHT(), LEFT(), and MID() functions	**Chapter 11**: Additional Specialized Functions	Use the LEFT, RIGHT, and MID Functions
4.3.2	Format text by using UPPER(), LOWER(), and LEN() functions	**Chapter 11**: Additional Specialized Functions	Use the PROPER, UPPER, and LOWER Functions
4.3.3	Format text by using the CONCAT() and TEXTJOIN() functions	**Chapter 11**: Additional Specialized Functions	Use the CONCAT and TEXTJOIN Functions

5. Manage Charts

MOS Obj #	MOS Objective	Exploring Chapter	Exploring Section Heading
5.1	**Create charts**		
5.1.1	Create charts	**Chapter 3**: Charts	Creating a Basic Chart Using Other Methods to Create a Chart Creating Other Charts
5.1.2	Create chart sheets	**Chapter 3**: Charts	Move a Chart
5.2	**Modify charts**		
5.2.1	Add data series to charts	**Chapter 3**: Charts	Change the Data Source
5.2.2	Switch between rows and columns in source data	**Chapter 3**: Charts	Switch Row and Column Data
5.2.3	Add and modify chart elements	**Chapter 3**: Charts	Chart Elements
5.3	**Format charts**		
5.3.1	Apply chart layouts	**Chapter 3**: Charts	Apply a Quick Layout
5.3.2	Apply chart styles	**Chapter 3**: Charts	Applying a Chart Style and Colors
5.3.3	Add alternative text to charts to accessibility	**Chapter 3**: Charts	Include Alt Text

Microsoft Office 2019 Expert Excel

Online Appendix materials can be found in the Student Resources located at **www.pearsonhighered.com/exploring**.

MOS Obj #	MOS Objective	Exploring Chapter	Exploring Section Heading
I.	**Manage Workbook Options and Settings**		
1.1	**Manage workbooks**		
1.1.1	Copy macros between workbooks	Online Appendix	
1.1.2	Reference data in other workbooks	**Chapter 9**: Multiple-Sheet Workbook Management	Linking Workbooks
1.1.3	Enable macros in a workbook	**Chapter 12**: Templates, Workbook Inspection, and Macros	Run a Macro
1.1.4	Manage workbook versions	Online Appendix	
1.2	**Prepare workbooks for collaboration**		
1.2.1	Restrict editing	**Chapter 9**: Multiple-Sheet Workbook Management	Lock and Unlock Cells
1.2.2	Protect worksheets and cell ranges	**Chapter 9**: Multiple-Sheet Workbook Management	Lock and Unlock Cells Protect a Worksheet
1.2.3	Protect workbook structure	**Chapter 9**: Multiple-Sheet Workbook Management	Protecting a Workbook
1.2.4	Configure formula calculation options	Online Appendix	Online Appendix
1.2.5	Manage comments	**Chapter 12**: Templates, Workbook Inspection, and Macros	Annotate a Workbook
1.3	**Use and configure languate options**		
1.3.1	Configure editing and display languages	Online Appendix	Online Appendix
1.3.2	Use language-specific features	Online Appendix	Online Appendix
2.	**Manage and Format Data**		
2.1	**Fill cells based on existing data**		
2.1.1	Fill cells by using Flash Fill	**Chapter 1**: Introduction to Excel **Chapter 11**: Additional Specialized Functions	TIP Flash Fill Use Flash Fill
2.1.2	Fill cells by using advanced Fill Series options	**Chapter 6**: What If Analysis	Set Up One Variable Substitution Values
2.2	**Format and validate data**		
2.2.1	Create custom number formats	**Chapter 1**: Introduction to Excel	TIP Custom Number Formats
2.2.2	Configure data validation	**Chapter 9**: Multiple-Sheet Workbook Management	Creating a Data Validation Rule
2.2.3	Group and ungroup data	**Chapter 5**: Subtotals, PivotTables, and PivotCharts	Grouping and Ungrouping Data

MOS Obj #	MOS Objective	Exploring Chapter	Exploring Section Heading
2.2.4	Calculate data by inserting subtotals and totals	**Chapter 5**: Subtotals, PivotTables, and PivotCharts	Subtotaling Data
2.2.5	Remove duplicate records	**Chapter 4**: Datasets and Tables	Remove Duplicate Rows
2.3	**Apply advanced conditional formatting and filtering**		
2.3.1	Create custom conditional formatting rules	**Chapter 4**: Managing Large Volumes of Data	Create a New Conditional Formatting Rule
2.3.2	Create conditional formatting rules that use formulas	**Chapter 4**: Managing Large Volumes of Data	Use Formulas in Conditional Formatting Rules
2.3.3	Manage conditional formatting rules	**Chapter 4**: Managing Large Volumes of Data	Manage Rules
3.	**Create Advanced Formulas and Macros**		
3.1	**Perform logical operations in formulas**		
3.1.1	Perform logical operations by using nest functions including the IF(), IFS(), SWITCH(), SUMIF(), AVERAGEIF(), COUNTIF(), SUMIFS(), AVERAGEIFS(), COUNTIFS(), MAXIFS(), MINIFS(), AND(), OR(), and NOT() functions	**Chapter 2**: Formulas and Functions **Chapter 7**: Specialized Functions	Using the IF Function Use the IFS Function Use the SWITCH Function Use the SUMIF Function Use the AVERAGEIF Function Use the COUNTIFS Function Use the COUNTIFS, SUMIFS, and AVERAGEIFS Functions Use the MAXIFS and MINIFS Functions Use AND, OR, and NOT Functions
3.2	**Look up data by using functions**		
3.2.1	Look up data by using the VLOOKUP(), HLOOKUP(), MATCH(), and INDEX() functions	**Chapter 2**: Formulas and Functions **Chapter 11**: Additional Specialized Functions	Use the VLOOKUP Function Use the HLOOKUP Function Use the INDEX Function Use the MATCH Function
3.3	**Use advanced date and time functions**		
3.3.1	Reference date and time by using the NOW() and TODAY() functions	**Chapter 2**: Formulas and functions	Use Date Functions
3.3.2	Calculate dates by using the WEEKDAY() and WORKDAY() functions	**Chapter 7**: Specialized Functions	Use the WEEKDAY Function Use Other Date Functions (WORKDAY in a table)
3.4	**Perform data analysis**		
3.4.1	Summarize data from multiple ranges by using the Consolidate feature		
3.4.2	Perform what-if analysis by using Goal Seek and Scenario Manager	**Chapter 6**: What If Analysis	Determine Optimal Input Values Using Goal Seek
3.4.3	Forecast data by using the AND(), IF(), and NPER() functions	**Chapter 7**: Use AND, OR, or NOT Functions	Use AND, OR, and NOT Functions Use the NPER and RATE Functions
3.4.4	Calculate financial data by using the PMT() function	**Chapter 2**: Formulas and Functions	Use the PMT Function

MOS Obj #	MOS Objective	Exploring Chapter	Exploring Section Heading
3.5	**Troubleshoot formulas**		
3.5.1	Trace precedence and dependence	**Chapter 9**: Multiple-Sheet Workbook Management	Trace Precedents and Dependents
3.5.2	Monitor cells and formulas by using the Watch Window	**Chapter 9**: Multiple-Sheet Workbook Management	Setting Up a Watch Window
3.5.3	Validate formulas by using error checking rules	**Chapter 9**: Multiple-Sheet Workbook Management	Creating a Data Validation Rule
3.5.4	Evaluate formulas	**Chapter 9**: Multiple-Sheet Workbook Management	Check for and Repair Errors
3.6	**Create and modify simple macros**		
3.6.1	Record simple macros	**Chapter 12**: Templates, Workbook Inspection, and Macros	Use the Macro Recorder
3.6.2	Name simple macros	**Chapter 12**: Templates, Workbook Inspection, and Macros	Edit a Macro
3.6.3	Edit simple macros	**Chapter 12**: Templates, Workbook Inspection, and Macros	Edit a Macro
4.	**Manage Advanced Charts and Tables**		
4.1	**Create and modify advanced charts**		
4.1.1	Create and modify dual axis charts	Online Appendix	Online Appendix
4.1.2	Create and modify charts including Box & Whisker, Combo, Funnel, Histogram, Map, Sunburst, and Waterfall charts	**Chapter 7**: Specialized Functions **Chapter 8**: Statistical Functions Online Appendix	Inserting a Map Create a Histogram Online Appendix
4.2	**Create and modify PivotTables**		
4.2.1	Create PivotTables	**Chapter 5**: Subtotals, PivotTables, and PivotCharts	Creating a PivotTable
4.2.2	Modify field selections and options	**Chapter 5**: Subtotals, PivotTables, and PivotCharts	Add Rows, Values, and Columns Modifying a PivotTable
4.2.3	Create slicers	**Chapter 5**: Subtotals, PivotTables, and PivotCharts	Insert a Slicer
4.2.4	Group PivotTable data	**Chapter 5**: Subtotals, PivotTables, and PivotCharts	Group PivotTable Data
4.2.5	Add calculated fields	**Chapter 5**: Subtotals, PivotTables, and PivotCharts	Creating a Calculated Field
4.2.6	Format data	**Chapter 5**: Subtotals, PivotTables, and PivotCharts	Change the Value Field Settings
4.3	**Create and modify PivotCharts**		
4.3.1	Create PivotCharts	**Chapter 5**: Subtotals, PivotTables, and PivotCharts	Creating a PivotChart
4.3.2	Manipulate options in existing PivotCharts	**Chapter 5**: Subtotals, PivotTables, and PivotCharts	Modify the PivotChart
4.3.3	Apply styles to PivotCharts	**Chapter 5**: Subtotals, PivotTables, and PivotCharts	Modify the PivotChart
4.3.4	Drill down into PivotCharts details	**Chapter 5**: Subtotals, PivotTables, and PivotCharts	Modify the PivotChart

Glossary

100% stacked bar chart A chart type that places (stacks) data in one bar per category, with each bar the same width of 100%.

100% stacked column chart A chart type that places (stacks) data in one column per category, with each column the same height of 100%.

3-D reference A reference within a formula or function on one worksheet that includes the name of another worksheet, column letter, and row number located within the same workbook. The three dimensions include the worksheet name, the column, and the row.

Absolute cell reference A designation that indicates a constant reference to a specific cell location; the cell reference does not change when you copy the formula.

Accessibility Checker A tool that reviews a workbook to detect potential issues that could hinder the ability of users who access your public files and then alerts you to these issues so that you can address them.

Accounting Number Format A number format that displays $ on the left side of a cell, formats a value with a comma for every three digits on the left side of the decimal point, and displays two digits to the right of the decimal point.

Active cell The current cell in a worksheet. It is indicated by a dark green border, and the Name Box shows the location of the active cell.

Active sheet The currently displayed worksheet.

Add-in A program that can be added to Excel to provide enhanced functionality.

Alignment The placement of data within the boundaries of a cell.

Alt text Also known as *alternative text*, an accessibility compliance feature where you enter text and a description for an objective, such as a table or a chart. A special reader can read the alt text to a user.

Analysis ToolPak An add-in program that contains tools for performing complex statistical analysis, such as ANOVA, correlation, and histogram.

AND function A logical function that returns TRUE when all arguments are true and FALSE if any one of the conditions is false.

ANOVA stands for Analysis of Variance and is a statistical tool that compares the means between two data samples to determine if they were derived from the same population.

Area chart A chart type that emphasizes magnitude of changes over time by filling in the space between lines with a color.

Argument A positional reference contained within parentheses in a function such as a cell reference or value, required to complete a function and produce output.

Auto Fill A feature that helps you complete a sequence of months, abbreviated months, quarters, weekdays, weekday abbreviations, or values. Auto Fill also can be used to fill or copy a formula down a column or across a row.

AutoComplete A feature that searches for and automatically displays any other text in that column that matches the letters you type.

AVERAGE function A statistical function that calculates the arithmetic mean, or average, of values in a range of cells.

AVERAGEIF function A statistical function that calculates the average, or arithmetic mean, of all cells in a range that meet a specific condition.

AVERAGEIFS function A statistical function that returns the average (arithmetic mean) of all cells in a range that meet multiple criteria.

Axis title A label that describes either the category axis or the value axis. Provides clarity, particularly in describing the value axis.

Backstage view A component of Office that provides a concise collection of commands related to an open file.

Bar chart A chart type that compares values across categories using horizontal bars where the length represents the value; the longer the bar, the larger the value. In a bar chart, the horizontal axis displays values and the vertical axis displays categories.

Binding constraint A rule that Solver enforces to reach the objective value.

Bins Data ranges in which values can be categorized and counted.

Border A line that surrounds a cell or a range of cells to offset particular data from the rest of the data in a worksheet.

Breakpoint The lowest value for a category or in a series.

Calculated field A user-defined field that performs a calculation based on other fields in a PivotTable.

Cancel A command to the left of the Formula Bar that is used to cancel data being entered or edited into the active cell. The Cancel command changes from gray to red when you position the pointer over it.

Category axis The chart axis that displays descriptive labels for the data points plotted in a chart. The category axis labels are typically text contained in the first column of worksheet data (such as job titles) used to create the chart.

Cell The intersection of a column and row in a Word table, PowerPoint table, or Excel worksheet.

Cell address The unique identifier of a cell, starting with the column letter and then the row number, such as C6.

Cell style A collection of format characteristics (font, font color, font size, borders, fill colors, and number formatting) to provide a consistent appearance within a worksheet and among similar workbooks.

Changing variable cell A single cell or range of cells containing variables whose value changes until Solver optimizes the value in the objective cell.

Chart A visual representation of numeric data.

Chart area A container for the entire chart and all of its elements, including the plot area, titles, legends, and labels.

Chart element A component of a chart that helps complete or clarify the chart.

Chart filter A setting that controls what data series and categories are displayed or hidden in a chart.

Chart sheet A sheet within a workbook that contains a single chart and no spreadsheet data.

Chart style A collection of formatting that controls the color of the chart area, plot area, and data series, as well as the font and font size of the titles.

Chart title The label that describes the entire chart. The title is usually placed at the top of the chart area.

CHOOSE function A lookup function that returns a value from a list using an index number between 1 and 254.

Circular reference A situation that occurs when a formula contains a direct or an indirect reference to the cell containing the formula.

Cloud storage A technology used to store files and to work with programs that are stored in a central location on the Internet.

Clustered bar chart A type of chart that groups, or clusters, bars displayed horizontally to compare several data points among categories.

Clustered column chart A type of chart that groups, or clusters, columns set side by side to compare several data points among categories.

Collaboration A process that occurs when multiple people work together to achieve a goal by using technology to edit the contents of a file.

Color scale A conditional format that displays a particular color based on the relative value of the cell contents to the other selected cells.

Column chart A type of chart that compares values vertically in columns where the height represents the value; the taller the column, the larger the value. In a column chart, the vertical axis displays values and the horizontal axis displays categories.

Column heading The alphabetical letter above a column in a worksheet. For example, B is the column heading for the second column.

Column index number The column number in the lookup table that contains the return values.

Column width The horizontal measurement of a column in a table or a worksheet. In Excel, it is measured by the number of characters or pixels.

Columns area A section within the PivotTable Fields task pane used to display columns of summarized data for the selected field(s) that will display labels to organize summarized data vertically in a PivotTable.

Combo chart A chart that combines two chart types, such as column and line, to plot different types of data, such as quantities and percentages.

Comma separated values (CSV) file Uses commas to separate data into columns and a newline character to separate data into rows.

Comma Style A number format that formats a value with a comma for every three digits on the left side of the decimal point and displays two digits to the right of the decimal point.

Command A button or area within a group that you click to perform tasks.

Comment A note or annotation to ask a question or provide a suggestion to another person about content in a worksheet cell.

Comment indicator A red triangle that appears in the top-right corner of a cell containing a comment.

Compatibility Checker A tool that evaluates the workbook's contents to identify what data and features are not compatible with previous versions.

CONCAT function A text function that joins up to 253 text strings into one text string.

Conditional formatting A set of rules that applies specific formatting to highlight or emphasize cells that meet specific conditions.

Constraint A limitation that imposes restrictions on a spreadsheet model as Solver determines the optimum value for the objective cell.

Contextual tab A tab that contains a group of commands related to the selected object.

Copy A command used to duplicate a selection from the original location and place a copy in the Office Clipboard.

CORREL function A statistical function that determines the strength of a relationship between two variables.

COUNT function A statistical function that tallies the number of cells in a range that contain values you can use in calculations, such as numeric and date data, but excludes blank cells or text entries from the tally.

COUNTA function A statistical function that tallies the number of cells in a range that are not blank—that is, cells that contain data, whether a value, text, or a formula.

COUNTBLANK function A statistical function that tallies the number of cells in a range that are blank.

COUNTIF function A statistical function that counts the number of cells in a range when a specified condition is met.

COUNTIFS function A statistical function that counts the number of cells in a range that meet multiple criteria.

Covariance Measure of how two sample sets of data vary simultaneously.

Criteria range A group of two or more adjacent cells that specifies the conditions used to control the results of a filter.

CUMIPMT function A financial function that calculates the cumulative interest through a specified payment period.

CUMPRINC function A financial function that calculates the cumulative principal through a specified payment period.

Currency format A number format that displays $ to the immediate left of the value, formats a value with a comma for every three digits on the left side of the decimal point, and displays two digits to the right of the decimal point.

Cut A command used to remove a selection from the original location and place it in the Office Clipboard.

Data bar Data bar formatting applies a gradient or solid fill bar in which the width of the bar represents the current cell's value compared relatively to other cells' values.

Data label An identifier that shows the exact value of a data point in a chart. Appears above or on a data point in a chart. May indicate percentage of a value to the whole on a pie chart.

Data mining The process of analyzing large volumes of data using advanced statistical techniques to identify trends and patterns in the data.

Data model A collection of related tables that contain structured data used to create a database; enables you to integrate data from multiple sources within a workbook.

Data point An individual value in a cell that is plotted in a chart.

Data series A group of related data points that displays in rows or columns in a worksheet.

Data shaping The process of editing information from one or more data sources to desired parameters before importing into an application.

Data structure The organization method used to manage multiple data points within a dataset.

Data table A grid that contains the data source values and labels to plot data in a chart. A data table may be placed below a chart or hidden from view.

Data validation rule A set of rules that must be followed in order to allow data to be entered in a cell.

Data visualization A method of summarizing data visually to better understand the significance of the information.

Database function A function that analyzes data for selected records in a dataset using a criteria range.

DATE function A date function that displays the date when provided with the numeric year, month, and date arguments.

DAVERAGE function A database function that calculates the arithmetic mean, or average, of values in a column that match specified conditions in a criteria range.

DAY function A date function that displays the day (1–31) within a given date.

DAYS function A date function that calculates the number of days between two dates, where the most recent date is entered in the end_date argument and the older date is entered in the start_date argument.

DAYS360 function A date function that calculates the number of days between two dates based on a 360-day year, using 30 days per month.

DCOUNT function A database function that counts the cells that contain numbers in a column that matches specified conditions in a criteria range.

Delimiter A special characters (such as a tab or space) that separate data.

Dependent cell A cell containing a formula that relies on other cells to obtain its value.

Destination file A file that contains a link to receive data from a source file.

DGET function A database function that extracts a single value from a dataset that matches specified conditions.

Dialog box A box that provides access to more precise, but less frequently used, commands.

Dialog Box Launcher A button that when clicked opens a corresponding dialog box.

Dimension Attributes that contribute to the visualization of data.

DMAX function A database function that identifies the highest value in a column that matches specified conditions in a criteria range.

DMIN function A database function that identifies the lowest value in a column that matches specified conditions in a criteria range.

Document Inspector A feature that reviews a workbook for hidden or personal data stored in the workbook or personal document properties, such as author, and then informs you of these details so that you can select what data to remove.

Document properties Data elements that are saved with a document but do not appear in the document as it is shown onscreen or is printed.

DSUM function A database function that adds the values in a column that match specified conditions in a criteria range.

EDATE A date function that displays the serial number representing a date X number of months in the future or past from a given date.

Embed The act of importing external data into Excel but not maintaining a link to the original data source.

Enhanced ScreenTip A small message box that displays when you place the pointer over a command button. The purpose of the command, short descriptive text, or a keyboard shortcut, if applicable, will display in the box.

Enter A command to the left of the Formula Bar that is used to accept data typed in the active cell and keep the current cell active. The Enter command changes from gray to blue when you position the pointer over it.

EOMONTH A date function that displays the serial number representing the last day of a month that is X number of months from a given date.

Error alert A message that displays when a user enters invalid data in a cell that contains a validation rule.

Error bars Visual that indicates the standard error amount, a percentage, or a standard deviation for a data point or marker in a chart.

Exploded pie chart A chart type in which one or more pie slices are separated from the rest of the pie chart for emphasis.

External Data property Setting that controls how imported data connects to the external data source.

Field The smallest data element contained in a table, such as first name, last name, address, and phone number.

Fill color The background color that displays behind the data in a cell so that the data stand out.

Fill handle A small green square at the bottom-right corner of the active cell. You can position the pointer on the fill handle and drag it to repeat the contents of the cell to other cells or to copy a formula in the active cell to adjacent cells down the column or across the row.

Filtering The process of specifying conditions to display only those records that meet those conditions.

FILTERS area A section within the PivotTable Fields task pane used to place a field so that the user can then filter the data by that field. Displays top-level filters above the PivotTable so that you can set filters to display results based on conditions you set.

FIND function A text function that identifies the starting position of one text string within another text string.

Fixed-width Text File A file in which each column contains a specific number of characters.

Flash Fill A feature that fills in data or values automatically based on one or two examples you enter using anther part of data entered in a previous column in a dataset.

Footer Information that displays at the bottom of a document page.

Forecast Sheet A business intelligence feature that creates a forecast worksheet to detail trends based on historical data.

FORECAST.LINEAR function A statistical function that calculates, or predicts, a future value along a linear trend by using existing values.

Format Painter A feature that enables you to quickly and easily copy all formatting from one area to another in Word, PowerPoint, and Excel.

Formula A combination of cell references, operators, values, and/or functions used to perform a calculation.

Formula auditing Tools that enable you to display or trace relationships for formulas, show formulas, check for errors, and evaluate formulas.

Formula AutoComplete A feature that displays a list of functions and defined names that match letters as you type a formula.

Formula Bar A bar below the ribbon and to the right of the Insert Function command that shows the contents (text, value, date, formula, or function) stored in the active cell. You enter or edit cell content here.

FORMULATEXT function A lookup function that returns the formula as a string that is stored in another cell.

Freezing The process of keeping rows and/or columns visible onscreen at all times, even when you scroll through a large dataset.

FREQUENCY function A statistical function that determines the number of occurrences of numeric values in a dataset based on predetermined bins.

Fully qualified structured reference A structured formula that contains the table name.

Function A predefined computation that simplifies creating a complex calculation and produces a result based on inputs known as *arguments*.

Function ScreenTip A small pop-up description that displays the function's arguments.

FV function A financial function that calculates the future value of an investment, given a fixed interest rate, term, and identical periodic payments.

Gallery An Office feature that displays additional formatting and design choices.

Go To Navigation feature to go to a specific page in Word or a specific cell in Excel.

Goal Seek A tool that identifies the necessary input value to obtain a desired goal by changing one variable.

Gridline A horizontal or vertical line that extends from the tick marks on the value axis across the plot area to guide the reader's eyes across the chart to identify values.

Group A subset of a tab that organizes similar tasks together.

Grouping (data) The process of joining rows or columns of related data into a single entity so that groups can be collapsed or expanded for data analysis.

Grouping (worksheets) The process of selecting two or more worksheets so that you can perform the same action at the same time on all selected worksheets.

Header An area with one or more lines of information at the top of each page.

Histogram A chart that is similar to a column chart. The category axis shows bin ranges (intervals) where data are aggregated into bins, and the vertical axis shows frequencies.

HLOOKUP function A lookup and reference function that accepts a value, looks the value up in a horizontal lookup table with data organized in rows, and returns a result.

Horizontal alignment The placement of cell data between the left and right cell margins. By default, text is left-aligned, and values are right-aligned.

Hyperlink An electronic link that, when clicked, goes to another location in the same or a different worksheet, opens another file, opens a webpage in a Web browser, or opens an email client and inserts an email address into the To box.

Icon set A set of symbols or signs that classify data into three, four, or five categories, based on values in a range.

Ideas feature A task pane that provides intelligent analysis of a dataset to recommend potentially useful charts.

IF function A logical function that evaluates a condition and returns one value if the condition is true and a different value if the condition is false.

IFERROR function A logic function that checks a cell to determine if that cell contains an error or if a formula will result in an error. If no error exists, the function returns the value of the formula. If an error exists, the function returns the type of error.

IFS function A logical function that evaluates up to 127 conditions and returns a result that corresponds to the first logical test that is true.

Importing The process of inserting external data—data created or stored in another format—into the current application.

Indent A format that offsets data from its default alignment. For example, if text is left-aligned, the text may be indented or offset from the left side to stand out. If a value is right-aligned, it can be indented or offset from the right side of the cell.

INDEX function A lookup and reference function that returns a value at the intersection of a specified row and column within a given range.

Input area A range of cells in a worksheet used to store and change the variables used in calculations.

Input message Descriptive text or instructions that inform a user about the restrictions for entering data in a cell.

Insert Function A command that displays the Insert Function dialog box to search for and select a function to insert into the active cell. The Insert Function command changes from gray to green when you position the pointer over it.

INTERCEPT function A statistical function that calculates the point at which a line will intersect the y-axis by using a best-fit regression line plotted through the known x-values and y-values.

IPMT function A financial function that calculates the periodic interest for a specified payment period on a loan or an investment given a fixed interest rate, specified term, and identical periodic payments.

ISOWEEKNUM function A date function that returns the number of the week within the year for the specified date.

Keyboard shortcut A combination of two or more keys pressed together to initiate a software command.

Keyword A special programming syntax that has special meaning within the programming language and must be used for the intended purposes.

Landscape orientation A document layout when a page is wider than it is tall.

LARGE function A statistical function that returns the kth largest value in a dataset.

LEFT function A text function that extracts the specified number of characters from the left side of a text string.

Legend A key that identifies the color or pattern assigned to each data series in a chart.

LEN function A text function that identifies the number of characters in a text string.

Line chart A chart type that displays lines connecting data points to show trends over equal time periods, such as months, quarters, years, or decades.

Linear Trendline A least squares line to best fit simple linear datasets.

Linking The process of creating external cell references from worksheets in one workbook to cells on a worksheet in another workbook.

Live Preview An Office feature that provides a preview of the results of a selection when you point to an option in a list or gallery. Using Live Preview, you can experiment with settings before making a final choice.

Loan amortization table A schedule showing monthly payments, interest per payment, amount toward paying off the loan, and the remaining balance after each payment for a loan.

Locked cell A cell that prevents users from editing the contents or formatting of that cell in a protected worksheet.

Logic error An error that occurs when a formula is syntactically correct but logically incorrect, which produces inaccurate results.

Logical test An expression that evaluates to true or false.

Lookup table A range that contains data for the basis of the lookup and data to be retrieved.

Lookup value The cell reference of the cell that contains the value to look up.

LOWER function A text function that converts all uppercase letters in a text string to lowercase.

Macro A set of instructions that execute a sequence of commands to automate repetitive or routine tasks.

Macro Recorder A feature that records your commands, keystrokes, and mouse clicks to store Excel commands as VBA code within a workbook.

Map chart A chart that displays data by geographic region based on a dataset containing countries, states, counties, or postal codes.

Margin The area of blank space that displays to the left, right, top, and bottom of a document or worksheet.

MATCH function A lookup and reference function that searches through a range for a specific value and returns the relative position of that value within the range.

MAX function A statistical function that identifies the highest value in a range.

MAXIFS function A statistical function that returns the highest value in a range that meets multiple criteria.

MEDIAN function A predefined formula that identifies the midpoint value in a set of values.

Microsoft Access A relational database management system in which you can record and link data, query databases, and create forms and reports.

Microsoft Excel An application that makes it easy to organize records, financial transactions, and business information in the form of worksheets.

Microsoft Office A productivity software suite including a set of software applications, each one specializing in a particular type of output.

Microsoft PowerPoint An application that enables you to create dynamic presentations to inform groups and persuade audiences.

Microsoft Word A word processing software application used to produce all sorts of documents, including memos, newsletters, forms, tables, and brochures.

MID function A text string that extracts the characters from the middle of a text string, given a starting position and length.

MIN function A predefined formula that displays the lowest value in a range.

MINFIS function A statistical function that returns the lowest value in a range that meets multiple criteria.

Mini Toolbar A toolbar that provides access to the most common formatting selections, such as adding bold or italic, or changing font type or color. Unlike the Quick Access Toolbar, the Mini Toolbar is not customizable.

Mixed cell reference A designation that combines an absolute cell reference with a relative cell reference. The absolute part does not change but the relative part does when you copy the formula.

Module A file in which macros are stored.

MONTH function A date function that displays the month (1–12), where 1 is January and 12 is December, for a specific date.

Name Box A rectangular area located below the ribbon that displays the address (or name) of the active cell, selected chart, or selected table. Use the Name Box to go to a cell or table; select a range; or assign a name to one or more cells.

Nested function A function that is embedded or "nested" within an argument of another function.

NETWORKDAYS function A date function that calculates the number of work days (excluding weekends) between two dates; can optionally exclude federal and state holidays as well as other nonwork days.

New sheet A button used to insert a new worksheet to the right of the current worksheet.

Newline Character A special character that designates the end of a line and separates data for the next line or row.

Nonadjacent range A collection of multiple ranges (such as D5:D10 and F5:F10) that are not positioned in a contiguous cluster in an Excel worksheet.

Nonbinding constraint A constraint that does not restrict the target value that Solver finds.

Normal view The default view of a worksheet that shows worksheet data but not margins, headers, footers, or page breaks.

NOT function A logical function that returns TRUE if the argument is false and FALSE if the argument is true.

Note A basic documentation tool that annotates a cell but does not display as a discussion thread.

NOW function A date and time function that calculates the current date and military time that you last opened the workbook using the computer's clock.

Nper Total number of payment periods.

NPER function A financial function that calculates the number of payment periods for an investment or loan given a fixed interest rate, periodic payment, and present value.

NPV function A financial function that calculates the net present value of an investment, given a fixed discount rate (rate of return) and future payments that may be identical or different.

Number format A setting that controls how a value appears in a cell.

Object An element that contains both data and code and represents an element of Excel such as Range or Selection.

Objective cell The cell that contains the formula-based value that you want to maximize, minimize, or set to a value in Solver by manipulating values of one or more variables.

Office Clipboard An area of memory reserved to temporarily hold selections that have been cut or copied and allows you to paste the selections.

OneDrive Microsoft's cloud storage system. Saving files to OneDrive enables them to sync across all Windows devices and to be accessible from any Internet-connected device.

One-variable data table A structured range that contains different values for one variable to compare how the different values affect one or more calculated results.

Optimization model A model that finds the highest, lowest, or exact value for one particular result by adjusting values for selected variables.

OR function A logical function that returns TRUE if any argument is true and returns FALSE if all arguments are false.

Order of operations A set of rules that controls the sequence in which arithmetic operations are performed. Also called the *order of precedence*.

Outline A hierarchical structure of data that you can group related data to summarize. When a dataset has been grouped into an outline, you can collapse the outlined data to show only main rows (such as subtotals) or expand the outlined data to show all the details.

Output area The range of cells in an Excel worksheet that contain formulas dependent on the values in the input area.

Output range A range of cells that contains the list of records from a dataset that meets the conditions specified in the criteria range.

Page break An indication of where data will start on another printed page.

Page Break Preview A view setting that displays page breaks within the worksheet.

Page Layout view A view setting that displays the worksheet data, margins, headers, and footers.

Paste A command used to place a cut or copied selection into another location.

Paste Options button A button that displays near the bottom-right corner of the pasted data immediately after using the Paste command. It enables the user to apply different paste options.

Percent Style A number format that displays a value as if it was multiplied by 100 and with the % symbol. The default number of decimal places is zero if you click Percent Style in the Number group or two decimal places if you use the Format Cells dialog box.

PERCENTILE.EXC function A statistical function that returns the percentile of a range excluding the 0 or 100% percentile.

PERCENTILE.INC function A statistical function that returns the percentile of a range including the 0 or 100% percentile.

PERCENTRANK.EXC function A statistical function that identifies a value's rank as a percentile, excluding 0 and 1, of a list of values.

PERCENTRANK.INC function A statistical function that identifies a value's rank as a percentile between 0 and 1 of a list of values.

Personal Macro Workbook A hidden workbook containing macros that can be used in any workbook on the local workstation.

Picture A graphic file that is retrieved from storage media or the Internet and placed in an Office project.

Pie chart A chart type that shows each data point in proportion to the whole data series as a slice in a circle. A pie chart depicts only one data series.

PivotChart An interactive graphical representation of data in a PivotTable.

PivotTable An interactive table that uses calculations to consolidate and summarize data from a data source into a separate table to enable a person to analyze the data in a dataset without altering the dataset itself. You can rotate or pivot the data in a PivotTable to look at the data from different perspectives.

PivotTable Fields task pane A window that displays the fields in a dataset and enables a user to specify what fields are used to create a layout to organize the data in columns, rows, values, and filters in a PivotTable.

PivotTable style A set of formatting that controls bold, font colors, shading colors, and border lines.

PivotTable timeline A small window that starts with the first date and ends with the last date in the data source. It contains horizontal tiles that you can click to filter data by day, month, quarter, or year.

Plot area The region of a chart containing the graphical representation of the values in one or more data series. Two axes form a border around the plot area.

PMT function A financial function that calculates the periodic loan payment given a fixed rate, number of periods (also known as *term*), and the present value of the loan (the *principal*).

Pointing The process of using the pointer to select cells while building a formula. Also known as *semi-selection*.

Population A dataset that contains all the information you want to evaluate.

Portrait orientation A document layout when a page is taller than it is wide.

Power BI An online application suite designed to help users manage, supplement, visualize, and analyze data.

Power Pivot A built-in add-in that offers the key functionality that is included in Excel's stock Pivot Table options, plus a variety of useful features for the power user.

Power Query Editor A business intelligence tool that can connect and shape data from multiple sources.

PPMT function A financial function that calculates the principal payment for a specified payment period on a loan or an investment given a fixed interest rate, specified term, and identical periodic payments.

Precedent cell A cell referred to by a formula in another cell.

Print area The range of cells within a worksheet that will print.

Print order The sequence in which the pages are printed.

Procedure A named sequence of statements stored in a macro.

PROPER function A text function that capitalizes the first letter of each word in a text string, including the first letter of prepositions and articles.

Pv An argument in the PMT function representing the present value of the loan.

PV function A financial function that calculates the total present (current) value of an investment with a fixed rate, specified number of payment periods, and a series of identical payments that will be made in the future.

Quartile A value used to divide a range of numbers into four equal groups.

QUARTILE.EXC function A statistical function that identifies the value at a specific quartile, exclusive of 0 and 4.

QUARTILE.INC function A statistical function that identifies the value at a specific quartile.

Quick Access Toolbar A toolbar located at the top-left corner of any Office application window; provides fast access to commonly executed tasks such as saving a file and undoing recent actions.

Quick Analysis A set of analytical tools you can use to apply formatting, create charts or tables, and insert basic functions.

Radar chart A chart type that compares aggregate values of three or more variables represented on axes starting from the same point.

Range A group of adjacent or contiguous cells in a worksheet. A range can be adjacent cells in a column (such as C5:C10), in a row (such as A6:H6), or a rectangular group of cells (such as G5:H10).

Range name A word or string of characters assigned to one or more cells.

Range_lookup An argument that determines how the VLOOKUP and HLOOKUP functions handle lookup values that are not an exact match for the data in the lookup table.

RANK.AVG function A statistical function that identifies the rank of a value, providing an average ranking for identical values.

RANK.EQ function A statistical function that identifies the rank of a value, omitting the next rank when tie values exist.

Rate The periodic interest rate; the percentage of interest paid for each payment period; the first argument in the PMT function.

RATE function A financial function that calculates the periodic rate for an investment or loan given the number of payment periods, a fixed periodic payment, and present value.

Record A group of related fields representing one entity, such as data for one person, place, event, or concept.

Refresh Updates the linked data in an Excel workbook with the most up to date information.

Relationship An association or connection between two related tables where both tables contain a related field of data, such as IDs.

Relative cell reference. A designation that indicates a cell's relative location from the original cell containing the formula; the cell reference changes when the formula is copied.

Ribbon The command center of Office applications. It is the long bar located just beneath the title bar, containing tabs, groups, and commands.

RIGHT function A text function that extracts the specified number of characters from the right side of a text string.

Row heading A number to the left side of a row in a worksheet. For example, 3 is the row heading for the third row.

Row height The vertical measurement of the row in a worksheet.

Rows area A section within the PivotTable Fields task pane used to place a field that will display labels to organize data horizontally in a PivotTable. It groups the data into categories in the first column, listing each unique label only once regardless how many times the label is contained in the original dataset.

RSQ function Short for *R*-square, the RSQ function is a statistical function that returns the square of the Pearson product moment correlation coefficient through the given data points.

Run-time error An error that occurs when a syntactically correct formula or function contains a cell reference with invalid or missing data; an error that occurs when there is a problem with software or hardware while executing a program.

Sample A smaller portion of the population that is easier to evaluate.

Scenario A detailed set of values that represent different possible situations.

Scenario Manager A tool that enables you to define and manage scenarios to compare how they affect results.

Scenario Manager A what-if analysis tool that enables you to define and manage up to 32 scenarios to compare their side effects on calculated results.

Scenario Summary report An organized structured table of the scenarios, their input values, and their respective results.

Scene An animated segment within a Tour.

Select All The triangle at the intersection of the row and column headings in the top-left corner of the worksheet used to select everything contained in the active worksheet.

Semi-selection The process of using the pointer to select cells while building a formula. Also known as *pointing*.

Sheet tab A label that looks like a file folder tab, located between the bottom of the worksheet and the status bar, that shows the name of a worksheet contained in the workbook.

Sheet tab scroll button Button to the left of the sheet tabs used to scroll through sheet tabs; not all the sheet tabs are displayed at the same time.

Shortcut menu A menu that provides choices related to the selection or area at which you right-click.

Sizing handle One of eight circles that display on the outside border of a chart—one on each corner and one on each middle side—when the chart is selected; enables the user to adjust the height and width of the chart.

Slicer A small window containing one button for each unique item in a field so that you can filter the PivotTable quickly.

Slicer caption The text or field name that appears as a header or title at the top of a slicer to identify the data in that field.

SLOPE function A statistical function that returns the slope of the linear regression line through the given data points.

SMALL function A statistical function that returns the *k*th smallest value in a dataset.

Smart Lookup A feature that provides information about tasks or commands in Office and can also be used to search for general information on a topic, such as *President George Washington*.

Solver An add-in application that searches for the best or optimum solution to a problem by manipulating the values for several variables within restrictions that you impose.

Sorting The process of arranging records by the value of one or more fields within a table or data range.

Source file The file that contains the original table or data used or copied to create a linked or embedded object, such as an Excel worksheet.

Sparkline A small line, column, or win/loss chart contained in a single cell to provide a simple visual illustrating one data series.

Split bar The vertical or horizontal line that frames a split window. A vertical split bar splits the window into left and right panes. A horizontal split bar splits the window into top and bottom panes.

Splitting The process of dividing a worksheet window into two or four resizable panes so you can view separate parts of a worksheet at the same time. Any changes made in one pane affect the entire worksheet.

Spreadsheet An electronic file that contains a grid of columns and rows used to organize related data and to display results of calculations, enabling interpretation of quantitative data for decision making.

Stacked bar chart A chart type that places stacks of data in segments in one bar, with each category in the data series represented by a different color.

Stacked column chart A chart type that shows the relationship of individual data points to the whole category by stacking data in segments in one column, with each segment represented by a different color.

Standard Deviation A statistic that measures how far the data sample is spread around the mean.

Standard Error The level of accuracy of the forecast.

Status bar A bar located at the bottom of the program window that contains information relative to the open file. It also includes tools for changing the view of the file and for changing the zoom size of onscreen file contents.

STEYX function A statistical function that returns the standard error of the predicted *y*-value for each *x* in a regression.

Stock chart A chart type that shows fluctuation in stock prices.

Structured reference A tag or use of a table element, such as a field label, as a reference in a formula. Field labels are enclosed in square brackets, such as [Amount], within the formula.

Sub procedure Visual Basic code that performs actions on a workbook but does not return a specific value.

SUBSTITUTE function A text function that substitutes, or replaces, an old text string with a new text string.

Substitution value A value that replaces the original value of a variable in a data table.

Subtotal A summary calculation, such as a total or an average, of values for a category.

SUBTOTAL function A predefined formula that calculates an aggregate value, such as totals, for displayed values in a range, a table, or a database. The first argument is a number that indicates the function. For example, the argument 9 represents the Sum function. The second argument represents a range of values to subtotal.

Subtotal row A row that includes one or more aggregate functions for each category within a dataset.

SUM function A statistical function that calculates the total of values contained in one or more cells.

SUMIF function A statistical function that calculates the total of a range of values when a specified condition is met.

SUMIFS function A statistical function that calculates the cells in a range that meet multiple criteria.

Surface chart A chart type that displays trends using two dimensions on a continuous curve.

SWITCH function A logical function that evaluates an expression, compares it to a list of values, and returns the first corresponding result.

Syntax A set of rules that governs the structure and components for properly entering a function.

Syntax error An error that occurs when a formula or function violates construction rules; for example, by containing a misspelled a function name.

Tab Located on the ribbon, each tab is designed to appear much like a tab on a file folder, with the active tab highlighted.

Tab-delimited file A technique that uses tabs to separate data into columns.

Table A structured range that contains related data organized in a method that increases the capability to manage and analyze information.

Table array The range that contains the lookup table.

Table style A named collection of color, font, and border designs that can be applied to a table.

Tag A data element or metadata that is added as a document property. Tags help in indexing and searching.

Task pane A window of options specific to a feature in an Office application. The task pane name and options change based on the selected range, object, or feature.

Tell me box A box located to the right of the last tab that enables you to search for help and information about a command or task you want to perform and also displays a shortcut directly to that command.

Template A predesigned file that contains suggested content, formatting, and other elements that can be modified to conform to the user's specific needs.

Template A predesigned file that incorporates formatting elements, such as a theme and layouts, that you can use as a model to create other documents that have the same structure and purpose; may include content that can be modified.

Text Any combination of letters, numbers, symbols, and spaces not used in Excel calculations.

Text File A data file that contains characters, such as letters, numbers, and symbols, including punctuation and spaces.

TEXTJOIN function A text function that combines up to 252 text strings using a delimiter specified as an argument.

Theme A collection of design formats that include colors, fonts, and special effects used to give a consistent appearance to a document, workbook, presentation, or database form or report.

Title bar The long bar at the top of each window that displays the name of the folder, file, or program displayed in the open window and the application in which you are working.

TODAY function A date and time function that displays the current date.

Toggle command A button that acts somewhat like a light switch that you can turn on and off. You select the command to turn it on, then select it again to turn it off.

Total row (Excel) A table row that appears below the last row of records in an Excel table and displays summary or aggregate statistics, such as a sum or an average.

Tour A time-based animation that can display a 3D Map from different perspectives.

Tracer arrow A colored line that shows relationships between precedent and dependent cells.

TRANSPOSE function A function that transposes or rearranges the data from columns to rows and rows to columns.

Trend Analysis A method of analyzing historical data to gain insight into predicting potential future outcomes.

Trendline A line that depicts trends or helps forecast future data in a chart. For example, if the plotted data includes 2015, 2020, 2025, and 2030, a trendline can help forecast values for 2030 and beyond.

TRIM function A text function that removes leading and trailing spaces in a text string and extra spaces between words but maintains one space between words in a text string.

Truth table A matrix that provides the results (TRUE or FALSE) for every possible combination for an AND, OR, or NOT criteria combination.

Two-variable data table A structured range that contains different values for two variables to compare how these differing values affect the results for one calculated value.

Ungrouping The process of deselecting grouped worksheets so that actions performed on one sheet do not affect other worksheets.

Unqualified reference The use of field headings without row references in a structured formula.

UPPER function A text function that converts text strings to uppercase letters.

Validation criteria The rules that dictate the type of data that can be entered in a cell.

Value A number that represents a quantity or a measurable amount.

Value axis The chart axis that displays incremental numbers to identify approximate values, such as dollars or units, of data points in a chart.

Value_if_false The value that is returned if Logical_test is FALSE, if omitted, the word FALSE is returned.

Value_if_true The value that is returned if Logical_test is TRUE, if omitted, the word TRUE is returned.

Values area A section within the PivotTable Fields task pane used to place a field to display summary statistics, such as totals or averages, in a PivotTable.

Variable An input value that you can change to see how that change affects other values.

Variance A measure of a dataset's dispersion, such as the difference between the highest and lowest points in the data.

VBA Comments Indicated by an apostrophe and appear in green; provide information about the macro, but do not affect its execution and are considered documentation.

Vertical alignment The placement of cell data between the top and bottom cell margins.

View controls Buttons on the right side of the status bar that enable you to change to Normal, Page Layout, or Page Break view to display the worksheet.

View The various ways a file can appear on the screen.

Visual Basic Editor An application used to create, edit, execute, and debug Office application macros using programming code.

Visual Basic for Applications (VBA) A robust programming language that is the underlying code of all macros.

VLOOKUP function A lookup and reference function that accepts a value, looks the value up in a vertical lookup table with data organized in columns, and returns a result.

Watch Window A separate window from the worksheet window that displays cell addresses, values, and formulas so you can monitor and examine formula calculations involving cells not immediately visible on the screen.

WEEKDAY function A date function that returns an integer that represents the day of week, such as for 6 Friday and 7 for Saturday.

What-if analysis The process of experimenting with different variables or assumptions so that you can observe and compare how these changes affect a related outcome.

Workbook A collection of one or more related worksheets contained within a single file.

WORKDAY function A date function that calculates a serial number of a date, given a specified number of days before or after a date, excluding specified holidays.

Worksheet A single spreadsheet that typically contains descriptive labels, numeric values, formulas, functions, and graphical representations of data.

Wrap text An alignment option that word-wraps data on multiple lines within a cell.

X Y (scatter) chart A chart type that shows a relationship between two variables using their X and Y coordinates. Excel plots one coordinate on the horizontal X-axis and the other variable on the vertical Y-axis. Scatter charts are often used to represent data in education, scientific, and medical experiments.

X-axis Also known as the *horizontal axis*; the horizontal border that provides a frame of reference for measuring data left to right on a chart.

Y-axis Also known as the *vertical axis*; the vertical border that provides a frame of reference for measuring data up and down on a chart.

YEAR function A date function that displays the year (such as 2021) for a specific date.

YEARFRAC function A date function that calculates the fraction of a year between two dates based on the number of whole days using the start_date and end_date arguments.

Zoom slider A feature that displays at the far right side of the status bar. It is used to increase or decrease the magnification of the file.

Index

Compress Pictures, 36
Computer Job Outlook case study,
    192–193
CONCAT function, 661–663
Conditional Formatting feature, 544
conditional formatting in tables, 290–296,
    297–301
conditional math and statistical functions
    evaluating multiple condition, 455–456
    evaluating one condition, 453–455
    inserting a map, 457, 463
connections. *see* Queries & Connections
    group
constraints, defining with Solver, 413–414,
    416, 420
contextual tabs, 10
copy/move worksheet, 120–121, 128–129
copy ranges of cells, 99–100, 107
copy text, 30, 40–41
CORREL function, 497–498, 507
COUNT functions, 162, 167
COUNTIF function, 454, 458–459, 499
COUNTIFS function, 455–456, 461–462
COVARIANCE function, 511–512, 517
criteria argument, 673
criteria range, 670–671, 676
Crop tool, 36
CUMIPMT function, 470
CUMPRINC function, 471
cumulative financial functions, 470–471,
    475–476
Currency format, 113
custom filters in tables, 279–280
cut text, 30, 40–41

D

data. *see also* one-variable data table
    bars in tables, 293, 300
    chart labeling, 218–219, 225–226
    copy/paste ranges of cells, 99–100
    external data properties, 620, 625
    filtering data tables, 276–280
    find/replace in, 81, 86
    grouping/ungrouping, 317–318
    importing data, 610–618
    moving ranges of cells, 99
    Paste Options button, 100–102, 108
    selecting range of cells, 98–99
    sorting data in tables, 274–276
    source selection, 195–196, 234
    transform data, 616–618, 623–624
data model and Power Pivot, 626–627,
    631
data modeling, 353–355
data point, 195, 221–222, 226–227
data series, 195, 220–221
data shaping, 616
data source, 229–230
Data Tools group, 354
data validation, 567–568, 572–575,
    579–580

data visualization, 635–638
data_array, 498
database filtering and functions
    advanced filtering, 670–672, 677
    criteria and output ranges, 670–671,
        676
    introduction to, 670
    lookup functions, 680–688
    manipulating data with, 673–675
database functions, defined, 673
datasets
    freezing rows and columns, 253,
        257–258
    large datasets, 252
    page breaks, 254–255, 258–259
    print area, 255–256, 259–260
    print page order, 256
    print titles, 256, 260–261
    printing large datasets, 254–256
dates
    entering in Microsoft Excel, 80, 85–86
    filters in tables, 278, 287
    functions, 436–439, 446–448
DAVERAGE function, 674, 678
DAY function, 436
DAYS function, 437
DCOUNT function, 674, 679
DCOUNTA function, 674
decimal places, 114, 118
delimiters, defined, 611
dependent cells, 568–569, 576
destination file, 560, 561
Developer tab, 726
DGET function, 675, 679
Dialog Box Launcher, 10
dialog box, 10–11, 48, 75
dimensions, defined, 637, 640
DMAX function, 674, 679
DMIN function, 674, 679
Document Inspector, 711–713, 719–720
document properties Microsoft Excel
    Accessibility Checker, 714–716,
        720–721
    annotating worksheet, 716–718, 722
    checking for issues, 711–715
    Compatibility Checker, 714–715,
        721–722
    Document Inspector, 711–713,
        719–720
    editing/deleting comments, 716 717,
        723
    introduction to, 711
    printing comments, 717
    show/hide comments, 718, 724
document properties Microsoft Office,
    50–51, 56
document properties Microsoft Word,
    50–51
document views, 45, 46
DSUM function, 674, 678
duplicate rows, removing in tables,
    265–266, 271

E

education evaluation case study, 494–495
embedding data, 610
encrypting a workbook file, 585
Enhanced ScreenTips, 17
error alert, 574–575
error feedback, 713
Evaluate Formula dialog box, 570
expanding subtotals, 316–317, 321
exploded pie chart, 221–222
external data properties, 620, 625

F

F4 Key, 152
field argument, 673
fields in tables. *see* PivotTables; tables
File Explorer, 6, 612
files/folders in Microsoft Office
    creating new file, 6
    open saved file, 7–8, 20–21
    previewing and printing, 51–52, 57
    saving file, 7, 19–20
    working with, 6–9
Fill Across Worksheets, 543–544, 551–552
fill color in Microsoft Excel, 112, 117–118
fill handle, 78
filters in PivotTables, 340–341, 348–349
financial functions
    cumulative financial functions, 470–471,
        475–476
    loan amortization table, 467–469
    using, 464–465
find data in Microsoft Excel, 81, 86
fixed-width text file, 612
Flash Fill, 79, 262, 658–659, 666
Font Dialog Box Launcher, 10
Font group, 9
footers
    Microsoft Excel, 124–125, 130–131
    Microsoft Office, 49–50, 55
Forecast Sheet, 513–514, 519
FORECAST.LINEAR function, 523–524,
    528
Format Cells dialog box, 582
Format Painter, 17
formatting in Microsoft Excel, 76, 113–114,
    118, 393–394, 398–399
formatting in Microsoft Office, 28 29,
    39–40
formula audits, 567–571
Formula AutoComplete, 134, 157
formulas in Microsoft Excel
    absolute cell references in, 151–152,
        155–156
    adding to one-variable data table,
        391–392, 397
    adding to two-variable data table, 395
    cell references in, 87–88
    conditional formatting in tables,
        295–296

Windows-based Office applications, 4
word wrap feature, 111
worksheets
  annotating worksheet, 716–718, 722
design of, 76
  Fill Across Worksheets, 543–544,
    551–552
  grouped worksheets, 542–545, 551–553
  management of, 119–122
  protected worksheets, 738–739
  protection of, 581–586, 588–590

renaming tables/worksheets, 121–122,
  128–129, 264–265, 269
ungrouped worksheets, 542–543
wrap text, 111, 116

XLSTART folder, 726